The Cambridge Handbook of World Englishes

The plural form "Englishes" conveys the diversity of English as a global language, pinpointing the growth and existence of a large number of national, regional, and social forms. The global spread of English and the new varieties that have emerged around the world has grown to be a vast area of study and research, which intersects multiple disciplines. This *Handbook* provides a comprehensive and authoritative survey of World Englishes from 1600 to the present day. Covering topics such as variationist sociolinguistics, pragmatics, contact linguistics, linguistic anthropology, corpus and applied linguistics, and language history, it combines discussion of traditional topics with a variety of innovative approaches. The chapters, all written by internationally acclaimed authorities, provide up-to-date accounts of the evolution of different Englishes around the globe, a comprehensive coverage of different models and approaches, and some original perspectives on current challenges.

DANIEL SCHREIER is Professor of English Linguistics at the University of Zurich, Switzerland. He is author of several books on English in the South Atlantic, has published some sixty articles, and has served as co-editor of the journal *English World-Wide* (2013–19).

MARIANNE HUNDT is Professor of English Linguistics at the University of Zurich, Switzerland. She is the coordinator of the *International Corpus of English* (since 2017), wrote *New Zealand English Grammar* (1998), and is co-editor of the journal *English World-Wide* (since 2013).

EDGAR W. SCHNEIDER is Chair Professor of English Linguistics at the University of Regensburg, Germany. His many books include *Postcolonial English* (2007) and *English Around the World* (2011), both published by Cambridge University Press.

Genuinely broad in scope, each handbook in this series provides a complete state-of-the-field overview of a major sub-discipline within language study and research. Grouped into broad thematic areas, the chapters in each volume encompass the most important issues and topics within each subject, offering a coherent picture of the latest theories and findings. Together, the volumes will build into an integrated overview of the discipline in its entirety.

Published titles

The Cambridge Handbook of Phonology, edited by Paul de Lacy

The Cambridge Handbook of Linguistic Code-switching, edited by Barbara E. Bullock and Almeida Jacqueline Toribio

The Cambridge Handbook of Child Language, Second Edition, edited by Edith L. Bavin and Letitia Naigles

The Cambridge Handbook of Endangered Languages, edited by Peter K. Austin and Julia Sallabank

The Cambridge Handbook of Sociolinguistics, edited by Rajend Mesthrie

The Cambridge Handbook of Pragmatics, edited by Keith Allan and Kasia M. Jaszczolt

The Cambridge Handbook of Language Policy, edited by Bernard Spolsky

The Cambridge Handbook of Second Language Acquisition, edited by Julia Herschensohn and Martha Young-Scholten

The Cambridge Handbook of Biolinguistics, edited by Cedric Boeckx and Kleanthes K. Grohmann

The Cambridge Handbook of Generative Syntax, edited by Marcel den Dikken

The Cambridge Handbook of Communication Disorders, edited by Louise Cummings

The Cambridge Handbook of Stylistics, edited by Peter Stockwell and Sara Whiteley

The Cambridge Handbook of Linguistic Anthropology, edited by N.J. Enfield, Paul Kockelman and Jack Sidnell

The Cambridge Handbook of English Corpus Linguistics, edited by Douglas Biber and Randi Reppen

The Cambridge Handbook of Bilingual Processing, edited by John W. Schwieter

The Cambridge Handbook of Learner Corpus Research, edited by Sylviane Granger, Gaëtanelle Gilquin and Fanny Meunier

The Cambridge Handbook of Linguistic Multicompetence, edited by Li Wei and Vivian Cook

The Cambridge Handbook of English Historical Linguistics, edited by Merja Kytö and Päivi Pahta

The Cambridge Handbook of Formal Semantics, edited by Maria Aloni and Paul Dekker

The Cambridge Handbook of Morphology, edited by Andrew Hippisley and Greg Stump

The Cambridge Handbook of Historical Syntax, edited by Adam Ledgeway and Ian Roberts

The Cambridge Handbook of Linguistic Typology, edited by Alexandra Y. Aikhenvald and R. M. W. Dixon

The Cambridge Handbook of Areal Linguistics, edited by Raymond Hickey

The Cambridge Handbook of Cognitive Linguistics, edited by Barbara Dancygier

The Cambridge Handbook of Japanese Linguistics, edited by Yoko Hasegawa

The Cambridge Handbook of Spanish Linguistics, edited by Kimberly L. Geeslin

The Cambridge Handbook of World Englishes

Edited by

Daniel Schreier
University of Zurich

Marianne Hundt
University of Zurich

Edgar W. Schneider
University of Regensburg

CAMBRIDGE
UNIVERSITY PRESS

University Printing House, Cambridge CB2 8BS, United Kingdom

One Liberty Plaza, 20th Floor, New York, NY 10006, USA

477 Williamstown Road, Port Melbourne, VIC 3207, Australia

314-321, 3rd Floor, Plot 3, Splendor Forum, Jasola District Centre, New Delhi - 110025, India

103 Penang Road, #05-06/07, Visioncrest Commercial, Singapore 238467

Cambridge University Press is part of the University of Cambridge.

It furthers the University's mission by disseminating knowledge in the pursuit of
education, learning and research at the highest international levels of excellence.

www.cambridge.org
Information on this title: www.cambridge.org/9781108441957
DOI: 10.1017/9781108349406

First published 2020
First paperback edition 2022

A catalogue record for this publication is available from the British Library

Library of Congress Cataloging in Publication data
Names: Schreier, Daniel, 1971– editor. | Hundt, Marianne, editor. | Schneider, Edgar
W. (Edgar Werner), 1954– editor.
Title: The Cambridge handbook of world Englishes / edited by Daniel Schreier,
Marianne Hundt, Edgar W. Schneider.
Description: 1. | New York : Cambridge University Press, 2019. | Series: Cambridge
handbooks in language and linguistics | Includes bibliographical references and
index.
Identifiers: LCCN 2019041190 (print) | LCCN 2019041191 (ebook) | ISBN
9781108425957 (hardback) | ISBN 9781108441957 (epub)
Subjects: LCSH: English language – Foreign countries. | English language – Variation –
Foreign countries. | English language – Social aspects – Foreign countries.
Classification: LCC PE2751 .C36 2019 (print) | LCC PE2751 (ebook) | DDC 427–dc23
LC record available at https://lccn.loc.gov/2019041190
LC ebook record available at https://lccn.loc.gov/2019041191

ISBN 978-1-108-42595-7 Hardback
ISBN 978-1-108-44195-7 Paperback

In memory of Alex Kautzsch (1969–2018)

Contents

Figures

Maps

Tables

Notes on Contributors

Michael Aceto is Professor of Linguistics at East Carolina University, USA. His research has mostly presented primary data gathered in the field in Panama, Barbuda, St Eustatius, and Dominica. His articles have appeared in *Language in Society*, *English World-Wide*, *American Speech*, and the *Journal of Pidgin and Creole Languages*, and he is the co-editor (with Jeff Williams) of the book *Contact Englishes of the Eastern Caribbean* (2003). Aceto aspires to bring the discipline of linguistics in contact with the millennia of works and thought by Buddhist scholars. He is also exploring the relationship between vernacular and standard Englishes in his manuscript *Everyday Language Every Day*.

Carolin Biewer is the Chair of English Linguistics at the University of Würzburg, Germany, where she teaches corpus linguistics, historical linguistics, sociolinguistics, and World Englishes. Her research focuses on language variation and change in East Asia, Australasia, and the Pacific, particularly on non-native varieties of English, which are an integral part of the linguistic repertoire of speech communities in remote places, such as Fiji, or megacities, such as Hong Kong. She is the author of the monograph *South Pacific Englishes: A Sociolinguistic and Morphosyntactic Profile of Fiji English, Samoan English and Cook Islands English* (2015), which won the 2016 European Society for the Study of English (ESSE) book award for the category of language and linguistics.

Brook Bolander is a lecturer in the School of Languages, Literatures, Cultures and Linguistics at Monash University, Australia. Core research interests are the sociolinguistics of globalization, English as a transnational language, and language use online. Major publications include a monograph on *Language and Power in Blogs* (2013); articles on language and transnationalism in *Language in Society* (2016), the *International Journal of the Sociology of Language* (2017), and *Language Policy* (2018); and a special issue (co-edited with Till Mostowlansky), "Language and globalization in South and Central Asian spaces," for the *International Journal of the Sociology of Language* (2017).

David Britain has been Professor of Modern English Linguistics at the University of Bern in Switzerland since 2010, having previously worked in New Zealand and the UK. His research interests embrace language variation and change, varieties of English (especially in southern England, the southern hemisphere, and the Pacific), dialect contact and attrition, dialect ideologies, and the dialectology–human geography interface, especially with respect to space/place, urban/rural, and the role of mobilities. He is editor of *Language in the British Isles* (Cambridge University Press, 2007), co-editor (with Jenny Cheshire) of *Social Dialectology* (2003), and co-author of *Linguistics: An Introduction* (with Andrew Radford, Martin Atkinson, Harald Clahsen, and Andrew Spencer) (Cambridge University Press, 2nd edition, 2009). He is also co-author (with Laura Rupp) of a forthcoming book *Let's Talk About – s: Linguistic Perspectives on a Variable English Morpheme*. He was Associate Editor of the *Journal of Sociolinguistics* between 2008 and 2017.

Kate Burridge is Professor of Linguistics at Monash University, Australia, and Fellow of the Australian Academy of the Humanities. Her main areas of research are language change, the Pennsylvania German of Anabaptist communities in North America, the notion of linguistic taboo, and the structure and history of English. Her most recent books are *Forbidden Words: Taboo and the Censoring of Language* (with Keith Allan, 2006), *Gift of the Gob: Morsels of English Language History* (2010), *Wrestling with Words and Meanings* (with Réka Benczes, 2014), *For the Love of Language* (with Tonya Stebbins, 2016), *Understanding Language Change* (with Alex Bergs, 2018), and *Introducing English Grammar* (with Kersti Börjars, 2019). She is a regular presenter of language segments for radio and TV.

Sarah Buschfeld is a full professor of English linguistics (multilingualism) at the Technical University of Dortmund, Germany, after previous appointments at the universities of Regensburg and Cologne. She has worked on postcolonial and non-postcolonial varieties of English (e.g. English in Cyprus, Greece, Namibia, and Singapore) and in the field of language acquisition and multilingualism. She has written and edited several articles and books on these topics, including *English in Cyprus or Cyprus English: An Empirical Investigation of Variety Status* (2013) and *Children's English in Singapore: Acquisition, Properties, and Use* (2019), and explores the boundaries between such disciplines and their concepts.

Alexandra D'Arcy is Professor of Linguistics at the University of Victoria, Canada, where she is Director of the Sociolinguistics Research Lab. She is a co-editor of the *Journal of English Linguistics* and the author of *Discourse-Pragmatic Variation in Context: Eight-Hundred Years of* LIKE (2017). Her research focuses on language variation and change and the mechanisms that support these innate aspects of linguistic systems, with an emphasis on varieties of settler-colonial English in both diachronic and synchronic perspectives.

Alison Edwards is a research affiliate at the Leiden University Centre for Linguistics, the Netherlands. She received her PhD from the University of Cambridge in 2014 and is the author of the book *English in the Netherlands: Functions, Forms and Attitudes*. Her research interests include sociolinguistics, corpus linguistics, critical discourse analysis, multilingualism, and language policy and planning.

Sue Fox is a senior lecturer in Modern English Linguistics at the University of Bern, Switzerland. She is a sociolinguist whose research interests are language variation and change (especially in urban multicultural contexts), multi-ethnolects, language and dialect contact, the impact of immigration on language change, multilingualism, and language attitudes. She is also interested in the language of adolescents from a variationist perspective. Her research has mainly focused on the social and historical contexts that have led to the variety of English that is spoken in London today.

Raymond Hickey is Professor of English Linguistics at the University of Duisburg-Essen, Germany. He has written and edited several books on varieties of English, including *Dublin English: Evolution and Change* (2005), *Irish English: History and Present-day Forms* (Cambridge University Press, 2007), *A Dictionary of Varieties of English* (2014), *Sociolinguistics in Ireland* (2016), *Listening to the Past: Audio Records of Accents of English* (Cambridge University Press, 2017), *The Cambridge Handbook of Areal Linguistics* (Cambridge University Press, 2017), and *English in Multilingual South Africa* (Cambridge University Press, 2019). On the Irish language, he has published *The Dialects of Irish* (2011) and *The Sound Structure of Modern Irish* (2014).

Magnus Huber is Professor of English Linguistics and the History of English at the University of Giessen, Germany, and has taught 130 courses in a wide variety of subjects in English linguistics. He is an expert on varieties of English in West Africa, including English-lexicon pidgins and creoles, and is interested in these languages' present structure, sociolinguistics, and their historical evolution. He is the author of *Ghanaian Pidgin English in Its West African Context* (1999) and co-edited *The Atlas and Survey of Pidgin and Creole Languages* (2013). His research interests include (historical) sociolinguistics, dialectology, corpus linguistics, and historical linguistics, particularly at the levels of phonetics/phonology, morphology, and syntax.

Marianne Hundt is Professor of English Linguistics at the University of Zurich, Switzerland. Her research interests range from grammatical change in contemporary and late modern English to varieties of English as a first and second language (New Zealand, British, and American English; English in Fiji and South Asia) and language in the Indian diaspora. She has been involved in various corpus compilation projects and is the coordinator of the *International Corpus of English*. She has also explored the use of the World Wide Web as a corpus and for corpus building. She is the author of *New Zealand English Grammar* (1998) and co-editor of the journal *English World-Wide* (since 2013).

Alexander Kautzsch† was a *Privatdozent* (Associate Professor) of English Linguistics at the University of Regensburg, Germany, until his sudden and tragic death in March 2018. His book publications include *The Historical Evolution of Earlier African American English: An Empirical Comparison of Early Sources* (2002) and *The Attainment of an English Accent: British and American Features in Advanced German Learners* (2017). His most recent research focused on Namibian English and on modeling World Englishes.

Merja Kytö is Professor of English Language at Uppsala University, Sweden, specializing in English historical linguistics, corpus linguistics, historical pragmatics, and manuscript studies. She has investigated developments in early American English, among them modal auxiliaries, the third-person present singular verb inflection, and the use of the conjunction *and* in documents from the Salem witch trials. She participated in the compilation of the *Helsinki Corpus of English Texts* and *A Corpus of English Dialogues 1560–1760*. She was associate editor of the *Records of the Salem Witch-hunt* (2009) as well as co-editor of *Corpus Linguistics: An International Handbook* (2008) and *The Cambridge Handbook of English Historical Linguistics* (2016). Her recent co-authored books include *Early Modern English Dialogues: Spoken Interaction as Writing* (2010) and *Testifying to Language and Life in Early Modern England* (2011).

James Lambert is a lexicographer and World Englishes scholar, formerly at the National Institute of Education (NIE), Singapore. He is currently teaching English in Australia and working on a comprehensive dictionary of ornithology and birdwatching.

Claudia Lange holds the chair of English Linguistics at Dresden University of Technology, Germany. Her research interests cluster in the area of language variation and change, with a focus on Postcolonial Englishes – a field where language contact, language ideologies, and structural change intersect in the emergence of new varieties. Over the years, her work on Indian English has benefitted from close ties to the University of Pune, the University of Mumbai, the English and Foreign Languages University, Hyderabad, and others.

Lisa Lim is an associate professor at the University of Sydney, Australia, having held positions previously at the National University of Singapore, the University of Amsterdam, and the University of Hong Kong. Her interests center around New Englishes, especially Asian varieties in multilingual ecologies, such as Singapore and Hong Kong; issues of language shift, endangerment, revitalization, and post-vernacular vitality in minority and endangered language communities, such as the Peranakans in Singapore and the Malays of Sri Lanka; and the sociolinguistics of globalization, with interests in mobility, urban multilingualism, computer-mediated communication, and their impact on contact dynamics. She is co-author of *Languages in Contact* (Cambridge University Press, 2016), co-editor of *The Multilingual Citizen* (2018), and founding co-editor (with Umberto Ansaldo) of the journal *Language Ecology*. One of her most engaging projects, since 2016, is her fortnightly "Language Matters" column for the *South China Morning Post*'s *Sunday Post Magazine*.

Christian Mair, a graduate of the University of Innsbruck, Austria, was appointed to a chair in English Linguistics at the University of Freiburg, Germany, in 1990, where his research has focused on the corpus-based description of modern English grammar and variation and ongoing change in standard Englishes worldwide, resulting in the publication of several monographs (among them, with Cambridge University Press, *Twentieth-Century English: History, Variation, and Standardization*, 2006) and more than 100 contributions to scholarly journals and edited works. Several of these have been devoted to the use of Jamaican Creole and Nigerian Pidgin in computer-mediated communication.

Christiane Meierkord holds the chair of English Linguistics at the Ruhr-University of Bochum, Germany, and has previously taught at the universities of Erfurt, Münster, and Stockholm, where she was a visiting professor. She is the author of *Interactions across Englishes: Linguistic Choices in Local and International Contact Situations* (2012) and has published extensively on English as a lingua franca. She has also edited *Ugandan English: Its Sociolinguistics, Structure and Uses in a Globalising Post-Protectorate* (2016), together with Bebwa Isingoma and Saudah Namyalo. Her current research focuses on the forms and functions of English in post-protectorates and on the recent spread of English at the grassroots of societies.

Andrew Moody is Associate Professor of English at the University of Macau, China, where he teaches courses in sociolinguistics and World Englishes. He has also worked and studied in the USA, the People's Republic of China, and Japan. While working in Japan he began investigating the role of English in Japanese popular culture, generally, and, especially, in "J-Pop music." He has published in *World Englishes*, *ELT Journal*, and *English Today* and has contributed essays to several collections focusing on language in the media, popular culture, and World Englishes. He is currently the editor of the journal *English Today* (Cambridge University Press).

Salikoko S. Mufwene is the Frank J. McLoraine Distinguished Service Professor of Linguistics at the University of Chicago, USA, where he also serves on the Committee of Evolutionary Biology. His current research is in evolutionary linguistics, which he approaches from an ecological perspective, focused on the phylogenetic emergence of languages and language speciation, especially the emergence of creoles and other forms of the indigenization of European languages in the colonies, as well as language vitality. His books include *The Ecology of Language Evolution* (Cambridge University Press, 2001), *Language Evolution: Contact, Competition and Change* (2008), and *Iberian Imperialism and Language Evolution in Latin America* (2014). He is the founding editor of the *Cambridge Approaches to Language Contact* series.

Pam Peters is a fellow of the Australian Academy of the Humanities and Emeritus Professor of Macquarie University, Australia. She was a member of the editorial committee of the *Macquarie Dictionary* from 1991 to 2006 and Director of Macquarie University's Dictionary Research Centre (2000–7). She led the compilation of sample corpora for researching Australian English and developed an evidence-based approach to usage description in two major reference works: the *Cambridge Guide to English Usage* (2004) and the *Cambridge Guide to Australian English Usage* (2007). She currently coordinates an international research network on Varieties of English in the Indo-Pacific (VEIP).

Bertus van Rooy has been with the North-West University, South Africa, since April 1999 and has been Professor of English Linguistics since 2007. His current research focuses on grammatical variation and change that result from the influences of English and Afrikaans on each other, alongside a wider interest in varieties of English across the world and the factors that play a role in constraining language change in complex settings, such as bilingual language contact, translation, and online communication. He is a past president of the International Association for World Englishes and deputy president of the Linguistics Society of South Africa.

Melanie Röthlisberger is a senior research and teaching assistant at the English Department, University of Zurich, Switzerland, having gained her PhD at KU Leuven, Belgium, in 2018. Her main research focus is on morphosyntactic and phonological variation and change in World Englishes and dialects of English within the framework of cognitive sociolinguistics. She has published in *Cognitive Linguistics*, *Corpus Linguistics and Linguistic Theory*, *English World-Wide*, and *Glossa* and is currently co-editing a volume on ditransitives in Germanic and a special series on lectometry. She has been actively involved in the compilation of various corpora and has a keen interest in the move toward open science.

Mario Saraceni is a reader in English Language and Linguistics at the University of Portsmouth, United Kingdom. His main research interest is the political and ideological implications of English outside its traditional "cultural base" (i.e. the UK, the USA, etc.). In particular, he is interested in the ways in which English is decolonized, denationalized, renationalized, and transnationalized; in the ways in which it is idealized, fetishized, and criticized; and how all these narratives interface with the lives and the identities of those who use this language. He is also interested in the ways in which English is used translingually and how this invites us to reconceptualize the very notion of "a language."

Among his publications in this area is *World Englishes: A Critical Analysis*, which was awarded the 2016 BAAL Book Prize.

Erik Schleef is Professor of English Linguistics at the University of Salzburg, Austria. His research focuses on variation and change in dialects of the British Isles, the acquisition of variation, sociolinguistics and perception, and language and gender in educational settings. He is co-editor of the *Routledge Sociolinguistics Reader* (2010) and co-author of *Doing Sociolinguistics: A Practical Guide to Data Collection and Analysis* (2015).

Edgar W. Schneider is Chair Professor of English Linguistics at the University of Regensburg, Germany, after previous appointments in Bamberg and Berlin, Germany, and Athens, GA, USA. He has written and edited about twenty books, including the *Handbook of Varieties of English* (2004/2008), *Postcolonial English* (Cambridge University Press, 2007), and *English Around the World* (Cambridge University Press, 2011), and edited the scholarly journal *English World-Wide* for many years. He has published and lectured on all continents on topics in the dialectology, sociolinguistics, history, and semantics of English and its varieties. In World Englishes research he is known widely for his "Dynamic Model" of the evolution of Postcolonial Englishes.

Daniel Schreier is Professor of English Linguistics at the University of Zurich, Switzerland. His research interests include English sociolinguistics, varieties of English around the world, language variation and change, and contact linguistics. He has written several books on English in the South Atlantic, published in international journals such as *English World-Wide*, *Language Variation and Change*, *Diachronica*, *American Speech*, *Journal of Sociolinguistics*, *Language in Society*, and the *Journal of English Linguistics* and contributed chapters to half a dozen handbooks and a dozen edited volumes. From 2013 to 2019, he served as co-editor for *English World-Wide: A Journal of Varieties of English*.

Philip Seargeant is Senior Lecturer in Applied Linguistics at the Open University, UK. He is the author of several books, including *Exploring World Englishes* (2012) and *The Idea of English in Japan* (2009), and is editor of the *Routledge Handbook of English Language Studies* (2018, with Ann Hewings and Stephen Pihlaja), *English in the World* (2012, with Joan Swann), and *English in Japan in the Era of Globalization* (2011).

Benedikt Szmrecsanyi is Associate Professor of linguistics at the Department of Linguistics of KU Leuven, Belgium. His research interests include variation studies (synchronic and diachronic), probabilistic grammar, language complexity, geolinguistics, and dialect typology. Recent books include *Grammatical Variation in British English Dialects* (2013, Cambridge University Press) and *Aggregating Dialectology, Typology, and Register Analysis* (2014, co-edited with Bernhard Wälchli). He has published some thirty papers in international, peer-reviewed journals, including *Language*, *Language Variation and Change*, the *Journal of Linguistic Geography*, the *International Journal of Corpus Linguistics*, and

English World-Wide. He is an associate editor of the journal *Cognitive Linguistics* and is currently directing two Research Foundation Flanders–funded projects.

Lionel Wee is Provost's Chair Professor in the Department of English Language and Literature and Vice-Dean (Research Division) at the Faculty of Arts and Social Sciences at the National University of Singapore. His latest books include *The Singlish Controversy* (Cambridge University Press, 2018) and *Language, Space and Cultural Play: Theorizing Affect in the Semiotic Landscape* (with Robbie Goh, Cambridge University Press, 2019). He is currently working with Nidya Shanthini Manokara and Nora Samosir on *Representing the Female in Staged Performances*, a project that investigates the intersection between gender politics and theatre.

Lena Zipp is a postdoctoral teaching and research associate in the English Department at the University of Zurich, Switzerland. She is a sociolinguist with interests in identity construction in diaspora settings and language attitudes. Her work includes studies on intra-speaker variation, socio-phonetics, lexico-grammar, and World Englishes. She is the author of *Educated Fiji English: Lexico-Grammar and Variety Status* (2014) and is the co-editor of a forthcoming volume on *Research Methods in Language Attitudes.*

1

World Englishes: An Introduction

Daniel Schreier, Marianne Hundt, and Edgar W. Schneider

The field generally labeled *World Englishes* (WEs) is rich and diverse, as research into structural, typological, and sociological aspects of varieties of English around the world has come a long way over the last forty years. The field has moved from the description of individual varieties, general modeling, and an overlap with traditional disciplines such as historical linguistics to highly dynamic topics requiring interdisciplinary approaches: transnationalism, language acquisition, identity formation, indexicality, and the role of new media and cyberspace. The complexity of the WEs paradigm (if indeed it is one single paradigm, a question that will be addressed repeatedly throughout the volume) derives from the fact that there are countless forms of English across the globe. These are difficult to classify: from informal and localized types to formal and supra-regional varieties, from internationally recognized to newly emerging local standards, from language-shift varieties to contact-derived pidgins and creoles, from second-language to learner varieties, and so on. English is now so widely spoken that it truly represents "the language on which the sun never sets." While this has given rise to processes of linguistic diversification that are unparalleled on a global scale, there are also consequences for language hegemony, the overall balance of world languages and local (applied) issues that affect the daily lives of hundreds of millions of speakers: English is the language of a global economy, substantial parts of public discourse, and, for many of its speakers, it provides access to education, wealth, and so on.

The sheer diversity of WEs poses a challenge for attempts to model forms and functions of English as a world language. Traditional (synchronic) models (Kachru 1985; Görlach 1990) have recently been complemented by more dynamic (diachronic) ones (Schneider 2007), where identity (as a postcolonial local construct) is posited as the driving force that operates in a multistep cyclical development. Indeed, the term *Englishes*, once contested but now standard usage, has been adopted to emphasize the diversity of English as a global language with various regional forms

and the decreasing influence of one prestigious variety as an internationally recognized and accepted norm.

A serious academic discussion and a growing awareness of the special
challenges posed by emerging Englishes have developed since the 1980s,
mainly starting with work on Singapore English (Platt and Weber 1980;
Platt, Weber, and Ho 1984; Foley 1988). The exact focus of the very general
term WEs (which has largely replaced the earlier term "New Englishes") is
difficult to pin down, as it comprises various variety types. McArthur
(2003: 56) suggested the label "English Language Complex," which was
fleshed out by Mesthrie and Bhatt (2008: 3–6) into the following typology:

- metropolitan standard varieties (England, USA)
- "colonial" standard varieties in the former British Empire, e.g. in
  Australia, New Zealand, Canada (Extraterritorial Englishes; Lass 1990)
- regional dialects of metropolitan and extraterritorial Englishes (with
  the latter being emergent)
- social dialects of metropolitan and extraterritorial Englishes, i.e. variation across class, ethnicity, gender, etc. (e.g. Cockney, the cline from
  Broad via General to Cultivated accents in Australia and New Zealand,
  African American English, Aboriginal English, Māori English)
- pidgins (restricted linguae francae with limited lexicons and simplified
  morphosyntax, particularly common in, and yet not limited to, the
  equatorial belt, where there was extensive trade and slavery)
- creoles (further refined and elaborated contact-derived systems, often
  with English as a lexifier, and spoken natively)
- English as an institutionalized Second Language (ESL), spoken in bi- and
  multilingual nations where English has an important social or political
  function (in education, commerce, jurisdiction, etc.)
- English as a Foreign Language (EFL), where English is learned as an
  additional language in regions where English has had no historical
  (colonial) roots
- immigrant Englishes resulting from the migration of large numbers of
  people to English-speaking countries (e.g. Chicano English in the USA or
  Polish English in the UK)
- shift varieties of English in communities characterized by high contact,
  bilingualism, and multilingualism (the historical origins of Hiberno
  English)
- unstable jargons or pre-pidgins (with greater individual variation than
  what would be expected in a true pidgin)
- hybrid Englishes, i.e. varieties that emerged in urban centers such as
  Singapore out of code-mixing and that have the potential to develop into
  local markers of identity

This typology can be extended, of course, and it will be shown in this volume
that new forms are constantly emerging (see, e.g., the "grassroots Englishes"
described by Schneider [2016] or multicultural varieties, studied by, e.g.,

Cheshire et al. [2011]). Attempts to model such astounding heterogeneity received the first major boost by Braj B. Kachru's (1985) suggestion that English(es) can be grouped into three concentric circles: an *Inner Circle*, i.e. countries of historical continuity which in a sense represent the traditional bases of English (the UK, the USA, Australia, etc.), where the language is spoken natively by the majority of speakers (English as a Native Language, or ENL); the *Outer Circle*, which includes countries where English is important for historical reasons and where it is spoken mostly as a second language (e.g. as the legacy of political expansion or colonization by the British Empire) and where it plays a part in the nation's institutions (ESL countries include India, Nigeria, Pakistan, Kenya, Singapore, etc.); and, finally, the *Expanding Circle*, in which we find those countries where English plays no historical or governmental role but where it is widely used as a foreign language or lingua franca (EFL countries such as China, Russia, Japan, much of continental Europe). Speaker numbers are notoriously difficult to estimate for obvious reasons (lack of population statistics in many countries, especially on multilingualism and language usage; unclear definitions of proficiency levels as a yardstick), but recent estimates quote ca. 350–400 million native speakers, ca. 600–800 million ESL speakers, and between 500 million and perhaps 1.5 billion or more EFL speakers and learners (Crystal 2008; Schneider 2011: 56).

Though Kachru's model was by far the most influential approach, a number of problems have been identified and these have given rise to extensive discussions in the literature (for an overview, see Buschfeld and Kautzsch, Chapter 3, this volume, or Mesthrie and Bhatt 2008). For one, the concentric model is static rather than dynamic (not leaving much room for transition from one circle to the other); based on geography, nation-states, history, and ancestry rather than on perceptions of identity or shared linguistic features; and also struggles to account for linguistic diversity within individual varieties. The model also triggered rather emotional debates on issues of norm orientation. Kachru (1985) called the Inner Circle (UK, USA, Australia, New Zealand) "norm-providing," the Outer Circle "norm-developing," and the Expanding Circle "norm-dependent," thus relying on standards set by native speakers. Regional, social, and ethnic diversity, for example within South Africa, also contributes to blurring the lines and makes it difficult to assign many nations to specific variety types.

Schneider (2007) builds on all these criteria in his Dynamic Model of the evolution of postcolonial Englishes (PCEs). His main point is that, notwithstanding the fact that English develops in heterogeneous multilingual contexts around the world and despite all evident differences, a fundamentally uniform developmental process, shaped by consistent sociolinguistic and language-contact conditions, has operated in the individual instances of relocating and re-rooting the English language in another territory. This makes it possible to present individual histories of PCEs as manifestations of the same underlying process (Schneider

2007: 5). Each stage sees characteristic features and developments as caused by specific parameters: extralinguistic history determines identity definitions of the groups involved, which shapes their sociolinguistic conditions of interaction, and these, in turn, ultimately influence the structural properties of an emerging variety. Schneider's Dynamic Model has been widely discussed, frequently adopted, and largely accepted; for example, Seoane (in Seoane and Suárez-Gómez 2016: 4) stated that this "groundbreaking model fundamentally changed the way we approach World Englishes" (cf. Buschfeld et al. 2014; for some stocktaking and an overview of applications and discussions, see Schneider 2014). It is explicitly geared toward postcolonial varieties, however, and seems less suitable for an application to the expanding circle (cf. Schneider 2014) – though this has also been attempted (e.g. Ike 2012 on Japan).

Lately, the dynamism of the extension of WEs has reached out to new domains – a process that Schneider (2014) labeled "transnational attraction." For instance, a recent research trend has strongly questioned the strict distinction between ESL (or "Outer circle") and EFL (or "Expanding circle"), which seems much more a continuum than a dichotomy (see the papers and discussion in Mukherjee and Hundt 2011 or Davydova 2012). It has been shown that ESL countries can lose this status, as in the case of Cyprus (Buschfeld 2013), or that EFL countries can adopt properties which seem very close to ESL varieties, as in the Netherlands (Edwards 2016) or Namibia, which remarkably, at independence in 1990, established English as its sole national language despite the lack of a colonial past or much sociolinguistic backing (Buschfeld and Kautzsch 2014).

Buschfeld and Kautzsch (2017) reacted to this situation by proposing a new model, which is viewed as an expansion of the Dynamic Model and emphasizes the effect of "extra- and intra-territorial forces" in the emergence of both ESL and EFL varieties. Some innovative theorizing has questioned the earlier focus on English in specific nation-states, partly through the increasing importance of the Internet; Seargeant and Tagg (2011), for example, have suggested a "post-varieties approach" to the understanding of the current variability of global English. In a similar vein, Mair (2013) proposes a new hierarchy of global Englishes (with American English as the only "hypercentral" hub) and looks into the transnational dissemination of some varieties in cyberspace. Buschfeld and Schneider (2017) provide a comprehensive account of the history and current state of WEs theorizing (see also Buschfeld and Kautzsch, Chapter 3, this volume).

Early accounts of individual varieties of WEs used to be based on an author's intimate familiarity with the variety in question and tended to document and illustrate a selection of distinctive linguistic feature lists. Many broad sociohistorical accounts have followed suit, documenting the transportation of English to specific locales and the resultant sociolinguistic settings, often in multilingual communities. The majority of these studies are based on fieldwork on location, that is, systematic collections

of speech data. At the same time, a strictly sociolinguistic "language variation and change" paradigm, strongly employing quantitative techniques
in the post-Labovian tradition, has been growing, though it tends to mainly
focus on ENL countries. For example, the 1990s and after saw a strong wave
of quantitative sociolinguistic work in New Zealand (e.g. Holmes and Bell
1990); there has been some work in this tradition in Australia (notably
Horvath 1985) and South Africa (Wilmot 2014) – but, generally speaking,
this remains a research desideratum for most ESL countries (for
a programmatic outline of such research, see Sharma 2017).

For the last two decades, the field of WEs has received a major boost by its
association with corpus linguistics. A wide range of large-scale electronic text
collections representing individual national varieties of English and different
styles and genres is now readily available (see Hundt, Chapter 22, this volume)
and can be analyzed by means of specially designed software (e.g. the free-
ware program AntConc). Originally, this is to be credited to the vision of
Sidney Greenbaum, who originated the *International Corpus of English* (ICE)
project (Greenbaum 1996). Individual ICE corpora consist of one million
words of text from a given nation, sampled along the same lines. Notably,
60 percent of the data are transcripts of speech, which gives these corpora
a high degree of authenticity despite their focus on educated speech.
Subsequently, the work of Mark Davies of Brigham Young University (Utah)
has boosted the magnitude of corpora which represent WEs. He has culled
huge corpora automatically from the Internet, tremendous in size though
more restricted in representativeness as far as text types are concerned. Cases
in point are the *Global Web-Based English* (GloWbE) corpus with 1.9 billion
words and the *News on the Web* (NOW) corpus, which is a monitor corpus,
that is, it keeps growing every day and by now has reached almost 7 billion
words – both sampling data from twenty different nations.

For this particular handbook, we opted for a selection of what we regard
as important "must-have chapters" plus several chapters that address
recent developments and introduce innovative perspectives, partly touch-
ing on neighboring fields. Most notably, the former include a thorough
coverage of the expansion of English from its heartland in the British Isles
to the "New World" and the entire globe, first within the British Isles, then
across the North Atlantic into the Caribbean and North America, and,
finally, into Asia, Africa, and the Southern Hemisphere, including the
Pacific region. The common denominator to many (if not all) of the regionally oriented chapters is that a diachronic approach is quintessential to
retrace the historical dimension of English as a global language and to
understand why the different Englishes carry the ideological weight or
have a particular function in a now globalized world – or, quite simply,
why WEs are the way they are and how they have come to be so. We follow
the regional expansion step-by-step and use historical evolution as
a baseline for further explorations in other research fields, which in our
view have great potential and might develop into new hotspots or even

new subdisciplines. At the same time, we give room to important over-arching questions relating to the consequences of colonization and economic globalization via population movements and language contacts (cf. language shift in favor of an economically and politically dominant language), the survival of stigmatized forms, and immigrants' varieties whose present-day migration patterns are rapidly changing social and linguistic landscapes around the world, affecting the current role of English as a global language as well. Population structure(s) may produce various kinds of boundaries between the coexistent languages, through ethnic or religious segregation for instance, although we will see that such divisions are usually far from clear-cut.

As a reflection of the evolution of a vast and quickly diversifying research area, *The Cambridge Handbook of World Englishes* has been conceived to cover the state of the art of four decades' research on various issues related to English as a world language while at the same time inviting readers to critically assess what we perceive to be some of the most topical issues and research questions for the near future. It is not our intention to integrate all traditional fields here, as there is neither scope nor space (nor indeed need) for this; instead, we focus on some selected research areas, so some important and current topics (e.g. language contact involving English and other languages) are addressed from different and complementary perspectives, simply to show how densely connected and inter-disciplinary the field has become as the body of research has grown. Perhaps the principal aim of the handbook is to show how various disciplines are merging and intersecting in the broad field of WEs research, from the historical development of the language into multiple localized varieties to the relevance for linguistic disciplines such as historical linguistics, lexicography, or contact linguistics but also in terms of social applications, political thinking, media reflections, and the like.

The volume thus offers a comprehensive view of various fields, recent achievements, and current developments in the quickly expanding and highly productive area of WEs. In addition to the general introduction, it consists of twenty-eight chapters, all written by internationally acclaimed authorities, providing up-to-date discussions of timely and relevant themes. They place special focus on the analysis and contextualization of Englishes from theoretical and also methodological perspectives, thereby contributing to the appreciation and in-depth understanding of English as a global language. The handbook thus covers the major domains of contemporary research on WEs, including the history of individual varieties, the contact-based evolution of WEs, areal expansion and diffusion patterns, the formation of local extraterritorial forms, areal typology, and the function of English from a transnational perspective.

Part I, "The making of Englishes," consists of five contributions, each dealing with a general aspect of the role and function of English around the world. The expansion of English, the presentation and critical evaluation of theoretical models, and the contribution of language contact to the emergence of WEs are central concerns, along with the impact of sociodemographics, population structures, migration and language change in the diaspora, and ethnolectalization in super-diverse urban areas.

In Chapter 2, "The Colonial and Postcolonial Expansion of English," Raymond Hickey details the most crucial process as to why English has become a world language: its spread beyond the British Isles into various "new Worlds" between the early seventeenth and the early twentieth centuries. In several settlement waves, the colonists (who were by no means a homogeneous group) took various forms of English (mainly from England, Scotland, and Ireland) to the newly established colonies on all continents. Hickey shows that dialect transportation was diachronically layered over roughly three centuries, with the northern half of the globe being settled from approximately 1600 onward and the southern half from around 1800. With reference to a framework of dialect contact and principles of koinéization, Hickey shows the linguistic consequences of regional origins and layers of colonization for the shaping of varieties of English in overseas locations, for instance that non-rhoticity in Southern Hemisphere Englishes can be accounted for by relatively late settlement and ongoing change in the British Isles. With the end of the colonial period and de facto independence of nearly all the larger English-speaking countries, new developments affected both the continuation of settler English and the emergence of new second-language varieties. Hickey concentrates on the dialect-contact origins of varieties around the world and analyzes them within a framework of emerging varieties derived (but geographically separated from) their ancestral varieties in the British Isles.

In Chapter 3, "Theoretical Models of English as a World Language," Sarah Buschfeld and Alexander Kautzsch provide a critical assessment of various models and their implications for a classification of Englishes around the world. A range of theoretical frameworks and models have been developed and proposed to understand comparable types and developments of the different Englishes that have developed in virtually every corner of the world and to grasp similarities between forms and functions of native-language, second-language, and foreign-language varieties. Adopting a perspective which respects the evolution of subsequent, perhaps increasingly sophisticated frameworks within the field and distinguishing early static models from a later "diachronic turn," the chapter sketches major developments and theoretical trends in WEs research. It provides an overview and critical account of the most influential models of English as a world language, including the ENL/ESL/EFL distinction, Kachru's (1985), McArthur's (1987), and Görlach's (1990) circles, Gupta's (1997), Mesthrie and Bhatt's (2008), and Mair's (2013) classifications, as well as the diachronic approaches proposed by Moag (1992) and Schneider (2003, 2007). Moreover, Buschfeld and Kautzsch discuss some more recent developments, that is, they call for a more flexible handling of ostensibly clear-cut categories (e.g. ENL vs. ESL vs. EFL) and a stronger consideration of the Expanding Circle/EFL varieties; and they advocate an integrated theoretical approach to second-language and learner varieties of English. They argue that there is a need to develop more nuanced models to cope with the complex realities of speakers in a globally mobile and increasingly transnational world, notably the Extra- and Intra-territorial Forces Model (Buschfeld and Kautzsch 2017) and the notion of Transnational Attraction (Schneider 2014).

Chapter 4, "The Contribution of Language Contact to the Emergence of World Englishes," authored by Lisa Lim, focuses on contact-induced language change by discussing the contribution of language contact between English and other languages on local processes of transformation, transfer, and change. Lim shows that the emergence of WEs is a direct consequence of contact between communities and their language varieties, as the earlier spread of English, in the exploitation colonies of Asia and Africa in particular, entailed contact with numerous, typologically diverse, languages over some four centuries of British/American colonization. The local populations adopted English historically as a second language through education or via lingua franca use in trade situations, so this is presented as a major criterion in ongoing diversification processes. The Englishes that have evolved in all these locales thus reveal the social history of communities in contact alongside the structural peculiarities of linguistic systems that contributed to their emergence, which means that researchers need to focus on contact linguistic mechanisms by combining external and internal foci. With special focus on the Asian century, Lim highlights newly emerging dynamics in the era of globalization, such as computer-mediated communication, the global new economy, and popular culture, which, in turn, involve new roles of New Englishes and their speakers.

In Chapter 5, "Population Structure and the Emergence of World Englishes," Salikoko S. Mufwene highlights the notion of "population structure" to explain the ecologies of the global diffusion of English, the spread of innovations, and the evolution of new varieties of English. He sketches the colonization of the world by the English since the seventeenth century, beginning with the colonization of Ireland, and considers sociopolitical processes like industrialization and urbanization as crucial factors. In North America and the Caribbean, he traces the unintended consequences of varying colonization styles implemented there. Economic and cultural practices explain differences in the evolutionary trajectories between African American and European American dialects in the overall evolution of varieties of American English. In a similar vein, he considers the development of Australian English, including Aboriginal English, and of Southwest Pacific as well as West African pidgins, all of which ultimately were shaped by the socioeconomic and communicative conditions determined by their respective population structures. Exploitation colonies produced postcolonial (or "Outer Circle") varieties, with local population majorities and a significant impact of indigenous languages. Mufwene thus emphasizes that sociohistorical and language-ecological factors have been crucial in the differential evolution of Englishes around the world.

In Chapter 6, "World Englishes, Migration, and Diaspora," Lena Zipp focuses on the consequences of modern-day migration patterns for the emergence of new forms or types of WEs in the diaspora, a concept that has found renewed currency in sociological and sociolinguistic scholarship in the last two decades. Zipp advocates the addition of different analytic perspectives to WEs research, pushing the boundaries of the discipline toward a constructivist rather than an essentialist perspective, and toward foregoing static categories (such as "varieties") in favor of more fluid concepts ("diaspora as practice"). She uses third-wave variationist sociolinguistics as a baseline to address issues related to the creation and re-creation of identities through language practices: emerging forms of language mixing or hybridization with identity construction, the role of the immigrant generation in the flexible usage of ethnolinguistic repertoires, linguistic correlates of the factors of *homeland orientation* and *boundary maintenance* in secondary diaspora situations, and the overall contribution of multi-ethnic varieties of English to the WEs canon.

Part II, "World Englishes Old and New," consists of six contributions altogether, each dealing with one particular world region, highlighting sociohistorical evolution processes and current social or medial settings of WEs. Combined, these chapters offer a comprehensive outline of the history of English and provide an overview of the exportation of English within the British Isles into the New World and around the globe (North America, Caribbean, Africa, South and Southeast Asia as well as the Southern Hemisphere), thus complementing the chapters in Part I from the perspective of external language history.

In Chapter 7, "A Sociolinguistic Ecology of Colonial Britain," David Britain looks at what might be referred to as the "prehistory" of English as a world language: the sociolinguistic context of England and English society around 1600. His focus is not on the migrants or their linguistic profiles per se but on the social and linguistic ecology of Britain at the time when colonization and out-migration began as a concerted enterprise, so this chapter provides the sociohistorical backbone for an understanding of the linguistic and sociolinguistic processes that occurred in overseas settings. Britain concentrates on four aspects in particular: multilingualism and multidialectalism; social and geographical mobility and its causes; education, schooling, and literacy (including some reflections on ongoing standardization and language ideologies); and the role of social "identities" in British society at the time. The chapter characterizes the cultural and sociolinguistic baggage the migrants took with them to the New

World while also highlighting the cultural burdens, societal division, and emotional disruption from which the colonists would have wished to distance themselves during their colonial experiences.

In Chapter 8, "English in North America," Merja Kytö provides a detailed account of the evolution of US and Canadian English as well as African American English as an example of an ethnolect, drawing on previous research in dialectology, historical sociolinguistics, and corpus-based studies. Starting with a review of the sociohistorical background of North American Englishes, she critically discusses available evidence on the evolution of US, Canadian, and African American English and gives an overview of characteristic features of the varieties with respect to accent, morphosyntax, and vocabulary. Even though North American varieties of English are among the best-documented and most widely researched WEs, there is still considerable scope for further research, as Kytö points out in her conclusion.

Chapter 9, "English in the Caribbean and the Central American Rim," authored by Michael Aceto, shifts the geographical focus by discussing the emergence of "newer" (i.e. in the last 400 years or less) varieties of English spoken in the Caribbean and in Central America, focusing on a description of geographical locations and the social contexts in which they emerged and where they are now used. Aceto provides a short discussion of the sociolinguistic influences that have shaped contact-derived varieties and critically assesses some of the popular heuristics suggested for understanding the emergence of these same varieties. The chapter is complemented by a morphosyntactic profile of similarities and differences among specific varieties, which is both a description of varieties that have received less attention in the WEs canon and an illustration of the research potential for the field of contact linguistics and dialect typology.

In Chapter 10, "English in Africa," Bertus van Rooy explains how English came to Africa through the slave trade, exploitation colonization, and limited settlement colonization. After political independence, English continues to play a major role in the vast majority of former British colonies, where a majority of non-native African teachers of English are key role players in transmitting English to new users rather than native speakers. English shares its place in these linguistic ecologies with many other languages, which means that there has been a long-standing tradition of multilingualism in Africa. Van Rooy's chapter goes on to examine the history of transmission and diffusion of English in order to account for its present-day position and diversity. The chapter pays special attention to available linguistic descriptions and discusses new evidence from corpora, identifying patterns of correspondence and divergence among varieties within regions and countries. It also accounts for these patterns in terms of social history, contact, substrate languages, and processes of teaching and learning that all have contributed to the present state, exemplifying the processes at hand with in-depth discussions of various settings throughout the continent.

Chapter 11, "English in South Asia," contributed by Claudia Lange, shows how the English language has developed from a contested colonial legacy into an asset. The chapter defines the notion of South Asia and surveys the nation-states of the region, including its cultural and linguistic background, and then traces the historical development of English in the area from the beginning of British colonialism to the present day, with a main focus on English in India as the largest and most important nation-state to emerge on the subcontinent. Distinctive features of Indian English are outlined as opposed to those of Sri Lanka and other South Asian varieties. On that basis, the theoretically important notion is developed that Indian English has grown into the role of a regional epicenter in South Asia.

The course of English has taken a slightly different trajectory in Southeast Asia, and this provides complementary insights into the changing status and properties of English in this region. In Chapter 12, consequently, Lionel Wee focuses on four settings primarily: Singapore, Malaysia, the Philippines, and Thailand. His aim is to detail how local settings contributed to the emergence of indigenized varieties there, sketching out and comparing parallels and differences with reference to the wider Asian region generally. The chapter describes the sociolinguistic development of Englishes in various settings while also including recent processes that are a by-product of human traffic, the economy, and globalization: neoliberalism, migration, and commodification.

In Chapter 13, "World Englishes Old and New: English in Australasia and the South Pacific," Caroline Biewer and Kate Burridge cover a broad and diverse range of native and non-native varieties of English. They take as their starting point a critical discussion and redefinition of the notion of "areal feature" and survey arguments that speak in favor and those that speak against the existence of areal features in Australasia and the South Pacific (AuSP). Against this theoretical backdrop, they discuss three scenarios for the emergence of areal features in AuSP in more detail: (1) parallel developments in Australian and New Zealand English; (2) influence of settler varieties and outcomes of language contact in the region; and (3) similarities in the substrate languages and linguistic ecologies in the development of AuSP pidgins and creoles, illustrating each with examples on all linguistic levels from varieties such as Australian and New Zealand English, Māori English, and Tok Pisin. While they concede that "[g]enuine pan-AuSP features are hard to locate" (p. 301), their critical and comprehensive survey of regional varieties against this theoretical backdrop provides an interesting starting point for further research.

The eleven contributions in Part III, "Linguistics and World Englishes," focus on the contribution of WEs for various linguistic disciplines, with the aim of providing a detailed range of theoretical and methodological aspects involved in the application of WEs to linguistic research: the global grassroots growth of English, the persistence and local innovation of

dialect roots, methodological aspects underlying research on the diachrony of WEs, the general relevance of WEs for and their coverage in
lexicography, and relationships with neighboring disciplines such as multilingualism, variationist sociolinguistics, and language acquisition.
Moreover, Part III deals with the transition of Englishes between second-
language and foreign-language status and with English in cyberspace, and
it critically evaluates corpus-linguistic or dialect-typological methods
employed in researching WEs.

Chapter 14, "The Global Growth of English at the Grassroots," by
Christiane Meierkord, moves away from the conventional focus of the
field on educated speakers, individuals with secondary education, and
members of social elites to a recognition of an increasingly important
proportion of today's users of English (especially in postcolonial societies),
namely those who have acquired English with limited or no access to
formal instruction in the language. She looks into how grassroots emergence and diffusion have been growing in a wide range of contexts,
regions, and varieties, associating these with characteristic occupations
and settings that require some degree of expressive capacity in English
without access to formal education (but driven by high motivation). The
survey is supported by interesting figures on proficiency levels in different
countries and regions. "Englishes at the grassroots" are then illustrated,
drawing on examples from informal traders in Uganda, domestic workers
in Hong Kong, refugees in Europe, and informal eateries in Uganda and the
Maldives. Further aspects covered include interactions of Englishes at the
grassroots level and grassroots literacy (e.g. in linguistic landscapes). In
conclusion, the chapter critically assesses and shows how these so far
underrepresented varieties can be included in current models of English,
thus opening a fresh and important perspective on the discipline.

Chapter 15, "Beyond English as a Second or Foreign Language: Local Uses
and the Cultural Politics of Identification," by Alison Edwards and Philip
Seargeant, reacts to and further develops a strong trend in recent research,
motivated by the recognition that it is becoming increasingly difficult in
many contexts to neatly distinguish between ESL and EFL countries.
Consequently, the authors advocate a shift away from highlighting territorial varieties toward a sociocultural and ethnographic orientation. They
draw observations and case studies from Japan and the Netherlands, two
putatively "Expanding Circle" countries in which, however, English has
been gaining ground substantially in the recent past. Starting out from
sociolinguistic sketches of the functions and settings of current English in
these two countries and drawing on media examples from there, they
argue that English is seen as a flexible and creative mobile resource,
available for transcultural processes and practices and thus transcending
a neatly variety-based line of thinking. English is thus seen as a vehicle for
the enactment of localized but also transnational identities and for one's
own self-positioning.

Research on English as a commodity for communication on the Internet is a relatively recent field in WEs research. In Chapter 16, "World Englishes in Cyberspace," Christian Mair provides a state-of-the-art review of previous studies, within both more traditional discourse-analytical and recent sociolinguistic approaches, as well as research that straddles this distinction. He defines the scope of the field and uses two case studies, one on the prestige associated with nonstandard Englishes in computer-mediated communication (CMC) and one on multilingual practices in CMC. In the final section, these case studies are brought together in a discussion of the sociolinguistics of WEs as used on the World Wide Web, notably with respect to the notion of *languagescape* (Appadurai 1996), which Mair uses to single out existing biases in previous studies of WEs. The chapter closes with suggestions on how the notion of *languagescape(s)* could be fruitfully exploited in future research into WEs in cyberspace.

Chapter 17, "World Englishes and Their Dialect Roots," focuses on English historical linguistics and the role of dialect contact in particular. Daniel Schreier retraces how WEs gradually developed out of Englishes spoken throughout the British Isles. Dialects were transported all over the globe by speakers from different regions, social classes, and educational backgrounds, who migrated with distinct trajectories, for various periods of time, and in distinct chronological phases. It was these founder varieties that laid the foundation for emerging offspring varieties; some features either remained in more or less robust form or underwent far-reaching structural and systemic change under local linguistic-ecological contact conditions. Schreier traces some selected dialect roots of New Englishes, that is, features that can be retraced to regional dialects of the British Isles, what Hickey (2004: 1) has called "dialect input and the survival of features from a mainland source or sources." These "roots of English" (Tagliamonte 2012) are of equal importance for regionally confined contact scenarios (i.e. WEs in specific locales) and the widespread appearance of what Chambers (2009: 258) calls "vernacular roots." They are central to any reconstruction of the evolutionary formation of WEs in that they allow for an assessment of input strength and the impact of contact-induced mechanisms. Diffusion and feature adoption processes are exemplified with case studies from Newfoundland, the US Atlantic States, and the Caribbean.

While traditional lexicography has largely focused on mainstream "Inner Circle" varieties of English, in Chapter 18, "Lexicography and World Englishes," James Lambert redirects our attention and systematically covers and documents lexicographic efforts to collect and describe the vocabularies of new varieties of English in ESL and other countries. He starts out with a thorough survey of conceptual and methodological basics in lexicography, considering fundamental properties, subtypes, methodological issues, and user perspectives of dictionaries. The main part then consists of a first-time comprehensive survey of available dictionaries and glossaries that cover the English lexis in specific varieties, regions, and nation-states, with descriptive and characterizing annotations. For anybody interested in the lexicography of WEs, this chapter provides a wealth of information, documentation, and detail.

In Chapter 19, "The Relevance of World Englishes for Variationist Sociolinguistics," Alexandra D'Arcy shows the overlap of WEs research with variationist sociolinguistics and historical linguistics, arguing that many of the changes have operated diachronically but were, by necessity, reflected in synchronic grammars of individual varieties (D'Arcy 2015). The worldwide spread of English offers new research perspectives for variation and change processes, and these are demonstrated here with reference to external language history (e.g. patterns of colonization, stratification, contact and interaction) on both local and global scales. D'Arcy suggests that WEs ideally lend themselves to the scrutiny of central issues in sociolinguistic theory – the adoption, survival, and modification of inherited features and diffusion and innovation processes, to name but two – and shows how a study of WEs can be applied to language variation and change mechanisms, both as contact-induced and as structure-specific processes through an application of the comparative method (Tagliamonte 2002). The processes at hand are illustrated with case studies on individual features in WEs (e.g. quotative *like*) while special attention is given to non-native speakers and lingua franca varieties.

Since the foundations of English were laid in the British Isles, English has *always* existed within a context of multilingualism, a fact that is often overlooked in any discussion of global English or the "spread" of English. In Chapter 20, "Multilingualism and the World Englishes," Sue Fox shows the sociolinguistic consequences of the fact that English has continued to become more important in countries that have no links to a colonial history or where it has no official function. It is in these countries, she shows, that many speakers have acquired or are acquiring English for use as a lingua franca for communicating with people from many different linguistic backgrounds. English is often used within an individual's multilingual repertoire and tends to be modeled on one of the world's "standard" varieties, usually British or, increasingly, American English. Fox provides an overview of the way in which English has existed within a framework of multilingualism in different contexts. Drawing on Kachru's (1992) terms, she considers multilingualism in Inner, Outer, and Expanding Circle countries. Special focus is given to the British Isles, where the myth of English monolingualism probably persists most strongly. The chapter considers both historical and modern-day multilingualism within the British Isles and shows how multilingualism, as a consequence of the immigration of speakers from postcolonial contexts, has an impact on the English variety spoken in London.

The growing interest in the WEs paradigm has given rise to a rapidly increasing number of synchronic studies, yet diachronic investigations are still the exception. In Chapter 21, "Unearthing the Diachrony of World Englishes," Magnus Huber provides some attempts to unearth the structural history of New Englishes based on written and spoken data. His emphasis is on national standard varieties of English but reference is also made to the diachronic study of pidgin and creole Englishes, which started earlier, raising methodological and practical issues that are also relevant for New Englishes. Though some progress has been made with regard to the investigation of the development of a number of Inner Circle (mother tongue) varieties, Outer Circle (second language, or L2) varieties have not received much attention. One main reason for the lack of studies on the structural evolution of these varieties is that, in many cases, authentic historical language data are either nonexistent or have not yet been accessed by linguists. Huber locates and discusses the compilation of historical corpora and identifies sources that can be used to further our understanding of the diachrony of Outer Circle Englishes.

In Chapter 22, "Corpus-Based Approaches to World Englishes," Marianne Hundt traces the main developments in corpus-linguistic research from a WEs perspective, critically discussing methodological issues such as corpus size, sampling, and representativeness, and tracing the changing focus from metropolitan to PCEs and learner Englishes. The chapter also provides an overview of the various applications of corpora in WEs research, be it for theoretical or statistical modeling or as a testing bed for hypotheses concerning language contact and morpho-syntactic, sociolinguistic, or pragmatic variation, citing representative case studies for each area. Another section on corpus-based research into recent and diachronic change complements Huber's chapter: It looks at different approaches to the corpus-based study of change in WEs (apparent- vs. real-time, brachychronic vs. diachronic), surveys existing corpus resources, and provides an overview of the state of the art in the field on the basis of seminal studies in this subfield of corpus linguistics. The chapter concludes by pointing out lacunae in corpus-based research of WEs and the resources that would be necessary to fill these gaps.

In Chapter 23, Benedikt Szmrecsanyi and Melanie Röthlisberger approach "World Englishes from the Perspective of Dialect Typology." They look into language-internal factors that are used to distinguish different WEs (i.e. variety type, areality, and contact) and critically discuss different kinds of universals (ranging from genuine universals via areovensals to varioversals) and their usefulness for a dialect typology of WEs before moving on to parameters of structural diversity (i.e. parameters such as analyticity vs. syntheticity and complexity vs. simplicity). For each perspective, Szmrecsanyi and Röthlisberger show how the concepts have been used in empirical research, thus providing a survey of relevant and cutting-edge methodologies (such as NeighborNet clustering or Multiple

Correspondence Analysis) in the field. They conclude by pointing toward neighboring disciplines (in particular corpus-based statistical modeling of variation and language sociology) that could be brought to bear on research into dialect typology in the future.

Second-language and foreign-language WEs are ultimately products of second-language acquisition and sometimes language shift on a community basis. Fundamentally, thus, there should be an intrinsic relationship between the disciplines of language acquisition and WEs but, in practice, the methodologies and results of both branches are largely unrelated and unaware of each other – a fact that early research already identified as a "paradigm gap" (Sridhar and Sridhar 1986: 3). In Chapter 24, "Language Acquisition and World Englishes," Sarah Buschfeld sets out to bridge this gap and to work out similarities and relationships between both approaches, bringing in first-language acquisition as well and arguing that all these branches should work together closely to gain a better understanding of the phenomena in question. She briefly surveys earlier work in WEs, language acquisition, and learner Englishes, highlighting components that should be of interest for all these approaches. Based on some earlier contributions and on case studies (comparing English in Cyprus, a putative second-language setting, and Greece, a foreign-language context, or English in Singapore, Malaysia, and Indonesia where the language coexists with Malay in systematically differing relationships, for instance), she argues that there is no reason to posit ESL and EFL as fundamentally distinct variety types when considering and comparing contact and acquisitional settings and their outcomes. This perspective is then expanded to integrate also ENL contexts, based on research on the first-language acquisition of English by children in Singapore. Buschfeld's argument that these contexts should be regarded as a continuum rather than as distinct variety types and that sociolinguistic WEs approaches and psycholinguistic work in language acquisition need to collaborate more effectively and will strongly profit from such a collaboration constitutes an important theoretical advancement in the field.

Finally, Part IV, "Current Challenges," is dedicated to issues that we believe are contemporary hotspots in WEs research and which promise to be important and fruitful avenues for future exploration. The five chapters here deal with the questions of what the norms are for different WEs and by which processes new standards emerge, how WEs are subject to identity construction and indexicality, and also what role they play in language politics, the media, and transnationalism in a globalizing world.

In Chapter 25, "Norms and Standards in World Englishes," Pam Peters lays the conceptual basis by reviewing the linguistic issues inherent in the concepts of "norm" and "standard," distinguishing between language and usage norms as well as between different perspectives on standardization, including the evolution of new regional standards in a globalizing language. Having provided workable operationalizations of the core concepts, she uses two case studies to illustrate how theoretical modeling of WEs (in particular the notion of evolutionary stages from Schneider 2003, 2007) can be brought together with empirical (corpus- and survey-based) research into local norms of usage. In addition, available metalinguistic evidence is used to validate corpus- and survey-based results. Taken together, Peters convincingly argues, the different kinds of evidence allow us to assess the emergence of endonormativity in evolving WEs.

Identity construction is a key concept in WEs, as well as (but not only) in Schneider's evolutionary model. At the same time, it is a theoretically and empirically elusive concept. The aim of Chapter 26, "Identity and Indexicality in the Study of World Englishes," by Erik Schleef, is to provide a sound theoretical basis for the study of identity in WEs research and thus furnishes scholars of WEs interested in the concept of identity with an overview of the different ways that sociolinguistic variationist research has defined and applied the notion of "identity" (i.e. the move from macro-sociological to local definitions and a shift from quantitative to more qualitative research). Schleef also reviews previous research into WEs that has made use of the different perspectives on identity construction, critically discussing the choice of variables that has been used to tap into identity work in WEs. Schleef argues that indexicality theory is best suited to address the question of how linguistic usage and identity construction are connected and that the micro and macro level of variation need to be integrated in research by taking the meso and macro level of social structure into account. He also argues that evidence for the study of identity construction has to come from both usage and perception data.

Chapter 27, "The Politics of World Englishes," by Mario Saraceni, highlights the inherently and unavoidably political character of language practice in general and discussions of WEs in particular. Language usage is directly associated with questions of supremacy and power relationships (as is shown by a discussion of the fears of jeopardizing the purity of English by immigrants), and the same applies to the global diffusion of English to new territories, of course. As Saraceni shows, the legitimacy of new varieties of English has also been questioned in settler colonies (e.g. in Australia) and even more so in exploitation colonies in Africa and Asia. WEs as a research paradigm has always embraced an explicitly egalitarian stance, and the chapter discusses the political debates that have resulted from this attitude. Alternatively, the claim of "linguistic imperialism" has blamed global English as being essentially a tool in a neoliberal, capitalist agenda of perpetuating linguistic as well as sociopolitical inequalities. Saraceni navigates a reasonable intermediate position between these claims and concepts, questioning some aspects of the discourses on the political legitimacy of varieties of English. Like others in this handbook, he implicitly calls for viewing English not as a national property (which unavoidably introduces inequalities) but as a fluid set of semiotic resources available in a wide range of transnational contexts. He makes readers aware of the fact that inequalities and power imbalances need to be considered, however, when discussing WEs and the global functions of the language.

In Chapter 28, "World Englishes in the Media," Andrew Moody examines fundamental issues as well as a range of studies of media language conducted from a WEs perspective. He demonstrates that the examination of media Englishes has become a staple component of descriptions of WEs, listing many examples from different countries and contexts. As such, the chapter questions the validity of claims that some types of language usage (and, by implication, data in general) are "authentic" whereas others are not. The chapter shows that "authenticity" is often considered a characteristic feature of media Englishes that must be carefully balanced against the "authority" of the standard language. Within this framework of thinking, the Inner, Outer, and Expanding Circles of WEs show consistently different patterns of balancing concerns for "authenticity" and "authority" in media Englishes, an observation that is substantiated by case studies from different varieties. Moody thus thoroughly documents the important role that both media language in itself and its investigation and interpretation play in the context of WEs research.

Finally, in Chapter 29, Brook Bolander looks at "World Englishes and Transnationalism." She briefly traces the history of the concept to its current popularity in sociology and its adoption by sociolinguists, and provides a clear definition of the notion vis-à-vis related concepts such as globalization and across different disciplinary appropriations of the term (i.e. in anthropology, sociology, political science, and cultural studies). Bolander argues that transnationalism serves as an important concept to counter approaches that unduly focus on nation-states, borders, and centers, thus stressing that it has relevance beyond theory-building for methodological approaches in sociolinguistics, including research into WEs. Her survey of sociolinguistic studies, specifically on English, that have been informed by discussions about transnationalism includes studies with a metatheoretical focus, ethnographic research, investigation of migration and subjectivity, digital communication as a translocal space, and sociolinguistic investigation of language commodification. Importantly, as the author points out, transnationalism "should not deter from World Englishes research in national contexts. It should rather prompt for the concurrent problematizing of the nation as an ideological and historical construct in its own right, in connection with a focus on how localized and localizing uses and ideologies of English become pertinent to the enactment of transnationalism" (p. 695).

All in all, this handbook is intended to be a reference guide, a complete state-of-the-art overview and coherent picture of key findings (present and past) and theoretical ideas that jointly have created the dynamic and vibrant research field of WEs, seasoned with innovative ideas that will direct the future of the discipline. The sections are complementary and interlocking. We have done our best to minimize overlap yet at the same time show interdisciplinary connections as clearly as possible, pointing out related areas and topics so as to offer readers a clear, comprehensive, and authoritative approach to significant topics in the field. Our most important aim, other than retracing how English has grown into its current role as a global language, is to show the breadth, versatility, and immense research potential of WEs as a field in its own right.

References

Appadurai, Arjun. 1996. *Modernity at Large: Cultural Dimensions of Globalization.* Minneapolis: University of Minnesota Press.

Buschfeld, Sarah. 2013. *English in Cyprus or Cyprus English? An Empirical Investigation of Variety Status.* Amsterdam: John Benjamins.

Buschfeld, Sarah and Alexander Kautzsch. 2014. English in Namibia: A first approach. *English World-Wide 35*(2): 121–160.

Buschfeld, Sarah and Alexander Kautzsch. 2017. Towards an integrative approach to postcolonial and non-postcolonial Englishes. *World Englishes 36*: 104–126.

Buschfeld, Sarah, Thomas Hoffmann, Magnus Huber and Alexander Kautzsch, eds. 2014. *The Evolution of Englishes: The Dynamic Model and Beyond.* Amsterdam: John Benjamins.

Buschfeld, Sarah and Edgar W. Schneider. 2017. World Englishes: Postcolonial Englishes and beyond. In Ee Ling Low and Anne Pakir, eds. *World Englishes: Re-Thinking Paradigms.* London: Routledge, 29–46.

Chambers, J. K. 2009. *Sociolinguistic Theory.* Oxford: Wiley Blackwell.

Cheshire, Jenny, Paul Kerswill, Susan Fox and Eivind Torgersen. 2011. Contact, the feature pool and the speech community: The emergence of Multicultural London English. *Journal of Sociolinguistics 15*(2): 151–196.

Crystal, David. 2008. Two thousand million? Updates on the statistics of English. *English Today 93* 24: 3–6.

D'Arcy, Alexandra. 2015. Variation, transmission, incrementation. In Patrick Honeybone and Joe Salmons, eds. *The Oxford Handbook of Historical Phonology.* Oxford: Oxford University Press, 583–602.

Danet, Brenda and Susan C. Herring, eds. 2007. *The Multilingual Internet: Language, Culture, and Communication Online.* Oxford: Oxford University Press.

Davydova, Julia. 2012. English in the outer and expanding circles: A comparative study. *World Englishes 31*: 366–385.

Edwards, Alison. 2016. *English in the Netherlands: Functions, Forms and Attitudes.* Amsterdam: John Benjamins.

Foley, Joseph, ed. 1988. *New Englishes: The Case of Singapore.* Singapore: Singapore University Press.

Görlach, Manfred. 1990. The development of Standard Englishes. In Manfred Görlach, ed. *Studies in the History of the English Language.* Heidelberg: Carl Winter, 9–64.

Greenbaum, Sidney, ed. 1996. *Comparing English Worldwide: The International Corpus of English.* Oxford: Clarendon.

Gupta, Anthea Fraser. 1997. Colonisation, migration, and functions of English. In Edgar W. Schneider, ed. *Englishes Around the World, Vol. 1: General Studies, British Isles, North America.* Amsterdam: John Benjamins, 47–58.

Hickey, Raymond, ed. 2004. *Legacies of Colonial English: Studies in Transported Dialects.* Cambridge: Cambridge University Press.

Holmes, Janet and Allan Bell, eds. 1990. *New Zealand Ways of Speaking English.* Clevedon: Multilingual Matters.

Horvath, Barbara. 1985. *Variation in Australian English: The Sociolects of Sydney.* Cambridge: Cambridge University Press.

Ike, Saya. 2012. Japanese English as a variety: Features and intelligibility of an emerging variety of English. Unpublished doctoral dissertation, The University of Melbourne.

Kachru, Braj B. 1985. Standards, codification and sociolinguistic realism: The English language in the outer circle. In Randolph Quirk and H. G. Widdowson, eds. *English in the World: Teaching and Learning the Language and Literatures.* Cambridge: Cambridge University Press, 11–30.

Kachru, Braj B., ed. 1992. *The Other Tongue: English across Cultures.* Urbana: University of Illinois Press

Lass, Roger. 1990. Where do Extraterritorial Englishes come from? Dialect input and recodification in transported Englishes. In Sylvia M. Adamson, Vivien A. Law, Nigel Vincent and Susan Wright, eds. *Papers from the 5th International Conference on English Historical Linguistics.* Amsterdam: John Benjamins, 245–280.

Mair, Christian. 2013. The world system of Englishes: Accounting for the transnational importance of mobile and mediated vernaculars. *English World-Wide* 34(3): 253–278.

McArthur, Tom. 1987. The English languages? *English Today* 3(3): 9–13.

McArthur, Tom. 2003. World English, Euro-English, Nordic English? *English Today* 19(1): 54–58.

Mesthrie, Rajend and Rakesh M. Bhatt. 2008. *World Englishes: The Study of New Linguistic Varieties.* Cambridge: Cambridge University Press.

Moag, Rodney. 1992. The life cycle of non-native Englishes: A case study. In Braj B. Kachru, ed. *The Other Tongue: English across Cultures.* Urbana: University of Illinois Press, 233–252.

Mukherjee, Joybrato and Marianne Hundt, eds. 2011. *Exploring Second-Language Varieties of English and Learner Englishes: Bridging a Paradigm Gap.* Amsterdam: John Benjamins.

Platt, John and Heidi Weber. 1980. *English in Singapore and Malaysia: Status, Features, Functions*. Kuala Lumpur: Oxford University Press.

Platt, John, Heidi Weber and Mian Lian Ho. 1984. *The New Englishes*. London: Routledge & Kegan Paul.

Schneider, Edgar W. 2003. The dynamics of New Englishes: From identity construction to dialect birth. *Language 79*: 233–281.

Schneider, Edgar W. 2007. *Postcolonial English: Varieties around the World*. Cambridge: Cambridge University Press.

Schneider, Edgar W. 2011. *English around the World: An Introduction*. Cambridge: Cambridge University Press.

Schneider, Edgar W. 2014. New reflections on the evolutionary dynamics of World Englishes. *World Englishes 33*: 9–32.

Schneider, Edgar W. 2016. Grassroots Englishes in tourism interactions. *English Today 32*(3): 2–10.

Seargeant, Philip and Caroline Tagg. 2011. English on the internet and a "post-varieties" approach to language. *World Englishes 30*(4): 496–514.

Seoane, Elena and Cristina Suárez-Gómez, eds. 2016. *World Englishes: New Theoretical and Methodological Considerations*. Amsterdam: John Benjamins.

Sharma, Devyani. 2017. World Englishes and sociolinguistic theory. In Markku Filppula, Juhani Klemola and Devyani Sharma, eds. *The Oxford Handbook of World Englishes*. Oxford: Oxford University Press, 232–251.

Sridhar, Kamal, K. and Shikaripur N. Sridhar. 1986. Bridging the paradigm gap: Second language acquisition theory and indigenized varieties of English. *World Englishes 5*: 3–14.

Tagliamonte, Sali A. 2002. Comparative sociolinguistics. In J. K. Chambers, Peter Trudgill and Natalie Schilling-Estes, eds. *The Handbook of Language Variation and Change*. Malden, MA: Blackwell, 729–763.

Tagliamonte, Sali. 2012. *Roots of English: Exploring the History of Dialects*. Cambridge: Cambridge University Press.

Part I

The Making of Englishes

2

The Colonial and Postcolonial Expansion of English

Raymond Hickey

2.1   Introduction

The ensemble of varieties of English[1] found throughout the world today are the result of manifold developments. The historical impetus for what was to become an unprecedented spread of a European language overseas[2] was a largely commercial undertaking that began with a British presence in the Caribbean in the early seventeenth century and which continues to the present day. Britain was just one of several major maritime countries in Europe whose history was determined in large part by their participation in the colonial enterprise (Canny 1998: 1–4); Spain, Portugal, Holland,[3] and France were also involved, often in competition with each other. Many of the rival territorial claims of the major colonial powers were settled in treaties that were arranged in European cities, for example the famous Treaty of Utrecht (1713). About a century after the colonial enterprise began, the term "empire" came to be used[4] to refer to the sphere of commercial and political influence built up by Britain overseas. In terms of language spread during the colonial period, only Spain can rival England. Seen from the historical rise of their overseas colonies, it is Spain and Portugal that were the main movers in the colonial arena for the entire sixteenth century. Holland was also a major player as well, with

---

[1] It is beyond the scope of this chapter to offer comprehensive references for all varieties mentioned here. For good summaries of features with references, see the four volumes of Kortmann et al. (2008).

[2] For the current chapter, the expansion of English into Ireland and the development of Old English Anglian into Scots are not considered, as the term "overseas" is taken to refer to regions outside of Europe. This furthermore means that English in Gibraltar (Levey 2008), the Channel Islands (Ramisch 1989), Malta (Mazzon 1993), and Cyprus (Buschfeld 2013) is not considered.

[3] What is here termed "Holland" is the historical core of present-day Netherlands, that is, the provinces of North and South Holland that include the three major cities Amsterdam, The Hague, and Rotterdam. During the seventeenth century, this was the Dutch Republic and consisted of a union of seven provinces of which Holland was clearly the most dominant.

[4] It was first employed in a book title in 1708, in John Oldmixon's *The British Empire in America* (Canny, 1998: 25).

France occupying a more minor position, especially during the seventeenth century.

From the earliest stage of these activities there were population movements out of the British Isles. In order to provide labor for the colonies, the British government from the outset pursued a policy of resettlement, both voluntary and involuntary. In this respect, it differed from the other European colonial powers that had military and administrative presences in their colonies but did not follow the practice of resettling large numbers of local inhabitants overseas. The transportation of varieties of English began with British population movements across the Atlantic in the seventeenth century (Hickey 2004b).

2.1.1 The Spread of English

Although the New World had been discovered at the end of the fifteenth century, England did not get involved in the colonial enterprise until a good century later, if one neglects John Cabot's voyage to Newfoundland in 1497. What signals the beginning of English colonialism (Marshall 1996; Louis 1998) in the New World is the settlement of the east coast of the later United States, first with the unsuccessful attempt at Roanoke Island, North Carolina, in 1584 by Walter Raleigh and later with the settlement at Jamestown, Virginia, in 1607. These were followed by the establishment of other colonies, such as the Plymouth colony in 1620 in Massachusetts and the Maryland colony in 1634 (Algeo 2001: 9). Initially, the British were on a more or less equal footing with other European groups, such as Dutch and Germans, but they were later to become the predominant European group. The forms of English taken by voluntary settlers, such as the New England Puritans, meant that these provided an initial impetus for the development of the language in the region later to become the United States of America after the American Revolutionary War (1775–1783).

Parallel to forming a bridgehead on the mainland of America, the British established a presence in the Caribbean (Beckles 1998). During the early 1620s, they occupied the small Caribbean islands of St Kitts and Nevis as well as Barbados, a few years later. From these humble beginnings, the British colonial enterprise grew steadily, quickly outstripping the Spanish and the Dutch and becoming the leading European power engaged in colonial activities overseas. The individuals who were either deported by the British authorities to the Caribbean or left largely of their own accord, usually as so-called indentured laborers, came from various regions of England and Wales, from Scotland, and from Ireland (Cullen 1994). This fact is of significance for the British colonies in the Caribbean because it meant that the very first settlers were actually dialect speakers of English, representing the main linguistic actors of the so-called homestead phase (Hickey 2004a). It was not until a generation or so after the first English-speaking settlers that African slaves began to arrive in the Caribbean, especially after the "sugar revolution" of the 1640s (Beckles 1998).

2.1.2　Sources of Early Emigrants

Emigration was not originally connected with the rise of the British Empire (Lloyd 1984), although the two issues are closely related. Only in a few cases did emigration form part of the construction of the empire, for example where England sent administrative staff and military abroad or settlers with the specific goal of occupying and holding an overseas territory in the name of Britain. However, in many cases, the emigrants were anything but concerned with strengthening the empire (see Britain, Chapter 7, this volume). For instance, in Scotland, the reorganization of the northern parts of the country, known as the Highland Clearances, was a major reason for emigration to Canada and Australia well into the nineteenth century. Periods of exodus occurred in the early stages of these clearances, between 1763 and 1775, when thousands of Highlanders left for British North America.

2.1.3　Emigration and Colonies

The issues of emigration and the transportation of varieties of English often do not involve such central imperial concerns as was evidenced by the incorporation of India or parts of Southeast Asia into the British sphere of influence (Lange, Chapter 11, this volume). Nor do these issues concern to any significant extent essential elements of the commercial enterprise as the chartered companies, for example the East India Company (Lawson 1993), founded in the seventeenth century and active in Bengal in the eighteenth century (it also dominated English trade with China until it was disbanded after 1857). These organizations did not have a direct effect on the development of overseas varieties of English. In addition, in many parts of the empire, particularly in those sections accrued in the period from the second half of the nineteenth century to immediately after World War I, no new forms of native English arose. In many instances, the countries were not actually termed colonies, for instance Egypt, over which Britain took control in 1882. Mandated territories arose after the defeat of Germany in World War I. These were laid down in the Treaty of Versailles (1919) and held under the general supervision of the League of Nations but were only superficially administered by Britain, for example Iraq, Transjordan, and Palestine, which Britain gained from Turkey. Tanganyika, West Togoland, and south Cameroon were taken over from Germany. There may have been a minor amount of subsequent internal migration due to the supervision of colonies of

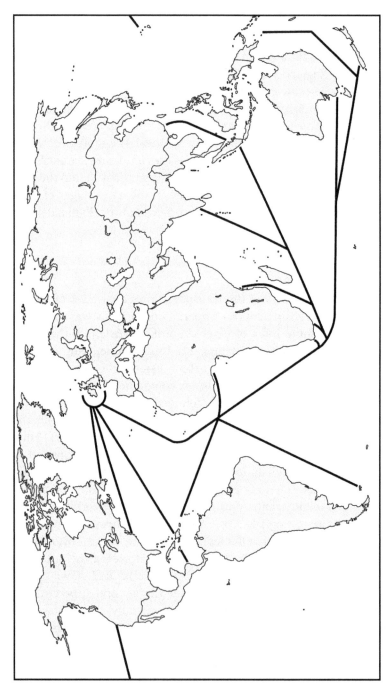

Map 2.1 The spread of English in the colonial period (from Hickey 2004c: 627)

defeated powers by (former) colonies of Britain, for example with the administration of New Guinea by Australia or Western Samoa by New Zealand. In the course of the twentieth century, these countries severed their ties with Britain, usually through independence, for instance Western Samoa in 1962 and New Guinea in 1973.

2.1.4 Regions of the Anglophone World

The anglophone world can be divided into two large regions, resulting from the timescales for initial emigration. The Northern Hemisphere, which consists essentially of the New World (the Caribbean, the USA, and Canada), was first settled in the early seventeenth century. The Southern Hemisphere was settled from the late eighteenth century onward. This fact accounts for essential differences between the two large areas, for example the generally non-rhotic nature of English in the Southern Hemisphere and the raising of short vowels along with the lower or more retracted articulation of diphthongs when compared to forms of English in the Northern Hemisphere.

Each of these large regions can be further subdivided. Within the Northern Hemisphere, the Caribbean forms a subregion of its own, not just by its pattern of initial English settlement but because of the larger number of African-origin slaves taken there from the mid-seventeenth century onward. Pidgins, and later creoles, arose there and have survived and shaped present-day varieties of Caribbean English (Williams 2012; see Mufwene, Chapter 5, and Lim, Chapter 4, this volume).

The Southern Hemisphere also shows distinct subregions. Southern Africa is one such region consisting of South Africa, Zimbabwe, Botswana, and Malawi. Geographically related to this continental region is the South Atlantic, which, in anglophone terms, consists of St Helena (Schreier 2008), Tristan da Cunha (Schreier 2003), and the Falkland Islands (Sudbury 2001). Two further subregions of the Southern Hemisphere are (1) Australia and New Zealand and (2) the Southwest and South Pacific, which consist of many Melanesian and Polynesian island states where English-lexified creoles are spoken along with indigenous languages.

2.1.5 Types of English Overseas

Traditionally, a distinction has been made between settler and non-settler English in the overseas colonies. This division has further been associated with the distinction between native and non-native forms of English, a distinction that is often ideologically overladen and has been challenged (Kachru 1990). Swan, Aboshiha, and Holliday (2015) see the distinction not just as unnecessary but as evaluative and divisive. For countries that have had significant numbers of settlers from Britain or

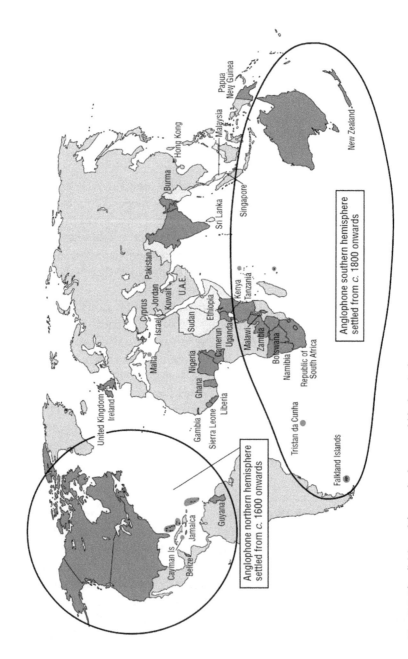

Map 2.2 The division of the anglophone world by hemisphere

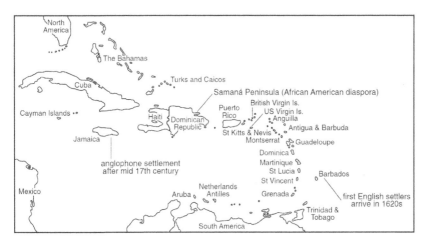

Map 2.3 The Caribbean

Ireland, for example Australia and New Zealand, the descendants of these initial European populations are undoubtedly native speakers. The classification becomes difficult when one considers countries such as Singapore where much of the recent Chinese-origin population has now grown up speaking English throughout their childhood, both at home and in school. This situation would justify labeling individuals brought up in such environments as native speakers (Lim, Chapter 4, this volume).

The geography of overseas locations has played a role in the development of varieties. Some isolated regions led to dialectally relic varieties, for example on Ocracoke Island, in the Ozarks, and the (southern) Appalachians, all in the USA. Otago in the south of the South Island of New Zealand, where many Scottish emigrants settled, is a further example. Related to relic regions are isolated locations, frequently islands with small anglophone populations. This holds for Caribbean and Pacific islands where English is in contact with indigenous languages. Other islands have entirely anglophone communities, notably those of the South Atlantic such as Tristan da Cunha (Schreier 2003) and the Falklands.

Diaspora forms of overseas varieties of English include the African American English in Nova Scotia and (formerly) in Samaná in the Dominican Republic. Within the anglophone world, there are also diaspora forms of indigenous groups. The most significant diaspora of the anglophone world is probably that of India (see Hundt, Chapter 22, this volume): Speakers of Indian languages (from either the Indo-European or Dravidian language families) are found in Singapore, Fiji, East Africa (formerly), South Africa, and on several islands of the Caribbean. At most of these locations, the Indian population has shifted to English entirely.

2.2   Dialect Areas Providing Input to Colonies

The origins of colonial English lie in the dialects of England (Ihalainen 1994) in the early modern and late modern periods respectively, specifically in the seventeenth century for the Northern Hemisphere and in the late eighteenth/early nineteenth century for the Southern Hemisphere. At both these times, the dialect landscape was determined by geographical distributions that stemmed from the dialect configuration of Middle English (see Britain, Chapter 7, this volume). In essence, the fivefold division of the country, (1) Northern, (2) West Midland, (3) East Midland, (4) Southern, (5) Kentish, was maintained into the early modern period (Lass 1987).

The closer one moves to the present day the more differentiated views of dialect divisions in England become, largely because of a greater amount of documentation. By the late nineteenth century, multivolume surveys of dialects were available, which continued into the twentieth century – see Ellis (1868–1889) and Orton and colleagues (1962–1971) as the main examples, alongside the dialect dictionary and grammar by Wright (1898–1905, 1905); see also the contemporary overview in Trudgill (1990). For instance, it becomes clear that the East Anglia area of the Middle English East Midland region was separate from the center of the country (Trudgill 2001) and the southwest, consisting of Devon, east and central Cornwall, and probably Somerset and Dorset, appeared as a dialectally distinct subregion of the south.

For the colonial expansion of English, the position of largely rural dialects in the early modern period is of central concern. Certainly for emigration to the New World in its formative years, cities[5] did not play the significant role which they did later, with the exception of London perhaps. By the time of the major emigration to the Southern Hemisphere, in the late eighteenth and early nineteenth centuries, cities had become more important and the population movements from London and the Home Counties provided the most significant inputs for the development of anglophone varieties (not least because of their social status) in the major locations of the Southern Hemisphere, that is, South Africa, Australia, and New Zealand.

2.2.1   Language Contact During the Colonial Period

Virtually all of the overseas locations saw contact between English settlers and other groups (Lim, Chapter 4, this volume). In most cases, the latter were indigenous populations and this may have had an effect on emerging

---

[5] But the ports of departure for emigration to the New World were already known for their linguistic diversity. For instance, George Puttenham (1532–1600) was of the opinion that certain forms of English (even in the south) were to be avoided. In his *Arte of English Poesie* (Puttenham 1589), he mentions the "marches and frontiers" (where contact with Welsh or Cornish would have occurred) and the "port townes" because of the high degree of language mixing there (Görlach 1999: 110).

varieties of English, at least in vocabulary, for example in Australia or New Zealand. The groups in contact may have consisted of two European languages, as in Canada with English and French, or South Africa with English and Afrikaans (Cape Dutch Vernacular). In other cases, groups were both English-speaking and of different regional origin, for example southwest English and southeast Irish settlers in Newfoundland (Clarke 2004).

Contact with indigenous populations did not always result in borrowing into varieties of English. In the USA and Canada, there are practically no traces of contact with Native American or First Nations groups, bar a few lexical items, usually for flora and fauna or artifacts typical of the native group in question, for example *moccasin*, *tomahawk* (Algonquin), *coyote* (Nahuatl via Mexican Spanish), *kayak* (Inuit).

2.2.2 New Dialect Formation Scenarios

The rise of new varieties in overseas locations depended on a number of factors, not least the dialectal composition of the early settler groups. According to the "founder principle" (Mufwene 1996), it is always the group initially present at a given location that determines the future shape of the variety arising there. Yet, in those instances where there was an initial mix of dialects, for example English English, Scottish English, and Irish English, as in both Australia and New Zealand, there has been much speculation about how, and to what extent, these inputs contributed to the shape of the present-day forms of English in these countries. Two prominent models in this area are suggested in Trudgill (see Trudgill 2004 and Hickey 2003a for a critical assessment) and Schneider (2003, 2007). The latter model highlights the reorientation from an exonormative model of English to an endonormative one, especially after a colony gained independence from Britain (see also Buschfeld and Kautzsch, Chapter 2, this volume).

2.2.3 Pidgins and Creoles

Contact forms the basis for two further related variety types, pidgins and creoles, which have been the focus of much research. The roots of these varieties lie in their contact origins involving colonial powers and native populations, frequently in a trade or slavery context. The pidgins that arose under these conditions could, and in many cases did, develop further into creoles. The essence of the latter varieties is that they were, and often still are, native varieties for a certain population. The development of a creole furthermore presumes a break in linguistic transmission across generations, or at least a highly fragmentary transmission, typically found in an early planta-tion scenario where slaves of differing linguistic backgrounds (sometimes deliberately mixed by their owners) lived in isolation with little or no exposure to native varieties of English and no schooling. English-lexifier creoles are found in two main arenas, the Atlantic and the Pacific, and across these locations they share common features in phonology, such as simplified syllable structure, non-rhoticity, and the lack of interdental fricatives. In grammar, creoles show subject–verb–object (SVO) word order, an almost complete lack of inflectional morphology, and a preference for parataxis over hypotaxis. Whether creoles represent a typological class on their own is a much-discussed issue (McWhorter 2000).

2.3   Transported English in the Colonial Period

During the three centuries from approximately 1600 to 1900 different forms of English were taken overseas by regional speakers from diverse parts of the British Isles. The role that this input played in the formative period of many overseas varieties has been the subject of much research (for North America, see Montgomery 2001 and Kirwin 2001; for Australia, Ramson, 1970) with opinions differing on the contribution of input to the shape of later varieties. The more recent the variety, the more vigorous this discussion has been, as can be clearly recognized in the case of New Zealand for which there are diverging opinions on the role of dialect input to later English in that country (see Section 2.2.2). In the following, the outcomes of dialect contact for the emergence of World Englishes are briefly illustrated with cases from phonetics/phonology, grammar, and lexicon.

2.3.1   Phonetics/Phonology

Without going into detail concerning individual varieties (see Schreier, Chapter 17, this volume) there are nonetheless certain prominent phonological developments across groups of varieties. Some of these constitute mergers present embryonically in Britain and/or Ireland, some constitute losses, and some further developments are more common overseas than in source varieties.

A well-known dictum regarding contact situations is that "mergers expand at the expense of distinctions" (Labov 1972: 300). The contact situations in the overseas locations of the colonial period include those between different languages and those between varieties of one language, here dialects of English. In the following, three instances of merger are listed that frequently occurred at overseas locations.

2.3.1.1   The *Which/Witch* Merger

Historically, words like *which* [wɪtʃ] and *witch* [ʍɪtʃ] were distinguished consistently, the merger being of late modern origin. In phonological terms, this loss is the removal of /h/ from the initial /hw/ cluster. There are no varieties of English that have *h*-dropping and the retention of [w], that is, /hw-/.[6] In conservative forms of English in the British Isles, such as Scottish and Irish English, a distinction in voice with these approximants is made but there are noticeable exceptions, for example Newfoundland English, which has only the voiced approximant, even for the Irish-based variety of English, which certainly had the distinction in its historical input. In all varieties, the distinction is recessive and there are no instances of increase or spread.

2.3.1.2 The *Cot/Caught* Merger

Traditionally, this merger has been typical of Canadian English, including Newfoundland English. Unrounding was characteristic of both English and Irish inputs (Boberg 2010: 126–130; Clarke 2004). A merger has not generally taken place in the British sources and vowel length is still distinctive, which is not always true for many varieties of North American English (hence the merger).

2.3.1.3 Mid-back Vowels Before /r/

Again, for many conservative varieties there may be a distinction among mid-back vowels before /r/, that is, the words *mourning* and *morning* may not be homophones, for example one has ['mornɪŋ] versus ['mɔrnɪŋ]. All such varieties are rhotic and it is difficult to predict just what lexical items show which vowel though there is a preponderance of French loanwords with the higher vowel, for example *force, port, fort*.

2.3.1.4 Palatal Glide Insertion

This feature is present in Northern Irish English and in Caribbean English (Hickey 2004a) and recessively in conservative varieties in the American South (Kurath and McDavid 1983 [1961]). It is manifested as a palatal glide after velars and before /a/. The feature is still well attested in the north of Ireland, e.g. *car* [kjær], *gap* [gjæp]. Harris (1987) concludes that there is compelling evidence for origins within mainland English (it has been attested in southern England) and rejects Irish English or African substrate languages in the Caribbean as a source. In this case, the demise of the feature in England has been countered by a few overseas locations retaining it.

2.3.1.5 Short Vowels Before /r/

The distinction between front and back short vowels before /r/ as in *term* / tɛrm/ and *burn* /bʊrn/ has been generally lost in English, and not just in non-rhotic varieties. However, conservative varieties (in Scotland and Ireland) may retain the distinction, at least in their vernacular forms,

---

[6] See Hickey (1984) for more detailed arguments.

perhaps even showing a further distinction between mid- and high-front vowels as in *fir* [fir] and *fern* [fɛrn]. In general, this distinction is not found in varieties of English overseas.

Assuming that regional speakers who emigrated in the early modern period took their local pronunciations of English with them, then the question arises as to how these came to be lost. At least two explanations can be offered here: (1) In a dialect mix situation, certain features were disfavored by the offspring of earlier dialect speakers; or (2) through the later imposition of more standard varieties, older regional features were supplanted (Hickey 2013). Deciding on whether option (1) or (2) was operative in the genesis of an overseas variety is sometimes difficult, but dialect mixture is likely to apply early on as different dialects were usually present at overseas locations (Hickey 2003a). Option (2) would require an external stimulus, that is, for a dialect to start replacing its salient features by more mainstream ones. The spread of general education for the majority population and the rise of an independent middle class in the eighteenth and nineteenth centuries are powerful factors in favor of (2).

2.3.1.6   The FOOT- STRUT Split

In the north of England, the southern split between words of the FOOT and STRUT lexical sets (Upton and Widdowson 2006: 26–27; Wells 1982: 196–199) is not found: a high back vowel [ʊ] is used in both lexical sets. Despite the numbers of northern English emigrants to overseas locations, this pronunciation does not occur in any overseas variety of English as a realization of the STRUT vowel (note that the [ʊ] in the FOOT class only occurs in words in which this pronunciation is lexicalized). This fact is quite remarkable, as emigration goes back to the seventeenth century. In North America, for instance, the early seventeenth century saw emigration to New England as well as the Caribbean and the eighteenth century experienced much emigration from Ulster and Scotland. The conclusion is that emigrants from the north of England did not have a dominant influence in overseas locations (Lass 1990; Montgomery 2001: 138) and hence their speech never became a model in the genesis of a new variety. The initial generations, with generalized [ʊ] in both the FOOT and STRUT lexical sets, did not succeed in passing this distribution to following generations, hence the presence of the FOOT/STRUT distinction throughout the anglophone world with the exception of the north of England (Hickey 2015: 8–11) and vernacular Dublin English (Hickey 2005: 35–37).

2.3.2   Morphosyntax

The morphosyntax of overseas varieties shows prominent nonstandard features that go back to initial input or to missing distinctions in the inputs. The examples discussed here are now typical of vernacular forms of varieties, given that in most anglophone countries more standard forms of English are found in official and public usage (Hickey 2012a).

2.3.2.1 Non-standard Verbal -*s*

A considerable body of literature has been produced on inflectional -*s* in present-tense verb paradigms in different varieties of English (Clarke 1997; Poplack and Tagliamonte 2004). A number of parameters condition the feature and the rules governing nonstandard verbal -*s* tend to be variable rather than categorical. Some scholars have proposed only one constraint, the *Type of Subject constraint* (Poplack and Tagliamonte 1989), whereas others, such as Montgomery (1997), recognize two constraints, *Type of Subject* and *Proximity to Subject*. In essence, the claim is that verbal -*s* is disfavored by an immediately preceding personal pronoun but that other types of subject can (but must not always) trigger verbal -*s* across the paradigm for the present tense. In addition, the distance between subject and verb form is considered relevant. Varieties vary according to person and number – for instance, in southern Irish English there is a strong tendency for the third-person plural to show inflection, irrespective of the type of subject, for example *They owns the whole street now* (Hickey 2007: 182). Subject weight (pronoun, noun, noun phrase) and the distance between subject and verb also influence the occurrence of verbal -*s* across varieties.

2.3.2.2 Second-Person Plural Pronouns

Although standard English does not distinguish number with second-person pronouns, since the loss of *thou/thee/thine* as second-person singular forms, most nonstandard varieties of English have some means of distinguishing between singular and plural in the second person. By and large, the form *you* is retained for the singular with plurality being indicated by one of a series of elements, for example *ye, y'all, you'uns, youse, unu* (for a detailed discussion, see Hickey, 2003b). The first form, *ye* (found in Scotland and Ireland), is a continuation of the historical second-person plural pronoun in the nominative (the form *you* is derived from an original accusative form). The formation *y'all* is generally taken to be an independent development that arose through the natural use of the quantifier *all* as a marker of plurality (though see Montgomery 1989, 1992, for a possible (Ulster) Scots origin). This view gains added credence from the fact that *y'all* has appeared independently in South African Indian English (Mesthrie 1992: 61). The form *you'uns* would seem to be of Ulster Scots provenance while *youse* is definitely of Irish English origin and has spread to a number of varieties of English in the Southern Hemisphere, especially in colloquial modes of speech. Forms similar to *unu* are confined to Caribbean creoles and Gullah (Turner 1971: 134). The West African language Ibo has been determined as the source of this form (Burchfield 1994: 10).

Another issue in the grammar of overseas varieties is the use of forms that occur in mainland English but that have a different function from their source (Schreier, Chapter this volume). Varieties as far apart as African American English and Newfoundland English offer attestations here. In the former, the past participle *been* is used for remote past (Rickford 1975) and an uninflected *be* is found in the present in an aspectual sense (Myhill 1988). In Newfoundland English, the verbs *have* and *do* are uninflected when they function as auxiliaries but inflected as lexical verbs (Clarke 2004).

2.3.3 Vocabulary

The retention of elements from the original input is perhaps clearest for overseas varieties in the area of vocabulary as this is a level of language of which speakers are clearly conscious (Schneider 2007). The continued use of items from early input is known by the term "colonial lag" and is often used to account for such preferences as *fall* for *autumn* or *mail* for *post* in American English. But this only accounts for a small fraction of vocabulary. Flora and fauna at the overseas location is responsible for many items and the sources of these words can be indigenous languages, for example *impala* (Zulu), but also a further European, or European-derived, language, for example *wildebeest* (Afrikaans) in South African English. Still other preferences do not necessarily represent earlier usage or borrowings, for example *movies* for *pictures*, *store* for *shop*, *elevator* for *lift*, in American English.

Vocabulary usage is an area of high permeability, which, in today's world, tends to be unidirectional with American English influencing forms of English elsewhere, as well as many other languages. Word pairs such as *truck* and *lorry*, *cookie* and *biscuit*, *apartment* and *flat* that in the past represented American and British English usage fairly exclusively no longer do so as many words from American English have become common usage in British English (see Read 2005 for a treatment of mutual borrowing between these varieties of English).

2.4   Postcolonial Scenarios in the Anglophone World

By the late nineteenth century, there were no more new varieties as a result of settlers moving to overseas locations (New Zealand was the last major colony where this happened). This means that in linguistic terms the period of colonial English, that is, one in which varieties arose due to transported forms from Britain and/or Ireland, was over by 1900 at the latest. Of course, varieties in existing overseas locations continued to develop and new varieties developed for a variety of reasons. Yet, in both these cases, varieties developed independently of the language of first-generation colonial settlers.

As a temporal reference, the term "postcolonial" refers to the time after former colonies of Britain gained independence. Yet the term has a much wider application in linguistics, literature, and cultural studies. It encompasses all the issues surrounding adaptation after the termination of official links to the former colonial power. This is a complex phenomenon, involving practical matters concerning the positioning of newly independent countries in the global network of nations but also changes in attitudes to the culture of the former colonial power and the release from its dominating influence. In this process, the political relationship of former colonies to Britain is key. Some of these remained in loose association with the original colonial power, for example Canada, Australia, and New Zealand, which, in the nineteenth/early twentieth century, had dominion status within the British Empire (from 1867, 1901, and 1907 onward, respectively). In the course of the twentieth century, these countries became more and more independent, although none of them became a republic and still have a public office for the representative of the British Crown, the governor general. Such countries have traditionally had an orientation toward British English for their public usage of English, often an uncodified standard of English (Hickey 2012b).

2.4.1 Independence from Britain

The timescale for the rise of postcolonial varieties of English has been shaped by the date of independence from Britain. Some countries attained independence very early, notably the USA with the successful conclusion of the American Revolutionary War by the Treaty of Paris in 1783. Partial independence was achieved in other cases (see previous paragraph) with greater degrees of national sovereignty being provided by the Statute of Westminster (1931). Full independence for British colonies only got underway in the twentieth century: Ireland (south) in 1922; India in 1947 (with the division of the country into largely Hindu India and Muslim Pakistan, the latter East and West until the independence of East Pakistan as Bangladesh in 1971). After World War II, the movement toward independence gained momentum and most of the African, Asian, and Caribbean colonies severed their political ties with Britain, for example Ghana in 1957, Nigeria in 1960, Malaysia in 1957, Sri Lanka in 1948, Jamaica in 1962, and Barbados in 1966. Some of these countries remained in the British Commonwealth of Nations, which was formally constituted by the London Declaration of 1949.

2.4.2 Changes in Exonormative Orientation

The movement away from a British model of English can be furthered by political independence but also by the increasing influence of American English, as is happening to a certain extent in Jamaica where the proximity to the USA and the large number of American visitors have meant greater exposure to, and influence from, American English (N. Gordon 2009; see Hackert and Deuber 2015 for a discussion of other locations in the Caribbean). The pervading influence of the USA can also be recognized in the linguistic influence of American English on young people's speech in Ireland (Hickey 2016).

Canada is another case in point with a traditional orientation toward British English but at present ever more under the influence from varieties of English spoken south of its long border with the USA. In addition, for many countries, political independence has meant the development of increasingly endonormative varieties of English. This is true of countries geographically close to Britain, like Ireland (Hickey 2017), but also those at a considerable distance, such as Australia (Blair and Collins 2001; Peters, Chapter 25, this volume) and New Zealand (E. Gordon et al. 2004).

2.4.3 Language Choice and Identity

From a linguistic point of view, postcolonialism involves making explicit language choices (Schleef, Chapter 26, this volume). For some countries, notably those in sub-Saharan Africa, such as Nigeria or Kenya, the choice of linguistic medium, especially for fictional literature, is often one between a local Bantu language and English. Yet, even if English is the uncontested language, there will have been a switch from an exonormative to an endonormative orientation as described in Schneider's Dynamic Model (Schneider 2003, 2007), at least initially and for the sound level of language. The projection of linguistic identity (Anchimbe 2007; Riley 2007) via pronunciation is a central aspect of language use and newly independent countries usually develop unique phonetic profiles for their English, irrespective of whether there is more than one recognizable variety in any given postcolonial country. The supraregional variety, that is, the nonstigmatized form maintained across a country for public and official domains (Hickey 2013), is never identical to an exonormative standard, although it may be viewed as a local standard within its own country. Despite prescriptive attitudes from official quarters, this will nonetheless be and remain the case, cf. Singapore where a government-sponsored push toward internationally accepted standard English has still not eliminated unique features of Singapore English, despite the dissociation of its speakers from Colloquial Singapore English (Wee 2013; Zhiming 1999).

2.4.4 New Epicenters for English

Regional epicenters for emerging varieties have arisen that rival Britain and the USA. Such epicenters can be found in the Southern Hemisphere and the Pacific arena. For example, South Africa plays a dominant role in southern Africa and its English has had an influence on that spoken in the other anglophone countries of this area, for example in Zimbabwe, Zambia, Malawi, Botswana, Lesotho, Swaziland, and, to a lesser extent, given its more complex language situation, in Namibia.

For the Southwest Pacific, both Australia and New Zealand function as regional epicenters (Peters 2009) with many small island nations gravitating toward the English of these countries as an exonormative model in the sense of Schneider's Dynamic Model (Schneider 2003, 2007). Linguistic similarities may reflect political ties as with New Zealand and Niue (Starks, Christie, and Thompson 2007), which is in free association with the former. They may derive from a common Polynesian substrate as in the case of New Zealand Maori English and Pasifika Englishes (Starks 2008) or Pacific inter-island connections as in the case of Norfolk and Pitcairn islands (Ingram and Mühlhäusler 2008; Mühlhäusler 2008).

2.4.5 Nativized Varieties of English

The association of native speakers and their language with cultural dominance over others has received academic treatment (see Phillipson 1992 and Canagarajah 1999), although not all scholars would necessarily agree with the stances adopted in such studies, which use the metaphor of imperialism to characterize the dominance of English over other languages in today's world. One resolution of the tension between local and English cultures is to view the English language as deculturized and released from an all-too-close connection with the large, traditionally first-language countries, notably Britain and the USA (Saraceni 2015). This would seem to have worked best in Asian countries with English as a foreign language, not least in those countries whose languages have freely incorporated elements from English, irrespective of whether the output corresponds to any structure or phrase found in native varieties of English (see Seargeant 2005 on the situation of English elements in Japanese; Eun-Young 2012 in Korean; see also Edwards and Seargeant, Chapter 15, this volume).

A further issue in this field is the status of varieties with respect to native speaker competence. The most prominent case in this regard is Singapore (Deterding 2007; Leimgruber 2013; Ooi 2001), which has an official policy of furthering English at all levels of society. Especially the Chinese-origin sector of Singapore (ca. 77 percent of the population) have, in many instances, adopted English as the home language with primary schooling already in English. Children who grow up in such an environment have a degree of exposure to English directly comparable to that of those in Australia or anglophone Canada, for instance, and hence attain proficiency in the language and a level of competence similar to native speakers from other countries, even though many features of Singapore English will not necessarily be shared by varieties outside of Singapore.

2.4.6   The Role of Second- and Foreign-Language Varieties in Today's World

It is a truism that there are more non-native speakers of English than there are native speakers. The sheer numbers alone demand that scholars take cognizance of second- and foreign-language varieties and analyze them linguistically. The number of countries with English as a second language is fairly limited and they are generally former colonies of Britain[7]. Such countries are known for a wide use of English along with indigenous languages across a range of societal domains. Those with English as a foreign language, that is, when English is only used if no common language is available between interlocutors, comprises, in this broad definition, virtually every non-anglophone country in today's world.

Both second- and foreign-language varieties of English are linguistically influenced by the first language(s) of their users. Furthermore, features may be common across many countries, irrespective of whether they share languages from the same family. For instance, a lack of rhoticity, of vowel length distinctions, and of consonant clusters is virtually universal in East and Southeast Asian non-native varieties of English. The use of basic English in commercial contexts, for example in tourism (Schneider 2016), has become the focus of research to analyze the manner in which basic English (often term "grassroots English"; see Meierkord, Chapter 14, this volume) is used in exchanges with clients and how this can develop into a domain- and function-specific register.

Lastly, the use of English across the Internet by individuals of highly diverse backgrounds should be stressed. Again, the degree to which English in cyberspace (Mair, Chapter 16, this volume) corresponds to traditional written forms of English in anglophone countries is not the issue for its users; comprehensibility is the key aim and prescriptive notions of normative language usage do not apply. A similar freedom from linguistic norms is found across the world for all the languages used for this purpose. Whether language usage in such non-prescriptive domains will have an influence in other spheres is a contested matter (Crystal 2009).

2.4.7   Transnational Influences and the Effects of Globalization

Since the end of the nineteenth century, it is not colonialization but rather globalization that is responsible for the rise of new varieties of English (Schneider 2014). It is true that precisely the same situations will probably not arise again, but similar situations will no doubt apply and processes of variation and change in former colonies will have parallels in the future, especially in the context of identity construction within frameworks of

---

[7] There are some exceptions, like Nepal, which was never formally a colony of Britain but was heavily influenced by the English presence in India during the British Raj between 1858 and 1947.

variety initiation and entrenchment. The focus of research on varieties has moved away from older forms of settler English toward more recent varieties, certainly in the African and Asian arenas. These varieties are largely forms that traditionally would be classified as non-native, that is, second-language or indeed foreign-language varieties of English. Especially with the former it has become increasingly difficult to draw a clear demarcation line between native and non-native varieties (cf. Chow 2014; Higgins 2003; Kachru 1990; Kachru and Nelson 2006; Vaish 2011). Furthermore, the interface between second-language and learner varieties of English has been recognized as a significant avenue of research (Mukherjee and Hundt 2011).

2.5 Conclusion

A more inclusive perspective on varieties of English has been explicitly pursued by scholars working broadly within the paradigm of "World Englishes" (Bolton and Kachru 2006; Crystal 2003, 2004; Hoffmann and Siebers 2009; Jenkins 2003; Kachru, Kachru, and Nelson 2006; Kirkpatrick 2007; Melchers and Shaw 2012; Mesthrie and Bhatt 2008; Saraceni, 2015; Seoane and Suárez-Gómez 2016). With this more embracing view, additional factors in the shaping of twentieth-first-century varieties of English can be identified, such as transnational contacts (Bolander, Chapter 29, this volume), interactions across the media, and in specific domains such as tourism (Schneider 2016). Further factors are language contact through migration (Collins, Baynham, and Slembrouck 2011; Geraghty and Conacher 2016) and the rise of urban vernaculars (McLoughlin 2011) with complex linguistic landscapes in locations of high population density producing a diversity in which many input strands are responsible for the shaping of language (see Cheshire et al. 2011).

The globalization of today's world has engendered a multiplicity of scenarios in which language variation and change can occur (Blommaert 2010; Saxena and Omoniyi 2010). This has meant that, for many mobile speakers involved in various alliances throughout their lives, there is a continual negotiation of linguistic identity (Blackwood, Lanza, and Woldemariam 2016), which contributes to the kaleidoscopic panorama of present-day varieties of English visible across the world.

References

Algeo, John. 2001. External history. In John Algeo, ed. *English in North America. The Cambridge History of the English Language*, Vol. 6. Cambridge: Cambridge University Press, 1–58.

Algeo, John. 2006. *British or American English? A Handbook of Word and Grammar Patterns*. Cambridge: Cambridge University Press.

Anchimbe, Eric A., ed. 2007. *Linguistic Identity in Postcolonial Multilingual Spaces*. Newcastle: Cambridge Scholars Publishing.

Beckles, Hilary McDonald. 1998. The "Hub of Empire": The Caribbean and Britain in the seventeenth century. In Nicholas Canny, ed. *The Origins of Empire: British Overseas Enterprise at the Close of the Seventeenth Century*. Oxford: Oxford University Press, 218–240.

Blair, David and Peter Collins, eds. 2001. *English in Australia*. Amsterdam: John Benjamins.

Blackwood, Robert, Elizabeth Lanza and Hirut Woldemariam, eds. 2016. *Negotiating and Contesting Identities in Linguistic Landscapes*. London: Bloomsbury.

Blommaert, Jan. 2010. *The Sociolinguistics of Globalization*. Cambridge: Cambridge University Press.

Boberg, Charles. 2010. *The English Language in Canada*. Cambridge: Cambridge University Press.

Bolton, Kingsley and Braj B. Kachru. 2006. *World Englishes: Critical Concepts in Linguistics*, 6 vols. London: Routledge.

Burchfield, Robert W. 1994. Introduction. In Robert Burchfield, ed. *The Cambridge History of the English Language, Vol. 5: English in Britain and Overseas: Origins and Development*. Cambridge: Cambridge University Press, 1–19.

Buschfeld, Sarah. 2013. *English in Cyprus or Cyprus English: An Empirical Investigation of Variety Status*. Amsterdam: John Benjamins.

Canagarajah, Suresh. 1999. *Resisting Linguistic Imperialism*. Oxford: Oxford University Press.

Canny, Nicholas. 1998. The origins of empire. In Nicholas Canny, ed. *The Origins of Empire. British Overseas Enterprise at the Close of the Seventeenth Century*. Oxford: Oxford University Press, 1–33.

Cheshire, Jenny, Paul Kerswill, Susan Fox and Eivind Torgersen. 2011. Contact, the feature pool and the speech community: The emergence of multicultural London English. *Journal of Sociolinguistics* 15: 151–196.

Chow, Rey. 2014. *Not Like a Native Speaker: On Languaging as a Postcolonial Experience*. New York: Columbia University Press.

Clarke, Sandra. 1997. English verbal -s revisited: The evidence from Newfoundland. *American Speech* 72(3): 227–259.

Clarke, Sandra. 2004. The legacy of British and Irish English in Newfoundland. In Raymond Hickey, ed. *Legacies of Colonial English: Studies in Transported Dialects*. Cambridge: Cambridge University Press, 242–261.

Collins, James, Mike Baynham and Stef Slembrouck, eds. 2011. *Globalization and Language in Contact: Scale, Migration, and Communicative Practices*. London: Bloomsbury.

Crystal, David. 2003. *English as a Global Language*. Cambridge: Cambridge University Press.

Crystal, David. 2009. *Txtng: The Gr8 Db8*. Oxford: Oxford University Press.

Cullen, Louis. 1998. The Irish diaspora and the seventeenth and eighteenth centuries. In Nicholas Canny, ed. *The Origins of Empire. British Overseas Enterprise at the Close of the Seventeenth Century*. Oxford: Oxford University Press, 113–149.

Deterding, David. 2007. *Singapore English*. Edinburgh: Edinburgh University Press.

Ellis, Alexander. 1868–1889. *On Early English Pronunciation*, 5 vols. London: Philological Society.

Eun-Young, Julia Kim. 2012. Creative adoption: Trends in Anglicisms in Korea. *English Today 28*(2): 15–17.

Geraghty, Barbara and Jean Conacher, eds. 2016. *Intercultural Contact, Language Learning and Migration*. London: Bloomsbury.

Gordon, Elizabeth, Lyle Campbell, Jennifer Hay, Margaret MacLagan, Andrea Sudbury and Peter Trudgill. 2004. *New Zealand English: Its Origins and Evolution*. Cambridge: Cambridge University Press.

Gordon, Nickesia Stacy Ann. 2009. Globalization and cultural imperialism in Jamaica. *International Journal of Communication 3*: 307–331.

Görlach, Manfred. 1999. *English in Nineteenth-Century England: An Introduction*. Cambridge: Cambridge University Press.

Hackert, Stephanie and Dagmar Deuber. 2015. American influence on written Caribbean English: A diachronic analysis of newspaper reportage in the Bahamas and in Trinidad and Tobago. In Peter Collins, ed. *Grammatical Change in English World-Wide*. Amsterdam: John Benjamins, 389–410.

Harris, John. 1987. On doing comparative reconstruction with genetically unrelated languages. In Anna Giacalone Ramat, Onofrio Carruba and Giuliano Bernini, eds. *Papers from the 7th International Conference on Historical Linguistics, Pavia, Italy*. Amsterdam: John Benjamins, 267–282.

Hickey, Raymond. 1984. Syllable onsets in Irish English. *Word 35*: 67–74.

Hickey, Raymond. 2003a. How do dialects get the features they have? On the process of new dialect formation. In Raymond Hickey, ed. *Motives for Language Change*. Cambridge: Cambridge University Press, 213–239.

Hickey, Raymond. 2003b. Rectifying a standard deficiency: Pronominal distinctions in varieties of English. In Irma Taavitsainen and Andreas H. Jucker, eds. *Diachronic Perspectives on Address Term Systems* (Pragmatics & Beyond New Series). Amsterdam: John Benjamins, 345–374.

Hickey, Raymond. 2004a. English dialect input to the Caribbean. In Raymond Hickey, ed. *Legacies of Colonial English: Studies in Transported Dialects*. Cambridge: Cambridge University Press, 326–359.

Hickey, Raymond. 2004b. Dialects of English and their transportation. In Raymond Hickey, ed. *Legacies of Colonial English: Studies in Transported Dialects*. Cambridge: Cambridge University Press, 33–58.

Hickey, Raymond, ed. 2004c. *Legacies of Colonial English: Studies in Transported Dialects*. Cambridge: Cambridge University Press

Hickey, Raymond. 2005. *Dublin English: Evolution and Change*. Amsterdam: John Benjamins.

Hickey, Raymond. 2007. *Irish English: History and Present-Day Forms*. Cambridge: Cambridge University Press.

Hickey, Raymond, ed. 2012a. *Areal Features of the Anglophone World*. Berlin: de Gruyter Mouton.

Hickey, Raymond. 2012b. Standard English and standards of English. In Raymond Hickey, ed. *Standards of English: Codified Varieties around the World*. Cambridge: Cambridge University Press, 1–33.

Hickey, Raymond. 2013. Supraregionalisation and dissociation. In J. K. Chambers and Natalie Schilling, eds. *Handbook of Language Variation and Change* (2nd ed.). Wiley-Blackwell, 537–554.

Hickey, Raymond, ed. 2015. *Researching Northern English*. Amsterdam: John Benjamins.

Hickey, Raymond. 2016. English in Ireland: Development and varieties. In Raymond Hickey, ed. *Sociolinguistics in Ireland*. Basingstoke: Palgrave Macmillan, 3–40.

Hickey, Raymond. 2017. Early recordings of Irish English. In Raymond Hickey, ed. *Listening to the Past: Audio Records of Accents of English*. Cambridge: Cambridge University Press, 199–231.

Higgins, Christina 2003. "Ownership" of English in the Outer Circle: An alternative to the NS-NNS dichotomy. *TESOL Quarterly* 37(4): 615–644.

Hoffmann, Thomas and Lucia Siebers, eds. 2009. *World Englishes: Problems, Properties and Prospects. Selected Papers from the 13th IAWE Conference*. Amsterdam: John Benjamins.

Ihalainen, Ossi. 1994. The dialects of England since 1776. In Robert Burchfield, ed. *The Cambridge History of the English Language, Vol. 5: English in Britain and Overseas: Origins and Development*. Cambridge: Cambridge University Press, 197–274.

Ingram, John and Peter Mühlhäusler. 2008. Norfolk Island-Pitcairn English: Phonetics and phonology. In Kate Burridge and Bernd Kortmann, eds. *Varieties of English: The Pacific and Australasia*. Berlin: Mouton de Gruyter, 267–291.

Jenkins, Jennifer. 2003. *World Englishes: A Resource Book for Students*. London: Routledge.

Kachru, Braj. 1990. *The Alchemy of English: The Spread, Functions, and Models of Non-Native Englishes: English in a Global Context*. Chicago: University of Illinois Press.

Kachru, Braj B., Yamuna Kachru and Cecil L. Nelson, eds. 2006. *The Handbook of World Englishes*. Oxford: Blackwell.

Kachru, Yamuna and Cecil L. Nelson. 2006. *World Englishes in Asian Contexts*. Hong Kong: Hong Kong University Press.

Kirkpatrick, Andy. 2007. *World Englishes: Implications for International Communication and English Language Teaching*. Cambridge: Cambridge University Press.

Kirwin, William J. 2001. Newfoundland English. In John Algeo, ed. *English in North America: The Cambridge History of the English Language*, Vol. 6. Cambridge: Cambridge University Press, 441–455.

Kortmann, Bernd et al., eds. 2008. *Varieties of English*. 4 vols. Berlin: Mouton de Gruyter.

Kurath, Hans and Raven I. McDavid, Jr. 1983 [1961]. *The Pronunciation of English in the Atlantic States: Based upon the Collection of the Linguistic Atlas of the Eastern United States*. Tuscaloosa: University of Alabama Press.

Labov, William. 1972. *Sociolinguistic Patterns*. Philadelphia: University of Pennsylvania Press.

Lass, Roger. 1987. *The Shape of English: Structure and History*. London: Dent.

Lass, Roger. 1990. Where do extraterritorial Englishes come from? Dialect input and recodification in transported Englishes. In Sylvia Adamson et al., eds. *Papers from the 5th International Conference on English Historical Linguistics*. Amsterdam: John Benjamins, 245–280.

Lawson, Philip. 1993. *The East India Company: A History*. London: Longman.

Leimgruber, Jakob R. E. 2013. *Singapore English: Structure, Variation and Usage*. Cambridge: Cambridge University Press.

Levey, David. 2008. *Language Change and Variation in Gibraltar*. Amsterdam: John Benjamins.

Lloyd, Trevor Owen. 1984. *The British Empire, 1558–1983*. Oxford: Oxford University Press.

Louis, William Roger, ed. 1998. *The Oxford History of the British Empire*. Oxford: Oxford University Press.

Marshall, P. J., ed. 1996. *The Cambridge Illustrated History of the British Empire*. Cambridge: Cambridge University Press.

Mazzon, Gabriella. 1993. English in Malta. *English World-Wide* 14: 171–208.

McWhorter, John. 2000. *Defining Creole*. Oxford: Oxford University Press.

McLaughlin, Fiona. 2011. *The Languages of Urban Africa*. London: Bloomsbury.

Melchers, Gunnel and Philip Shaw. 2012. *World Englishes* (2nd ed.). London: Arnold.

Mesthrie, Rajend. 1992. *English in Language Shift: The History, Structure and Sociolinguistics of South African Indian English*. Cambridge: Cambridge University Press.

Mesthrie, Rajend and Rakesh M. Bhatt. 2008. *World Englishes: An Introduction to New Language Varieties*. Cambridge: Cambridge University Press.

Montgomery, Michael. 1989. Exploring the roots of Appalachian English, *English World-Wide* 10: 227–278.

Montgomery, Michael. 1992. The etymology of y'all. In Joan H. Hall, Nick Doane and Dick Ringler, eds. *Old English and New: Studies in Language and Linguistics in Honor of Frederic G. Cassidy*. New York: Garland Press, 356–369.

Montgomery, Michael. 1997. Making transatlantic connections between varieties of English: The case of plural verbal -s. *Journal of English Linguistics* 25(2): 122–141.

Montgomery, Michael. 2001. British and Irish antecedents. In John Algeo, ed. *English in North America: The Cambridge History of the English Language*, Vol. 6. Cambridge: Cambridge University Press, 86–153.

Mufwene, Salikoko. 1996. The founder principle and creole genesis. *Diachronica* 13: 83–134.

Mühlhäusler, Peter. 2008. Norfolk Island – Pitcairn English (Pitkern Norfolk): Morphology and syntax. In Kate Burridge and Bernd Kortmann, eds. *Varieties of English: The Pacific and Australasia*. Berlin: Mouton de Gruyter, 568–582.

Mukherjee, Joybrato and Marianne Hundt, eds. 2011. *Exploring Second-language Varieties of English and Learner Englishes: Bridging a Paradigm Gap*. Amsterdam: John Benjamins.

Myhill, John. 1988. The rise of *be* as an aspect marker in Black English Vernacular. *American Speech* 63, 304–325.

Ooi, Vincent B. Y. ed. 2001. *Evolving Identities: The English Language in Singapore and Malaysia*. Singapore: Times Academic Press.

Orton, Harold et al. 1962–1971. *Survey of English Dialects: The Basic Materials*, 4 vols in 3 parts. Leeds: E. J. Arnold & Son.

Peters, Pam. 2009. Australian English as a regional epicentre. In Thomas Hoffmann and Lucia Siebers, eds. *World Englishes: Problems, Properties and Prospects. Selected Papers from the 13th IAWE Conference*. Amsterdam: John Benjamins, 385–406.

Phillipson, Robert. 1992. *Linguistic Imperialism*. Oxford: Oxford University Press.

Poplack, Shana and Sali Tagliamonte. 1989. There's no tense like the present: Verbal -s inflection in Early Black English. *Language Variation and Change* 1: 47–84.

Poplack, Shana and Sali Tagliamonte. 2004. Back to the present: Verbal -s in the (African American) English diaspora. In Raymond Hickey, ed. *Legacies of Colonial English: Studies in Transported Dialects*. Cambridge: Cambridge University Press, 203–223.

Puttenham, George. 1589. *Arte of English Poesie*. London: Richard Field.

Ramisch, Heinrich. 1989. *The Variation of English in Guernsey/Channel Islands*. Bern: Peter Lang.

Ramson, William S., ed. 1970. *English Transported: Essays on Australian English*. Canberra: National University Press.

Read, Allen Walker. 2005. Words crisscrossing the sea: How words have been borrowed between England and America. *American Speech* 80(2): 115–134.

Rickford, John R. 1975. Carrying the new wave into syntax: The case of Black English BIN. In Ralph W. Fasold and Roger W. Shuy, eds. *Analyzing*

Variation in Language. Washington, DC: Georgetown University Press, 162–183.

Riley, Philip. 2007. *Language, Culture and Identity: An Ethnolinguistic Perspective*. London: Bloomsbury.

Saraceni, Mario. 2015. *World Englishes: A Critical Analysis*. London: Bloomsbury.

Saxena, Mukul and Tope Omoniyi, ed. 2010. *Contending with Globalization in World Englishes*. Clevedon: Multilingual Matters.

Schneider, Edgar W. 2003. The dynamics of New Englishes: From identity construction to dialect birth. *Language* 79(2): 233–281.

Schneider, Edgar W. 2007. *Postcolonial English: Varieties around the World*. Cambridge: Cambridge University Press.

Schneider, Edgar W. 2014. New reflections on the evolutionary dynamics of World Englishes. *World Englishes* 33(1): 9–32.

Schneider, Edgar W. 2016. Grassroots Englishes in tourism interactions. *English Today* 32(3): 2–10.

Schreier, Daniel. 2003. *Isolation and Language Change: Contemporary and Sociohistorical Evidence from Tristan da Cunha English*. Houndsworth: Palgrave Macmillan.

Schreier, Daniel. 2008. *St Helenian English: Origins, Evolution and Variation*. Amsterdam: John Benjamins.

Seargeant, Philip. 2005. Globalisation and reconfigured English in Japan. *World Englishes* 24(3): 309–319.

Seoane, Elena and Cristina Suárez-Gómez, eds. 2016. *World Englishes: New Theoretical and Methodological Considerations*. Amsterdam: John Benjamins.

Starks, Donna. 2008. National and ethnic identity markers: New Zealand short front vowels in New Zealand Maori English and Pasifika Englishes. *English World-Wide* 29(2): 176–193.

Starks, Donna, Jane Christie and Laura Thompson. 2007. Niuean English: Initial insights into an emerging variety. *English World-Wide* 28(2): 133–146.

Sudbury, Andrea. 2001. Falkland Islands English: A southern hemisphere variety?. *English World-Wide* 22: 55–80.

Swan Anne, Pamela Aboshiha and Adrian Holliday, eds. 2015. *(En)Countering Native-speakerism: Global Perspectives*. Basingstoke: Palgrave Macmillan.

Trudgill, Peter. 1990. *The Dialects of England*. Oxford: Blackwell.

Trudgill, Peter. 1999. *The Dialects of England* (2nd ed.). Oxford: Blackwell.

Trudgill, Peter. 2001. Modern East Anglia as dialect area. Jacek Fisiak and Peter Trudgill, eds. *East Anglian English*. Cambridge: D. S. Brewer, 1–12.

Trudgill, Peter. 2004. *New Dialect Formation: The Inevitability of Colonial Englishes*. Edinburgh: Edinburgh University Press.

Turner, Lorenzo D. 1971. Notes on the sounds and vocabulary of Gullah. In Juanita V. Williamson and Virginia M. Burke, eds. *A Various Language: Perspectives on American Dialects*. New York: Holt, Rinehart and Winston, 121–135.

Upton, Clive and John D. A. Widdowson. 2006. *An Atlas of English Dialects* (2nd ed.). Oxford: Oxford University Press.

Vaish, Viniti. 2011. *Globalization of Language and Culture in Asia: The Impact of Globalization Processes on Language*. London: Bloomsbury.

Wee, Lionel. 2013. Language policy in Singapore: Singlish, national development and globalization. In Elizabeth Erling and Philip Seargeant, eds. *English and Development: Policy, Pedagogy and Globalization*. Clevedon: Multilingual Matters, 204–219.

Wells, J. C. 1982. *Accents of English*. 3 vols. Cambridge: Cambridge University Press.

Williams, Jeffrey P. 2012. English varieties in the Caribbean. In Raymond Hickey, ed. *Standards of English: Codified Varieties around the World*. Cambridge: Cambridge University Press, 133–160.

Wright, Joseph. 1898–1905. *English Dialect Dictionary*, 5 vols. London: Henry Frowde.

Wright, Joseph. 1905. *English Dialect Grammar*. Oxford: Clarendon Press.

Zhiming, Bao. 1999. The sounds of Singapore English. In J. A. Foley, T. Kandiah, Bau Zhiming, A. F. Gupta, L. Alsagoff, Ho Chee Lick, et al., eds. *English in New Cultural Contexts*. Singapore: Oxford University Press, 152–174.

3

Theoretical Models of English as a World Language

Sarah Buschfeld and Alexander Kautzsch[†]

3.1 Introduction

Ever since decolonization had taken place in most colonies of the former British Empire and at the latest since Kachru's publication of his Three Circles Model (1985), World Englishes (WEs) research has been developing into one of the most flourishing and vibrant fields of linguistic inquiry. To capture the sociolinguistic diversification of the English language, researchers have investigated a multitude of English varieties spoken around the globe as native or second languages. Together with different labels and terms for the different varieties of English, scholars have developed, applied, discussed, and refined different models of and approaches to WEs to account for the spread, forms, and functions of the language worldwide.

The chapter at hand gives an overview of the most important research developments in the field and introduces the most prominent models, that is, the ENL/ESL/EFL distinction (English as a Native Language, English as a Second Language, English as a Foreign Language; Quirk et al. 1972: 3–4), Kachru's (1985) Three Circles of World Englishes, McArthur's (1987) Circle of World English, Görlach's ([1988] 1990) Circle of International English, Gupta's (1997) classification of "output types" (Schneider 2011: 54), Mesthrie and Bhatt's (2008) classification of the English Language Complex, Moag's ([1982] 1992) Life Cycle of Non-Native Englishes, and Schneider's (2003, 2007) Dynamic Model, as well as the most recent approaches and developments in the field, viz. Meierkord's (2012) conception of Interactions across Englishes, Mair's (2013) World System of Standard and Non-Standard Englishes, Schneider's (2014) notion of Transnational Attraction, Onysko's (2016) Language Contact Typology, and – most recently – Buschfeld and Kautzsch's (2017) Extra- and Intra-territorial Forces (EIF) Model.

[†] 2018.

Given the wealth of different taxonomies, it is not possible to present the individual details of each model within the confines of this chapter. Instead, we will outline the developmental route the research field has taken in the last four decades by focusing on how WEs researchers have reacted to, built on, and complemented earlier models of the discipline, with a special focus on the most recent developments in the field. Accordingly, and often summarizing details into overarching conceptual considerations, we will look into important paradigm changes in the discipline: In the 1980s, Kachru initiated the first crucial steps toward an equal analysis and standing of native and non-native varieties of English by questioning the alleged superiority of native speaker standards (e.g. Kachru 1976, 1985, 1992a); in the first decade of the twenty-first century, Schneider's Dynamic Model introduced what we decided to call "the diachronic turn"; and the most recent approaches again suggest a change in orientation in WEs research, this time toward an enhanced analysis and stronger integration of Expanding Circle Englishes, that is, non-postcolonial Englishes (non-PCEs), and any other type of English developing beyond national boundaries (cf. Seargeant and Tagg's 2011 notion of a "post-varieties" approach; see also Blommaert 2010; Meierkord 2012). Accordingly, we divide the development of WEs theorizing and thus the structure of this chapter into three main phases. We first outline and discuss "The Early Years: 1970s to 1990," most prominently the ENL/ESL/EFL distinction as well as Kachru's Three Circles Model (Section 3.2.1); we subsequently account for "Advancements in the Development of World Englishes Theorizing: 1990 to 2010," focusing on the diachronic turn and Schneider's Dynamic Model (Section 3.2.2); we finally present a discussion and critical evaluation of the latest developments in the field, "Opening Up New Perspectives: Recent Approaches to World Englishes" (Section 3.2.3), including a brief description and evaluation of Meierkord's (2012) Interactions across Englishes framework, Mair's (2013) World System of Standard and Non-Standard Englishes, Schneider's (2014) notion of Transnational Attraction, and focusing on Buschfeld and Kautzsch's (2017) EIF Model.

3.2 Approaches to and Models of World Englishes: A Developmental Perspective

When approaching the major developments and theoretical trends in WEs studies by providing an overview, critical evaluation, and discussion of the most influential models of English as a world language, it makes most sense to do so in (mostly) chronological order. Often new taxonomies arose as responses to shortcomings or conceptual problems identified in earlier approaches, as complements to earlier approaches, or simply as reactions to theoretical reorientations in the field due to changing linguistic realities. To give a comprehensive and at the same time clear account of these developments, we have identified the three major developmental phases introduced in the previous section to which we will attend in turn.

3.2.1   The Early Years: 1970s to 1990

The field of WEs research built momentum in the 1970s and especially the 1980s as a response to and reaction against the monolithic view of the English language (cf. McArthur 1987: 9, 1998: 56–77) still prevalent then, despite the ongoing formation of different varieties of English around the globe. Researchers began looking into the sociolinguistic status and linguistic characteristics of these varieties and the 1980s brought forth several models (e.g. Görlach [1988] 1990; Kachru 1985; McArthur 1987) that approach the linguistic diversity of the English language(s) from a pluralistic angle (cf. McArthur 1998: 93–95).

3.2.1.1   The ENL/ESL/EFL Distinction

In line with this reorientation, one of the most stable and still most widely used categorizations of different types of WEs is the distinction between ENL, ESL, and EFL, respectively. It has been traced back to the first formal attempts to classify and characterize different varieties of English, namely to Barbara M. H. Strang's (1970) classification of the worldwide English speaking community into what she called A, B, and C speakers (cf. McArthur 1998: 42; see also Schneider 2007: 12). Two years after Strang's (1970) contribution, Quirk et al. (1972: 3–4) introduced "[a]n influential variant of her classification" (McArthur 1998: 43), viz. that of "native language," "second language," and "foreign language" use, which largely corresponds to the earlier tripartite distinction introduced by Strang. This terminology has then been adopted, used, and systematized in later approaches to and publications on the topic under the labels "English as a Native Language / ENL," "English as a Second Language / ESL," and "English as a Foreign Language / EFL" (see, among many others, Görlach [1988]1990, 1998; Graddol 1997; Moag [1982] 1992; Strevens 1992). Accordingly, the group of ENL countries consists of those territories where English is spoken as a native language by the vast majority of the population (e.g. the USA, Great Britain, and Australia). This does, however, not necessarily exclude multilingualism, that is, other languages might exist alongside English (Schneider 2007: 12). In ESL countries (e.g. India and Nigeria), English fulfills prominent intranational functions in a variety of possible contexts, for example in the education sector, the media, the political domain, and jurisdiction, and it is used as the language of interethnic communication between groups of different language backgrounds. It typically coexists with other languages, most often one or more indigenous languages of the local population. In EFL countries, on the other hand, English does not fulfill special intranational functions but is normally restricted to international communication and is mainly if not solely learned through formal education (cf. Quirk et al. 1985: 4–5; see also Schneider 2007: 12; Strevens 1992: 36).

3.2.1.2 Kachru's (1985) Three Circles of World Englishes

Next to the direct and explicit adoption and use of the ENL/ESL/EFL distinction in early as well as recent approaches, the classification finds implicit application as the conceptual basis of Kachru's (1985) Three Concentric Circles of WEs (cf. Schneider 2011: 31). Like the ENL/ESL/EFL distinction, this model has been widely recognized, adopted, and discussed, with scholars both pointing out its merits and discussing potential disadvantages and shortcomings (e.g. Crystal 2003a: 107, 2003b: 60–61; Mesthrie and Bhatt 2008: 28–31; Schneider 2007: 13–14, 2011: 31–33). The model, often visualized as three overlapping ovals or concentric circles, suggests a classification into Inner Circle, Outer Circle, and Expanding Circle countries, basically along the lines of the ENL/ESL/EFL distinction (cf. McArthur 1998: 59, 97–98).

In Inner Circle countries, English is (one of) the de facto if not de jure official and primary language(s) and the native language for the majority of the inhabitants. This holds for what Kachru (1985:12) calls "the traditional bases of English," that is, the UK, the USA, Australia, Canada, and New Zealand. The different Englishes spoken in the Inner Circle are typically endonormative in orientation and norm-providing since they serve as models for the Expanding Circle and partly also for the Outer Circle (hence the label "norm-providing varieties"; Kachru 1985: 16, 1992b: 5).

The Outer (or Extended) Circle traditionally comprises non-native English countries like India, Kenya, and Singapore. English was basically taken there as a by-product of extended (British) colonization. After having been transplanted, the English language typically went through the processes of nativization and institutionalization, which were driven by political, socio-cultural, and linguistic changes. In such regions, English is spoken as one of two or more languages of a bi- or multilingual society and often is the de jure second language for most of the inhabitants. With respect to function and use, institutionalized varieties in Outer Circle contexts have "an extended functional *range* in a variety of social, educational, administrative, and literary domains" (Kachru 1985: 13; emphasis in original), they are used across subgroups of the population, and have hence "acquired an important status in the language policies of most of such multilingual nations" (Kachru 1985: 12–13). They have been referred to as "norm-developing varieties" (Kachru 1985: 17) since some of them have experienced acceptance as local norms – at least by some of its speakers.

As opposed to the Outer Circle, the Expanding Circle consists of countries to which English has not been transported as the result of British (or American)[1] imperialism. Examples are China, Indonesia, Greece, Japan,

---

[1] This most prominently applies to the case of the Philippines (cf. Schneider's [2007: 140–144] case study).

and Saudi Arabia (Kachru 1985: 13). Accordingly, English does not have special status in such countries (Crystal 2003a: 107–108) but serves as a lingua franca, especially in international business. It is mainly spoken as a foreign language, is thus taught through formal education, and is "not passed on to infants naturalistically across generations" (Bruthiaux 2003: 160). In addition, speakers in EFL countries are normally not oriented toward a local model that reflects local usage of English (Graddol 1997: 11). Instead, they are exonormatively oriented toward and depend on norms of the Inner Circle, mostly British and American English, as assumed standard varieties, and they are consequently often referred to as "norm-dependent varieties" (Kachru 1985: 17). Since English is nowadays taught in most nations of the world, it can be argued that almost every country not belonging to either the Inner or the Outer Circle belongs to the Expanding Circle (cf. Bruthiaux 2003: 160).

Turning to the academic reception of these first two approaches, their importance for the field of WEs research cannot be overestimated, as they were the first to account for the pluralistic and diverse nature of English, which until then had been basically considered a monolithic whole (cf. McArthur 1987: 9, 1998: 56–77). The fact that they challenged this view of the English language brought them favorable attention and they have been widely adopted ever since by researchers around the globe. An additional major achievement of Kachru's approach back then was to bring about a change in scholarly (and also public) attitudes by challenging the outstanding importance often ascribed to ENL countries. In this respect, his main aim was to resolve the inequalities in perception of native and non-native varieties of English by questioning the alleged superiority of native speaker standards (Kachru 1976, 1985, 1992a). Nevertheless, when facing more recent linguistic realities and scientific demands, a number of problems and shortcomings become apparent with these approaches.

What is conceptually problematic with respect to both the ENL/ESL/EFL distinction and Kachru's Three Circles Model – a very similar line of criticism has been applied to both taxonomies – is that they do not account for the heterogeneity of speech groups and the multilingual setup of nations (e.g. different levels of proficiency, the linguistic setup of a country) and other aspects such as identity construction or language attitudes and use (e.g. Bruthiaux 2003: 162–167 on Kachru's model). They hence "ignore . . . certain facets of complex realities" (Schneider 2007: 12–13 on the ENL/ESL/ EFL distinction). We would like to address the three major aspects of criticism that have prominently been discussed in the literature and are more topical than ever.

The first important aspect here is that recent studies have revealed clear overlaps between the three categories, that is, the simultaneous existence of ENL, ESL, or EFL speakers in one territory (e.g. Mesthrie and Bhatt 2008: 31; Schneider 2007: 13 on the coexistence of ENL and ESL in South Africa).

The second major issue, as some case studies show, is that certain varieties are undergoing transition from one category to the other (e.g. Buschfeld 2013 on the ESL to EFL transition of English in Cyprus; Buschfeld forthcoming on the change from ESL to ENL in Singapore; Buschfeld and Kautzsch 2014 on the EFL to ESL development of English in Namibia; Edwards 2016 on the change from EFL to ESL in the Netherlands). This strongly suggests that a static handling of these categories does not reflect linguistic realities. It has consequently and repeatedly been argued that the strict ENL/ESL and ESL/EFL distinctions (and the Inner Circle–Outer Circle/Outer Circle–Expanding Circle divides, respectively) are imprecise taxonomies for many sociolinguistic situations (cf. Schneider 2007: 13), at least when considered as dichotomic constructs, and should better be viewed as two ends of a continuum (e.g. Biewer 2011; Buschfeld 2013; Gilquin and Granger 2011). Related to this aspect and ultimately leading the way to further developments in WEs research (cf. Section 3.2.2), it has often been pointed out that the older approaches almost completely lack a diachronic dimension of the development of different Englishes and are "products mainly of twentieth-century synchronic scholarship" (McArthur 1998: 98).[2]

3.2.1.3   Further Circle Models: McArthur (1987) and Görlach (1990)

Shortly after Kachru's (1985) model, McArthur (1987) and Görlach (1990) proposed further circle models to capture the diversity of WEs. Both models explicitly focus on membership assignment along geographical boundaries and issues of standardization. They originate in an allegedly homogeneous hub (a "World Standard English" in McArthur's conception and an "International English" in Görlach's model), branching out into geographically more distinct, regional, and less standard subvarieties in a spoke-wise fashion.

   The criticisms of McArthur's and Görlach's models have been less elaborate and less frequent in the literature, and, in fact, their influence and reception have been much less prominent than that of Kachru's three circles and the ENL/ESL/EFL distinction. Apart from their certain contribution to the discussion of notions such as "standard," criticism on the two models (e.g. in Mesthrie and Bhatt 2008) mostly does not address larger conceptual aspects of categorizing WEs or aspects that seem to have strongly influenced the development of the overall WEs research paradigm. Yet, in retrospect, critics of these models (e.g. Mesthrie and Bhatt

---

[2] With all due criticism, it has to be noted, however, that the gist of today's criticism of Kachru's model had been recognized by Kachru himself. He had commented on the inaccuracies identified long before most criticism came up. When he introduced his approach in 1985, he already conceded that the boundary between the Outer and the Expanding Circle is not clear-cut (Kachru 1985: 13–14, 17), and that "[g]rey areas between the . . . two do exist" (Kachru 1985: 17). For one thing, he acknowledged that ESL countries may develop EFL status and vice versa, due to changing language policies in the respective countries (Kachru 1985: 14). For another, he also conceded that complex linguistic situations as to be found in South Africa and Jamaica cannot be easily accounted for by his circle model (Kachru 1985: 14).

2008: 27–28) have at least indirectly referred to issues that are particularly relevant in most recent debates on modeling WEs (cf. Section 3.2.3). One such issue is the question of membership assignment, that is, what should and should not be included in the WEs paradigm, more precisely the role of, for example, Englishes in Europe, EFLs in general, pidgins and creoles, mixes, and other related languages involving English and their relationship to each other and to other varieties of English.

3.2.1.4 An Evaluative Summary of the Early Years

Despite the advancements these early models brought about, all of them employ rather superficial, imprecise, and static perspectives. They identify solely the functional and political roles the English language plays in the respective country or focus on geographical aspects for classification (cf. McArthur's [1998: 98] cover term "geopolitical models"). One important aspect that is almost completely lacking in most of these models is the diachronic dimension of the development of different Englishes (see also McArthur 1998: 98).

3.2.2 Advancements in the Development of World Englishes Theorizing: 1990 to 2010

After the first important step in WEs studies had been taken by generally acknowledging the pluricentricity[3] of the English language and devising first models to account for this development, other scholars suggested further, refined ways to capture the ever-increasing and ever-complexifying spread and entrenchment of the English language worldwide. Schneider's (2003, 2007) Dynamic Model is certainly the most influential approach of that time as it meets the essentials of many of the shortcomings of the earlier approaches and has experienced wide acceptance and application since its introduction in 2003/2007, sometimes with suggestions for slight modifications (e.g. Buschfeld 2013; Evans 2009; Mukherjee 2007; Weston 2011; cf. Schneider 2014 for a detailed stocktaking). It will consequently be at the heart of this section, but let us first briefly turn to two other approaches that clearly deserve some attention.

3.2.2.1 Gupta's (1997) Classification of "Output Types" and Mesthrie and Bhatt's (2008) English Language Complex

Pursuing a similar conceptual approach to classifying different types of WEs, both Gupta (1997)[4] and Mesthrie and Bhatt (2008) group different Englishes according to characteristics shared by certain countries, especially with respect to general conditions of usage. They both meet some of

---

[3] For a detailed account of the notion of "pluricentricity," see Leitner (1992).

[4] Schneider (2011: 54) refers to Gupta's (1997) classification of Englishes as "output types" since they are "produced by their historical origins."

the shortcomings identified for the earlier models in that they add socio-linguistic details to the classification scheme, such as degree of bi- or multilingualism of the respective country and the prevalent ways of language transmission. Along these lines, Gupta (1997) distinguishes five variety types, viz. (1) monolingual ancestral English countries (e.g. the UK, the USA, New Zealand, and Australia), (2) monolingual contact variety countries (e.g. Jamaica), (3) multilingual scholastic English countries (e.g. India and Pakistan), (4) multilingual contact variety countries (e.g. Papua New Guinea and Singapore), and (5) multilingual ancestral English countries (e.g. Canada and South Africa) (for further details, see Gupta 1997: 53–56). Yet she concentrates solely on native and non-native indigenized varieties of English and thus leaves out countries in which English is supposed to have EFL status since they have a non-postcolonial background (she cites France, Japan, and Korea as examples; Gupta 1997: 48). However, the 1990s were the decade in which English started to exert great influence even in countries without a postcolonial background, most importantly via the spread and growth of the Internet, other modern media, and globalization in general.

This aspect, however, seems to have been addressed in Mesthrie and Bhatt (2008), who adapt McArthur's notion of "the English Language Complex" and provide a list of twelve different subtypes. Their account is much more detailed than Gupta's classification, especially in that it is not restricted to indigenized non-native and native varieties of English but also includes types of English that cannot be classified in terms of Gupta's (1997) categories, for example EFLs, immigrant Englishes, and mixed codes. The classification catalogue (Mesthrie and Bhatt 2008: 3–6) can be summarized as follows, with 1–4 as native varieties and 5–12 as non-native Englishes: (1) metropolitan standards (British and American English), (2) colonial standards (e.g. Australia, New Zealand, South Africa), (3) regional dialects (i.e. regional variants of the USA and the UK, and potentially Australia, New Zealand, and the other colonial standards), (4) social dialects (i.e. the socially and/or ethnically stratified variants of colonial standards), (5) Pidgin Englishes (e.g. West African Pidgin English), (6) Creole Englishes (e.g. Jamaican Creole), (7) English as a Second Language (ESL) (cf. Section 3.2.1.1), (8) English as a Foreign Language (EFL) (cf. Section 3.2.1.1), (9) Immigrant Englishes (e.g. Chicano English), (10) Language-Shift Englishes (i.e. varieties that occur in contexts in which English has [largely] taken the position of a former native language of that territory, e.g. in Ireland), (11) Jargon Englishes (e.g. the South Seas Jargon), and (12) Hybrid Englishes (e.g. the Indian mixed code "Hinglish").

When turning to a critical evaluation of the two accounts, they both appear useful when classifying different types of Englishes according to their historical origins and their actual status (cf. Schneider 2011: 54). When compared to, for example, Kachru's Three Concentric Circles model, Gupta's approach is a lot more precise since, even if it still approaches a classification from a nation-state perspective, it clearly takes into account the internal linguistic heterogeneity of the respective country and at least some relevant developmental aspects. On the other hand, Gupta's approach is more limited in that it only considers countries in which English is spoken as a native or indigenized second-language variety of English. In this respect, Mesthrie and Bhatt's (2008) classification appears to be more comprehensive and better suited for capturing the realities of the worldwide spread of the English language today since it offers a larger set of options and does not presuppose indigenization as a criterion for inclusion. Nevertheless, their classification is not as clear-cut as it might appear at first sight and raises a number of important questions. Its weak spots seem to be the criteria of membership assignment, again the issue of potential overlaps of categories (cf. the discussion in Section 3.2.1.2), and still the general question of which forms of English to include at all (cf. Mesthrie and Bhatt 2008: 6–7). What is even more important is that, even though both models take into consideration the historical origin and at least some developmental aspects of the respective type of English, they both still operate synchronically, that is, categorization mainly works on the basis of current status rather than offering a comprehensive picture of the emergence of the different Englishes. We consider the latter aspect of crucial importance when trying to account for the unprecedented spread, entrenchment, and the many different manifestations of the English language worldwide.

3.2.2.2 The Diachronic Turn: Schneider's (2003, 2007) Dynamic Model
Since the diachronic dimension is fully offered by Schneider's Dynamic Model, we decided to introduce it in some more detail here as it constitutes the major advancement of this era and initiated what we suggest to call the diachronic turn in WEs studies.

Drawing on Moag's ([1982] 1992) four-stages Life Cycle of Non-Native Englishes[5] and others, Schneider (2007) proposes that "there is an underlying uniform process which has driven the individual historical instantiations of PCEs growing in different localities" (Schneider 2007: 21).[6] According to Schneider, this development typically proceeds along five major stages: (1) foundation, (2) exonormative stabilization, (3) structural nativization, (4) endonormative stabilization, and (5) differentiation. It

---

[5] It has to be noted here that Moag ([1982] 1992), in turn drawing on Hall's (1962) Life Cycle of Pidgin Languages, actually made the much earlier diachronic contribution to WEs theorizing but, even though the approaches are similar in many respects, Moag's model was not nearly as successful as Schneider's. This is certainly because it is not as detailed and well-conceived as the Dynamic Model but, more importantly, it may well be that, back in the early 1980s, the focus and demands of WEs research were on something different, viz. first acknowledging the pluricentricity of the English language. Moag's ideas were therefore probably just far ahead of the times. The model will not be described here as Schneider continues most of Moag's underlying ideas and expands and refines them. For a detailed description of the model, see, for example, Buschfeld (2011: 61–63).

[6] A similar observation has already been put forward by Kachru, who argued that "there is an underlying pattern and a shared direction in the linguistic nativization of English" (Kachru 1985: 21).

thus starts out with the translocation of the English language to a new territory, followed by major changes in social as well as linguistic realities, resulting in linguistic nativization and stabilization, and finally the potential for internal differentiation (Schneider 2007: 29–30). Also part of the Dynamic Model and operating within each of the five phases are four parameters, viz. (1) "Extralinguistic factors," that is, the historical and political development of a country, which leads to (2) "characteristic identity constructions," which influence (3) the "sociolinguistic determinants of the contact setting," that is, language contact conditions, and language attitudes and use, in turn resulting in (4) "structural effects," that is, lexical, phonological, and grammatical characteristics (Schneider 2007: 30–35).

At the heart of this overall process are the conceptualization and realignments of identity constructions as well as "their symbolic linguistic expressions" (Schneider 2007: 28) that manifest in the interaction, perspectives, and experiences of two major groups, the STL (settler) and IDG (indigenous) strands. In the initial stage of contact these are mutually exclusive but they experience gradual convergence while passing through the individual phases (Schneider 2007: 31). The Dynamic Model predicts that, in the course of time, the two strands become more and more intertwined, while gradual assimilation of identity constructions takes place. This in turn leads to linguistic accommodation of the two groups. In other words, they gradually merge into a single speech community, ultimately sharing a large set of linguistic features and norms (Schneider 2007: 32; for more details on the different phases, see Schneider 2007: 33–35, or one of the many summarizing accounts such as Buschfeld et al. 2014).

With respect to its scientific reception, it has been widely and mostly positively received, applied, and sometimes adapted; some contributions have suggested and discussed modifications (e.g. Buschfeld 2013, 2014; Buschfeld and Kautzsch 2017; Evans 2009, 2014; Huber 2014; Mukherjee 2007; Thusat et al. 2009; Weston 2011; cf. Schneider 2014 for a detailed stocktaking). Its clear advantage lies in the fact that it captures the development and characteristics of varieties of English in their entirety, that is, from the original transportation up to the current point of investigation. Next to modifications called for by specific case studies, some aspects of the model have received criticism from a more theoretical perspective (e.g. Mesthrie and Bhatt, 2008: 35–36; see Buschfeld 2013: 191–192 and Schneider 2014: 16–17 for details and some discussion). What has, however, been of crucial interest for WEs theorizing is the ongoing debate on the relevance of identity in the emergence of new varieties.

While identity figures prominently in Schneider's Dynamic Model, its impact is categorically denied by Trudgill's (2004) fully deterministic and mechanical model of "new-dialect formation." In Trudgill's view, the outcome of dialect contact in "tabula rasa colonial situations" (Trudgill 2004: 26) is predictable and dialect formation is seen as a purely mechanical process (e.g. Trudgill 2004: 28), based on certain input factors such as mixing, leveling, and unmarking (Trudgill 2004: 84–86). This controversy is discussed in a special issue of *Language in Society* (Trudgill 2008; for further discussions, see, e.g., Schneider 2018; van Rooy 2010). Besides some doubts about Trudgill's claim of tabula rasa situations in colonial settings, the most relevant part of the debate centers on the relative importance of accommodation and identity. In all contributions, there is wide agreement about the crucial role played by accommodation in the emergence of new varieties. Yet, while for Trudgill accommodation is mechanical, or, in his words, "is most often an automatic consequence of interaction" (Trudgill 2004: 28) that excludes identity as the driving force behind these processes, Schneider (2008) defines accommodation as "a process of linguistic approximation with the social goal of signaling solidarity by diminishing symbolic distance" and consequently postulates that accommodation and identity cannot be seen separately. For Schneider (e.g. 2018), these two views, however, are not necessarily mutually exclusive as they refer to different stages in the evolution of colonial varieties, that is, "the mechanistic strength of input factor weights is strongest in early dialect contact … while the role of identity kicks in effectively much later" (Schneider 2018: 54).

What should also be considered is that the applicability of the Dynamic Model is to some degree limited by its restriction to Englishes having emerged from (post)colonial contexts. However, in recent years, various studies have pointed to territories in which indigenized second-language varieties of English seem to be emerging even without an English colonial background (e.g. Buschfeld and Kautzsch 2014 and Buschfeld 2014 on Namibia; Davydova 2012 on Russia; Edwards 2016 on the Netherlands; Bolton 2003 on China; Modiano 2003 on Sweden) but mainly due to general forces of globalization (e.g. Bruthiaux 2003: 165–167; Buschfeld 2013, 2014; see also Blommaert 2010; Coupland 2010). The model does not address such developments. As Seargeant (2012: 155) puts it, "it is primarily varieties-based, and thus does not examine some of the ways in which the language exists in other parts of the world (i.e. the Expanding Circle)." Even though the model is deliberately restricted to PCEs, recent contributions to WEs theorizing have addressed the question whether the model can be applied to such non-postcolonial countries (e.g. Schneider 2014; Buschfeld and Kautzsch 2017; Edwards 2016). Whereas the answer is comparatively unanimous, viz. that what Edwards (2016: 187) calls "the colonial trappings of the model"[7] are hard to overcome, the reactions to

---

[7] These show in the lack of colonial background, which accounts for the following interrelated differences between postcolonial and non-postcolonial societies that are essential for the Dynamic Model to work: differences in "transplantation," lack of both a settler strand and an external colonizing power governing and influencing the colony from the outside, the type(s) of language contact, and the development of identity constructions and consequently linguistic accommodation between the two strands as observed in postcolonial societies (for details, see Buschfeld and Kautzsch 2017).

this insight vary: Schneider concludes that "[i]n essence, the Dynamic Model is not really, or only to a rather limited extent, a suitable framework to describe this new kind of dynamism of global Englishes" (2014: 27–8); Edwards demands that "the parallels [between PCEs and non-PCEs] should be salvaged, but placed in a new framework" (2016: 187); and, reacting to these earlier conclusions, Buschfeld and Kautzsch "stick to the idea of finding a solution that integrates PCEs and non-PCEs in a unified framework, salvaging the parallels but also accounting for the differences in form of a higher-level framework" (2017: 113).

3.2.3 Opening Up New Perspectives: Recent Approaches to World Englishes

We suggest that the theoretical offspring of this discussion has introduced yet another era of WEs studies, which will be described in the following section. We focus on Buschfeld and Kautzsch's (2017) EIF Model, paying tribute to the influence Schneider's Dynamic Model and his notion of Transnational Attraction have had on the World Englishes paradigm, with especially the first having developed so much well-deserved authority and recognition that it clearly has resonated into most recent developments of WEs theorizing. Before this, however, brief mention should also be made of Meierkord's (2012) Interactions across Englishes (IaE), Mair's (2013) World System of Standard and Non-Standard Englishes, and Onysko's (2016) Language Contact Typology, all of which have been recently suggested (within the present decade) to account for the current forces, mechanisms, and manifestations of English worldwide.

Meierkord's framework is the chronologically first of these three approaches and offers a welcome contribution to the topic from the English as a lingua franca perspective. She suggests to replace or rather complement the lingua franca notion by her conception of Interactions across Englishes, adding important perspectives to the general discussion of how to best capture the global realities of the use and spread of English worldwide. Most importantly, Meierkord brings in a focus on the interactional character of English-language conversations and emphasizes the fuzzy boundaries between the different varieties of English in today's ever globalizing conversations. The core assumption of the IaE concept is "that the different Englishes potentially merge in these interactions," resulting in "the development of new emergent varieties" and not "one stable or even codified variety, but rather a heterogeneous array of new linguistic systems" (Meierkord 2012: 2; emphasis in original).

Mair approaches the English Language Complex from yet another perspective, somewhat reminiscent of the earlier suggestions by Görlach and McArthur (cf. Section 3.2.1.3). Transferring de Swaan's (2002, 2010) language systems theory, a hierarchical categorization of the world's languages, to English, Mair (2013) proposes a theoretical framework aimed at grasping the relationships between standard and nonstandard varieties of English. To that end, he identifies Standard American English as the "hyper-central variety" or "hub," while other standard and nonstandard varieties are classified as "super-central," "central," or "peripheral." Despite its intuitive validity, its claim to "shed ... light on the differential power of non-standard varieties of English, particularly in the post-colonial world" (Mair 2013: 262), and its attempt to tackle new ways of communicating beyond nation-state boundaries, for example in Internet forums, this model does not serve the needs envisaged in the current contribution as we seek to account for the development and current manifestations of English in its worldwide entirety. From our perspective, it seems somewhat static in its synchronic orientation and addresses neither current issues such as the integration of EFLs nor diachronic developments, nor potential transformations in status (e.g. from "central" variety to "peripheral" variety or vice versa).

Another fairly recent contribution to the debate comes from Alexander Onysko (2016), who proposes to approach the topic from the perspective of language contact "as an underlying mechanism for all Englishes" (196). Grounded in this assumption, he proposes a "language contact circle of world Englishes ... [that] categorizes the plurality of Englishes in the world according to five major contact settings" (212), viz. "Global Englishes," "Learner Englishes," "Englishes in multilingual constellations," "English-based Pidgins and Creoles," and "Koiné Englishes" (212–215). His idea is convincing in principle, yet not really new – we doubt that anyone would actually deny the influence of language contact on the development of varieties of English. In fact, contact is indeed one of the core parameters in the formation and development of different Englishes but far from the only one. As elaborated on in more detail later in this section, we assume that we must take into consideration a variety of factors (cf. our notion of forces, operating on the formation and development of Englishes at different times and to different extents, depending on the particular context). Before we turn to the EIF Model in more detail, we briefly introduce Schneider's notion of transnational attraction, as it has inspired much of our theoretical work.

It is certainly much less detailed than any of the other approaches introduced in the present chapter, yet it conceptually addresses the most recent developments in the spread and entrenchment of the English language, viz. the ever-increasing use of English in the Expanding Circle as well as any kind of English emerging as the result of "poststructuralist diffusion" (Schneider 2014: 25), including speech forms developing beyond national boundaries as, for example, in Internet and new media communication. In this conceptual framework, English is seen as an attractor for both individuals and communities, who learn and use it "'as an economic resource' (Kachru 2005: 91), a symbol of modernity and a stepping stone toward prosperity." The concept thus tries to capture "the [resulting] appropriation of (components of) English(es) for whatever communicative purposes at hand, unbounded by distinctions of norms, nations or varieties" (Schneider 2014: 28). Even though this conceptual framework has not yet been carved out in every detail[8] and remains rather vague concerning its practical application, the general ideas, that is, English as worldwide attractor as well as its transnational appeal and use, have proven valuable and pivotal for the conception of a more broadly conceived, higher-level framework aiming to capture the recent linguistic developments in the English-speaking world.

Building on the general conception of Schneider's (2003, 2007) Dynamic Model as well as on the intriguing notions of Transnational Attraction (Schneider 2014) and "foundation-through-globalisation" (Edwards 2016), Buschfeld and Kautzsch developed the EIF Model. It specifically aims at integrating PCEs and non-PCEs in a unified framework of WEs, preserving the parallels but also accounting for the differences between the two linguistic scenarios (see Edwards, 2016 for a similar reasoning). To that end, Buschfeld and Kautzsch (2017) introduce the notion of extra- and intra-territorial forces as constantly operating on the development of both PCEs and non-PCEs. Being at the heart of the development of any kind of English around the world (e.g. ENL, ESL, EFL, but also English for Specific Purposes, English as a Lingua Franca), they assume that such forces operate both on the national level and on the different groups of speakers within (and ultimately also across) particular countries,[9] be they ethnic, social, vocational, or stratified by any other secondary variable like proficiency level or age.

In this respect, the extra-territorial forces manifest as any factor entering the country (and potentially community, which deliberately is meant to reach beyond national boundaries) from the outside and intra-territorial forces are such that mainly operate on a local, that is, national or regional, level and therefore influence the cultural and linguistic development from within the country. As we cannot elaborate on each of these forces in detail, Table 3.1 illustrates the five major potential subcategories of these extra- and intra-territorial forces identified so far, viz. colonization (extra)/ attitudes toward colonization (intra), language policies (both extra and intra), globalization (extra)/"acceptance" of globalization (intra), tourism (as a major manifestation of globalization but to be treated separately here due to its immense impact and influence in many parts of the world), foreign policies (both extra and intra), and the sociodemographic background of a country (mostly intra-territorial but with clear extra-territorial dimensions). In addition, Table 3.1 indicates whether or not the individual

---

[8] Personal communication with Edgar Schneider, December 2015.

[9] In principle, the authors have an approach in mind that goes beyond PCEs and non-PCEs and also includes scenarios not delimited by the boundaries of nation-states. Yet, due to its recency, the model has not been explicitly applied to such contexts. Thus, future research is needed to test and evaluate its applicability to these scenarios and to identify potential revisions or conceptual enhancements.

Table 3.1 *An overview of extra- and intra-territorial forces (after Buschfeld and Kautzsch 2017: 114)*

Extra-territorial force	PCE	Non-PCE	Intra-territorial force	PCE	Non-PCE
Colonization	✓	✗	Attitudes toward colonizing power	✓	✗
Language policies	✓	✓	Language policies	✓	✓
Globalization	✓	✓	"Acceptance" of globalization	✓	✓
Tourism	✓	✓	Tourism	✓	✓
Foreign policies	✓	✓	Foreign policies	✓	✓
Sociodemographic background	✓	✓	Sociodemographic background	✓	✓

forces theoretically apply to both PCE and non-PCE contexts, suggesting that colonization (and its intra-territorial side) is actually the only, admittedly very relevant, factor that truly sets the two scenarios apart (for further details on the forces, see Buschfeld and Kautzsch 2017), a finding that again reveals the necessity of an integrated analytical framework for PCEs and non-PCEs.

In the light of this EIF framework, extra- and intra-territorial forces have always been the driving forces behind the (socio)linguistic developments of both PCEs and non-PCEs alike, viz. in their foundation phases but also throughout their further developments, in colonial as well as postcolonial times (as indicated by the arrows in Figure 3.1), certainly at different paces, with exact manifestations differing from context to context. Yet Buschfeld and Kautzsch (2017) hold on to the idea of some kind of uniform development underlying the evolution of Englishes as finds expression in the five phases of the Dynamic Model (cf. Schneider 2003, 2007). As Figure 3.1 illustrates, both the phases and the four parameters of the Dynamic Model are preserved in the EIF Model, since they all can be accounted for in terms of extra- and intra-territorial forces.

The EIF Model sees the development from EFL to ESL and potentially ENL (as well as the potential for reverse development) as running parallel to the progression of the five phases, even though the latter step – as well as the movement to phases 4 and 5 – have so far apparently never been taken by non-PCEs and it remains questionable but theoretically conceivable and certainly interesting to see if such development is possible for a territory without a (post)colonial background at all (for a detailed account of the EIF Model and the rationale behind it, see Buschfeld and Kautzsch 2017).

As the third dimension in Figure 3.2 illustrates, the model also accounts for the variety-internal heterogeneity found in almost every regionally defined type of English to a greater or lesser extent. The main idea here is that capturing the sociolinguistic realities as well as the status,

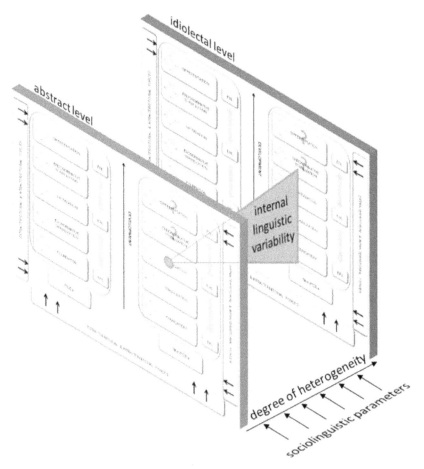

Figure 3.1 The Extra- and Intra-territorial Forces (EIF) Model (after Buschfeld and Kautzsch 2017: 117; Buschfeld et al. 2018: 24)

functions, and uses of English requires a higher level of granularity, that is, zooming in to possible differences between speaker groups and – in its most detailed form – the idiolects of individual speakers than are often found in accounts of varieties of English. As illustrated by the arrows at the bottom of the abstraction in Figure 3.2, such heterogeneity is mainly motivated by sociolinguistic variables such as age, ethnicity, social status, gender, and so on. This heterogeneity is visualized by the triangle in Figure 3.2, in which the starting node constitutes the highest level of abstraction and the vertical plane in the back the highest level of detail (viz. language use of the individual). As Buschfeld et al. (2018: 26) elaborate: "Within the triangle, the different sub-varieties can be located closer toward the node or closer toward the outside plane, depending on the level of granularity one aims at. The more heterogeneous a variety, the more widely spread the external points of the fan are at the level of the individual" (for further details, see Buschfeld et al. 2018).

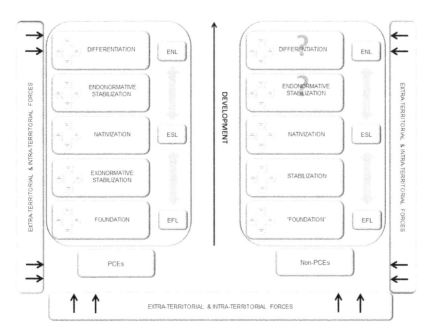

Figure 3.2 Depicting internal linguistic variability in the EIF Model (after Buschfeld et al. 2018: 25)

As the EIF Model is one of the most recent contributions to WEs theorizing, no criticism exists to date. It has so far just been applied to speech forms that have developed within national boundaries (e.g. Buschfeld and Kautzsch, 2017, on the case of Namibia) and it remains to be seen whether it can also account for Englishes emerging and developing beyond such borders, as, for example, in lingua franca communication, Englishes for Specific Purposes, and also mixed codes and other speech forms and modes developing in so-called emergent contexts (cf. Schneider 2014). This demand has recently been postulated as the so-called post-varieties approach (Seargeant and Tagg 2011) and clearly constitutes one of the most topical and upcoming challenges for WEs researchers.

3.3 Conclusion and Future Prospects

As this chapter has shown, the field of WEs studies has gone through some vigorous and most interesting changes despite its comparatively short history and constitutes one of the major, most vibrant research fields of modern linguistics. We have started by outlining some of the early approaches to the field that clearly initiated the development of the discipline into what it constitutes today. Since the English language has been experiencing an ever-increasing spread and entrenchment as well as unprecedented developments in usage conditions, WEs research has been faced with remarkably fast changes in linguistic realities and theoretical challenges since its very beginnings. Consequently, controversial discussions, criticism, and the development of new taxonomies reacting to the shortcomings identified in earlier approaches and complementing them have ever since determined the development of the discipline. We have outlined some of these major developments, from the early days of Kachru and his contemporaries, to Schneider's Dynamic Model initiating yet another crucial turn in the advancement of WEs studies, to most recent approaches such as Buschfeld and Kautzsch's (2017) EIF Model, making the case for yet another reorientation in the field. Yet one has to consider that this survey constitutes just a snapshot in time. Current and future developments in WEs will create new and exciting challenges for researchers and current approaches to the pluricentricity and functional, conceptual, and linguistic diversity of Englishes around the world; and further reorientations and models are certainly to be expected.

References

Biewer, C. 2011. Modal auxiliaries in second language varieties of English: A learner's perspective. In J. Mukherjee and M. Hundt, eds. *Exploring Second-Language Varieties of English and Learner Englishes: Bridging a Paradigm Gap*. Amsterdam: John Benjamins, 7–33.

Blommaert, J. 2010. *The Sociolinguistics of Globalization*. Cambridge: Cambridge University Press.

Bolton, K. 2003. *Chinese Englishes: A Sociolinguistic History*. Cambridge: Cambridge University Press.

Bruthiaux, P. 2003. Squaring the circles: Issues in modeling English worldwide. *International Journal of Applied Linguistics* 13(2), 159–178.

Buschfeld, S. 2011. The English language in Cyprus: An empirical investigation of variety status. Unpublished doctoral dissertation, University of Cologne.

Buschfeld, S. 2013. *English in Cyprus or Cyprus English? An Empirical Investigation of Variety Status*. Amsterdam: John Benjamins.

Buschfeld, S. 2014. English in Cyprus and Namibia: A critical approach to taxonomies and models of World Englishes and Second Language Acquisition research. In S. Buschfeld, T. Hoffmann, M. Huber and A. Kautzsch eds. *The Evolution of Englishes: The Dynamic Model and Beyond*. Amsterdam: John Benjamins, 181–202.

Buschfeld, S. Forthcoming. *Children's English in Singapore: Acquisition, Properties, and Use* [Routledge Studies in World Englishes]. London: Routledge.

Buschfeld, S., T. Hoffmann, M. Huber and A. Kautzsch. 2014. The evolution of Englishes: The Dynamic Model and beyond. In S. Buschfeld, T. Hoffmann, M. Huber and A. Kautzsch eds. *The Evolution of Englishes: The Dynamic Model and Beyond*. Amsterdam: John Benjamins, 1–17.

Buschfeld, S. and A. Kautzsch. 2014. English in Namibia: A first approach. *English World-Wide 35*(2), 121–60.

Buschfeld, S. and A. Kautzsch. 2017. Towards an integrated approach to postcolonial and non-postcolonial Englishes. *World Englishes 36*(1), 104–126.

Buschfeld, S., A. Kautzsch and E. W. Schneider. 2018. From colonial dynamism to current transnationalism: A unified view on postcolonial and non-postcolonial Englishes. In S. C. Deshors, ed. *Modelling World Englishes: Assessing the Interplay of Emancipation and Globalization of ESL varieties*. Amsterdam: John Benjamins, 15–44.

Coupland, N., ed. 2010. *The Handbook of Language and Globalization*. Malden, MA: Wiley-Blackwell.

Crystal, D. 2003a. *The Cambridge Encyclopedia of the English Language* (2nd ed.). Cambridge: Cambridge University Press.

Crystal, D. 2003b. *English as a Global Language* (2nd ed.). Cambridge: Cambridge University Press.

Davydova, J. 2012. English in the outer and expanding circles: A comparative study. *World Englishes 31*(3), 366–385.

de Swaan, A. 2002. *The World Language System: A Political Sociology and Political Economy of Language*. Cambridge: Polity.

de Swaan, A. 2010. Language systems. In N. Coupland, ed. *The Handbook of Language and Globalization*. Malden, MA: Wiley-Blackwell, 56–76.

Edwards, A. 2016. *English in the Netherlands: Functions, Forms and Attitudes*. Amsterdam: John Benjamins.

Evans, S. 2009. The evolution of the English-language speech community in Hong Kong. *English World-Wide 30*(3), 278–301.

Evans, S. 2014. The evolutionary dynamics of postcolonial Englishes: A Hong Kong case study. *Journal of Sociolinguistics 18*(5), 571–603.

Gilquin, G. and S. Granger. 2011. From EFL to ESL: Evidence from the International Corpus of Learner English. In J. Mukherjee and M. Hundt, eds. *Exploring Second-Language Varieties of English and Learner Englishes: Bridging a Paradigm Gap*. Amsterdam: John Benjamins, 55–78.

Görlach, M. [1988] 1990. The development of Standard Englishes. In M. Görlach, ed., *Studies in the History of the English Language*. Heidelberg: Carl Winter, 9–64.

Görlach, M. 1998. The origins and development of emigrant Englishes. In M. Görlach, ed. *Even More Englishes. Studies 1996–1997*. Amsterdam: John Benjamins, 19–38.

Graddol, D. 1997. *The Future of English: A Guide to Forecasting the Popularity of English in the 21st Century*. London: British Council.

Gupta, A. F. 1997. Colonisation, migration, and functions of English. In E. W. Schneider, ed. *Englishes Around the World, Vol. 1: General Studies, British Isles, North America* (Studies in Honour of Manfred Görlach). Amsterdam: John Benjamins, 47–58.

Hall, R. A. 1962. The life cycle of pidgin languages. *Lingua 11*, 151–156.

Huber, M. 2014. Stylistic and sociolinguistic variation in Schneider's Nativization Phase: T-affrication and relativization in Ghanaian English. In S. Buschfeld, T. Hoffmann, M. Huber and A. Kautzsch eds. *The Evolution of Englishes: The Dynamic Model and Beyond*. Amsterdam: John Benjamins, 86–106.

Kachru, B. B. 1976. Models of English for the Third World: White man's linguistic burden or language pragmatics? *TESOL Quarterly 10*(2), 221–239.

Kachru, B. B. 1985. Standards, codification and sociolinguistic realism: The English language in the outer circle. In R. Quirk and H. G. Widdowson, eds. *English in the World: Teaching and Learning the Language and Literatures*. Cambridge: Cambridge University Press for The British Council, 11–30.

Kachru, B. B. 1988. The sacred cows of English. *English Today 16* 4(4), 3–8.

Kachru, B. B. 1992a. Models for non-native Englishes. In B. B. Kachru, ed. *The Other Tongue: English across Cultures* (2nd ed.). Urbana: University of Illinois Press, 48–74.

Kachru, B. B. 1992b. World Englishes: Approaches, issues and resources. *Language Teaching 25*(1), 1–14.

Kachru, B. B. 1992c. Teaching World Englishes. In B. B. Kachru, ed. *The Other Tongue: English across Cultures* (2nd ed.). Urbana: University of Illinois Press, 355–365.

Kachru, B. B. 2005. *Asian Englishes Beyond the Canon*. Hong Kong: Hong Kong University Press.

Leitner, G. 1992. English as a pluricentric language. In M. Clyne, ed. *Pluricentric Languages: Differing Norms in Different Nations*. Berlin: Mouton de Gruyter, 179–237.

Mair, C. 2013. The world system of Englishes: Accounting for the transnational importance of mobile and mediated vernaculars. *English World-Wide 34*(3), 253–278.

McArthur, T. 1987. The English languages? *English Today 11* 3(3), 9–11.

McArthur, T. 1998. *The English Languages*. Cambridge: Cambridge University Press.

Meierkord, C. 2012. *Interactions across Englishes: Linguistic Choices in Local and International Contact Situations*. Cambridge: Cambridge University Press.

Mesthrie, R. and R. M. Bhatt. 2008. *World Englishes: The Study of New Varieties*. Cambridge: Cambridge University Press.

Moag, R. F. [1982] 1992. The life cycle of non-native Englishes: A case study. In B. B. Kachru, ed. *The Other Tongue: English across Cultures* (2nd ed.). Urbana: University of Illinois Press, 233–252.

Modiano, M. 2003. Euro-English: A Swedish perspective. *English Today 74* 19(2), 35–41.

Mukherjee, J. 2007. Steady states in the evolution of New Englishes: Present-day Indian English as an equilibrium. *Journal of English Linguistics 35*(2), 157–187.

Onysko, A. 2016. Modeling world Englishes from the perspective of language contact. *World Englishes 35*(2), 196–220. doi:10.1111/weng.12191.

Quirk, R., S. Greenbaum, G. Leech and J. Svartvik. 1972. *A Grammar of Contemporary English*. London: Longman.

Quirk, R., S. Greenbaum, G. Leech and, J. Svartvik. 1985. *A Comprehensive Grammar of the English Language*. London: Longman.

Schneider, E. W. 2003. The dynamics of New Englishes: From identity construction to dialect birth. *Language* 79(2), 233–281.

Schneider, E. W. 2007. *Postcolonial English: Varieties around the World*. Cambridge: Cambridge University Press.

Schneider, E. W. 2008. Accommodation versus identity? A response to Trudgill. *Language in Society* 37(2), 262–267.

Schneider, E. W. 2011. *English around the World: An Introduction*. Cambridge: Cambridge University Press.

Schneider, E. W. 2014. New reflections on the evolutionary dynamics of World Englishes. *World Englishes* 33(1), 9–32.

Schneider, E. W. 2018. English and colonialism. In P. Seargeant and A. Hewings, eds. *The Routledge Handbook of English Language Studies*. Malden, MA: Routledge, 42–58.

Seargeant, P. 2012. *Exploring World Englishes: Language in a Global Context*. London: Routledge.

Seargeant, P. and C. Tagg, 2011. English on the internet and a "post-varieties" approach to language. *World Englishes* 30(4), 496–514.

Strang, B. M. H. 1970. *A History of English*. London: Methuen.

Strevens, P. 1992. English as an international language: Directions in the 1990s. In B. B., Kachru, ed. *The Other Tongue: English across Cultures* (2nd ed.). Urbana: University of Illinois Press, 27–47.

Thusat, J., E. Anderson, S. Davis, M. Ferris, A. Javed, A. Laughlin et al. 2009. Maltese English and the nativization phase of the dynamic model. *English Today 97* 25(2), 25–32.

Trudgill, P. 2004. *New-Dialect Formation: The Inevitability of Colonial Englishes*. Edinburgh: Edinburgh University Press.

Trudgill, P. 2008. Colonial dialect contact in the history of European languages: On the irrelevance of identity to new-dialect formation. *Language in Society* 37(2), 241–254.

Van Rooy, B. 2010. Societal and linguistic perspectives on variability inworld Englishes. *World Englishes* 29(1), 3–20.

Weston, D. 2011. Gibraltar's position in the dynamic model of postcolonial English. *English World-Wide* 32(3), 338–367.

4

The Contribution of Language Contact to the Emergence of World Englishes

Lisa Lim

4.1 Preamble: On Attention to Language Contact in World Englishes Scholarship

To contemplate the emergence of World Englishes is really to contemplate the phenomenon of contact between communities and languages. This is, of course, not exclusive to World Englishes; after all, it has been widely noted that "[m]ost, if not all, languages have been influenced at one time or another by contact with others" (Winford 2003: 2) and that "language contact is everywhere: there is no evidence that any languages have developed in total isolation from other languages" (Thomason 2001: 8). That the English language itself is contact-derived from its very beginnings – that is, from the emergence of Old English from the contact of the Germanic dialects – has been explicitly recognized by scholars and foregrounded, for example, in collections such as that of Schreier and Hundt (2013) and in Onysko (2016), who argues that language contact be considered an underlying mechanism for all Englishes. Already, the first language varieties on the British Isles were shaped as a result of contact between Germanic, Celtic, and Romance varieties, characterizing present-day, standardized, and non-standardized English dialects as contact languages (Filppula 2008; Venneman 2011).

This chapter concerns itself with the evolution of Englishes outside the British Isles, in the first place as a consequence of Britain's colonization ventures in the seventeenth through the nineteenth centuries, which brought the English language (as it was then) into contact with diverse communities and languages and resulted in the emergence of numerous varieties of English around the globe, now well known as World Englishes. By doing so, attention is given in particular to the non-settler, exploitation colonies, in many ways viewed as the epitome of language contact dynamics, for reasons that will be outlined in the following sections. The international diversification of English has indeed been noted (e.g. Kachru 1992: 6), mostly due to its contact with other languages, creating different Englishes that have become functionally adapted in settings that are often multilingual. These World Englishes still continue to evolve in new sites of contact in this current global age (see Mair, Chapter 16, this volume) and this chapter concludes by evaluating the current and future evolution of English as a result of contemporary contact ecologies.

4.2 Historical Spread and Contact

4.2.1 Colonies

The usual story of the earlier stages of the emergence of World Englishes is by now not particularly unfamiliar to most, with several kinds of colonization regularly recognized. They are dealt with throughout the volume (see Hickey, Chapter 2; Mufwene, Chapter 5; Schreier, Chapter 17, this volume), so a short summary suffices here. The earliest movements – the first diaspora – saw Britain venturing to new lands to settle, involving large-scale group migrations to form the first kind of colonies – the settlement colonies. The early seventeenth century saw settlements in North America, the late eighteenth century Australia, and the early nineteenth century New Zealand and South Africa. For the most part, this precluded any return to the home country and such geographical and psychological distance, as well as the adaptation to life in a new environment, brought about strong internal group coherence and a desire to continue traditional cultural and social norms (Schneider 2013: 137). This led to accommodation among speakers of different regional and social dialects, with this group-internal dialect contact resulting in koineization and the emergence of a compromise variety – which, of course, was one of the most important dimensions of language contact in these colonies. The other dimension involved contact with the indigenous populations – the Native Americans in North America, the Aboriginal peoples in Australia, the Maori in New Zealand. Because of disproportions in demographic and/ or power relationships, such contact was relatively restricted. In general, select members of the indigenous group acquired the English language, as a learner's variety, in order to serve as translators and mediators; on the other hand, the indigenous languages had low prestige in the eyes of the colonizers, so these, with few exceptions, were generally not learned by the settlers. The contact situation was thus characterized by incipient unilateral bilingualism. Linguistic impact was mostly constrained to lexical borrowings in specific semantic domains, such as place names, words for fauna and flora, and terms for objects and concepts of indigenous cultures (Schneider 2007).

The second type of colonization involved the setting up of trade colonies for the exchange of commodities with indigenous peoples. In these scenarios, contact tended to be short-lived and limited to fulfilling specific goals, resulting in trade jargons or pidgins. This occurred in the seventeenth century along the West African coast, as well as on the Indian subcontinent, and in Southeast Asia and the Pacific in the eighteenth and nineteenth centuries; some trade colonies developed into exploitation colonies.

The exploitation colonies were the outcome of Britain's drive, during the agrarian and industrial revolution in the late eighteenth century, to establish new locales for finding and extracting new resources of raw materials in order to service the rapidly growing industries of a burgeoning capitalist economy. This enterprise led to their control of sea routes and the establishment of trading posts, the emergence of markets for goods that allowed for the investment of surplus capital overseas. In contrast to the settler colonies of the first diaspora, this second diaspora of expansion involved sparser British settlement, with very little displacement of the native population but subjugation and rule by long distance from the home country instead. The push to Asia was particularly successful as the British East India Company was granted a Royal Charter by Elizabeth I in 1600 with the intent to favor trade privileges in India, effectively giving it a monopoly on all trade with the East Indies.

In the exploitation colonies, while English would also have been introduced to the local populations in various informal, at times illegitimate, settings, including Christian missionaries, smugglers, and pirates, and communication would have involved predominantly dialectal varieties, L2 varieties, and foreigner talk modes (see, e.g., Bolton 2003; Ansaldo 2009), the English language was largely introduced through formal channels of English-medium education. This can be traced back to the historic Macaulay's Minute on Education, promulgated in India in 1835, in which Lord Macaulay, President of the Committee of Public Instruction, Calcutta, India, advocated the central place of English in education because "English is better worth knowing than Sanscrit [Sanskrit] or Arabic; [as] the natives are desirous to be taught English . . . we must . . . do our best to form a class of interpreters between us and the millions whom we govern – a class of persons, Indian in blood and colour, but English in taste, in opinion, in morals and in intellect."[1] Absolute primacy was consequently given to teaching English and teaching in English and, within fifty years, by the late 1800s, a majority of Indian primary schools were English-medium institutions (Kachru 1994: 507). This policy was also extended to British Malaya (i.e. present-day Malaysia and Singapore), where, in the latter, it has been said that it was "exclusively through the schools that English spread" (Bloom 1986: 348), as well as to Hong Kong. There, the first English-medium schools were set up in the nineteenth century, accessible to an elite minority during colonial rule, though enrolment gradually increased over the decades as the population recognized the value of such a resource.

---

[1] "Minute by the Hon'ble T. B. Macaulay, dated the 2nd February 1835." See www.columbia.edu/itc/mealac/pritchett/00generallinks/macaulay/txt_minute_education_1835.html.

4.2.2 Post-Independence Policies

Owing to nation-building and political independence, countries enacted different language policies. This resulted in different World Englishes, in particular regarding the position of English in wider society. With Singapore's independence in 1965 came ratification of some local languages: Malay, Mandarin, and Tamil were identified as official languages to represent the Malay, Chinese, and Indian founding races of Singapore, alongside the maintenance and support of English as a neutral language and the language of progress (Lim 2010a). India, too, made English coequal with Hindi in the Official Languages Act in 1967; thus English has also retained and strengthened its place there as the lingua franca, in government, education, literature, influence, and development (Kachru and Nelson 2006: 155–156). This contrasts with Malaysia and Sri Lanka, who chose to promote their indigenous languages as national language and medium of education – Bahasa Malaysia and Sinhala,[2] respectively – to restore balance to the groups viewed as having been disadvantaged by former colonial practices of English-language education. These different post-independence political choices have meant that English has taken different paths (see Mufwene, Chapter 5, this volume). In Singapore, the language was accessed by all in the education system and swiftly became a primary working language and interethnic lingua franca, in intimate contact with the vernaculars, resulting in a local variety of English that went beyond nativization to endonormative stabilization and recent generations of Singaporeans being native speakers of English. In Malaysia and Sri Lanka, however, the language is still commanded by a small minority, with the English language not nativizing in any real or stable manner throughout the community as a whole. In sum, sociopolitical choices have significant implications for how English has evolved in the different countries.

4.3 The Dynamics of Contact

Several factors have been identified as relevant for the evolution of World Englishes, most primarily: the variety/-ies of the English lexifier that entered the local context; the nature of transmission of English to the local population; and the local, that is, substrate, languages of the community in which the New English emerges (Hickey 2005: 506; Lim and Gisborne 2009).[3] As noted by Lim and Gisborne (2009: 124), an evaluation of the factors relevant to the evolution of a variety must of course also involve the recognition, first, that there are other important parameters

---

[2] Tamil was eventually made the other official language, albeit with much less internal recognition.

[3] As pointed out by Schneider (2007: 25), settlement and transmission types are clear-cut and important mostly for the early phases of settlement but tend to become increasingly blurred with time in the increasing complexity in the development of society.

involved, such as historical and political events, sociolinguistic determinants, and identity constructions, and, next, that these may be and often are distinct across the different phases or eras in evolution, which affect the dynamics of contact and the structural features that emerge in the evolving English differently at different points in time (see, e.g., Schneider 2007 for a model for Postcolonial Englishes; Lim 2007, 2010a, for Singapore English; Gonzales 2017 for Hokaglish). As a case in point, we look more closely now at the emergence of Englishes in exploitation colonies, with particular focus on those in the Asian region.

4.3.1   Players and Positionings in the Transmission of English

Even while Asia's initial contacts with English date back to the 1600s, with the trade and explorations of the British East India Company (Mesthrie 2008: 24), it is usually via the formal introduction of English via education (i.e. after formal colonization) that marks the beginnings of New Englishes in exploitation colonies.

In the territories in British India, British Malaya, and the Pearl River Delta, English-medium mission schools comprised headmasters (or headmistresses) and senior staff from Britain, while, in the Philippines, teachers were American. At the same time, much regional and dialectal variation would have been present, for example in Irish priests and nuns in the mission schools, as well as many teachers who in fact originated from more regional bases; some of the earliest teachers of English – as well as clerks in the civil service – in Singapore, Malaysia, Brunei, and Hong Kong were South Asians, employees in the British-administered government from India or Sri Lanka (then Ceylon) (Platt and Weber 1980: 23; Gupta 1994: 44; Mesthrie and Bhatt 2008: 19). In Singapore, until the early 1920s, the largest single racial group of teachers comprised the Eurasians, followed by roughly equal numbers of Europeans (comprising a majority of English, Irish, and Scottish; Gupta 1994: 43) and South Asians.

In addition to these "official" sources of English via education, some communities in Singapore and Malaysia very early on had (or soon acquired) English as their dominant language. These tended to be the non-European elite to whom the English-medium schools primarily catered and included the Eurasians, originally from Malacca, who shifted from Portuguese creole to (Eurasian) English (Gupta 1994: 43; Lim 2010a: 25–6), and the Straits-born Chinese or Peranakans who shifted from their vernacular Baba Malay to (Peranakan) English (Lim 2010a: 24–5; Lim, 2010b). Additionally, Christian Malayalis from Kerala in India and Tamils from Jaffna in Sri Lanka were English-educated and worked in the civil and educational services. These early English adopters in the region had significant influence on the emerging New Englishes in other communities of the territory. For example, more recent work has argued for Peranakan English (PerE) having a persistent influence on Singapore English (SgE), since it was the language of one of the founder populations in Singapore's ecology (Lim 2011). In SgE prosody, H tones are found word- and phrase-finally, rather than on accented syllables as in the prosodies of all other contact and learner varieties with tone-language vernaculars. This influence can be ascribed to PerE and, in turn, to the prosodic patterns found in Malay/Indonesian varieties with prominence on the penultimate and/or final syllable of the word and phrase-finally, including Singapore's Baba Malay (Lim 2010b, 2011). More generally, this highlights the significance of considering lesser-known varieties of English (Schreier et al. 2010) in investigations of influence on World Englishes.

4.3.2   Substrates

The substrate languages of the indigenous communities have been argued to be more germane when compared to input varieties, and settlement and transmission types when accounting for the features and typologies of New Englishes emerging in contact situations (Lim and Gisborne 2009: 124). The vernaculars of Asia, in particular, comprise a range of languages, notable for their quantity and diversity, coming from, inter alia, the Austronesian, Dravidian, Indo-Aryan, and Sinitic families, thus offering a wide scope in which to view the dynamics of typologies in contact. These languages are, for the most part, genetically unrelated to English and have typologically different grammars. The English varieties that develop in these contexts thus have the potential for displaying features typologically distinct from those of English, typically developed through transfer of substrate grammar in the acquisition process. This contrasts with a large swathe of the earlier history of English when it was in contact with primarily Germanic or Romance languages (thus with language typologies much closer to that of English).

4.3.3   Chains of Contact

As outlined thus far, most accounts of language contact in the evolution of World Englishes take their cue from the colonization situations, whether settler or exploitation, and the outcome of contact of substrate languages on the English language introduced. What is sometimes overlooked are other situations of contact that took place before British colonization, involving a chain of contact, with a feature initially transmitted from one language into another, and only later into a language of the European colonizer, usually first the Portuguese and from there into English. A substantial swathe of lexicon, such as *congee*, *godown*, and *shroff*, for example, is characteristic of Asian Englishes. Yet their origins do not always stem directly from contact between the English language in the territories and the language(s) of the local peoples but are in fact a few times removed.

Consider *shroff*, a word that is no longer in modern English usage – but for two Asian English exceptions (Lim 2017a). Indian English still uses *shroff*, with its original meaning – in colonial writings on India dating back to the early 1600s, it refers to a local, that is, Asian, banker or money changer in the British East Indies. In Hong Kong, a *shroff* in the nineteenth century was a police court official to whom monies were paid but the word underwent semantic narrowing and, in contemporary Hong Kong English (also Sri Lankan English and, previously, Singapore English), refers to a cashier, cashier's office or payment booth, in government offices, hospitals, or, especially, car parks. The word's origins ultimately lie in Arabic صَرَّاف *ṣarrāf* "money changer," entering Persian as *ṣarrāf*, and Gujarati as *šaraf*, in the large-scale Perso-Arabic influence on the language during the mid-thirteenth through mid-nineteenth centuries of Persian Muslim rule – the Delhi Sultanate and the Mughal Empire – on the Indian subcontinent. It thence also entered Portuguese – during that European colonizer's long occupation in India from the mid-sixteenth century – as *xaraffo*, referring to customs officers and money changers, also giving *xarafaggio*, meaning *shroff-age* – the xaraffo's commission – noted in a 1585 colonial report from Goa. With Indo-Portuguese, the lingua franca not only between the Portuguese and locals but also widely adopted by subsequent European travelers and colonizers, including the British, numerous words would have been introduced into Anglo-Indian English, subsequently entering British English, including *sharaf*, via this Portuguese contact language variety.

Another such example is found in *congee* (Lim 2017b). A staple dish across Asia, it is a preparation of – depending on where you live – rice (though there are versions that use other grains or legumes) boiled in water (though some versions use milk or coconut milk), using grains that may be long or short, whole or broken, which is served plain and accompanied by side dishes (ranging from salted duck egg or seafood to pickled vegetables to braised meat) or is cooked together with ingredients (such as chicken, preserved egg, or herbs), with as many names in Asian languages as varieties. As a dish, it is documented in ancient East and South Asian texts. The earliest reference to the dish is in the Zhou Dynasty (first century BCE); it is also mentioned in the Chinese *Record of Rites* (*c.* first century CE) as well as noted of India in Pliny's seventh-century CE writings. As a word in English – "congee houses" are ubiquitous across Hong Kong, for instance – *congee* has its origins in Tamil *kanji* (also Telugu and Kannada *gañji*, Malayalam *kaṇṇi*, Urdu *ganji*), from *kañjī* "boilings," referring to the water in which rice has been boiled. The word was encountered by the Portuguese in their colonies, first documented in Portuguese by the physician and botanist Garcia de Orta's 1563 *Colóquios dos simples e drogas da India* – the earliest treatise on the medicinal and economic plants of India – as *canje*. And it was via Portuguese that the word entered English: early English documentation is found in the 1698 *A New Account of East-India and Persia* and the 1800 English translation (from the German translation of the original Italian) of *A Voyage to the East Indies*, Carmelite missionary Paolino da San Bartolomeo's 1796 observations in India, which describes "Cagni, boiled rice water, which the Europeans call Cangi."

As these examples – just two of many – illustrate, investigations of contact must also involve a consideration of the contact of communities and languages beyond and before the usual groups of English-speaking and indigenous peoples for a richer, fuller appreciation of contact histories in World Englishes.

4.4   What Can Emerge Through Contact

Rather than providing a blow-by-blow description of features that evolve in World Englishes through contact, a number of such features are high-lighted in exemplary fashion: tone, particles, and mixed codes generally. These features have traditionally been considered as an outcome of imper-fect learning, and not as features of "English," but they are in fact most instructive because they demonstrate, as a consequence of contact, the extent to which restructuring is possible – that is, the reorganization of any part or parts of a linguistic system – to develop what are pointedly non-Indo-European–type features. Shared across a number of Asian Englishes, however, these features may actually be considered widespread, common developments and look set to continue their influence on the development of English.

4.4.1   Tone
The feature of tone is often acquired in a non-tonal language by borrowing or imitation due to the presence of tone in the broader linguistic environ-ment. Several creole language varieties have, for some time now, been recognized as having tone, acquired from their tone-language substrates, mostly in contact situations involving European accent languages and African tone languages. Textbook examples include Saramaccan, an Atlantic maroon creole spoken mostly in Surinam, generally classified as an English-based creole, though its lexicon shows substantial Portuguese influence, with Gbe and Kikongo as substrates. There is evidence for a split lexicon in Saramaccan where the majority of its words are marked for pitch accent, with an important minority marked for true tone (Good 2004a, 2004b, 2006). Similarly, Papiamentu spoken in the Netherlands Antilles, with superstrates of Spanish, Portuguese and Dutch, and West African Kwa and Gbe languages as substrates, shows use of both contras-tive stress and contrastive tonal features that operate independently from stress (Kouwenberg 2004; Rivera-Castillo and Pickering 2004; Remijsen and van Heuven 2005). Pichi, also known as Fernando Po Creole English, an Atlantic English-lexicon creole spoken on the island of Bioko,

Equatorial Guinea, which is an offshoot of Krio from Sierra Leone, and shares many characteristics with its West African sister language Aku from Gambia, as well as Nigerian, Cameroonian, and Ghanaian Pidgin, has also been documented as having a mixed prosodic system that employs both pitch accent and tone (Yakpo 2009). The Austronesian language Ma'ya is also documented as a hybrid system involving both contrastive stress and tone, a result of contact with tonal Papuan languages (Remijsen 2001).

Scholarship has also, more recently, recognized the emergence of tone in World Englishes. Nigerian English, for example, has been described as a mixed prosodic system that stands "between" an intonation/stress language and a tone language (Gut 2005); its pitch inventory is described as reduced compared to British English and the domain of pitch appears to be the word, with high pitch triggered by stress, thus resembling a pitch accent language.

New Englishes that have emerged in ecologies where Sinitic languages are dominant have also been shown to have developed lexically based tone. In Singapore, Hokkien was prominent as the Chinese intra-ethnic lingua franca and a widely used inter-ethnic lingua franca in colonial and early independence eras. Then, Mandarin gained importance as one of the nation's four official languages and Cantonese saw a resurgence in the late 1980s and 1990s, thanks to Cantonese popular culture and significant immigration from Hong Kong (see details in Lim 2010a). Hong Kong, during colonial rule and after the handover in 1997, has always been dominantly Cantonese-speaking. Tone languages have thus been in the majority and dominant, making tone salient in the feature pool (Mufwene, Chapter 5, this volume), so Hong Kong English (HKE) and SgE both exhibit (Sinitic-type) tone at the level of the word and phrase (Examples (1)–(4))[4] (Lim 2009a, 2011).

(1)	in'tend	LH	(HKE, Wee 2008: 488)
	'origin, 'photograph	HLL	
	o'riginal	LHLL	

(2)	'manage, 'teacher	MH	(SgE, Wee 2008: 490)
	in'tend, a'round	LH	
	'origin, bi'lingual	LMH	
	o'riginal, se'curity	LMMH	

| (3) | I saw the manager this morning | LHHHHHHHL! (HKE, K. K. Luke p.c.) |

| (4) | I think happier | LHLLM | (SgE, Lim 2004: 44) |

---

[4] Here, tone accents are used as in the sources for Examples (1) to (4), where L = Low tone, M = Mid tone, and H = High tone.

Consequently, linguistic features, however "exotic" they may appear in "the English language," may well emerge in World English varieties – as long as their ecologies support it.

4.4.2 Particles

Particles have long been recognized as a discourse-prominent feature and, consequently, are very easily transferred in contact-induced change (Matras 2000). Not surprisingly, where substrate typologies include particles in their grammars – languages such as Cantonese, Hokkien, Mandarin, Malay, Tagalog, and Hindi abound with discourse particles,[5] which are used widely in those languages to communicate pragmatic functions of various types (see Lim 2007; Lim and Borlongan 2011) – as a consequence of contact, particles figure as a characteristic feature in the New Englishes, notably the emerging Asian Englishes (Lim and Ansaldo 2012).

The *lah* and *ah* particles – whose origins lie in Malay and/or Hokkien (Gupta 1992; Lim 2007; Platt 1987) – are common both in MalE and in SgE (5–8), with *lah* as a SgE particle already included in the *Oxford English Dictionary* almost two decades ago. In the Singapore component of the International Corpus of English (ICE-SIN), the frequencies of *lah* and *ah* are well above 1,000 (Ler 2006) and a count of the particle *lah* in ICE- SIN's "direct conversation" subsection gives 1,605 tokens in sixty-five texts, that is, a frequency occurrence of 6.11 per 1,000 words, with *lah* occurring in all but four of the files (Lange 2009).

(5)   I don't know *lah*, I very blur *lah*. (SgE; Lim 2004: 46)
        "I don't know, I'm very confused."

(6)   Please, *lah*, come home early (MalE, Baskaran 2008: 619)
        "For heaven's sake, come home early"

(7)   Then you got to do those papers again *ah*? (SgE, Lim 2004: 46)

(8)   Where on earth you went *ah*? (MalE, Baskaran 1994: 28)

As Cantonese is particularly rich in discourse particles, it is also not surprising that New Englishes with Cantonese in their ecology have evolved to include such particles in their emergent English. HKE displays numerous Cantonese particles (Examples (9), (10)). SgE also encompasses a second, larger set of particles – *hor, leh, lor, ma,* and *meh* (11, 12) – that emerged in SgE in a later period than the earlier particles *lah* and *ah* (Lim 2007) and, notably, were the result of contact from a different source, viz. Cantonese.

---

[5] Here, tones are represented as pitch level numbers 1 to 5 where, in the Asianist tradition, the larger the number the higher the pitch; thus, for example, *55* represents a high-level tone and *24* represents a rising tone.

(9)   may be LG1 [Lower Ground 1st Floor] is much better *wor* ... noisy *ma* ... at G/F ... also u seem used to study there *ma* (HKE, James 2001)

(10)   K: How are you *a33*? (HKE, Multilingual Hong Kong Corpus, K. Chen p.c.)

(11)   My parents old fashion *a21*? Then your parents *le55*? (SgE, Lim 2007: 451)
        "Are you saying that my parents are old-fashioned? Then what about your parents?"

(12)   No *la21*! He's using Pirelli, you don't know *mε55*? (SgE, Lim 2007: 451)
        "No, he has Pirelli tyres; didn't you know that?" [incredulously]

Particles have also of late been noted in more formal contexts of SgE and are now considered more acrolectal or standard SgE (Lim 2012), suggesting that they are crossing the divide and obtain wider sociolinguistic currency.

    With Tagalog having some eighteen enclitic particles, it is not surprising that some of these occur frequently in PhE also. The Philippine component of the International Corpus of English (ICE-PH) attests to consistent usage of particles (in decreasing order of frequency) such as *na*, which signals a relatively new or altered situation; *pa*, which denotes a relatively old or continuing situation (Example (13)); and *ba*, a question marker obligatory in formulaic yes-no questions (Example ((14)) (Lim and Borlongan 2012).

(13)   We have an idea *na* of who we'll get yeah pero we're waiting *pa* for the approval. (Lim and Borlongan 2011: 68)
        "We already have an idea of who we'll get yeah but we're still waiting for the approval."

(14)   You find this fulfilling *ba* (Lim and Borlongan 2011: 62)
        "Do you find this fulfilling?"

Indian English (IndE) exhibits the particles *yaar* and *na* (15, 16), from Hindi, documented in the Indian component of the International Corpus of English (ICE-IND) and used in IndE by speakers regardless of their mother tongue (i.e. not constrained to Hindi mother-tongue speakers) (Lange 2009), thus appearing to be a robust feature of IndE (Lim and Ansaldo 2012).

(15)   You'll you must be really having good patience *yaar* (IndE, Lange 2009: 216)

(16)   Sunday will be more convenient *na* (IndE, Lange 2009: 213)

In their ubiquity, particles comprise one of the features most likely to spread not only from the substrates to the English language but, subsequently, also horizontally across Englishes in Asia (Lim and Ansaldo 2012).

4.4.3 Mixed Codes, or the Translingual Turn

The translingual turn, as it is now referenced, has emerged as one of the major areas of development in sociolinguistic scholarship in the past two decades. Numerous conceptual paradigms and a plethora of terms have been broached, including (roughly chronologically) translanguaging (Cummins 2008; Garcia 2009; Creese and Blackledge 2010; Baker 2011; Garcia and Li Wei 2014); codemeshing (Young 2004; Canagarajah 2006); polylingual languaging (Jørgensen 2008); fragmented multilingualism (Blommaert 2010); metrolingualism (Otsuji and Pennycook 2010; Pennycook 2010; Pennycook and Otsuji 2015); translingual dispositions (Horner et al. 2011; Canagarajah 2013; Lee and Jenks 2016); translingual practice (Canagarajah 2013); transglossic language practices (Sultana et al. 2015); and postmultilingualism (Gramling 2016). A common characteristic is the explicit concern with the fluidity of language boundaries, premised on the possibility that language is never normative but instead always negotiable.

This movement has seen its impact in World Englishes too, even if translingual scholarship is often positioned at odds with the World Englishes paradigm, which traditionally sees manifestation in discrete, usually national, varieties of English. That said, given that World Englishes have, by definition, emerged via contact with other language varieties, such a paradigm shift was perhaps overdue. What in earlier, more traditional approaches would have been analyzed as code-switching, code-mixing, or borrowing between English and some other language(s) is now considered as one manifestation of a New English (Lim 2009b). As has been pointed out by scholars such as Canagarajah (2009), hybrid varieties, mixed codes, or plurilingual practices have been natural and embraced in regions such as South Asia since precolonial times. It is noteworthy that, before the 2000s, scholars had already described such hybrid codes (e.g. Canagarajah 1995; Li Wei 1998; illustrated in the following paragraphs).

Canagarajah (1995) documents what is a now-classic illustration of plurilingual English, also referred to as "Englishised Tamil" – the unmarked everyday code in Jaffna, in northeast Sri Lanka (which was under the control of the Liberation Tigers of Tamil Eelam (LTTE) until 2009). This situation arose after independence in 1948 from British colonial rule. As a result, there was strong social pressure among Tamils against the excessive use of English, but the speaking of Tamil on its own could be considered excessively formal. Through this, Canagarajah (2009: 15) provides an instructive account of how plurilingual practices are wielded to one's advantage. The senior professor (P), for instance, who is comfortable with prestige varieties of English (having done his graduate work in the UK), is interviewing a junior lecturer (L) for a faculty position in English and begins the interview in the unmarked code. L, being locally trained and lacking advanced proficiency in English, draws from the plurilingual tradition to negotiate the conversation in his favor. He is able to understand P's questions because of his receptive multilingualism and continues the interaction confidently. He strategically uses the English tokens at his disposal, mostly technical or scholarly vocabulary common in academia, to shift the conversation in his favor. Although L lacks the ability to form complete sentences in English, his mixing is effective – in fact better than using Tamil only, as "the mixed language, particularly its vocabulary, conceals the social and regional identity of the speaker and thus has a standardizing (i.e. neutralizing) function" (Annamalai 2001: 174). Canagarajah argues that, although initially P continues to speak English and maintains a certain amount of distance (perhaps deliberately, as English provides him power and confirms his identity as a senior scholar), he is eventually forced to take L seriously because of his successful strategies, with P finally converging to L's plurilingual English (in line 5), after which they speak as equals.

(17)   1 P: So you have done a masters in sociology? What is your area of research?

       2 L: **Naan** sociology of religion-**ilai taan** interested. **enTai** thesis topic **vantu** the rise of local deities in the Jaffna peninsula. "**It is in** the sociology of religion **that I am** interested. **My** thesis topic **was** the rise of local deities in the Jaffna peninsula."

       3 P: Did this involve a field work?

       4 L: **oom, oru** ethnographic study-**aai taan itay ceitanaan. kiTTattaTTa** four years-**aai** field work **ceitanaan.** "**Yes, I did this as an** ethnographic study. **I did** field work **for roughly** four years."

       5 P: **appa kooTa** qualitative research **taan ceiyiraniir?** "**So you do mostly** qualitative research?"

A similarly mixed code is also described by Li Wei (1998) in second-generation bilinguals, such as younger generation British-born Chinese in the north of England, originally from Ap Chau, a small island near Hong Kong, as seen in Example (18), which Li Wei argues constitutes a distinctive linguistic mode (Chinese, English).

(18)   A: *Yeo hou do yeo* contact
             Have very many have contact
             "We have many contacts"

       G: We always have opportunities *heu xig kei ta dei fong gaowui di yen. Ngodei xixi dou* keep in contact   will know that other place
             church POSS person We time always
             "We always have opportunities to get to know people from other churches. We always keep in contact."

In other multilingual contexts of Asia, where English has become part of the linguistic fabric, similar mixed codes involving English have become commonplace too, viewed as single codes in their own right (Lim 2009b; Lim and Ansaldo 2012). Examples (19), (20), and (21), all varieties of Singapore English, illustrate the range observed in such mixed codes. In Example (19), taken from Lim (2009b: 58–59) and the Grammar of Spoken Singapore English Corpus (GSSEC; Lim and Foley 2004), comprising data of naturally occurring spontaneous speech of young Singaporeans), linguistic features from the local languages have evolved in the restructured New English, such as zero copula, *kena* passive, absence of inflection on third-person singular and past tense verbs, *is it* question tag, use of *one*, reduplication, and Malay/ Sinitic particles, all considered features of colloquial Singapore English. Significantly, such a code is used by Singaporeans of all ethnicities; here, A is ethnically Chinese, while B and C are ethnically Indian. Example (20) from Tay (1993: 139, cited in Kachru and Nelson 2006: 256) and Example (21) from Lim (2009b: 60)[6] exemplify the tight and fluid mix involving English, *Mandarin*, and **Hokkien** – commonly used by ethnically Chinese Singaporeans, exemplified in Example (21), in characters Mei and Seng who are representative of the younger generation of Singaporeans, and in the older generation father, Pa (Lim 2008, 2009b). (Here, only the English idiomatic gloss is provided: **Hokkien**, *Mandarin*, English, *Sinitic particles*.)

(19) B: So just go down ... ya just go down go straight down
      C: Go straight down and turn into Zion Road *ah* (Bazaar Malay / Hokkien particle)
      A: Careful! The *ah pek!* (Hokkien "old man")
      B, C: (laughter)
      C: You remember that guy that was running across the other day?
                 {Just run across like that. (laughter)
      B: {****
      A: Hey, you know that Razid in Pizza Hut, right?
      B: Which one?
      C: Razid *ah*, Razid ... the other {*mat*. (Malay (slang) "a Malay male")
      A: {Razali ... Razali's friend ... you know what he was doing or not?
      B: The one who always like to *kow peh* {is it? (Hokkien "complain")
      A, C: {Ya ya ...
      C: The one who always making {noise ...
      B: {I don't like him, you know ... he *ah* ... like *macam* (Malay "like")

---

[6] Example (21) derives from the script of the award-winning Singapore film *Singapore Dreaming* (Woo, Goh and Wu 2006) whose dialogues are vouched for by Singaporeans as being completely authentic.

C: The *botak botak* {fella (Malay "bald bald" = "very bald")

B: {*Ah* ... the like ****

A: The fella centre *botak* three side hair {*one* (Malay "bald")
          "The fellow is (has the quality of being) bald in the centre
          with hair on three sides"

C: {Eh, that guy got
          problem *ah*, that fella ...

(20)   Oh I see, *guai bu de* ("no wonder" Mandarin) ... *wo xie xing wen bi jiao*
        kuai ("I write faster in English" Mandarin), **gua sia eng boon luan jut**
        u luan ju sia ("when I write English, I simply scribble and write,
        carelessly" Hokkien), *jiaru* ("if" Mandarin) move *de* (particle
        Mandarin) fast, **bo tek khak o** ("not sure" Hokkien) *Dui bu qi*
        ("sorry" Mandarin). I got to go.

(21)   Mei: Seng *a21*, time to get a job *ho24*? Pa and Irene spend all their
                  savings on you already *le21*. Are you waiting for Pa *to buy Toto*
                  [the lottery] and get it all back *me55*?

        Pa: You say other people for what? You are just a secretary.

        Irene: *Aiya*, never mind, never mind. Anyway Seng already has
                  a job interview on Monday.

        Pa: *Wah*, real or not?

        Seng: I arranged the meeting through email. Now American
                  degrees *all in demand*.

        CB: *Wah*, congratulations, man.

        Seng: Thanks.

        Ma: **What did they just say?**

        Mei: *Seng said that on Monday* ...

        Pa: Now you've come back, you can't play the fool anymore,
                  okay? *What if* you end up selling insurance like this guy?
                  Don't make me lose face!

In the Philippines, a mixed code encompassing English and the local
languages is extensively used by urban Filipinos comfortable in both
languages (Bautista and Gonzales 2009: 137), and, as in the case of
Singapore's plurilingual code, the mix of English and Tagalog, often
referred to as Taglish, is even said to be the usual code among
Filipinos, with "pure" (sic) – i.e. what is considered unmixed –
Tagalog or English seldom heard (McFarland 2009: 144); see Example
(22)). Most recently, such a mixed code has even been observed in
domains that usually do not exhibit it, including newspaper reports
such as an article for *Yahoo! News Philippines* on territorial disputes in
the South China Sea (Tordesillas 2013). While predominantly in
English, a Filipino item is used in the first sentence along with
a sentence in Filipino to end the article.

(22)   Then they ask me, *ano pa daw* capabilities *ko* in singing . . . I did not
       told them . . . *gusto ko sila mag* find out.
       "Then they ask me, what other capabilities I have in singing . . . I did
       not tell them . . . I wanted them to find out for themselves"

(23)   Never have I felt so *kawawa* reading the statements of Defense
       Secretary Voltaire Gazmin justifying his plan to allow American
       and Japanese military access to military facilities in the Philippines
       to deter China's aggressive moves in the South China Sea.
       [Entire article in English]
       Ano ba naman tayo?

4.5 Contemporary Sites for Contact

In considering the continuing impact of language contact on World
Englishes, this section focuses on the Asian region for two main reasons
(e.g. Lim and Ansaldo 2016). The first factor regards the phenomenon that,
with the persistence of certain demographic and economic trends, the
twenty-first century will be dominated by Asian politics and culture. The
idea of the "Asian Century," a term attributed to a 1988 meeting between
the People's Republic of China leader Deng Xiaoping and the Indian prime
minister Rajiv Gandhi, is in contrast/counterpoint to the preceding
"American Century," coined by *Time* publisher Henry Luce used to describe
the dominance of the USA throughout much of the twentieth century (cf.
the preceding nineteenth century as the "British Century"). Indeed, as is
well recognized, there has been a great shift in the global economy's
center of gravity from West to East, which entails various phenomena of
globalization and economic growth in Asia, such as the pursuit of linguistic capital, mobility, trade, communication technology, and so on, all of
which have significant implications for language contact in terms of bringing together communities and their languages in new dynamics as well as
providing new sites and potential for consequences of contact. The second
factor is Asia's position as the site for the largest and most rapidly growing
number of users of English: The total English-using population in Asia is
some 600 million, far more than English speakers in the "Inner Circle."
Taken together, these factors mean that Asian English speakers are interacting with other Asian Englishes or speakers of other New Englishes, for
example African Englishes, in ways more numerous and more meaningful
than with "Inner Circle" or "native" English speakers.

   In what follows, a number of phenomena in World Englishes today are
identified, which involve sites comprising new dynamics of contact –
either contact that is even more diverse than before or sites that, by their
very nature, prompt contact of greater scope and intensity than would
have occurred under earlier circumstances.

4.5.1 Computer-Mediated Communication

Already some two decades ago, scholarship started to recognize the emergence of new ways of expression as a consequence of the rise in electronic media: new literacies shaped by the opportunities and constraints of the electronic medium. The platform has afforded flexibility and creativity of expression, including the exploiting of multilingual repertoires, notably in situations involving an emergent English and languages using different orthographic traditions. This is because, although advances have certainly been made and continue to be made in developing keyboards for various scripts, such as Chinese characters or Devanagari script, users very often prefer to use a Latin-based keyboard, and/or English, due to the constraints of the keyboard or the comparative efficacy compared to using character keystrokes. This presents not so much a challenge but opportunities for language contact.

Young Hongkongers, for instance, who are normally Cantonese-dominant in non-CMC (computer-mediated communication) domains, overwhelmingly agree that English is easier as an input (74.3 percent) than Chinese (25.7 percent), and report a significant preference for using English, or English and Cantonese (60.6 percent), rather than Chinese (Lin 2005). Clearly, CMC promotes significantly greater English usage than what there would normally be for a community dominant in another language and this has two major consequences.

First, because CMC platforms comprise a site quite distinct from the community's usual communicative practices, where there is more widespread use of English than in non-CMC contexts, there is more frequent mixing of codes – in the case of Hong Kong, of Cantonese and English – and impact on the New English variety. We see much evidence of this in the online chat of young Hongkongers, illustrated in the following examples (from Wong 2009), where a number of linguistic practices clearly demonstrating the outcome of language contact are noted. Common Cantonese phrases are used in romanized form, such as *mafan* "troublesome" for 麻煩 *maa4faan4* (Example (27), turn 5), and morpheme-for-morpheme translation or relexification, such as *gum is you dun ask* (Example (28), turn 3), and *or … gum you continue lo* (Example (28), turn 5).

(27)   1 R: head ask for resume??
               "the department head asked you for your resume?"
        2 R: how come ge
               "how come [ge2]?"
        3L: yes ar
               "yes [aa3]"
        3L: he said he ask all people la wor
               "he said he had asked everyone for their resume already
               [aa3 wo5]"

4 R: what for
"what is that for?"

5 R: ma fan
"it's so troublesome"

6L: not my head
"he is not my supervisor"

7L: programmer head
"my supervisor is the head of the programming
department"

(28)   1A: did u ask Wilson to pick you up in the train station?
2B: ah . . . not yet . . . hahaaa
3A: gum is u dun ask . . . .
咁   係   你   唔   問
gam2 hai6 nei5 ng4 man6
"then it's you who don't ask him to pick you up"
4A: dun say wt danger later ar . . . ghaa
唔   好   話   咩   危   險   一   陣   呀
ng4 hou2 waa6 me1 ngai4 him2 jat1   zan6 aa3
"don't say it is dangerous later (*laugh)"
[. . .]
5A: or . . . gum u continue lo
哦   咁   你   繼   續   囉
ngo4 gam2 nei5 gai3 zuk6 lo1
"ok . . . then you continue working on your assignment [lo1]"

One expression is worth a closer look, the direct translation or calquing of Cantonese expression 加油 ga1yau4 "add oil," into English "add oil," by younger Cantonese-English bilingual Hongkongers. As a general exhortation or cheer to persevere or to work hard, Cantonese加油 ga1yau4 is widely used, as seen in spoken Cantonese discourse in Example (29) and in CMC in Example (30) (Lim 2015).

(29)   A: *Ngo chin gei yat sin tong kui lao yuen gao*
"I argued with him just a few days ago"
B: *Hah? Again? For what?*
A: You know, just like *zi chin gor d lor*
"You know, just like what happened before"
B: *Ai, kui d* temper really . . . **gayau ah!**
"Sigh, his temper is really bad . . . be strong!"

(30)   A: Doin *meh?*
"What are you doing?"
B: *Hea gun ah, u?*
"Just taking some rest, and you?"

A: Gonna finish some readings. Need slp earlier, tmr *faan gong*
"I'm going to finish some readings and need to sleep earlier.
I need to work tomorrow."

B: Oh *hai wor, ho chur ah,* **gayau!**
"Oh right, you're so busy. Just hang in there!"

In a study on young Cantonese-English bilingual Hongkongers (Lim 2015), it is found that, in CMC, Cantonese 加油 is used less regularly than in spoken communication; however, the use of the English calque *add oil* increases significantly to quite often whether texting in Cantonese or in English or Cantonese-English – in fact, more than its original Cantonese expression – illustrated in Examples (31) (Wong 2009) and (32) (Lim 2015).

(31)   A: 7.00am . . .
"I have to work at 7.00am"

A: very sh*t le
"it's very bad [ne]"

B: ahaha ~~~ **add oil!**
"[laugh] work hard!"

B: Then goodnight and sweet dreams la

A: talk to you next time

(32)   A: Are you ready for tomorrow's Chinese test?

B: Not yet. Mom's forcing me to drink bedtime milk.

A: Then you should probably sleep too. **Add oil** for the test.

B: Yeah.

This is a significant finding in itself – a CMC platform does enable language contact and prompt the development of HKE, in this case, in the use of particular HKE phrases, here calqued from Cantonese. An examination of microblogging sites such as Instagram, Twitter, and Tumblr for the hashtag #addoil turns up a huge number of posts. Clearly such an innovation is already widely used in the community, in CMC.

Second, and even more significantly, more English-dominant bilinguals – for example, Hongkongers who emigrated several years ago and then returned to Hong Kong or Hongkongers of mixed parentage – exhibit a different pattern, where English *add oil* is used significantly more often when speaking. In other words, this feature appears to have spread from CMC to non-CMC domains. In effect, the increased use of English in the CMC domain comprises a drive in the direction of the community employing English in the bilingual mix to a greater extent, first in that domain and then in others, which is the road to further nativization of a restructured New English in a contact context, and subsequent endonormative stabilization. CMC is identified as one of the forces in this knowledge economy that can drive the evolution of a new variety (Lim 2015).

4.5.2 Language Teaching Industry

In the globalized new economy, the language teaching industry is a major thrust in the continuing spread of English in the twenty-first century. In contrast to previous centuries, this involves the traditional Expanding Circle countries as major consumers and Asian English communities as main distributors. This has implications for creating new contact sites for Asian Englishes with other Asian Englishes. For example, with Singapore drawing students from Asia as an educational hub, and the Japan Exchange and Teaching (JET) program bringing teachers of English from diverse backgrounds to Japan, these contexts of contact reinforce common features in regional language ecologies and the horizontal transmission of Asian English features (Lim and Ansaldo 2016).

4.5.3 Trading Places

The twenty-first century has witnessed increasingly strong economic ties between the two parties, through Sino-African trade relations, investments, and aid on the African continent. China is currently Africa's largest trade partner and the biggest investor in Africa. One million Chinese citizens are residing in Africa and some 500,000 Africans are working in China, with the largest African diaspora found in Guangzhou, the commercial and trading center of south China; it is estimated that there are some 100,000 Africans living and doing business in Guangzhou (Bodomo 2010). Recent research on language use in these communities shows that, in a survey of 120 Africans and Chinese in Guangzhou, the most frequently used language between the two communities is overwhelmingly English (80.3 percent), with the majority saying they use English most (50 percent) or all of the time (3 percent) (Liu 2013).

Significantly, African and Chinese varieties of English are documented in use (Bodomo 2010, 2012; Liu 2013) and one of the linguistic features that was observed prominently was reduplication – a feature that is common cross-linguistically, found in African and Sinitic languages, which has emerged in these New Englishes.

(33)   big-big
       same-same
       talk-talk
       chop-chop

Yet the impact of language contact extends further than the impact of substrates on a lexifier. The reduplicated phrase *chop-chop* has long been accepted in English, meaning "quickly," with its origins in Chinese Pidgin English meaning "quick" (Holm 1988: 516), from Cantonese 急急 *gāp-gāp* "quick." In the linguistic practices observed among the traders in Guangzhou, however, it is used, by both Africans and Chinese alike, to mean "to eat" (Liu 2013). In various West African Pidgin English varieties, such as Nigerian Pidgin English, Ghanaian Pidgin English, and Pichi, the meaning of (non-reduplicated) *chop* is "to eat, food" (Faraclas 1996; Blench 2006; Yakpo 2009), whose origin is suggested to lie in the obsolete English verb *chap* or *chop* "to take in the chops and eat" (Huber 1999: 99). It would appear that in the contemporary contact situation, the more stabilized African English varieties may be exerting more influence on the newer Chinese Englishes. This is the perception among the communities themselves, where the Chinese comment on picking up linguistic patterns such as *now-now* from the Africans and, more generally, that "some Chinese follow African speaking" (Liu 2013). In an opposite direction of impact of contact, accommodation strategies are also observed in the linguistic practices, with Africans exhibiting accommodation toward Chinese, as seen in Example (34) (Liu 2013).

(34)   African: How many pieces?
       Chinese: Ten piece.
       African: Oh, ten piece.

4.6 Concluding Remarks

Language contact comprises a critical, defining dimension in the emergence of World Englishes, as this chapter has shown. Three aspects are particularly underscored. First, while the evolution of World Englishes is usually ascribed primarily to the outcome of contact between the English-speaking community and the indigenous language communities during trade and colonization, there are other circumstances that should not be overlooked. One important circumstance comprises the contact that predates the usual periods of the historical spread of English in the colonies, where contact among a larger group of players, in a chain of contact, has made significant contributions to the emergence of World English varieties. In the Asian context, for example, the contact of various Asian communities with each other, and with the Portuguese, has shaped Asian Englishes substantially. Second, there are no constraints on the typology of the emergent World English varieties: If certain features are dominant in a feature pool of a given ecology, those features may well, and often do, develop in the emergent World English even if they are not traditionally considered features in Indo-European. Third, and following on this, as many of the examples in the chapter have alluded to, the dynamics and outcome of contact in World Englishes are not distinct from those commonly observed in creole languages (see also, e.g., Lim and Ansaldo 2016). It is now almost a truism to claim that the World Englishes have always been shaped by contact; at the same time, they continue to represent an ideal repository for extensive evolutionary histories and continuing research on language contact and change, regionally distinctive language ecologies, and translanguaging practices – whose importance is likely to increase as the "Asian century" progresses.

References

Annamalai, E. 2001. *Managing Multilingualism in India: Political and Linguistic Manifestations*. New Delhi: Sage.

Ansaldo, Umberto. 2009. *Contact Languages: Ecology and Evolution in Asia*. Cambridge: Cambridge University Press.

Baker, Colin. 2011. *Foundations of Bilingual Education and Bilingualism* (5th ed.). Clevedon: Multilingual Matters.

Baskaran, Loga. 1994. The Malaysian English mosaic. *English Today* 37(10): 27–32.

Baskaran, Loga. 2008. Malaysian English: Phonology. In Rajend Mesthrie, ed. *Varieties of English, Vol. 4: Africa, South and Southeast Asia*. Berlin: Mouton de Gruyter, 278–291.

Bautista, M. Lourdes S. and Andrew B. Gonzalez. 2009. Southeast Asian Englishes. In Braj B. Kachru, Yamuna Kachru and Cecil L. Nelson, eds. *Handbook of World Englishes*. Oxford: Wiley-Blackwell, 130–144.

Blench, Roger. 2006. *Archaeology, Language, and the African Past*. Lanham, MD: AltaMira Press.

Blommaert, Jan. 2010. *The Sociolinguistics of Globalisation*. Cambridge: Cambridge University Press.

Bloom, David. 1986. The English language and Singapore: A critical survey. In Basant K. Kapur, ed. *Singapore Studies*. Singapore: Singapore University Press, 337–458.

Bolton, Kingsley. 2003. *Chinese Englishes: A Sociolinguistic History*. Cambridge: Cambridge University Press.

Bodomo, Adam. 2010. The African trading community in Guangzhou: An emerging bridge for Africa–China relations. *China Quarterly 203*: 693–707.

Canagarajah, A. Suresh. 1995. The political-economy of code choice in a revolutionary society: Tamil/English bilingualism in Jaffna. *Language in Society* 24(2): 187–212.

Canagarajah, A. Suresh. 2006. The place of World Englishes in composition: Pluralization continued. *College Composition and Communication 57*: 586–619.

Canagarajah, A. Suresh. 2009. The plurilingual tradition and the English language in South Asia. In Lisa Lim and Ee-Ling Low, eds. *Multilingual, Globalising Asia: Implications for Policy and Education, AILA Review 22*: 5–22.

Canagarajah, Suresh. 2013. *Translingual Practice: Global Englishes and Cosmopolitan Relations*. London: Routledge.

Creese, Angela and Adrian Blackledge. 2010. Translanguaging in the bilingual classroom: A pedagogy for learning and teaching. *Modern Language Journal* 94: 103–115.

Cummins, Jim. 2008. Teaching for transfer: Challenging the two solitudes assumption in bilingual education. In Jim Cummins and Nancy Hornberger, eds. *Encyclopaedia of Language and Education* (2nd ed). New York: Springer, 65–76.

Faraclas, Nicholas. 1996. *Nigerian Pidgin*. London: Routledge.

Filppula, Markku. 2008. The Celtic hypothesis hasn't gone away: New perspectives on old debates. In Marina Dossena, Richard Dury and Maurizio Gotti, eds. *English Historical Linguistics*. Amsterdam: John Benjamins, 153–170.

García, Ofelia. 2009. *Bilingual Education in the 21st Century*. Oxford: Wiley Blackwell.

García, Ofelia and Li Wei. 2014. *Translanguaging: Language, Bilingualism and Education*. Basingstoke: Palgrave Macmillan.

Gonzales, Wilkinson Daniel Wong. 2017. Language contact in the Philippines: The history and ecology from a Chinese Filipino perspective. *Language Ecology* 1(2): 185–212.

Good, Jeff. 2004a. Tone and accent in Saramaccan: Charting a deep split in the phonology of a language. *Lingua* 114: 575–619.

Good, Jeff. 2004b. Split prosody and creole simplicity: The case of Saramaccan. *Journal of Portuguese Linguistics* 3: 11–30.

Good, Jeff. 2006. The phonetics of tone in Saramaccan. In Ana Deumert and Stephanie Durrleman, eds. *Structure and Variation in Language Contact*. Amsterdam: John Benjamins, 9–28.

Gramling, David. 2016. *The Invention of Monolingualism*. London: Bloomsbury.

Gupta, Anthea Fraser. 1992. The pragmatic particles of Singapore Colloquial English. *Journal of Pragmatics* 18: 31–57.

Gupta, Anthea Fraser. 1994. *The Step-Tongue: Children's English in Singapore*. Clevedon, UK: Multilingual Matters.

Gut, Ulrike. 2005. Nigerian English prosody. *English World-Wide* 26(2): 153–177.

Hickey, Raymond. 2005. Englishes in Asia and Africa: Origins and structure. In Raymond Hickey, ed. *Legacies of Colonial English: Studies in Transported Dialects*. Cambridge: Cambridge University Press, 503–535.

Holm, John. 1988. *Pidgins and Creoles, Vol. 1: Theory and Structure*. Cambridge: Cambridge University Press.

Horner, Bruce, Lu Min-Zhan, Jacqueline Jones Royster and John Trimbur. 2011. Language difference in writing: Toward a translingual approach. *Faculty Scholarship*, Paper No. 67. http://ir.library.louisville.edu/faculty/67

Huber, Magnus. 1999. *Ghanaian Pidgin English in Its West African Context*. Amsterdam: John Benjamins.

James, Gregory. 2001. Cantonese particles in Hong Kong students' emails. *English Today* 17(3): 9–16.

Jørgensen, J. N. 2008. Polylingual languaging around and among children and adolescents. *International Journal of Multilingualism* 5(3): 161–176.

Kachru, Braj B., ed. 1992. *The Other Tongues: English across Cultures* (2nd ed.). Urbana: University of Illinois Press.

Kachru, Braj B. 1994. English in South Asia. In Robert Burchfield, ed. *The Cambridge History of the English Language, Vol. 5: English in Britain and Overseas: Origins and Development*. Cambridge: Cambridge University Press, 497–553.

Kachru, Yamuna and Cecil L. Nelson. 2006. *World Englishes in Asian Contexts: Asian Englishes Today*. Hong Kong: Hong Kong University Press.

Kouwenberg, Silvia. 2004. The grammatical function of Papiamentu tone. *Journal of Portuguese Linguistics* 3: 55–69.

Lange, Claudia. 2009. Discourse particles in Indian English. In Thomas Hoffmann and Lucia Siebers, eds. *World Englishes: Problems, Properties, Prospects*. Amsterdam: John Benjamins, 207–226.

Lee, Jerry Won and Christopher Jenks. 2016, Doing translingual dispositions. *College Composition and Communication* 68(2): 317–344.

Ler, Vivien Soon Lay. 2006. A relevance-theoretic approach to discourse particles in Singapore English. In Kerstin Fischer, ed. *Approaches to Discourse Particles*. Amsterdam: Elsevier.

Li, Wei. 1998. The "why" and "how" questions in the analysis of conversational code-switching. In Peter Auer, ed. *Code-Switching in Conversation: Language, Interaction and Identity*. London: Routledge, 156–179.

Lim, JooHyuk and Ariane M. Borlongan. 2011. Tagalog particles in Philippine English: The cases of *ba, na, no,* and *pa. Philippine Journal of Linguistics* 42: 59–74.

Lim, Lisa. 2004. Sounding Singaporean. In Lisa Lim, ed. *Singapore English: A Grammatical Description* (Varieties of English Around the World G33). Amsterdam: John Benjamins, 19–56.

Lim, Lisa. 2007. Mergers and acquisitions: On the ages and origins of Singapore English particles. *World Englishes* 27(4): 446–473.

Lim, Lisa. 2008. Dynamic multilingual ecologies of Asian Englishes. *Asian Englishes* 11(1): 52–55.

Lim, Lisa. 2009a. Revisiting English prosody: (Some) New Englishes as tone languages? The typology of Asian Englishes, Special Issue. *English World-Wide* 30(2): 218–239.

Lim, Lisa. 2009b. Beyond fear and loathing in SG: The real mother tongues and language policies in multilingual Singapore. In Lisa Lim and Ee-Ling Low, eds. *Multilingual, Globalising Asia: Implications for Policy and Education, AILA Review* 22: 52–71.

Lim, Lisa. 2010a. Migrants and "mother tongues": Extralinguistic forces in the ecology of English in Singapore. In Lisa Lim, Anne Pakir, and Lionel Wee, eds. *English in Singapore: Modernity and Management* (Asian Englishes Today) Hong Kong: Hong Kong University Press, 19–54.

Lim, Lisa. 2010b. Peranakan English in Singapore. In Daniel Schreier, Peter Trudgill, Edgar W. Schneider, and Jeffrey P. Williams, eds. *The Lesser-Known Varieties of English: An Introduction*. Cambridge: Cambridge University Press. 327–347.

Lim, Lisa. 2011. Revisiting English prosody: (Some) New Englishes as tone languages? In Lisa Lim and Nikolas Gisborne, eds., *The Typology of Asian Englishes*, Amsterdam: John Benjamins, 97–118.

Lim, Lisa. 2015. Catalysts for change: On the evolution of contact varieties in the multilingual knowledge economy. Unpublished manuscript. The University of Hong Kong.

Lim, Lisa. 2017a. Money minded. Language Matters. *Post Magazine, South China Morning Post*. March 19. (Online version: Where the word "shroff" came from, and its many meanings. *Post Magazine*, 17 March. www.scmp.com/magazines/post-magazine/short-reads/article/2079497/where-word-shroff-came-and-its-many-meanings)

Lim, Lisa. 2017b. Boiling point. Language Matters. Post Magazine, *South China Morning Post*. November 1. (Online version: Where the word congee comes from – the answer may surprise you, *Post Magazine*, November 10. www.scmp.com/magazines/post-magazine/article/2119163/where-word-congee-comes-answer-may-surprise-you)

Lim, Lisa and Umberto Ansaldo. 2012. Contact in the Asian arena. In Terttu Nevalainen and Elizabeth Closs Traugott, eds. *The Oxford Handbook of the History of English*. New York: Oxford University Press, 560–571.

Lim, Lisa and Umberto Ansaldo. 2016. *Languages in Contact*. Cambridge University Press.

Lim, Lisa and Joseph A. Foley. 2004. English in Singapore and Singapore English: Background and methodology. In Lisa Lim, ed. *Singapore English: A Grammatical Description* (Varieties of English Around the World G33.) Amsterdam: John Benjamins, 1–18.

Lim, Lisa and Nikolas Gisborne. 2009. The typology of Asian Englishes: Setting the agenda (The Typology of Asian Englishes, Special Issue). *English World-Wide 30*(2): 123–132.

Lim, Lisa, Anne Pakir and Lionel Wee. 2010. English in Singapore: Policy and prospects. In Lisa Lim, Anne Pakir and Lionel Wee, eds. *English in Singapore: Modernity and Management*. Hong Kong: Hong Kong University Press, 3–18.

Lin, Angel M.Y. 2005. New youth digital literacies and mobile connectivity: Text messaging among Hong Kong college students. *Fibreculture*, Issue 6. http://journal.fibreculture.org/issue6/index.html

Liu, Yucong. 2013. Marketplace communication between Africans and Chinese in Guangzhou: An emerging pidgin? Unpublished master's dissertation, University of Hong Kong.

Matras, Yaron. 2000. How predictable is contact-induced change in grammar? In Colin Renfrew, April McMahon and Larry Trask, eds. *Time Depth in Historical Linguistics*, Vol. 2. Oxford: MacDonald Institute for Archaeological Research, 563–583.

McFarland, Curtis D. 2008. Linguistic diversity and English in the Philippines. In Maria Lourdes S. Bautista and Kingsley Bolton, eds. *Philippine English: Linguistic and Literary Perspectives.* Hong Kong: Hong Kong University Press, 131–155.

Mesthrie, Rajend and Rakesh M. Bhatt. 2008. *World Englishes: The Study of New Linguistic Varieties.* Cambridge: Cambridge University Press.

Onysko, Alexander. 2016. Language contact and World Englishes. *World Englishes 35*(2): 191–195.

Otsuji, Emi and Alastair Pennycook. 2010. Metrolingualism: Fixity, fluidity and language in flux. *International Journal of Multilingualism 7*(3): 240–254.

Pennycook, Alastair. 2010. Popular cultures, popular languages, and global identities. In Nikolas Coupland, ed. *Handbook of Language and Globalisation.* Malden, MA: Wiley-Blackwell, 592–607.

Pennycook, Alastair and Emi Otsuji. 2015. *Metrolingualism: Language in the City.* Abingdon: Routledge.

Platt, John. 1987. Communicative functions of particles in Singapore English. In Ross Steele and Terry Threadgold, ed. *Language Topics: Essays in Honour of Michael Halliday*, Vol.1. Amsterdam: John Benjamins, 391–401.

Platt, John and Heidi Weber. 1980. *English in Singapore and Malaysia.* Kuala Lumpur: Oxford University Press.

Remijsen, Bert. 2001. *Word Prosodic Systems of Raja Ampat Languages.* Utrecht: LOT.

Remijsen, Bert and Vincent van Heuven. 2005. Stress, tone and discourse prominence in Curacao Papiamentu. Unpublished manuscript. Leiden University.

Rivera-Castillo, Yolanda and Lucy Pickering. 2004. Phonetic correlates of stress and tone in a mixed system. *Journal of Pidgin and Creole Languages 19*: 261–284.

Schneider, Edgar. 2007. *Postcolonial Englishes.* Cambridge: Cambridge University Press.

Schneider, Edgar. 2013. English as a contact language: The "New Englishes." In Daniel Schreier and Marianne Hundt, eds. *English as a Contact Language.* Cambridge University Press, 131–148.

Schreier, Daniel and Marianne Hundt, eds. 2013. *English as a Contact Language.* Cambridge: Cambridge University Press.

Schreier, Daniel, Peter Trudgill, Edgar W. Schneider and Jeffrey P. Williams, eds. 2010. *The Lesser Known Varieties of English: An Introduction.* Cambridge: Cambridge University Press.

Sultana, Shaila, Sender Dovchin and Alastair Pennycook. 2015. Transglossic language practices of young adults in Bangladesh and Mongolia. *International Journal of Multilingualism 12*(1): 93–108.

Thomason, Sarah. 2001. *Language Contact.* Cambridge: Cambridge University Press.

Tordesillas, Ellen. 2013. Gazmin makes the Philippines look pathetic. *Yahoo! News Philippines*, July 1. http://ph.news.yahoo.com/blogs/the-inbox/gazmin-makes-philippines-look-pathetic-163745294.html

Venneman, Theo. 2011. English as a contact language: Typology and comparison. *Anglia* 129(3–4): 217–257.

Wee, Lian-hee. 2008. More or less English? Two phonological patterns in the Englishes of Singapore and Hong Kong. *World Englishes* 27: 480–501.

Winford, Donald. 2003. *An Introduction to Contact Linguistics*. Oxford: Blackwell.

Wong, Y.T. 2009. The linguistic function of Cantonese discourse particles in the English medium online chat of Cantonese speakers. Unpublished master's dissertation, University of Wollongong.

Yakpo, Kofi. 2009. *A Grammar of Pichi*. Berlin: Isimu Media.

Young, Vershawn. 2004. Your average Nigga. *College Composition and Communication 55*: 693–715.

5

Population Structure and the Emergence of World Englishes

Salikoko S. Mufwene

5.1 Introduction

Population structure is a term used in population studies in reference to the typically nonuniform way in which populations are organized. The concept helps address the question of whether members of a given population can interact freely or regularly with each other. This depends on whether they are distributed according to factors such as nation or place of origin, race or ethnicity, or socioeconomic class. They can account for the nonuniform way in which the relevant population's language or culture has evolved.

Since Mufwene (1996), I have found the notion useful to explain differences between the socioeconomic structures of the colonies in which European languages have evolved into "creoles" and those in which they have simply speciated into new "dialects" of, for all intents and purposes, the same lexifiers. The former are the settlement colonies whose economic development relied on plantations, especially of sugar cane, rice, or coffee, and in which the enslaved or contract laborers became majority populations, such as in the Caribbean. Residential segregation was instituted early in such colonies, preventing most slave and contract laborers from interacting regularly with the European colonists whose language their contact ecology forced them to appropriate as a vernacular.

In contrast, the non-plantation settlement colonies are those where the European colonists became the majority and the language of the dominant colonizing nation (e.g. English in the USA and Canada) spread as the primary vernacular. This evolution is the consequence of a cultural assimilationist tendency that was enabled by the gradual collapse of residential segregation based on national origins among European immigrants. The new socioeconomic world order would eventually exert pressure on other residents of the polity to shift to the prevailing vernacular.

In linguistics, the notion of POPULATION STRUCTURE also accounts for the age-based fashion in which some features, such as quotative *like*, have spread. Likewise, ethnic barriers explain why, for instance, according to Labov (2001) and Wolfram and Schilling-Estes (2016), the Northern City Vowel Shift has spread especially among White American urbanites but not among their African American counterparts. In a nutshell, POPULATION STRUCTURE directs our attention to patterns of socialization among members of a population, viz. who is likely to interact with whom, who one is likely to identify socially with, who is expected to accommodate whom linguistically, and, among other things, whose language one is likely to shift to in a contact ecosystem.

As explained in Mufwene (2001), POPULATION STRUCTURE does not explain everything; it must be complemented with other ecological factors that I will also invoke in some of my explanations in the following sections. These include the FOUNDER EFFECT/PRINCIPLE, PERIODIZATION (viz. which population arrived earlier than which other population in the colony – and did they constitute an important critical mass that can affect the current evolutionary trajectory of things?), and patterns of POPULATION GROWTH (viz. whether the population grew significantly or not and whether the growth was abrupt or incremental). How a population grows can cause a population structure to change, as happened during the transition from the "homestead phase" to the "plantation phase" of Caribbean and Indian Ocean plantation settlement colonies (Chaudenson 2001), which not only produced the slave majority but also fostered residential segregation (Wood 1974). This population structure change was a critical actuator of the emergence of creoles in especially the Caribbean and the Indian Ocean plantation colonies. In North America, the Louisiana Purchase (1803) was another such a critical actuator, as the anglophone European immigrants eventually eclipsed the francophones economically and demographically in the former French colony. The change undermined the vitality of both French and French Creole in the present state of Louisiana in favor of English as the vernacular (Mufwene 2016).

Quite relevant also to understanding the impact of population structure on language evolution are attitudes that speakers display to each other's language varieties and their own. For instance, some may find the others too distant or cold from a social perspective and despise their way of speaking. Others may feel that their own language makes them less competitive on the job market and shift from it. Still others may identify the way they speak as an identity marker they must maintain, as in the case of some regional and/or ethnic varieties that are resilient despite their stigmatization. Interestingly, the responses are not always identical, especially if the population structure itself can change too, toward either integration or an alternative segregation pattern. I show in the following sections that both of these occurred in the USA.

In this chapter, I invoke POPULATION STRUCTURE to explain why English has evolved differentially around the world, since it spread from England in the seventeenth century. I submit that this factor accounts more adequately for this aspect of the spread of English than VARIATION IN STYLES OF COLONIZATION alone (viz. exploitation, settlement, and trade colonization) that I have often invoked since Mufwene (2001) as an explanation, although the latter factor is responsible for the variation in population structure itself. The present approach provides a perspective that complements, for instance, Schneider's (2007, 2011) account of the different Englishes worldwide.

Like Kachru (2017), I use *World Englishes* as an umbrella term for all English varieties, especially in the Inner and Outer Circles (Kachru 1985). My approach is theoretical, intended both to elaborate a particular fold of my ecological approach to language evolution (Mufwene 2001, 2008) and to provoke more thinking on the differential evolution of English. It is informed by especially what I know about the colonization of various places around the world by England or the UK and by my research on the emergence of creoles and pidgins, which I also consider as natural offspring of their lexifiers. The overall approach is uniformitarian, intended to debunk the apparent exceptionalism of, in this case, English creoles and pidgins, as well as indigenized Englishes (Mufwene 2001; DeGraff 2003).

5.2   The Spread of English Since the Seventeenth Century

5.2.1   The Irish Colony

Accounts of the spread of English around the world since the seventeenth century have often overlooked the fact that the English also colonized Ireland in earnest during the same period they conquered much of the New World. This is when Oliver Cromwell ended the Irish Confederate Wars in 1650, although, to be sure, the conquest had started in the sixteenth century, with the "Tudor Conquest." From the point of view of population structure, English would not spread rapidly in Ireland before the eighteenth century. Until then, the majority of the Irish population was rural and the English colonists' presence was primarily in the urban centers and the plantations surrounding them. According to Corrigan (2010), most of the workers had been brought from the Scotland Lowlands and the English North and North Midlands. They spoke English already and were considered more suitable for the plantation work than the Irish.

Odlin (2003) hypothesizes that the plantations provided an incentive for those who wanted jobs on the plantations to learn the colonizers' language. However, one may also argue that there was then no general pressure on the Irish to shift to English as their vernacular, as long as they were at home, were the majority, and socialized primarily among themselves. The English planters and their Scottish and Northern English workers presumably lived separately from them, as typically occurred in other colonies.

I consider the introduction of the textile industry in the eighteenth century as a catalyst, as it brought the Irish more in contact with the anglophone manufacturers and employees. Situated in the Industrial Revolution, this socioeconomic development contributed to changing Ireland's population structure, with many Irish migrating out of their rural areas to places where the industry was developing (Corrigan 2010). Ireland was thus both urbanizing and anglicizing linguistically, as more Englishmen also relocated to the same places. These demographic changes must have prompted the Irish to communicate more and more in English even among themselves, in the industrial centers. The creation of English-medium schools must have facilitated the shift.

No less significant in this history is definitely the integration of Ireland in the United Kingdom of Great Britain and Ireland in 1801. Urbanization, which is also invoked by Dolan (2008), does not fully explain the linguistic anglicization of Ireland if the urban centers were residentially segregated and the rural areas also did not develop urban-like economic and political structures. A complementary explanation must lie in the anglicization-cum-British cultural assimilation of the colony. This process includes the pressure that the colonizers exerted since before the seventeenth century on the indigenous elite to anglicize. The pressure itself can be correlated with the fact that all sectors of Irish modern economy have functioned in English ever since. Consequently, Irish gradually became redundant in indigenous lives, as the working class emulated the elite. No less signifi-cant is also the succession of famines in 1740–1741, 1845–1852, and 1879, which caused massive deaths and emigration to urban centers and to outside Ireland; they reduced the size of the Irish-speaking population.

Since the Irish started communicating in the foreign tongue even among themselves too, English in Ireland has evolved in an ecology that favors substrate influence. The scenario is similar to that of contact settings where "indigenized Englishes" and creoles emerged. Competing with no other substrate language, Irish has thus exerted some incontrovertible influence on English in Ireland. This is the case of, for instance, the bilabial fricative substituting for /w/ in words such as *well* and the consuetudinal *be* V-*ing*, which is invariant and is negated with *don't*.

This evolution prompts in particular the question of why there is no evidence of such extensive Celtic substrate influence on Old English. Could it be that the Celts in England socialized minimally with the Germanic invaders until about the time of the Norman Conquest? Could their coex-istence have been similar to that of Native Americans with the European colonists in anglophone North America? As discussed in Section 5.2.2, the newcomers kept conquering lands from Native Americans and relegating the latter to the margins of the new socioeconomic world order, where they had little use for the foreign tongue. Except in a few ethnolects such as Lumbee English (see also Section 5.2.2), Native American languages have exerted little influence on structures of American Englishes largely because they have shifted quite late to English as a vernacular.

5.2.2 The American and Caribbean Colonies

The New World colonies call for a distinction between two kinds of settlement colonies. The first kind consists of those where the European colonists eventually became the demographic majority while instituting economic and political systems that marginalized the Natives to "reservations." The second kind, more typical of the Caribbean but applying also to coastal South Carolina and Georgia in the USA, consists of territories where the enslaved Africans brought to work on the plantations of especially sugarcane or rice became the overwhelming majorities. Although English prevailed as the only or dominant vernacular in both kinds of colonies, the racially segregated population structure of the plantation settlement colonies, following the homestead phase, produced an early divergence of English into varieties disfranchised as creoles. There is so far no evidence that they have evolved in any unusual way (Mufwene 2000, 2001, 2008), except that, like Irish English, their structures bear significant selective influence from the substrate languages of the majority populations that appropriated English as their vernacular. For instance, serial verb constructions in them have typically been claimed to reflect substrate influence.

The creoles differ from each other (see also Aceto, Chapter 9, this volume) primarily because the lexifier itself, which was koineizing from the contact of different metropolitan nonstandard dialects, was not identical from one colony to another. In addition, the gradual mix of the substrate languages was not uniform, for instance, from the point of view of demographic significance of speakers of particular (families of) languages. Cross-colony variation in the local dynamics of population structure, hence of language contact, explains why the creoles are no more identical than the different dialects of English that emerged in the other settlement colonies.

As shown in Mufwene (2009), the European-majority colonies were also segregated, by nationality, all the way into the twentieth century. Until the American Revolution, English in the colonies was the vernacular of the English colonists and indentured servants and slaves who worked for and lived with them. Note that the slaves were negligible minorities in colonies north of Virginia, between 2 percent and 4 percent of the colonial populations, though in Virginia they reached close to 40 percent in the eighteenth century (Perkins 1988), like in the cotton-plantation colonies, such as Mississippi and Alabama. The ratio was even lower in the interior of South Carolina and Georgia, where the settlers were small farmers.

These had to wait until the nineteenth century and the explosion of the textile industry to see a new population mix, including immigrants from Europe and migrants from other parts of the USA (Bailey 1997; McNair 2005).

As explained by Bailey and Thomas (1998), the history suggests that African American Vernacular English (AAVE, different from Gullah on the coast of South Carolina and Georgia) and American White Southern English were one and the same language until after the institution of Jim Crow in the late nineteenth century (Mufwene 2015a). The indentured servants had constituted 50–75 percent of the White colonial population (Kulikoff 1986, 1991) and had lived side by side with the Africans on the tobacco and cotton plantations.[1] The White farmers who had some slaves could not afford many and lived in small homesteads with them. McNair (2005) shows that, in the hinterland of Georgia, small farmers and the few African Americans that lived with them in the same mill villages inter- acted regularly in the nineteenth and even the early twentieth centuries, though they probably did not socialize together. The institution of Jim Crow drove many African Americans to the North and elsewhere, espe- cially during the Great Migration (late nineteenth and first half for the twentieth centuries), in search of better living conditions.

I submit that Jim Crow fostered AAVE by enabling the divergence of White and African American ethnolects, owing to decreasing interactions between their respective speakers in the American South and to the emergence of Black ghettos in American cities, which kept African Americans from socializing with European Americans even outside the South. It also led non-Southern White Americans, who were not familiar with the contact history of the South, to characterize as African American the Southern variety of English spoken by the in-migrants.

Metropolitan English who traveled to the South also drew the same hasty conclusion. According to them, the enslaved Africans had not only misshaped English but also influenced the way White Southerners speak through the nannies that had looked after them as children. However, Coleman (1978) points out that only 5–10 percent of Whites, especially the planters, could afford a nanny in the southern colonies, consistent with the demographics provided by Kulikoff (1986, 1991).

In any case, as is evident from writers such as Ambrose Gonzales, who grew up among the slaves, the children of the White plantocracy grew up bilingual or bilectal, and many of them had opportunities to attend school outside of the South and did not speak the relevant African American ethnolect as their vernacular. Similarities between AAVE and the varieties spoken by descendants of indentured servants, who had no Black nannies,

[1] One should not confuse race *segregation*, which was institutionalized late in the nineteenth century, in the American southern hinterland (though much earlier, in the early eighteenth century, in coastal South Carolina), with race *discrimination*. The latter had sustained the distinction between slaves and indentured servants in colonial America and the Caribbean.

need not be attributed to the influence of the latter, especially if only a negligible part of their structural features can be traced to African substrate languages. A more plausible conclusion is that, given the time of the institutionalization of Jim Crow, toward the end of the nineteenth century, the White indentured servants and the Africans on the tobacco and cotton plantations developed American Southern English jointly (Schneider 1995; Bailey and Thomas 1998; Mufwene 2015a). They started to diverge too late, after almost 250 years of living together, for their varieties to become clearly distinct from each other.

The above account instantiates the Founder Principle, according to which it takes significant new ecological factors, such as the arrival of a critical mass of newcomers, to change the linguistic legacy of the founder population (Mufwene 1996, 2001). McNair (2005) shows how this appears to have happened in the textile mill town of Griffin, Georgia, when "mill villagers" who had moved from the Appalachian mountains brought features that competed with those of the local farmers, while racial barriers apparently kept the local African Americans from participating in this local/regional evolution.

Overall, the story of the spread of English among free non-Anglo White Americans is different from its evolution among African Americans. As observed in Mufwene (2009), it really took German (Salmons 2003; Wilkerson and Salmons 2008), Norwegian (Haugen 1953), and Italian (Guglielmo and Salerno 2003) quite a long time to die. Along with the White indentured servants, the enslaved Africans were among the first to give up their heritage languages, forced by their lack of socioeconomic freedom to anglicize during the colonial period. One may also say that the French in Louisiana are exceptional compared to other continental European immigrants in having kept their "national" language to date.[2]

It was the weakening of their parochial economic practices starting in the nineteenth century and their gradual cultural assimilation, concurrent with residential desegregation, that led the non-Anglo European Americans to shift to English. More specifically, the shift was a consequence of their seeking employment in the Anglo economic system, their children attending Anglo schools, marriages across national cultural boundaries, and the integration of national neighborhoods into general White neighborhoods, in contrast to the emergence of "ethnic ghettos" such as African American and Hispanic neighborhoods.[3]

Because White Americans of continental European descent are now the majority, in contrast with 15–20 percent of people of English descent

---

[2] To be sure, as explained by Dubois (2014), it has been in attrition since the world wars, as numerous francophones have been leaving their isolated rural communities for the city, where English is the dominant vernacular and the language of the economy and politics.

[3] In American history, the term *ghetto* has not always been associated with poverty, especially when it applied earlier to European American communities identified by nationality, such as German, Irish, and Italian. It had previously also been used in Europe to distinguish between urban residential neighborhoods, for instance in Frankfurt.

(Doyle 1994), the question arises of why White American English varieties do not sound like the English varieties spoken in continental Europe. The answer is not that continental European immigrants were better learners of English than the enslaved Africans, who produced creoles in territories where they emerged as majorities. Continental Europeans today speak second-language English varieties that are distinct from American and British Englishes, which suggests that non-Anglo European Americans could have contributed substantial substrate elements to American English. The explanation for the limited amount of their influence appears to lie in PERIODIZATION, viz. the time of their shift to American English as a vernacular, rather late and incrementally (during the nineteenth and twentieth centuries), and in the interaction of the Founder Principle with changes in population structure.

The essence of American English, with its traditional dialectal distinctions in the original thirteen English American colonies (viz. New England, Midland, and Southern), whose boundaries have remained stable to date (Wolfram and Schilling 2016), was in place already by the time of the American Revolution, as hypothesized by American dialectologists such as Kurath (1928, 1949). Since then, continental European immigrants have been shifting to it, after the American Revolution, like recent immigrants have, with the adults dying with most of their xenolectal features while their children acquired the local English variety as faithfully as any mother-tongue speaker can (Mufwene 2009).

Thanks to children as the agents of selection in the competition between native and non-native features (Mufwene 2001, 2008), the continental European influence on especially the grammar and phonology of the umbrella construct AMERICAN ENGLISH has thus remained negligible. One may of course invoke a feature such as rhoticity as a congruence of English retroflection and the European pronunciation of trilled /r/ in pre-consonantal and word-final position (Mufwene and Pargman 2002).[4] However, such features are so few that the contribution of continental European languages to the grammar of American English may be considered negligible and certainly less significant than the contribution of the same languages to its lexicon.

To be sure, German, Italian, and Yiddish/Jewish English varieties *did* emerge but they appear to have been transitions to the Americanization of European immigrants. They have basically died as a consequence of the sociocultural assimilation of the non-Anglo Whites to the Anglos. As noted above, the evidence for this lies in the disappearance of, for instance, German, Italian, and Jewish neighborhoods in American cities. In the meantime, AAVE and Gullah have survived, consistent

---

[4] Literacy may also have played a role in this case, though one should not overlook the fact that some British English varieties had the same feature in the seventeenth century (Wolfram and Schilling 2016), which is still evident in Scots today but lost in the Received Pronunciation.

with the continuing residence of their speakers in segregated urban neighborhoods (like Southside Chicago) and in isolated communities (on the coast of South Carolina and Georgia), respectively.[5] In contrast, small island varieties such as Martha's Vineyard and Ocracoke are endangered by the migrations of mainland White Americans, with whom some of the locals have socialized (intimately) and whose varieties they have learned (Labov 1963; Wolfram and Schilling-Estes 1995).

Population structure accounts for this differential evolution of English in the USA, stopping divergence through the sociocultural assimilation of some White communities, while fostering or sustaining it through social and/or spatial segregation. In other words, residential segregation has sustained African American ethnolects (among others), whereas the deghettoization of European Americans has caused the loss of ethnolects once identified as German, Italian, Jewish/Yiddish Englishes, and so on.

Other evidence of the role of population structure in sustaining a particular ethnolect can be found in Wolfram and Dannenberg's (1999) and Dannenberg's (2002) account of Lumbee English, a Native American English vernacular spoken in North Carolina. Although it is difficult to determine when this Native American population shifted to English as their vernacular, it has evolved into an ethnolect thanks to race segregation in their county, thus fostering ethnic-specific elements in it. Generally, the Lumbees have socialized with neither the White Americans nor the African Americans in their geographical environment; and their English now functions as a marker of ethnic identity.

Non-integration in the vernacular-English population in the USA has certainly fostered greater substrate influence on some other English ethnolects, including Hispanic vernaculars identified as Chicano English, spoken in southwestern USA, and Puerto Rican English, spoken especially in New York City. They both bear influence from Spanish, though, as noted by Robert Bailey (2008), Puerto Rican English bears some legacy from AAVE. This connection reflects who the Puerto Rican immigrants could interact most easily with in the host country. However, as also explained by Santa Ana (1993), these varieties remain different and can function as ethnic markers not only because of race segregation in American cities but also because even native speakers have to be (somewhat) bilingual in Spanish too, in order to communicate with family members that are either Spanish monolinguals or less fluent in English.

---

[5] As pointed out in Mufwene (1997a), the numerous affluent, mostly White Americans who have relocated to these coastal areas since the mid-twentieth century have developed communities of practice that are separate from those of Gullah speakers. Although they see each other in the grocery store, situated on the highway that separates their segregated communities, they do not socialize together. They do not even attend the same churches.

5.2.3   English in Australia

Australia was a settlement colony, in which the Europeans also became the majority population, minoritizing the Aborigines and marginalizing most of them to Aboriginal "reserves." English became its dominant vernacular, under conditions similar to anglophone North America, although it was settled in earnest in the late eighteenth century (see Biewer and Burridge, Chapter 13, this volume). English spread among non-Anglo European immigrants in a way similar to its adoption by continental European immigrants in North America, once their parochial national economic practices became less competitive, especially after World War II (Clyne 2003). That also meant gradually adopting the Anglo model, with the non-native elements being weeded out by children. Trudgill (2004) underscores the significance of the features from the British Isles during the early settlements, instantiating the Founder Principle. Other immigrants, especially from Asia and Africa, who were admitted only since the 1970s (ignoring Chinese immigrations during the Gold Rush of the mid-nineteenth century), have assimilated to the preceding anglophone populations in ways similar to their counterparts in anglophone North America.

Equally noteworthy is the emergence of Australian Aboriginal English (AAbE) and the varieties in the northern part of the country identified as creole. The creole, also called *Kriol*, was born in Queensland sugarcane plantations, under contact conditions similar to those that produced creoles in the Caribbean, although the labor consisted of people recruited from different parts of Australia itself and from parts of Asia.

According to Malcolm (2000), AAbE evolved from a pidgin-like variety in which the Aborigines communicated with the colonists in the Sidney area. It spread to other urban centers and farms where the Aborigines interacted with the colonists. As more and more Aborigines from different ethnolinguistic groups in Australia migrated to the urban centers and used it for communication among themselves, it expanded into a vernacular, presumably because they mixed across their ethnic boundaries. Residential segregation from the White population also has fostered its divergence from the Australian White vernacular. The education of children and literacy in English have putatively made it less pidgin-like, while permanent residence in the city turned it into an ethnolect that would take the place of their indigenous vernaculars.

Queensland Kanaka or Canefields English is apparently a pidgin that developed on the sugarcane plantations in Northeast Australia in the early nineteenth century. According to Baker (1993), it developed earlier than Melanesian pidgins, from the same Sidney variety that evolved into AAbE. It is likewise related to Torres Strait Creole, spoken on the archipelago between Australia and Papua New Guinea, though the latter has also been linked to Jamaican Creole and Pacific pidgins, owing to the origins of the laborers that worked on the plantations.

In addition to the above, one must include Kriol, which is spoken in the Northern Territory and Western Australia and appears to be the northern counterpart of AAbE. According to Munro (2000), it evolved into an ethnic vernacular during the 1930s and 1940s, when the Aborigines chose the towns, farms, missions, and army camps to which they had relocated as their permanent residences and identified with them culturally, though they did not abandon their Aboriginal identity. However, their children acquired it natively while they were also being schooled in White Australian English and told that their ethnolect was bad English. Although these native speakers did not give it up, for reasons of ethnic identity, it bears influence from the Australian English learned in school, which they use to communicate with non-Aborigines.

Regardless of whether they are called *Creole*, *Pidgin*, *Broken*, or *English* (among other names), these non-White English varieties are by-products of emergent, nontraditional population structures in which the non-Europeans interacted with Europeans but did not socialize with them. It is also telling that those that evolved into vernaculars did so rather late, after their Aboriginal speakers had relocated to the new multilingual contact communities in which they did not have a common indigenous vernacular and could not resort to their traditional multilingual practices.

5.2.4 English Pidgins

The population-structure approach developed in this chapter also helps us account better for the emergence of English pidgins in the Pacific, especially in Melanesia, where, the vast majority of them are attested. The "three dialects" of "Melanesian Pidgin" identified by Siegel (2010), viz. Tok Pisin (in Papua New Guinea), Bislama (in Vanuatu), and Pijin (in Solomon Islands), have been linked to Queensland Pidgin (e.g. Baker 1993), though Keesing (1988) traces their origins to a maritime English jargon spoken aboard the whaling ships. The two accounts may not be mutually exclusive. Siegel (2010) identifies earlier contacts between, on the one hand, Melanesians and, on the other, American and Australian whalers and traders in the early 1800s, during which transactions were conducted in English foreigner talk, New South Wales Pidgin English (an ancestor of Queensland Pidgin English), and Chinese Pidgin English.

Queensland is conspicuous because Melanesian contract laborers had been recruited to work on its sugarcane plantations. They not only brought several mutually unintelligible languages but also constituted a disproportionally large population relative to the White owners and employees; and they adopted Queensland English (Pidgin) as their lingua franca. After their contracts expired, many of them were recruited to work on Melanesian sugarcane plantations (see also Keesing 1988) and eventually would settle in the emerging urban centers. In both contact ecologies, the English pidgin brought from Queensland apparently continued to function as a lingua franca. It was influenced by the local substrate languages and, owing to differences among them, speciated into the "three dialects" identified by Siegel (2010).

From the point of view of population structure, the Melanesian contract laborers worked in nontraditional socioeconomic ecologies in which, together with the Australian Aborigines, they were the overwhelming majority, were residentially segregated from the heritage speakers of English, did not socialize with them, but had to communicate in some approximation of this foreign language. The processes that produced its divergence can certainly be compared to those that produced the Romance languages from Vulgar Latin (Schlieben-Lange 1977; Mufwene 2015b) or Irish English in especially the eighteenth and nineteenth centuries, at least in the following respect: the new speakers were the majority and indigenous to the birth place of the new varieties.[6]

The contact ecologies of the English varieties that evolved on Pitcairn and Norfolk (in the South Pacific) and are identified as creoles are only remotely comparable to those where creoles emerged in, for instance, the Caribbean and Hawaii. Ignoring the Genoese and Danish castaways in the case of Norfolk, these then uninhabited islands were settled, the first by nine and the second by three anglophones and a slightly larger population of especially Tahitians. Power asymmetry imposed English as the lingua franca. Most of the original English native speakers did not survive but the lingua franca evolved into the vernacular of the surviving communities. As their small populations grew on the islands (more by birth than by immigration), new local English varieties emerged that bear influence from the relevant Polynesian languages. The ways in which the populations grew also underscore the significance of the Founder Principle, because the contact varieties of the first settlers paved the way for the subsequent evolution of English locally. All the women settlers were non-European and the children inherited most of the non-native features from them.

In contrast, although traditionally claimed to have evolved from pidgins that emerged from the contact of English traders with Africans on the eastern Atlantic coast in the seventeenth century, the emergence of Cameroon and Nigerian Pidgin Englishes shows little resemblance to that of Melanesian English pidgins. Until late in the eighteenth century, the Europeans used Portuguese to trade with the African rulers (Huber 1999), and this language remained the exclusive lingua franca of trade with Europeans in Dahomey until the nineteenth century. The trade itself was conducted through interpreters,[7] who, according to the sources cited

---

[6] To be sure, the Melanesians were not indigenous in Queensland but they certainly were in Melanesia, where Tok Pisin, Bislama, and Pijin emerged as new linguae francae and subsequently vernacularized in the emergent urban centers of Papua New Guinea, Vanuatu, and Solomon Islands, respectively.

[7] The interpreters are unlikely to have spoken flawless Portuguese (or any other European language in which they developed competence). However, they must have spoken it well enough to assume their function, considering the financial significance of the transactions in which they were involved (e.g. large numbers of slaves and extensive

in Mufwene (2014), became important power brokers all the way till the exploitation colonization of sub-Saharan Africa in the late nineteenth century. King Dom Afonso of the Kongo himself (early sixteenth century) learned Portuguese and wrote to his "brother" King Dom Manuel I of Portugal and to the Pope in this language. As is illustrated by the following examples, the putatively early attestations of a "West African Pidgin English" adduced by Dillard (1972, 1992) date from the eighteenth century, are closer to English than to Nigerian or Cameroon Pidgin English, and are minimally comparable to the sample utterances cited by Siegel (2010) for early Melanesian Pidgin:

(1)   [. . .] and we nebber see our mudders any more (1732, Dillard 1992: 62)

(2)   By-and-by you die, and go to the bad place, and after a while Cuff die and go and knock at the good gate (mid-eighteenth century, Dillard 1992: 62)

(3)   Only he got using all the same pigeon (Gilbert Islands, 1860; Siegel 2010: 819)

(4)   Canoe too little, by and by broke – All man go away, canoe gone, very good me stop (Lifu Loyalty Islands, 1850; Siegel 2010: 819).

It is difficult to resist the conclusion that the evidence cited by Dillard may represent interlanguages but not any communal English pidgin that may have emerged so early in the colonial history of Africa. The origins of both Cameroon and Nigerian Pidgin Englishes appear to lie in Krio, spoken in Sierra Leone, from which the first Baptist missionaries came in the mid-nineteenth century. Warner-Lewis (2018) also mentions missionaries from Jamaica that came to the region around the same time. Thus Cameroon and Nigerian Pidgin Englishes appear to have emerged around the same time as their counterparts of the Pacific (Mufwene 2014), just like Pichi,[8] which evolved from the Krio spoken by settlers from Free Town (Sierra Leone) who relocated to Bioko Island (in Equatorial Guinea) in 1827 (Yapko 2009).

These varieties undoubtedly reflect influence from the local languages, just like Krio itself bears influence from the local substrate languages, which account partly for its divergence from Jamaican Creole, its primary ancestor. According to Yakpo (2009: 186), Pichi has borrowed 50 percent of nouns, 62 percent of numerals, and 57 percent of conjunctions, among other lexical categories, from Spanish, its new superstrate. It has borrowed less from the indigenous languages because it has a higher social status

---

amounts of gold and ivory) and also the role they would play in the early stages of the exploitation colonization of the land. Many of them learned the European languages in Europe by immersion (Mufwene 2014).

[8]   The name is, tellingly, a distortion of the word *pidgin*, which is locally used to designate the language, just like Hawaiians use *Pidgin* in reference to what linguists call Hawaiian English Creole.

than them.[9] Population structure appears to have influenced variously, under the pressure of local contact ecosystems, the evolutionary trajectories of English, in this case to the point where it is harder to recognize the outcomes as genetically related to the lexifier.

5.2.5 Outer Circle Englishes (OCE)

I am deliberately avoiding the term *indigenized Englishes*, which has traditionally been used to designate varieties of English outside the Inner Circle, because all English varieties that evolved outside England have indigenized in one way or another (Mufwene 2009). They are the outcomes of adaptations of English to the local natural ecologies and to the previous or current communicative habits (including structural and pragmatic features) of its new, non-heritage speakers. Creoles are the epitome of "indigenization," a word also used by Hall (1966) as an alternative to *nativization*, according to his position that creoles evolved from antecedent pidgins.

I use the term *Outer Circle Englishes* (OCE) strictly in reference to the varieties that emerged in former British exploitation colonies and American unincorporated territories.[10] Unlike in the settlement colonies, the Europeans did not intend to settle new homes or to found new Europes (Crosby 1986) in the exploitation colonies. Their primary goal was to amass raw materials needed to fuel the Industrial Revolution.

In exploitation colonies, the European colonizers did not mix with the indigenous populations; nor did they intend to anglicize the totality of the indigenous populations culturally, thus linguistically. The often-cited *Minute on Education in India*, by Thomas Babington Macaulay (1835), was intended to produce a small elite class of indigenous colonial auxiliaries that would interface as intermediaries between the colonizers and the masses of the colonized people. As a matter of fact, the first ones were recruited from elite families of indigenous rulers, who would enjoy some privileges in the new socioeconomic world order. There thus emerged a three-tier population structure: (1) the top tier included the British colonizers, living in their own separate quarters and speaking English as a vernacular; (2) the bottom one consisted of the masses of the populations, who seldom interacted directly with the colonizers and continued to speak their heritage languages and often another indigenous language as a lingua franca; while (3) the middle tier comprised the colonial auxiliaries, who

---

[9] This is a phenomenon typical of sub-Saharan Africa, where borrowings from the superstrate into indigenous languages are better accepted than the other way around, although the former colonial languages, now the official languages, have indigenized too.

[10] I will not discuss English in the Expanding Circle because no local communal norms have emerged there, despite similarities in the xenolectal features of speakers when they share (typologically related) native languages. English is learned there for communication with people from different polities.

became multilingual in indigenous languages and in English, which they spoke as a non-native lingua franca.[11]

This same socioeconomic world order has been maintained since Independence: 1947 for India but much later, in the late 1950s and early 1960s, for the other colonies, especially in Africa. The former colonial auxiliaries then stepped into the shoes of the former colonizers and adopted English not only as a (co-)official language but also as an emblem of their political and social distinction.

English has also become accessible to all those who can attend school, the primary means of its transmission (Mufwene 2001). Very few children acquire it as a mother tongue. On the other hand, teachers have increasingly been indigenous, speaking it non-natively (Bamgbose 1992). The chain of transmission from non-native speakers to learners has produced what Chaudenson (2001) characterizes as "approximations of approximations of the lexifier," regarding creoles. An important difference is that the lexifier is a nonstandard vernacular in case of latter varieties, whereas it is a scholastic variety for OCEs (Mufwene 2001).

We can thus conclude that, although the colonial auxiliaries did not replicate faithfully the English taught to them by the colonizers and Eurasians (Gupta 1994), the OCEs really emerged after Independence, when the class of speakers expanded and when national norms emerged as a consequence of Natives using the European language for communication primarily among themselves. To be sure, continua emerged, as elsewhere (see also Aceto, Chapter 9, this volume), with the variation correlated with the extent to which a particular speaker's idiolect diverges from the Inner Circle's educated norms. Noteworthy factors include the level of education (Kachru 1983, 1994, 2005), the kinds of teachers a speaker has had (Bamgbose 1992), their native vernacular (Bamgbose 1992), and whether or not they have interacted significantly with Inner Circle speakers, notwithstanding their particular language learning skills.

One important factor that explains the extensive amount of substrate influence on OCEs is the fact that, as in the case of Irish English, the new speakers are the overwhelming majority at home, in contrast to Inner Circle English speakers. Also, like in the case of the emergence of creoles, the fact that they communicate more among themselves than with heritage speakers fosters more extensive indigenization in the sense of both meeting the cultural peculiarities of the speakers' communicative needs and being affected by the speakers' communicative practices shaped by their heritage languages. Although they speak different vernaculars, new national or regional norms emerge from their interactions with one another, through competition and selection between the substrate features (Mufwene 2001, 2008). Those who acquire it as their mother tongue are likewise almost exclusively exposed to their parents' features, which are typically not from

---

[11] Non-British Europeans were conveniently assimilated to the British colonists, though they did not matter politically.

the Inner Circle. It is typically features of such Natives that new learners target, even if they sometimes interact with Inner Circle English speakers; and it is not unusual to find children of expatriates from the Inner Circle that speak OCE-influenced idiolects.

Equally relevant in this context is the fact that English in the Outer Circle remains the "other tongue" and coexists with ancestral languages, even if it functions as a vernacular, as is evident from, for example, Kachru (1992, 2005), Kachru and Nelson (2006), Kachru et al. (2006), and Bao (2015). With the economies of most of the relevant countries evolving mostly in the blue-collar sector and functioning in indigenous linguae francae, English has remained the working language of a minority elite, in the white-collar sector. The overwhelming majority of its speakers are at least bilingual, even if they are native speakers, and communicate frequently with extended family members and helpers, both of whom are more fluent in their heritage languages. Such ecologies of multilingualism in English and indigenous languages favor local or national norms (corresponding to Schneider's 2007 endonormativity) that diverge from those of both the Inner Circle and the other OCEs.

5.3 Conclusions

In this chapter, I have focused on the role of POPULATION STRUCTURE, a fold of Mufwene's (2001) ecological approach to language evolution, in determining why English has not evolved uniformly everywhere and how. I have sometimes discussed why it has also prevailed as a (dominant) vernacular in some colonies but not in others. To be sure, POPULATION STRUCTURE does not explain everything, as indeed no particular ecological factor does alone. I have usually also explained how it interacts with other ecological factors, such as PERIODIZATION (in relation to which the Founder Principle must be understood), and the DEMOGRAPHIC PROPORTIONS of the populations in contact in causing the changes. Space limitations have not made it possible to discuss other factors such as AGE differences within the relevant population, differences in LEVELS OF EDUCATION, means of language transmission, and TYPOLOGICAL DIFFERENCES between the languages in contact, which would make for an elaborate and fine-grain analysis of the differential evolution of English.

Thus this chapter is strictly an initial sketch of an approach to the history of English that can enrich some accounts (such as Schneider 2007, 2011), assuming, in agreement with Kachru (2017), that *World Englishes* subsumes all English varieties spoken around the world.[12] My

---

[12] Naturally, determining which varieties (do not) count as English involves an ideological stand. My research on the emergence of creoles and pidgins argues against disfranchising them as "illegitimate offspring of English" (Mufwene 1997b). Therefore, this approach, which I consider uniformitarian, should include them (see also Aceto, Chapter 9, this volume) and has actually been inspired by my research on them.

primary objective was to show that POPULATION STRUCTURE is an important ecological factor, which can perhaps also explain the differential evolution of English in its earlier Old English and Middle English phases. This would entail looking into the different layers of the colonization of England, starting with the first Germanic invaders (the Jutes, the Angles, and the Saxons), then moving on to how the Norse and Norman French colonizers interacted with the populations they conquered. The study would have to include patterns of segregation, looking into the extent to which the Natives were integrated in, or excluded from, the new socioeconomic world order. This would also explain the nature and frequency of social interactions with the native speakers of the prevailing language and the extent to which the Natives felt pressured by the new socioeconomic ecology to appropriate it as their vernacular.

I propose this approach, which is fundamentally sociohistorical, not to dispute all extant accounts of the evolution of English but rather to provide an alternative perspective that can help determine which ones are (more) plausible and which ones are less or not. This remains an open agenda proposed to practitioners in a research area on which I am primarily a constructive critic.

References

Bailey, Guy. 1997. When did southern American English begin? In Edgar W. Schneider, ed. *Englishes Around the World: Vol. 1: General Studies, British Isles, North America* (Studies in honor of Manfred Görlach). Amsterdam: John Benjamins, 255–275.

Bailey, Guy, and Erik Thomas. 1998. Some aspects of African-American vernacular English phonology. In Salikoko S. Mufwene, John R. Rickford, Guy Bailey, and John Baugh, eds. *African-American English: Structure, History and Use*. London: Routledge, 85–109.

Bailey, Robert. 2008. Latino varieties of English. In Momma, Haruko and Michael Mato, eds. *A Companion to the History of the English Language*. Malden, MA: Wiley-Blackwell, 521–530.

Baker, Philip. 1993. Australian influence in Melanesian Pidgin English. *Te Reo* 36.3–67.

Bamgbose, Ayo. 1992. Standard Nigerian English: Issues of identification. In Braj Kachru, ed. *The Other Tongue: English across Cultures*. Urbana: University of Illinois Press, 148–161.

Bao, Zhiming. 2015. *Contact, Ecology, and New Englishes: The Making of Singapore English*. Cambridge: Cambridge University Press.

Chaudenson, Robert. 2001. *Creolization of Language and Culture*. London: Routledge.

Clyne, Michael. 2003. *Dynamics of Language Contact: English and Immigrant Languages*. Cambridge: Cambridge University Press.

Coleman, K. 1978. *Georgia History in Outline* (rev. ed.). Athens: University of Georgia Press.

Corrigan, Karen P. 2010. *Irish English, Vol. 1: Northern Ireland*. Edinburgh: Edinburgh University Press.

Crosby, Alfred W. 1986. *Ecological Imperialism: The Biological Expansion of Europe, 900–1900*. Cambridge: Cambridge University Press.

Dannenberg, Clare J. 2002. *Sociolinguistic Constructs of Ethnic Identity: The Syntactic Delineation of an American Indian English* (Publication of the American Dialect Society 87). Durham, NC: Duke University Press.

DeGraff, Michel. 2003. Against creole exceptionalism: Discussion note. *Language 79*: 391–410.

Dillard, J. L. 1972. *Black English; Its History and Usage in the United States*. New York: Random House.

Dillard, J. L. 1992. *A History of American English*. London: Longman.

Dolan, Terence Patrick. 2008. English in Ireland. In Haruko Momma and Michael Mato, eds. *A Companion to the History of the English Language*. Malden, MA: Wiley-Blackwell, 366–375.

Doyle, Rodger. 1994. *Atlas of Contemporary America: Portrait of a Nation*. New York: Facts On File.

Dubois, Sylvie. 2014. Autant en emporte la langue: La saga louisianaise du français. In Salikoko S. Mufwene and Cécile B. Vigouroux, eds. *Colonisation, gloablisation et vitalité du français*. Paris: Odile Jacob, 155–178.

Guglielmo, Jennifer and Salvatore Salerno, eds. 2003. *Are Italians White? How Race Is Made in America*. New York: Routledge.

Gupta, Anthea F. 1994. *The Step-Tongue: Children's English in Singapore*. Clevedon: Multilingual Matters.

Hall, Robert A., Jr. 1966. *Pidgin and Creole Languages*. Ithaca, NY: Cornell University Press.

Haugen, Einar. 1953. *The Norwegian Language in America: A Study in Bilingual Behavior*. Philadelphia: University of Pennsylvania Press.

Huber, Magnus. 1999. Atlantic creoles and the Lower Guinea Coast: A case against Afrogenesis. In Magnus Huber and Mikael Parkvall, eds. *Spreading the Word: The Issue of Diffusion among the Atlantic Creoles*. London: University of Westminster Press, 81–110.

Kachru, Braj B. 1983. *The Indianization of English: The English Language in India*. New Delhi: Oxford University Press.

Kachru, Braj B. 1985. Standards, codification, and sociolinguistic realism: The English language in the outer circle. In Randolph Quirk and Henry Widdowson, eds. *English in the World: Teaching and Learning the Language and Literatures*. Cambridge: Cambridge University Press, 11–30.

Kachru, Braj B., ed. 1992. *The Other Tongue: English across Cultures*. Urbana: University of Illinois Press.

Kachru, Braj B. 1994. English in South Asia. In Robert Burchfield, ed. *The Cambridge History of the English Language*. Cambridge: Cambridge University Press, 497–553.

Kachru, Braj. 2005. *Asian Englishes beyond the Canon*. Hong Kong: Hong Kong University Press.

Kachru, Braj B. 2017. *World Englishes and Culture Wars*. Cambridge: Cambridge University Press.

Kachru, Braj B., Yamuna Kachru, and Cecil L. Nelson, eds. 2006. *The Handbook of World Englishes*. Malden, MA: Blackwell.

Kachru, Yamuna and Cecil L. Nelson. 2006. *World Englishes in Asian Contexts*. Hong Kong: Hong Kong University Press.

Keesing, Roger M. 1988. *Melanesian Pidgin and the Oceanic Substrate*. Stanford: Stanford University Press.

Kulikoff, A. 1986. *Tobacco and Slaves: The Development of Southern Cultures in the Chesapeake, 1680–1800*. Chapel Hill: University of North Carolina Press.

Kulikoff, A. 1991. Colonial economy. In E. Foner and J. A. Garaty, eds. *The Reader's Companion to American History*. Boston: Houghton Mifflin, 201–203.

Kurath, Hans. 1928. The origin of dialectal differences in spoken American English. *Modern Philology 25*: 385–395.

Kurath, Hans. 1949. *A Word Geography of the Eastern United States*. Ann Arbor: University of Michigan Press.

Labov, William. 1963. The social motivation of a sound change. *Word 19*: 273–309. (Reprinted in Labov, William. 1972. *Sociolinguistic Patterns*. Philadelphia: University of Pennsylvania Press.)

Labov, William. 2001. *Principles of Linguistic Change: Social Factors*. Malden, MA: Blackwell.

Macaulay, Thomas Babington. 1835 (February). Minute on Indian Education. In William Ferguson and Laurie Beatson, eds. *Sketches of Some Distinguished Anglo-Indians: Including Lord Macaulay's Great Minute on Education in India* (Second Series). London: J. B. Day [1875].

Malcolm, Ian G. 2000. Aboriginal English: From contact variety to social dialect. In Jeff Siegel, ed. *Processes of Language Contact: Studies from Australia and the South Pacific*. Saint-Laurent, QC: Fides, 123–144.

McNair, Elizabeth DuPree. 2005. *Mill Villages and Farmers: Dialect and Economics in a Small Southern Town* (Publication of the American Dialect Society 90). Durham, NC: Duke University Press.

Mufwene, Salikoko S. 1996. The founder principle in creole genesis. *Diachronica 13*: 83–134.

Mufwene, Salikoko S. 1997a. The ecology of Gullah's survival. *American Speech 72*: 69–83.

Mufwene, Salikoko S. 1997b. The legitimate and illegitimate offspring of English. In Michael L. Forman and Larry Smith, eds. *World Englishes 2000*. Honolulu: University of Hawai'i Press, 182–203. (Slightly revised in Mufwene [2001].)

Mufwene, Salikoko S. 2000. Creolization is a social, not a structural, process. In Ingrid Neumann-Holzschuh and Edgar W. Schneider, eds. *Degrees of Restructuring in Creole Languages*. Amsterdam: John Benjamins, 65–84.

Mufwene, Salikoko S. 2001. *The Ecology of Language Evolution*. Cambridge: Cambridge University Press.

Mufwene, Salikoko S. 2008. *Language Evolution: Contact, Competition and Change*. London: Continuum Press.

Mufwene, Salikoko S. 2009. The indigenization of English in North America. In Thomas Hoffmann and Lucia Siebers, eds. *World Englishes: Problems, Properties, Prospects. Selected Papers from the 13th IAWE Conference*. Amsterdam: John Benjamins, 353–368.

Mufwene, Salikoko S. 2014. Globalisation économique mondiale des XVIIe–XVIIIe siècles, émergence des créoles, et vitalité langagière. In Arnaud Carpooran, ed. *Langues créoles, mondialisation, éducation*. Vacoas, Mauritius: Éditions le Printemps, 23–79.

Mufwene, Salikoko S. 2015a. The emergence of African American English: Monogenetic or polygenetic? Under how much substrate influence? In Sonja Lanehart, ed. *The Oxford Handbook of African American Language*. Oxford: Oxford University Press, 57–84.

Mufwene, Salikoko S. 2015b. L'émergence des parlers créoles et l'évolution des langues romanes: Faits, mythes et idéologies. *Etudes Créoles* 33: 1–29.

Mufwene, Salikoko S. 2016. Évolution différentielle du français: Une interprétation écologique. In Annette Boudreau, ed. *Langue et légitimation: La construction discursive du locuteur francophone*. Saint-Nicolas, QC: Les Presses de l'Université Laval, 211–235.

Mufwene, Salikoko S. and Sheri Pargman. 2002. Competition and selection in the development of American Englishes. *World Englishes* 22: 367–375.

Munro, Jennifer M. 2000. Kriol on the move: A case of language spread and shift in Northern Australia. In Jeff Siegel, ed. *Processes of Language Contact: Studies from Australia and the South Pacific*. Saint-Laurent, QC: Fides 245–270.

Odlin, Terence. 2003. Language ecology and the Columbian exchange. In Brian Joseph, Johanna DeStefano, Neil Jacobs and Ilse Lehiste, eds. *When Languages Collide: Perspectives on Language Conflict, Language Competition, and Language Coexistence*. Columbus: Ohio State University Press, 71–94.

Perkins, Edwin J. 1988. *The Economy of Colonial America* (2nd ed.). New York: Columbia University Press.

Salmons, Joseph. 2003. The shift from German to English, World War I and the German-language press in Wisconsin. In Walter G. Rädel and Helmut Schmahl, eds. *Menschen zwischen zwei Welten: Auswanderung, Ansiedlung, Akkulturation*. Trier: Wissenschaftlicher Verlag, 179–193.

Santa Ana, Otto. 1993. Chicago English and the nature of the Chicano language setting. *Hispanic Journal of Behavioral Sciences* 15: 3–35.

Schlieben-Lange, Brigitte. 1977. L'origine des langues romanes: Un cas de créolisation? In Jürgen M. Meisel, ed. *Pidgins – creoles – Languages in Contact*. Tübingen: Narr, 81–101.

Schneider, Edgar W. 1995. Black-White language contact through the centuries: Diachronic aspects of linguistic convergence or divergence in the United States of America. In Jacek Fisiak, ed. *Linguistic Change under Contact Conditions*. Berlin: Mouton de Gruyter, 237–252.

Schneider, Edgar W. 2007. *Postcolonial English: Varieties Around the world*. Cambridge: Cambridge University Press.

Schneider, Edgar W. 2011. *English Around the World: An Introduction*. Cambridge: Cambridge University Press.

Siegel, Jeff. 2010. Contact languages of the Pacific. In Raymond Hickey, ed. *The Handbook of Language Contact*. Malden, MA: Wiley-Blackwell, 814–836.

Trudgill, Peter. 2004. *New-Dialect Formation: The Inevitability of Colonial Englishes*. Oxford: Oxford University Press.

Warner-Lewis, Maureen. 2018. The African diaspora and language: Movement, borrowing, and return. In Ericka A. Albaugh and Kathryn M. de Luna, eds. *Tracing Language Movement in Africa*. Oxford: Oxford University Press, 321–341.

Wilkerson, Miranda E. and Joseph Salmons. 2008. "Good old immigrants of yesteryear" who didn't learn English: Germans in Wisconsin. *American Speech 83*: 259–283.

Wolfram, Walt and Clare J. Dannenberg. 1999. Dialect identity in a tri-ethnic context: The case of Lumbee American Indian English. *English World-Wide 20*: 79–116.

Wolfram, Walt and Natalie Schilling-Estes. 1995. Moribund dialects and the endangerment canon: The case of Ocracoke Brogue. *Language 71*: 696–721.

Wolfram, Walt and Natalie Schilling. 2016. *American English: Dialects and Variation* (3rd ed.). Malden, MA: Wiley-Blackwell.

Wood, Peter H. 1974. *Black Majority: Negroes in Colonial South Carolina from 1670 Through the Stono Rebellion*. New York: Alfred A. Knopf.

Yapko, Kofi. 2009. Complexity revised: Pichi (Equatorial Guinea) and Spanish in contact. In Nicholas Faraclas and Thomas B. Klein, eds. *Simplicity and Complexity in Creoles and Pidgins*. London: Battlebridge Publications, 184–216.

6

World Englishes, Migration, and Diaspora

Lena Zipp

6.1 Introduction

The World Englishes (WEs) paradigm rests on a pluricentric view of the language, evident in its use of plural *Englishes* to index different national varieties, sociocultural backgrounds, and localized identities (e.g. Bhatt 2001). While this focus has always foregrounded varieties that resulted from language contact during the historical spread of English around the world, more recent WEs research has embraced the "mobility turn" observed in the social sciences (Urry 2012), which called for a changed perspective on increased levels and new forms of social mobility. The focus is now on smaller-scale movements of people, ideas, and things, conceptualized as facts "that lie at the centre of ... the creation of identities and the micro-geographies of everyday life" (Cresswell 2011: 551) and on the convergence of migrant and sedentary forces as the locus of linguistic variation and change (cf. Kerswill 2006; see also Britain 2004, 2016; Blommaert 2016; Canagarajah 2017). As Blommaert and Jie (2010: 367) put it, "[w]e now see that the mobility of people also involves the mobility of linguistic and sociolinguistic resources, that 'sedentary' patterns of language use are complemented by 'trans-local' forms of language use, and that the combination of both often accounts for unexpected sociolinguistic effects."

The present chapter gauges the contribution of these modern-day migration patterns to the emergence of new forms or types of WEs "in the diaspora," a concept that has found renewed currency in sociological as well as sociolinguistic scholarship in the last two decades. It advocates the addition of different analytic perspectives to WEs research, pushing the boundaries of the discipline toward a constructivist rather than an essentialist perspective, and toward foregoing static categories (such as "varieties") in favor of more fluid concepts ("diaspora as practice," see Section 6.2). Third wave variationist sociolinguistic thinking (see also Schleef,

Chapter 26, this volume) runs like a red thread through the following sections that each touch on the creation and re-creation of identities through language practices: Section 6.3.1 links forms of language mixing or hybridization with identity construction. Section 6.3.2 addresses the role of the immigrant generation in the flexible usage of ethnolinguistic repertoires. Section 6.3.3 homes in on the linguistic correlates of the factors of *homeland orientation* and *boundary maintenance* in secondary diaspora situations; and Section 6.3.4 introduces research on multi-ethnic varieties of English to the WEs canon. As all of these scenarios draw on language contact situations that have been described as diasporic in the broadest sense, Section 6.2 first locates the concept of *diaspora* in current sociological scholarship and endeavors to provide a working definition for linguistic disciplines by considering the more established but increasingly proliferating uses of the term in the social sciences.

6.2 Diaspora as Linguistic Practice

The term *diaspora* generally denotes "any group of people who have spread or become dispersed beyond their traditional homeland or point of origin."[1] Sociological writing, however, draws a distinction between diasporas and other migrant communities, as "diasporas comprise special kinds of immigrants because they have retained a memory of, a cultural connection with, and a general orientation toward their homelands" (Safran 2004: 10). Originally stemming from the Jewish experience of catastrophic dispersion, the term *diaspora* carries connotations of persecution, loss, and longing for a return to the homeland (also for other "victim diasporas" like those from Armenia, Africa, or Palestine). However, post-1990 interest in the complexity of migration patterns spawned a body of research that resulted in what Brubaker (2005: 1) termed the "diaspora diaspora": "a dispersion of the meanings of the term in semantic, conceptual and disciplinary space." More inclusive definitions (e.g. Tölölyan 1996; Cohen 2008) thus capture trade diasporas (e.g. Chinese, Indian, Lebanese), colonial (e.g. British), or labor diasporas (e.g. Filipino, Mexican, Polish). Not only did academic disciplines witness a proliferation in the use of this broadened *diaspora* concept (Safran 2004; Tölölyan 2007), but it also spread to popular culture and media (Brubaker 2005: 4) and is increasingly adopted by individuals as a means of self-identification. In consequence, "[n]otions of ethnicity, immigration, settlement and race are all found to intersect and dissect conceptualizations of the diaspora" (Kalra, Kaur, and Hutnyk 2005: 9). However, "not all ethnic communities are diasporic" (Tölölyan 2007: 649) – in fact, most migrant communities are made up of members with varying levels of ethnic and diasporic self-identification and behavior. As Vertovec (2005) notes,

---

[1] "diaspora, n." *Oxford English Dictionary Online*, Oxford University Press, June 2017, www.oed.com/view/Entry/52085

"[b]elonging to a diaspora entails a consciousness of, or emotional attach-ment to, commonly claimed origins and cultural attributes associated with them." A lot of this emotional attachment in diasporic identity has been claimed to draw on the heritage language(s) as a core cultural value: "The defining characteristics of diasporas are, first, a culture and a collective identity that preserves elements of the homeland's language, or religious, social, and cultural practice, either intact or, as time passes, in mixed, bicultural forms ... denoted by the term *hybridity*" (Tölölyan 2007: 649).

In previous linguistic research, the term *diaspora* is widely used (see, e.g., Poplack and Tagliamonte 2001; Hackert and Huber 2007; Hazen and Hamilton 2008; Kachru, Kachru, and Nelson 2009; Canagarajah and Silberstein 2012; Mair 2013; Hinrichs 2014; Hundt 2014a, 2014b; Hundt and Sharma 2014; Rathore-Nigsch and Schreier 2016; Hickey 2017; Rosa and Trivedi 2017; Zipp 2017) but mostly remains theoretically underspe-cified. It thus appears justified and necessary to make definitions from the sociological tradition accessible and applicable to linguistic work on dia-spora situations, and ultimately to WEs research. The following criteria have been isolated as characteristics of diasporas (adapted from Cohen 2008: 17):

1) a) Dispersal from an original homeland, often traumatically, to two or more foreign regions;

   b) alternatively or additionally, the expansion from a homeland in search of work, in pursuit of trade or to further colonial ambitions;

2) a collective memory and myth about the homeland, including its loca-tion, history, suffering and achievements;

3) an idealization of the real or imagined ancestral home and a collective commitment to its maintenance, restoration, safety and prosperity, even to its creation;

4) the frequent development of a return movement to the homeland that gains collective approbation even if many in the group are satisfied with only a vicarious relationship or intermittent visits to the homeland;

5) a strong ethnic group consciousness sustained over a long time and based on a sense of distinctiveness, a common history, the transmis-sion of a common cultural and religious heritage and the belief in a common fate;

6) a troubled relationship with host societies, suggesting a lack of accep-tance or the possibility that another calamity might befall the group;

7) a sense of empathy and co-responsibility with co-ethnic members in other countries of settlement even where home has become more vestigial; and

8) the possibility of a distinctive creative, enriching life in host countries with a tolerance for pluralism.

In this list, items (1.b), (7), and (8) are additions provided by Cohen (2008: 6–8) to the classic definition (e.g. by Safran 1991). They capture more positive notions of the diaspora construct characteristic of today's most pertinent migration type, long-distance, long-term labor migration (Kerswill 2006: 2274).

On the basis of this definition, diasporic languages can now be defined as the varieties spoken by self-identified members of diasporic communities. In addition, Cohen's multifaceted diaspora description allows us to fine-tune the definition. First, a diasporic language variety is one that is dispersed across more than one location apart from its homeland and therefore related to localized varieties in other places. Second, it is part of a collective cultural memory of a homeland and as such is often idealized. Third, its speakers commit to the variety's maintenance also in consideration of sustained or envisaged relationships with the homeland. Fourth, the heritage variety – or a hybrid or localized version – is employed to index ethnic group consciousness and distinctiveness from the host society, as a means of identification and as carrier of notions of belonging. Fifth, the diasporic variety is used to connect with members of diasporic communities in other countries of settlement or on the Internet. And, lastly, diasporic varieties often exhibit hybrid, localized characteristics that are indicative of both heritage and local influences. Diasporic language varieties are thus different from generally ethnic varieties in that their use entails a consciousness of shared history, interests, and identity. This consciousness can be interpreted as self-ascribed diasporic membership, which is the most crucial part of the diasporic definition:

> Such a definition cuts through questions around the number of generations passed, degree of linguistic competence, extent of co-ethnic social relations, number of festivals celebrated, ethnic meals cooked, or style of dress worn. That is, just "how ethnic" one is does not affect whether and to what extent someone might feel themselves part of a diaspora. With such an understanding, we can appreciate how diasporic identification may be lost entirely, may ebb and flow, be hot or cold, switched on or off, remain active or dormant.   (Vertovec 2005)

Such an emic view of diaspora as a process or practice rather than as a descriptive tool (Clifford 1994; Kalra, Kaur, and Hutnyk 2005: 3–4) reveals the potential the concept has for linguistic study; as Canagarajah and Silberstein (2012: 82) put it: "once we stop treating diaspora as bounded, territorialized, static, and homogenous, we begin to appreciate the role language and discourse play in its construction." This view resonates with the third wave of variationist study in sociolinguistics, which marked the same shift away from static category membership as an explanatory factor for linguistic variation (e.g. Eckert 2012; Schleef, Chapter 26, this volume). Research in this tradition sees variation not as a reflection of social identities but as an expression of speakers' linguistic agency in constructing social meaning: "the linguistic practice in which speakers place them-selves in the social landscape through stylistic practice" (Eckert 2012: 94).

Scholarship in English linguistics has a long tradition of researching topics revolving around diasporic varieties, for example with a focus on questions of heritage-language maintenance or shift, accommodation, second-language or second-dialect acquisition, the sociolinguistics of communities of practice or networks, in addition to questions of indexicality and identity construc-tion. However, the WEs paradigm has been slow in incorporating research on "new diasporic situations" (Hinrichs 2014: 170) as locations of systematic language contact, focusing traditionally more on larger-scale postcolonial and national language contact scenarios. In the following, this chapter presents four different scenarios of contemporary diasporicity and sets them in relation to WEs studies.

6.3 New Scenarios of WEs Research Influenced by Migration and Diaspora

6.3.1 Code-Mixing as Diasporic Identity Construction

The role of bilingual language use, such as code-switching or code-mixing, has traditionally been underestimated for the study of WEs, despite the fact that WEs have been claimed to be code-mixed varieties "by definition" (McLellan 2010: 425) because they undergo processes of localization in prolonged situations of language contact. Although, of course, not all speakers in WEs contexts have multilingual resources at their disposal, Bullock, Hinrichs, and Toribio (2017) point out a wide range of different types of code-switching in WEs, which are governed by societal, individual, and situational constraints. For example, alternating (AB) or insertional (ABA) code-switching (Muysken 2000) are frequent phenomena particular to language contact situations around the world, the former usually asso-ciated with "settings in which languages are separately maintained in a state of stable bilingualism" (Bullock, Hinrichs, and Toribio 2017: 217), while the latter "occurs in social contexts where there is an apparent asymmetry in the power relations between the languages, as is often the case in immigrant settings, where the heritage language has a much more socially restricted place in the wider community" (Bullock, Hinrichs, and Toribio 2017: 217). Our focus here, however, is on a particular type of bilingual language use that has been termed *language mixing* (Auer 1999), *congruent lexicalization* (Muysken 2000), *intra-sentential switching* (Poplack 1980) or *unmarked code-switching* (Myers-Scotton 1993). Alternatively, it is framed as *translanguaging* or *translingual practice* in the "superdiversity" paradigm (for a critical discussion of both framework and terms, see Pennycook 2016; see also Section 6.3.4). The phenomenon is defined as a bilingual style consisting of "a largely . . . shared structure, lexicalized by elements from either language" (Muysken 2000: 5), in which the switch between codes is unmarked and does not serve discourse- or participant-related functions. Such a practice is illustrated in Example (1), which is taken from a radio host's moderation of her Brit-Gujarati show on the BBC Asian Network.

(1)   *Ane* villains *nu aaje talkie chhe, karan ke* as you know, sadly, *gaya* Friday we lost one of the greatest villains from Bollywood. ("And tonight, we are talking about villains, because as you know, sadly, last Friday we lost one of the greatest villains from Bollywood.") (Alpa Pandya Show, BBC, 14 July 2013)

Practices like this that seem to freely mix codes have been traced to highly proficient bilingual speakers as well as second-generation diasporic migrants, as embodied by our radio show host, in publications in the code-switching tradition (e.g. Auer 1999, 2005; Muysken 2000). They have, however, also acquired salience with speakers in WEs contexts, where they gained notoriety at least partly due to a popular misconception, as the following quote about Singlish (Colloquial Singaporean English) shows: "Many laypersons assume that speakers of so-called *Singlish* … or indeed any other '-glish' that arises when English is in contact with a local language, cannot help but mix the languages because they cannot speak the normative or 'pure' form of English" (Bullock, Hinrichs, and Toribio 2017: 212). Recent overview articles have homed in on the "multitude of *-lishes*" (Lambert 2018), stating that "the amount of language mixing and the number of truly mixed (hybrid) varieties involving English is one of the most striking, and perhaps surprising, findings when comparing the ecologies of world Englishes" (Schneider 2016: 341). However, mixed language practices are often termed "basilectal" or "colloquial" in the WEs tradition, and few (e.g. Schneider 2016: 342) recommend to consider them "new contact varieties in their own right," which might be due to great differences in their status, structural properties, stability, and level of documentation. In agreement with Schneider's notes on a poststructuralist perspective that challenges the very notion of "variety," this section aims to bridge the paradigm gap between research on WEs/varieties and research on language mixing as a process. After all, both WEs and mixed language varieties have been closely linked to the issue of identity construction. Our radio show host in Example (1) prides herself on presenting her show in what she refers to as "Gujlish," a mixture of English and Gujarati. In doing so, she negotiates local, hybrid identity construction and shapes the communicative practices of her audience, younger-generation diasporic Gujarati Asians in the UK (Zipp 2017: 45). Auer (1999: 318) explains this specific role of language mixing: "The fact that [language mixing], other than [code-switching], sometimes has a folk name can be attributed to its identity-related functions." It thus seems appropriate to draw parallels between these identity-related functions in language mixing on the individual, the community (diaspora), and the variety level in the -*lishes* tradition.

The phenomenon known as *Spanglish* is probably one of the best researched instances of language mixing, albeit not necessarily seen as a contact variety in the WEs canon of postcolonial varieties. This umbrella term refers to a range of different manifestations (Toribio 2011) of which an example is given in Sentence (2), taken from Poplack's (1980: 589) New York City Puerto Rican data:

(2)   He was sitting down *en la cama, mirandonos peleando, y* really, I don't remember *si el nos separo* or whatever, you know. ("He was sitting down in bed, watching us fighting and really, I don't remember if he separated us or whatever, you know.")

Of course, a number of different linguistic strategies characterize *Spanglish* in addition to code-mixing, such as phonological, morphological, and semantic adaptations. Attitudes toward the practice range from positive appropriation of the term (e.g. Morales 2002) to programmatic rejection (e.g. Lipski 2008). What should be noted here is that positive attitudinal accounts of language mixing practices are more often than not linked with processes of group identity construction, as Morales (2002: 33) puts it: "just as Spanglish folks might have made a transition to a more conventional American identity, they pulled back and consolidated their position. They found a third option, the Spanglish way." The plural "folks" in this quote can be taken to indicate a multitude of Latin American origins, while the quote at the same time emphasizes the shared aspects of the (pan-)Latin American experience across different national provenience and places of settlement. This perspective lends itself to an interpretation of diasporicity, which is special because the shared heritage language unites people of different Latin American origins (as opposed to, e.g., the Chinese or Indian diasporas in which a single national country of origin subsumes different linguistic backgrounds). Language mixing between heritage and host languages is one of the practices found to be employed throughout diasporas in in-group discourse for reasons of solidarity and covert prestige, even if openly disavowed: It is "frequent among recent immigrants, or even among those long-standing immigrants who maintain tangible or strong psychological ties with their original community; after all, immigrants are persons with one foot in each of two camps" (Myers-Scotton 1993: 482).

However, in diasporas as well as in traditional WEs settings, care should be taken to "avoid the pitfalls of the old essentialist view" (Auer 2005: 407) that sees an inherent relationship between mixed language and hybrid social identity: Not all use of mixed languages necessarily indicates identity work. Similarly, not all language contact between minority and majority languages in migration settings results in the meaningful use of mixed languages. First, some migrant groups attach less cultural value to the maintenance of their heritage languages, as research into language shift has shown (Clyne and Kipp 1997). Second, even if language is used for ethnic self-identification, levels of ethnic identification change both within the individual and across community members, calling for an emic approach to ethnic self-identification (Hoffman and Walker 2010: 40). Third, a range of different linguistic codes – going beyond the binary of host and heritage languages – can be employed to index ethnic identity, commonly grouped under the label of *ethnolects* (Clyne, Eisikovits, and Tollfree 2002). Yet, overall, new and increased forms of migration to English-speaking countries present fruitful scenarios to study multilingual practices in second- or third-generation migrant groups, opening up the potential to link localized or hybrid styles in diasporic settings with WEs studies (also see Section 6.3.4 on "superdiverse" hybrid language use and Section 6.3.2 on generational language practices in diasporic communities).

6.3.2 The Role of the Immigrant Generation for the Flexible Use of Ethnolinguistic Identity Construction

Some of the new and increased migration patterns that have influenced English throughout its history are marked by less than straightforward movements of speakers, such as back-and-forth, sustained, or onwards migration. They oftentimes result in prolonged language contact between first- and second-language varieties of English, rendering the issue an increasingly important subject of study in WEs. The present and the following section each look at two recent strands of research on migration and language contact in diasporic Englishes. The present section discusses work focused on generational language use of both ethnic and non-ethnic features in ethnolinguistic repertoires by members of diasporic minority language communities, looking at the North American Chinese and British Asian diasporas. This direction of research has provided a means of modeling agentive in-group and intra-speaker strategies of using first- and second-language varieties of English in the diaspora. Section 6.3.3 relates how studies of secondary or double diaspora situations have shed light on the influence of social and attitudinal parameters on language use and identity construction. Both of these directions are again indicative of the current trend of integrating the process- and agency-based perspective from current third wave variation research with the study of WEs. As Sharma (2017) points out in an article on the importance of sociolinguistic theory for WEs, a number of analytic shifts have taken place in the WEs paradigm that move the field forward, for example the inclusion of smaller-scale locations of linguistic variation such as networks or communities of practice, the consideration of language attitudes toward variation, and an acknowledgment of language practice and dynamic social positioning as influential processes.

Sharma's own work (2011; Sharma and Rampton 2015) has made headway in modeling subtle socio-indexical changes in the speech of members of diasporic communities by accounting for the use of ethnolinguistic features in discourse. It is based on Benor's construct of *ethnolinguistic repertoire*, which "shifts the analytic focus from ethnic 'language varieties' to individuals, ethnic groups, and their distinctive linguistic features" (Benor 2010: 159). The ethnolinguistic repertoire construct thus accounts for intra-group and intra-speaker variation, presenting a theoretical milestone in research on diasporic varieties and WEs, which have traditionally conceptualized localized varieties as ethnolects, polylectal continua, or diglossic language roles. Most importantly, it foregrounds the agentive linguistic construction of group membership that is seen as inherent to recent diaspora scholarship. Studies by Hoffman and Walker (2010), Nagy, Chociej, and Hoffman (2014), Zipp and Staicov (2016), and Hundt and Staicov (2018) have used questionnaire and interview methods to show the link between ethnolinguistic variation and ethnic orientation (EO); moreover, they have contributed to an understanding of how EO can be measured, quantified, and compared across diasporas. Hoffman and Walker (2010), for example, find that different ethnic groups in Toronto have different degrees of EO despite sharing similar demographic representation, institutional support, and strong ethnolinguistic vitality: The Toronto Italians exhibit lower mean EO scores than the Toronto Chinese across all immigrant generations, even if ethnic affiliations are generally stronger in the first than the following generations for both groups. This leads the authors to suggest that overall inter-group differences are linked to settlement history and visible-minority status. At the same time, they interpret in-group differences in the use of ethnolinguistic features as evidence for strategic variation in "the way in which speakers actively construct and express ethnic identity" (Hoffman and Walker 2010: 59) rather than as a static expression of ethnolects that could be traced to "imperfect second-language acquisition, substrate transfer, or lack of exposure to mainstream Canadian English" (Hoffman and Walker 2010: 58).

Nagy, Chociej, and Hoffman (2014) come to similar conclusions with regard to the influence of EO on linguistic variation in diasporic contexts, and emphasize the role of the immigrant generation: "ethnic orientation measures must be interpreted differently depending on the generation of the speaker" (Nagy, Chociej, and Hoffman 2014: 23). It has been noted, though, that, as migrant communities across the globe grow older and more diverse, theorizing of immigrant generation will have to be modified accordingly. In this vein, Hall-Lew and Starr (2010) take a look at Chinese Americans "beyond the 2nd generation" and list a number of problematic issues pertaining to the interpretation of diaspora settings. First, the immigrant generation as a social variable often is conflated with first language and/or age of acquisition, but it no longer seems to be the case that second- and third-generation immigrants acquire English earlier and with fewer heritage language features, as was shown with the case of the long-established, dense-knit Chinese immigrant community in the San Francisco Bay Area (Hall-Lew and Starr 2010: 16–17). Second, demographic changes in prolonged diaspora situations throw up new questions with regard to the meaning of immigrant generation and diasporic or ethnic self-identification: For the Chinese diaspora in the USA, increasing immigration leads to greater exposure to recent immigrants with strong homeland ties and to a decrease of interracial marriage, changing the previously observed generational pattern of integration and Americanization. These recent immigrants are more likely to uphold the diasporic group boundaries in that they will choose to take up residence in areas with concentrated Chinese populations; they are also more likely to return to China, and they exhibit different patterns of English-language acquisition. As Hall-Lew and Starr (2010: 18) note:

> This change in immigrant population has profound cultural and linguistic implications for Chinese Americans. Unlike previous waves of Chinese American immigrants, 1.5- and second-generation children in this population are often culturally oriented toward China and greater East Asia ... This cultural identity, sometimes referred to as FOB ("fresh off the boat"), is quite distinct from the culture of the children of the first- and second-wave immigrants, sometimes referred to as ABC ("American-born Chinese"), which is oriented primarily towards mainstream American culture ... Intriguingly, although these terms appear to refer to the length of time that an individual has lived in the United States, today they are often used to refer to cultural identities that are independent of immigration history – even fourth-generation Chinese Americans can participate in FOB culture ... For Chinese Americans in particular, orientations to Chinese cultural practices are gaining frequency and value, and FOB styles are losing stigma and gaining currency.

This scenario of evolving migration patterns and subsequent changes in cultural values is an impressive reminder of the fact that future WEs research should account for shifts in language status, prestige, and ethnolinguistic orientation, as well as for in-group variation in diasporic varieties.

Sharma's (2011) study on social change in British Asian English provides more support for a differentiated perspective on diasporic varieties, arguing that "'second generation' is not a unitary category. When continually replenished through ongoing migration, the second generation can be internally heterogeneous, encompassing several stages of social and linguistic change" (Sharma 2011: 487). By factoring in community history (hostile or welcoming toward immigrants in different decades), gender roles (working or home-based), and network types (diverse or local), Sharma shows that second-generation Punjabi British speakers draw on two different types of stylistic repertoires (differentiated or fused). Her results question the justification of monolithic ethnolects in this community as well as of "broad claims of fluidity and individual agency" in the use of ethnolinguistic features, suggesting instead "differing degrees of agentive indexical use among equally 'hybrid speakers'" (Sharma 2011: 465). How these ethnolinguistic features are ultimately used in an agentive manner in the same community is the focus of Sharma and Rampton's (2015) method paper on quantitative discourse analysis, that is, lectal focusing in interaction. Confronted with data such as Example (3), the authors track the fluctuations in Anwar's (a middle-class, middle-aged British Asian Muslim businessman) spontaneous speech, which comprises "a complex mix of linguistic elements … : Punjabi language and London vernacular (glottalling, th-fronting, segmental deletion, and syntactic ellipsis) mixed in with Standard British English (-*ing*, h-retention) and even some Jamaican (*yard*) and other vernacular (*old lady*) vocabulary pronounced with Punjabi retroflexion" (Sharma and Rampton 2015: 4).

(3)   *tennu pata hai yaar*
        ("you know how it is man")
        hor kiddan? wa[?]s goi[n] [d]own man? every[f]i[ŋ] coo[w]?
        ('what else is up?')
        [h]ow's [ø]ings a[?] [ø]e yar[d]?
        [d]e o[l][ø] l[e][d]y a[w]righ[?]?
        (adapted from Sharma and Rampton 2015: 4)

Their analysis shows that not all instances of ethnolinguistic features are employed to index general ethnic identity. Rather, older second-generation male speakers in this community use their full range of ethnic and non-ethnic features for finely tuned interactional work, suggesting "continual reinscription of specific social and ethnopolitical commitments" (Sharma and Rampton 2015: 21). Younger second-generation speakers on the other hand exhibit a restricted range of lectal focusing for discourse work, which signals the emergence of a fused lect that is claimed to index a more unified British Asian identity (see Section 6.3.1). In sum, recent work on (ethno-)linguistic repertoires and (ethnic or diasporic) identity construction lends itself well to a more fine-grained, deep-level analysis in the study of WEs, in particular by taking on the task of theorizing the factor of immigrant generation. These methodological and theoretical approaches have proven to open new ways of working with variation along a cline of lectal continua in language contact situations in general, of quantifying intra-speaker variation, and of modeling the role of linguistic variables to create meaning in discourse.

6.3.3   The Effects of Multiple Migration: Language Contact in Secondary Diaspora Situations

Whereas Section 6.3.2 reported on the characteristics of diasporas with repeated or increasing migration (the Chinese diaspora in the USA and the Punjabi diaspora in the UK), the type of diasporas discussed here involve patterns of onward migration from already established diasporas to new diaspora locations. These multiple migration movements are at the center of research into the spread of linguistic features through language or dialect contact in scenarios of *relocation diffusion*, which "tends to have more dramatic linguistic consequences than expansion diffusion. This is largely because it usually involves greater social upheaval, and a greater likelihood of contact with structurally distinct dialects, causing much more dramatic accommodation in contexts of greater linguistic diversity" (Britain 2004: 40). In this section, we look at these successive forms of English-language contact in the Indian diaspora in order to highlight two cornerstones of the diaspora definition introduced in Section 6.2, *homeland orientation* and *boundary maintenance* (Brubaker 2005: 5).

Most long-standing diasporas, such as the Chinese or Indian diasporas, have a history of migration that is commonly conceptualized as different waves or periods. Mesthrie (2014: 172–174) identifies three different periods and types in the history of Indian migration: pre–seventeenth-century emigration out of South Asia in the course of trade and settlement movements, Imperialist-era forced migration of slaves and indentured workers from the seventeenth to the nineteenth centuries, and postcolonialist or globalization migration of working professionals (see also Lal 2006). Each of these periods is characterized by different parameters of homeland orientation and boundary maintenance. An example of the linguistic consequences of these parameters is provided by the case of indentured labor migration from the Indian subcontinent to South Africa from around 1860, which led to the formation of a distinct variety of South African Indian English (Mesthrie 2006): "The distinctiveness of this variety was partly due to South Africa's rigid policy of segregation or apartheid, and the fact that not many Indians could afford to travel to India" (Mesthrie and Chevalier 2014: 89). Thus, the enforced boundary maintenance of the indenture scenario prohibited linguistic contact with other South African indigenous languages or English varieties, whereas limited homeland contact ruled out any influence of Indian English as a potential normative orientation variety. Parallel local processes of dialect leveling and variety-internal language change linked to social variables such as gender or social class (Mesthrie and Chevalier 2014) further contributed to the emergence of South African Indian English, which is now a WEs variety in its own right.

A very similar history of indentured labor migration and diaspora formation, along with racial segregation and the formation of a linguistic koine of Fiji Hindi, can be observed for the Indian diaspora in Fiji (Siegel 1987; Zipp 2014a). However, Fiji's sociohistory changed with subsequent decolonization and local political independence, leading to redefinitions of belonging and identity for members of the Indian diaspora that can be seen as a renegotiation of both homeland orientation and boundary maintenance. Societal changes such as the loss of the Indian caste system as well as continued professional migration from India brought about the rise of a new Indian-heritage middle class with considerable economic influence in the mid-twentieth century, and previous studies have argued that this localized identity is mirrored linguistically in the formation of a multi-ethnic variety of Fiji English rather than a diasporic variety of Fiji Indian English (Zipp 2014a, 2014b). Persisting ethnic tensions and political unrest, however, remain a cause for emigration for Fiji Indians. As Raghuram and Sahoo (2008: 9) point out, members of indenture diasporas often "have tenuous links with India. When faced with racialised targeting they have migrated again, but often not to India." This weak degree of (original) homeland orientation also holds for Indo-Fijians, whose main migration movements are directed toward English-speaking countries of the Pacific rim, such as New Zealand, Australia, the USA, and Canada rather than toward India.

In her study of Fiji Indians in Wellington, New Zealand, Hundt (2014a, 2018) shows how questions of boundary maintenance and homeland orientation take on another dimension in the case of secondary diasporas. First, homeland orientation for the Fiji Indian diaspora signifies Fiji rather than (or at least in addition to) India as the mother country, particularly when it comes to transnational activities such as maintaining social networks with family and friends, back-and-forth visits, or continued migration (Hundt 2014b: 138–141). Note, however, that not all diasporic identifications entail transnational behavior, for example when exchanges with the homeland do not take place (Vertovec 2005; Sharma 2014; Bolander, Chapter 29, this volume): Some of Hundt's (2014a: 131–132) informants nevertheless see India, their "ancestral home," as central to their ethnic identity construction. Second, boundary maintenance in the secondary diaspora situation can be measured against two yardsticks, the New Zealand host society and the local Indian diaspora consisting of direct migrants from the Indian subcontinent. On the one hand, Hundt (2014b: 139) reports on Fiji Indians' experiences of "being 'othered' by Indians from India," based on different trajectories of sociohistory as well as on linguistic differences (the heritage language of Fiji Indians being the local koine, Fiji Hindi). On the other hand, she finds that, linguistically, second-generation Fiji Indians with weak maintenance of transnational ties have shifted toward New Zealand English with regard to the use of definite and indefinite zero articles (Hundt 2014b). Thus, while there is high boundary maintenance between the Indian and Fiji Indian diasporas in New Zealand, there also appears to be linguistic assimilation as a result of contact between the second-language variety of Fiji Indian English and New Zealand English (although a more fine-grained analysis of speakers' indexical use of ethnolinguistic features as discussed in Section 6.3.2 might show a more differentiated picture).

In an interview-based study of East African Indian twice migrants in Leicester, Rathore (2014: 61) also argues that first-generation informants "express strong affiliation with East Africa and a clear sense of distinctiveness vis-à-vis direct migrants from South Asia." However, both aspects of diasporic identification tend to disappear in her second-generation group, which report a more general British Asian identity. These particular characteristics of diasporic identity construction in a double migration situation are at the heart of Rathore's (2014; Rathore-Nigsch and Schreier 2016) examination of their linguistic correlates through different migrant generations. The East African diaspora began through indentured labor migration similar to the diasporas in South Africa and Fiji but was soon followed by voluntary/proactive migration, that is, professional/labor migration, the opposite extreme on the axis of force and choice in migrational motivation (Van Hear 1998: 40–61). The small and lively community of East African Indians exhibited strong voluntary boundary maintenance throughout the twentieth century, with residence in ethnically segregated communities, rare intermarriages, and limited contact to the African population mostly conducted in Kiswahili, not English. This diasporic setting resulted in a close-knit community with a distinct sense of localized Indian identity among its participants that was carried over to the secondary diaspora location after their economic success and political influence made them a target of Africanization policies and ultimately led to their second dispersion through exodus and expulsion. As regards the linguistic correlates, the first diaspora did not adopt East African English features but retained variants of Indian English (rhoticity, central vowel system) over generations in the East African diaspora, and subsequently transferred them to the secondary diaspora in the UK. The second generation of diasporic East African Indians in Leicester, on the other hand, exhibit far less ethnolinguistic features than hypothesized, which the authors argue is due in parts to their strong affiliation with Leicester and the East Midlands local dialect. In sum, Rathore-Nigsch and Schreier's (2016; Rathore 2014) studies are an impressive example of how homeland orientation, boundary maintenance, and local diasporic identity construction both in a first and in a second diaspora setting lay the foundation for linguistic variation in complex migration situations. At the same time, they resonate with the work presented in Sections 6.3.1 and 6.3.2 in their layered approach to generational language use in the diaspora. Any study of WEs therefore seems well-advised to take their speakers' migration histories and resulting multiple identifications and orientations into account.

6.3.4 Beyond Diaspora: Migration and Multi-ethnolectalization in Urban Centers

Recent sociolinguistic scholarship has prioritized the impact of migration on the demographic and linguistic makeup of urban populations. As such it is heavily influenced by the "superdiversity" paradigm shift that has taken hold in a number of fields in the humanities and social sciences since about the turn of the century (Vertovec 2007). This paradigm shift occurred in response to globalization and the perceived increase in and complexification of migration patterns since the early 1990s. Originally defined in the context of the UK, superdiversity is described as a condition "distinguished by a dynamic interplay of variables among an increased number of new, small and scattered, multiple-origin, transnationally connected, socio-economically differentiated and legally stratified immigrants" (Vertovec 2007: 1024). One of these variables in dynamic interplay is language (see, e.g., Creese and Blackledge 2010; Duarte and Gogolin 2013; Arnaut et al. 2016; Blommaert and Rampton 2016; Canagarajah 2017), although it has to be noted that questioning or "denaturalizing" entities such as "language," "speakers," and "communication" is a defining part of the paradigm shift (Blommaert and Rampton 2016). Instead, the superdiversity approach is ethnographic, concerned with communicative practices, multimodality, political dynamics, and historical embedding, and challenges most predetermined categories and starting assumptions of traditional linguistic scholarship. In all its methodological, theoretical, and terminological disruptiveness (Britain 2016; Pennycook 2016), the superdiverse turn has pushed more traditional strands of urban sociolinguistics to scrutinize and challenge notions of and connections between variables such as migration, mobility, origin, citizenship, and residence; ethnicity, race, and ethnolinguistic identity; and class, gender, and other social categories.

At the intersection of variationist sociolinguistics, superdiversity, and WEs studies we find a research area of heightened interest since the turn of the century: multi-ethnolectalization in urban centers across Europe (e.g. Cheshire, Nortier, and Adger 2015). The name of its most prominent variety, Multilingual London English (MLE), was coined by research groups led by Kerswill and Cheshire, after early types of ethnic crossing in inner-city London were described by Sebba (2013) and Rampton (1991, 1995, 2011); the phenomenon of "Multicultural English" has since been extended to Birmingham (Fox, Khan, and Torgersen 2011). From its beginnings, crossing and multi-ethnolectalization were seen as belonging to the realm of youth language; later studies focus on acquisition, network structure, and feature selection (Cheshire et al. 2011; Kerswill et al. 2013). In this process, described as *group second-language acquisition*, "where minority linguistic groups form part of a larger host community and acquire the target language mainly through unguided informal second-language acquisition in their friendship groups" (Cheshire et al. 2011: 153), parents' language use does not constitute a target model even for the youngest speakers. With a high percentage of heritage speakers and a striking diversity of languages spoken in multi-ethnic urban communities, native English models are only partially available. On the basis of this complex language contact situation, the authors observe variable use of a range of feature types: adoption of global trends, increase in latent minority forms, divergent distributions of existing forms, but also the "development of a set of innovative features" (Cheshire et al. 2011: 190), such as the new quotative *this is* + *speaker* (Example 4), the pragmatic marker *you get me* (Example 5), the new pronoun *man* (Example 6), or syllable-timed rhythm (Torgersen and Szakay 2013).

(4)   *This is them* "what area are you from. What part?" *This is me* "I'm from Hackney." (adapted from Cheshire et al. 2011: 172)

(5)   [...] I would not go jump out of the window because ... my parents will find out, *you get me*, my mum goes to work, right? (adapted from Torgersen et al. 2011: 96)

(6)   Before I got arrested *man* paid for my own ticket to go Jamaica you know [...] (adapted from Cheshire 2013: 2)

The emergence of MLE is then conceptualized as selection from a feature pool that forms the linguistic repertoire for speakers of various ethnic and language backgrounds. This notion of a non–ethnically specific feature pool is why Cheshire et al. (2011: 190) avoid labels such as *variety* or *lect* for the "variety space" MLE (also see Cheshire, Nortier, and Adger 2015). Britain (2016: 236), on the other hand, questions the motivations behind viewing the speakers as a homogeneous group despite the possibility of discovering ethnicity-based usage patterns, that is, behind de-specifying the ethnic while using the term *multi-ethnolect*:

> we could ask why we need labels like "multiethnolect", when we already have well-established terms that capture the relevant linguistic process and outcome, such as koine and koineisation. To label them as distinct fetishizes the ethnic other in ways reminiscent of claims of creole exceptionalism.

It is undisputed, however, that research into urban multi-ethnolectalization needs to be considered both as a process and as a result of language contact in a complex diasporic situation, as well as on grounds of the variety's potential as a younger member of the WEs family.

6.4 Conclusions

This chapter on the growth and role of immigrant varieties has touched on a number of issues pertaining to the study of varieties of English around the world. It has demonstrated how smaller-scale migration movements in general and diasporic identity in particular are central to the analysis of global versus local forces in the WEs paradigm, and how a focus on processes and practices holds great promise for future study. The chapter argued the value of intersections with recent sociolinguistic scholarship on identity construction, raised questions around the existence of mixed codes, (multi-)ethnolects and linguistic repertoires, and problematized the role of the immigrant generation. Englishes in the diaspora (or diasporas within WEs) remain one of the most vibrant and exciting areas of linguistic research into language variation and change.

References

Arnaut, Karel, Jan Blommaert, Ben Rampton and Massimiliano Spotti, eds. 2016. *Language and Superdiversity*. New York: Routledge.

Auer, Peter. 1999. From codeswitching via language mixing to fused lects: Toward a dynamic typology of bilingual speech. *International Journal of Bilingualism* 3(4): 309–332.

Auer, Peter. 2005. A postscript: Code-switching and social identity. *Journal of Pragmatics* 37: 403–410.

Benor, Sarah Bunin. 2010. Ethnolinguistic repertoire: Shifting the analytic focus in language and ethnicity. *Journal of Sociolinguistics* 14(2): 159–183.

Bhatt, Rakesh M. 2001. World Englishes. *Annual Review of Anthropology* 30(1): 527–550.

Blommaert, Jan. 2016. From mobility to complexity in sociolinguistic theory and method. In Nikolas Coupland, ed. *Sociolinguistics: Theoretical Debates*. Cambridge: Cambridge University Press, 242–259.

Blommaert, Jan and Dong Jie. 2010. Language and movement in space. In Nicolas Coupland, ed. *The Handbook of Language and Globalization*. Oxford: Wiley-Blackwell, 364–384.

Blommaert, Jan and Ben Rampton. 2016. Language and superdiversity. In Karel Arnaut, Jan Blommaert, Ben Rampton, and Massimiliano Spotti, eds. *Language and Superdiversity*. New York: Routledge, 21–48.

Britain, David. 2004. Geolinguistics: Diffusion of language. In Ulrich Ammon, Norbert Dittmar, Klaus J. Mattheier and Peter Trudgill, eds. *Sociolinguistics/ Soziolinguistik: An International Handbook of the Science of Language and Society*. Berlin: Mouton de Gruyter, 34–48.

Britain, David. 2016. Sedentarism and nomadism in the sociolinguistics of dialect. In Nicolas Coupland, ed. *Sociolinguistics: Theoretical Debates*. Cambridge: Cambridge University Press, 217–241.

Brubaker, Rogers. 2005. The "diaspora" diaspora. *Ethnic and Racial Studies* 28(1): 1–19.

Bullock, Barbara E., Lars Hinrichs and Almeida Jacqueline Toribio. 2017. World Englishes, code-switching, and convergence. In Markku Filppula, Juhani Klemola and Devyani Sharma, eds. *The Oxford Handbook of World Englishes*. Oxford: Oxford University Press, 211–231.

Canagarajah, Suresh, ed. 2017. *The Routledge Handbook of Migration and Language*. Oxon: Routledge.

Canagarajah, Suresh and Sandra Silberstein. 2012. Diaspora identities and language. *Journal of Language, Identity and Education* 11(2): 81–84.

Cheshire, Jenny. 2013. Grammaticalisation in social context: The emergence of a new English pronoun. *Journal of Sociolinguistics* 17(5): 608–633.

Cheshire, Jenny, Paul Kerswill, Sue Fox and Eivind Torgersen. 2011. Contact, the feature pool and the speech community: The emergence of Multicultural London English. *Journal of Sociolinguistics* 15(2): 151–196.

Cheshire, Jenny, Jacomine M. Nortier and David Adger. 2015. Emerging multiethnolects in Europe. *Queen Mary's Occasional Papers Advancing Linguistics* 33: 1–27.

Clifford, James. 1994. Diasporas. *Cultural Anthropology* 9(3): 302–338.

Clyne, Michael and Sandra Kipp. 1997. Trends and changes in home language use and shift in Australia, 1986–1996. *Journal of Multilingual and Multicultural Development* 18(6): 451–473.

Clyne, Michael, Edina Eisikovits and Laura Tollfree. 2002. Ethnolects as ingroup varieties. In Anna Duszak, ed. *Us and Others: Social Identities across Language, Discourses and Cultures*. Amsterdam: John Benjamins, 133–158.

Cohen, Robin. 2008. *Global Diasporas: An Introduction* (2nd ed.). Oxon: Routledge.

Creese, Angela and Adrian Blackledge. 2010. Towards a sociolinguistics of superdiversity. *Zeitschrift für Erziehungswissenschaft* 13(4): 549–572.

Cresswell, Tim. 2011. Mobilities I: Catching up. *Progress in Human Geography* 35(4): 550–558.

Duarte, Joana, and Ingrid Gogolin, eds. 2013. *Linguistic Superdiversity in Urban Areas: Research Approaches*. Amsterdam: John Benjamins.

Eckert, Penelope. 2012. Three waves of variation study: The emergence of meaning in the study of variation. *Annual Review of Anthropology* 41: 87–100.

Fox, Sue, Arfaan Khan, and Eivind Torgersen. 2011. The emergence and diffusion of Multicultural English. In Friederike Kern and Margret Selting, eds. *Ethnic Styles of Speaking in European Metropolitan Areas*. Amsterdam: John Benjamins, 19–44.

Hackert, Stephanie, and Magnus Huber. 2007. Gullah in the diaspora: Historical and linguistic evidence from the Bahamas. *Diachronica* 24(2): 279–325.

Hall-Lew, Lauren, and Rebecca L. Starr. 2010. Beyond the 2nd generation: English use among Chinese Americans in the San Francisco Bay area. *English Today* 26(3): 12–19.

Hazen, Kirk, and Sarah Hamilton. 2008. A dialect turned inside out: Migration and the Appalachian diaspora. *Journal of English Linguistics* 36(2): 105–128.

Hickey, Raymond. 2017. Retention and innovation in settler Englishes. In Markku Filppula, Juhani Klemola, and Devyani Sharma, eds. *The Oxford Handbook of World Englishes*. Oxford: Oxford University Press, 657–675.

Hinrichs, Lars. 2014. Diasporic mixing of World Englishes: The case of Jamaican Creole in Toronto. In E. Green and C. Meyer eds. *The Variability of Current World Englishes*. Berlin: De Gruyter, 169–194.

Hoffman, Michol F., and James A. Walker. 2010. Ethnolects and the city: Ethnic orientation and linguistic variation in Toronto English. *Language Variation and Change 22*(1): 37–67.

Hundt, Marianne. 2014a. Home is where you're born: Negotiating identity in the diaspora. *Studia Neophilologica 86*(2): 125–137.

Hundt, Marianne. 2014b. Zero articles in Indian Englishes: A comparison of primary and secondary diaspora situations. In Marianne Hundt and Devyani Sharma, eds. *English in the Indian Diaspora*. Amsterdam: John Benjamins, 131–170.

Hundt, Marianne. 2018. "My language, my identity": Negotiating language use and attitudes in the New Zealand Fiji-Indian diaspora. *Asian Englishes 21*(1). https://doi.org/10.1080/13488678.2018.1463148

Hundt, Marianne and Devyani Sharma, eds. 2014. *English in the Indian Diaspora*. Amsterdam: John Benjamins.

Hundt Marianne and Adina Staicov. 2018. Identity in the London Indian diaspora: Towards the quantification of qualitative data. *World Englishes 37*, 166–184.

Kachru, Braj, Yamuna Kachru and Cecil Nelson, eds. 2009. *The Handbook of World Englishes*. Malden, MA: Blackwell.

Kalra, Virinder, Raminder Kaur, and John Hutnyk. 2005. *Diaspora and Hybridity*. London: Sage.

Kerswill, Paul. 2006. Migration and language. In Klaus Mattheier, Ulrich Ammon and Peter Trudgill, eds. *Sociolinguistics/Soziolinguistik: An International Handbook of the Science of Language and Society*, Vol 3. (2nd ed.). Berlin: De Gruyter, 2271–2285.

Kerswill, Paul, Jenny Cheshire, Sue Fox and Eivind Torgersen. 2013. English as a contact language: The role of children and adolescents. In Daniel Schreier and Marianne Hundt, eds. *English as a Contact Language*. Cambridge: Cambridge University Press, 258–282.

Lal, Brij V. 2006. *The Encyclopedia of the Indian Diaspora*. Singapore: Editions Didier Millet.

Lambert, James. 2018. A multitude of "lishes." *English World-Wide 39*(1): 1–33.

Lipski, J. 2008. *Varieties of Spanish in the United States*. Washington, DC: Georgetown University Press.

Mair, Christian. 2013. The World System of Englishes: Accounting for the transnational importance of mobile and mediated vernaculars. *English World-Wide 34*(3): 253–278.

McLellan, James. 2010. Mixed codes or varieties of English. In Andy Kirkpatrick, ed. *The Routledge Handbook of World Englishes*. Oxon: Routledge, 425–441.

Mesthrie, Rajend. 2006. *English in Language Shift: The History, Structure and Sociolinguistics of South African Indian English* (2nd ed.). Cambridge: Cambridge University Press.

Mesthrie, Rajend. 2014. A lesser globalisation: A sociolexical study of Indian Englishes. In Marianne Hundt and Devyani Sharma, eds. *English in the Indian Diaspora*. Amsterdam: John Benjamins, 171–186.

Mesthrie, Rajend and Alida Chevalier. 2014. Sociophonetics and the Indian diaspora: The NURSE vowel and other selected features in South African Indian English. In Marianne Hundt and Devyani Sharma, eds. *English in the Indian Diaspora*. Amsterdam: John Benjamins, 85–104.

Morales, Ed. 2002. *Living in Spanglish: The Search for Latino Identity in America.* New York: St Martin's Press.

Muysken, Pieter. 2000. *Bilingual Speech: A Typology of Code-Mixing.* Cambridge: Cambridge University Press.

Myers-Scotton, Carol. 1993. Common and uncommon ground: Social and structural factors in codeswitching. *Language in Society* 22(4): 475–503.

Nagy, Naomi, Joanna Chociej and Michol F. Hoffman. 2014. Analyzing Ethnic Orientation in the quantitative sociolinguistic paradigm. *Language and Communication 35*: 9–26.

Pennycook, Alastair. 2016. Mobile times, mobile terms: The trans-super-poly-metro movement. In Nikolas Coupland, ed. *Sociolinguistics: Theoretical Debates*. Cambridge: Cambridge University Press, 201–216.

Poplack, Shana. 1980. Sometimes I'll start a sentence in Spanish Y TERMINO EN ESPAÑOL: Toward a typology of code-switching. *Linguistics 18*(7–8): 581–618.

Poplack, Shana and Sali Tagliamonte. 2001. *African American English in the Diaspora*. Malden, MA: Wiley-Blackwell.

Raghuram, Parvati and Ajaya Kumar Sahoo. 2008. Thinking "Indian Diaspora" for our times. In Parvati Raghuram, Ajaya Kumar Sahoo, Brij Maharaj and Dave Sangha, eds. *Tracing an Indian Diaspora. Contexts, Memories, Representations*. New Delhi: Sage, 1–20.

Rampton, M. B. H. 1991. Interracial Panjabi in a British adolescent peer group. *Language in Society 20*(3): 391–422.

Rampton, Ben. 1995. Language crossing and the problematisation of ethnicity and socialisation. *Pragmatics 5*(4): 485–513.

Rampton, Ben. 2011. From "multi-ethnic adolescent heteroglossia" to "contemporary urban vernaculars." *Language and Communication 31*(4): 276–294.

Rathore, Claudia. 2014. East African Indian twice migrants in Britain. In Marianne Hundt and Devyani Sharma, eds. *English in the Indian Diaspora*. Amsterdam: John Benjamins, 55–83.

Rathore-Nigsch, Claudia and Daniel Schreier. 2016. "Our heart is still in Africa": Twice migration and its sociolinguistic consequences. *Language in Society 45*(2): 163–191.

Rosa, Jonathan and Sunny Trivedi. 2017. Diaspora and language. In Suresh Canagarajah, ed. *The Routledge Handbook of Migration and Language*. Oxon: Routledge, 330–346.

Safran, William. 1991. Diasporas in modern societies: Myths of homeland and return. *Diaspora: A Journal of Transnational Studies* 1(1): 83–99.

Safran, William. 2004. Deconstructing and comparing diasporas. In Waltraud Kokot, Khachig Tölölyan and Carolin Alfonso, eds. *Diaspora, Identity and Religion: New Directions in Theory and Research*. London: Routledge, 9–29.

Schneider, Edgar W. 2016. Hybrid Englishes: An exploratory survey. *World Englishes* 35(3): 339–354.

Sebba, Mark. 2013 [1993]. *London Jamaican: Language Systems in Interaction*. Oxon: Routledge.

Sharma, Devyani. 2011. Style repertoire and social change in British Asian English. *Journal of Sociolinguistics* 15(4): 464–492.

Sharma, Devyani. 2014. Transnational flows, language variation, and ideology. In Marianne Hundt and Devyani Sharma, eds. *English in the Indian Diaspora*. Amsterdam: Benjamins, 215–242.

Sharma, Devyani. 2017. World Englishes and sociolinguistic theory. In Markku Filppula, Juhani Klemola and Devyani Sharma, eds. *The Oxford Handbook of World Englishes*. Oxford: Oxford University Press, 232–251.

Sharma, Devyani and Ben Rampton. 2015. Lectal focusing in interaction: A new methodology for the study of style variation. *Journal of English Linguistics* 43(1): 3–35.

Siegel, Jeff. 1987. *Language Contact in a Plantation Environment: A Sociolinguistic History of Fiji*. Cambridge: Cambridge University Press.

Tölölyan, Khachig. 1996. Rethinking diaspora(s): Stateless power in the transnational moment. *Diaspora: A Journal of Transnational Studies* 5(1): 3–36.

Tölölyan, Khachig. 2007. The contemporary discourse of diaspora studies. *Comparative Studies of South Asia, Africa and the Middle East* 27(3): 647–655.

Torgersen, Eivind Nessa, Costas Gabrielatos, Sebastian Hoffmann and Susan Fox. 2011. A corpus-based study of pragmatic markers in London English. *Corpus Linguistics and Linguistic Theory* 7(1): 93–118.

Torgersen, Eivind Nessa and Anita Szakay. 2012. An investigation of speech rhythm in London English. *Lingua* 122(7): 822–840.

Toribio, Almeida Jacqueline. 2011. Code-switching among US Latinos. In Manuel Díaz-Campos, ed. *The Handbook of Hispanic Sociolinguistics*. Oxford: Wiley-Blackwell, 530–552.

Urry, John. 2012. *Sociology Beyond Societies: Mobilities for the Twenty-First Century* (2nd ed.). London: Routledge.

Van Hear, Nicholas. 1998. *New Diasporas: The Mass Exodus, Dispersal and Regrouping of Migrant Communities*. Padstow: UCL Press.

Vertovec, Steven. 2005. The political importance of diasporas. *Migration Information Source*, Migration Policy Institute, Washington, DC; Migration

Policy Institute Europe, Brussels. www.migrationpolicy.org/article/political-importance-diasporas, 1 June.

Vertovec, Steven. 2007. Super-diversity and its implications. *Ethnic and Racial Studies 30*(6): 1024–1054.

Zipp, Lena. 2014a. Indo-Fijian English: Linguistic diaspora or endonormative stabilization? In Marianne Hundt and Devyani Sharma, eds. *English in the Indian Diaspora*. Amsterdam: John Benjamins, 187–213.

Zipp, Lena. 2014b. *Educated Fiji English: Lexico-Grammar and Variety Status*. Amsterdam: John Benjamins.

Zipp, Lena. 2017. Code-switching in the media: Identity negotiations in a Gujarati diaspora radio program. *International Journal of the Sociology of Language 247*: 33–48.

Zipp, Lena and Adina Staicov. 2016. English in San Francisco Chinatown. In Elena Seoane and Cristina Suárez-Gómez, eds. *World Englishes: New Theoretical and Methodological Considerations*. Amsterdam: John Benjamins, 205–228.

Part II

World Englishes
Old and New

7

A Sociolinguistic Ecology of Colonial Britain

David Britain

7.1 Introduction

In our attempts to understand how particular linguistic outcomes emerged in colonial settings, where European languages and dialects encountered those of indigenous peoples, in communities where different forms of slavery and forced migration had shaped the new demographic, in new tabula rasa contexts, and in contexts where colonial intervention had different degrees of intensity and settlement, we rightly have been urged to consider very carefully the sociolinguistic ecology of language (and dialect) contact. Mufwene (1996: 85) argued that in every colony, metropolitan varieties had to adapt to new (and often very different) socio-ecological circumstances, so their structural linguistic material came into contact with that of other varieties in the community. As a consequence, adaptations resulted and new varieties came into being. The task for linguists interested in the genesis of these new varieties has included establishing the nature of and influences on contact-induced linguistic change, the influence of acquisition mechanisms, and the structures of the varieties – metropolitan, local, and other – that actually came into contact in the colonial setting often centuries in the past. As part of this endeavor, Mufwene (1996), Trudgill (1986, 2004), Montgomery (1989), and many others have made clear the importance of establishing the structures of the *nonstandard* varieties of the metropolitan languages used in the colonial settings, and others have pointed to problematic cases where this has not been heeded (Britain 2008; Kuo 2005). A sensitivity to the colonial ecology has enabled us to successfully tease apart how, in different places, at different times, in different contexts, different types of linguistic outcome have emerged. Focusing on the Anglo colonial context, I aim here to discuss the sociolinguistic ecology not of the *destinations* of colonists and settlers but of the Great Britain they *left behind*. To do so, I examine a few of the many factors that would have shaped the sociolinguistic ecology of

Britain during the colonial era and thereby influenced the language and dialect backgrounds of those who left to permanently settle elsewhere.

Many social and historical linguists uphold the uniformitarian principle as it applies to language change, a principle on which the sociolinguistic approach of using the present to explain the past relies. In considering the sociolinguistic ecology of colonial Britain, this principle is borne in mind, and I will adopt lessons and principles from contemporary sociolinguistics to speculate about the types of linguistic change that the social ecology will have engendered. We must remember, however, that the same principle cannot be upheld for the social ecology itself. We must not, obviously, operate according to what has come to be known as the Flintstones Principle that "today's cultural constructions [can be] projected back in time as quasi-historical confirmation for today's practices" (Bradburne 2000: 44). Bradburne (2000: 44) points, for example, to the way that the apparently Stone Age cartoon characters Fred, Wilma, and Pebbles from *The Flintstones* depict the nuclear family as "an age-old constellation," presenting an ideological frame through which we could believe society were ever thus. One aim of this chapter, then, is to simply remind ourselves that the British Isles of two, three hundred years ago was, in some respects, rather different from now and, in others, actually and, perhaps surprisingly, rather similar. We must remind ourselves, for example, that during most of the colonial period education was not compulsory or free; literacy was (therefore) at considerably lower rates than now; the only media were the print media; and so mechanisms for the dissemination of standard ideologies were fewer and less intensive and invasive on everyday life, and patterns of internal mobility and migration were different, as a result of the dominance of the primary sector of the economy (and, following the Industrial Revolution, the secondary sector) and as a result of different and more limited public and private transport – even the bicycle did not become a widely owned transportation option until the late nineteenth century. Nevertheless, mobility was significant, even dramatic. Britain was also linguistically diverse, like today, but in very different ways (see Fox, Chapter 20, this volume).

I pick up a number of these themes in order to sketch some aspects of the sociolinguistic lives of ordinary Britons that might be relevant to explain the development of English and Englishes overseas. Although early colonial emigration began from the British Isles in the sixteenth century, most of my focus in what follows is on the eighteenth and nineteenth centuries, since these are the centuries of mass emigration – half a million in the eighteenth century, twenty-five million in the nineteenth are the figures suggested by Belich (2009: 126). The themes I will touch on in the sections that follow are multilingualism and multidialectalism, mobility, education and literacy, and language ideology. Doing so helps us to understand some of what Belich (1997: 330) called the "cultural baggage" that migrants took with them when they left Britain. I begin by looking at each in turn before considering their impact on English as it was spoken during this period.

7.2 Multilingualism and Multidialectalism

Today, with the exception of Welsh, the languages other than English that are widely spoken in Britain are immigrant languages – Polish, Punjabi, Urdu, Bengali/Sylheti, for example – with 7.7 percent of the population of England and Wales having a "main" language that is not English or Welsh (ONS 2011). While we do not have precise figures on language choice through the colonial period, the degree of the population that was "of foreign birth" was at about 1 percent in 1901, as it was also in 1440[1]. Any significant societal multilingualism in the British Isles during the period of colonial emigration, then, did not come as a result of immigration. However, the Celtic languages of the British Isles had much more vitality then than now. In 1750, most areas of Wales were majority Welsh-speaking, and there were, well into the late twentieth century, communities of Welsh speakers in parts of England near Oswestry in Shropshire, for example (Williams 1988). In the 2011 Census, 115 residents of Oswestry (population 17,000) claimed Welsh as their main language (Bevan 2016: 132). Gaelic was still robustly used in the north and west of Scotland and was the majority language in these areas in the 1881 census. Irish, too, was the majority language of Ireland nearly until the end of the eighteenth century (Fox, Chapter 20, this volume). British colonial settlers, therefore, were by no means all anglophone, with significant populations of Irish speakers in Newfoundland, and Gaelic speakers in Nova Scotia and even the Falkland Islands (Sudbury 2000). Jupp (2001: 800) points to the significance of the Gaelic, Irish, and Welsh speaking populations in nineteenth-century Australia: In Britain, he says, "it is probable that there were well over two million Irish speakers in the 1840s, 250,000 Scottish Gaelic speakers by the 1860s, and perhaps 20,000 Manx speakers, Welsh continued . . . to a peak of 1 million in 1911. Within the Australian population, there were undoubtedly considerable numbers of Celtic speakers for over a century" (p. 800).

Even with conservative estimates of the number of Celtic speakers, it is probable that around 10 percent of the population of the British Isles in the mid-nineteenth century spoke a first language other than English, considerably *higher*, therefore, than today's figure of 7.7 percent.

It is hard to overestimate the diversity of varieties of English across the British Isles during the colonial period. First, and in light of the multilingualism discussed earlier in this section, there will have been many hundreds of thousands of speakers of English who spoke L2 or language

---

[1] www.historyextra.com/article/international-history/medieval-immigrants-moving-england-middle-ages

shifted or substrate influenced varieties of English, especially in the Celtic areas of the British Isles (see Filppula, Klemola, and Paulasto 2012; for Ireland, see, e.g., Hickey 2012; for Scotland, Sabban 1985, Shuken 1985, and Clayton 2017; for Wales, Thomas 1997, Paulasto 2006, Penhallurick 2004, and Mayr et al. 2017). Ellis (1889), in the most significant early account of accent variation in the British Isles, wished to account for the use of English among

> uneducated people, speaking an inherited language, in all parts of Great Britain where English is the ordinary medium of communication between peasant and peasant. This limitation excludes those parts of Wales and Scotland where Celtic is habitually spoken by the natives. Ireland has also been excluded, except in the south-east of Co. Wexford – an old English colony – because it has otherwise a comparatively recently imported speech. (p. 92)

In fact, virtually all of Wales was excluded, except for a small area along the border with England, and very small parts of Pembrokeshire and Gower. In Ireland, only Bargy and Forth in Wexford are briefly mentioned. In Scotland, most of the Highlands and Islands to the north and west are excluded. The Isle of Man is included in the same dialect area as Blackpool in Lancashire, but Ellis (1889: 351) states that "of course the Isle of Man is not an independent English dialect. It is entirely imported and indeed recently acquired ... But I could find no better place for it than this." Ellis's survey of the English dialects of the rest of the country showcases the massive variability – phonological, morphosyntactic – of the early nineteenth century and he included cities as well as rural areas. Wright (1898–1905) presents a multivolume account of lexical variation. There is no space here to do justice to the dialectology of British English in the colonial period (for an excellent summary, see Ihalainen, 1994). We will consider the impact on this variation of factors such as mobility in Section 7.5. There was, it must be said, variability on a scale incomparable with today. Colonial migrants from the British Isles left dialectally extremely diverse communities.

7.3 Mobility

The effect of mobility on language variability has been recognized for centuries – recognized by the traditional dialectologists conducting large surveys (like Ellis mentioned in the previous section), by variationist sociolinguists focusing on variation within individual speech communities, and by contact linguists examining what happens when different linguistic systems collide. For a long time, the dramatic effects of mobility were seen as so significant that mobile residents were simply excluded from traditional and variationist studies. Orton (1962: 14–16), for example, in explaining the criteria for inclusion of informants in the Survey of English Dialects in the mid-twentieth century, noted that "dialect speakers whose residence in the locality had been interrupted by significant absences were constantly regarded with suspicion."

Given that this volume examines what happened when Britons engaged in probably the most significant act of mobility of their entire lives – moving to settle in another country – it is, however, important to examine how mobile people were in Britain during that period, and how that mobility would have affected their language use. One rather uncritical view that we read all too often in today's sociolinguistic literature, furthermore, is that the world today is way more mobile than it ever was, that certain societies today are superdiverse, and that this superdiversity is a societally recent phenomenon. This supermobility discourse is now being critiqued – for example, by Pavlenko (2018), Piller (2014), Britain (2016), and others – but, in order to not unwittingly reinforce such discourses, an inspection of colonial mobility within Britain also enables us to contextualize the extent to which mobility has changed between the colonial period and today.

Games (2009: 35) has claimed that "migration was a fundamental feature of English life" even before the colonial period and that "migration occurred regularly over the course of the life cycle, for both women and men. It was not aimless, and regularly occurred within a narrow geographic field of 10–15 miles, thus ... reinforcing not undermining regional cultures" (pp. 35–36). She reminds us, first, of the fact that the population was much more rural at the start of the colonial period – just 3.1 percent of the population of England and Wales lived in towns with populations greater than 10,000 in 1500, and this rose to 20.3 percent by 1800 (Games 2009: 36). Second, it was young men who were the most mobile and the most responsible for urbanization. Cities had their own "demographic regimes." Fed by huge numbers of rural in-migrants, they continued to grow, despite having "their own unique disease environments" (Games 2009: 37) – plague and other epidemic diseases – to which migrants were more likely to succumb. Cities grew despite deaths outnumbering births at some points by 65 percent. Games puts it bluntly – "for migrants, children and the poor, cities were death traps" (2009: 37).

Looking at internal migration within especially nineteenth-century Britain, the most intense period of the Industrial Revolution, we see especially high levels of mobility. Nicholas and Shergold (1987: 160), in their investigation of internal migration in the first half of the nineteenth century, found that 32 percent of their sample had moved out of their county of birth and half of the migrants had moved between 30 and 110 miles (48–177 km). They argue that "during the 19th century, the English were the most mobile people of Europe, at least as regards internal migration" (1987: 161). Friedlander and Roshier (1966) also show high levels of internal migration, with certain areas gaining throughout the nineteenth century – notably the southeast and London, Yorkshire, and Lancashire – and others losing (e.g. the rural south of England but most dramatically rural Wales).

Pooley and Turnbull (1998: esp. 93–146), in a detailed account of mobility in Britain since the 1700s, demonstrate that, while there is, throughout the eighteenth and nineteenth centuries, an overall migratory shift from rural to urban, movement up the urban hierarchy only narrowly outstrips movement down, there was considerable mobility within rural areas, and overall shifts were predominantly of a relatively local, relatively short-distance kind. The English countryside during the period of colonial emigration was neither static nor straightforwardly or wholeheartedly depopulating, therefore. More important for our purposes here is that the overall net shift to urban areas hides the very large number of moves in both directions (Pooley and Turnbull 1998: 97) – short-distance moves and moves to places of the same size dominated in the eighteenth and early nineteenth centuries. Belich (1997: 289) summed up the situation nicely when he stated that Victorian Britain was "changing: shrinking, growing, shifting, mixing, merging, separating and reshuffling." Mobility, of course, was in practical terms more difficult then than it is today. Significant improvements to make transportation affordable for most people – Pooley and Turnbull (1998: 303) claim that many people could simply not afford even third-class rail fares until the end of the nineteenth century – were not seen for most of the period of mass colonial emigration. Networks of turnpike roads, navigation canals, and eventually railways "contracted England by a factor of about ten in terms of travelling time in the century before 1880," says Belich (1997: 289). For most of the colonial emigration period, however, travel was simply more difficult than it is today, but people did it all the same.

7.4 Education and Literacy

Considering levels of education and literacy for the sociolinguistic ecology of colonial Britain is important, not only because of education's enduring status as one of the strongest influences on language variation but also because it provides us with an indication of people's access to other potentially significant influences, such as the print media and the supra-local transmission of ideologies that such media make possible. Throughout the period of colonial settlement, "media" were synonymous with printed text – there was of course no radio or TV until well into the twentieth century. Newspapers became increasingly popular in the UK in the eighteenth century, particularly in the cities, alongside pamphlets and magazines. They were the most direct route by which the people could hear about news and events outside of their communities, beyond chance word of mouth, but also became an additional mechanism for the dissemination of their proprietors' ideological perspectives.

Right throughout the overseas colonial settlement period, however, the provision of a free education system that might systematically equip *all* people to actually read these newspapers was extremely patchy. Free compulsory education was only introduced in the UK as a whole in 1880 and only then up to the age of ten. A free education of sorts had been available to some, especially in the cities, before this time, in Sunday and day schools attached to the Church, in so-called ragged schools for destitute children, and in a range of other more local settings. There was, throughout the nineteenth century, considerable opposition from many sides to compulsory education, in fact – from parents who needed their children at work rather than at school, from some groups who felt that educating the working classes could prove dangerous, and from the Church who wanted to maintain their grip on the education system and on their opportunity to ensure that religion continued to play a major role in the curriculum. Attendance was therefore patchy right up until the end of the nineteenth century.

As a result, literacy levels, not surprisingly, remained stubbornly low well into the 1800s. The measurement of literacy before the modern era is notoriously difficult, and many measures of it require just the very most basic abilities. The Marriage Act of 1754 brought into effect a ruling that no wedding would be valid if the parish register were not signed with a signature or a mark by the bride and groom and two witnesses. Since parish registers were accessible, this became an extremely basic measure of extremely basic literacy before the twentieth century. In 1839, for example, 33 percent of grooms and 49 percent of brides signed the register with a mark, rather than a signature (Vincent 1989: 3). Given that signing one's name is probably the or one of the first and most basic acts of literacy, these figures probably quite significantly *underestimate* the degree of illiteracy at the time. There was naturally also considerable variation within these figures. Vincent (1989: 97) shows that among skilled workers literacy rates were lower for miners and potters, for example, than for among handicraft workers, and were considerably lower among unskilled workers. Just 27 percent of unskilled manual workers were able to sign their name in 1839 (p. 97). As Roberts (1990: 222) has argued, "Most men struggling for a living knew well enough that for them literacy brought no bread." Nicholas and Shergold (1987: 162) found, furthermore, that Britons who had moved home were more likely to be literate than nonmobile ones.

By the end of the nineteenth century, as a result of a combination of formal schooling and informal teaching within the family and neighborhood, these literacy figures had dramatically improved, though again, as with improvements in transportation, this was occurring just as settler migration was tailing off in many parts of the country. Belich (1997: 289) claims that "the population read a dozen times more books and wrote a dozen times more letters to each other in 1900 than in 1800."

7.5 Linguistic Ramifications

I look now at some of the potential linguistic consequences of these earlier outlined aspects of the sociolinguistic ecology that reigned during the colonial era in the British Isles, beginning with the effects of mobility on language variation and dialect diversity, before moving on to the effects of education, literacy, and the media landscape (or the paucity of one).

The British Isles during the colonial period were multilingual, multi-dialectal, and mobile, and such a combination is a recipe for linguistic change and language shift. Friedlander and Roshier (1966), for example, show a dramatic population exodus in the second half of the nineteenth century from the rural Welsh-speaking heartlands to the growing cities of Glamorgan in the south of the country. While this urbanization of the population coincided with a brief increase in the number of Welsh speakers over that period, fewer and fewer remained monolingual, and so began a decline in Welsh-speaking throughout the twentieth century.

We can consider the effects of mobility on the dialects of English during the colonial period from two perspectives – first, in terms of social network strength and the impact of network strength on susceptibility to change and, second, in terms of the linguistic outcomes of dialect contact that ensue from mobility. James and Lesley Milroy (e.g. L. Milroy 1980; J. Milroy and L. Milroy 1985; J. Milroy 1992) in their sociolinguistic investigations in Belfast were the first to demonstrate convincingly that social network links of greater time depth, intimacy, and functional reciprocity tend to resist linguistic innovations emanating from outside of the network: "Many studies," J. Milroy argued, "both urban and rural, have shown that a close-knit network structure functions as a conservative force, resisting pressures for change originating from outside the network; conversely those speakers whose ties to the localized network are weakest approximate least closely to localized vernacular norms, and are most exposed to external pressures for change" (J. Milroy 1992: 176–177). Strong multifunctional social networks also serve as norm-enforcement mechanisms since, within such a strong network, behaviors (including linguistic ones) that are alien to that group are sanctioned. Giddens (1984) has framed this effect in a related way, emphasizing the role of routinization – "the habitual, taken for granted character of the vast bulk of activities of day-to-day social life, the prevalence of familiar styles and forms of conduct" (p. 376) – in the perpetuation of social structures and in norm enforcement (p. 64). Routines, he argues, are the "material grounding of the recursive nature of social life" (p. xxiii). As we engage in highly routine activities, the structure of these activities is reproduced by their very performance. In this sense, routines (like strong networks in the work of the Milroys) lead to system preservation. Mobility, however, not infrequently leads to the "large-scale disruption of close-knit, localized networks which have historically maintained highly systematic and complex sets of socially structured linguistic norms" (L. Milroy 2002: 565). The social networks of internal migrants during the colonial period therefore would potentially have been weaker than those of the people they left behind, with, following Milroy, a consequent effect on their patterns of linguistic variation.

Some have argued that the friction of distance would have been stronger then than now, too, with short-distance moves more disruptive for social network cohesion than now, because those distances were less easily traveled and social network ties were therefore harder to nurture. "It should not be assumed that a move of, for instance, 20kms, short by present-day standards, was necessarily perceived as a local move in the late eighteenth century . . . even short distance moves could . . . alter established patterns of social interaction" (Pooley and Turnbull 1998: 301–302). In these circumstances, even though average mobilities appear relatively modest, such moves would have weakened social network ties and broken routines in more impactful ways than is probably the case today.

Granovetter (1973: 1378), especially, is keen to explain the *strength* of weak ties, which he argues are "often denounced as generative of alienation [but are] . . . indispensable to individuals' opportunities and to their integration into communities." Urry (2007: 213), likewise, has reiterated the importance of weak ties in creating "network capital . . . the capacity to engender and sustain social relations with those people who are not necessarily proximate, and which generate emotional, financial and practical benefit" (p. 197). Networks may be broken as a result of mobility but they are reformed anew (Belich 1997: 412) and new routines are created – and this is important in the focusing of new dialect forms (see Britain 1997).

We would expect, in the circumstances thus described, to see rather rapid linguistic change. Games (2009: 37) flags up dramatic urbanization as especially important in the early colonial period – London grew from 40,000 people in 1500 to 900,000 in 1801 – with Pooley and Turnbull (1998) emphasizing the size of the overall demographic churn – rural and urban – as well as the overall shift to the city. It would be hard to argue against a claim that koineization and new dialect formation must have been at work in many of the larger cities of this period (Hickey, Chapter 2, this volume) – the dialect of Liverpool, a particularly prominent port during the colonial period, has indeed been analyzed within this framework (Honeybone 2007). Dialect leveling must also have been an active process, just as it is today, though we do not possess adequate records of the spoken dialect of English in the period before the beginning of the nineteenth century that would enable us to show this with any degree of precision. Ellis (1889) demonstrates an acute consciousness of the prevalence of dialect leveling around London as late as in the nineteenth century, and Sayers (2009) argues articulately that the seeds for the dramatic leveling and supralocalization of the twentieth century were sown in the turbulent demographic upheaval of the eighteenth and especially nineteenth centuries.

The extent to which leveling and koineization were already underway *before* the dialects of the British Isles were shipped or transported to the colonial context is an issue that has been frequently raised in accounts of the formation of postcolonial varieties. In the case of Australian English, for example, Collins argued as early as 1975 that some of the mixing and leveling that ultimately shaped early Australian English actually took place in England, before emigration. We must be cautious, therefore, when using early dialect surveys to establish which dialects and dialect variants were transported from where and in what quantities to the settlement colonies, since these surveys very often explicitly and consciously excluded mobile people from their attention.

We saw earlier that, although the colonial period saw an increased dissemination of newspapers, a good number of ordinary Britons had no or few means to access the print media because of a lack of functional literacy. The repercussions of this are rather significant and not only in terms of what it might tell us about the degree of the population's non-standardness at the time.

In contemporary society, the mass media – newspapers, radio, TV, social media – are one of the most important mechanisms by which people learn about the world and by which ideologies, including language ideologies, are circulated and reproduced. Coupland (2010: 69) states that it is "inconceivable" to suggest that the broadcast media today have no effect "on the evaluative and ideological worlds in which language variation exists in late modernity ... mass media are changing the terms of our engagement with language and social semiosis ... and with linguistic variation and dialect as part of that." In these media, we hear particular language varieties being deployed (and evaluated, stereotyped, etc.) in different ways for different purposes – more standard accents for serious news broadcasts and a range of different social, regional, and national accents to "perform" characterizations in film, drama, and comedy, for example. We come to recognize these varieties via our media engagement with them, to link these varieties with the social information we glean from these contacts and contexts, and to sow indexical fields with the clusters of associations that we attach to varieties and to individual variants (Eckert 2008).

During the colonial period being addressed in this chapter, these mediated means by which language ideologies could be circulated were extremely limited. Whereas today we can, sitting in our, say, British living rooms, routinely hear a wide variety of, say, American accents, there is a good chance that many British people during the eighteenth and nineteenth centuries went their whole lives without ever hearing one. As Kroskrity (2005: 507) says: "language users' ideologies bridge their sociocultural experience and their linguistic and discursive resources by constituting those linguistic and discursive forms as indexically tied to features of their sociocultural experience." It is important, then, to establish what sociocultural experiences of language variation people may have had during that period and how ideologies about these varieties would have been circulated in the absence of a mass broadcast media. As we have seen, the people of the British Isles were relatively mobile and the country was both multilingual and multidialectal, more so than today. At that time, a more focused Standard English was emerging but in its morphosyntactic guise more than its phonetic one. The means to disseminate particular elite ideologies about this standard were relatively weak, however. For very many, schooling during this time was geographically patchy, occurring only late in the relevant period as a compulsory mechanism, and it was brief. The Church may well have been the more powerful and influential, yet indirect, conduit of the view that Standard English was to be seen as something "better." We should be skeptical, then, of assuming that standard ideologies were as well internalized in the eighteenth and nineteenth centuries as they apparently were in the twentieth. Just as people's mobilities tended to be rather more local, especially in the earlier part of the colonial period – Games (2009) suggested that mobilities at that time reinforced regional cultures rather than broke them down – the language ideologies of many, brewed as a result of their sociocultural experiences (and in the absence of a long education or access to broadcast media), would similarly have been shaped more intensively at the local and regional levels than the national. I am not arguing here that they had in some way "restricted" ideological perspectives but that they were influenced more by highly diverse local and regional complexes of variation since the kinds of exposure to distant geographical varieties that we take for granted today were much less intensive.

Why is this important? Just as linguistic analyses of settler colonial communities have to examine the dialectal adjustments that take place as a result of the mixture of different regional and social metropolitan varieties, so the speakers of these varieties would also have brought with them a diverse range of language ideologies and indexical associations, many of which they would not have had in common, thereby adding a sociolinguistic dimension to the dialectological diffuseness of the very early colonial ecology (see Britain 2005). This diversity also suggests that any strong standard ideologies that emerged in the colonial context were probably "repackaged" and disseminated there by the new local colonial elite rather than having been imported wholesale and intact among the mass settler population and merely in need of a little polishing.

7.6 Closing Words

Tens of millions left the British Isles during the colonial period of the eighteenth and nineteenth centuries. What they sounded like, their grammars, their lexis have all become important evidence in our attempts to understand how colonial languages and dialects emerged as they did. In this chapter, I have attempted to consider a few of the main factors that will have shaped these languages and dialects before they set sail with their users. Colonial migrants, on the whole, did not have the luxury of a long and free education behind them, nor, therefore, did they have high levels of literacy either. The media that today beams voices and ideologies about those voices into our homes was in its printed infancy. Language ideologies circulated largely, therefore, within communities, by word of mouth. Unlike for the Flintstones, there existed, of course, no TV, no radio, no drive-in movie theaters, no electricity, no cars … Nevertheless, the population was, perhaps surprisingly, mobile, and this mobility will have engendered the same processes of leveling and koineization that we experience in many communities today. Perhaps also surprisingly, the Islands were also more multilingual than today. This meant that multilingualism was exported too, though ultimately it fared worse than it did at home.

References

Belich, James. 1997. *Making Peoples: A History of the New Zealanders from Polynesian Settlement to the End of the Nineteenth Century*. Auckland: Penguin.

Belich, James. 2009. *Replenishing the Earth: The Settler Revolution and the Rise of the Anglo-World, 1783–1939*. Oxford: Oxford University Press.

Bevan, Robert. 2016. Oswestry, Hay-on-Wye and Berwick-upon Tweed: Football fandom, nationalism and national identity across the Celtic borders. Unpublished doctoral dissertation, Cardiff University.

Bradburne, James. 2000. Changes of art: The changing role of art and museums in contemporary society. In Deutsche Bank ed., *Visuell*, London and Frankfurt: Deutsche Bank, 44–48.

Britain, David. 1997. Dialect contact and phonological reallocation: "Canadian Raising" in the English Fens. *Language in Society 26*: 15–46.

Britain, David. 2005. Where did New Zealand English come from? In Allan Bell, Ray Harlow and Donna Starks, eds. *The Languages of New Zealand*. Wellington: Victoria University Press, 156–193.

Britain, David. 2008. When is a change not a change?: A case study on the dialect origins of New Zealand English. *Language Variation and Change 20*: 187–223.

Britain, David. 2016. Sedentarism, nomadism and the sociolinguistics of dialect. In Nikolas Coupland ed., *Sociolinguistics: Theoretical Debates*. Cambridge: Cambridge University Press, 217–241.

Clayton, Ian. 2017. Preaspiration in Hebrides English. *Journal of the International Phonetic Association 47*.

Cohen, Ira. 1989. *Structuration Theory: Anthony Giddens and the Constitution of Social Life*. London: Macmillan.

Collins, Henry. 1975. The sources of Australian pronunciation. Working Papers of the Speech and Language Research Centre, Macquarie University, No. 1, 115–128.

Coupland, Nikolas. 2010. Language, ideology, media and social change. In Karen Junod and Didier Maillat eds., *Performing the Self*. Tübingen: Gunter Narr Verlag, 127–151.

Eckert, Penelope. 2008. Variation and the indexical field. *Journal of Sociolinguistics 12*: 453–476

Ellis, Alexander. 1889. *On Early English Pronunciation: Part V*. London: Truebner and Co.

Filppula, Markku, Juhani Klemola and Heli Paulasto. 2012. *English and Celtic in Contact*. London: Routledge.

Friedlander, Daniel and Robert Roshier. 1966. A study of internal migration in England and Wales: Part I. *Population Studies 19*: 239–279.

Games, Alison. 2009. Migration. In David Armitage and Michael Braddick eds., *The British Atlantic World 1500–1800* (2nd ed.). London: Palgrave Macmillan, 33–52.

Giddens, Anthony 1984. *The Constitution of Society: Outline of the Theory of Structuration*. Cambridge: Polity Press.

Granovetter, Mark. 1973. The strength of weak ties. *American Journal of Sociology 78*: 1360–1380.

Hickey, Raymond. 2012. *Irish English: History and Present-Day Forms*. Cambridge: Cambridge University Press.

Honeybone, Patrick. 2007. New-dialect formation in nineteenth century Liverpool: A brief history of Scouse. In Anthony Grant and Clive Grey eds. *The Mersey Sound: Liverpool's Language, People and Places*. Liverpool: Open House Press. 106–140.

Ihalainen, Ossi. 1994. The dialects of England since 1776. In Robert Burchfield ed. *The Cambridge History of the English Language, Vol. 5: English in Britain and Overseas: Origins and Development*. Cambridge: Cambridge University Press. 197–276.

Jupp, James. 2001. The making of the Anglo-Australian. In James Jupp ed. *The Australian People*. Cambridge: Cambridge University Press, 796–803.

Kroskrity, Paul. 2005. Language ideologies. In Alessandro Duranti ed. *A Reader in Linguistic Anthropology*. Oxford: Blackwell, 496–517.

Kuo, Yun-Hsuan. 2005. New dialect formation: The case of Taiwanese Mandarin. Unpublished doctoral dissertation, University of Essex.

Mayr, Robert, Jonathan Morris, Ineke Mennen and Daniel Williams. 2017. Disentangling the effects of long-term language contact and individual bilingualism: The case of monophthongs in Welsh and English. *International Journal of Bilingualism 21*: 245–267.

Milroy, James 1992. *Linguistic Variation and Change*. Oxford: Basil Blackwell.

Milroy, James and Lesley Milroy. 1985. Linguistic change, social network and speaker innovation. *Journal of Linguistics 21*: 339–384.

Milroy, Lesley 1980. *Language and Social Networks*. Oxford: Basil Blackwell.

Milroy, Lesley 2002. Social networks. In Jack Chambers, Peter Trudgill and Natalie Schilling-Estes eds., *Handbook of Language Variation and Change*. Oxford: Blackwell, 549–572.

Montgomery, Michael 1989. Exploring the roots of Appalachian English. *English World-Wide 10*: 227–278.

Mufwene, Salikoko 1996. The founder principle in creole genesis. *Diachronica 8*: 83–134.

Nicholas, Stephen and Peter Shergold. 1987. Internal migration in England, 1818–1839. *Journal of Historical Geography 13*: 155–168.

ONS (Office for National Statistics). 2011. *2011 Census: Quick Statistics for England and Wales, March 2011*. www.ons.gov.uk/peoplepopulationandcommunity/populationandmigration/populationestimates/bulletins/2011censusquickstatisticsforenglandandwales/2013-01-30#main-language

Orton, Harold. 1962. *Survey of English Dialects: Introduction*. Leeds: E J Arnold and Son.

Paulasto, Heli. 2006. *Welsh English Syntax: Contact and Variation*. Joensuu: Joensuu University Press.

Pavlenko, Aneta. 2018. Superdiversity and why it isn't: Reflections on terminological innovation and academic branding. In Barbara Schmenk, Stephan Breidbach and Lutz Küster eds., *Sloganization in Language Education Discourse*. Clevedon: Multilingual Matters, 142–168.

Penhallurick, Robert. 2004. Welsh English: Phonology. In Edgar Schneider, Kate Burridge, Bernd Kortmann, Rajend Mesthrie and Clive Upton eds., *A Handbook of the Varieties of English, Vol. 1: Phonology*. Berlin: De Gruyter. 98–112.

Piller, Ingrid. 2014. Superdiversity: Another Eurocentric idea? *Language on the Move*, June 4. www.languageonthemove.com/language-globalization/superdiversity-another-eurocentric-idea

Pooley, Colin and Turnbull, Jean. 1998. *Migration and Mobility in Britain since the 18th Century*. London: UCL Press.

Roberts, Robert. 1990. *The Classic Slum: Salford Life in the First Quarter of the Century*. London: Penguin.

Sabban, Annette. 1985. On the variability of Hebridean English syntax. In Manfred Görlach ed., *Focus On: Scotland*. Amsterdam: John Benjamins. 125–44.

Sayers, Dave. 2009. Reversing Babel: Declining linguistic diversity and the flawed attempts to protect it. Unpublished doctoral dissertation, University of Essex.

Shuken, Cynthia. 1985. Variation in Hebridean English. In Manfred Görlach ed., *Focus On: Scotland*. Amsterdam: John Benjamins, 145–158.

Sudbury, Andrea. 2000. Dialect contact and koineization in the Falkland Islands: Development of a southern hemisphere variety? Unpublished doctoral dissertation, University of Essex.

Thomas, Alan. 1997. English in Wales. In Hildegard Tristram ed., *The Celtic Englishes*. Heidelberg: Universitätsverlag Carl Winter, 55–85.

Trudgill, Peter. 1986. *Dialects in Contact*. Oxford: Blackwell.

Trudgill, Peter. 2004. *New Dialect Formation: The Inevitability of Colonial Englishes*. Edinburgh: Edinburgh University Press.

Urry, John. 2007. *Mobilities*. London: Polity.

Vincent, David. 1989. *Literacy and Popular Culture: England 1750–1914*. Cambridge: Cambridge University Press.

Williams, Colin. ed. 1988. *Language in Geographic Context*. Clevedon: Multilingual Matters.

Wright, Joseph. 1898–1905. *English Dialect Dictionary*. Oxford: Oxford University Press.

8

English in North America

Merja Kytö

8.1 Introduction: New Settings, New Varieties

The emergence and subsequent history of English in North America makes an intriguing case for the study of language change. It was in the early seventeenth century that commentators began to point out features distinguishing the varieties used in the colonies from British English (BrE). Lexical borrowings were noticed first when words such as *maize, canoe, raccoon, wampum,* and *tomahawk* became part of the settlers' lexical repertoire (Mathews 1936: 4; Montgomery 2001: 92–93; Cassidy and Hall 2001: 188–189). Some 150 years later, in the 1770s, early commentators marveled at the similarity of speech habits and the uniformity of language among the settlers in the New World when comparing their language use with the different dialects characterizing language use in contemporaneous England (Read 1933: 323). Yet the issue of homogeneity in the early colonial days and today is more complex than one might think. By comparison, in Canada, British visitors found nothing distinctively different from the dialects of England as late as the early 1800s, after the massive influx of immigrants to the area from the British Isles in the late 1700s (Chambers 2004: 226).

There is indeed all reason to acknowledge the plurality of what could be referred to as North American Englishes (see Mufwene 1996), which comprise the main regional varieties and their local subvarieties used in the Northern, Southern, and Middle states of the current USA, and in Canada. A further variety in the family of North American Englishes with a history going back to the eighteenth century is African American English (AAE) (also referred to as African American Vernacular English, AAVE). The tension between linguistic conservatism and innovation in the new sociodemographic environment of an emerging variety readily gives rise to geographical and social variation promoting or discouraging unification or diversification tendencies (see, e.g., Marckwardt 1958; Görlach 1987).

A situation characterized by input from various local dialects often leads to leveling phenomena (Trudgill 1986) whereby linguistic features impeding mutual understanding fade away in the interest of those promoting communication.

The questions raised by the language-change mechanisms involved in the emergence of new transported varieties are many; for instance, what kind of extralinguistic and/or language-internal factors may lie behind the developments; what were the settler inputs like; what was the role played by the leveling phenomena and language contact with foreigners; how to value the evidence of convergent or divergent developments in the new varieties and the mother country (see Lass 1990)? Attempting to answer these questions sets considerable demands to language-theoretical reasoning and empirical methodology. Schneider's (2007) Dynamic Model seeks to systematize these questions into a fundamental framework where five stages are distinguished in any new variety formation, that is, foundation, exonormative stabilization, nativization, endonormative stabilization, and differentiation. Once the settlers' home variety and the possible indigenous varieties or languages in the new country are brought together, the structure and meanings in both are likely to go through a period of change at several levels of language use (Schneider 2007: 32–55).

This chapter focuses on Anglo-American Englishes, Canadian English (CanE), and AAE. It describes the sociohistorical background of these varieties (Section 8.2), paying attention to the relevant aspects of settlement history (Section 8.2.1), to settlers and their sociodemographic and educational background (Section 8.2.2), and to the settler input (Section 8.2.3). The sources of linguistic evidence will be surveyed in Section 8.3, with subsections on Anglo-American Englishes (Section 8.3.1), CanE (Section 8.3.2), and AAE (Section 8.3.3). Section 8.4 is devoted to the linguistic features and their trajectories of development in the early varieties. Phonetic and phonological features will be highlighted in Section 8.4.1, morphosyntax in Section 8.4.2, and vocabulary in Section 8.4.3. Section 8.5 concludes the chapter.

8.2 Sociohistorical Background

8.2.1 Settlement History: Chronology and Migration Routes

The first permanent English settlement in the Americas was Jamestown in the Colony of Virginia (1607). This enterprise was followed by the Plymouth Colony settled by Puritan Separatist Pilgrims (1620). A decade later, the Massachusetts Bay Colony was formed in Boston by influential Puritans. In addition to the Southern and Northern colonies established by settlers from England, the Middle colonies were founded by settlers from other countries in Europe, for example New Netherland (1624), New Sweden (1638), and Quaker Pennsylvania (1681), which all added diversity to the multilingual setting. It has been estimated that the half a century that followed the establishment of the first colonies was a key period regarding the regional differences in linguistic usage in the area (Kurath et al. 1939; Kurath 1972). As for Canada, English-speaking settlers gained access to the former French colonies as a result of the Treaty of Utrecht (1713) and to the rest of mainland Canada fifty years later as a result of the Treaty of Paris (1763).

A number of factors played a decisive role in the formation of the new varieties, among them the chronology of the settlement history, the routes of migration, and the origins and the demographic and sociocultural characteristics of the population flooding to the colonies. Most colonies were populated by migrants from various parts of the British Isles, often aiming at regions that would provide them daily contacts and support from networks of family, compatriots, or religious leaders (Montgomery 2001: 89). There is evidence of the early settlement areas and migration routes in the present configuration of American English (AmE) dialects (Wolfram and Schilling-Estes 1998: 26–27).

8.2.2   Settlers and Their Sociodemographic and Educational Background

The earliest settlers to the English colonies came from England, Scotland, Wales, and Ireland and tended to land in different parts of America. Eastern New England and Tidewater Virginia drew emigrants from south-eastern England, in particular, and the New Jersey and Delaware area drew population from northern and western parts of England. Scots-Irish settlers from Ulster ended up in western New England, upper New York, and parts of Appalachia. By the 1700s, the numbers of incoming settlers for New England had increased to 90,000, out of the 250,000 estimated for all the colonies (Greene and Harrington 1966: 3–4, 9–10). At the same time, some 16,000 settlers were populating New France at the shores of the Saint Lawrence River and parts of Nova Scotia. By the mid-1700s, however, English settlers in Newfoundland, Nova Scotia, and the Thirteen Colonies had outnumbered the French ten to one (Porter 1994: 60). From 1816 to 1857, close to 1.2 million immigrants came from the British Isles to Canada, with the sparsely populated inland territories in Lower Canada and Upper Canada. The immigrants came from ports in England, Scotland, and Ireland mainly comprising British Loyalists along with Germans and Scandinavians.

It has not always been possible to establish the exact origin of the early individual settlers on the basis of, for example, surname research; it has been estimated that perhaps one-fifth were Irish (Montgomery 2001: 89). According to another estimate, most of the early settlers to the New England area came from a socioeconomically and educationally leading area in England comprising five eastern counties, Lincolnshire, Norfolk, Suffolk, Cambridgeshire, and Essex (Thompson 1994: 14, 17). In Virginia, the majority of colonists also arrived from England while Scots and Scots-Irish settled on the frontier (Chalkey 1912: 3). As for Canada, after the outbreak of the American Revolution in 1776, thousands of refugees from New England flooded into the Maritime Provinces and either headed toward England or stayed in Nova Scotia, and, toward the end of the century, further refugees came from the Midland and northern states, especially Pennsylvania, New York, New Jersey, and western Vermont, staying in Quebec and Ontario (Chambers 2004: 225).

The early immigrants mainly represented middling and lower ranks and also comprised thousands of indentured servants who had exchanged years of labor for passage or training. London paupers and orphans were also transported to the colonies, along with military transportees and convicts (Montgomery 2001: 86). Social distinctions were evident (Campbell 1959: 68) and the social stratification continued once the settlers had found their way to the colonies. In the Massachusetts Bay Colony, a decade after the founding of the colony, five social classes have been distinguished: a number of high-rank colonists, a limited number from the ranks of the English squires, farmers and skilled tradesmen, tenants of inferior position, and indentured servants (Pomfret and Shumway 1970). Of these the latter two groups were only poorly educated. There was a great interest in instruction and formal education in the New England area and personal achievement in one's education was a way of obtaining upward social mobility. The colonies reached a nearly universal male literacy toward the end of the colonial period; women remained disadvantaged in basic education and hence also literacy (McDavid 1958: 510; Lockridge 1974: 4–5, 13–43).

The regional and social mobility, often promoted by the possibility of gaining wealth through purchase of land in the colonies, facilitated a loosening up of social structures in ways unavailable in the mother country (Handlin 1959: 5–7). This contributed to variation and enrichment in dialects and registers (Halliday 1978; Fairclough 1988), potentially leading to changes from below and from above. Yet there were boundaries that rather discouraged than promoted diffusion of linguistic change. Hierarchy and order were characteristics of social networks and the early colonial family life, especially among the Puritans, who believed in the dual relationship of superiority and inferiority (parents vs. children, husband vs. wife, master vs. servants) and restraint and distance in their mutual relationships. In these close-knit communities, the cultural climate of restrained contacts hampered diffusion of linguistic change (for further discussion, see Kytö 1991: 26–27).

8.2.3 Settler Input

Considering the multifaceted dimensions of sociodemographic and sociocultural circumstances, and the constant influx of new speakers in the early settlements, linguistic change was characterized by the complexity of contact phenomena and other factors at work. While acknowledging the crucial role that the settler input must have played in the differentiation of American Englishes, scholars have found it difficult to pin down precisely in what ways and to what extent the settlers' speech habits can be traced in the subsequent varieties; some have even doubted that the settler input played any significant role in the development of the new varieties (Montgomery 2001: 87–88). In his study of the English dialect heritage of the Southern USA, Schneider (2004: 262) surveys the conflicting views presented to account for the myth and the overall development of AmE varieties, especially of Southern AmE: On the one hand, it has been acknowledged that the new American varieties are offshoots of early modern BrE with concurring geolinguistic evidence presented by Kurath (1977 [1949]); but, on the other hand, it has been shown that many features in AmE need not descend from the mother variety directly (Görlach 1987) or can even be later innovations (Bailey 1997).

The linguistics of early modern England were already complex at the time of early migration: In addition to the "London English" supported by political, commercial, and literary prestige, the gentry and populace in the countryside used local dialects characterized by distinct features in, for example, Kent, the south-west, the west Midlands, and the north (Barber 1976/1997: 13; Görlach 1999a, 1999b). Speakers of the prestige variety and local dialects from all walks of life with varying degrees of formal education were represented among the migrants. Many of those arriving in New England were well educated and mastered the London prestige variety or supraregional features of southern England varieties while the emigrants from lower ranks used local vernacular varieties. It would be futile to try to establish systematic correspondences between the varieties in the early colonies and the settlers' speech habits (Krapp 1925: 1:53; for discussion, see Kytö 2004: 125–126). Instead, heterogeneous speech communities with fluid borderlines between regional and sociolectal varieties fed into the unifying and diversifying tendencies in the colonies and also promoted leveling tendencies in the use made by settlers of their dialect-specific phonological and morphosyntactic features (cf. Trudgill 1986). In Boston and many other fashionable coastal towns, it was the features of prestige varieties from southern England that made their way to the new emerging varieties at the expense of more conspicuously dialectal features (Kurath 1949/1977: 4–5). The result of this development has been referred to as an American "koiné" (see, e.g., Read 1938: 79; Trudgill 1986; Montgomery 1989a: 236–237). Understandably enough, after the American Revolution, direct influence on American popular speech from regional and social varieties of the British Isles has been estimated to be of only minor significance (Montgomery 2001: 92–93; for an overall survey of the linguistics of the early colonies, see Laird 1970, chaps. 7–8; Wood 1977; and Cassidy 1982: 177–178).

In the South, the transportation of Africans during the period of slavery was a significant factor influencing dialect formation to a greater extent than has perhaps been traditionally assumed (Lipski 1993; Feagin 1997; see Schneider 2004: 265). There is limited evidence on the similarities and differences between African American and White vernaculars (Wolfram 1974; Dorrill 1986; Wolfram and Thomas 2002; see Schneider 2004: 265). The role played by the British input dialects, the African and creole languages, and the internal developments has been debated intensively in the recent literature on the history of AAE (for references, see Schneider 2004: 265). The leading theories are the Anglicist and Creolist Hypotheses, the former advocating descendance of AAE mainly from BrE dialects and the latter postulating that AAE developed from a creole resulting from the vocabulary of one primary language having been imposed on an adapted and restricted grammatical structure (Wolfram and Schilling-Estes 1998: 175–177; Wolfram 2000; for historical insights into the conflicting theories on the development of AAE, see Mufwene 2001: 311–321). Comparisons across linguistic features shared by AAE and varieties of BrE and AmE, especially Southern AmE, have also been considered in the literature (see, e.g., Schneider 1989). By and large, features found in AAE and in Southern and other American vernaculars are more frequent and used in a wider range of linguistic contexts in AAE than in Southern White vernacular speech in general (Rickford 1999: 11).

The roots of CanE go back to British dialects in the first half of the eighteenth century (Chambers 2004: 224). When transported to Canada, the original British dialects had already undergone leveling processes contributing to homogenization of speech habits over the first generations (Chambers 2004: 224). In practical everyday life, these newcomers conformed to the established societal patterns and local norms developed by the descendants of the Loyalists. Accordingly, they also conformed to local speech habits, which meant that the linguistic input of the British immigrants remained only limited and that the Loyalist accent persisted (Chambers 2004: 226–228).

8.3 Sources of Evidence

The specimens of early writing from the colonies reflect the harsh circumstances experienced by the settlers. The texts they produced in the seventeenth and early eighteenth century are mostly of utilitarian nature, comprising history writing; travel narratives; town records; court documents, including, for example, appeals and answers, wills, records of hearings and examinations, and witness depositions; notes of sermons; and, importantly, ego documents such as private and official letters and diaries. Private letters, in particular, are a valuable source of evidence as they can often be taken to reflect the colloquial, everyday language considered as a crucial register for language change (Schneider and Montgomery 2001; Nevalainen and Raumolin-Brunberg 2003; Culpeper and Kytö 2010; Schneider 2013). Considering the vast areas covered by geographical labels such as "northern" and "southern colonies" and the rapidly increasing numbers of potential authors, it has been customary to treat these varieties in their own right, characterized by a set of linguistic features typical of a region itself and found in the texts produced in the area (Schneider 2004: 263; see, further, Montgomery 1989b: 761; Montgomery and Melo 1990: 201; Montgomery 2001: 102–104). In addition to textual evidence, four further types of evidence have been distinguished (Montgomery 2001: 97–102): commentators' reports of aspects of language use in the early colonies (among them clergymen, explorers, journalists, and other visitors), grammarians' and lexicographers' accounts, instances of literary dialect in drama and fiction, and rhyme evidence in colonial poetry.

8.3.1   Anglo-American Englishes

Recent corpus compilation projects have meant a boost for the study of World Englishes and significantly facilitated the study of the formation of American Englishes by providing access to collections of texts representative of a period and various genres. For example, we now have access to the *Corpus of Historical American English* (COHA) released in 2010 (Davies 2012a, 2012b) extending from 1810 to the 2000s and comprising 400 million words, making it the largest structured corpus of historical AmE. Further late modern English material is available in *A Representative Corpus of English Historical Registers* (ARCHER). ARCHER is a multi-genre corpus of BrE and AmE covering the period 1600–1999. The AmE texts have been sampled for five subperiods from 1750 to 1999 and total 1,350,000 words (version 3.2). In addition to stratified multi-genre corpora, there are single-genre text collections available in electronic form such as the *TIME Magazine Corpus* (1923–2006) and also online newspaper collections, for example *Nineteenth-Century U.S. Newspapers* and *America's Historical Newspapers*. Major newspapers along with those published by African Americans, Native Americans, and other interest groups have been included in the collections.

For dialectologists interested in evidence of vernacular and untutored language use, reliable records of historical dialectal speech are practically nonexistent as literate language users wrote in the standard variety they had been tutored to use while those who spoke their local dialect were not able to write (Schneider 2004: 268). In this respect, the above-mentioned ego documents comprising letters by untutored or modestly educated writers have increasingly started to attract attention among researchers (see, e.g., McCafferty and Amador-Moreno 2014). Such sources are valuable as they can be assumed to come closer to the vernacular owing to their private context and informal circumstances of writing. Examples of studies based on early letters are those by Montgomery on the Appalachian dialect (e.g. Montgomery 1989a) and AAE (e.g. Montgomery et al. 1993; Montgomery 1999). Recently, at least three letter corpora containing material from the American South have been compiled, that is, Southern plantation overseers' letters and letters by Civil War Soldiers and African Americans between 1760 and 1910 (Schneider and Montgomery 2001; Ellis and Montgomery 2012, n.d.; Siebers 2015). These sources provide opportunities to learn more about the origin of AAE and the connections between this variety and Southern vernacular English.

A further source for indirect access to the vernacular is the representation of dialects in fiction. Literary dialects are not records of authentic language use (cf. Schneider's 2013 classification of "spoken" vs. "written" sources) but can nevertheless serve as a basis for the study of language variation in the past (Kautzsch 2012: 1794–1796). Other unusual sources have also been the object of study, among them the *Tennessee Civil War Veterans Questionnaires*, a collection of Confederate veterans' responses from the post-1915 period (for details, see Schneider 2004: 268). Yet another source of unconventional data revelatory of the history of the Southern AmE is the speech island of Americana in Brazil with a daughter variety of nineteenth-century Southern AmE, which is still spoken by the descendants of Confederates (Montgomery and Melo 1990; Schneider 2004: 268).

8.3.2 Canadian English

Reconstruction of earlier CanE has been based on a variety of sources. Sociolinguistic interviews have served as the basis for linguistic corpora of transcribed speech as in, for example, the *Toronto Corpus* (Tagliamonte 2008), in the ethnolectic study of linguistic variation in urban Toronto English (Hoffman and Walker 2010), and in the *Quebec English Corpus* (Poplack et al. 2006). On the other hand, the tradition of historical corpus compilation in the sense it has been applied to, for example, the historical varieties of BrE, is only in its beginnings in Canada (Dollinger 2012: 1865). However, there are a number of important exceptions to this, among them the *Corpus of Early Ontario English* (CONTE) with its pre-Confederation section (CONTE-pC) (Dollinger 2006, 2008: 99–119). The compilation principles and the design of the corpus make the material comparable to corpora such as ARCHER. Further, the *Bank of Canadian English* database has served as the source for the revised and extended online version of the *Dictionary of Canadianisms on Historical Principles*, or DCHP-2. Further sources of historical CanE include the self-report surveys that go back to the 1950s (Chambers 1994; Dollinger 2012: 1864–1865), fictional representation of early folk speech, and the external language history, extrapolating with what is known of the input varieties to CanE (Dollinger 2008: 55–56).

8.3.3   African American English

Assessing the value of potential sources containing AAE has proved a particularly challenging area in the study of early American Englishes, and bones of contention have been many (for an overview, see Wolfram 2000; Lanehart 2012). Most use has perhaps been made of ex-slave narratives comprising (1) written documents and (2) original audio material (the useful survey in Kautzsch 2012: 1797–1801 has been consulted for the information given in this section; see also Wolfram 2000 and Schneider 2015 for further insights). Among the written narratives, we find autobiographical accounts, many of them available in digitized form. The second source of written narratives comprises records of interviews with former slaves. These records have a complex production history going back to the 1920s, with varying practices in subsequent editorial policies adopted (see, e.g., Brewer 1974; Perdue et al. [1976]1992; Schneider 1989; Kautzsch 2002).

The type (2) narratives, original audio material, comprise early record-ings on aluminum cylinders. These are mostly referred to as the "ex-slave recordings." The centrality of this source lies in it representing the earliest available spoken evidence of early AAE to date and enabling research on speech instead of written records (Bailey et al. 1991). As with written records, these recordings suffer from limitations that hamper their full use for linguistic study; for instance, the sound quality of the recordings is bad and the sample relatively small and, among the interviewees, house servants are overrepresented (for discussion, see Kautzsch 2002: 1799; see, also Bailey et al. 1991: 16). However, they have value in mirroring realisti-cally the language contact contexts in the South after the emancipation of slaves in 1863; they are now available online from the Library of Congress. Subsequent recordings comprise interviews with "hoodoo" doctors and other individuals involved in such practices, conducted as of the 1930s onwards (Kautzsch 2012: 1799–1800). Further material can be found in sociolinguistic interviews of descendants of former slaves from present-day enclave communities, among them Samaná in the Dominican Republic and in Nova Scotia in Canada, and in Liberia as the home of a "diaspora variety" (see, e.g., Poplack and Tagliamonte 2001; Kautzsch 2012: 1801).

Further sources of evidence comprise various types of letters written by former slaves (Siebers 2015). The extent to which these sources can be used for linguistic study depends on the kind of editorial practices adopted for the distribution versions. Worth mentioning are also the early blues lyrics corpus (BLUR) from the 1920s to the 1940s (Miethaner 2005).

8.4 Linguistic Features: Glimpses at Trajectories of Development

This section turns to the development of linguistic features of interest to the history of North American Englishes. Note that singling out a linguistic feature in the development of a variety need not mean that this feature would not be of interest to some other World Englishes as well. For instance, the sentence-final *eh? /ei/* has been diagnosed as an icon characteristic of Canadian English but is also common in, for example, Maori English (Warren and Britain 2000: 166).

8.4.1 Phonetic and Phonological Features

By the time the settlers arrived in the colonies, the regional variation that was undoubtedly there in spoken language was covered by the emerging standard language applied in writing and based to a noticeable extent on the Middle English dialect of the East Midlands and its later south-eastern forms used in the prestigious London area and the court. Yet dialectal features made their way to writing, and early texts from the colonies allow us to take a glimpse at the kind of dialectal and sociolectal features that the settlers brought with them (Görlach 1991: 13–18). Of the levels of language, pronunciation has been considered to be most likely to preserve conservative features as there were no more prestigious models easily available to the first two or three generations (Görlach 1987: 47). However, along with retention, innovation has also been a characteristic of early speech habits in the American colonies. Using colonial and early national sources, Krapp (1925) provides the most comprehensive description of early American vowels, diphthongs, and consonants compared with their counterparts in BrE. The material revealed the persistence of English pronunciations in the American records (Montgomery 2001: 137).

A number of features have caught researchers' attention, among them the pronunciation of [aː] (*glass*), postvocalic /r/ (*barn, bar, thirty*), and the merger of /w/ and /hw/ (*witch/which*). The history of these features in the USA is complex, displaying retention, adherence to British norms, and independent development. While areas in New England adopted London [aː], later eighteenth-century immigrants went for the by then common AmE [æː], a retention or an independent development of the early modern English sound. The early settlers apparently brought with them the retroflex [r] in postvocalic position, a sound lost in BrE around the 1800s but retained in the American North and West. Evidence of the New England *r*-less pronunciation from 1700 are recorded spellings such as *libity* for *liberty* and *patchis* for *purchase* (Wakelin 1988: 18), and although *r*-full forms dominate in, for example, the records of the Salem witchcraft trials from 1692, the documents also contain *r*-less forms in mid- and end-positions (e.g. *Geale* for "girl," *nuss* for "Nurse," *Googe* for "George," *uging* for "urging" *doe* for "door") and even instances of *r*-insertion in spellings such as *parth* for "path," *worter* for "water," *Dearth* for "death" (Grund et al. 2009: 74; for further discussion of the repertoire of pronunciation features displayed by the Salem records, see Kytö 2004: 134–137). Parts of the American South also adopted the new pronunciation fashion, a trend supported by wealthy plantation owners and aristocrats in Charleston sending their children to be educated in the best British schools. However, Western New England and New York State became *r*-full areas by virtue of their *r*-pronouncing settlers, reduction of dialect differences induced by dialect and language contact, and relative lack of contact with the home country (Wolfram and Schilling-Estes 1998: 94–95). Between the 1700s and 1900s two million Scots-Irish immigrants flooded especially to Pennsylvania and spread throughout the Middle states and the highlands of the American South. They contributed to the retention of the *r*-full pronunciation, a characteristic of Scots-Irish (Wolfram and Schilling-Estes 1998: 98–99). As for the *witch/which* merger, the distinction must have been carried to the colonies by the speakers of dialects other than Southern BrE, where the two sounds had merged well before colonization started (Görlach 1987: 46–47). A further pronunciation distinction kept in the USA is the stress in polysyllabic Latinate words (*secretary*). Variation in stress patterns was there in early modern English and unstressing reached its peak at the turn of the eighteenth and nineteenth centuries. This development was not echoed in the colonies, possibly after the recommendations put forth by Noah Webster in his *Spelling Book* in 1783 (Görlach 1987: 47).

As for Southern AmE, the so-called Southern drawl has been considered perhaps the "best-known characteristic of southern pronunciation" (Wells 1982: 529). Montgomery and Melo (1990: 210) have surmised it could go back to mid-nineteenth-century Southern AmE, but lack of mention made of it in the literature prevents one from drawing any firm conclusions; for this and other features typical of Southern AmE pronunciation, see Schneider (2004: 269–283).

Turning to CanE, this variety has been characterized by conservatism and adherence to the BrE norms across most of its history. In the Victorian era, schoolchildren and white-collar workers were not only encouraged to "enunciate clearly" but also to use British equivalents such as *schedule* with /ʃ/, *rather* with /ɑ:/, and *student* with "yod" (/ˈstju: dent/) for certain native pronunciations. Such reverence felt for forms used by upper-middle-class speakers in England led to speech patterns referred to as the "Canadian Dainty" (Chambers 2004: 232–233; Dollinger 2012: 1872). For instance, yod-retention became considered a "stereotypical Canadianism." Even though speakers displaying these patterns were in the minority, the prestige of British pronunciation was influential and fostered criticism against American pronunciation.

It is only relatively recently that evidence has been presented on the decline of such Briticisms (see, e.g., Chambers 2014: 233–240).

Although the final solutions accounting for change may still be pending, a number of features in the phonology and pronunciation of present-day CanE can be traced back in history. The merger homophony in low-back vowels of words such as *cot* and *caught*, *stock* and *stalk*, or *collar* and *caller* is among the most salient of them. There is historical evidence of it having been imported from the USA prior to 1830; the feature is still spreading in parts of North America today (Dollinger 2012: 1869). Language contact with Scots-Irish immigrants has also been offered as an explanation to account for what within this framework would appear as a source of independent development (Boberg 2010: 102, 128). Another distinctively Canadian phenomenon, possibly triggered by the *cot–caught merger*, is the Canadian Shift by which is meant a lowering and retraction of the TRAP, DRESS, and KIT vowels; this development follows the opposite path compared with the Northern Cities Shift in the USA (for discussion, see Dollinger 2008: 32–33 and 2012: 1869).

Yet a further distinctive Canadian feature is the so-called Canadian Raising, which affects the pronunciation of diphthongs with open-vowel starting points. CanE can have raising in words with both /aɪ/ (*height*, *life*, *psych*, *type*, etc.) and /aʊ/ (*clout*, *house*, *south*, *scout*, etc.), while most dialects of US English when they have raising only have it in /aɪ/. Various theories of the origin of the phenomenon have been presented. It has been considered a Canadian innovation, perhaps the majority opinion today, but also a result of dialect mixing and reallocation of features in CanE (for references and discussion, see Dollinger 2008: 29–32; Dollinger 2012: 1868–1869).

In relation to comparable Anglo-American varieties, that is, the speech of low-status Anglo-American and African American groups in the South, Fasold (1981) identified a number of unique features in AAE. Those pertaining to pronunciation include devoicing of voiced stops in stressed syllables ([bit] for *bid*, [bæk] for *bag*) and reduction of final consonant clusters when followed by a word beginning with a vowel or a suffix beginning with a vowel (*lif' up* for *lift up*, *bussing* for *busting*); however, the plural marker *-s* is pronounced even in a word-final cluster (*pets*). In his account, Rickford (1999: 4–5) lists eighteen distinctive phonological (pronunciation) features, with references to further sources. Among the other features that have become shibboleths of AAE is, for example, transposition of adjacent consonants as in *aks* for *ask*, condemned by gatekeepers of standard English (Rickford 1999: 5).

8.4.2 Morphosyntax

A mixture of nonstandard and emerging standard forms and usage patterns was transported to the colonies, making seventeenth- and eighteenth-century American records echo the morphosyntactic features found in contemporaneous BrE varieties. For instance, double negation and variant forms of the principal parts of verbs are distinguished rather in social than geographical terms in both varieties. Comparing early grammatical patterns in American and British records is complicated by features continuing to develop in the colonies at the same time as they continued evolving in the British Isles and Ireland (Montgomery 2001: 144).

Only relatively little empirical research has been done on the morpho-syntactic features of early Anglo-American Englishes. A survey based on textual evidence and previous work of verb forms and syntax, nouns, pronouns, adjectives, and numerals and expressions of quantity in the formative years of the New England area can be found in Kytö (2004); for developments in the use of modal auxiliaries, see Kytö (1991); for adjective comparison and standardization processes, see Kytö and Romaine (2000). As for verb forms, the use of *was* with the second-person pronoun *you* was common in the colonies throughout the seventeenth century, curiously regarded to represent finer usage (Krapp 1925: 2:261; Marckwardt 1958: 75–6; Kytö 2004: 138–139). There was also variation in the use of the principal parts of irregular verbs (e.g. Abbott 1953, 1957; Kytö 2004: 140–143; Hundt 2009: 20–27; Anderwald 2014). To mention a well-known example, *got* is the standard form in BrE today while *gotten* is considered an Americanism (see Krapp 1925: 2:259). By the time the early settlers left for the colonies, *got* still prevailed in their writings; *gotten* apparently fell from use in the mid- or late seventeenth century in England (Marckwardt 1958: 76). According to Hundt (2009: 20–22), who investigated evidence from ARCHER and previous empirical studies, the use of *gotten* in AmE is rather a case of postcolonial revival than a development induced by colonial lag. Finally, forms of irregular verbs are often regularized in dialects (*tell-telled-telled*), a feature transported to AmE varieties (for references, see Peitsara 1996: 296). Despite the forceful prescriptive trends having removed most of such variation from present-day standard English, there is still vacillation in the use of the forms, even with irregular forms being introduced in the paradigms of originally regular verbs (cf. *sneak/snuck/snuck*; Romaine 2013). Toward the end of the eighteenth century, as predicted by Schneider's Dynamic Model, most changes and innovations are of a lexico-grammatical nature, with words having developed new grammatical uses as in, for example, complementation patterns of verbs (for examples, see Schneider 2007: 297).

In his substantial investigation of Southern AmE, Schneider (2004) focuses on the hallmarks of the variety, including in his discussion the second-person plural pronoun *y'all*, double modals (*might could*), the preverbal form *done* with perfective meaning, and counterfactual *liketa* (or *like to*) (pp. 284–289; for a number of further features, see pp. 290–292). The origin of *y'all* has raised a good deal of discussion among researchers but the general agreement is that it represents a new plural form (Görlach

1987: 54; Schneider 2004: 284–285), first attested in 1824 (Bailey 1997: 268). Several theories have been put forth to account for the emergence of the form, among them the interplay of language contact (Scots-Irish, Gullah, and Caribbean creoles); it is evident that transported dialects alone cannot be the source for the form. Instead, indigenous evolution influenced by linguistic and extralinguistic factors must have led to the emergence of the form, among them contact with early AAE (Schneider 2004: 285–287). Double modals, as in *I might could do it*, are a Southern feature par excellence. They are difficult to investigate as they are rare and restricted to certain types of informal face-to-face interactions (Montgomery 1998: 96). Even though some double modals also occur in Scotland and northern England, as well as the Caribbean, they can hardly be considered transported features owing to lexical variation in the modal combinations. The preverbal form *done* with perfective meaning as in *I am dun cutting, I done all that I knowed what to Do, I done planting of corn* is a feature of Southern AmE shared with AAE (this instance is given in Eliason [1956: 249] from plantation overseers' letters, Rockingham county, North Carolina, 1829–1860; the use is cited and discussed in Schneider [2004: 287]). The perfective function derives from earlier English (*have done* + present participle) and the structure has probably developed as a result of contact with AAE (Schneider 2004: 287–288). Counterfactual *liketa* (or *like to*) meaning "nearly," "almost" in, for example, *It was so cold out there, I liketa died* (Wolfram and Schilling-Estes 1998: 45) is another Southernism. The form as such goes back to BrE dialects but the construction was modified in terms of semantics and syntactic uses in the New World (Schneider 2004: 288–289; see also Feagin 1979).

Turning to CanE, in his real-time study of modals in the history of the variety, Dollinger (2008) focused on data drawn from the CONTE-Pc corpus. As for the apparent time approach, the post-1950s developments of features such as future *will* and *going to*, deontic *have got to* and *have to*, possessive *have got* and *have*, intensifiers *very*, *really*, and *so*, and the sentence tags *you know*, *whatever*, *so*, and *stuff like that* have been investigated using the *Toronto English Corpus* (Tagliamonte 2006). Many of the nonstandard past tense and past participle forms of verbs such as *dive*, *sneak*, *get*, *drink*, *write*, *see*, and *eat* have exhibited variation in CanE and in other varieties of English since the 1700s (Dollinger 2008: 46). Among verbs with double forms such as *spelt/spelled*, *dreamt/dreamed*, *learnt/learned*, and *knelt/kneeled*, the early and shorter forms have been reported to be more common than the longer forms in current CanE usage (Brinton and Fee 2001: 432). Among expressions indexing various degrees of standardness (from the more nonstandard toward the more standard end of the cline) in CanE are the *after+V+ing* construction, the positive *anymore* construction, and sentence-initial *as well* (Chambers 1986). The *after+V+ing* constructions indicate that the action in question has just been completed, as in *He's after coming home from the mainland*. The use occurs in Irish English and has been considered to be of Celtic influence. The positive *anymore* constructions, as in *He complains a lot anymore*, convey the "nowadays" meaning. The use also occurs in Northern Irish English and in some Midland American Englishes and in parts of the Ontario area. The origin of the construction, which is gaining ground regionally in the USA (Brinton and Fee 2001: 432), has been debated among researchers: the construction's origin has been attributed to loyalists but also considered to represent an independent development (for discussion, see Dollinger 2008: 47–48). Sentence-initial *as well* functioning as a conjunctive adverb has been considered typical of CanE only but US American instances are also attested (Chambers 1986; see also Brinton and Fee 2001: 432; and Dollinger 2008: 47–48). Finally, survey evidence has been used for investigating the above-mentioned sentence-final *eh?* /eɪ/, a highly distinctive Canadian feature used in a variety of functions (Woods [1979] 1999).

Regarding AAE, the linguistic features distinctive to the variety are mostly grammatical, according to Rickford (1999: 11). His inventory (based on information drawn from a wide range of studies) comprises thirteen features of preverbal markers of tense, mood, and aspect, six features related to other aspects of verbal tense marking, seven types of noun and pronoun uses, four types of negation and two types of questions, three types of existential and locative constructions, and the use of complementizer or quotative *say* (Rickford 1999: 6–9; for a treatment of the most often cited features, see Mufwene 2001: 297–308). Among the verbal markers are, for instance, the absence of present tense copula or auxiliary *is* and *are*, as in *They Ø running* for *They **are** running*, the use of stressed BIN to mark that the action happened a long time ago, as in *He **BIN** ate it* for *He **ate** it a long time ago*, and the use of *done* to indicate the completion of an action, as in *He **done did** it* for *He's already done it*. A number of the features listed are shared with Southern AmE or other transported varieties, for example double modals, absence of third-person singular present tense -*s*, or use of *don't* for *doesn't*, and second-person plural *y'all*. Research on AAE has shown that, as with most varieties, inherent variability is typical of the use made of the language (Rickford 1999: 12).

8.4.3 Vocabulary

Vast numbers of new terms flooded into the English language during the colonization of North America ever since the late 1400s, with European explorers introducing names for animals, plants, birds, and so forth or new uses for old terms, for example *corn* for "maize," the original term in England having denoted grains in general (Cassidy and Hall 2001: 188–189). Utilitarian reasons were often behind the "Americanisms," especially the additions to the lexical resources of the language. Native American place names underwent phonetic assimilation and simplification, for example *Milwaukee* < *mahnah-wauk-seepe* "council ground near a river"

(Mencken1919/1963: 644). However, a good share of the vocabulary came from the dialects the settlers brought along with them. Yet many of the local expressions originating in Britain fell into oblivion, among them, for example, *frimicate* "to put on airs" and *golde* "to shout," originally from East Anglia (Bailey 2012: 1813). Differences in present-day usage, for example *fall* in the USA and *autumn* in Britain, can often be traced back to the period of colonization (Cassidy and Hall 2001: 191). The expansion of the early colonies northward, westward, and southward gave rise to region-specific Americanisms such as *cymbal* "a doughnut" and *dooryard* "the grounds around the house" in New Hampshire, Maine, Vermont, Connecticut, and Rhode Island (for further examples, see Cassidy and Hall 2001: 193–195).

As for CanE, the influence of aboriginal languages (e.g. *kayak, Saskatoon* "Pacific/western serviceberry," *muskeg* "swamp, bog") and also French (e.g. *capelin, coulee* "deep ravine," *shanty* "a primitive dwelling") is obvious in "Canadianisms," usually defined as "a word, expression, or meaning which is native to Canada or which is distinctively characteristic of Canadian usage though not necessarily exclusive to Canada" (Avis 1967: xiii; for discussion, see Brinton and Fee 2001: 434–439; Dollinger 2008: 24–25). Research has pointed to the influence of AmE lexis exerted increasingly on CanE (e.g. Boberg 2005) but evidence has also been presented on the influence of CanE lexis on AmE (McDavid 1951). Archaisms, rural, fishing, fur trade, or rare uses dominate in the more than 10,000 Canadianisms included in the *Dictionary of Canadianisms* (Avis 1967; for extensive lists of terms representative of subject categories, see Brinton and Fee 2001: 434–438). There are also other historical dictionaries of CanE, for example the *Dictionary of Newfoundland English* (Story et al. [1982] 1990) for "Newfoundlandisms" and a systematic approach to the word-stock (for a survey, see Fee 1992; Dollinger 2008: 25–26).

The lexical resources and semantics of AAE have not received much attention. Mufwene (2001: 308–309) mentions dictionaries and Smitherman's (1977) study where the terms used to denote African Americans since the colonial period are treated. Smitherman draws attention to "Black semantics," or the tradition to use English for contrary meanings, African American and White, as in *He is a bad dude* for "a person of undesirable character" or "a person of highly desirable character" (Smitherman 1977: 58–59). Further examples are *clean, cool, hang,* and *attitude*. It is often difficult for outsiders to decipher such "counter-language" (Morgan 1989, 1993). Yet some of the uses have been adopted into AmE, for example *hip* "up-to-date on a trend" and *cool* "acceptable."

8.5 Concluding Remarks

In the global perspective, AmE was the first postcolonial English to develop into a national variety, today claiming a success story with more than 400 years of history behind it (Schneider 2007: 251–252).

Tracing that history back to the extant records, whether published or penned down for private or official use, is a complex challenge, which involves the use of eclectic methodology and understanding mechanisms of language change. This chapter has painted a picture of aspects of the development in North American Englishes in broad brushstrokes, hinting to areas that offer further puzzles to solve. The discussion has also highlighted the need for researchers to turn to empirical, textual evidence, and make use of corpus linguistic, variationist, sociolinguistic, and other modern analytical frameworks to collect and organize the data and make sense of the findings. Clearly, interdisciplinary approaches are also called for so as to allow historical linguists to appreciate the information that historians, social historians, and experts in demographics, cultural studies, and other areas have been able to unearth about the early North American colonies and their subsequent development. All such information is needed to help assess the tension between the roles played by the settler input, linguistic innovation, and postcolonial revivals in the developments.

There are a number of desiderata in sight in terms of future work on North American Englishes. To start with, there is a need to compile further stratified language corpora containing textual evidence drawn from (ego) documents produced by, for example, women or untutored writers, or from sources containing speech-related language. One would also welcome further work on North American and contemporaneous British grammar books and on the potential role played by the precept on the actual language use in the colonial period (see Anderwald 2016). Of major interest would be the empirical study of relationships between Northern and Southern American Englishes, on the one hand, and of those between African American and Southern American Englishes, on the other hand. There is also a need for further mapping and accounting for developments in CanE, along the lines of the initiatives taken by, for example, Stefan Dollinger and Sali Tagliamonte, and for making comparisons between the developments in this variety and those attested for the Anglo-American varieties. Within this framework, looking further into the ego documents such as private letters can be expected to lead to exciting results. There are also gaps in what we know about the development of various morphosyntactic and pragmatic features across the North American varieties. The developments that took place in the North American Englishes are of major interest to the research done on the evolution of other World Englishes. The North American varieties are well documented and have enabled researchers to explore numerous aspects of their history. From this perspective, studies on North American Englishes can be considered to serve as reference points for other research on World Englishes, inviting further explorers to stake their lots.

References

Abbott, Orville Lawrence. 1953. A study of verb forms and verb uses in certain American writings of the seventeenth century. Unpublished doctoral dissertation, Michigan State College of Agriculture and Applied Science.

Abbott, Orville Lawrence. 1957. The preterit and past participle of strong verbs in seventeenth-century American English. *American Speech 32*: 31–42.

Anderwald, Lieselotte. 2014. *Burned, dwelled, dreamed*: The evolution of a morphological Americanism and the role of prescriptive grammar writing. *American Speech 89*(4): 408–440.

Anderwald, Lieselotte. 2016. *Language Between Description and Prescription: Verbs and Verb Categories in Nineteenth-Century Grammars of English*. Oxford: Oxford University Press.

Avis, Walter S. 1967. Introduction. In Walter S. Avis, Charles Crate, Patrick Drysdale, Douglas Leechman, Matthew H. Scharill and Charles L. Lovell, eds. *A Dictionary of Canadianisms on Historical Principles*. Toronto: Gage, i–xiixv.

Bailey, Guy. 1997. When did Southern English begin? In Edgar Schneider, ed. *Englishes Around the World, Vol. 1: General Studies, British Isles, North America*. Amsterdam: John Benjamins, 255–275.

Bailey, Guy, Natalie Maynor and Patricia Cukor-Avila, eds. 1991. *The Emergence of Black English: Text and Commentary*. Amsterdam: John Benjamins.

Bailey, Richard W. 2012. Varieties of English: Standard American English. In Laurel J. Brinton and Alexander Bergs, eds. *English Historical Linguistics: An International Handbook*. Berlin: De Gruyter Mouton, 1809–1826.

Barber, Charles. 1976/1997. *Early Modern English*. Edinburgh: Edinburgh University Press.

Boberg, Charles. 2005. The North American regional vocabulary survey: New variables and methods in the study of North American English. *American Speech 80*(1): 22–60.

Boberg, Charles. 2010. *The English Language in Canada: Status, History and Comparative Analysis*. Cambridge: Cambridge University Press.

Brewer, Jeutonne P. 1974. The verb *be* in early Black English: A study based on the WPA ex-slave narratives. Unpublished doctoral dissertation, University of North Carolina at Chapel Hill.

Brinton, Laurel J. and Margery Fee. 2001. Canadian English. In John Algeo, ed. *The Cambridge History of the English Language, Vol. IV: English in North America*. Cambridge: Cambridge University Press, 422–440.

Campbell, Mildred. 1959. Social origins of some early American. In James Morton Smith, ed. *Seventeenth-Century America. Essays in Colonial History*. Chapel Hill: University of North Carolina Press, 63–89.

Cassidy, Frederic G. 1982. Geographical variation of English in the United States. In Richard W. Bailey and Manfred Görlach, eds. *English as a World Language*. Ann Arbor: University of Michigan Press, 177–209.

Cassidy, Frederic G. and Joan Houston Hall. 2001. Americanisms. In John Algeo, ed. *The Cambridge History of the English Language, Vol. IV: English in North America*. Cambridge: Cambridge University Press, 184–218.

Chalkey, Lyman. 1912. *Chronicles of the Scotch-Irish Settlement in Virginia: Extracted from the Original Court Records of Augusta County, 1745–1800*. Rosslyn, VA: The Commonwealth Printing Company.

Chambers, Jack K. 1986. Three kinds of standard in Canadian English. In W. C. Lougheed, ed. *In Search of the Standard in Canadian English* (Strathy Occasional Papers on Canadian English 1). Kingston, ON: Queen's University, 1–15.

Chambers, Jack K. 1994. An introduction to dialect topography. *English World-Wide 15*: 35–53.

Chambers, Jack K. 2004. "Canadian Dainty": The rise and decline of Briticisms in Canada. In Raymond Hickey, ed. *Legacies of Colonial English. Studies in Transported Dialects*. Cambridge: Cambridge University Press, 224–241.

Chambers, Jack K. 2014. Canadian English and identity. *Annual Review of Canadian Studies 34*: 57–65.

Culpeper, Jonathan and Merja Kytö. 2010. *Early Modern English Dialogues: Spoken Interaction as Writing*. Cambridge: Cambridge University Press.

Davies, Mark. 2012a. The 400 million word Corpus of Historical American English (1810–2009). In Irén Hegedus and Alexandra Fodor eds. *English Historical Linguistics 2010*. Philadelphia: John Benjamins, 217–250.

Davies, Mark. 2012b. Expanding horizons in historical linguistics with the 400 million word Corpus of Historical American English. *Corpora 7*(2): 121–157.

Dollinger, Stefan. 2006. Oh Canada! Towards the Corpus of Early Ontario English. In Antoinette Renouf and Andrew Kehoe, eds. *The Changing Face of Corpus Linguistics*. Amsterdam: Rodopi, 7–25.

Dollinger, Stefan. 2008. *New-Dialect Formation in Canada: Evidence from the English Modal Auxiliaries*. Amsterdam: John Benjamins.

Dollinger, Stefan. 2012. Varieties of English: Canadian English in real-time perspective. In Laurel J. Brinton and Alexander Bergs, eds. *English Historical Linguistics: An International Handbook*. Berlin: De Gruyter Mouton, 1858–1879.

Dorrill, George Townsend. 1986. *Black and White Speech in the Southern United States: Evidence from the Linguistic Atlas of the Middle and South Atlantic States*. Frankfurt am Main: Peter Lang.

Eliason, Norman E. 1956. *Tarheel Talk: An Historical Study of the English Language in North Carolina to 1860*. Chapel Hill: University of North Carolina Press.

Ellis, Michael and Michael Montgomery. 2012. LAMSAS, CACWL, and the South-South Midland dialect boundary in nineteenth-century North Carolina. *American Speech 87*(4): 470–490.

Ellis, Michael and Michael Montgomery. N.d. *The Corpus of American Civil War Letters* (CACWL). See www.ehistory.org/projects/private-voices.html.

Fairclough, Norman. 1988. Register, power and socio-semantic change. In David Birch and Michael O'Toole, eds. *Functions of Style*. London: Pinter Publishers, 111–125.

Fasold, Ralph W. 1981. The relation between black and white speech in the South. *American Speech* 56(3): 163–189.

Feagin, Crawford. 1979. *Variation and Change in Alabama English: A Sociolinguistic Study of the White Community*. Washington, DC: Georgetown University Press.

Feagin, Crawford. 1997. The African contribution to Southern States English. In Cynthia Bernstein, Thomas Nunnally and Robin Sabino, eds. *Language Variety in the South Revisited*. Tuscaloosa: University of Alabama Press, 123–139.

Fee, Margery. 1992. Canadian dictionaries in English. In Tom McArthur, ed. *The Oxford Companion to the English Language*. Oxford: Oxford University Press, 178–179.

Görlach, Manfred. 1987. Colonial lag? The alleged conservative character of American English and other "colonial" varieties. *English World-Wide 8*: 41–60.

Görlach, Manfred. 1991. *Introduction to Early Modern English*. Cambridge: Cambridge University Press.

Görlach, Manfred. 1999a. Regional and social variation. In Roger Lass, ed. *The Cambridge History of the English Language, Vol. III: 1476–1776*. Cambridge: Cambridge University Press, 459–538.

Görlach, Manfred. 1999b. Towards a historical dialectology of English. In Manfred Görlach, *Aspects of the History of English*. Heidelberg: Universitätsverlag C. Winter, 94–161.

Greene, Evarts B. and Virginia D. Harrington. 1966 [1932]. *American Population before the Federal Census of 1790*. Gloucester, MA: Peter Smith.

Grund, Peter, Risto Hiltunen, Leena Kahlas-Tarkka, Merja Kytö, Matti Peikola and Matti Rissanen. 2009. Linguistic introduction. In Bernard Rosenthal, Gretchen A. Adams, Margo Burns, Peter Grund, Risto Hiltunen, Leena Kahlas-Tarkka et al., eds. *Records of the Salem Witch-Hunt*. Cambridge: Cambridge University Press, 64–90.

Handlin, Oscar. 1959. The significance of the seventeenth century. In James Morton Smith, ed. *Seventeenth-Century America: Essays in Colonial History*. Chapel Hill: University of North Carolina Press, 3–12.

Halliday, M.A.K. 1978. *Language as Social Semiotic. The Social Interpretation of Language and Meaning*. London: Edward Arnold.

Hoffman, Michol F. and James A. Walker. 2010. Ethnolects and the city: Ethnic orientation and linguistic variation in Toronto English. *Language Variation and Change 22*(1): 37–67.

Hundt, Marianne. 2009. Colonial lag, colonial innovation or simply language change? In Günter Rohdenburg and Julia Schlüter, eds. *One Language, Two Grammars? Differences Between British and American English.* Cambridge: Cambridge University Press, 13–37.

Kautzsch, Alexander. 2002. *The Historical Evolution of Earlier African-American English: An Empirical Comparison of Early Sources.* Berlin: Mouton de Gruyter.

Kautzsch, Alexander. 2012. English in contact: African American English (AAE) early evidence. In Laurel J. Brinton and Alexander Bergs, eds. *English Historical Linguistics: An International Handbook.* Berlin: De Gruyter Mouton, 1793–1807.

Krapp, George Philip. 1925. *The English Language in America,* Vols. 1–2. New York: Frederick Ungar.

Kurath, Hans. 1972. *Studies in Area Linguistics.* Bloomington: Indiana University Press.

Kurath, Hans. 1977 [1949]. *A Word Geography of the Eastern United States.* Ann Arbor: University of Michigan Press.

Kurath, Hans, et al. 1939. *The Linguistic Atlas of New England.* New York: AMS Press.

Kytö, Merja. 1991. *Variation and Diachrony, with Early American English in Focus.* Frankfurt am Main: Peter Lang.

Kytö, Merja. 2004. The emergence of American English: Evidence from seventeenth-century records in New England. In Raymond Hickey, ed. *Legacies of Colonial English: Studies in Transported Dialects.* Cambridge: Cambridge University Press, 121–157.

Kytö, Merja and Suzanne Romaine. 2000. Adjective comparison and standardisation processes in American and British English from 1620 to the present. In Laura Wright, ed. *The Development of Standard English 1300–1800: Theories, Description, Conflicts.* Cambridge: Cambridge University Press, 171–194.

Laird, Charlton. 1970. *Language in America.* New York: Basil Blackwell.

Lanehart, Sonja L. 2012. Varieties of English: Re-viewing the origins and history of African American language. In Laurel J. Brinton and Alexander Bergs, eds. *English Historical Linguistics: An International Handbook.* Berlin: De Gruyter Mouton, 1826–1839.

Lass, Roger. 1990. Where do extraterritorial Englishes come from? Dialect input and recodification in transported Englishes. In Sylvia M. Adamson, Vivien A. Law, Nigel Vincent and Susan Wright, eds. *Papers from the 5th International Conference on English Historical Linguistics.* Amsterdam: John Benjamins, 245–280.

Lipski, John M. 1993. *Y'all* in American English: From black to white, from phrase to pronoun. *English World-Wide* 14: 23–56.

Lockridge, Kenneth A. 1974. *Literacy in Colonial New England: An Enquiry into the Social Context of Literacy in the Early Modern West.* New York: W.W. Norton.

Marckwardt, Albert H. 1958. *American English*. New York: Oxford University Press.

Mathews, Mitford McLeod. 1936. Notes and comments made by British travelers and observers upon American English, 1770–1850. Unpublished doctoral dissertation, Harvard University.

McCafferty, Kevin and Caroline P. Amador-Moreno. 2014. "[The Irish] find much difficulty in these auxiliaries ... putting *will* for *shall* with the first person": The decline of first-person *shall* in Ireland, 1760–1890. *English Language and Linguistics* 18(3): 407–429.

McDavid, Jr., Raven I. 1951. Midland and Canadian words in upstate New York. *American Speech* 26(4): 248–256.

McDavid, Jr., Raven I. 1958. The dialects of American English. In W. Nelson Francis, ed. *The Structure of American English*. New York: The Ronald Press Company, 480–543.

Mencken, Henry L. 1963 [1919]. *The American Language*, Vol. 1 (abridged ed.; ed. by Raven I. McDavid and David W. Maurer). New York: Knopf.

Miethaner, Ulrich. 2005. "*I Can Look Through Muddy Water*": *Analyzing Earlier African American English in Blues Lyrics (BLUR)*. Frankfurt am Main: Peter Lang.

Montgomery, Michael M. 1989a. Exploring the roots of Appalachian English. *English World-Wide 10*: 227–278.

Montgomery, Michael M. 1989b. English language. In Charles Reagan Wilson and William Ferris, eds. *Encyclopedia of Southern Culture*. Chapel Hill: University of North Carolina Press, 761–767.

Montgomery, Michael M. 1998. Multiple modals in LAGS and LAMSAS. In Michael M. Montgomery and Thomas Nunnally, eds. *From the Gulf States and Beyond: The Legacy of Lee Pederson and LAGS*. Tuscaloosa: University of Alabama Press, 90–122.

Montgomery, Michael M. 1999. Eighteenth-century Sierra Leone English: Another exported variety of African American English. *English World-Wide 20*: 1–34.

Montgomery, Michael M. 2001. British and Irish antecedents. In John Algeo, ed. *The Cambridge History of the English Language, Vol. IV: English in North America.*Cambridge: Cambridge University Press, 86–153.

Montgomery, Michael, Janet M. Fuller and Sharon DeMarse. 1993. "The black men has wives and Sweet harts [and third person plural -*s*] Jest like the white men": Evidence for verbal -*s* from written documents of 19th-century African American speech. *Language Variation and Change* 5(3): 335–354.

Montgomery, Michael and Cecil Ataide Melo. 1990. The phonology of the lost cause: The English of the Confederados in Brazil. *English World-Wide 11*: 195–216.

Morgan, Marcyliena. 1989. From Down South to Up South: The language behavior of three generations of black women residing in Chicago. Unpublished doctoral dissertation, University of Pennsylvania.

Morgan, Marcyliena. 1993. The Africanness of counterlanguage among Afro-Americans. In Salikoko S. Mufwene, ed. *Africanisms in Afro-American Language Varieties* Athens: University of Georgia Press, 423–435.

Mufwene, Salikoko S. 1996. The development of American Englishes: Some questions from a creole genesis perspective. In Edgar W. Schneider, ed. *Focus on USA* Amsterdam: John Benjamins, 231–264.

Mufwene, Salikoko S. 2001. African-American English. In John Algeo, ed. *The Cambridge History of the English language, Vol. 4: English in North America.* Cambridge: Cambridge University Press, 291–324.

Nevalainen, Terttu and Helena Raumolin-Brunberg. 2003. *Historical Sociolinguistics: Language Change in Tudor and Stuart England.* London: Pearson Education.

Peitsara, Kirsti. 1996. Studies on the structure of the Suffolk dialect. In Juhani Klemola, Merja Kytö and Matti Rissanen, eds. *Speech, Past and Present: Studies in English Dialectology in Memory of Ossi Ihalainen.* Frankfurt am Main: Peter Lang, 284–306.

Perdue, Charles L., Thomas E. Barden and Robert K. Phillips. [1976] 1992. *Weevils in the Wheat: Interviews with Virginia Ex-Slaves.* Charlottesville: University Press of Virginia.

Pomfret, John E. and Floyd M. Shumway. 1970. *Founding the American Colonies, 1583–1660.* New York: Harper and Row.

Poplack, Shana and Sali Tagliamonte. 2001. *African American English in the Diaspora.* Oxford: Blackwell.

Poplack, Shana, James A. Walker and Rebecca Malcolmson. 2006. An English "like no other"?: Language contact and change in Quebec. *Canadian Journal of Linguistics* 51(2–3): 185–213.

Porter, Andrew Neil. 1994. *Atlas of British Overseas Expansion.* Abingdon: Routledge.

Read, Allen Walker. 1933. British recognition of American Speech in the eighteenth century. *Dialect Notes* 6: 313–334.

Read, Allen Walker. 1938. The assimilation of the speech of British immigrants in colonial America. *The Journal of English and Germanic Philology* 37: 70–79.

Rickford, John R. 1999. *African American Vernacular English.* Malden, MA: Blackwell.

Romaine, Suzanne. 2013. "It snuck in so smooth and slippery we didn't even hear it": How *snuck* snuck up on *sneaked. Anglistica* 15(1–2): 127–145.

Schneider, Edgar W. 1989. *American Earlier Black English: Morphological and Syntactic Variables.* Tuscaloosa, AL: University of Alabama Press.

Schneider, Edgar W. 2004. The English dialect heritage of the southern United States. In Raymond Hickey, ed. *Legacies of Colonial English: Studies in Transported Dialects.* Cambridge: Cambridge University Press, 262–309.

Schneider, Edgar W. 2007. *Postcolonial English: Varieties Around the World.* Cambridge: Cambridge University Press.

Schneider, Edgar W. 2013. Investigating historical variation and change in written documents: New perspectives. In J. K. Chambers and Natalie Schilling, eds. *The Handbook of Language Variation and Change* (2nd ed.). Oxford: Wiley-Blackwell, 57–81.

Schneider, Edgar W. 2015. Documenting the history of African American English: A survey and assessment of sources and results. In Jennifer Bloomquist, Lisa J. Green and Sonja L. Lanehart, eds. *The Oxford Handbook of African American Language*. Oxford: Oxford University Press, 125–139.

Schneider, Edgar W. and Michael Montgomery. 2001. On the trail of early nonstandard grammar: An electronic corpus of Southern U.S. antebellum overseers' letters. *American Speech* 76: 388–410.

Siebers, Lucia. 2015. Assessing heterogeneity. In Anita Auer, Daniel Schreier and Richard Watts, eds. *Letter Writing and Language Change* Cambridge: Cambridge University Press, 240–263.

Smitherman, Geneva. 1977. *Talkin and Testifyin: The Language of Black America*. Boston: Houghton Mifflin. (Reprint: Detroit: Wayne State University Press, 1988).

Story, G. M., W. J. Kirwin and J. D. A. Widdowson, eds. 1990 *Dictionary of Newfoundland English* (2nd ed.). Toronto: University of Toronto Press. (First edition published in 1982.)

Tagliamonte, Sali. 2006. "So cool, right?": Canadian English entering the 21st century. *Journal of Linguistics* 51(2–3): 309–332.

Tagliamonte, Sali. 2008. So different and pretty cool: Recycling intensifiers in Toronto. *English Language and Linguistics* 12(2): 361–394.

Thompson, Roger. 1994. *Mobility and Migration: East Anglian Founders of New England, 1629–1640*. Amherst: University of Massachusetts Press.

Trudgill, Peter. 1986. *Dialects in Contact*. Oxford: Blackwell.

Wakelin, Martyn. 1988. Tracing the English in American. *Righting Words* 1988(May–June): 16–23.

Warren, Paul and David Britain. 2000. Intonation and prosody in New Zealand English. In Allan Bell and Koenraad Kuiper, eds. *New Zealand English*. Amsterdam: John Benjamins, 146–172.

Wells, John C. 1982. *Accents of English*. Cambridge: Cambridge University Press.

Wolfram, Walt. 1974. The relationship of white Southern speech to vernacular Black English. *Language* 50: 498–527.

Wolfram, Walt. 2000. Issues in reconstructing earlier African-American English. *World Englishes* 19: 39–58.

Wolfram, Walt and Natalie Schilling-Estes. 1998. *American English: Dialects and Variation*. Oxford: Blackwell.

Wolfram, Walt and Erik Thomas. 2002. *The Development of African American English*. Oxford, Malden: Blackwell.

Wood, Gordon R. 1977. English language and the westward movement. In Howard R. Lamar, ed. *The Reader's Encyclopedia of the American West*, New York: Harper and Row, 349–353.

Woods, Howard B. [1979] 1999. *The Ottawa Survey of Canadian English*. Kingston: Queen's University.

9

English in the Caribbean and the Central American Rim

Michael Aceto

This chapter discusses "newer" (i.e. in the last 400 years or less) varieties of English spoken in the Caribbean, in particular the relationship between the Caribbean and Central American varieties on the western edge of the Caribbean. It also presents a short discussion of the influences that have shaped these varieties and various popular heuristics for imagining their emergence as well as a description of the geographical locations in the Caribbean where these varieties are spoken. The social contexts of their emergence are also discussed as well as a grammatical sketch pointing out similarities and differences and a discussion of several theoretical issues of relevance to the field.

9.1 Introduction

English varieties have been spoken in various locations in the Caribbean and along its Atlantic rim for approximately 400 years (e.g. in Antigua, Barbados, Jamaica, Providencia, the Miskito Coast of Nicaragua), 300 years in others (e.g. Guyana), 200 years in locations received by the British from other colonial powers (e.g. Trinidad, St Lucia, and Dominica from France), and about 100 plus years in several locations on the eastern rim of Central America (e.g. Panama, Costa Rica). There is no reason to assume that new varieties in new geographical and social spaces will not continue to emerge as anglophone West Indians continue to move about the Caribbean/Atlantic rim in search of work (see Zipp, Chapter 6, this volume).

The terms "Englishes," "English varieties," "Caribbean Englishes," or "restructured Englishes" are used here as generally synonymous with other terms found in the linguistics literature: English(-derived, -based) creoles and even dialects of English, though not without some controversy (see the concluding discussion in Section 9.5; Mufwene, 2001, 2008).

Creolists have never agreed on a typologically distinct linguistic definition in terms of common structures, features, or processes that demarcate so-called creole languages from other natural human languages (Aceto 1999a; DeGraff 1999; Mufwene 1994, 1996, 2008; cf. Bakker 2014; McWhorter 1998). Neumann-Holzschuh and Schneider (2000) also suggest that there is not even a generally accepted definition of what constitutes "restructuring" and how it is sufficiently different from the areal contact phenomena that all human languages experience to a lesser or greater degree.[1] If we assume, following Mufwene (see Mufwene, Chapter 5, this volume), that the term "creole" derives more from the sociohistorical circumstances of colonization surrounding the earliest genesis of these "new(er)" varieties in specific spaces than from any single linguistic feature (or cluster of features) that might prove to be diagnostic of this group of languages, then we have a definition that covers many of these younger languages that have emerged mostly within the crucible of European colonization.[2] Accordingly, owing to colonial competition in some areas of the Caribbean, largely between the French and British, restructured varieties of English coexist within relatively small, well-defined geographical spaces (e.g. St Lucia, Carriacou, Dominica) alongside chronologically older "creoles" that do not share the same lexical base (in these cases, French-derived forms). Even in Latin America today, the term "criolla" in Spanish means "local" or "native" to the area (e.g. *comida criolla* or "local food"). Calling locally born native languages sharing similar features "creoles" is useful and accurate in a sociohistorical sense, even though less precise in its linguistic application. Differences in syntax, phonology, and lexicon suggest that colonial varieties of a European language became, emerged into, and were changed into "creole" in situ varieties over successive generations of native speakers. The similarities suggest some sort of intervening factor(s), two of which are suggested in the literature: (1) a historically prior pidgin stage (McWhorter 1998; Bakker et al. 2011; Bakker 2014) or (2) a genetically specified factor, either the Language Bioprogram Hypothesis (LBH) à la Bickerton (1984) or the Universal Grammar (UG) à la Chomsky.

Most of these new, restructured or "creole" varieties in the Atlantic (and Pacific) regions seem to be the result of a disproportionate social/power relationship in which speakers of one language or, more commonly, a set of languages (e.g. the Kwa and Bantu languages from west and southern Africa in the Atlantic region) are dominated socially, economically, and/or militarily by politically (but, crucially, not numerically) more powerful

---

[1] Since all living languages change each time a new grammar or "idiolect" is constructed or created by a child one may view each creation of a native language grammar as a "restructured" language, to a greater or lesser degree.

[2] Of course, a "creole" with an English-derived lexical base is just one possible outcome of linguistic/cultural contact between and among peoples who originally spoke other languages. That is, there are "creoles" with French, Spanish, Portuguese, Dutch as well as Arabic, and African languages (e.g. Kikongo in Kituba) as the source of most of the basic morphemes of the language and most likely some other syntactic and phonological features as well.

speakers of another language (in this case, European languages spoken by colonists and settlers involved in the colonization of the Americas). These new varieties emerged within the crucible of European colonization and its lopsided power dynamic with many of the basic lexemes derived from the socially more powerful or dominant language.

One of the unintended consequences of European-styled slavery in the Americas is that it dislocated and brought together Africans from across 3,000 miles of West African coastline, who ordinarily would have never heard each other's languages. A multilingual context, over successive generations, encouraged the emergence of a European-derived lingua franca (or superordinate form associated with social, economic, and political power on the ground) to bridge communication gaps within and among African language communities as well as among Europeans. For example, within the anglophone context, children born into these multilingual settings grappled with whatever local varieties of English they heard from colonists, settlers (see Britain, Chapter 7, this volume), and slaves who had varying degree of familiarity with the colonial language of power. These children used forms heard in situ as the basis of the grammars they were creating, restructuring the local varieties even further, enforcing structural regularity on the second-language varieties (in the form of a pidgin or otherwise) heard by the adults in their communities, drawing on processes made available through the common genetic endowment of the language faculty for naturally uncovering grammatical units.

Some specific words and phonemes heard in Caribbean varieties are derived from substrate original languages spoken by Africans. For example, *dokunu* "dumpling" is derived from Twi, a language of Ghana (the Gold Coast during the colonial period) and is heard in several varieties in the Atlantic region; the coarticulated stops /kp/ and /gb/ heard in Saramaccan, a mixed English- and Iberian-derived language of Suriname in northern South America, are also articulated in several West African languages and conspicuously absent from any European languages spoken by colonists. However, the source(s) of any creole language's structure or syntax is a subject of some healthy debate: substrate, superstrate, and/or language universals. The substratist position has dominated Creole Studies since the 1970s (see Holm 1988/1989 and Parkvall 2000 as just two of many examples). The superstrate influence of dialects spoken by European colonists on emerging Caribbean varieties has most definitely been a persistent but minority voice (see Hancock 1994; Mufwene 2001; Niles 1980; Winford 2000). Others insist that syntactic features of these new languages are largely influenced by principles of first-language acquisition/creation (see Bickerton 1984; cf. DeGraff 1999 for a different perspective; cf. discussion in Mufwene, Chapter 5, this volume).

These processes most likely entail components of all of the above categories (substrates, superstrates, universals in first language creation, and even processes in second-language acquisition; Andersen 1983) and have played a role in shaping these varieties. For example, post-nominal /dem/ appears to be a feature added to the grammars of specific anglophone varieties several generations after the variety's genesis, namely when Africans who had similar pluralization strategies in their native languages arrived (see Section 9.4.1.8).

9.2 Geographical Locations of English Varieties of the Caribbean

Contact between colonizers speaking regional dialects of British English and subsequently colonized peoples (whether Amerindians or later dislocated African slaves and their descendants) occurred largely along coastal shipping and sailing routes during the period of European expansion and colonization in the seventeenth through the twenty-first centuries.[3] Whether we call these new European varieties dialects or creoles, all natural human languages display the effects of cultural/language contact, even if population dislocation and slavery are not significant factors in a given language's ecology (slavery is just one trigger for language contact in that it often brought speakers colliding into each other; see Lim, Chapter 4, this volume). Even if one disagrees with the assessment that these new varieties are in fact "dialects," they are the latest instantiations of colonial varieties dispersed about the globe. Every former British colonial territory in the Caribbean reveals an English variety spoken today.[4]

Why some varieties in the Caribbean are designated either a "dialect" or a "creole" is often not based on specific language features but rather on who the speakers are in terms of their ancestry (see the work of Williams 1985, 1987, 1988, 2003). Many of these languages are distributed across the islands of the Caribbean: Trinidad and Tobago, Grenada, Barbados, St Vincent, St Lucia, Dominica (Aceto 2010a), Montserrat, St Kitts and Nevis, Antigua and Barbuda (Aceto 2002), Jamaica, and the Cayman Islands. The British Virgin Islands of Tortola, Virgin Gorda, Anegada, and Jost Van Dyke contain largely undocumented varieties. The Dutch Windward Islands of Saba, St Martin, and St Eustatius (Aceto 2015) also reveal English dialects. The varieties heard on the US Virgin Islands of St Croix, St John, and St Thomas have received relatively little attention from linguists.

By contrast, English varieties have been spoken for more than a century by minority populations in several Latin American countries associated with Spanish as a national language: the Dominican Republic; Providencia and San Andres Islands (politically controlled by Colombia); and the Central American nations – Panama, Costa Rica, Nicaragua, Honduras,

---

[3] The recent neglectful treatment of Puerto Rico and US Virgin Islands as territories of the USA when it comes to hurricane relief suggest the vestiges of colonialism are still at play even in this century.

[4] Differing yet similar varieties have emerged in (nearly) all former colonial locations in Africa, Asia and the Pacific Rim in general.

and Guatemala. Puerto Rico (a territory of the USA as are the US Virgin Islands) has had local varieties of English in contact with Spanish since 1898. Relatively little research has documented these varieties. Belize is the only nation in Central America in which English varieties are widely spoken and where a standard form associated with literacy is the official language.

Central American varieties of English are related to two general trajectories. First, British colonial competition for land, cash crops, and supplies for larger colonial plantation projects gave rise to Belize; Bluefields, Nicaragua; and even the Bay Islands of Honduras to some small degree, which are as old as other British colonial locations in the Caribbean. Second, a post-emancipation pattern emerges when West Indians began to move about the Caribbean and western Atlantic rim in search of employment. Varieties along the Caribbean edge of Panama (as well as in Panama City on the Pacific) are largely related to the large-scale work project on the Panama Canal in the early twentieth century and earlier railroad projects in the nineteenth century. Immigrants from several anglophone locations (e.g. Trinidad, Jamaica) relocated and stayed in Panama after the completion of the canal in 1914. This economic/employment event lies behind the history of the restructured varieties heard in Colón and Panama City (Aceto 1995) (but does not include the many second-language speakers of English who live in Panama today). The English varieties heard on the Caribbean edge of the Bocas del Toro region as well as Puerto Limón in Costa Rica share a similar history rooted in the attraction of employment opportunities on fruit plantations and earlier railroad projects.

In situ names for these varieties vary widely. Unfortunate qualifiers such as *bad*, *flat*, *raw*, and *broken* (all such terms reflect negative speaker attitudes mistakenly and prescriptively encouraged by sites of institutional literacy) often qualify, what many speakers also simply call, English.[5] Discrete names such as *Patois*, *Guari-Guari*, and *Kokoy* are used, respectively, in Jamaica, Panama, and Dominica. In the eastern Caribbean, particularly in Antigua and Barbuda, the term "dialect" is used for the local vernacular. To my knowledge, Belize is the only anglophone location where the term "creole" is regularly applied.

9.3 Scenarios for the Emergence of English Varieties in the Atlantic Region

Some scholars (e.g. Thomason and Kaufman 1988; Bickerton 1984) insist that many new English varieties largely spoken by the descendants of Africans are "creoles" because they represent cases of what is called

---

[5] In St. Eustatius speakers call their variety, appropriately if not vaguely, simply *English*. "Just like yours," one consultant informed me.

"broken" transmission between the superstrate language and subsequently emerging English varieties. However, definitions as to what constitutes "broken" are conspicuously lacking in research models and this raises the question of how any language may come from nothing, that is, without some (cognitive or innate) models. In Suriname, a regular English source was withdrawn when the British traded that colony to the Dutch in the late seventeenth century. From then on, *Sranan*, an English-derived variety spoken today, became the source of anglophone forms for the other emerging maroon varieties *Ndyuka* and *Saramaccan*. Perhaps the case of "broken" transmission is only accurate and appropriate (if even) when access to native speakers is dramatically closed off in isolated maroon scenarios. The other former British colonies have had English varieties spoken consistently (but often among other languages too) by colonists, settlers, Amerindians, and slaves of African descent (with varying degrees of access, contact, and familiarity, of course). They have persisted as the ambient language of institutional power (and thus one source of linguistic influence) before, during, and well after the emergence of local vernaculars in all the former British colonies. Standard varieties associated with sites of institutional literacy continue to exert influence even today.

Clearly the Surinamese varieties are exceptional cases. However, they are often considered as the baseline against which other varieties are measured. Not surprisingly, other varieties that differ considerably are considered lacking in the same "creole" features even if no reliable typological inventory of features has been established. The distorted assumption that all anglophone varieties spoken by the descendants of slaves today once sounded more like one of the Surinamese creoles (or Jamaican or Guyanese, in some research paradigms) is problematic, easily falsified, and (was in the past) often asserted with little corroborating data (Dillard 1973).

Some cases of language emergence resist being classified within the plantation experience. Barbuda, an island to the north of Antigua, was populated by slaves raising food crops and manufacturing goods to supply plantations off the island. Barbudan slaves often came into contact with no more than a handful of Europeans (see Aceto 2002). In West Africa, neither Krio nor Liberian English emerged on plantations. Several anglophone varieties spoken by Africans and their descendants emerged on small-scale farms and homesteads, working alongside perhaps a handful of other Africans and alongside Europeans and their descendants in the field. The role of immigration and in-migration in search of work since emancipation in the Caribbean is an important factor for our understanding of the earliest emergence of local varieties, which still has been largely ignored by most researchers in Creole Studies.

Central American Englishes are the result of intra-Caribbean migration since the nineteenth century (Holm 1983; Aceto 1995), for example Panama, Costa Rica, and Guatemala. Even Trinidadian English is the result of immigration by a variety of ethnic groups who already spoke preexisting Englishes among other varieties such as French and Spanish. Out of this matrix, a new variety emerged. Clearly any discussion of so-called creole genesis is moot here since immigrants arrived to the respective locations in Spanish- or French-speaking areas with fully formed grammars of their respective varieties. What variety emerged over time as representative of a specific geographical and cultural space would manifest the same leveling and convergence processes like any immigrant populations speaking largely mutually intelligible varieties. I have called these varieties "immigrant varieties" (Aceto 2003).

Several former French colonial territories ultimately came under British control in the nineteenth century. In St Lucia, Dominica, Grenada, and Carriacou, a French-derived language had previously emerged. British dominion over these territories for the last two centuries has resulted in new anglophone varieties significantly influenced by the earlier French varieties, which are declining in terms of speaker numbers (see Garrett 1999, 2003 for the case of St Lucia). In these locations, the emergence of English varieties has been significantly influenced by institutional sites of literacy where Bajan teachers modeled Bajan-like forms for students (see Aceto 2010a for the case of Dominica).

European Anglo-Caribbean varieties (i.e. those varieties spoken mostly among the descendants of Irish, Scots, and English colonists and settlers) have been neglected in most research paradigms except for the work of Williams (1985, 1987, 1988, 2003). These Englishes (rarely, if ever, called "creoles"), largely spoken by Euro-Caribbeans on Saba, Bequia, the Cayman Islands, Barbados, and Anguilla (see Williams 2003), may shed light on the European-derived component heard by Africans or Afro-Caribbeans who worked alongside indentured servants (and often were treated no differently than slaves), colonists, and settlers.

9.4 Generalized Basic Features

This section provides a brief generalized grammatical and phonological sketch of restructured Caribbean varieties (though, despite general similarities, it reveals synchronic differences in terms of lexicon, phonology, morphology, and syntax). Features presented here are not exclusively associated with any specific variety (i.e. from Jamaican, often representative of the western varieties, or Guyanese, often representative of the eastern varieties) but a synthesis of possible features based on personal research in Panama, Barbuda, St Eustatius, and Dominica and my published works unless otherwise stated. This treatment does not in any way pretend to be exhaustive. For syntactic features associated with specific varieties, including the Surinamese creoles (ignored here), readers should consult the survey presented in Hancock (1987). For a discussion of accent variation in the Atlantic varieties, see Wells (1982).

The varieties of English heard by Africans and their descendants were originally regional, social, and ethnic dialects of British spoken in the seventeenth through the nineteenth centuries. From a diachronic perspective, English-derived Caribbean varieties are more British-oriented in not only their histories but especially their phonologies, though, in the last century, American and Canadian influence is documented (Van Herk 2003).

Initially, anglophone forms with lingua franca functions were acquired as second-language varieties by adults speaking African languages. In subsequent generations, these forms would have been embedded in first-language varieties of English. These were created and expanded by children and at the same time influenced by the second-language forms spoken by adults. The two stages – second-language forms spoken by adults and subsequent nativization by children – may also have been influenced by whatever anglophone forms were heard along the western coast of Africa among slave forts or at subsequent Caribbean entrepôts as slaves were distributed to onward buyers or by whatever immigration patterns occurred locally. Both St Kitts and Nevis (Baker and Bruyn 1998) and St Eustatius (Aceto 2015) had this function as sources of slaves for onward destination in the Americas. Whether pidgin forms and/or second-language varieties emerged in these locations is a matter of debate.

The Caribbean regions are generally divided into western and eastern varieties on the basis of comparative phonology and syntax (see Holm 1988–1989: 445; Wells 1982, 1987; Le Page 1957–8; Hancock 1987). However, the grounds for this division are largely abstract and impressionistic since few specific features are exclusively heard in one region but not in the other (see Section 9.5.3). Creolists are often comfortable with the (highly questionable) assumption that earlier Anglophone Caribbean varieties were monolithic and that contemporary synchronic variation is a more recent (i.e. post-emancipation) phenomenon. Whether the overlapping patterns between eastern and western varieties represent parallel developments or are due to intra-Caribbean migration is an open topic for future research (however, it is a bundle of features rather than individual structures that are diagnostic of typological affiliations).

9.4.1 Syntax

9.4.1.1 Copula

The verbal complex has received significant attention from linguists (see Winford 1993) and the form and distribution of the copula have often been central here. The three basic functions of the copula (attributive, locative, nominal) are heard in the following forms.

Attributive constructions:

/ʃi de gʊd/, /ʃi aarait/, /ʃi iz gʊd/ "she's good, she's alright, she's doing fine"

The verb /de/ or /iz/ is often the copula form but no overt verb may appear with only a predicate adjective appearing.

The locative form is often /de/ as in:

/we im de/, /we im iz/, "where is she/he/it?"

Inversion between the copula and the noun is not required for interrogatives in these varieties. Rising intonation alone often indicates questions.

The nominal form of the copula displays /a/, /iz/, /bi/, and no overt realization at all:

/ʃi a mi sista/, /ʃi iz mi sista/, /ʃi bi mi sista/, /ʃi mi sista/ "she's my sister"

9.4.1.2   Past

The past tense marker, as is the case with most overt grammatical markers in Caribbean varieties is a discrete, free morpheme before the main verb of a clause. Unmarked non-stative (or dynamic) verbs often have a [+past] interpretation, e.g. /mi iit aaredi/ "I ate already." Nonetheless, both stative and non-stative verbs may be preverbally marked [+past] with a range of forms. Depending on the context, an utterance may be interpreted as conveying both simple past and what is sometimes called the past perfect:

/mi bin iit/, /mi woz iit/, /mi di(d) iit/, /mi min iit/ "I have eaten"
(or even "I ate")

The utterance /mi dʌn iit/ with the completive marker /dʌn/ would more closely match "I already ate, I have already eaten, I'm done eating." This is heard in Southern American English as well as in nearly all varieties of Caribbean English.

9.4.1.3   Future

The preverbal future marker is some reflex of either /go/, /a go/, /goin/, or sometimes /wi/ < *will*:

/dem go dans/, /dem wi dans/, /dem gwain dans/, /dem goin dans/, /dem a go dans/ and even /dem wan dans/
"They're going to dance."

In the last instance, the future marker *wan* seems to be a grammaticalized form of the verb *want*. The form *gwain* is often associated with the western Caribbean and is heard robustly there.

9.4.1.4   Progressive Aspect

The preverbal markers /de/, /da/ or /a/ as well as the bound morphological suffix /-in/ are those features most commonly associated with progressive aspect in Anglophone Caribbean varieties:

/di gyal a kaal yu/, /di gyal de kaal yu/, /di gyal kaalin yu/, "The girl's calling you"

9.4.1.5 Pronouns

Most pronouns below take subject, object, and possessive functions, with the following exceptions: both /ai/ and /a/ are only subject pronouns; /ar/ "her" is an object pronoun with exclusive reference to females; /om/ may refer to "him/her/it" in object position (largely limited to the eastern Caribbean). The pronoun /(h)im/ indicates males or females or even nonhuman referents in either subject or object position. The plural pronouns /aayu/ and /aawi/ are heard in the eastern Caribbean, while /unu/ is more common in western varieties. An important exception is Barbados, which reveals a reflex of /unu/.

The use of the same pronoun with dual distributions as both subjects and objects as well as possessive pronouns is illustrated by the following:

/dem no stie laik dem/ "They're not like them"
/ʃi doz sii ʃi sista everi en da wik/ "She sees her sister every weekend"

The common habitual marker /doz/ is often associated with eastern varieties. Many Caribbean varieties lack this overt distinction and instead rely on /de/ (see Section 9.4.1.4) to mark this function or simply a bare verb marked by an adverbial (e.g. every day, every week).

For those researchers who insist that lexemes from the superstrate were "creolized" with little or no grammatical information, the pronoun set is problematic since /unu/ is the only pronoun not derived from a superstrate source. Its appearance in the Jamaican texts, along with post-nominal *dem* as a plural marker occurring only in the nineteenth century, suggests it is a relatively late addition to the grammar or reflects lacunae in the earlier texts (Lalla and D'Costa 1990: 78).

9.4.1.6 Possession

Possession is solely marked by word order, not by inflectional morphology:

/mi brada uman de de/ "My brother's wife/woman is/was there"

Table 9.1 *Pronouns in Caribbean English*

	Singular	Plural
1st	/mi/, /a, ai/ (subject only)	/wi, aawi/
2nd	/yu/	/unu, aayu, yaal/
3rd	/(h)i(m)/ 'he, she, it'	/de, dem/
	/ʃi/, /ar/ 'she' (object)	
	/om, am/ 'he, she it' (object)	
	/i(t)/	

9.4.1.7 Infinitival Marker

Anglophone Caribbean varieties often mark infinitives with some reflex of *for*, /fu/ or /fi/:

/unu hafu du it/ "You (pl.) have to do it."
/a fiil fi smuok/, "I feel like smoking."

The marker *to* is used as well.

9.4.1.8 Pluralization

Pluralization is most often marked by a post-nominal /dem/ rather than a bound inflectional morpheme (the marker may occur in pre-nominal position as well), unless a number of more than one has been established previously within the phrase or clause:

/di daag dem/ "the dogs"
/di daag an dem/ "the dogs (and the other dogs)"
/dem daag/ "those dogs"
(cf. /di tʃri daag/ "the three dogs," in which no redundant plural marker is necessary once a plural number has been established.)

Nouns like "people" and "children," which aren't usually pluralized in other varieties of English, are often pluralized in Caribbean Englishes:

/hau di pipl dem trai fi liv/ "How do the people manage to live?"

9.4.1.9 Negation

Negation in the Anglophone Caribbean is designated by a preverbal negator, which is usually some reflex of "no," "not," or "never":

/ʃi no siŋ/, /ʃi na(t) siŋ/, /ʃi neva siŋ/ "she didn't sing"

Other negators are derived from "don't" and "ain't":

/ʃi duon iit/, /ʃi en iit/ "she didn't eat"

9.4.1.10 Serial verbs

One of the most heavily researched areas of English varieties of the Caribbean (though, again, this feature is not structurally diagnostic) is serial verb constructions (see Winford 1993). Verbs may occur serially with no intervening coordinator or infinitival marker:

/dem gaan iit/, "They went to eat/they went and ate."
/yu waan paas di die wi mi/, "Do you want to spend the day with me?"

Many other dialects of English reveal similar constructions, especially with imperative forms with motion verbs: "Come bring me my food" and "Go get my car."

9.4.2 Lexicon

An English-derived or English-based variety implies that the greatest part of its everyday vocabulary was drawn from colonial varieties of English spoken between the seventeenth and twentieth centuries (see Hancock 1994; Mufwene 2001; Niles 1980; Winford 2000). Consequently, Caribbean varieties maintain archaic words such as:

/krabit/ "mean, disagreeable, rough, cruel" (can be traced to Old English and to more recent usage in Scotland)
/fieba/ (< favor) "to resemble" (e.g. /ʃi fieba yu/ "she resembles you"; is also heard robustly in the American South)
/beks/ (< vex) "to anger" (e.g. /wa mek yu beks so/ "Why are you so angry?")
/beg/ "to ask" (e.g. /a wan beg yu wan tiŋ/ "I want to ask you something") which is preserved in many other English dialects in the frozen expression "I beg your pardon."

Other lexemes reflect the historical usage of sailor jargon, which arguably influenced passengers (slaves, colonists, settlers, immigrants) and thus the varieties that emerged at these destinations in the Americas:

/haal/ (< haul) "to pull"
/gyali/ (< galley) "the kitchen of any household"

African-language–derived words are also found in the lexicon of Caribbean English varieties. More than a few words derive from Twi, a language spoken in Ghana or the Lower Guinea Coast (see Aceto 1999b):

/koŋgosa/ "gossip"
/fufu/ "common food of yam and plantains"
/mumu/ "dull, dumb, silent"
/potopoto/ "mud, muddy" are common but there are many others.

Other African languages are represented as well: /dʒuk/ "to stab, to poke, to have sex with" appears to be from Fulani, a language spoken in Nigeria among other locations on the Guinea Coast.

The influence of African words goes beyond borrowing and many expressions in the Caribbean seem to be calques or word-for-word translations: *big-eye* "greedy" and *day-clean* "daybreak," for example, have a number of correspondences with languages spoken on the Guinea Coast.

9.4.3 Morphology

It is often claimed that creoles display few (if any) bound morphemes. McWhorter (1998: 792) qualifies his claim by stating that creole languages rarely have more than one or two inflectional affixes. Regardless of his generalization, one can find historical attestations of /-in/ < -ing as progressive marker attached to verbs, /-a/ < -er as a comparative marker attached to adjectives, and /-is/ < -*est* as a superlative marker also attached to adjectives (see Lalla and D'Costa 1990). The standard practice in Creoles Studies is to dismiss such textual examples as evidence of earlier "decreolization." Nonetheless, the relative lack of inflectional morphology is not diagnostic of creoles since non-creole languages may reveal few inflectional affixes as well, e.g. Mandarin, and Modern English has only eight.

In the Anglophone Caribbean, bound morphology includes progressive /-in/, e.g. /kaalin/ "calling," /go/ + /-in/, which may also function as future marker, respectively:

/mama kaalin me/, "Mama is calling me"
and /mi goin iit/, "I'm going to eat."

Comparative and superlative inflections are commonly formed with inflections as well: /fas(t)a/ (< fast + -er) "faster" and /fastIs/ "fastest."

Derivational forms also make use of bound morphemes /wikidnis/ (< wicked + -ness). These bound morphemes (among others) are robust in the Anglophone Caribbean and they are part of the grammars of nearly all varieties (standard and vernacular alike) of English today. There is no evidence that Jamaican or Gullah ever had comparative or superlative forms different from, for example, *big/biga/bigis*.[6]

Many Caribbean Englishes have also created phrasal verbs not heard in contributing dialects of British English nor in British or American varieties today: *kiss up* "to kiss or make out," *wet up* "to soak"; cf. with *show up* "to appear," *cook up* "to cook" heard in other dialects today.

9.4.4 Phonology

This section is largely based on Holm (1988–1989), Wells (1982), and Aceto and Williams (2003), various specific articles referenced in this section, and the author's own notes from fieldwork.

9.4.4.1 Vowels

Long vowels. Off-glides in [ei] and [ou] diphthongs are not common in the eastern Caribbean, corresponding to [e:] and [o:]. However, Childs, Reaser, and Wolfram (2003) suggest that in some Bahamian communities [ei] can be heard, perhaps due to influence from the USA. In the Leeward Islands, specifically Montserrat (Wells 1982: 587), words that historically had long vowels have been shortened and have no off-glides, e.g. /de/ "day." There are on-glides in many western Caribbean varieties, /fies/ "face" and /guot/ "goat."

Unreduced vowels. Caribbean varieties of English often display a preference for unreduced vowels, e.g. /abɪlɪtɪ/ "ability" and /tawil/ "towel,"

---

[6] I'm indebted to Ian Hancock for pointing this out.

where other dialects have a schwa. Many varieties in the eastern Caribbean (except Bajan) lack mid-central vowels.

Other vowels. The low front vowel /æ/ is often realized further back as /aː/ /kyat/ "cat." There is often an off-glide after velar consonants and before this vowel, e.g. /gyaadin/ "garden." However, some varieties of English in the Turks and Caicos (as well as Bermuda) do have /æ/.

There are also remnant forms due to the preservation of older regional British pronunciations, e.g. /spail/ "spoil," /bail/ "boil," especially in the western Caribbean.

9.4.4.2 Consonants

Rhoticity. Except for varieties of English in Barbados, and to some degree in Jamaica and Guyana, postvocalic /r/ is uncommon. Bajan English is recognized by full rhoticity at all levels of society. Other dialect areas of the Caribbean are non-rhotic after vowels (e.g. Trinidad, the Bahamas), while others are highly variable (e.g. Guyana). In the non-rhotic dialects, additional phonemes are often created, e.g. /nea/ "near," /foa/ "four."

/v/-/w/ merger. Many dialects of Caribbean English (e.g. Bahamian, Bermudan, Vincentian) may alternate [w], [β] (the voiced bilabial fricative) or [ʋ] (the voiced labiodental approximate) for words with initial /v/, e.g. [wɪlidʒ] "village." This could be related to contributing dialect varieties spoken by colonists in the eighteenth century that contain this same alternation (e.g. Cockney, dialects from the southwest or Cornish regions of England) or possibly to early speakers of African languages. Some communities may reveal /b/ where other varieties display /v/, e.g. /bɛks/, "angry," /riba/ "river."

Word-initial /h/. In the Leeward Islands (Antigua, Barbuda, St Kitts and Nevis, Montserrat, Anguilla), unlike in Jamaican and other western varieties, /h/ is often realized at the beginnings of words. So-called /h/-dropping or deletion is common in Jamaica and the Bahamas. It also occurs in British Cockney, which is often cited as the source of this feature. In dialects with this feature, new homophones are sometimes created, e.g. /iɛr/ "hair/air," / uol/ "whole," /aaf/ "half." On the other hand, dialects with "h-dropping" often have inserted /h/ (or /w/), e.g. /heg/ "egg," /wogli/ "ugly."

Th-stopping. The neutralization of /θ/ and /ð/ as /t/ and /d/ (e.g. /tiŋ/ "thing" and /fada/ "father") is common. Any dialect with this feature creates new homonyms, e.g. /tɪn/ "thin-tin," /fet/ "faith-fate," /do/ "though-dough," /brid/ "breathe-breed," /triː/ "three-tree," /tru/ "through-true." Words with an /r/ following the alveolar stop are often palatized, e.g. [tʃrii] "three," [tʃru] "true." In Kokoy, a variety spoken in Dominica, /θ/ often corresponds to /f/ not /t/, e.g. /fri/ "three," /fru/ "through" (Aceto 2010a). In St Eustatius, many speakers display both interdental fricatives and stops (Aceto 2015). Cutler

(2003) and Williams (2003) make similar observations about the English varieties spoken on Grand Turk Island and Anguilla.

Consonant clusters. In many Caribbean varieties, word-final /t/ and /d/ preceded by an obstruent in clusters is often not realized, e.g. / lɛf / "left," /nɛs/ "nest," /ak/ "act," /sɛn/ "send," /bɪl/ "build." However, word-final clusters of nasal and a voiceless consonant are stable, e.g. /lamp/ "lamp," /tɛnt/ "tenttenth," /bank/ "bank." In rhotic dialects, clusters in codas are also realized in combination with liquids, e.g. /mɪlk/ "milk," /ʃɛlf/ "shelf," /part/ "part," /hard/ "hard." Other consonant cluster combinations occur freely, e.g. /aks/ "ask," /baks/ "box," /sɪks/ "six." In some varieties, word-initial clusters are dispreferred, e.g. /taat/ "start," /tan/ "stand," /tap/ "stop."

9.5 Discussion and Conclusions

By means of a general discussion and to embed the feature presentation, I would like to briefly take up some theoretical issues that have emerged from the analysis of Caribbean English. I will discuss the status of creoles, the nature of variation in the form of continua, and the uniqueness of features attributed to creoles.

9.5.1 Creoles or Dialects?

The first one is whether Creole Studies represents a separate field from Dialect Studies in general. Put differently: Is it necessary to distinguish "creoles" as separate from "dialects" in the sense referred to above (see Hickey, Chapter 2; Schreier, Chapter 17, this volume)? Recent volumes in English dialectology and creoles (Hickey 2014 is just one example; this case is expanded on in Section 9.5.2) demonstrate that there are very few, if any, concepts (except perhaps the idiosyncratic and largely falsified terms such as *decreolization* and *recreolization*)[7] used in Creole Studies that cannot be accurately applied to speech communities elsewhere, regardless of their contact history. Terms that emerged while first studying "marginal" languages (à la Reinecke 1937 in terms of socioeconomic, political, and military power) were a first step toward validation as natural, native languages and the usefulness of these terms and their application *outside* of Creole Studies make them more vital and influential (e.g. the abstractions: basilect, acrolect).

Bakker et al. (2011) insists that so-called creoles are typologically distinct ("typologically similar" would probably be uncontroversial); yet the conclusions of that work seem unfalsifiable under any circumstances, at least in the usual Popperian (Popper 1984) sense. Bakker et al. (2011: 19) admit

---

[7] How *creolization* is different from language emergence in general has never been clearly articulated except to insist on *broken transmission* with little or no evidence.

that "it is not possible to specify which individual features are responsible for the clusterings." Viewing "dialects" and "creoles" as separate does not seem to be advantageous, though it does make it more rarified and exotic (and the "cult of uniqueness" is very seductive and pervasive in academia; see Aceto 2010b: 281) – but marginalization is the peril when separating Creole Studies from the study of other vernaculars.

What would be the loss to Creole Studies today if it were unified with Dialect Studies? The varieties spoken historically by the ancestors involved in colonizing the Americas (both those speaking African languages and those speaking European languages) as spoken by their descendants today are fascinating not only because of what linguists can infer about socio-historical events and cognitive patterns as reflected in language. The end result of first-language emergence and preceding earlier varieties spoken as non-native varieties by adults reflect the infinitely creative ways in which humans organize, process, and use language. Connecting, for example, Guari-guari or Kokoy (or any English-derived variety) as one possible quantum (i.e. statistically probable) output among other possibilities (and many other lexically related varieties have been realized by other speech communities) creates a web of interconnected varieties that, though different from each other, exemplifies that all languages are connected if data allow sufficient time depth. If creoles are organic, naturally occurring varieties, then they must be connected historically to other varieties.

In some creole-speaking areas like Haiti, nearly every inhabitant speaks *Kreyol*. This has pragmatic and political consequences as speakers are trying to maintain a kind of linguistic distance from "French," which they perceive as the language with a standard that emerged out of Paris and its environments. This breaks with the folk idea that it is merely a "deviant" variety of "real" French. This point is important for political and educational bodies who make decisions for implementing ortho-graphic standards and language.

I am not only proposing a traditional diachronic view of eastern and western varieties for understanding how varieties have changed in the last several centuries. This is useful but what we should highlight is that, for a group of "new" varieties, whether they are called Englishes, dialects, or creoles, it seems odd that linguists are still insisting that they came mostly from "nothing" (i.e. that "broken transmission" is responsible). I am skep-tical as to whether only the phonetic forms of free morphemes survive in creole languages (but none of the grammatical meanings associated with function words or bound morphemes) or whether a language should be more influenced by a set of genetically predetermined parameters à la Chomsky or Bickerton, but not from the varieties spoken by colonists, settlers, overseers, straw bosses, and so on, with whom the subordinated masses interacted with and whose vernaculars they maintained, changed, and innovated, ultimately making them their own. This perspective is not to dismiss the influence of the first languages spoken by the earliest speakers of a given variety, as it emerged in situ and their second-language approximations (whether pidgins or otherwise) that arose out of these earliest contacts. Certainly there has been a swing back to dialectology, yet mostly for African American English (AAE; see Schneider 1989; Wolfram and Thomas 2002). In previous decades, creolists struggled hard to fit AAE into a creole paradigm (see Dillard 1973; Baugh 1983) but the evidence was so slight that the hypothesis that AAE used to be more creole-like, having decreolized subsequently, has now mostly been abandoned.

9.5.2 Decreolization and Continua

Related to the unifying issue is the second question, namely whether it is necessary for Creole Studies to have its own unique terminology. Are these terms necessary? The short answer is no, but one notices that some of the terms are now applied beyond creole-speaking communities, so perhaps the generation and initial usage of unique terms (decreolization, continuum) have some usefulness. Mufwene (2008) makes the case that Creole Studies should be used to inform other linguistic histories since the colonial artifacts shedding light on language emergence are often much richer than language varieties going back 1,000 years or more. Yet the trend is for Creole Studies and the dynamics of language contact to be considered as exceptional cases rather than regular examples.

The concept of *decreolization* deserves special attention here. It is the result of a (highly questionable) assumption that uniformity was once the norm among anglophone colonial varieties and that any differences in varieties today are the result of a shift toward the norms of the institutional standard associated with literacy. Clearly these institutional norms play a role in language contact, variation, and change, especially among speakers of related dialects, but any human language has options for variation and change unrelated to such pressures (see Aceto 1999a; Satyanath 2006). Even if the effects of so-called decreolization could be rigorously distinguished from what is regular contact and variation (and possibly shift), which all languages exhibit everywhere (whether "creoles" or not), unquestioned acceptance of this concept often obscures the fact that all living languages vary and change, whether it be in the direction of the lexically related variety associated with institutional literacy or not. Speakers cannot undo "creolization" (even if that were clearly understood as a linguistic process), so consequently we have no examples of "recreolization," except as circularly applied to languages classified as *creoles*. Why should normal language change in the Caribbean be considered unique from all other human languages? (see Mufwene, Chapter 5, this volume). There seems no justification for a new (and problematic) term like *decreolization* that has never been coherently defined.

Creolists in the 1970s and 1980s used to insist that the variation of the purported post-creole continuum was due to "decreolization," perceived as a unilateral force affecting all Caribbean Englishes. Once this strong view of decreolization was questioned and criticized with data that showed change not to be unidirectional, creolists began to largely reject the concept of decreolization but still held on to the useful notion of "continuum" (even if decreolization was *the* explanatory factor). Le Page (1998: 91) makes several points on the subject of the continuum: "I came to realize – too late, unfortunately, to stop David DeCamp and others from taking up the 'continuum' model – that it was a false representation." Le Page also writes that DeCamp wrote him that he "regretted the concept had been taken up with such enthusiasm, since he [DeCamp] had never found that it could provide an account of more than 30% of his Jamaican data" (p. 92). The insistence by many creolists that something unique and qualitatively different from the rest of the language-speaking world (both past and present) occurred is troubling. Le Page (1998: 48) is worth quoting again:

> I have come to realize more and more the extent to which academics, as they become authorities on subjects, are at the same time creating the universe which they study, the subject matter of their discourse. They evolve their own perceptual framework and then fill it with their percepts.

"Decreolization" as an expired term in the field should be used to remind linguists that all living languages change and that there are dangers in innovating unique terms exclusively for narrowly examined speech communities, except as a first step in understanding languages that had received little attention from linguists until the last several decades.

Variation is built into all communities. Early creolists like David DeCamp and R. B. Le Page (among others) prompted the move away from the impossibility of the early Chomskyan theoretical paradigm that "Linguistic theory is concerned primarily with an ideal speaker-listener in a completely homogeneous speech community" (Chomsky 1965: 3). Le Page (1998: 157) describes this premise as "inherently absurd" merely because it has never existed as a precondition among humans, though hiving off messy natural variation is a useful strategy for focusing exclusively on cognitive features of language. Yet that does not mean that so-called creole languages necessarily exhibit more variation than other natural languages. It must be remembered that the Jamaican variety found in Bailey (1966) represented an abstract bundle of features (i.e. the bundle is abstract, not any individual feature) associated with the so-called basilect, and DeCamp (1971) considered this type of abstraction to be a necessary first step in understanding variation in creole-speaking communities.

This abstraction suggests very strongly that, both from a diachronic and from a synchronic perspective, there have always been few if any speakers of the purported "basilect" with its associated features (see Section 9.5.3); in other words, few individual speakers can be said to have ever exclusively displayed all the features of the "basilect." The reification "basilect" is an abstract compilation of all the features that are considered typologically as the furthest away from standard or metropolitan English varieties, often associated with institutional literacy in the last two centuries. Furthermore, any human language, including so-called creole languages, can change in ways left unexplored by the assumptions of the creole continuum, even if the effects of internally induced change have been left largely unexplored by researchers studying creole-speaking societies (see Aceto 1999a). In addition, some types of change, whether they are externally or internally motivated, may occur that do not resemble metropolitan varieties of English. I am in complete agreement with Mufwene (2008), who argues that so-called creole languages are the latest stage of the dispersal of a subgroup of the Indo-European family of languages that began 10,000–12,000 years ago. In other words, the English-derived, French-derived, and so on varieties spoken in the Americas, Africa, and Asia are "daughters" (and perhaps even *dialects*, as objectionable as that may be to some) of their lexifiers in a similar manner that French and Spanish, for example, are "daughters" of the Vulgar Latin varieties spoken by the Romans in the administration of their empire in different epochs and geographical spaces.

The "family" or "mother-daughter" metaphor for the descent of one language from another is simplistic and one-dimensional (as all metaphors are) in that it only considers a single language as influencing the newer "offspring" language. This partial or incomplete view as to the history of any specific variety reminds us that every language has what Mufwene (2008: 54) calls its own specific language ecology (i.e. the history of who came into contact with whom, the linguistic variants available, whatever social factors are attached to those variants, as well as the specific ethnographic circumstances). "Languages evolve in non-uniform ways" (p. 14), so *decreolization* is not necessary for explanation.

Hickey (2014) uses terms commonly used in creole across research in dialectology and linguistics in general. The purported "creole" continuum (as exclusively applied to anglophone communities in the Caribbean) and its associated terms "basilect" and so on are applied well beyond the Caribbean or traditional areas associated with creole languages. For example, the entry for Singaporean English (p. 85) reveals "a continuum of varieties found in Singapore, the acrolectal of which is fairly close to general English." There is a "continuum of Scottish Standard English to Scots, which are very different from forms to the south in England" (p. 52; see also p. 276 and the entry for "Orkney and Shetland English as well" [p. 225]). Hickey also writes of "basilectal English" (p. 170) in regards to varieties spoken in India as well as in the entry for "Chicano English" (p. 66). The entry for "continuum" (p. 79) makes no mention of either pidgins or creoles: "A scale on which one can locate varieties ranging from a strongly vernacular to a near-standard form of a language." Hickey writes that varieties of English that are listed individually are not always clearly separated from each other (p. vii). It is more common for speakers to position themselves on a continuum whose extremes are represented by the most vernacular and the least vernacular forms of their English. Indeed, many speakers deliberately move along this continuum depending on the nature or purpose of a specific situation.

Not only does Hickey make clear that this applies to all varieties in his dictionary, not just so-called creoles, but one could easily take his useful generalization one small step further and apply it to all human languages, perhaps especially those in some kind of sustained contact with a literacy-based institutional standard whether or not the varieties in question are lexically related or not.

If creolists want to demonstrate through data that there is *more* variation in the Anglophone Caribbean than other communities throughout the world that may be possible (but doubtful): The "creole continuum" has always assumed there is a vague, unspecified degree of quantitative and qualitative variation in the Caribbean that is not heard elsewhere in the language-speaking world. This hypothesis seems easily falsified from any number of directions, especially when examining rural and isolated language varieties in which access to institutional literacy is mostly encountered during hours at school and in media, where poverty is endemic, and literacy is largely a practice that students are forced to engage in while participating in these same institutions.

Mufwene (2014: 158) points out that scholars such as DeGraff have asserted that Caribbean creoles should be historically grouped with their lexifier without calling them dialects of the same language. That is, they should be seen as part of the latest (in the last 500 years) distribution (or descent) of this subfamily (DeGraff's points are in relation to Haitian vis-à-vis French). Mufwene then states that "this position does not entail that Haitian Creole is a 'dialect' of French" (p. 158). But why not? He provides no reasons for suggesting that *dialect* should not be a coherent term for designating a regional, ethnic, or socially constructed variety of a language. He then goes on to state "Haitian Creole is as much a descendant of nonstandard French as French is accepted to be a daughter of Vulgar Latin" (p. 158). My feeling is that his equivocating on the term "dialect" has more to do with pragmatic issues regarding language planning in Haiti (described in Section 9.5.1) than linguistic issues.

9.5.3 Feature Uniqueness

The third and last question addressed here is whether creoles have their own unique features. The answer seems to be negative. Even Bakker (2014: 189), one of the biggest proponents of creole typology, states:

> Is there a single structural feature that is shared by all creoles? No, there is
> not a single one. In fact, some of the supposedly typical traits, such as
> serial verbs, are only found in a minority. Is there a single structural
> feature that is found in any one creole, or a set of creoles, that is not
> found in a non-creole? Nil. None has been discovered. Creoles are perfectly
> ordinary languages, in line with the languages of the world.

Other researchers have made similar observations. Michaelis (2000: 163)
makes clear that "there are restructuring processes in creole languages
that do not differ in principle from diachronic change in non-creole languages." Rizzi (1999: 466) states: "creole languages do not look different
from other natural languages in any qualitative sense. We may find, at
most, a relatively high concentration of unmarked options." Perhaps these
"unmarked options" could explain the clustering that Bakker is so unable
to identify specifically. Bakker (2014: 189) goes on to suggest, "if a language
has no tense-aspect inflection and if it has an indefinite article [derived]
from 'one', it is very likely a creole language." Yet many of the Romance
languages have forms such as *un homme*, *un hombre*, *un uomo*, and so on,
which seem to blur the distinction between "a man" and "one man" so
perhaps even that feature may have to be revised.[8]

A study of immigrant varieties of Caribbean Englishes in particular such
as Panamanian and Costa Rican reminds creolists that speakers familiar
with these varieties have often been mobile, especially during but not
limited to post-emancipation eras (see also Britain, Chapter 7, this
volume). Thus, when we discuss issues such as creole genesis, we must
be careful since these languages have changed (as all living grammars have
changed) since their earliest emergence. The earliest periods of so-called
creole genesis are lost. There is a suggestion that "ontogeny recapitulates
phylogeny," which is an often falsified or more nuanced notion in biology
and still leaves unquestioned whether any one group of languages offers
a *unique* insight into the human species and its ability to create and uncover
meaningful units of language. Bickerton's Language Bioprogram
Hypothesis sounds little different from Chomsky's notion of Universal
Grammar. Yet neither are essential theories for understanding the nature
of the issues discussed here except insofar as all humans have a species-
specific brain/mind that is prespecified for uncovering the meaningful
units of grammar exposed to as a child with idiolectal creativity (an ability
that is likely genetically specified even if related to other cognitive abilities; see Evans 2014) folded in as well. All living languages are approximations of the approximations that came before them.

References

---

[8] I am indebted again to Ian Hancock for making this point as well.

Aceto, Michael. 1995. Variation in a secret Creole language of Panama. *Language in Society 24*: 537–560.

Aceto, Michael. 1999a. Looking beyond decreolization as an explanatory model of language change in Creole-speaking communities. *Journal of Pidgin and Creole Languages 14*: 93–119.

Aceto, Michael. 1999b. The Gold Coast contribution to the Atlantic English creoles. In M. Huber and M. Parkvall, eds. *Spreading the Word: The Issue of Diffusion among the Atlantic Creoles* (Westminster Creolistics Series 6). London: University of Westminster Press, 69–80.

Aceto, Michael. 2002. Barbudan Creole English: Its history and some grammatical features. *English World-Wide 23*: 223–250.

Aceto, Michael. 2003. What are creole languages? An alternative approach to the Anglophone Atlantic World with special emphasis on Barbudan Creole English. In Michael Aceto and Jeffrey P. Williams, eds. *Contact Englishes of the Eastern Caribbean* (Varieties of English around the World Series). Amsterdam: John Benjamins, 121–140.

Aceto, Michael. 2010a. Dominican Kokoy. In D. Schreier, P. Trudgill, E. W. Schneider, and J. P. Williams, eds. *The Lesser-Known Varieties of English: An Introduction* (Studies in English Language Series). Cambridge: Cambridge University Press, 171–194.

Aceto, Michael. 2010b. Review of Salikoko Mufwene. Language Evolution: Contact, competition and change (London, New York: Continuum International Publishing Group, 2008). *Language in Society 39*: 276–281.

Aceto, Michael. 2015. St. Eustatius English. In D. Schreier, P. Trudgill, E. W. Schneider, and J. P. Williams, eds. *The Lesser-Known Varieties of English*, Vol. 2. (Studies in English Language Series). Cambridge: Cambridge University Press, 165–197.

Aceto, Michael and Jeffrey P. Williams, eds. *Contact Englishes of the Eastern Caribbean* (Varieties of English around the World Series). Amsterdam: John Benjamins.

Andersen, Roger, ed. 1983. *Pidginization and Creolization as Language Acquisition*. Rowley, MA: Newbury House.

Bailey, Beryl L. 1966. *Jamaican Creole Syntax: A Transformational Approach*. Cambridge: Cambridge University Press.

Baker, Philip and Adrienne Bruyn, eds. 1998. *St Kitts and the Atlantic Creoles: The Texts of Samuel Augustus Mathews in Perspective* (Westminster Creolistics Series 4). London: University of Westminster Press.

Bakker, Peter. 2014. Creolistics: Back to square one? *Journal of Pidgin and Creole Languages 29*: 177–194.

Bakker, Peter, Aymeric Daval-Markussen, Mikael Parkvall and Ingo Plag. 2011. Creoles are typologically distinct from non-creoles. *Journal of Pidgin and Creole Languages 26*: 5–42.

Baugh, John. 1983. *Black Street Speech: Its History Structure and Survival*. Austin: The University of Texas Press.

Bickerton, Derek. 1984. The Language Bioprogram Hypothesis. *The Behavioral and Brain Sciences 7*: 173–221.

Childs, Becky, Jeffrey Reaser and Walt Wolfram. 2003. Defining ethnic varieties in the Bahamas: Phonological accommodation in Black and White enclave communities. In Michael Aceto and Jeffrey P. Williams, eds. *Contact Englishes of the Eastern Caribbean* (Varieties of English around the World Series). Amsterdam: John Benjamins, 1–28.

Chomsky, Noam. 1965. *Aspects of the Theory of Syntax*. Cambridge, MA: MIT Press.

Cutler, Cecilia. 2003. English in the Turks and Caicos Islands: A look at Grand Turk. In Michael Aceto and Jeffrey P. Williams, eds. *Contact Englishes of the Eastern Caribbean* (Varieties of English around the World Series). Amsterdam: John Benjamins, 51–80.

DeCamp, David. 1971. Toward a generative analysis of the post-creole continuum. In Dell Hymes, ed. *Pidginization and Creolization of Languages*. Cambridge: Cambridge University Press, 349–370.

DeGraff, Michel, ed. 1999. *Language Creation and Language Change: Creolization, Diachrony, and Development*. Cambridge, MA: MIT Press.

Dillard, J. L. 1973. *Black English*. New York: Random House.

Evans, Vyvyan. 2014. *The Language Myth: Why Language Is Not an Instinct*. Cambridge: Cambridge University Press .

Garrett, Paul. 1999. Language socialization, convergence, and shift in St Lucia, West Indies. Unpublished doctoral dissertation, New York University.

Garrett, Paul. 2003. An English Creole that isn't: On the sociohistorical origins and linguistic classification of the vernacular English in St. Lucia. In Michael Aceto and Jeffrey P. Williams, eds. *Contact Englishes of the Eastern Caribbean* (Varieties of English around the World Series). Amsterdam: John Benjamins, 155–210.

Hancock, Ian. 1987. A preliminary classification of the anglophone Atlantic Creoles with syntactic data from thirty-three representative dialects. In Glenn G. Gilbert, ed. *Pidgin and Creole Languages*. Honolulu: University of Hawai'i Press, 264–333.

Hancock, Ian. 1994. Componentiality and the Creole matrix: The south-west English contribution. In Michael Montgomery, ed. *The Crucible of Carolina: Essays in the Development of Gullah Language and Culture*. Athens: University of Georgia Press, 95–114.

Hickey, Raymond. 2014. *A Dictionary of Varieties of English*. Malden, MA: Wiley Blackwell.

Holm, John, ed. 1983. *Central American English* (Varieties of English around the World, Text Series 2). Heidelberg: Julius Groos Verlag.

Holm, John, ed. 1988–1989. *Pidgins and Creoles*, Vols. 1 and 2. Cambridge: Cambridge University Press.

Lalla, Barbara and Jean D'Costa. 1990. *Language in Exile: Three Hundred years of Jamaican Creole*. Tuscaloosa: The University of Alabama Press.

Le Page, Robert. B. 1957–8. General outlines of Creole English dialects in the British Caribbean. *Orbis 6*: 373–391; 7: 54–64

Le Page, Robert. B. 1998. *Ivory Towers: The Memoirs of a Pidgin Fancier. A Personal Memoir of Fifty Years in Universities around the World.* St Augustine, Trinidad: Society for Caribbean Linguistics.

McWhorter, John H. 1998. Identifying the creole prototype: Vindicating a typological class. *Language* 74: 788–818.

Michaelis, Susanne. 2000. The fate of subject pronouns: Evidence from creole and non-creole languages. In Ingrid Neumann-Holzschuh and Edgar W. Schneider, eds. *Degrees of Restructuring in Creole Languages.* Amsterdam: John Benjamins, 163–183.

Mufwene, Salikoko S. 1994. On decreolization: The case of Gullah. In Marcyliena Morgan, ed. *Language and the Social Construction of Identity in Creole Situations.* Los Angeles: Center for Afro-American Studies, UCLA, 63–99.

Mufwene, Salikoko S. 1996. The founder principle in creole genesis. *Diachronica 12:* 83–134.

Mufwene, Salikoko S. 2001. *The Ecology of Language Evolution.* Cambridge: Cambridge University Press.

Mufwene, Salikoko S. 2008. *Language Evolution: Contact, Competition and Change.* London: Continuum International Publishing Group.

Mufwene, Salikoko S. 2014. The case was never closed: McWhorter misinterprets the ecological approach to the emergence of creoles. *Journal of Pidgin and Creole Languages* 1: 157–171.

Neumann-Holzschuh, Ingrid and Edgar W. Schneider, eds. 2000. *Degrees of Restructuring in Creole Languages.* Amsterdam: John Benjamins.

Niles, Norma A. 1980. Provincial English dialects and Barbadian English. Unpublished doctoral dissertation, University of Michigan.

Parkvall, Mikael. 2000. *Out of Africa: African Influences in the Atlantic Creoles.* London: Battlebridge Publications.

Popper, Karl. 1984. *The Myth of the Framework: In Defence of Science and Rationality.* London: Routledge.

Reinecke, John. E. 1937. Marginal languages: A sociological survey of the creole languages and trade jargons. Unpublished doctoral dissertation, Yale University.

Rizzi, Luigi. 1999. Broadening the empirical basis of Universal Grammar models: A commentary. In Michel DeGraff, ed. *Language Creation and Language Change: Creolization, Diachrony, and Development.* Cambridge, MA: MIT Press, 453–472.

Satyanath, Shobha. 2006. English in the New World: Continuity and change, the case of personal pronouns in Guyanese English. In Parth Bhatt and Ingo Plag, eds. *The Structure of Creole Words: Segmental, Syllabic and Morphological Aspects.* Tubingen: Max Niemeyer, 179–199.

Schneider, Edgar W. 1989. *American Earlier Black English.* Tuscaloosa: The University of Alabama Press.

Thomason, Sarah G. and Terrence Kaufman. 1988. *Language Contact, Creolization, and Genetic Linguistics.* Berkeley: University of California Press.

Van Herk, Gerard. 2003. Barbadian lects: Beyond Meso. In Michael Aceto and Jeffrey P. Williams, eds. *Contact Englishes of the Eastern Caribbean* (Varieties of English around the World Series). Amsterdam: John Benjamins, 241–264.

Wells, John C. 1982. *Accents of English, Vol. 3: Beyond the British Isles.* Cambridge: Cambridge University Press.

Wells, John C. 1987. Phonological relationships in Caribbean and West Africa English. *English World-Wide* 8: 61–68.

Williams, Jeffrey P. 1985. Preliminaries to the study of the dialects of White West Indian English. *New West Indian Guide* 59: 27–44.

Williams, Jeffrey P. 1987. Anglo-Caribbean English: A study of its socio-linguistic history and the development of its aspectual markers. Unpublished doctoral dissertation, University of Texas at Austin.

Williams, Jeffrey P. 1988. The development of aspectual markers in Anglo-Caribbean English. *Journal of Pidgin and Creole Languages* 3: 245–263.

Williams, Jeffrey P. 2003. The establishment and perpetuation of White enclave communities in the Eastern Caribbean: The case of Island Harbor, Anguilla. In Michael Aceto and Jeffrey P. Williams, eds. *Contact Englishes of the Eastern Caribbean* (Varieties of English around the World Series). Amsterdam: John Benjamins, 95–119.

Winford, Donald. 1993. *Predication in Caribbean English Creoles.* Amsterdam: John Benjamins

Winford, Donald. 2000. "Intermediate" creoles and degrees of change in creole formation: The case of Bajan. In Ingrid Neumann-Holzschuh and Edgar W. Schneider, eds. *Degrees of Restructuring in Creole Languages.* Amsterdam: John Benjamins, 215–246.

Wolfram, Walt and Erik Thomas. 2002. *The Development of African American English.* Malden, MA: Wiley Blackwell.

10

English in Africa

Bertus van Rooy

10.1 Introduction

English was transplanted to Africa through different types of colonial engagement by the British with the continent. This came in three main forms and contributed to the diversity of Englishes to be found in Africa today. The first type of contact was trade contact, which started out along the African West Coast from the fifteenth century onward. The main linguistic consequence of this first type of contact is a set of early West African pidgin varieties of English, although much of the early traders' English was used in contexts of short-lived contact and did not stabilize beyond lexis (Huber 1999: 132). Later developments, including the influence of Krio from Sierra Leone, contributed to the development of the more expanded pidgins that are widely used in contemporary West Africa (Huber 1999: 119–129).

The second type of colonialism was settlement by speakers of English in various parts of Africa: in Sierra Leone and Liberia in West Africa; and in South Africa, from where native speakers moved inland to Zimbabwe in southern Africa; and Kenya in East Africa. This resulted in a number of native-speaker Englishes that are spoken in Africa (Angogo and Hancock 1980: 71), although the total number of speakers is relatively small.

This chapter relies extensively on the research of African and international scholars who have added their insights into varieties of English from across the content, often conducting their research under very trying circumstances. Conversations about African English with a number of scholars have shaped my understanding and I would like to acknowledge the following who have taken the time to share their insights with me over many years: Ayo Bamgbose, Susan Coetzee-Van Rooy, Luanga Kasanga, Haidee Kotze Rajend Mesthrie, Daniel Nkemleke, and Josef Schmied, as well as former PhD students from across the continent, including Debra Adeyemi, Ian Bekker, Keoneng Magocha, Thadeus Marungudzi, and Ronel Wasserman. I would also like to acknowledge the feedback of the editors on an earlier draft of this chapter. I acknowledge the support of the National Research Foundation (NRF) of South Africa (Grant Number 109369) and also acknowledge that opinions, findings, and conclusions or recommendations expressed in any publication generated by the NRF-supported research are those of the author and that the NRF accepts no liability whatsoever in this regard.

The third type of colonial contact was the diffusion of English as second language among large segments of the indigenous African population in countries incorporated into the British Empire from the late nineteenth to mid-twentieth century, in the first instance via formal education. This wave of diffusion was strengthened further after the independence of African states in the second half of the twentieth century, as the educational provision expanded across these countries and English came to play a central role in the educational system. Angogo and Hancock (1980: 71) distinguish two kinds of non-native Englishes: that used by fluent speakers and that used by speakers who acquired it imperfectly, which should perhaps best be viewed as two opposite ends of a continuum.

The chapter adopts a chronological line of argumentation, looking at each new transplantation of English to a particular region and following the route of diffusion of the language, before assessing the current state of English in Africa and attempts to make sense of it. English is also used as a foreign language in many African countries with no historical association with the British Empire, including former French and Belgian colonies like the Democratic Republic of the Congo and Côte d'Ivoire, as well as Arab countries in the North, such as Morocco and Algeria. A very recent development in this group is the adoption of English as an official language in countries like Namibia (Haacke 1994) and Rwanda (Samuelson and Freedman 2010). Owing to limitations of space, the use of English outside the former British Empire is not considered further in this chapter.

10.2 Trade and Pidgins in West Africa

European contact with Africa south of the Mediterranean started with Portuguese explorers and traders from the fifteenth century, proceeding along the west coast, round the southern tip, and up the east coast from there (Nöthling 1989: 264–267). After sporadic involvement in the fifteenth and sixteenth centuries, the English maintained consistent involvement from the seventeenth century (Nöthling 1989: 295). The English followed the Portuguese and the Dutch in establishing trade posts along the West African coast for purposes of trade in gold, ivory, slaves, and local produce. The traders set up forts and other trading posts, but did not travel extensively inland (Huber 1999: 31–40; Nöthling 1989: 264–297). The most important linguistic consequence of this early contact phase is the development of a range of related West African pidgins with English as significant lexifier language, alongside traces of Portuguese.

Huber (1999: 42) identifies the earliest recorded evidence for Africans speaking English as 1564, with documented samples of actual English usage dating from 1686. He argues that, on the basis of available evidence, a restructured English with stabilized features can be traced to the early eighteenth century and must have been in fairly widespread use along the

West African coast by 1800 (Huber 1999: 44–45). The West African pidgins show considerable similarity – not due to common ancestry but rather due to similarities in their origin and function (Huber 1999: 69). However, Huber (1999: 46–47) points out that contact between Europeans and Africans, and hence proficiency in English among Africans, remained restricted to the intermediaries that facilitated trade and did not extend much beyond that. The formation of English-based pidgins was also restricted to West Africa and did not have counterparts elsewhere on the continent. Peter and Wolf (2007: 18–19) point out, however, that the West African Pidgin Englishes in the different countries are still mutually intelligible today and are growing closer to the local West African Englishes as part of an ongoing process of convergence.

10.3 Native Speaker Settlements

A small number of native speakers of English are found in West Africa, East Africa, and southern Africa and descend from settlements in the nineteenth and early twentieth century. Their effect on the development of other African varieties of English is limited due to the segregated nature of the societies in which they lived, except for the influence of Krio in West Africa and the recent influence of native speakers of English in South Africa.

The largest settlement in Africa took place in South Africa from 1820 until the first half of the twentieth century, in three waves. The 1820 settlers settled in the Eastern Cape and numbered around 5,000, followed by the Natal settlement in the mid-nineteenth century of similar size, and eventually a much more extensive settlement of about 250,000 in the late nineteenth to mid-twentieth century as diamonds, gold, and other precious metals were discovered and commercial mining got off the ground (Giliomee and Mbenga 2007). A degree of convergence between the varieties of these different settlements took place during the course of the twentieth century (Bekker 2012). The present-day descendants of the British settlers (and other Europeans who were incorporated into the speech community) numbered 1.6 million in the 2011 national census (Stats SA 2012) but their ranks were further strengthened by an extensive language shift in the Indian population from the middle of the twentieth century (Mesthrie 1995), adding a further million speakers to the language. However, until the last decade of the twentieth century, the native-speaker descendants of the European settlers were isolated from all other speech communities except from White Afrikaans speakers due to apartheid policies. This contributed to the development of distinct ethnolects during the course of the twentieth century in the various communities (Van Rooy 2014), with some convergence at the top end of the social spectrum only beginning to take place after the political transition of 1994 (Mesthrie 2010).

The native-speaker settlement in Zimbabwe is mainly an offspring of the South African settlement; the majority of Europeans migrating to Zimbabwe from 1890 to the mid-twentieth century were South African–born (Fitzmaurice 2010: 269). At its height, Europeans constituted only about 5 percent of the Zimbabwean population but, since the 1970s, the vast majority left Zimbabwe (Fitzmaurice 2010: 270–272) and the dialect that Fitzmaurice (2010) calls Rhodesian English is a fossilized dialect that is no longer transplanted to children of the "Rhodesian diaspora." The attitude and political choices of White Rhodesians were in general such that they sought little social integration with the indigenous population, further strengthened by the polarization brought about by the civil war in the 1970s (Fitzmaurice 2010: 271), while some of the domestic interaction between Whites and Blacks during the Rhodesian years also took place in a contact variety that is related to South African Fanagalo (Fitzmaurice 2010: 283). Individuals who were born after independence in 1980 and remained in Zimbabwe no longer use the Rhodesian dialect, according to Fitzmaurice (2010: 272), but speak a variety of Zimbabwean English that bears testimony to contact with the indigenous majority of the country.

British interest in Kenya goes back to the sixteenth century but settlement only started at the beginning of the twentieth century (Hoffmann 2010: 288). Compared to the rest of Africa, the settlers were decidedly more upper-class, including a relatively large proportion of the aristocracy and senior military officers (Hoffmann 2010: 288). Census figures from 1931 show that approximately half of the European residents at the time were British-born, and mainly English at that, while a fifth were of South African origin and another fifth were locally born (Hoffmann 2010: 289). During most of the twentieth century, native speakers of English, who settled in Kenya, did very little to spread the language to the indigenous population, but largely used a simplified version of Kiswahili with their laborers (Michieka 2005: 176). Following the Mau Mau rebellion and a liberation struggle in the 1950s, Kenya became an independent country in 1963. In the wake of independence, the majority of settlers left, with only a core group of 10,000 to 15,000 staying, although new European migrants have continued to arrive in small numbers (Hoffmann 2010: 290–291). However, contact between White and Black Kenyans remains limited, with the White population living together in particular areas, sending the children to expat schools and continuing to send children to the UK or South Africa for secondary and tertiary education (Hoffmann 2010: 293). In consequence, the English of the native-speaker and indigenous populations of Kenya does not exert strong mutual influences, and accommodation in both directions is limited.

There were two West African settlements of native English speakers in the nineteenth century. These settlements are different from the ones in southern and East Africa: The settlers were of African descent, that is, liberated slaves, who returned to Africa from North America, alongside Africans (mainly from the Congo River area) who were liberated from slave ships by the British or the US navy.

The Liberian settlers, while a distinct minority, were the most powerful political force since the establishment of the independent state of Liberia until 1980 (Breitborde 1988: 19; Singler 2008: 107). They remained largely on the coast and did not integrate with the indigenous population. In consequence, their language was influenced relatively little by the African languages and the local English-based pidgin, whereas the pidgin (Vernacular Liberian English) was influenced extensively by Settler English, which has caused the Liberian pidgin to diverge sharply from the other West African pidgins (Singler 2008: 103). Singler (2008: 102) notes that the language of the settlers remained largely North American and therefore represents an isolated instance on the African continent. Breitborde (1988: 20–21) points out that, after the coup of 1980, mesolectal English of the non-native speakers started to be used more widely in public spaces, although the prestige of the settler variety of English remained intact.

The other West African settlement of African returnees is Sierra Leone, where Krio, an English-lexified creole, developed. Huber (1999), based on a range of archival and older sources, traces the settlement of Sierra Leone by the "Black Poor," liberated slaves (from Jamaica and Americans that came via Nova Scotia) and liberated Africans from 1787 to 1863. Huber (1999: 63) notes that, when slaving was made illegal for British subjects, British ships started to patrol the African West Coast to intercept slave ships. Between 1808 and 1840, about 60,000 recaptives were also settled in Sierra Leone, a much larger number than the original returnees from North America (Huber 1999: 63). In the early nineteenth century, liberated Africans occupied a much lower position within the society than the returnees from Nova Scotia and Jamaica but, gradually, from the 1830s, the distinction between the settlers from North America and the liberated Africans blurred and marriages across group boundaries were recorded (Huber 1999: 71–72).

On the basis of a historical comparison of Krio features with older evidence from West African Pidgin Englishes (WAPE) and New World Creoles, particularly Gullah and Jamaican, Huber (1999: 114–119) comes to the conclusion that Krio is in the first instance descendent from New World Creoles, and stabilized into Krio during the nineteenth century: "All this indicates that the origins of Krio are quite distinct from those of 18th- and 19th-century WAPE" (Huber 1999: 115). When liberated slaves migrated as laborers or missionaries from Sierra Leone to other parts of West Africa from 1839 onward, their language influenced existing WAPEs and contributed to their stabilization, mainly in the late nineteenth and early twentieth century (Huber 1999: 128–129).

While Africa does have a number of native English–speaking groups, the majority of which are in South Africa, contact with the indigenous populations has been consistently limited from the onset of colonial occupation and settlement right through the twentieth century. The one notable exception is Krio in Sierra Leone, whose speakers came into contact with other West Africans and influenced West African pidgins extensively (Huber 1999). It is through interaction between local pidgins and a subsequent transplantation of English that Krio has had an indirect influence on African varieties of English. On the whole, native-speaker settlers were not the principal agents of the transmission of English across the African continent. Rather, the colonial expansion since the late nineteenth century and, particularly, the postcolonial phase from the middle of the twentieth century were the key developments that have given rise to the present use of the language.

10.4   Colonial Expansion and Elite Diffusion

The English language, as it is used in Africa today, can mainly be traced back to various late nineteenth-century colonial developments rather than West African pidgins that resulted from earlier trade contact (Banjo 1993: 261). Pakenham (1991: xv) points out that, by the mid-1870s, Africa was still quite unknown to Europeans but, within the next decade, European powers claimed and occupied the vast majority of the African continent. From November 15, 1884 to February 27, 1885, the German chancellor Bismarck convened a conference in Berlin, at which the European powers carved up Africa into difference territories and assigned the various territories to the control of different European powers (Ajala 1983; Pakenham 1991: 239–255). Britain was not, initially, in the "scramble for Africa" by European powers, the most aggressive or enthusiastic; nor did they prioritize the teaching of English to indigenous Africans (Schmied 1991: 11–12; Simo Bobda 2004: 20). They were rather guided by commercial opportunities (Schmied 1991: 13). The British government tried to contain the expense of colonial administration by trying to raise revenue from settlers to pay for the cost of administration, or else leave the administration to chartered companies (Schmied 1991: 13). Where settlement did not happen, as in most of West and East Africa, a strategy of indirect rule was adopted, in terms of which a limited colonial superstructure was imposed on the traditional governance practices, which were encouraged to continue from below (Wolf 2010: 198). This had the consequence that the imperial government left (formal, school-based) education of the indigenous Africans in the hands of missionaries (Schmied 1991: 13). Prior to the mid-twentieth century, only a relatively small portion of the African population thus received formal education that included sufficient opportunity to acquire proficiency in English, as will be set out below with reference to different countries and regions.

In southern Africa, the British occupied the Cape of Good Hope in 1795 and again in 1806 to prevent its fall into French hands, before it was

permanently "awarded" to them in 1814 (Giliomee and Mbenga 2007: 85).
As the British expanded their interests inland, three protectorates – the
precursors to contemporary Lesotho, Botswana, and Swaziland – were
established in the nineteenth and early twentieth century, as indigenous
groups entered into unstable agreements with the British and Afrikaner
governments to protect their territories and maintain a degree of self-rule
in their own areas (Arua 2004: 256; Giliomee and Mbenga 2007: 152–154,
171–172; Kamwangamalu 1996: 295). Europeans did not settle in these
territories in the nineteenth century and, consequently, much of the
traditional lifestyle and political organization continued until mining
and industrialization in South Africa attracted migrant laborers across
the border from the late nineteenth century onward (Giliomee and
Mbenga 2007: 200–202). The expansion further north into modern-day
Zimbabwe was driven by the British South Africa Company, where agriculture was the main commercial activity for settlers (Fitzmaurice 2010:
268–269; Schmied 1996: 302). This was also the case for the expansion into
Zambia, which picked up momentum after the discovery of large reserves
of copper there. The commercial activities were gradually connected by
railways, and settlers (temporary or permanent) were responsible for the
exploitation of the mines, with indigenous Africans largely incorporated
as manual laborers (Schmied 1996: 302–303). Otherwise, arrangements
were made, partly by treaties, partly by coercion, to separate access to
land for European farmers and traditional African societies.

The commercial dimension of colonial expansion was complemented by missionary activity, which started in the late eighteenth century in the Eastern Cape of South Africa (Hodgson 1997: 69–70) and
gradually moved further east and north to cover most of contemporary
southern Africa by the end of the nineteenth century. The missionaries were the principal agents of the transmission of English
(Schmied 1996: 302). Elphick (1997: 1) and Hirson (1980: 220) observe
that, in South Africa, until the early 1950s, almost all schools for
Africans were mission schools. This only changed from 1953 when
the government took over education from the churches through the
Bantu Education Act (Elphick 1997: 9).

Mission schools were quite diverse in the scope and quality of their
education. Among the Batswana,[1] Beck (1997: 118) reports that most
children in the major villages had access to primary education by 1860.
Simeja and Mathangwane (2010: 215), however, argue that nineteenth-
century education in Botswana was mainly reserved for the chiefs and
their offspring and that gradual expansion of the school system only took
place from the beginning of the twentieth century. Beck (1997: 119) and

[1] It is customary, especially in southern Africa, to denote languages and people, with names that respect the grammatical
structure of the indigenous languages, specifically to the extent that different class prefixes distinguish between
languages and the speakers of those languages. Thus, Setswana or isiZulu are names of languages, while their speakers
are identified as the Batswana or amaZulu respectively, also with different capitalization rules.

Etherington (1997: 97–99) report that, among the Basotho and amaZulu, participation in education in the nineteenth century was quite limited. Hirson (1981: 220) reports that the total enrollment of Africans in South African schools in the 1920s was below 20 percent.

A few elite schools, using English as medium of education, developed in various parts of South Africa in the latter part of the nineteenth century, such as Lovedale in the Eastern Cape, established in 1841 (Hodgson 1997: 80). This led to the emergence of a local elite that articulated a moderate voice of protest against colonialism (Etherington 1997: 105; Hodgson 1997: 82). Some schools were staffed by British teachers in the first half of the twentieth century and offered a very traditional British curriculum (Barnett 1983: 12). These "great mission institutions" fostered the acquisition of English at a high level of proficiency, even including interaction with native-speaker peers who also attended the schools (Lanham 1996: 22; Hodgson 1997: 80).

The situation in West Africa differs from southern Africa insofar as English was introduced twice, in different forms, in the region (Anchimbe 2006: 54; Omoniyi 2006: 174): The period of trade colonization gave rise to West African Pidgin Englishes, as noted earlier, while "educated English" was introduced separately from the nineteenth century onward by missionaries. Anchimbe (2006: 54) argues that the modern indigenized varieties of English in West Africa are the consequence of the second introduction through missionary education and not a development from the WAPEs. Bamgbose (1992) and Banjo (1995), in their discussion of models of English in Nigeria, also agree that pidgins do not have their origins in the indigenized varieties of West Africa. Hence, although the prior existence of pidgins may have been of some support in the acquisition of English, the second introduction of English in West Africa actually corresponds in many ways with the introduction in southern Africa, with the difference that native speakers, apart from missionaries themselves, were even fewer. Wolf (2010: 198) explains this as a consequence of a policy of indirect rule in West Africa. In consequence, education was left to the missions prior to the mid-twentieth century, with very limited reach into remote rural areas (see also Banjo 1993: 262). Wolf's generalization is supported by studies that looked at individual West African countries.

As far as Ghana is concerned, Sey (1973: 4) notes that English was introduced to the territory by the British through education, with the first known school established in 1788. Huber (2014: 87) adds that English-medium government and missionary schools were established in larger numbers from the 1880s. Furthermore, Sey (1973: 5) adds that, until independence, most schools were run by Christian missionaries. The need for education was mainly to train a class of clerks that acted as intermediaries between the British administrators and traders and the indigenous population. Hence, the aspiration of an educated Ghanaian was to attain proficiency in British Standard English right from the beginning, even if the attempts fell short of this expectation (Sey 1973: 5).

The diffusion of English in Nigeria is very similar to that in Ghana. English was introduced by missionaries in education from the mid-nineteenth century (Banjo 1993: 261–262) but the reach was restricted initially. As the demands for intermediaries increased, the government became more involved and more schools were set up from the 1880s, where increased emphasis was put on the teaching of English (Gut 2008: 36–37). Banjo (1995: 205–206) points out that missionary schools increased the number of speakers of English in Nigeria, leading to an increase in the intranational use of the language. It attained the position of lingua franca among the educated classes after the amalgamation of Southern and Northern Nigeria in 1914 and has since then become the "undeclared" national language and principal language of education. During the missionary education phase, a small number of elite institutions offered a very British curriculum (Achebe 1993: 21), similar to what happened in South Africa.

Similarly, the transmission of English by missionaries also happened in Cameroon in the nineteenth century (Anchimbe 2006: 54; Kouega 2006: 37). However, from 1884 to the end of World War I, Cameroon fell under German control and was partitioned into a larger French sector in the South and smaller British second in the North at the end of the War, at which point the centrality of English was reestablished in the North (Kouega 2006: 37–38; Simo Bobda 2010: 653). The educated elite of the British Cameroons continued to use English as its language of administration after the end of colonial rule, leaving the modern state of Cameroon in a unique bilingual position with both French and English as its national languages but differentiated by region (Anchimbe 2006: 55–57; Simo Bobda 2010: 654–656).

English was introduced to East Africa later than to the other two major English-using regions, West Africa and southern Africa. A small number of missions were founded along the Indian coast in the 1860s, with the first inland mission established a decade later (Schmied 2006: 190). Schmied (2006: 188–189) points to some differences in colonial history, especially a period of German rule in what is now Tanzania between the Berlin conference of 1884 and the end of World War I, but argues that the three major English-using countries in East Africa – Kenya, Tanzania, and Uganda – form a relatively homogeneous group (see also Wolf 2010: 197). Kiswahili is widely used across East Africa and, in consequence, for most of the colonial period, Kiswahili performed functions in East Africa within the missions and civil service that English performed in West Africa and southern Africa (Michieka 2005: 176; Schmied 2006: 190). As such, access to English was restricted to a small elite during the colonial period (Schmied 2006: 191). German obtained almost no foothold at all in German East Africa (Tanzania) because the Germans ended up using Kiswahili (Schmied 1985: 23–28).

In the earliest years of missionary education, teachers were not all standard English users (Banjo 1993: 262; Mesthrie 1996), and some features in African varieties also reveal the continued use of archaic features that had fallen into disuse in contemporary varieties, as Mesthrie (1999) demonstrates for unstressed *do* in Cape Flats English. However, by and large, the enduring image of missionary education is that of elite institutions, often staffed by native speakers who commanded the standard variety, and whose students went on to become prominent newspaper editors and politicians (De Kock 1996, McGinley 1987).

10.5 Independence and Mass Diffusion

After World War II, the tide turned and the colonies of the nineteenth-century empires started to demand their independence. Where the British were reluctant to invest in education during the colonial era (Simo Bobda 2004: 20), they adopted a policy to "prepare colonies for independence" through "modernization," which included economic development in the field of agriculture and industry, but also an expansion of education (Schmied 1991: 17). However, Pakenham (1991: 673) points out that, by the end of World War II, development and educational provision were not yet making significant progress and, after the war, the calls for independence were so rapid that there was too little time to implement a systematic development program.

English was central to the mid-twentieth-century educational expansion, not only because of the importance the UK attached to the language as a vehicle for modernization and inter-ethnic communication but also due to the value attached to it by African liberation movements themselves. These movements were usually pan-ethnic and wanted to address an international audience, which further strengthened the position of English (Schmied 1991: 18). Banda (1996: 110–111) notes, with reference to Zambia, that concerns about tribalism and the perception that some indigenous groups/languages were promoted at the expense of others also supported the choice of English, both in government and in education, a situation that was true for many newly independent African countries.

At the same time, English was regarded as the language of modernity and upward mobility among large segments of the African population, which created a very receptive environment for an education system that afforded a central role for English. Withholding English from the population was, and still is, regarded with extreme suspicion (Kamwangamalu 2013: 329; Mfum-Mensah 2005: 72). This attitude was perhaps most striking in the case of Bantu education in South Africa (Hartshorne 1995: 309–314), but the same suspicion extended even to a country like Tanzania, where the use of an indigenous language, Kiswahili, was implemented in primary education (Rubagumya 1991).

However, at the time of independence in the third quarter of the twentieth century, the typical situation in most English-using countries in

Africa was that a very small elite with access to sufficient education in English was fully proficient and a very small number of secondary schools existed in any particular country, with universities just about being founded. Thus, the overall supply of teachers for the task at hand was limited as native speakers (some of whom acted as teachers) were a rarity in most African countries even in the colonial period (Achebe 1993: 16). Moreover, many left the countries in the wake of political upheavals, as was the case in Kenya (Hoffmann 2010: 291) in the early 1960s, Uganda (Tembe 2006: 858) in the 1970s, and Zimbabwe in the early 1980s (Fitzmaurice 2010: 272). In South Africa, with potentially the highest number of native speakers, there were still not enough to form an extensive native-speaker teaching cohort; this was partly due to government policies that were not attractive for teaching English to indigenous children, leading Lanham (1967) to propose all kinds of steps to compensate for the lack of exposure to native speakers in the schools of Soweto, the most urbanized Black township in the country.

At this point in history, then, a much larger proportion of the indigenous populations of Africa started to receive English-language education. With the exception of Tanzania, who chose Swahili as medium of instruction for the entire of primary school education (Rubagumya 1991: 70), African countries opted for a model with an indigenous language for the first part of primary school only (three to four years), after which a switch is made to English as the medium of instruction; but English is taught right from the first year in preparation for the transition into the medium of instruction (Bamgbose 2003).

The wider diffusion of English in Africa has to be attributed to post-independence educational expansion rather than to any of the earlier initiatives, all of which were of narrow scope and only reached a small elite. Obviously, this phase built on the teachers who were trained by the missionaries, but the low number of teachers with adequate English proficiency has been a problem across Africa (Bamgbose 2003: 427; Gough 1996: 54; Lanham 1996: 27; McGinley 1987: 160; Tembe 2006: 857). Brosnahan (1958: 97) writes, with reference to data from 1951, that only one-seventh of all teachers employed in Nigerian education at the time had professional certificates. Tembe (2006: 859–860) points out that, until the 1990s, Ugandans who have only completed seven years of primary education were allowed to enroll in teacher-training colleges to become primary school teachers themselves, a situation that was also true of Ghana after independence (Huber 2008a: 69). In Zimbabwe, the number of enrollments in secondary schools increased from 73,540 to 417,450 in the space of five years from 1979 to 1984 in the wake of its political liberation, clearly showing the all but impossible demand put on the provision of teachers (McGinley 1987: 16).

One of the consequences of this type of system, as Bamgbose (2003: 423–424) and Kamwangamalu (2013: 330) point out, is that an elite group is maintained, with access to good schools and good teachers, while the majority of children are accommodated in schools with poor facilities and teachers and do not have similar access to the employment opportunities and upward social mobility that their elite peers do. In consequence, Kamwangamalu (2013: 331–332), Manyike (2007), Simo Bobda (2004: 22), and others point to the low literacy and limited proficiency of English in many parts of Africa, a situation that also coincides with the urban/rural divide, in that access to English and eventual attainment of proficiency are even more restricted in rural areas (Michieka 2005: 179). Even where students do progress through the school system and make it into tertiary education, their chances of success are not as high as those for students from the elite schools, as has been established in South Africa, a country with an above-average number of students with postsecondary education (Van Rooy and Coetzee-Van Rooy 2015).

Where the elite diffusion of English in Africa resulted in forms of English that were quite close to the native-speaker input, the consequence of mass diffusion in the second half of the twentieth century was forms of English that displayed more extensive transfer from the indigenous languages, as well as other learner language features, such as overgeneralization and analogical extension. In many cases, the proficiency level attained was much lower than in the earlier phase of elite diffusion (Banjo 1993: 267; Lanham 1996: 31; Mesthrie and Bhatt 2008: 165; Schneider 2007: 99–109). Some of these features, which may be viewed as learner errors in their origin, nevertheless came to gain a widespread foothold and a degree of acceptance within the various speech communities (Bamgbose 1998; Van Rooy 2011).

10.6 Models, Acceptability, and Standardization

Exactly how the various input factors interact and what the eventual variety of English is that a particular user commands as an adult has been captured by a number of models and these models in turn have implications for how innovations are viewed in African Englishes. Some of the earliest discussions took place in Nigeria. Brosnahan (1958: 99) bases his classification on levels of education and distinguishes Nigerian Pidgin English as Level 1, which is available to Nigerians without any formal education (and, hence, does not represent a "New English" or "Institutionalized Variety of English" – BvR), and then from Levels 2–4, speakers with increasing levels of education, whose English is increasingly fluent.

A more influential early model is Banjo's (1971, 1993), which builds on Brosnahan (1958) but adds a number of further dimensions to the classification: the extent of transfer from the mother tongue, the approximation to a world standard, and the degree of acceptability that a particular variety enjoys within Nigeria. Banjo does not include pidgin in his model. Variety I is characterized most strongly by transfer and is least intelligible to international users, while Variety III is characterized by relatively less transfer and greater approximation to international use, with Variety II somewhere in between. Variety IV is the form of English acquired by Nigerians living in England and then returning and is not regarded as a home-grown model. Bamgbose (1992) argues against the inclusion of Variety IV in the description of Nigerian English, a point that Banyo (1995: 209) concedes, adding that this variety does not enjoy social acceptance within Nigeria (Banyo 1993: 273). Variety III is the variety that Banjo (1993: 272–273) proposes as cornerstone of an endonormative Nigerian English. It is phonologically and syntactically reasonably similar to other Englishes, internationally, but differs both phonetically and lexically. Banjo (1993: 269–270) argues that the language of African fiction, as penned by writers like Achebe and Soyinka, draws on Variety III to stamp their African experience on the English language. Bokamba (2015: 333) argues that the lexical and semantic dimension is the primary area of creative extension in African Englishes, while grammatical usage in creative writing is largely in correspondence with the conventions of standard English.[2]

Schmied (1991: 47–49) proposes a cline with three broad regions – basilect, mesolect, and acrolect – that has since been adopted very widely in discussions of African Englishes. This classification largely overlaps with Varieties I–III in Banjo's classification. Schmied (1991: 47) emphasizes the role of education and occupation as key determinants of the kind of English a particular individual acquires. Like Banjo's Variety III, Schmied (1991: 49) notes that the acrolect is similar to standard English as far as pronunciation, grammar, and lexis are concerned but different in terms of phonetics, semantics, discourse, and content. The mesolect is more divergent in phonological and grammatical domains, with simplification and transfer playing a role, while the basilect differs to such an extent that it might not be intelligible to outsiders. A key motivation behind this line of modeling is to arrive at a selection of a local variety that can be used as the basis for endonormative standardization (Bamgbose 1998, Banjo 1993). However, before considering the issue of a local standard in African Englishes, there is a more recent, influential model that requires consideration.

Schneider's (2003, 2007) Dynamic Model of postcolonial Englishes also extends to Africa and has gained considerable traction among scholars since its publication. Schneider (2007: 31–32) identifies two parties to every colonial encounter, the group of settlers (the STL strand) and the

---

[2] The issue of African literature in English is an important one that has implications for the study of the language but it is not possible to do justice to the extensive scholarship in the field of African literature (or the subpart of African literature written in English) within the confined scope of this chapter. In a paper, though, Bokamba (2015: 315) points out the study of the linguistic resources that creative writers draw on to convey that an African experience has not received much attention. He offers an analysis of a number of passages from novels by leading West African and East African authors and concludes that the authors rely in the main on standard English but adjust language skillfully for the purposes of characterization and draws extensively on imagery and direct translations of proverbs from African languages to convey the African settings and mindset of their characters.

indigenous inhabitants of a particular geographical space (the IDG strand).[3] If viewed as static categories, these correspond roughly to the Inner and Outer Circle users of English in Kachru's (1986) model. However, Schneider (2007: 30–55) proposes a Dynamic Model in which the two strands gradually come to engage more frequently and, eventually, language change happens to the varieties of both groups until they reach the point of convergence. The dynamic process is conceptualized along five stages, where each stage is characterized by typical historical, sociolinguistic, and, ultimately, linguistic effects. An important aspect that receives much more prominence in Schneider's (2007: 44–45) proposal than other proposals is the occurrence of nativization at a grammatical level, especially lexico-grammatical change, where the restructuring of the English language is an option due to the gradual diffusion of innovative grammatical structures that originated in the IDG strand to the wider speech community (in both stages 2 and 3 of the model; see D'Arcy, Chapter 19, this volume). By stage 4, endonormative stabilization, the nativized forms come to enjoy widespread acceptance across the speech community (Schneider 2007: 49–52).

Africa is in some ways a prototypical environment for the discussion of colonial language transmission; yet the local ecologies differ in one very important way from the generalized picture offered by the Dynamic Model. As pointed out earlier in this chapter, the STL strand was a relatively insignificant presence in most of the colonial linguistic encounters. The missionaries were the main representatives of the STL strand but were quite few in number and, except in South Africa, Zimbabwe, and Kenya, did not become permanent, or even long-term, residents of the African territories. Colonial administrators were likewise not settlers. Moreover, as has been pointed out in the discussion of Zimbabwean (Rhodesian), Kenyan, and South African settlers, they did not become part of an integrated, multi-ethnic local polity. The only exception, and this is a quite recent one, is the South African context after 1994, which will be discussed in the next section.

Thus, with the caveat that the progression along the stages of the Dynamic Model is essentially the story of the IDG strand in the absence of contact with the STL strand, the question of endonormative standards can be considered. Where Schneider (2003, 2007) views endonormativity in terms of identity rewriting, and as a sign of convergence between the STL and IDG strands in the colonial encounter, much of the discussion of endonormativity in Nigeria takes its cue from educational concerns (Bamgbose 1998: 5, 8–10; Banjo 1993: 263). A related debate ignited in South Africa in the wake of the political transition, with two clear camps:

---

[3] Schneider (2007) also provides for a third party in some settings where postcolonial Englishes develops, which he terms the adstrate (ADS), who speak a language that enjoys higher status than the indigenous languages. This might apply to other European languages or Arabic in some African countries, but generally, such languages have not received extensive consideration in research on African Englishes.

pro-restandardization (Chick and Wade 1997; Ndebele 1987; Webb 1996) and anti-restandardization (Lanham 1995; Titlestad 1996; Wright 1995). Different visions of the goals of education occupied a central position in the debate, although Ndebele (1987: 13) raises questions related to decolonization and nativization of English, when he claims:

> South African English must be open to the possibility of its becoming a new language. This may happen not only at the level of vocabulary (notice how the word "necklace" has acquired a new and terrible meaning), but also with regard to grammatical adjustments that may result from the proximity of English to indigenous African languages.

Evidence about the acceptability of putative nativized features of African Englishes has been sought in a number of surveys, such as Alo and Igwebuke (2010) in Nigeria, Burugeya (2006) in Kenya, and Van der Walt and Van Rooy (2002) in South Africa. However, Bamgbose (1998: 4–5) makes the point that, while acceptance of an innovative feature is an important step, it ultimately requires codification of the new norms, otherwise examiners (in West Africa but by implication elsewhere too) will continue to be guided by an exonormative codified metropolitan model when evaluating work in high-stakes exams. Gut (2011: 102–103) explains one dimension of the historical route an innovation takes to become a feature of a new variety: After an innovation enters the language of second-language learners, the speakers' proficiencies develop further but some features remain in their language production after they have acquired a high level of proficiency. If these features are then transmitted as part of the language to a next generation of speakers, it can be regarded as entrenched. Van Rooy and Kruger (2016) report evidence of exactly this kind in a study of Black South African English, where certain features of learner language are present at lower proficiency levels but disappear with increased proficiency. Other features remain in the language production of highly proficient writers and these features should be considered as better candidates for the status of conventionalized innovations.

Van Rooy (2011: 195) adds a further requirement for conventionalized innovation, which is that a feature is only likely to gain acceptance if it has come to occupy a systematic place in the emergent grammar of individuals in the speech community, with a regular function association for the form. Schneider (2007: 52) points out, however, that grammatical innovations, unlike lexical ones, find it harder to gain recognition in codifying grammars, in part due to concerns with international currency of all Englishes. As a proxy for such codification, Kruger and Van Rooy (2017) explore the extent to which the text editors of published books contribute to the legitimization of innovative features. These gatekeepers do weed out certain innovative features but only to the extent that they are salient and socially stigmatized, while they let through innovations that operate below the level of conscious awareness.

The acceptability of lexical innovations (borrowings, the use of indigenous idioms, and metaphors in translations) seems unproblematic in African Englishes, in both literary (Bokamba 2015; Bamgbose 1998) and nonliterary writing (Van Rooy and Terblanche 2010; Wolf and Polzenhagen 2009). The status of grammatical innovations is less certain. Corpus evidence of the use of a range of innovative features has been uncovered by researchers working on corpora of various African Englishes, such as ICE-Nigeria (Akinlotan and Housen 2017; Fuchs et al 2013, Gut 2012), ICE-East Africa (Mwangi 2003, Skandera 2003, Schmied 2004); and various corpora of Black South African English (De Klerk 2006; Makalela 2013; Van Rooy 2013). However, codification has, in general, not been attempted and evidence about their acceptability remains ambiguous, which suggests that endonormative stabilization, of the kind envisaged by Banjo (1995), Bamgbose (1998), or Schneider (2007), is still some way off for most African Englishes.

10.7 Recent Trends

The early parts of the twenty-first century show the signs of two incipient changes, both in part related to urbanization and changing socioeconomic conditions. There is some evidence of a small-scale but growing language shift to English as the home language in affluent families in the big cities of Africa. In the specific case of South Africa, there is also evidence of a convergence between the STL strand and a small but growing group of middle-class users from the IDG strand. Furthermore, in the contact situations of the cities, new forms of hybrid language usage emerge, further strengthened by the possibilities offered by mobile communication. Parallel to the emergence of hybrid codes, pidgin in West Africa has been reappraised since the late twentieth century.

Schneider (2007) reviews evidence about (mainly affluent) urban, African families that adopt English as their home language in South Africa (2007: 188), Kenya (2007: 194), and Nigeria (Schneider 2007: 207; Udofot 2013: 12), while Ofori and Albakry (2012) make a similar claim for Ghana. Quantitative evidence of the extent of such shift is hard to come by, though, as most researchers draw on case studies. The most comprehensive census data on this phenomenon come from the 2011 national census in South Africa, where more than a million, or 2.9 percent of the Black African population, claims English as home language (Stats SA 2012: 26–27). Coetzee-Van Rooy (2014) shows that this phenomenon is particularly prevalent among upwardly mobile urban university students, although it does not result in monolingualism. Ofori and Albakry (2012: 171) report that 13.8 percent of their respondents in upper-class neighborhoods in the Ghanaian capital Accra claim English as their first language but, similar to South Africa, none claims to be monolingual in English.

Nonetheless, language shift that results in the loss of community languages has been observed in the Indian community of South Africa, as detailed by Mesthrie (1995). Some of the circumstances were different from the present-day shift in African cities but there are shared features, such as the multilingual contact setting and the absence of another widely shared language, as well as the importance of English as a language of school education from the primary school level (Mesthrie 1995: 119, 126–127). Thus, English is the native language for the vast majority of the Indian community of South Africa today (Stats SA 2012: 26). Language shift has also been observed in the Colored community in South Africa, where English came to be favored increasingly as medium of education, although bilingualism in English and Afrikaans remains the norm (McCormick 2002: 24–32, 55–61).

These various South African communities, to the extent that they engage with one another more frequently in an open society, have started to show evidence of convergence in their pronunciation. Although some differences still characterize the Colored and Indian communities (e.g. Mesthrie and Chevalier 2014), Mesthrie (2010) and Mesthrie et al. (2015) report evidence of convergence on the STL speech norms by Black students from middle-class families with a non-racial education background. Conversely, there are indications of increasing acceptance, especially of lexical innovations that originated in the IDG strand (see, e.g., Branford and Venter 2016).

A related phenomenon, although not as extensive as language shift, is the extended range of contexts in which English is used in African cities (Michieka 2005: 179). This is in part a question of identity, where the urban space is associated with a modern identity, which is particularly liberating for women from traditional rural societies, as De Kadt (2004) reports. Such use of English does not imply the use of the standard language, however, but a degree of mixing between English and other languages that the speakers possess (De Kadt 2005). The most extensive of these developments is arguably a variety called Sheng, a mixed code incorporating English and Kiswahili, which is widely used in urban areas across Kenya (Meierkord 2012: 81), although a number of mixed codes have also developed in South Africa (Flaaitaal, Tsotsitaal, Iscamto; see Mesthrie and Hurst 2013). These codes carry covert prestige within the multilingual urban settings in which they are used (Meierkord 2009). Of particular interest is the more recent development of Engsh (Meierkord 2009: 6–10), which is a mixed language with a much stronger English base, used by English-dominant younger speakers in affluent areas of Nairobi and which finds its way to the printed media directed at this audience.

The rapid growth in the use of mobile communication devices in Africa serves as further support for the expansion of linguistic creativity, in which English plays an important role but remains one of the many resources that speakers have available (Deumert 2014). In a case study, Deumert and Masinyana (2008) find that, while the use of English in SMSs

by speakers of isiXhosa adopts many of the international trends characteristic of digital communication, it also infuses the English with local
(English) idiom and short or longer incorporations of elements from
isiXhosa. Udofot and Mbarachi (2016) find that an internationally shared
jargon emerges in Nigerian Internet language, similar to Deumert (2014:
122–145), but elements from local languages, Nigerian Pidgin English, and
Nigerianisms combine to lead to a variety of language use that is distinctively Nigerian (see also Mair and Heyd 2014).

A recent change very specific to West Africa has been recorded since the
final decades of the twentieth century. The traditional view of West
African pidgins is that they are used by uneducated people and have
been regarded in negative attitudinal terms in the middle to latter parts
of the twentieth century, possibly even as a potential barrier to the acquisition of standard English (see Huber 1999: 2–3 for a review of Ghanaian
Pidgin English). Jibril (1995: 232–233) notes that Nigerian Pidgin English
had a similar association with uneducated speakers until it started to be
used in a wider range of contexts from the 1980s and by a wider range of
speakers, including elite users of English. Dolphyne (1995: 32) and Huber
(1999: 147–152) refer to the rapid expansion of use of Ghanaian Pidgin
English by university students, giving it prestige through the nickname
"Harvard" (Dolphyne 1995: 32) used by students. It serves as a register with
covert prestige and expression of solidarity by males in particular (Huber
2008b: 95). Kamtok, the Cameroonian Pidgin English, is used very widely
in society, a bridging language often between the anglophone and francophone communities, but, even there, Menang (2008: 138) reports innovative uses among the youth that draw more extensively on French and the
indigenous languages, leading to the possible emergence of a new mixed
code, "Camfranglais."

English has therefore been appropriated increasingly by urban Africans
since the final decades of the twentieth century, leading to innovative
forms characterized by hybridity, but also to more widespread adoption
as the language of interpersonal and even private communication, as
opposed to its more traditional role in the formal domains of education,
government, and commerce. However, current changes appear to be
restricted to urban settings, with the rural areas in many countries not
yet drawn into the cycle of ongoing social change and linguistic innovation. These areas continue to have limited access to education.

10.8 Conclusion

English in its various forms is firmly rooted in Africa, although it is not
the unqualified carrier of civilization and economic development that it
might be conceived of in many circles. The earliest transplantation was in
the form of a contact language along the West African trade routes,

which gave rise to the contemporary West African pidgins. These pidgins are widely used by uneducated people in inter-ethnic communication but also gained a new life recently as a medium of in-group solidarity for educated, younger West Africans, especially students and secondary school pupils.

The second transplantation to Africa came in the wake of the nineteenth-century British colonial expansion as part of the European scramble for Africa, where English settlers went to South Africa, and later to Zimbabwe and Kenya, while the English colonial administrators and merchants imposed themselves on West Africa, East Africa, and southern Africa. Within this context, missionaries came to Africa, in the first instance with the goal of converting Africans to the Christian faith, but, at the same time, set up schools where English was taught and a form of standard English was transmitted to a small group of Africans. Not all mission schools were elite schools, and not all missionaries were native speakers of English, but a small number of Africans acquired good education and considerable proficiency in standard English from the late nineteenth to mid-twentieth century.

Mission education only reached a small minority of indigenous Africans. Only after the independence of African "colonies" from the mid-twentieth century did education become more widely available. Since English was given such a prominent role in education, the third transplantation of English was by African teachers, themselves not always fully proficient in standard English, which led to the more typical African Englishes that are characterized by a more extensive transfer of linguistic properties of the indigenous languages, as well as all kinds of simplification and regularization phenomena.

In recent years, English has been embedded so thoroughly in the language repertoires of urban Africans that, on the one hand, it is becoming a home language to a (still small, elite) minority and it is being used in more playful ways to assert an African identity beyond the confines of the educational setting, which has been the seat of acquisition for most of its history.

Future research needs to take a more substantial comparative perspective within the three major English-using regions of Africa but also across them. Corpus-building is ongoing but much still needs to be done to provide an adequate basis for the description of the linguistic features of African Englishes. In particular, corpora are required that capture a wider cross-section of the English-using population, to trace the diffusion of linguistic features in the entire speech community, while more historical corpora are also needed. Finally, there is also a need for support and opportunity to enable more researchers on the African continent itself to add their voices to the global attempt to understand the forms and the use of English in Africa more comprehensively.

References

Achebe, Chinua. 1993. The education of a British-protected child. In Chinua Achebe, *The Education of a British-Protected Child: Essays*. New York: Anchor Books, 3–24.

Ajala, Adekunle. 1983. The nature of African boundaries. *Africa Spectrum* 18(2): 177–189.

Akinlotan, Mayowa and Alex Housen. 2017. Noun phrase complexity in Nigerian English. *English Today* 33(3): 31–38.

Alo, Moses A. and Ebuka E. Igwebuike. 2012. The grammaticality and acceptability of Nigerianisms: Implications for the codification of Nigerian English. *Journal of the Nigerian English Studies Association* 15(1): 13–35.

Anchimbe, Eric A. 2006. *Cameroon English: Authenticity, Ecology and Evolution*. Frankfurt am Main: Peter Lang.

Angogo, Rachel and Ian F. Hancock. 1980. English in Africa: Emerging standards or diverging regionalisms? *English World-Wide* 1: 67–96.

Arua, Arua E. 2004. Botswana English: Some syntactic features. *English World-Wide* 25(2): 255–272.

Bamgbose, Ayo. 1992. Standard Nigerian English: Issues of codification. In Braj B. Kachru, (ed.) *The Other Tongue: English across Cultures* (2nd ed.) Urbana: University of Illinois Press, 99–111.

Bamgbose, Ayo. 1998. Torn between the norms: Innovations in world Englishes. *World Englishes* 17(1): 1–14.

Bamgbose, Ayo. 2003. A recurring decimal: English in language policy and planning. *World Englishes* 22(4): 419–431.

Banda, Felix. 1996. In search of the lost tongue: Prospects for mother tongue education in Zambia. *Language, Culture and Curriculum* 9(2): 109–119.

Banjo, Ayo. 1971. Towards a definition of standard Nigerian spoken English. In *Actes du 8e Congres de la Société Linguistique de l'Afrique Occidental* (pp. 165–174).

Banjo, Ayo. 1993. An endonormative model for the teaching of English in Nigeria. *International Journal of Applied Linguistics* 32(2): 261–275.

Banjo, Ayo. 1995. On codifying Nigerian English: Research so far. In Ayo Bamgbose, Ayo Banjo, and Andrew Thomas, eds. *New Englishes: A West African Perspective*. Trenton, NJ: Africa World Press, 203–231.

Barnett, Ursula A. 1983. *A Vision of Order: A Study of Black South African Literature in English (1914–1980)*. Cape Town: Maskew Miller Longman.

Beck, Roger B. 1997. Monarchs and missionaries among the Tswana and Sotho. In Richard Elphick and Rodney Davenport, eds. *Christianity in South Africa: A Political, Social and Cultural History*. Cape Town: David Phillip, 107–120.

Bekker, Ian. 2012. South African English as a late 19th-century extraterritorial variety. *English World-Wide* 33(2): 127–146.

Bokamba, Eyamba G. 2015. African Englishes and creative writing. *World Englishes* 34(3): 315–335.

Bretborde, Lawrence B. 1988. The persistence of English in Liberia: Sociolinguistic factors. *World Englishes* 7(1): 15–23.

Brosnahan, Leonard F. 1958. English in southern Nigeria. *English Studies* 39(1–6): 97–110.

Buregeya, Alfred. 2006. Grammatical features of Kenyan English and the extent of their acceptability. *English World-Wide* 27: 199–216.

Chick, J. Keith and Rodrik, Wade. 1997. Restandardisation in the direction of a new English: Implications for access and equity. *Journal of Multilingual and Multicultural Development* 18(4): 271–284.

Coetzee-Van Rooy, Susan. 2014. Explaining the ordinary magic of stable African multilingualism in the Vaal Triangle region in South Africa, *Journal of Multilingual and Multicultural Development* 35(2): 121–138.

De Kadt, Elizabeth. 2004. Gender aspects of the use of English on a South African university campus. *World Englishes* 23(4): 515–534.

De Klerk, Vivian. 2006. *Corpus Linguistics and World Englishes: An Analysis of Xhosa-English.* London: Continuum

De Kock, Leon. 1996. *Civilising Barbarians: Missionary Narrative and African Textual Response in Nineteenth-Century South Africa.* Johannesburg: Witwatersrand University Press.

Deumert, Ana. 2014. *Sociolinguistics and Mobile Communication.* Edinburgh: Edinburgh University Press.

Deumert, Ana and Sibabalwe O. Masinyana. 2008. Mobile language choices – The use of English and isiXhosa in text messages (SMS): Evidence from a bilingual South African sample. *English World-Wide* 29(2): 117–147.

Dolphyne, Florence. 1995. A note on the English language in Ghana. In Ayo Bamgbose, Ayo Banjo, and Andrew Thomas, eds. *New Englishes: A West African Perspective.* Trenton, NJ: Africa World Press, 27–33.

Elphick, Richard. 1997. Introduction: Christianity in South African history. In Richard Elphick and Rodney Davenport, eds. *Christianity in South Africa: A Political, Social and Cultural History.* Cape Town: David Phillip, 1–15.

Etherington, Norman. 1997. Kingdoms of this world and the next: Christian beginnings among Zulu and Swazi. In Richard Elphick and Rodney Davenport, eds. *Christianity in South Africa: A Political, Social and Cultural History.* Cape Town: David Phillip, 89–106.

Fitzmaurice, Susan. 2010. L1 Rhodesian English. In Daniel Schreier, Peter Trudgill, Edgar W. Schneider, and Jeffrey P. Williams, eds. *The Lesser-Known Varieties of English: An Introduction.* Cambridge: Cambridge University Press, 263–285.

Fuchs, Robert, Ulrike Gut, and Taiwo Soneye. 2013. "We just don't even know": The usage of the pragmatic particles *even* and *still* in Nigerian English. *English World-Wide* 34(2): 123–145.

Giliomee, Herman and Bernard Mbenga. 2007. *Nuwe geskiedenis van Suid-Afrika.* (New history of South Africa.) Cape Town: Tafelberg.

Gough, David, 1996. Black English in South Africa. In Vivian De Klerk, ed. *Focus on South Africa*. Amsterdam: Benjamins, 53–77.

Gut, Ulrike. 2008. Nigerian English: Phonology. In Rajend Mesthrie, ed. *Varieties of English, Vol. 4: Africa, South and Southeast Asia*. Berlin: Mouton de Gruyter, 35–54.

Gut, Ulrike. 2011. Studying structural innovations in New English varieties. In Joybrato Mukherjee and Marianne Hundt (eds.) *Exploring Second-Language Varieties of English and Learner Englishes: Bridging a Paradigm Gap*. Amsterdam: Benjamins, 101–124.

Gut, Ulrike. 2012. Towards a codification of Nigerian English: The ICE Nigeria project. *Journal of the Nigerian English Studies Association* 15(1): 1–12.

Haacke, Wilfrid. 1994. Language policy and planning in independent Namibia. *Annual Review of Applied Linguistics* 14: 240–253.

Hartshorne, Ken, 1995. Language policy in African education: A background to the future. In Rajend Mesthrie, ed. *Language and Social History: Studies in South African Sociolinguistics*. Cape Town: David Phillip, 306–318.

Hirson, Baruch. 1981. Language in control and resistance in South Africa. *African Affairs 80*: 219–37.

Hodgson, Janet. 1997. A battle for sacred power: Christian beginnings among the Xhosa. In Richard Elphick and Rodney Davenport, eds. *Christianity in South Africa: A Political, Social and Cultural History*. Cape Town: David Phillip, 68–88.

Hoffmann, Thomas. 2010. White Kenyan English. In Daniel Schreier, Peter Trudgill, Edgar W. Schneider, and Jeffrey P. Williams, eds. *The Lesser-Known Varieties of English: An Introduction*. Cambridge: Cambridge University Press, 286–310.

Huber, Magnus. 1999. *Ghanaian Pidgin English in Its West African Context*. Amsterdam: John Benjamins.

Huber, Magnus. 2008a. Ghanaian English: Phonology. In Rajend Mesthrie, ed. *Varieties of English, Vol. 4: Africa, South and Southeast Asia*. Berlin: Mouton de Gruyter, 67–92.

Huber, Magnus. 2008b. Ghanaian Pidgin English: Phonology. In Rajend Mesthrie, ed. *Varieties of English, Vol. 4: Africa, South and Southeast Asia*. Berlin: Mouton de Gruyter, 93–101.

Huber, Magnus. 2014. Stylistic and sociolinguistic variation in Schneider's nativization phase: T-affrication and relativization in Ghanaian English. In Sarah Buschfeld, Thomas Hoffmann, Magnus Huber, and Alexander Kautzsch, eds. *The Evolution of Englishes: The Dynamic Model and Beyond*. Amsterdam: John Benjamins, 86–106.

Jibril, Munzali. 1995. The elaboration of the functions of Nigerian Pidgin. In Ayo Bamgbose, Ayo Banjo, and Andrew Thomas, eds. *New Englishes: A West African Perspective*. Trenton, NJ: Africa World Press, 232–247.

Kamwangamalu, Nkonko M. 1996. Sociolinguistic aspects of siSwati-English bilingualism. *World Englishes* 15(3): 295–305.

Kamwangamalu, Nkonko M. 2013. Effects of policy on English-medium instruction in Africa. *World Englishes* 32(3): 325–337.

Kouega, Jean-Paul. 2006. *Aspects of Cameroon English Usage: A Lexical Appraisal.* Munich: Lincom.

Kruger, Haidee and Van Rooy, Bertus. 2017. Editorial practice and the distinction between error and conventionalised innovation in New Englishes: The progressive in Black South African English. *World Englishes* 36(1): 20–41.

Lanham, L. W. 1967. *Teaching English in Bantu Primary Schools: Final Report on Research in Johannesburg Schools.* Johannesburg: Wits University.

Lanham, L. W. 1995. Which English? In L. W. Lanham, David Langhan, Arie Blacquière, and Laurence Wright. *Getting the Message in South Africa: Intelligibility, Readability, Comprehensibility.* Howick: Brevitas, 12–43.

Lanham, L. W. 1996. A history of English in South Africa. In Vivian De Klerk, ed. *Focus on South Africa,* Amsterdam: John Benjamins, 19–34.

Mair, Christian and Theresa Heyd. 2014. From vernacular to digital ethno-linguistic repertoire: The case of Nigerian Pidgin. In Jabok Leimgruber and Thiemo Breyer, eds. *Indexising Authenticity: Sociolinguistics Perspectives.* Berlin: Mouton de Gruyter, 244–268.

Makalela, Leketi. 2013. Black South African English on the radio. *World Englishes* 32(1): 93–107.

Manyike, T.V. 2007. The acquisition of English academic language proficiency among grade 7 learners in South African schools. Unpublished D. Ed. thesis, University of South Africa.

McCormick, Kay. 2002. *Language in Cape Town's District Six,* Oxford: Oxford University Press.

McGinley, Kevin. 1987. The future of English in Zimbabwe. *World Englishes* 6(2): 159–164.

Meierkord, Christiane. 2009. *It's kuloo tu*: Recent developments in Kenya's Englishes. *English Today* 25(1): 3–11.

Meierkord, Christiane. 2012. *Interactions across Englishes: Linguistic Choices in Local and International Contact Situations.* Cambridge: Cambridge University Press.

Menang, Thaddeus. 2008. Cameroon Pidgin English (Kamtok): Phonology. In Rajend Mesthrie, ed. *Varieties of English, Vol. 4: Africa, South and Southeast Asia.* Berlin: Mouton de Gruyter, 133–149.

Mesthrie, Rajend. 1995. Language change, survival, decline: Indian languages in South Africa. In Rajend Mesthrie, ed. *Language and Social History: Studies in South African Sociolinguistics.* Cape Town: David Phillip, 116–128.

Mesthrie, Rajend. 1996. *Imagint excusations*: Missionary English in the nineteenth century Cape Colony, South Africa. *World Englishes* 15(2): 139–157.

Mesthrie, Rajend. 1999. Fifty ways to say "I do": Tracing the origins of unstressed do in Cape Flats English, South Africa. *South African Journal of Linguistics* 17(1): 58–71.

Mesthrie, Rajend. 2010. Sociophonetics and social change: Deracialisation of the GOOSE vowel in South African English. *Journal of Sociolinguistics* 14(1): 3–33.

Mesthrie, Rajend and Alida Chevalier. 2014. Sociophonetics and the Indian diaspora: The NURSE vowel and other selected features in South African Indian English. In Marianne Hundt and Devyani Sharma, eds. *English in the Indian Diaspora*. Amsterdam: John Benjamins, 85–104.

Mesthrie, Rajend, Alida Chevalier, and Timothy Dunne. 2015. A regional and social dialectology of the BATH vowel in South African English. *Language Variation and Change* 27(1): 1–30.

Mesthrie, Rajend and Ellen Hurst. 2013. Slang registers, code-switching and restructured urban varieties in South Africa: An analytic overview of tsotsitaals with special reference to the Cape Town variety. *Journal of Pidgin and Creole Languages* 28(1): 103–130.

Mfum-Mensah, Obed. 2006. The impact of colonial and postcolonial Ghanaian language policies on vernacular use in two northern Ghanaian communities. *Comparative Education* 41(1): 71–85.

Michieka, Martha Moraa. 2005. English in Kenya: A sociolinguistic profile. *World Englishes* 24(2): 173–186.

Mwangi, Serah. 2003. *Prepositions in Kenyan English: A Corpus-Based Study in Lexico-Grammatical Variation*. Aachen: Shaker Verlag.

Ndebele, Njabulo S. 1987. The English language and social change in South Africa. *English Academy Review* 4(1): 1–17

Nöthling, F. J. 1989. *Pre-colonial Africa: Her Civilisations and Foreign Contacts*. Johannesburg: Southern Book Publishers.

Ofori, Dominic M. and Mohammed Albakry. 2012. I own this language that everybody speaks: Ghanaians' attitude toward the English language. *English World-Wide* 33(2): 165–184.

Omoniyi, Toye. 2006. West African Englishes. In Braj B. Kachru, Yamuna Kachru, and Cecil L. Nelson, eds. *The Handbook of World Englishes*. Oxford: Blackwell, 172–187.

Pakenham, Thomas. 1991. *The Scramble for Africa*. London: Weidenfeld and Nicolson.

Peter, Lothar and Hans-Georg Wolf. 2007. A comparison of the varieties of West African Pidgin English. *World Englishes* 26(1): 3–21.

Rubagumya, Casmir, M. 1991. Language promotion for educational purposes: The example of Tanzania. *International Review of Education* 37(1): 67–85.

Samuelson, Beth L. and Freedman, Sarah W. 2010. Language policy, multilingual education, and power in Rswana. *Language Policy* 9(3): 191–215.

Schmied, Josef J. 1985. *Englisch in Tansania*. Heidelberg: Julius Groos Verlag.

Schmied, Josef. 1991. *English in Africa*. London: Longman.

Schmied, Josef. 1996. English in Zimbabwe, Zambia and Malawi. In Vivian De Klerk, ed. *Focus on South Africa*, Amsterdam: John Benjamins, 301–321.

Schmied, Josef. 2004. Cultural discourse in the Corpus of East African English and beyond: Possibilities and problems of lexical and collocational research in a one million-word corpus. *World Englishes* 23(2): 251–260.

Schmied, Josef. 2006. East African Englishes. In Braj B. Kachru, Yamuna Kachru, and Cecil L. Nelson, eds. *The Handbook of World Englishes.* Oxford: Blackwell, 188–202.

Schneider, Edgar W. 2003. The dynamics of New Englishes: From identity construction to dialect birth. *Language 79*: 233–281.

Schneider, Edgar W. 2007. *Postcolonial English: Varieties around the World.* Cambridge: Cambridge University Press.

Sey, K.A. 1973. *Ghanaian English: An Exploratory Study.* London: Macmillan.

Simeja, Brigit and Joyce T. Mathangwane. 2010. The development of English in Botswana: Language policy and education. In Andy Kirkpatrick, ed. *The Routledge Handbook of World Englishes.* Oxford: Routledge, 212–218.

Simo Bobda, Augustin. 2004. Linguistic apartheid: British language policy in Africa. *English Today* 20(1): 19–26.

Simo Bobda, Augustin. 2010. Cameroon: Which language, where and why? In Andy Kirkpatrick, ed. *The Routledge Handbook of World Englishes.* Oxford: Routledge, 653–670.

Singler, John V. 2008. Liberian Settler English: Phonology. In Rajend Mesthrie, ed. *Varieties of English, Vol. 4: Africa, South and Southeast Asia.* Berlin: Mouton de Gruyter, 102–114.

Skandera, Paul. 2003. *Drawing a Map of Africa: Idiom in Kenyan English.* Tübingen: Narr, 2003.

Stats SA. 2012. *Census 2011 in brief.* Pretoria: Statistics South Africa. www .statssa.gov.za/census/census_2011/census_products/Census_2011_ Census_in_brief.pdf)

Tembe, Juliet. 2006. Teacher training and the English language in Uganda. *TESOL Quarterly* 40(4): 857–860.

Titlestad, Peter. 1996. English, the Constitution and South Africa's language future. In Vivian De Klerk, ed. *Focus on South Africa.* Amsterdam: John Benjamins, 163–173.

Udofot, Inyang. 2013. The English language and politics in Nigeria. *Journal of the Nigeria English Studies Association* 13(1): 8–16.

Udofot, Inyang and Chibuike S. Mbarachi. 2016. Social media English in Nigeria. *Research Journal of English Language and Literature* 4(2): 775–784.

Van der Walt, Johann L. and Bertus van Rooy. 2002. Towards a norm in South African Englishes. *World Englishes* 21(1): 113–128.

Van Rooy, Bertus. 2011. A principled distinction between error and conventionalised innovation in African Englishes. In Joybrato Mukherjee and Marianne Hundt, eds. *Exploring Second-Language Varieties of English and Learner Englishes: Bridging a Paradigm Gap.* Amsterdam: John Benjamins, 191–209.

Van Rooy, Bertus. 2013. Corpus linguistic work on Black South African English. *English Today* 29(1): 10–15.

Van Rooy, Bertus. 2014. Convergence and endonormativity at Phase Four of the Dynamic Model. In Sarah Buschfeld, Thomas Hoffmann, Magnus Huber and Alexander Kautzsch, eds. *The Evolution of Englishes: The Dynamic Model and Beyond*. Amsterdam: John Benjamins, 21–38.

Van Rooy, Bertus and Coetzee-Van Rooy, Susan. 2015. The language issue and academic performance at a South African University. *Southern African Journal for Linguistics and Applied Linguistics* 33(1): 1–16.

Van Rooy, Bertus and Kruger Haidee. 2016. The innovative progressive aspect of Black South African English: The role of language proficiency and normative processes. *International Journal of Learner Corpus Research* 2(2): 205–228.

Van Rooy, Bertus and Lize Terblanche. 2010. Complexity in word-formation processes in new varieties of South African English. *Southern African Linguistics and Applied Language Studies* 28(4): 357–374.

Webb, Vic. 1996. English and language planning in South Africa: The flip-side. In Vivian De Klerk, ed. *Focus on South Africa*. Amsterdam: John Benjamins, 175–190.

Wolf, Hans-Georg. 2010. East and West African Englishes: Differences and commonalities. In Andy Kirkpatrick, ed. *The Routledge Handbook of World Englishes*. Oxford: Routledge, 197–211.

Wolf, Hans-Georg and Polzenhagen, Frank. 2009. *World Englishes: A Cognitive Sociolinguistic Approach*. Berlin: Mouton de Gruyter.

Wright, Laurence. 1995. English in South Africa: Effective communication and the policy debate. In L. W. Lanham, David Langhan, Arie Blacquière, and Laurence Wright, eds. *Getting the Message in South Africa: Intelligibility, Readability, Comprehensibility*. Howick: Brevitas, 1–8.

11

English in South Asia

Claudia Lange

From a bird's-eye perspective, the English language in South Asia has developed from a contested colonial legacy into an asset within the linguistic ecology of the region, both intra-nationally and pan-regionally. With more and more speakers and contexts of use in a population of well over a billion, English has become a firmly entrenched South Asian language with distinctive characteristics, effectively the third-largest variety of English worldwide.

This chapter will outline the sociohistorical background to the development of English in South Asia from the beginning of British colonialism in the area to the present day. The main focus will be on English in India as the largest state to emerge out of the former British Raj and arguably the historical input variety to other South Asian Englishes. In presenting distinctive features of Indian English vis-à-vis other South Asian Englishes, the notion of Indian English as the regional epicenter will also be taken into account.

11.1 Introduction

The modern geopolitical entity "South Asia" may be delineated in different ways. Political organizations such as the United Nations take Afghanistan, Bangladesh, Bhutan, India, Iran, Maldives, Nepal, Pakistan, and Sri Lanka to jointly constitute South Asia (Mann 2015: 1) while the South Asian Association for Regional Cooperation (SAARC) excludes Iran from this list. The magisterial survey *South Asian Languages and Linguistics* (Hock and Bashir 2016) excludes both Iran and Bhutan; the late Braj Kachru, in his influential overview of "English in South Asia" (Kachru 1994), referred to the seven states of India, Pakistan, Bangladesh, Sri Lanka, Nepal, Bhutan, and the Maldives. Kachru's chapter in a way set a trend in focusing mostly on Indian English (IndE) as representing South

Asian English (SAE), or even summarily equating SAE with IndE. There are several good reasons for doing so, even if it may cause some raised eyebrows in the Sri Lankan English (SLE) speech community: first of all the time-depth of the arrival of English on the scene, secondly the current socioeconomic status of India as the most populous and most influential country within South Asia – a fact that contributes to the third reason, namely the abundance of studies on IndE as compared to other South Asian varieties of English.

Table 11.1 captures information about the South Asian states that is relevant in the context of this chapter. The label "small" or even "micro states" for Bhutan and the Maldives appears justified when considering their population size (see Misra 2004a, 2004b). The final column notes whether an account of the variety in question has found its way into the *Handbook of Varieties of English* (HVE) (Kortmann et al. 2004) and/or its update, the *Electronic World Atlas of Varieties of English* (eWAVE; Kortmann and Lunkenheimer 2013), and whether it is represented in the ICE-project (*International Corpus of English*). As the table shows, only SLE and Pakistani English (PakE) are treated in standard reference handbooks (in addition to IndE; compare also Mendis and Rambukwella 2010 for SLE); there are only a handful of papers on English in Bangladesh (BanE) and Nepal (NepE), and none on English in Bhutan and the Maldives.[1]

This overview will proceed as follows. To begin with, a sketch of South Asia as a (socio-)linguistic area will focus on the shared cultural and linguistic heritage of this vast region with its long-standing traditions of literacy and multilingualism. The next section will be devoted to the history of English in the area, intimately tied up with the unfolding of British colonialism in what came to be known as the "British Raj." A subsequent section will be concerned with individual South Asian Englishes. Pride of place will be given to IndE, for the reasons outlined at the beginning of the chapter, as well as SLE. Finally, a section on the global impact of IndE brings up the rear: IndE in global diasporic contexts followed by a brief look at the available evidence for assigning the status of South Asian epicenter to IndE.

11.2   South Asia as a (Socio-)Linguistic Area

South Asia frequently figures as the prime example of a *Sprachbund* or convergence area: "South Asia is a linguistic area with one of the longest histories of contact, influence, use, and teaching and learning of English-in-diaspora in the world" (Kachru and Nelson 2006: 153). Contact between speakers representing four language families (Indo-Aryan, Dravidian, Austro-Asiatic, and Tibeto-Burman) goes back some 3,500 years. A lot of

---

[1] Except for articles based on the SAVE-corpus (*South Asian Varieties of English*), cf. Section 11.5.1.

Table 11.1 *Overview of South Asian countries*

Country	(Post)colonial History: Independence	Population	National/Official Languages, Main Language Families	Included in (a) HVE, (b) eWAVE, (c) ICE
Bangladesh (part of "British Raj")	1947 (as East Pakistan) 1971 (from Pakistan)	154 million (2013 census)	Bangla (IA)	(a) no (b) no (c) no
India Crown colony since 1858 ("British Raj")	1947	1.2 billion (2011 census)	Hindi (IA, official language), English (associate official language); DR, AA, TB	(a) yes (b) yes (c) yes
Nepal	n/a (2008: Republic rather than Monarchy)	26.5 million (2011 census)	Nepali (IA)	(a) no (b) no (c) no
Pakistan (part of "British Raj")	1947	132.3 million (1998 census)	Urdu (IA)	(a) yes (b) yes (c) no
Sri Lanka British Crown colony since 1802	1948 (Dominion status within the Commonwealth until 1972)	20.3 million (2012 census)	Sinhala (IA) Tamil (DR) English "link language"	(a) no (b) yes (c) yes
Bhutan	n/a	672,425 (2005 census)	Dzongkha (TB)	(a) no (b) no (c) no
Maldives British protectorate since 1887	1965	407,660 (2014 census)	Dhivehi (IA)	(a) no (b) no (c) no

Note. Abbreviations: IA: Indo-Aryan; DR: Dravidian; TB: Tibeto-Burman; AA: Austro-Asiatic.

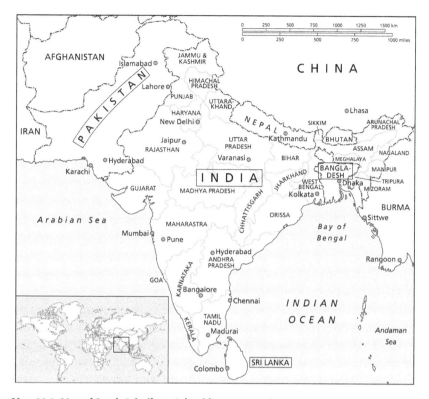

Map 11.1 Map of South Asia (from Schneider 2011: 152)

attention has been directed to the contact scenario involving Indo-Aryan (mainly situated in the north) and Dravidian (mainly located in the south) languages, arguing for the most likely candidates for contact-induced features (e.g. Emeneau 1956; Masica 1976; Hock and Bashir 2016: 241–260). From these lists of shared areal features, one common phonological trait of South Asian languages emerges as relevant for Indian English as well, namely the contrastive set of dental and retroflex consonants (cf. Section 11.4.1.1).

   The sacred Indo-Aryan texts, the earliest dating back to around 1500 BC, were composed in Sanskrit and transmitted orally for centuries; what is even more astonishing from a Western perspective dominated by "print-capitalism" (Anderson 2006) is that the first grammar of Sanskrit was likewise composed in verse form and committed to memory. The first written records of Sanskrit appeared in AD 150 but they do not mark a turning point in what was to remain an essentially oral culture. When Kachru (2008: 4) lists "Sanskritization" along with "Persianization" (in the wake of Mughal rule in north India from 1526 to 1707; cf. Abidi and Gargesh 2008) and "Englishization" as the major successive influences on the South Asian communicative space, he does not imply that Sanskritization is restricted to the distant past. In contemporary India, the shared cultural heritage of Sanskrit is sometimes appropriated for political agendas of quite different stripes, as will be discussed in Section 11.4.1.

However, the emphasis on South Asia as a convergence area should not mask the fact that the subcontinent is characterized by great linguistic diversity: Modern India alone is home to 122 languages (according to the 2001 census) or 462 (according to *Ethnologue*), depending on one's definition of "language." Grassroots multilingualism is the norm rather than the exception, as is a domain-specific allocation of languages, with, for example (in a middle-class family in northern India), colloquial Hindi-Urdu reserved for the bazaar, English for white-collar jobs, a regional language for family and friends, and yet another (minority) regional language for the childminder and domestic help. "In short, one of the defining features of South Asia is long-term stable bilingualism and linguistic accommodation" (Bhatia and Ritchie 2013: 858). Even though quite a number of the more vulnerable tribal languages are endangered, South Asia's multilingual ethos continues to thrive.[2]

Since the South Asian contact scenario extends well beyond the linguistic, scholars have proposed the notion of a "sociolinguistic area" with a shared "grammar of culture" (d'Souza 1987; Khubchandani 1991). The concept aims to capture shared norms of social interaction, translating into shared norms of politeness impacting on communicative exchanges regardless of linguistic boundaries. Such common, culturally rooted discursive practices will also surface in South Asian Englishes, as will be exemplified in Section 11.4.1.3.

11.3 English in South Asia: The Colonial Experience

South Asia's "Englishization" began in the early seventeenth century with the endeavors of the British East India Company (EIC) to compete with other European powers for the riches and markets of the East. The Portuguese had followed up Vasco da Gama's successful voyage to India in 1498 with the conquest of Goa on the west coast in 1510; the Dutch East India Company was founded in 1602 and likewise established trading outposts along the Indian coast, as did the French after the foundation of the French East India Company in 1642, acquiring Pondicherry on the east coast in 1673 from a local ruler. The EIC, founded in 1600, was granted a Royal Charter for the Asian trade; the Company's third voyage in 1606/7 took it to the port city of Surat (in today's Gujarat) (Farrington 1999: 726). In 1617, Sir Thomas Roe, the British ambassador to the Mughal emperor

---

[2] According to *Ethnologue*, "55 [Indian languages] are in trouble, and 13 are dying" (www.ethnologue.com/country/IN); the *UNESCO Interactive Atlas of the World's Languages in Danger* (Moseley 2010) lists 197 endangered languages, of which 42 are considered "critically endangered," 7 "severely endangered," and 5 "extinct" (www.unesco.org/languages-atlas/index.php?hl=en&page=atlasmap&lid=362).

Jahangir's court in Delhi, obtained permission for the Company to set up a trading post ("factory") in Surat (Metcalf and Metcalf 2006: 47). From these humble and haphazard beginnings, the EIC morphed from being one player among many both in the Indian Ocean trade and in the South Asian political arena to the de facto ruler of a subcontinent, a development that continues to baffle historians: "How so few Britons, as servants of a private business enterprise, could have conquered so huge an area and so many people, so far away, has never ceased to amaze or embarrass. Neither British nor national historiography has proven satisfactory" (Frykenberg 1999: 200).

In the following, the history of English in the Indian subcontinent, a by-product of British colonialism, will be charted until the end of the colonial period, reserving the postindependence developments in the separate states that emerged from former British India for the next section. This history has been laid out many times, providing different points of view (e.g. Kachru 1994; Krishnaswamy and Burde 1998: 79–144; Sailaja 2009: 96–112; Sedlatschek 2009: 8–24; Sharma 2012b). In the context of this volume, it is expedient to focus on the development of English in the area from the perspective of the Dynamic Model as out-lined in Schneider (2007: 161–173) and Mukherjee (2010). Figure 11.2 combines a timeline with their alignment of relevant events with the five stages posited by the Dynamic Model (see Buschfeld and Kautzsch, Chapter 3, this volume). Both scholars agree that the foundation stage lasted until 1757, when the troops of the EIC won the battle of Plassey and established control over Bengal, a secure and highly profitable bridgehead for its further expansion. This date also features in historians' accounts as the beginning of the "Company Raj" (e.g. Bose and Jalal 2004: 53–69), a century of brokering and consolidating power until the advent of "Crown Raj" in 1858, when British control over India was transferred from the EIC directly to the British government in the wake of the revolt unfolding over the previous year. However, British concerns about lan-guage – the languages of indigenous learning, of administration, and of modern education – predate the realm's official integration into the British Empire. The Charter Act of 1813 conferred responsibility for Indian education on the EIC, leading to prolonged arguments about the kind of institutions to be funded, as well as the medium of instruction. It has become customary to use the labels "Orientalists" and "Anglicists" for the contestants in this debate: Horace Hayman Wilson as the most articulate spokesperson for the "extreme" Orientalist cause (cf. Sirkin and Sirkin 1971: 415) was squarely in favor of indigenous learning – that is, of continuing an elitist Brahmanical tradition of imparting the classical canon of Sanskrit learning on the select few (Sirkin and Sirkin 1971: 411–412). The Anglicists, on the other hand, most likely had ulterior imperialist motives in mind in opting for modern subjects but they were also well aware of local support and the rising demand for

English education: Ram Mohan Roy, a well-known Bengali intellectual, already took the Anglicist side in the debate when he protested against the establishment of a further Sanskrit college in 1823:

> the Sanskrit system of education would be the best calculated to keep this country in darkness, if such had been the policy of the British legislature. But as the improvement of the native population is the object of the government, it will consequently promote a more liberal and enlightened system of instruction; embracing mathematics, natural philosophy, chemistry, anatomy, with other useful sciences.
>
> (cited in Zastoupil and Moir 1999: 113)

What is generally highlighted as a turning point for the establishment of English in India can be pinpointed to the year 1835 and Thomas Babington Macaulay's *Minute on Education* (cf. Zastoupil and Moir 1999: 161–173). The *Minute* is credited with establishing the Anglicist victory and thus with turning the tide for English in India: "The comprehensive implementation of English in India via Macaulay's Minute was a transformative moment in India's linguistic history. The 19th century witnessed a steady increase in English use in education, press, printing, and bureaucracy" (Sharma 2012b: 2079). It has to be noted that English as the medium of instruction does not necessarily follow from the focus on modern subjects, as the shorthand "Anglicist" readily insinuates. English was eventually favored over the vernacular Indian languages out of practical reasons: It would have been too time-consuming to translate everything that was to be taught into (not yet standardized) Indian languages. Thus, if considered out of context, Macaulay's assessment as the imperialist incarnate is certainly justified, for example "The 'Minute' constitutes an example of colonialist and imperialist attitude of superiority" (Sailaja 2009: 106). However, in retrospect the "extreme Orientalist" position was perhaps more condescending than Macaulay's – the liberating potential of a modern education did eventually unfold itself, to the detriment of the colonial rulers (Evans 2002: 279). Nevertheless, the impact of all colonial language policies was also always limited to the territories under direct British control, omitting the princely states that covered about a quarter of India (cf. Hock and Bashir 2016: 648). Finally, "in 1854, the largest part of educational enterprise in India (indigenous schools apart) was provided, not by the Company, but by the missionaries" (Nurullah and Naik 1951: 101).

As Figure 11.2 shows, only Mukherjee (2010) acknowledges 1835 as the beginning of the nativization phase for IndE; Schneider (2007) takes the period from 1757 up to 1905 as the phase of exonormative stabilization and doubts whether IndE has since then progressed from nativization to endonormative stabilization. Neither Schneider nor Mukherjee integrate decolonization in 1947 into their accounts; in the Dynamic Model, independence is a necessary but not a sufficient condition for moving toward endonormative stabilization. On Mukherjee's timeline, IndE's progression

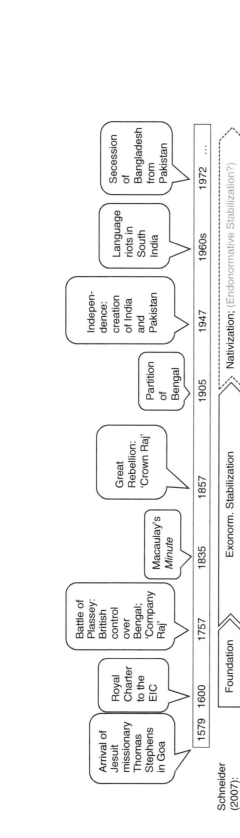

Figure 11.1 A timeline for the establishment of English in the Indian subcontinent

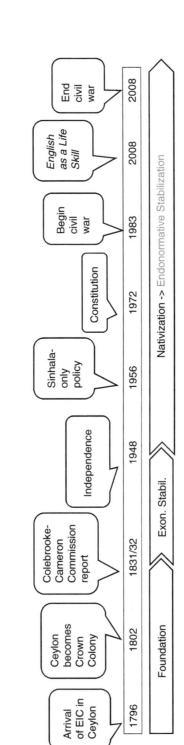

Figure 11.2 A timeline for the establishment of English in Sri Lanka (after Bernaisch 2015: 19–54)

on the cycle is linked to postindependent events, which will be treated in the next section.

Independence from British colonial rule in 1947 went along with Partition, creating India and Pakistan as sovereign states. Pakistan, in turn, comprising East and West Pakistan, experienced language conflicts almost from its inception, with the Bangla-speaking population of East Pakistan fiercely opposing the imposition of Urdu as the national language (cf. Rahman 2006: 79–102). The tension between the two discontinuous parts of the country finally erupted into open civil war, which eventually led to the secession of East Pakistan to become Bangladesh in 1971.

Thus, the label "Indian English" has changed its reference in 1947, from denoting English in colonial British India to Indian English(es) only. When the two and later three sovereign states emerging from the independence process were free to negotiate their own language policies, the differences in the role accorded to English led to markedly different evolutionary trajectories for English in the individual South Asian countries, to be sketched in Section 11.4.

11.3.1 The Colonial Complaint Tradition

English in colonial India is the historical input variety to IndE, PakE, and BanE alike and came into focus of what may be called the "colonial complaint tradition." Nineteenth- and early twentieth-century writings on IndE testify both to the increasing role of English in Indian society and to the expats' condescending attitude toward it, a reflection of the overall shift from admiration for the ancient culture to a supremacist perspective. Collections such as *Baboo English as 'tis Writ: Being Curiosities of Indian Journalism* (Wright 1891) both generated and fed the stereotype of the "bookish" character of Indians' writing in English (cf. Sedlatschek 2009: 49), which can be traced back to its nativization phase: "English education and bureaucracy emerge almost simultaneously and become a decisive combination for the use of English in India" (Krishnaswamy and Burde 1998: 89). The stereotypical designation "Babu" or "Baboo" for an Indian clerk working for the British colonial administration originated in Bengal but came to be extended to all Indians who staffed the extensive bureaucracy and promoted a "bureaucratic register with its officialese and the formulaic use of English within and outside the bureaucratic domain" (ibid.: 96).

Early twentieth-century writings on colonial IndE display a shift away from the mere collection of "curious specimens" (Wright 1891: 53) toward a more systematic comparative approach. While these (e.g. Whitworth 1907; Goffin 1934; Kindersley 1938) capture features of IndE mainly in terms of "deviance" from its historical input variety, they still serve as our only access to historical IndE, until a diachronic corpus of IndE becomes available.

11.4 Postcolonial South Asian Englishes

11.4.1 Indian English

English is more entrenched in the sociocultural fabric of modern India than in any other South Asian society. Still, IndE's position on Schneider's evolutionary trajectory remains open to discussion: Schneider (2007: 172–173) himself sees IndE as oddly poised between stage 3 and 4, assuming that it might not become a marker of identity for the speech community. Mukherjee (2007), on the other hand, relates the advent of endonormative stabilization to political events triggered by postcolonial India's legislation concerning the official languages of the Union: Article 343 of the Indian constitution (1949) stipulated Hindi as the Union's official language, with English in place as the second official language for another fifteen years. This period of time was deemed long enough for the transition from the colonizer's language in government and administration to an indigenous language, and also for this language to become a symbol of national unity as envisaged by Gandhi, even though it was unevenly distributed: Hindi was – and still is – mostly confined to the north and the language with the largest number of speakers but it is not the majority language.

Gandhi had campaigned relentlessly for Hindustani – colloquial Hindi-Urdu – as the national language. For him, getting rid of English was vital for thorough decolonization:

> The highest development of the Indian mind must be possible without a knowledge of English. It is doing violence to the manhood and specially the womanhood of India to encourage our boys and girls to think that an entry into the best society is impossible without a knowledge of English. It is too humiliating a thought to be bearable. To get rid of the infatuation for English is one of the essentials of swaraj [self-rule]. (Gandhi [1921] 1999)

His project of propagating Hindustani for the whole country was not only to unify the northern Hindi-belt with the southern Dravidian states but also to bridge the ever widening gap between Hindus and Muslims. After the national trauma of Partition and the foundation of Pakistan as a separate Muslim state, his vision lost all support.

In the 1960s, shortly before Hindi was to become the sole official and national language, the issue became a rallying point for the grievances of the Dravidian south against the Indo-Aryan north, culminating in violent upheavals protesting against the phasing-out of English. After months of unrest and a high death toll, the Union government backed out of the commitment to Hindi: English was to remain the second official language indefinitely.

Estimates about the number of proficient speakers of English in India vary: Crystal (2008: 4) estimates that "around a third of the population were these days capable of carrying on a domestic conversation in

English," that is "around 350 million people"; according to Graddol (2010: 66), "the 2001 census data (released in late 2009) reports that 10.4% of the population claimed to speak English as a second or third language – that equates to around 126 million speakers in 2010." Still, Kachru's (1994: 509) notion of a "cline of proficiency" has not lost its significance. On the one hand, there are Indians identifying as native speakers of English, with English as their sole or (more commonly) one of their home languages, and typically clustering in affluent metropolitan milieus (as well as in those states that have chosen English as their official language, e.g. Nagaland in the northeast). On the other hand, around 270 million Indians live below the poverty line, with hardly any access to basic amenities and services, let alone English education.[3] Even though English is mostly no longer framed as a colonial imposition, it sparks ambivalent attitudes: Students coming up from rural colleges to metropolitan universities acutely feel the class and caste connotations attached to lingering on the wrong end of the cline of proficiency. English is a highly prized commodity, with countless English-medium institutions from playschools to colleges cashing in on the demand. This ambivalence is also apparent in the Dalit community itself, with a tendency to pit English against other Indian languages. The people marginalized by the Hindu caste system, who prefer to rally round the designation "Dalit" ("downtrodden") rather than "untouchables," are aware of the advantages of English as a neutral language within a highly stratified society:

> For the privileged sections, English could be a language of achievement, or they could have a choice between languages. But for the disadvantaged and marginalized people like the Dalits, mastering English would mean liberation. They do not have a choice because mainstream languages, being the medium of instruction in education, are equally oppressive.
>
> (Uma et al. 2014: 2)

"Sanskritization," as mentioned in Section 11.2, equally contributes to the marginalization of large sections of society: Sanskrit as the holy Vedic language was the sole prerogative of Brahmin pundits and had to be kept apart from women and lower castes. Eventually, the slow but steady broadening of the social base for the acquisition of English will accelerate the development of innovative forms and functions of English as a truly Indian language.

In a sense, this whole volume in general as well as this chapter in particular are a tribute to the legacy of the late Braj Kachru, who, in fighting for the recognition of Indian English as a variety in its own right, also established the whole field of World Englishes. Many of the points Kachru made about English in South Asia still stand, even though his empirical basis was remarkably thin: Krishnaswamy and Burde (1998:

---

[3] This figure is based on the World Bank's definition of poverty as having to subside on less than $1.90 a day, cf. http://www.worldbank.org/en/news/infographic/2016/05/27/india-s-poverty-profile.

35) rather scathingly criticize him for equating "literary writing in [Indian] English with the use of English in everyday life" and concomitantly (mis-) representing his examples of "Indianisms" as everyday IndE. Slightly gentler criticism comes from Sedlatschek (2009: 30), who attributes the "feature list approach" to Kachru, among others, and notes:

> The major weakness of feature-list descriptions of IndE lies in their presentation of data in a decontextualized fashion without documenting the stability of individual items, their domains of use and their overall relevance for IndE as a linguistic entity. (p. 40)

Today, with this criticism in mind, concentrating on empirical studies of South Asian varieties of English is no big feat: Studies on the lexicogrammar and/or morphosyntax of South Asian varieties of English are now typically corpus-based – that is, if a corpus for a particular variety is available. IndE is represented with the Kolhapur Corpus (modeled on the Brown family; cf. Hundt 2015) released in 1986 as well as with ICE-India, released in 2002; the written part of ICE-Sri Lanka has been released previously and the spoken part is now also available. PakE, BanE, and NepE are caught in a vicious circle: There exist only a few studies to begin with, and the absence of corpora effectively discourages scholars to contribute to further research on their distinctive features. One notable exception has to be mentioned: The *South Asian Varieties of English* (SAVE) corpus provides access to the register of newspaper language across six South Asian Englishes (cf. Bernaisch et al. 2011). However, studies based on this corpus typically assume a comparative perspective, frequently with the notion of IndE as a regional epicenter at issue (cf. Section 11.5.1), and do not single out the lesser-known South Asian Englishes.

11.4.1.1 IndE Phonology

The inevitability of defining a nativized standard for the pronunciation of General Indian English has been acknowledged early on, notably by R. K. Bansal (widely circulated as Bansal and Harrison [1988] 2009). Nihalani et al. (1979: 203, 205) summarize the tacit consensus:

> We believe that BRP [British RP], because it is unattainable and in many other ways unsuitable for India, does not represent a realistic model. . . . Any language model to be followed in instruction and learning has to be a living model and one which is physically present.
>
> . . .
>
> Indian learners general feel that they would sound rather "foreign" – unnatural and affected – if they imitated BRP.

More recent acoustic studies have confirmed the range of variation in spoken IndE as a reflection of speakers' L1 (Wiltshire 2005; Wiltshire and Harnsberger 2006; Maxwell and Fletcher 2009). A comprehensive summary of current research on IndE phonology can be found in Fuchs (2016: 20–25).

Table 11.2 *The phoneme inventory of educated Indian English compared to*
British English (after Fuchs: 2016: 23, 25)

Lexical Set	IndE	BrE	Lexical Set	IndE	BrE
GOAT, NORTH	o	əʊ, ɔ	THIN	t̪ʰ	θ
LOT	ɔ	ɒ	THUS	d̪	ð
STRUT, COMMA, NURSE	ʌ~ɐ~ə	ʌ, ə, ɜ	COOL, SCHOOL	k̚	kʰ ~k̚
FACE	e	ɛɪ	POOL, SPOOL	p̚	pʰ ~ p̚
CURE	u(ə)	ʊə	TOOL, STOOL	t̚~t̪	t̪ʰ~ t̚
VILLAGE, WILL	ʋ~w	v, w	DULL	d~d̪	d
LIP, PILL	l	l, ɫ	ROLL	ɹ~ɾ~r~ɭ	ɹ
			CAR	∅~ ɹ~ɾ~r~ɭ	∅

The most conspicuous pan-regional pronunciation features include the
monophthongization of the FACE and GOAT diphthongs, the retroflex
realization of the dental plosives /t/ and /d/, and the realization of the dental
fricatives as dental plosives. Another typical feature concerns the retention
of the vowel in unstressed syllables.

Fuchs's study is also the first to go beyond the general pronouncement
that IndE is syllable-timed rather than stress-timed. His investigation confirmed empirically that the phonology of IndE can indeed be characterized
as syllable-timed in comparison to British English (BrE), and "[g]iven how
robust the differences between IndE and BrE are, it is likely that a more
syllable-timed rhythm will remain part and parcel of IndE in the future"
(Fuchs 2016: 207).

11.4.1.2 IndE Lexicogrammar

One of the unequivocal indicators of endonormative stabilization, namely
a dictionary of the local variety, is not in evidence for IndE. Lambert (2012:
312) reviews the available dictionaries and concludes:

> As the situation currently stands, the lexicography of Indian English
> provides an unsatisfactory and insufficient description of the variety.
> There are a number of dictionaries purporting to cover Indian English
> in one way or another, but these incorporate a great number of
> deficiencies that detract from their overall worth. In short, they tend
> to present Indian English as nothing more than "standard" English
> with a select collection of lexical peculiarities tacked on, as it were,
> many of which would be regarded as "errors" by prescriptivist lan-
> guage scholars.

At the time of writing, Lambert did not register much enthusiasm in the
speech community for the laborious and time-consuming project of codifying IndE in a national dictionary. There has been no change in attitude

since then – a project application to include IndE in a new *Linguistic Survey of India* was shelved (Malekar 2010; see also Lange 2012a: 271). *The People's Linguistic Survey of India* has published a volume on *English and Other International Languages* (Kumar 2018). Meanwhile, at least the number of IndE entries in the *Oxford English Dictionary* continues to grow;[4] recent examples include *yaar* (added June 2015, first attestation 1963), *filmi* (added December 2016, first attestation 1965), and *chana dal* (added June 2017, first attestation 1895).

The situation for lexicogrammar/morphosyntax is markedly different. The numerous studies available can be broadly assigned to two directions: First are studies that take Schneider's (2007: 86) dictum as their point of departure that "grammatical innovations, also in the process of structural nativization, typically start out where the regular meets the chaotic, i.e. at the intersection of grammar and lexis" and look at a morphosyntactic feature from a comparative perspective. Examples include verb complementation patterns, ditransitives, light verbs (cf. Kashyap 2014: 260). Other studies return to the much-maligned "feature list approach" (see Section 11.4.1) and try to substantiate the claims concerning typical "Indianisms" empirically. For the latter approach, Sedlatschek (2009) stands out as the most comprehensive corpus-based investigation of a wide range of IndE features. Some of the "typical Indianisms" covered above are also attested across many other Postcolonial Englishes (PCEs), as already noted by Platt et al. (1984) and discussed by Sharma (2012c). The most conspicuous of these will be presented in turn.

No account of IndE fails to mention that "[IndE] speakers tend to use articles where they are not necessary and leave them out where they are" (Sailaja 2009: 52), e.g.

(1) A; I think the movie has started <,>
     B: Yeah <,>
     A: Which movie
     B: *It is good movie* you know <,> (ICE-IND:S1A-070#223–226)

(2) No exception could be taken to that approach but the fact that cannot be denied is that during *the recent years* a situation was brought about to make the Governors merely dummies of the powers that be at the Centre. (ICE-IND:W2E-009#71:3)

The IndE patterns of article use are frequently correlated with substrate influence, since Indian languages lack articles. However, if substrate influence were the only factor, then we would expect fewer articles in IndE generally than in other varieties, as Sedlatschek (2009: 199) observed. His quantitative study revealed a higher frequency of definite articles in IndE than in BrE or American English (AmE), which calls a simplistic explanation

---

[4] *Oxford English Dictionary* (OED) online: www.oed.com.

in terms of substrate influence into doubt. Platt, Weber, and Ho (1984: 54) already suggested that many PCEs operate with a different system governing the use of articles: They "appear to make the specific/non-specific distinction rather than follow the definite/indefinite division of the more established Englishes." Sharma empirically verified and extended this account for IndE: "the markedly different article system seems to be sensitive not only to specificity but also to the relative discourse familiarity of the NP [noun phrase]" (2005: 561). There is further evidence that innovative patterns of article usage are stabilizing in both spoken and written language: IndE speakers who consider English as one of their native languages retain nonstandard patterns of article use (Sharma 2005: 544), and set phrases such as *the recent years*, as in Example (2), firmly belong to the repertoire of Indian broadsheet newspapers (Sedlatschek 2009: 214).

Another feature deemed typical of IndE is the so-called overuse of the progressive, that is, the progressive supposedly occurs with a higher frequency in IndE and is also extended to new contexts, namely to stative verbs as illustrated in Example (3).[5]

(3) A: Un by any chance uh <,> *you were uh knowing* the police <,> uh officers of Bandra Police station <,,> ? [...]
     C: *I'm not having* any acquaintance with the police officers of Bandra police station (ICE-IND:S1B-062#38–41)

Stative verbs in the progressive are indeed more frequent in IndE (Balasubramanian 2009: 90), as is the progressive form overall (Sharma 2009). This again may be explained by the complex interaction of substrate and superstrate: Since languages such as Hindi require the marking of (im-)perfectivity, "IndE speakers have a pervasive substrate pressure to mark imperfectivity overtly," falling back on the polysemous –*ing*-form "as a global imperfectivity marker." Thus, a system that is "typologically distinct from both input systems" emerges (Sharma 2005: 185).

The "feature list" for IndE further contains the lack of inversion in questions, as in Example (4), and its mirror image, that is, inversion in embedded interrogatives, as in Example (5).

(4) A: Uh Mr Angale <,>
     B: Yes <,,>
     A: Uh in the year nineteen eighty-one what business <,> *you were* <,,> *doing* <,,> ? (ICE-IND:S1B-062#1–3)

(5) Could you kindly let me know *what exactly was the understanding* with USEFI about the purchase of our published proceedings?[6] (ICE-IND: W1B-012#10:1)

---

[5] Sharma (2012a: 527) provides the ranking "pervasive" for IndE for the two eWAVE-categories related to the "wider range of uses of progressive *be* +*V-ing*," namely "extension to stative verbs" and "extension to habitual contexts."

[6] USEFI: *United States Educational Foundation in India*.

Both Sedlatschek (2009: 289–296) and Hilbert (2008) have shown that this construction is much rarer than the feature lists would have it and largely confined to unmonitored speech and nonprofessional writing.

The most conspicuous feature of spoken IndE is the "invariant non-concord tags" (eWAVE) *isn't it* (Example (6)) and *no/na* (Example (7)), the latter derived from the Hindi negative particle *na* that also functions as a question tag.

(6)   Okay okay <,> Indian culture says that women should work <,> *isn't it?* (ICE-IND:S1A-087#165:1:B)

(7)   No I'm do not fall in the problem <,> because I like like this <,> because *na* whenever we are coming from outside *no* <,> then get we fever and all *no* <,> someone should look after *no* then only <,> we can look after others <,> like this I'm doing the work *no* <,> I'll I can't do all the work (ICE-IND:S1A-049#188:1:A)

It has frequently been claimed that *no/na* constitutes "bad (Indian) English" and is restricted to speakers with low proficiency, but the empirical evidence suggests otherwise: In the ICE-India direct conversation files, indigenous *no/na* massively outnumbers the English-derived tags, both invariant and canonical. The indigenous tag is overrepresented with younger female speakers, hinting at a possible change from below: "We are dealing, then, with the established borrowing of a bilingual discourse marker" (Lange 2012b: 231).

Another feature found in spoken IndE is labeled "non-initial existential *there*," a misnomer in several respects: The main function of the existential construction is not to assert the existence of some entity but to introduce new referents into the discourse while preserving the old-before-new pattern of structuring information. Since this pattern is reversed in the IndE construction, this discourse meaning is lost entirely, as in Example (8). Example (9) is even further remote from the function of the existential in the more traditional varieties of English: discourse-deictic *that* refers to the preceding turn. Rather than establishing new information in the discourse, *that is there* acknowledges the preceding speaker's turn by "elliptical repetition," a South Asian politeness device (cf. Lange 2012b: 121)

(8)   This Saturday I think one <,> lecture *is there* <,> (ICE-IND:S1A-086#206:1:A)

(9)   B: You have heavy rains
       A: Yeah Goa it's raining very heavily and you can't go anywhere out also <,> uhm
       B: Yeah *that is there* in Goa also (ICE-IND:S1A-065#19–21)

Finally, the focus markers *also* (cf. Fuchs 2012), *only*, and *itself* typically found in spoken IndE have to be mentioned. Example (10) displays *only* in its innovative IndE use as a presentational focus marker:

(10)   Anyway I <,> I have in fact planned about <,> doing IAS now[7]
        My parents wanted it <,,> and in fact first I was thinking of becom-
        ing a lecturer *only* <,> but then something happened and now <,>
        I am going to sit for IAS (ICE-IND:S1A-062#152–153)

A *lecturer* **only** does not indicate a negative evaluation (in contrast to a career
in the IAS); *only* simply serves to emphasize, as *itself* does in Example (11).

(11)   Sarich and Wilson were not new to announcing provocative the-
        ories on human evolution. Their initial salvo in the field was fired *in*
        the 1960s itself with results similar to the reactions they were getting
        now. (ICE-IND:W2B-038#18–19)

Presentational *only* is much more common than *itself* and largely restricted
to spoken language, while *itself* has already stabilized in written IndE and
beyond (cf. Lange 2007). Both forms are calques of Hindi clitics; this origin
in an invariant particle might also go some way toward explaining invariant *itself* with a plural antecedent in Example (11) (cf. Bernaisch and Lange
2012: 11–12).

11.4.1.3   IndE pragmatics

Compared to lexicogrammar, the pragmatics of IndE appears underre-
searched, a condition shared with other PCEs (Schneider 2007: 47). Kashyap
(2014: 263–266) provides an overview of work done so far. An important
landmark in the field is d'Souza's (1987, 1988) notion of a "grammar of
culture" (cf. Section 11.2), extending to the South Asian convergence area.
Its linguistic reflexes are most prominent in the field of politeness. For example, elaborate kinship terminology as well as the use of *auntie* and *uncle* as
honorifics for persons older than oneself testify to the importance of the
extended family. Within this extended family, saying "thank you" would be
impolite, as it creates social distance (Lange 2012b: 63). Discourse-pragmatic
patterns such as the non-initial existential *there* described in Section 11.4.1.2
also serve to express politeness by "elliptical repetition," thus creating topic
continuity in discourse (Subbarao et al. 1991; Lange 2012b: 239).

   As English continues to be nativized in India, the emergence of a new hybrid
"grammar of culture" will prove a particularly interesting field of study.

11.4.2   Sri Lankan English

English in Sri Lanka underwent a checkered history following the country's
independence. Figure 11.3 displays the development of SLE since the arrival
of the EIC (in what was then Ceylon). Despite being much younger than IndE,
there is a noteworthy overlap in the two countries' colonial language policies:
The Colebrooke-Cameron commission report did for Sri Lanka what

---

[7] IAS: (entrance exam for) the *Indian Administrative Service*.

Macaulay's *Minute* did for India (cf. Section 11.3). After independence in 1948, English continued to be the official language until 1956, when the Official Language Act made Sinhala, the dominant language of the population, the only official language – to the detriment of English-medium education, and much more to the detriment of the Tamil-speaking minority:

> In the years preceding Sinhala as the sole official language, the English language, either as a shared privilege or a common enemy, had a unifying effect for the various ethnic groups in Sri Lanka. However, when English was relegated to the status of a second language, this unifying effect ceased to exist accordingly, which lead to each ethnic group fighting for niches in the social hierarchy.   (Bernaisch 2015: 35)

As always, language conflicts are only the surface manifestations of social conflicts, which erupted into a bitter civil war between Tamil separatists and the Sinhala majority that lasted from 1983 until 2008.

The constitution of 1987 already went some way toward alleviating the grievances of the Tamil minority: Both Sinhala and Tamil became official languages and English was designated "the link language," leaving open "what English is supposed to link" (Mendis and Rambukwella 2010: 182). Since 2008, the government campaign *English as a Life Skill* aims at improving English competence throughout the country's educational institutions. Teacher training modules and textbooks were designed in cooperation with the Indian *English and Foreign Languages University* (EFL-U), which gave rise to a heated public discussion about the relative status and value of the indigenous variety of English vis-à-vis IndE and BrE (Lim 2013; Bernaisch 2015: 51–53). Public opinion does not necessarily follow most linguists' pronouncement that SLE constitutes a variety in its own right.

Empirical studies on SLE are few; Bernaisch (2015) stands out as a detailed investigation of selected aspects of the lexicogrammar of SLE. Michael Meyler (2007), whose *Dictionary of Sri Lankan English* ignited the debate in the country whether SLE was really distinct from BrE, places SLE on a cline between IndE and BrE: On the one hand, "Indian English and Sri Lankan English have much in common" (Meyler 2012: 541) but, on the other, he acknowledges "how close Sri Lankan English is to the British standard, when compared with other varieties" (p. 542).

At the time of writing, both the written and spoken part of ICE-Sri Lanka are available from the corpus compilers at Justus-Liebig University Giessen (Germany). Now that ICE-Sri Lanka is complete, researchers will have ample opportunity to probe into the specific forms and functions of SLE.

11.5 Supraregional and Global South Asian Englishes

Speakers of South Asian Englishes have long moved beyond the subcontinent, sometimes involuntarily (as indentured servants to South Africa, cf. Mesthrie 1992) but frequently permanently, establishing diasporic communities in areas as diverse as the USA, the UK, East Africa, South Africa, Guyana, and Fiji – to name but a few that have been subject to research (cf. Hundt and Sharma 2014; Zipp, Chapter 6, this volume). Sharma's studies of British Asian English spanning three generations of speakers indicate that speakers' repertoires comprise standard BrE, local London English as well as IndE to different degrees in different contexts; some heritage language forms acquire new social meanings in the process of forging a distinct British Asian identity (Sharma 2011). "Chutnefying English" or "Hinglish" (Kothari and Snell 2011) represents another note-worthy aspect of global South Asian Englishes: Mixed codes, especially in urban settings and with younger speakers, seem to be on the rise, testify-ing to the creative exploitation of multilingual repertoires (cf. Schneider 2016). Phenomena such as these will continue to mount a challenge to the established categories and tools of variationist studies.

11.5.1   IndE as Regional Epicenter

It has some intuitive plausibility to assume that IndE plays a prominent role within South Asia: India is the largest, most populous, and economic-ally most powerful country in the area, with a well-established tradition of literary creativity in English. The booming Bollywood film production attracts fans across South Asia and beyond. Indian universities provide English and/or teacher training courses for thousands of students from neighboring countries. However, in order to transform a mere hunch into a testable hypothesis, the concept of an "epicenter" has to be more rigor-ously defined. According to Hundt (2013: 185),

> a variety can be regarded as a potential epicentre if it shows endonorma-tive stabilization (i.e. widespread use, general acceptance and codifica-tion of the local norms of English) on the one hand, and the potential to serve as a model of English for (neighboring?) countries on the other hand.

Table 11.3 draws together the available studies tackling the epicenter question: These are typically corpus-based and quantify the occurrence of a specific feature or construction across South Asian Englishes. All studies demonstrate that a particular feature is more frequent in IndE than in the neighboring varieties, hinting at a possible "trickle-down effect" for the spread of features. Unfortunately, the sheer presence of a feature, even if with higher frequency, is only a necessary but not a sufficient condition for stipulating epicenter status. Diachronic studies would be needed to verify the spread of features, as well as attitudinal studies that test the acceptance of IndE features outside of India (cf. Hundt 2013: 201). As it stands, the issue must remain unresolved until a diachronic corpus of South Asian Englishes can be scrutinized.

Table 11.3 *Overview of studies testing the potential epicenter status for IndE*

Study, Feature Under Discussion	Results
Light verbs, e.g. *have a look, take rest, give a boost* (Hoffmann, Hundt, and Mukherjee 2011)	IndE has a higher frequency of LVC than all other varieties No conclusive evidence for epicenter status
Hypothetical subjunctive, e.g. *if I were you; as if that* would *achieve the desired results* (Hundt, Hoffmann, and Mukherjee 2012)	No conclusive evidence for epicenter status
Presentational focus marker *itself*, e.g. *there itself, on Monday* itself (Bernaisch and Lange 2012)	IndE has highest frequency of focus marker *itself*, followed by Nepal and Sri Lanka No conclusive evidence for epicenter status
Dative alternation with GIVE, e.g. *John gave a book to Mary* vs. *John gave Mary a book* (Bernaisch, Gries, and Mukherjee 2014; Gries and Bernaisch 2016)	"IndE is the variety from which the others are predicted with the smallest summed deviation, followed by Maldivian and then Pakistani English" (Gries and Bernaisch 2016: 19) "synchronic data are sufficient to identify linguistic epicenters, but diachronic data are needed to study their seismic waves." (Gries and Bernaisch 2016: 23)
Complex-transitive complementation with "intrusive *as*," e.g. *People call it* as *city of garden* (Lange 2016; Koch, Lange, and Leuckert 2016)	India and Sri Lanka have highest frequency of "intrusive *as*," Nepal the lowest No conclusive evidence for epicenter status

11.6   Conclusion and Outlook

The long history of English in South Asia gave rise to a multitude of South Asian Englishes, most of which still remain largely beyond the focus of research. This chapter has aimed at a historical, sociocultural, and linguistic sketch of English in South Asia, with a strong but unavoidable bias toward English in India. Thus, the unfortunate situation that more is known about IndE than about all other South Asian Englishes combined persists. These Englishes – with the exception of SLE – mainly occur in accounts of language policies and planning (e.g. Simpson 2007; Chand 2013), leaving ample scope for further research on their linguistic properties. A further bias concerns the almost exclusive choice of educated SAE as the object of investigation, a bias that emerged as a by-product of the development of the field: As already mentioned, establishing PCEs as a legitimate field of study entailed acknowledging the legitimacy of PCEs as varieties in their own right – rather than learner Englishes riddled with "deviations." This more or less naturally led to an emphasis on educated L2 usage, which became reified with the advent and the eager adoption of the ICE-corpora with their focus on standard(izing) varieties of English. Now that the ideological skirmishes over PCEs are long over, researchers are free to turn their attention to grassroots Englishes and to (re-)turn to learner Englishes in South Asia and elsewhere (see Meierkord, Chapter 14; Edwards and Seargeant, Chapter 15, Buschfeld, Chapter 24, this volume). In doing so, they will eventually arrive at a more inclusive representation of South Asian communicative spaces. Further, the study of multilingualism and language contact (see Fox, Chapter 20, this volume), leading to contact languages and contact-induced language change (see Lim, Chapter 4, this volume) would receive a massive boost if more contributions came from multilingual members of the very speech communities under scrutiny.

The intricate interplay of convergence vs. divergence, globalization vs. localization on both a micro- and a macrolinguistic level will continue to manifest itself in individual speech communities as well as across the South Asian linguistic area as a whole. After all, English has been, is, and will be an Asian language, matching the dynamism that drives South Asian societies.

References

Abidi, S. A. H. and Gargesh, R. 2008. Persian in South Asia. In B. B. Kachru, S. N. Sridhar, and Y. Kachru, eds. *Language in South Asia*. Cambridge: Cambridge University Press, 103–120.

Anderson, B. 2006. *Imagined Communities: Reflections on the Origin and Spread of Nationalism* (rev. ed.). London: Verso.

Balasubramanian, C. 2009. *Register Variation in Indian English*. Amsterdam: John Benjamins.

Bansal, R. K., and Harrison, B. [1988] 2009. *Spoken English: A Manual of Speech and Phonetics*. New Delhi: Orient BlackSwan.

Bernaisch, T. 2015. *The Lexis and Lexicogrammar of Sri Lankan English*. Amsterdam: Benjamins.

Bernaisch, T., Gries, S. T. and Mukherjee, J. 2014. The dative alternation in South Asian English(es): Modelling predictors and predicting prototypes. *English World-Wide* 35: 7–31.

Bernaisch, T., Koch, C., Schilk, M. and Mukherjee, J. 2011. *Manual to the South Asian Varieties of English (SAVE) Corpus*. Giessen: Justus Liebig University, Department of English.

Bernaisch, T. and Lange, C. 2012. The typology of focus marking in South Asian Englishes. *Indian Linguistics* 73: 1–18. http://nbn-resolving.de/urn: nbn:de:bsz:14-qucosa-224747.

Bhatia, T. K. and Ritchie, W. C. 2013. Bilingualism and multilingualism in South Asia. In T. K. Bhatia and W. C. Ritchie, eds. *The Handbook of Bilingualism and Multilingualism* (2nd ed.). Malden, MA: Wiley-Blackwell, 843–870.

Bose, S. and Jalal, A. 2004. *Modern South Asia: History, Culture, Political Economy.* London: Routledge.

Chand, V. 2013. Language policies and politics in South Asia. In R. Bayley, R. Cameron, and C. Lucas, eds. *The Oxford Handbook of Sociolinguistics.* Oxford: Oxford University Press, 587–608.

Crystal, D. 2008. Two thousand million? Update on the statistics of English. *English Today 93*(24): 3–6.

D'Souza, J. 1987. South Asia as a sociolinguistic area. Unpublished doctoral dissertation, University of Illinois.

D'Souza, J. 1988. Interactional strategies in South Asian languages: Their implications for teaching English internationally. *World Englishes 7*: 159–171.

Emeneau, M. B. 1956. India as a linguistic area. *Language 32*: 3–16.

Evans, S. 2002. Macaulay's Minute revisited: Colonial language policy in nineteenth-century India. *Journal of Multilingual and Multicultural Development 23*: 260–281.

Farrington, A. 1999. *Catalogue of East India Company Ships' Journals and Logs, 1600–1834.* London: British Library, Oriental India Office Collections.

Frykenberg, R. E. 1999. India to 1858. In R. W. Winks, ed., *The Oxford History of the British Empire, Vol. 5: Historiography.* Oxford: Oxford University Press, 194–213.

Fuchs, R. 2012. Focus marking and semantic transfer in Indian English: The case of also. *English World-Wide 33*: 27–53.

Fuchs, R. 2016. *Speech Rhythm in Varieties of English: Evidence from Educated Indian English and British English.* Singapore: Springer.

Gandhi, M. K. [1921] 1999. "Young India," February 9, 1921. In *The Collected Works of Mahatma Gandhi* (eBook), 98 vols. New Delhi: Publications Division Government of India. www.gandhiashramsevagram.org /gandhi-literature/collected-works-of-mahatma-gandhi-volume-1-to-98 .php.

Goffin, R. C. 1934. *Some Notes on Indian English.* Oxford: Oxford University Press.

Graddol, D. 2010. *English Next India: The Future of English in India.* British Council. https://englishagenda.britishcouncil.org/sites/default/files/ attachments/books-english-next-india-2010.pdf

Gries, S. T. and Bernaisch, T. 2016. Exploring epicentres empirically: Focus on South Asian Englishes. *English World-Wide 37*: 1–25.

Hilbert, M. 2008. Interrogative inversion in non-standard varieties of English. In P. K. N. Siemund, ed., *Language Contact and Contact Languages.* Amsterdam: John Benjamins, 262–89.

Hock, H. H. and Bashir, E., eds. 2016. *The Languages and Linguistics of South Asia: A Comprehensive Guide.* Berlin: De Gruyter Mouton.

Hoffmann, S., Hundt, M. and Mukherjee, J. 2011. Indian English: An emerging epicentre? A pilot study on light verbs in web-derived corpora of South Asian Englishes. *Angliae 129*: 258–280.

Hundt, M. 2013. The diversification of English: Old, new and emerging epicentres. In D. Schreier and M. Hundt, eds. *English as a Contact Language*. Cambridge: Cambridge University Press, 182–203.

Hundt, M. 2015. World Englishes. In D. Biber and R. Reppen, eds. *The Cambridge Handbook of English Corpus Linguistics*. Cambridge: Cambridge University Press, 362–380.

Hundt, M., Hoffmann, S. and Mukherjee, J. 2012. The hypothetical subjunctive in South Asian Englishes: Local developments in the use of a global construction. *English World-Wide 33*: 147–164.

Hundt, M. and Sharma, D., eds. 2014. *English in the Indian Diaspora*. Amsterdam: John Benjamins.

Kachru, B. B. 1994. English in South Asia. In R. Burchfield, ed., *The Cambridge History of the English Language, Vol. 5: English in Britain and Overseas: Origins and Developments*. Cambridge: Cambridge University Press, 497–553.

Kachru, B. B. 2008. Introduction: Languages, contexts, and constructs. In B. B. Kachru, Y. Kachru, and S. N. Sridhar, eds. *Language in South Asia*. Cambridge: Cambridge University Press, 1–28.

Kachru, B. B., Kachru, Y., and Sridhar, S. N., eds. 2008. *Language in South Asia*. Cambridge: Cambridge University Press.

Kachru, Y. and Nelson, C. L. 2006. *World Englishes in Asian Contexts*. Hong Kong: Hong Kong University Press.

Kashyap, A. K. 2014. Developments in the linguistic description of Indian English: State of the art. *Linguistics and the Human Sciences 9*: 249–275.

Khubchandani, L. M. 1991. India as a sociolinguistic area. *Language Sciences 13*: 265–288.

Kindersley, A. F. 1938. Notes on the Indian idiom of English: Style, syntax, and vocabulary. *Transactions of the Philological Society 37*: 25–34.

Koch, C., Lange, C. and Leuckert, S. 2016. This hair-style called as "Duck Tail": The "intrusive *as*"- construction in South Asian varieties of English and Learner Englishes. *International Journal of Learner Corpus Research 2*: 151–176.

Kortmann, B., Burridge, K., Mesthrie, R., Schneider, E. W. and Upton, C., eds. 2004. *A Handbook of Varieties of English, Vol. 2: Morphology and Syntax*. Berlin: De Gruyter Mouton.

Kortmann, Bernd and Lunkenheimer, Kerstin, eds. 2013. *The Electronic World Atlas of Varieties of English*. Leipzig: Max Planck Institute for Evolutionary Anthropology. http://ewave-atlas.org

Kothari, R. and Snell, R. 2011. *Chutnefying English: The Phenomenon of Hinglish*. New Delhi: Penguin Books.

Krishnaswamy, N. and Burde, A. S. 1998. *The Politics of Indians' English: Linguistic Colonialism and the Expanding English Empire*. New Delhi: Oxford University Press.

Kumar, T. V. ed. 2018. *Peoples' Linguistic Survey of India, Vol. 37: English and Other International Languages*. Hyderabad: Orient BlackSwan.

Lambert, J. 2012. Beyond Hobson Jobson: Towards a new lexicography for Indian English. *English World-Wide 33*: 292–320.

Lange, C. 2007. Focus Marking in Indian English. *English World-Wide 28*: 89–118.

Lange, C. 2012a. Standards of English in South Asia. In R. Hickey, ed. *Standards of English: Codified Varieties around the World*. Cambridge: Cambridge University Press, 256–273.

Lange, C. 2012b. *The Syntax of Spoken Indian English*. Amsterdam: John Benjamins.

Lange, C. 2016. The "intrusive *as*"-construction in South Asian Varieties of English. *World Englishes 35*: 133–146.

Lim, L. 2013. Kaduva of privileged power, instrument of rural empowerment? The politics of English (and Sinhala and Tamil) in Sri Lanka. In L. Wee, R. B. H. Goh, and L. Lim, eds. *The Politics of English: South Asia, Southeast Asia and the Asia Pacific*. Amsterdam: John Benjamins, 61–80.

Malekar, A. 2010. The case for a linguistic survey. *Info Change India*. http://infochangeindia.org/component/content/article/310-media/languages-of-india/8218-the-case-for-a-linguistic-survey.

Mann, M. 2015. *South Asia's Modern History: Thematic Perspectives*. Abingdon: Routledge.

Masica, C. P. 1976. *Defining a Linguistic Area: South Asia*. Chicago: University of Chicago Press.

Maxwell, O. and Fletcher, J. 2009. Acoustic and durational properties of Indian English vowels. *World Englishes 28*, 42–69.

Mendis, D. and Rambukwella, H. 2010. Sri Lankan Englishes. In A. Kirkpatrick, ed. *The Routledge Handbook of World Englishes*. London: Routledge, 181–196.

Mesthrie, R. 1992. *English in Language Shift: The History, Structure and Sociolinguistics of South African Indian English*. Cambridge: Cambridge University Press.

Metcalf, B. D. and Metcalf, Th. R. 2006. *A Concise History of Modern India*. Cambridge: Cambridge University Press.

Meyler, M. 2007. *A Dictionary of Sri Lankan English*. Colombo: Mirisgala.

Meyler, M. 2012. Sri Lankan English. In B. Kortmann and K. Lunkenheimer, eds. *The Mouton World Atlas of Variation in English*. Berlin: De Gruyter Mouton, 540–547.

Misra, A. 2004a. An introduction to the "small" and "micro" states of South Asia. *Contemporary South Asia 13*: 127–131.

Misra, A. 2004b. Theorising "small" and "micro" state behaviour using the Maldives, Bhutan and Nepal. *Contemporary South Asia 13*: 133–148.

Moseley, C., ed. 2010. *Atlas of the World's Languages in Danger* (3rd ed.). Paris: UNESCO Publishing. www.unesco.org/culture/en/endangeredlanguages/atlas.

Mukherjee, J. 2007. Steady states in the evolution of New Englishes: Present-day Indian English as an equilibrium. *Journal of English Linguistics 35*: 157–187.

Mukherjee, J. 2010. The development of the English language in India. In A. Kirkpatrick, ed. *The Routledge Handbook of World Englishes*. London: Routledge, 167–180.

Nihalani, P., Tongue, R. K., and Hosali, P. 1979. *Indian and British English: A Handbook of Usage and Pronunciation*. New Delhi: Oxford University Press.

Nurullah, S. and Naik, J. P. 1951. *A History of Education in India (During the British Period)*. Bombay: Macmillan. https://ia801902.us.archive.org/26/items/in.ernet.dli.2015.513884/2015.513884.History-of.pdf

Platt, J., Weber, H. and Lian, H. M. 1984. *The New Englishes*. London: Routledge and Kegan Paul.

Rahman, T. 2006. *Language and Politics in Pakistan*. New Delhi: Orient Longman.

Sailaja, P. 2009. *Indian English*. Edinburgh: Edinburgh University Press.

Schneider, E. W. 2007. *Postcolonial English: Varieties around the World*. Cambridge: Cambridge University Press.

Schneider, E. W. 2016. Hybrid Englishes: An exploratory survey. *World Englishes 35*: 339–354.

Schneider, E. W. 2011. *English around the World: An Introduction*. Cambridge: Cambridge University Press.

Sedlatschek, A. 2009. *Contemporary Indian English: Variation and Change: Varieties of English around the World*. Amsterdam: John Benjamins.

Sharma, D. 2005. Language transfer and discourse universals in Indian English article use. *Studies in Second Language Acquisition 27*: 535–566.

Sharma, D. 2009. Typological diversity in New Englishes. *English World-Wide 30*: 170–195.

Sharma, D. 2011. Style repertoire and social change in British Asian English. *Journal of Sociolinguistics 15*: 464–492.

Sharma, D. 2012a. Indian English. In B. Kortmann and K. Lunkenheimer, eds. *The Mouton World Atlas of Variation in English*. Berlin: De Gruyter Mouton, 523–530.

Sharma, D. 2012b. Second-language varieties: English in India. In A. Bergs and L. Brinton, eds., *English Historical Linguistics*. Berlin: De Gruyter Mouton, 2077–2091.

Sharma, D. 2012c. Shared features in New Englishes. In R. Hickey, ed. *Areal Features of the Anglophone World.* Berlin: De Gruyter Mouton, 211–232.

Simpson, A., ed. 2007. *Language and National Identity in Asia.* Oxford: Oxford University Press.

Sirkin, N. R. and Sirkin, G. 1971. The battle of Indian education: Macaulay's opening salvo newly discovered. *Victorian Studies* 14(4): 407–428.

Subbarao, K. V., Agnihotri, R. K. and Mukherjee, A. 1991. Syntactic strategies and politeness phenomena. *International Journal of the Sociology of Language 92*: 35–53.

Uma, A., Rani, S. and Manohar, D. M., eds. 2014. *English in the Dalit Context.* New Delhi: Orient Blackswan.

Whitworth, G. C. 1907. *Indian English: An Examination of the Errors of Idiom Made by Indians in Writing English.* Letchworth: Garden City Press.

Wiltshire, C. R. 2005. The "Indian English" of Tibeto-Burman language speakers. *English World-Wide 26*: 275–300.

Wiltshire, C. R. and Harnsberger, J. D. 2006. The influence of Gujarati and Tamil L1s on Indian English: A preliminary study. *World Englishes 25*: 91–104.

Wright, A. 1891. *Baboo English as 'tis Writ: Being Curiosities of Indian Journalism.* London: T. Fisher Unwin. https://babel.hathitrust.org/cgi/pt?id=hvd .hn3byx;view=1up;seq=11.

Zastoupil, L. and Moir, M., eds. 1999. *The Great Indian Education Debate. Documents Relating to the Orientalist-Anglicist Controversy, 1781–1843.* Richmond: Curzon.

12

English in Southeast Asia

Lionel Wee

12.1 Introduction

The historical emergence of English in Southeast Asia is interesting given the fact that it has managed to establish a foothold in the region both because of colonization as well as without it. The presence of English in Malaysia and Singapore, for example, is due to these two countries being former British colonies. The presence of English in the Philippines is a result of American colonization following an earlier wave of colonization by Spain. Finally, Thailand decided on embracing English as a political stratagem precisely in order to avoid being taken by the British. Thus, it was the actual fact of colonization or its likely possibility and the steps taken to prevent it from happening that contributed in no small manner to the language's historical insertion into the Southeast Asian region.

Since the early days of English's presence, the language has been embraced in different Southeast Asian countries with varying degrees of enthusiasm and officially recognized in some while having the status of a de facto working language in others. Indeed, the contemporary status of English has become even more varied. The language is arguably far more institutionalized in Singapore and the Philippines than Malaysia or Thailand. For example, it is an official language as well as the working language in Singapore and it has institutional support in the Philippines' Constitution though it is less widely used throughout the country. On the other hand, it has no official recognition in either Malaysia or Thailand. Even here, the notion of institutionalization is only a rough descriptor that covers a broad range of issues so that it is necessary to recognize that there are in fact far more significant differences between these four countries regarding the status and properties of English. Of course, across the entire Southeast Asian region, many countries (and not just these four) continue to grapple in different ways with the challenges posed by a language that has spread globally and that is as a consequence not easily ignored. One significant development, for example, has been the adoption of English as the official language of ASEAN (the Association of Southeast Asian Nations).

It would not be possible to discuss in detail all the different issues faced by the different Southeast Asian countries within a single chapter given the space constraints. Nevertheless, a focus on Malaysia, Singapore, the Philippines, and Thailand should make for a sufficiently comprehensive coverage that provides us with a sense of the major issues involving the development of English today, such as neoliberalism, migration, and commodification. Retaining the connection with colonization mentioned at the beginning of the chapter, the discussion that follows will close by considering possible strategies of decolonization as different Southeast Asian countries attempt to evolve beyond the constraints of exonormativity and linguistic insecurity.

12.2 English in Malaysia, Singapore, the Philippines, and Thailand: Early Colonial Policies

12.2.1 Malaysia

What we know today as Malaysia actually started off as a collection of independent states ruled by sultans. These states were consolidated by the British colonial administrators in 1896 as the Federated Malay States and, latterly, as the Federation of Malaya in 1948 when the number of member states was expanded. The Federation became independent in 1957 and in 1963 and was reconstituted as the Federation of Malaysia when North Borneo, Sarawak, and Singapore joined as members.

The British began taking serious interest in the region around the middle of the nineteenth century, seeing it as a territory for establishing trading posts as well as a place that was rich in resources. Where language education was concerned, Kok (1978: 12–13) points out that the Colonial Office in London gave the Residents or regional governors a great deal of autonomy in deciding on local education policies. This resulted in great disparities across the various Malay states on how much of the local vernacular and how much English ought to be taught in the schools.

Stevenson (1975) points out that English was in actual fact only sparingly taught because the British government was worried that learning the language would alienate local children from their own heritage. Even where vernacular education was made available, the goal here was to "promote loyalty, obedience and acceptance of colonial rule" (Pennycook 1998: 100) by letting "the people see that the Government has really their welfare at heart in providing them with this education, free, without compulsion, and with the greatest consideration for their mohamedan sympathies" (Perak Government Gazette, January 4, 1895: 4–7).

Around 1897, however, there was a change in policy, prompted probably by the colonial government's realization that there was a greater need for local clerical and administrative staff that had at least some basic competence in English (Kok 1978: 16). This led to the formalization of the Education Code of 1899, which had as one of its goals (cited in Chan 2012: 151):

> To emphasize the importance of teaching English by making English Vocabulary and Composition one of the "elementary subjects" with reading, writing and arithmetic, and strengthening it further by making "English grammar and construction" a class subject to be taken with it.

These policies were targeted mainly at the ethnic Malays. The Chinese and Indians were largely left to themselves and, because of this, their own exposure to English-language education came mainly from schools that were set up by Christian missionaries. According to Gaudart (1987, n.p.):

> In government schools, teachers were of poor calibre, and many were untrained. Interviews with educators who were pupils in schools at that time indicated that many principals of girls' schools, for example, were wives of expatriate officers. In comparison, teachers in mission schools seemed more dedicated to the education of their pupils ...
>
> The only exception to the education of Malays was the setting up of a special English medium school to train the upper echelons of Malay society. The British believed that as these upper-class Malay children were to be the leaders of the people, they should receive special training.

Thus, somewhat ironically, the quality of English-language education provided by the colonial government to the Malays did not compare well at all with that provided by their missionary counterparts to the Chinese and Indians. The teachers in the government schools lacked the pedagogical interest and even professional commitment that the missionaries possessed in no small part because of the latter's religious motivation. The exception here was the educational experience of upper-class Malay children. This relationship between English, ethnicity, and social class is an important sociolinguistic issue that needs to be kept in mind when we consider modern-day Southeast Asia.

12.2.2 Singapore

Singapore became the focus of attention for the British after parts of the region were handed over to the Dutch in the early 1800s, as part of an agreement, ultimately formalized in 1824, between the rival colonial powers on how to divide up the region among themselves. In particular, the British governor Stamford Raffles had foreseen Singapore's potential as an alternative trading post and he moved to acquire the island from the

Sultan of Johor in 1819. Singapore's status as a free port "soon attracted Chinese, Malay, and Arab traders, travelers, and others, and the population grew rapidly" (Schneider 2007: 153).

Early colonial policy regarding the government of Singapore focused primarily on urban resettlement. Variously referred to as the Jackson Plan or the Raffles Town Plan, this was the work of a town committee appointed by Stamford Raffles in 1822. Raffles instructed that "separate quarters or *kampungs* be demarcated for specific racial and occupational groups" (Yeoh 2003: 71, emphasis in original). The committee's proposal thus allocated different locales to distinct ethnic groups. For example, "the Chinese and Indians occupied South Bridge Road and New Bridge Road, while the residence of the Malay royals was located north of the proposed European town between the coast and Rochore River, and next to the Bugis and Arab *kampongs* (Malay for 'villages')."[1]

Such ethnic segregation was less pronounced at the upper echelons of Singapore society, whose members were more or less united by a shared knowledge of English and love of British culture, an attitude no doubt fostered also by the fact that English had gained prestige as the language of government and business. There was a strong exonormative orientation toward learning the language of the colonizers as a marker of high status. Those individuals who were competent in the language also endeavored to adopt various aspects of the British lifestyle as ways of signaling this status, such as enjoying afternoon high tea and playing cricket. This led to the formation of an Asian elite that comprised Chinese, Malay, and Indian professionals. In this regard, Eurasians (defined under colonial rule as persons of mixed British and Asian heritage though modern definitions have broadened to include persons of mixed European and Asian heritage) formed a particularly significant segment of the local teachers up until the early 1920s and, thereafter, Chinese teachers were increasingly common, being former students who had since graduated and entered the teaching profession (Lim 2010: 27, citing Gupta 1994: 39–40).

In 1965, however, Singapore left the Federation of Malaysia due to political differences with the central government over the management of ethnic diversity. As we will see in Section 12.3.2, this departure from the Federation allowed Singapore to pursue a different and more pragmatic policy regarding the English language.

12.2.3 The Philippines

Unlike Malaysia and Singapore, English came to the Philippines by way of American rather than British colonization but, even then, only after an earlier wave of colonization by Spain. Spanish rule over the Philippines

---

[1] HistorySG: An Online Resource Guide. http://eresources.nlb.gov.sg/history/events/d489ee4f-a03b-42df-a88d-c924c24ac720

ended in 1898 when the USA won the Spanish-American War and acquired the Philippines as a result. American rule over the Philippines in turn ended in 1946 when the former recognized the latter's independence, giving rise to the Republic of the Philippines in that same year.[2]

The American takeover of the Philippines from the Spanish was marked by an aggressive push to institutionalize English and to remove as far as possible traces of Spanish. Consequently, unlike the British rule in Malaysia and Singapore, the goal of the Americans was to make English in the Philippines widely available. English was made the language of government and education and it was "the main and only language of instruction in public schools in 1901" (Sibayan and Gonzalez 1996: 139). Teachers from America were even brought in to teach in the elementary school system. English in the Philippines has therefore tended to be modeled on American English. However, about ten years before being granted independence by the Americans, the government decided in 1937 to develop Tagalog as a national language, relabeling it Filipino, so that there was in effect a bilingual education policy that emphasized the importance of both Filipino and English.

The period of American rule therefore did not result in English being associated with any sense of elitism. This can be attributed to two factors: one, the American desire to have English as widely used in Philippine society as possible so as to supplant the use of Spanish; and, two, the American ideology of egalitarianism that saw elitism as undemocratic. In fact, as Schneider (2007: 141) points out, it was only much later that English would become "associated with colonialism and an undemocratic elitism" due in no small part to the feudal nature of Philippine politics (Rappa and Wee 2006). Thus, the emergence of English in the Philippines – at least during colonization and in the early aftermath of independence – differs from the experiences of Malaysia and Singapore in that there was no elitist connotation.

Yet, as with Malaysia and Singapore, both of which had highly demarcated ethnic populations, ethnicity in the Philippines has also been an issue of contention. While the history of inter-ethnic marriage has resulted in many mixed-race individuals, widely referred to as Filipino mestizo, there are many who claim more traditional ethnic affiliations, such as Chinese, Tagalog, Ilocano, Bisaya, and Kapampangan, to name but a few. The issue of ethnicity tends to carry greater ramifications for the status of Filipino than English. This is because, as mentioned, the former was based on Tagalog, one of many indigenous languages that could have been selected to be the national language, thus breeding controversy and resentment among other ethnic groups whose languages were not chosen (Asuncion-Lande, 1971: 677).

---

[2] The Philippines currently celebrates June 12, 1898 (and not 1946), when it first gained independence from the Spanish colonizers, as its Independence Day. Immediately after acquiring independence from the USA, the Philippines marked July 4 as its Independence Day because the treaty that gave rise to the Republic was signed on July 4, 1946; however, in 1962, President Macapagal changed the date to June 12 and renamed July 4 as Philippine Republic Day.

12.2.4 Thailand

Masavisut, Sukwiwat, and Wongmontha (1986) provide a concise summary of how English came to Thailand, despite the kingdom never having been colonized. As they point out (1986: 198), during the reign of King Rama III (1824–1851), knowledge of English was pursued as a means of accessing Western science and technology. Yet, following the British attack on China, the kingdom became acutely aware of its own vulnerability to European powers. When King Rama's successor, King Mongkut (1851–1868), ascended the throne, he therefore decided to open up communications with the West "to prove to them that Siam was a civilized nation, and the equal of any foreign powers" (Masavisut, Sukwiwat, and Wongmontha 1986: 198):

> King Mongkut and his ministers were quite well prepared for this task. They had been exposed to Western culture through their contact with American missionaries during King Rama III's reign, and some had already adopted the language and lifestyle of the West. Indeed the British were, in their own words, amazed to find the Siamese to be so civilized and to speak English so well. When Sir John Bowring (1959) arrived in Bangkok in 1855 to negotiate the famous Bowring's Treaty he observed: "It is amazing to find that the Siamese who live so far away from us can speak English so well."

This strategy of proactively learning English in order to deal with the European powers was largely continued by later kings as well, even as the goal shifted from one of trying to preempt a foreign takeover to one of showing "the West that Siam could survive and could become the equal of Western nations" (Vella, 1955: 336).

Thus, Thai royals early on appreciated the strategic value of English, both as a tool for accessing Western knowledge and as an instrument of diplomacy. Initially, knowledge of English was largely limited to the royals and other members of the ruling class and, moreover, the variety of English being acquired was primarily British English. However, knowledge of the language gradually became more widely distributed throughout Thai society (albeit with highly varying degrees of competence) and American English in particular became more dominant after World War II. This is due to the fact that, especially during the Vietnam War, "thousands of Americans came to Thailand and thousands of Thais recognized the value of the English language to obtain jobs and run businesses which would attract the American soldiers" (Masavisut et al. 1986: 205).

12.3 Contemporary Positionings of English

On gaining independence, Malaysia, Singapore, and the Philippines had to make important decisions about how to position English vis-à-vis the other languages in their respective societies. Even Thailand, despite it not having been colonized, still had to make decisions about English given that the language was gaining importance not just in international trade and diplomacy but also as a cultural marker of sophistication and cosmopolitanism.

12.3.1 Malaysia

Malaysia introduced the *bumiputra* policy in the 1970s under the New Economic Policy (NEP) in order to increase the participation and ownership of ethnic Malays in the national economy relative to that of other ethnic groups. The rationale, according to the Malaysian government, was that there was a need to provide special recognition of the rights of the ethnic Malays, on the basis that, as the "*original or indigenous people of Malaya*" (Mahathir 1970: 133, emphasis in original), they were entitled to specific consideration and privileges in relation to other ethnic groups. The government's reasoning was that Malay control over their homeland had been weakened by British colonial policy, which had preferred to employ non-Malay workers, especially the Chinese, thus accounting for the Malays' relative lack of economic power in comparison to the other ethnic groups. The bumiputra policy was thus intended to redress this historical imbalance.

In 1970, a refinement was implemented in the form of the NEP, under which "Malays were not only given special rights in administration and education but also in terms of language and culture" (Rappa and Wee 2006: 33). In 1971, an amendment to the Constitution further stated that the status of Malay as the official language and the status of other languages – including English – as nonofficial but merely tolerated "may no longer be questioned, it being considered that such a sensitive issue should for ever be removed from the arena of public discussion."

Educationally, Malaysia then switched from English to Malay as the medium of instruction in its national schools from 1968 and expanded the switch to encompass the universities in 1983. Yet, since Chinese and Indians were worried about their children being disadvantaged, vernacular schools – using Chinese and Tamil as the languages of instruction – were allowed to exist alongside the national schools. One consequence of this preference for Malay, Chinese, or Tamil as the medium of instruction has been the production of Malaysian graduates with questionable proficiency in English, with many of them unable to find employment. Pennycook (1998: 201) points out that "those educated in the Malaysian university system tend to be regarded as second-class students, and thus have more difficulty finding top jobs, especially in the private sector, while the overseas-educated remain a social and economic elite." Furthermore, it has been estimated that more than 50,000 of the country's graduates are unemployed – many of whom are "poor, female, Malay and cannot speak enough English to hold a two-minute conversation in the language" ("Good sense held hostage to politics," *The Straits Times*, January 14, 2009).

To address this problem, in 2003, the Malaysian government introduced a policy where only mathematics and science were to be taught in English. Yet even this limited role for English has been met with resistance, as some Malaysian states have lobbied for mathematics and science to be taught in Malay, on the grounds that using English was "a blow to the 'sanctity of Bahasa Malaysia' as the national language" and has "created problems for both teachers and students, especially from the rural areas" ("Pakatan states oppose English in class," *The Straits Times*, January 14, 2009). Even members of the ruling coalition have called for a move toward the "mother tongue": The Malaysian Chinese Association and the Malaysian Indian Congress, respectively, want Chinese and Tamil to be used for teaching mathematics and science ("Six years later, language debate rages on," *The Straits Times*, January 16, 2009).

The problem of how to improve the standard of English in the country is not likely to disappear anytime soon. There have been renewed expressions of concern about poor proficiency affecting the Malaysian workforce ("Finger pointing over poor English in Malaysia textbooks," *The Straits Times*, July 23, 2015). Further, most recently, the Sultan of Johor has even urged the government to consider implementing a single-stream education system ("Johor Sultan moots single-stream education system to improve Malaysians' English skills," *The Straits Times*, December 28, 2015).

The challenge for Malaysia, then, is to improve the standard of English without being seen to undermine the bumiputra policy, while at the same time also remaining sensitive to the language concerns of the Chinese and Indian communities.

12.3.2 Singapore

Unlike Malaysia, which is grappling with the question of how to accommodate English, Singapore had from the outset embraced English for its pragmatic value. Singapore became independent in 1965 when it was ejected from Malaysia. The Singapore government disagreed with the federal government on whether ethnic Malays ought to be granted special rights. Singapore's position was that the bumiputra policy would do little to improve the status of the Malays and would, instead, create more problems for ethnic relations.

Singapore's objections to the bumiputra policy were articulated by Lee Kuan Yew (the country's first prime minister) in a 1965 speech to the Federal Parliament (Rappa and Wee 2006: 78):

> This is a very dangerous thing, leading people to believe that if we just switch in 1967 from talking English in the courts, and in business, to speaking Malay, therefore the imbalance in social and economic development will disappear. It will not disappear ... If we delude people into believing that they are poor because there are not Malay rights or because

opposition members oppose Malay rights – where are we going to end up? You let people in the kampongs believe that they are poor because we don't speak Malay, because the government does not write in Malay, so he expects a miracle to take place in 1967. The moment we all start speaking Malay, he is going to have an uplift in the standard of living, and if it doesn't happen, what happens then?

Singapore's separation from Malaysia meant that its leaders were faced, quite suddenly, with the task of building a nation out of an ethnolinguistically diverse population and with developing the nation's economy without access to any natural resources. This emphasis on economic development motivated Singapore's strong emphasis on learning English. Yet, because of the country's ethnic and linguistic diversity, the promotion of English has had to take into account the presence of Singapore's other languages as well as the feelings of the speakers of those languages. In order to do this, the government has consistently encouraged Singaporeans to be bilingual in English and a mother tongue that is officially assigned to them on the basis of their ethnic identity. Given Singapore's ethnically diverse society, three official mother tongues are recognized for each of the major ethnic groups: Mandarin for the Chinese, Malay for the Malays, and Tamil for the Indians.

So, although the government recognizes English as an official language, it does not wish to accord the language the status of an official mother tongue for a number of reasons. One, English is to serve as an inter-ethnic lingua franca. Two, as the major language of socioeconomic mobility, maintaining an ethnically neutral status for English helps ensure that the distribution of economic advantages is not seen as being unduly associated with a specific ethnic group, which would otherwise raise the danger of inter-ethnic tension. Lastly, English is treated as a language that is essentially Western and thus unsuitable to be a mother tongue for an Asian society such as Singapore. English and the mother tongue are therefore expected to play different roles in the lives of Singaporeans. The former is to serve a pragmatic function of facilitating mobility, while the latter is expected to aid in the preservation of cultural heritage and ethnic identity. However, this particular positioning of English is problematic since, for many Singaporeans, the language of the home is English rather than one of the official mother tongues. This raises the question of whether it is feasible for the government to continue denying English the status of a mother tongue.

The challenge for Singapore, then, is to come to terms with the fact that one consequence of successfully encouraging the learning of English is that it cannot any longer be relegated to a purely pragmatic realm. The language will have to be acknowledged as serving an identity and cultural function as well. This also means recognizing that English is not a monolithic entity but rather that there can be many different varieties of English even within a single country (see Section 12.4).

12.3.3 The Philippines

The 1987 Constitution of the Republic of the Philippines makes an explicit provision for bilingualism in Filipino, the national language, and English. The Philippine Bilingual Education Policy mandates the separate use of Filipino and English (Espiritu 2015). The former is to be used as the medium of instruction in the social sciences, music, arts, physical education, home economics, and character education (a cover term for initiatives aimed at cultivating civic-mindedness and social responsibility). The latter is to be the medium of instruction for science, mathematics, and technology subjects (Department Order No. 52). Other "regional languages" can be used as supplementary aids in the lower grades of education, specifically, Grades I and II.

While not intended as an outcome, this division of linguistic labor has tended to breed an association between English and socioeconomic status and success, and, given the context of President Marcos's rule, cronyism and nepotism as well. Thus, when Corazon Aquino succeeded Marcos as president, this was seen as "a backlash to English" (Schneider 2007: 143) and a willingness to give greater social and political prominence to Filipino. In this regard, Espiritu (2015: n.p.) points out that Aquino ordered that there be greater use of Filipino in official administrative domains:

> On August 25, 1988, then President Corazon Aquino signed Executive Order No. 335 enjoining all departments/bureaus/offices/agencies/instrumentalities of the government to take such steps as are necessary for the purpose of using the Filipino language in official transactions, communications, and correspondence. The order was issued on the belief that the use of Filipino in official transactions, communications and correspondence in government offices will result to a greater understanding and appreciation of government programs, projects and activities throughout the country, thereby serving as an instrument of unity and peace for national progress.

The promotion of Filipino as the national language, according to Sibayan and Gonzales (1996), has led to a general decline in English-language proficiency. The challenge for the Philippines, though, is that English is still widely seen as the language that opens up pathways for greater prosperity, especially for many Filipinos who see better prospects for themselves in overseas markets. Even the Philippine education seems to be geared toward producing graduates whose English skills are intended for an externally defined labor market (Lorente 2013: 194). This means any attempt to position Filipino as being equal to English is faced with an uphill battle. This battle is compounded by the fact that any attempt to push for wider acceptance of Filipino will also have to overcome suspicion not only from speakers of other ethnic languages but also from the non-Tagalog elites. This dispute, in turn, is less an inter-ethnic matter than an intra-elite one, between "the Tagalog-speaking elites who nevertheless were conversant in English and who took up the fight for Pilipino as the national language, and the non-Tagalog elites who were likewise conversant in English, but who feared that the imposition of Pilipino as the national language would put them at a disadvantage over resources necessitating competence in Pilipino" (Tupas 2004: 20).

12.3.4 Thailand

Thailand's language policy recognizes only Thai as the national language even though the society is in fact linguistically and ethnically diverse. As Noss (1984: 92) points out,

> neither the nature nor the role of the national language has ever been seriously questioned. Whether this has something to do with the country's non-colonial history, or whether it merely reflects some kind of ethnic accident, there has been no serious challenge to the national language of Thailand. It is the standard version of the Central Plains variety of Thai that is officially used in all domains and which is also the most important lingua franca of the country ... No concessions are going to be made to the other Thai varieties, any more than they are going to be made to speakers of Malay in the South, to speakers of Khmer in the East, to speakers of Chinese varieties in the cities, or to speakers of minority languages in the mountains.

In addition to Thai, however, Thailand's National Education Council makes mention of English as "the most widely used international language for academic and occupational purposes" (Noss 1984: 11), a clear continuation of the monarchy's earlier strategic approach and pragmatic attitude toward the language.

As a consequence, in contemporary Thai society, all languages except for Thai are only available as taught subjects and not used as a medium of instruction. However, there has been a growing number of international schools that use English as the language of instruction (Wongsothorn 2000: 309), thus prefiguring the possibility that the link between English and socioeconomic status might come to be entrenched within Thai society.

For the time being, however, English continues to be considered valuable mainly for international rather than domestic purposes. Both the monarchy and the military have consistently stressed the value of English in the context of globalization, international diplomacy, and economic competition. Within Thai society itself, it is knowledge of Thai that has greater value since "The conduct of local business agreements or simply the search for gainful employment depends on knowing the language well" (Rappa and Wee 2006: 107).

In fact, in rural parts of Thailand, English has little or no appeal. Thus, Smalley (1994: 23) comments that

> In poor rural areas English does not even have much snob appeal ... The need to use English for international communication likewise cannot

compete with the family need to remove children from school to harvest rice, care for the younger children, or fulfill other responsibilities … Standards of teaching English in the schools, especially in country areas, frequently remain low, as well. Teaching materials may not be available, or may be inadequate in poor schools. Although their own average education has improved markedly in recent years, some Thai teachers themselves have little command even of Thai English, since they have not had much more education than their pupils.

The absence of appeal that English might hold for Thais living in the rural areas contrasts with the essential role the language plays in the daily lives of their urban counterparts. As Masavisut et al. (1986: 202) point out, "educated Thais from the higher echelon of society have to resort to English-language newspapers" for more incisive analyses as well as coverage of issues beyond the domestic. English-language magazines dealing with topics such as housing, sports, travel, and business are also popular; and, where possible, "Thais have deliberately chosen to use the English language to develop their opportunities for international education, business and communication, to broaden their horizons and those of their children" (Masavisut et al. 1986: 203)

In the long run, even English's lack of appeal in rural Thailand is likely to change given that Thai advertising tends to favor English brand names for a variety of products, even for those that happen to be made in Thailand. This means that the media's fostering of aspirational consumption and the desire for a better life need not only be linked to a migratory shift from rural to urban parts of the country. Concomitant with this cultivated imaginary is the indexical association between a cosmopolitan identity and the English language. In this sense, the challenge faced by Thailand regarding its positioning of English is not much different from those confronting the other Southeast Asian countries discussed in the chapter. It will have to address rising expectations about prosperity, consumption, and the development of a cosmopolitan identity, all of which tend to be bound up with the English language, while still ensuring that the critical role the Thai language plays in fostering the national identity is not undermined.

12.4 English: Changing Status and Properties

The spread of English across Southeast Asia has resulted in multiple varieties of English being identified (Schneider 2016). There are references to Manglish in Malaysia (Muniandy et al. 2010), Singlish in Singapore (Rubdy 2001), Taglish in the Philippines (MacArthur 1998), and Tinglish or Thaiglish in Thailand (Kong 2012; Lee and Nadeau 2011: 1124).

As Bruthiaux (2003: 168) has pointed out, "The question of what constitutes a variety of a language is a thorny one" since premature scholarly claims that new varieties have emerged indicate careless uses of the notion, raising the danger that it risks losing its value as an analytical concept (see also Park and Wee 2013: 341). However, the situation is different when the names of varieties are being evoked in popular usage (Wee, 2018). The issue here is not about trying to provide various criteria by which the analyst can determine with some degree of objective certainty the putative varietal status of the various Englishes. Rather, it is to recognize the role that language ideology can play in fostering the development of different varieties of English. For example, the nativized variety of English in Singapore, commonly known as Singlish, is fairly well established. In contrast, claims in Thailand regarding the existence of Thaiglish or Tinglish are made on somewhat more tenuous grounds. Regardless, what cannot be dismissed is the possibility that the very existence (presumed or otherwise) of a variety such as Singlish fuels the belief that a similar or analogous variety exists in Thailand.

Constituting an opposition to the emergence of these nativized varieties of English, however, is the often highly conservative stance adopted by government and education authorities, many of whom tend to stigmatize such varieties as both lacking in prestige and being detrimental to the learning of standard English (Siegel 1999). For example, the concern about standards of English in Malaysia is linked to the emergence of a nativized variety sometimes referred to as Manglish[3] (Muniandy et al. 2010), which shows influences from the local languages, including Malay in particular. Examples of Manglish lexis include *kapster* (from the Malay verb *cakap* "to speak") to describe a talkative person ("He is so kapster"), *gostan* "to reverse a vehicle" (a conflation of *go* and *astern*), and *maluation* "embarrassment" (a combination of the Malay adjective *malu* "embarrassed" and the English suffix -*ation*).

Singapore represents perhaps the clearest such case of official concerns about nativized varieties of English, the vehemence of the government's anti-Singlish stance no doubt being proportional to the perceived popularity and widespread usage of Singlish (Chng 2003; Rudby 2001). Not surprisingly, there are strong similarities between Manglish and Singlish. For example, *gostan* is also found in Singlish, though perhaps the best known shared feature is the particle *lah* that has been described as a solidarity marker ("Join us, lah!") though it can also be used to express annoyance ("Don't disturb me, lah!") (Wee 2004: 118–119). Other features of Singlish include reduplication (*hot-hot*, *cough-cough*) and the pluralizing of noncount nouns (e.g. *staffs*). This is because Singlish, much like Manglish, is known to show a high degree of influence from other local languages, particularly Hokkien, Cantonese, Malay, and Tamil (Platt and Weber, 1980: 18).

---

[3] While I use labels such as "Manglish" and "Singlish," it is important to note that such labels oversimplify the range and variability in language practices, not just in terms of implying "more homogeneity than is warranted" (Schneider 2011: 155) but also in suggesting that Manglish and Singlish – and, for that matter, Konglish, Taglish, and so on – all enjoy the same varietal status in their respective countries. It is therefore important not to take such cases of linguistic baptism (Park and Wee 2013) at face value.

While the Singapore government has recently toned down its earlier harsh criticism of Singlish (Bruthiaux 2010), this does not so much indicate an acceptance of the variety's legitimacy as a sense of resignation that Singlish is not something that can be easily eradicated. Official pronouncements in the late 1990s and early 2000s were unequivocal in their condemnation. For example, Goh Chok Tong (then prime minister) during the 1999 National Day Rally Speech made clear that Singlish was an obstacle to the country's efforts to globalize:

> We cannot be a first-world economy or go global with Singlish … The fact that we use English gives us a big advantage over our competitors. If we carry on using Singlish, the logical final outcome is that we, too, will develop our own type of pidgin English, spoken only by 3 m Singaporeans, which the rest of the world will find quaint but incomprehensible. We are already half way there. Do we want to go all the way?

In much the same vein as Goh Chok Tong, the following extract from a speech by Lee Hsien Loong, deputy prime minister, also makes clear that, at least as far as the government is concerned, there is no place for Singlish in Singapore society:

> The course of least resistance is to end up with Singlish, because that is what we get when the English language is mixed with Malay words, Chinese grammar, and local slang. But once we are stuck with Singlish, and children grow up learning Singlish as their first language, it will be very difficult to get them to learn standard English in schools. Singlish will not be cute or amusing, because those speaking Singlish will consider Singlish sentences and words quite normal, and not even know that they are using the words wrongly. And it will be even harder later on to get our whole society to switch languages a second time, from Singlish to English.[4]
> We must consciously and deliberately strive to avoid this outcome.

Somewhat problematic for the Singapore government's anti-Singlish stance, however, is the fact that the *Oxford English Dictionary* (OED) has only just recently included more than 500 Singapore English words and phrases in its 2016 update.[5] Words like *blur* "slow in understanding," *ang moh* "a light-skinned person, especially of Western origin," *sotong* "squid or cuttlefish," and *shiok* "cool, delicious, superb" are now official entries in the OED. This has even led *The Independent* to point out that these words "can now be officially used in an English sentence … [making] 'That ang mo is blur like sotong' a perfect English sentence."

---

[4] Speech given at the 2001 launch of the Speak Good English Movement, 5 April 2001: www.nas.gov.sg/archivesonline/ speeches/view-html?filename=2001040502.htm

[5] "Oxford English Dictionary confirms: 'That ang mo is blur like sotong' is a perfect English sentence," *The Independent*, May 11, 2016: http://theindependent.sg/oxford-english-dictionary-confirmsthat-ang-mo-is-blur-like-sotong-is -a-perfect-english-sentence/

In contrast to Malaysia and Singapore, the authorities in the Philippines and Thailand (so far) seem to show little to no signs of anxiety about their own nativized varieties of English. Taglish, the nativized variety of English in the Philippines, shows substratal influences from Tagalog, Cebuano, Ilocano, and other local languages. Perhaps not surprisingly, Taglish also has Spanish loans (*asalto* "surprise party" and *bienvenida* "welcome party") and neologisms such as *carnap* ("to steal a car") and *hold-upper* ("someone who engages in hold-ups") (MacArthur 1998: n.p.). In Thailand, Tinglish or Thaiglish is far less established than any of the other three nativized varieties of English, as indicated by the variation in naming convention as well as attempts to argue that the variation in name reflects distinct subvarieties in Thai society. There are nevertheless multiple popular websites that seem to assume that the existence of Tinglish or Thaiglish can be taken for granted, as shown by the following examples.

One website states that "Tinglish" "can also be know (sic) as Thaiglish" and is "the non-standard form (on) English used by native Thai speakers due to language interference."[6] Another site describes "Tinglish" as the "Thai version of English" where sentences "are simplistic but still easily understandable": For instance, "I didn't want to go yesterday" would likely be said instead as "Yesterday I not want go." There's also the doubling of a few English words where it happens in Thai, for example "same same," "near near," and so on.[7]

A final example asks rhetorically:

> Ever heard of the word *Tinglish* or *Thaiglish*? They are the unofficial terms used to describe the fusion of the Thai language with the English language often producing a new word with a meaning that may or may not be grammatically correct ... When a Thai person says that *"These pants are fit"*. What they really do mean is that, *"These pants are too small"*. Fit is Thaiglish for *small.*[8]

In contrast, Lee and Nadeau (2011: 1123) suggest that:

> Tenglish (pronounced "tinglish") is characterized as the English spoken by Thais, while Englithai refers to the Thai spoken by Anglophones, or native English-speakers. The third form, Thaiglish, is characterized as a bonfide hybrid language, which conflates the Thai and English language structure and vocabulary ...
>
> Tenglish is merely an adaptation of English and will generally lack particles, articles and/or correct grammar conjugation ...
>
> Thai Americans will often try to speak in the Thaiglish form, which adapts the Thai language rhythm, tone, and pattern. Thaiglish speakers will retain Thai pronunciation, tonality, and question tags like "na" and

"ja" and particles like "krub" and "ka" to soften their tone, indicate respect, a request, encouragement or other moods ... Another characteristic of Thaiglish is adding suffixs (sic) like "-ing" when words cannot be directly translated or clearly described in one English word. For example, the term "wai-ing" as in "I am wai-ing my aunt" is often used amongst Thai Americans when one is referring to the traditional Thai form of greeting someone.

These examples reinforce the point made about the importance of attending to language ideologies. Regardless of whether there is any objective structural evidence for the existence of a nativized variety of English, the sociolinguistic dynamics are such that speakers often assume its existence and, as a consequence of this very assumption, consciously or otherwise, over time may collectively will it into existence by virtue of their linguistic and metalinguistic practices.

12.5 Conclusion

Pennycook (1998: 4) has observed that the "long term conjunction between English and colonial discourses has produced a range of linguistic-discursive connections between English and colonialism," connections that persist even today. The most glaring indication of this long-term connection is the valuing of English while insistently positioning English as the language of the Western Other. The implication, then, is that nativization of English devalues the language.

A good example of this can be seen in September 2011, when the Singapore government launched the English Language Institution of Singapore. The guest of honor, Lee Kuan Yew (Singapore's first prime minister and main architect of the country's language policy), suggested that English-language teaching in Singapore might want to shift its normative target to American English, given the cultural and political influence of the USA:[9] "I believe we will be exposed more and more to American English, and it might be as well that we accept and teach our students to recognise and, (if) need be, to speak American English," he said. What remains unquestioned here is the assumption that there is some exonormative variety of English that needs to be treated as the reference for proper usage. The specific exonormative variety may change over time but the assumption of exonormativity itself remains unquestioned.

A key challenge for the development of English in Southeast Asia (and certainly by no means a challenge that is unique to this region), then, is convincing governments that the emergence of nativized varieties of

---

[9] See "LKY: English gave S'pore its edge," September 7, 2011, schang@sph.com.sg, http://www.asiaone.com/News/AsiaOne+News/Singapore/Story/A1Story20110907-298079.html; accessed 16 January 2012.

English is both sociolinguistically natural as and a phenomenon that need not compromise any efforts toward cultivating competence in standard English. That is, the relationship between Manglish, Singlish, Taglish, and Tinglish or Thaiglish, on the one hand, and standard English, on the other, is not a zero-sum game. In this regard, Kumaravadivelu (2003: 540, cited in Rubdy 2015: 50) makes an important and useful distinction between nativization and decolonization:

> In the context of world Englishes nativization may be seen as an attribute of a language whereas decolonization is an attitude of the mind. Nativization is a relatively simple process of indigenizing the phonological, syntactic and pragmatic aspects of the linguistic system of the English language – a target that has been largely achieved. Decolonization is a fairly complex process of taking control of the principles and practices of planning, learning, and teaching English – a task that has not been fully accomplished.

Nativization is a sociolinguistically natural and indeed inevitable result of the spread of English. Decolonization, in contrast, is an attitudinal issue that lags behind nativization (Rudby 2015: 50):

> For Kumaravadivelu, then, nativization marks only the beginning, not the end of the process of decolonization. He believes that to erase the lingering traces of English imperialism and to claim ownership of the language learning and teaching enterprise, it is imperative to move from nativization to decolonization.

Yet exactly how to bring about this decolonization of the mind remains a difficult question (see Jain and Wee 2018 for further discussion on this matter). It seems clear, though, that nativization without decolonization will only serve to penalize speakers of nativized varieties of English.

References

Asuncion-Lande, N. 1971. Multilingualism, politics, and "Filipinism." *Asian Survey* 11(7): 677–692.

Bowring, John. 1959. Diary 1856. Bangkok: Trironasarn Printing House.

Bruthiaux, Paul. 2003. Squaring the circles: Issues in modeling English worldwide. *International Journal of Applied Linguistics* 13(2): 159–178.

Bruthiaux, Paul. 2010. The Speak Good English Movement: A web-user's perspective. In Lisa Lim, Anne Pakir and Lionel Wee, eds. *English in Singapore: Modernity and Management*. Hong Kong: Hong Kong University Press, 91–108.

Chan, Swee Heng. 2012. Defining English language proficiency for Malaysian tertiary education. *Advances in Language and Literary Studies* 3(2): 150–160.

Chng, Huang Hoon. 2003. "You see me no up": Is Singlish a problem? *Language Problems and Language Planning* 27(1): 45–62.

Espiritu, Clemencia. 2015. Language policies in the Philippines. April 30. http://ncca.gov.ph/subcommissions/subcommission-on-cultural-disseminationscd/language-and-translation/language-policies-in-the-philippines/

Gaudart, Hyacinth. 1987. English Language Teaching in Malaysia: A historical account. *The English Teacher, Vol XVI.* www.melta.org.my/index.php/11-melta-articles/128-english-language-teaching-in-malaysia-a-historical-account

Gupta, Anthea Fraser. 1994. *The Step-Tongue: Children's English in Singapore.* Clevedon: Multilingual Matters.

Jain, Ritu and Lionel Wee. 2018. Diversity management and the presumptive universality of categories: The case of the Indians in Singapore. *Current Issues in Language Planning* 20(1): 16–32.

Kok, Loy Fatt. 1978. *Colonial Office Policy Towards Education in Malaya (1920–1940).* Kuala Lumpur: FaKulti Pendidikan.

Kong, Rithdee. 2012. Davos, Tokyo and clueless Tinglish. *Bangkok Post*, October 3.

Kumaravadivelu, B. 2003. A postmethod perspective on English language teaching. *World Englishes* 22(4): 539–550.

Lee, Jonathan and Kathleen Nadeau. 2011. Thai Americans: Vernacular language, speech and manner. In *Encyclopedia of Asian American Folklore and Folklife*, Vol. 3, 1122–1126. Santa Barbara, CA: ABC-CLIO.

Lim, Lisa. 2010. Migrants and "mother tongues": Extralinguistic forces in the ecology of English in Singapore. In Lisa Lim, Anne Pakir and Lionel Wee, eds. *English in Singapore: Modernity and Management.* Hong Kong: Hong Kong University Press, 19–54.

Lorente, Beatriz. 2013. The grip of English and Philippine language policy. In Lionel Wee, Robbie Goh and Lisa Lim, eds. *The Politics of English: South Asia, Southeast Asia and the Asia Pacific*, 187–204. Amsterdam: John Benjamins.

MacArthur, Tom. 1998. Philippine English. In *Concise Oxford Companion to the English Language.* www.encyclopedia.com/doc/1O29-PHILIPPINE ENGLISH.html

Mahathir, M. 1970. *The Malay Dilemma.* Singapore: Times Books International.

Masavisut, Nitaya, Mayuri Sukwiwat and Seri Wongmontha. 1986. The power of the English language in Thai media. *World Englishes* 5(2–3): 197–207.

Muniandy, Mohan K., Gopala Krishnan Sekharan Nair, Shashi Kumar Krishnan Shanmugam, Irma Ahmad and Norashikin Binte Mohamed Noor. 2010. Sociolinguistic competence and Malaysian students' English language proficiency. *English Language Teaching* 3(3): 145–151.

Noss, R. B. 1984. *An Overview of Language Issues in South-East Asia 1950–1980.* Singapore: Oxford University Press.

Park, Joseph and Wee, Lionel. 2013. Linguistic baptism and the disintegration of ELF. *Applied Linguistics Review* 4(2): 339–359.

Pennycook, Alastair. 1998. *English and the Discourses of Colonialism*. London: Routledge.

Platt, John and Heidi Weber. 1980. *English in Singapore and Malaysia*. Kuala Lumpur: Oxford University Press.

Rappa, A. and L. Wee. 2006. *Language Policy and Modernity in Southeast Asia: Malaysia, Philippines, Singapore and Thailand*. New York: Springer.

Rubdy, Rani. 2001. Creative destruction: Singapore's Speak Good English Movement. *World Englishes 20*: 341–355.

Rubdy, Rani. 2015. Unequal Englishes, the native speaker, and decolonization in TESOL. In T. Ruanni Tupas, ed. *Unequal Englishes: The Politics of Englishes Today*. Basingstoke: Palgrave, 42–58.

Schneider, Edgar. 2007. *Postcolonial English*. Cambridge: Cambridge University Press.

Schneider, Edgar. 2011. English into Asia: From Singaporean ubiquity to Chinese learners' features. In Michael Adams and Anne Curzan, eds. *Contours of English and English Language Studies*. Ann Arbor: University of Michigan Press, 135–156.

Schneider, Edgar. 2016. Hybrid Englishes: An exploratory survey. *World Englishes 35*(3): 339–354.

Sibayan, Bonifacio and Andrew Gonzales. 1996. Post-imperial English in the Philippines. In Joshua A. Fishman, Alma Rubal-Lopez and Andrew W. Conrad, eds. *Post-imperial English*. Berlin: Mouton, 139–72.

Siegel, J. 1999. Stigmatized and standardized varieties in the classroom: Interference or separation. *TESOL Quarterly 33*(4): 701–728.

Smalley, W. A. 1994. *Linguistic Diversity and National Unity: Language Ecology in Thailand*. Chicago: University of Chicago Press.

Stevenson, Rex. 1975. *Cultivators and Administrators: British Educational Policy Towards the Malays 1875–1906*. Kuala Lumpur: Oxford University Press.

Tupas, Topsie Ruanni F. 2004. Back to class: The medium of instruction debate in the Philippines. Paper presented at the *Language, Nation and Development in Southeast Asia Roundtable*.

Vella, Walter F. 1955. *The Impact of the West on Government in Thailand*. Berkeley: University of California Press.

Wee, Lionel. 2004. Reduplication and discourse particles. In Lisa Lim, eds. *Singapore English: A Grammatical Perspective*. Amsterdam: John Benjamins, 105–126.

Wee, Lionel. 2018. *The Singlish Controversy: Language, Culture and Identity in a Globalizing World*. Cambridge: Cambridge University Press.

Wongsothorn, A. 2000. Thailand. In Wah Kum Ho and Ruth Y. L. Wong, eds., *Language Policies and Language Education*. Singapore: Times Academic Press, 307–320.

Yeoh, Brenda. 2003. *Contesting Space in Colonial Singapore*. Singapore: NUS Press.

13

World Englishes Old and New: English in Australasia and the South Pacific

Carolin Biewer and Kate Burridge

13.1 Introduction

Australasia and the Pacific encompass a range of very diverse native and non-native varieties of English, including English-based contact varieties such as pidgins and creoles. While varieties such as Australian English (AusE), New Zealand English (NZE), Māori English, and Tok Pisin have been described in various publications, information on the structure and use of English as a second or foreign language in Polynesian, Melanesian, and Micronesian island states remains much more limited. This chapter aims to provide a new approach to these varieties by focusing on their geographical closeness: Can we find structural patterns that are typical of many if not all English varieties in this region, that is, areal features of Australasian and (South) Pacific Englishes? Such features are not only difficult to define but also difficult to trace (due to the interaction of conditioning factors in language evolution, as well as the lack of detailed studies on function and frequency of relevant individual features). We therefore reserve a larger section of the chapter to a theoretical discussion on areal features in Australasia and the South Pacific (AuSP).[1]

In this chapter, we focus on the most significant Englishes currently spoken in Australasia and the Pacific (comprising Australia, New Zealand, and neighboring islands in the Pacific). Our account covers a range of very different variety types that have evolved as a consequence of the spread of English into these regions.

It is impossible to do justice to the linguistic diversity here, particularly when it comes to second-language varieties (L2) and contact

---

[1] Since data on English in Micronesia are still scarce, our linguistic discussion in Section 13.3 will concentrate on Australasia and the South Pacific rather than the Pacific, which is why we introduce the abbreviation AuSP here. The arguments stated for/against areal features in Section 13.2, however, partly also apply to Micronesia.

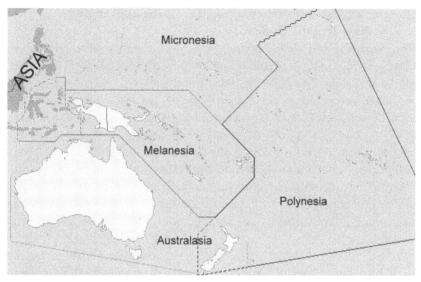

Map 13.1 Australasia and the Pacific (Wikipedia Commons)
Oceania's Regions. https://commons.wikimedia.org/wiki/File:Oceanias_Regions.png

varieties and the very different outcomes that arise from contact (Winford 2003).[2] Two main linguistic factors contribute to the rich regional, social, and idiolectal variation: (1) the influence of local vernacular languages (which may or may not be the first language of the speakers) and (2) contact with standard English – for certain (especially urban) groups a growing force of influence. We also need to emphasize the complex nature of the multilingualism that characterizes many of these speech communities. In addition to knowing one or more of the local indigenous languages, speakers of creoles or L2 varieties typically have some command of a range of varieties (depending on situation and audience) along a continuum, from those at the "acrolectal" end close to the superstrate language (standard English) through to those at the "basilectal" end that are quite distinct from the standard.

The inadequacy of labels such as ENL (English as a native language) versus ESL (English as a second language), pidgin versus creole, and so on is readily acknowledged (e.g. Schneider 2007; Biewer 2011; see also Buschfeld and Kautzsch, Chapter 3, this volume) and, as we go on to discuss, capturing this diversity in any current model of World Englishes is problematic. Nonetheless, for convenience we draw on the traditional nomenclature to introduce and to initially organize the varieties spoken in the area of Australasia and the Pacific.

[2] In this chapter, we will use the term *contact variety* to refer to pidgin and creole languages, mixed languages in Australasia and the Pacific, and the more extreme ends of the Aboriginal and Māori English continua. Since L2 varieties of English have equally been shaped through intensive language contact with the local substrate, we will occasionally include these under the label "contact varieties in a broad sense."

13.1.1   "English as a Native Language": Australian English, New Zealand English

Both Australia and New Zealand have in common a relatively recent history of European settlement and both share transplanted Englishes. For Australia, the date coincides with the arrival of Captain Cook in 1770 but, on the other side of the Tasman, English got off to a later and somewhat slower start. Though Cook charted the islands around the same time he visited Australia, the official colony was not established until nearly the middle of the 1800s. Before then, the number of English speakers in New Zealand was small but, in the second half of the century, immigration from Australia and Britain increased dramatically and, in terms of dialectal evolution (Schneider, 2007), both varieties now find themselves at Stage 5 (internal differentiation – continuing codification, social and regional diversification).

As Bauer (2017: 422) describes, "[t]here are good reasons why most of the world has difficulty in distinguishing between Australian and New Zealand Englishes: they have a great deal in common. They are not, however, identical." Factors such as settlement dates and patterns, contact with indigenous languages, and mix of original dialects have created differences between the two varieties. Their physical separation from other English-speaking regions is allowing this distinctiveness to flourish.

13.1.2   Ethnic Varieties: Māori, Aboriginal, Pasifika Englishes

Aboriginal and Māori English are ethnolects that grew out of the original contact situation between English and indigenous languages and they now provide a distinctive dimension to the extraterritorial Englishes in the Antipodes. In the face of the disappearance of local languages in both countries, these ethnic varieties have become an important means of projecting their speakers' cultural identity. For the Aboriginal and Torres Strait Islander speech communities, language contact with the accompanying imposition of colonization has brought about wholesale extinction of many languages – only around 120 of the original 200–250 languages exist today, and even the remaining robust languages are under threat, despite vigorous efforts to maintain them (Marmion et al. 2014). In New Zealand, few contexts remain where Māori is the natural means of communication. However, as Maclagan (2010) describes, Māori revitalization has led to increased numbers of children being raised bilingually and adults speaking Māori as a second language. She also describes Māori English as the fastest growing variety of NZE (p. 159).

New Zealand now has well over 200,000 people whose families immigrated from the South Pacific Islands, largely from the Cook Islands, Tonga, Samoa and Niue. As these communities shift from their Polynesian languages to English, we see again the potential for speakers to start signaling ethnic identity through a distinctive form of English.

Pasifika Englishes share features with Māori English (some through Polynesian substrate commonalities) and – as we go on to discuss – a number of them are spreading beyond the Pasifika communities.

13.1.3 South Pacific Englishes: Fiji English, Samoan English, Cook Islands English; English in Micronesia (Palau, Kosrae, Saipan, Kiribati and the Marshall Islands)

While research on pidgin and creole languages in the South Pacific abounds, information on ESL in this region is much more limited. The term *South Pacific Englishes* (SPEs) was introduced in Biewer (2008a, 2008b) for institutionalized non-native varieties of English used in postcolonial settings in the South Pacific, following the definition of *New Englishes* by Platt et al. (1984: 2–3). Fiji English is the only variety belonging to this group that has gained wider attention in academic publications, for example in Tent and Mugler (2008), Schneider and Hundt (2012), Zipp (2014), Biewer (2015). The grammatical structure and sociolinguistic profile of two other emerging varieties, Samoan English and Cook Islands English, have been described by Biewer (2015). The structure and use of ESL in other island groups such as Tonga, Niue, Tokelau, and so on, have not yet been explored.

SPEs show very interesting characteristics that differentiate them from standard British English (BrE) or standard NZE. Looking at the development of these features not only enhances our overall understanding of the evolution and dynamics of L2 English but also reveals intriguing influences of the local substrate and local cultural conventions of language use (e.g. Biewer 2015: 218), thus justifying the label SPEs. As norm-developing varieties, SPEs are also likely to be influenced by their geographical neighbors, for example NZE. Concerning the question of areal features in AuSP, they are therefore an interesting group of contact varieties (in a broad sense) drawing from Oceanic languages as well as local superstrate languages, just as ethnic varieties or pidgins and creole languages in AuSP do – albeit to a different degree. They deserve more academic attention, particularly in this context.

The University of Bern has launched a project on English in Micronesia with special focus on previously undescribed varieties of English that are developing in Palau, Saipan (in the Northern Mariana Islands), Kosrae (in the Federated States of Micronesia), and the Republic of Kiribati (see Bürki 2016; Britain & Matsumoto 2016 ; Leonhardt 2016; Lynch 2016).[3] Another project at the University of Duisburg-Essen investigates the language contact situation on the Marshall Islands (see Buchstaller 2016). While interesting results are to be expected from these projects, the description of the structure of these varieties remains a little sketchy and the status of the

---

[3] Presentations given at the *Sociolinguistic Symposium* 21 at the University of Murcia on June 15–18, 2016.

varieties not entirely clear. Yet, whether second-language varieties or learner varieties, they deserve their place in future studies on areal features of AuSP varieties. In this chapter, we concentrate on SPEs.

13.1.4   English-Based Contact Languages: Australian Creole Varieties, Tok Pisin, Bislama, Solomon Islands Pijin, Hawai'i Creole, Norfuk (and Pitkern), Palmerston Island English

In the early 1880s, a "foreigner-talk" system known as South Seas Jargon was used in various parts of the Pacific primarily between European whalers and indigenous crew members, some of whom were Māori. In New Zealand, this variety developed into Māori Pidgin English and was used for early contact between Māori and Pākehā (European) groups. However, the pidgin never stabilized enough to evolve further and the New Zealand pidgin was short-lived. In Australia, pidgins based on English appeared not long after the arrival of the Europeans and became increasingly important for contact, not only between Aboriginal speakers and English speakers but also as a lingua franca between speakers of different Aboriginal languages. Creoles later evolved in the Kimberley Region, the Roper River area, and parts of North Queensland (the two major varieties being Kriol and Torres Strait Creole). These various English-based creoles have much in common but they also show regional differences, depending on the Aboriginal languages of the community and also influences from other contact varieties brought into Australia from outside.

We should also point out that extensive language contact in Australia has seen the rise of new languages created via bilingual speakers' code-switching between an English-based creole and an Australian traditional language. Two new mixed varieties, Gurindji Kriol (Victoria River District) and Light Warlpiri (Lajamanu), have now conventionalized into autonomous languages acquired by children as a first language. These intertwined languages are clearly not varieties of English – their unique development sets them apart. However, they are genetically related to two (or more) languages, one of which is an English-lexifier creole (Meakins and O'Shannessy 2012). In Gurindji, Kriol nouns and main verbs can come from either Gurindji (the traditional Aboriginal language) or Kriol but there is a structural split between the noun phrase and verb phrase grammar – Gurindji contributes the noun structure (including case-marking) and the verb structure (including auxiliaries) comes from Kriol. Light Warlpiri draws most verbs and verbal morphology from Kriol, nouns from Warlpiri and English, and nominal morphology from Warlpiri.

The multilingualism in these two indigenous speech communities is complex and multilayered. In addition to the traditional languages Warlpiri and Gurindji, the linguistic repertoires of these speakers vary along a continuum (reminiscent of the creole continuum). At one end of the continuum, the way of talking is close to the English of many people in rural Australia and at the other end are the mixed languages, which contain words and structural features of the different parent languages. In the middle are varieties of an English-based creole. It is still early days – these hybrid languages may well be stabilizing or else they could be in the process of a more dramatic shift toward Kriol.

Other contact languages we consider include Bislama (Vanuatu), Solomon Islands Pijin, and Tok Pisin (Papua New Guinea), which have their roots in Melanesian Pidgin and share lexical patterning and a number of structural characteristics. However, different external influences (e.g. contact with French for Bislama and with German for Tok Pisin) and interaction with different local languages have given rise to distinct developments within these varieties.

Even though the Hawai'ian Islands have been politically part of the USA since 1958, their geographical location in the northern Pacific means Hawai'i Creole is included as another English-lexifier contact language of this region (one that also draws vocabulary from Hawai'ian and Japanese). Although its story is very different, it does have features in common with the creoles from the southwestern Pacific: (1) early links with South Seas Jargon (as mentioned at the beginning of this section, a jargon variety used for short-term communication by crews on ships and by individuals on shore in various locations around the Pacific Islands) and (2) input from Melanesian Pidgin spoken by laborers recruited for the sugarcane plantations in the early 1800s. These four Pacific creoles have, since the beginning of the twentieth century, undergone substantial functional and structural expansion.

Norfolk Island is a small Australian territory that sits in the South Pacific Ocean between Australia (1,700 km to the west) and New Zealand (1,100 km to the south) and is the only Australian territory where a language other than English shares official status with English. Norfolk Island/Pitcairn English (or Pitkern-Norf'k) is the linguistic outcome of contact between the BrE of the *Bounty* mutineers and Tahitian. It is a remarkable example of a contact language since we know precisely the number of speakers who originally settled on Pitcairn in 1790, the origin of these speakers, and even their names. However, its subsequent development has not yet been fully established and although there are clear early influences from the Pacific Pidgin English of the Melanesian islanders, the exact relationship of Norfolk Island-Pitcairn English to other contact varieties is problematic (Mühlhäusler 2008 suggests the diffusion of creole features from St Kitts places this variety linguistically closer to Atlantic creoles rather than neighboring Pacific varieties).

Palmerston Island English is a variety of English used by a tiny isolated community in the Cook Islands (its total land area is only around 1 square mile, or 2.6 square km); in August 2009, its population numbered only fifty-four. The island is divided three ways and each third belongs to one of three families Akakaingara, Matavia, and Tepou (named after the three

Cook Island wives of William Marsters, the man who settled the island in the early 1800s). Given its isolation, it is not surprising that over the past 140 years it has developed a unique linguistic and cultural identity, with distinctive phonetic and grammatical influences from a northern English dialect (based on the nineteenth-century speech patterns of Marsters), Cook Islands Māori, and Polynesian English (Hendery 2015).

Older static models of World Englishes are seriously lacking when it comes to these AuSP varieties, their acknowledgment, their categorization, and the visualization of their genetic relation to each other (cf. Strevens 1980; Kachru 1985; McArthur 1987; Görlach 1990). Individual varieties such as Samoan English or whole groups like South Pacific pidgin and creole languages are not considered. Areal categorization takes a back seat while status distinctions are at the forefront. A common supranational Australasian standard is postulated although highly unlikely (cf. Görlach 1990). Areal subcategorizations are restrictive and faulty (cf. Strevens 1980). In our approach, we include many more AuSP varieties: ethnic varieties, EFL varieties, pidgins and creoles, as well as native varieties and ESL varieties. Rather than focusing on status differences, we want to focus on their geographical closeness and investigate the shared linguistic characteristics that may set these varieties apart from other World Englishes. Without a precategorization of previous models and with a closer look at intralinguistic similarities, we may be able to give a more accurate description of what we truly mean when we talk about "varieties of English in Australasia and the South Pacific."

13.2   How Likely Are Areal Features in AuSP Varieties?

13.2.1   Defining "Areal Feature": A Challenge

What we hope to find is a better way to describe AuSP varieties as a group sharing certain extra- and intralinguistic characteristics that set them apart from English varieties spoken in other regions. As such, we are less interested in universals of the English language or common features of ESL all over the world (see definition of *angloversal* in Mair 2003: 85) than in common features specific to the AuSP region. We are trying to identify so-called *areal features* for AuSP.

It is not easy, however, to express what is meant by "areal" features. In a strict sense, these are linguistic features that emerge through a contact situation "within a given habitat," following the definition of Haugen (1972: 38–39) and Mühlhäusler (1996) (see also Peters and Burridge 2012: 233). In this sense, we would consider only linguistic features that have emerged through language contact in the AuSP region. As the discussion in Section 13.2.3 shows, however, contact-induced areality is hard to prove. We would like to apply a broader definition of "areal" that includes parallel developments within a given habitat without claiming any causal links. Such a definition then embraces the phenomenon of drift, inherited trends that can be witnessed in the colonial Englishes. For example, front vowel raising was a sound change well on its way in nineteenth-century British English spoken in the south-east of England and this "intralinguistic tendency" (Bussmann 1996: 139) was transported "downunder" and further developed in the new habitat.

A broader definition would also include parallel developments in AuSP varieties due to similarities in their language ecology (both internal and external). Internal ecology refers to the language system and includes all sources of an emerging variety, including possible substrate languages. External ecology covers sociolinguistic, sociocultural, and historical aspects of the setting in which the language is used and therefore refers to such things as social identity, language attitudes, language policies, immigration patterns, and so on (Mufwene 2001: 207; Lim 2009: 199). It is likely that we find a number of linguistic features shared by AuSP varieties, not because they are all influenced by the same variety of English but because parallels can be found in their substrates or the cultural practices in their community. Sociocultural motivations of language use, in particular, cannot be overemphasized and Pacific culture is one aspect that differentiates AuSP communities from other communities. Suffice to say, that, while "areal" features here refer to linguistic characteristics, they are partly the result of extralinguistic influences. We should also add that, when describing varieties of English, we rarely find features that only occur in one variety or group of varieties but never in another. We therefore look for relative features, that is, a particular high or low proportion of a particular feature in AuSP varieties in contrast to other World Englishes. We will also not restrict the view to features that occur in all AuSP varieties under observation but will be satisfied with its occurrence in a substantial number of varieties that do not all belong to the same status group as identified by Kachru (1985) or Görlach (1990). Moreover, as we will demonstrate, on the surface a given feature may not look different from a feature in a variety outside the AuSP region but there may be a special local function of that feature, which as such makes it "areal."

Even with such a more open definition of "areal," it is still very difficult to prove the existence of truly areal features. We therefore allow for a theoretical discussion of arguments for and against the perceptibility of areal features in AuSP varieties before looking more closely at potential candidates.

13.2.2   Arguments for Areal Features in AuSP

For a number of reasons, areal features as defined in the previous section are absolutely plausible for the AuSP varieties. First, in terms of the internal ecology, we find similarities in the local substrate, that is, in the native languages of the indigenous population of New Zealand and the Pacific

Islands. The Pacific tends to be subdivided into three "culture-areas," Melanesia, Polynesia, and Micronesia. Language-wise the native languages of Polynesia, of Micronesia (apart from Palauan and Chamorro), and of parts of Melanesia all belong to the Oceanic language family. This includes Māori, the indigenous language of New Zealand (hence New Zealand is often listed as part of the Polynesian triangle). Although there is no typological unity among Oceanic languages, "there are certain patterns and structures which tend to recur over large geographical and genetic groupings of Oceanic languages" (Lynch et al. 2002: 34); features include the CV syllable structure, contrastive vowel length, the distinction between inclusive and exclusive for first-person plural pronouns, no gender distinction for third-person pronouns, the use of reduplication as a process in verb morphology and noun derivation, the use of preverbal tense and aspect markers (whether as a free morpheme or prefixed) (Lynch et al. 2002: 34–35, 44–45), and the list goes on. Similarities in the substrate may cause similarities in EFL or ESL spoken in the Pacific. They may also account for similarities between SPEs, Pasifika Englishes, and Māori English. In addition to their common origins, Pacific languages have frequently influenced each other. Some have, from early on, been used as a lingua franca by European missionaries, for example Bauan Fijian in Fiji or Samoan in Tokelau (Lynch et al. 2002: 26–27). Given the seafaring skills of Pacific Islanders, particularly in Eastern Oceania, there has been long-standing contact between Oceanic languages (e.g. see Besnier 1992: 249).

When it comes to English-based pidgin and creole languages in the Pacific, we must bear in mind that Bislama, Pijin, and Tok Pisin have a common ancestor, Melanesian Pidgin (Lynch et al. 2002: 27). Naturally these creoles share many of the common features of Oceanic languages through this common origin (e.g. a gender-neutral pronoun system with inclusive and exclusive distinctions for first-person plural; Burridge 2008: 593).

Areal features in AuSP may also arise through parallels in the external ecology. First of all, the Melanesian and Polynesian culture share various concepts and practices: the preparation of food in earth ovens, dress codes, the role of story-telling, family ties, tribal hierarchies (see Pitt and Macpherson 1974; Bruno and Schade 1993); some Polynesian communities show interesting parallels in the concept of transgender (for information, see Besnier 1994). Successful communication in English in Pacific communities requires a local form of English that can adequately express cultural needs (see also Biewer 2015: 106). Local cultural constructs will most certainly influence local language use: Transfer from the native language will be linked to cultural conventions of how to tell a story, how to express social class distinctions, how to construct the identity of a *fa'afafine* or *fakaleiti* (men displaying female gender traits in Samoa/Tonga). Wherever cultural similarities exist in the South Pacific, SPEs are likely to acquire similar features to address similar cultural needs.

Another similarity in the external ecology is the fact that, in many Pacific Islands, English will have been implemented during colonial times as the language of administration and education, while being spoken as a native language only by a minority (e.g. Fiji, Samoa). Language attitudes toward English in such postcolonial settings are usually positive. Partly through its historical spread, proficiency in English will always be seen as the mark of an educated speaker. Moreover, as both a lingua franca for the Pacific and a language of wider communication, English makes the Western economic market accessible to those with the linguistic skills. Siegel (1996: 241) calls English "the most important language of intercultural communication in the Pacific Basin." Such connotations and amenities at least guarantee that English use remains widespread enough in AuSP that a search for similarities between AuSP varieties beyond national borders is not a far-fetched endeavor.

Particularly interesting in this context is the impact of NZE and AusE in AuSP territory – a result not just of geographical closeness but also of political and economic power. A number of islands remain politically associated with either Australia or New Zealand. The Cook Islands and Niue are in free association with New Zealand, that is, the local governments are in charge of all internal affairs while New Zealand takes responsibility for all external affairs, in particular military defense (Campbell 1989: 198). Tokelau is still a New Zealand territory; Norfolk is equally considered an external territory of Australia.[4] Nauru is legally independent but heavily dependent on aid from Australia, so much that it is considered a "client state" of Australia that cannot say "no" to any requests from the Australian government (Doherty 2016).

Historically, responsibilities in many colonies in the South Pacific were shifted to Australian and New Zealand authorities around the time of World War I.[5] As a reaction to the outbreak of World War I, German New Guinea and German Samoa were seized and then administered by Australia and New Zealand, respectively, under a League of Nations mandate (for Samoa, see Meleisea et al. 1987: 126); and, though Fiji remained under British rule until 1970, New Zealand took over responsibility of education in the 1920s and thus fundamentally influenced its educational system (Tent 2000: 17). Even Tonga, a former British protectorate that became independent in 1970, felt political pressure from Australia and New Zealand in 2006 when they interfered in a political turmoil in the capital to smooth the way to greater democracy in the country (Fraenkel 2012).

Economically speaking, New Zealand and Australia do much more business with China, the USA, and with each other than they do with the Pacific Islands.[6] Nevertheless, for many Pacific Islands, these two global

---

[4] See *CIA – The World Factbook* (www.cia.gov/library/publications/the-world-factbook/).
[5] See *Colonialism in the South Pacific* (www.southpacific.org/history/colonialism. html).
[6] See *The Treasury – Kaitohutohu Kaupapa Rawa* (www.treasury.govt.nz).

players are major trading partners[7]. Moreover, the islands are important tourist destinations, especially for New Zealanders, and this considerably strengthens New Zealand's economic power in AusP territory (Crocombe 1992: 237–244). A number of the Pacific Islands are also heavily dependent on foreign aid from New Zealand and Australia (e.g. Niue, Tokelau, the Cook Islands receive substantial economic aid from New Zealand).[8] In addition, New Zealand and Australia are favored migration destinations for Pacific Islanders, with more Cook Islanders, Niueans, and Tokelauans living in New Zealand than in their home countries (Crocombe 1992: 237, 241, 243); and, while the Pacific community in Australia is smaller than in New Zealand, it is "rapidly growing" (Ravulo 2015: 11).

Clearly, Australia and/or New Zealand have considerable political and economic clout over at least some of the Pacific Islands, with New Zealand being particularly influential in Polynesia. Such an external impact makes it plausible that AusE or NZE may influence the locally emerging varieties of English. The so-called "epicentre theory" popularized by Leitner (1992) suggests that new national standards such as standard NZE can replace standard BrE or AmE "as external norms for other newly emerging varieties" (Biewer 2015: 69). Geopolitical power and geographical closeness of those countries where these national standards have been established are seen as important prerequisites for such standards to gain epicentric status in a region (Biewer 2015: 71). AusE and NZE could be such new "centres of radiating influence" (term from Bailey 1990: 85) for at least some SPEs. Studies on Cook Islands English mention the use of New Zealandisms such as *jandals* for *flipflops*, and front vowel raising in DRESS and TRAP as in NZE (Biewer 2015: 280). Areal features may, therefore, emerge due to an influence of AusE and NZE on newly emerging varieties of English in the region. Moreover, if the notion of epicentric influence were widened to include the take-up of vernacular features, then we might also count the appearance of *youse* in Palmerston Island English, which Hendery (2015: 273) describes as a transfer from NZE (though additional impetus would come from historical diffusion and normal processes of change).

13.2.3   Arguments against Areal Features in AuSP

Section 13.2.2 lists a number of good arguments for the existence of areal features for the AuSP territory. However, such features may be less common than expected – and, if they do exist, they are not necessarily verifiable. Revisiting our earlier arguments, we need to point out several things. With respect to internal ecology, beside a number of crucial similarities between the substrate languages, there are also decisive differences. While

---

[7] In 2004, for instance, 61 percent of the imports to the Cook Islands came from New Zealand (www.cia.gov). Crocombe (1992: 237–244) names New Zealand as an important partner in trade for the Cook Islands, Fiji, French Polynesia, New Caledonia, Niue, Tokelau, Vanuatu, Norfolk Island and Pitcairn Island.

[8] See *CIA – The World Factbook* (www.cia.gov/library/publications/the-world-factbook/).

Melanesian languages tend to have many different dialects, Polynesian and Micronesian languages are comparatively more homogeneous (Schütz 1972: 2, Lynch 1998: 30). Before predicting the existence of areal features due to common transfer patterns, one has to check closely which features are really similar in the Oceanic substrate languages – and whether they are the ones likely to resurface in L2 Englishes, pidgins and creoles, or ethnic varieties (on this issue, see also Siemund 2008: 8–9).

Relevant here is also Andersen's *Transfer to somewhere principle*. Studies show that grammatical transfers from the local substrate into L2 English are only likely if similar structures can be found in the ENL target language (Andersen 1983: 178). Types of reduplication (for intensification, iteration, and distribution), for example, are common in Oceanic languages and they will find their way from the substrate language into a creole (Kouwenberg 2003). Yet they are unlikely to become areal features in AuSP English encompassing L2 Englishes and ethnic varieties of English since this is not a morphological process common in the English language system. The expected result of transfer is a reproduction or modification of what is already there in the target language. Andersen's principle in a way assures the production of L2 features on the basis of Oceanic structure; similarities in the Oceanic input will point us in the right direction to search for areal features for AuSP varieties; but, since an overlap of ENL patterns with Oceanic patterns has to be guaranteed to find areal features across various types of contact varieties of English (in a broad sense), the occurrence of areal features for AuSP automatically becomes less obvious and less verifiable. This is related to the very interesting question of what kind of a contact scenario is required to suddenly find more marked differences between contact and noncontact varieties of English.

With respect to external ecology, we must again acknowledge that, alongside similarities between various cultural conventions and habits, there is also cultural diversity in the Pacific. In terms of hierarchies and gender roles, for instance, some island groups have matrilineal land tenure (e.g. on the Marshall Islands, the Solomon Islands, and Vanuatu; Huffer 2008), while others do not. In terms of identity constructions, Pacific Islanders will, when working and living abroad, possibly see themselves first and foremost as Pacific Islanders (in contrast to Europeans or Caucasians) but, within the Pacific, they clearly distinguish themselves as Tongans, Samoans, or Cook Islands Māori. Within the Cook Islands, people will not only refer to cultural distinctions between communities from the Southern (island) group and the more remote Northern group; they will select an island, whose community they feel strongly connected to. In terms of cultural needs and practices, we have to be careful not to oversimplify matters. Communities all over the world will always develop the language they need to express their cultural habits and necessities. As such, sociocultural motivations of language use are extremely influential in the evolution of areal features; they guarantee that in the emergence of a new non-native variety of English we do not get a 1:1 replication of an ENL. Yet just as with the general question of when to expect visible areal features through transfer, the question remains which cultural practices have such an enormous influence beyond national borders that they create new Pacific forms of English usage.

Added to that, politics and national borders make it highly unlikely that a supranational standard of English will emerge for the AuSP territory. While English certainly plays an important role in the Pacific as a means of intercultural communication, the type of English used by different ethnic groups as a lingua franca or as the language of wider communication (business, technology, and science) may be some form of an English used on an international scale with few features displaying local identification. On the supranational level, we may find a number of similar features, then, but they could not be counted as "areal." This supports our argument that we should not restrict the term "areal" to features occurring in all AuSP varieties under observation but broaden the definition to include features occurring in a substantial number of varieties.

Coming back to the impact of NZE and AusE, we also have to add that this impact has certainly been felt on a number of island nations but not all over the Pacific. Island groups in Micronesia tend to have a closer bond with the USA (see, e.g., Britain and Matsumoto 2016 on Palau; Bürki 2016 on Saipan) – not to mention the fact that American Samoa is a US territory and Hawai'i is a US state.[9] Again, while some supranational areal features for AuSP varieties are possible, we should not expect the same areal features present in all AuSP varieties. Moreover, while epicentric influence of NZE and/or AusE on some Pacific island varieties of English is plausible, it is hard to prove. Early studies on epicentric influence in World Englishes (e.g. Leitner 2004) focus on extralinguistic factors, while linguistic variables tend to be neglected. More recent work (e.g. Hundt 2013) has shown skepticism as to whether epicentric influence can ever be proved using current methodology; and, as Biewer (2015: 282–306) demonstrated, even if epicentric influence occurs on the structural level, substrate influence and the impact of second-language acquisition are the stronger factors, which in a multivariate analysis cover up evidence of norm reorientation (p. 304). External evidence points at norm reorientation toward the two AuSP ENL varieties for some Pacific island states, and there is some anecdotal evidence, but the existence of areal features due to epicentric influence is hardly verifiable (for a reassessment of the "epicentre theory," see Biewer 2015: 303–304). Moreover, the direction of influence is often uncertain. For a number of features that are shared across NZE, Māori English, Pasifika Englishes, and SPEs, it remains unclear who influences whom.

Clearly, on the theoretical level areal features for AuSP varieties (as in our definition) are perfectly plausible but difficult to trace in practice. This

---

[9] See *CIA – The World Factbook* (www.cia.gov/library/publications/the-world-factbook/).

is also partly due to the highly complex dynamic nature of L2 Englishes and contact varieties in general. Detailed information is lacking on various levels. We need more publications on the theory of language contact that also consider aspects of cultural motivations of language reorganization; publications that look more closely at the external ecology and discuss which features are likely to be modified in which contact scenarios; and we need more (detailed) publications on individual AuSP varieties to learn more about local functions of individual structures and their frequency of use. It is well possible that a number of features that resemble standard BrE are in fact areal since they are used in a different manner with a different frequency. Our discussion has also shown that, though it makes perfect sense to look for evidence of areality in the AuSP territory, we should not expect, for the moment, to find an abundance of features that qualify as "areal."

Ignoring epicentric influence (for reasons just outlined), we see three likely scenarios when it comes to potential candidates for areal features in AuSP varieties (our definition of "areal" as in Section 13.2.1):

Scenario 1: Areal features emerge in NZE and AusE due to parallel developments in these two varieties.

Scenario 2: Areal features emerge for Māori English, Pasifika Englishes, SPEs, and NZE due to an influence of immigrant Englishes and the Māori language in New Zealand on other varieties.

Scenario 3: Areal features emerge for a number of AuSP varieties including pidgin and creole languages due to similarities in the substrate languages, the cultural practices, and the external ecology.

13.3   Areal Features in AuSP: Three Scenarios

13.3.1   Scenario 1: Distinctive Features Shared between NZE and AusE

Many shared phonological traits are the products of the colonial dialect melting pot and represent the continuation of variation in the original dialects that fed into these dialects (see Hickey, Chapter 2, this volume). As described in Section 13.2.1, southern hemisphere varieties of English exhibit short front vowel raising. For NZE, historical evidence suggests a "push-chain" effect; Gordon et al. (2004: 453) conclude that the already raised TRAP vowel was part of the colonial input in the nineteenth century and then went on to influence the vowels in DRESS and KIT. Certainly, there is good evidence for TRAP raising in nineteenth-century AusE, and subsequent front vowel raising generally; however, over the past few decades, there has been a reversal of this trend with the Australian changes moving in the opposite direction to the NZE vowels (Cox and

Palethorpe 2008: 344). It is one of a number of points of divergence (rather than convergence), as we show in Section 13.3.2.

In his account of phonological variation in English worldwide, Schneider (2004: 1122) concludes that vowel mergers are regionally restricted. Certainly, prelateral vocalic mergers are not a general feature of the northern hemisphere and appear to be an innovative areal feature of the L1s of the southern region. In NZE and AusE, one shared sociolinguistic variable is the neutralization of DRESS and TRAP before laterals (making *celery* and *salary* indistinguishable). In Australia, this change has been attested in both (urban and regional) Victoria and Queensland (Loakes et al. 2014). There is a parallel phenomenon for the LOT and GOAT vowels; hence, *doll* and *dole* are not distinguished for many speakers. The FOOT and GOOSE vowels are also neutralizing before laterals in words such as *fool* and *full*. In NZE, this merging is extending to the vowels of KIT and FOOT before final [l], so that *pill* and *pull* are indistinguishable.

Many other shared phonological features are common in vernacular forms around the world and are more likely the fallout of historical diffusion coupled with the regular (usually reductive) processes of phonological change. For example, vocalization of /l/ is increasing in both dialects; the variant is a back vowel [u] (which may or may not be rounded or labialized). The contexts that promote vocalized /l/ involve backness (of adjacent consonants and vowels), syllable position (e.g. end position as in *pill*), and syllabic environment (*buckle*). It is hard to assess the areal significance of this feature. Lateral consonants have a long and complicated history of dropping out and reappearing in the English language, dating back to at least the seventeenth century – indeed, forms of L-vocalization occur throughout the anglophone world.

A striking prosodic feature of both varieties is the high rising contour on declarative clauses, especially common in narratives and descriptions (known variously as high rising terminal (HRT), Antipodean Uptalk, or Australian Questioning Intonation). There is evidence it was around in early AusE and in all likelihood NZE too, given the close contact during their evolutionary stages. Certainly Desmond's (1911: 15) early condemnation of "the extraordinary intonation that the Australian imparts to his phrases" suggests something interesting intonation-wise, especially when she describes how "everybody sings his remarks." However, this distinctive prosody is making appearances well beyond this geographical area; among younger speakers, it is reported to occur in British, American, Caribbean, and occasionally African and Asian Englishes (Schneider 2004: 1126). Clearly, this is one feature that requires more research before we can establish its status but it provides another interesting lead in the search for areal features in AuSP territory.

Using historical dictionaries to trace vocabulary over time, Peters (2009: 115) describes a body of shared Australian and New Zealand items that are "demonstrably Australian in origin." While dating expressions is notoriously difficult (especially when they are of a colloquial nature), chronology also suggests that formations specifically using the colloquial hypocoristic suffixes (*-ie/-y* as in *bushie/bushy* "bushman," *-o* as in *arvo* "afternoon" and, to a lesser extent, *-a/-eroo* as in *bossaroo* "king kangaroo") were bred in Australia and moved into New Zealand during the nineteenth century.

Lexical items are always the most easily transferred – but for those features more than skin-deep, evidence of diffusion is scarce. Peters and Burridge (2012) conclude that these hypocoristic suffixes are the only aspects of a morphosyntactic nature that qualify as areal features in the strict sense – their distinctive southern hemisphere use seems to have been stimulated by contact between AusE and NZE speakers at home and abroad in the nineteenth and early twentieth centuries. On the other hand, taking the broader view of *areal* described in Section 13.2.1, corpus-based research reveals a productivity of certain syntactic elements in these two varieties (e.g. *get*-passives), and this they attribute to the more informal character of the Australian and New Zealand culture and its greater willingness to embrace colloquial styles of discourse. It is worth emphasizing that many vernacular forms routinely appear in the everyday speech of standard speakers (e.g. invariant tags *You're going home soon,* **isn't it**? and **eh**?). While corpus-based research is still lacking on these grammatical forms, colloquial usage has always been the earmark of these Antipodean Englishes, and, as Peters and Burridge (2012: 253) describe, this cultural context or linguistic habitat supports the take-up of what are elsewhere spoken of as "vernacular universals" of English, as well as "angloversals," or colloquial variants of standard English. As described in Section 13.2.1, the ability of the language habitat to reshape the structural traits of a variety in this way makes it, together with borrowing, inheritance, and natural forces, a key element in any account of areality.

13.3.2   Scenario 2: Possible Influence of Pasifika Englishes and the Māori Language

Though the exact relationship between Pasifika English and Māori English has not yet been established, a number of features are known to be shared (including DH-stopping, where /ð/ is pronounced [d], and TH-fronting where /θ/ is pronounced [f]; non-aspiration of some stops; low rates of linking /r/ and other sandhi phenomena; rhoticity after the NURSE vowel); some are clearly transfers from Polynesian substrates. A number of these features are acquiring social meaning and, as Bell and Gibson (2008) describe, are being picked up by younger speakers, not just Pasifika and Māori people but Pākehā. Also important here is the significance of Māori English as a solidarity marker and the practice of "crossing" (sometimes referred to as "bro talk"). Speakers are no longer confined to those who are ethnically Māori – Pākehā growing up or identifying with Māori groups may also speak the variety and, as Bell and Gibson (2008: 52) conclude, the expansion of these ethnolectal features is very important to the overall development of NZE.

Relevant here is also the expansion of syllable timing, a widespread feature in the region (indeed around the world; Schneider 2004: 1126). Unlike the stress-timed quality of standard English, syllables in these varieties show more equal force in terms of loudness and duration (due to the comparative lack of reduced vowels in function words and unstressed syllables; Deterding 2012). As with the other features, there are signs that syllable-based speech is becoming a marker of style in the phonological repertoires of younger NZE speakers, also due to the influence of Māori, or the more syllable-timed Māori-influenced varieties of English (Hay et al. 2008; Maclagan 2010). Aiding the spread of this feature is the fact that there are already elements of syllable-based rhythms in L1 varieties. Crystal (1994: 175–176), for example, describes the use of staccato rhythms in child-directed language, emotional language, TV and radio commercials, types of popular music, and the language of air and sea services.

It is interesting that the incorporation of all these very "unEnglish-looking" structures in NZE is contributing to the divergence of Australia and New Zealand. Regional chauvinism can be a major incentive for people to start highlighting their distinctiveness linguistically and perhaps the rivalry between the two countries has a role to play here (also in the deviating front vowel trends, as described in Section 13.3.1). It is also true that New Zealand is lessening its British ties more and more and embracing its Polynesian heritage. Since the 1990s, in a form of identity reconstruction, both Māori and Pākehā have started to perceive their nation more and more as a Pacific nation (Crocombe 1992: 152–153). Convergence/divergence in any language-contact situation will always be a complex process involving the interaction of linguistic, sociocultural, and psychological factors, and it reminds us that areal features are never constant; as Hickey (2012: 12) emphasizes, "[t]he assessment of areality is always based on a snapshot at a particular point in time."

Before we conclude this section, it is worth pointing out another shared feature of interest, namely the realization of /tr/ and /str/ as [tʃɹ] and [ʃtɹ] respectively; e.g. tree [tʃɹi] and street [ʃtɹit]. The variant is attested in at least NZE, AusE, and Hawai'i Creole (see Burridge 2008) and is spreading to other contexts (in younger speakers S-retraction can also be heard for the /stj/ cluster in such words as student [ʃtju-dent]). Is this a case of NZE/AusE influencing other varieties or is it another influence from Pasifika Englishes? There is also the chance of parallel but independently motivated change – after all, the phenomenon represents a well-attested assimilatory process to [r] (the bunching of the tongue and lip-rounding) and is reported elsewhere (AmE and varieties of BrE; see Gylfadottir 2015). This example speaks to the perennial difficulty of ascertaining the causes behind areality.

13.3.3 Scenario 3: Distinctive Features Shared by Contact Varieties, Ethnolects, and L2s

The contact varieties in question (pidgins, creoles, mixed languages in Australasia and the Pacific, and the more extreme ends of the Aboriginal and Māori English continua) show striking resemblances in their phonology and grammar (many of which they share of course with creoles worldwide). These are the fallout of a number of factors, some of which we have described in Section 13.3.1: similar historical and sociological conditions that gave rise to these offsprings of English, coupled with common input early on from nautical jargon, and combined with the fact that their repertoires pattern on the systems of the relevant substrate languages; additionally, some have been argued to be the outcome of genetically programmed innate faculties (though Bickerton's Language Bioprogram Hypothesis remains a controversial idea; see Bickerton 1975; Velupillai 2015).

In this context, however, we are looking for features that are not restricted to one varietal type. The following phonological features attested in English-based contact varieties in Australasia and the Pacific also occur in one way or another in South Pacific L2 varieties of English (i.e. Fiji English, Samoan English, Cook Islands English):

(1) The Oceanic languages, just as the local pidgin and creole languages, show a preference for a CVCV structure. This preference in the mother tongue also leaves its traces in a high frequency of consonant cluster reductions in SPEs; e.g. pronunciations of *island* and *past* as [aɪlən] and [pɑːs]. (Note too, English is typologically unusual in allowing complex consonant clusters of up to four consonants.)

(2) Previous studies on Pacific pidgin and creole languages note a reduction in the phoneme system with respect to fricatives. Often no fricatives are used but /s/. Where they do occur, voicing contrasts are not consistently maintained. Interestingly, SPEs also show a tendency to reduce the number of fricatives (e.g. with the occasional pronunciation of the palato-alveolar fricative /ʃ/ as [s] in words like *shorts*).

(3) With the exception of a lenis dental fricative in Fijian (Tent and Mugler 2008: 239), dental fricatives do not seem to occur in Oceanic languages (typologically the sounds are rare). TH-stopping, the substitution of dental fricatives with stops, is attested to some extent for basilectal Fiji English and Māori English and has also been found occasionally in Cook Islands English conversations (Biewer, in preparation).

(4) As described in Section 13.3.2, syllable timing is a widespread and striking feature of the region and one easily attributable to substrate influence. Recordings of Samoans, Fijians, and Cook Islanders show that syllable timing appears on and off in SPE spoken data (e.g. words like *moment* show each syllable equally stressed).

The difficulty certainly arises here that syllable timing, consonant cluster reduction, and the replacement of the dental fricative with other consonants articulated close by are also attested in contact Englishes around the world. Common substrate influence unites contact varieties with L2 varieties in AuSP territory, which is an important point, as it questions Kachru's strict separation of pidgin and creole languages from other non-native varieties of English. Yet similarities of the Oceanic substrate with other (substrate) languages in the world (in their distinction from ENL) make it difficult to identify these features as truly areal. This would only be justified if a special local use of these features could be verified. That they are relevant for this area, in the current definition of "areal," is not enough. More research is needed in this respect. And the fact that syllable timing appears to be diffusing into the L1s of the area (Scenario 2) certainly makes this a promising feature for future studies on areality.

There are a number of grammatical features attested in English-based contact varieties in Australasia and the Pacific that also emerge in one way or another in SPEs. Like other contact varieties, SPEs tend to sometimes omit bound morphemes in favor of free morphemes to indicate plurality, tense, or aspect (see Biewer 2015). As L2 varieties, SPEs are highly dynamic. They are also closer to the English input than pidgins, creoles, or mixed languages. Morpheme omission, therefore, does not occur in absolutely every possible context but there are some interesting regularities that point at the influence of second-language acquisition, substrate influence, and cultural motivations of language use. The loss of endings is widely attested in L2 Englishes around the world, unsurprisingly, given that second-language learners in early stages of language acquisition always have difficulties with bound morphemes and tend to leave them out (Winford 2003: 218). However, a closer look at the function of these features may uncover interesting candidates for areality, for example verbal past tense non-marking in the South Pacific, which reflects the cultural perception of time hidden underneath this form of language use (on local narrative techniques and culture-specific conceptualizations of time, see Biewer 2015: 218).

Other striking resemblances of SPEs with Pacific pidgins, creoles, mixed languages, and some ethnolects are the following: (1) omission of gender distinction on pronouns (*my mother he is a teacher*); (2) repetition as a stylistic device; (3) invariant tag questions – in SPEs (and Māori English) often but not exclusively *eh*; and (4) the elaborate pronoun system, distinguishing dual and plural and inclusive and exclusive first person.[10]

Again some of these features are shared with other Englishes and English-based creoles worldwide. Besides similarities in substrate influence, Andersen's *Transfer to somewhere principle* predicts that with English

---

[10] For the pronoun system, compare for example Fiji English (Mugler and Tent 2008: 549), Palmerston Island English (Hendery 2015: 273–274), Aboriginal English, and Māori English (Burridge 2008: 584).

as the superstrate we will see features in the emerging L2 Englishes that are replications and slight modifications of features already existing somewhere in the English-language system rather than something completely new. The key once more lies in the local functions of these features, their cultural implications, and possibly in frequencies differing from the rate of use in other variety types or regions. Differences of such a kind would certainly point at areality. Once again, more research is needed but it would be a rewarding pursuit, in particular for verb phrase and pronominal systems. A productive research avenue would be to compare characteristics of ESL varieties with pidgin and creole languages as two extremes of a continuum.

13.4   Shared Features across the AuSP Region? A Conclusion

In this chapter, we presented a large number of AuSP varieties demonstrating the immense diversity of Englishes and English-based pidgins and creoles in the region with the view to promoting a model that goes beyond a pigeonholing of variety types. We discussed and extended the definition of "areal feature" to include regional parallel developments and features that occur not in all but in a number of AuSP varieties across variety type. In our theoretical framework, we demonstrated that areal features of the AuSP region are plausible but difficult to verify. We then isolated three different possible scenarios in which areal features may occur: parallel developments in AusE and NZE, parallel developments in ESL and pidgins and creoles, and the potential influence of Pasifika Englishes and the Māori language on NZE, SPEs, and Māori English.

Genuine pan-AuSP features are hard to locate – as yet there are none routinely occurring across all groups. In our discussion, however, we did identify a number of features that "have legs." Concerning forms shared between NZE and AusE, hypocorisms and the enthusiastic take-up of informal features are two aspects in which the local habitat has reshaped the structural traits found in other Englishes around the world.

We also find a few features in the process of crossing variety types. For example, the appearance of a distinctive syllable-timed rhythm and other Pasifika features in NZE; here, younger speakers seem to be seizing on this variation and attributing social meaning to it. This is a fascinating development, which reminds us to look closely at where budding areal features originate. While much has been published on epicentric influence of standard ENL on newly emerging varieties worldwide, little has been said about subcultures and the influence of immigrant Englishes on ENL in this region.[11]

---

[11]   There is one study by Hundt and Vogel (2011) on the high frequency of progressives in NZE, in which they argue that this result might, in part, be attributed to contact with ESL speakers.

Moreover, there are a number of features occurring both in pidgins and in creoles and to a lesser extent in L2 Englishes. Similarities in cultural practices and similarities in substrate influence show that we should consider similarities between the two variety types rather than hide their commonalities as in previous models (e.g. the tense and aspect system, perceptions of time, and storytelling techniques). It also becomes clear when looking at tense and aspect systems and pronominal systems that areality may rather be a matter of function than structure. More research is required along these lines.

Another prosodic feature that may be extending across variety types is the high rising terminal. As described, the rising intonation at the end of statements is pervasive in NZE and AusE but it is also reported for some creoles in the area and ethnic varieties such as Aboriginal English and Māori English; however, it is difficult to know what to make of this feature given its global pervasiveness and the fact that details differ (see Malcolm 2008: 135; Hay et al. 2008: 108).

The question of areal features for the AuSP region has not been an easy one to answer but we have gained a number of valuable insights and ideas for where to search for future variants. Siegel (2013: 769) suspects that varieties in the AuSP region cluster "according to variety type rather than region" and to some extent this is true. However, Siegel's valuable quantitative study could not consider local functions of language use and his database at the time only included Fiji English but no other L2 variety of the area. Since many other studies on Fiji English only consider basilectal Fiji English (e.g. Moag 1992), and a few erroneously believe the basilect to have been derived from a pidgin (e.g. Geraghty 1997), Siegel's results may be misread as demonstrating Fiji English to be a rather unusual ESL variety. In reality, Fiji English aligns with other SPEs and it is rather our habit of putting pidgin and creole languages into different categories that makes their commonalities with SPEs seem surprising. We hope that both our study and Siegel's approach will encourage researchers to think more about varietal versus regional differences for Australasia, the South Pacific, and beyond.

References

Andersen, Roger W. 1983. Transfer to somewhere. In Susan Gass and L. Selinker, eds. *Language Transfer in Language Learning: Issues in Second Language Research*. Rowley, MA: Newbury House, 177–201.

Bailey, Richard W. 1990. English at its twilight. In Christopher Ricks and Leonard Michaels, eds. *The State of the Language*. London: Faber and Faber, 83–94.

Bauer, Laurie. 2017. Australian and New Zealand Englishes. In Markku Filppula, Juhani Klemola and Devyani Sharma, eds. *The Oxford Handbook of World Englishes*. Oxford: Oxford University Press, 409–424.

Bell, Allan and Andy Gibson. 2008. Stopping and fronting in New Zealand Pasifika English. *University of Pennsylvania Working Papers in Linguistics* 14(2): 42–53.

Besnier, Niko. 1994. Polynesian gender liminality through time and space. In Gilbert Herdt, ed. *Third Sex, Third Gender: Beyond Sexual Dimorphism in Culture and History*. New York: Zone, 285–328.

Besnier, Niko. 1992. Polynesian languages. In William Bright, ed. *International Encyclopedia of Linguistics*, Vol. 3. Oxford: Oxford University Press, 245–251.

Bickerton, Derek. 1975. *Dynamics of a Creole System*. Cambridge: Cambridge University Press.

Biewer, Carolin. 2008a. South Pacific Englishes: Unity and diversity in the usage of the present perfect. In Terttu Nevalainen, Minna Korhonen, Paivi Pahta and Irma Taavitsainen, eds., *Dynamics of Linguistic Variation: Corpus Evidence on English Past and Present*. Amsterdam: John Benjamins, 203–219.

Biewer, Carolin. 2008b. Concord patterns in South Pacific Englishes: The influence of New Zealand English and the local substrate. In Klaus Stierstorfer, ed. *Anglistentag 2007 Münster, Proceedings*. Trier: Wissenschaftlicher Verlag, 331–343.

Biewer, Carolin. 2011. Modal auxiliaries in second language varieties of English: A learner's perspective. In Joybrato Mukherjee and Marianne Hundt, eds. *Exploring Second-Language Varieties of English and Learner Englishes. Bridging a Paradigm Gap*. Amsterdam: John Benjamins, 7–33.

Biewer, Carolin. 2015. *South Pacific Englishes. A Sociolinguistic and Morphosyntactic Profile of Fiji English, Samoan English and Cook Islands English*. Amsterdam: John Benjamins.

Biewer, Carolin. in preparation. Cook Islands English: Structure and use.

Britain, David and Kazuko Matsumoto. 2016. When substrate and super-strate collide: The case of (d) in Palauan English. Presentation given at the Sociolinguistic Symposium 21 at the University of Murcia, June 15.

Bruno, Sabine and Anette Schade. 1993. *Fiji, Samoa, Tonga*. Munich: Beck.

Buchstaller, Isabelle. 2016. Language contact at the date line: Investigating Marshallese English. Presentation given at the Sociolinguistic Symposium 21 at the University of Murcia, June 15.

Bürki, Dominique. 2016. A case study of the future tense in Saipan: Mobility as a window on the emergence of a new Pacific variety. Presentation given at the Sociolinguistic Symposium 21 at the University of Murcia, June 15.

Burridge, Kate. 2008. Synopsis: Morphological and syntactic variation in the Pacific and Australasia. In Kate Burridge and Bernd Kortmann, eds. *Varieties of English: The Pacific and Australasia*. Berlin: Mouton de Gruyter, 583–600.

Bussmann, Hadumod. 1996. *The Routledge Dictionary of Language and Linguistics* (trans. and ed. G. P. Trauth and K. Kazzazi). London: Routledge.

Campbell, Ian. 1989. *A History of the Pacific Islands*. Christchurch: University of Canterbury Press.

Cox, Felicity and Sallyanne Palethorpe. 2008. Reversal of short front vowel raising in Australian English, *Proceedings of Interspeech*, September 22–26, Brisbane, 342–345.

Crocombe, Ron. 1992. *Pacific Neighbours: New Zealand's Relations with Other Pacific Islands. Aotearoa me Nga Moutere o te Moana Nui a Kiwa*. Christchurch: Centre for Pacific Studies.

Crystal, David. 1994. Documenting rhythmical change. In J. Windsor Lewis ed., *Studies in General and English Phonetics*. London: Routledge, 174–179.

Desmond, Valerie. 1911. *The Awful Australian*. Sydney: John Andrew & Co.

Deterding, David. 2012. Variation across Englishes: Phonology. In Andy Kirkpatrick, ed., *The Routledge Handbook of World Englishes*. London: Routledge, 385–399.

Doherty, Ben. 2016. A short history of Nauru, Australia's dumping ground for refugees. *The Guardian*, August 9. www.theguardian.com/world/2016/aug/10/a-short-history-of-nauru-australias-dumping-ground-for-refugees

Fraenkel, Jon. 2012. Pacific Islands and New Zealand – Fiji and Tonga. In *Te Ara – the Encyclopedia of New Zealand*. www.teara.govt.nz/en/ pacific-islands -and-new-zealand/page-6

Geraghty, Paul. 1997. The ethnic basis of society in Fiji. In Brij V. Lal and Tomasi R. Vakatora, eds., *Fiji Constitution Review Commission Research Papers, Vol. 1: Fiji in Transition*. Suva: USP, 1–23.

Gordon, Elizabeth, Lyle Campbell, Jennifer Hay, Margaret Maclagan, Andrea Sudbury and Peter Trudgill. 2004. *New Zealand English: Its Origins and Evolution*. Cambridge: Cambridge University Press.

Görlach, Manfred. 1990. The development of Standard Englishes. In Manfred Görlach, ed. *Studies in the History of the English Language*. Heidelberg: Carl Winter, 9–64. (Revised paper based on a German version from 1988.)

Gylfadottir, Duna. 2015. Shtreets of Philadelphia: An Acoustic Study of /str/-retraction in a Naturalistic Speech Corpus. *University of Pennsylvania Working Papers in Linguistics* 21(2), 89–97. http://repository.upenn.edu/pwpl/vol21/iss2/11

Haugen, Einar. 1972. *The Ecology of Language: Essays*. Stanford: Stanford University Press.

Hay, Jennifer, Margaret Maclagan and Elizabeth Gordon. 2008. *New Zealand English*. Edinburgh: Edinburgh University Press.

Hendery, Rachel. 2015. Palmerston Island English. In Jeffrey P. Williams, Edgar W. Schneider, Peter Trudgill and Daniel Schreier, eds. *Further Studies in the Lesser-Known Varieties of English*. Cambridge: Cambridge University Press, 267–287.

Hickey, Raymond, ed. 2012. *Areal Features of the Anglophone World*. Berlin: Mouton de Gruyter.

Huffer, Elise, ed. 2008. *Land and Women: The Matrilineal Factor. The Cases of the Republic of the Marshall Islands, Solomon Islands and Vanuatu.* Fiji: Pacific Islands Forum Secretariat.

Hundt, Marianne. 2013. The diversification of English: Old, new and emerging epicentres. In Daniel Schreier and Marianne Hundt, eds. *English as a Contact Language.* Cambridge: Cambridge University Press, 182–203.

Hundt, Marianne and Katrin Vogel. 2011. Overuse of the progressive in ELS and learner Englishes – fact or fiction? In Joybrato Mukherjee and Marianne Hundt, eds. *Exploring Second-Language Varieties of English and Learner Englishes. Bridging a Paradigm Gap.* Amsterdam: John Benjamins, 145–165.

Kachru, Braj B. 1985. Institutionalized second-language varieties. In Sidney Greenbaum, ed. *The English Language Today.* Oxford: Pergamon Press, 211–226.

Kouwenberg, Silvia. 2003. Introduction. In Silvia Kowenberg, ed. *Twice as Meaningful: Reduplication in Pidgins, Creoles and Other Contact Languages.* London: Battlebridge, 1–6.

Leitner, Gerhard. 1992. English as a pluricentric language. In Michael Clyne, ed. *Pluricentric Languages: Differing Norms in Different Nations.* Berlin: de Gruyter, 179–237.

Leitner, Gerhard. 2004. *Australia's Many Voices: Australian English – the National Language.* Berlin: Mouton de Gruyter.

Leonhardt, Tobias. 2016. Kiribati and English: Bridging linguistic and cultural obstacles with alveolar plosives. Presentation given at the Sociolinguistic Symposium 21 at the University of Murcia, June 16.

Lim, Lisa. 2009. Not just an "Outer Circle", "Asian" English: Singapore English and the significance of ecology. In Thomas Hoffmann and Lucia Siebers, eds. *World Englishes: Problems, Properties and Prospects.* Amsterdam: John Benjamins, 183–206.

Loakes, Debbie, Josh J. Clothier, John Hajek and Janet Fletcher. 2014. An investigation of the /el/-/ael/ merger in Australian English: A pilot study on production and perception in south-west Victoria. *Australian Journal of Linguistics* 34(4): 436–452.

Lynch, John. 1998. *Pacific Languages: An Introduction.* Honolulu: University of Hawai'i Press.

Lynch, John, Malcom Ross and Terry Crowley. 2002. *The Oceanic Languages.* Richmond: Curzon.

Lynch, Sara. 2016. Cases of epenthesis and deletion in the Pacific: The intriguing realization of /h/ in Kosraen English. Presentation given at the Sociolinguistic Symposium 21 at the University of Murcia, June 16.

Maclagan, Margaret. 2010. The English(es) of New Zealand. In Andy Kirkpatrick, ed. *The Routledge Handbook of World Englishes.* London: Routledge, 152–164.

Mair, Christian. 2003. Kreolismen und verbales Identitätsmanagement im geschriebenen jamaikanischen Englisch. In Elisabeth Vogel, Antonia Napp and Wolfram Lutterer, eds. *Zwischen Ausgrenzung und Hybridisierung – Zur Konstruktion von Identitäten aus Kulturwissenschaftlicher Perspektive*. Würzburg: Ergon Verlag, 79–96.

Malcolm, Ian G. 2008. Australian creoles and Aboriginal English: phonetics and phonology. In Kate Burridge and Bernd Kortmann, eds. *Varieties of English: The Pacific and Australasia*. Berlin: Mouton de Gruyter, 124–141.

Marmion, Doug, Obata, Kazuko and Troy, Jakelin. 2014. *Community, identity, wellbeing: The report of the Second National Indigenous Languages Survey*. Australian Institute of Aboriginal and Torres Strait Islander Studies (AIATSIS). Canberra: Australia.

McArthur, Tom. 1987. The English languages? *English Today* 3(3): 9–13.

Meakins, Felicity and Carmel O'Shannessy. 2012. Typological constraints on verb integration in two Australian mixed languages. *Journal of Language Contact* 5: 216–246.

Meleisea, Malama, Penelope Schoeffel Meleisea, Isalei Va'ai and I'iga Suafole. 1987. New Zealand Samoa 1914–1944. In Malama Meleisea and Penelope Schoeffel Meleisea, eds. *Lagaga: A Short History of Western Samoa*. Suva: Oceania Printers, 125–144.

Moag, Rodney F. 1992. The life cycle of non-native Englishes: A case study. In Braj B. Kachru, ed. *The Other Tongue: English across Cultures*. Urbana: University of Illinois Press, 233–252.

Mufwene, Salikoko S. 2001. *The Ecology of Language*. Cambridge: Cambridge University Press.

Mugler, France and Jan Tent. 2008. Fiji English: Morphology and syntax. In Kate Burridge and Bernd Kortmann, eds. *Varieties of English: The Pacific and Australasia*. Berlin: Mouton de Gruyter, 546–567.

Mühlhäusler, Peter. 1996. *Linguistic Ecology: Language Change and Linguistic Imperialism in the Pacific Rim*. London: Routledge.

Mühlhäusler, Peter. 2008. Norfok Island-Pitcairn English (Pitkern Norfolk): Morphology and syntax. In Kate Burridge and Bernd Kortmann, eds. *Varieties of English: The Pacific and Australasia*. Berlin: Mouton de Gruyter, 568–582.

Peters, Pam. 2009. Australian English as a regional epicenter. In Thomas Hoffmann and Lucia Siebers, eds. *World Englishes: Problems, Properties and Prospects*. Amsterdam: John Benjamins, 107–124.

Peters, Pam and Kate Burridge. 2012. English in Australia and New Zealand. In Raymond Hickey, ed. *Areal Features of the Anglophone World*. Berlin: Mouton de Gruyter, 233–260.

Pitt, David and Cluny Macpherson. 1974. *Emerging Pluralism: The Samoan Community in New Zealand*. Auckland: Longman Paul.

Platt, John, Heidi Weber and Mian Lian Ho. 1984. *The New Englishes*. London: Routledge and Kegan Paul.

Ravulo, Jioji. 2015. *Pacific Communities in Australia*. Sydney: School of Social Sciences and Psychology, University of Western Sydney.

Schneider, Edgar W. 2004. Global synopsis: Phonetic and phonological variation in English worldwide. Edgar W. Schneider, Kate Burridge, Bernd Kortmann, Raj Mesthrie and Clive Upton, eds. *A Handbook of Varieties of English, Vol. 1: Phonology*. Berlin: Mouton de Gruyter, 1111–1138.

Schneider, Edgar W. 2007. *Postcolonial English: Varieties around the World*. Cambridge: Cambridge University Press.

Schneider, Gerold and Marianne Hundt. 2012. "Off with their heads": Profiling TAM in ICE corpora. In Marianne Hundt and Ulrike Gut, eds. *Mapping Unity and Diversity World-Wide: Corpus-based Studies of New Englishes*. Amsterdam: John Benjamins, 1–34.

Schütz, Albert J. 1972. *The Languages of Fiji*. Oxford: Clarendon Press.

Siegel, Jeff. 1996. The English language in the Asia Pacific region. In Stephen A. Wurm, Peter Mühlhäusler and Darrell T. Tryon, eds. *Atlas of Languages of Intercultural Communication in the Pacific, Asia, and the Americas*, Vol. 2.1. Berlin: Mouton de Gruyter, 241–250.

Siegel, Jeff. 2013. Regional profile: Australia Pacific Region. In Bernd Kortmann and Kerstin Lunkenheimer, eds. *Mouton World Atlas of Variation in English*. Berlin: Mouton de Gruyter, 765–782.

Siemund, Peter. 2008. Language contact: Constraints and common paths of contact-induced language change. In Peter Siemund and Noemi Kintana, eds. *Language Contact and Contact Languages*. Amsterdam: John Benjamins, 3–11.

Strevens, Peter. 1980. *Teaching English as an International Language*. Oxford: Pergamon Press.

Tent, Jan. 2000. The dynamics of Fiji English: A study of its use, users and features. Unpublished doctoral dissertation, University of Otago.

Tent, Jan and France Mugler. 2008. Fiji English: Phonology. In Kate Burridge and Bernd Kortmann, eds. *Varieties of English: The Pacific and Australasia*. Berlin: Mouton de Gruyter, 234–266.

Velupillai, Viveka. 2015. *Pidgins, Creoles and Mixed Languages: An Introduction*. Amsterdam: John Benjamins.

Winford, Donald. 2003. *Introduction to Contact Linguistics*. Oxford: Blackwell Publishing.

Zipp, Lena. 2014. *Educated Fiji English: Lexico-grammar and Variety Status*. Amsterdam: John Benjamins.

Part III

Linguistics and World Englishes

14

The Global Growth of English at the Grassroots

Christiane Meierkord

14.1 Introduction

The last decades have witnessed an enormous increase of publications discussing the spread of English worldwide and the various Englishes that have developed as well as the processes that today seem to characterize interactions conducted in English. Varieties of English around the world have received an enormous amount of attention, particularly following Kachru's pioneering work on Indian English (see Kachru 1965, 1976, 1983). Their sociolinguistics and their linguistic features have been described extensively, and today corpora such as the International Corpus of English (ICE) allow for their linguistic comparison.

However, most corpora and descriptions of innovations and deviations as characteristics of individual varieties are based on what have been called "educated speakers." ICE "is investigating 'educated' or 'standard' English" (Greenbaum 1996: 6) through spoken and written language of "adults (18 or over) who have received formal education through the medium of English to the completion of secondary school" (ibid.) and, for example, politicians, broadcasters, or writers who do not meet these education criteria but have a status that renders them "educated" speakers.[1]

The "educated speaker" was established as a notion by Braj Kachru to put forward his argument that native and non-native speakers of English have equal communicative competence in English. With reference to India, Kachru (1976: 7) equated "educated" with standard Indian English, explaining that "[t]he standard variety of Indian English is used by those bilinguals who rank around the central point on the cline of bilingualism" (1976: 10). He refers to Quirk (1972: 49), who, as early as then, observed

---

[1] Given the fact that one of the ultimate goals of ICE is to serve as a model for teaching English in Outer Circle countries, unstable forms of English, i.e. interlanguage English, would fail to serve the purpose.

that "[i]n the Indian and African countries, we find an even spectrum of kinds of English, which extends from those most like Pidgin to those most like standard English, with imperceptible gradations the whole way along." The following quote by Strevens (1977: 140–141) is illustrative of these uses and of the perceived cline in proficiency:

> The Indian (or Pakistani) doctor who communicates easily in English with professional colleagues at an international medical conference is using a type of "Indian English" similar to those mentioned above [i.e. "educated" second-language varieties; CM] in which Standard English dialect is spoken with a regional accent. The Indian clerk who uses English constantly in his daily life for communication with other Indians, by correspondence or telephone, may employ an "Indian English" in which the dialect is not Standard English and the accent is regional or local. The lorry-driver who uses English occasionally, as a lingua franca, may be using an "Indian English" which is for all practical purposes a pidgin.

Often, however, the label "educated" has proven difficult. For example, Schmied (1996: 187) points out that "in a sociolinguistic context where English is learnt only as a second (or third, etc.) language it is difficult to determine where an interlanguage ends and educated English starts." Nevertheless, "non-educated" forms of English have typically been excluded from models of World Englishes, mainly based on the argument that they lack systematicity. This is also frequently the case for pidginized varieties,[2] which feature in, for example, Mesthrie and Bhatt's (2008) "English Language Complex,"[3] but which they exclude from their further account of World Englishes on grounds that they "are studied as a field in their own right" (2008: 19). In fact, as Schneider (2011: 29) explains, "[e]arly creolist theory vigorously held that creoles are new languages" (see the discussion in Aceto, Chapter 9, this volume). As Mufwene (1997: 182) has pointed out, it has frequently seemed that pidgins and creoles, that is, varieties "spoken primarily by populations that have not fully descended from Europeans" are considered "illegitimate offspring of English." Today, in fact, a growing number of English linguists follow Mufwene (1997, 2001) in arguing that English-based pidgins and creoles are varieties of English. Integrating the various "non-educated" forms of English that spread at the grassroots is timely, since, although precise figures do not exist, their speakers constitute a number that is just as high as, or maybe even higher than, that of elite speakers following the spread of English through work migration, tourism, forced migration/refugees, and, to some degree, the Internet.

This chapter aims to describe the use of English outside the elite domains such as corporate business, politics and administration, and higher education. It looks at how English spread at the grassroots of societies in countries

---

[2] Crucially, such varieties are also typically disregarded in most research conducted in the framework of English as a Lingua Franca, with Guido (2008, 2014, 2016) being a noticeable exception.

[3] This is actually based on McArthur (2003).

traditionally located in the Outer and Expanding Circle, and aims to assess the size of such spread. The chapter then describes the forms that English assumes in such contexts, both in speech and in writing. Drawing on examples from informal traders in Uganda, domestic workers in Hong Kong, refugees in Europe, and informal eateries in Uganda and the Maldives, it discusses how these can be accounted for in, or incorporated into, models of English.

14.2   The Grassroots: An Attempt at a Definition

Grassroots is a term that most of us are familiar with from phrases such as *grassroots movement* or *grassroots democracy*, referring to local people's political activities. The word *grassroots* itself has been defined by Webster (Merriam-Webster 2016) as "the basic level of society or of an organization especially as viewed in relation to higher or more centralized positions of power," "the ordinary people in a society or organization," and "the people who do not have a lot of money and power."[4]

In linguistics, the term gained currency at the turn of the millennium, when Khubchandani and Hosali (1999: 254) talked of "grassroots English among those who spontaneously acquire certain rudimentary characteristics of the language in plurilingual settings (and not through formal education)" and "are in a position to handle rudimentary tasks in English" (p. 255), citing Hinglish and Tamlish as two examples.

Definitions have also been offered from within the field of sociolinguistics. Blommaert (2008) discusses grassroots literacy and uses the term for "a wide variety of 'non-elite' forms of writing" (2008: 7), thus clearly demarcating the boundaries of grassroots as ending where "elites" begin. Similarly, Meierkord (2012) uses the label to refer to contexts outside of international organizations, education and academia, and the business world.[5] Somewhat more narrowly, Schneider (2016a: 3) defines grassroots Englishes as typically having been learned "in direct interactions rather than through formal education" by individuals of poor backgrounds and with little or no access to formal education.

For the remainder of this chapter, I will conceive of the grassroots as comprising all societal groups that are non-elite, following Blommaert (2008). Their individual members may have learned English in school and/or acquired it informally.

---

[4] According to the *Oxford English Dictionary Online* (OED 2016), the above uses are figurative extensions of the original eighteenth-century literal meaning "the root of a plant of grass," which has been documented to denote "the fundamental level; the source or origin" from the early twentieth century onward, frequently with reference to politics.

[5] There is some disagreement about the social class background and the acquisitional context of English: While Erling, Hamid, and Seargeant (2013) do not explicitly define what they call "grassroots attitudes," implicitly grassroots seems to refer to local communities (pp. 89, 92) and to include "participants from different socio-economic backgrounds and those living in both urban and rural areas" (p. 92). The grassroots level is conceived as the bottom-up level, as opposed to the "top-down, policy level" (p. 106).

14.3 The Territorial Spread of English at the Grassroots

The spread of English at the grassroots of many societies worldwide seems to be the result of various factors: the spread of English through colonialism starting in the sixteenth century, leading to the imposition of English as a language of administration in the colonies, protectorates and UN mandates; the rise of English as a foreign language taught in schools, together with the provision of free education in most countries of the world and amendments of school curricula, often following political developments; and the spread of English through increasing factual and virtual migration, for example through work migration, tourism, and the Internet.

The spread of English at the grassroots, that is, beyond the elite strata of society in the fields of business, administration, and education, is, of course not a new phenomenon. English spread throughout the various parts of societies ever since it was taken beyond its original habitat in the British Isles.

14.3.1 The Grassroots in the History of the Spread of English in the Outer Circle

During colonization, British and American settlers, missionaries, and administrative as well as military personnel spread English in various forms. English was used informally with servants and workers, while, in many cases, an elite of the indigenous population was also taught English formally, to eventually serve the colonial administration. Typically, the informal spread involved nonstandard varieties of English, which were spoken by the English-speaking settlers, while formal teaching followed the British or American standard. A prime example is India, where functionally restricted and linguistically simplified varieties developed through interaction between the British settlers and their local staff, for example Butler English or Boxwalla English (see Kachru 1983: 70; 1994: 511–513), which were spoken by head servants and door-to-door sellers respectively. At the same time, following Macaulay's Minute in 1835, the English Education Act of the same year provided the ground for a national language-in-education policy, that is, the use of English as a medium of instruction, which implied teaching of and in standard English to those who could afford an education.

14.3.1.1 Differences in Different Types of Colonies

The different types of exposure to English yield different outcomes. As Mesthrie and Bhatt (2008: 20) emphasize, "[w]hether speakers come up with a pidgin, EFL, ESL or ENL depends on factors such as the following: (a) the relative number of speakers of the different languages, including the TL; (b) the social relationships between them; (c) the duration of the contact; and (d) educational opportunities in the TL." These factors, in turn, depended on the type of colony that the British and Americans established. Mufwene (2001) distinguishes between trade colonies, exploitation colonies, and settlement colonies. While, in the latter case, the English/British settled in very large numbers, trade colonies typically were not permanent and involved sporadic contact between traders and the local population. In exploitation colonies, set up to exploit the natural resources of a colonized area, English was typically taught to a local elite, either by the colonial administrators or by missionaries (see Mufwene, Chapter 5, this volume). Crucially, the majority of the population were, if at all, taught in a local language (e.g. the British aimed at spreading Kiswahili as the local lingua franca in East Africa) and were denied access to English (cf. Brutt-Griffler 2002). Restricted, sporadic, and informal contacts typical of the sixteenth-century trade colonies or slavery scenarios along the West African coast typically resulted in pidginized varieties of English, while extensive formal instruction, for example in India, raised a group of speakers who spoke a variety very close to the exonormative standard. In all cases, however, the grassroots will also have been involved, albeit to varying degrees and numbers. Even though English was typically acquired by an elite in the exploitation colonies, "[m]ost likely this was not the only form of English – underneath the surface less educated soldiers, traders, and so on brought nonstandard forms of English as well, influenced lower-rank indigenous speakers through daily contact, and got influenced linguistically by them as well" (Schneider 2011: 46). Once stably established, the purposes for which the colonies were originally established "require a growing consumption of land and result in an expansion of the region under foreign dominance, and typically they entail an ever increasing range of contacts with members of the indigenous population" (Schneider 2007: 37). In the trade colonies, individual locals were taken to Europe and trained as interpreters and would "probably have used ESL" (Mesthrie and Bhatt 2008: 17–18) on their return. As a result, "there is a large gap between the middle-class varieties of New Englishes and their jargon, pidgin or basilectal counterparts" (Mesthrie and Bhatt 2008: 36).

Toward independence, typically the original settlers left the country in large numbers (Uganda being a case in point). As a result, contact to English first-language (L1) speakers and, thus, informal acquisition declined drastically.

14.3.1.2 Post-independence Grassroots in the Outer Circle

Following independence, attitudes toward English were at times negative, with it being regarded as the language of the previous colonizer. This was the case, for example, in Tanzania, from 1967 to the 1990s, while a swing toward a more positive attitude toward English can be observed following these decades (see Ochieng 2015).

In general, English now mainly spread through formal education to those who could afford it. Different from what is the case in many countries today, education was not typically free, even at primary school level in very many countries. At secondary and tertiary level, fees tend to be typical even today, and, in addition, there are differences between public and private schools as well as between urban and rural areas. Frequently, schools in rural areas teach little English and do not attract well-skilled teachers (cf. Michieka 2009 for Kenya; Ssentanda 2016 for Uganda). Also, for most individuals living in rural areas, English is not a prerequisite for their professions. However, ongoing urbanization in search for employment has increased the demand for English.

Wornyo (2015: 41) describes the use of English by individuals who leave the rural areas of Ghana to work "as artisans, casual workers in factories, labourers, taxi drivers and others engage in all sorts of petty trading" in the capital Accra. Here, they acquire English in informal settings to communicate with individuals who do not speak their L1. Wornyo investigated carpenters, masons, painters, electricians, steel benders, and laborers on an Accra construction site. As he explains (p. 54), code-switching frequently makes up for limited competence in English, while foremen often insist on giving instructions in English as the prestige language.

Similar observations have been made for South Africa, where work migration has a long history, for example in the mining industry. However, Deumert and Mabandla (2009) point out that, although a knowledge of English is mostly a prerequisite for jobs, English is not a guarantee factor: Positions in Cape Town's construction industry or as domestic workers in the area frequently require Afrikaans.

In several countries of the Outer Circle, English is now also used for intranational interactions with individuals who have recently come to reside in the country. A case in point is Chinese workers in Africa, who arrive with construction companies but also to set up private trades. Akhidenor (2013) explains that, while code-switching frequently, Chinese traders interact in English with their Botswana customers, and Deumert and Mabandla (2013) make similar observations for rural South Africa.

In South Africa, English is also used for interactions across blacks, who speak one of the Bantu languages as L1, and coloreds, who traditionally spoke Afrikaans. Interestingly, it seems that, at the grassroots, colored speakers seem to accommodate to Black South African English (Meierkord 2012: 116–128), while upper-middle-class speakers orient toward White South African English (Mesthrie 2010).

In Uganda, particularly in the north, peasants and informal traders offering produce at local markets, butchers, and hairdressers report to frequently communicate in English, which functions as the lingua franca outside of the central region, where Luganda is used in this function (cf. Namyalo et al. 2016).

Uses of Englishes at the grassroots also occur when locals or immigrants engage in small businesses. In Cebu, as Regala-Flores (2009) explains, these include local jeepney drivers, nannies, janitors, and market vendors. These "marginalized voices," as she labels them, use English to negotiate with their business partners from various parts of the world. Similarly, in Hong Kong, traders from the Indian subcontinent and various African countries use English to conduct their businesses in downtown Kowloon, particularly in Chungking Mansions, a "low-rise (seventeen-story) building housing a labyrinth of market stalls and small shops trading in electrical goods, mobile telephones, luggage, African artifacts, clothing and snacks" (Knowles and Harper 2009: 117).

In the Philippines (and more recently also in Indonesia), women attempting to seek employment as domestic workers in Hong Kong learn English, since interaction with the Cantonese-speaking employers takes place in English. Kwan and Dumworth (2016) found that, although the different English pronunciation and language structures were held to be the most frequent challenges for successful interaction, they were not deemed to be the most important challenges. Rather, etiquette, understanding the implied meaning, and notions of politeness were considered more important. However, Hong Kong's population at large has limited proficiency in English: In areas outside of Central and Kowloon, interactions in English are uncommon, and most taxi drivers require Chinese (written) instructions.

14.3.2 The Spread of English in the Expanding Circle Countries

While there is a considerable body of research describing uses of English in the education sector, business, and international organizations, little is known about the grassroots of the Expanding Circle. This is, at least partly, due to the fact that several factors limited the spread of English to the grassroots in the past.

First, in the countries of the Expanding Circle, English was typically not acquired informally through interactions with native speakers but learned in school, mainly for interactions with English speakers from the Inner Circle. As such, interactions were not commonly envisaged to occur outside the elite; teaching of English to the grassroots was not common until the recent past. In Germany, for example, English was typically learned in private schools during the eighteenth century. Only in the nineteenth century did the subject make inroads into the curricula of public schools. Initially, it was included into the curriculum for *Realschule* (secondary modern school/junior high school; schools frequented by the offspring of the bourgeoisie) for reasons of profession, travel, and potential emigration to America, while most *Gymnasiums* (grammar schools) taught French or a classical language, that is, Greek or Latin (Klippel 1994). *Volksschulen* (elementary schools), attended by the masses, were not obliged to teach a foreign language, until it became a compulsory subject in the newly founded *Hauptschulen* (secondary modern schools) in 1964. Up until then, the majority of the population did not learn English, and the limited use of English at the grassroots has been a result of this.

Second, in many countries, the first foreign language to be taught was not English until recently. Often, it was the language of a neighboring country, with which there existed trade relations, or another language of wider communication. For example, in Bosnia and Herzegovina, "[p]reviously favoured foreign or additional languages include Turkish, Arabic, German, French and Russian" (Buckingham 2016a: 1). However, following the disintegration of what used to be Yugoslavia, the country's new political orientation and its becoming a candidate for membership in the European Union involved a switch to teaching English as the first foreign language in order to comply with the regulations of the European Union.

Finally, political developments after World War II led many countries to ban English teaching from their schools, as was the case in, for example, Cambodia during the Pol Pot regime, the areas occupied by Japan (Korea, Malaya, and North Borneo) during the first half of the twentieth century, Libya during the conflict between Qaddafi and the UK and USA, Romania during the Ceausescu regime, and Spain during the reign of Franco. Anti-Western and anti-English attitudes still pertain today, in individual countries, such as the Islamic Republic of Iran, which, since its formation in 1979, "has consciously distanced itself from the West and the English language" (Baumgardner and Brown 2012: 294). Similarly, as Figureido (2015: 458) states, Brazil has debated over the past fifteen years "whether English should be prohibited (or at least restricted) in public discourses," while the number of private English schools has been growing.

However, English has recently come to be taught in the majority of those countries that previously, for political or economic reasons, did not teach the language. As a result, English is today being used in the Maghreb states and sub-Saharan Africa, Central and South America, Central and East Asia and the Far East, the Gulf region, and in the postcommunist countries. Unfortunately though, publications are still scarce for many regions, for example Southern and Eastern Europe, the Middle East, North Africa, large parts of Central and South America, and countries previously under Soviet control or influence; and accounts of uses at the grassroots or research into this are almost nonexistent.

A general spread of English as a link language has been reported for the Maghreb states (particularly Tunisia, Algeria, and Morocco; see Battenburg 1997). While English has been part of the linguistic ecologies of many sub-Saharan African countries from the sixteenth century onward (see Section 14.3.1), not much research has been conducted on the spread of English into those nations that were not colonized by the British, for example Benin, the Ivory Coast, Mozambique, Angola, or Gabon. A case in point is Rwanda, where English is spoken by a well-educated middle class, who fled to Uganda during and following the 1994 genocide and now return to the country.

In Central and South America, where, with the exception of Brazil, Spanish has been used in most parts, English seems to be largely a language used on signage, in advertising, and in the media. In Brazil, Rajagopalan (2003: 92) explains that English "is all over the place – on neon signs, shop windows, television commercials, popular magazines and newspapers." However, as Vélez-Rendón (2003: 189) states for Colombia, "[t]he role of English as a link language in Colombia is limited" (2003: 192). A concise picture of the uses and users of English at the grassroots in this huge area does not exist to date.

English has also spread fast in Asia and the Far East. While its use in diverse genres, ranging from advertising, to Internet and email, the media, and popular and youth culture, has been discussed frequently for China (e.g. Bolton and Botha 2015), Korea, and Japan (e.g. D'Angelo 2005; or the papers collected in Seargeant 2011), the grassroots do not explicitly figure in these accounts. In Cambodia, there is a "pervasive presence of English, be it in the signage of streetscapes, in various media or as the default language of choice in dealings between Cambodians and visiting non-Cambodians" (Moore and Bounchan 2010: 114). In the upper middle class, Cambodians also use English to chat with their friends and to exchange SMSs or sing karaoke, and of course at work (Moore and Bounchan 2010: 119). Moreover, in urban areas, it is used at home, for watching television and listening to the radio, for using the Internet, and even for interactions with one's children. Again, however, we do not know about the grassroots. Also, nations such as Bhutan, Burma, North Korea, and Laos have not been covered by research at all.

In Europe, English is strongly promoted by the European Council, and interactions between Europeans, on business or holiday alike, are frequently conducted in English as a lingua franca rather than in the language(s) of the people involved. It is, however, mainly in the Scandinavian countries and the Netherlands that English has also made inroads into the private domains of citizens (see e.g. Edwards 2016). As regards Europe's East, exact descriptions are not available for countries such as Belarus, Kosovo, Latvia, Lithuania, Montenegro, Romania, Serbia, Slovakia, Slovenia, and Ukraine, while a full volume has been dedicated to English in Bosnia and Herzegovina (Buckingham 2016b). However, uses at the grassroots appear to be limited: Hasanova (2007: 281) reports that "English is vital especially for those involved in business, academia and commerce" in Uzbekistan. At the same time, the situation in Russia seems to be changing fast. While Proshina (2006: 437) pointed out that "the predominant role of English is primarily that in education," the papers collected in Proshina and Eddy (2016) document its growing use in the mass media, popular culture, and tourism.

While uses at the grassroots have not been documented frequently, it is difficult to tell whether this reflects the fact that uses of English are scarce and restricted outside the elite or whether research has failed to account for these. At the same time, there are detailed reports for individual areas, in which English has clearly been observed at the grassroots, in Central America, in Asia, Europe, and the Gulf region.

Gonçalves (2016) describes the use of English by domestic migrants working in a cleaning company in New Jersey, among Portuguese- and Spanish-speaking domestic workers from Europe and the Americas, their driver, their English-speaking company owner, and their anglophone clients. While their private domains are accommodated to Portuguese- and Spanish-speaking immigrants, English is used at the workplace.

Snodin (2014: 101) states that, following the presence of American soldiers during the Vietnam war, "[i]n recent years, English has been used by people of all levels of Thai society – business people, academics, government leaders, waiters, tour guides, hotel officers, taxi drivers and bar girls – to fulfil their own objectives, whether they were to obtain technical knowledge, enhance career opportunities, develop the tourism industry of simply to improve their family's economic wellbeing."

In Europe, typically, interactions conducted in English involve either immigrants or tourists from various social and regional backgrounds. For many of the former, English is an alternative to the local language when they have acquired English before or during their migration. Often, however, immigrants' use of English is restricted to their early years in the new country of residence, as the results of Bolton and Meierkord (2013) reveal. In Sweden, many immigrants are unable to speak or learn Swedish before their status has been confirmed but shift to Swedish fast, especially in the second generation. English is also chosen by locals who wish or need to interact with individuals who do not speak Swedish, for example volunteers in church communities. Tourism had been identified by Fishman (1977) as a context for the use of English among an "international elite." However, recent developments, particularly the increase of low-budget travel options and accommodation sharing, have resulted in changes in many parts of the world, albeit not in all. Bruyèl-Olmedo and Juan-Garau (2009) found that, in S'Arenal on Mallorca, a location that tends to attract budget tourists, although Germans make up the majority of tourists in this area, there is a huge variety of nineteen other mother tongues among 79 percent of the investigated tourists,[6] who predominantly stated to have expected to find English in hotels, restaurants, shops, leisure provisions, transportation, and also in local government notices. Tourism scenarios have also been investigated by Schneider (2016a). His examples from Outer and Expanding Circle countries document that linguistically apt[7] individuals acquire English largely through informal interaction to

---

[6] In decreasing frequency, their informants spoke English, Dutch, French, Polish, Russian, Swedish, Norwegian, Danish, Turkish, Icelandic, Italian, Japanese, Romanian, Portuguese, Arabic, Armenian, Gaelic, Chinese, and Soninke.

[7] Aptitude refers to those cognitive abilities predicted to facilitate foreign language learning: phonetic coding ability, grammatical sensitivity, rote learning ability, and inductive language learning ability (cf. Carroll 1981).

find employment in one of the better paid positions, for example as drivers or tour guides.

It may be the regions of the Persian Gulf, particularly the United Arab Emirates, where English is increasingly used as a lingua franca at the grassroots rather than the traditionally used Arabic. This is in large parts due to the large amount of foreign workers, such as the South East Asians and Filipinos, who work in the retail business, the construction industry, and in the medical services (Randall and Samimi 2010). In Kuwait, most people speak some English (cf. Dashti 2015: 28). Since the language is a compulsory school subject from primary school onward, young Kuwaitis confidently use the language extensively, not only in business, science, and technology but also in banks, hospitals, restaurants, cafés, shops, and at home, frequently also mixing English and Kuwaiti Arabic. Particularly in fast-food restaurants, "English is mainly used, even if the salesperson comes from an Arabic-speaking country" (p. 32). In the Gulf state of Oman, as Buckingham (2015: 411) finds,

> [t]he generation of wealth through the petroleum industry, increasingly consumer-oriented societies and expansive infrastructure projects have brought greater numbers of expatriate workers to the region than at any other time in history. Street-level commercial establishments provide a rich context for the study of language contact, as oral interactions between ethnically-diverse customers and staff frequently employ English and Arabic-based lingua francas. This is particularly true of Oman, where the proportion of expatriate workers has traditionally been lower than in states such as Qatar or the United Arab Emirates (UAE).

Large numbers of migrant workers originate from Southeast Asia, particularly from the Philippines, and English is used in the health sector, services industries, and also by small-scale street vendors and manual workers, leading to the use of Philippine English but also Indian English in spoken interactions as well as in informal signage. Mahboob and Elyas (2014) explain that English is considered similarly important in the Kingdom of Saudi Arabia, since the country relies on foreign companies to contribute to its economy and on the many expatriates working in the hospitals, restaurants, and shops.

In some cases, historical grassroots uses have also been attested: González Cruz (2012: 22) reports that the Canary Islands received sizable numbers of British settlers from after 1880, particularly in Las Palmas de Gran Canaria, which "demanded a variety of English-style services, such as hotels, restaurants, bars, bazaars, milliners etc." In this case, as a result of regular and intensive culture and language contact, a pidgin, *Pichingly*, in which English and Spanish mixed, developed and was spoken in the islands' ports, by dockers, traders, harbor peddlers, and guides. Similarly, Dashti (2015: 28) explains that the older Kuwaiti generations "who worked in the [oil, CM] fields side-by-side with English people found themselves obliged to learn some English, though they learnt it informally through communicating with them."

While uses of English at the grassroots per se are, thus, a historical as well as a current phenomenon, what is different today, however, is the amount of individuals using English at the grassroots.

14.3.3   The Spread of English at the Grassroots in Figures

Figures reflecting the realities of English uses at the grassroots are hard to come by and often not up to date, reducing individual figures to mere "guesstimates." The Ethnologue (Eberhard et al. 2019) reports that some form of English is spoken in 126 countries. Wikipedia contributors (2016) have compiled a list of English-language speakers per country, which, however, needs to be treated with great caution. While individual figures were taken from fairly recent Eurobarometer reports, others rely on Crystal (2003), due to a lack of more recent studies. As Crystal (2003: 55) himself points out, his own figures are only seldom based on sociolinguistic studies but rely on statistical data, censuses, or the Ethnologue estimates. Despite these caveats, a clear picture seems to emerge from the figures: English is spoken by large parts of the population in North and Central Europe, in individual West and Southern African countries, on Cuba and most Caribbean Islands, in the Philippines, and in Papua New Guinea. The majority of the Outer Circle Asian and African countries, as well as Central and Southern America do not have large shares of English speakers – that is, below 20 percent, despite the fact that English is a, if not *the*, official language of the country. However, the figures refer to the population as a whole, and the situation may be crucially different if younger citizens only were investigated, especially since the provision of free education or the introduction of English as a school subject has been a somewhat recent development in many nations.

Nevertheless, English is not a language spoken by vast majorities in postcolonial nations and as a result uses at the grassroots are restricted, with the notable exception of pidginized varieties. Mufwene (2010: 57) finds that "in most countries of the Outer Circle, the proportion of actual speakers of English remains very small (at best between 20% and 30% of the total population)." Similarly, Bamgbose (2006: 646) is skeptical about more optimistic figures for users of standard(izing) Englishes and argues that

> in Nigeria, as in all other former British colonies, English remains a minority, but powerful, language used by an elite. Given the fact that literacy in English is acquired through formal education, and that a sizable percentage of children have no access to formal education, it is not surprising that the English-using population is not a large one.

Although proficiency in English need not necessarily involve literacy in it, the link to education is crucial. Universal free primary education had been identified as one of the Millennium Goals of the United Nations in 2000; but, as the United Nations (2015) need to admit,

> [f]ifty-two percent of countries achieved this goal; ten percent are close and the remaining thirty-eight percent are far or very far from achieving it. This leaves almost 100 million children not completing primary education in 2015. A lack of focus on the marginalized has left the poorest five times less likely to complete a full cycle of primary education than the richest.

Besides the enormous social differences, in urban areas, on average, schools are better equipped, and rural areas tend to lose out. Of course, primary education does not always involve English, and, even if it does, the proficiency levels attained vary considerably.

The EF English Proficiency Index aims to assess the average English proficiency of individual countries' populations. EF Education First, a private, globally operating, company carries out annual English tests online. According to their findings (EF Education First 2018), very high proficiency levels are currently found mostly in Europe, particularly Northern Europe but also Slovenia, and in Singapore and South Africa. This is only partially reflected in the figures established by the European Commission (2012), where respondents were asked whether they could hold a conversation in English. In the Netherlands, 90 percent stated to be able to do so, in Denmark and Sweden 86 percent, in Austria 73 percent, in Germany 56 percent, and in Poland a mere 33 percent. Very low proficiency levels, on the other end of the scale, are found, typically, in most Arabic states and Central and Southern Americas (with the exception of Argentina, where the level is high).[8]

As we know, however, the use of nonstandard English is not an obstacle in interactions across Englishes. As Section 14.4 will document, interactions at the grassroots are highly diverse and successful despite particularities at all levels of language structure.

14.4 Input and Output Englishes at the Grassroots

14.4.1 The Spread of Nonstandard Englishes

Just as soldiers, traders, and so on spread nonstandard Englishes to the colonies in the past, a vast variety of Englishes travel around the globe today, either factually with their users or virtually via the Internet. As Mair (2013) argues, individual nonstandard varieties today enjoy sufficient prestige to be acquired outside of their original habitats. He holds that African American Vernacular Creole, Jamaican Creole, and popular London make

---

[8] Since participants in the index are self-selected voluntary participants, the index is not representative, and the figures need to be interpreted carefully. Also, the tests underlying the calculated proficiency levels assess grammar, vocabulary, reading and listening, i.e. the traditional four skills. Low levels calculated for a particular country thus do not imply that individuals are not successful in interacting in English but that their English does not conform to the standards.

a transnational impact similar to that of British English or Australian English, through transnational diasporic uses and mediated or commodified forms in hip-hop. In fact, for the Croatian context, Drljača Margić and Širola (2014) mention that students participating in a study on attitudes toward varieties of English claim to find Jamaican and Irish English fun to learn, but there are no accounts of speakers factually using these varieties.

At times, immigrants introduce creolized Englishes to their new home countries. Although they typically have a high command in these vernacular varieties of English, the grammar of these Englishes may not be easily comprehensible to individuals who have not been exposed to it. This is the case, for example, with immigration officers in Italy, who frequently interact with refugees from the West African coast who speak one of the creoles or pidgins of the area (cf. Guido 2008).

At the output side, speakers at the grassroots show an enormous variability of restructuring, as Examples (1) and (2)[9] reveal. Example (1) is an interaction between a craftswoman (engaged in basket weaving) and the author, recorded during a visit to a shop in downtown Kampala, which sells craftwork produced by members of disadvantaged communities. The conversation between two Indonesian domestic workers, the author and one of her research assistants, documented in Example (2), was recorded at Kowloon Park in Hong Kong, one of the places where Filipina and Indonesian domestic workers typically spend their Sundays. While the Ugandan lady, Carol, in Example (1) constructs utterances that are close to the standard, the two Indonesian domestic workers in Hong Kong (in Example (2)) construct more basic sentences and seem to use a more simplified grammar.

Example (1)

ANJA: Is this a local radio station?
CAROL: It is a what?
ANJA: Eh Local radio station? Ugandan radio?
CAROL: Yuh it is a Uganda radio.
ANJA: It sounds very (.) British @.
CAROL: Yuh yuh, because there you see it is just (.) it talks in English.
ANJA: Mhm
CAROL: American English, so_
ANJA: So what is more popular here, American English or British English?
CAROL: It is eh it is the: it is eh local language.
ANJA: Mhm
CAROL: Yeah. Because sometimes (.) that type of English (.) You see, there are some people who didn't go to school. So, they are used to the

[9] In addition to standard orthography, the following symbols are used in the examples to represent spoken language: […] indicates that passages from the interview have been left out, italics are used to highlight non-English words, – means that an utterance was cut off or restarted, (.) indicates a brief pause, @ represents laughter, a colon signifies lengthening, and capitals increased volume. To preserve interviewees' anonymity, all names used here are nicknames.

local one. So that one that one, just we put on. For us, we are international, so, sometimes we put that that yeah the radio. But it is not a government radio.

ANJA: Private

CAROL: It is a private, not a government.

While Carol's utterances include several features of Ugandan English, such as the use of *radio* instead of *radio station*, her utterances largely comply with the grammatical rules of standard Englishes. By contrast, the productions of the two Indonesian ladies, Putri and Intan, contain numerous features, for example lack of a copula or a particular use of the definite article, which seem to be results of simplification and transfer from their first language.

Example (2)

JOYCE: So eh when you speak to the children, what language do you use?

PUTRI: Ehm, we using English language and Cantonese language.

JOYCE: You use Cantonese language?

PUTRI: Yes, also the- (.) Sometime, grandma also teach me, because every day, we uh having a chat with them. Ehm some time we using the Cantonese, Most of (.) use in everyday is English. But I LOVE to learn other language.

ANJA: So, but you don't use any Indonesian with them?

INTAN: No, because in the house I only one person working with them.

JOYCE: How many children does your master have?

INTAN: One children. It's the boy: three and a half years.

The two examples give a first impression of how heterogeneous the English productions of speakers at the grassroots are. While in these two cases speakers draw exclusively on English, in many other situations, particularly when interlocutors share more than one language, speakers exploit their full linguistic repertoire.

14.4.2 Translanguaging, Hybrid Englishes, and the "New Speaker"

At the grassroots, English does not so much spread as an alternative to one's other language(s) but often as an addition to one's linguistic repertoire, which one can draw on how ever one sees fit. Often, this takes place in the form of code-mixing or of what has recently been called translanguaging.

Following García and Wei (2013), translanguaging refers to "the use of language … of bilinguals not as two autonomous language systems as has been traditionally the case, but as one linguistic repertoire with features that have been societally constructed as belonging to two languages." As Canagarajah (2013) has pointed out, such practices are not new. However, they have been found to increasingly characterize language behavior in times of migration, resulting in what Vertovec (2007) has called superdiversity. Translanguaging has also been reported from those countries of the Outer Circle in which English is increasingly spreading at the grassroots, giving rise to new codes, which often draw on more than two languages. One such example is *kasi taal*, which draws on Sotho, Nguni, and English and has been observed by Makalela (2015) as spoken in the townships in and around Johannesburg.[10] Translanguaging also occurs among individuals who bring these practices to diasporic contexts, for example West African immigrants in Germany. First-generation English-speaking West Africans in the Ruhr Area seem to continue to use language(s) in the way they would do in their home countries. Example (3), which is an exchange recorded during a drive to a festival, is illustrative of this.

> Example (3)
> JOYCE: A beg lower the radio small ja Rockie a di wan hear you,
>   ("I beg turn down the radio, yes, Rockie, I want to hear you,")
>   a di struggle, lower am small a beg.
>   ("I am struggling to do so, turn it down I beg.")
> ROCKIE: Na mi a wan lower am, a know place we dem di lower am?
>   ("Oh, I want to turn it down, do I know the place where they turn it down?")
> JOYCE: Tantie please can you lower it just a little bit?
> ROCKIE: I said I went to that wake keeping eh?
> AIMÉE: Oga madame! You know that am driving?
>   ("Boss madame!")
> *Note*: Orthography in this example follows Kouega (2008).

In this example, the first exchange between Joyce and Rockie, who both originate from the anglophone part of Cameroon, is largely in Cameroon Pidgin English. However, Joyce integrates a German discourse marker, *ja*, into her request to Rockie. When she realizes that Joyce does not know how to decrease the volume of the radio, she addresses Aimée. Aimée is francophone and does not command Cameroon Pidgin English so that Joyce now employs Cameroon English. To address Aimée, however, she uses a word that is peculiar to the German diaspora community, *Tantie*. Although it is likely to be related to the French *tante*, it is the German *Tante* as well as the diminuitive *-i(e)* that have been combined into this novel construction. Aimée reproaches her using the phrase *oga madame!* (roughly translating into "You bossy thing!") meant to signify that she considers Joyce's request imperious, particularly as she herself is driving the car. The phrase combines the Nigerian Pidgin English *oga*, which typically implies a male referent, and the French *madame* to refer to Rockie as a "female boss."

---

[10] However, the informants included in Makalela's study are students at the University of the Witswatersrand, South Africa's leading university. The fact that they reside in townships is not sufficient to infer their socioeconomic status. During South Africa's Apartheid era, black South Africans had to reside in these segregated areas, regardless of their profession or socioeconomic status. While large parts of South Africa's growing black middle class have moved out of these areas, others have remained in their original communities.

As Meierkord, Fonkeu, and Zumhasch (2015) report, many of the multilingual individuals are highly aware of their practices. Example (4), which has been recorded during our fieldwork in the North Rhine-Westfalia's Ruhr area illustrates this very clearly. It captures the comments of a female Nigerian in her thirties, who is a shop attendant in an African food store. Italics in the example indicate German and Cameroon Pidgin English words.

Example (4)
And then they don't, I don't really know *Deutsch*, I'm just (.) I, I bite it. I just learn to say half, half *Deutsch*, I don't- @@@@ this *cot an nail Deutsch*. @@@ I *wollen lernen Deutsch* for my, my, little, this little girl
[…]
Yea, that's why I said I do *kot an nail*. You know how they call *kot an nail* this (.) they call it eh street *Deutsch* @@@ half half *Deutsch* that you pick here and there. Sometimes it doesn't really make meaning, but they can really understand.   (Leyla, Nigerian female)

As our informant here explains, speakers draw on Pidgin English, standard(ized) English, and German, which she describes with the expressions *I bite it*, and the Pidgin English *kot an nail*. The former is a calque, originating from the indigenous cultures and languages and derived via the Pidgin English *a jus bit am here an de* ("I just bite it here and there"), which indicates an act of "selecting things randomly." Similarly, *kot an nail* (Pidgin English for *cut and nail*) *German* is a label meant to indicate that she picks up and combines German words and phrases indiscriminately rather than acquiring the new language systematically. Evidently, the Nigerian lady finds that this practice suffices for her daily communicative needs.

In several areas, translanguaging or code-mixing has resulted in hybrid, or mixed Englishes, in which English blends with one or more of the local languages. Individual forms of these have been labeled as, for example, Singlish, Hinglish, or Taglish for codes used in Singapore, India, or the Philippines, respectively (Meierkord 2012: 71–72, 77–82; Schneider 2016b). Example (5), adapted from McCormick (2002: 169), illustrates how Afrikaans and English combine into such a new code in Cape Town's former District Six, a traditionally multiethnic working-class neighborhood. It has been taken from a meeting at a rugby club in the neighborhood, during which the chairperson describes the role of the team's manager. Afrikaans words are in italics.

Example (5)

Ek dink dat die-die manager *se* duties *sal wees om te* manage *die* team
("I think that the the manager's duties shall be to manage the
    team")

op die veld on the field. Also, once a team has been picked *dan*
    vat hy
("on the field on the field. Also, once a team has been picked then
    he takes")
die team *oor.* From then on *hy is* responsible *vir daai.*
("the team over. From then on he is responsible for those.")

14.4.3   Interactions across Englishes at the Grassroots

Many interactions at the grassroots take place across speakers of diverse
L1s who, hence, speak different Englishes. As a result, they are Interactions
across Englishes (IaEs; Meierkord 2012) and many have been discussed as
English as a lingua franca interactions. For the Outer Circle, IaEs are
typically reported in the context of work migration.

The trend to increasingly use English outside of elite work domains
has, for example, been attested for Ghana. Wornyo (2015: 41) points out
that migrant labourers who move to the capital Accra to work as artisans,
casual workers in factories, labourers, taxi drivers or to engage in petty
trade may have had no formal education. His study of construction workers (carpenters, masons, painters, electricians, still benders and
labourers) who originate in various parts of Ghana and hence speak
different L1s, demonstrates that interactions involve concurrent uses of
English when participants do not share a Ghanaian language, such as
Akan or Ewe.

In Asia, it is particularly Hong Kong from where very similar interactions have been reported. Besides the interactions between traders
in Chunking Mansion, mentioned in Section 14.3.1.2, IaEs frequently
occur between domestic workers and their employers. As Kwan and
Dunworth (2016) explain, more than 250,000 of Hong Kong's 7 million
population are foreign domestic workers, of which 70 percent originate from the Philippines, 25 percent from Indonesia, and 3 percent
from Thailand. Recently, it seems that "newer migrants may lack the
desired level of English language competence," (ibid.: 14) resulting in
an increasing number of reported domestic disputes and language-
related tensions. Kwan and Dunworth's (2016) study of twelve employers and fourteen employees, residing in Hong Kong Island, Kowloon,
and the New Territories, revealed, through questionnaires and semi-
structured interviews, that the most frequent challenges met in interactions were pronunciation or language structure and vocabulary difference. However, these were not seen as the most important
challenges, which were perspectives on etiquette, understanding of
implied meaning, notions of politenes, and differing expectations.
The most frequent strategies to redress these were repetition, clarification, self-correction, and direct questions.

Currently, "significant numbers of Indians, Parsees, and Eurasians still live in the territory, as do Indonesians, Filipinos, Japanese, Malaysians, Nepalis, Pakistanis, and Thais" (Bolton 2000: 276). As a result, many different Englishes add to Hong Kong's ecology, but precise descriptions of these diasporic varieties do not yet exist. Recently, informal traders from various African countries have also been introducing their Englishes to Hong Kong.

From Europe, Cutting (2012: 3) describes work migration of ground staff in European airports, including "security guards (who carry out document and baggage checks and metal screenings of individuals), ground handlers (who ensure safe and timely movement of aircraft, drive the 'push-back' truck, communicate with pilots and load and unload baggage airside), catering staff (who work in bars, fast food outlets and restaurants) and bus drivers (who handle the loading and unloading of both passengers and crew)."

Another context in which IaEs take place at the grassroots is that of forced migration. Weyns (2013) investigates the use of English by refugees and asylum seekers from a wide range of cultural and linguistic backgrounds with their Flemish social workers at the *Transithuis* in Ghent, an institution offering social welfare services. Guido (2016) investigates encounters between tourists visiting voluntary-work camps in Italian seaside resorts affected by migrant arrivals, where they interact with the migrants who often originate from West African countries and use Nigerian Pidgin English. In an earlier paper (Guido 2014), she describes how English is also used in Italy for interactions between the local Catholic clergy, in an attempt to make Roman Catholic beliefs accessible and acceptable to West African (in this case Liberian) refugees. However, as Blommaert (2010: 8) points out for the Brussels context, these interactions are seldom conducted in English only, as not all immigrants speak English at high levels of proficiency. As a result, "when a Nigerian woman goes to buy bread in a Turkish-owned bakery, the code for conducting the transaction will, for both, be a clearly non-native and very limited variety of local vernacular Dutch, mixed with some English, or German, words." When interacting with local native Belgians, as Blommaert (2010: 8) explains, "when the Nigerian woman goes to her daughter's school for consultation on her child's progress, she will have to revert to her non-native English. This will then be met by a Belgian-Flemish variety of English from the teachers."

14.4.4 Grassroots English Literacy

The oral uses of English at the grassroots also find reflection in writing. As Blommaert (2008: 7) explains, grassroots literacy remains rooted in orality and is characterized by nonstandard spelling and punctuation, corrections and additions, and code-switching, reflecting limited exposure to standard, normative language use and formal text genres.

Uses of grassroots literacy are typically found in more informal genres of writing, that is, not necessarily in letters but in what has been called and extensively discussed as bottom-up signage (see, e.g., the papers in Shohamy and Gorter 2009). The following are illustrative of such usage.

The example in Figure 14.1, however, is mostly in line with standard orthography – only the apostrophe in *today's* is missing. The notice also mixes English and Luganda, using the word *offal* for intestines in combination with the Luganda word *katogo*, which refers to cooking bananas, typically prepared with a sauce, for breakfast. In this case, *offal* is furthermore treated as a count noun and pluralized, which is common in Ugandan English but in contrast to what is the case in standard Englishes, where *offal* is a mass noun.

As explained above, writing in English at the grassroots often defies standard(ized) orthography, which is the case in Figure 14.2, from Maafushi, Maldives. The signage, composed by a local, operating a small café on the beach, is aimed at tourists from various linguistic, educational, and social backgrounds. Currently, the island is often visited by Chinese middle-class tourists with a low-to-intermediate level of English (from participant observation).

While the lexical items are largely spelled according to standard English conventions, individual words disregard this, as is the case with *chees* ("cheese"), *oder* ("order"), *befor* ("before") and *tirp* ("trip").

Figure 14.1 Notice outside a roadside restaurant in Kira, Uganda

Figure 14.2 Signposts outside a local café on Maafushi Island, Maldives

14.6 Conclusion: Englishes at the Grassroots and Models of English

While the spread of English at the grassroots is not a new phenomenon as such, it gained momentum after World War II and then again following the breakdown of communist regimes. As a result of migrations, forced or voluntary, and of the teaching of English to all parts of societies, English has made inroads into the lives of individuals all around the world, many of whom have fallen outside of the traditional description of World Englishes that were based on "elite" speakers of the language. Not surprisingly, the Englishes used at the grassroots are highly heterogeneous as regards their form. While some users' Englishes reflect processes associated with interlanguage but approximate standard Englishes, others involve complex processes of restructuring and simplification, at times resembling jargons. Frequently, users also combine English with other languages in their linguistic repertoire, leading to what has been described as translanguaging and code-mixing.

Discussions of the grassroots are necessarily about social class, which is a factor crucially missing from many models of World Englishes, as Mesthrie and Bhatt (2008) criticize. In fact, the grassroots and their Englishes do not figure in Kachru's Three Circles Model. Pidginized varieties, albeit only stable Pidgins and Creoles such as Tok Pisin, Krio, and Jamaican Creole, were, however, included in McArthur's (1987) and Görlach's (1988) models. The grassroots are implicitly considered in Schneider's (2007) accounts of the contact scenarios between the indigenous population and the settlers during the early time of the various colonies. However, social variation of the postcolonial Englishes is said to only emerge during Phase 5 of the Dynamic Model, after a Phase 4, in which the variety would undergo endonormative stabilization, and most postcolonial Englishes are held to not have reached this stage. Yet, if we conceive of the Englishes at the grassroots as also being a class-related phenomenon, social variation seems to occur. As Mesthrie and Bhatt (2008) have suggested, it may be useful to consider that individual varieties may skip a stage of the model.

The grassroots are decidedly discussed in Meierkord's (2012) model of Interactions across Englishes, and Mair (2013) seems to explicitly account for varieties spoken at the grassroots in his discussion of the impact made by nonstandard Englishes. However, neither of these accounts for hybrid Englishes and translanguaging practices.

Whether the extremely low engagement with behaviors at the grassroots is due to a lack of scholars' contact with and thus access to the lower social classes or whether it reflects a sheer lack of interest and ignorance is difficult to tell. However, engaging with the grassroots is a necessity for linguists to (1) not lose contact with the realities of English usage and hence with the further development of the language and (2) to readdress models that had been conceived based on data obtained from observing "the elite" more or less exclusively. Clearly, given the fact that contexts of English uses as well as the individuals involved will continue to change, there is a need to further integrate grassroots uses of English and their structural characteristics, as well as the translanguaging strategies and hybrid Englishes that often go along with these, into models of World Englishes. Arguably, this is best achieved in a post-varieties approach (cf. e. g. Leimgruber 2013; cf. Buschfeld and Kautzsch, Chapter 3, this volume).[11]

---

[11] Another very recent approach is that of the "new speaker" These are "multilingual citizens who, by engaging with languages other than their 'native' or 'national' language(s), need to cross existing social boundaries, re-evaluate their own levels of linguistic competence and creatively (re)structure their social practices to adapt to new and overlapping linguistic spaces" (New Speakers Network 2014), in particular regional minorities, immigrants, and transnational workers. As summarized in Duchêne and Pietikainen (undated), a variety of individuals emerge as new speakers in present-day contexts of globalization, including Philippine nurses in Switzerland; coalminers in, e.g., Belgium; Eastern European workforce in the secondary sector; staff and customers in local supermarkets, e.g. in the Netherlands.

References

Akhidenor, Anthonia Eboseremen. 2013. Code-switching in the conversations of the Chinese trading community in Africa: The case of Botswana. *English Today* 29(4): 30–36.

Bambgbose, Ayo. 2006. A recurring decimal: English in language policy and planning. In Braj B. Kachru, Yamuna Kachru and Cecil L. Nelson, eds. *The Handbook of World Englishes*, Oxford: Wiley-Blackwell, 645–660.

Battenburg, John. 1997. English versus French: Language rivalry in Tunisia. *World Englishes* 16(2): 281–290.

Baumgardner, Robert J. and Kimberley Brown. 2012. English in Iranian magazine advertising. *World Englishes* 31(3): 292–311.

Blommaert, Jan. 2008. *Grassroots Literacy: Writing, Identity and Voice in Central Africa*. London: Routledge.

Blommaert, Jan. 2010. *The Sociolinguistics of Globalization*. Cambridge: Cambridge University Press.

Bolton, Kingsley. 2000. The sociolinguistics of Hong Kong and the space for Hong Kong English. *World Englishes* 19(3): 265–285.

Bolton, Kingsley and Werner Botha. 2015. Researching English in contemporary China. *World Englishes* 34(2): 169–174.

Bolton, Kingsley and Christiane Meierkord. 2013. English in contemporary Sweden: Perceptions, policies, and narrated practices. *Journal of Sociolinguistics* 17(1): 93–117.

Bruyèl-Olmedo, Antonio and Maria Juan-Garau. 2009. English as a lingua franca in the linguistic landscape of the multilingual resort of S'Arenal in Mallorca. *International Journal of Multilingualism* 6(4): 386–411.

Brutt-Griffler, Janina. 2002. *World English: A Study of Its Development*. Bristol: Multilingual Matters.

Buckingham, Louisa. 2015. Commercial signage and the linguistic landscape of Oman. *World Englishes* 34(3): 411–435. doi:10.1111/weng.12146

Buckingham, Louisa. 2016a. Introduction. In Louisa Buckingham, ed. *The Status of English in Bosnia and Herzegovina*. Bristol: Multilingual Matters, 1–6.

Buckingham, Louisa, ed. 2016b. *The Status of English in Bosnia and Herzegovina*. Bristol: Multilingual Matters.

Canagarajah, A. Suresh. 2013. *Translingual Practice: Global Englishes and Cosmopolitan Relations*. London: Routledge.

Carroll, John B. 1981. Twenty-five years of research on foreign language aptitude. In Karl C. Diller, ed. *Individual Differences and Universals in Language Learning Aptitude*. Rowley, MA: Newbury House, 83–118.

Crystal, David. 2003. *English as a Global Language* (2nd ed.). Cambridge: Cambridge University Press.

Cutting, Joan. 2012. English for airport ground staff. *English for Specific Purposes*, 31: 3–13.

D'Angelo, James F. 2005. Educated Japanese English: Expanding oral/aural core vocabulary. *World Englishes* 24(3): 329–349.

Dashti, Abdulmohsen. 2015. The role and status of the English language in Kuwait. *English Today* 31(3): 28–33.

Deumert, Ana and Nkululeko Mabandla. 2009. I-dollar *eyi* one! Ethnolinguistic fractionalization, communication networks and economic participation: Lessons from Cape Town, South Africa. *Journal of Development Studies 45*: 412–40.

Deumert, Ana and Nkululeko Mabandla. 2013. "Everyday a new shop pops up": South Africa's "new" Chinese diaspora and the multilingual transformation of new towns. *English Today* 29(1): 44–52.

Duchêne, Alexandre and Pietikainen, Sari. undated. COST Action IS1306. Workers as new speakers (WG3). Collaborative final report. www.nspk.org.uk/images/WG3.pdf

Eberhard, David M., Gary F. Simons and Charles D. Fennig, eds. 2019. *Ethnologue: Languages of the World.* (20th ed.) Dallas, TX: SIL International. www.ethnologue.com.

Edwards, Alison. 2016. *English in the Netherlands: Functions, Forms and Attitudes.* Amsterdam: John Benjamins.

EF Education First. 2018. *EF English Proficiency Index 2015.* Cambridge, MA: EF Education First. www.ef.edu/epi/

Erling, Elizabeth J., Hamid, M. Obaidul and Philip Seargeant. 2013. Grassroots attitudes to English as a language for international development in Bangladesh. In Elizabeth J. Erling and Philip Seargeant, eds. *English and Development: Policy, Pedagogy and Globalisation.* Bristol: Multilingual Matters, 88–110.

European Commission. 2012. *Special Eurobarometer 386: Europeans and Their Languages.* Brussels: Commission of the European Communities. ec.europa.eu/public_opinion/archives/ebs/ebs_386_en.pdf

Fishman, Joshua. 1977. Knowing, using and liking English as an additional language. In Joshua A. Fishman, Robert L. Cooper and Andrew W. Conrad, eds. *The Spread of English: The Sociology of English as an Additional Language.* Rowley, MA: Newbury House, 302–310.

García, Ofelia and Li Wei. 2013. *Translanguaging: Language, Bilingualism and Education.* Basingstoke: Palgrave.

Gonçalves, Kellie. 2016. The pedagogical implications of ELF in a domestic migrant workplace. In Hugo Bowles and Alessia Cogo, eds. *International Perspectives on English as a Lingua Franca: Pedagogical Insights.* Houndsmills: Palgrave Macmillan, 136–158.

González Cruz, Isabel. 2012. English in the Canaries: Past and present. *English Today* 28(1): 20–28.

Görlach, Manfred. 1988. Sprachliche Standardisierungsprozesse im englischsprachigen Bereich. *Sociolinguistica* 2: 131–85. (Also available in

English as: Görlach, Manfred. 1990. The development of Standard Englishes. In Manfred Görlach, ed. *Studies in the History of the English Language*. Heidelberg: Winter: 9–64.)

Greenbaum, Sidney. 1996. Introducing ICE. In Sidney Greenbaum, ed. *Comparing English Worldwide: The International Corpus of English*. Oxford: Clarendon Press, 3–12.

Guido, Maria Grazia. 2008. *English as a Lingua Franca in Cross-Cultural Immigration-Domains*. Bern: Lang.

Guido, Maria Grazia. 2014. New-Evangelization discourse in ELF immigration encounters: A case study. *Lingue e Linguaggi* 12: 111–126.

Guido, Maria Grazia. 2016. ELF in responsible tourism: Power relationships in unequal migration. In Marie-Luise Pitzl and Ruth Osimk-Teasdale, eds. *English as a Lingua Franca: Perspectives and Prospects: Contributions in Honour of Barbara Seidlhofer*. Berlin: Walter de Gruyter.

Hasanova, Dilbarhon. 2007. Broadening the boundaries of the Expanding Circle: English in Uzbekistan. *World Englishes* 26(3): 276–290.

Kachru, Braj B. 1965. The Indianness in Indian English. *Word* 21: 391–400.

Kachru, Braj B. 1976. Indian English: A sociolinguistic profile of a transplanted language. *Studies in Language Learning* 1(2): 139–189.

Kachru, Braj B. 1983. *The Indianization of English: The English Language in India*. New Delhi: Oxford University Press.

Kachru, Braj B. 1994. English in South Asia. In Robert Burchfield, ed. *The Cambridge History of the English Language, Vol. 5: English in Britain and Overseas: Origins and Development*. Cambridge: Cambridge University Press.

Khubchandani, Lachman M. and Hosali, Priya. 1999. Grassroots English in a communication paradigm. *Language Problems and Language Planning* 23(3): 251–272.

Klippel, Friederike. 1994. *Englischlernen im 18. und 19. Jahrhundert. Die Geschichte der Lehrbücher und Unterrichtsmethoden*. Münster: Nodus Publikationen. www .google.de/url?sa=t&rct=j&q=&esrc=s&source=web&cd= 5&cad=rja&uact= 8&ved=0ahUKEwi00vvguenPAhWGvxQKHcmHDncQFghAMAQ&url=https %3A%2F%2Fepub.ub.uni-muenchen.de%2F8653%2F1%2F8653.pdf&usg= AFQjCNGbpRQc8S3iI9qgU4iTClnhLmtajw

Knowles, Caroline and Douglas Harper. 2009. *Hong Kong: Migrant Lives, Landscapes, and Journeys*. Chicago: The University of Chicago Press.

Kouega, Jean Paul. 2007. *A Dictionary of Cameroon English*. Berne: Peter Lang.

Kwan, Noel and Katie Dunwort. 2016. English as a lingua franca communication between domestic helpers and employers in Hong Kong: A study of pragmatic strategies. *English for specific Purposes* 43: 13–24.

Leimgruber, Jakob R. E. 2013. The trouble with World Englishes. *English Today* 29(3): 3–7.

Mahboob Ahmar and Tariq Elyas. 2014. English in the Kingdom of Saudi Arabia. *World Englishes* 33(1): 128–142.

Mair, Christian. 2013. The World System of Englishes: Accounting for the transnational importance of mobile and mediated vernaculars. *English World-Wide 34*: 253–278.

Makalela, Leketi. 2015. Translanguaging practices in complex multilingual spaces: A discontinuous continuity in post-independent South Africa. *International Journal of the Sociology of Language 234*: 115–132. doi:10.1515/ijsl-2015-0007

Margić, Branka Drljača and Dorjana Širola. 2014. "Jamairan and Irish for fun, British to show off": Attitudes of Croatian university students of TEFL to English Language Varieties. *English Today 30*(3): 48–53.

McArthur, Tom. 1987. The English languages? *English Today 3*(3): 9–13.

McArthur, Tom. 2003. World English, Euro English, Nordic English? *English Today 19*(1): 54–58.

McCormick, Kay. 2002. *Language in Cape Town's District Six*. Oxford: Oxford University Press.

Meierkord, Christiane. 2012. *Interactions across Englishes. Linguistic Choices in Local and International Contact Situations*. Cambridge: Cambridge University Press.

Meierkord, Christiane, Bridget Fonkeu and Eva Zumhasch. 2015. Diasporic second language Englishes in the African communities of Germany's Ruhr Area. *International Journal of English Linguistics 5*(1): 1–13.

Merriam-Webster. 2016. Grassroots. *Merriam-Webster Dictionary*. www .merriam-webster.com/dictionary/grass%20roots

Mesthrie, Rajend. 2010. Socio-phonetics and social change: Deracialisation of the GOOSE vowel in South African English. *Journal of Sociolinguistics 14*(1): 3–33.

Mesthrie, Rajend and Rakesh M. Bhatt. 2008. *World Englishes: The Study of New Linguistic Varieties*. Cambridge: Cambridge University Press.

Michieka, Martha. 2009. Expanding circles within the outer circle: The rural Kisii in Kenya. *World Englishes 28*(3): 352–364.

Moore, Stephen H. and Suksiri Bounchan. 2010. English in Cambodia: Changes and challenges. *World Englishes 29*(1): 114–126.

Mufwene, Salikoko. 1997. The legitimate and illegitimate offspring of English. In Larry Smith and Michael L. Forman, eds. *World Englishes 2000*. Honolulu: University of Hawai'i Press.

Mufwene, Salikoko. 2001. *The Ecology of Language Evolution*. Cambridge: Cambridge University Press.

Mufwene, Salikoko. 2010. Globalization and the spread of English: What does it mean to be Anglophone? *English Today 26*(1): 57–59.

Namyalo, Saudah, Bebwa Isingoma and Christiane Meierkord. 2016. Towards assessing the space of English in Uganda's linguistic ecology: Facts and issues. In Christiane Meierkord, Bebwa Isingoma and Saudah Namyalo, eds. *Ugandan English: Its Sociolinguistics, Structure and Uses in a Globalising Post-Protectorate*. Amsterdam: John Benjamins, 19–49.

New Speakers Network. 2014. *About COST Action IS1306 on New speakers*. www.nspk.org.uk/about/

Ochieng, Dunlop. 2015. The revival of the status of English in Tanzania. *English Today 31*(2): 25–31.

OED (Oxford English Dictionary). 2016. "grass root, n." In *Oxford English Dictionary*. Oxford: Oxford University Press.

Proshina, Zoya G. 2006. Russian Englishes. Introduction. *World Englishes 24*(4): 437–438.

Proshina, Zoya G. and Anna A. Eddy, eds. 2016. *Russian English: History, Functions, and Features*. Cambridge: Cambridge University Press.

Quirk, Randolph. 1972. *Linguistic Bonds across the Atlantic: The English Languages and Images of Matter*. London: Oxford University Press.

Rajagopalan, Kanavillil. 2003. The ambivalent role of English in Brazilian politics. *World Englishes 22*(2): 91–101.

Randall, Mick and Mohammad Amir Samimi. 2010. The status of English in Dubai. *English Today 26*(1): 43–50.

Regala-Flores, Eden. 2009. An exploratory study of the phonological features of basilectal Philippine English: A case of some Cebuano speakers. Paper presented at the 15th International Conference of the International Association for World Englishes (IAWE), Cebu, October 22-24.

Schneider, Edgar. 2007. *Postcolonial English: Varieties Around the World*. Cambridge: Cambridge University Press.

Schneider, Edgar. 2011. *English Around the World: An Introduction*. Cambridge: Cambridge University Press.

Schneider, Edgar. 2016a. Grassroots Englishes in tourism interactions. *English Today 32*(3): 2–10.

Schneider, Edgar. 2016b. Hybrid Englishes: An exploratory survey. *World Englishes 35*(3): 339–354.

Schmied, Josef. 1996. Second-Language corpora. In Sidney Greenbaum, ed. *Comparing English Worldwide: The International Corpus of English*. Oxford: Clarendon Press.

Seargeant, Philip, ed. 2011. *English in Japan in the Era of Globalization*. London: Palgrave Macmillan.

Shohamy, Elana and Durk Gorter, eds. 2009. *Linguistic Landscape: Expanding the Scenery*. London: Routledge.

Snodin, Navaporn Sanprasert. 2014. English naming and code-mixing in Thai mass media. *World Englishes 33*(1): 100–111.

Ssentanda, Medadi. 2016. Tensions between English medium and mother tongue education in rural Ugandan primary schools: An ethnographic investigation. In Christiane Meierkord, Bebwa Isingoma and Saudah Namyalo, eds. *Ugandan English: Its Sociolinguistics, Structure and Uses in a Globalising Post-Protectorate*. Amsterdam: John Benjamins, 95–117.

Strevens, Peter. 1977. *New Orientations in the Teaching of English*. Oxford: Oxford University Press.

United Nations. 2015. Education for all report. www.un.org/youthenvoy/ 2015/04/education-2000-2015-third-countries-reached-global-education-goals/

Vélez-Rendón, Gloria. 2003. English in Colombia: A sociolinguistic profile. *World Englishes 22*(2): 185–198.

Vertovec, Steven. 2007. Super-diversity and its implications. *Ethnic and Racial Studies 30*(6): 1024–1054.

Weyns, Babette. 2013. English as a lingua franca in service encounters with migrants in Belgium: Moving away from the social vacuum. Unpublished master's dissertation, University of Gent.

Wikipedia contributors. 2016. List of countries by English-speaking population. *Wikipedia, The Free Encyclopedia.* https://en.wikipedia.org/w/index .php?title=list_of_countries_by_english-speaking_population &oldid=746761575

Wornyo, Albert Agbesi. 2015. English lingua franca (ELF) as a means of communication among construction workers in Ghana. *International Journal of Language Learning and Applied Linguistics World (IJLLALW)* 9(4): 41–56.

15

Beyond English as a Second or Foreign Language: Local Uses and the Cultural Politics of Identification

Alison Edwards and Philip Seargeant

15.1 Introduction

In this chapter, we explore the ways in which English forms an integral part of local language practices in what, in the field of World Englishes (WEs), has traditionally been referred to as the Expanding Circle: those countries in which English is neither a native (ENL) nor a postcolonial language and thus has not, traditionally, had an official presence. Conventional ways of categorizing English around the world have distinguished between countries where, for mostly historical reasons, English has an established role in society and those where it is considered a foreign or (more recently) an international language. The boundary between the Outer and Expanding Circle countries in Kachru's (1985) Three Circles Model, or contexts in which English predominantly serves as a second (ESL) or foreign (EFL) language respectively, has provided a useful shorthand for mapping how English is used and perceived around the world. This categorization is inevitably a simplification, however, and there are contexts in which a more complex identity for English exists. This chapter examines the blurring of this boundary between ESL and EFL contexts and the increasing recognition that, by investigating the ways in which English resists such neat categorizations, we can arrive at a more nuanced picture of the actuality of English use around the globe.

The chapter begins by investigating the space discursively carved out in the study of English as a global language for the use and users of the language in societies traditionally seen as belonging to the Expanding

Circle. As noted, English in these contexts has typically been constructed as a foreign or international language – thereby precluding consideration of the increasingly complex and multifarious ways in which it is mobilized for local interpersonal functions and in producing and performing identity. Different strands of recent research are challenging this, advocating a shift from a traditional WEs approach focusing on territorialized varieties toward a more sociocultural and ethnographic orientation, studying English as a situated social practice wherever it is found (see Bolander, Chapter 29, this volume). We focus, as illustrative case studies, on Japan and the Netherlands, exploring the ways in which English is becoming a fundamental resource in these countries despite having limited official status, or, in the case of Japan, no significant role in transactional communication at all.

The first half of the chapter discusses these contexts in general terms, before turning to two analytic examples from the mediascapes (Appadurai, 1990) of the two countries where, as we shall see, English is tied up with the construction of the self and the other in different, profound, and sometimes unexpected ways. Analyzing these transcultural media products from a sociolinguistic and discourse-analytic perspective, we show how the use of English as a global linguistic resource creates new semiotic opportunities for social actors to negotiate and revise their identities and strategically construct the local. The use of English – or English-related linguistic resources – thus becomes an integral part of the linguistic repertoire and cultural makeup of these societies, counter to the prevailing discourse that often still positions it as "merely" a foreign language.

Let us first make a brief note about terminology. In the chapter, we employ both the traditional Kachruvian terminology of the Three Circles (Kachru, 1985) and the conventional distinction between EFL and ESL, as well as English as an international language (EIL). We use these terms as useful starting points for the discussion, acknowledging that all are simplifications and are colored by the traditions that have used them. The very premise of the chapter is that these conceptual categorizations should not be taken as givens and that discussing the ongoing reconsideration of such classifications enables us to highlight important issues about how the English language exists in diverse world contexts.

15.2   English as a Global Language and the Expanding Circle

English in the Expanding Circle has typically been constructed as a foreign language drawing on native-speaker models, or as a tool for international communication purposes. This conceptualization is mirrored in education policy and the English-language classroom, where a focus on EFL and native-speaker norms is still very much in evidence and insights from academic discussions that challenge this have not filtered through to any great extent. Paradigms such as EIL, English as a Lingua Franca, Lingua Franca English (Canagarajah, 2013) and Interactions across Englishes (Meierkord, 2012), which have developed to challenge traditional EFL approaches, all focus on the use of English between people with different linguistic backgrounds; and, given that transnational communication is one of the major functions of English today, such models are undoubtedly valuable. However, these paradigms have less to say about the roles and uses of English *within* individual Expanding Circle societies.

In contrast to lingua franca approaches, the concept of WEs draws attention to the appropriation of English within local contexts. The term WEs was initially associated with the Kachruvian paradigm, based on his foundational Three Circles Model (Kachru, 1985). An early aim of proponents of the paradigm was to legitimize the status of postcolonial Englishes, which were often seen as inferior or deficient versions of center varieties. By analyzing empirical evidence of local English-language use, researchers sought to construct these Englishes as valid varieties in their own right. In this process, however, the rootedness of English in local language practices has typically been considered characteristic of the Outer Circle (where the language has an official status of some sort) rather than the Expanding Circle. Thus, certain analytical conceptualizations came to be treated as canonized schemas in WEs, in particular the mapping onto the Three Circles of the tripartite distinction between ENL, ESL, and EFL. Much literature reiterates a dichotomized and rather simplified account of Outer and Expanding Circles societies, whereby the former are construed as norm-developing second-language users and active agents of English innovation and the latter as foreign-language learners who defer to Inner Circle norms and for whom English plays little role in their daily lives and identity constructions.

This discursive account has faced criticism from commentators within and outside WEs. Ironically, precisely as this account was becoming entrenched orthodoxy, English was developing an ever greater role in the Expanding Circle due to the forces of globalization, accelerated by technological developments. Within WEs research, there were calls for more attention to be paid to Expanding Circle contexts (Berns 2005) and suggestions that various societies, especially in northern and western Europe, were potentially transitioning from EFL to ESL status (Graddol 1997). In-depth studies illustrating the depth of English use in such settings emerged, such as Hilgendorf (2001) and Erling (2004) on Germany and Edwards (2016) on the Netherlands. At the same time, Buschfeld (2013), investigating the case of Cyprus, showed that traditionally ESL societies can also "revert" to EFL status. This growing body of research emphasizes that, on the ground, the categorizations are far from clear-cut (see also the contributions in Mukherjee and Hundt, 2011).

Meanwhile, scholars working from a "critical linguistics" perspective have challenged the exclusionary and essentializing nature of the WEs approach. Pennycook described WEs research as "insistently exclusionary" for privileging some contexts and varieties over others and discounting nonstandard(izing) forms, such as creoles and "all those language forms used in the 'expanding circle'" (2003: 521). Others criticized the field's apparent penchant for "broad-brush," top-down categorizations at the level of nation-states as reflecting twentieth-century discourse patterns (Bruthiaux, 2003). The conception of territorialized speech communities and the a priori ascription of identity (e.g. exonormatively oriented "learner") appears essentialistic and out of step with the social-constructivist and discursive turns in the broader social sciences, which see concepts such as language, community, and identity not as predetermined and stable but rather as discursively constructed, strategically (re)produced, and continually revised (Heller, 2008; Tusting and Maybin, 2007).

In response to such criticisms, it has been argued that "the Kachruvian model of the three circles was never intended to be monolithic and unchanging" (Bolton, 2005: 75) and that, beyond the varieties-based studies criticized by Pennycook and others, there has long been a much broader range of research falling under the umbrella of WEs (Bolton, 2005, 2012). A look through the journal *World Englishes* over the last decade reveals a small, eclectic, but growing collection of literature on diverse Expanding Circle contexts from Brazil to Russia, Finland to South Korea, which explores the role of English as a locally embedded resource for meaning-making. These studies show how the dialectical relationship between the local and the global in Expanding Circle contexts is more complex than can be accounted for by essentialized discourses about English as either simply a foreign language or a tool for international communication.

Such studies are in line with the recent impetus (Bolton, 2013; James, 2016; Mair, 2016) for WEs research to move toward the more sociocultural and ethnographic approaches represented by notions such as transcultural flows (Pennycook, 2007), translanguaging (García, 2009), translingual practice (Canagarajah, 2013), and the sociolinguistics of globalization (Blommaert, 2010). These approaches are interested in situated language practice, whereby "the contexts for communication should be investigated rather than assumed" (Rampton, 2007: 585). They emphasize the notion of linguistic resources rather than languages (Blommaert, 2010) and the study of issues such as intersubjective identity construction and language ideology at the intersection between language, culture, and society (Bucholtz and Hall, 2005, 2008).

This chapter contributes to bringing together these sociolinguistic/sociocultural approaches with WEs, investigating the ways in which English serves as a fundamental linguistic and semiotic resource in canonically Expanding Circle settings where it has little or no official status and is still positioned institutionally as EFL (and/or EIL). Specifically, we aim to explore the use of English as a vehicle for social positioning and the enactment of localized identities in Japan and the Netherlands, illustrating how the existence of English in these contexts is more complex than traditional categorizations suggest. In the next section, we introduce these two settings in more detail.

15.3   Japan and the Netherlands as Sites of English-Language Practice

15.3.1   The Context of Japan

Japan is often viewed as having an ambiguous relationship with English (McVeigh, 2002). As a society it is relatively ethnically homogeneous and Japanese is the overwhelmingly dominant language (Hino, 2009), viewed as an essential marker of cultural identity (Heinrich, 2012). English is on prominent display around the built environment on signs and in advertising, and is a frequent topic in public discourse about education and internationalization, but the language has no real official status and few citizens need to communicate in it either in their everyday or working lives (Terasawa, 2012; Yano, 2011). Although there has been a great deal of investment in language education since World War II, fluency in English remains low: in the Test of English as a Foreign Language (TOEFL), Japan ranked second to bottom among thirty Asian countries in 2009 (Hongo, 2013). According to one policy document, "Today's Japanese are lacking . . . basic skills . . . The Japanese themselves are painfully aware of the inadequacy of their communication skills" (CJGTC, 2000: 4). There is no suggestion that English has anything near ESL status, nor is it likely to move in that direction. Nonetheless, the language is regularly stressed as being essential for the country's status and success on the international stage, especially economically (Yoshida, 2013). English is therefore positioned in political discourse as an important skill that will contribute to Japanese national identity, yet its functional use within society as a language of communication is minimal.

The history of English in Japan explains a great deal about its current status. Unlike many countries in Asia, Japan was never colonized by a Western power, and thus English was never integrated into Japanese society in the way it has been in Outer Circle countries. English has a relatively short existence in Japan compared to many other countries. During the long period of self-imposed isolation begun by the Tokugawa shogunate in the 1600s, all relations with the international community became highly regulated and the need for foreign-language skills was minimal. It was not until the Meiji Restoration of 1868 and the ensuing modernization that continued international relations with the West began in earnest and English began to have a sustained role.

During World War II, the learning of English was officially discouraged (Koike and Tanaka, 1995). Educational reforms were enacted during the seven-year American occupation following the war and English again became an important school subject. Further important reforms came about in the 1980s as part of the Nakasone administration's program of *kokusaika* (internationalization), aiming to boost English teaching at school and foster a communicative approach, which marked a shift from the traditional grammar-translation method. For example, a subject called "Oral Communication" was implemented in secondary schools in 1994 and the subject of "Foreign Languages" (which in practical terms meant English) became compulsory in junior high schools from 1998. In 2003, the "Action Plan to Cultivate 'Japanese with English Abilities'" was introduced, followed in 2011 by "Five Proposals and Specific Measures for Developing Proficiency in English for International Communication," both emphasizing the need for communicative language teaching (CLT). For many within the teaching profession, however, CLT is incompatible with other elements of the education system, most notably the importance accorded to the exam system, which operates as a form of gatekeeping for the job market.

As can be seen, there is a divide between the aspiration to embed English more deeply in society and the reality of a society in which the language has limited actual use value. There are a couple of recent but isolated examples of corporations that have adopted English as their official working language (Rakuten, Fast Retailing). Yet, unlike in Outer Circle countries, a local variety with its own identifiable forms and cultural identity ("Japanese English") is unlikely to develop given the lack of contexts where the language has official, and thus sustained, status. In this sense, Japan is a stereotypically EFL country in the traditional sense, "where English ... will function only as a means of communication with non-Japanese in international settings. It will probably never be used within the Japanese community and form part of the speaker's identity repertoire" (Yano, 2001: 127).

Nonetheless, the presence and influence of English in Japan is such that relegating it to the status of simply "foreign" is to underestimate its actual existence within society. One way in which English has been absorbed into Japanese culture is in the form of loanwords. Estimates suggest that loanwords make up some 10 percent of the lexicon (Hogan, 2003). Among the different types are "pseudo-loans" (Hogan, 2003: 44), in which the original English form is adapted, its meaning or range of use altered, or in which elements from both English and Japanese are combined to create a term unique to both languages. Such words, referred to as *wasei eigo* ("Japanese-made English"), show clear signs of nativization (Honna, 1995) and are thus a form of linguistic appropriation, albeit at the level of individual lexical items rather than the code as a whole.

Another significant way in which English has become absorbed in Japanese society is by means of its decorative use in domains such as the media, advertising, and popular culture (Seargeant, 2009; Dougill, 2008). English words and phrases, often written in the Roman alphabet rather than

katakana, frequently appear on adverts, signs, clothes, and pop culture artifacts (Hyde, 2002), often in ways that confuse or baffle English speakers. The
language here functions as a vehicle of association (Piller, 2003): It is not
intended for any obvious denotational function but is instead predominantly
ornamental, its purpose typically being to tap into "symbolic cool" (Furukawa,
2014: 199).

Finally, the appropriation of English in local pop culture has led to
suggestions that competence may not in fact be as low as commonly
claimed. In their study of Japanese popular music (J-Pop), Moody and
Matsumoto (2003: 4) contend that song lyrics assume a widespread ability
to understand English and describe J-Pop English as "an emerging form of
bilingual creativity." Pennycook drew attention to a similar trend with his
examination of the Japanese rappers Rip Slyme, who use code-mixed and
blended language forms in a way "that cannot be predefined as a
first, second or foreign language" (2003: 528). In such ways, English operates as an important touchstone in Japanese society and culture and has
a rootedness within everyday life despite its limited use for transactional
communicative purposes.

15.3.2 The Context of the Netherlands

The entrenchment of English in the Netherlands has grown in recent
decades to such an extent that, like several other western and northern
European countries, it is frequently described as transitioning from its
traditional EFL to ESL status. Historically – and quite unlike Japan – the
Netherlands has long been said to have one of the most "open" economies
in world, dating back to its days as a maritime power during the Dutch
Golden Age of the seventeenth century. It has a long tradition of foreign-
language learning, necessitated by its status as a small country at the
crossroads of three major language areas – German, French, and
English – and of accommodating and adapting to different cultures and
languages (Ammon and McConnell, 2002; McArthur, 1998).

Until the nineteenth century, English was mostly used instrumentally, for
example in ports. It became a compulsory school subject in 1863, although
French and German still predominated. Only in the second half of the
twentieth century did it acquire the status of "first" foreign language in
Dutch education, spurred on by the popularity of Anglo-American popular
culture. World War II was a major turning point: "English was the language
of the liberators, the money providers and progress" (Ridder, 1995: 44), and
Dutch foreign policy ever since has been characterized as anglophile and
Atlanticist (Asbeek Brusse, 2007). Since the 1990s, European Union policies
and initiatives have further strengthened the position of English. For
instance, as Erasmus[1] students in the Netherlands are unlikely to have an

---

[1] Erasmus (or Erasmus+ since 2014) is the name of the European Union's student exchange program.

adequate command of Dutch, their presence in the university classroom often triggers a wholesale switch to English (Berns et al., 2007: 28).

Thus, European developments combined with the global spread of new media technologies have drastically increased contact with and acquisition of English in the Netherlands. Ordinarily, English is introduced as a subject in the last two years of primary school. However, recent decades have seen rapid growth in (1) early foreign-language education, which introduces English in the form of EFL at age four or five, and (2) bilingual secondary education. Some 25 percent of grammar school students now follow bilingual Dutch-English education, in which 50 percent of lessons are taught in English for the first three years (Verspoor, De Bot, and Xu, 2011).[2] At higher education level, the Netherlands has developed into an English education "destination," offering the highest absolute number of English-medium programs in continental Europe (Wächter and Maiworm 2014). Moreover, most Dutch universities now bill themselves as officially bilingual; indeed, some view the recent internationalization process in higher education as more or less synonymous with Englishization (Zegers and Wilkinson, 2005).

Nortier (2011) has suggested that the position of English in the education system means that virtually all Dutch citizens under the age of fifty speak English. This was confirmed by the latest Eurobarometer survey, indicating that some 90 percent of the Dutch population are conversant in English (European Commission 2012). The high proficiency levels are often attributed, besides education, to the practice of subtitling rather than dubbing foreign films and television programs. This widespread competence is reflected in the *assumption* in diverse societal domains of English-language competence; consider the creative wordplay in advertising, which draws on knowledge of both Dutch and English. Advertising materials such as TV commercials created for anglophone audiences are, for cost-cutting reasons, not uncommonly reused in the Netherlands without subtitles. Furthermore, English quotes and passages in the print media are often left untranslated. This is not to say such usages are always entirely understood (Gerritsen, 1996; Gerritsen et al., 2007) – yet this situation seems to be a point of pride for some. Letters to the editor about the use of English in newspapers seem to concern the *mis*use as frequently as they do the *over*use of English, such as spelling mistakes in English code-switches (Klaassen 2002). Complaints about heavy code-switching elicit tongue-in-cheek responses, such as a 2010 headline in the NRC: "*Te veel Engelse woorden in de krant*? Point taken!" ("Too many English words in the newspaper? Point taken!").[3]

The sheer spread and multifarious uses of English in the Netherlands call into question its traditional EFL status. Given the evident expansion in roles, including intranationally, Edwards (2016) concluded that English serves

---

[2] Bilingual education is not restricted to grammar schools, but is increasingly employed in lower school streams as well.

[3] For the NRC article, see www.nrc.nl/nieuws/2010/10/23/te-veel-engelse-woorden-in-de-krant-point-taken -11960780-a129317

functionally as a second language in the Netherlands. It forms an integral part of the linguistic repertoire even when not strictly necessary to accommodate foreigners; consider its use in professional and academic conferences, for example, despite all attendees understanding Dutch (Nortier, 2011), or during the gay pride parade by the national police float, which sought to attract new (Dutch) recruits under the English-language banner "Never be afraid to be different, join us" (Schrauwers, 2006). Such uses serve as markers of status and internationalism and allow users to construct cosmopolitan, academic, or subculture identities. In this way, English is used not purely instrumentally but also as a language of identification.

Ideologically, however, English in the Netherlands retains the characteristics of a foreign language. Educational curricula remain largely Anglocentric and overt attitudes firmly exonormatively oriented. Attitudinal research shows that British English remains the most popular target model, with young people also open to American English (Edwards 2016; Van der Haagen 1998). "Dutch English" does not serve as a target model. Its basilectal counterpart, Dunglish (*Steenkolenengels* or "coal English"), is widely acknowledged and ridiculed but Dutch English does not appear to be recognized at all as a potentially legitimate variety. Further, structural nativizations, although often highly salient (such as the prominent "Welcome at Schiphol" signs at Amsterdam's airport), are generally not seen as acceptable. In a grammaticality judgment survey of the progressive aspect in Dutch English, certain nonstandard uses were rated as relatively acceptable, but the higher the respondent's proficiency level, the lower the acceptance of nonstandard uses, reflecting a typically exonormative orientation (Edwards 2016).

In public discourse, there is a noticeable sense that English should properly be used only when "necessary" and not when there is "a perfectly good Dutch alternative" (Edwards, 2018). That this is a common gripe is testament to just how numerous and salient such apparently superfluous uses are. English is positioned in public discourse as a tool, its "proper" use being purely instrumental – yet its actual use often far exceeds this. This tension between perception and practice is indicative of the complex status of English in the Netherlands.

15.4 Examples from the Mediascapes of Japan and the Netherlands

With the strikingly different approaches to internationalization and to their place in the world, and with their traditional EFL status being either contested (the Netherlands) or overly simplistic (Japan), these two contexts make for a compelling comparative case study about the place of English in the Expanding Circle. To illustrate the ways in which English is positioned ambiguously as both part of and separate from local cultural identity in these two countries, we analyze two language objects from their respective mediascapes. The examples are from data collected as part of two large-scale earlier projects: a study of the conceptualization of English in Japan (Seargeant, 2009) and a macrosociolinguistic study of the roles and status of English in the Netherlands (Edwards, 2016). Both are translocal cultural products that reflect at once the local and the global, mobilizing the global language of English for the purposes of local meaning-making in different ways. We approach these from a sociolinguistic and discourse-analytic perspective, informed by a poststructural understanding of identity as "performed in the doing rather than reflecting a prior set of fixed options" (Pennycook, 2007: 115). As our examples show, social and linguistic resources such as humor, mocking, and cultural references can serve as important discoursal means of self-assertion and (dis)identification (Vásquez, 2014: 86).

15.4.1   Karakuri Funniest English

"Karakuri Funniest English" was a regular segment on the popular Japanese television variety show *Sanma no Karakuri Terebi* (TBS). It consists of the host – a bilingual Japanese–American English speaker who, as a blond Caucasian, is a prototypical "native speaker" in the idealized Japanese version of English and its speakers – eliciting brief anecdotes in English from members of the public, who inevitably stumble or make mistakes, providing rich comedy for the studio audience. The segment mimics an education setting, as is common in Japanese variety shows (Furukawa 2014: 222), thus positioning English as being most naturally associated with the classroom and learning context. In this excerpt, the host (H) asks the interviewee (M) to recount a personal tragedy (adapted from Seargeant, 2009: 147–148).

Dialogue	Comments
H: What what is your (.) job? *Shokugyô* [job]?	
M: *Kajitetsudai* [housekeeper]	
H: *Kajitetsudai* [housekeeper]? English please	
M: (2) **Health** keeper	Marked Japanese English pronunciation
(laughing)	
H: Please tell me your *watashi no higeki* [my tragedy] story	
M: *Kanojo no tame ni daietto wo shitan desu yo. Soshitara 140 kiro made yaseta noni furarechaimashita.* [I went on a diet for my girlfriend. Although I managed to slim down to 140 kg, she ditched me]	
H: Okay. English please	Hand gesture summoning M to reply

M:	I am (2) one hundred forty (3) kilogram (2) and (3) my girlfriend (5) shaking me (laughing)	Spoken with katakana pronunciation, very slowly
H:	Do do you have me … message to er … before girlfriend?	H's speech accommodating to M's
	Hai [yes]	Turns to camera
M:	*Koibito yo modotte oide.* [Please come back to me, my sweetheart.]	Bows
H:	Na (.) English please	
M:	*'Koibito' tte eigo de nan to iun desu ka ne?* [How do you say *koibito* in English?]	
H:	*Koibito?* Erm, 'lover'	
M:	Please come back (1) my (1) **lebâ** [liver]	
H:	(laughs)	Holds head in hand

Transcription conventions
- (.) = pause
- (2) = two-second pause
- (laugh) = transcription of a sound etc. that forms part of the utterance
- words in italics = Japanese
- words in square brackets = translations of the Japanese
- words in bold = specific mispronunciations

Such media representations tap into the ideology of the Japanese as non–English-knowing, in particular the popular trope that English is an "impossible" language for the Japanese, who as a consequence will always be ineffective users of it. The host is positioned as the authorized power, the embodiment of "proper" English. Throughout the transcript he responds to M's marked uses of English ("health keeper" for *house keeper*, "lebâ" for *lover*) by laughing and putting his head in his hands, pragmatically constructing M's language use as deviant. As the segment always follows this same format, the very setup of the show is designed to inevitably reinforce the notion of the Japanese as incompetent and illegitimate users of English.

Paradoxically, however, the humor relies on viewers understanding the English mistakes made and being able to appreciate the resulting word play. When M says "health" instead of "house," the audience must perceive this as a mistake and realize the resulting term is nonsensical. When he is confounded by the multiple meanings of the verb *furu* and, instead of picking the figurative meaning "to ditch one's girlfriend," opts for the literal meaning "to shake," the audience must appreciate that this polysemy does not exist in English, thus rendering the image ridiculous. In this way, a substantial amount of English-language knowledge is required for the encounter to be interpreted as funny, whereas the segment as a whole is predicated on the prejudice that such sophistication with English is beyond most Japanese.

This type of display indicates that English plays a crucial role in imagining and performing identity and envisaging Japan and the West, the Japanese and the Other. It mirrors a type of self-critical humor found in many countries, where the ways in which locals are purported to use English are exaggerated and ridiculed through the medium of English itself (Higgins, 2014). A typical instance in the Netherlands is the book *I always get my sin: Het bizarre Engels van Nederlanders* ("The bizarre English of the Dutch"; Rijkens, 2005), a collection of comical transliterations of Dutch expressions. The title itself is derived from the Dutch *ik krijg altijd mijn zin*, meaning "I always get my own way." As with Karakuri, such examples can be seen as a response to the changes brought about by globalization and, with it, the English language: This is "humour that relies on knowledge of English as a way to critically and humorously interrogate local identities in relation to global flows" (Higgins, 2014: 22). We explore this further as we turn to our second example, from the Dutch media landscape.

15.4.2   The World Spins Through

Figure 15.1 is a post from November 2015 in *De Speld*, a Dutch-language satirical online news magazine comparable to the English-language *The Onion*.[4] It consists only of a screenshot from a (presumably) fictional Facebook thread, followed by a title and subtitle by one of *De Speld*'s writers. Readers see a status update in English by a user called Tjeerd: *Just something to think about: I watched The World Spins Through with Matthew from Newchurch and the annoyments of John Mulder yesterday. What do you guys think?*

Readers are to understand that "The World Spins Through" is a literal rendering of the title of a popular Dutch talk show, *De Wereld Draait Door*, and the names Matthew from Newchurch and John Mulder are anglicized versions of those of the host, Matthijs van Nieuwkerk, and a panelist, Jan Mulder. "The annoyments of John Mulder" refers to *De ergernissen van Jan Mulder*, a segment in which Mulder recounts things that have recently irritated him. A contact named Willem Jan has replied to the status update and Tjeerd responds in turn (referring to him as "William John"). Below the screenshot is the *Speld* title (or caption): *Tjeerd's Facebook updates are in English*, followed by the subtitle *Man supposedly has international friends*.

Like the Karakuri segment in Japan, this figure presents a challenge to academic and "official" discourses surrounding English in the Netherlands. Not only is the entire language object itself in English but it also presents a specific critique of people who purport to use English for the benefit of foreigners, while the "ulterior motive" is apparently to make oneself appear sophisticated and cosmopolitan. It shows acute awareness on the part of the *Speld* writer that, far from serving as merely a transnational communicative code, English is also deployed as

---

[4] See http://speld.nl/2015/11/17/tjeerds-facebook-updates-are-in-english/

Tjeerd de Haan

Just something to think about: I watched The World Spins Through with Matthew from Newchurch and the annoyments of John Mulder yesterday. What do you guys think?

Vind ik leuk · Reactie · 37 min. ·

👍 Marieke Mol en 2 anderen vinden dit leuk.

Willem Jan Tollenaar I respect your opinion, but I disargee with you, Tjeerd.

25 min. · Vind ik leuk · 👍 1

Tjeerd de Haan I understand your point of view William John, thank you. Let's have a drink sometimes soon, it's been to long!! How are things going in Bunnik? Is Tineke still pregnant?

24 min. · Vind ik leuk · 👍 1

Tjeerd's Facebook updates are in English

Man supposedly has international friends

17 november 2015 door Rudolf Julius

Figure 15.1 Tjeerd's Facebook updates are in English

a symbolic code for identity construction and social positioning. There is an additional layer of tongue-in-cheek humor in that the *Speld* post is itself in English, despite appearing in a magazine targeted at a Dutch audience and requiring knowledge of the Dutch language and context to appreciate the cultural references. Thus it presents a commentary on the "unnecessary" use of English through the (equally unnecessary) means of English.

Like Karakuri, the *Speld* post relies on a measure of English-language competence among its audience. However, the two examples are very different in terms of the ideology on which they are premised. While Karakuri taps into the popular ideology of the Japanese as English-incompetent, the *Speld* example references a broadly shared English-knowing identity among the Dutch and the ensuing eagerness to use it, even when not "necessary." A class-based element comes into play here, whereby the *Speld* author uses specific linguistic devices to portray Tjeerd and Willem Jan as unsophisticated and laughable:

– The inaneness of Tjeerd's status update – *Just something to think about . . . what do you guys think?* – followed by Willem Jan's response *I respect your opinion but I disargee* [sic] *with you*, when Tjeerd's post contained little of substance to either agree or disagree with.
– The absurd literal renderings of proper nouns.
– The use of spelling mistakes (e.g. *disargee, to* instead of *too*) and an unusually formal register for a Facebook thread (*I respect your opinion, I understand your point of view*), indicating a lack of pragmatic fluency despite being entirely standard in form.

– The references to Bunnik, a small town in the Netherlands, and Tineke, a female name stereotypically associated with a rural setting, which place the characters in the periphery geographically.

In this way, the author constructs a highly stylized "unsophisticated" English for Tjeerd and Willem Jan, designed to cast doubt on whether they (and the people they are supposed to represent) are really as worldly as they seek to present themselves. Juxtaposed with this is the standard English of the title and subtitle, which demonstrates the strategic manipulation of English by the writer and constructs him (and his readers) as "legitimate" users of English.

The "unsophisticated" English designed for Tjeerd and his friend recalls Furukawa's (2014) concept of "uncool English," in which certain users of English in Japan are discursively constructed as uncool and unsophisticated by means of parody. Dandy Sakano, for example, is a highly stylized comedic character who wears gaudy tuxedos, is pictured with a disco ball in the background, and points at people with both index fingers while saying "Gets!" As Furukawa explains, Sakano is supposed to represent those who consider themselves cool and slick:

> The general public has a metalinguistic awareness of the fact that English can be viewed as cool which some people then try too hard to achieve, making themselves appear un-cool. This combined with his other high performance stylizations of the character type mocks these types of people as a critique of their overuse of symbolic cool such as English to seem more appealing.   (Furukawa, 2014: 199)

Such exaggerated uses of English testify to recognition of the ways in which the language can be mobilized not just as a communicative tool but also as a symbolic code to construct in- and out-groups and voice resistance as English comes to play an increasingly prominent role in diverse local contexts.

15.5 Conclusion

In the two Expanding Circle settings explored in this chapter, vastly different though they are, English appears to serve "distinctively local needs," constructing "both a new world order and a sense of the local" (Higgins, 2009: 18) through its mobilization in different (but related) ways as a commodified and creative resource. This entrenchment of English-language social practices contributes to the unsettling of essentialized discourses on English in the Expanding Circle as primarily either a foreign language or a tool for international communication. Rather, it can be seen as an additional (or "co-available"; Cromdal 2005 cited in Leppänen and Nikula, 2007: 335) linguistic resource that is put to use in the form of translingual practice (Canagarajah, 2013) for local meaning-making in various ways.

First, far from being restricted to instructional contexts, English plays an important role in globalized mediascapes, whereby ludic media products such as those discussed here represent "a distinct form of cultural production in their own right and an integral part of the local cultural landscape" (Seargeant, 2009: 146). Further, while traditional discourses do not license Expanding Circle users to have English in their identity repertoire (Pennycook, 2003), we have seen here how it is harnessed (as both idea and linguistic resource; Seargeant, 2009) in complex, layered ways to produce as well as to critique identity constructions.

To start with Japan, the prevailing ideology is of the Japanese as English-incompetent, yet simultaneously English obsessed (which also reflects an ambiguity about Japan's identity within the global community, as at once isolated and internationally outward looking). That the non–English-knowing identity is defined in negative terms – an identity revolving around what it is not (and juxtaposing English-speaking knowledge with Japanese-speaking knowledge) – makes it no less crucial as a component of local cultural identity. Further, the construction of what counts as English and who counts as a licensed user of it can also be seen as a powerful assertion of Japanese cultural identity. Seargeant (2009) comments on cultural practices that amount to ideological erasure of unsanctioned English users and uses, establishing English as "forever foreign" vis-à-vis Japanese society. These include the insistence on hiring stereotypically Caucasian-looking teachers and the resistance to perceiving as "real" English anything that is not presented in sanctioned contexts, such as English on commercial signage that is not "read" as such but rendered invisible or merely decorative.

What is interesting is that, in this way, the public and "official" imaginary reflects academic discourses on English as a foreign language in Japan. Yet, given that the word "foreign" has particular and powerful connotations within Japanese society, the local positioning of English as a foreign language is itself, ironically, an important element of Japanese identity. Moreover, our discussion of ludic transcultural media products such as Karakuri Funniest English and comedic characters such as Dandy Sakano suggests that, paradoxically, performing and maintaining the identity of illegitimate English users requires quite "sophisticated and innovative exploitation of English language resources" (Seargeant, 2009: 147), thus giving the lie to the national mythology of the Japanese as perpetually helpless when it comes to English.

The collective identity in the Netherlands is, quite in contrast to the Japanese context, one of English-knowing. However, this assumed competence exists in tandem with the common trope that many Dutch overestimate their skills in English (Booij, 2001; Nortier, 2011), which manifests itself in a complaint tradition and criticism of anything perceived as deviant (i.e. excessive or markedly Dutch-influenced) English use. As noted in the previous section, such critique often has a class-based element, the belief that less well-educated people slavishly pepper their talk with English words in an effort to sound intelligent or sophisticated. This was apparent in the *Speld* case study, where Tjeerd's language use was held up for ridicule both in terms of linguistic form and for attempting to tap into the global indexicals of English that he was perceived as unlicensed to access.

In this way, English is implicated in Expanding Circle contexts, just as it is in other settings, in the (re)production of social hierarchies. Here we can draw on Blommaert's (2010) notion of low- and high-mobility linguistic resources. Those who have access to and the capacity to deploy high-mobility linguistic resources are able to mobilize the "power-and-identity tactics of exclusion and hierarchical ranking" (Blommaert, 2007: 7). As a consequence, others can be "outscaled" (Blommaert, 2007: 7) or disempowered: In the *Speld* example, the deliberate juxtaposition of marked (i.e. localized) and standard English resources allowed the writer to strategically construct local and global identities and (re)position himself and others in the social hierarchy, effectively denying Tjeerd a legitimate English-using identity within a global context.

Still, the picture is more nuanced than a simple societal divide between the "haves" and "have-nots" of English (Preisler, 1999). Tjeerd and his peer group were rendered laughable only when their supposedly unsophisticated English work was contrasted with purportedly more worldly usages. Read on its own terms, it affords them the opportunity to create and demonstrate linguistic and cultural capital within their own communities and to fashion their identities in their own favor (Canagarajah, 2013: 29). Indeed, such local usages are often perfectly adequate (and highly creative) within the context for which they were designed (much like seemingly nonsensical English slogans on T-shirts in Japan); it is only when they are critiqued from the perspective of wider norms that they become disqualified.

In this chapter, we have aimed to contribute to the emerging rapprochement between WEs approaches and those with a more situated and socio-cultural orientation to linguistic analysis (see also Bolton, 2013; Bolton and Meierkord, 2013; Gritsenko and Laletina, 2016; James, 2016; Leppänen and Nikula, 2007; Mair, 2016). Rather than focusing on the linguistic aftermath of colonization – the traditional focus of WEs scholars interested in "non-native" settings – these studies seek to take better account of the effects of globalization in local contexts and shed more nuanced light on notions such as identity and community, and the way in which English as a global resource plays an increasing part in their expression and negotiation. Of interest "is not so much whether or not one is born in a particular type of community but rather what one does with the language" (Pennycook, 2003: 527). In place of modernist ideas of fixed language varieties spoken by bounded, homogeneous communities and the top-down ascription of identities ("learner" versus "user"), the "new" sociolinguistics is concerned with linguistic resources, processes and practices, transcultural flows, heterogeneous social networks, language ideologies, and mixed and multiple identities (Blommaert and Rampton, 2011; Heller, 2008). By adopting such a perspective, we can see how English in the Expanding Circle offers new opportunities for people to claim agency, signify global participation, and perform identity work in ways that transcend traditional second- or foreign-language categories.

References

Ammon, U. and G. D. McConnell. 2002. *English as an Academic Language in Europe*. Frankfurt: Peter Lang.

Appadurai, A. 1990. Disjuncture and difference in the global cultural economy. *Theory, Culture and Society* 7: 295–310.

Asbeek Brusse, W. 2007. Dutch-British commercial relations in a European context. In N. Ashton and D. Hellema, eds. *Unspoken Allies: Anglo-Dutch Relations since 1780*. Amsterdam: Amsterdam University Press, 203–222.

Berns, M. 2005. Expanding on the expanding circle: Where do WE go from here? *World Englishes* 24(1): 85–93.

Berns, M., K. De Bot and U. Hasebrink. 2007. *In the Presence of English: Media and European Youth*. New York: Springer.

Blommaert, J. 2007. Sociolinguistic scales. *Intercultural Pragmatics* 4(1): 1–19.

Blommaert, J. 2010. *The Sociolinguistics of Globalization*. Cambridge: Cambridge University Press.

Blommaert, J. and B. Rampton. 2011. Language and superdiversity. *Diversities* 13(2): 1–21.

Bolton, K. 2005. Where WE stands: Approaches, issues, and debate in world Englishes. *World Englishes* 24(1): 69–83.

Bolton, K. 2012. World Englishes and linguistic landscapes. *World Englishes* 31(1): 30–33.

Bolton, K. 2013. World Englishes, globalisation, and language worlds. In N.-L. Johannesson, G. Melchers and B. Björkman, eds. *Of Butterflies and Birds, of Dialects and Genres*. Stockholm: Acta Universitatis Stockholmiensis, 227–251.

Bolton, K. and C. Meierkord. 2013. English in contemporary Sweden: Perceptions, policies, and narrated practices. *Journal of Sociolinguistics* 17(1): 93–117.

Booij, G. 2001. English as the lingua franca of Europe: A Dutch perspective. *Lingua E Stile* 36(2): 347–357.

Bruthiaux, P. 2003. Squaring the circles: Issues in modeling English worldwide. *International Journal of Applied Linguistics* 13(2): 159–178.

Bucholtz, M. and K. Hall 2005. Identity and interaction: A sociocultural linguistic approach. *Discourse Studies* 7(4–5): 585–614.

Bucholtz, M. and K. Hall 2008. All of the above: New coalitions in sociocultural linguistics. *Journal of Sociolinguistics* 12(4): 401–431.

Buschfeld, S. 2013. *English in Cyprus or Cyprus English*. Amsterdam: John Benjamins.

Canagarajah, S. 2013. *Translingual Practice*. London: Routledge.

CJGTC (Prime Minister's Commission on Japan's Goals in the Twenty-First Century). 2000. *The Frontier Within: Individual Empowerment and Better Governance in the New Millennium*.

Edwards, A. 2016. *English in the Netherlands*. Amsterdam: John Benjamins.

Edwards, A. 2018. "I'm an Anglophile, but . . .": A corpus-assisted discourse study of language ideologies in the Netherlands. In S. C. Deshors, ed., *Modelling World Englishes in the 21st Century*. Amsterdam: John Benjamins, 163–186.

Erling, E. J. 2004. Globalization, English and the German university classroom. Unpublished doctoral dissertation, Freie Universität Berlin.

European Commission. 2012. Europeans and their languages: Special Eurobarometer 386. Brussels. http://ec.europa.eu/public_opinion/archives/ebs/ebs_386_en.pdf

Furukawa, G. K. 2014. The use of English as a local language resource for identity construction in Japanese television variety shows. Unpublished doctoral dissertation, University of Hawaii at Manoa.

García, O. 2009. *Bilingual Education in the 21st Century*. Malden, MA: Blackwell.

Gerritsen, M. 1996. Engelstalige productadvertenties in Nederland: Onbemind en onbegrepen. In R. Van Hout and J. Kruijsen, eds. Taalvariaties: Toonzettingen en modulaties op een thema. Dordrecht: Foris, 67–83.

Gerritsen, M., C. Nickerson, C. Van den Brandt, R. Crijns, N. Dominguez, F. Van Meurs and U. Nederstigt. 2007. English in print advertising in Germany, Spain and the Netherlands: Frequency of occurrence, comprehensibility and the effect on corporate image. In G. Garzone and C. Ilie, eds., *The Use of English in Institutional and Business Settings: An Intercultural Perspective*. Bern: Peter Lang, 79–98.

Graddol, D. 1997. *The Future of English*. London: British Council.

Gritsenko, E. and A. Laletina 2016. English in the international workplace in Russia. *World Englishes* 35(3): 440–456.

Heinrich, P. 2012. *The Making of Monolingual Japan*. Bristol: Multilingual Matters.

Higgins, C. 2009. *English as a Local Language*. Bristol: Multilingual Matters.

Higgins, C. 2014. When scapes collide: Reterritorializing English in East Africa. In R. Rubdy and L. Alsagoff, eds. *The Global-Local Interface and Hybridity*. Bristol: Multilingual Matters, 17–42.

Hilgendorf, S. K. 2001. Language contact, convergence, and attitudes: The case of English in Germany. Unpublished doctoral dissertation, University of Illinois at Urbana-Champaign.

Hino, N. 2009. The teaching of English as an international language in Japan. *AILA Review 22*: 103–119.

Hogan, J. 2003. The social significance of English usage in Japan. *Japanese Studies 23*(1): 43–58.

Hongo, J. 2013. Abe wants TOEFL to be key exam, *Japan Times*, 25 March. www.japantimes.co.jp/news/2013/03/25/national/abe-wants-toefl-to-be-key-exam/#.Vd2iUMR4WrU

Honna, N. 1995. English in Japanese society: Language within language. *Journal of Multilingual and Multicultural Development 16*(1–2): 45–62.

Hyde, B. 2002. Japan's emblematic English. *English Today 18*(3): 12–16.

Heller, M. 2008. Language and the nation-state: Challenges to sociolinguistic theory and practice. *Journal of Sociolinguistics 12*(4): 504–524.

James, A. 2016. From code-mixing to mode-mixing in the European context. *World Englishes 35*(2): 259–275.

Kachru, B. B. 1985. Standards, codification and sociolinguistic realism: The English language in the outer circle. In R. Quirk and H. Widdowson, eds. *English in the World*. Cambridge: Cambridge University Press, 11–30.

Klaassen, J. 2002. Volkskrant aan kop bij het gebruik van Engels. *Volkskrant*, October 19. www.volkskrant.nl/vk/nl/2844/Archief/archief/article/detail/629418/2002/10/19/Volkskrant-aan-kop-bij-het- gebruik-van-Engels.dhtml

Koike, I. and H. Tanaka. 1995. English in foreign language education policy in Japan: toward the twenty-first century, *World Englishes 14*: 13–25.

Leppänen, S. and T. Nikula. 2007. Diverse uses of English in Finnish society: Discourse-pragmatic insights into media, educational and business contexts. *Multilingua 26*(4): 333–380.

Mair, C. 2016. Englishes beyond and between the three circles: World Englishes research in the age of globalisation. In E. Seoane and C. Suárez-Gómez, eds. *World Englishes*. Amsterdam: John Benjamins, 17–36.

McArthur, T. 1998. *The English Languages*. Cambridge: Cambridge University Press.

McVeigh, B. 2002. *Japanese Higher Education as Myth*. New York: M. E. Sharpe.

MECSST: Ministry of Education Culture Sports Science and Technology. 2002. Developing a strategic plan to cultivate "Japanese with English Abilities." www.gifu-net.ed.jp/kyoka/eigo/CommunicativeEnglish/RegardingtheEstablishmentofanActionPlantoCultivate%A1%C8JapanesewithEnglishAbilities%A1%C9.htm

Meierkord, C. 2012. *Interactions across Englishes*. Cambridge: Cambridge University Press.

Moody, A. 2006. English in Japanese popular culture and J-Pop music. *World Englishes 25*(2): 209–222.

Moody, A. and Y. Matsumoto. 2003. "Don"t Touch My Moustache": Language blending and code ambiguation by two J-Pop artists. *Asian Englishes* 6(1): 4–33.

Mukherjee, J. and M. Hundt. 2011. *Exploring Second-Language Varieties of English and Learner Englishes*. Amsterdam: John Benjamins.

Nortier, J. 2011. The more languages, the more English? A Dutch perspective. In A. Houwer and A. Wilton, eds. *English in Europe Today*. Amsterdam: John Benjamins, 113–132.

Norton, B. 2000. *Identity and Language Learning*. Harlow: Pearson.

Pennycook, A. 2003. Global Englishes, Rip Slyme, and performativity. *Journal of Sociolinguistics* 7(1992): 513–533.

Pennycook, A. 2007. *Global Englishes and Transcultural Flows*. London: Routledge.

Piller, I. 2003. Advertising as a site of language contact. *Annual Review of Applied Linguistics* 23: 170–183.

Preisler, B. 1999. Functions and forms of English in a European EFL country. In T. Bex and R. Watts, eds., *Standard English*. London : Routledge, 239–267.

Rampton, B. 2007. Neo-Hymesian linguistic ethnography. *Journal of Sociolinguistics* 11(5): 584–607.

Ridder, S. 1995. English in Dutch. *English Today* 11(4): 44–50.

Rijkens, M. H. 2005. *I always get my sin*. The Hague: BZZToH.

Schrauwers, A. 2006. *Stichting Nederlands*, News Brief No. 17, November 8. www.stichtingnederlands.nl/nieuwsbrief17.pdf.

Seargeant, P. 2009. *The Idea of English in Japan*. Bristol: Multilingual Matters.

Seargeant, P. 2011. The symbolic meaning of visual English in the social landscape of Japan. In P. Seargeant, ed. *English in Japan in the Era of Globalization*. Basingstoke: Palgrave Macmillan, 187–204.

Terasawa, T. 2012. "Ninety percent of Japanese do not need English"? Statistical analysis of workers' needs to use English. *Kantokoshinetsu Association of Teacher of English (KATE) Journal* 27(71–83): 71–83.

Tusting, K. and J. Maybin. 2007. Linguistic ethnography and interdisciplinarity: Opening the discussion. *Journal of Sociolinguistics* 11(5): 575–583.

Van der Haagen, M. 1998. *Caught Between Norms: The English Pronunciation of Dutch Learners*. The Hague: HAG.

Van der Horst, H. 2012. *The Low Sky: Understanding the Dutch*. Schiedam: Scriptum.

Van Goor, J. 2007. The colonial factor in Anglo-Dutch relations 1780–1820. In N. Ashton and D. Hellema, eds. *Unspoken Allies: Anglo-Dutch Relations since 1780*. Amsterdam: Amsterdam University Press, 17–32.

Vásquez, C. 2014. "Usually not one to complain but … ": Constructing identities in user-generated online reviews. In P. Seargeant and C. Tagg, eds. *The Language of Social Media*. Basingstoke: Palgrave Macmillan, 65–90.

Verspoor, M., K. De Bot and X. Xu. 2011. The role of input and scholastic aptitude in second language development. *Toegepaste Taalwetenschap 86(2):* 93–107.

Wächter, B. and F. Maiworm. 2014. *English-Taught Programmes in European Higher Education.* Bonn: Lemmens.

Woodward, K. 1997. Concepts of identity and difference. In K. Woodward, ed. *Identity and Difference.* London: Sage, 8–48.

Yano, Y. 2011. English as an international language, and "Japanese English." In P. Seargeant, ed. *English in Japan in the Era of Globalization.* Basingstoke: Palgrave Macmillan, 125–142.

Yano, Y. 2001. World Englishes in 2000 and beyond. *World Englishes 20(2):* 119–132.

Yoshida, R. 2013. Conflict between learners' beliefs and actions: Speaking in the classroom. *Language Awareness 22(4):* 371–388.

Zegers, V. and R. Wilkinson. 2005. Squaring the pyramid: Internationalization, plurilingualism, and the university. Paper presented at the Bi- and Multilingual Universities: Challenges and Future Prospects Conference, University of Helsinki, September 1–3, 2005.

16

World Englishes in Cyberspace

Christian Mair

Before mobile phones became a thing, there was a very clear distinction between "online" and "offline". You went on the Internet to go and hang out with people in cyberspace, the space that is no space, a realm of ideas and representations. The online world has since begun colonizing the offline world – software is eating the world.

http://visakanv.com/reviews/information-superhighway/[1]

16.1   Introduction

By the time the Internet and the World Wide Web started taking off as mass phenomena in the mid-1990s, English had been established as the global *lingua franca* for several decades. This of course did not mean that the world was headed for a monolingual English future, nor even that the majority of the world's population was on the way to becoming fluent in English as a Second Language (ESL). What it meant was that, for the first time in human history, a "World Language System" (de Swaan 2002, 2010) had come into being that integrated the world's several thousand languages on four hierarchical layers:

- **hyper-central language:** English
- **super-central languages:** Arabic, Chinese, English, French, German, Hindi, Japanese, Malay, Portuguese, Russian, Spanish, and Swahili[2]

---

[1] This philosophy blogger, physically apparently based in Singapore, is "on a quest to write 1,000,000 words in 1,000 essays of 1,000 words each. Updated (hopefully) 1–2 times a day" (https://twitter.com/1000wordvomits).

[2] In the updated 2010 version, de Swaan (2010: 57) adds Turkish to this list, presumably in recognition of the growing importance of the Turkish migrant diaspora and the role of Turkish as a regional lingua franca in the Turk-speaking zones of post-Soviet Central Asia.

- **central languages:** e.g. Dutch, Finnish, Korean
- **peripheral languages:** the remaining 6,000 plus languages of the world

According to de Swaan (2010: 56), the World Language System constitutes "a surprisingly efficient, strongly ordered, hierarchical network, which ties together – directly or indirectly – the 6.5 billion inhabitants of the earth at the global level." Alongside the political, economic, ecological, and cultural dimensions, it can be said to represent the linguistic dimension of globalization, drawing attention to the impact of globalization on language use and at the same time recognizing the partial autonomy of the linguistic dynamics of globalization from the other dimensions.

In de Swaan's system, English, as the single hyper-central language, acts as the hub of the World Language System. It is thus a potentially relevant contact language for all other languages in the system. Super-central languages are major standard languages with transnational reach. Central languages are also standardized and usually institutionally recognized at the national level. Peripheral languages tend to be spoken by demographically small communities and often lack a written standard and other institutional support. As we move down the hierarchy, the number of languages tends to get larger: one at the top, a dozen or so on the second tier, around 150 on the third, and the vast majority at the bottom. Borderline cases exist. For example, in the first half of the twentieth century, Yiddish had transnational reach, a written form (based on the Hebrew script), a lively press, and a vibrant literary tradition. Nevertheless, it would have sat somewhat uneasily among the super-central languages because, with an estimated ten million speakers at the time, its demographic weight was more in line with what one would expect from a central language. In fact, one could argue that its lack of full institutional recognition in any and all of the nation-states in which it was spoken even pushed it toward the peripheral category. Such borderline cases notwithstanding, the system as a whole serves as a generally reliable and robust guide to power relations among languages – or rather, among their communities of speakers.

Computer-mediated communication (CMC) first became popular in the English-speaking world, which raised fears that English might monopolize this new domain of communication. As we now know (e.g. Danet and Herring 2007; Gao 2006; Williams 2009), this has not happened. Table 16.1 shows the top-ten Internet languages (as of June 30, 2017).

With the exception of Japanese and German, all languages have registered faster growth rates than English, which corroborates the trend toward selective multilingualism on the Web. Table 16.1 shows that the hierarchies of the World Language System apply to cyberspace, as well. English does not monopolize the Internet but, in the shape of Standard American English, it currently clearly serves as its default language. This

Table 16.1 *Top ten Internet languages*

	Users	User growth (2000–2017)
English	984,703,501	599.6%
Chinese	770,797,306	2,286.1%
Spanish	312,069,111	1,616.4%
Arabic	184,631,496	7,247.3%
Portuguese	158,399,082	1,990.8%
Malay	157,580,091	2,650.1%
Japanese	118,453,595	151.6%
Russian	109,552,842	3,434.0%
French	108,014,564	800.2%
German	84,700,419	207.8%

Source: www.internetworldstats.com/stats7.htm

can easily be demonstrated from web-sourced corpora such as GloWbE, which show that British spellings (e.g. *fibre, honour*) and lexical Briticisms (e.g. *blokes*) are broadly confined to the historical British sphere of colonial influence, whereas the corresponding American forms (*fiber, honor, dudes*) register a significant presence in all varieties, including British English itself. Consider, by way, of example, the distribution of *bloke(s)* and *dude(s)* in this corpus (Figures 16.1 and 16.2).

As can be seen (Figure 16.1), *bloke(s)* does not have much currency beyond the UK, Australia, and New Zealand (not even in Ireland), whereas *dude(s)* (Figure 16.2) shows considerable seepage into other varieties, with Nigeria and Singapore, two historically British English–using nations, coming close to US levels of usage.

Yet, from the web of varieties of English back to the multilingual web, all of the top-ten languages on the Internet are from the hyper-central and super-central layers. Of course, we do not expect the multilingualism of cyberspace to mirror that of the real world exactly, such that all the world's 6,000 plus languages receive proportional representation in this new medium. Dor (2004) studied the complex cluster of demographic, cultural, and economic factors that make the world's central languages fit or unfit for the Internet. Note, however, that the connection between modernity, technological progress, and loss of linguistic diversity is not absolute and inevitable: among the languages **benefiting** from the Web are some of the world's most peripheral and endangered ones (Eisenlohr 2004; Cormack 2007).

What Table 16.1 does not show is another dimension of growth that is very important for the study of World Englishes in cyberspace, namely growth in the volume of Internet traffic. For the first fifteen years of mass Internet use, growth in volume largely meant growth in textual data and

US	CA	GB	IE	AU	NZ	IN	LK	PK	BD	SG	MY	PH	HK	ZA	NG	GH	KE	TZ	JM
414	79	5234	504	4296	1019	174	79	65	19	76	140	35	97	121	87	72	75	40	27
1.07	0.59	13.50	4.99	28.99	12.52	1.80	1.70	1.27	0.48	1.77	3.36	0.81	2.40	2.67	2.04	1.86	1.83	1.14	0.68

Figure 16.1 [bloke] (lemma search) in GloWbE, absolute number of occurrences (row 2) and normalized frequencies per million words (row 3)

US	CA	GB	IE	AU	NZ	IN	LK	PK	BD	SG	MY	PH	HK	ZA	NG	GH	KE	TZ	JM
10649	1980	3172	602	1744	719	879	240	601	196	712	489	455	270	669	959	319	586	238	446
27.53	14.69	8.18	5.96	11.77	8.83	9.12	5.15	11.70	4.96	16.57	11.74	10.52	6.67	14.75	22.49	8.23	14.27	6.77	11.27

Figure 16.2 [dude] (lemma search) in GloWbE, absolute number of occurrences (row 2) and normalized frequencies per million words (row 3)

images. From around 2010, this started to change. The amount of text and images has continued to increase in a steady, linear fashion, whereas the amount of audiovisual and multimodal language data has exploded. Two separate estimates of mobile Internet traffic undertaken in 2014 put the share of YouTube at 17 and 18 percent, respectively, in March and September of that year.[3] Unfortunately, this wealth of audiovisual data tends to elude linguists who search the Internet for written forms (but, for an exploratory assessment of the value of YouTube for the study of World Englishes, see Schneider 2016).

16.2 Scope

In view of the pervasive presence of the English language in the world's linguistic ecology, it is important to define the focus of the present survey on "World Englishes in cyberspace" clearly and narrowly. One type of work that I cannot review in detail is that produced in the still-dominant paradigm, the discourse analysis of CMC (see, e.g., Maynor 1994; Collot and Belmore 1996; Dürscheid 2004; Crystal 2006; Baron 2008). Such studies tend to be based on data produced by mainstream speakers of the major natively spoken varieties. The emphasis is less on geographical, social, and ethnic variation than on questions such as whether or not the language of the Internet should be seen as a coherent register ("Netspeak") or how language use in CMC positions itself with regard to the traditional spoken and written modalities (see, e.g., Sand 2013). Note, however, that there is a latent sociolinguistic dimension even in the discourse analysis of CMC (Bolander and Locher 2014). For example, the boundary between informality and nonstandardness is fuzzy and language ideologically motivated processes of enregisterment (Squires 2010) are common online and offline.

Its central role in the World Language System makes English universally available as a contact language for other languages – probably online even more so than offline – which has led to a fascinating range of multilingual practices and hybrid repertoires (e.g. Androutsopoulos 2006c; Fung and Carter 2007; Williams 2009; Zhang 2012; Ooi and Tan 2014; Montes-Alcalá 2016). This phenomenon cannot be documented exhaustively in this survey, either; however, as the Web has become an almost perfect showcase for the multilingual contexts in which English functions as a global language, exemplary illustration of the phenomenon will be provided in Section 16.3.

While the discourse analysis of CMC is about twenty-five years old, the sociolinguistics of CMC has consolidated during the past ten years (for an

---

[3] Sandvine consultancy gives the share of YouTube as 17.26 percent of peak time mobile Internet traffic in North America for March 2014. BI (Business Intelligence) has 18 percent, measured on the same criteria, for September.

early outlier, see Paolillo 2001; for the inauguration of the trend, see Androutsopoulos 2006a, 2006b). The first textbook on the sociolinguistics of digital Englishes (Friedrich and Diniz de Figueiredo, 2016) was only published in 2016. In addition to studying how speakers and languages adapt to the demands of the new medium, the sociolinguistic approach also concentrates on how communities of practice (Meyerhoff 2002) use linguistic resources to express social identities in CMC. To illustrate this shift of emphasis, the following is a simple example: Nonstandard spellings have been listed among the salient linguistic features of CMC from the very start but only in more recent sociolinguistically oriented studies (e.g. Hinrichs 2006; Deuber and Hinrichs 2007, Rajah-Carrim 2009; Hinrichs and White-Sustaíta 2011; Moll 2015) is their full importance beginning to be recognized. They are not studied in their own right, as mere linguistic features, but as the constitutive elements of coherent digital literacy practices, which are partly autonomous from offline sociolinguistic orders but certainly not totally disconnected from them. This is nowhere more obvious than in postcolonial constellations, where currents of migration in the real world frequently combine with the flow of nonstandard language in the new media and the business activities of the global entertainment industry. The study of World Englishes in cyberspace therefore has its core and its most immediate frame of reference at the intersection of the sociolinguistics of globalization (Blommaert 2010, Coupland, ed. 2010), the sociolinguistics of CMC, and postcolonial cultural studies.

This intersection will be explored by means of two case studies, with the first (Section 16.3) focusing on prestige change of standard and nonstandard varieties in CMC and the second (Section 16.4) presenting CMC as a powerful agent in the democratization of multilingual writing practices. Building on work on cultural globalization by Appadurai (1996), the concluding Section 16.5 will propose the concept of *languagescapes* as the appropriate tool to understand the use of (nonstandard) varieties of English in CMC.

16.3 Nonstandard Englishes: Crossing and Prestige Change on the Web

In studies of postcolonial diasporic web forums from Nigeria and Jamaica,[4] I have repeatedly noted a tendency toward change of sociolinguistic prestige of the following type: A nationally prestigious new standard, such as Jamaican Standard English and Nigerian Standard English, tends to "dissipate" in CMC, whereas the corresponding nonstandard forms, Jamaican Creole and Nigerian Pidgin, continue to thrive in the new medium. In the

---

[4] See Mair 2013b for a survey of the project.

heterogeneous transnational and diasporic "communities of practice" (Meyerhoff 2002) that support the forum communication, the stigma that still attaches to pidgins and creoles offline ceases to matter, while their strong covert prestige ensures them a continuing role as potent symbols of identification with one's own community and, simultaneously, as efficient rhetorical devices for negotiating the boundaries between the in-group and various out-groups. This latter function, it should be added, stimulates extensive "crossing" (Rampton 1995, 2006) by out-group members.

I will briefly illustrate the phenomenon with data from the "Corpus of Cyber-Nigerian (CCN)." Published work on this corpus (e.g. Mair 2013a; Heyd and Mair 2014) is based on a preliminary version containing ca. 17.3 million words produced by 11,718 forum contributors (covering the years from 2005 to 2008). This is a lot of material but still insufficient to investigate some of the less common features of Nigerian Standard English. For the present study, I will therefore rely on the expanded version (CCN2), which is still under development and currently features 843.1 million words from 302,714 members (covering the years from 2005 to 2014).

A well-known feature of noun-phrase grammar in Nigerian Standard English is the use of plural forms for what are non-count collective or abstract nouns in International English. Examples mentioned in Alo and Mesthrie (2004: 821) include *advice, aircraft, behaviour, blame, deadwood, equipment, information, personnel* and *underwear*. Similar cases are *stuffs* and *supports*, as illustrated in Examples (1) and (2):

(1)   hmmmmmmmmmmmmmmmmmmmmmmmmmmmm. i have heard **all sort of bad stuffs** about the dude. who am i to judge so i wldn't say anything about the dude. (CCN2, 2005)

(2)   But this time he/she needs **your supports** more than ever. (CCN2, 2005)

To give a quantitative picture of the dissipation of Standard Nigerian English in cyberspace, Table 16.2 lists the number of documents (i.e. single posts to the Web) containing instances of *stuffs, supports, equipments* and compares these findings with the use of some variety-neutral English vocabulary, some well-known British and American spelling and lexical variants, and – finally and most importantly – with three indicators of the use of Nigerian Pidgin. The data have not been manually post-edited but the impact of these minor issues of precision and recall in the corpus searches on the overall trends are negligible.[5]

---

[5] The most obvious source of statistical noise is, of course, the fact that the frequencies refer to the number of documents containing the searched-for form at least once rather than the frequencies of the forms themselves. In addition, there are problems specific to the individual searches. The widest margin of error has to be taken into account for *stuffs*. First, the plural form *stuffs* is fully acceptable in International English in compounds such as *food stuffs* (also written as *food-stuffs*,

Table 16.2 *Corpus of Cyber-Nigerian (CCN) – Nigerian English, British and American English, and Nigerian Pidgin forms used by top 200 posters*

User based in→ Variable ↓	Nigeria	USA	UK
get	275,763	100,958	105,459
thing	115,396	45,953	43,069
mother	20,068	10,392	8,663
mum	8,589	2,230	4,446
mom	4,327	4,293	1,373
travelling	2,779	733	1,392
traveling	1,238	510	606
equipments	718	222	146
stuffs	3,494	1,354	1,246
my|your|his|her|our|their supports	36	10	9
abi	43,737	10,397	14,580
na wa	16,923	5,010	5,738
wetin be	2,521	703	976

The frequencies for *get* and *thing* can serve as pointers to the average distribution of text produced in the three regions. They show that, for regionally and socially unmarked search items such as these, somewhat more than half of the forum data (57 and 56 percent, respectively) come from Nigeria itself. A clear deviation from this expectation is observed for *mother* and its local British and American variants *mum* and *mom*. Nigeria and the UK show the historically expected preference for the British form *mum*, whereas the forum data from the USA show the informal American term *mom* to dominate, caused by Nigerian Americans' readiness to assimilate to prevailing norms in the USA. The most interesting fact about the spelling of the double <l> in *travel(l)ing* is not the preference, however slight in the USA, for the historically expected British spelling but rather how widely current the American spelling has become in Nigeria itself and among Nigerians resident in the UK. This is a case of American norms and conventions being imposed on the traditional variability within the global "English Language Complex" (to use the term introduced by McArthur 2003 and popularized through its use in Mesthrie and Bhatt 2008) as a

foodstuffs). The three spellings account for 2,226 out of a total of 31,638 cases, which is a margin of error that should be borne in mind (note that the figures 31,638 and 2,226 refer to the total concordance output and are therefore considerably larger than the geolocalized posts produced by the top 200 posters in Table 16.2). Second, as CCN is not tagged for part of speech at the moment, another potential source of error is the overcollection of verbal third-person singular forms. Here, there is consolation in the fact that a mere forty-seven cases instantiate the sequences *he\|she\|it stuffs* (with even some of these containing nominal plurals: e.g. "anything dat comes out of **it, stuffs** like 'i dont want u anymore', 'stop calling me', 'it cant work out anymore'." – CCN2, 2005). The margin of error is somewhat greater for *supports*, which is why Table 16.2 gives the frequencies for the specific nominal forms *my\|your\|his\|her\|our\|their supports*.

globally operating homogenizing force – a development that is spear-headed by the Internet and the World Wide Web.

For *equipments* and *stuffs*, 66 and 62 percent of the cases are produced by contributors from Nigeria, which is above the expected default distribution. A similar value (65 percent) is obtained, on the basis of a much smaller but qualitatively tidier sample, for *supports*. Nigeria, as the territorial base of Nigerian Standard English, is over-represented.

It seems plausible to expect a similar erosion of Pidgin beyond its territorial home base. A lot of factors work against the use of Pidgin on the forum, starting with the forum guidelines, which strongly discourage it.[6] Specifically with regard to the diaspora, knowledge of Pidgin is expected to decline, particularly among second- and third-generation Nigerian immigrants, so that the pool of competent users would be smaller in the USA and the UK. In this light, the fact that 37, 39, and 40 percent, respectively, of the instances of *abi*, *na wa*, and *wetin be* do not come from Nigeria but from the UK and the USA, is definitely worth noting. This strongly suggests that Pidgin retains its function also in the diaspora and we have at most slow erosion, where, in the case of Nigerian Standard English, we have immediate loss of prestige in contact with British and American Standard English and, hence, almost instantaneous loss of function. What maintains Nigerian Standard English among the participants based in the UK and the USA is the inertia of first-generation users, whose old linguistic habits die hard. Pidgin, on the other hand, continues to be cultivated actively.

In a qualitative analysis of the data, the persistent attractiveness of Nigerian Pidgin in the digital diaspora becomes evident in numerous ways, for example in the "Pidgin English Thread,"[7] which turns the forum into a classroom for the teaching and learning of Pidgin. Participant *mruknaijaboy*, who indicates his dual affiliation to the UK and Nigeria (here represented in its hypocoristic form *Naija*) even in his name, deplores his lack of competence and invites fellow contributors to the thread to correct him (Example (3):

(3)   nairaland wetin dey, i no sabi blow pidgin like una sake of say dem born me for jand na im make me no sabi am well, i go try sha, i dey learn am small small from una for dis thread, mak una correct me if una see mistake for my pidgin, how una dey? (CCN2, 2009)
[*Nairaland, what's happening? I can't speak pidgin like you, because I was born in England. That's why I don't know it well. I'll try though, and I am learning it slowly from you on this thread. Let's you correct me if you see mistakes in my pidgin. How are you?*]

---

[6] "**Nairaland** is an English-language forum. English happens to be our official language in Nigeria. [I]t also happens to be the language of the web. Please make every effort to use clear English at all times: [. . .] Avoid pidgin English, but 'put am inside italics' if you need to use pidgin English." (www.nairaland.com/6/nairaland-forum-participation-guidelines)

[7] See www.nairaland.com/246047/pidgin-english-thread for the original version in the Nairaland forum. This thread was active with about 700 contributions between March 2009 and July 2012.

Participant *talina*, who according to her profile is based in Canada, joins the conversation in a Pidgin that is rudimentary by comparison – restricted to the phrase *wetin dey* ("what's happening?"). Realizing her limitations, she announces her intention to withdraw from the conversation. Another participant, however, encourages her to stay on and learn on the Web, providing a first simple and helpful rule (Example (4)):

(4)   @talina, Yessoo but for authenticity jus sprinkle it with o . . . so u can
       say *fine o* (CCN2, 2009)

Clearly, talina's is not a case of fluent spoken Pidgin being reduced to writing in CMC but rather a case of building up a viable digital/visual ethnolinguistic repertoire from the resources that happen to be at hand – a situation that I expect to be very common wherever nonstandard varieties of languages are used in digital communication.

Such exchanges are made possible by the community structure of the forum as a meeting place for Nigerian locals – who are usually viewed as the authorities on proper Pidgin usage – and other, more heterogeneous participants in the diaspora: first- and second-generation emigrants and people whose affiliation with Nigeria is even more indirect, for example through a spouse or people in their peer group. Based on such CMC data, we can investigate the transformation of a previously oral vernacular into a written ethnolinguistic repertoire (Benor 2010; Heyd and Mair 2014).

16.4 Multilingual Digital Repertoires: English–Spanish Code-Switching on the Web

The two world languages English and Spanish have been in contact in many parts of the world: in the Philippines a little more than a century ago, when the USA took over from Spain as the colonial power, or today in Belize (Central America) or Gibraltar. For a number of reasons, however, English–Spanish bilingualism in the USA is a special site of contact. For one thing, the number of speakers involved is very high. The 2010 US Census puts the "Hispanic" population at slightly more than 50 million, which represents about 16 percent of the national total. Not every person identifying as "Hispanic" will speak Spanish fluently and there will be regular speakers of Spanish who do not identify as "Hispanic" for census purposes. Nevertheless, the figures are a good first indicator of the possible extent of Spanish–English bilingualism. What is more important for the present purpose (the sociolinguistics of cyberspace) is that both American English and US Spanish wield significant transnational media power, not least on the Internet. This has long been obvious for English but is only beginning to be acknowledged for US Spanish. The US-based

Spanish-language media industry is commercially and culturally influential throughout Latin America – to the extent that it has become a force in shaping contemporary language standards (Hofmann 2007).

Web-based communities of practice may be dispersed geographically but, in the case of US Latinos, there are also strong corresponding communities on the ground. This becomes apparent from an innovative and dynamic map of multilingualism in New York City produced by British geographer James Cheshire, based on large open digital datasets.[8] The raw data for this map are a multilingual corpus of tweets collected from the New York region, which is put through automatic language recognition in order to identify the top-ten languages. These are English, Spanish, Portuguese, Japanese, Russian, Korean, French, Turkish, Arabic, and Italian (in that order). After the elimination of eight million tweets in English (the local default language), the remaining nine languages are color-coded and tweets are mapped on geographical space. As reproduction of this multicolored, graphically complex, and interactive map in black and white does not do full justice to the cartographer's achievement, the interested reader is referred to the original website.[9]

For the present discussion, it will suffice to summarize the two main conclusions that can be drawn from the blue blots and webs on this map that represent the spatial distribution of 228,000 Spanish-language tweets collected in this experiment. Manhattan emerges as an intensely multilingual modern Babylon, in which the blue dots are mixed with all the other colors. This multilingualism combines the multilingualism of the permanent resident population and the workforce commuting in and out of Manhattan daily, but, of course, more so the even greater linguistic diversity of a cosmopolitan and transient mass of visitors. Outside of Manhattan, however, the blue dots fall into a different pattern, a web of thin blue lines radiating from the center. Spanish speakers/tweeters are found along the major thoroughfares of Brooklyn and the Bronx and, across the Hudson River, in New Jersey. In such a constellation, it makes sense to also consider language use in the social media when investigating communities on the ground, and it makes even more sense to discuss English–Spanish code-switching on the Web with reference to the offline sociolinguistic order (Silva-Corvalán 1994; Otheguy and Zentella 2012; Escobar & Potowski 2015). This is the approach taken in a study by Montes-Alcalá (2016), who studies Spanish–English code-switching in a corpus covering the three CMC genres of blogs, email, and social media. She points out that:

> most of the stylistic and social functions traditionally displayed in (conversational) oral code-switching may also be present in CMC given the fact that this mode of communication, despite being written, shares many similarities with oral, face-to-face, interaction.   (p. 29)

[8] See http://spatial.ly/   [9] See http://spatial.ly/2013/02/mapped-twitter-languages-york/

Montes-Alcalá distinguishes five functional types of switching, which I illustrate with one typical example each:[10]

(1) Quotes:

Y me pregunta "Does it look corny?"

(2) Emphasis:

Qué relación más rara [. . .] muy *WEIRD!*

(3) Elaboration:

[. . .] my cousins (*primos segundos*) who I didn't know

(4) **Culturally bound switches: Isolated nouns and idiomatic expressions, discourse and identity markers, and linguistic routines:**

Tuve una linda sorpresa de *Valentine's Day love u*

(5) Triggered switches:

Los Angeles and Colorado will be the only *recuerdos de lo que hubo anteriormente*

Obviously, all five types occur in offline and online communication but I have printed type (4) in bold because it is the one that Montes-Alcalá finds to be more common online than offline. She also notes that speakers are more likely to switch in blogs and email than in social media.

The higher frequency of switches in blogs may have to do with what Keefe and Padilla (1987), in a study of Mexican Americans, have referred to as selective acculturation and situational ethnicity:

> For native-born Mexican Americans, the ethnic community is made up of Mexican Americans who have **selectively acculturated** and inter-act with Anglos, as well as other Mexican Americans. However, the content and degree of interethnic interaction is governed by time and place and reflects a **situational ethnicity**. At times, some of our respondents are Mexican *Americans*, part of the larger society, knowl-edgeable about American culture and interacting with the mainstream population. At other times, the same respondents are American *Mexicans*, carrying on traditional culture, taking pride in their heritage, and tied intimately to others of similar ethnicity. At still other times, they are Chicanos, practicing new and emergent cultural patterns and sustaining an ethnic community set apart from both Anglos and recent immigrant Mexicans. (p. 190, emphases added)

Written vernacular performances featuring culturally motivated code-switches between Spanish and English did not originate in digital communication, of course. They have clear analogues in print. Consider the following extract from Puerto Rican poet Tato Laviera's "my graduation speech," published in the collection *La carreta made a u-turn* ("The car made a u-turn," the title itself an example of a cultural switch):

---

[10] The examples are Montes-Alcalá's, although I have abridged them to save space here.

> i think in spanish
> i write in english
> i want to go back to puerto rico,
> but i wonder if my kind could live
> in ponce, mayagüez and carolina
> tengo las venas aculturadas
> escribo en spanglish
> abraham in español
> abraham in english
> tato in spanish
> "taro" in english
> tonto in both languages
> how are you?
> ¿cómo estás?
> i don't know if i'm coming
> or si me fui ya
>
> (Laviera 1992: 17)

Although the poet may have seen bilingual writing as the path to wide popular appeal in his community, the readership of poetry collections tends to remain limited in number. Clearly, CMC has provided an environment in which similar practices have been taken up by large numbers of grassroots writers, who can thus be said to have truly democratized a formerly elite cultural practice. Similar trends can be observed for several pidgin and creole languages, which too were not widely used in writing before the advent of CMC but have gained a significant digital presence (see, e.g., Deuber and Hinrichs 2007; Hinrichs 2006; Moll 2015 for Jamaican Creole; Heyd and Mair 2014 for Nigerian Pidgin; Rajah-Carrim 2009 for Mauritian Creole).

16.5 Conclusion

As the case studies presented in Sections 16.3 and 16.4 have shown, the World Wide Web and CMC have become domains that need to be included in any comprehensive study of the forms and functions of World Englishes today: "A look at the sociolinguistics of digital Englishes is crucial to the understanding of the sociolinguistics of globalization, since Englishes and the Internet are such a big part of how we experience globalization in today's age" (Friedrich and Diniz de Figueiredo 2016: 168). The New Englishes, including many nonstandard forms, have a massive presence in cyberspace, and this is not just the result of speakers' arbitrary individual choices and experimental playfulness. Rather, cyberspace has been developing a sociolinguistic order of its own, which – though partly autonomous and innovative in the way in which speakers respond to the demands and opportunities of the new medium – nevertheless remains connected to the sociolinguistic norms that regulate language use in the "English Language Complex" (McArthur 2003; Mesthrie and Bhatt 2008) as a whole. The specific role of CMC is as one of several potent mobilizing forces for the linguistic resources available in World Englishes.

World Englishes have long been mobile on the ground, through currents of migration, colonization, and the creation of diaspora communities. Even the traditional media, whether print or audiovisual, have intensified this mobility, for example by making American books available for British readers or by showing Hollywood movies and US television series to global audiences. No doubt, the Internet has weakened the links between "variety," "territory," and "speech community" even more – sometimes drastically. Indeed, it might seem that, as far as cyberspace is concerned, all Englishes are now everywhere (which, of course, is not saying that cyberspace is a linguistic democracy in which all varieties are equal).

One consequence of this new textual mobility is that the very notion of "variety of English" has come under scrutiny. Seargeant and Tagg (2011), for example, present their study of Thai–English code-switching in CMC under the heading of "a post-varieties approach." Similarly, Heyd and Mair (2014) consider language practices on the Nigerian diasporic Web as "digital ethnolinguistic repertoires" that draw on real-word languages such as English (in its many varieties), Nigerian Pidgin, and Yoruba and Igbo but combine these linguistic resources in ways that do not always have straightforward analogues in face-to-face interaction. Use of nonstandard language on the Internet is best seen as "mediated performance" (Coupland 2009) of the vernacular, which – in combination with the anonymity frequently afforded by the World Wide Web – encourages "crossing" (Rampton 1995, 2006), particularly of the disaffiliative and hostile kind.

Another notable feature of cyber-dialects is prestige change. What is a stigmatized vernacular on the ground may become a hot commodity (in the material and immaterial senses of the term) on the Web – particularly in the context of the linguistic and cultural "hyper-awareness" provided by postcolonial contexts. As (Bhatt 2010: 520) puts it,

> One of the defining features of globalisation is the increasingly complex and multifaceted interactions of localism and globalism. The post-colonial contexts present us with a vibrant site where local linguistic forms – inflected by the nexus of activities taking place elsewhere in time and space – are constantly transforming in response to asymmetric exchanges, pluralized histories, power plays, and battles over polysemous signs. The transformation makes available a semiotic space where a repertoire of identities evolves in the inter-animation of the colonial-global and of the indigenous local.

As I have shown, speakers do not invest in Nigerian Standard English in the diaspora for very long but keep Nigerian Pidgin going into the second and third generations.[11] Similarly, the transnational reach and media power of Jamaican Creole far exceeds that of Standard Jamaican English. "Thus, in the case of digital Englishes ... sociolinguistic scales and orders of indexicality are being negotiated by individuals most – if not all – of the time" (Friedrich and Diniz de Figueiredo 2016: 168).

Friedrich and Diniz de Figueiredo invoke Zygmunt Bauman's notion of "liquid modernity" to explore what might be happening to languages in CMC. Bauman (2007: 1) defines the passage from the "solid" to the "liquid" phase of modernity as a move to

> social forms (structures that limit individual choices, institutions that guard repetitions of routines, patterns of acceptable behaviour) [which] can no longer (and are not expected) to keep their shape for long, because they decompose and melt faster than the time it takes to cast them, and once they are cast for them to set. Forms, whether already present or only adumbrated, are unlikely to be given enough time to solidify, and cannot serve as frames of reference for human actions and long-term life strategies because of their short life expectation: indeed, a life expectation shorter than the time it takes to develop a cohesive and consistent strategy, and still shorter than the fulfilment of an individual "life project" requires.

At first sight, it seems tempting to take this metaphor to account for the massive and unpredictable ebbs and flows of the most varied linguistic resources that we can witness in cyberspace. Friedrich and Diniz de Figueiredo (2016: 164) ask whether "Englishes in the digital social formation (i. e. **digital Englishes**) are indeed in a liquid state, as they do not seem to have a regular shape that is based on specific norms and institutions, or regular patterns that can be expected" but do not answer their own question in an unreserved affirmative. Their main argument is a practical one: As the digital age is still very young, we simply cannot tell yet whether the suspected liquefaction of language will go on unchecked or come to a halt (or even be reversed).

To this, I would like to add some more principled reservations. Empirical sociolinguistic case studies of CMC show again and again that cyberspace is not the protean "space that is no space" in which all languages can be encountered everywhere and no single language manifests itself in a definable and stable (i.e. "solid") form. As long as the buying power that the speakers of a language command in the real world continues to have an impact on its presence on the Web, cyberspace will not be completely

---

[11] In diasporic contexts, this process will result in structural simplification (in comparison to the "model" spoken vernacular in Nigeria), particularly in situations in which CMC writing assumes an important role in transmission.

detached from the offline sociolinguistic orders. Many linguistic norms may have become fluid in CMC but some remain surprisingly solid. To give a trivial but obvious example: Despite automatically generated search suggestions and corrections, deep learning, and robots responding to the human voice, reliable keyboard skills and familiarity with the orthography of Standard American English still help enormously when searching and using the World Wide Web.

The concept that I would like to propose as the most helpful one in the task of integrating the sociolinguistics of cyberspace and the sociolinguistics of globalization is that of the *languagescape* – a term that has no general currency yet but which I am not the first to use, either. Mary Louise Pratt (2011: 279) has defined it as follows:

> In the global languagescape, new forms of linguistic distribution are in play. In electronic form, any language can travel anywhere any time. With access to tools, anyone can appropriate, broadcast, download, study any language they want, for any purpose they want, without asking permission.

Although Pratt does not explicitly point this out, the term *languagescape* is serendipitously consistent with five other *-scape* neologisms, suggested by Appadurai (1996) to account for the various dimensions of the transnational flows of cultural globalization. The model for the words is the term *landscape*, which connects the objectivity of the physical/geographical territory with the subjectivity and history of the human observer, who assigns meaning to its features. The global *technoscape* and the global *financescape* refer to the hardwiring of the integrated circuits of globalization. The world's changing *ethnoscapes*, *mediascapes*, and *ideoscapes*, on the other hand, are shaped by the intensifying transnational flows of people and ideas and thus cover the psychological, social, and cultural dimensions of globalization.

With direct reference to Appadurai, the term *languagescape* was introduced in an ethnographic study of television viewing habits in contemporary Indonesia by Klarijn Loven (2009: 104–105):

> The term "languagescape" is coined on the model by [sic] Appadurai (1996), who attached the scape suffix to keywords that represented certain universal phenomena he wanted to describe ... Applying the landscape metaphor to the phenomenon of language opens interesting perspectives on language use.
>
> One may for instance speak of a languagescape because like a natural landscape, the silhouette of a languagescape too may be fluid and irregular. The Indonesian languagescape, for instance, consists of hundreds of tongues from different language groups and language families, some of which have as little resemblance to each other as Dutch and Russian or English and Bengali do ... Furthermore, like Appadurai's -scape terms, a languagescape is experienced differently by different people and

institutions. The national language Indonesian will have different connotations for a primary school teacher of this language who lives and works
in the capital Jakarta, for example, than for an uneducated pedicab driver
in Central Java, or for a Papuan politician . . . The languagescape is furthermore like a natural landscape in that its composition changes over time.
Whereas Dutch was an important language of communication in the
colonized archipelago, it has little significance as such for contemporary
Indonesians, who would rather learn English or Japanese.

Although dealing with the old and established medium of television,
Loven (2009: 105) herself mentions the role of the Internet and the
new media for diasporic networks in the postcolonial world in a brief
aside:

> Presently, communities of speakers of an Indonesian language are not
> only found within the boundaries of the archipelago, but also far
> beyond. Examples are the numerous Indonesians who work as domestic
> servants in Arabic [sic] countries and the Philippines, students and
> professors of Indonesian at universities outside Indonesia, and
> Internet communities that centre around weblogs in a local
> Indonesian language.

Alongside *languagescape*, the term *linguascape* has gained some currency.
The first to use it in the context of World English studies was apparently Pennycook (2003: 523), who coined it with explicit reference to
Appadurai's five other *-scapes* and to his cultural-anthropological model
of globalization. In this specific sense, the term figures prominently in
Dovchin's (2017) study of mixed language practices involving English
in Mongolian hip-hop.[12] In other recent publications, however, the
term seems to have been cut loose from this clear theoretical framework and become a synonym for many kinds of linguistic-landscaping
analysis (Gorter 2006). Thus, Jaworski and Piller (2008) use it without
explicit reference to either Pennycook or to Appadurai in a critical
discourse analysis of British tourist discourse about Switzerland. For
Liebscher and Dailey-O'Cain (2013: 35), the "linguascape" merely
denotes the bilingual repertoires of their German-Canadian informants. In the context of the sociolinguistics of globalization, and as
a technical term anchored in Appadurai's model, the term *languagescape* thus seems preferable.

To summarize the advantages of the concept of languagescape(s) for the
sociolinguistic analysis of CMC, we can say that it helps redress four
potential biases in existing approaches to World Englishes:

---

[12] Steyaert, Ostendorp and Gaibrois (2011), organizational psychologists working in business studies, use the notion of *linguascape* "as inspired by the transnational anthropology developed by Appadurai" (p. 276) in their study of employees' response to the introduction of English as a working language in multinational companies.

(i) Territorial bias: Dialect maps have isoglosses and most of the prevailing classifications of World Englishes – from Kachru's (1992) "Three Circles" to Schneider's (2007) "Dynamic Model" – are organized around national varieties, hence based on nation-states and their clearly defined geographical boundaries. Languagescapes acknowledge the territorial factor but accept that boundaries can be shifting and fuzzy. There is only one type of English that we can expect to encounter everywhere on the Web: Standard American English, the Web's default lingua franca and the hub of the World Language System, in its online as well as its offline manifestation.[13] The extent and reach of all other Englishes are limited to varying extent in comparison; these limitations must be described and yet none of them can be plotted on a map.

(ii) Vernacular bias: For the pioneering "First Wave" (Eckert 2012) sociolinguists, the only authentic data were to be obtained from spontaneous face-to-face interaction in closely knit vernacular communities. Spontaneous speech of this kind provides the baseline of any languagescape as well. Yet languagescapes are also shaped by stylized, performed, and mediated language. One fascinating task for the sociolinguist studying World Englishes in cyberspace is, therefore, to separate ephemeral individual creativity and playfulness from language use that establishes digital extensions and transformations of offline sociolinguistic orders supporting web-based communities of practice.

(iii) Colonial bias: The study of "varieties of English around the world" took shape under the long shadow of colonialism and in the era of early postcolonial nation-building. Initially, it was colonial expansion that made English one important world language among several others. Subsequently, decolonization made English a pluricentric language with several coexisting standards. Neither colonialism nor decolonization, however, has made English the lingua franca of cyberspace. Languagescapes are agnostic with regard to whether a particular use of English on the Web has a colonial history or not. This makes them appropriate for the study of Englishes in CMC, a domain where much of what is going on with regard to the use of English is situated beyond or between the "Three Circles" (for illustration, see Mair 2013a, 2016).

(iv) Monolingual bias: The study of World Englishes has always recognized the sedimented traces of language contact – in the shape of lexical borrowings or of substrate influence in pronunciation and grammar. There has been relatively little interest, by comparison, in the multilingual settings in which varieties of English are used – and

---

[13] This obviously does not mean that American English forms will become statistically dominant or even replace local variants – merely that they are used alongside them.

even less in the multilingual practices of their speakers. This bias is redressed in the languagescapes, which are multilingual by default and monolingual only in the marked case.

An additional serendipitous association is that between *linguistic landscape* and *languagescape*. Research in the linguistic landscape paradigm (e.g. Gorter, ed. 2006) deals with (mostly written) language in public spaces, such as official public signs, names and signs of commercial establishments, and informal "bottom up" activities such as graffiti. It is easy to see how this approach can be carried over to the study of language design in the more static and text-led components of the World Wide Web, such as institutional self-representations on websites. To study language use in the multimodal components of the Web (e.g. YouTube, Tumblr) and in social media, on the other hand, *languagescapes* are the better conceptual tool.

The observations made in the case studies presented in Sections 16.3 and 16.4 add up to the defining features of two fairly typical types of Internet languagescape – that of the bilingual immigrant minority within the nation-state (Latinos in the USA) and that of the postcolonial diaspora ("cyber-Nigeria"). Both have a transnational foundation but with a different emphasis. In the immigrant-minority scenario, the priority is on expressing a stance toward the dominant national linguistic and cultural mainstream, whereas, in the postcolonial diaspora, it is on maintaining the link to the original homeland (and the other centers of the global diaspora).

An obvious way of testing the explanatory power of the concept further would be to ask whether different CMC genres, such as email, blogs, and social networks, develop different languagescapes. Other applications will take us beyond linguistic description into cultural studies. Through its stylized subvariety of hip-hop nation language, African American Vernacular English (AAVE), for example, has become the one truly global nonstandard variety of English and, in its own subculture, has embedded itself as deeply in the world's multilingual ecology as standard English has as the lingua franca of choice in the global mainstream. As Coleman (2014) has pointed out, AAVE has become the powerhouse for innovation in the varied languagescapes of global youth slang (Coleman 2014) – in English as in many other languages, in the Global North as well as in the South. As in the spread of standard English, migrations, a globally operating entertainment industry, and the Internet and the social media have colluded to bring this situation about. In their own ways, other highly stigmatized and nonstandard language forms such as Jamaican Creole or Nigerian Pidgin have been following in the wake of AAVE. The wide dissemination of their resources throughout the global English Language Complex and beyond holds a final irony: These languages now share in the global power of the language that was their main historical lexifier and still is their sociolinguistic antagonist on their own home ground.

References

Alo, Moses A., and Rajend Mesthrie. 2004. Nigerian English: Morphology and syntax. In Bernd Kortmann, Edgar Schneider, Kate Burridge, Rajend Mesthrie, and Clive Upton, eds. *A Handbook of varieties of English*, Vol 2. Berlin: Mouton de Gruyter, 813–827.

Androutsopoulos, Jannis. 2006a. The sociolinguistics of computer-mediated communication. *Journal of Sociolinguistics* 10(5) [Special Issue].

Androutsopoulos, Jannis. 2006b. Introduction: Sociolinguistics and computer-mediated communication. *Journal of Sociolinguistics* 10: 419–438.

Androutsopoulos, Jannis. 2006c. Multilingualism, diaspora, and the internet: Codes and identities on German-based diasporic websites. *Journal of Sociolinguistics* 10: 520–547.

Appadurai, Arjun. 1996. *Modernity at Large: Cultural Dimensions of Globalization*. Minneapolis: University of Minnesota Press.

Baron, Naomi S. 2008. *Always On: Language in an Online and Mobile World*. Oxford: Oxford University Press.

Bauman, Zygmunt. 2007. *Liquid Times: Living in an Age of Uncertainty*. Malden, MA: Polity.

Benor, Sarah Bunin. 2010. Ethnolinguistic repertoire: shifting the analytic focus in language and ethnicity. *Journal of Sociolinguistics* 14: 159–183.

Bhatt, Rakesh M. 2010. Unraveling post-colonial identity through language. In Nikolas Coupland, ed. *Handbook of Language and Globalization*. Malden, MA: Blackwell, 520–539.

Blommaert, Jan. 2010. *The Sociolinguistics of Globalization*. Cambridge: Cambridge University Press.

Bolander, Brook and Miriam Locher. 2014. Doing sociolinguistic research on computer-mediated data: A review of four methodological issues. *Discourse, Context and Media* 3: 14–26. http://dx.doi.org/10.1016/j.dcm.2013.10.004

Coleman, Julie. 2014. Understanding slang in a global context. In Julie Coleman, ed. *Global English Slang: Methodologies and Perspectives*, London: Routledge, 1–14.

Collot, Milena and Nancy Belmore. 1996. Electronic language: A new variety of English. In Susan Herring, ed. *Computer-Mediated Communication: Linguistic, Social and Cross-Cultural Perspectives*. Amsterdam: John Benjamins, 147–170.

Cormack, Mike. 2007. The media and language maintenance. In Mike Cormack and Niamh Hourigan, eds. *Minority Language Media: Concepts, Critiques and Case Studies*. Clevedon: Multilingual Matters, 52–68.

Coupland, Nikolas. 2009. Response: The mediated performance of vernaculars. *Journal of English Linguistics* 37: 284–300.

Coupland, Nikolas, ed. 2010. *The Handbook of Language and Globalization*. Oxford: Blackwell.

Crystal, David. 2006. *Language and the Internet* (2nd ed.). Cambridge: Cambridge University Press.

Danet, Brenda and Susan C. Herring, eds. 2007. *The Multilingual Internet: Language, Culture, and Communication Online*. Oxford: Oxford University Press.

de Swaan, Abram. 2002. *The World Language System: A Political Sociology and Political Economy of Language*. Cambridge: Polity.

de Swaan, Abram. 2010. Language systems. In Nikolas Coupland, ed., *The Handbook of Language and Globalization*. Malden, MA: Blackwell, 56–76.

Deuber, Dagmar and Lars Hinrichs . 2007. Dynamics of orthographic standardization in Jamaican Creole and Nigerian Pidgin. *World Englishes* 26: 22–47.

Dor, Daniel. 2004. From Englishization to imposed multilingualism: Globalization, the Internet, and the political economy of the linguistic code. *Public Culture* 16: 97–118.

Dovchin, Sender. 2017. Translocal English in the linguascape of Mongolian popular music. *World Englishes* 36: 2–19.

Dürscheid, Christa. 2004. Netzsprache – ein neuer Mythos. *Osnabrücker Beiträge zur Sprachtheorie* 68: 141–157.

Eckert, Penelope. 2012. Three waves of variation study: The emergence of meaning in the study of variation. *Annual Review of Anthropology* 41: 87–100.

Eisenlohr, Patrick. 2004. Language revitalization and new technologies: Cultures of electronic mediation and the refiguring of communities. *Annual Review of Anthropology 33*: 21–45.

Escobar, Anna Maria and Kim Potowski. 2015. *El español de los Estados Unidos*. Cambridge: Cambridge University Press.

Friedrich, Patricia and Eduardo H. Diniz de Figueiredo. 2016. *The Sociolinguistics of Digital Englishes*. London: Routledge.

Fung, Loretta and Ronald Carter. 2007. Cantonese E-discourse: A new hybrid variety of English. *Multilingua 26*: 35–66.

Gao, Liwei. 2006. Language contact and convergence in computer-mediated communication. *World Englishes* 25: 299–308.

Gorter, Durk, ed. 2006. *Linguistic Landscape: A New Approach to Multilingualism*. Clevedon: Multilingual Matters.

Heyd, Theresa and Christian Mair. 2014. From vernacular to digital ethnolinguistic repertoire: The case of Nigerian Pidgin. In Véronique

Lacoste, Jakob Leimgruber and Thiemo Breyer, eds. *Indexing Authenticity: Sociolinguistic Perspectives*. Berlin: Mouton de Gruyter, 242–266.

Hinrichs, Lars. 2006. *Codeswitching on the Web: English and Jamaican Creole in E-mail Communication*. Amsterdam: John Benjamins.

Hinrichs, Lars and Jessica White-Sustaíta. 2011. Global Englishes and the sociolinguistics of spelling: A study of Jamaican blog and email writing. *English World-Wide 32*: 46–73.

Hofmann, Sabine. 2007. Construir el espacio latinoamericano: el caso de CNN en español. In Sabine Hofmann, ed. *Medios, espacios comunicativos y comunidades imaginadas*. Berlin: Tranvía, 69–84.

Jaworski, Adam and Ingrid Piller. 2008. Linguascaping Switzerland: Language ideologies in tourism. In Miriam Locher and Jürg Strässler, eds. *Standards and Norms in the English Language*. Berlin: Mouton de Gruyter, 301–332.

Kachru, Braj. B., ed. 1992. *The Other Tongue: English across Cultures*. Urbana, IL: University of Illinois Press.

Keefe, Susan E. and Amado Padilla. 1987. *Chicano Ethnicity*. Albuquerque, NM: University of New Mexico Press.

Laviera, Tato. 1992. *La Carreta Made a U-Turn* (2nd ed.). Houston, TX: Arte Publico Press.

Liebscher, Grit and Jennifer Dailey-O'Cain. 2013. *Language, Space and Identity in Migration*. Basingstoke: Palgrave Macmillan.

Loven, Klarijn. 2009. *Watching* Si Doel*: Television, Language and Cultural Identity in Contemporary Indonesia*. Leiden: KITLV Press.

McArthur, Tom. 2003. World English, Euro-English, Nordic English. *English Today 19*(1): 54–58.

Mair, Christian. 2013a. The World System of Englishes: Accounting for the transnational importance of mobile and mediated vernaculars. *English World-Wide 34*: 253–278.

Mair, Christian. 2013b. Corpus-approaches to the vernacular web: Post-colonial diasporic forums in West Africa and the Caribbean. In Katrin Röder and Ilse Wischer, eds. *Anglistentag 2012: Proceedings*. Trier: Wissenschaftlicher Verlag, 397–406. (Expanded version reprinted in *Covenant Journal of Language Studies* (Ota, Nigeria) 1 (2013): 17–31. http://journals.covenantuniversity.edu.ng/jls/published/Mair2013.pdf)

Mair, Christian. 2016. Beyond and between the Three Circles: World Englishes research in the age of globalisation. In Elena Seoane and Cristina Suárez-Gómez, eds. *World Englishes: New Theoretical and Methodological Considerations*. Amsterdam: John Benjamins, 17–36.

Maynor, Natalie. 1994. The language of electronic mail: written speech? In Greta D. Little and Michael Montgomery, eds. *Centennial Usage Studies*. Tuscaloosa: University of Alabama Press, 48–54.

Mesthrie, Rajend and Rakesh M. Bhatt. 2008. *World Englishes: The Study of New Varieties*. Cambridge: Cambridge University Press.

Meyerhoff, Miriam. 2002. Communities of practice. In Jack Chambers, Peter Trudgill and Natalie Schilling-Estes, eds. *Handbook of Language Variation and Change*. Oxford: Blackwell, 526–548.

Moll, Andrea. 2015. *Jamaican Creole Goes Web: Sociolinguistic Styling and Authenticity in a Digital Yaad*. Amsterdam: John Benjamins.

Montes-Alcalá, Cecilia. 2016. *iSwitch*: Spanish-English mixing in computer-mediated communication. *Journal of Language Contact 9*: 23–48.

Ooi, Vincent and Peter K.W. Tan. 2014. Facebook, linguistic identity and hybridity in Singapore. In Rani Rubdy and Lubna Alsagoff, eds. *The Global-Local Interface and Hybridity*. Bristol: Multilingual Matters, 225–244.

Otheguy, Ricardo and Ana Celia Zentella. 2012. *Spanish in New York: Language Contact, Dialectal Leveling and Structural Continuity*. Oxford: Oxford University Press.

Paolillo, John. 2001. Language variation on Internet Relay Chat: A social network approach. *Journal of Sociolinguistics 5*(2): 180–213.

Pennycook, Alastair. 2003. Global Englishes, Rip Slyme, and performativity. *Journal of Sociolinguistics 7*: 513–533.

Pratt, Mary Louise. 2011. Comparative literature and the global languagescape. In Ali Behdad and Dominic Thomas, eds. *A Companion to Comparative Literature*. Malden, MA: Blackwell, 273–295.

Rajah-Carrim, Aaliya. 2009. Use and standardisation of Mauritian Creole in electronically mediated communication. *Journal of Computer-Mediated Communication 14*: 484–508.

Rampton, Ben. 1995. *Crossing: Language and Ethnicity Among Adolescents*. London: Longman.

Rampton, Ben. 2006. *Language in Late Modernity: Interaction in an Urban School*. Cambridge: Cambridge University Press.

Sand, Andrea. 2013. Singapore weblogs: Between speech and writing. In Magnus Huber and Joybrato Mukherjee, eds. *Corpus Linguistics and Variation in English: Focus on Non-native Englishes*. Helsinki: Research Unit for Variation, Contacts and Change in English. www.helsinki.fi/varieng/journal/volumes/13/sand/

Schneider, Edgar. 2007. *Postcolonial English: Varieties Around the World*. Cambridge: Cambridge University Press.

Schneider, Edgar. 2016. World Englishes on YouTube: Treasure trove or nightmare? In Elena Seoane and Cristina Suárez-Gómez, eds. *World Englishes: New Theoretical and Methodological Considerations*. Amsterdam: John Benjamins, 253–282.

Seargeant, Philip and Caroline Tagg. 2011. English on the internet and a "post-varieties" approach to language. *World Englishes 30*: 496–514.

Silva-Corvalán, Carmen. 1994. *Language Contact and Change: Spanish in Los Angeles*. Oxford: Clarendon Press.

Squires, Lauren. 2010. Enregistering internet language. *Language in Society 39*: 457–492.

Steyaert, Chris, Anja Ostendorp and Claudine Gabrois. 2011. Multilingual organizations as "linguascapes": Negotiating the position of English through discursive practices. *Journal of World Business 46*: 270–278.

Williams, Bronwyn. 2009. Multilingual strategies in online worlds. *JAC 29*: 255–259.

Zhang, Wei. 2012. Chinese-English code-mixing among China's netizens. *English Today 28*(3): 40–52.

17

World Englishes and Their Dialect Roots

Daniel Schreier

World Englishes developed out of English dialects spoken throughout the British Isles. These were transported all over the globe by speakers from different regions, social classes, and educational backgrounds, who migrated with distinct trajectories, for various periods of time and in distinct chronological phases (Hickey, Chapter 2, this volume; Britain, Chapter 7, this volume). The dialects they spoke formed a foundation for the offspring varieties; some features either remained in more or less robust form or underwent far-reaching structural and systemic change under local linguistic-ecological contact conditions. In this chapter, I will trace the dialect roots of New Englishes, that is, features that can clearly be retraced to regional dialects of the British Isles – what Hickey (2004: 1) has called "dialect input and the survival of features from a mainland source or sources." These "roots of English" (Tagliamonte 2012: 1) manifest themselves in regionally specific new-dialect formation processes (i.e. the emergence of World Englishes around the world) but also in the regional persistence of what Chambers (2009: 258) calls "vernacular roots." They are central for any reconstruction of the evolutionary formation of World Englishes in that they allow for an assessment of input strength and the impact of contact-induced mechanisms. I will discuss the importance of dialect roots for the formation of World Englishes (in terms of direct [conservative] legacies as well as contact-dynamic [e.g. camouflaged] forms), look into the diagnostic value of roots (suggesting a taxonomy of features) in what I would like to call first- and second-window transplantation scenarios, and, finally, present some reasons to account for why some dialect features take root whereas others disappear.

17.1 Introduction: Picking the Roots

This chapter deals with the legacy of British English in offspring varieties around the world, with a focus on the historical evolution and sociolinguistic implications of localized Englishes and their spread (Crystal 2003; Schneider 2011; Kachru, Kachru, and Nelson 2006). It looks into the emergence of new varieties indexed to certain social strata and speech communities (Schneider 2007, Mesthrie and Bhatt 2008), including ideology, identity construction, and globalization issues (Blommaert 2010). The question is to what extent these legacies of British varieties (Hickey 2004), in the form of dialect roots, come to be embedded into new language ecologies and how they develop on transplantation and subsequent adoption by speakers around the world (Lim and Ansaldo 2015).

One important misconception probably needs to be done away with right away. The input strength of dialect roots alone is not responsible for why World Englishes form the way they do. Contact-induced processes and interaction between systems may change the evolution of local varieties in addition to ongoing internal change, attesting to their dynamic and innovative character. Yet feature retention, as a consequence of dialect contact, is only one possible outcome of dialect transplantation, and Hickey (2004: 1–2) singles out a conglomerate of five factors that shape the sociolinguistic outcome of World Englishes:

> "1. Dialect input and the survival of features from a mainland source or sources.
> 2. Independent developments within the overseas communities, including realignments of features in the dialect input.
> 3. Contact phenomena where English speakers co-existed with those of other languages.
> 4. An indirect influence through the educational system in those countries in which English arose without significant numbers of native-speaker settlers.
> 5. Creolisation in those situations where there was no linguistic continuity and where virtually the only input was a pidgin, based on English, from the preceding generation."

This chapter primarily deals with complex 1 ("Input and survival"), whereas other factors (interaction, mixing, substratal effects, and the like) are kept to a minimum here (see Lim, Chapter 4; Hickey, Chapter 2; Fox, Chapter 20; D'Arcy, Chapter 19, all this volume). I will discuss features that have been transported outside the British Isles and that thus represent a legacy of the roots of (British) dialectal Englishes on a global scale (Tagliamonte 2012; see Britain, Chapter 7, this volume). In doing so, I partly follow Tagliamonte's (2012: 3) approach by focusing on "the historically embedded explanation that comes from tracing their roots back to their origins in the British Isles ... the study of British dialects is critical to disentangling the history and development of varieties of English everywhere in the world." Though this may be rather general, I will approach roots as dialectal features that are permanently adopted in the emerging World Englishes (see taxonomy in Section 17.2).

The first question in this context is what features are most likely to be transported and to which original dialects these are attributed. As Hickey (2004: 1) claims, it is "probably true to say that mainly regional forms of English were taken to the colonies which England founded in the core 200-year period between the early seventeenth and the early nineteenth centuries." Regional forms were certainly important, yet not the only strand of language use in former British society. The majority of speakers who left the British Isles and migrated to overseas territories came from lower social ranks (lower middle and working classes); they brought their regional varieties to the new settings, so these featured as primary input varieties. This stock of low-strata social and regional varieties (which arguably reinforced each other, as many inhabitants of regional areas were from the working classes and had little or no education) combined to found a solid basis of the newly emerging local varieties (as shown in selected case studies in this chapter). One may even go as far as to say that the foundations of these Englishes were firmly entrenched in nonstandard varieties (see Schreier 2008 on "nonstandardization" and its consequences), even though this assessment is probably too general. The focus on nonstandard heritage has been advocated by Watts and Trudgill (2002: 27), who go as far as to claim that

> Non-standard dialects have histories too, and these histories are sometimes especially helpful because, as a result of the absence of standardisation, many of the forces of linguistic change are played out in these varieties in a much more unfettered and revealing way than in a standard dialect.

This has triggered documentation of and research on so-called lesser-known varieties of English (Schreier et al. 2010; Williams et al. 2015), that is, mostly peripheral varieties that now have an important place in studies on dialect transplantation and produced fresh insights into the export and survival of dialect roots. Generally speaking, two questions are particularly important here, namely (1) identification and localizability of roots and (2) survival vs. loss on the new-dialect contact scenario. I will address these in Section 17.3.

One important question is how "roots" should be approached in the first place. There are various ways to describe and classify the dialectal contributions of World Englishes; the concentration of the overall distribution of features has some currency here. Such a classificatory attempt would include what Chambers (2004: 19) called "vernacular roots," a set of dialect features considered as universals that comprise

> a small number of phonological and grammatical processes [that] recur in vernaculars wherever they are spoken ... not only in working class and rural vernaculars, but also in ... pidgins, creoles and interlanguage varieties.
>
> (Chambers 2004: 128, quoted in Szmrecsanyi and Kortmann 2009: 37)

Though the concept has given rise to criticism and engaged debates in the field (see the contributions to Filppula, Klemola, and Paulasto 2009), Chambers originally regarded these universals as "primitive features of vernacular dialects" (2003: 243), emphasizing that they were unlearned and innate: consonant cluster reduction, (-ing), past *be* leveling to *was*, multiple negation, and leveling of irregular verb forms.

Trudgill (2004), on the other hand, criticized the notion of vernacular universals when arguing that there was no such a thing as a major divide between standard and nonstandard (or vernacular) varieties of English (as Chambers suggested). Rather, he argued in favor of a "true typological split" (2004: 315) between high- and low-contact world Englishes; high contact led to simplification, which he believed to be the main distinguishing factor between the two ends of the divide (Trudgill 2009: 312). Trudgill shifted the focus to contact-induced language change and brought in contact intensity as an alternative explanation for dialect diversification (see Schreier 2016 for a detailed discussion on such a strict dichotomy).

Kortmann and Szmrecsanyi (2011: 68–74) analyzed the sociolinguistic reality of vernacular universals from the viewpoint of dialect typology. They advocated the adoption of implicational, not absolute, principles and suggested focusing on nonstandard features with a wide areal and/or social reach, including pidgins and creoles, and to factor in genetic, areal, and historical relationships between different varieties. Distributional patterns of features in a World Englishes context thus should be classified in a more fine-grained system that includes typological categories such as (1) *genuine universals*, (2) *typoversals* (i.e. features that are common to languages of a specific typological type; e.g. postpositions in SOV languages), (3) *phyloversals* (i.e. features shared by a family of genetically related languages (e.g. languages belonging to the Indo-European language family that distinguish masculine and feminine gender), (4) *areoversals* (features common in languages that are in geographical proximity; e.g. finite complement clauses in languages in the Balkan *sprachbund*), (5) *angloversals* (i.e. features that tend to recur in vernacular varieties of a specific language), and (6) *varioversals* (features recurrent in language varieties with a similar sociohistory, historical depth, and mode of acquisition; e.g. resumptive pronouns in relative clauses found in English L2 varieties; Szmrecsanyi and Kortmann 2009; see Szmrecsanyi and Röthlisberger, Chapter 23, this volume).

As for a general taxonomy of dialect roots, the question is which of these categories should be most influential for the distribution of current patterns – or how the interplay of criteria combines to shape an ultimate outcome. In a cross-varietal study, Kortmann and Szmrecsanyi (2011: 276) found that the "varieties cluster very nicely according to whether they are L1 varieties ..., L2 varieties ..., or English-based pidgins and creoles ... – and indeed better than geographically," concluding that "it is the variety type ... which is of towering importance" in the distribution of linguistic features among World Englishes (p. 274). Winford (2009: 208), in contrast, stressed that typological universals should not be offered as "explanatory principles." Referring to Kiparsky (2008), he claimed that there was a need to "reconcile research that seeks to uncover typological generalizations, which are the result of recurrent processes of language change, with research directed at uncovering the universal principles underlying such processes" (Winford 2009: 209). In other words, principles of contact-induced language change (on a more micro-oriented level) accounted for distribution patterns among World Englishes, not the typological generalizations on a macro level per se. Similarly, Thomason (2009) discussed the interplay of contact-induced change and typological universals in historical language change. She rejected Trudgill's view of simplification as a result of contact-induced change and claimed that "linguistic changes involve both kinds of process – that is, various processes of contact-induced change and also universal tendencies of various kinds" (Thomason 2009: 349). In other words, the local-specific origin of features had to be taken into consideration along with universal criteria.

The second question, survival vs. loss of (English) dialect roots on the new-dialect contact scenario, draws on dialect typology, sociolinguistics, contact linguistics, dialectology, and English historical linguistics. Perhaps the major issue one needs to address is "why all of this has happened and whether there is an underlying scheme that has continued to drive and motivate the evolution of new varieties of English" (Kortmann and Schneider 2004: 1). The task here is to find out what features are selected where and why, why some are common, found all over the English-speaking world, whereas others are restricted to particular varieties, and so on. This is a complex issue: The diachrony of World Englishes, including diachronic corpora and data sources, are discussed by Huber (Chapter 21, this volume) and principles of dialect typology from a World Englishes perspective are sketched by Szmrecsanyi and Röthlisberger (Chapter 23, this volume), who introduce the electronic World Atlas of Varieties of English (eWAVE) in full detail. As this is referred to in much more detail in Chapter 23 in this volume, it suffices to say that the eWave can be used as a research tool for the study of World Englishes and learner Englishes generally. It distinguishes between Traditional L1 varieties (Orkney and Shetland English, Ozark English, etc.), High-Contact L1 varieties (Irish English, African American English, etc.), Indigenized L2 varieties (Chicano English, Pakistani English), English-Based Pidgins (Ghanaian Pidgin English, Tok Pisin) and English-based Creoles (Gullah, Krio, Hawai'i Creole) and there is (admittedly rather basic) variationist classification between features in terms of whether they are pervasive/obligatory, neither pervasive nor rare, extremely rare, or nonexistent.

The frequency ratings used in eWave allow us to affiliate British and overseas dialects, to establish links and offer sociohistorically informed explanations why some British dialect features are adopted and gain ground in World Englishes, whereas others do not. Based on historical evidence, we can reconstruct the history of dialect features and pinpoint their place of origin, which is instrumental in understanding their evolution via competitive interaction processes with other dialects and their features. Following Hickey and others, it is clear that roots do not remain static and are subject to change themselves, which means that there are high-contact scenarios that involve unprecedented interaction patterns of dialects from distinct regions and social classes (see Section 17.3).

17.2 The Diagnosticity of Dialect Roots

One of the most thorough attempts to reconstruct the legacy of dialect patterns is Montgomery's (1989) analysis of the formation of US Appalachian English, an isolated variety of American English that has a strong ancestral heritage of Irish, Northern Irish, and Scottish English. Based on sociohistorical data (see Schneider 2002) and data collected from ego documents such as emigrant letters (Auer, Schreier and Watts 2013), Montgomery asked rather holistically what evidence was necessary so that researchers could firmly establish a link between Appalachian English, Scottish, and Irish Englishes. He called for methodological, descriptive, historical, and analytical considerations as a detailed description of synchronic data needed to be entrenched in a historical corpus so as to assess present-day forms of English – Irish and Appalachian – and to reconstruct them at the time of emigration from the British Isles to Appalachia (see Britain, Chapter 7, this volume).

From a methodological point of view, the majority of migrations that gave rise to current World Englishes took place before the advent of permanent speech recordings. The oldest *spoken* data available are thus from speakers born around the mid-nineteenth century. This makes it challenging to localize sufficient quantities of data in order to not only have sporadic, often anecdotal reports of given features (as in logbooks or traveler diaries) but also have sufficient information on the context of grammatical features under study (Tagliamonte 2012; the Origins of New Zealand English (ONZE) corpus is a notable exception; Gordon et al. 2004). As data often come from written sources, there is always the possibility that grammatical forms are screened out or avoided, particularly when they are salient or sociolinguistically stigmatized (Schneider 2013). In other words, features may have been in existence but we might simply lack hard evidence of this fact.

From an analytical and interpretative perspective, we need to have as much information as possible on two points A and B of a temporal axis so as to retrace dialect evolution and feature inheritance. Two principal factors need to be considered: the overall proportions and relationships of the founding populations and their input varieties; and koineization

and general contact effects between varieties before and during departure, on arrival, and in the inceptive phases of settlement (see Gordon
et al. 2004 for a detailed discussion of these issues in the New Zealand
context). Moreover, one also should account for other types of contact,
such as between multilingual settlers and the native Amerindian ones in
North America (Schneider 2007). We also need to filter in social information, namely how society was structured in both home and host environments and what sort of strata the early settlers came from: mobility and
settlement patterns, social relationships, language attitudes, and so on.
Retracing dialect roots is a complex task, depending on the availability of
social, sociolinguistic, and historical data – which are often not sufficiently available. Sources typically offer information on certain aspects
(e.g. language use, attitudes) but not necessarily all the background
information required.

Nevertheless, it is possible to identify and pinpoint such features, sometimes even in minute detail, and I would suggest that they be placed along
a localizability continuum, ranging from high to low. Obviously, the most
important features in this context have high diagnostic value in that they
are restricted to a small set of varieties. The exact positioning can be
established by checking ratings and dialect maps on eWave, and a few
selected features will serve to illustrate localizability in more detail.

17.2.1   Root 1: The '*after*' Perfect in Irish and Newfoundland English

To start with a show-case scenario, the "*after*" perfect, as in

(1)   Brazil is after winning the World Cup ("Brazil has just won the
        World Cup")

provides a particularly clear example of how roots may be replanted
successfully, without undergoing much change. The eWave lists merely
two varieties where the feature is classified as pervasive or obligatory: Irish
English and Newfoundland English (it is also attested in Sri Lankan
English, which needs further substantiation; see the discussion in
Kortmann and Szmrecsanyi 2004).

Historically, it has been suggested that Irish constructions such as

(2)   Tha Iain air a bhith ag ithe an arain ("is Iain after COMP been at
        eating the bread")

were transferred via language contact when Irish English emerged, and
here they survive and are stable in present-day varieties (Hickey 2013). The
"*after*" construction, once it had taken hold in Ireland, was brought across
the North Atlantic to Newfoundland from the seventeenth century
onward. The Newfoundland population developed when the local cod
fishery became a lucrative business; it involved major settlement groups
from south-western England (Devon and Dorset) and the south-east

counties of Ireland (Wexford and Waterford). Only small numbers of settlers arrived, and many of them arrived as part of a workforce with little intention to stay permanently. Most of the Irish settlers came in the eighteenth century, but there was a dramatic decline of immigration from the 1850s onward (see the social history provided by Clarke 2010: 72–75).

Given these contact patterns and sociohistorical relationships, the "morphosyntactic structure of vernacular NfldE [Newfoundland English] displays many conservative features inherited from its regional source varieties in southwest England and southeast Ireland" (Clarke 2004: 316), thus representing a quasi-laboratory setting to study long-term effects of dialect contact and interaction. Further evidence for the Irish English (IrE) roots of NfldE come from the area of lexis ... (*sleveen* "rascal," *scrob* "scratch").

17.2.2 Root 2: Conjunction *do* in East Anglian and African American English

Trudgill (2002) provided a reconstruction of conjunction *do* in East Anglian English (semantically equivalent to "otherwise"), as in

(3)   Sing out, do we shall get drowned! ("Call out, or we shall be drowned")

and claimed that it underwent complex stages of phonological reduction, loss of lexical *because if* + pronoun, loss of tense marking of *do* and *don't*, grammatical extension to other environments, and, finally, loss of negative/positive polarity (Trudgill 2002: 13). Crucially in this context, conjunction *do* is

> not found anywhere in the British Isles outside East Anglia. Nor, as far as I know, is it found anywhere else in the English-speaking world, with one exception – in the South-eastern United States.   (Trudgill 2002, 13)

Citations from the work of Zora Neal Hurston in the *Dictionary of American Regional English* (*DARE*) rendered several instances of conjunction *do* in literary African-American English usage:

(4)   Dat's a thing dat's got to be handled just so, do it'll kill you ("that's a thing that has te handled just so, if you don't it will kill you")

The explanation provided in *DARE* (that this was an abbreviation of *if you do*) accounted for some of the examples, but Trudgill (2002) argued that conjunction *do* in AAVE showed "progress towards the fully completed grammaticalisation also typical of East Anglia in that *do* is employed where *don't* might have been expected" (p. 13). In other words, AAVE would have collapsed polarity and neutralization in favor of *do* instead of *don't*. Trudgill quoted evidence from fieldwork notes and personal observations that the feature was currently found in spoken varieties (both African-American and Anglo-American) in coastal North Carolina. The possibility of independent developments was excluded; rather, *do* in East Anglia and AAVE was interpreted as a direct legacy, representing a feature with high diagnostic value for dialect roots:

> this feature . . . was brought to eastern North Carolina by settlers who were speakers of East Anglian dialects. In (at least some parts of) the southeastern United States, it was then not only retained in White nonstandard dialects of English but also acquired by speakers of AAVE . . . It is undoubtedly true, however, that there is at least one nonstandard dialect feature with its origins in the British Isles . . . which has been retained by some AAVE speakers.   (Trudgill 2002: 14–15).

As such, features like conjunction *do* may be important pieces of evidence for the sociolinguistic reconstruction of AAVE more generally (see Poplack and Tagliamonte 2001).

17.2.3   Root 3: "Sequential" or "Irrealis" *be done* in African American and Liberian English

Dialect roots are not restricted to the British Isles alone and it is certainly possible that features are transported from earlier established colonies to later offspring varieties, a process I would like to label "second-window transplantation." Once a colony with a distinctive variety is established, it may in turn come to serve as a focus for other settlements founded at a later stage, a process inherent in the discussion of emerging epicenters of English as world language (Hundt 2013). The Caribbean serves as a good case in point, as the earliest colonial possessions (e.g. St Kitts and Nevis [Baker and Bruyn 1998] or the Bermudas [Eberle 2017]) subsequently became donor varieties in their own right as settlers moved on to other locations. A good example of second-window exportation is the use of *be done* for resultatives or the future/conditional perfect (Rickford 1999: 6), as in

(5)   My ice cream be done melted by the time we get there

The combination of *be* and *done* as a preverbal tense/aspect marker indicates a resultative or a future conditional state, semantically similar to the standard-type English future perfect *will have Ved*-construction.

The origins of sequential *be done* are not well understood but it is reported with low frequency in Urban AAVE (eWave rating B) and Rural AAVE (eWave rating C). Other than in the case of completive *done*, as in

(6)   I done finish supper

there is no attestation of *be done* in historical British English, which strongly suggests that this is in fact a local African American English innovation. There are some claims (Labov 1998; discussed in Wolfram 2004) that the construction has recently taken on the function of a future resultative-conditional, referring to an inevitable consequence of a general condition or a specific activity, as in

(7)   If you love your enemy, they be done eat you alive in this society

Dayton (1996) argued that this meaning, often pragmatically associated with direct speech acts (insults and warnings), is a semantic-aspectual development in twentieth-century AAVE (see discussion in Schneider 2008: 765; Wolfram 2004).

Crucially for the present purpose, only one other variety of World English also has *be done*: Liberian Settler English (eWave rating B), a variety transported to Liberia by African Americans in the early nineteenth century, so that it was "the Liberian cohort of African-American English" (Singler 2004: 231). There is a sociohistorical explanation: sequential *be done* was most likely brought to West Africa by speakers of early nineteenth-century AAVE, where it was adopted as a dialect root.

17.2.4   Root 4: Remote *yon/yonder*

Remote *yon/yonder* represents a more complex scenario than those presented so far. In the "after" perfect, conjunction *do* and remote sequential *be done*, there were few (British and American) varieties involved, which is evidence of first- (from the British Isles to the colonies) and second-window (from the first to offspring colonies) transplantation processes. Given the complexity of contact-induced change, there are cases where a simple one-on-one mapping is not accurate. The case of remote (or distal) *yonder* as a locative illustrates this well. It is found in

(8)   Der a boat hoose yonder (Shetland and Orkney English; Melchers and Sundkvist 2013: 30)

(9)   see that hill that be on the side – it all up top yonder (St Helenian English; Schreier 2008: 186)

An eWave search indicates that *yonder* is reported (with varying frequencies) in a total of sixteen varieties of English around the world: in the British Isles (the northern varieties, to be more specific), America (the Southeast and the Appalachians), the Caribbean, the South Atlantic, Africa, and also in the Pacific. It is found in Traditional L1 varieties, English-based Pidgins and Creoles and also in High-Contact L1 Varieties (see Table 17.1).

Yonder is globally spread and has taken hold firmly. As its British origins are more diverse (north of England, Isle of Man, Scotland, Shetland and Orkney Islands), it is less diagnostic and cannot with confidence be pinpointed to one particular area, making multiple inputs plausible (see Section 17.3). In American English, it is found in southeastern enclave varieties and in the Appalachians, the latter having been strongly

Table 17.1 *Donor source attribution for* yonder *(eWave ratings)*

A (feature pervasive or obligatory)		
Variety	Region	Type
Orkney and Shetland English	British Isles	Traditional L1 varieties
Gullah	America	English-Based Creoles
Barbadian Creole (Bajan)	Caribbean	English-Based Creoles
Eastern Maroon Creole	Caribbean	English-Based Creoles
Palmerston English	Pacific	English-Based Creoles
B (feature neither pervasive nor extremely rare)		
North English dialects	British Isles	Traditional L1 varieties
Manx English	British Isles	Traditional L1 varieties
Scottish English	British Isles	Traditional L1 varieties
Appalachian English	America	Traditional L1 varieties
Southeast American enclave	America	Traditional L1 varieties
Guyanese Creole	Caribbean	English-Based Creoles
Vincentian English	Caribbean	English-Based Creoles
St Helenian English	South Atlantic	High-Contact L1 varieties
C (feature exists but is extremely rare)		
Rural African American English	America	High-Contact L1 varieties
Tristan da Cunha English	South Atlantic	High-Contact L1 varieties
Vernacular Liberian English	Africa	English-Based pidgins

influenced by the Ulster Scots (thus suggesting a direct link, as we had in Liberia as well). *Yonder* also made its way into the Caribbean (from the British Isles presumably, though a secondary American input cannot be excluded), the South Atlantic, Africa (again via the settlers that influenced Liberian Settler English), and the Pacific (notably Palmerston English, Hendery 2015a, 2015b; see the following section). While it is still possible to retrace its diffusion, the patterning is much more widespread so that the overall diagnostic value of the feature is lower than in the cases previously discussed (particularly in what regards the Caribbean).

17.2.5   Root 5: Negator *ain't*

The last root discussed in detail here is *ain't*, which, though highly stigmatized, is "used world-wide as the negative form of both *be* and (auxiliary) *have*" (Anderwald 2012: 312) and also functions as a generic negator before main verbs. *Ain't* is a merged negator used for the auxiliaries *be, have* as well as *didn't*, as in Examples (9)–(14), all taken from Kortmann and Lunkenheimer (2013):

(9)   I ain't really thinking about getting with J. or any other guy. (Chicano English; ain't = *be*)

(10)   Them fellas ain't doing nothing. (Trinidadian Creole; ain't = *be*)

(11)   I ain't got no money. (Australian English; ain't = *have*)

(12)   Sister Ruth ain't come yet o. (Liberian Settler English; ain't = *have*)

(13)   They ain't tell me. (Liberian Settler English; ain't = *didn't*)

(14)   He ain't live too far. (Bahamian Creole; ain't = *didn't*)

Ain't as the negated form of *be* is attested in thirty-three varieties included in the eWave (ca. 40 percent): in all American and South Atlantic varieties, in nine out of twelve British varieties, as well as in most Australian and Caribbean dialects (see Figure 17.1). However, it features less often in Africa (where it is attested in Liberian Settler English, Vernacular Liberian English, and White Zimbabwean English) and the Pacific (Norfolk Islands/Pitcairn English) and is completely absent in South and Southeast Asia. There is thus a clear areal concentration in America and the South Atlantic, followed by the British Isles and to a lesser extent Australia and the Caribbean (Bahamian Creole, Barbadian Creole, and Vincentian Creole). *Ain't* mostly occurs in L1 varieties and high-contact L1 varieties have a slightly higher attestation than traditional L1 varieties. This is to be expected as the regions with the highest attestation rates (America, South Atlantic, and the British Isles) include a majority of L1 varieties. The low percentages for indigenized L2 varieties and English-based Pidgins can be explained by the fact that most L2 varieties and Pidgins occur in the regions that have the lowest attestation, namely

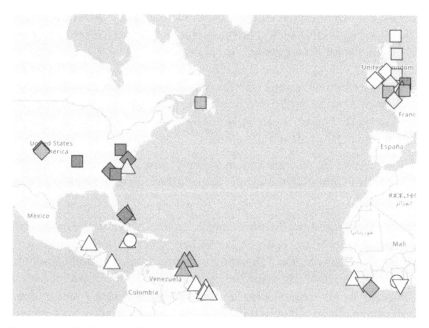

Figure 17.1 *ain't* for negated *be* in eWAVE

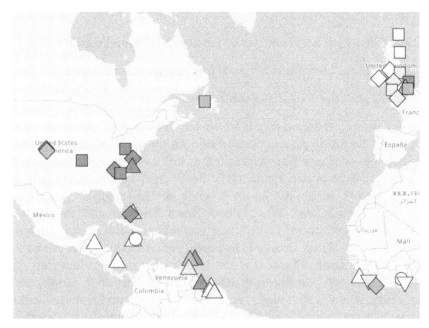

Figure 17.2 *ain't* for negated *have* in eWAVE

Africa, Asia, and the Pacific. Thus, variety type distribution very much correlates with regional distribution.

The overall attestation of *ain't* as the negated form of *have* in eWAVE is ca. 40 percent (see Figure 17.2), thus slightly lower than for negated *be*, yet the attestations in the individual world regions are quite similar. It is more common in America and in the Caribbean than in the British Isles and Australia, rare in the Pacific, and inexistent in Asia. With regard to variety types, the feature is frequent in high-contact L1 and traditional L1 varieties.

Ain't as a common negator, finally, is least frequent, reported in only ca. 21 percent of all varieties, and one of the most infrequent negation features in World Englishes generally (Anderwald 2012: 312). It is most common in America, particularly in AAVE:

(15)   I hop' ya ain't wanna kno' much mo' 'cause I 'bout through. (Earlier African American Vernacular English) (Kortmann and Lunkenheimer 2013)

and in the Caribbean (Bahamian English, Bajan, Guyanese Creole) but has attested absence in the British varieties and Africa (with the exception of the two Liberian varieties). Figure 17.3 shows that it is entirely absent in Asia, Australia, the Pacific, and the South Atlantic.

In other words, general negator use is restricted to the American and Caribbean varieties but absent in the British donor varieties, even though *ain't* is historically attested for both *have* and *be* (the one exception is

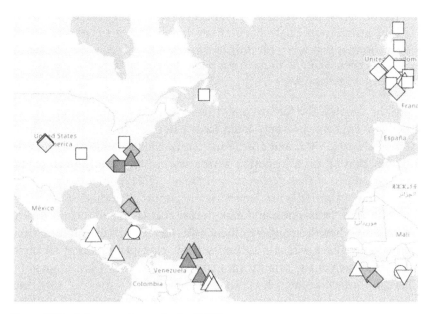

Figure 17.3 *ain't* as generic negator in eWAVE

Channel Island English, where it is reported to be rare: "in the JersE [Jersey English] data, there is just a single occurrence of *ain't* in the interview with a 48-year old male speaker"; Rosen 2014: 167).

The distribution of this particular dialect root in World Englishes can be summarized as follows: *ain't* for *be* and *have* is mostly found in the British Isles (with a predominance in the south), in the Caribbean, and in nearly all American varieties. It is also found in Africa, though only in the Liberian Settler English and Vernacular Liberian English. *Ain't* for *be* is the most widespread usage, with attestations in the South Atlantic and in the Pacific also (Palmerston Island English). The overall hierarchy with regard to widespread distribution is:

> *ain't* for *be*
> > *> ain't* for *have*
> > > *> ain't* as general negator

This hierarchy finds support in the overall number of varieties (thirty-three, thirty-two, sixteen) and – as a corollary – also in regional spread and variety type. This suggests that a dialect root (*ain't*) was transplanted out of the British Isles (or, to be more specific, the southern varieties) into the transatlantic colonies. Both usages (*be* and *have*) were common at the time of colonization. The general usage as a negator, however, represents an independent local phenomenon, restricted to America and the Caribbean and not found in the donor sources. Following Anderwald (2012: 312):

It is unclear which world region influenced which, but it is not completely implausible to speculate that in the evolution of creoles in the Caribbean, the negator that was frequently employed by the slave holders to negate the frequent verbs *have* and *be* was overextended by the slaves themselves to a more general use.

From the Creoles, the feature might have "spread to Gullah and African American English, and may later have extended to Chicano English" (Anderwald 2012: 312) and other American varieties. Anderwald goes on to claim that "[t]he distribution across variety types only mirrors the distribution inside these geographical areas" (p. 312). Importantly, most high-contact L1 varieties are American and almost all of the Creoles are in the Caribbean. Thus, one could make a case that areal and sociohistorical factors might have a stronger influence on the feature's distribution than variety type. There was also second-window transplantation of all three usages back across the Atlantic into Liberia (where they were adopted by Liberian Vernacular English via the Liberian Settler Varieties). *Ain't* thus took a life of its own, so to speak; it originated as a negator for *have* and *be* in the British Isles and later took on an additional function. Roots may develop further semantic/pragmatic usages or change to adopt more general usages induced by extensive language and dialect contact (perhaps via ongoing grammaticalization).

To sum up, the discussion of five selected features, the "after" perfect, conjunction *do*, sequential *be done*, remote *yon/yonder*, and negator *ain't*, has shown how dialect features may differ in terms of donor source attribution, regional spread, and potential for additional developments. The first three features were characterized by a high degree of localizability; they were assigned to one region of origin and one place in the newly established overseas colonies (America and the Caribbean). The "after" perfect is a direct legacy of Southern Irish English, brought to Newfoundland by fishermen in the eighteenth century; conjunction *do*, though the historical connections are somewhat sketchy, could have been brought to coastal North Carolina by East Anglian settlers (Trudgill argued against the possibility of independent innovation). Similarly, *be done* had both a donor and a recipient variety but the process represented indirect legacy, or rather, second-window transplantation, as it was a colonial (Caribbean or American) innovation brought to Liberia by slaves, speaking forms of nineteenth-century African American English. Both first- and second-window transplantation provide showcase scenarios that allowed us to investigate dialect change and outcomes of contact types in new linguistic-ecological environments (see Poplack and Tagliamonte 2001 on the development of African American English in diasporic settings; see Zipp, Chapter 6, this volume).

However, as the discussion of remote *yon/yonder* and *ain't* has shown, one-on-one mapping of dialect features from donor to recipient variety is not usually straightforward. There are several reasons. First (and perhaps most importantly), the same feature may be present in several input varieties: *yon/yonder* is reported throughout the English North, Scotland, the Orkneys, and Shetlands, as well as on the Isle of Man, so pinpointing one particular donor source is not possible in these cases. Generally speaking, Trudgill (1986) already claimed that settlement by speakers of one donor variety is the exception rather than the norm. As the analysis of varieties such as Tristan da Cunha English (Schreier 2002) has shown, selection chances are likely to be higher when features are present in dialects spoken by several founding populations. Second, the interaction of dialects may give rise to additional developments. One good example here is linguistic camouflaging, when "a vernacular form resembles a standard or different vernacular form so closely that it is simply assumed to be identical to its apparent structural counterpart" (Wolfram 2004: 114). Wolfram (1994) suggested that, in an example such as "They call themselves dancing," camouflaging may involve syntactic expansion and a subsequent semantic-pragmatic reorientation. While counterfactual *call oneself* is common with noun phrases (e.g. "They call themselves experts") or adjective phrases (e.g. "They call themselves cheap"), its structural expansion to include *Verb+ing* complements sets African American English apart from most other American English dialects (see also Spears 1982), who argued that the semi-auxiliary *come* has acquired a specific semantic-pragmatic role of indicating speaker indignation).

Though this is personal speculation, camouflaging processes may arguably increase and intensify due to second-window transplantation. Accordingly, quantitative analyses to uncover language-internal constraints should ideally accompany feature-based analyses that are qualitative in nature.

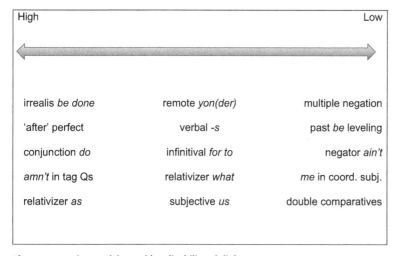

High		Low
irrealis *be done*	remote *yon(der)*	multiple negation
'after' perfect	verbal *-s*	past *be* leveling
conjunction *do*	infinitival *for to*	negator *ain't*
amn't in tag Qs	relativizer *what*	*me* in coord. subj.
relativizer *as*	subjective *us*	double comparatives

Figure 17.4 Diagnosticity and localizability of dialect roots

Figure 17.4 summarizes the diagnostic value of dialect features and suggests a continuum, ranging from high to low degrees of localization. Features toward the left end are ideal for an analysis of founder effects (Mufwene 2001), as they can be clearly demarcated regionally, both in donor and in recipient varieties. Toward the right end there are general features, characterized by wide regional diffusion, both in donor and in recipient dialects. In their extreme form, they are what Chambers (2009: 258) has classified as "vernacular roots" (multiple negation, past *be* leveling, etc.; see Section 17.2).

The dialect roots of World Englishes thus differ in their distribution and regional affiliation, and this leads to the second question that needs to be considered here: why some features thrive whereas others do not.

17.3   The Growth of Roots

Recent debates on the principal motivation of feature selection have primarily focused on the roles of (1) input strength and (2) identity. Whereas Trudgill (2004) has categorically denied any influence of identity, Hickey (2004) and Schneider (2007) have included an indexical function of dialect features in their models. The question is too complex to go into much detail here (see Schreier 2013 for a more thorough critique), so it is sufficient to state that attempts to explain feature selection should consider the following factors: the concentration and frequency of features in the input varieties, the social relationships and settlement patterns of the migrant populations, the social meaning of features (particularly when it comes to overt sociolinguistic stigmatization), and the intensity of connections (including human traffic) with the homeland (e.g. via transnational ties; Bolander, Chapter 29, this volume).

As for input strength, features with wider distribution patterns and frequent usage across speech communities have an overall advantage, so the concentration of dialects throughout the wider sociolinguistic ecology of founder communities is an important criterion to consider (see Section 17.1). A good example comes from New Zealand English, where Schreier et al. (2003) showed that new-dialect formation processes were a direct reflection of local feature proportions in transplanted dialects. They analyzed the maintenance of voiceless labiovelar /hw-/ fricatives (minimal pairs *Wales* ~ *whales*, *witch* ~ *which*) in three selected regions (Otago/Southland, Canterbury, and the North Island) and found that there was considerable regional variation in early twentieth-century New Zealand English. Whereas New Zealanders from the North Island and Canterbury were predominantly using /w/ (here the /hw/ ~ /w/ merger was practically completed by 1950), speakers from the Southland and

Table 17.2 */hw- ~ w-/ variation in early twentieth-century New Zealand English (from Schreier et al. 2003: 258)*

	/hw/	/w/	percent /hw/
Southland	441	666	40.0% (441/1107)
Canterbury	51	596	7.9% (51/647)
North	21	369	5.4% (21/390)

Otago regions had high levels of /hw-/ well into the second half of the twentieth century (Table 17.2).

The regional distribution of the variable was linked to population demographics and ancestral effects, thus correlating with the input strength of /hw-/ retaining donor dialects. /hw-/ survival in the Otago/Southland dialect region was explained by high input frequency and the disproportionally high input of Scottish and Irish settlers, where a /hw-/ and /w-/ distinction survives until today. In the other regions, the social configuration and the local contact and mixture situations were substantially different, so /hw-/ was not adopted. Here the inputs mainly came from the south of England, where /hw-/ was a minority feature, and this enhanced leveling-out in the local forms of NZE. A high overall presence of /hw-/ variants in the inputs had an enhancing effect on adoption and maintenance, an effect that was arguably even stronger given that the feature was regionally marked (see Hickey 2003a, 2004). These effects may have correlated with settler numbers and may in fact be more persistent in small communities, where founder populations have a particularly high impact. On Palmerston Island, for instance, Henry Marsters, who came from the Midlands or the English North and established the community in the 1850s, left dialect roots such as a STRUT vowel that has FOOT, or unetymological /h/ before vowels with initial-stress vowels (*helse*, *hunderstand*), a conservative British dialect feature that also has taken root elsewhere (e.g. on Tristan da Cunha; Schreier 2019).

Similarly, Hickey (2003a) argued that the numerical proportions between colonizers and their degree of social organization are important factors in the new-dialect formation process. Based on a chronology of Irish settlements in New Zealand, Hickey suggested that the earliest settlement forms were socially stratified and that the donor dialects' prestige was a decisive factor for the adoption of dialect features. Accordingly, this might possibly explain why Irish English, though present early and sociodemographically prominent in large settlements such as Auckland, disappeared without having much of an impact, simply because the social stigma of the speakers and their dialects was too strong. According to Hickey, supraregionalization ("an historical process whereby varieties of a language lose specifically local features and becomes less regionally bound"; Hickey 2003b: 351) is a key factor in feature adoption and selection: "[D]ialect speakers progressively adopt more and more features of a non-regional variety which they are in contact with. There does not have to be direct speaker contact" (2003a: 236), so that the new variety can "be seen as a product of unconscious choices made across a broad front in a new society to create a distinct linguistic identity" (Hickey 2003a: 215). A supraregional form, according to Hickey, would emerge in the melting pot settlements first, where there were mixed populations of high density and size, and then spread to rural settlements that subsequently would become dialectally distinctive. On the other hand, sustained contacts with the "mother country" are also crucial. Close links, bidirectional migration patterns and high levels of human traffic enable interaction between donor and recipient dialects. As a result, innovations may be passed on and picked up; a good example here is non-rhoticity, which was "transplanted" to coastal American settings (Boston, Savannah) but did not take root further inland where there was little contact with British colonists.

The issue of identity has become central in recent approaches to the emergence of World Englishes. For instance, it is central in Schneider's (2007) model of the evolution of postcolonial Englishes (e.g. in the maintenance of transnational ties), and

> represents an individual stance with respect to the social structures of one's environment, an attitude that also contributes to group formation and group delimitation through establishing an "us vs. them" construct of human alignments and through establishing relationships of similarity or difference – that is, social classification and individual affiliation.
>
> (Schneider 2007: 264)

In sum, feature adoption, or the survival of dialect roots, is a complex process that depends on the sociolinguistic nature of a contact setting, its social structuring and amount of stratification, the amount of dialects in dialect contact situations, and of course also on indexical values such as stigma and prestige. These have to be assessed independently in each setting.

17.4 Conclusion

This chapter has looked into selected aspects of dialect roots in World Englishes. Complementing other chapters in this volume, particularly the methodological demands of diachronic reconstruction (Huber, Chapter 21), earlier accounts of British English during colonization (Britain, Chapter 7), and the impact of contact-induced language and dialect change (Britain, Chapter 7; Mufwene, Chapter 5; Hickey, Chapter 2; Zipp, Chapter 6), the focus here has been on individual dialect roots: their adoption, selection, and subsequent development in newly forming colonial environments.

There are various reasons why dialect roots, that is, dialectal features that are permanently adopted in emerging World Englishes (ranging from traditional L1 varieties to pidgins and creoles), thrive and develop under dialect transportation and contact conditions. The originally British varieties that represent a substantial input in colonial settings are in a process of competition, as a result of which some features survive whereas others disappear. Criteria such as concentration and frequency of features, their regional distribution, and sociolinguistic significance all have to be taken into account in such an analysis. There is evidence that roots with wider usage have higher selection chances in the formation of World Englishes (even though frequency alone is not deterministic, in the sense of Trudgill [2004], for the ultimate outcome).

More often than not, it is difficult to map the dialectal origins of features. Though one-on-one mapping exists, as in the "after" perfect or conjunction *do*, ideally enabling a case study of dialect transplantation and also of change under potential dialect contact conditions (with potential morpho-syntactic or semantic/pragmatic effects), the picture is usually less clear, particularly when roots are brought to the colonies via several donor varieties (e.g. multiple negation). As a result, features that have high attestation levels in the eWave (*Me* instead of *I* in coordinate subjects) are less important for research on dialect roots (though of course they are valuable for dialect typology and the regional distribution of angloversal features).

Roots should be classified with regard to their degree of localizability, ranging from high to low, which emerged as an important criterion for research on contact-induced language change. Moreover, first- vs. second-window transportation may offer insights into typological affiliations of World Englishes and also help explain changes that originate as local innovations (e.g. *done been*). Offspring varieties can develop and spread their roots as well (exemplified by the connection between African American English and the Liberian varieties). As for survival rate, roots may persist and survive for generations (/hw-/ in New Zealand, verbal *–s* agreement in Appalachia) before they gradually disappear (conjunction *do* has all but disappeared in coastal North Carolina). To sum up, dialect roots provide an ideal background for research on the diversification of World Englishes. They allow a better understanding of the origins and development of these features, of variation and change processes, and help pinpoint potential donor sources from a historical perspective. They have been integrated into the research canon in diverse fields, from pidgin and creole studies, dialect typology, language variation and change to regional dialectology and contact linguistics.

References

Anderwald, Lieselotte. 2012. Negation in varieties of English. In Raymond Hickey, ed. *Areal Features of the Anglophone World*. Berlin: de Gruyter, 299–328.

Auer, Anita, Daniel Schreier and Richard J. Watts, eds. 2015. *Letter Writing and Language Change*. Cambridge: Cambridge University Press.

Baker, Philip and Adrienne Bruyn, eds. 1998. *St. Kitts and the Atlantic Creoles: The Texts of Samuel Augustus Mathews in Perspective*. London: Battlebridge Publications.

Blommaert, Jan. 2010. *The Sociolinguistics of Globalization*. Cambridge: Cambridge University Press.

Chambers, J. K. 2004. Dynamic typology and vernacular universals. In Bernd Kortmann, ed. *Dialectology Meets Typology*. Berlin: Mouton de Gruyter, 127–145.

Chambers, J. K. 2009. *Sociolinguistic Theory: Linguistic Variation and Its Social Significance* (3rd ed.). Oxford: Blackwell.

Clarke, Sandra. 2004. Newfoundland English: Phonology. In Edgar W. Schneider, Kate Burridge, Bernd Kortmann, Rajend Mesthrie and Clive Upton, eds. *A Handbook of Varieties of English*, Vol. 1. Berlin: de Gruyter, 366–382.

Clarke, Sandra. 2010. Newfoundland and Labrador English. In Daniel Schreier, Peter Trudgill, Edgar W. Schneider and Jeffrey P. Williams, eds. *The Lesser-Known Varieties of English. An Introduction*. Cambridge: Cambridge University Press, 72–91.

Crystal, David. 2003. *English as a Global Language* (2nd ed.). Cambridge: Cambridge University Press.

Dayton, Elizabeth. 1996. Grammatical categories of the verb in African-American Vernacular English. Unpublished doctoral dissertation, University of Pennsylvania.

Eberle, Nicole. 2017. "They're trying to hear English, which they are hearing, but it's Bermudian English": Bermudian English – Origins and Variation. Unpublished doctoral dissertation, University of Zurich.

Filppula, Markku, Juhani Klemola and Heli Paulasto, eds. 2009. *Vernacular Universals and Language Contacts: Evidence from Varieties of English and Beyond*. New York: Routledge.

Gordon, Elisabeth, Lyle Campbell, Jennifer Hay, Margaret Maclagan, Andrea Sudbury and Peter Trudgill. 2004. *New Zealand English: Its Origins and Evolution*. Cambridge: Cambridge University Press.

Hendery, Rachel. 2015a. Palmerston Island English. In Jeffrey P. Williams, Edgar W. Schneider, Peter Trudgill and Daniel Schreier, eds. *The Lesser-Known Varieties of English: Further Case Studies*. Cambridge: Cambridge University Press, 267–287.

Hendery, Rachel. 2015b. *One Man Is an Island: The Speech Community William Marsters Begat on Palmerston Island*. London: Battlebridge Publications.

Hickey, Raymond, ed. 2003a. *Motives for Language Change*. Cambridge: Cambridge University Press.

Hickey, Raymond. 2003b. How and why supraregional varieties arise. In Marina Dossena and Charles Jones, eds. *Insights into Late Modern English*. Frankfurt: Peter Lang, 351–373.

Hickey, Raymond, ed. 2004. *Legacies of Colonial English: Studies in Transported Dialects*. Cambridge: Cambridge University Press.

Hickey, Raymond. 2013 English as a contact language in Ireland and Scotland. In Daniel Schreier and Marianne Hundt, eds. *English as a Contact Language*. Cambridge: Cambridge University Press, 88–105.

Hundt, Marianne. 2013. The diversification of English: Old, new and emerging epicentres. In Daniel Schreier and Marianne Hundt, eds. *English as a Contact Language*. Cambridge: Cambridge University Press, 182–203.

Kachru, Braj B., Yamuna Kachru and Cecil Nelson. 2006. *The Handbook of World Englishes*. Oxford: Wiley.

Kiparsky, Paul. 2008. Universals constrain change; change results in typological generalizations. In Jeff Good, ed. *Language Universals and Language Change*. Oxford: Oxford University Press, 333–356.

Kortmann, Bernd and Kerstin Lunkenheimer, eds. 2013. *The Electronic World Atlas of Varieties of English*. Leipzig: Max Planck Institute for Evolutionary Anthropology. http://ewave-atlas.org

Kortmann, Bernd and Edgar W. Schneider. 2004. General introduction. In Bernd Kortmann and Edgar W. Schneider, eds. *A Handbook of Varieties of English: A Multimedia Reference Tool*. Berlin: de Gruyter, 1–9.

Kortmann, Bernd and Benedikt Szmrecsanyi. 2004. Global synopsis: Morphological and syntactic variation in English. In Edgar W. Schneider, Kate Burridge, Bernd Kortmann, Rajend Mesthrie and Clive Upton, eds. *A Handbook of Varieties of English, Vol. 2: Morphology and Syntax*. Berlin: Mouton de Gruyter, 1142–1202.

Kortmann, Bernd and Benedikt Szmrecsanyi. 2011. Parameters of morphosyntactic variation in World Englishes: Prospects and limitations of searching for universals. In Peter Siemund, ed. *Linguistic Universals and Language Variation*. Berlin: de Gruyter, 264–290.

Labov, William. 1998. Co-existent systems in African-American Vernacular English. In Salikoko Mufwene, John R. Rickford, Guy Bailey and John Baugh, eds. *The Structure of African-American English: Structure, History and Use*. London and New York: Routledge, 110–153.

Lim, Lisa and Umberto Ansaldo. 2015. *Languages in Contact*. Cambridge: Cambridge University Press.

Melchers, Gunnel and Peter Sundkvist. 2013. Orkney and Shetland. In Daniel Schreier, Peter Trudgill, Edgar W. Schneider and Jeffrey P. Williams, eds. *The Lesser-Known Varieties of English. An Introduction*. Cambridge: Cambridge University Press, 17–34.

Mesthrie, Rajend and Rakesh Bhatt. 2008. *World Englishes: The Study of New Linguistic Varieties*. Cambridge: Cambridge University Press.

Montgomery, Michael. 1989. Exploring the roots of Appalachian English. *English World-Wide 10*: 227–278.

Mufwene, Salikoko. 2001. *The Ecology of Language Evolution*. Cambridge: Cambridge University Press.

Poplack, Shana and Sali Tagliamonte. 2001. *African American English in the Diaspora*. Oxford: Blackwell.

Rickford, John E. 1999. Phonological and grammatical features of African American Vernacular English. In John R. Rickford, ed. *African American English*. Malden, MA: Blackwell, 3–14.

Rosen, Anna. 2014. *Grammatical Variation and Change in Jersey English*. Amsterdam: Benjamins.

Schneider, Edgar W. 2002. Investigating variation and change in written documents. In Jack K. Chambers, Peter Trudgill and Natalie Schilling-Estes, eds. *The Handbook of Language Variation and Change*. Oxford: Blackwell, 67–96.

Schneider, Edgar W. 2007. *Postcolonial English: Varieties Around the World*, Cambridge: Cambridge University Press.

Schneider, Edgar W. 2008. Synopsis: Morphological and syntactic variation in the Americas and the Caribbean. In Edgar W. Schneider, ed. *Varieties of English, Vol. 2: The Americas and the Caribbean*. Berlin: de Gruyter, 763–776.

Schneider, Edgar W. 2011. *English Around the World: An Introduction*. Cambridge: Cambridge University Press.

Schneider, Edgar W. 2013. Investigating historical variation and change in written documents: New perspectives. In Jack K. Chambers and Natalie Schilling, eds. *The Handbook of Language Variation and Change* (2nd ed.). Oxford: Blackwell, 57–81.

Schreier, Daniel. 2002. *Terra incognita* in the Anglophone world: Tristan da Cunha, South Atlantic Ocean. *English World-Wide 23*: 1–29.

Schreier, Daniel. 2008. *St Helenian English: Origins, Evolution and Variation*. Amsterdam: John Benjamins.

Schreier, Daniel. 2009. Language in isolation, and its implications for variation and change. In *Blackwell Language and Linguistics Compass 3*. Oxford: Blackwell Publisher.

Schreier, Daniel. 2013. English as a contact language: Lesser-known varieties. In Daniel Schreier and Marianne Hundt, eds. *English as a Contact Language*. Cambridge: Cambridge University Press, 149–164.

Schreier, Daniel. 2016. Contact histories and simplification: Some typological and sociolinguistic considerations. In Guido Seiler and Raffaela Bächler, eds. *Complexity, Isolation and Variation*. Berlin: Mouton de Gruyter, 139-157.

Schreier, Daniel. 2019. /h/ insertion as a "camouflaged archaism"? Dialect contact, colonial lag and the feature pool in South Atlantic English. *Diachronica 36*(1): 36–64.

Schreier, Daniel, Peter Trudgill, Edgar W. Schneider and Jeffrey P. Williams, eds. 2010. *The Lesser-Known Varieties of English. An Introduction*. Cambridge: Cambridge University Press.

Schreier, Daniel, Elizabeth Gordon, Jennifer Hay and Margaret Maclagan. 2003. The regional and sociolinguistic dimension of /hw-/ maintenance and loss in early 20th-century New Zealand English. *English World-Wide* 24: 245–69.

Singler, John V. 2004. The morphology and syntax of Liberian settler English. In Bernd Kortmann and Edgar W. Schneider, eds. *A Handbook of Varieties of English: A Multimedia Reference Tool*. Berlin: de Gruyter, PAGES.

Spears, Arthur K. 1982. The Black English semi-auxiliary come. *Language* 58(4): 850–872.

Szmrecsanyi, Benedikt and Bernd Kortmann. 2009. Vernacular universals and angloversals in a typological perspective. In Markku Filppula, Juhani Klemola and Heli Paulasto, eds. *Vernacular Universals and Language Contacts: Evidence from Varieties of English and Beyond*. London: Routledge, 33–53.

Tagliamonte, Sali A. 2012. *Roots of English: Exploring the history of dialects.* Cambridge: Cambridge University Press.

Thomason, Sarah G. 2009. Why universals versus contact-induced change? In Markku Filppula, Juhani Klemola and Heli Paulasto, eds. *Vernacular Universals and Language Contacts: Evidence from Varieties of English and Beyond*. London: Routledge, 349–64.

Trudgill, Peter. 1986. *Dialects in Contact*. Oxford: Blackwell.

Trudgill, Peter. 2002. *Sociolinguistic Variation and Change*. Edinburgh: Edinburgh University Press.

Trudgill, Peter. 2004. *New Dialect Formation: The Inevitability of Colonial Englishes*. Edinburgh: Edinburgh University Press.

Trudgill, Peter. 2009. Vernacular universals and the sociolinguistic typology of English dialects. In Markku Filppula, Juhani Klemola and Heli Paulasto, eds. *Vernacular Universals and Language Contacts: Evidence from Varieties of English and Beyond*. London: Routledge, 302–320.

Watts, Richard J. and Peter Trudgill. 2002. *Alternative Histories of English*. London and New York: Routledge.

Williams, Jeffrey P., Edgar W. Schneider, Peter Trudgill and Daniel Schreier, eds. 2015. *The Lesser-Known Varieties of English: Further Case Studies*. Cambridge: Cambridge University Press.

Winford, Donald. 2009. The interplay of 'universals' and contact-induced change in the emergence of World Englishes. In Markku Filppula, Juhani Klemola and Heli Paulasto, eds. *Vernacular Universals and Language Contacts: Evidence from Varieties of English and Beyond*. London: Routledge, 206–30.

Wolfram, Walt. 1994. On the sociolinguistic significance of obscure dialect structures: NPi call NPi V-ing in African American Vernacular English. *American Speech 69*: 339–360.

Wolfram, Walt. 2004. The grammar of urban African American Vernacular English. In Bernd Kortmann and Edgar W. Schneider, eds. *A Handbook of Varieties of English: A Multimedia Reference Tool*. Berlin: de Gruyter, 111–32.

18

Lexicography and World Englishes

James Lambert

This chapter discusses dictionaries from the point of view of World Englishes (WEs). The first section describes what dictionaries are, provides some relevant categorizations of dictionary types, and discusses the importance of dictionaries for WEs. For those considering compiling a dictionary, advice and caveats are given. The second section provides an overview of the dictionaries currently available for the various anglophone regions around the world. The paucity of dictionaries for many varieties, not to mention the absence of dictionaries for many others, highlights the need for more lexicographical work to be done in the field of WEs.

18.1 Basic Issues

18.1.1 What Is a Dictionary?

For most people, the word "dictionary" brings a particular conceptualization to mind, namely the traditional, monolingual, standardizing, synchronic, alphabetically ordered, print dictionary – what we can call the *traditional dictionary*. It is the traditional dictionary that is invoked in the common expression "Look it up in the dictionary." Even today, with so many dictionaries available electronically, the usual idea of "dictionary" is the traditional dictionary and, indeed, many online dictionaries are little more than traditional print dictionaries that have been put on the Internet. So to start, let us explore this idea, for even though the traditional dictionary is the most common type by sheer number, there are many other dictionary types not covered by this conceptualization. Of course it is well known that dictionaries need not be monolingual and that in our electronically advanced world they no longer need to be printed. Yet dictionaries also do not need to be standardizing, nor synchronic, nor alphabetically ordered (thematic dictionaries, for instance, are not). At its barest minimum, the dictionary format consists of relatively uniform entries, each of which is headed with a term (i.e. a word or expression, a "lexical item" or "lexeme") followed by some linguistic information about that lexical item. In other words, the concept of dictionary in its simplest form is defined by structure (term + explication/information) and topic (items of language). Encyclopedias have the same structure but differ essentially in that the headwords are not wholly restricted to items of language, explications are longer, and information given extends beyond the linguistic: Once we move away from linguistic information, we move away from lexicography.

Expanding on this simple lexicographical structure we arrive at a great variety in dictionary types. Indeed, so great is the variety that lexicography theoretician Béjoint, after struggling with the question of dictionary typology, concluded that "it is impossible to classify dictionaries in a way that would be both orderly and applicable to all societies" (2010: 45). The innumerate variety of dictionary types is a result of (1) the selection of lexical items, (2) the categories of linguistic information presented for each lexical item, and (3) the method of presentation, all of which are determined by the imagined target audience. The most common types of linguistic information provided in dictionaries are definition of senses, orthography, pronunciation, grammatical category, illustrative sentences, and etymology, but there are no restrictions on the types of linguistic information that can be presented in the dictionary format. In this aspect of lexicography, there are no actual rules as such: The lexicographer has the ultimate free hand. Other information types that have been included are common collocations (both pre- and post-), visual information (diagrams, graphs, line drawings, illustrations, photos, video, etc.), usage notes (especially for disputed usages), quotations from famous authors and/or other texts, pragmatic information, frequency data, and syntactic information, but essentially the list is unrestricted so long as the information is linguistic or serves to illustrate some linguistic feature. For example, a recent dictionary of Indian English (Carls 2017), uniquely, incorporates a vast amount of data about the word-formation patterns of the lexis covered. Thus, I am suggesting here that the most useful way to view "the dictionary" is as an amazingly versatile and highly adaptable platform for the presentation of linguistic information, and in this respect dictionaries offer a valuable avenue for WEs scholars to display research.

18.1.2   Some Major Dictionary Types

The conventional method of dictionary compilation is to collect a large body of linguistic evidence of the target lexis, which is then analyzed in order to detect the linguistic features of interest (denotation, connotation, grammatical category, morphology, pronunciation, etc.). Most frequently this evidence is textual, but oral evidence has also been used extensively for some dictionaries (and, naturally, oral evidence provides the basis of dictionary pronunciations). Traditionally, the collection of text-based evidence was done through reading (specially selected) texts and collecting relevant data by excerpting sentences containing target vocabulary and writing those sentences on slips of paper or, later, inputting them into a database. Today's technology allows for the creation of (increasingly larger) electronic corpora of language that can then be searched for relevant lexicographical information. This has brought about two changes: First, corpora make searching for target vocabulary easier and, second, lexicographers are confronted with many more lexical items to deal with. However, apart from these changes, there has been little change from pre-computer days in terms of lexicographic techniques.

While dictionaries come in a multitude of forms, most can be categorized according to the following dichotomies.

18.1.2.1   Synchronic vs. Diachronic

Synchronic dictionaries treat the lexis current at the time of compilation and publishing. A standard commercial desk dictionary is a good example, as are learner dictionaries and dictionaries for the school market. Naturally, as language changes over time, synchronic dictionaries have a limited lifespan, and successful titles necessarily go through multiple editions. Obsolete lexis and obsolete linguistic features (e.g. senses, pronunciations, spellings) are generally omitted unless they still exist as archaisms in current language (e.g. *'tis* for *it is*). Synchronic dictionaries are generally published by commercial publishers with the primary goal of making a profit. In contrast, diachronic dictionaries attempt to cover the history of a language from a specific date in the past up to the time of its compilation and publishing. The most recognized example of the historical dictionary is the multivolume *Oxford English Dictionary* (hereafter *OED*), the first edition of which covered English from the twelfth century until the Victorian era. Such lexicographical undertakings are known by the somewhat unwieldy title "dictionaries on historical principles" and typically display a selection of the citational evidence amassed for the project, from the earliest discovered examples to the latest, and with senses chronologically listed from oldest to most recent, so that reading an entry from the beginning gives an overview of the term's development over time. Dictionaries on historical principles are large scholarly undertakings, requiring decades to produce, and are often subsidized by institutional funding since they are infrequently profitable as a publishing venture. Both the diachronic and the synchronic types are suitable for dictionaries of WEs.

18.1.2.2   Inclusive vs. Exclusive

This terminology is useful when describing regional or varietal dictionaries. An inclusive dictionary is one that takes the entire lexis (or at least the core vocabulary) of the variety as its target lexis, while an exclusive dictionary only focuses on the lexical items that are specific to that variety. While the *OED* was inclusive, attempting to cover all British English, other Oxford publications in the same style are exclusive, such as Orsman (1997), which only treats New Zealandisms, Silva (1996), restricted to South Africanisms, and Moore (2016), treating Australianisms. Most WEs dictionaries are exclusive. Examples of inclusive dictionaries treating a specific variety of English are *Webster's* (for American English) and *Macquarie* (for Australian English). There also exist standard dictionaries with an appended glossary of regionalisms. A crossover category consists of traditional inclusive dictionaries (of British or American English) with an exclusive glossary attached as an appendix. Both inclusive and exclusive approaches are suitable for dictionaries of WEs.

18.1.2.3 Professional vs. Amateur

The use of the words "professional" and "amateur" is not meant to imply any automatic value judgment but these adjectives are commonly used as a convenient way to refer to two different types of dictionary, each of which occupy one end of a spectrum. Professional lexicography is involved in compiling both traditional and scholarly historical dictionaries such as the *OED*, and generally tends to employ a higher standard of lexicographical rigor, resulting in a more balanced and consistent treatment. In contrast, amateur lexicographers usually produce short works, commonly between 300 and 2,000 entries, aimed at the popular market. Most have brightly illustrated covers, humorous cartoon illustrations, and occasionally comic/punning titles, for example *The Coxford Singlish Dictionary* (Goh and Woo 2009) or *The Queen's Hinglish: How to Speak Pukka* (Mahal 2006). While not scholarly in approach, these are nevertheless generally reliable sources for localized lexis and they certainly should not be dismissed out of hand. However, amateur works do tend to include at least some terms that would be excluded by professional lexicographers. Examples include typical but non-idiomatic phrases, such as *aveagoodweegend* for "have a good weekend" (McInnes 2014: 10), and concocted spellings meant to represent local pronunciations, such as *immeelly* for "immediately" (Goh and Woo 2009: 98). They also frequently mismatch the grammatical class of headword and definition. For example, Aw (2016) labels the headword *siao* a "verb," defines it as a noun, "[a]n act of being fanatical towards," and then provides an illustrative phrase in which the word is an adjective: "My sister is a little *siao* collecting these limited edition Hello Kitty toys" (this last being the correct part of speech). Another feature is the inclusion of lexical items thought to be locally restricted but that occur right across the anglophone world, such as *gimme* for "give me" (Christian 1993: 16).

Amateur works often consist of only headword and definition, though illustrative phrases are also common. Pronunciation information is usually absent or, if present, only applied intermittently rather than systematically, and via an unexplained respelling system rather than the

International Phonetic Alphabet (IPA). Not uncommonly, amateur works feature comic definitions, such as "**clackers**: Dentures – remember, always be true to your teeth and they'll never be false to you!" (Blackman 1990: 22). Etymologies are usually given sparingly and offer only very basic details, often just the source language, and it is safest not to rely on them without further confirmation. Folk etymologies are occasionally put forward as genuine but these are generally few in number (and neither are folk etymologies entirely absent from professional lexicography). An exonormative stance (which typically posits British English as the prestige/target form) is present in some amateur dictionaries, though the bulk of them are written as celebrations of localized lexis, native inventiveness, and unique local culture. Amateur dictionaries, true to etymology, are normally the result of a labor of love and are usually written *in toto* before a publisher is sought. Larger-scale scholarly works normally require financial and institutional backing in order to come to fruition, and there are many cases of such works being abandoned. Clearly both "professional" and "amateur" types are suitable for dictionaries of WEs, though academics will of course tend toward the former.

18.1.3   Caveats for WEs Lexicographers

There is nothing special about any of the so-called new varieties of English that requires any special innovation in lexicography. That said, there are a number of aspects that may be more salient for scholars in the field of WEs. One area is etymology, especially for those varieties of English that are strongly influenced by local languages. Traditionally dictionaries have devoted much etymological endeavor to words borrowed into English from the major donor languages Greek, Latin, and French but have generally accorded less effort to borrowings from other languages. One step forward in lexicography for those Englishes that exist in multilingual environments would be to provide more etymological detail for borrowed lexis. At present the common practice is to only give etymons in transliteration, often using a system that is neither standardized nor universally known. For example, the Hindi etymon of the word *chutney* appears in various dictionary etymologies as *chatni*, *chatnī*, or *caṭnī*, based on some phonemic equivalence system that is not explained anywhere in the front matter of the dictionary in question. In a dictionary of Indian English, for whom a good deal of the intended audience would know Hindi, it would be better to give the original script form चटनी, followed by the transliteration. Similarly, transliterations of Cantonese etymons of borrowings in Hong Kong English, such as *baahk choi* or *baak6 coi3* for *bok choy*, are practically meaningless to local Honkongers who are generally unfamiliar with transliteration systems. It is much better to give the original script form, 白菜, which can then be followed by a transliteration, or even a rendering in IPA /paːk˥ tsʰɔːi˩/. For electronic dictionaries, it would be preferable to accompany the native script etymon with a recorded pronunciation, which could be optionally supported by a transliteration or IPA rendering. As a general rule, when transliteration systems are used, a table of equivalence to IPA phonemes should be supplied to the dictionary-user as well.

Pronunciation is another aspect that requires careful consideration. Apart from scholarly dictionaries for Inner Circle varieties, WEs lexicographers have generally omitted pronunciations from their dictionaries, and some compilers openly throw their hands up at the task (e.g. Lewis 1991: vi; Sengupta 1996: 1431; Mahal 2006: xii). There are exceptions, for instance, the various Asian English dictionaries produced by the *Macquarie Dictionary* publishers, and Lee (2004–2015) for Singapore English. Difficulty arises from the fact that many varieties of English have quite variable pronunciation, dependent on a number of factors, and, while some varieties have a recognized standard form, many others do not. Nevertheless, none of these factors absolutely preclude adding pronunciations to a dictionary; it just makes the task more complex. Indeed, American English dictionaries have always had pronunciations despite the fact that pronunciation is very variable across the speech community and the fact that there is no single standard pronunciation ("general American" being best viewed as "an idealization over a group of accents"; Carr 2012: 19).

18.1.4   How Are Dictionaries Useful to WEs?

There are a number of ways in which dictionaries can contribute significantly to the WEs field. First, varietal dictionaries can play an important role as a resource for later lexicographers, not only in alerting them to various items of localized lexis they may not be aware of (and hence informing corpus searches) but also in providing crucial evidence of a term's existence at a certain time. This is especially true for lexical items from the colloquial, taboo, and other nonformal registers of a language. All historical lexicographers are well aware of the value of early glossaries and dictionaries to the historical record of a language. In the case of Australian English, for example, the lexicographical works of Sidney J. Baker in the 1940s still today provide the earliest evidence for a long list of words that are commonplace in contemporary Australian English.

Second, those dictionaries that already exist can be used for further academic inquiry. Contemporary publications offer a window on contemporary lexis, while earlier works provide a historical perspective. For example, Sey (1973) offers about 300 items of Ghanaian English from more than four decades ago, which, aside from the lexical and sociolinguistic interest such a wordlist provides, could be assessed against current Ghanaian English sources in order to determine the stability of the variety over time, which in turn comments on the endo-/exonormativity of the variety. The assumption here is that, if a large body of lexis is stable in a particular variety over a long period, this points to an endonormative vigor that has withstood any exonormative pressures the variety has been subjected to over the same period. Other possibilities are to analyze the dictionary lexis in terms of cultural linguistics, or to take a discourse analysis approach.

Finally, the production of a lexicon can assist in the validation and valorization of a variety. The important place of dictionaries in language standardization is well known (e.g. Kachru 1980: 72), but dictionaries are not restricted to recording standard varieties and their potential to valorize varieties that are not considered standard is still powerful. Winer, compiler of the *Dictionary of the English/Creole of Trinidad & Tobago* (2009), reports that the most common response she received from members of the public on publication of her dictionary was a statement equivalent to "Thank you for validating our language" (personal communication, July 29, 2016). That said, to date, detailed studies that seek to investigate the role of lexicography in the emergence of varieties of English, or to quantify or otherwise explicate the impact of dictionaries on language validation, are lacking, and research in this area is a clear desideratum as the important question of whether dictionaries are leaders or followers in this respect has not been answered.

18.1.5   A Call for More Dictionaries

Given the versatility of the dictionary format, and the interest in lexis that can be seen in the field of WEs, it is surprising that so few dictionaries exist for the numerous varieties of English globally present. Especially lacking are scholarly dictionaries compiled by experts in the field of WEs.

Some explanations for the dearth of dictionaries come to mind. First, linguists familiar with a particular variety of English may nonetheless be unfamiliar with the process of lexicography, having never worked on a dictionary project, and this may lead to apprehension about tackling the task. Second, there apparently exists a notion that dictionaries, as publications, are not as academically worthwhile as other book publications. This negative assessment of the academic worth of dictionaries is not codified or officially sanctioned anywhere. Beltrami has noted in academia a tendency to treat lexicography as a "clerical job separated from research" (2013: 529), and anecdotally I know this to be a widely held point of view, having heard it expressed on many occasions. However, this point of view is quite untrue. Although dictionary entries are typically brief, they are based on significant academic research that belies their brevity. Extreme concision is a hallmark of lexicography, and even such a seemingly trivial statement as "origin unknown" in an etymology was very likely arrived at through a thorough collection, collation, and investigation of early citations, together with many hours of research on proposed etymons, including several wild goose chases, and much back-and-forth correspondence with experts for input on possible origins.

Dictionaries are the result of thousands of hours of rigorous research, analysis, and synthesis. They typically involve entirely new discoveries about hundreds or even thousands of lexical items and are, in short, enormous contributions to knowledge. In any case, whatever the reasons for this unwarranted negative bias, scholars interested in dictionary compiling would do well to assay the perspective of any relevant promotion and tenure bodies on dictionaries as academic publications before any work commences. At the same time, efforts need to be made to counter the erroneous view that devalues lexicography as an academic pursuit.

The opposite side of the coin is that very successful dictionaries have been produced under the aegis of institutional academic support, for example the *Middle English Dictionary* (Kurath et al. 1956–2001) with the University of Michigan and the *Dictionary of American Regional English* (Cassidy and Hall 1985–2012) with the University of Wisconsin-Madison (among other funding sources). Indeed, a number of productive academic careers have flourished with dictionary editorship. However, large-scale historical dictionaries are time-consuming, labor-intensive, and hence costly, and smaller-scale dictionaries on a more modest plan may be more feasible for many scholars. One way to achieve this is through narrowing the scope of the lexis to be covered. A dictionary has a greater chance of coming to fruition and being published if it only treats words borrowed from a single source language, or is restricted to a certain subject area, or to a particular author's works, or for a particular period of time, or if it focuses on a specific corpus of texts, and so on. Such restrictions are readily workable within the already-restricted context of a particular variety of English. For those scholars interested in dictionary compilation, useful resources are Zgusta (1971), Landau (2001), Görlach (1990), and Atkins (1992).

Finally, by observing what already exists, we consequently get to see what is missing and, in this way, the following section amply illustrates the need for more, and better, dictionaries of WEs.

18.2 Overview of Current World Englishes Dictionaries and Glossaries

The overview presented here provides a snapshot of the current dictionaries and glossaries available for various varieties of English, beginning with dictionaries having worldwide coverage and then proceeding by continent, in alphabetical order. All Englishes from Inner, Outer, and Expanding Circles are treated, though with emphasis on the latter two. Websites, though abundant, are not discussed unless they are of academic quality (very rare) or the only resource available.

Since my working bibliography of dictionaries and glossaries for varieties of English (omitting Internet-only works) amounts to more than 600 items, this overview cannot treat each text in detail. Additionally, although my personal dictionary/glossary collection is quite extensive and online resources allow many texts to be inspected, I have not been able to obtain access to all the works in my bibliography. This means that it is not possible to assess each text in the same manner. However, this seeming downside to the assessment actually alerts us to a more important practical consideration, namely availability and accessibility. To exemplify, even though Yule and Burnell's *Hobson-Jobson* (primarily covering Indian English) was published as long ago as 1903, today it is widely available in both modern reprint editions and electronically (e.g. Google Books, Internet Archive). In contrast, a more recent work, the *Anvil-Macquarie Dictionary of Philippine English for High School* (Macquarie 2000), is not in print, nor available electronically, and, according to WorldCat,[1] appears to be held in only four libraries worldwide. Furthermore, I could only locate a single second-hand copy for sale, and that for the princely sum of USD \$75.[2] Thus, although the *Anvil-Macquarie* has more than 540 entries for Philippine English vocabulary, those entries are today practically out of reach for anyone interested in that variety. This lack of availability applies to numerous titles, many of which were published by local publishing houses that are now defunct. In some instances, I have been in direct email contact with editors of various dictionaries and even *they* were unable to assist me in obtaining copies.

In constructing the list, care was taken to exclude any text that was not in dictionary format with terms accessible by headwords. Thus, while Xu (2010) has a chapter on the lexis of China English, the lexis is not presented in a dictionary format and so this text was excluded. Texts before 1960 are omitted from the overview unless they are highly significant. Also omitted, for space reasons, are glossaries that occur in the back of Lonely Planet and similar guidebooks (albeit for many varieties these are often the most substantial glossaries currently available).

18.2.1 Worldwide

The first edition of the *OED* (Murray et al. 1888–1933), using the historical principles approach, covered British English comprehensively and British dialects to a lesser extent, including Scottish English. It also covered American, Australian, and Indian English. The *OED Supplements* (Burchfield 1972–1986) extended the original coverage, brought much material up to date, and increased coverage of other varieties of English. The so-called third edition of *OED*, available online by subscription (2000 to present),[3] is a gradual updating and re-editing of the entire work. An effort is being made to extend coverage of WEs lexis (see Salazar 2014), but, while the quality of *OED* entries is high, coverage is far from comprehensive, or even representative, with numbers of new entries quite low: Recent updates added

---

[1] WorldCat: www.worldcat.org   [2] AddALL: www.addall.com   [3] *OED*: www.oed.com

seventy items for Indian English, forty for Philippine English, nineteen for Singapore English, and a mere thirteen for Hong Kong English.

Partridge (1937; 7th ed. 1970) and Partridge and Beale (1984) provide some coverage of Australian, Canadian, New Zealand, and South African English, but only in the slang register. All editions are out of print though easily obtainable second-hand. The two-volume *New Partridge* (Dalzell and Victor 2005) is a reimagining of the original based on wholly new scholarship; treatment is on historical principles; it has good material on British, American, Australian, and New Zealand English, though coverage of other varieties is not extensive.

Webster's Third New International Dictionary (Gove 1961) has reasonable coverage and reliable etymologies for many words borrowed into English from other languages but has not been updated since the 1960s. Bolton and Butler (2008: 187) note that the Philippine English lexis therein was "archaic and scanty" and this characterization is likely to pertain to the lexis of other varieties. More recent editions of *Webster's*, including the free online offerings, are essentially concerned with core English vocabulary.

Green's Slang Dictionary (2010), a massive three-volume work on historical principles, is the best slang dictionary currently available (and ever likely to be). It primarily covers British, American, Australian, and New Zealand English, and to a lesser extent Irish, Caribbean, and South African English.[4] Some expansion into other varieties of English is anticipated, with more than 100 entries for Anglo-Indian slang recently added (see Lambert 2018).

Wiktionary, unlike many crowd-sourced dictionaries, generally has a high standard of quality control, policed by a small body of dedicated editors/contributors. Part of the quality control is the "criteria for inclusion," which stipulates that a term only warrants inclusion if it can be found in at least three separate sources spanning more than one year in time and that those sources are durably archived (i.e. not a Facebook page, Twitter feed, or other ephemeral website). The best entries have etymologies, pronunciations in various varieties of English (not just British and American), synonyms, citational evidence, illustrations or pictures, translation equivalents in other languages, variant spellings, and lists of derived terms. To give an idea of the extent of coverage, at present there are 182 for Singapore English, 648 for Indian English, more than 800 for Irish English, more than 1,000 for New Zealand English, and more than 2,000 for Australian English. At the same time, there are only forty-two entries labeled Hong Kong English, seventy-five for Jamaican English, and merely a handful of terms for most African Englishes. However, coverage of all varieties will increase over time.

---

[4] *Green's Slang Dictionary* is now also available, and regularly updated, online (greensdictofslang.com).

18.2.2 Africa

English is spoken widely throughout Africa and many regional varieties exist. There are forty-two entries in my bibliography covering African Englishes (plus a further fifteen online glossaries). However, no printed dictionaries could be located for varieties of the Englishes of Botswana, Burundi, Gambia, Eritrea, Ethiopia, Kenya, Lesotho, Malawi, Mauritius, Namibia, Rwanda, the Seychelles, Sierra Leone, South Sudan, Sudan, Swaziland, Tanzania, Zambia, or Zimbabwe. Any Internet glossaries found were of limited scope and quality.

Pan-Africa. Dalgish (1982) covers more than 1,100 loanwords from African languages for the entire continent excepting the Maghreb, most of which appear nowhere else. Citations are provided for about half the entries and pronunciations are in IPA; a review by Hancock (1984) highlights, but unfairly magnifies, some failings.

West Africa. Anchimbe (2006) covers only sixty-four terms, while Leonard and Longbottom (2000) is restricted to the vocabulary of land tenure.

Cameroon English. A number of lexicons were published in the 1950s and 1960s; all out of print now. The exception is Kouega (2007), a scholarly work covering some 1,890 entries based on written and spoken data.

Gambian English. No dictionaries, but Richmond (1989) has a short glossary of ninety-two entries.

Ghanaian English. Three dictionaries. Dako (2003) is a scholarly work of some 2,500 entries with definition, etymology, and citational evidence, but no pronunciations. Kirby (1998) has some 2,500 very concise entries that include pronunciations in respelling, sample sentences, source languages of borrowings, and some cartoon illustrations. Sey (1973) lists about 300 items.

Liberian English. Two out-of-print dictionaries from the 1970s (d'Azevedo and Gold 1979; Wheeler 1979). An Internet glossary, the *Liberian English Dictionary*,[5] covers about 120 terms.

Nigerian English. Igboanusi (2002) is a scholarly work of more than 1,500 entries with definitions, illustrative phrases, 228 etymologies (source language only), and 306 pronunciations; second edition 2010. Other works include Adegbite et al. (2014) and Oluikpe and Anasadu (2006). Asomugha (1981) is out of print. Rundell and Fox (2009) is a synchronic inclusive dictionary for primary school.

Sierra Leone English. No dictionaries, but Pemagbi (1989) has a short glossary of 188 entries.

---

[5] Available at universaloutreachfoundation.org/liberian-english/

South Africa English. Well covered. Earlier admirable works by Beeton and Dorner (1975) and Branford (1991) have largely been superseded by Silva (1996), a comprehensive scholarly dictionary on historical principles with ca. 5,000 entries supported by 47,000 citations. Two dictionaries that cover lexis excluded by Silva are Mesthrie (2010), a competent scholarly work on South African Indian English, and Cage and Evans (2003) for South African gay slang. Inclusive dictionaries for the South African market began with Branford and Allen (1987), a localized edition of the *Pocket Oxford*, and are now produced by several reputable publishers, such as Collins, Oxford, and Pharos.

Ugandan English. One dictionary, Sabiiti (2014); about 200 entries sorted alphabetically within thematic sections; numerous color photographs of newspaper cuttings, street signage, and so on, displaying localized lexis; attitudinally exonormative. Isingoma (2014) has a short glossary of thirty-two entries.

Zambian English. No dictionaries as such, though some localized lexis was recorded in an online magazine column entitled *The Chrysalis Dictionary of Zanglish* (Mzyece 1998–1999).

Zimbabwean English. No dictionaries. A few Internet glossaries of limited scope, for example Baker (2015), which covers about 120 terms.

18.2.3 The Americas

American English. Well covered. Leaving aside numerous high-quality synchronic inclusive dictionaries (e.g. Gove 1961), a number of dictionaries on historical principles are available covering a range of lexis, especially slang (Lighter 1994, 1997, sadly stalled at two of three volumes) and regionalisms, the most important of which is the five-volume *Dictionary of American Regional English* (Cassidy and Hall, 1985–2012).[6] Also important for American English are *OED* and, for slang lexis, *Green's Dictionary of Slang*. Dictionaries also exist for various dialectal regions, such as the **Appalachians** (e.g. Montgomery and Hall 2004, with more than 6,000 entries), the **South** (Hendrickson 1993), and the **West** (e.g. the much reprinted Adams 1936, and Potter 1986). McMillan and Montgomery (1989: 163–215) list 560 "lexical studies" for "Southern American English" alone! For the English in **Hawaii**, there are numerous editions of Simonson, Sakata, and Sasaki (from 1981 onwards), comic in tone, with cartoon illustrations. These cover colloquial lexis, though the titles misleadingly use the term "pidgin."

African American Vernacular English. Dictionaries began appearing in the 1970s, with the underlying goal of establishing Black English as a valid variety of language; the bulk of these are now out of print. Recent

---

[6] The *Dictionary of American Regional English* is also available via subscription online (www.daredictionary.com).

works include Major (1994) and Smitherman (1994). The online *Green's Dictionary of Slang* records more than 4,600 items of US Black slang. Cassidy and Hall (1985–2012) is strong on historical Black English of rural America. Much rap lexis (which is white as well as black) can be found on *The Right Rhymes* website, backed up with citations from rap song lyrics.[7] A scholarly dictionary on historical principles devoted solely to AAVE is wanting.

Canadian English. Avis et al. (1967), a comprehensive dictionary on historical principles covering more than 9,000 lexical items, has now been superseded by the excellent and up-to-date Dollinger and Fee (2017).[8] Dictionaries also exist for various dialectal regions, such as **Newfoundland English** (Story et al.) [9] **Cape Breton English** (Davey and Mackinnon 2016), and **Prince Edward Island** (Pratt 1988): these three dictionaries are all scholarly works on historical principles based on both written and spoken data. Inclusive dictionaries have been produced for Canada by various reputable dictionary publishers, beginning with Gage in the 1960s, thence followed by Winston, Funk and Wagnalls, and, latterly, Collins and Oxford.

18.2.3.1 Caribbean Englishes

As a region, the Anglophone Caribbean is reasonably well covered, with more than sixty entries in my bibliography, including a number of substantial academic works. However, many titles are amateur productions for the local and tourist markets. No dictionaries for the Englishes of Antigua and Barbuda, Dominica, Montserrat, St Lucia, or Turks and Caicos could be located.

Pan-Caribbean. Allsopp (1996) covers the Anglophone Caribbean based on written and spoken data, treating more than 20,000 words and phrases; scholarly in approach but not historical; has etymologies, pronunciations, and citations for many but not all entries. Updated by a supplement of 590 new entries (Allsopp 2010). Allsopp (2003) is a multilingual lexicon on the lexis of flora, fauna, and cuisine. The online *Green's Dictionary of Slang* records more than 1,700 items of Caribbean slang.

Anguilla. One dictionary, Christian (1993); covers some 300 entries.

Bahamas. Three popular-market dictionaries, Glinton-Meicholas (1994, 1995), Henry and Harris (2007), and Roberts (2015). Holm and Shilling (1982) is a large-scale scholarly dictionary.[10]

Barbados. Three dictionaries, Collymore (2005), academic in style with more than 1,000 entries, the pamphlet-sized Davis (2009), and Ward (2013), written for the tourist market.

---

[7] See *The Right* Rhymes: *A Hip-hop Dictionary*: www.therightrhymes.com/
[8] Available online at www.dchp.ca/dchp2   [9] Available online at www.heritage.nf.ca/dictionary
[10] An updated version is available online: www.cobses.info/EDBEWW

Belize. One dictionary, McKesey (1974), focuses on localized pronunciation spellings. Dayley (1979) is an English-to-Creole and Creole-to-English glossary.

British Virgin Islands. One dictionary, Hull (2015), has more than 1,700 entries.

Cayman Islands. Fuller (1967) has a glossary of 173 terms. The more recent Goring (2011) and (2012) are now out of print, though work on a third larger dictionary by the author is currently underway.

Grenada. A sole dictionary, Francis (2016) is 126 pages in length; definitions are accompanied by etymologies and illustrative phrases. Additionally, Chase and Chase (2011) has a dictionary section. A quite basic online *Dictionary of Grenadianisms* covers more than 650 terms.[11]

Guyana. Two dictionaries. Seymore (1975), has more than 660 basic entries. Yansen (1993) covers more than 2,000 words, idioms, expressions, and proverbs.

Jamaica. Reasonably well covered with more than twenty-five titles in my bibliography. Cassidy and Le Page (1967, 2nd edition 1980) is the classic text, reprinted in paperback as recently as 2002. It is scholarly and historical in approach, based on oral and written sources, though now in need of updating. More recent works include Chen (1994); two glossaries of Rastafarian slang, Jendah (2008) and Slone (2003); and one dictionary of dancehall slang, Francis-Jackson (1995). A recent range of amateur dictionaries by Henry and Harris, beginning with the *LMH Official Dictionary of Sex Island Style* (2001), leverage the popular appeal of Jamaican speech.

Panama. A sole dictionary exists: Thomas-Brereton (2001).

Saba. A sole dictionary, Johnson (2016); a competent dictionary of more than 1,600 entries.

St Kitts and Nevis. A sole dictionary, Baker and Pederson (2013); a competent dictionary of about 3,400 entries.

St Vincent and the Grenadines. Meyerhoff and Walker (2013) has a small glossary of about sixty-five terms.

Trinidad and Tobago. Winer (2009) is a comprehensive scholarly dictionary on historical principles of more than 1,000 pages and covering some 12,200 entries. Other smaller and less scholarly works for the popular market include Baptiste (2011), Haynes (1987), Mendes (2012), and Orda (2010).

US Virgin Islands. A small number of non-scholarly dictionaries exist, largely aimed at the popular market. Out-of-print works include Roy (1975), Valls (1981), and Sterns (2008).

---

[11] Available online at www.bigdrumnation.org/dictionary_link.htm

18.2.4 Asia

The long history of English in Asia has resulted in a correspondingly long tradition of lexicography. Many colonial-era lexicons are available today, freely downloadable as scans, though these do not tell us much about present-day English varieties. In the modern era, many varieties have not had any lexicographical treatment. No dictionaries could be located for varieties of English in Afghanistan, Bangladesh, Brunei, Cambodia, China (excepting Hong Kong), Indonesia, Japan, Korea, Laos, Mongolia, Myanmar, Nepal, Pakistan, Thailand, or Vietnam. Similarly there are no dictionaries for Central Asia (Kazakhstan, Kyrgyzstan, Tajikistan, Turkmenistan, Uzbekistan). Any Internet glossaries found were of limited scope and quality.

Regional Southeast Asia. The *Grolier International Dictionary* (Macquarie 2000) is a synchronic inclusive dictionary with more than 9,000 entries, about a third of which have British English pronunciations in IPA. In descending coverage, it treats Philippine English (445 items), Malaysian English (291 items), Singapore English (163 items, though 153 overlapping with Malaysian English), Hong Kong English (108 items), Thai English (40 items), and Taiwanese English (31 items); a further 93 terms are labeled "Asian English," indicating they are common to all regional varieties; out of print.

Hong Kong English. Bolton (2003) has an appendix with 320 entries. Cummings and Wolf (2011) covers slightly more than 460 entries, with pronunciations in IPA for words from Chinese languages (239 entries), citations, illustrations, and some indication of frequency based on Google.com.hk hits (though accuracy of these figures is questionable). See also *Grolier* (Macquarie 2000).

Indian English. This has the best lexicographical coverage of the Asian Englishes. Yule and Burnell's famous *Hobson-Jobson*, in its second edition edited by William Crooke in 1903, is still being reprinted and even today is widely held as a good source of information on Indian English. In truth, it is (naturally) wildly out of date and, due to its having been written with all the expectations of Victorian-era upper-class erudition, not very user-friendly, though, for the most part, it is based on solid and reliable research. A recent reprint (Teltscher 2013) is a cut-down version. Hankin's (2003) imitatively titled *Hanklyn-Janklin* is more up to date but not especially reliable, while Lewis (1991) and Hawkins (1984) are primarily concerned with colonial-era lexis. Muthiah (1991), Sengupta (1996), and Nihalani et al. (2004) cover more recent lexis but all are out of print and difficult to obtain. An underlying exonormative stance is detectable in Nihalani et al. (2004) despite its protestations to the contrary (Lambert 2014: 376–380). Lonely Planet's (2008) *Indian English: Language and Culture* has an index enabling it to be used as a dictionary; treatment is limited to headword and gloss. The recent Carls (2017) has ca. 3,900 entries with citations and basic etymologies. It breaks new ground by giving Indian English pronunciations in IPA and recording copious compound noun forms.

In terms of inclusive dictionaries, there is the *Macmillan* range of dictionaries for the Indian market. The most comprehensive of these, the *Macmillan Comprehensive Dictionary* (Macmillan 2006), has more than 98,000 headwords, of which 2,175 are specific to Indian English. Pronunciations are adapted from those of the base dictionary, the *Macquarie Dictionary* (1997 edition) but retain Australian English stress patterns that are frequently not those of Indian English. Etymologies for Hindi borrowings are based on McGregor (1993).

Malaysian English. Kim (1998) is an amateur offering, ordered thematically, with humorous cartoons; covers some 270 lexical items. The *Macquarie Junior Dictionary* (Macquarie 1999), for primary school, covers some 250 Malaysian English items. For Higgleton and Ooi (1997), see "Singapore English" section. See also *Grolier* (Macquarie 2000).

Philippine English. The *Anvil-Macquarie Dictionary* (2000) is a synchronic inclusive dictionary for the primary school market; more than 8,500 entries and 2,000 American English pronunciations in IPA; more than 540 entries relating to the Philippines. Cruz and Bautista (1995) is a small booklet with 623 entries with definitions, part of speech labels, and pronunciations in a respelling system. See also *Grolier* (Macquarie 2000), discussed in the "Regional Southeast Asia" section.

Singapore English. Reasonably well covered. Higgleton and Ooi (1997) is a synchronic inclusive dictionary aimed at the school market; Singapore English is lumped with Malaysian English, of which around 1,000 lexical items are treated, with pronunciations representing "educated local speakers" (p. vii), though all other lexis in the dictionary is in Received Pronunciation; an appendix contains 111 terms proscribed by the authors. The *Macquarie Junior Dictionary* (1999), for primary school, covers some 160 Singapore English items. Brown (1999) is partially arranged as a dictionary (many terms covered do not have their own headword and there is no index); covers 840 lexical items in about 500 discursive entries, especially comparing local usage against British and American English. Lee (2004–2015) is an online dictionary on historical principles; more than 1,200 entries, 1,000 well-researched etymologies, more than 2,500 citations, and Singapore English pronunciations in both respelling and IPA. Aside from these, other texts focus on the highly colloquial register of Singapore English known locally as "Singlish." Hanna (2003) has 225 entries, with cartoon illustrations; aimed at the popular market. Goh and Woo (2009) covers 1,115 lexical items, with numerous etymologies and pronunciations (in respelling) and has cartoon illustrations. Shelley (1995) is primarily a usage guide but covers much Singapore English lexis. Aw

(2015) is a privately published arty visual dictionary covering 150 items of Singapore English. See also *Grolier* (Macquarie 2000), discussed in the "Regional Southeast Asia" section.

Sri Lankan English. Covered only by Meyler (2007), privately published. A sound piece of lexicography treating more than 2,500 lexical items (including nested entries), numerous etymologies and pronunciations, plus more than 150 illustrations; a website has updates with additions, deletions, and corrections.[12]

18.2.5   Australia, Oceania, and Atlantic Islands

English is spoken widely throughout the Pacific and many regional varieties exist. However, no printed dictionaries could be located for varieties of the Englishes of American Samoa, the Cook Islands, Guam, Kiribati, the Marshall Islands, Nauru, Niue, the Northern Mariana Islands, Palau, Samoa, the Solomon Islands, Tokelau, Tonga, Tuvalu, or Vanuatu. Any Internet glossaries found were of limited scope and quality.

Antarctic English. Hince (2000) is a well-researched scholarly work on historical principles, with just less than 2,000 entries illustrated by more than 15,000 citations. It covers, inter alia, some of the lexis specific to Falkland Islands English and Tristan da Cunha English (though it has nothing specific for Ascension or Saint Helena).

Australian English. Well covered, with more than 100 titles published since the beginning of the nineteenth century, including a number of dictionaries on historical principles (Morris 1898; Wilkes 2008; Moore 2016) and a comprehensive range (all sizes and age levels) of inclusive dictionaries from Macquarie Dictionary publishers, beginning with the successful *Macquarie Dictionary* (Macquarie 1981), now regarded as the standard for Australian English. Oxford and Collins also produce synchronic inclusive dictionaries of similar quality. There is an abundance of smaller lexicons for slang (including rhyming slang), various jargons (criminal, military, occupational), and regionalisms. The online *Green's Dictionary of Slang* records more than 6,300 items of Australian slang.

Australian Aboriginal English. Apart from the excellent Arthur (1996), now out of print, nothing has been published.

Falklands Island English. See Antarctic English.

Fiji English. Covered by one synchronic inclusive dictionary (Geraghty et al. 2006), covering some 15,000 lexical items; based ultimately on the *Macquarie Dictionary* with extensive incorporation of localized lexis; pronunciations in a respelling system especially devised for the dictionary.

---

[12] Meyler (2007): www.mirisgala.net

New Zealand English. Traditionally less well covered than Australian English, with about thirty titles since the beginning of the nineteenth century, many of which focus on NZ slang. However, well covered since the publication of Orsman (1997), a comprehensive scholarly dictionary on historical principles. Deverson (2010) is a shortening and updating of Orsman, removing the historical apparatus but adding new coinages. Macalister (2005) focuses on loanwords from Maori, and Bardsley (2009) on rural lexis. Synchronic inclusive dictionaries have been published by Oxford, Collins, and Macquarie publishing houses since the 1980s. The online *Green's Dictionary of Slang* records more than 1,600 items of New Zealand slang.

Norfolk Island English. Three dictionaries available: Buffett (1999), Mühlhäusler et al. (2012), and Nobbs-Palmer (1992).

Papua New Guinea. A small number of standard synchronic inclusive dictionaries have been adapted for the PNG school market (for an overview, see Taylor 1994). No exclusive dictionaries specifically covering localized lexis.

Pitcairn Island English. Two dictionaries: Ross and Moverly (1964) and Kallgard (1991).

Tristan da Cunha English. See Antarctic English.

18.2.6 Europe

In the WEs literature many varieties of English in Europe have been identified and written about, for example Dutch English (Edwards 2011), Swedish English (Ferguson 1994), Eastern European English (Salakhyan 2012), Polish English (Kasztalska 2014), Turkish English (Çelik 2008), and so on; yet little if anything in terms of lexicography has been published. An exception is Kabakchi's *Dictionary of Russia: English-English Dictionary of Russian Cultural Terminology* (2002), though this is out of print and difficult to obtain.

18.2.7 Great Britain and Ireland

British dialects. *The English Dialect Dictionary* (Wright 1898–1905) provided extensive coverage of British dialect lexis (and grammar and phonology) up to the end of the nineteenth century; it is still the authority, despite its age.[13] Upton, Widdowson and Parry (1994) is more up to date, covering 17,000 items. More recent works are available for the urban dialects of larger cities, such as **Birmingham** (Chinn and Thorne 2001), **Liverpool** (Briscoe 2003; Fazakerley 2001), and **Newcastle** (Fazakerley and Douglas

---

[13] Available online: eddonline-proj.uibk.ac.at/edd

2001), but these are nonacademic publications for the popular market. For **Cockney**, the bulk of publications focus solely on rhyming slang, for which more than twenty-five dictionaries were published from 1970 to 2018, most covering the same ground, now all superseded by Lillo and Victor (2017), an excellent comprehensive dictionary on historical principles. **Orkney English** has two modern dictionaries (Flaws and Lamb 1997; Lamb 1988), **Shetland** has one (Graham 1993), as does the **Isle of Wight** (Lavers 1988).

British Indian English. One dictionary, Mahal (2006); well written, covering about 380 terms.

British Black English. No dedicated dictionaries. Sutcliffe (1982) has a glossary of some 320 terms. *Green's Dictionary of Slang* records more than 800 items of British Black slang.

Scottish English and Scots. Historically well covered, for example Jamieson (1808), Wright (1898–1905), and *OED*. Now well served by Craigie et al. (1937–2002) and Grant and Murison (1927–1976), both scholarly dictionaries on historical principles together treating lexis from the twelfth century onward and available combined online for free.[14]

Welsh English. A number of recent works for the popular market, including Charles (1982), Edwards (1985, 2003), Scourfield and Johnson (2008), Lewis (2008), Jones (2016), and Jandrell (2017).

Irish English. One of the better recorded varieties with eleven dictionaries (though one is only published as a doctoral thesis). Some are specific to certain areas, such as **Cork** (Beecher 1983) or **Donegal** (Traynor 1953). Some are nonprofessional in nature, as evidenced by their titles, such as *The Book of Feckin' Irish Slang that's Great Craic for Cute Hoors and Bowsies* (Murphy and O'Dea 2004). The best is Dolan (2004), which provides pronunciations, part of speech labels, etymologies, citational evidence (based on written and spoken sources), and information on regional restrictions. The second edition (2004) also includes lexis from Ulster Scots. The online *Green's Dictionary of Slang* records more than 1,100 items of Irish slang.

Northern Irish English. In addition to Dolan (2004), noted above for "Irish English," there are four current glossaries of Ulster Scots/English (for considerations of whether this is actually "English," see Görlach 2002: 69–86), namely Fenton (2001), Macafee (1996), O'Kane (1991), and Pepper (1981). Two dictionaries by Todd (1989, 1990) specifically treat Northern Irish English. The online *Green's Dictionary of Slang* records more than 250 items of Ulster slang.

---

[14] *Dictionary of the Scots Language:* dsl.ac.uk

References

Adams, Ramon F. 1936. *Cowboy Lingo*. Boston: Houghton Mifflin.

Adegbite, Wale, Inyang Udofot, and Kehinde Ayoola. 2014. *A Dictionary of Nigerian English*. Ile-Ife: Obafemi Awolowo University Press.

Allsopp, Jeanette. 2003. *The Caribbean Multilingual Dictionary of Flora, Fauna and Foods: In English, French, French Creole and Spanish*. Kingston: Arawak Publications.

Allsopp, Richard. 1996. *Dictionary of Caribbean English Usage*. Jamaica: University of the West Indies Press.

Allsopp, Richard. 2010. *New Register of Caribbean English Usage*. Kingston, Jamaica: University of the West Indies Press.

Anchimbe, Eric. 2006. Local meaning in the English of West Africa. *English Today* 22: 50–54.

Arthur, J. M. 1996. *Aboriginal English: A Cultural Study*. Melbourne: Oxford University Press.

Asomugha, C. N. C. 1981. *Nigerian Slangs: Dictionary of Slangs and Unconventional English Used in Nigeria*. Onitsha: Abic Publishers.

Atkins, B. T. S. 1992. Theoretical lexicography and its relation to dictionary-making. In Thierry Fontenelle, ed. *Practical Lexicography: A Reader*. Oxford: Oxford University Press, 31–50.

Avis, Walter S., Charles Crate, Patrick Drysdale, Douglas Leechman, and M. H. Scargill. 1967. *A Dictionary of Canadianisms on Historical Principles*. Toronto: W.J. Page.

Aw, Zinkie. 2016. *Singaporelang: What the Singlish?* Singapore: Zinkie Aw.

Baker, Philip and Lee Pederson. 2013. *Talk of St Kitts and Nevis*. London: Battlebridge Publications.

Baker, Rod. 2015. *An Introductory Vocabulary in Zimblish*. www.rhodesia.com /docs/other/zimblish.htm

Baptiste, Rhona. 2011. *Trini Talk: A Dictionary of Words and Proverbs of Trinidad and Tobago*. Port of Spain: Caribbean Information Systems and Services.

Bardsley, Dianne. 2009. *In the Paddock and on the Run: The Language of Rural New Zealand*. Dunedin: Otago University Press.

Beecher, Seán. 1983. *A Dictionary of Cork Slang*. Cork: Goldy Angel Press.

Beeton, D. and Helen Dorner. 1975. *A Dictionary of English Usage in South African*. Cape Town: Oxford University Press.

Béjoint, Henri. 2010. *The Lexicography of English*. Oxford: Oxford University Press.

Beltrami, Pietro G. 2013. Theory of dictionary management. In Rufus H. Gouws, Ulrich Heid, Wolfgang Schweickard, and Herbst Ernst Weigand, eds. *Dictionaries. An International Encyclopedia of Lexicography. Supplementary Volume: Recent Developments with Focus on Electronic and Computational Lexicography*. Berlin: de Gruyter Mouton, 524–530.

Blackman, John. 1990. *The Aussie Slang Dictionary*. Sydney: Sun Books.

Bolton, Kingsley. 2003. Appendix 5: The vocabulary of Hong Kong English. In Kingsley Bolton, *Chinese Englishes: A Sociolinguistic History*. Cambridge: Cambridge University Press, 288–297.

Bolton, Kingsley and Susan Butler. 2008. Lexicography and the description of Philippine English vocabulary. In Ma. Lourdes S. Bautista and Kingsley Bolton, eds. *Philippine English: Linguistic and Literary*. Hong Kong: Hong Kong University Press, 175–200.

Branford, Jean. 1991. *A Dictionary of South African English*. Cape Town: Oxford University Press.

Branford, William and R. E. Allen. 1987. *The South African Pocket Oxford Dictionary*. Cape Town: Oxford University Press. (Second edition published in 1994.)

Briscoe, Diana. 2003. *Wicked Scouse English*. London: Michael O'Mara.

Brown, Adam. 1999. *Singapore English in a Nutshell: An Alphabetical Description of its Features*. Singapore: Federal.

Buffett, Alice Inez. 1999. *Speak Norfolk Today: An Encyclopaedia of the Norfolk Island Language*. Norfolk Island: Himii Publishing Company.

Burchfield, Robert. 1972–1986. *A Supplement to the Oxford English Dictionary*, 4 vols. Oxford: Clarendon Press.

Cage, Ken and Moyra, Evans. 2003. *Gayle: The Language of Kinks and Queens: A History and Dictionary of Gay Language in South Africa*. Houghton: Jacana.

Cassidy, Frederic G. and Joan Houston Hall. 1985–2012. *Dictionary of American Regional English*, 5 vols. Cambridge, MA: Belknap Press.

Cassidy, Frederic G. and R. B. Le Page. 1967. *Dictionary of Jamaican English*. Cambridge: Cambridge University Press. (Second edition published in 1980; later "editions" are reprints of 1980 edition without changes.)

Çelik, Mehmet. 2008. A description of Turkish-English phonology for teaching English in Turkey. *Journal of Theory and Practice in Education* 4(1): 159–174.

Carls, Uwe. 2017. *A Dictionary of Indian English with a Supplement on Word-formation Patterns*. Leipzig: Leipziger Universitätsverlag.

Carr, Philip. 2012. *English Phonetics and Phonology: An Introduction*. Malden, MA: John Wiley & Sons.

Charles, Berti G. 1982. *The English Dialect of South Pembrokeshire*. Aberystwyth: Pembrokeshire Record Society.

Chase, Thomas R and Chase, Zarah A. 2011. *Abridged Handbook of Grenadian Creole English and French Names: A Dictionary of Grenadian Creole English with Grammar and Syntax*. St. George: West Indies Academic Communications Linguistic and Integrated Media Services.

Chen, Ray. 1994. *The Jamaica Dictionary: A Is Fi Aringe*. Ontario: Periwinkle.

Chinn, Carl and Steve Thorne. 2001. *Proper Brummie: A Dictionary of Birmingham Words and Phrases*. Studley: Brewin Books.

Christian, Ijahnya. 1993. *Dictionary of Anguillian Language*. Anguilla: Government of Anguilla, Adult and Continuing Education Unit.

Collymore, F. A. 2005. *Notes for a Glossary of Words and Phrases of Barbadian Dialect* (7th ed.). Bridgetown: Advocate Co.

Craigie, W. A., Aitken, A. J., Stevenson, J. A. C., Watson, H. D. and Dareau, M. G. 1937–2002. *A Dictionary of the Older Scottish Tongue.* Aberdeen: Aberdeen University Press.

Cruz, Isagani R. and Lourdes S. Bautista. 1995. *A Dictionary of Philippine English.* Manila: Anvil Publishing.

Cummings, Patrick J. and Wolf Hans-Georg. 2011. *A Dictionary of Hong Kong English: Words from the Fragrant Harbour.* Hong Kong: Hong Kong University Press.

Dako, Kari. 2003. *Ghanaianisms: A Glossary.* Accra: Ghana University Press.

Dalgish, Gerard M. 1982. *A Dictionary of Africanisms: Contributions of Sub-Saharan Africa to the English Language.* Westport, CT.: Greenwood Press.

Dalzell, Tom and Terry Victor. 2005. *The New Partridge Dictionary of Slang and Unconventional English.* 2 vols. London: Routledge.

Davey, William John and Richard P. Mackinnon. 2016. *Dictionary of Cape Breton English.* Toronto: University of Toronto Press, Scholarly Publishing Division.

Davis, Jerome E. 2009. *Understanding Bajan Dialect for Tourists and Visitors to Barbados.* Barbados: Davis.

Dayley, Jon P. 1979. *Belizean Creole: Glossary.* Brattleboro, VT: The Experiment in International Living.

d'Azevedo, Warren L. and Michael Evan Gold. 1979. *Some Terms from Liberian Speech.* Monrovia: Michael Evan Gold.

Deverson, Tony. 2010. *The Oxford Dictionary of New Zealandisms.* Auckland: Oxford University Press.

Dolan, Terence. 2004. *A Dictionary of Hiberno-English.* Dublin: Gill and Macmillan.

Dollinger, Stefan and Margery Fee. 2017. *DCHP-2: The Dictionary of Canadianisms on Historical Principles* (2nd ed.). Vancouver, BC: University of British Columbia. www.dchp.ca/dchp2

Edwards, Alison. 2011. Introducing the Corpus of Dutch English. *English Today* 27(3): 10–14.

Edwards, John. 1985. *Talk Tidy: The Art of Speaking Wenglish.* Cowbridge: D. Brown and Sons.

Edwards, John. 2003. *More Talk Tidy: Further to the Art of Speaking Wenglish.* Creigiau: Tidyprint.

Fazakerley, Fred. 2001. *Scouse-English Glossary.* Bristol: Abson Books.

Fazakerley, Fred and Percy Douglas. 2001. *Geordie-English Glossary.* Bristol: Abson Books.

Fenton, James. 2001. *The Hamely Tongue: A Personal Record of Ulster-Scots in County Antrim.* London: Athlone Press.

Ferguson, Charles A. 1994. Note on Swedish English. *World Englishes* 13(3): 419–424.

Flaws, Margaret and Gregor Lamb. 1997. *The Orkney Dictionary*. Kirkwall: Orkney Language and Culture Group.

Francis, C. W. 2016. *Popular Phrases in Grenada Dialect*. San Bernardo, CA: CreateSpace Independent Publishing Platform.

Francis-Jackson, Chester. 1995. *The Official Dancehall Dictionary: A Guide to Jamaican Dialect and Dancehall Slang*. Kingston: Kingston Publishers.

Fuller, Robert Sevier. 1967. *Duppies Is: An Expose of the Caprices of Ghosts of Grand Cayman and a Dictionary of Words and Phrases of the Islanders*. Grand Cayman, BWI: Cayman Authors.

Geraghty, Paul, France Mugler, and Jan Tent. 2006. *The Macquarie Dictionary of English for the Fiji Islands*. Sydney: The Macquarie Library.

Glinton-Meicholas, Patricia. 1994. *Talkin' Bahamian: A Useful Guide to the Language of the Islands*. Nassau: Guanima Press.

Glinton-Meicholas, Patricia. 1995. *More Talkin' Bahamian*. Nassau: Guanima Press.

Goh, Colin and Y. Y. Woo. 2009. *The Coxford Singlish Dictionary* (2nd ed.). Singapore: Angsana Books.

Goring, Kevin M. 2011. *Cayman Islands Dictionary: A Collection of Words used by Native Caymanians*. George Town: Gap Seed.

Goring, Kevin M. 2012. *Caymanian Expressions: A Collection of Sayings and Expressions Used in the Cayman Islands*. George Town: Gap Seed.

Görlach, Manfred. 1990. The Dictionaries of Transplanted Varieties of Languages: English. In F. J. Hausmann, O. Reichmann, H. E. Wiegand and L. Zgusta, eds. *Wörterbücher: Dictionaries: Dictionnaires: An International Encyclopedia of Lexicography*, Vol. 2. Berlin: de Gruyter, 1475–1499.

Görlach, Manfred. 2002. *Still More Englishes*. Amsterdam: John Benjamins Publishing.

Gove, Philip B. 1961. *Webster's Third New International Dictionary of the English Language*. Springfield, MA: Merriam-Webster.

Graham, John J. 1993. *The Shetland Dictionary*. Lerwick: The Shetland times.

Grant, William and David D. Murison. 1927–1976. *The Scottish National Dictionary*. 10 Vols. Edinburgh: The Scottish National Dictionary Association.

Green, Jonathon. 2010. *Green's Dictionary of Slang*. 3 vols. London: Chambers Harrap Publishers. (Online, 2016–present: greensdictofslang.com)

Macquarie. 2000. *The Grolier International Dictionary*. Sydney: Macquarie Library.

Hancock, Ian. 1984. Review of Gerard M. Dalgish. A Dictionary of Africanisms: Contributions of Sub-Saharan Africa to the English Language. *Research in African Literatures* 15(2): 312–315.

Hankin, Nigel. 2003. *Hanklyn-Janklin: A Stranger's Rumble-Tumble Guide to some Words, Customs and Quiddities Indian and Indo-British*. New Delhi: Tara Press.

Hanna, Samantha. 2003. *An Essential Guide to Singlish*. Singapore: Gartbooks.

Hawkins, R.E. 1984. *Common Indian Words in English*. Delhi: Oxford University Press.

Haynes, Martin. 1987. *Trinidad and Tobago Dialect (Plus)*. San Fernando: M. Haynes.

Hendrickson, Robert. 1993. *Whistlin' Dixie: A Dictionary of Southern Expressions*. New York: Facts on File.

Henry, L. Mike and K. Sean Harris, 2001. *LMH Official Dictionary of Sex Island Style*. Kingston, Jamaica: LMH Publishing.

Henry, L. Mike and K. Sean Harris. 2007. *LMH Official Dictionary of Popular Bahamian Phrases*. Kingston: LMH Publishing.

Higgleton, Elaine and Vincent B.Y. Ooi. 1997. *Times-Chambers Essential English Dictionary* (2nd ed.). Singapore: Chambers-Harrap and Federal.

Hince, Bernadette. 2000. *The Antarctic Dictionary: A Complete Guide to Antarctic English*. Collingwood: CSIRO Publications and the Museum of Victoria.

Holm, John and Alison W. Shilling. 1982. *Dictionary of Bahamian English*. Cold Spring, NY: Lexik House.

Hull, Kareem-Nelson. 2015. *The Virgin Islands Dictionary: A Collection of Words and Phrases So You Could Say It Like We*. Bloomington, IN: AuthorHouse.

Igboanusi, Herbert. 2002. *A Dictionary of Nigerian English Usage*. Ibadan: Enicrownfit Publishers.

Isingoma, Bebwa. 2014. Lexical and grammatical features of Ugandan English. *English Today 30*: 51–56.

Jamieson, John. 1808. *An Etymological Dictionary of the Scottish Language*. Edinburgh: W. Creech.

Jandrell, David. 2017. *Welsh Valleys Phrasebook: Get by in Valleys-Speak!* Talybont: Y Lolfa.

Jendah, Jesse. 2008. *Rasta Talk: A Guide to Rastafarian Dialect*. Kingston: LMH Publications.

Johnson, Theodore R. 2016. *A Lee Chip: A Dictionary and Study of Saban English*. [Raleigh]: North Carolina State University.

Jones, Benjamin A. 2016. *Welsh English Dialect: A Selection of Words and Anecdotes from Around Wales*. Sheffield: Bradwell Books.

Kabakchi, Victor V. 2002. *The Dictionary of Russia: English-English Dictionary of Russian Cultural Terminology*. St. Petersburg: Soyuz.

Kallgard, Anders. 1991. *Fut yoli noo bin laane aklen? A Pitcairn Word-list*. Gothenburg: University of Gothenburg.

Kasztalska, Aleksandra. 2014. English in contemporary Poland. *World Englishes 33*(2): 242–262.

Kim, Su Lee. 1998. *Manglish: Malaysian English at Its Wackiest!* Kuala Lumpur: Times Books International.

Kirby, Jon P. 1998. *Igo Talk Da Broken English Proper: A North American's Guide to Ghanaian English*. Tamale: Tamale Institute of Cross-Cultural Studies.

Kouega, Jean-Paul. 2007. *A Dictionary of Cameroon English Usage*. Bern: Peter Lang.

Kurath, Hans, Kuhn, Sherman A., Reidy, John, and Lewis, Robert. 1956–2001. *The Middle English Dictionary*. Ann Arbor: University of Michigan Press.

Lamb, Gregor. 1988. *Orkney Wordbook: A Dictionary of the Dialect of Orkney*. Orkney: Byrgisey.

Lambert, James. 2014. Beyond Hobson-Jobson: Towards a new lexicography for Indian English. Unpublished doctoral dissertation, City University of Hong Kong.

Lambert, James. 2018. Anglo-Indian slang in dictionaries on historical principles. *World Englishes* 1–13. doi:10.1111/weng.12291

Landau, Sidney I. 2001. *Dictionaries: The Art and Craft of Lexicography* (2nd ed.). Cambridge: Cambridge University Press.

Lavers, Jack. 1988. *The Dictionary of Isle of Wight Dialect*. Dorset: Dovecote.

Lee, Jack Tsen-Ta. 2004–2015. *A Dictionary of Singlish and Singapore English*. www.singlishdictionary.com

Leonard, Rebecca and Judy Longbottom. 2000. *Land Tenure Lexicon: A Glossary of Terms from English and French Speaking West Africa*. London: International Institute for Environment and Development.

Lewis, Ivor. 1991. *Sahibs, Nabobs and Boxwallahs: A Dictionary of the Words of Anglo-India*. Delhi: Oxford University Press.

Lewis, Robert E. 2008. *Wenglish: The Dialect of the South Wales Valleys*. Talybont: Y Lolfa.

Lighter, J. E. 1994/1997. *Historical Dictionary of American Slang*. 2 vols. New York: Random House.

Lillo, Antonio and Terry Victor. 2017. *A Dictionary of English Rhyming Slangs*. Berlin: De Gruyter Mouton.

Lonely Planet. 2008. *Indian English: Language and Culture*. Melbourne: Lonely Planet.

Macafee, Caroline. 1996. *A Concise Ulster Dictionary*. Oxford: Oxford University Press.

Macquarie. 2000. *The Anvil-Macquarie Dictionary of Philippine English for High School*. Sydney: Macquarie Library.

Macalister, John. 2005. *A Dictionary of Maori Words in New Zealand English*. Oxford: Oxford University Press.

McGregor, R.S. 1993. *The Oxford Hindi-English Dictionary*. New Delhi: Oxford University Press.

McInnes, Dianne. 2014. *Aussie Phrases Down Under*. Brisbane: Pictorial Press Australia.

McKesey, G. 1974. *The Belizean Lingo*. Belize: National Printers Ltd.

Macmillan. 2006. *The Macmillan Comprehensive Dictionary*. Bangalore: Macmillan Publishers India.

McMillan, James B. and Michael Montgomery. 1989. Lexical studies. In *Annotated Bibliography of Southern American English*. Tuscaloosa: University of Alabama Press, 163–215.

Macquarie. 1981. *The Macquarie Dictionary*. Sydney: Macquarie Library. (Seventh edition published in 2016.)

Macquarie. 1999. *The Macquarie Junior Dictionary*. Sydney: Macquarie Library.

Mahal, Baljinder K. 2006. *The Queen's Hinglish: How to Speak Pukka*. Glasgow: HarperCollins.

Major, Clarence. 1994. *Juba to Jive: The Dictionary of African-American Slang*. New York: Viking.

Mendes, John. 2012. *Côté ci Côté la: Trinidad and Tobago Dictionary* (3rd ed.). Arima: John Mendes.

Mesthrie, Rajend. 2010. *A Dictionary of South African Indian English*. Cape Town: University of Cape Town Press.

Meyerhoff, Miriam and James A. Walker. 2013. *Bequia Talk (St Vincent and the Grenadines)*. London: Battlebridge Publications.

Meyler, Michael. 2007. *A Dictionary of Sri Lankan English*. Colombo: Meyler.

Montgomery, Michael and Joseph S. Hall. 2004. *Dictionary of Smoky Mountain English*. Knoxville: University of Tennessee Press.

Moore, Bruce. 2016. *The Australian National Dictionary: A Dictionary of Australianisms on Historical Principals*. 2nd edition. Melbourne: Oxford University Press.

Morris, Edward E. 1898. *Austral English: A Dictionary of Australasian Words, Phrases and Usages*. London: Macmillan and Co.

Mühlhäusler, Peter, Rachel Nebauer-Borg, and Piria Coleman. 2012. *Ucklun's Norf'k: Words as a Memory of Our Past*. Kingston: Norfolk Island Museum Trust.

Muthiah, S. 1991. *Words in Indian English: A Reader's Guide*. Delhi: HarperCollins.

Murphy, Colin and Donal O'Dea. 2004. *The Book of Feckin' Irish Slang that's Great Craic for Cute Hoors and Bowsies*. Dublin: O'Brien Press.

Murray, James A.H., Henry Bradley, William Craigie, and C. T. Onions. 1888–1933. *The Oxford English Dictionary on Historical Principles*, 11 vols. Oxford: Clarendon Press.

Mzyece, Mjumo. 1998–1999. *The Chrysalis Dictionary of Zanglish*. web.archive.org/web/*/http://www.chrysalis.co.zm:80

Nihalani, Paroo, R. K. Tongue, Priya Hosali, and Jonathan Crowther, 2004. *Indian and British English: A Handbook of Usage and Pronunciation*. New Delhi: Oxford University Press.

Nobbs-Palmer, Beryl. 1992. *A Dictionary of Norfolk Words and Usages*. Norfolk Island: Photopress International.

O'Kane, William. 1991. *You Don't Say? The Tyrone Crystal Book of Ulster Dialect*. Dungannon, Tyrone: Irish World.

Oluikpe, Benson A. Omenihu and B. Anasadu. 2006. *Dictionary of Nigerian English Slang*. Nigeria: Rex Charles and Patrick.

Orda, Martin. 2010. *Trinnie Talk: A Handbook of Trinidad and Tobago Dialect, Traditions, Tours and Travel*. Trinidad and Tobago: Papellon Enterprises.

Orsman, H. W. 1997. *The Dictionary of New Zealand English: A Dictionary of New Zealandisms on Historical Principals*. Auckland: Oxford University Press.

Partridge, Eric. 1937. *A Dictionary of Slang and Unconventional English*. London: Routledge and Kegan Paul. (Seventh edition published in 1970.)

Partridge, Eric and Paul Beale. 1984. *A Dictionary of Slang and Unconventional English*. (8th ed.). London: Routledge and Kegan Paul.

Pemagbi, Joe. 1989. A glossary of Sierra Leonean English. *English Today* 5(1): 22–24.

Pepper, J. 1981. *Ulster-English Dictionary*. Belfast: Blackstaff Press.

Potter, Edgar R. 1986. *Cowboy Slang*. Phoenix: Golden West Publishers.

Pratt, T.K. 1988. *Dictionary of Prince Edward Island English*. Toronto: University of Toronto Press.

Richmond, Edmun B. 1989. African English expressions in The Gambia. *World Englishes* 8: 223–228.

Roberts, Nicole. 2015. *Bahamian Dictionary of Dem Old Essential Words and Phrases* (2nd ed.). Nassau: Suffolk House Books.

Ross, Alan Strode Campbell and A. W. Moverly. 1964. *The Pitcairnese Language*. London: Oxford University Press.

Roy, John D. 1975. *A Brief Description and Dictionary of the Language Used in the Virgin Islands*. St. Thomas: Virgin Islands Department of Education.

Rundell, Michael and Gwyneth Fox. 2009. *Premier Dictionary for Nigerian Primary Schools*. Oxford: Macmillan.

Sabiiti, Bernard. 2014. *UgLish: A Dictionary of Ugandan English*. Arlington, MA: Jean-Claude Muganga.

Salakhyan, Elena. 2012. The emergence of Eastern European English. *World Englishes* 31(3): 331–350.

Salazar, Danica. 2014. Towards improved coverage of Southeast Asian Englishes in the *Oxford English Dictionary*. *Lexicography* 1(1): 95–108.

Scourfield, Robert and Keith Johnson. 2008. *Below the Landsker: An Introduction to the Dialect, Place Names and Folklore of South Pembrokeshire*. Kilgetty: Jackydando Books.

Sengupta, Indira Chowdhury. 1996. Indian English supplement. In Jonathan Crowther, ed. *The Oxford Advanced Learner's Dictionary of Current English*. Delhi: Oxford University Press, 1429–1475.

Sey, K. A. 1973. *Ghanaian English: An Exploratory Survey*. London: Macmillan.

Seymore, A. J. 1975. *Dictionary of Guyanese Folklore*. Georgetown, Guyana: National History and Arts Council.

Shelley, Rex. 1995. *Sounds and Sins of Singlish and Other Nonsense*. Singapore: Times Books International.

Silva, Penny. 1996. *A Dictionary of South African English on Historical Principles*. Oxford: Oxford University Press.

Simonson, Douglas, Ken Sakata, and Pat Sasaki. 1981. *Pidgin to da Max*. Honolulu: Peppovision.

Slone, Thomas H. 2003. *Rasta is Cuss: A Dictionary of Rastafarian Cursing*. Oakland, Calif.: Masalai Press.

Smitherman, Geneva. 1994. *Black Talk: Words and Phrases from the Hood to the Amen Corner.* Boston: Houghton Mifflin. (Second edition published in 2000.)

Sterns, Robin. 2008. *Say it in Crucian! A Complete Guide to Today's Crucian for Speakers of Standard English.* St. Croix: Antilles Press.

Story, G. M., W .J. Kirwin, and J. D. A. Widdowson. 1982. *The Dictionary of Newfoundland English.* Toronto: University Press of Toronto. (Second edition published in 1990.)

Sutcliffe, David. 1982. *British Black English.* Oxford: Basil Blackwell.

Taylor, Andrew. 1994. English dictionaries for Papua New Guinea. In Sibayan Boniface and Leonard Newell, eds. *Papers from the First Asia International Lexicography Conference, Manila, Philippines – 1992.* Manila: Linguistic Society of the Philippines, 161–177.

Teltscher, Kate, ed. 2013. *Hobson-Jobson: The Definitive Glossary of British India.* Oxford: Oxford University Press.

Thomas-Brereton, Leticia C. 2001. *Dictionary of Panamanian English.* 3rd ed. Brooklyn: Leticia C. Thomas Brereton.

Todd, Loreto. 1989. *A Short History and Dictionary of Northern Irish English.* London: Athlone Press.

Todd, Loreto. 1990. *Words Apart: A Dictionary of Northern Ireland English.* London: Colin Smythe.

Traynor, Michael. 1953. *The English Dialect of Donegal: A Glossary.* Dublin: Royal Irish Academy.

Upton, Clive, John D. A. Widdowson, and David Parry. 1994. *Survey of English Dialects: The Dictionary and Grammar.* London: Routledge.

Valls, Lito. 1981. *What a Pistarkle: A Dictionary of Virgin Islands English Creole.* Cruz Bay, VI: Prestige Press.

Ward, Nicholas M. L. 2013. *Bajan Slang Dictionary.* [Bridgetown]: Nicholas Ward.

Wheeler, Tom. 1979. *A Small Collection of Expressions from Liberian Speech.* Portales, NM: Eastern New Mexico University.

Wilkes, G. A. 2008. *Stunned Mullets and Two-pot Screamers: A Dictionary of Australian Colloquialisms.* Melbourne: Oxford University Press.

Winer, Lise. 2009. *Dictionary of the English/Creole of Trinidad & Tobago: On Historical Principles.* Montreal: McGill-Queen's University Press.

Wright, Joseph. 1898–1905. *The English Dialect Dictionary*, 6 vols. Oxford: Henry Frowde.

Xu, Zhichang. 2010. *Chinese English: Features and Implications.* Hong Kong: Open University of Hong Kong Press.

Yansen, C. A. 1993. *Random Remarks on Creolese.* [London]: Chameleon Press.

Yule, Henry, Arthur Coke Burnell, and William Crooke. 1903. *Hobson-Jobson: A Glossary of Anglo-Indian Colloquial Words and Phrases.* London: John Murray.

Zgusta, Ladislav. 1971. *Manual of Lexicography.* Prague: Academia.

19

The Relevance of World Englishes for Variationist Sociolinguistics

Alexandra D'Arcy

19.1 Introduction

Language change unfolds constantly, rendering explicit the seminal value of diachrony to language science. Within variationist sociolinguistics, the analytical lens is often focused on some current state of a language or variety, yet the roots of the field are grounded in matters of historical linguistics. Chief among these is the *Uniformitarian Principle*, the proposition that "knowledge of processes that operated in the past can be inferred by observing ongoing processes in the present" (Christy 1983: ix). As a consequence, the operating premise is that processes can be modeled and are inherently explicable on the basis of past events. The baseline methodologies of variationist sociolinguistics operate overtly on this foundation and the central questions of the discipline emerged from debates concerning the very nature of sound change (phonemic or lexical, gradual or abrupt, regular or erratic), the conditions of change (phonetic or also grammatical or semantic), the object of study (langue or parole, idiolect or group lect), and the appropriate scope of observation (past stages or a current stage). Likewise, the discipline can be traced to earlier dialectological work and the ways in which it shed light on some of the issues with which historical linguists were grappling (e.g. Gauchat 1905; Hermann 1929; Fónagy 1956). The advances of pioneering sociolinguists such as Steinholt (1964) and linguistic anthropologists such as Fischer (1958) pervade the current state of the field and its associated disciplines as well. In short, while the social underpinnings of language variation have necessarily had a central role in variationist research, as essentials of the speech community (e.g. Labov 1972, 2001), the field is crucially anchored in diachrony as reflected by synchronic grammars.

World Englishes, which emerge through particular sociohistorical factors (e.g. settlement, colonialization, imperial expansion, land reclamation, indentured servitude), and particular sociolinguistic factors (e.g. language contact, dialect mixing, pigdinization, creolization, koineization, leveling, simplification, focusing, reallocation), provide an ideal window for examining questions that are central to the variationist mission, such as the inheritance of shared features (see Schreier, Chapter 17, this volume), ongoing evolutionary trajectories, and pathways of innovation as dialects interact and settle within new local linguistic ecologies (e.g. Schneider 2003, 2007; Mufwene, Chapter 5, this volume). As a result, these varieties shed light on the underlying mechanisms of language variation and change, and they expose the interaction between external social forces and internal linguistic ones on linguistic forms and functions. What makes this possible is the formative assumption that the natural state of language (and hence linguistic structure) is *orderly heterogeneity*. Variable features, whether they be involved in change or not, are systematically constrained by a matrix of linguistic and extralinguistic factors. Interpretation of data in terms of stability, continuity, shared history, parallel change, or divergence thus depends on the entire sociolinguistic structure (Weinreich, Labov, and Herzog 1968: 177).

To ascertain points of similarity and divergence – and thus hypothesize about their theoretical status and import across varieties – the most important heuristic in the variationist toolkit is the comparative method (Tagliamonte 2002). As will be explored throughout this chapter, although two varieties may share a feature, mere overlap in occurrence is not particularly insightful. Moreover, frequencies of use may differ across varieties for many reasons (e.g. point of development, restricted contexts of use, genre, discourse type, topic, setting, speaker-specific characteristics). As in historical linguistics, the comparative method is invoked to ascertain the historical relationship between varieties. As instantiated in variationist sociolinguistics, the method also enables insight to the underlying variable grammar. Because this "choice mechanism" constrains predictors on variation and their direction of effect, elucidating the details of its operation provides key evidence of development and lineage, regardless of surface patterns in vernacular use. If the full architecture of the variable grammar is shared by two or more varieties, then they likely derive from a common ancestor (Poplack and Tagliamonte 2001; Tagliamonte 2002).

In this chapter, I review variationist research of spoken language, since speech is the primary hub of variation and change and the primary carrier of indexical stances and values (see Schleef, Chapter 26, this volume). The primary foci are varieties in which English may be the primary and native language of most speakers and where it holds official recognition as an official or national language (de facto or de jure) – British, Southern Hemisphere, and North American varieties in particular – not because these hold special heuristic value but because they represent the bulk of variationist literature.[1] There is a large research tradition in the World Englishes paradigm that examines English as used in non-native, mixed-language, and lingua franca contexts (e.g. Shaub 2000; Bolton 2003; Kachru, Kachru, and Nelson 2006; Björkman 2008), but variationist work targeting these varieties is less robust (but see, for example, Höhn 2011; Durham 2014; Biewer 2015).[2] The aim of this chapter is not to engage in debates concerning the privileging of traditional native speakers in the theoretical, ideological, and analytical apparatus of English studies but to outline the gains that are possible by harnessing the synergistic energies of World Englishes through a variationist lens. My intention is to link, overtly, the diachronic and the synchronic in the ongoing evolution and diversification of the English language. In pursuit of this goal, the references in this chapter represent a diversity of varieties and contexts, including English in continental Europe, Egypt, Jamaica, Fiji, Samoa, Singapore, Kenya, and Hong Kong.

19.2 Linguistic Perseverance and the Family Tree

A set of features has come to be relied on in variationist sociolinguistics to explore fundamental questions about the nature of language variation as illustrated by English. This sampling includes such variables as be, (t,d), and (ng). For example, (t,d) has helped expose the role of the group and the individual, the inherent nature of variation and linguistic conditioning, the relevance of cell size in statistical analysis, and the uniformity of constraint effects across speakers (e.g. Guy 1980), alongside the acquisition of social and linguistic constraints on variation and the role of parental variety in the mastery of local norms (e.g. Roberts 1997; Smith, Durham, and Fortune 2009). In conjunction with contraction and deletion of be in African American English, central to arguments on the systemacity and rule-governed nature of variation (e.g. Labov 1969; Rickford et al. 1991), (t,d) was also important in early work establishing (and debating) the operation of variable rules, as well as in later discussions about their demise as the state of art advanced (e.g. Labov 1969; Cedergren and Sankoff 1974; Kay and McDaniel 1979; Sankoff and Labov 1979; Fasold 1991). Like (t,d), variable (ng) has also been critical to uncovering patterns of acquisition (Roberts 1997) and it has been pivotal to formalizing the roles of social factors as determinants of variation and in refuting variation as unconstrained (e.g. Fischer 1958; Trudgill 1974). Variable (ng) has been

---

[1] English-based creoles have been central to discussions concerning the origin, history, and development of African American English; see, for example, Baugh (1980), Winford (1997, 1998), Mufwene et al. (1998), Rickford (2015), and references therein. For discussion of pidgins and creoles in the context of World Englishes, see Biewer and Burridge, Chapter 13, and Szmrecsanyi and Röthlisberger, Chapter 23, this volume.

[2] For discussion of sociolinguists' general exclusion of English lingua franca from the research agenda, see Seidlhofer (2011).

foundational to explorations of the cognitive status of variables and variants as social objects, alongside the contributions of speaker agency, listener agency, and social perceptions in the deployment and interpretation of variants in situated practice (e.g. Campbell-Kibler 2008, 2010). This feature has also been seminal to explorations of the sociolinguistic monitor, a psychological process for tracking, storing, and evaluating information on variation (Labov et al. 2011; Levon and Fox 2014). It is the roles of (t, d) and (ng) relative to linguistic perseverance, however, that are most relevant to the question of World Englishes and what they offer to variationist sociolinguistics (and vice versa).

Labov (1989) argued that children are linguistic historians: They inherit the history of a language as they acquire it, systematically reproducing residue from earlier historical stages as part of synchronic grammar. It is not only language change that opens a window on language history, then, but also the persistence of older, stable patterns of variation. This is robustly illustrated by (ng). Variation between velar and alveolar realizations is attested across varieties (e.g. Fischer 1958; Trudgill 1974; Houston 1985; Bell and Holmes 1992), and its linguistic conditioning applies in parallel, reflecting a historical morphological alternation between –*inge*, a verbal noun suffix, and –*inde*, the present participle suffix (velar realizations are favored in nominal contexts; alveolar realizations remain favored in verbal ones). Two factors precipitated the contemporary situation. First, both suffixes were affected by regular sound changes: reduction of the final vowel to schwa, rendering it vulnerable to apocope, followed by simplification of the final, unstressed consonant cluster in the verbal suffix, from /nd/ to /n/; the nominal one underwent phonologization of the velar element. Second, there is historical evidence of partial merger between the two suffixes, such that participial –*inde* was replaced by –*inge*, beginning in the south of England during the Middle English period. As summarized by Houston (1985: 287), synchronic patterns are a reflex historical ones, with "categorical differences in the past being preserved in noncategorical variation in the present."

Like variable (ng), variable (t,d) is a long-standing and widely attested feature of English (e.g. Guy 1980; Khan 1991; Patrick 1991; Bayley 1994; Hansen Edwards 2015), with the same conditions on variation (more or less) operating across the board. For example, deletion is probabilistically more likely when the following or preceding segment is an obstruent, in monomorphemes, in unstressed syllables, in trimorphemic clusters, and so on. The only apparent exception operates in the effect of a following pause, which either promotes or inhibits deletion, depending on the dialect (e.g. Guy 1980; Santa Ana 1996). Within communities, however, the stability of constraint effects and their predictive patterns across speakers of all ages are uniform.

In short, variable (t,d) and (ng) provide evidence of both stable longevity and cross-variety parallelism, leading to their characterization as vernacular primitives of English (e.g. Chambers 2004; but see Szmrecsanyi and Kortmann 2009; Trudgill 2009). The uniformity of their constraint effects across time and space provides compelling evidence of intergenerational transmission, the foundation of the family tree model of historical linguistics. Linguistic descent refers to continuous cross-generational native-language acquisition by children. The attestation of long-term dialect uniformity thus derives from repeated and ongoing intergenerational replication of variable patterns, resulting in preservation across historical stages of a language regardless of geographical locale. Indeed, recent work on the incrementation of linguistic change is premised on intergenerational transmission (i.e. replication of the adult model), followed by an active period of vernacular reorganization whereby features undergoing change are systematically advanced along the appropriate vector of change (e.g. frequency, F1, F2, duration, voice onset time). The constraints underlying variable features remain intact, however (Labov 2001; Tagliamonte and D'Arcy 2009). Linguistic descent is thus continuous, even in cases of language change. This creates a critical distinction between transmission, in which lineage is constant, and diffusion, in which lineage is interrupted via contact-induced transfer across branches of a family tree.

In the model proposed by Labov (2007), transmission and incrementation map to the family tree view of diachrony, whereas diffusion maps to a wavelike model of differentiation. The former is seen as the primary mechanism of diversity. The latter, a consequence of contact between adults and therefore of a "very different character" (2007: 347), is the secondary mechanism. Applied to World Englishes (or to any cross-variety comparisons), the following predictions are made: Transmission, via children, will result in the replication of abstract features of language structure, including constraints on variation, whereas diffusion, via adults, will lead to breakdowns in variable patterns and loss of structure (see also Kerswill 1996: 199–200). Theorizing from outside the variationist frame, Blommaert (2003: 612) notes that "whenever sociolinguistic items travel across the globe, they travel across *structurally different* spaces, and will consequently be picked up differently in different places" (emphasis in original). Crucially, the distinction between transmission and diffusion applies not strictly to Euclidean space (e.g. short-*a* in New York, Albany, North Plainfield, Cincinnati, and New Orleans) but also to social space as features diffuse across community groups (e.g. short-*a* among European Americans and African Americans).

It is clear that even in cases of diffusion, however, the outcomes can be vastly different depending on the degree and type of contact between speakers. Superficial innovations may spread with little personal contact, but tacit knowledge about variants, including their social meanings and linguistic predictors, requires "highly local contact" between speakers (Meyerhoff and Niedzielski 2003: 538). Ultimately, density of contact is a primary determinant of diffusion – the more interaction, the higher the likelihood that high-context information will spread (Labov 2001: 19). Similarly, Milroy (2007: 151–152) differentiated between *off the shelf* changes, features that are "relatively freely available to appropriately positioned social actors as a stylistic and social resource, regardless of the structure and location of their primary social networks," and *under the counter* changes, those that are "by definition restricted to locales which define the boundaries of particular speech communities." The former type diffuses in the absence of unambiguous evidence for sustained face-to-face contact, while the latter characterizes the regular social interaction of close-knit networks.

Crucial for these types of arguments are features that are attested across multiple varieties, such as vocalization of coda /l/, /θ,ð/ fronting, /t/ lenition, and /u/ fronting (e.g. Holmes 1995; Sudbury 2001; Horvath and Horvath 2002; Mesthrie 2010; Hay and Foulkes 2016). Yet, is the presence of a feature in distinct regional varieties sufficient motivation for assuming that diffusion has occurred? In a word: no. An alternate diachronic explanation is available for synchronically similar pathways of change. Through drift, a change may occur in two or more places as independent developments. Where the former is exogenous, the latter is endogenous and has the effect that "languages long disconnected will pass through the same or strikingly similar phases" (Sapir 1921: 150). As summarized by Trudgill (2014: 217), varieties that have derived from some common source may evolve in similar directions because they have "inherited a shared propensity to the development of the same characteristics, even after separation." In short, *drift* adds another dimension to historical pathways of change: parent to child transmission, adult-to-adult diffusion, and also parallel development.[3] Transmission is differentiated from shared innovation in that drift entails cases in which "parallel constraints are evident, but no contact can be inferred" (Tagliamonte and Denis 2014: 92). Variationist sociolinguistics thus provides an important analytical framework for teasing apart the spread of features but, again, the roots of the field in historical linguistics are relevant. For the features mentioned at the start of this paragraph, for example, the challenge for diffusionist arguments is that they are unmarked sound changes. They are also common cross-linguistic diachronic changes and are not particular to Germanic languages.

Notably, a single change may advance via multiple pathways. For example, Trudgill (2014: 218) argues that, within Britain, the fronting of /θ,ð/ has diffused spatially from London, while the presence of this change outside of Britain, in New Zealand English and African American English, for example, has emerged through independent and parallel developments. This case

---

[3] Drift is not fully explicative, nor is it a mechanism of change. It has little theoretical status on its own. Rather, its value comes in providing, in a uniformitarian sense, a historically consistent interpretation of synchronic facts that requires no post hoc rationalization. There is currently no way to disambiguate between changes that were perhaps incipient and those that emerged separately as a consequence of shared tendencies (see Trudgill 2004). The force of any argued case of drift thus lay in the structural conditions that lead to the propensity for parallel development.

thus raises the question of more local processes of diffusion, where contact is long-standing and facilitated by geographical proximity. Tagliamonte and Denis (2014) uncover a complex interplay between historical depth of a change, the age of the respective layers within a variable system, and the latent effects of the founder varieties. On the one hand, changes with a common root, such as possessive *have* and deontic *have to*, are transmitted with parallel structure. Replication is consistent across locales, with minor perturbations evident not in the structural architecture of variation but in the frequency of forms. This result, they argue, derives from distinct English-speaking settler populations (in this case, Loyalist vs. Ulster-Scots). On the other hand, older variable systems that contrast conservative forms with more recent innovations, such as intensifying adverbs, provide evidence for divergent pathways of development, evident in different diachronic trajectories, different frequencies of use, and different social associations. For example, intensifying *pretty* and *so* follow distinct patterns across locales. In the hinter region, *pretty* exhibits the hallmarks of transmission (expected for a longitudinally present feature) but, in the urban context, its progress diverges across genders as *so* makes inroads among women. The net result is that *so* is stable outside the urban center but increasing in the city. There is also evidence that diffusion may advance via collocations or constructions that reflect frequent or favored contexts for innovating forms, supporting the hypothesis that "recurrent patterns in discourse tokens exert pressure on linguistic types" (Du Bois 1985: 359–360). In short, imperfect replication may take many forms across linguistic structure, even when dealing with diffusion over relatively short, contiguous distances.

In cases of transmission, which preserves linguistic descent and informs the family tree model of language change, "the wheels of change just keep moving on" (Tagliamonte and Denis 2014: 131). Cases of diffusion reveal nuances of imperfect replication, affecting not strictly constraints on variation but also frequencies of use and collocational tendencies: Frequent contexts may transfer while less frequent ones lag behind or fail to be adopted. In contrast to diffusion over relatively proximate geographical regions, in which forms are argued to be propagated following either wavelike or hierarchical pathways (e.g. Trudgill 1986; Britain 2004), diffusion over vast geographical distances has come to herald globalization, by which "traveling" linguistic resources spread to distal places and subsequently have some impact in those places (see, e.g., Urry 2003). Britain (2002: 618) argued that contact between a supra-local innovation and regional, in situ norms could minimally result in one of three outcomes: wholesale adoption of the innovation, its outright rejection, or some degree of interaction between the innovation and the local system. Globalization (in the variationist sense of feature spread) is thus a specialized case of diffusion.

19.3 Challenging Diffusion in Globalization

Setting aside lexical features, which diffuse quite easily (and sometimes quite ephemerally), the repertoire of global variants is quite small. The flagship feature has long been quotative *be like*, attested in varieties of English worldwide (e.g. Bislama, Fiji, Filipino, Hong Kong, Indian, Jamaican, Kenyan, Malaysian, Singaporean, Vincentian English; e.g. Kortmann and Lunkenheimer 2013). Tagliamonte and Hudson (1999: 168) suggested that its diffusion "may be a very good linguistic indicator of the types of developments and changes we might expect from the putative ongoing globalization of English." Variationist examination has revealed that *be like* is not exceptional for its ability to transcend national boundaries but for the way in which it appears to have done so. Until recently, the assumption was that *be like* spread from an American epicenter (e.g. Blyth, Recktenwald, and Wang 1990; Romaine and Lange 1991; Ferrara and Bell 1995; Tagliamonte and Hudson 1999), a position that was supported by two elements of its literature. The first was an editor's note reporting on *be like* as an innovative collocation in American English to introduce quoted thought (Butters 1982). The second was an apparent early restriction to the USA (Romaine and Lange 1991). However, more recent research challenges the American naissance story as a strictly diffusion-based narrative. The structural conditions to support the emergence of *be like* were in place prior to its development and it arose in parallel across major national varieties of English. In other words, its candidacy as a case of globalization is in doubt.

The discourse surrounding much recent work on direct quotation, both variationist and otherwise, is embedded in the assumption that the English quotative system is undergoing rapid and large-scale change via the emergence of new quotatives (e.g. Blyth et al. 1990; Cheshire et al. 2011). This view is consistent with synchronic analyses, which have revealed a robust variable system undergoing rapid change. Longitudinal analyses do not contradict this interpretation but they do expose a diachronic lack of stability. Specifically, *be like* and other new competitors (e.g. *this is me*; Cheshire et al. 2011) have evolved through structural reorganization of direct quotation over (minimally) the past century and a half (Buchstaller 2011; D'Arcy 2012, in press).

The historical function of direct quotation was to introduce reconstructed speech. In the latter half of the nineteenth century, for example, direct quotation was almost categorically used to introduce realist talk and *say* accounted for almost all instances of speech reconstruction (D'Arcy 2012). Only a handful of forms accounted for the remainder of direct quotation in spontaneous discourse. In short, the reporting of thought, attitudes, and other context types was exceedingly rare in vernacular use. Further, quotation primarily encoded the speech of others – it was exceptional to quote oneself. There was also little elaboration of the quotative context, whether through voicing effects, tense shifts, aspectual nuances, verb movement, valency, and so on (D'Arcy 2012: 350).

Variationist research has consistently demonstrated that across varieties of English in northern England, Australia, New Zealand, and Canada this status quo began to break down with speakers born around the middle of the twentieth century, when lexical competition emerged. Importantly, it did so as a consequence of the changing function of quotation. The surface distributions of forms shifted only subtly but the underlying architecture of the system had been shifting since the late nineteenth century, with multiple constraints affected. The most fundamental change concerned the pragmatic constraint: the content of the quote. Beginning in the twentieth century, the generalization of quotation to new content types became discernible, developing into a regular and incremental increase of thought reporting across time (D'Arcy 2012, in press). In other words, speakers began to quote first-person internal dialogue with increasing frequency and the expansion of thought was not fully coterminous with the expansion of *think* as a reporting verb in vernacular practice.

Against this backdrop, the timing of *be like* is important. It was first attested across dialects of English with speakers born in the late 1950s and 1960s (Tagliamonte, D'Arcy, and Rodríguez Louro 2016). This places its development subsequent to reorganization of the quotative system. It did not cause the changes; rather, it filled an emergent niche. The reporting of first-person inner states and monologues was developing into a productive narrative genre, creating the slot that ultimately emerged as the nucleus of *be like*. By the end of the twentieth century, the system of direct quotation had developed an active and richly articulated variable grammar, in which a host of primary forms, such as *say*, *think*, *go*, and the null form, had a distinct role to play. It is clear, then, that underlying systemic shifts were ongoing and that these shifts were not regionally restricted. In other words, the structural preconditions were in place across varieties and they were moving in parallel. It is also clear that the preconditions for *be like* arose in parallel.

Romaine and Lange (1991) proposed that the quotative function of *like* emerged when it generalized from preposition to complementizer, allowing it to take sentential complements. Buchstaller (2014) argued that it was actually *like* in its function as a discourse marker, established in English since the eighteenth century (D'Arcy 2017), that filled the slot adjacent to *be* to form the quotative construction. That is, *be* was available within the quotative system independent of *like*. As Examples (1) and (2) show, both are attested in quotative frames since the early twentieth century, though they did not appear together until roughly the middle of the century (D'Arcy 2017, forthcoming). As a marker, *like* originally signaled exemplification, clarification, and elaboration and only subsequently came to be reanalyzed with *be* as a quotative construction in its own right.

1. a. It was one of those things where you *feel like* "Gosh, I'm kind of glad it happened that way." (Victoria/male/b. 1919)
   b. You'd get that late call Friday evening about seven o'clock and *say*, you know, *like* "I'm sorry. I can't play tomorrow." (New Zealand/female/b. 1947)
   c. What do you call out to a guy? Do you ever *say like* "Make a meat"? (Philadelphia/male/b. 1959)
2. a. It's *like* "Okay, I don't care. Don't believe me." (Victoria/male/b. 1948)
   b. It's kind of *like* "No, I don't want to toss him out of the house." (New Zealand/female/b. 1955)
   c. It's *like* "[sound effect]." (New Zealand/female/b. 1968)

The diachronic trajectory thus suggests that *be like* emerged from preexisting linguistic resources within the system and that it was able to capitalize on underlying changes already underway. As a quotative verb, *be* was pragmatically flexible from the outset, able to occur with all content types. This set it apart from the traditional locutionary verbs – *dicendi* (speech), *sentiendi* (perception), *scribendi* (writing) – that tend to encode fixed interpretations; special manipulations are required to change their pragmatic implicatures (e.g. *said* > speech, but *said to myself* > thought). The ongoing reconfiguration was bringing context types beyond speech into the foreground of direct quotation, setting the scene for flexibility in a previously regimented and rather fixed system. Moreover, *be* typically occurred with non-referential *it*, a context repeatedly exposed by variationist research to be a (near) categorical context for *be like* (Ferrara and Bell 1995; Tagliamonte and Hudson 1999; Tagliamonte and D'Arcy 2004, 2007; D'Arcy 2012; Tagliamonte et al. 2016). In short, it was not coincidental that early literature linked *it* with *be like*: *be* was the entry point and, when *like* first collocated with this verb, it necessarily followed the established patterns for *be*. In other words, its ability to occur with *it* is vestigial, an inheritance from its origins in the quotative system.

The evidence to this point is more in line with drift than it is with diffusion. A further challenge to globalization accounts is that *be like* exhibits parallel linguistic structure across time and space, especially among settler colonial varieties (e.g. Tagliamonte and D'Arcy 2007; Buchstaller and D'Arcy 2009; Tagliamonte et al. 2016): its variable grammar has been remarkably stable. In particular, four constraints condition its use, both in apparent time and in real time: grammatical person (first), mimesis (with voicing effects), content of the quote (internal monologue), and tense (historical present). For tense, the trajectory entails gradual differentiation of the simple present and the historical present but the main effect is continuously present and it does not wholly reorganize (i.e. the past tense has consistently disfavored *be like*).

Finally, cross-variety examination has revealed that *be like* rose to prominence in the same age cohorts on a global scale – speakers born in the 1950s and 1960s were the first to use it, those born in the 1970s promoted and accelerated it, and speakers born in the following decades have successively continued its uptake (Tagliamonte et al. 2016). If we assume diffusion, such a trajectory is undocumented in the literature and it is not predicted by current epistemologies about language change, which are inductive (cf. Uniformitarianism). If we assume drift, the temporal parallelism continues to require an interpretation (on this, see Tagliamonte et al. 2016: 838–840) but the structural parallelism is rendered explicable on both theoretical and empirical grounds. If we accept the premise that diffusion and drift entail distinct predictions concerning the structure and operation of the variable grammar, then variationist sociolinguistics provides a methodological toolkit for distinguishing between genuine effects of globalization and those that may merely benefit from social and technological advances that enhance contact between speakers from diverse regional backgrounds (see, e.g., Tagliamonte et al. 2016).

19.4   Contact In Situ and Language Shift

The family tree model and linguistic transmission set the scene for a model of language and dialect continuity in which the linguistic system is passed seamlessly from one generation to the next. It gives rise to predictions about parallel structural development, whether in situ or through drift, in which change is enacted via generational incrementation of innovation (Labov 2001, 2007; Tagliamonte and D'Arcy 2009). Diffusion, on the other hand, accounts for shared innovation that cannot be tied to shared structural properties (Labov 2007; Tagliamonte and Denis 2014). In colonial and new town settings, dialect mixture leads to the formation of new dialects of a common language (e.g. Kerswill and Williams 2000; Gordon et al. 2004; Trudgill 2004; Britain and Trudgill 2005; Schneider 2007; Dollinger 2008; Schreier 2017); these may or may not also involve contact with local Indigenous languages. Another typological scenario is also possible, one in which distinct dialects emerge as a consequence of disrupted, limited, or unavailable intergenerational transmission. In such cases, it is not adults who provide the initial target model but the peer group. That is, although – for English contexts – local "Anglo" models are available in the community, a high enough proportion of children acquire the language in a context where second-language speakers are sufficiently common that the "standard" model of intergenerational transmission is disrupted. The result is a local repertoire, or pool of features, derived from multiple input varieties or languages (cf. Siegel 1997; Mufwene 2001; Winford 2003). From this pool, what can cautiously be labeled a *multi-ethnolect* emerges (see also Fox, Chapter 20, this volume). A multi-ethnolect is a highly variable and possibly transient variety formed by large-scale group second-language acquisition (Cheshire et al. 2011). In this sense, multi-ethnolects are the consequence of rapid and large-scale community-wide language shift – not from one language but from multiple languages (see Fox, Chapter 20, this volume).

As outlined by Cheshire et al. (2011), a specific (but perhaps increasingly common) set of social and linguistic circumstances is required for the emergence of multi-ethnolects: large-scale immigration from developing countries to an urban – and typically underprivileged – neighborhood, a restriction on the availability of native-language models for the host language, and an abundance of languages and varieties within the community (see also Kerswill 2013).

Multi-ethnolects have been discussed in multiple European settings (e.g. Quist 2008; Svendsen and Røyneland 2008; Wiese 2009; but see Bodén 2010). Kerswill (2013: 133–124) defines Multicultural London English (MLE) as a feature pool, comprising elements from a variety of sources: "learners' varieties of English, Englishes from the Indian subcontinent and Africa, Caribbean creoles and Englishes along with their indigenised London versions (Sebba 1993), local London and south-eastern vernacular varieties of English, local and international youth slang, as well as more leveled and standard-like varieties from various sources." Acquisition and mastery of English in such a setting, in which many children are bilingual and the home language may not be English, assumedly takes place at school and in friendship groups, from peers and older siblings. With robust competition between forms, the question of which is chosen is not straightforward. Overall frequency is a known predictor of variant selection in language and dialect contact; yet, in MLE, there is evidence that frequency of representation also plays a role, such that a low-frequency form that occurs in multiple input varieties may be selected (Cheshire et al. 2011: 177). Regularity, transparency, ease of perception, and saliency also appear to be relevant (cf. Siegel 1997: 139). As in cases of dialect formation generally, the on-the-ground details of the language-contact situation are implicated as well: different mixes lead to different pools.

As in any group usage, locally salient identity is also central. Multi-ethnolects are used by speakers to "collectively ... express their minority status and/or [react] to that status to upgrade it" (Clyne 2000: 87), and factors that typically influence practice are surely relevant also (e.g. friendship groups, network structures, communities of practice, alignment, context, topic). That is, multi-ethnolects are both linguistic and social constructs, and in this latter respect they are inherently intersectional, sitting at the crossroads of ethnicity, culture, age, socioeconomic status, and place.[4] In MLE, it seems that lexis patterns along ethnic lines, while socio-phonetic and discourse-pragmatic variation are predominantly place-based

---

[4] On the challenges of operationalizating variationist sociolinguistics for the analysis of youth lects, see Kerswill (2013).

and socioeconomic (Kerswill 2013), though, perceptually, sociophonetic cues are strongly linked to ethnicity. Yet to what extent are these identity-based patterns of variation? In one borough (Hackney), it seems there is a weak (and potentially emergent) sense of self as "non-Cockney" among MLE speakers but this is largely restricted to non-Anglos; Anglos are less likely to reject a Cockney identity. In the other borough (Havering), the primary distinction is "not London" and thus "Essex," an identity rooted in place that is shared across ethnic groups, despite the belief that there is a distinction between Anglo and non-Anglo speech.

That children should quickly adjust their speech model toward their local peer cohort is well established in variationist studies of dialect acquisition (e.g. Labov 1972; Payne 1980; Kerswill and Williams 2000; Smith et al. 2009), and differences between the home and the peer dialects are greatest when the languages are not shared. In such cases, non-native dialect features may emerge as important sociolinguistic resources of ethnolinguistic repertoires. As noted by Sharma and Sankaran (2011: 402), "foreign traits can become a source of new raw material in dialect change, to mark affiliation or to inscribe new social boundaries." It is therefore not uncommon to find variable patterns of retention and reallocation of non-native parental language features (e.g. Penfield and Ornstein-Galicia 1985; Zentella 1997; Alam and Stuart-Smith 2011).

A matter of some debate concerns the question of when such reallocation occurs, assuming ancestral features are not simply cast aside. Sharma and Sankaran (2011) reported an important lag in the reallocation of retroflex /t/, an exogenous and salient South Asian feature, in Southall, West London. The continuous influx of immigrants has created a large range in the ages and experiences of first generation native English speakers. The oldest (i.e. "older Gen 2"), who grew up at a time when Asians were a (sizable) minority demographic and faced open racial tension, exhibited lower frequencies of retroflex pronunciations overall, yet they maintained the internal linguistic conditioning of their parents' second-language speech. Social and structural reallocation occurred only among younger generation 2 speakers, individuals who grew up part of the majority Punjabi group and experienced less racial tension. The cumulative effect is that the founding model persisted an entire generation after native English-speaking British Asians first appeared in the community. This result is nontrivial: It reveals that nativeness is not the trigger for structural reallocation.

At the same time, there was a significant effect of time of residence among the native Punjabi-speaking generation. Specifically, retroflexion was least frequent among speakers who had been in England for three to twelve years and was most frequent among those with fewer than three years of residency. While this result may relate to sociodemographic factors (e.g. long-term settlement plans, readjustment, employment (in)security, network strength), it is informative with respect to the home variety the British-born children would have encountered. It also suggests that declines in overall frequency of use are traceable to the non-native speakers themselves and the negotiation of meaning and form in locally based social practices (Sharma and Sankaran 2011: 418). Meanwhile, the whole of the second-generation cohort exhibited native-like competence in /t/-glottaling, the local variant.

The broader generalization that variationist sociolinguistics gains from World Englishes is that intergenerational transmission in immigrant communities appears to unfold in parallel with pathways already examined in the contexts of new dialect formation and creolization. In other words, the pathways are not strictly intralanguage phenomena; they apply across different kinds of contact situations. Focused varieties emerge gradually within the second generation of native speakers (and beyond), with increased demographic density playing a key role in the formation of varieties and lects (cf. Trudgill 2004). These processes may also be layered, in that diaspora communities may experience large-scale immigration more than once (e.g. Hundt 2014; Nigsch Rathore and Schreier 2016), where degrees and kinds of contact with the local language, as well as ideological affiliations in each region, leave indelible footprints on the linguistic model (English or otherwise).

19.5 The Non-native Speakers: English as a Lingua Franca

Within this larger backdrop of nativization, an important aspect of English varieties worldwide that remains relatively untapped is English as an additional language and contexts in which it functions as a lingua franca. As noted by Durham (2014: 3), English is unique:

> Never before has one language been spoken by such a high proportion of people across the world and in so many different contexts. ... English is a *global* lingua franca, the de facto choice across numerous bilingual and multilingual communities all over the world.   (emphasis in original)

This renders English lingua franca highly valuable to variationist socio-linguistics and to the development of an empirical theory of language variation and change. Lingua franca contexts, where English is "the other tongue" (Kachru 1982: 1), provide direct evidence of the ways in which the language is adapted to new environments and uses, including the treatment of its (variable) structural elements. This is all the more pressing given that native speakers do not "set the linguistic agenda" in lingua franca settings (Durham 2014: 8). The primary speaker is non-native, meaning that all interlocutors, regardless of linguistic background, must make adjustments within the interaction. The variationist sociolin-guistics and World Englishes paradigms both have much to gain from disentangling acquisitional phenomena from native/non-native usage difference (i.e. *target-based variation*; Durham 2014). In this case, the emphasis of variationist methods on usage patterns (as opposed to simply the existence or grammaticality of linguistic structures) is particularly useful.

The comparative method allows variable structures to be targeted directly, without assumptions that "different" entails speaker error. Three evidentiary indicators are relevant: the hierarchy of effects within a predictor, the magnitude of effect of a predictor, and the statistical significance of a predictor. Of these, significance carries the least interpretive weight, since it is sensitive to the number of tokens in the analysis (which may be insufficient for attaining significance but which may nonetheless provide evidence for constraint ordering and effects). Using Switzerland as a test case, Durham (2014: 63–64) proposed a three-way model for interpreting results in a lingua franca context. In the first instance, if the English variable grammar for a feature is parallel across speaker groups and replicates what is found in native-speaker use, then the same rule operates across native and non-native use; for that feature, lingua franca speakers have achieved sociolinguistic competency. In the second instance, if the variable grammar for a feature is parallel across speaker groups but distinct from native-speaker use, then either a new, focused feature has emerged in English as a lingua franca within the region (potentially distinguishing English in Switzerland from other lingua franca contexts) or it points to a common acquisitional pathway. In the third instance, if the variable grammar is distinct across (and potentially within) speaker groups and it is inconsistent with native-speaker use, then neither sociolinguistic competency nor focusing has occurred. Instead, practice reflects cross-linguistic interference of some sort (e.g. transfer).

Durham's examination of four features (future temporal reference, relative pronouns, complementizer *that*, additive adverbials) revealed characteristics of all three pattern types but, not surprisingly, the reality is nuanced.[5] That is, the evidence for an individual feature rarely falls neatly into a single category. Lingua franca speakers may or may not acquire native-like stylistic variation, they may or may not exhibit limited use of certain variants, and some non-native-speaker groups may pattern together yet contrast with another, but they also acquire some native-like variable constraints on use. What unites this range is two important insights. The first concerns the types of features that lingua franca speakers are more likely to learn to use natively. Syntactically conditioned variants most closely mirror the evidence from major native-speaker varieties while those with any lexical conditioning prove less native-like in lingua franca use. At the same time, features with primarily linguistic conditioning (as opposed to extralinguistic conditioning) more closely

---

[5] In a multilingual country, we would expect that different contact-induced patterns will obtain, depending on the first language of individual speakers (e.g. Italian, French, Romansch, Swiss German) and variation in language policies across regions.

approximate native-speaker patterns of variation. It also appears that formal variants are acquired before informal, vernacular ones (Durham 2014: 149). The second insight concerns the role of the source language, which may support learnability but does not necessarily hinder it when the structures are not parallel (e.g. complementation patterns). Mismatched structures across source and target do not interfere with native-like acquisition of variable rules (Durham 2014: 110) and yet syntactic structures do not simply map from source to target (e.g. the periphrastic future). This is all the more noteworthy when the variation in question entails neither conscious nor taught mastery of English patterns (e.g. through formal education, though variable patterns are acquired through ambient language exposure rather than taught).

Ultimately, whether native-like or not, English as a lingua franca is marked by inherent variation. As noted by Durham (2014: 153), the acquisition of variable patterns by non-native speakers provides "testament to the strength of variable patterns and their potential for transmission that they are maintained by users who do not predominantly use English with native speakers." The mechanism in this case can only be diffusion, which leads to the prediction that replication of the variable system will be imperfect. This is supported by the Swiss data but that is not the main point here. Rather, variation cannot be scrubbed out of the language model, regardless of the context, manner, or motivation for acquisition. English lingua franca contexts thus hold rich potential for exposing new understandings of general linguistic processes, including the versatility of speakers to manage and subsequently model variation as part of sociolinguistic competency. For variationist sociolinguistics and World Englishes, this will surely be important, enabling insight into possible developmental and evolutionary pathways as English varieties spread and diversify.

19.6 Conclusion

If we accept that languages change constantly and that overarching general constraints govern the transition from one synchronic state to the next, the diversity of Englishes amounts to a hotbed for theory testing and development across multiple contexts and linguistic landscapes. From contact phenomena to shared structural properties to ongoing evolutionary pathways of change, the global status of English is a critical access point in the development of an empirical theory of language change (cf. Weinreich et al. 1968). In short, variationist sociolinguistics has grown exponentially in terms of the scope and nature of the questions it can address, directly as a result of the myriad of English varieties available for study and by the growth of World Englishes as source input for analysis. At the same time, the field must necessarily push its boundaries beyond its primary focus on native-speaker varieties and monolingualism (cf. Meyerhoff and Nagy 2008; Stanford and Preston 2009) if it is to uncover the full linguistic ecology of possible constellations of language variation and change.

References

Alam, Farhana and Jane Stuart-Smith. 2011. Identity and ethnicity in /t/ in Glasgow-Pakistani high-school girls. In Wai-Sum Lee and Eric Zee *Proceedings of the 17th International Congress of Phonetics Sciences (ICPhS XVII)*. Hong Kong: City University of Hong Kong, 216–219.

Baugh, John. 1980. A re-examination of the Black English copula. In W. Labov, ed. *Locating Language in Time and Space*. New York: Academic Press, 83–106.

Bayley, Robert. 1994. Consonant cluster reduction in Tejano English. *Language Variation and Change* 6: 303–326.

Bell, A. and J. Holmes. (1992). H-droppin': Two sociolinguistic variables in New Zealand English. *Australian Journal of Linguistics* 12: 223–248.

Biewer, Carolin. 2015. *South Pacific Englishes: A Sociolinguistic and Morphosyntactic Profile of Fiji English, Samoan English and Cook Islands English*. Amsterdam: John Benjamins.

Björkman, Beyza. 2008. So where are we? Spoken lingua franca English at a technical university in Sweden. *English Today* 24: 35–41.

Blommaert, Jan. 2003. Commentary: A sociolinguistics of globalization. *Journal of Sociolinguistics* 7: 607–623.

Blyth, Carl, Sigrid Recktenwald and Jenny Wang. 1990. I'm like, 'Say what ?!'. A new quotative in American oral narrative. *American Speech* 65: 215–227.

Bodén, Petra. 2010. Pronunciation in Swedish multiethnolect. In P. Quist and B. A. Svendsen, eds. *Multilingual Urban Scandinavia: New Linguistic Practices*. Bristol: Multilingual Matters, 65–78.

Bolton, Kingsley. 2003. *Chinese Englishes: A Sociolinguistic History*. Cambridge: Cambridge University Press.

Britain, David. 2002. Space and spatial diffusion. In J. K. Chambers, P. Trudgill and N. Schilling-Estes, eds. *The Handbook of Language Variation and Change*. Oxford: Blackwell, 603–637.

Britain, David. 2004. Geolinguistics and linguistic diffusion. In U. Ammon, N. Dittmar, K. J. Mattheier and P. Trudgill (eds.), *Sociolinguistics: International Handbook of the Science of Language and Society*. Berlin: Mouton de Gruyter. 34–38.

Britain, David and Peter Trudgill. 2005. New dialect formation and contact-induced reallocation: Three case studies from the Fens. *International Journal of English Studies* 5: 183–209.

Buchstaller, Isabelle. 2011. Quotations across the generations: A multivariate analysis of speech and thought introducers across 5 decades of Tyneside speech. *Corpus Linguistics and Linguistic Theory* 7: 59–92.

Buchstaller, Isabelle. 2014. *Quotatives: New Trends and Sociolinguistic Implications*. Malden, MA: Wiley-Blackwell.

Buchstaller, Isabelle and Alexandra D'Arcy. 2009. Localized globalization: A multi-local, multivariate investigation of be like. *Journal of Sociolinguistics* 13: 291–331.

Butters, Ronald. 1982. Editor's note [on be like "think"]. *American Speech* 57: 149.

Campbell-Kibler, Kathryn. 2008. I'll be the judge of that: Diversity in social perceptions of (ING). *Language in Society* 37: 637–659.

Campbell-Kibler, Kathryn. 2010. The effect of speaker information on attitudes toward (ING). *Journal of Language and Social Psychology* 29: 214–223.

Cedergren, Henrietta J. and David Sankoff. 1974. Variable rules: Performance as a statistical reflection of competence. *Language* 50: 333–355.

Chambers, J. K. 2004. Dynamic typology and vernacular universals. In B. Kortmann, ed., *Dialectology Meets Typology*. Berlin: Mouton de Gruyter. 127–145.

Cheshire, Jenny, Paul Kerswill, Sue Fox and Eivind Torgersen. 2011. Contact, the feature pool and the speech community: The emergence of Multicultural London English. *Journal of Sociolinguistics* 15: 151–196.

Christy, Craig. 1983. *Uniformitarianism in Linguistics*. Amsterdam: John Benjamins.

Clyne, Michael. 2000. Lingua franca and ethnolects in Europe and beyond. *Sociolinguistica* 14: 83–89.

D'Arcy, Alexandra. 2012. The diachrony of quotation: Evidence from New Zealand English. *Language Variation and Change* 24: 343–369.

D'Arcy, Alexandra. 2017. *Discourse-pragmatic Variation in Context: Eight-hundred years of* like. Amsterdam: John Benjamins.

D'Arcy, Alexandra. Forthcoming Reconfiguring direct quotation over time and the system-internal rise of *be like*. In P. Grund and T. Walker, eds. *The Dynamics of Speech Representation in the History of English*. Oxford: Oxford University Press.

Dollinger, Stefan. 2008. *New-Dialect Formation in Canada: Evidence from the Modal Auxiliaries*. Amsterdam: John Benjamins.

Du Bois, John W. 1985. Competing motivations. In J. Haiman, ed. *Iconicity in Syntax*. Amsterdam: John Benjamins, 343–365.

Durham, Mercedes. 2014. *The Acquisition of Sociolinguistic Competence in a Lingua Fraca Context*. Bristol: Multilingual Matters.

Fasold, Ralph W. 1991. The quiet demise of variable rules. *American Speech* 66: 3–21.

Ferrara, Kathleen and Barbara Bell. 1995. Sociolinguistic variation and discourse function of constructed dialogue introducers: The case of *be + like*. *American Speech 70*: 265–290.

Fischer, John L. 1958. Social influences on the choice of a linguistic variant. *Word 14*: 47–56.

Fónagy, Ivan. 1956. Über den Verlauf des Lautwandels. *Acta Linguistica 6*: 173–278.

Gauchat, Louis. 1905. L'unité phonétique dans le patois d'une commune. *Aus Romanischen Sprachen und Literaturen: Festschrift Heinrich Morf*. Halle: Max Niemayer. 175–232.

Gordon, Elizabeth, Lyle Campbell, Jennifer Hay, Margaret Maclagan, Andrea Sudbury and Peter Trudgill. 2004. *New Zealand English: Its Origins and Evolution*. Cambridge: Cambridge University Press.

Guy, Greg. 1980. Variation in the group and the individual: The case of final stop deletion. In W. Labov, ed. *Locating Language in Time and Space*. New York: Academic Press, 1–36.

Hansen Edwards, Jette G. 2015. The deletion of /t,d/ in Hong Kong English. *World Englishes 35*: 60–77.

Hay, Jennifer and Paul Foulkes. 2016. The evolution of medial /t/ over real and remembered time. *Language 92*: 298–330.

Hermann, Eduard. 1929. Lautveränderungen in der Individualsprache einer Mundart. *Nachrichten der Gesellsch. der Wissenschaften zu Göttingen. Philosophisch-Historische Klasse 11*: 195–214.

Höhn, Nicole. 2011. Quotatives in the Jamaican acrolect: Corpus-based variationist studies of vernacular globalisation in World Englishes. Unpublished doctoral dissertation, University of Freiburg.

Holmes, Janet. 1995. Two for /t/: Flapping and glottal stops in New Zealand English. *Te Reo 38*: 53–72.

Horvath, Barbara M. and Ronald J. Horvath. 2002. The geolinguistics of /l/ vocalization in Australia and New Zealand. *Journal of Sociolinguistics 6*: 319–346.

Houston, Ann C. 1985. Continuity and change in English morphology: The variable (ING). Unpublished doctoral dissertation, University of Pennsylvania.

Hundt, Marianne. 2014. Home is where you're born: Negotiating identity in the diaspora. *Studia Neophilologica 86*: 125–137.

Kachru, Braj B., ed. 1982. *The Other Tongue*. Oxford: Pergamon Institute of English.

Kachru, Braj. B., Yamuna Kachru and Cecil L. Nelson. 2006. *The Handbook of World Englishes*. Malden, MA: Blackwell Publishing.

Kay, Paul and Chad K. McDaniel. 1979. On the logic of variable rules. *Language in Society 8*: 151–187.

Kerswill, Paul. 1996. Children, adolescents, and language change. *Language Variation and Change 8*: 177–202.

Kerswill, Paul. 2013. Identity, ethnicity and place: The construction of youth language in London. In P. Auer, M. Hilpert, A. Stukenbrock and B. Szmrecsanyi, eds. *Space in Language and Linguistics: Geographical, Interactional, and Cognitive Perspectives*. Berlin: de Gruyter. 128–164.

Kerswill, Paul and Ann Williams. 2000. Creating a new town koine: Children and language change in Milton Keynes. *Language in Society 29*: 65–115.

Khan, Farhat. 1991. Final consonant cluster simplification in a variety of Indian English. In Jenny Cheshire, ed. *English Around the World: Sociolinguistic Perspectives*. Cambridge: Cambridge University Press, 288–298.

Kortmann, Bernd and Kerstin Lunkenheimer, eds. 2013. *The Electronic World Atlas of Varieties of English*. Leipzig: Max Planck Institute for Evolutionary Anthropology. http://ewave-atlas.org

Labov, William. 1969. Contraction, deletion and inherent variability of the English copula. *Language 45*: 715–762.

Labov, William. 1972. *Sociolinguistic Patterns*. Philadelphia: University of Pennsylvania Press.

Labov, William. 1989. The child as linguistic historian. *Language Variation and Change 1*: 85–94.

Labov, William. 2001. *Principles of Linguistic Change, Vol. 2: Social Factors*. Malden, MA: Blackwell.

Labov, William. 2007. Transmission and diffusion. *Language 83*: 344–387.

Labov, William, Sharon Ash, Maya Ravindranath, Tracey Weldon, Maciej Baranowski and Naomi Nagy. 2011. Properties of the sociolinguistic monitor. *Journal of Sociolinguistics 15*: 431–463.

Levon, Erez and Sue Fox. 2014. Social salience and the sociolinguistic monitor: A case study of ING and TH-fronting in Britain. *Journal of English Linguistics 42*: 185–217.

Mesthrie, Rajend. 2010. Socio-phonetics and social change: Deracialisation of the GOOSE vowel in South African English. *Journal of Sociolinguistics 14*: 3–33.

Meyerhoff, Miriam and Naomi Nagy, eds. 2008. *Social Lives in Language: Sociolinguistics and Multilingual Speech Communities. Celebrating the work of Gillian Sankoff*. Amsterdam: John Benjamins.

Meyerhoff, Miriam and Nancy Niedzielski, 2003. The globalisation of vernacular variation. *Journal of Sociolinguistics 7*: 534–555.

Milroy, Lesley. 2007. Off the shelf or under the counter? On the social dynamics of sound changes. In C. M. Cain and G. Russom, eds. *Studies in the History of the English Language, Vol. 3: Managing Chaos: Strategies for Identifying Change in English*. Berlin: Mouton de Gruyter, 149–172.

Mufwene, Salikoko S. 2001. *The Ecology of Language Evolution*. Cambridge: Cambridge University Press.

Mufwene, Salikoko S., John R. Rickford, Guy Bailey and John Baugh, eds. 1998. *African American English: Structure, History and Use*. London: Routledge.

Nigsch Rathore, Claudia and Daniel Schreier. 2016. "Our heart is still in Africa": Twice migration and its sociolinguistic consequences. *Language in Society 45*: 163–191.

Patrick, Peter L. 1991. Creoles at the intersection of variable processes: -t,d deletion and past-marking in the Jamaican mesolect. *Language Variation and Change 3*: 171–189.

Payne, Arvilla C. 1980. Factors controlling the acquisition of the Philadelphia dialect by out-of-state children. In W. Labov, ed. *Locating Language in Time and Space*. New York: Academic Press, 143–178.

Penfield, Joyce and Jacob Ornstein-Galicia, 1985. *Chicano English: An Ethnic Contact Dialect*. Amsterdam: John Benjamins.

Poplack, Shana and Sali Tagliamonte. 2001. *African American English in the Diaspora*. Oxford: Blackwell.

Quist, Pia. 2008. Sociolinguistic approaches to multiethnolect: Language variety and stylistic practice. *International Journal of Bilingualism 12*: 43–61.

Rickford, John R. 2015. The creole origins hypothesis. In S. Lanehart, ed. *The Oxford Handbook of African American Language*. Oxford: Oxford University Press, 35–56.

Rickford, John R., Arnetha Ball, Renee Blake, Raina Jackson and Nomi Martin. 1991. Rappin on the copula coffin: Theoretical and methodological issues in the analysis of the copula variation in African-American Vernacular English. *Language Variation and Change 3*: 103–132.

Roberts, Julie. 1997. Acquisition of variable rules: A study of (-t,d) deletion in preschool children. *Journal of Child Language 24*: 351–372.

Romaine, Suzanne and Deborah Lange. 1991. The use of *like* as a marker of reported speech and thought: A case of grammaticalization in progress. *American Speech 66*: 227–279.

Sankoff, David and William Labov. 1979. On the uses of variable rules. *Language in Society 8*: 189–222.

Santa Ana, Otto. 1996. Sonority and syllable structure in Chicano English. *Language Variation and Change 8*: 63–89.

Sapir, Edward. 1921. *Language*. New York: Harcourt Brace.

Schneider, Edgar W. 2003. The dynamics of New Englishes: From identity construction to dialect birth. *Language 79*: 233–281.

Schneider, Edgar. 2007. *Postcolonial English: Varieties Around the World*. Cambridge: Cambridge University Press.

Schreier, Daniel. 2017. Dialect formation in isolated communities. *Annual Review of Linguistics 3*: 347–362.

Sebba, Mark. 1993. *London Jamaican*. London: Longman.

Seidlhofer, Barbara. 2011. *Understanding English as a Lingua Franca*. Oxford: Oxford University Press.

Sharma, Devyani and Lavanya Sankaran. 2011. Cognitive and social forces in dialect shift: Gradual change in London Asian speech. *Language Variation and Change 23*: 399–428.

Shaub, Mark. 2000. English in the Arab Republic of Egypt. *World Englishes 19*: 225–238.

Siegel, Jeff. 1997. Mixing, leveling and pidgin/creole development. In A. K. Spears and D. Winford, eds. *The Structure and Status of Pidgins and Creoles*. Amsterdam: John Benjamins, 111–149.

Smith, Jennifer, Mercedes Durham and Liane Fortune. 2009. Universal and dialect-specific pathways of acquisition: Caregivers, children, and t/d deletion. *Language Variation and Change 21*: 69–95.

Stanford, James N. and Dennis R. Preston, eds. 2009. *Variation in Indigenous Minority Languages*. Amsterdam: John Benjamins.

Steinholt, Anders. 1964. *Målbryting i Hedrum*. Oslo: Universitetsforlaget.

Sudbury, Andrea. 2001. Falkland Islands English: A southern hemisphere variety? *English World-Wide 22*: 55–80.

Svendsen, Bente Ailin and Unn Røyneland. 2008. Multiethnolectal facts and functions in Oslo, Norway. *International Journal of Bilingualism 12*: 63–83.

Szmrecsanyi, Benedikt and Bernd Kortmann. 2009. Vernacular universals and angloversals in a typological perspective. In M. Filppula, J. Klemola and H. Paulasto, eds. *Vernacular Universals and language Contacts: Evidence from Varieties of English and Beyond*. London: Routledge, 33–53.

Tagliamonte, Sali A. 2002. Comparative sociolinguistics. In J. K. Chambers, P. Trudgill and N. Schilling-Estes, eds. *The Handbook of Language Variation and Change*. Malden, MA: Blackwell, 729–763.

Tagliamonte, Sali A. and Alexandra D'Arcy. 2007. Frequency and variation in the community grammar: Tracking a new change through the generations. *Language Variation and Change 19*: 199–217.

Tagliamonte, Sali A. and Alexandra D'Arcy. 2009. Peaks beyond phonology: Adolescence, incrementation, and language change. *Language 85*: 58–108.

Tagliamonte, Sali A., Alexandra D'Arcy and Celeste Rodríguez Louro. 2016. Outliers, impact, and rationalization in linguistic change. *Language 92*: 824–849.

Tagliamonte, Sali A. and Derek Denis. 2014. Expanding the transmission/diffusion dichotomy: Evidence from Canada. *Language 90*: 90–136.

Tagliamonte, Sali and Rachel Hudson. 1999. Be like et al. beyond America: The quotative system in British and Canadian Youth. *Journal of Sociolinguistics 3*: 147–172.

Torgersen, Eivind, Costas Gabrielatos, Sebastian Hoffmann and Sue Fox. 2011. A corpus-based study of pragmatic markers in London English. *Corpus Linguistics and Linguistic Theory 7*: 93–118.

Trudgill, Peter. 1974. *The Social Differentiation of English in Norwich*. Cambridge: Cambridge University Press.

Trudgill, Peter. 1986. Dialects in Contact. Oxford: Blackwell Publishing.

Trudgill, Peter. 2004. *New-dialect Formation: The Inevitability of Colonial Englishes*. Edinburgh: Edinburgh University Press.

Trudgill, Peter. 2009. Vernacular universals and the sociolinguistic typology of English dialects. In M. Filppula, J. Klemola and H. Paulasto, eds. *Vernacular Universals and language Contacts: Evidence from Varieties of English and Beyond*. London: Routledge, 304–322.

Trudgill, Peter. 2014. Diffusion, drift, and the irrelevance of media influence. *Journal of Sociolinguistics* 18: 214–222.

Urry, John. 2003. *Global Complexity*. Cambridge: Polity Press.

Weinreich, Uriel, William Labov and Marvin I. Herzog. 1968. Empirical foundations for a theory of language change. In W. P. Lehmann and Y. Malkiel, eds. *Directions for Historical Linguistics: A Symposium*. Austin: University of Texas Press, 95–195.

Wiese, Heike. 2009. Grammatical innovation in multiethnic urban Europe: New linguistic practices among adolescents. *Lingua 119*: 782–806.

Winford, Donald. 1997. On the origins of African American Vernacular English: A creolist perspective. Part 1: The sociohistorical background. *Diachronica 14*: 305–344.

Winford, Donald. 1998. On the origins of African American Vernacular English: A creolist perspective. Part II: Linguistic features. *Diachronica 15* : 99–155.

Winford, Donald. 2003. *An Introduction to Contact Linguistics*. Oxford: Blackwell.

Zentella, Ana Celia. 1997. *Growing Up Bilingual: Puerto Rican Children in New York*. Oxford: Blackwell.

20

Multilingualism and the World Englishes

Sue Fox

20.1 Introduction: Multilingualism with English

Since the foundations of English were laid in the British Isles, English has *always* existed within a context of multilingualism (Schreier and Hundt 2013), a fact that is often overlooked in any discussion of global English or the "spread" of English. In Britain, the multilingual elements consisted of the indigenous Celtic languages: Irish Gaelic, Scottish Gaelic, Welsh, Cornish, and Manx. As English was taken beyond the shores of Britain, it was always introduced to contexts where indigenous populations and their languages already existed (Schneider 2007). At first, these contexts were countries where English speakers settled, in America, Canada, Australia, and New Zealand for example, countries that became known as ENL (English as a Native Language) countries or, in Kachru's (1992) model of World Englishes, "Inner Circle" countries. In these contexts, the indigenous populations were put under pressure to conform to the English language of the settlers (see Lim, Chapter 4; Hickey, Chapter 2; Mufwene, Chapter 5; all this volume). Ultimately, this led to the demise of many of the indigenous languages in North America and Australia but, nevertheless, some survived and are still in existence today, although most are under threat of language death. The fact that the indigenous populations were marginalized in these early settlements of English-speaking communities also meant that the variety of English (for the majority of speakers) that emerged in these places was not influenced to a great extent by the indigenous languages, with the exception of lexical items adopted, such as toponyms, flora, fauna, and cultural concepts for which there was no direct translation into English. Later, as English was taken to the continents of Africa and Asia, English rose to importance in those countries that were colonized by the British, countries such as Nigeria and India, where English was used early on for official functions in domains such as law, government, and education. These are the ESL (English as a Second

Language) or "Outer Circle" countries according to Kachru's (1992) "Three Circles Model" of English. Here, then, English added to the multilingual patterns that already existed in those places. Since the independence of those countries, English has continued to function in those same domains and is used by a considerable number of speakers for a variety of functions, including, for some, English as their first language. In these varieties, it is often very clear that the emergent English has been influenced by the substrate languages, not only in terms of lexical constructions but also in phonological and morpho-syntactic constructions.

Of course, English has continued to rise in importance in countries that have no links to a colonial history or where it has no official function – Kachru's (1992) "Expanding Circle" – and this continuing spread of English to the vast numbers of countries around the world is often linked to the processes of globalization in the twentieth and twenty-first centuries (see Buschfeld and Kautzsch, Chapter 3, this volume). In these countries, many speakers have acquired, or are acquiring, English for use as a lingua franca for communicating with people from many different linguistic backgrounds. English, in this case, is often used within an individual's multilingual repertoire and tends to be modeled on one of the world's "standard" varieties, usually British or, increasingly, American English.

The rest of this chapter will provide an overview of the way in which English has existed within a framework of multilingualism in each of these different contexts. Drawing on Kachru's (1992) terms, I will consider multilingualism in Inner Circle countries, where English is the majority language, Outer Circle countries where English is used for a range of different functions and Expanding Circle countries where English has no official function. Finally, I will return to Britain, where the myth of English monolingualism probably persists the most. I will consider both historical and modern-day multilingualism within the British Isles and I will also attempt to show how multilingualism has impacted on the English variety spoken in London today.

20.2 Multilingualism with English in Inner Circle Countries

Omitting Britain for the moment, let us consider the countries that Kachru (1992) defines as Inner Circle countries, namely America, Canada, Australia, and New Zealand, those countries where the myth of monolingualism is the strongest. Often described as the "New World," the label hides the fact that there were already indigenous peoples and their languages in existence in these countries long before the European colonizers arrived. Although exact figures are unknown, there were well over 300 Native American languages across America and Canada (Krauss 1992) and between 200 to 250 Aboriginal languages in Australia alone (Romaine 1991). The impact of colonization was devastating for many of these languages as populations were wiped out through conflict with the Europeans or death from the introduction of new diseases. The indigenous languages that survived tended to be ignored and "English-only" policies were promoted, causing further language death. According to current figures in the *Ethnologue*, it is estimated that there are 196 living indigenous languages in the USA, 145 of which are dying and the remainder endangered. Canada does not fare much better, with most of its 77 living indigenous languages either dying or seriously endangered. Worst by far, though, is the situation in Australia. Of the 330 known Aboriginal languages, only 13 (4 percent) are spoken natively by children (Zuckermann, Shakuto-Neoh, and Quer 2014). The dilemma for all of these endangered languages is that many of them only have relatively few speakers, rendering language maintenance and revival efforts nearly impossible. The picture is somewhat better in New Zealand, perhaps because Te Reo Māori is the only indigenous language. Te Reo Māori is an Eastern Polynesian language spoken by the Māori people and it was the predominant language of New Zealand until the mid-1800s (King 2001). After this time, it was overshadowed by the English of the many settlers and those who came as missionaries or gold diggers. Policies of the colonial governments of New Zealand in the late nineteenth century introduced an English-only schooling system for all New Zealanders, often separating children from their parents and placing them in residential boarding schools, with the aim of filtering out the Māori language. The results of these measures led to Māori children failing to learn their ancestral language and, by the 1980s, it was estimated that fewer than 20 percent of the Māori could speak the language well enough to be considered native speakers, and linguists identified it as an endangered language. Since that time there has been an intense effort, both by Māori leaders and subsequently the New Zealand government, to reverse that situation. One of the first responses to the situation was the introduction of "language nests" (*kohunga reo*) set up by the Māori community. These were preschools for younger children where the children were taught Māori by older Māori speakers who were members of the community and worked voluntarily on the project (King 2001). The children were immersed in Māori during their formative years from infancy to school age. These were so successful that they led to the establishment of primary and secondary schools where Māori is the primary language of instruction. The Māori Language Act was passed in 1987, which gave Māori the status of an official language in New Zealand. It also established the Māori Language Commission, which was set up to promote the language and provide linguistic advice. The latest 2013 Census statistics show that 148,395 people (3.7 percent) can speak Te Reo Māori, whether as their only language or as one of several languages. Encouragingly, for the future vitality of the language, is the fact that almost a quarter (24.6 percent) of those who could hold a conversation in Māori were children and only one in ten (10.1 percent) were aged sixty-five years or over.

Apart from indigenous languages, there are other established languages in the Inner Circle countries. French and Spanish, for example, are both long-established colonial languages in North America (Edwards 2004). French colonization of the Americas began in the sixteenth century and resulted in French settlements stretching from Hudson Bay in the North to the Mississippi in the South, with cities such as Quebec and Montreal in Canada and Detroit and New Orleans in America developing from these early settlements. Although France eventually relinquished these colonies, the French language remained. In the 2009–2013 sampling period, US Census statistics show that more than 2 million people reported that French (including Cajun and Patois) or French Creole is spoken in the home in the USA. In Canada, the 2016 Census recorded more than 7.3 million francophones, representing around 21 percent of the total population. Of these, 85 percent live in the province of Quebec. The concentration of the French population in and around Quebec, together with sustained language planning measures taken by the Quebec government to promote the use of French in Quebec, would seem to secure its place in Canada's multilingual landscape, at least for the present.

Spanish has also had a long history with the USA. The Spanish were, in fact, the first European settlers of the Americas (Edwards 2004) and held territories in Mexico, Florida, and western parts of America as well as the Caribbean islands of Cuba and Puerto Rico. The ties between Spain and these territories were severed in the nineteenth century. The Mexican War of Independence (1810–1811) ended the rule of Spain and led to the independence of Mexico, and the end of the Spanish-American War in 1898 led to the independence of Cuba and the incorporation of the American colonies and Puerto Rico into the USA. The legacy of Spanish colonization is, of course, the language, and the number of Spanish speakers has continued to grow throughout the twentieth and twenty-first centuries, with large numbers of new arrivals from Cuba and Central and South America. Today, Spanish is the second most widely spoken language in the USA after English, with more than 37.5 million people of the population five years old and over in the USA reporting that they speak Spanish at home, almost 13 percent of the total population. Faced with these figures, one can hardly concede that the USA is a monolingual English-speaking country.

If the figures thus far are not convincing enough to dispel the myth of English monolingualism in the Inner Circle countries, let us add to this the more recent languages that have arrived in these countries due to large-scale immigration from the second half of the twentieth century onward. According to the 2016 Current Population Survey (CPS), immigrants and their US-born children number approximately 84.3 million people, or 27 percent of the total population. In 2015, Mexicans accounted for approximately 27 percent of immigrants in the USA, making them the largest foreign-born group in the country, followed by Indians (6 percent), Chinese (including Hong Kong but not Taiwan), and Filipinos, close to

5 percent each. Further groups from El Salvador, Vietnam, Cuba (about 3 percent each), the Dominican Republic, Korea, and Guatemala (around 2 percent each) represent 58 percent of the US immigrant population. Table 20.1 lists the top ten ethnic languages spoken at home in the USA excluding English and Native American languages.

Canada admitted 271,845 new permanent residents in 2015, with the highest proportion coming from the Philippines (18.7 percent), followed by India (14.5 percent), the People's Republic of China (7.2 percent), Iran (4.3 percent), and Pakistan (4.2 percent). Smaller numbers were admitted from Syria, the USA, France, the UK, and Nigeria (Government of Canada, 2016 Annual Report to Parliament on Immigration). Table 20.2 provides the top ten ethnic languages spoken in Canada, excluding the indigenous and official languages (English and French).

Table 20.1 *Top ten ethnic languages spoken at home in the USA, excluding English and Native American languages*

Language	Number of speakers
Spanish	37,458,470
Chinese (incl. Cantonese, Mandarin, and other Chinese languages)	2,896,766
French (incl. Patois, Cajun and French Creole)	2,047,467
Tagalog	1,613,346
Vietnamese	1,399,936
Korean	1,117,343
German (incl. Luxembourgian)	1,063,773
Russian	879,434
Italian	739,725
Portuguese (incl. Portuguese Creole)	693,469

Source: United States Census Bureau. www.census.gov/data/tables/2013/demo/2009–2013-lang-tables.html

Table 20.2 *Top ten ethnic languages spoken at home in Canada, excluding indigenous and official languages (English and French)*

Language	Number of speakers
Chinese (Mandarin and Cantonese)	1,204,865
Punjabi	543,495
Tagalog (Pilipino, Filipino)	510,420
Spanish	495,090
Arabic	486,525
Italian	407,455
German	404,745
Urdu	243,090
Portuguese	237,000
Persian (Farsi)	225,155

Source: Statistics Canada 2016. www12.statcan.gc.ca/census-recensement /2016/as-sa/98–200-x/2016010/98–200-x2016010-eng.cfm

The cultural and linguistic diversity of Australia has also been reshaped by immigration in recent years. The 2016 Census of Population and Housing showed that more than a quarter (26 percent) of Australia's population (6,163,667 people) were born overseas, a slight increase when compared with 2011 (25 percent). This figure has continually been increasing since the first Census in 1911 (excluding periods during both world wars when migration to Australia halted). Notably, nearly one in five (18 percent) of the overseas-born population had arrived since 2012. The top countries of birth for those born overseas continue to be the UK (15 percent of the overseas-born population) and New Zealand (8.4 percent) but there have also been increases in the proportion born in China (from 6.0 to 8.3 percent in the period 2011 to 2016) and India (from 5.6 to 7.4 percent) (Australian Bureau of Statistics). The 2016 Census also identified more than 300 languages spoken at home. While English continues to be the main language spoken at home, the data revealed that 21 percent of Australians spoke a language other than English at home. The top ten languages spoken at home in 2016 are listed in Table 20.3.

The number of people living in New Zealand who were born overseas has also risen rapidly in recent years, increasing from 19.5 percent in 2001 to 25.2 percent (1,001,787 people) of the total population in 2013. England remained the most common country of birth for overseas-born people living in New Zealand (at 21.5 percent of overseas-born people) followed by the People's Republic of China (8.9 percent). India, however, had overtaken Australia for third place, with Australia in fourth place and followed by South Africa, Fiji, Samoa, Philippines, Korea, and Scotland (Stats NZ). There is much less linguistic diversity in New Zealand, with English spoken by 96.1 percent of the total population. However, there were big increases in the number of people who could hold a conversation about everyday things in Hindi (66,309 people in 2013, up from 22,749 in 2001)

Table 20.3 *Top ten ethnic languages spoken at home in Australia, excluding English and Aboriginal languages*

Language	Number of speakers
Mandarin	596,711
Arabic	321,728
Cantonese	280,943
Vietnamese	277,400
Italian	271,597
Greek	237,588
Hindi	159,652
Spanish	140,817
Punjabi	132,496

Source: Australian Bureau of Statistics 2016. www.abs.gov.au/aus stats/abs@.nsf/Lookup/by%20Subject/2071.0~2016~Main% 20Features~Cultural%20Diversity%20Article~20

and northern Chinese (including Mandarin) (52,263 people in 2013, up from 26,514 in 2001).

So far, there has been no mention of South Africa. It is difficult to determine where South Africa fits into Kachru's concentric circles of English because, in this context, Englishes of the Inner and Outer Circles "co-exist in close proximity" (Coetzee-van Rooy and van Rooy 2005: 3). In some ways, South Africa would seem to fit the criteria of an Inner Circle country in that English fulfills the function of lingua franca and is the dominant language in education and government institutions. Its native speakers of English, however, form a minority of the population, estimated at just less than 10 percent of the population (Ibid.: 3), and these speakers exist and interact alongside a majority who are proficient second-language English speakers (van der Walt and van Rooy 2002). The minority "White South African English" exists alongside what is usually called "Black South African English" (van Rooy 2000; van der Walt and van Rooy 2002), with some identifying a third variety as "South African Indian English" (Mesthrie 1996). These labeling practices for English in South Africa have been the topic of scholarly debate (see Coetzee-van Rooy and van Rooy 2005 for a discussion of these issues) but perhaps what is important here is that the different varieties of English in use in this one context illustrate, as de Kadt (2000) argues, that South Africa fits neither the Inner Circle nor the Outer Circle components of Kachru's (1992) model. Furthermore, these varieties of English exist amid a complex multicultural and multilingual framework. If any country dispels the myth of English monolingualism it is South Africa, where more than twenty different languages are spoken and where there are no less than eleven official languages: nine languages from four major African language groups along with English and Afrikaans.

A further group of languages that often get forgotten in discussions of monolingualism/multilingualism are sign languages. Each of the countries mentioned so far has its own sign language. The US Census Bureau does not collect information about American Sign Language (ASL) users. There are no accurate records for the number of users of ASL but estimates range from 500,000 to two million users (Harlan, Hoffmeister, and Bahan 1996: 42). At the higher figure, it would be the fifth most widely used language after English, Spanish, Chinese, and French. The Canadian Association of the Deaf – Association des Sourds du Canada – states that there are two legitimate Sign languages: ASL and la Langue des Signes Quebecoise (LSQ); there is also a regional dialect, Maritimes Sign Language (MSL). No accurate figures appear to be available for the number of sign language users in Canada and the Census does not collect data about sign language. Auslan is the sign language of the Australian Deaf Community. The 2011 Census population of Auslan users in Australia was 9,723. The 2016 Census form offered assistance to deaf or hard of hearing people in Auslan, and Auslan was included in the languages spoken in the home. In New Zealand, 2013

Census data showed that 20,235 people reported the ability to use New Zealand Sign Language, a decrease of 16 percent from the 2006 Census. New Zealand Sign Language has official language status in New Zealand.

20.3   Multilingualism with English in Outer Circle Countries

As English was taken to the continents of Africa and Asia, English rose to importance in the countries that were colonized by the British, countries such as Nigeria, India, and Singapore (Buschfeld and Kautzsch, Chapter 3, this volume). Here, then, English added to the multilingual patterns that already existed in those places. During colonial times, English was used for higher-level administration and education and this often led to an "elite" class of English speakers forming among the indigenous population, led by those who aspired for economic or political success and encouraged by those who saw the benefits of the promotion of English for the British Empire (see Schneider 2007 for a historical and theoretical account for many of these settings). After the independence of most of those countries, English was fully established and many African and Asian states took the pragmatic decision to retain English but often alongside one or more of its vernacular languages. In the case of India, after independence in 1947, English was officially recognized in the Indian Constitution but it was only meant to be for a transition period until 1965, after which time it was intended that Hindi would replace English as the national language. However, this proved to be impracticable and, in the Official Languages Act 1967, English was deemed to have co-official status for an indefinite period of time. Many other countries adopted English as a tool to maintain cohesion among ethnically diverse members of the state (Stavans and Hoffman 2015). English in these contexts has usually continued to function in the same domains of higher-level administration, education, the media, and business and technology; and, of course, in more recent years, English has continued to spread at the "grassroots" level, particularly in contexts of tourism (Schneider 2016).

As the decades have passed, then, the influence of English has usually increased rather than declined and it is now used by a considerable number of speakers for a variety of functions, including, for some, English as their first language. Pakir (2001), for example, argues that Singapore is moving into Kachru's Inner Circle. The growing use of English in the home in Singapore (and therefore its use as a first language) has led to occasional calls for English to be officially recognized as a mother tongue for Singaporeans but the government insists that English must continue to serve only a purely instrumental role and that it is not acceptable as a mother tongue, of course keeping in mind that terms such as "mother tongue" can often be politically loaded rather than used in a purely linguistically descriptive sense. In these varieties, it is often very clear that the emergent English has been influenced by the substrate languages, not only in terms of lexical constructions but also in phonological and morpho-syntactic constructions (see Lim, Chapter 4, this volume). In other words, over time, English has undergone a process of "structural nativization," first proposed by Kachru in reference to what he called "institutionalised second-language varieties" that have a long history of "acculturation in new cultural and geographical contexts" (Kachru 1985: 211) and theorized by Schneider as being the "emergence of locally characteristic linguistic patterns and thus the genesis of a new variety of English" (Schneider 2007: 5–6).

20.4 Multilingualism with English in Expanding Circle Countries

English has continued to rise in importance in countries that have no links to a colonial history or where it has no official function. This continuing spread of English to the vast numbers of countries around the world is often linked to the processes of globalization and the rise of America as a superpower in the twentieth and twenty-first centuries. Here, then, English is taught as a foreign language (EFL). It should be noted that these countries are only separated here because of this distinction in their historical past but, of course, many countries in this category may be considered to be ESL settings in terms of the users of English as well as its forms and functions. The boundaries between ESL and EFL settings are becoming increasingly blurred, particularly in countries such as the Netherlands (Edwards 2014, 2016), with the result that various World Englishes scholars have argued that ESL and EFL (or Outer and Expanding Circle varieties) can best be seen as a continuum rather than as a dichotomy (Buschfeld 2013; Buschfeld and Kautzsch 2017; Gilquin and Granger 2011) and that ESL and EFL varieties should be studied in analogy (Davydova 2012). Notwithstanding these blurred distinctions and the valid scholarly arguments, it is, however, in this category where we can clearly see that English has truly reached global status, with most countries around the world adopting it as their first choice for foreign-language teaching, increasingly introduced at primary school level or even younger. In China, for instance, official policy since 2001 has stated that English should be taught from the age of eight or nine onward, in Grade 3 of the national education system. English was also required in the National University Entrance exam (called *gaokao*); and, in a society where examinations are accorded high importance, the university entrance exam has had a ripple effect on younger children whose parents want to give their children an educational advantage through arranging early English tuition for children as young as kindergarten age. There is today an expectation that children in China should be familiar with English before they even start their formal education; and, although this might be considered a feature of middle-class aspirations, the middle classes themselves have been growing strongly over the last ten years, with the consequence that more and more children are being exposed to English. These attitudes toward English teaching can be found perhaps even more strongly in South Korea, where a series of governmental policies in the early 1990s has led to "English Fever," resulting in an increasing number of young children being sent abroad for the main purpose of learning English (Shim and Park 2008; Park 2009).

In these countries, many speakers have acquired, or are acquiring, English for use as a lingua franca (ELF) for communicating with people from many different linguistic backgrounds (Edwards and Seargeant, Chapter 15, this volume). Such is the extent of the use of English in these contexts that the field of ELF has grown to become an established subdiscipline of English linguistics, with an annual conference series, a journal, and many journal articles and textbooks (cf. Jenkins 2007, 2014; Seidlhofer 2011) published on the topic. English, in this case, is often used within an individual's multilingual repertoire and tends to be modeled on one of the world's "standard" varieties, usually British or, increasingly, American English, particularly if it is learned within the formal context of a classroom. However, English is acquired in these contexts in a variety of settings and from many different sources and may not necessarily use native speaker models (see Edwards and Seargeant, Chapter 15, this volume). The media and Internet have become useful tools for acquiring language skills; English is prominent in the music industry as well as in films and television channels to which many people are exposed. Tourist locations also provide opportunities for language learning, although the use of English may be limited to this setting. The learning outcomes and the varieties of English acquired are therefore very diverse but there is no doubt that, for many people around the world, English is seen as the language of social and economic advancement.

20.5   Multilingualism with English in the British Isles

Let us return then to the British Isles, where the myth of English monolingualism perhaps has the strongest hold. Partly, this vision of a monolingual Britain may lie in the fact that this is where the foundations of English were laid during the Anglo-Saxon invasions of around AD 450. It is generally considered that the roots of English began with the languages spoken by the Angle, Saxon, and Jute settlers and it is therefore seen as the birthplace of English. It may also partly be because the British have a poor track record when it comes to language learning. According to Eurostat, the statistical office of the European Commission, in 2013 the UK had the highest proportion (52 percent) in Europe of upper secondary school students who were not learning any foreign language. A third factor may be because, according to 2011 Census data, 92 percent (49.8 million) of the usual residents of England and Wales reported English as their main language (Office for National Statistics, ONS). Nevertheless, as outlined in Section 20.1, English was not always spoken in the British Isles; previously, the British Isles was inhabited by the Celts who, after the Anglo-Saxon and Viking invasions, retreated to the western fringes of Britain to what is now Ireland, Scotland, the Isle of Man, Wales, and Cornwall.

20.6 The Celtic Languages

Some scholars have argued that the Celtic languages have had much more of a substratum influence on the formation of English than was once thought. The assumption that there had been little Celtic influence was based on the fact that both Old English and Modern English contain very few Celtic loanwords (Lutz 2009). However, recent years have seen the rise of scholarly works that have traced Celtic influence in English at the level of syntax (mostly) but also at the morphological and phonological levels (Filppula et al. 2002; Filppula et al. 2008) and at the level of usage (Vennemann 2009). Let us turn, then, to the different Celtic languages that were in use and their current status in the British Isles.

Manx, along with Irish and Scottish Gaelic, is a member of the Goidelic/ Gaelic branch of the Celtic languages. Until the thirteenth century, they formed a single speech community but subsequent sociopolitical developments fragmented the community and, thereafter, substantial morphological and phonological differences developed (Ó'Riagáin 2007). From approximately AD 500 to the mid-nineteenth century, Manx was the native language of the majority of the people who lived on the Isle of Man, a self-governing dependent island of the British Crown off the west coast of Britain (Clague 2009). The last known native speaker of Manx died in 1974. Revival efforts have ensured that the language continues to survive and is used by some as a second language. From its lowest point of just twenty speakers in 1946 (Clague 2009: 168), the number of people who are now able to speak Manx is 1,662 according to the most recent 2011 Census figures (ONS). Today, the language is supported at the institutional level and the language is very visible in the public domain: bilingual street signs, bilingual government department names, bilingual public bus time-tables, and, occasionally, bus destinations in Manx only (Clague 2009: 174). Language revival attempts have escalated in recent years with the introduction of Manx-medium playgroups, nurseries, and *Bunscoill Ghaelgagh* (Manx Gaelic primary school) (Clague 2009: 195). It seems that adult second-language (L2) learners of Manx consider the language to be a projection of their heritage and nationality but they are in the minority. For the majority of Manx people, the language "is not a badge of identity" (ibid.: 194). For now, then, Manx is stable and support for the language among the population is strong, but the social and economic pressures of English are never far away.

Cornish, along with Welsh, is a member of the Brythonic (or British) branch of the Celtic languages. Tradition has it that the last known native speaker of Cornish, Dolly Pentreath, died in 1777 (Payton 2000) and whether or not this is true it seems unlikely that the language survived much beyond the eighteenth century (Thomas 1993). Revival attempts started at the beginning of the twentieth century with the work of Henry Jenner (Everson [1904] 2010). The language has since undergone reconstruction and the most popular versions are Common Cornish or Unified Cornish Revised or UCR (*Kernowek Unys Amendys*) (Omniglot). The 2011 Census figures show that 600 people reported Cornish to be their main language, with just 83 percent (500) of those people living in Cornwall (ONS). The language has support at the institutional level; BBC Radio Cornwall has regular broadcasts in Cornish, there are a number of magazines published solely in Cornish and the language is taught at some schools and at the University of Exeter. In 2010, a bilingual Cornish/ English crèche or *Skol dy'Sadorn Kernewek* (Cornish Saturday School) was set up. Children between the ages of two and five years old are immersed in Cornish in one room, while their parents attend Cornish lessons in another. The first ever feature film entirely in Cornish *Hwerow Hweg* (Bitter Sweet) was released in 2002, followed by a number of others since then (Omniglot).

Scottish Gaelic continues as one of Scotland's living indigenous languages although it, too, is struggling for survival under the pressure of English. Its origins date from the fifth century AD but, after a number of Acts of the Scottish and British parliaments aimed at promoting English literacy, Gaelic had, by the seventeenth century, retreated into the Highlands, Hebrides, and Clyde Islands, comprising the *Gaidhealtachd*, or Gaelic-speaking area (MacKinnon 2007). The Highland Clearances of the nineteenth century forced many Gaelic speakers to move away from the Highlands, and legislation in 1872, which virtually banned the use of Gaelic in schools, also had a devastating effect on the language. There was a general decline throughout the twentieth century, with numbers dwindling from 254,415 speakers reported in the 1891 Census to just 58,969 in the 2001 Census (Mackinnon 2007: 201). The questions relating to the use of Scottish Gaelic in the 2011 Census were quite detailed, related to home use but also to details of skills in speaking, writing, listening, and reading. Nationally, 25,000 people (0.49 percent of the total population) reported using Gaelic at home. This figure represented 40.2 percent of all Gaelic speakers in Scotland. The total number of people aged three and above who reported some Gaelic skills was 87,100. The number of people aged three and above who reported being able to speak Gaelic was 57,600 (66 percent), a decline from the 2001 figure. There were 23,400 (27 percent) people who said they could understand Gaelic but could not speak, read, or write it (Scotland's Census). Since 1975, there has been a concerted effort to revive Gaelic in Scotland. Bilingual schooling schemes are in place and, in 1985, Gaelic-medium schooling was introduced. Gaelic can be heard on radio and television and, in 1997, a Minister for Gaelic was appointed (Mackinnon 2007: 201–202).

Irish Gaelic dates back to around AD 500 and scholars generally divide its historical development into four periods, *Old Irish* (500–900), *Middle Irish* (900–1200), *Early Modern Irish* (1200–1600), and *Modern Irish*. Until the beginning of the Modern Irish period, Gaelic was the dominant language spoken in Ireland (Ó'Riagáin 2007). The early part of the seventeenth century saw large numbers of English speakers establishing plantations in Ireland and language shift toward English began. The Great Famine (1846–48) also took its toll on the language, with many Irish-speaking families having to move away to seek employment and avoid starvation. The population of Ireland was depleted by two and a half million during this time, hitting the Irish-speaking areas the hardest. Article 8 of the Constitution of Ireland states that "The Irish Language as the national language is the first official language" and, as with the other Celtic languages discussed so far, there have been vigorous revival attempts in Ireland. Particularly, strong efforts have been made to maintain Irish Gaelic in those areas where it is still considered to be the community language to some extent (the *Gaeltacht*). A study of the Gaeltacht was undertaken by the National University of Ireland, Galway, and, in 2007, the research report suggested creating three linguistic zones within the Gaeltacht region: Category A, where 67 percent or more are daily Irish-speaking and Irish is dominant as the community language, and Category B, where 44–66 percent are speaking Irish daily. Here, English is dominant but with a large Irish-speaking minority. Finally is Category C, where 43 percent or less are daily Irish-speaking. Here, English is dominant but with an Irish-speaking minority much higher than the national average. The report suggested that Category A districts should be the state's priority in providing services through Irish and development schemes, and that Category C areas that show a further decline in the use of Irish should lose their Gaeltacht status. The report seems to suggest that the best hope to stem the tide toward English is in the strongest Irish footholds but its pessimistic message is that "it is clear that the threat of language shift [to English] is intensifying" (Ó'Giollagáin et al. 2007). A further report published in 2015 *Nuashonrú ar an Staidéar Cuimsitheach Teangeolaíoch ar Úsáid na Gaeilge sa Ghaeltacht: 2006–2011* (Ó'Giollagáin and Charlton 2015) stated that, on present indicators, Irish will have ceased to be used as a community language in the Gaeltacht within ten years.

These views are also reflected in the number of speakers claiming the ability to speak Irish in the Republic of Ireland. From 1851 to 2002, the numbers consistently went up, from 29.1 percent in 1851 to 41.9 percent in 2002, but the 2011 Census reported a decline in that figure to 41.4 percent, representing 1,774,367 speakers from a total population of 4,370,631 (Central Statistics Office). However, it is clear that the Irish language receives a great deal of governmental support, as evidenced in the *20-year strategy for the Irish Language 2010–2030* (Department of Education and Skills). There are statements in this document setting out the government's aim to increase the number of daily speakers of Irish outside of the education system to 250,000 and to increase the number of daily speakers in the Gaeltacht by 25 percent overall. There are also strategies in place to increase the number of people that use state services through the Irish language and to ensure that television, radio, and print media can be accessed through Irish. Education would also appear to be a prime domain for maintaining Irish according to the twenty-year plan. The document states that all-Irish education is to be provided to those pupils whose parents so wish and that education through Irish is to be developed up to third-level college education. Irish is also taught as an obligatory subject from primary to Leaving Certificate level throughout Ireland, ensuring its continuity if only through its use as a second-language. Only time will tell how successful these measures will be.

Like the other languages, Welsh has undergone a decline but it is the most robust (predominantly in northern Wales) of the Celtic languages in the British Isles. Before the Act of Union between Wales and England in 1536, Welsh was the main language spoken in Wales but the Act of Parliament resulted in the loss of political and legal domains for Welsh (Ball 2007). The development of coal fields in Wales during the Industrial Revolution attracted many English speakers to the country and English was the language of the pit owners and the professional classes (Ibid.: 249). Education policies in the nineteenth century led to the suppression of Welsh and schools taught in English. Welsh became restricted to the home, chapel, and *eisteddfod* (literary competition) (Ibid.: 249). The estimated number for the percentage of Welsh speakers in 1801 is around 80 percent and the first Census recorded 54.5 percent in 1891. There was then a rapid decline to just 18.6 percent in 1991 (Ibid.: 250). Revival programs in Wales have been the most rigorous, and organizations such as the Welsh Language Society, the Welsh League of Youth, the Welsh Women's Organization, and the *Eisteddfod Genedlaethol* (the National Eisteddfod) have campaigned tirelessly to achieve equality for Welsh. There are now Welsh-language radio and television stations, bilingual road signs, and Welsh-medium schools at the kindergarten, primary, and secondary levels as well as a large number of adult learners' classes across Wales (Ibid.: 251). These tremendous efforts appeared to be rewarded when the 2001 Census reported that the number of Welsh speakers had risen to 20.8 percent (582,000 people). However, the most recent 2011 Census results show that the figure has again gone down to just 19 percent (562,000) (Statistics for Wales). Once more, it seems that *survival* rather than *revival* seems to be the most appropriate way to describe the current situation for Welsh.

20.7 British Sign Language

The British Deaf Association reports that British Sign Language (BSL) is used by 151,000 individuals in the UK, 87,000 of whom are deaf. The figure does not include professional BSL users such as translators and interpreters unless they use it at home. In the 2011 Census, 22,000 people living in England and Wales reported using a sign language as their main language, with 15,000 of those people using BSL as their main language (ONS). The origins of BSL can be traced back hundreds of years and, although it was recognized by the British Government as a language in its own right in 2003, it does not have any legal status. Similarly, BSL and Irish Sign Language (ISL) were officially recognized as minority languages in Northern Ireland in 2004 but there is no legal status for either. BSL was also officially recognized as a minority language for about 4,000 deaf people living in Wales but again it has no legal status. The British Deaf Association has been campaigning for the legal recognition of BSL and ISL on an official level since the 1980s (British Deaf Association). In Scotland, the British Sign Language (Scotland) Act 2015 puts a duty on Scottish Ministers to promote the use and understanding of BSL and requires Scottish Ministers to prepare and publish BSL national plans. The first BSL National Plan 2017–2023 was published in October 2017. The National Plan reflects the views and needs of the BSL Community in Scotland and what the Scottish Government and national public bodies can realistically deliver. The document sets out Scotland's aim "to make Scotland the best place in the world for BSL users to live, work and visit" (p. 4). A BSL National Advisory Board has also been set up to help develop the National Plan (Deaf Sector Partnership).

20.8 Immigrant Languages in England and Wales

Mass migration in the twentieth and twenty-first centuries has also led to a great deal of linguistic diversity in the British Isles, particularly concentrated in the large cities. Of course, the large cities of Europe and beyond have always been a destination for immigrants; but perhaps the scale and diversity of migration over the past sixty years or so is unprecedented, with a result that it has had a vast impact on multilingualism in our cities. The perception that Britain is an English-monolingual country could be forgiven when one reads the Census statistics that 92.3 (49.8 million) percent of people aged three and above reported English (English or Welsh in Wales) as their main language. On reflection, though, it would be difficult

Table 20.4 *Top ten main languages other than English spoken in England and Wales*

Language	Number of speakers
Polish	546,000
Punjabi	273,000
Urdu	269,000
Bengali (with Sylheti and Chatgaya)	221,000
Gujarati	213,000
Arabic	159,000
French	147,000
"All other" Chinese (an aggregate of Chinese languages excluding those who wrote Mandarin and Cantonese)	141,000
Portuguese	133,000
Spanish	120,000

Source: Office for National Statistics 2011. www.ons.gov.uk/peoplepopulationandcom munity/culturalidentity/language/articles/languageinenglandandwales/2013–03-04

as a resident *not* to use English as a main language, given that it is used in all walks of public life. Nevertheless, 7.7 percent (4.2 million) of people reported a language other than English as their main language, with Polish coming out top at 1.0 percent (546,000 people). Overall, 1.3 percent (726,000) of people said that they could not speak English well and 0.3 percent (138,000) said that they could not speak English at all. Those that could not speak English well or at all were concentrated in London and the West Midlands (where the city of Birmingham is situated) (ONS). Table 20.4 shows the top ten main languages (excluding English) spoken in England and Wales.

What these figures do not show, of course, is the languages that people use *in addition* to English nor how English is used within the diverse and rich multilingual repertoires of individual speakers.

20.9 A Case in Point: Multilingualism in London

Let us now, by means of an example, zoom in and consider the situation in London. London is Europe's largest city and has one of the highest proportions of foreign-born residents across cities globally, with 3 million (34.9 percent) of its 8.6 million population being foreign-born (Fox and Sharma 2017). In 2013, more than a third of the foreign-born population in the UK were living in London and about 1.3 million foreign-born people were living in inner London, an increase from just over 800,000 in 1995 (Migration Observatory 2016). Inner and outer London boroughs have the highest number of immigrants in terms of percentage of the whole population in the UK. The 2011 Census results show that London had the highest proportion of people who reported their main language as other than English at 22.1 percent. London also had the highest proportion of people who could not speak English well or not at all at 4.1 percent (320,000 people). While the overall picture of London, then, is one of great diversity, these figures mask the fact that the situation is not uniform all over the Greater London area. London is divided into thirty-three boroughs and the demographics of the different populations can vary considerably. For example, in Havering (the borough further east), there is a predominantly White British population, whereas Newham (another borough east of the City of London) is the most ethnically diverse, with 44.4 percent of people reporting a main language other than English. Newham also has the highest proportion of people who either cannot speak English well or not at all at 8.7 percent. It should also be noted that even *within* boroughs the situation may not be uniform. In Tower Hamlets, for example, (the borough directly to the east of the City of London), there is a high proportion of Bangladeshi residents – 32 percent (81,488 people) of the total population; but the Bangladeshi community tends to be concentrated in the west of the borough so that some neighborhoods are made up of 75 percent Bangladeshi residents (Fox 2015). More than half of inner London school children are known or believed to have a first language other than English (Department for Education) and well over 300 languages are spoken within the Greater London area.

What effect can this level of multilingualism have on an existing variety of English such as that spoken in London? Most handbooks of English (cf. Schneider et al. 2004) deal with a range of newly emerging Englishes around the world and generally consider the substrate effects of the languages involved (as indeed does this volume). However, when there are so many languages involved as is the case in London, it is difficult to pinpoint what role individual languages play in language change. Nevertheless, language contact is considered to be the driving force in changes that have been documented recently for London English (Cheshire and Fox 2009; Cheshire et al. 2011; Fox 2015). Indeed, London is not the only place where such changes have been documented. In the last fifty years or so, the amount and diversity of immigration across many cities, particularly in Europe, has increased massively, and this in turn has affected the amount of multilingualism within those cities. In high migration, multilingual areas of cities, new forms and styles of languages have been reported, commonly referred to as *multiethnolects* (cf. Nortier and Svendsen 2015), a term used to refer to varieties spoken by young people (mainly) from different ethnic backgrounds, including those with a background in the dominant host language. As early as the mid-1980s, Kotsinas (1988) reported what she called *Rinkebysvenska* "Rinkeby-Swedish" to refer to Swedish spoken by immigrant children and similar ways of speaking have since been reported in Oslo (Svendsen and Røyneland (2008), Copenhagen (Quist 2008), the Netherlands (Nortier and Dorleijn 2008), and Berlin (Wiese 2009, Freywald et al. 2011). All of these varieties arise in multiethnic language contact situations.

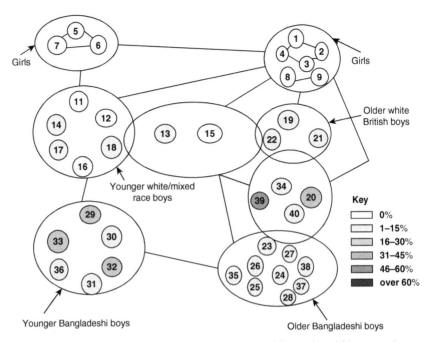

Figure 20.1 Distribution of the PRICE variant [æ] among different friendship groups in an East London youth club

In London, Fox (2015) argues for the effects of language contact and the impact of non-UK varieties on the language of London. In her study of Bangladeshi adolescent males and White British adolescents attending a youth club in the traditional East End of London, she found that the Bangladeshi males had not acquired the traditional Cockney variety of London English and were leading in innovative variants of FACE and PRICE vowels not previously documented for London. They were also leading in changes in the allomorphy system of the definite and indefinite articles. Furthermore, she found that friendship networks are a conduit for the diffusion of innovations. Figure 20.1 is a representation of the youth club members' friendship groups. It shows the distribution of the [æ] variant of the PRICE vowel among the participants in the study. It can clearly be seen that the Bangladeshi males are the most frequent users of this innovative variant but that it is also used by the younger and older White British males to some extent, seemingly reflecting the fact that these groups engage in some of the same social practices. The White British girls did not use this variant at all and this appears to correlate with the fact that they did not interact socially with the Bangladeshi males. The same pattern held for the innovations found for the FACE vowel and for changes occurring in the article system (see Fox 2015 for more details).

Many innovations have been found in the English of young people in another part of inner London. The emerging variety has been referred to as *Multicultural London English* to reflect the fact that the variety spoken by many young people in London today contains innovations that are not traditional Cockney features associated with London. It also captures the idea that it is spoken by young people regardless of their ethnicity and includes both young people of recent immigrant background as well as their peers from the (monolingual) majority background of the host community (Cheshire, Nortier, and Adger 2015). The innovations are often led by non-Anglo (the children of recent immigrants to London) male adolescents. For example, non-Anglos have extreme fronting of the GOOSE vowel (Cheshire et al. 2008). Diphthong shift reversal has also been documented in London. It involves the backing of the onset of the MOUTH vowel and again the non-Anglos are in the lead. Non-Anglos also have a more raised onset for the FACE vowel compared to Anglos. The non-Anglos also lead in fronting and lowering for the PRICE vowel and they have a more raised GOAT vowel compared to Anglo speakers (Fox and Torgersen 2017). Overall, then, the results show that the non-Anglos are innovative in vowel change processes.

A number of consonantal features show the same pattern. H-dropping, a traditional London feature, appears to be receding among young speakers in London but, once more, the non-Anglos have even less H-dropping than their Anglo peers. DH-stopping, the realization of [d] in words such as *this* and *that,* appears frequently in the speech of young people in inner London, with non-Anglos in the lead here again (Cheshire et al. 2011).

The pattern holds for some morphological and syntactic innovations, too. The use of *a* [ə] instead of *an* [ən] and *the* [ðə] instead of *the* [ði] in front of words beginning with vowel sounds has been reported by Fox (2015) and Cheshire et al. (2011). In both studies, the innovations are led by the non-Anglo groups. Cheshire and Fox (2009) found innovative leveling to a *was/wasn't* pattern in the past tense BE paradigm in line with contact varieties around the world, led specifically by male speakers of Black and Afro-Caribbean background. Their Anglo counterparts tended to follow the nonstandard southeast England pattern of leveling to *was/weren't.* Interestingly, for many of the innovations, Anglos in dense multicultural friendship networks were often the second highest users of the innovations, supporting Fox (2015) in the role that friendship networks play in the adoption of innovations.

For London, then, multilingualism and language contact are prevalent and have a major role to play in linguistic variation and change. This may have always been the case. Indeed, Nevalainen and Raumolin-Brunberg (2003: 162) have argued that waves of migration have had a significant effect on the language of London historically and point to the sixteenth and seventeenth centuries, when no more than 15 percent of the population had been born there (Ibid.: 164). It seems that the old adage that history repeats itself is never more true than it is today in the "world within a city" (Greater London Authority 2005) and the "super-diversity" (Vertovec 2007) that is London's population in the twenty-first century (Fox 2012).

20.10 Conclusion

English has established its place as a global language on the world stage and, in some ways, this focus on multilingualism seems rather at odds with that concept. Current estimates put English speakers anywhere between one to two billion (cf. Crystal 2008) and there are no signs that interest in learning English is dwindling. However, what we have seen is that the many different English varieties that have emerged around the world have all arisen in contact settings and have been influenced by the different languages or other English varieties with which they have come into contact (Lim, Chapter 4, this volume). Even established varieties such as London English can change as a result of multilingualism and language contact. What I have attempted to show here is that English always exists within a context of multilingualism and that multilingualism has been of major importance to the emergence of Englishes around the world, not only to those outlined in Outer and Expanding Circle countries but also to the different varieties of English spoken in places like the British Isles. Multilingualism continues to play an important role in the emergence of multi-ethnolects and is a major contributory factor to the process of language variation and change. Even in those countries where English is spoken by the majority of the population, different languages and cultures can, and do, exist side by side. The efforts of revivalists to keep languages alive reveal the importance that people attach to their language and that it is part of our social identity, who we are and where we come from. Bilingual/multilingual and bicultural/multicultural individuals may potentially be the links between minority and majority communities, leading to better relations between different groups. Certainly, the London studies have shown us that social interaction takes place in multicultural friendship networks and this in turn has informed our understanding of processes of language change. Perhaps the overriding message here is that multilingualism is something to be embraced and should be viewed as an asset that contributes to the development of communication between different cultures.

References

Ball, Martin. 2007. Welsh. In David Britain, ed. *Language in the British Isles.* Cambridge: Cambridge University Press, 237–254.

Buschfeld, Sarah. 2013. *English in Cyprus or Cyprus English: An Empirical Investigation of Variety Status.* Amsterdam: John Benjamins.

Buschfeld, Sarah and Alexander Kautzsch. 2017. Towards an integrated approach to postcolonial and non-postcolonial Englishes. *World Englishes* 36(1): 104–126.

Cheshire, Jenny and Sue Fox. 2009. Was/were variation: A perspective from London. *Language Variation and Change 21*(1): 1–23.

Cheshire, Jenny, Susan Fox, Paul Kerswill and Eivind Torgersen. 2008. Ethnicity, friendship network and social practices as the motor of dialect change: Linguistic innovation in London. *Sociolinguistica 22*: 1–23.

Cheshire, Jenny, Paul Kerswill, Susan Fox and Eivind Torgersen. 2011. Contact, the feature pool and the speech community: The emergence of Multicultural London English. *Journal of Sociolinguistics 15*(2): 151–196.

Cheshire, Jenny, Jacomine Nortier and David Adger. 2015. Emerging multi-ethnolects in Europe. Queen Mary's Opal No. 33, Occasional Papers Advancing Linguistics.

Clague, Marie. 2009. Manx language revitalization and immersion education. *e-Keltoi-Journal of Interdisciplinary Celtic Studies 2*: 165–1198.

Coetzee van Rooy, Susan and Bertus van Rooy. 2005. South African English: Labels, comprehensibility and status. *World Englishes 24*(1): 1–19.

Crystal, David. 2008. Two thousand million? *English Today 24*(1): 3–6.

de Kadt, Elizabeth. 2000. English language proficiency in South Africa at the turn of the millennium. *Southern African Linguistics and Applied Language Studies 18*: 25–32.

Davydova, Julia. 2012. Englishes in the Outer and Expanding Circles: A comparative study. *World Englishes 31*(3): 366–385.

Edwards, Alison. 2014. The progressive aspect in the Netherlands. *World Englishes 33*(2): 173–194.

Edwards, Alison. 2016. *English in the Netherlands: Functions, Forms and Attitudes*. Amsterdam: John Benjamins.

Edwards, V. 2004. *Multilingualism in the English-speaking World*. Oxford: Blackwell.

Everson, Michael. [1904] 2010. *Henry Jenner's Handbook of the Cornish Language*. Co. Mhaig: Evertype.

Filppula, Markku, Juhani Klemola and Heli Pitkänen, eds. 2002. *The Celtic Roots of English* (Studies in Languages 37). Joensuu: University of Joensuu, Faculty of Humanities.

Filppula, Markku, Juhani Klemola and Heli Paulasto. 2008. *English and Celtic in Contact* (Routledge Studies in Germanic Linguistics 13). New York: Routledge.

Fox, Susan. 2012. Cockney. In Alex Bergs and Laurel Brinton, eds. *Historical Linguistics of English: An International Handbook*. Berlin: Mouton de Gruyter, 2013–2031.

Fox, Susan. 2015. *The New Cockney: New Ethnicities and Adolescent Speech in the Traditional East End of London*. Basingstoke: Palgrave Macmillan.

Fox, Susan and Devyani Sharma. 2017. The language of London and Londoners. In Dick Smakman and Patrick Heinrich, eds. *Urban Sociolinguistics: The City as a Linguistic Process and Experience*. Abingdon: Routledge, 115–129.

Fox, Sue and Eivind Torgersen. 2017. Language change and innovation in London: Multicultural London English. In Natalie Braber and Sandra Jansen, eds. *Sociolinguistics in England*. Basingstoke: Palgrave Macmillan, 189–214.

Freywald, Ulrike, Katharina Mayr, Tiner Özçelık and Heike. Wiese. 2011. Kiezdeutsch as a multiethnolect. In Friederike Kern and Margret Selting, eds. *Ethnic Styles of Speaking in European Metropolitan Areas*. Amsterdam: John Benjamins, 45–73.

Gilquin, Gaëtanelle and Sylviane Granger. 2011. From ESL to EFL: Evidence from the International Corpus of Learner English. In Joybrato Mukherjee and Marianne Hundt, eds. *Exploring Second-Language Varieties of English and Learner Englishes: Bridging a Paradigm Gap*. Amsterdam: John Benjamins, 55–78.

Greater London Authority 2005. *London – the World in a City: An Analysis of the 2001 Census Results*. London: Greater London Authority Data Management and Analysis Group Briefing 2005/6.

Harlan, Lane, Robert Hoffmeister and Ben Bahan. 1996. A *Journey into the Deaf-World*. San Diego: DawnSignPress.

Jenkins, Jennifer. 2007. *English as a Lingua Franca: Attitude and Identity*. Oxford: Oxford University Press.

Jenkins, Jennifer. 2014. *English as a Lingua Franca in the International University: The Politics of Academic English Language Policy*. Abingdon: Routledge.

Kachru, Braj. 1985. Standard, codification and sociolinguistic realism: The English language in the outer circle. In Randolph Quirk and H. G. Widdowson, eds. *English in the World: Teaching and Learning the Language and Literatures*. Cambridge: Cambridge University Press, 11–30.

Kachru, Braj. 1992. *The Other Tongue: English across Cultures*. Urbana: University of Illinois Press.

King, J. 2001. Te Kōhanga Reo: Māori Language Revitalization. In Leanne Hinton and Ken Hale, eds. *The Green Book of Language Revitalization*. San Diego: Academic Press, 119–132.

Kotsinas, Ulla-Britt. 1988. Immigrant children's Swedish: A new variety? *Journal of Multicultural and Multilingual Development* 9(1–2): 129–140.

Lutz, Angelika. 2009. Celtic influence on Old English and West Germanic. *English Language and Linguistics* 13(2): 227–249.

MacKinnon, Kenneth. 2007. Gaelic. In David Britain, ed. *Language in the British Isles*. Cambridge: Cambridge University Press, 200–217.

Mesthrie, Raj. 1996. Language contact, transmission, shift: South African Indian English. In Vivian de Klerk, ed. *Focus on South Africa*. Amsterdam: John Benjamins, 79–98.

Nevalainen, Terttu and Helena Raumolin-Brunberg. 2003. *Historical Sociolinguistics: Language Change in Tudor and Stuart England*. Harlow: Longman.

Nortier, Jacomine and Margreet Dorleijn. 2008. A Moroccan accent in Dutch: A sociocultural style restricted to the Moroccan community? *International Journal of Bilingualism* 12(1–2): 125–142.

Nortier, Jacomine and Bente. A. Svendsen, eds. 2015. *Language, Youth and Identity in the 21st Century: Linguistic Practices across Urban Spaces.* Cambridge: Cambridge University Press.

Ó Giollagáin, Conchúr and Martin Charlton. 2015. *Nuashonrú ar an Staidéar Cuimsitheach Teangeolaíoch ar Úsáid na Gaeilge sa Ghaeltacht: 2006–2011.* Co. Galway: Údarás na Gaeltachta (Gaeltacht Development Authority).

Ó'Giollagáin, Conchúr, Seosamh Mac Donnacha, Fiona Ní Chialáin, Aoife Ní Shéaghdha and Mary O'Brien. 2007. Comprehensive Linguistic Study of the use of Irish in the Gaeltacht: Principal Findings and recommendations 2007. A Research Report prepared for the Department of Community, Rural and Gaeltacht Affairs.

Ó'Riagáin, Pádraig. 2007. Irish. In David Britain, ed. *Language in the British Isles.* Cambridge: Cambridge University Press.

Pakir, Anne. 2001. The voices of English-knowing bilinguals and the emergence of new epicentres. In Vincent Ooi, ed. *Evolving Identities: The English Language in Singapore and Malaysia.* Singapore: Times Academic Press, 1–11.

Park, Jin-Kyu. 2009. "English Fever" in South Korea: Its history and symptoms. *English Today* 25(1): 50–57.

Quist, Pia. 2008. Sociolinguistic approaches to multiethnolect: Language variety and social practice. *International Journal of Bilingualism* 12(1–2): 43–61.

Romaine, Suzanne. 1991. *Language in Australia.* Cambridge: Cambridge University Press.

Schneider, Edgar. 2007. *Postcolonial English: Varieties Around the World.* Cambridge: Cambridge University Press.

Schneider, Edgar. 2016. Grassroots Englishes in tourism interactions. *English Today* 32(3): 2–10.

Schneider, Edgar, Kate Burridge, Berndt Kortmann, Raj Mesthrie and Clive Upton, eds. 2004. *A Handbook of Varieties of English,* 2 vols. Berlin: Mouton de Gruyter.

Schreier, Daniel and Marianne Hundt. 2013. *English as a Contact Language.* Cambridge: Cambridge University Press.

Seidlhofer, Barbara. 2011. *Understanding English as a Lingua Franca.* Oxford: Oxford University Press.

Shim, Doobo and Joseph Sung-Yul Park. 2008. The Language Politics of "English Fever" in South Korea. *Korea Journal*: 136–159.

Stavans, Anat and Charlotte Hoffmann. 2015. *Multilingualism: Key Topics in Sociolinguistics.* Cambridge: Cambridge University Press.

Svendsen, Bente. A. and Unn Røyneland. 2008. Multiethnolectal facts and functions in Oslo, Norway. *International Journal of Bilingualism* 12: 63–83.

Thomas, Alan. R. 1993. The Cornish language. In Donald MacAulay, ed. *The Celtic Languages*. Cambridge: Cambridge University Press, 346–370.

van der Walt, J. L. and Bertus van Rooy. 2002. Towards a norm in South African Englishes. *World Englishes 21*(1): 113–128.

van Rooy, Bertus. 2000. Introduction. *South African Journal of Linguistics*. Suppl. 38: i–vii.

Vennemann, Theo. Celtic influence in English? Yes and no. *English Language and Linguistics 13*(2): 309–334.

Vertovec, Steven. 2007. Super-diversity and its implications. *Ethnic and Racial Studies 29*(6): 1024–1054.

Wiese, Heike. 2009. Grammatical innovation in multiethnic urban Europe: New linguistic practices among adolescents. *Lingua 119*(5): 782–806.

Zuckermann, Ghil'ad, Shiori Shakuto-Neoh and Giovanni Matteo Quer. 2014. Native tongue title: Proposed compensation for the loss of Aboriginal languages. *Australian Aboriginal Studies (AAS) 1*: 55–71.

Online References

Australian Bureau of Statistics. Cultural Diversity in Australia, 2016. www.abs.gov.au/ausstats/abs@.nsf/Lookup/by%20Subject/2071.0~2016~Main%20Features~Cultural%20Diversity%20Article~20

British Deaf Association. https://bda.org.uk

The Canadian Association of the Deaf-Association des Sourds du Canada. www.cad.ca

Central Statistics Office – An Phríomh-Oifig Staidrimh www.cso.ie/en/census/census2011reports/census2011thisisirelandpart1/

Deaf Sector Partnership. http://deafsectorpartnership.net/bsl-scotland-act/

Department of Education and Skills. *20-year Strategy for the Irish Language 2010 – 2030.* www.education.ie/en/Publications/Policy-Reports/20-Year-Strategy-for-the-Irish-Language-2010-2030.pdf *Accessed 24th June 2018.*

Department for Education (2015). *Statistics: Schools, pupils and their characteristics: January 2015.* www.gov.uk/government/collections/statistics-school-and-pupil-numbers

Department for Education (2015). *Statistics: Schools, pupils and their characteristics: January 2017.* www.gov.uk/government/statistics/schools-pupils-and-their-characteristics-january-2017 Accessed 1st October 2017

Ethnologue: Languages of the World. www.ethnologue.com

European Commission Eurostat. http://ec.europa.eu/eurostat

Government of Canada. 2016 Annual Report to Parliament on Immigration. www.cic.gc.ca/english/resources/publications/annual-report-2016/index.asp#s4.3

Isle of Man Census Report 2011. www.gov.im/media/207882/census2011reportfinalresized_1_.pdf

The Migration Observatory. www.migrationobservatory.ox.ac.uk

New Zealand Census statistics www.stats.govt.nz/Census/2013-census/pro
file-and.../quickstats.../languages.aspx

Office for National Statistics. www.ons.gov.uk/

Omniglot www.omniglot.com

Scotland's Census www.scotlandscensus.gov.uk/

Scottish Government British Sign Language (BSL) National Plan 2017–2023
www.gov.scot/Resource/0052/00526382.pdf

Statistics Canada www12.statcan.gc.ca/census-recensement/2016/dp-pd
/hlt-fst/lang/Table.cfm?Lang=E&T=11&Geo=00

Statistics Canada. Linguistic Diversity and Multilingualism in Canadian
homes. www12.statcan.gc.ca/census-recensement/2016/as-sa/98–200-x/
2016010/98–200-x2016010-eng.cfm

Statistics for Wales – *ystadegau ar gyfer cymru.* http://gov.wales/docs/statis
tics/2012/121211sb1182012en.pdf

Stats NZ. 2013 Census Quickstats about culture and identity. www
.stats.govt.nz/Census/2013-census/profile-and-summary-reports/quick
stats-culture-identity/birthplace.aspx

United States Census Bureau www.census.gov/data/tables/2013/demo/
2009–2013-lang-tables.html

21

Unearthing the Diachrony of World Englishes

Magnus Huber

21.1 Introduction

The present chapter presents projects, trends, and methods of unearthing the structural history of selected types of World Englishes. The history of the two "supervarieties" (to use Collins's [2015: 1] term) of British and American English is well documented and discussing related research would go far beyond the scope of this chapter (see Britain, Chapter 7; Hickey, Chapter 2; Kytö, Chapter 8; all this volume). The focus here will therefore be on the other native standard varieties, like Canadian English, as well as on non-native national standard varieties of English, like Singapore English. Reference will also be made to the diachronic study of pidgin and creole Englishes, which started earlier than that of New Englishes and which raised a number of methodological and practical issues that are relevant for the investigation of World Englishes. Nonstandard regional or social subvarieties, such as dialects, sociolects, and ethnolects, are not covered here.

While the growing interest in World Englishes has been accompanied by a rapidly increasing number of synchronic studies, diachronic investigations of postcolonial Englishes still remain the exception. So far, diachronic analyses have mostly adopted a macro-sociolinguistic perspective and focused on the external history of (post)colonial Englishes, while linguistic structure has been neglected. When studies do investigate structural developments, they often take an apparent-time approach and base their findings on recent data. For example, Schneider's (2007: 113–250) case studies, illustrating his Dynamic Model of the evolution of New Englishes and describing postcolonial Englishes at different stages of their development, are based mainly on synchronic data.

While we have only recently seen the first historical (=synchronic, i.e. investigation of one earlier language stage) or diachronic approaches (several developmental stages) to the structural evolution of New Englishes, the collection and analysis of older linguistic data started earlier in pidgin and creole linguistics (see Lim, Chapter 4, this volume). This is because the central questions in creolistics concern the mechanisms of emergence of contact languages. These questions are inherently diachronic in nature and can only be answered with recourse to early data (cf. the overview of formation theories in Thomason 2008 and Velupillai 2015: 171–189). The idea of a developmental path of contact languages, spanning parts or all of the continuum from makeshift jargons to full-fledged languages, was already mentioned in passing by the father of creolistics, Hugo Schuchardt (1909: 442–443), who said that the American "slave languages … developed from contact languages to mother tongues … they developed into full-fledged languages." The notion was taken up by Bloomfield (1933: 473–475), and Hall (1962) labelled it "life cycle." The idea that contact languages follow evolutionary trajectories has been current (and debated) in creolistics ever since (see the overview in Velupillai 2015: 189–191).

In the study of New Englishes, some progress has recently been made in the study of the development of a number of Inner Circle (mother-tongue) varieties, including phonetics and phonology. For example, for the investigation of the development of the New Zealand English sound system, studies have been based on the 1940s recordings of the Mobile Unit of the New Zealand Broadcasting Service, which recorded recollections of early settlers, born as early as 1851 (e.g. Hay, MacLagan and Gordon 2008: 89–92; Sóskuthy et al. 2017). However, when it comes to Outer Circle (L2) Englishes, one main reason for the scarcity of studies on the structural evolution of these varieties is that, in many cases, authentic historical language data are either nonexistent or have not yet been accessed by linguists. Nevertheless, the compilation of a number of historical or diachronic corpora of New Englishes has started recently, based on written data. However, for many Outer Circle Englishes, few if any early spoken data have been located and analyzed so far.

21.2   Research on the History of English-Lexicon Contact Languages

Interest in pidgins and creoles predated that in New Englishes. There are descriptions of contact languages dating back to the early eighteenth century (e.g. Herlein 1718) and the academic discipline now called creolistics emerged in the second half of the nineteenth century, a period dominated by historical linguistics. It was (and still is) felt that, being relatively young languages with a accelerated development, contact languages presented test cases for one of the central assumptions of the historical framework, that is, that languages can be grouped into a tidy *Stammbaum*, suggesting neat splits of daughters from one mother language. Accordingly, the evolution of these languages was of major interest from the beginning. There are numerous early individual historical studies, like those by Hugo Schuchardt, starting in the 1880s (cf. his list of publications in the Hugo Schuchardt Archiv).[1] Overviews of the external histories of a large number of contact languages can be found in Reinecke's (1937) pioneering doctoral dissertation, including the English-lexicon varieties of Suriname and Guyana, Gullah, West African Pidgin English, and Chinese Pidgin English. Half a century later, Holm (1989) presented a survey of the external histories and structural characteristics of more than 120 contact languages (of which thirty-seven are English-lexified) including their external histories. In more recent publications, the sociohistory of twenty-four English-lexicon contact languages is summarized in, for example, Volume 1 of the *Survey of Pidgin and Creole Languages* (Michaelis et al. 2013) and five more overviews can be found in the *Mouton World Atlas of Variation in English* (Kortmann and Lunkenheimer 2012).

21.3   Research on the History of English Mother-Tongue Varieties

There is a long tradition and a large body of research on the history of the two supervarieties, that is, English in Britain (BrE) and the USA (AmE). Standard textbooks such as Baugh and Cable's (2012) *History of the English Language* typically give an account of both the external and the internal language history of these varieties. External language history focuses on nonlinguistic aspects that are thought to have influenced the development of a language. This includes settler groups (e.g. the arrival of the Angles, Saxons, and Jutes in England), settlement patterns (e.g. the strong Scandinavian presence in northeast England following the Viking raids), and social relationships between settler and indigenous groups (e.g. the relationship between francophone Normans and anglophone Anglo-Saxons after the Norman Conquest). It also involves cultural and societal trends (e.g. Christianization, the Renaissance) or technological innovations (e.g. the printing press, the railway, radio and television, the Internet). Internal language history is based on the conception of language as a closed system in the Saussurean sense and looks at structural developments on the levels of, for example, phonetics and phonology (e.g. the Great Vowel Shift), morphology (e.g. the loss of case inflections), and syntax (e.g. the shift from infinitival to gerundial complements). Many approaches consider both external and internal factors, for example historical sociolinguistics with its emphasis on structural co-variation with

---

[1] See Hugo Schuchardt Archiv, compiled by Berhard Hurch, https://schuchardt.uni-graz.at

social parameters or sociohistorical linguistics with its emphasis on the functional aspects of language use.

The histories of the other major mother-tongue varieties of Irish (IrE), Canadian (CanE), Australian (AusE), and New Zealand English (NZE) have also received a fair bit of attention (cf., among others, the studies in Hickey 2004), though by far not as much as those of BrE and AmE. So far, research on the evolution of IrE, CanE, AusE, and NZE has been based mostly on written material and has therefore primarily focused on developments in the areas of morphology, syntax, and the lexicon. Research in this area is facilitated by the availability of a number of corpora documenting the present-day states but also earlier stages of these varieties (cf. e.g. the corpora described in the Corpus Resource Database, CoRD).[2] In addition, analysis has also begun in recent years of a number of resources of early spoken data of these varieties, with a focus on phonetics and phonology. The still comparatively few studies in this area include Gordon et al. (2004), Trudgill (2004), and Sóskuthy et al. (2017), who base their investigation of the evolution of NZE pronunciation on the 1946–1948 recordings of the Mobile Unit of the New Zealand Broadcasting Service: Of the more than 300 speakers recorded in the 1940s, some were born as early as the 1850s, at the very beginning of NZE. Rodriguez-Louro (2015) uses oral history recordings of speakers born between 1874 and 1983 to investigate the grammaticalization of epistemic verbs in AusE. For CanE, Baxter (2010) looks at the *merry-marry* merger in Quebec English, using interviews with speakers born between 1895 and 1915.

Written sources have also been used for the investigation of earlier CanE sound systems, for example by Dollinger (2010), who explores the possibilities of a phonetic reconstruction of the low-back vowel merger based on pre–twentieth-century literary and authentic written data. A recent volume devoted to early audio records of accents of English (Hickey 2017) includes eight studies on mother-tongue varieties outside of Britain and the USA: IrE (Hickey 2017), CanE (Boberg 2017; Clarke, De Decker, and Van Herk 2017), AusE (Cox and Palethorpe 2017), NZE (Sóskuthy et al. 2017), South African English (Bekker 2017), Tristan da Cunha English (Schreier 2017), as well as the creoles of Trinidad and Jamaica (Gooden and Drayton 2017).

21.4 Research on the History of New Englishes

While the internal and external histories of (the major) mother-tongue varieties of English are thus tolerably well researched, it is only since the 1980s that the popularity of New Englishes as objects of study has increased. Today, there is a large number of synchronic studies, both on the written and spoken

---

[2] CoRD: www.helsinki.fi/varieng/CoRD/index.html

mode and on all descriptive levels (phonology, morphology, syntax, semantics, pragmatics, etc.). The comparatively few diachronic investigations in this field approach the development of New Englishes mainly from a language-external perspective. Settlement patterns, language-contact situations, or the functions of English and indigenous languages in the speech communities are reasonably well-documented for many Outer Circle Englishes and there are good overviews in the first volume of the *Handbook of Varieties of English* (Kortmann and Schneider 2004), in the *Mouton World Atlas of Variation in English* (Kortmann and Lunkenheimer 2012) or in *The Lesser-Known Varieties of English* (Schreier et al. 2010). Descriptions of the language-internal evolution of New Englishes are rarer as the structural history of these varieties has come into focus only recently. Volumes such as Collins's (2015) *Grammatical Change in English World-Wide* or Calabrese, Chambers, and Leitner's (2015) *Variation and Change in Postcolonial Contexts* and special journal issues like Noël, van Rooy, and van der Auwera's (2014) *Diachronic Approaches to Modality in World Englishes* are very recent additions to the academic discipline, as are workshops such as "Diachronic Change in New Englishes" at the 4th Conference of the International Society for the Linguistics of English (ISLE 4), Poznań (Poland), September 18–21, 2016, and "Morphosyntactic Variation in World Englishes: Apparent-Time and Diachronic Studies" at the 7th Biennial International Conference on the Linguistics of Contemporary English, Vigo (Spain), September 28–30, 2017.

Of the comparatively few studies looking at structural developments in New Englishes, most choose what in sociolinguistics is termed an apparent-time approach, taking synchronic generational differences as indications of language change. This framework is applied variety-internally, as, for example, by Hansen and Heller (2017), who "use information about the speakers' age from the metadata of ICE-HK, ICE-IND and ICE-PHI to construct apparent-time scenarios about the development of genitive choice." It can also be extended to the comparison of different text types or modes, some of which are supposed to be developmentally more advanced than others, for example written (conservative = earlier language stage) vs. spoken (progressive = later stage; see Collins 2015: 3). Another application of the apparent-time framework is cross-varietal, for example in the synchronic comparison of New Englishes with their parent varieties, as, for instance, in Mair and Winkle (2012), who show that New Englishes are "less advanced" than BrE or AmE in the adoption of the unmarked infinitive in cleft sentences. The assumption here is that New Englishes once were like their parent variety but then developed at a slower speed (leading to, e.g., colonial lag) and/or diverged from the parent (leading to innovations; cf. Mair and Winkle 2012: 258–259). Real-time studies include, for example, Hackert and Deuber (2015), who compare negative contractions, the *be*-passive, *that~which* relativizer variation, and pseudotitles in Bahamian and Trinidad and Tobagan newspapers from the 1960s with the respective rates in contemporary news report corpora. Another real-time study is that by Gries, Bernaisch, and Heller (2018), who look at the development of the genitive alternation in Singapore English from the 1950s to the 1990s.

The majority of the studies investigating language-internal developments in real time rely on written data because they are more readily available. For instance, the eight articles on the diachrony of Outer Circle varieties in Collins (2015) are all based on written sources. Studies of historical spoken data of New Englishes are very rare: Of the twenty analyses in the volume on early audio records mentioned in the previous section (Hickey 2017), just one is on a so-called New English (i.e. Ghanaian English; Huber 2017).

The state of research can thus be summed up as follows: While the history of the two supervarieties is well-documented, there are fewer studies on the mother-tongue varieties outside Britain and the USA and even fewer on the history of New Englishes. As a rule, the external language histories of these Englishes are reasonably well-researched but there is comparatively little on language-internal, structural developments. Diachronic research for the most part relies on written data and tends to investigate the lexicon, morphology, or syntax, while analyses of earlier spoken data remain the rare exception.

21.5 Model-Building and the Histories of World Englishes

That the internal histories of World Englishes were neglected for so long is surprising since, from the beginning, the models proposed for the classification of World Englishes were diachronically motivated. One of the earliest models (Strevens 1980: 86) in fact superimposed a family tree of Englishes on a world map deriving the varieties of English around the world from a common ancestor. Kachru's (1985, 1988) well-known Three Circles Model, though primarily concerned with the different synchronic functions of standard Englishes around the world, is also partly historically motivated:

> The outer (or extended) circle needs a historical explanation: it involves the earlier phases of the spread of English and its institutionalization in non-native contexts ... [T]hese regions have gone through extended periods of colonization ... The linguistic and cultural effects of such colonization are now a part of their histories.   (Kachru 1985: 12)

More recent models like Moag's (1982) Life Cycle of Non-Native Englishes and Schneider's (2003, 2007) Dynamic Model are even more explicitly diachronic, proposing different consecutive stages in the development of new varieties of English: transportation > indigenization > expansion in use and function > institutionalization > restriction of use and function in the case of Moag, and foundation > exonormative stabilization >

nativization > endonormative stabilization > differentiation in the case of Schneider (see Buschfeld and Kautzsch, Chapter 3, this volume).

Schneider's influential Dynamic Model is based on the belief that there are "fundamentally uniform developmental processes, shaped by consistent sociolinguistic and language-contact conditions" (2003: 233). The model abstracts away from the idiosyncrasies of individual varieties and proposes a universal evolutionary trajectory of New Englishes. The emphasis is more on general language-external factors shaping the history of these Englishes, not so much on their structural evolution. The case studies in the seminal (Schneider 2003) *Language* article thus focus more on the historical social, cultural, and political factors determining the evolution of selected New Englishes (Fiji, Hong Kong, Malaysia, the Philippines, Singapore, Australia, and New Zealand). Reference to linguistic innovations is primarily based on recent descriptions of the varieties, not so much on historical data. Similarly, Schneider (2007: 113–250) lists lexical and structural innovations from a present-day perspective, as compared to today's BrE or AmE. By comparing varieties at different stages of evolution today and by relying on synchronic linguistic descriptions, the structural component of this diachronic model was developed in an apparent-time approach.

Model-building plays an important role in theorizing in that it attempts to identify general trends applicable to a large number of cases. Once released, models need to be tested and refined and/or revised in the light of further empirical data. This has started with regard to the Dynamic Model, where scholars are now looking in detail at the structural development of individual varieties and comparing it with the model's predictions. For example, Peters (2014) demonstrates that AusE, in conformity with the model's predictions, exhibits the first signs of differentiation of social and ethnic groups, whereas Huber (2014) shows that there is sociolinguistic variation in Ghanaian English even though the Dynamic Model predicts this only for a later evolutionary phase.

21.6 Early Data in the Diachronic Study of World Englishes: Theoretical and Methodological Considerations

In historical approaches to New Englishes, it is often tacitly assumed that, at one point in time, usually during colonization or shortly after decolonization, a New English split off and subsequently diverged from the English of the colonizer. This is obviously an oversimplification, based on the nineteenth-century notion of neat splits in a language tree. More often than not, New Englishes did not evolve away from their colonial input varieties in complete isolation but instead have a history of ongoing – constant or fluctuating, direct or indirect – contact with the parent variety. Rather than progressively distancing itself from the input variety, there may be periods in the history of a New English where the gap with the parent language was closing again. In present research, the structural characteristics of the new variety are usually described in terms of their divergence from today's parent variety. In their contribution to the *Oxford Handbook of the History of English*, Mukherjee and Schilk (2012: 190) point out one shortcoming of such a method:

> In almost all descriptive approaches to New Englishes, their linguistic features are usually analyzed against the background of the present-day state of the parent variety ...
>
> However, while such comparisons may capture the synchronic distance between old and new varieties of English, they cannot explain to what extent a new postcolonial variety of English has diverged across time from the historical input variety.

That is, to assess the degree of divergence between the two varieties, we need corpora of earlier stages of the colonial input variety (BrE for most New Englishes; AmE only in a few cases like Liberian or Philippine English). This is because the synchronic distance between the two varieties may not necessarily be due to innovations in the New English: Rather than developing away from it, the New English may have preserved features from an earlier stage of the input variety ("colonial lag") that got lost in the latter.

Some large corpora are available for nineteenth- and twentieth-century AmE and BrE, for example Mark Davies's web-derived corpora,[3] including the 1.6 billion word Hansard Corpus of British parliamentary debates between 1803 and 2005, the 400 million word Corpus of Historical American English with texts from the 1810–2009 period, and the 100 million word TIME Magazine Corpus (1923–2006). In addition, the compilation of smaller, more structured corpora of written texts from earlier stages of the historical input varieties has started recently. The Lancaster-Oslo-Bergen Corpus (LOB) of British English[4] and the Standard Corpus of Present-Day Edited American English (Brown),[5] both containing one million words, are being extended into the first half of the twentieth century, in thirty-year steps. For BrE, work is progressing on the BLOB-1931 and the BLOB-1901 corpora (see Leech and Smith 2005). For AmE, there is the 1930s BROWN Corpus (B-Brown, see the entries in CoRD). Late modern English speech-related data are available in the Old Bailey Corpus,[6] a corpus of proceedings at London's Central Criminal Court from 1720 to

---

[3] See https://corpus.byu.edu

[4] The Lancaster-Oslo/Bergen Corpus (LOB; original version [1970–1978] compiled by Geoffrey Leech, Lancaster University, Stig Johansson, University of Oslo (project leaders), and Knut Hofland, University of Bergen (head of computing). http://clu.uni.no/icame/manuals/LOB/INDEX.HTM.

[5] Brown (compiled by W. N. Francis and H. Ku era, Brown University [1964, 1971, 1979]): http://clu.uni.no/icame/brown/bcm.html.

[6] See the Old Bailey Corpus 2.0 (compiled by Magnus Huber, Magnus Nissel, and Karin Puga): http://fedora.clarin-d.uni-saarland.de/oldbailey/index.html.

1913. It contains 24 million words of direct speech as taken down by the shorthand scribes.

In addition, what is urgently required for a diachronic, real-time investigation of the evolution of New Englishes is written and spoken data from their earlier stages. Only if we have parallel historical or diachronic corpora of the input variety *and* the New English will we be able to answer the crucial questions with a higher degree of certainty: At which developmental stage of the New English and to what extent were particular linguistic features present and do they present retentions or innovations? (For a classification of cases of retention, innovation, and language change, see Hundt 2009.)

21.7 Corpora of Earlier Stages of New Englishes

At the time of writing, very little progress has been made in the compilation of corpora of earlier stages of New Englishes but there are some first attempts. For instance, Fuchs (2017) looks at the development of the progressive in Indian English (IndE) over the last 200 years, using CoHind, a 400,000-word parallel newspaper corpus of nineteenth- and twentieth-century Indian and British English. Fuchs and Borlongan (2016) investigate the change in the use of the present perfect and past tense in Philippine English (PhilE) and IndE, based on two Brown-style corpora of PhilE and IndE from the 1970s and two components of the International Corpus of English (ICE)[7] from the 1990s. However, such studies are still rare. As Mukherjee and Bernaisch (2015: 413) put it, "[t]he lack of historical corpora for most of the colonial and postcolonial settings world-wide is one of the most severe challenges for research into New Englishes." This lack is not a result so much of the absence of early data but of the fact that locating, accessing, and compiling authentic historical language data is costly, time-consuming, often difficult, and is thus shunned by many researchers. However, work has started on a few historical or diachronic corpora of World Englishes with the aim to describe their evolution on an empirical basis. These corpora will also make it possible to test models of the evolution of Englishes. For the Inner Circle Englishes, these include, among several others:

- The Corpus of Oz Early English (COOEE, Fritz 2007), a two-million-word corpus covering the years 1788–1900 and including books, letters, diaries, proclamations, and newspaper reports from Australia, New Zealand, and Norfolk Island. Because of copyright reasons, the corpus is not freely available but can be accessed on request from the compiler.
- The comparatively small (220,000 words) Corpus of Early New Zealand English (see Hundt 2012; Hundt and Szmrecsanyi 2012), covering the

---

[7] ICE: www.ice-corpora.uzh.ch/en.html.

1860s to 1920s and including the text categories newspaper, science, fiction, and letters.

Corpora of earlier stages of a number of Outer Circle varieties are also being compiled. They are often based on the design of existing corpora of Inner Circle varieties (mostly Brown/LOB or the ICE) to allow for a direct comparison with the historical input variety:

- Phil-Brown is a corpus of PhilE texts published between the late 1950s and early 1960s (see Collins, Borlongan, and Yao 2014; Borlogan and Dita 2015). Compiled by Ariane Borlongan at De La Salle University, Manila, the corpus is modeled on the Brown corpus. Phil-Brown includes text types from the press, fiction, and nonfiction registers.
- Also based on the design of the Brown corpus is the Diachronic Corpus of Singapore English (see Hoffman, Sand, and Tan 2012). It includes general and academic prose, fiction, newspapers, and periodicals as well as speeches. The Diachronic Corpus of Singapore English is a truly diachronic project, spanning fifty years from 1951 to 2011 and sampled in ten-year intervals.
- The Historical Corpus of English in Ghana (see Brato 2018, 2019) is a historical synchronic corpus that covers publications in the period 1966–1975 and follows the design of the written-printed component of ICE. It includes the ICE categories academic writing, popular writing, press reportage, instructional writing, opinion, and creative writing. With 600,000 words, the Historical Corpus of English in Ghana includes almost twice as much material as the respective text categories in ICE written-printed because it was compiled for the study of the lexicon.
- The Diachronic Corpus of Hong Kong English (see Biewer et al. 2014) parallels the LOB corpus with regard to sample years (five-year spans around 1930, 1960, 1990, with possible extensions to 1910 and 2010) and includes five of the fifteen text categories in the LOB Corpus: press reportage, press editorials, press reviews, nonacademic writing, and academic writing. The aim is 120,000 words per period for the press section. The Diachronic Corpus of Hong Kong English lacks the six fiction categories in LOB, since most of these turned out to be translations from Cantonese, but it has the additional categories of private correspondence and diaries.

Some of the above corpora were compiled for specific studies and are not publicly available or can be accessed only by special arrangement with the compilers. This is also often the case with single-genre compilations like diachronic newspaper corpora, for example those of earlier Bahamian, Jamaican, and Trinidadian and Tobagan English (all reaching back to the 1960s) as well as Indian English (reaching back as far as 1939), described and analyzed in Hackert (2014, 2015), Hackert and Deuber (2015), Hackert and Wengler (2016, 2017). A number of more easily accessible, first-generation synchronic corpora of New Englishes are so old by now that they offer a glimpse into earlier language stages and can be used for diachronic studies, even though they only allow for a time depth of about twenty to thirty years. These include a number of corpora on the original ICAME CD:[8] The Kolhapur Corpus of Indian English (Shastri 1986), modeled on Brown/LOB, includes texts from 1978 and has been used in the analysis of the recent history of Indian English (e.g. in Sedlatschek 2009). The ICAME collection also includes one early ICE corpus component from the 1990s, ICE-East Africa with texts from between 1990 and 1996 (see Hudson-Ettle and Schmied 1999). The Australian Corpus of English (ACE) consists of material from 1986 and is paralleled by the Wellington Corpus of Written New Zealand English, most of whose texts were published in 1986 and 1987. The texts in ICE-Australia (not in the ICAME collection) date from 1992 to 1995. In some cases, the nonavailability of younger corpora of a comparable design means that a diachronic approach is only possible if such a corpus is compiled by the investigator.

Almost all of these corpora include written texts only,[9] since they are more readily available, sometimes already in digitalized form (e.g. electronic newspaper archives, ebooks in digital archives), whereas the inclusion of spoken material in a corpus is logistically much more difficult and by far more laborious and costly. Nevertheless, early recordings are invaluable since it is in the spoken mode that New Englishes tend to show more pronounced departures from the input variety.[10] One of the few projects that aims at creating a corpus of a spoken earlier New English, that is, spoken Ghanaian English from the 1950s and 1960s, is conducted by the present author together with Mikael Okyerefo of the Department of Sociology, University of Ghana. The material consists of radio broadcasts (public speeches, radio announcement and reportage) stored in the audio archives of the Ghana Broadcasting Corporation (GBC). A pilot corpus of forty-eight audio files and their transcripts has been compiled and phonologically analyzed (cf. Huber 2017). The GBC has an exceptionally large and well-organized archive, with thousands of recordings starting in the 1950s. The drawback is that many early radio recordings were scripted and fall within the most formal end of educated speech, which in morphosyntax was closely oriented toward the exonormative standard of the colonizer's language. This makes the material suitable mainly for phonetic or phonological studies. Finding recordings of spontaneous speech (e.g. interviews or discussions) therefore remains a desideratum. Such a large amount of

---

[8] Compare the manuals at http://clu.uni.no/icame/manuals.

[9] The Diachronic Corpus of Singapore English includes contemporary transcripts of speeches, but these were not produced by linguists and – as other such texts – are not a 100 percent faithful reproduction of the spoken word.

[10] Huber (2014: 89) observes that "nativization in GhE – and other Outer Circle varieties for that matter – proceeds at a differential pace. Speakers of postcolonial Englishes seem to be readier to accept (or even expect) local innovations and endogenous norms in the areas of pronunciation and the lexicon than in (especially written) morphology or syntax."

early data as in the GBC archives may not be available for all New Englishes but this does not mean that a systematic investigation of their historical phonological systems is impossible. Other, more unconventional, and as yet underused, data include early popular music sung in English. For Ghana, the present author has a collection of more than fifty so-called Highlife songs from the 1950s and 1960s, which has been used to reconstruct phonological variation in Ghanaian English around independence in 1957 (Huber and Schmidt 2011).

The specific problems encountered in the analysis of early audio records pertain, among others, to the identification of speakers and to the quality of the recordings. Biographical information may be incomplete or lacking, making it difficult or impossible to say whether we are actually dealing with a speaker of a particular variety. Also, depending on the quality of the original analogue recording, on recording practices, on the age of the record, and on storage conditions before digitization, the sound signal may be so impaired that an acoustic or auditory analysis is severely hampered: The sound may have been clipped or otherwise distorted in the original recording, the analogue media (wax or tin cylinders, reel-to-reel tape, etc.) may have deteriorated considerably over time, and there may be ambient noise and voiceovers that make transcription and phonetic or phonological analysis impossible (cf. Huber 2017: 449–451).

21.8   Problems in Corpus Compilation

The compilation of corpora of earlier stages of New Englishes faces several challenges that concern the existence, accessibility, and nature of texts. A general issue in diachronic research relates to the comparability of linguistic material available for different periods, and New Englishes present no exception here. Some modern text types were not in existence at an earlier period or vice versa. For example, electronic communication has largely superseded private letters. Moreover, even if the text type existed, it may have changed its character, for example become more or less formal.

In addition, local text production was quite low for many New Englishes and it may be difficult, if not impossible, to fill the required text categories with material from that period.[11] Brato (2018: 27) illustrates this with regard to his Historical Corpus of English in Ghana:

> Just how small the number of books and other material is, can be illustrated by this quotation from Apponsah (1968: 4): "[I]n 1966, Ghana

---

[11] Incidentally, this problem is also encountered in the major mother-tongue varieties. The sampling time frame of the Brown and LOB prequels had to be extended beyond the one year in the original Brown and LOB corpora (see Hundt and Leech 2012); and Bauer (1993) reports that "not enough suitable material was published in New Zealand in 1986, and in practice the Wellington Corpus . . . covers the years 1986–1990."

produced a total of 225 books and pamphlets." Of this figure we must deduct publications in Ghanaian languages, which further decreases the figure. Except for newspaper articles, these problems were also encountered for the 1970–72 period. In addition, over the whole time frame there is a strong bias towards the social sciences and humanities, whereas local publications in the natural sciences and technology are rare.

In the interest of authenticity of the linguistic material included, a historical or diachronic corpus of any New English should ideally contain texts produced by authors that were locally educated and that did not spend much time abroad. The difficulty is that, for some varieties, the number of early authors was rather small and that few of them were actually locally educated: In some (post)colonial societies, literary activity and text production in general were (and still are) sustained mainly by the well-educated, privileged, and thus internationally mobile classes. It is part of the above-mentioned continued contact of an ex-colony with its former colonizer that members of the local economic and educational elite spend part of their lives in the parent country (or in other Inner Circle countries) and acquire their further education there. In the compilation of corpora documenting the early stages of a new variety, the ideal of text production by nonmobile, locally educated writers may thus have to be abandoned. The same goes for speakers of the variety – a sufficient proficiency in English would only have been acquired by the privileged, Western-oriented classes.

Added to this are access difficulties, for example because of copyright limitations or restricted access to archival material. For instance, Hoffmann (2013) describes the huge problems in accessing the data for the Diachronic Corpus of Singapore English as "a corpus compiler's nightmare."

21.9 Beyond Corpora: The Usefulness of Individual Sources

Sometimes the small number, limited availability, and/or heterogeneity of early texts does not allow for the compilation of balanced corpora that can be analyzed within a quantitative-variationist framework (see D'Arcy, Chapter 19, this volume). However, even scattered early texts, casual observations by contemporaries on phonological or grammatical "peculiarities" of Englishes, early pedagogical material, or scholarly descriptions can be helpful in the reconstruction of earlier language stages.

In the field of creolistics, where for many contact languages there are often only few and very short early texts – sometimes amounting to the mention of one word only – Philip Baker (e.g. 1987, 1993) has pioneered the collection of first attestations of lexical and structural features by way of an extensive and systematic analysis of travel accounts, missionaries' reports, traders' memoirs, and the like. Such data is helpful in the investigation of, for example, grammaticalization processes, and it can even be used quantitatively for the construction of affinity networks between several varieties (e.g. Baker and Huber 2001). The *Database of Early Pidgin and Creole Texts* (DEPiCT)[12] brings together early texts collected by various creolists and makes them searchable through a standardized annotation scheme.

Scouring early publications and manuscripts is laborious but can bring to light interesting evidence on the linguistic situation as well as structural features of the emerging English. To give just a few examples from my own West Africa collection, a passage referring to the early 1830s shows that Pidgin English was the established lingua franca in inter-ethnic communication:

> Amid all the dialects spoken by the various Negro tribes and inhabitants in the colony, English is the language generally understood and made use of in every degree of imperfection. Poor Quamino, in giving utterance to our civilized dialect, falls into many diverting errors of style, as well as pronunciation, and our countrymen here seem to think that it is necessary he should not improve in this respect, as they all make use of the same defective and incongruous jargon in speaking to every one of dingy exterior, conceiving, no doubt, that the blacks understand better what is said to them when spoken to in their own broken imperfect English.
>
> (Anon. 1833: 37–38)

As far as structural features of early West African English are concerned, Kemp (1898: 179) has an entertaining remark on the pronunciation of English by speakers of Fante in the Gold Coast (modern Ghana):

> A somewhat amusing little accident occurred at the annual school examination. Our scholars, for some inexplicable reason, invariably pronounce the letter "u" as "e," and will insist, for example, in calling "butter" "better." The senior scholars were asked to name the principal seaports of England. One little lad thought of "Hull." But in consequence of the difficulty just mentioned the examiner did not recognise the name, and somewhat absent-mindedly asked in which part of England "Hell" was.

That this observation is phonetically accurate is supported by the fact that the fronting of the STRUT vowel is still a minority variant in modern Ghanaian English (see Huber 2017: 457ff). For English in Nigeria, Temple (1918: 246–247) provides an observation on the TRAP-BATH/PALM merger (which still holds today):

> on my first arrival in Northern Nigeria I was supplied by Government with a quite reasonably well-intentioned honest interpreter …, only he pronounced the "a" short, thus "kant." "Tell him he kant do it" was what he

---

[12] DEPiCT: www.unigiessen.de/faculties/f05/engl/ling/staff/professors/mhuber/depict

used to say in place of the usual pidgin English "Tell him he no fit to do it." ... Newly arrived from England ... I used to convey permission by using the ordinary term, "Tell him he can do it." The interpreter failing to detect the omission of the final "t" always, I discovered about six months later, mistook my "can" for ... "kant." The administration of the Province was somewhat complicated by this slight difference.

Quasi-phonetic spellings by Western authors mimicking local pronunciations can also be helpful. Banbury's (1888: 88) "De kitchen on bode de man-ob-war is called de galley" attests *th*-stopping (*de* "the"), non-rhoticity (*bode* "board") and v>b (*ob* "of") substitution in late nineteenth-century Sierra Leonean English.

Early teaching material, like Brown and Scragg's (1938) *Common Errors in Gold Coast English* or Schachter's (1962) *Teaching English Pronunciation to the Twi-speaking Student*, can also be a rich source of features of earlier stages of New Englishes. For some varieties, scholarly interest goes back quite a while, and articles like Strevens's (1953–1954) "Spoken English in the Gold Coast" or his (1965) "Pronunciations of English in West Africa" are helpful resources, as is Sey's (1973) *Ghanaian English*, one of the earliest book-length descriptions of a New English.

In a few lucky cases, early texts written by speakers of the varieties themselves survive, as, for example, the diary of Antera Duke, a semi-literate, late eighteenth-century Nigerian slave trader (Behrendt, Latham, and Northrup 2010). Early local literary works written by colonial subjects, like the 1942 *Eighteenpence* (Obeng 1998), the first Gold Coast novel, may also provide evidence on linguistic features.

21.10 Conclusion

While there is a long tradition and a large body of research on the internal and external histories of the two major mother-tongue varieties of BrE and AmE, the diachrony of the other L1 Standard Englishes (like CanE or AusE) and of New Englishes has only relatively recently received an increased attention of linguists. The external histories of the minor mother-tongue varieties and of the New Englishes are usually well-described, but studies of their structural development (in particular that of New Englishes) are comparatively rare. The reason for this is that early language data have either not been located yet or are difficult or costly to access and time-consuming in their compilation. In the worst case, there may simply be no early material. Nevertheless, the recent decades have seen an increased activity in analyzing early linguistic data: For the mother-tongue varieties, these studies are mostly based on written material and thus focus on the diachrony of their morphology and syntax. There is, however, also a growing number of projects investigating developments of the sound systems of these Englishes, in some cases even based on early recordings. As far as the New Englishes are concerned, the last few years have seen the compilation of the first corpora of earlier written texts, often modeled on existing corpora of the historical input varieties of BrE and AmE. However, for most varieties, early spoken data still need to be tracked down, digitalized, and transcribed.

In the investigation of the diachronies of World Englishes, apparent-time approaches may currently seem the only convenient option for many varieties. Nevertheless, the potential of early linguistic data of giving us a real-time glimpse of the development of these Englishes should encourage us to increase our efforts in locating early written texts and recordings. This is by no means an easy task, but not impossible, as the first attempts mentioned in this chapter show. The analysis of real-time early data holds a great potential for the description of the structural history of World Englishes.

References

Anon. 1833. *The Western Coast of Africa. Journal of an Officer under Captain Owen.* + *Leonard, Peter Records of a Voyage in the Ship* Dryad, *in 1830, 1831, and 1832.* Philadelphia: Edward C. Mielke.

Apponsah, K. 1968. African writers must be up and doing. The Evening News, February 20, p. 4.

Banbury, G. A. Lethbridge. 1888. *Sierra Leone: or, the White Man's Grave.* London: Swan Sonnenschein, Lowrey & Co.

Baugh, Albert C. and Thomas Cable. 2012. *A History of the English language* (6th ed.). London: Routledge.

Baker, Philip. 1993. Australian influence on Melanesian Pidgin English. *Te Reo* 36(3): 67.

Baker, Philip. 1987. Historical developments in Chinese Pidgin English and the nature of the relationships between the various Pidgin Englishes of the Pacific region. *Journal of Pidgin and Creole Languages* 2: 163–207.

Baker, Philip and Magnus Huber. 2001. Atlantic, Pacific, and world-wide features in English-lexicon contact languages. *English World-Wide* 22: 157–208.

Bauer, Laurie. 1993. Manual of information to accompany the Wellington Corpus of Written New Zealand English. http://clu.uni.no/icame/man uals/WELLMAN/INDEX.HTM

Baxter, Laura. 2010. Lexical diffusion in the early stages of the *merry-marry* merger. *University of Pennsylvania Working Papers in Linguistics* 16(2). http://repository.upenn.edu/pwpl/vol16/iss2/3

Behrendt, Stephen D., A. J. H. Latham and David Northrup. 2010. *The Diary of Antera Duke, an Eighteenth-Century African Slave Trader.* Oxford: Oxford University Press.

Bekker, Ian. 2017. Earlier South African English. In Raymond Hickey, ed. *Listening to the Past: Audio Records of Accents of English*. Cambridge: Cambridge University Press, 464–483.

Biewer, Carolin, Tobias Bernaisch, Mike Berger, and Benedikt Heller. 2014. Compiling the Diachronic Corpus of Hong Kong English (DC-HKE): Motivation, progress and challenges. Poster presented at the 35th ICAME Conference, Nottingham, England, April 30–May 5 2014.

Bloomfield, Leonard. 1933. *Language*. New York: Holt, Rinehart & Winston.

Boberg, Charles. 2017. Archival data on earlier Canadian English. In Raymond Hickey, ed. *Listening to the Past: Audio Records of Accents of English*. Cambridge: Cambridge University Press, 375–394.

Borlongan, Ariane Macalinga and Shirley N. Dita. 2015. Taking a look at expanded predicates in Philippine English across time, Asian Englishes. *Asian Englishes 17*: 240–247.

Brato, Thorsten. 2019. The Historical Corpus of English in Ghana (HiCE Ghana): Motivation, compilation, opportunities. In Alexandra Esimaje, Ulrike Gut and Bassey E. Antia, eds. *Corpus Linguistics and African Englishes*. Amsterdam: John Benjamins, 119–141.

Brato, Thorsten. 2018. "Outdooring" the Historical Corpus of English in Ghana: Insights from the compilation of a historical corpus of New English. *English Today 34*(2): 25–34.

Brown, Philip Penton and John Scragg. 1938. *Common Errors in Gold Coast English* (2nd ed.). Accra: Scottish Mission Book Depot.

Calabrese, Rita, J. K. Chambers and Gerhard Leitner, eds. 2015. *Variation and Change in Postcolonial Contexts*. Newcastle: Cambridge Scholars Publishing.

Clarke, Sandra, Paul De Decker and Gerard Van Herk. 2017. Canadian Raising in Newfoundland? Insights from early vernacular recordings. In Raymond Hickey, ed. *Listening to the Past: Audio Records of Accents of English*. Cambridge: Cambridge University Press, 395–413.

Collins, Peter, ed. 2015. *Grammatical Change in English World-Wide*. Amsterdam: John Benjamins.

Collins, Peter, Ariane Macalinga Borlongan and Xinyue Yao. 2014. Modality in Philippine English. *Journal of English Linguistics 42*: 68–88.

Cox, Felicity and Sallyanne Palethorpe. 2017. Open vowels in historical Australian English. In Raymond Hickey, ed. *Listening to the Past: Audio Records of Accents of English*. Cambridge: Cambridge University Press, 502–528.

Dollinger, Stefan. 2010. Written sources for Canadian English: Phonetic reconstruction and the low-back vowel merger. In Raymond Hickey, ed. *Varieties of English in Writing: The Written Word as Linguistic Evidence*. Amsterdam: John Benjamins, 197–221.

Fritz, Clemens W. A. 2007. *From English in Australia to Australian English 1788–1900*. Frankfurt: Peter Lang.

Fuchs, Robert. 2017. The progressive in 19th- and 20th-century Indian English: A pilot study. Paper presented at the 7th Biennial

International Conference on the Linguistics of Contemporary English, Universidade de Vigo (Spain), September 28–30, 2017.

Fuchs, Robert and Ariane Borlongan. 2016. Recent diachronic change in the use of the present perfect and past tense in Philippine and Indian English. Paper presented at the 4th conference of the International Society for the Linguistics of English (ISLE 4), Poznań (Poland), September 18–21, 2016.

Gooden, Shelome and Kathy-Ann Drayton. 2017. The Caribbean: Trinidad and Jamaica. In Raymond Hickey, ed. *Listening to the Past: Audio Records of Accents of English*. Cambridge: Cambridge University Press, 414–443.

Gordon, Elizabeth, Lyle Campbell, Jennifer Hay, Margaret Maclagan, Andrea Sudbury and Peter Trudgill. 2004. *New Zealand English: Its Origins and Evolution*. Cambridge: Cambridge University Press.

Gries, Stefan Th., Tobias Bernaisch and Benedikt Heller. 2018. A corpus-linguistic account of the history of the genitive alternation in Singapore English. In Sandra C. Deshors, ed. *Modeling World Englishes: Assessing the Interplay of Emancipation and Globalization of ESL Varieties*. Amsterdam: John Benjamins.

Hackert, Stephanie. 2015. Pseudotitles in Bahamian English: A case of Americanization? *Journal of English Linguistics* 43: 143–167.

Hackert, Stephanie. 2014. Recent grammatical change in Caribbean English: A corpus-based study of Bahamian newswriting. Paper presented at the 3rd conference of the International Society for the Linguistics of English (ISLE3), Zurich (Switzerland), August 24–27, 2014.

Hackert, Stephanie and Dagmar Deuber. 2015. American influence on written Caribbean English: A diachronic analysis of newspaper reportage in the Bahamas and in Trinidad and Tobago. In Peter Collins, ed. *Grammatical Change in English World-Wide*. Amsterdam: John Benjamins, 389–410.

Hackert, Stephanie and Diana Wengler. 2017. Genitive variation and change in postcolonial Englishes: Focus on semantic relations. Paper presented at the 7th Biennial International Conference on the Linguistics of Contemporary English, Universidade de Vigo (Spain), September 28–30, 2017.

Hackert, Stephanie and Diana Wengler. 2016. Recent grammatical change in postcolonial Englishes: A real-time study of genitive variation in Caribbean and Indian newswriting. Paper presented at the 19th International Conference on English Historical Linguistics, Essen (Germany), August 22–26, 2016.

Hay, Jennifer, Margaret MacLagan and Elizabeth Gordon. 2008. *Dialects of English: New Zealand English*. Edinburgh: Edinburgh University Press.

Hall, Robert A. 1962. The life cycle of pidgin languages. *Lingua 11*: 151–156.

Hansen, Beke and Benedikt Heller. 2017. Expansion of the s-genitive in World Englishes. Paper presented at the 7th Biennial International

Conference on the Linguistics of Contemporary English, Universidade de Vigo (Spain), September 28–30, 2017.

Herlein, J. D. 1718. *Beschrijvinge van de volksplantinge Zuriname*. Leeuwarden: Injema.

Hickey, Raymond, ed. 2004. *Legacies of Colonial English: Studies in Transported Dialects*. Cambridge: Cambridge University Press.

Hickey, Raymond. 2017. Early recordings of Irish English. In Raymond Hickey, ed. *Listening to the Past: Audio Records of Accents of English*. Cambridge: Cambridge University Press, 199–231.

Hoffmann, Sebastian. 2013. The Corpus of Historical Singapore English – Practical and methodological issues. Paper presented at UCREL Corpus Research Seminar, Lancaster University, March 26, 2013. http://ucrel .lancs.ac.uk/crs/attachments/UCRELCRS-2013–03-26-Hoffmann-Slides.pdf

Hoffmann, Sebastian, Andrea Sand and Peter Tan. 2012. The Corpus of Historical Singapore English: A first pilot study on data from the 1950s and 1960s. Paper presented at the 33 ICAME Conference. Belgium: University of Leuven.

Holm, John. 1989. *Pidgins and Creoles*, Vol. 2: *Reference survey*. Cambridge: Cambridge University Press.

Huber, Magnus. 2017. Early recordings from Ghana. A variationist approach to the phonological history of an Outer Circle variety. In Raymond Hickey, ed. *Listening to the Past: Audio Records of Accents of English*. Cambridge: Cambridge University Press, 444–463.

Huber, Magnus. 2014. Stylistic and sociolinguistic variation in Schneider's Nativization Phase. T-affrication and relativization in Ghanaian English. In Sarah Buschfeld, Thomas Hoffmann, Magnus Huber and Alexander Kautzsch, eds. *The Evolution of Englishes: The Dynamic Model and Beyond*. Amsterdam: John Benjamins, 86–106.

Huber, Magnus and Sebastian Schmidt. 2011. New ways of analysing the history of varieties of English. Early Highlife recordings from Ghana. Paper presented at the second conference of the International Society for the Linguistics of English (ISLE2), Boston (USA), June 17–21, 2011.

Hudson-Ettle, Diana M. and Josef Schmied. 1999. Manual to accompany the East African component of the International Corpus of English (ICE-EA): Background information, coding conventions and lists of source texts. http://clu.uni.no/icame/manuals/ICE_EA.PDF

Hundt, Marianne. 2012. Towards a corpus of early written New Zealand English: News from Erewhon? *Te Reo 55*: 51–74.

Hundt, Marianne. 2009. Colonial lag, colonial innovation, or simply language change? In Günter Rohdenburg and Julia Schlüter, eds. *One Language, Two Grammars: Morphosyntactic Differences between British and American English*. Cambridge: Cambridge University Press, 13–37.

Hundt, Marianne and Geoffrey Leech. 2012. Small is beautiful: On the value of standard reference corpora for observing recent grammatical change. In Terttu Nevalainen and Elizabeth Traugott Closs, eds. *The Oxford Handbook of the History of English*. Oxford: Oxford University Press, 175–188.

Hundt, Marianne and Benedikt Szmrecsanyi. 2012. Animacy in early New Zealand English. *English World-Wide 33*: 241–263.

Kachru, Braj B. 1988. The sacred cows of English. *English Today 4*: 3–8.

Kachru, Braj B. 1985. Standards, codification and sociolinguistic realism: The English language in the outer circle. In Randolph Quirk and H. G. Widdowson, eds. *English in the World: Teaching and Learning the Language and Literatures*. Cambridge: Cambridge University Press, 11–30.

Kemp, Dennis. 1898. *Nine Years at the Gold Coast*. London: MacMillan and Co.

Kortmann, Bernd and Lunkenheimer, Kerstin, eds. 2012. *The Mouton World Atlas of Variation in English*. Berlin: Mouton de Gruyter.

Kortmann, Bernd and Edgar W. Schneider, eds. 2004. *A Handbook of Varieties of English: A Multimedia Reference Tool, Vol. 1: Phonology*. Berlin: Mouton de Gruyter.

Leech, Geoffrey and Nick Smith. 2005. Extending the possibilities of corpus-based research on English in the twentieth century: A prequel to LOB and FLOB. *ICAME Journal 29*: 83–98.

Mair, Christian and Claudia Winkle. 2012. Change from to-infinitive to bare infinitive in specificational cleft sentences: Data from World Englishes. In Marianne Hundt and Ulrike Gut, eds. *Mapping Unity in Diversity Worldwide: Corpus-Based Studies of New Englishes*. Amsterdam: John Benjamins, 243–262.

Michaelis, Susanne Maria, Philippe Maurer, Martin Haspelmath and Magnus Huber, eds. 2013. *The Survey of Pidgin and Creole Languages, Vol 1: English-Based and Dutch-Based Languages*. Oxford: Oxford University Press.

Moag, Rodney F. 1982. The life cycle of non-native Englishes: A case study. In Braj B. Kachru, ed. *The Other Tongue: English across Cultures*. Urbana: University of Illinois Press, 270–290.

Mukherjee, Joybrato and Tobias Bernaisch. 2015. Cultural keywords in context. A pilot study of linguistic acculturation in South Asian Englishes. In Peter Collins, ed. *Grammatical Change in English World-Wide*. Amsterdam: John Benjamins, 411–435.

Mukherjee, Joybrato and Marco Schilk. 2012. Exploring variation and change in New Englishes. Looking into the International Corpus of English (ICE) and beyond. In Terttu Nevalainen and Elizabeth Traugott Closs, eds. *The Oxford Handbook of the History of English*. Oxford: Oxford University Press, 189–199.

Noël, Dirk, Bertus van Rooy and Johan van der Auwera, eds. 2014. *Diachronic approaches to modality in World Englishes* (Special edition). *Journal of English Linguistics 42*(1).

Obeng, Richard Emmanuel. 1998. *Eighteenpence*. Ed. Kari Dako. Accra: Sub-Saharan Publishers.

Peters, Pam. 2014. Differentiation in Australian English. In Sarah Buschfeld, Thomas Hoffmann, Magnus Huber and Alexander Kautzsch, eds. *The Evolution of Englishes: The Dynamic Model and Beyond*. Amsterdam: John Benjamins, 107–125.

Reinecke, John. 1937. Marginal languages: A sociological survey of the creole languages and trade jargons. Unpublished doctoral dissertation, Yale University.

Rodríguez Louro, Celeste. 2015. The evolution of epistemic marking in West Australian English. In Peter Collins, ed. *Grammatical Change in English World-Wide*. Amsterdam: John Benjamins, 205–220.

Schachter, Paul 1962. *Teaching English Pronunciation to the Twi-Speaking Student*. Legon: Ghana University Press.

Schneider, Edgar W. 2003. The dynamics of New Englishes: From identity construction to dialect birth. *Language 79*: 233–281.

Schneider, Edgar W. 2007. *Postcolonial English: Varieties Around the World*. Cambridge: Cambridge University Press.

Schreier, Daniel. 2017. Early twentieth-century Tristan da Cunha h'English. In Raymond Hickey, ed. *Listening to the Past: Audio Records of Accents of English*. Cambridge: Cambridge University Press, 484–501.

Schreier, Daniel, Peter Trudgill, Edgar W. Schneider and Jeffrey P. Williams, eds. 2010. *The Lesser-Known Varieties of English: An Introduction*. Cambridge: Cambridge University Press.

Schuchardt, Hugo. 1909. Die Lingua Franca. *Zeitschrift für Romanische Philologie 33*: 441–461.

Sedlatschek, Andreas. 2009. *Contemporary Indian English. Variation and Change*. Amsterdam: John Benjamins.

Sey, Kofi A. 1973. *Ghanaian English. An Exploratory Survey*. London: Macmillan.

Shastri, S.V. 1986. Manual of information to accompany the Kolhapur Corpus of Indian English, for use with digital computers. http://clu.uni.no/icame/kolhapur/kolman.htm.

Sóskuthy, Márton, Jennifer Hay, Margaret Maclagan, Katie Drager and Paul Foulkes. 2017. Early New Zealand English: The closing diphthongs. In Raymond Hickey, ed. *Listening to the Past: Audio Records of Accents of English*. Cambridge: Cambridge University Press, 529–561.

Strevens, Peter. 1980. *Teaching English as an International Language: From Practice to Principle*. Oxford: Pergamon Press.

Strevens, Peter 1965. Pronunciations of English in West Africa. In Peter Strevens, ed. *Papers in Language and Language Teaching*. London: Oxford University Press, 110–122.

Strevens, Peter. 1953–1954. Spoken English in the Gold Coast. *English Language Teaching 8*: 81–89.

Temple, Charles Lindsay. 1918. *Native Races and Their Rulers: Sketches and Studies of Official Life and Administrative Problems in Nigeria*. Cape Town: Argus Printing & Publishing Company.

Thomason, Sarah G. 2008. Pidgins/creoles and historical linguistics. In Silvia Kouwenberg and John Victor Singler, eds. *The Handbook of Pidgin and Creole Studies*. Oxford: Blackwell, 242–262.

Trudgill, Peter. 2004. *New-Dialect Formation: The Inevitability of Colonial Englishes*. Oxford: Oxford University Press.

Velupillai, Viveka. 2015. *Pidgins, Creoles and Mixed Languages. An Introduction*. Amsterdam: John Benjamins.

22

Corpus-Based Approaches to World Englishes

Marianne Hundt

22.1 Introduction

Research into World Englishes (WEs) draws on various methods, including linguists' intuitions, elicitation experiments, and anecdotal evidence. When it comes to describing and modeling variation in WEs, data from corpora add important detail. Bao and Wee (1999), for instance, report that Singapore English (SingE) has a nativized (adversative) passive construction combining a loan word from Malay (*kena*, "to strike/suffer") with a past participle:

(1)   I mean they're like there is guy who must be about sixty over then always kena teased by this other guy uhm. (ICE-SG, S1A-079)

When we look at corpus evidence from the Singapore component of the *International Corpus of English* (ICE) we see that this construction is extremely rare in standard SingE, even in spontaneous spoken usage, where the *be*-passive and the *get*-passive prevail (Bao 2010: 801–804).[1]

Almost from the very beginning, corpus-based research on the English language has taken regional variation into account: the first standard reference corpus for English – a one-million-word sample of printed American English (AmE) text extracts from 1961 – was soon to be followed by a matching corpus of British English (BrE). These two corpora – named Brown (AmE) and Lancaster-Oslo-Bergen (BrE) corpus after the universities involved in their compilation – were then followed by corpora that made use of more or less identical sampling criteria to enable usage-based investigation of Australian (AusE), New Zealand (NZE), and Indian English (IndE). Since its beginnings in the 1960s, when computer storage capacity was still very limited and usage-based research went against the dominant approach in the field (i.e. introspection-based grammaticality judgments), English corpus linguistics has come a long way. This chapter looks at developments in corpus linguistics in the WEs context in various subdisciplines, including both synchronic and diachronic approaches.

Generally speaking, Biber et al. (1998: 4) characterize the corpus-based approach by the following key components:

- it is empirical, analysing the actual patterns of use in natural texts;
- it utilizes a large and principled collection of natural texts, known as a "corpus," as the basis for analysis;
- it makes extensive use of computers for analysis, using both automatic and interactive techniques;
- it depends on both quantitative and qualitative analytical techniques.

As this chapter will show, studies of WEs have made use of corpus evidence in the ways described by Biber et al. (1998). They have been used to describe variation within and across WEs, that is, for both intra- and intervarietal research. Occasionally they limit their methodology to qualitative description. This is not necessarily a shortcoming of such studies as not all theoretical perspectives on WEs might be amenable to statistical modeling of variation in the first place. Also, what exactly constitutes a corpus might need some discussion. Thus, Section 22.2 will introduce different types of corpora and approaches to corpus compilation. Corpus-based research into WEs has progressed from a focus on first-language varieties to institutionalized second-language varieties and learner varieties of English, as the overview of synchronic corpora in Section 22.3 shows. As corpus linguistics is first and foremost just a methodology, Section 22.4 looks into the application of synchronic corpus evidence in WEs research. This is followed by an overview of studies with a focus on variation and change in Section 22.5. The outlook in the final section considers open challenges, research lacunae, and possible future developments in corpus-based studies of WEs. The focus of this chapter is on studies based on publicly available corpora.

22.2 From Standard Reference Corpora to Web-Based Databases: Small and Beautiful vs. Big and Messy?

Following Biber et al.'s (1998: 4) definition, a corpus needs to be of a specific size ("large") as well as a "principled" collection of naturally used language. What precisely "large" and "principled" can mean varies greatly when we consider existing corpora of WEs. In the 1960s, a one-million-word corpus was considered "large." Twenty years later, the *British National Corpus* (BNC) already ran to 100 million words. In the days of "big data," electronic databases of WEs such as the *Global Web-Based English* (GloWbE) and *News on the Web* (NOW) corpora comprise 1.9 billion and more than 6 billion words, respectively. The significant increase in corpus size was made possible by technical

Table 22.1 *Comparison of the fiction components in standard written corpora (number of text excerpts per corpus)*

Text category	Brown	ACE	WWC	Kolhapur
General fiction	29	29	29	59
Mystery and detective fiction	24	15	24	24
Science fiction	6	7	6	2
Western and adventure fiction	29	8	29	15
Romantic fiction	29	15	29	18
Humor	9	15	9	9
Historical fiction	–	22	–	–
Women's fiction	–	15	–	–

developments. However, in the WEs context, corpus size can still be restricted by the availability of certain text categories. Literary production in a particular country may be limited, for instance. This can be the case with respect to specific literary genres even in countries where English is the first or "native" language (ENL) of the majority of speakers, such as Australia and New Zealand. Literary production in English typically tends to be limited in contexts where English is only used as an institutionalized second language (ESL) variety competing with other national languages in the area of creative language use, as is the case in India, where more specialized literary genres proved difficult to obtain. Table 22.1 illustrates the point by giving the different numbers of text samples included in the fiction component of the Brown-type corpora in Australia (ACE), New Zealand (WWC), and India (Kolhapur).

Availability of texts for a given sampling frame becomes even more problematic in much smaller ESL countries such as Fiji, where not only local text production (e.g. the limited number of local newspapers and magazines) posed a problem for corpus compilation but also the political situation between 2006 and 2015 (i.e. at a period when parliament was resolved, making the sampling of parliamentary debates impossible for a time; see Biewer et al. 2010).

With respect to corpus size, the bigger is not necessarily always the better. For a study of prepositional complements in WEs, for instance, a corpus of one million words already provides too much information for comprehensive and detailed analysis, especially seeing that Prepositional Phrase (PP) attachment is notoriously difficult to model in both qualitative and computational approaches (e.g. Schütze 1995; Volk 2001; Agire et al. 2008).[2] The counts in Table 22.2 therefore give only a very rough indication of prepositional complements in the various components of ICE.

---

[2] PP attachment is difficult, among other things, because of ambiguity: In a sentence like *He opened the box with the knife*, the PP *with the knife* could be attached to *open* (and would therefore be an argument of the main clause) or to *the box* (as a post-modifier and thus not an argument). Moreover, the distinction between arguments and adjuncts is not clear-cut, either (see Hoffmann 2007 for detailed discussion). Automatic parsing, finally, may identify prepositional complements correctly, as in *I'll come and deliver it to you* (ICE-GB, S1A-064) or incorrectly, as in *I kept it in case he wanted to see it* (ICE-GB, S1A-065).

Table 22.2 *Automatically retrieved PP complements from syntactically parsed ICE corpora*

ICE component	GB	CAN	IRE	NZ	IND	SG	HK	PHI
PP complements	21,316	20,935	20,954	23,918	21,083	20,058	21,825	20,556

Table 22.3 *Complementation patterns of* enter *in ICE (figures in brackets report concrete spatial use of* into*)*

	absolute	NP/nominal clause	into/onto	in	other P	NP + P	total
ICE-GB	10	58	11 (1)	1	1	0	81
ICE-NZ	15	89	13 (1)	1	1	3	122
ICE-IND	11	88	29 (14)	2	1	1	132
ICE-SG	13	47	9 (1)	1	3	3	76
ICE-HK	15	104	18 (7)	1	3	3	144
ICE-PHI	6	93	20 (1)	3	1	1	124

The same corpora can be too small for a related study on lexico-grammatical variation. The verb *enter* can have a bare Noun Phrase (NP) as complement or a PP, as in *He entered (into) the room*. The frequencies for these and other complements are rather small in individual ICE components, as Table 22.3 shows. In other words, the size of a corpus required for a particular study always depends on the specific research question(s) and the level of granularity that the analyses aim to provide. The small and carefully compiled corpora may therefore be complemented with large (often web-based) databases (see, e.g., De Clerck and Vanopstal 2015). Where even these fail to provide sufficient evidence they can be combined with other data, for example from experiments. Horch (2019) uses web-based psycholinguistic experimentation (an online maze task) to verify the more widespread use of conversion for deverbal nouns in ESL varieties. Her study shows that corpus and experimental evidence converge, which in turn validates the usefulness of web-based corpora like GloWbE.

The question of what constitutes a "principled" text collection is similarly difficult to answer. In order for statistical modeling to be applied at a later stage, sampling should, in principle, be representative of the "population." For any living language at large, this means that much more spontaneous spoken interaction would have to be included in order to reflect the fact that people use language more often in the spoken than in the written medium. Since spoken corpora have been extremely costly to compile, most corpora are skewed toward the written mode. However, even for printed AmE texts published in a single year, truly representative sampling is impossible to achieve in the theoretical sense.[3] In practice, corpus compilers therefore

---

[3] Strictly speaking, one would first have to compile a list of all texts printed during that year and then enter this list using a random number table to select individual texts, the page on which to start sampling, etc. (for a more detailed discussion and the pragmatic solution to sampling in linguistic research, see Woods et al. 1986, chap. 4).

apply judgment sampling to arrive at a balanced selection of various spoken and written text categories, where "judgment" "refers to the ability professionally competent members of a speech community seem to have in recognizing the relative prevalence of different genres" (Leech, 2007: 140).[4] The Brown-type corpora and the components of ICE are based on such judgment samples. However, a sampling frame that provides a good selection of spoken and written material in a largely monolingual ENL country may not necessarily provide a suitable sampling frame for ESL countries where English is used with varying competence and alongside other languages.

Finally, there is a connection between size and sampling principles: Typically, smaller corpora tend to be subjected to stricter sampling criteria and the careful selection of individual text extracts or speakers, including the collection of socio-economic background data for the latter, whereas large mega-corpora often use more coarse-grained sampling frames and a more generous policy on the inclusion of individual samples, on the assumption that a single specimen is unlikely to skew the results from a sufficiently large corpus.[5] Again, however, the question whether preference should be given to a small and carefully compiled corpus or a "messy" mega corpus cannot be answered without reference to the research question. While for a study on mandative subjunctives across different Englishes, the one-million-word ICE components yield just about enough evidence for a general assessment of usage patterns, more fine-grained analyses with respect to individual trigger expressions such as *demand* or *require* necessitate larger amounts of data from less rigorously compiled databases. Web-based corpora such as GloWbE have to be used advisedly, however: In their manual postediting of the data, linguists may want to remove individual instances from their data sets. GloWbE, for instance, contains blogs in order to represent informal language use on the Internet. These occasionally include data from expatriate bloggers, which could have a skewing effect for the study of low-frequency phenomena (see Hundt 2018).[6] When they are used with the necessary degree of caution, web-based data may usefully complement evidence from smaller corpora.

The GloWbE and NOW corpora are examples of how the World-Wide Web can be used for corpus compilation. Similarly, web-based versions of the original Brown and LOB corpora have been compiled in Lancaster for the study of recent change (see Section 22.5). Researchers have also explored the web-as-corpus approach, either with the help of freely available search engines or on the basis of specifically developed meta-crawlers (see Hundt et al. 2007). Hundt (2013a) uses the progressive passive, as a case

---

[4] For more detailed discussions of representativeness, see, e.g., Biber (1993) or Leech (2007).

[5] See Hundt and Leech (2012) and Davies (2012) for a discussion of the "small and beautiful" vs. the "size matters" approach to sampling.

[6] The GloWbE and its potential uses are introduced in more detail in Davies and Fuchs (2015). The advantages and potential pitfalls involved in using this resource are discussed in a number of responses by Christian Mair, Joybrato Mukherjee, Gerald Nelson, and Pam Peters in the same journal.

study to compare the web-as-corpus and web-for-corpus building approach in the context of WEs research. Both approaches are found to provide useful evidence on a low-frequency phenomenon that supplement findings on standard reference corpora. In addition, the web-as-corpus approach returns interesting meta-linguistic comments on the issue of grammaticality, that is, the question whether nonfinite (*having been being Ved*) or present perfect modal progressive passives (*could have been being Ved*) are viable constructions of English. The web-as-corpus approach provides evidence of such very rare verb phrases:

(2)   The 2017 Australian PrEP Guidelines have the benefits of *having been being written* and edited by clinicians, epidemiologists and representatives of peak Australian HIV community organisations who have significant experience of PrEP in the clinical, research and real-world settings.

(3)   Most physicians believed that the quality targets had improved patient care by focussing attention on necessary clinical activities that *might have been being neglected.*[7]

In 2007, when new web-based mega-corpora were making an appearance on the scene, Geoffrey Leech – one of the founding fathers of English corpus linguistics – asked whether linguists should use these "[n]ew resources or just better old ones?" Ten years later, Guillaume Desagulier (2017) finds that there is still quite a bit of mileage in the old resources, not least to replicate the results of earlier research with new methodologies such as correspondence analysis. In a blog entry that reports on a replication of Hirschmüller's (1989) study on complex prepositions in IndE, he concludes that "comparatively speaking, the older corpora have the kind of spick-and-span internal structure that makes them pleasant to use."

22.3 From Metropolitan Varieties to Learner Englishes: The Broadening Scope of Corpus-Based Research

The study of regional variation in a number of standard WEs was made possible early on through the compilation of Brown-type reference corpora. With the exception of the Kolhapur Corpus, however, they provided evidence for ENL varieties only. The scope of corpus-based research into WEs broadened significantly in 1990 with the inception of ICE (Greenbaum 1988, 1996). This resource provides not only a substantial amount of spoken language (60 percent) but also a wide range of ENL

---

[7] The examples were retrieved with a simple google search and come from the following websites: Example (2) – https://siren.org.au/post-1294/ (accessed 3 October 2018); Example (3) – www.annfammed.org/content/6/3/228 .full.pdf (accessed 3 October 2018).

and ESL varieties as well as samples of English from countries like Jamaica, where standard English is used as a second dialect (ESD) alongside an English-based creole.

The 500 samples of approximately 2,000 words each in the ICE components are spread across four macro text categories: dialogues, monologues, nonprinted, and printed. The largest subsample (a fifth of the material) comes from spontaneous conversations (including telephone conversations). The second largest subsample is drawn from public dialogues (including classroom lessons and broadcast interviews but also more formal interactions such as parliamentary debates). Half of the corpus (250 samples) represent unscripted spoken usage. The sampling frame thus takes into account the fact that the majority of language production happens online and in the spoken medium. It does not, however, aim at a representative sampling of all speakers but intentionally focuses on educated usage.[8] Moreover, only production in English is part of the corpus, that is, all contributions to a spoken exchange that are in one of the local languages in ESL countries are marked as "extra-corpus" material.[9]

Not all of the eighteen ICE components originally envisaged as part of the project (Greenbaum 1996: 3) were compiled or completed (using material produced between the late 1980s and early 1990s); additional ICE corpora have been compiled (or are being compiled) from more recent material, resulting in a (varying) diachronic bias.[10] These include varieties such as Malaysian and Malta English, which straddle the divide between ESL and foreign language. While this broadens the regional scope for the corpus-based investigation across WEs, intervarietal research has to take the diachronic dimension into account in the comparison of older with ICE-age II corpora. The diachronic incompatibility of the older and the more recent ICE components is less of a problem with relatively stable regional variation that we would expect to find for instance with the so-called dative alternation than in the investigation of phenomena that underwent rapid change, such as the development of quotative *be like*.

In addition to the diachronic gap between the early and later ICE corpora, comparability across ICE components is likely to be influenced by stylistic variation that, so far, remains under-researched. Multidimensional (MD) analysis of register variation (see Biber 1985, 1988) is required to gauge the extent to which component parts of ICE are comparable in this respect.

---

[8] Corpora of nonstandard WEs are rarer and often not publicly accessible, as is the case with the corpus of colloquial SingE (Lim, 2004).

[9] See Mair (2018: 117) for a critical discussion of the "monolingual" bias of the ICE sampling frame and Lange (2018).

[10] The ICE component for Fiji, for instance, was supposed to be part of the original set of ICE corpora but work on the corpus only started in 2005. ICE-US, to the present day, is limited in that only the written component was completed. For a list of available corpora, see www.ice-corpora.uzh.ch/en.html.

In an early attempt at applying the MD approach to ICE components, Xiao (2009) found comparability in some areas (e.g. academic prose and creative writing) and differences in others (e.g. spontaneous spoken conversation). While this study adds useful ideas to expand the original MD approach, it is limited to only one ENL variety (BrE) and four contact varieties of English (Indian, Hong Kong, Singapore, and Philippine English). Kruger and van Rooy (2018) broaden the MD approach considerably by applying it to the written part of sixteen ICE components (both ENL and ESL). While they find that, overall, written registers across ICE components are comparable, they point out that this might not apply to spontaneous conversations: "There may be more extensive differences between varieties in spoken language, especially in face-to-face conversation" (Kruger and van Rooy 2018: 237).

In the last decade, corpus-based research has systematically challenged the traditional divide between ESL and EFL countries. As the contributions to Mukherjee and Hundt (2011) show, usage data frequently do not support the traditional ENL/ESL/EFL divide but provide evidence of some EFL usage coming close to patterns found in ENL varieties (see Section 22.4.1). Moreover, usage patterns considered typical of contact varieties (such as the extended use of the progressive to stative verbs like *know*) need to be integrated with discussions about conditions on language learning and norm developments. In other words, factors such as the role of second-language learning in the classroom (and beyond) need to be considered as a variable as well as the question whether ESL (but not EFL) varieties are likely to ever start orienting toward an endo-normative model of usage (see Hundt and Mukherjee 2011). The line of research that challenges the ESL/EFL divide has been enabled by the compilation of learner corpora, notably the *International Corpus of Learner English* (ICLE), which provides a uniform sampling frame for written academic usage. The *Louvain International Database of Spoken English Interlanguage* (LINDSEI) complements ICLE with spoken data from interviews with advanced learners (see Gilquin 2015). These learner corpora were compiled on the assumption that English as a Foreign Language (EFL) emerges under fundamentally different conditions from those that play a role in the formation of ESL varieties. By contrast, the *Corpus of Dutch English* takes the sampling frame for the written section of the ICE corpora as its model, that is, focuses on educated written English in a country where the language is not institutionalized but where a large proportion of the population are exposed to English from an early age and use it extensively in their everyday lives (Edwards 2011, 2016, 2017; Edwards and Laporte 2015). Evidence from this corpus even further challenges the divide between ESL and EFL and, together with findings from studies on English in Cyprus or Namibia, has led to recent renegotiations of how WEs should be modeled (see Buschfeld and Kautzsch, Chapter 2, this volume).

22.4 From Description to Theoretical and Statistical Modeling

Corpora can be used for the description of a single variety or varieties in the same region, as is the case in Sand's (1999) study of Jamaican English (JamE) or the papers on SingE collected in Lim (2004). Most of the time, however, descriptions of a single variety use other WEs as a backdrop. Deuber (2014) compares spoken evidence from the Jamaican and Trinidadian ICE components in her study of Caribbean English. The analysis of a range of creole-influenced grammatical features allows her to arrive at a typology of different stylistic connotations. These are then used for a reinterpretation of the creole continuum (pp. 241–243). While Deuber focuses on regional evidence, Zipp (2014) assesses the variety status of educated Fiji English (FE) on the basis of comparisons with BrE, NZE, and IndE. Drawing additionally on evidence from learner corpora allows her to arrive at a fine-grained analysis and interpretation of prepositional usage, also with respect to variety-internal differences between Indo-Fijian and Fijian FE. Intra-varietal comparisons like Deuber (2014) and Zipp (2014) take a local variety or regional usage as their starting point and provide case studies on several features. This approach differs from the focus of most papers in Hundt and Gut (2012): these aim at broad regional coverage for one phenomenon. Finally, individual studies differ in their treatment of variety types: They may juxtapose ENL and ESL varieties (e.g. Collins and Yao, 2012) or use corpus data to test the distinction (e.g. Hundt 2009a).

It is important to note that not only the size and the composition of a corpus determine its usefulness for a specific research question. Developments in the annotation of corpora – notably Part-of-Speech (PoS) tagging and parsing – have also opened up new avenues for research.[11] Automatic retrieval of passives and corresponding transitive actives, for instance, is only possible once both kinds of meta-information (word class and syntactic function) have been added to the raw text (see Section 22.4.3). Annotation beyond grammatical categories cannot be done automatically and is therefore not universally applied to existing corpus resources.[12] Ideally, corpus research can also draw on metadata for each sample in the corpus, such as a speaker's age, ethnicity, gender, and so on (cf. Section 22.4.4).

Once a corpus has been enriched by grammatical annotation, it can be fruitfully employed for both top-down and bottom-up approaches to data retrieval. The former takes an existing research hypothesis as its starting point and uses the corpus to verify it. The bottom-up approach uses corpus

---

[11] The British ICE component has been annotated with the ICE parser (see Nelson et al. 2002). At Zurich, available ICE corpora have been annotated with a probabilistic dependency parser (Pro3Gres, Schneider 2008). The latter version is searchable to holders of an ICE license through the Dependency Bank jointly developed by Hans Martin Lehmann and Gerold Schneider (see the ICE website).

[12] The pragmatically annotated ICE-IRE (Kirk 2016) is an exception.

data in a more explorative fashion. An example would be Schneider and Hundt's (2009) attempt at exploring corpus annotation as a discovery tool for nativization in ESL varieties. The working assumption for this study was that parser output would be erroneous more often in the case of novel patterns typically found in such varieties. However, as it turns out, the parser is too robust for this approach to work. This, in turn, means that automatically annotated data from both ENL and ESL can be taken as a reliable starting point for investigation. Schneider and Hundt (2012) explore an intermediate annotation state between PoS and parsing (called "chunking") to arrive at a bottom-up description of variation in TAM across different WEs.

Corpus-based research into WEs increasingly makes use not only of richer, annotated data but also of various kinds of statistical modeling, thus moving beyond the significance testing characteristic of research from the 1990s.

The studies discussed in the following sections have been selected to reflect these developments in the field.

22.4.1   Corpora as a Testing Bed for Models of World Englishes

Corpus evidence has provided a testing ground for the typologies of different WEs (including Kachru's Three Circles Model), Schneider's (2003, 2007) Dynamic Model, and the Epicenter Hypothesis. With respect to Kachru's (1985) Three Circles Model, numerical evidence on individual grammatical patterns does not necessarily support the distinction between ENL, ESL, and EFL varieties: Taking a grassroots perspective, Hundt and Vogel (2011) show that not all ESL varieties share with learner Englishes a propensity to overuse the progressive. Szmrecsanyi and Kortmann's (2011) bird's-eye view does provide evidence of an ESL/EFL divide. They compare evidence from the BNC, ICE, and ICLE on a set of features to characterize grammatical syntheticity and analyticity, respectively. Their study shows that learner varieties systematically differ from ESL varieties when compared with a single ENL (BrE): Learner Englishes are more analytic than ESL varieties, which in turn are more analytic than comparable BrE writing (Szmrecsanyi and Kortmann, 2011: 182).

Synchronic corpora of WEs have also been used to test the validity of Schneider's Dynamic Model of the evolution of WEs, in particular different degrees of nativization.[13] In doing so, corpus linguists have followed the explicit suggestion by Schneider (2004: 227) that "[t]he most promising road to a possible detection of early traces of distinctive features is a principled comparison of performance data collected along similar lines, i.e. systematically elicited corpora." Early examples are Mukherjee and Gries (2009) and Gries and Mukherjee (2010). While Mukherjee and

---

[13] For a diachronic approach, see Section 22.5.

Gries' (2009) collostruction analysis reveals that a variety's divergence from BrE tallies well with its respective developmental stage, Gries and Mukherjee's (2010) study of lexical bundles did not provide additional evidence that the more advanced a variety is in the evolutionary cycle, the more it will have developed region-specific usage patterns. Gries and Mukherjee (2010: 537) conclude that developmental stages are "less likely to be reflected in lexical differences because lexis-related differences are topic-dependent and volatile."

Corpus data have also been used to test the hypothesis that new Englishes may develop into regional standard varieties and eventually become local norm-providing centers (Bailey 1990: 85). While it is relatively easy to empirically verify that a variety has diverged enough from its original input variety and stabilized to the degree that it can now be considered a new (regional) standard variety of English, it is more difficult to prove exclusively through corpus evidence that this variety is also serving as a new local epicenter (see Hundt 2013b). Existing corpus-based research (e.g. Hoffmann et al. 2011; Biewer 2015) does not normally go beyond testing for relative structural closeness of the varieties in question, that is, it provides indirect evidence of potential epicenter status. Gries and Bernaisch (2016) and Heller et al. (2017) use two well-tried alternations (the dative alternation with GIVE and the genitive alternation) and Multifactorial Prediction and Deviation Analysis with Regression (MuPDAR) to argue that underlying patterns of usage are sufficient to test epicenter status. According to their data, this can be supported for IndE in South Asia but not for SingE in Southeast Asia. These studies still need to be supplemented with evidence on whether language users in countries like Sri Lanka or Bangladesh actually accept IndE as a local norm-providing variety.

22.4.2   Corpus Evidence, Language Contact, and Typology

Corpus data have served to model the influence of language contact on different types of Englishes. Szmrecsanyi (2009), for instance, combines the data from various ICE components and compares them with data from the Brown family, the BNC, a corpus of traditional British dialects, and a corpus of spoken AmE. He finds not only that ENL varieties exhibit a significantly higher degree of syntheticity than ESL varieties but also that there is a marked difference between varieties in Southeast Asia (SingE, PhilE, HKE) and non-Southeast Asian varieties (IndE, JamE, East African English; Szmrecsanyi 2009: 328–329). The observation that Southeast Asian varieties use less overt grammatical marking in general aligns well with typological differences of the underlying substrate languages described in Bisang (2009), as Szmrecsanyi (2009: 331) observes.

Brunner (2014) provides a close-up of the role that substrate influence might have for noun phrase complexity in just two WEs with typologically different substrates, SingE and Kenyan English (KenE), using BrE as the ENL yardstick. This allows him to consider the specifics of NP structure in various substrate languages in Kenya and Singapore in more detail (i.e. African languages from three different branches of African languages and three varieties of Chinese as well as Malay, respectively). He predicts two potential outcomes for KenE and SingE – a greater frequency of head-initial NPs in KenE (p. 29) and overall simpler NPs in the ESL than in the ENL variety (p. 30) – and tests these hypotheses on random samples of NPs from the spontaneous conversations in the respective ICE components.[14] Corpus data confirm that KenE has a strong preference for head-initial NPs and disprefers head-final structures, whereas SingE has the opposite preference (p. 37). With respect to NP complexity in ESL and ENL varieties, Brunner's results show that BrE and KenE occupy two endpoints on a cline with SingE in the middle. According to Brunner (2014: 44), the results for hypothesis 1 provide a good argument in favor of substrate language effects, whereas the results for hypothesis 2 tie in with predictions from Schneider's (2003, 2007) Dynamic Model.

22.4.3 Modeling Morpho-syntactic Variation across World Englishes

Comparative studies of variable morphology across WEs are relatively rare, mostly because English is a morphologically impoverished language. One of the possible phenomena that has been studied is the (re)regularization of irregular verb morphology.[15] Table 22.4 provides information on the proportion of irregular {-t} and regular {-ed} in verbs such as *burn*, *dream*, and *learn* across ENL and ESL varieties in ICE.[16]

While the figures in Table 22.4 obviously abstract away from a more complex situation in that they only give information on overtly marked past tense/participle forms (i.e. ignore the potentially unmarked past forms in, e.g., ICE-SG or ICE-HK), they provide interesting data for the typology that groups WEs according to their matrilect: NZE and AusE are more conservative in this ongoing change than BrE, while IrE is more advanced (pair-wise significance tests with BrE as a yardstick prove that only the difference between AusE and BrE is significant). Canadian English (CanE), the variety that derives from BrE but is geographically closest to US English, is significantly more advanced in the (re)regularization of regular past tense forms (also than IrE). With respect to ESL varieties, Philippine

---

[14] The East African component of ICE comprises both Kenyan and Tanzanian samples. Brunner includes only NPs from Kenyan conversations in his dataset (2014: 30).

[15] The change from {-t} to {-ed} is a case of (re)regularization because the irregular forms were only introduced from the Middle English period onwards and then re-regularized in the nineteenth century (see Hundt 2009b and Anderwald 2014 for details).

[16] The totals are based on a search for the variable forms of the verbs *burn, dream, kneel, lean, leap, learn, spell, spill* and *spoil*. Figures for ICE-AUS, ICE-NZ and ICE-GB are from Peters (2009: 23). The study by De Clerck and Vanopstal (2015) only uses the written part of the ICE corpora and is limited to ICE-GB, ICE-US and ICE-IND. Adjectival uses of the past participle (as in *a learned woman* or *a burnt piece of toast*) are excluded from the counts.

Table 22.4 *Relative frequency of –t and –ed forms across ICE corpora*

	{-t}	{-ed}	% {-ed}
ICE-GB	55	62	53
ICE-NZ	79	68	46.3
ICE-AUS	85	42	33.1
ICE-CAN	19	131	87.3
ICE-IRE	43	67	60.9
ICE-IND	116	28	19.4
ICE-SG	91	33	26.6
ICE-HK	59	40	40.4
ICE-PHI	4	164	97.6
Total	551	635	53.5
			(average)

English (PhilE) is almost categorical in its use of regular forms and thus closest to US English (see, e.g., De Clerck and Vanopstal 2015). IndE and SingE are even more conservative than AusE (IndE significantly so), whereas the proportion of regular forms in ICE-HK is close to those in ICE-NZ but still significantly different from ICE-GB. The results in Table 22.4 only serve as an initial starting point for a study that would need to rely on larger corpora to dig deeper into the marked differences between lexical items where ICE does not provide sufficient evidence.[17] Larger amounts of data could then be subjected to the kind of statistical modeling that De Clerck and Vanopstal (2015) apply to the Brown-family corpora, Kolhapur, and supplementary data from GloWbE.

Corpus-based research on syntactic variation greatly benefits from syntactic annotation. Studying the active:passive alternation across WEs has only become feasible with the parsing of the ICE corpora. Hundt et al.'s (2016) study of the parsed academic writing sections in ICE shows that US English is the regional variety which is markedly different from all other Englishes (both ENL and ESL) in avoiding the passive. However, regression analysis reveals that differences across academic subdisciplines are even more marked than regional differences. This demonstrates the need for multifactorial analysis to gauge the relative importance of regional variety as a predictor variable in variationist research into WEs. Similarly, when testing for the role that language-internal factors play in the voice alternation, Hundt et al. (2018) show that there is no general difference across ENL and ESL varieties. However, differences in the effect size that some factors have provide evidence of subtle regional variation across academic Englishes, some of which find an explanation in substrate influence even in a highly edited register such as academic writing. In the Philippine ICE

---

[17] The most frequent alternating verb is LEARN. The regular form of this verb may function as an adjective, a use that is particularly frequent in ICE-IND, ICE-SG and ICE-HK.

data, for instance, GIVENNESS of the subject has a stronger effect on the choice of a passive, which fits in well with the requirement of the main substrate language, Tagalog, where sentences are required to have at least one given argument (Hundt et al. 2018: 9, 26).

The application of sophisticated statistical modeling to WEs is a relatively recent phenomenon. A good example is Szmrecsanyi et al.'s (2016) study of the dative, genitive, and particle placement alternations. They use two multivariate models, a conditional inference tree and a random forest analysis.[18] Their aim is to investigate whether the three alternations provide evidence of "probabilistic indigenization" (2016: 133), which they define as

> the process whereby stochastic patterns of internal linguistic variation are reshaped by shifting usage frequencies in speakers of post-colonial varieties. To the extent that patterns of variation in a new variety A, e.g. the probability of item x in context y, can be shown to differ from those of the mother variety, we can say that the new pattern represents a novel, if gradient, development in the grammar of A. These patterns need not be consistent or stable ..., but they nonetheless reflect the emergence of a unique, region-specific grammar.

Szmrecsanyi et al. (2016: 133) find that regional variety is the most important predictor for the particle placement alternation, whereas the genitive alternation is the least subject to regional variation. They suggest that regional variety is the more likely to have an effect on speakers' choices the more individual lexical items play a role in the alternation.

22.4.4 Corpus-Based Modeling of Sociolinguistic and Pragmatic Variation across World Englishes

Systematic use of publicly available corpora for sociolinguistic research into WEs is still rare, partly because the metadata for the ICE corpora that provide information on speaker background are not readily available.[19] Mair (2009) is as an early proponent of this approach. Having been involved in the compilation of ICE-JAM himself, he compares educated JamE with BrE, IndE, SingE, HKE, and PhilE. However, in his case studies on lexical, syntactic, and pragmatic features, he does not include speaker variables. Zipp (2014) systematically takes ethnicity into account in her study of educated Fiji English but, like Mair (2009), does not include

---

[18] This statistical approach was developed by psychologists and later applied to the modeling of linguistic data. The most comprehensive comparison of more traditional multivariate analyses and the tree-and-forest approach can be found in Tagliamonte and Baayen (2012).

[19] For an overview of ICE corpora with metadata on individual speakers, see Lang (2018: 23). Sharma (2017) provides a thorough discussion of the theoretical underpinnings for the sociolinguistics of WEs. A workshop at the 38th ICAME conference in Prague (2017) on genderlectal variation across ESL and EFL varieties is indicative of a growing interest in sociolinguistic exploration of WEs corpora. Some researchers (e.g. Sigley and Holmes 2002) have used corpora to investigate sexist language use across WEs, which also falls under the heading of sociolinguistic corpus-based research.

information on the speaker level in her investigation. Gut and Fuchs (2014) set out to study speaker fluency across two phonologically annotated ICE corpora. Despite the title of their paper, they only compare speaker fluency (in terms of mean length of utterance) in Nigerian and Scottish English without reference to the individual speaker.[20]

Höhn (2012) uses multivariate analysis on the spoken components of ICE-JAM and ICE-IRE for a socio-pragmatic study on the developmental trajectory of quotative *be like*, dividing the data into two collection periods (1990–1994 and 2002–2005). With respect to the speaker variable "gender," she finds that "the corpus is too skewed in favour of women in the period 2002 to 2005 to allow a firm statement" (2012: 288). Höhn's study thus nicely illustrates the problem inherent in the ICE corpora for the study of socio-pragmatic variation: The corpora were primarily designed to study variation across WEs. This means that speaker variables such as age, gender, ethnicity, first language, and so on were not necessarily controlled for in the sampling of the data.

Studies of socio-phonetic variation based on ICE corpora are even rarer than sociolinguistic studies generally, mostly because the recordings themselves are not available to the academic community at large. Rosenfelder's (2009) study on rhoticity in educated JamE is therefore particularly unusual as she combines variation at the speaker level with a socio-phonetic variable. She finds that contextual variables are significant in predicting rhoticity; somewhat surprisingly, "gender" and "age" as speaker variables are not significant (Rosenfelder, 2009: 73).

Vine (2000) is an early publication that critically discusses the methodological challenges involved in using ICE data for the study of pragmatic phenomena. One of the main problems in her comparative study of directives in ICE-GB and ICE-NZ turned out to be corpus comparability:

> [T]he same section in each component contained different types of interactions. ICE-NZ's demonstrations include cooking and Tupperware demonstrations, while ICE-GB's are mostly academic ... These different types of demonstrations yield very different types of directives.
>
> (Vine, 2000: 379)

Despite these challenges, ICE corpora have regularly been used to study aspects of pragmatics across WEs, such as discourse particles (Lange 2009) or invariant *isn't it* (Parviainen 2016). ICE corpora are also used to study pragmatic variation in individual varieties, as in Wong (2010), Heine et al. (2017), and Unuabonah and Gut (2018). These studies can serve as starting points for cross-varietal comparisons.

---

[20] Note, however, that the purpose of their case study is primarily to demonstrate the added value that phonologically annotated corpora provide.

22.5 Synchronic, "Brachryonic," and Diachronic Evidence: Corpus-Based Investigation of Change in World Englishes

Since genuine diachronic data are missing for most ESL varieties of English,[21] Fuchs and Gut (2015) use the apparent-time approach and regression analysis on their ICE-Nigeria data to study the spread of the progressive in this variety: "The results show that younger speakers use more progressives than older speakers, which we interpret as evidence for ongoing language change" (Fuchs and Gut, 2015: 373). Interestingly, the spread cannot be attributed to an increase in extended uses of the progressive to stative verbs (as in Example (4)), so often associated with ESL and EFL varieties (ibid.).

(4)   we *are* believing that erm in three years' time there will be a railway. (ICE-NIG, S1B-32)

Similarly, Hansen (2017: 479–481) is able to use apparent-time data to demonstrate how *must* gives way to *have to* in HKE, with female speakers leading the change (p. 482).

   The apparent-time concept is applied in a much looser fashion in Mair and Winkle's (2012) study of the shift from *to*-infinitive to bare infinitive in specificational cleft sentences (e.g. *What she did was (to) call him on her mobile*). Having established that there is a real-time change in two reference varieties (BrE and US English), they use synchronic evidence from different ICE components and interpret differences between varieties as indicative of regional differences in this ongoing change:

> It is highly likely that these varieties also share in the drift toward the bare infinitive, so that a higher frequency of this form in comparison to ICE-GB should be interpreted as a sign of faster diachronic change, while a lower frequency would be a sign of a relatively more retarded stage in the development.   (Mair and Winkle, 2012: 247)

In a similar vein, van der Auwera et al. (2012) establish recent real-time change in the use of *need (to)* in BrE and AmE as their baseline before moving on to interpret synchronic ICE data as evidence of convergence and divergence of ESL varieties from the reference varieties. In particular, they argue that change is more advanced in speech than in writing, that is, they take stylistic variation in present-day English as a proxy for ongoing change. They are cautious in interpreting their results as hard evidence of diachronic developments, though, not only because they use synchronic data as a proxy for change but also because of low token frequencies (van der Auwera et al. 2012: 72).

---

[21] The focus in this section is on morpho-syntactic change in WEs. For available evidence on accent evolution, see Huber, Chapter 21, this volume. This section also refers to diachronic corpora that are not (yet) in the public domain.

Both Mair and Winkle (2012) and van der Auwera et al. (2012) use real-time evidence from the Brown-family corpora[22] to establish their diachronic benchmark, that is, the earlier and later replica corpora sampled from material published thirty years prior and after the publication of the original Brown and LOB evidence. Mair (1994: 130–131) adopts Lehmann's (1991) term "brachychronic" (literally "short-time") both for recent change and for the corpus-based description of it. Initially, Brown-family corpora were used to study brachychronic change in BrE and AmE (Leech et al., 2009).[23]

More recently, the brachychronic approach has been extended beyond ENL varieties. Collins et al. (2014) use evidence from a Brown-type corpus of PhilE from the 1950s/1960s and comparative data from ICE to study change in core and quasi-modals. According to this evidence, PhilE is seen as realigning itself with its matrilect, AmE. Gries et al. (2018) use brachychronic evidence on the genitive alternation from a Brown-type corpus of SingE and ICE-SG and comparative data from ICE-GB. Applying the MuPDAR approach (see Section 22.4.1), their aim is to verify Schneider's (2007: 155) claim that SingE transitioned from stage 3 (nativization) into stage 4 (endonormative stabilization) in the 1970s. Their results do not provide unambiguous proof of structural divergence (2018: 273), if structural divergence is what the model indeed predicts in this case. They go on to discuss the issues involved in operationalizing Schneider's model for corpus-linguistic research (2018: 273–276) and conclude that additional corpus-based research based on real-time evidence is needed for each of the WEs to test the hypotheses against a number of linguistic variables. Similar corpora for the study of recent change in ESL varieties are being compiled for HKE (Biewer et al. 2014) and Ghanaian English (Brato 2018).

Real-time diachronic change into varieties of English was first enabled by the compilation of ARCHER, *A Representative Corpus of Historical English Registers*.[24] The purpose behind the compilation of the corpus was to study diachronic shifts in registers but it can also be used to study differential change in BrE and AmE (for an ARCHER-based typology of change that goes beyond the "lag" vs. "innovation" dichotomy, see Hundt 2009b).

Corpora for other ENL varieties followed suit, such as the *Corpus of Oz Early English* (COOEE; Fritz 2007) and the *Corpus of Early New Zealand English*

---

[22] The original Brown family extended the time frame from 1961 to 1991/1992 (FLOB and Frown); the extended Brown family adds corpora from the 1930s (B-LOB and B-Brown). The web-based extensions into the twenty-first century are the AE06 and BE06 corpora compiled at Lancaster (see Hundt and Leech 2012).

[23] In his recent study that includes changes in spelling, word formation, and semantics, Baker (2017) draws on the extended Brown family (see Hundt and Leech 2012) and supplements these corpora with real-time evidence from the original BNC and its 2014 update. The brachychronic approach can also be pursued with the *Strathy Corpus* of CanE, which was originally sampled on the basis of the Brown sampling frame and since expanded to include more recent material as well as spoken data.

[24] Incidentally, the corpus was introduced at the same time that Mair (1994) adopted the term "brachychronic" for recent and ongoing change (see Biber et al. 1994).

(Hundt 2012).[25] Collins (2015) compares COOEE with evidence from ARCHER for a number of morpho-syntactic features, which enables him to chart how AusE has shifted away from its matrilect and toward AmE, the center of gravity for various (recent) changes in English. Hundt and Szmrecsanyi (2012) and Hundt (2015) provide case studies on the progressive, the genitive alternation, and *do*-support in early NZE and AusE vis-à-vis BrE and AmE. Their results show that the direction of change is not necessarily one away from BrE to an American model but that some changes can occur in tandem.

As with synchronic corpora of WEs, the Web has also been used to collect mega-diachronic corpora of AmE and BrE (the *Corpus of Historical American* English, COHA, and the *Corpus of Late Modern English Texts*, CLMET, respectively), but there are no matching corpora of other WEs to enable cross-varietal diachronic research yet. In addition to the stratified corpora, a number of single-genre corpora exist, such as the *Corpus of Irish English Correspondence* (CORIECOR).

One of the challenges for the compilation of historical corpora of WEs, especially for the early stages, is the question when an emigrant should count as a speaker of the new variety (see Hundt 2012 for a more detailed discussion). For ESL varieties, a more serious problem is the availability (or accessibility) of material from the colonial period. It is therefore not surprising that the compilation of genuine diachronic corpora for ESL varieties has been seen as one of the central requirements for corpus-based research into WEs (e.g. Mukherjee and Schilk, 2012: 190; Hundt, 2016a: 345; Mair, 2018: 118). While there are no resources comparable to ARCHER, for instance, for ESL varieties, progress can still be made on the basis of other materials. On the basis of Legislative Council proceedings, Evans (2015) charts the development of regional lexis to demonstrate that Hong Kong English (HKE) shows the effect of nativization later than predicted in previous research: "If indeed English is being nativized in Hong Kong, this process is likely to have commenced at least two decades later than Schneider (2007) claims. This points to the need for an alternative periodization" (Evans 2015: 189). However, he also concedes that investigating lexical nativization is only one piece in the jigsaw puzzle: "Thus, if we wish [to, MH] test the model, we need to examine the framework as a whole, not just one element (lexis) of one of the four parameters (linguistic effects)" (Evans 2015: 192).

22.6 Outlook

The inception of ICE was an important milestone for the corpus-based investigation of WEs. The corpora have resulted in a rich body of existing

---

[25] The *Corpus of Early Ontario English* (Dollinger 2005) uses a similar sampling frame as ARCHER but is regionally restricted rather than providing a sample of early CanE as a whole.

research, of which only a tiny fraction could be reviewed in this chapter. While ICE is an immensely useful resource, its full potential has not been exploited yet, especially with respect to sociolinguistic variationist approaches. Making existing metadata available in a user-friendly interface is one of the developments that will hopefully further advance corpus-based research into WEs in the near future. One of the original deliverables of the ICE project – alignment of the original recordings with the transcripts (Kirk 2017: 373) – has not been achieved (with a few exceptions). It would provide an important additional avenue, especially for systematic cross-varietal socio-phonetic studies. In combination with statistical approaches that can deal with small and skewed data sets, researchers would be able to arrive at more fine-grained intra- and intervarietal descriptions of variation.

Despite the technical advances, mega-corpora of natural conversations from a broad range of WEs and a representative sample of speakers are still not available. With recent developments in machine learning and speech recognition, the digitization of spontaneous spoken language has become much less costly. This will hopefully advance corpus building in the near future. However, bigger corpora of spoken language will only provide useful if they are sampled carefully and fully documented, particularly with respect to speaker variables.

It is advisable to supplement evidence from synchronic corpora with historical data since patterns that are identified as instances of nativization in ESL varieties (e.g. the extension of pluralization to non-counts) may also have precursors in earlier stages of English (Hundt 2016b, Schneider et al., 2019). In other words, for the historical study of WEs, researchers not only need stratified diachronic corpora of ESL varieties to fill in the gaps but ideally also diachronic evidence on regional and nonstandard varieties of English to gauge the effect that different input varieties may have had on the development of WEs. At the end of the day, however, any corpus-based investigation of WEs needs to start from theory-informed hypotheses and should, ideally, feed back into advancing theories of WEs.

References

Corpora

ACE   = *Australian Corpus of English* (Written Australian English, 1986)
AmE06   = Web-derived 2006 *Brown Corpus* (Written American English, 2006)
ARCHER   = *A Representative Corpus of Historical English Registers* [www .helsinki.fi/varieng/CoRD/corpora/ARCHER/updated%20ver sion/background.html#history]
B-Brown   = *Before Brown Corpus* (Written American English, 1930s)

BE06   = Web-derived 2006 *LOB Corpus* (Written British English, 2006)
B-LOB   = *Before LOB Corpus* (Written British English, 1930s)
BNC   = *British National Corpus* (Spoken and Written British English, 1991–1994; 2014) [www.natcorp.ox.ac.uk]
Brown   = *Brown Corpus* (Written American English, 1961)
CENZE   = *Corpus of Early New Zealand English* (see Hundt 2012)
CLMET   = *Corpus of Late Modern English Texts* [www.helsinki.fi/varieng/CoRD/corpora/CLMETEV/index.html]
COHA   = *Corpus of Historical American English* [https://corpus.byu.edu/coha/]
CONTE   = *Corpus of Early Ontario English* (see Dollinger 2005)
COOEE   = *Corpus of Oz Early English* (see Fritz 2007)
CORIECOR = *Corpus of Irish English Correspondence* (see McCafferty & Amador-Moreno 2012)
Frown   = *Freiburg Brown Corpus* (Written American English, 1992)
FLOB   = *Freiburg LOB Corpus* (Written British English, 1991)
GloWbE   = *Corpus of Global Web-based English* (web-based corpus of World Englishes, approximately 1.9 million words) [www.english-corpora.org/glowbe/]
ICE   = *International Corpus of English* [www.ice-corpora.uzh.ch]
ICLE   = *International Corpus of Learner English* (Corpus of argumentative essays from university learners of English as a foreign language, with various first language backgrounds) [https://uclouvain.be/en/research-institutes/ilc/cecl/icle.html]
Kolhapur   = The *Kolhapur Corpus of Indian English* (Written Indian English, 1978)
LINDSEI   = *Louvain International Database of Spoken English Interlanguage* (Spoken learner interview data, various first languages) [https://uclouvain.be/en/research-institutes/ilc/cecl/lindsei.html]
LOB   = *London-Oslo-Bergen Corpus* (Written British English, 1961)
NOW   = *News on the Web* (web-based monitor corpus of newspaper archives from twenty countries; since 2010) [www.english-corpora.org/now/]
Strathy   = *Strathy Corpus of Canadian English* (spoken and written Canadian English, 50 million words; data from the early 1980s until 2010; available at BYU) [www.queensu.ca/strathy/corpus]
WWC   = *Wellington Corpus of Written New Zealand English* (Written New Zealand English, 1986)

Secondary Sources

Agire, Eneko, Timothy Baldwin and David Martinez. 2008. Improving parsing and PP attachment performance with sense information. *Proceedings of ACL-08*: 317–325. www.aclweb.org/anthology/P08-1037

Anderwald, Lieselotte. 2014. Burned, dwelled, dreamed: The evolution of a morphological Americanism, and the role of prescriptive grammar writing. *American Speech 89*: 408–440.

Bailey, Richard W. 1990. English at its twilight. In Christopher Ricks and Leonard Michaels, eds. *The State of the Language*. London: Faber and Faber, 83–94.

Baker, Paul. 2017. *American and British English: Divided by a Common Language?* Cambridge: Cambridge University Press.

Bao, Zhiming. 2010. A usage-based approach to substratum transfer: The case of four unproductive features in Singapore English. *Language 86*(4): 792–820.

Bao, Zhiming and Lionel Wee. 1999. The passive in Singapore English. *World Englishes 18*(1): 1–11.

Biber, Douglas. 1985. Investigating macroscopic textual variation through multifeature/multidimensional analyses. *Linguistics 23*(2): 337–360.

Biber, Douglas. 1988. *Variation across Speech and Writing*. Cambridge: Cambridge University Press.

Biber, Douglas. 1993. Representativeness in corpus design. *Literary and Linguistic Computing 8*(4): 243–257.

Biber, Douglas, Susand Conrad and Randi Reppen. 1998. *Corpus Linguistics. Investigating Language Structure and Use*. Cambridge: Cambridge University Press.

Biber, Douglas, Finegan, Edward, and Atkinson, David. 1994. ARCHER and its challenges: Compiling and exploring A Representative Corpus of Historical English Registers. In Udo Fries, Gunnel Tottie and Peter Schneider, eds., *Creating and Using English Language Corpora*. Amsterdam: Rodopi, 1–14.

Biewer, Carolin. 2015. *South Pacific Englishes. A Sociolinguistic and Morphosyntactic Profile of Fiji English, Samoan English and Cook Islands English*. Amsterdam: Benjamins.

Biewer, Carolin, Marianne Hundt and Lena Zipp. 2010. "How" a Fiji corpus? Challenges in the compilation of an ESL ICE component. *ICAME Journal*, 34:5–23.

Biewer, Carolin, Tobias Bernaisch, Mike Berger and Benedikt Heller. 2014. Compiling the diachronic corpus of Hong Kong English: Motivation, progress and challenges. Poster presented at *ICAME* 35, Nottingham.

Bisang, Walter. 2009. On the evolution of complexity. Sometimes less is more in East and mainland Southeast Asia. In Geoffrey Sampson David Gil and Peter Trudgill, eds., *Language Complexity as an Evolving Variable*. Oxford: Oxford University Press, 34–49.

Brato, Thorsten. 2018. "Outdooring" the historical corpus of English in Ghana. *English Today 34*(2): 25–34.

Brunner, Thomas. 2014. Structural nativization, typology and complexity: Noun phrase structures in British, Kenyan and Singaporean English. *English Language and Linguistics 18*(1): 23–48.

Collins, Peter. 2015. Diachronic variation in the grammar of Australian English. Corpus-based explorations. In Peter Collins, ed. *Grammatical Change in English World-Wide*. Amsterdam: John Benjamins, 15–42.

Collins, Peter, Ariane Borlongan and Xinyue Yao. 2014. Modality in Philippine English: A diachronic study. *Journal of English Linguistics 42*(1): 68–88.

Collins, Peter and Xinyue Yao. 2012. Modals and quasi-modals in New Englishes. In Marianne Hundt and Ulrike Gut, eds. *Mapping Unity and Diversity World-Wide. Corpus-Based Studies of New Englishes*. Amsterdam: John Benjamins, 35–54.

Davies, Mark. 2012. Some methodological issues related to corpus-based investigations of recent syntactic changes in English. In Terttu Nevalainen and Elizabeth Closs Traugott, eds. *The Oxford Handbook of the History of English*. Oxford: Oxford University Press, 157–174.

Davies, Mark, and Robert Fuchs. 2015. Expanding horizons in the study of world Englishes with the 1.9 billion word Global Web-based English Corpus (GloWbE). *English World-Wide 36*: 1–28.

De Clerck, Bernard and Klaar Vanopstal. 2015. Patterns of regularisation in British, American and Indian English. A closer look at irregular verbs with *t/ed* variation. In Peter Collins, ed. *Grammatical Change in English World-Wide*. Amsterdam: Benjamins, 335–371.

Desagulier, Guillaume. 2017. The Indian exception: Complex prepositions in the Kolhapur Corpus. *Around the word*, December 20. https://corpling.hypotheses.org/284

Deuber, Dagmar. 2014. *English in the Caribbean: Variation, Style and Standards in Jamaica and Trinidad*. New York: Cambridge University Press.

Dollinger, Stefan 2005. Oh Canada! Towards the Corpus of Early Ontario English. In Antoinette Renouf and Andrew Kehoe, eds. *The Changing Face of Corpus Linguistics*. Amsterdam: Rodopi, 7–25.

Edwards, Alison. 2011. Introducing the corpus of Dutch English. *English Today 27*(3): 10–14.

Edwards, Alison. 2016. *English in the Netherlands: Functions, Forms and Attitudes*. Amsterdam: John Benjamins.

Edwards, Alison. 2017. ICE Age 3: The expanding circle. *World Englishes 36*(3): 404–426.

Edwards, Alison and Samantha Laporte. 2015. Outer and Expanding Circle Englishes: The competing roles of norm orientation and proficiency levels. *English World-Wide 36*(2): 135–169.

Evans, Stephen. 2015. Testing the Dynamic Model: The evolution of the Hong Kong English lexicon (1858–2012). *Journal of English Linguistics 43*(3): 175–200.

Fritz, Clemens W. A. 2007. *From English in Australia to Australian English 1788–1900*. Frankfurt: Peter Lang.

Fuchs, Robert and Ulrike Gut. 2015. An apparent time study of the progressive in Nigerian English. In Peter Collins, ed. *Grammatical Change in English World-Wide*. Amsterdam: John Benjamins, 373–387.

Gilquin, Gaëtanelle. 2015. At the interface of contact linguistics and second language acquisition research. New Englishes and Learner Englishes compared. *English World-Wide* 36(1): 91–124.

Greenbaum, Sidney. 1988. A proposal for an international computerized corpus of English. *World Englishes* 7(3): 315.

Greenbaum, Sidney, ed. 1996. *Comparing English Worldwide: The International Corpus of English*. Oxford: Clarendon Press.

Gries, Stefan and Joybrato Mukherjee. 2010. Lexical gravity across varieties of English: An ICE-based study of *n*-grams in Asian Englishes. *International Journal of Corpus Linguistics* 15: 520–548.

Gries, Stefan Th. and Tobias Bernaisch. 2016. Exploring epicentres empirically. Focus on South Asian Englishes. *English World-Wide* 37(1): 1–25.

Gries, Stefan Th., Tobias Bernaisch and Benedikt Heller. 2018. A corpus-linguistic account of the history of the genitive alternation in Singapore English. In Sandra C. Deshors, ed. *Modelling World Englishes. Assessing the Interplay of Emancipation and Globalization of ESL Varieties*. Amsterdam: Benjamins, 245–279.

Gut, Ulrike and Robert Fuchs. 2014. Exploring speaker fluency with phonologically annotated ICE corpora. *World Englishes* 36(3): 387–403.

Hansen, Beke. 2017. The ICE metadata and the study of Hong Kong English. *World Englishes* 36(3): 471–486.

Heine, Bernd, Gunther Kaltenböck, Tania Kuteva and Haiping Long. 2017. Cooptation as a discourse strategy. *Linguistics* 55(5): 813–855.

Heller, Benedikt, Tobias Bernaisch and Stefan Th. Gries. 2017. Empirical perspective on two potential epicentres: the genitive alternation in Asian Englishes. *ICAME Journal* 41: 111–144.

Hirschmüller, Helmut. 1989. The use of complex prepositions in Indian English in comparison with British and American English. In Gottfried Graustein and Wolfgang Thiele, eds. *Englische Textlinguistik und Varietätenforschung*. [Linguistische Arbeitsberichte 69]. Leipzig: Karl-Marx-Universität Leipzig, 52–58.

Hoffmann, Thomas. 2007. Complements versus adjuncts? A construction grammar account of English prepositional phrases. *Occasional Papers in Language and Linguistics* (University of Nairobi) 3, 92–119.

Hoffmann, Sebastian, Marianne Hundt and Joybrato Mukherjee. 2011. Indian English – an emerging epicentre? A pilot study on light-verbs in web-derived corpora of South Asian Englishes. *Anglia* 12(3–4): 258–280.

Höhn, Nicole. 2012. "And they were all like 'What's going on?'": New quotatives in Jamaican and Irish English. In Marianne Hundt and Ulrike Gut, eds. *Mapping Unity and Diversity World-Wide. Corpus-Based Studies of New Englishes*. Amsterdam: John Benjamins, 263–289.

Horch, Stephanie. 2019. Complementing corpus analysis with web-based experimentation in research on World Englishes. *English World-Wide* *40*(1): 24–52.

Hundt, Marianne. 2009a. Global feature – local norms? A case study on the progressive passive. In Thomas Hoffmann and Lucia Siebers, eds. *World Englishes: Problems, Properties and Prospects*. Amsterdam: John Benjamins, 287–308.

Hundt, Marianne. 2009b. Colonial lag, colonial innovation, or simply language change? In Günter Rohdenburg and Julia Schlüter, eds. *One Language, Two Grammars: Morphosyntactic Differences between British and American English*. Cambridge: Cambridge University Press, 13–37.

Hundt, Marianne. 2012. Towards a corpus of early written New Zealand English: News from Erewhon? *Te Reo: Journal of the Linguistic Society of New Zealand 55*: 51–74.

Hundt, Marianne. 2013a. Using web-based data for the study of global English. In Manfred Krug and Julia Schlüter, eds. *Research Methods in Language Variation and Change*. Cambridge: Cambridge University Press, 158–177.

Hundt, Marianne. 2013b. The diversification of English: Old, new and emerging epicentres. In Daniel Schreier and Marianne Hundt, eds. *English as a Contact Language*. Cambridge: Cambridge University Press, 182–203.

Hundt, Marianne. 2015. *Do*-support in early New Zealand and Australian English. In Peter Collins, ed. *Grammatical Change in English World-Wide*. Amsterdam: Benjamins, 65–86.

Hundt, Marianne. 2016a. Global spread of English: Processes of change. In Merja Kytö and Päivi Pahta, eds. *The Cambridge Handbook of English Historical Linguistics*. Cambridge: Cambridge University Press, 335–347.

Hundt, Marianne. 2016b. Error, feature, (incipient) change – or something else altogether? On the role of low-frequency deviant patterns for the description of Englishes. In Elena Seoane and Cristina Suárez-Gómez, eds. *World Englishes: New Theoretical and Methodological Considerations*. Amsterdam: John Benjamins, 37–60.

Hundt, Marianne. 2018. It is important that mandatives *(should) be studied* across different World Englishes and from a construction grammar perspective. In Paloma Núñez Pertejo, María José López Couso, Belén Méndez Naya and Ignacio Palacios Martínez, eds. *Crossing Linguistic Boundaries: Systemic, Synchronic and Diachronic Variation in English*. London: Bloomsbury, 211–238.

Hundt, Marianne, Carolin Biewer and Nadja Nesselhauf, eds. 2007. *Corpus Linguistics and the Web*. Amsterdam: Rodopi.

Hundt, Marianne and Ulrike Gut, eds. 2012. *Mapping Unity and Diversity World-Wide. Corpus-Based Studies of New Englishes*. Amsterdam: John Benjamins.

Hundt, Marianne and Geoffrey Leech. 2012. Small is beautiful – On the value of standard reference corpora for observing recent grammatical change. In Terttu Nevalainen and Elizabeth Closs Traugott, eds. *The Oxford Handbook of the History of English*. Oxford: Oxford University Press, 175–188.

Hundt, Marianne and Joybrato Mukherjee. 2011. Discussion forum: New Englishes and Learner Englishes – *quo vadis?* In Joybrato Mukherjee and Marianne Hundt, eds. 2011. *Exploring Second-Language Varieties of English and Learner Englishes: Bridging a Paradigm Gap*. Amsterdam: John Benjamins, 209–217.

Hundt, Marianne, Melanie Röthlisberger and Elena Seoane. 2018. Predicting voice alternation across academic Englishes. *Corpus Linguistics and Linguistic Theory*. doi:10.1515/cllt–2017–0050

Hundt, Marianne, Gerold Schneider and Elena Seoane. 2016. The use of the *be*-passive in academic Englishes: Local vs. global usage in an international language. *Corpora* 11(1): 31–63.

Hundt, Marianne and Benedikt Szmrecsanyi. 2012. Animacy in early New Zealand English. *English World-Wide* 33(3): 241–263.

Hundt, Marianne and Katrin Vogel. 2011. Overuse of the progressive in ESL and learner Englishes – Fact or fiction? In Joybrato Mukherjee and Marianne Hundt, eds. *Exploring Second-Language Varieties of English and Learner Englishes: Bridging a Paradigm Gap*. Amsterdam: John Benjamins, 145–166.

Kachru, Braj B. 1985. Standards, codification and sociolinguistic realism: The English language in the outer circle. In Randolph Quirk and H. G. Widdowson, eds. *English in the World: Teaching and Learning the Language and Literatures*. Cambridge: Cambridge University Press, 11–30.

Kirk, John. 2016. The pragmatic annotation scheme of the SPICE-Ireland corpus. *International Journal of Corpus Linguistics* 21(3): 299–323.

Kirk, John. 2017. Developments in the spoken components of ICE corpora. *World Englishes* 36(3): 371–386.

Kruger, Haidee and Bertus van Rooy. 2018. Register variation in written contact varieties of English. A multidimensional analysis. *English World-Wide* 39(2): 214–242.

Lange, Claudia. 2009. "Where's the party *yaar!*" Discourse particles in Indian English. In Thomas Hoffmann and Lucia Siebers, eds. *World Englishes: Problems, Properties and Prospects*. Amsterdam: Benjamins, 207–225.

Lange, Claudia. 2018. Indian English or Indian Englishes? Accounting for speakers' multilingual repertoires in corpora of postcolonial Englishes. In Arja Nurmi, Tanja Rütten and Päivi Pahta, eds. *Challenging the Myth of Monolingual Corpora*. Amsterdam: Brill, 16–38.

Leech, Geoffrey. 2007. New resources or just better old ones? The Holy Grail of representativeness. In Marianne Hundt, Nadja Nesselhauf and Carolin Biewer, eds. *Corpus Linguistics and the Web*. Amsterdam: Rodopi, 133–149.

Leech, Geoffrey, Marianne Hundt, Christian Mair and Nicholas Smith. 2009. *Change in Contemporary English. A Grammatical Study*. Cambridge: Cambridge University Press.

Lehmann, Christian. 1991. Grammaticalization and related changes in contemporary German. In Elizabeth Traugott and Bernd Heine, eds. *Approaches to Grammaticalization*, Vol. 2, Amsterdam: John Benjamins, 493–535.

Lim, Lisa, ed. 2004. *Singapore English: A Grammatical Description*. Amsterdam: John Benjamins.

McCafferty, Kevin and Amador-Moreno, Carolina P. 2012. A Corpus of Irish English Correspondence (CORIECOR): A tool for studying the history and evolution of Irish English. In Bettina Migge and Máire Ní Chiosáin, eds. *New Perspectives on Irish English*. Amsterdam: John Benjamins, 265–88.

Mair, Christian. 1994. Is *see* becoming a conjunction? The study of grammaticalisation as a meeting ground for corpus linguistics and grammatical theory. In Udo Fries, Gunnel Tottie and Peter Schneider, eds. *Creating and Using English Language Corpora*. Amsterdam: Rodopi, 127–137.

Mair, Christian. 2009. Corpus linguistics meets sociolinguistics: Studying educated spoken usage in Jamaica on the basis of the *International Corpus of English*. In Thomas Hoffmann and Lucia Siebers, eds. *World Englishes: Problems, Properties and Prospects*. Amsterdam: John Benjamins, 39–60.

Mair, Christian. 2018. World Englishes and corpora. In Markku Filppula, Juhani Klemola and Devyani Sharma, eds. *The Oxford Handbook of World Englishes*. Oxford: Oxford University Press, 103–122.

Mair, Christian and Claudia Winkle. 2012. Change from *to*-infinitive to bare infinitive in specificational cleft sentences: Data from World Englishes. In Marianne Hundt and Ulrike Gut, eds. *Mapping Unity and Diversity World-Wide: Corpus-Based Studies of New Englishes*. Amsterdam: John Benjamins, 243–262.

Mukherjee, Joybrato and Stefan Th. Gries. 2009. Collostructional nativisation in new Englishes: Verb-construction associations in the International Corpus of English. *English World-Wide* 30(1): 27–51.

Mukherjee, Joybrato and Marianne Hundt, eds. 2011. *Exploring Second-Language Varieties of English and Learner Englishes: Bridging a Paradigm Gap*. Amsterdam: John Benjamins.

Mukherjee, Joybrato and Schilk, Marco. 2012. Exploring variation and change in New Englishes: Looking into the International Corpus of English (ICE) and beyond. In Terttu Nevalainen and Elizabeth Closs Traugott, eds. *The Oxford Handbook of the History of English*. Oxford: Oxford University Press, 189–199.

Nelson, Gerald, Sean Wallis and Bas Aarts. 2002. *Exploring Natural Language: Working with the British Component of the International Corpus of English*. Amsterdam: John Benjamins.

Parviainen, Hanna. 2016. The invariant tag *isn't it* in Asian Englishes. *World Englishes 35*(1): 98–117.

Peters, Pam. 2009. Irregular verbs. Regularization and ongoing variability. In Pam Peters, Peter Collins and Adam Smith, eds. *Comparative Studies in Australian and New Zealand English. Grammar and Beyond*. Amsterdam: John Benjamins, 13–29.

Rosenfelder, Ingrid. 2009. Rhoticity in educated Jamaican English: An analysis of the spoken component of ICE-Jamaica. In Thomas Hoffmann and Lucia Siebers, eds. *World Englishes – Problems, Properties and Prospects*. Amsterdam: John Benjamins, 61–82.

Sand, Andrea. 1999. *Linguistic Variation in Jamaica – A Corpus-Based Study of Radio and Newspaper Usage*. Tübingen: Narr.

Schneider, Edgar W. 2003. The dynamics of New Englishes: From identity construction to dialect birth. *Language 79*(2): 233–281.

Schneider, Edgar W. 2004. How to trace structural nativization: Particle verbs in World Englishes. *World Englishes 23*(2): 227–249.

Schneider, Edgar W. 2007. *Postcolonial Englishes: Varieties around the World*. Cambridge: Cambridge University Press.

Schneider, Gerold. 2008. Hybrid long-distance functional dependency parsing. Unpublished doctoral dissertation. www.zora.uzh.ch/id/eprint/7188/;

Schneider, Gerold and Marianne Hundt. 2009. Using a parser as a heuristic tool for the description of New Englishes. Paper presented at the Fifth Corpus Linguistics Conference, Liverpool, UK, July 20–23.

Schneider, Gerold and Marianne Hundt. 2012. "Off with their heads": Profiling TAM in ICE corpora. In Marianne Hundt and Ulrike Gut, eds. *Mapping Unity and Diversity World-Wide: Corpus-Based Studies of New Englishes*. Amsterdam: John Benjamins, 1–34.

Schneider, Gerold, Marianne Hundt and Daniel Schreier. 2019. Pluralized non-count nouns across Englishes: A corpus-linguistic approach to variety types. *Corpus Linguistics and Linguistic Theory*. doi:10.1515/cllt-2018-0068

Schütze, Carson T. 1995. PP attachment and argumenthood. *MIT Working Papers in Linguistics 26*: 95–151.

Sharma, Devyani. 2017. World Englishes and sociolinguistic theory. In Markku Filppula, Juhani Klemola and Devyani Sharma, eds. *The Oxford Handbook of World Englishes*. Oxford: Oxford University Press, 232–251.

Sigley, Robert and Janet Holmes. 2002. Looking at *girls* in corpora of English. *Journal of English Linguistics 30*(2): 138–157.

Szmrecsanyi, Benedikt. 2009. Typological parameters of intralingual variability: Grammatical analyticity versus syntheticity in varieties of English. *Language Variation and Change 21*: 319–353.

Szmrecsanyi, Benedikt and Bernd Kortmann. 2011. Typological profiling. Learner English versus indigenized L2 varieties of English. In Joybrato Mukherjee and Marianne Hundt, eds. 2011. *Exploring Second-*

Language Varieties of English and Learner Englishes: Bridging a Paradigm Gap. Amsterdam: John Benjamins, 167–187.

Szmrecsanyi, Benedikt, Jason Grafmiller, Benedikt Heller and Melanie Röthlisberger. 2016. Around the world in three alternations: Modelling syntactic variation in varieties of English. *English World-Wide* 37(2): 109–137.

Tagliamonte, Sali A. and R. Harald Baayen. 2012. Models, forests, and trees of York English: *Was/were* variation as a case study for statistical practice. *Language Variation and Change* 24(2): 135–178.

Unuabonah, Foluke Olayinka and Ulrike Gut. 2018. Commentary pragmatic markers in Nigerian English. *English World-Wide* 39(2): 190–213.

Van der Auwera, Johan, Dirk Noël and Astrid de Wit. 2012. The diverging *need (to)*'s of Asian Englishes. In Marianne Hundt and Ulrike Gut, eds. *Mapping Unity and Diversity World-Wide. Corpus-Based Studies of New Englishes.* Amsterdam: John Benjamins, 55–75.

Vine, Bernadette. 2000. Getting things done: Some practical issues in a functional investigation of directives in spoken extracts from the New Zealand and British components of the International Corpus of English. In Christian Mair and Marianne Hundt, eds. *Corpus Linguistics and Linguistic Theory.* Amsterdam: Rodopi, 371–374.

Volk, Martin. 2001. Exploiting the WWW as corpus to resolve PP attachment ambiguities. In Paul Rayson, Andrew Wilson, Tony McEnery, Andrew Hardie and Shereen Khoja, eds. *Proceedings of the Corpus Linguistics 2001 Conference, Lancaster, 30 March – 2 April 2001.* Department of Linguistics. No pagination.

Wong, May L.Y. 2010. Expressions of gratitude by Hong Kong speakers of English: Research from the International Corpus of English in Hong Kong (ICE-HK). *Journal of Pragmatics* 42(5): 1243–1257.

Woods, Anthony, Paul Fletcher and Arthur Hughes. 1986. *Statistics in Language Studies.* Cambridge: Cambridge University Press.

Xiao, Richard. 2009. Multidimensional analysis and the study of World Englishes. *World Englishes* 28(4): 421–450.

Zipp, Lena. 2014. *Educated Fiji English. Lexico-grammar and Variety Status.* Amsterdam: John Benjamins.

23

World Englishes from the Perspective of Dialect Typology

Benedikt Szmrecsanyi and Melanie Röthlisberger

23.1 Introduction

LINGUISTIC TYPOLOGY is concerned with classifying human languages and with identifying structural similarities and differences between these languages. DIALECTOLOGY is the study of typically vernacular and regionally restricted and/or distinctive forms of language. The intersection between typology and dialectology has received considerable attention in recent years (see, e.g., the papers in Kortmann 2004; Szmrecsanyi and Wälchli 2014): DIALECT TYPOLOGY (also known as SOCIOLINGUISTIC TYPOLOGY) is interested in the "extent to which differences of linguistic structure, whether within or between languages, can be ascribed to or explained in terms of features of the society in which the dialects in question are spoken" (Trudgill 1996:3; see also Trudgill 2004; Trudgill 2009a; Trudgill 2011). The aim of this contribution is to survey work on World Englishes that takes a dialect typology perspective, the remit of which we define rather generously as also including, for example, areal patterns.

This chapter is structured as follows. In Section 23.2, we set the scene by reviewing the set of language-external factors (variety type, world region, exposure to contact) that has been used to categorize World Englishes. Section 23.3 summarizes what we know about (vernacular) universals, angloversals, and related notions in World Englishes. In Section 23.4, we synthesize work on parameters of structural diversity in World Englishes (analyticity versus syntheticity, complexity versus simplicity). Section 23.5 offers some concluding remarks.

23.2   Language-External Factors

23.2.1   Variety Type

Needless to say, there are many fine-grained distinctions to be made regarding different types and subtypes of varieties of English, and these distinctions are meticulously covered in this handbook (see Hickey, Chapter 2, this volume). From a dialect typology perspective, the most basic typology customary in the literature, which is also used in reference works such as Crystal (2004) and Kortmann and Lunkenheimer (2013), distinguishes the following variety types:[1]

- **Native L1 (or "English as a native language," ENL) varieties of English**, such as Canadian English or New Zealand English. This type roughly corresponds to the Inner Circle in Kachru (1992).
- **Indigenized L2 (or "English as a second language," ESL) varieties of English**, such as educated Jamaican English or Malaysian English. This type roughly corresponds to the Outer Circle in Kachru (1992).
- An inclusive typology will also recognize **English-based pidgin and creole languages**, such as Tok Pisin and Hawai'i Creole, as a third type.

This typology is primarily defined based on language-external facts – in terms of how and when English is acquired (first-language acquisition versus second-language acquisition) and with regard to whether or not we are dealing with a contact language. Against this backdrop, dialect typologists have been primarily concerned with establishing those linguistic features that are particularly diagnostic of specific types. Szmrecsanyi and Kortmann (2009a) refer to such features as "varioversals" (see also Section 23.3), that is, "features recurrent in language varieties with a similar socio-history, historical depth, and mode of acquisition" (p. 33).

How are varioversals identified empirically? A common way is to utilize survey databases, similar to the World Atlas of Language Structures (WALS) (Dryer and Haspelmath 2013), which have become an indispensable tool in the field of cross-linguistic typology. One popular survey in the World Englishes literature is the morphosyntax survey[2] that accompanies the *Handbook of Varieties of English* (Kortmann et al. 2004). This survey of nonstandard English morphosyntax was conducted by compiling a catalogue of seventy-six nonstandard features. The authors of the chapters in the morphosyntax volume of the *Handbook* were then asked to rate the features in the relevant variety according to the following categories:

---

[1] We acknowledge that an argument could be made to include Learner Englishes in this typology; however, in keeping with much of the dialect typology literature we take the liberty to not consider Learner Englishes and refer the reader to Edwards and Seargeant (Chapter 15, this volume) instead.

[2] See www.varieties.mouton-content.com/

A   pervasive (possibly obligatory) or at least very frequent

B   exists but a (possibly receding) feature used only rarely, at least not frequently

C   does not exist or is not documented

The survey covers forty-six varieties of English around the world, all of which are vernacular (see Kortmann and Szmrecsanyi 2004 for discussion).[3] The survey reveals that the top L1 varioversals (i.e. morpho-syntactic features that are particularly characteristic of L1 varieties of English) include existential/presentational *there's, there is, there was* with plural subjects (e.g. *There's two men waiting in the hall*); *me* instead of *I* in coordinate subjects (e.g. *Me and my brother*); and adverbs having the same form as adjectives (e.g. *Come quick!*). The top L2 varioversals are lack of inversion in main clause yes/no questions (e.g. *You get the point?*); irregular use of articles (e.g. *Take them to market, I had nice garden, about a three fields, I had the toothache*); and leveling of the difference between the present perfect and the simple past (e.g. *Were you ever in London?, Some of us have been to New York years ago*). Finally, distinctive varioversals for English-based pidgin and creole languages include lack of inversion/lack of aux-iliaries in *wh*-questions (e.g. *What you doing?*); lack of inversion in main clause yes/no questions (e.g. *You get the point?*); and special forms or phrases for the second-person plural pronoun (e.g. *youse, y'all, aay', yufela, you ... together, all of you, you ones/'uns, you guys, you people*). It is clear that feature profiles like this can be interpreted in terms of language simpli-city and complexity in connection with the mode of acquisition (see, e.g., Szmrecsanyi and Kortmann 2009b and Section 23.4).

Beside this rather feature-centric view of variety types, dialect-typological work on World Englishes has also occasionally adopted a more holistic, variety-centric perspective: What is the extent to which variety type shapes overall similarities and differences between varieties of English? Szmrecsanyi and Kortmann (2009c) propose to use a statistical technique called Multidimensional Scaling (MDS) to address this issue. MDS (Kruskal and Wish 1978) is a well-known dimension-reduction tech-nique that translates distances between objects (in our case, varieties of English) in high-dimensional space into a lower-dimensional representa-tion. To establish aggregate distances between varieties, we may use the well-known squared Euclidean distance measure, which calculates the distance between any two varieties as the number of feature classifications with regard to which the varieties differ. Applying the technique to the morphosyntax survey that accompanies the *Handbook of Varieties of English* and merging the A and B ratings into an "attested" category (while

---

[3] There is also an updated version, the Electronic World Atlas of Varieties of English (eWAVE) (see Kortmann and Lunkenheimer 2013).

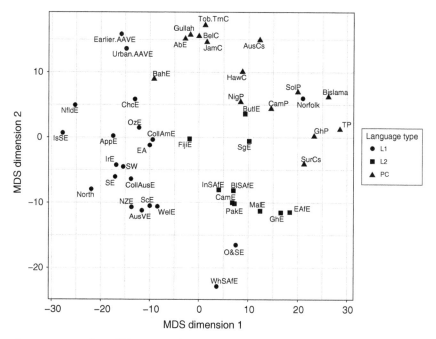

Figure 23.1 Metric Multidimensional Scaling (MDS) map, based on the morphosyntax survey from the *Handbook of Varieties of English* (see Kortmann and Szmrecsanyi 2004) Proximity between varieties in the plot is proportional to their aggregate morphosyntactic similarity.
Note. Abbreviations: E/R/UAAVE: Earlier/Rural/Urban African American Vernacular English; AbE/AborE: (Australian) Aboriginal English; AppE: Appalachian English; AusCs: Australian Creoles; AusVE: Australian Vernacular English; BahE: Bahamian English; BelC: Belizean Creole; BlSAfE: Black South African English; ButlE: Butler English; CamP/E: Cameroon Pidgin/English; ChcE: Chicano English; CollAmE: Colloquial American English; CollAusE: Colloquial Australian English; EA: East Anglian English; EAfE: East African English; FijiE: Fiji English; GhP/E: Ghanaian Pidgin/English; HawC/E: Hawai'ian Creole/English; InSAfE: Indian South African English; IrE: Irish English; IsSE/SEAmE: Isolated South Eastern American English; JamC/E: Jamaican Creole/English; MalE: Malaysian English; ManxE: Manx English; NfldE: Newfoundland English; NigP/E: Nigerian Pidgin/English; North: English dialects in the north of England; NZE: New Zealand English; O&SE: Orkney & Shetland English; OzE: Ozarks English; PakE: Pakistani English; ScE: Scottish English, Scots; SE: English dialects in the southeast of England; SgE: Singapore English; SolP: Solomon Islands Pidgin; SurC(s): Suriname Creoles; SW: English dialects in the southwest of England; TP: Tok Pisin, New Guinea Pidgin, Neomelanesian; Tob.TrnC: Creoles of Trinidad & Tobago; WelE: Welsh English; WhSAfE: White South African English.

C counts as "not attested") yields the MDS plot in Figure 23.1. In this plot, a nice three-way split emerges: The English-based pidgin and creole languages (e.g. Tok Pisin, Ghanaian Pidgin) are located in the right half of the plot, while native L1 varieties (e.g. Newfoundland English, dialects in the north of England) are located in the left half. Indigenized L2 varieties of English (e.g. Bahamian English, Fiji English, Malaysian English) are sandwiched in between, as it were. Therefore, in the big picture, variety type is clearly a major determinant of overall grammatical similarities and differences between varieties of English.

23.2.2 Areality

Areal patterns of linguistic similarity, possibly thanks to contact, is what takes center stage in both areal typology and in classical dialectology (see Murelli and Kortmann 2011), and so it is not surprising that areal effects in World Englishes have received attention as well: Do varieties of English spoken in, say, the British Isles share particular features that tend to be absent in varieties of English spoken in, say, North America? With regard to sound systems we know, for example, that British varieties of English tend to have an extensive system of diphthongs (Schneider 2004:1127), that West African varieties tend to have five-vowel systems, and that there is more generally speaking a list of sound features that are particularly diagnostic of regional accents, such as the TRAP vowel or yod-dropping (Schneider 2004:1129). In the realm of grammar, surveys such as Kortmann and Szmrecsanyi's (2004) show that British varieties tend to have, e.g., existential/presentational *there's, there is, there was* with plural subjects; that American varieties tend to have, e.g., special forms or phrases for the second-person plural pronoun; that Caribbean varieties often have, e.g., multiple negation; that Asian varieties regularly exhibit, e.g., irregular (from a standard English perspective) use of articles; and that African varieties more often than not attest a wider range of uses of the progressive.

More generally speaking, the areal null hypothesis is that geographical proximity between dialects or varieties should predict linguistic similarity between these dialects and varieties (Nerbonne and Kleiweg 2007:154 refer to this as the "Fundamental Dialectology Principle"). Yet precisely how important are such areal patterns, compared to other factors such as variety type? Consider Szmrecsanyi (2012), a study that is concerned with similarities and differences between thirty L1 varieties sampled in the World Atlas of Varieties of English (WAVE) (see Kortmann and Lunkenheimer 2012), a database that covers 235 morphosyntactic features. To shed light on relatedness patterns between those L1 varieties, the paper presents a NeighborNet diagram, which is reproduced in Figure 23.2. Originally developed in biometry and bioinformatics to map phylogenies and reticulate effects such as genetic recombination, NeighborNets are now quite popular in dialectology (e.g. McMahon et al. 2007) as well as in historical linguistics and in cross-linguistic typology (e.g. Dunn et al. 2008). Without insisting on a strictly phylogenetic interpretation, Figure 23.2 visually depicts – like the MDS map in Figure 23.1 – aggregate similarities and distances between L1 varieties of English. The diagram can be read like a family tree that is not rooted. Branch lengths are proportional to linguistic distance: Proximity in the plot broadly indicates morphosyntactic similarity. The most crucial split in Figure 23.2 we observe is between what Trudgill (2009b) would call "high-contact" L1 varieties (at the bottom of the diagram) and the other L1 varieties in the sample (more

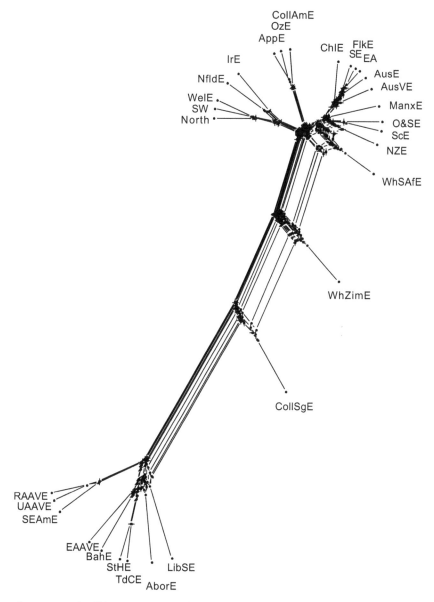

Figure 23.2 Visualizing aggregate similarities: NeighborNet diagram (after Szmrecsanyi 2012: figure 4, used with permission)
Distances (branch lengths) are proportional to cophenetic linguistic distances.
Note. Abbreviations: E/R/UAAVE: Earlier/Rural/Urban African American Vernacular English; AbE/AborE: (Australian) Aboriginal English; AppE: Appalachian English; AusCs:; AusVE: Australian Vernacular English; BahE: Bahamian English; ChlE: Channel Island English; CollAmE: Colloquial American English; CollSgE: Colloquial Singapore English; EA: East Anglian English; FijiE: Fiji English; IrE: Irish English; IsSE/SEAmE: Isolated South Eastern American English; LibSE: Liberian Settler English; ManxE: Manx English; NfldE: Newfoundland English; North: English dialects in the north of England; NZE: New Zealand English; O&SE: Orkney & Shetland English; OzE: Ozarks English; ScE: Scottish English, Scots; SE: English dialects in the southeast of England; SEAmE / IsSE: Southeastern US enclave dialects; StHE: St Helena English; SW: English dialects in the southwest of England; TdCE: Tristan da Cunha English; WelE: Welsh English; WhSAfE: White South African English; WhZimE: White Zimbabwean English.

on the distinction between high-contact and low-contact varieties in Section 23.2.3). In the "other" cluster to the top of the diagram, we find some areal subgroupings, such as Colloquial American/Ozarks/ Appalachian English (an American cluster) and Welsh/Southwest/North English (a British cluster). At the bottom of the diagram, we find another areal cluster consisting of Rural AAVE, Urban AAVE, and Southeastern American English. The upshot is that there are areal effects in World Englishes, but these are less important than other factors.

We note that the importance of geography and areality can be precisely quantified by correlating pairwise linguistic distances (as calculated by, for example, the number of feature classifications in WAVE with regard to which two varieties differ) with pairwise geographic distances (as the crow flies, in kilometers, calculated using a standard trigonometry formula). For the set of L1 varieties depicted in Figure 23.2, the correlation coefficient between morphosyntactic and geographical distances comes out as $r = 0.226$ ($p < 0.001$). In plain English, this means that there is a significant areal relationship, but geographical distance explains no more than 5.1 percent ($R^2 = 0.051$) of the morphosyntactic variability in the dataset. This is a comparatively modest share compared to dialectometry measurements in traditional dialects. Shackleton (2007), for example, finds that geographical distance explains about 49 percent of phonetic variation in traditional English dialects in England. We conclude that areal patterns and geography are not particularly powerful explanatory factors in the realm of World Englishes, and so we turn to alternative factors, such as exposure to language and dialect contact, next.

23.2.3   Exposure to Language and Dialect Contact

Typological work aiming at cross-linguistic comparisons has often taken an interest in the impact that language contact has on the systematic distribution of structural features across the world's languages (see, e.g., Aikhenvald and Dixon 2001; Siemund and Kintana 2008). Such research has focused on disentangling the mechanisms and principles of contact-induced change, specifically the constraints (linguistic as well as social) that influence the outcome of language contact (Siemund 2008:3). For instance, factors such as the degree of bilingualism, architecture, and prestige of the languages involved; the number of speakers; the length of contact; and numerous other parameters (see Siemund 2008:4) have been scrutinized with regard to their influence on contact-based structural similarities between languages. Research in areal typology (see previous section) has further shown that these structural similarities can also arise between genetically unrelated languages in what has been called "*Sprachbund*" or "linguistic areas" (see Matras 2009: 236, 266).

The typological literature on the mechanisms and principles involved in language contact has stimulated dialectological work on World Englishes.

Spearheading this line of research was Peter Trudgill, who argues that language and dialect contact was and is the driving force for the diversification and emergence of new varieties (see Trudgill et al. 2000; Trudgill 2006; Trudgill 2008). Crucially, Trudgill (2009b: 320) proposes a typological split between "low-contact" varieties – long-established mother-tongue dialects – and "high-contact" varieties including the following:

- Non-native indigenized L2 varieties: e.g. Indian English, Hong Kong English, Philippine English, or Jamaican English
- Transplanted L1 Englishes or (post)colonial standards: e. g. New Zealand English, White South African English, or Maltese English
- Language-shift Englishes: e. g. Irish and Welsh English
- Standard L1 varieties: e. g. British and American English
- Creoles: e.g. Hawai'i Creole or Tok Pisin (see also Kortmann and Szmrecsanyi 2011: 15–16)

Needless to say, it is "high-contact" varieties that are of particular interest when it comes to language and dialect contact. During colonization, transplanted varieties of English were in contact with indigenous languages and a range of European languages. As a consequence, newly emerging varieties of English borrowed linguistic elements from other languages, for example *cookie* from Dutch or *mana* from Maori (Trudgill 2006: 267). Most importantly, however, colonization inevitably led to contact between various speakers of different (British) English dialects.

While it is agreed that new varieties of English emerge out of contact with other dialects and languages, predicting the structural outcome of such contact is a challenging task (Siemund 2008: 3). Researchers have provided evidence for both complexification and simplification as results of contact-induced change (see Section 23.4.2). Schreier (2016) has challenged the binary distinction between high-contact and low-contact contact varieties. He argues that the degree of similarity between the languages/dialects in contact is more important than the degree of contact (Schreier 2016: 145), as simplification only seems to occur in high-contact situations if the two linguistic systems are maximally different from each other. This difference between linguistic systems in high-contact scenarios is a crucial one if one distinguishes between dialect (same language) and language (different languages) contact settings. According to Schreier, it is language contact settings that lead to simplification while dialect contact settings do not.

The difference between language and dialect contact varieties becomes even more evident in the acquisition process: In dialect contact scenarios, the majority of language learners are children who select various features from the heterogeneous input of the feature pool (Trudgill 2010). Childhood language acquisition results in an increase of linguistic variants and complexification, as in the case of New Zealand English, Canadian English, or American English. In language contact scenarios, adults acquire English as a second language, which inevitably leads to simplification due to the limited language-acquisition abilities of adult learners (e.g. India, Singapore, or Hong Kong English) (Trudgill 2010). Since we expect to find simplification in those varieties where English is spoken by adult learners, and to find signs of complexification in those varieties where English has been acquired by (bilingual) children, the prediction is that there is more simplification in indigenized L2 varieties of English compared to colonial L1 varieties. Whether this hypothesis matches the facts will be discussed in Section 23.4.2.

23.3 Dialect Universals, Implications, and Related Notions

The quest for generalizations, also known as universals – what is it that human languages in general, or languages belonging to particular types, tend to have in common? – is an important topic in cross-linguistic typology and so has also inspired work on the dialect typology of World Englishes. Against this backdrop, Szmrecsanyi and Kortmann (2009a) present the following typology of universals:

(i) GENUINE UNIVERSALS (e.g. *all languages have vowels*);

(ii) TYPOVERSALS, i.e. features that are common to languages of a specific typological type (e.g. *SOV languages tend to have postpositions*);

(iii) PHYLOVERSALS, i.e. features that are shared by a family of genetically related languages (e.g. *languages belonging to the Indo-European language family distinguish between masculine and feminine gender*);

(iv) AREOVERSALS, i.e. features common to languages which are in geographical proximity to each other (e.g. *languages belonging to the Balkan Sprachbund have finite complement clauses*);

(v) VERNACULAR UNIVERSALS, i.e. features that are common to spoken vernaculars (e.g. *spoken vernaculars tend to have double negation*);

(vi) features that tend to recur in vernacular varieties of a specific language: ANGLOVERSALS, FRANCOVERSALS, etc. (e.g. *in English vernaculars, adverbs tend to have the same morphological form as adjectives*);

(vii) VARIOVERSALS, i.e. features recurrent in language varieties with a similar socio-history, historical depth, and mode of acquisition (e.g. *L2 varieties of English tend to use resumptive pronouns in relative clauses*).   (Szmrecsanyi and Kortmann 2009a: 33)

Orthodox typologists tend to be concerned with (i) to (iv), while (v) to (vii) are the realm of dialect typology. In what follows, we take the liberty to discuss the relevant notions in more detail.

According to Jack Chambers (e.g. Chambers 2004), VERNACULAR UNIVERSALS comprise "a small number of phonological and grammatical processes [that] recur in vernaculars wherever they are spoken ... not only in working class and rural vernaculars, but also in ... pidgins, creoles and interlanguage varieties" (p. 128). Chambers has specifically suggested the following features as candidates for vernacular universalhood:

- (ng) or alveolar substitution in final unstressed –ing, as in *walkin'*, *talkin'* and *runnin'*.
- (CC) or morpheme-final consonant cluster simplification, as in *pos' office, han'ful*.
- final obstruent devoicing, as in *hundret* (for hundred), *cubbert* (for cupboard).
- conjugation regularization, or leveling of irregular verb forms, as in *Yesterday John seen the eclipse* and *Mary heared the good news*.
- default singulars, or subject-verb nonconcord, as in *They was the last ones*.
- multiple negation, or negative concord, as in *He didn't see nothing*.
- copula absence, or copula deletion, as in *She smart* or *We going as soon as possible*.   (Chambers 2004: 129)

Chambers himself notes that the examples might be from English but since they are "primitive features, not learned" (and thus part of the language faculty), they cannot be restricted to English only (Chambers 2004: 129).

The putative ubiquity of such features is claimed to be unlikely to be due to sociolinguistic diffusion. Therefore, they must be "primitive features of vernacular dialects" (Chambers 2003: 243), unlearned and thus innate. For more discussion, we refer the reader to the papers in Filppula et al. (2009).

A related notion is that of ANGLOVERSAL(S), a term that is used in two different ways in the literature. While Mair (2003) uses the notion to refer to universals of postcolonial Englishes, Szmrecsanyi and Kortmann (2009a) – whose usage we follow here – define angloversals as being recurrent features in *all* varieties and types of English. Angloversals in this sense include, for example, lack of inversion in main clause *yes/no* questions (e.g. *You get the point?*); *me* instead of *I* in coordinate subjects (e.g. *Me and my brother were late for school*); and *never* as preverbal past tense negator (e.g. *he never came*) (Kortmann and Szmrecsanyi 2004: table 3).

In this connection, we should mention the related notion of "rara," that is, features that are rather infrequent in the languages of the world (e.g. Wohlgemuth and Cysouw 2010). Numerous reasons have been suggested for the infrequency of rara, such as their increased processing difficulty, the rara's malfunction in communication, and the low probability of rara arising in the first place (Harris 2010). In the realm of World Englishes, rara include the *after*-Perfect (e.g. *She's after selling the boat*) and the relative particle *at* (e.g. *This is the man at painted my house*) (Kortmann and Szmrecsanyi 2004: table 2).

Beyond the quest for universals, cross-linguistic typology also often takes an interest in co-occurrence patterns of linguistic features, for the sake of learning more about how features evolve. The relevant patterns can be biconditional implications (for instance, "if in a language the genitive follows the noun, then the complement follows the adposition, and vice versa"; Greenberg 1963) or one-way implications (for instance, "if a language has a marked singular, it has also a marked plural, but not necessarily vice versa"; Greenberg 1966). Implications can be extended to what is known as "implicational hierarchies," which predict that if a language has a property at some point in the hierarchy it will also possess all properties further down the hierarchy (see Siemund 2013: 17). Again, these notions can be, and have been, fruitfully transferred to the study of World Englishes. To illustrate, Szmrecsanyi and Kortmann (2009c) study the morphosyntax survey coming with the *Handbook of Varieties of English* and find that 94 percent of the varieties covered in the survey either have both *ain't* as the negated form of *be* (e.g. *They're all in there, ain't they?*) as well as *ain't* as the negated form of *have* (e.g. *I ain't had a look at them yet*) or have neither. This biconditional implication is, needless to say, in line with the dialectological literature (Anderwald 2003: 149–150). Building on such observations, Szmrecsanyi (2017) puts the quest for co-occurrence patterns in World Englishes on a more solid quantitative footing and marshals multiple correspondence analysis (MCA) (Lê, Josse, and Husson 2008; Levshina 2015: 375–376) to study co-occurrence patters in the morphosyntax survey of the *Handbook of Varieties of English*. The technique explores how categorical variables (in our case, features) are associated with each other, and provides information about the behavior of individual observations (in our case, varieties): A particular variety will appear in the same part of the plot as the values of the features by which the variety is characterized. The World Englishes MCA plot is shown in Figure 23.3.

The picture that emerges from Figure 23.3 can be summarized as follows. In the upper left-hand quadrant, we find features such as serial verbs and *no* as preverbal negator, which are demonstrably characteristic of English-based pidgin and creole languages; and, indeed, the varieties that the MCA plot identifies as particularly attracted to these features (e.g. Australian Creoles) are all pidgins and creoles. In the upper right-hand quadrant three features are identified as particularly distinctive: *ain't* as generic negator before a main verb, *ain't* as the negated form of *have*, and *ain't* as the negated form of *be*. This co-occurrence pattern ties in with what was said already. Note additionally that the varieties located in this quadrant are all North American, indicating that – as is well-known – *ain't* is particularly characteristic of North American Englishes. In the lower right-hand quadrant the plot locates some British varieties as well as New Zealand English, a variety that is known to be fairly close to British English, at least in terms of grammar. Note that corpus-based studies can offer slightly different results in that they find New Zealand and Australian English often wedged between British and American English with diverging orientation toward one or the other depending on the part of grammar that one looks at (e.g. Hundt 1998). Distinctive features in this corner

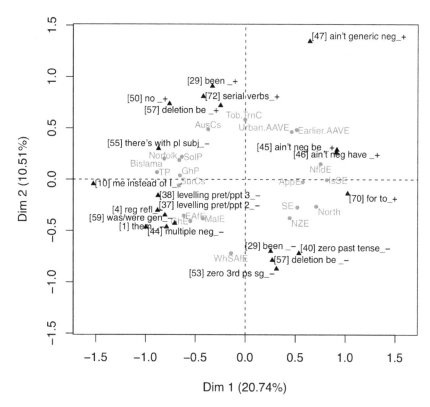

Figure 23.3 Multiple Correspondence Analysis (MCA) map, based on the morphosyntax survey from the *Handbook of Varieties of English* (from Szmrecsanyi 2017: figure 2) Proximity between features indicates co-occurrence patterns. Display is limited to the 20 features and varieties that have the highest contribution on the dimensions. "+" suffixed to a feature's label indicates presence of the feature, "–" indicates absence.
Note. Abbreviations: E/R/UAAVE: Earlier/Rural/Urban African American Vernacular English; AppE: Appalachian English; AusCs: Australian Creoles; EAfE: East African English; GhP/E: Ghanaian Pidgin/English; IsSE/SEAmE: Isolated South Eastern American English; MalE: Malaysian English; NfldE: Newfoundland English; North: English dialects in the north of England; NZE: New Zealand English; SolP: Solomon Islands Pidgin; SurC(s): Suriname Creoles; TobC: Tobagonian Creole; TP: Tok Pisin, New Guinea Pidgin, Neomelanesian; WhSAfE: White South African English.

include, e.g., unsplit *for to* in infinitival purpose clauses, while, e.g., deletion of *be* is typically absent. This distributional pattern is typical of British varieties of English (Kortmann and Szmrecsanyi 2004: 1162–1165). In the lower left-hand quadrant, we find primarily indigenized L2 varieties such as Malaysian English. MCA suggests that these varieties are characterized by the absence of features such as *them* instead of demonstrative *those*, and multiple negation. In all, therefore, the analysis would seem to suggest the following dialect typology: The most important dimension of variation (Dim 1) pits native varieties (right) against pidgins/creoles and L2 varieties (left). The vertical dimension (Dim 2) appears to be capturing a language–externally defined contrast between orientation toward North American English (top) versus orientation toward British English (bottom).

23.4 Parameters of Structural Diversity

Similarities between varieties of English are often discussed based on the trajectory of a variety's evolution (e.g. Schneider 2007), the status of English (e.g. the ENL/ESL/EFL distinction), the degree of contact (low vs. high), or shared linguistic (morphosyntactic) features (e.g. varioversals) as elucidated in Section 23.3. This section will introduce two sets of parameters to capture the structural diversity of World Englishes: analyticity vs. syntheticity (Section 23.4.1.), and complexity vs. simplicity (Section 23.4.2).

23.4.1 Analyticity vs. Syntheticity

The distinction between analytic and synthetic languages goes back to August Wilhelm von Schlegel (1818). Schlegel's original classification has been popular but has also received methodological criticism. Sapir (1921) proposes a classification that would allow languages to belong to more than one type and introduces a number of parameters along which languages should be categorized. Sapir's typology in turn influenced Greenberg (1960), who defined five indices to characterize languages, thus abolishing the need to assign languages categorically to one type (Greenberg 1960: 185). Greenberg proposed an essentially corpus-based method to classify languages and demonstrated that seemingly abstract typological notions are amenable to precise measurement through the calculation of text-based indices.

Drawing inspiration from Greenberg (1960), Szmrecsanyi (2009) and Szmrecsanyi and Kortmann (2009b) analyze the degree of grammatical analyticity and syntheticity, measured as an index of free versus bound grammatical markers per word, across a geographically widespread range of varieties of English. They define analyticity/syntheticity as follows:

– *Formal grammatical analyticity* includes all coding strategies where grammatical information is encoded with free grammatical markers defined as closed-class function words without any lexical meaning.
– *Formal grammatical syntheticity* includes all coding strategies where grammatical information is encoded with bound grammatical markers (see Szmrecsanyi 2009: 2).

A variety's degree of analyticity or syntheticity has been directly linked to mechanisms of simplification and complexification at work in dialect and language contact (see Section 23.2.3). According to Trudgill (2010), simplification results from widespread adult Second Language Acquisition (SLA) and manifests in two possible ways: regularization of irregularities and an increase in lexical and morphological transparency (Trudgill 2010: 307). Lexical and morphological transparency entails analytic structures where "the relation between form and meaning is as transparent as possible" and "every single meaning is expressed in a separate form" (Kusters 2003: 21). Languages that fall under Kuster's TRANSPARENCY PRINCIPLE are arguably more analytic and thus easier to learn for adult speakers (Trudgill 2010: 312). The most extreme cases where language contact results in simplification (and hence increased transparency/analyticity) are pidgins and creoles (see also Leufkens 2013; McWhorter 2001). On the other hand, it has been postulated that low-contact situations lead to complexification and arguably increased syntheticity. These hypotheses (namely that simplification leads to increased analyticity and complexification leads to increased syntheticity) have been tested using language data from varieties of English.

For example, Siegel et al. (2014) test the claim that we should find heightened analyticity in creole languages. Their study explores the coding of grammatical information (free vs. bound morphemes) in two English-lexified creoles (Tok Pisin and Hawai'i Creole) and – for benchmarking purposes – in a number of rural dialects of British English, non-native indigenized L2 varieties, transplanted L1 varieties around the world, and language-shift varieties. Using the Greenberg-inspired typological profiling method discussed in this section, their analysis shows that, indeed, creoles are significantly less synthetic than other varieties of English. That is, they exhibit a greater ratio of analytic versus synthetic structure. At the same time, however, it turns out that creoles are not necessarily more analytic (in absolute terms) than indigenized or native varieties of English. Figure 23.4 illustrates this by locating varieties in a two-dimensional syntheticity–analyticity space. As can be seen, both Tok Pisin and Hawai'i Creole use synthetic markers less often than other varieties of English but they do exhibit a similar degree of analyticity. We also see that L1 varieties and traditional British dialects exhibit more syntheticity and analyticity than some L2 varieties where zero marking is relatively frequent (see Kortmann and Szmrecsanyi 2011: 275). Hence, while low-contact scenarios in general seem to lead to more grammatical marking (the sum of both analytic and synthetic indices), high-contact scenarios typically level grammatical marking, especially of the synthetic kind.

A similar pattern has been observed by Callies (2016) regarding processes of structural innovations in New Englishes. Tapping into learner as well as indigenized L2 varieties of English, Callies (2016: 244) concludes that the processes at play in structural innovations rely on and result in increased morphological transparency and maximal "explicitness of form-meaning relations" in both variety types. A similar preference for transparent forms in structural innovations has been found by Laporte (2012) who explores the use of *to*-infinitives in causative constructions (e.g. *to make someone to laugh*) in some ESL and EFL varieties. Similarly, Steger and Schneider (2012) find an

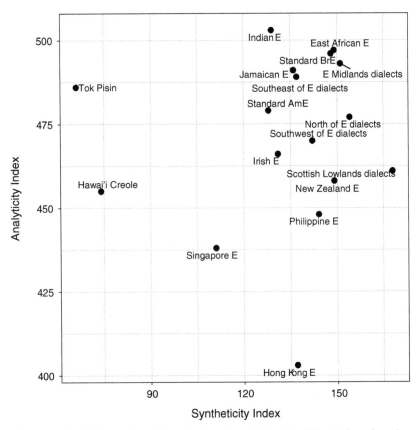

Figure 23.4 Tok Pisin and Hawai'i creole vis-à-vis varieties of English: total number of analytic types against total number of synthetic types (after Siegel et al. 2014: figure 2)

increase in the text frequency of overt complementizers in L2 varieties of English; Nesselhauf (2009) and Gilquin (2015) report usage of semantically redundant particles in (phrasal/prepositional) verbs in World Englishes (e.g. *enter into*) (see also Callies 2016: 246); and Mesthrie (2006) discusses "anti-deletion" in some L2 varieties, a tendency to use explicit markers where speakers of native varieties would omit them.

23.4.2 Complexity vs. Simplicity

Language complexity is a hot topic in both cross-linguistic typology and dialect typology. While twentieth-century structural linguists assumed all languages to be equally complex (see Sampson 2009 for an overview; also Newmeyer and Preston 2014), the issue of cross-linguistic and intra-lingual complexity differentials has increasingly received attention in the past few decades. The main idea behind the equi-complexity hypothesis had been the assumption of a trade-off between the different subsystems of a language: simplicity in one linguistic subsystem would be compensated by more complexity in another subsystem. This trade-off hypothesis has been challenged at the beginning of the twenty-first century (see, e.g., Gil 2008; Nichols 2009; Shosted 2006 whose empirical analyses give no indication of a trade-off; see, however, Sinnemäki 2014).

How is this relevant to (dialect) typology and World Englishes? In a seminal paper challenging the equi-complexity hypothesis, McWhorter (2001) argued that creoles are less complex grammatically than their lexifier languages

> by virtue of the fact that they were born as pidgins, and thus stripped of almost all features unnecessary to communication, and since then have not existed as natural languages for a long enough time for diachronic drift to create the weight of "ornament" that encrusts older languages. (McWhorter 2001: 125)

There is an emerging consensus that language complexity is indeed variable (see the papers in, e.g., Kortmann and Szmrecsanyi 2012; Miestamo, Sinnemäki and Karlsson 2008; Sampson, Gil and Trudgill 2009). Among other things, scholarship has sought to link observable complexity levels to language variation and change for the sake of understanding simplification or complexification as processes, as well as their language-external triggers. Moreover, the impact of sociolinguistic factors on language complexity has received special attention, as well as the ways in which complexity can be actually measured.

Researchers have been especially interested in the extent to which language-external factors fuel complexity variation. Trudgill (2001: 372) links complexity to adult language learning when he states that "[a]dult language contact means adult language learning; and adult language learning means simplification, most obviously manifested in a loss of redundancy and irregularity and an increase in transparency." Childhood bilingualism on the other hand results in complexification (Trudgill 2011: 42; see Section 23.2.3). Another important factor is intensity of language contact: Low-contact varieties seem to exhibit more complexity than those communities that are, or have been, subject to intense contact with other languages or dialects (Trudgill 2011). Other language-external factors whose impact on a linguistic system's complexity has been explored include age, sex, class (Sampson 2001), population size (Sinnemäki 2011), and geography (Nichols 1992; see also Trudgill 2016).

Analysts have proposed various measures according to which the complexity of *langue* or *parole* can be gauged. Most generally speaking, complexity measures can be dichotomized as follows (Miestamo 2008):

- *Global complexity measure* versus *local complexity measures*: global complexity quantifies the complexity of an entire language/dialect. Local complexity gauges the complexity of a domain-specific linguistic sub-system such as syntax or phonology.

– *Relative complexity measures* versus *absolute complexity measures*: measures of relative complexity assess subjective, user-oriented complexity (related to processing and learning). For instance, more complex linguistic phenomena are also more difficult to learn. Absolute complexity gauges objective, theory-oriented complexity by counting parts of the system such as the number of phonemes in a language.

More fine-grained categorizations would then go on to distinguish between, for example, absolute-quantitative complexity measures, where more material (bigger marker inventories etc.) equals "more complex," or redundancy-induced complexity, also called "ornamental complexity," where the amount of redundant linguistic material is counted toward a language's degree of complexity. SLA-based relative measures, too, are popular; they define language or dialect complexity as being proportional to the difficulty of learning the language or dialect in question.

In the World Englishes literature, the bulk of complexity-oriented research focuses on the difference in structural complexity between native and non-native varieties of English. For instance, Huber (2012) compares the results of structural nativization in the English relative clause system in Ghanaian English to present-day British English: The nativization of an already complex relativizer system can result in a similarly complex system where the structural factors that shape the choice of relativizer may have been assigned new importance but are still present overall. Also with regard to Ghanaian English, Schneider (2015) shows that future marker choice in Ghanaian English, an indigenized L2 variety, is less constrained by probabilistic factors (and thus, simpler) than it is in British English. Steger and Schneider (2012) explore the degree of iconicity and isomorphism in new varieties of English by looking at variable patterns in complement clause constructions. Adopting a cognitive-functionalist perspective, they define complexity as being a function of iconicity, that is, iconicity effects contribute to an increased transparency of grammatical encoding and hence an increase in simplicity. The authors find that iconic constructions are more popular in non-native than in native varieties and conclude that the cognitive principles at play during SLA lead to increased simplicity in second-language varieties of English (Steger and Schneider 2012: 187).

Kortmann and Szmrecsanyi (2009), finally, adopt a bird's-eye view and explore complexity patterns in, among other data sources, the morphosyntax survey that accompanies the *Handbook of Varieties of English* (Kortmann et al. 2004). They specifically inspect the seventy-six morphosyntactic features covered in the survey to identify (1) "simplifying features," that is, features or structures that simplify usage or the system, vis-à-vis standard English (an example would be leveling phenomena, such as leveling of preterite and past participle verb forms), and (2) "L2-simple features," that is features that are known to recur in interlanguage varieties, such as resumptive relative pronouns of the type *This is the house which I painted it yesterday* (see, e.g., Hyltenstam 1984). Subsequently, Kortmann and Szmrecsanyi establish the number of simplifying and L2-simple features attested per variety; the distributional pattern is visually depicted in Figure 23.5 (the *x*-axis, labeled "Rule simplicity," plots the number of simplifying features; the *y*-axis plots the number of L2-simple features). Two observations should be highlighted. First, on the whole, rule simplicity predicts L2 simplicity and vice versa. Second, there is a split between

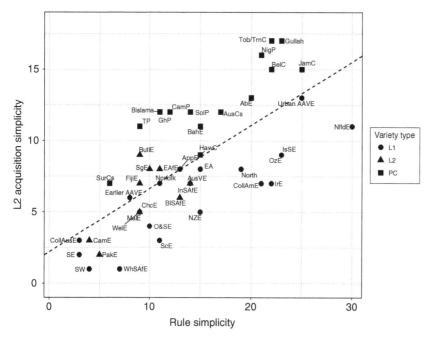

Figure 23.5 L2-simplicity by rule simplicity (after Kortmann and Szmrecsanyi 2009: diagram 1)
The dotted trend line represents linear estimate of the relationship.
Note. Abbreviations: E/R/UAAVE: Earlier/Rural/Urban African American Vernacular English; AbE/AborE: (Australian) Aboriginal English; AppE: Appalachian English; AusCs: Australian CreolesAusVE: Australian Vernacular English; BahE: Bahamian English; BelC: Belizean Creole; BlSAfE: Black South African English; ButlE: Butler English; CamP/E: Cameroon Pidgin/English; ChcE: Chicano EnglishCollAmE: Colloquial American English; CollAusE: Colloquial Australian English; EA: East Anglian English; EAfE: East African English; FijiE: Fiji English; GhP/E: Ghanaian Pidgin/English; HawC/E: Hawai'ian Creole/English; InSAfE: Indian South African English; IrE: Irish English; IsSE/SEAmE: Isolated South Eastern American English; JamC/E: Jamaican Creole/English; MalE: Malaysian English; NfldE: Newfoundland English; NigP/E: Nigerian Pidgin/English; North: English dialects in the north of England; NZE: New Zealand English; O&SE: Orkney & Shetland English; OzE: Ozarks English; PakE: Pakistani English; ScE: Scottish English, Scots; SE: English dialects in the southeast of England; SgE: Singapore English; SolP: Solomon Islands Pidgin; SurC(s): Suriname Creoles; SW: English dialects in the southwest of England; TobC: Tobagonian Creole; TrnC: Trinidadian Creole; TP: Tok Pisin, New Guinea Pidgin, Neomelanesian; WelE: Welsh English; WhSAfE: White South African English.

English-based pidgin and creole languages, which cluster in the upper right-hand quadrant (which means that they attest lots of simplifying and L2-simple features), and other varieties, which attest fewer simplifying and L2-simple features. What is surprising in this connection is that indigenized L2 varieties are not more clearly set apart from L1 varieties of English (see Kortmann and Szmrecsanyi 2009: 276 for more discussion).

23.5 Concluding Remarks

In this chapter, we have reviewed scholarship on World Englishes that is situated at the intersection between linguistic typology, a research field that is concerned with classifying human languages and with identifying structural similarities, and dialectology, which as a field is concerned with vernacular and regionally restricted and/or distinctive forms of language. Approaches that could not be discussed in this chapter but that are nonetheless relevant or at least neighboring to dialect typology include the extent to which variation patterns in particular varieties are rule-based or exemplar-based (see Baayen 2011 for some discussion); the potentially differential power of prescriptivism in different varieties (Hinrichs, Szmrecsanyi, and Bohmann 2015); and work that generates typologies of World Englishes by considering attitudes and transnational importance (Mair 2013). These are also topics whose interface with dialect typology would merit more attention in future research.

References

Aikhenvald, Alexandra Y. and Robert M. W. Dixon, eds. 2001. *Areal Diffusion and Genetic Inheritance: Problems in Comparative Linguistics*. Oxford: Oxford University Press.

Anderwald, Lieselotte. 2003. *Negation in Non-Standard British English: Gaps, Regularizations and Asymmetries* (Routledge Studies in Germanic Linguistics). London, New York: Routledge.

Baayen, R. Harald. 2011. Corpus linguistics and naive discriminative learning. *Revista Brasileira de Linguística Aplicada* 11(2): 295–328. doi:10.1590/S1984-63982011000200003.

Callies, Marcus. 2016. Towards a process-oriented approach to comparing EFL and ESL varieties: A corpus-study of lexical innovations. *International Journal of Learner Corpus Research* 2(2): 229–250. doi:10.1075/ijlcr.2.2.05cal.

Chambers, Jack K. 2003. *Sociolinguistic Theory: Linguistic Variation and Its Social Implications*. Oxford: Blackwell.

Chambers, Jack K. 2004. Dynamic typology and vernacular universals. In Bernd Kortmann, ed. *Dialectology Meets Typology: Dialect Grammar from a Cross-Linguistic Perspective*. Berlin: Mouton de Gruyter, 127–145.

Crystal, David. 2004. *The Cambridge Encyclopedia of the English Language* (2nd ed.). Cambridge: Cambridge University Press.

Dryer, Matthew S. and Martin Haspelmath, eds. 2013. *WALS Online*. Leipzig: Max Planck Institute for Evolutionary Anthropology. http://wals.info/

Dunn, Michael, Stephen C. Levinson, Eva Lindström, Ger Reesink and Angela Terrill. 2008. Structural phylogeny in historical linguistics: Methodological explorations applied in Island Melanesia. *Language* 84(4): 710–759.

Filppula, Markku, Juhani Klemola and Heli Paulasto, eds. 2009. *Vernacular Universals and Language Contacts: Evidence from Varieties of English and Beyond* (Routledge Studies in Germanic Linguistics 14). New York: Routledge.

Gil, David. 2008. How complex are isolating languages? In Matti Miestamo, Kaius Sinnemäki and Fred Karlsson, eds. *Language Complexity: Typology, Contact, Change*. Amsterdam: John Benjamins, 109–131.

Gilquin, Gaëtanelle. 2015. At the interface of contact linguistics and second language acquisition research: New Englishes and Learner Englishes compared. *English World-Wide* 36(1): 90–123.

Greenberg, Joseph H. 1960. A quantitative approach to the morphological typology of language. *International Journal of American Linguistics* 26(3): 178–194.

Greenberg, Joseph H. 1963. *The Languages of Africa*. Bloomington: Indiana University.

Greenberg, Joseph H. 1966. *Language Universals, With Special Reference to Feature Hierarchies*. The Hague: Mouton.

Harris, Alice C. 2010. Explaining typologically unusual structures: The role of probability. In Jan Wohlgemuth and Michael Cysouw, eds. *Rethinking Universals: How Rarities Affect Linguistic Theory*. Berlin: De Gruyter Mouton, 91–104.

Hinrichs, Lars, Benedikt Szmrecsanyi and Axel Bohmann. 2015. Which-hunting and the Standard English relative clause. *Language* 91(4): 806–836. doi:10.1353/lan.2015.0062.

Huber, Magnus. 2012. Syntactic and variational complexity in British and Ghanaian English: Relative clause formation in the written parts of the International Corpus of English. In Bernd Kortmann and Benedikt Szmrecsanyi, eds. *Linguistic Complexity: Second Language Acquisition, Indigenization, Contact*. Berlin: Mouton De Gruyter, 218–242.

Hundt, Marianne. 1998. *New Zealand English Grammar – Fact or Fiction? A Corpus-Based Study in Morphosyntactic Variation* (Varieties of English Around the World G23). Amsterdam: John Benjamins.

Hyltenstam, Kenneth. 1984. The use of typological markedness conditions as predictors in second language acquisition: The case of pronominal copies in relative clauses. In R. Andersen, ed. *Second Languages*. Rowley, MA: Newbury, 39–58.

Kachru, Braj B., ed. 1992. *The Other Tongue: English across Cultures* (2nd ed.). (English in the Global Context). Urbana: University of Illinois Press.

Kortmann, Bernd, ed. 2004. *Dialectology Meets Typology: Dialect Grammar from a Cross-Linguistic Perspective*. Berlin: Mouton de Gruyter.

Kortmann, Bernd and Kerstin Lunkenheimer. 2012. *The Mouton World Atlas of Variation in English*. Berlin: de Gruyter Mouton.

Kortmann, Bernd and Kerstin Lunkenheimer, eds. 2013. *eWAVE*. Leipzig: Max Planck Institute for Evolutionary Anthropology. http://ewave-atlas.org/

Kortmann, Bernd and Benedikt Szmrecsanyi. 2004. Global synopsis: Morphological and syntactic variation in English. In Bernd Kortmann, Edgar Schneider, K. Burridge, R. Mesthrie and C. Upton, eds. *A Handbook of Varieties of English*, Vol. 2. Berlin: Mouton de Gruyter, 1142–1202.

Kortmann, Bernd and Benedikt Szmrecsanyi. 2009. World Englishes between simplification and complexification. In Lucia Siebers and Thomas Hoffmann, eds. *World Englishes – Problems, Properties and Prospects: Selected Papers from the 13th IAWE Conference*. Amsterdam: John Benjamins, 265–285.

Kortmann, Bernd and Benedikt Szmrecsanyi. 2011. Parameters of morpho-syntactic variation in World Englishes: Prospects and limitations of searching for universals. In Peter Siemund, ed. *Linguistic Universals and Language Variation*. Berlin: Mouton de Gruyter, 264–290.

Kortmann, Bernd and Benedikt Szmrecsanyi. 2012. *Linguistic Complexity: Second Language Acquisition, Indigenization, Contact*. Berlin: Mouton de Gruyter.

Kortmann, Bernd, Edgar Schneider, Kate Burridge, Raj Mesthrie and Clive Upton, eds. 2004. *A Handbook of Varieties of English*. Berlin: Mouton de Gruyter.

Kruskal, Joseph B and Myron Wish. 1978. *Multidimensional Scaling (Quantitative Applications in the Social Sciences)*. Newbury Park, CA: Sage Publications.

Kusters, Wouter. 2003. *Linguistic Complexity: The Influence of Social Change on Verbal Inflection*. Leiden: Leiden University.

Laporte, Samantha. 2012. Mind the gap! Bridge between World Englishes and Learner Englishes in the making. *English Text Construction* 5(2): 265–292. doi:10.1075/etc.5.2.05lap.

Lê, Sébastien, Julie Josse and François Husson. 2008. FactoMineR: An R package for multivariate analysis. *Journal of Statistical Software* 25(1): 1–18.

Leufkens, Sterre. 2013. The transparency of creoles. *Journal of Pidgin and Creole Languages* 28(2): 323–362.

Levshina, Natalia. 2015. *How to Do Linguistics with R: Data Exploration and Statistical Analysis*. Amsterdam: John Benjamins.

Mair, Christian. 2003. Kreolismen und verbales Identitätsmanagement im geschriebenen jamaikanischen Englisch. In E. Vogel, A. Napp and W. Lutterer, eds. *Zwischen Ausgrenzung und Hybridisierung*. Würzburg: Ergon, 79–96.

Mair, Christian. 2013. The World System of Englishes: Accounting for the transnational importance of mobile and mediated vernaculars. *English World-Wide 34*(3): 253–278. doi:10.1075/eww.34.3.01mai.

Matras, Yaron. 2009. *Language Contact*. Cambridge: Cambridge University Press.

McMahon, April, Paul Heggarty, Robert McMahon and Warren Maguire. 2007. The sound patterns of Englishes: Representing phonetic similarity. *English Language and Linguistics 11*(1): 113–142.

McWhorter, John. 2001. The world's simplest grammars are creole grammars. *Linguistic Typology 5*: 125–166.

Mesthrie, Rajend. 2006. Anti-deletions in an L2 grammar: A study of Black South African English mesolect. *English World-Wide 27*(2): 111–145.

Miestamo, Matti. 2008. Grammatical complexity in a cross-linguistic perspective. In Matti Miestamo, Kaius Sinnemäki and Fred Karlsson, eds. *Language Complexity: Typology, Contact, Change*. Amsterdam: John Benjamins, 23–41.

Miestamo, Matti, Kaius Sinnemäki and Fred Karlsson, eds. 2008. *Language Complexity: Typology, Contact, Change*. Amsterdam: John Benjamins.

Murelli, Adriano and Bernd Kortmann. 2011. 28 Non-standard varieties in the areal typology of Europe. In Bernd Kortmann and Johan van der Auwera, eds. *The Languages and Linguistics of Europe*. Berlin: Mouton de Gruyter. www.degruyter.com/view/books/9783110220261/97831102202 61.525/9783110220261.525.xml

Nerbonne, John and Peter Kleiweg. 2007. Toward a dialectological yardstick. *Journal of Quantitative Linguistics 14*(2): 148–166.

Nesselhauf, Nadja. 2009. Co-selection phenomena across New Englishes. *English World-Wide 30*(1): 1–26.

Newmeyer, Frederick J and Laurel B. Preston, eds. 2014. *Measuring Grammatical Complexity*. Oxford: Oxford University Press.

Nichols, Johanna. 1992. *Linguistic Diversity in Space and Time*. Chicago: University of Chicago Press.

Nichols, Johanna. 2009. Linguistic complexity: A comprehension definition and survey. In Geoffrey Sampson, David Gil and Peter Trudgill, eds. *Language Complexity as an Evolving Variable*. Oxford: Oxford University Press, 64–79.

Sampson, Geoffrey. 2001. *Empirical Linguistics*. London: Continuum Press.

Sampson, Geoffrey. 2009. A linguistic axiom challenged. In Geoffrey Sampson, David Gil and Peter Trudgill, eds. *Language Complexity as an Evolving Variable*. Oxford: Oxford University Press, 1–18.

Sampson, Geoffrey, David Gil and Peter Trudgill, eds. 2009. *Language Complexity as an Evolving Variable*. Oxford: Oxford University Press.

Sapir, Edward. 1921. *Language: An Introduction to the Study of Speech*. New York: Harcourt, Brace and Company.

Schlegel, August Wilhelm von. 1818. *Observations sur la language et la littérature provençales*. Paris.

Schneider, Agnes. 2015. Aspect and modality in Ghanaian English: A corpus-based study of the progressive and the modal WILL. Unpublished doctoral dissertation, University of Freiburg.

Schneider, Edgar. 2004. Global synopsis: Phonetic and phonological variation in English world-wide. In Bernd Kortmann, Edgar Schneider, K. Burridge, R. Mesthrie and C. Upton, eds. *A Handbook of Varieties of English*, Vol. 1. Berlin: Mouton de Gruyter, 1111–1137.

Schneider, Edgar. 2007. *Postcolonial English: Varieties Around the World*. Cambridge: Cambridge University Press.

Schreier, Daniel. 2016. A true split? Typological and sociolinguistic considerations on contact intensity effects. In Raffaela Baechler and Guido Seiler, eds. *Complexity, Isolation, and Variation* (Linguae and Litterae 57). Berlin, Boston: Mouton de Gruyter, 139–157.

Shackleton, Robert G. Jr. 2007. Phonetic variation in the traditional English dialects: A computational analysis. *Journal of English Linguistics* 35(1): 30–102.

Shosted, Ryan. 2006. Correlating complexity: A typological approach. *Linguistic Typology* 10. 1–40.

Siegel, Jeff, Benedikt Szmrecsanyi and Bernd Kortmann. 2014. Measuring analyticity and syntheticity in creoles. *Journal of Pidgin and Creole Languages* 29(1): 49–85. doi:10.1075/jpcl.29.1.02sie.

Siemund, Peter. 2008. Language contact: Constraints and common paths of contact-induced language change. In Peter Siemund and Noemi Kintana, eds. *Language Contact and Contact Languages*. Amsterdam: John Benjamins, 3–11.

Siemund, Peter. 2013. *Varieties of English: A Typological Approach*. Cambridge: Cambridge University Press.

Peter Siemund and Noemi Kintana, eds. 2008. *Language Contact and Contact Languages*. Amsterdam: John Benjamins.

Sinnemäki, Kaius. 2011. *Language Universals and Linguistic Complexity: Three Case Studies in Core Argument Marking*. Helsinki: University of Helsinki.

Sinnemäki, Kaius. 2014. Complexity trade-offs: A case study. In Frederick J. Newmeyer and Laurel B. Preston, eds. *Measuring Grammatical Complexity*. Oxford: Oxford University Press, 179–201.

Steger, Maria and Edgar W Schneider. 2012. Complexity as a function of iconicity: The case of complement clause constructions in New Englishes. In Bernd Kortmann and Benedikt Szmrecsanyi, eds. *Linguistic Complexity: Second Language Acquisition, Indigenization, Contact*. Berlin: de Gruyter.

Szmrecsanyi, Benedikt. 2009. Typological parameters of intralingual variability: Grammatical analyticity versus syntheticity in varieties of English. *Language Variation and Change* 21(3): 319–353. doi:10.1017/S0954394509990123.

Szmrecsanyi, Benedikt. 2012. Typological profile: L1 varieties. In Bernd Kortmann and Kerstin Lunkenheimer, eds. *The Mouton World*

Atlas of Variation in English. Berlin: de Gruyter, 826–843. www
.degruyter.com/view/books/9783110280128/9783110280128.826/9783
110280128.826.xml

Szmrecsanyi, Benedikt. 2017. Featurometry. In Martijn Wieling,
Gosse Bouma and Geertjan van Noord, eds. *From Semantics to
Dialectometry: Festschrift in Honor of John Nerbonne*. Berlin: Language
Science Press.

Szmrecsanyi, Benedikt and Bernd Kortmann. 2009a. Vernacular universals
and angloversals in a typological perspective. In Markku Filppula,
Juhani Klemola and Heli Paulasto, eds. *Vernacular Universals and
Language Contacts: Evidence from Varieties of English and Beyond*. London:
Routledge, 33–53.

Szmrecsanyi, Benedikt and Bernd Kortmann. 2009b. Between simplification and complexification: Non-standard varieties of English around the
world. In Geoffrey Sampson, David Gil and Peter Trudgill, eds. *Language
Complexity as an Evolving Variable*. Oxford: Oxford University Press, 64–79.

Szmrecsanyi, Benedikt and Bernd Kortmann. 2009c. The morphosyntax of
varieties of English worldwide: A quantitative perspective. *Lingua*
119(11): 1643–1663.

Szmrecsanyi, Benedikt and Bernhard Wälchli, eds. 2014. *Aggregating
Dialectology, Typology, and Register Analysis: Linguistic Variation in Text and
Speech* (Lingua and Litterae 28). Berlin: Walter de Gruyter.

Trudgill, Peter. 1996. Dialect typology: Isolation, social network and pho-
nological structure. In Gregory R. Guy, Crawford Feagin,
Deborah Schiffrin and John Baugh, eds. *Towards a Social Science of
Language: Papers in Honor of William Labov, Vol. 1: Variation and Change in
Language and Society*. Amsterdam: John Benjamins, 3–22.

Trudgill, Peter. 2001. Contact and simplification: Historical baggage and
directionality in linguistic change. *Linguistic Typology* 5: 371–374.

Trudgill, Peter. 2004. Linguistic and social typology: The Austronesian
migrations and phoneme inventories. *Linguistic Typology* 8: 305–320.

Trudgill, Peter. 2006. Dialect mixture versus monogenesis in colonial
varieties: The inevitability of Canadian English? *Canadian Journal of
Linguistics-Revue Canadienne De Linguistique 51*: 265–286. doi:10.1353/
cjl.2008.0002.

Trudgill, Peter. 2008. The role of dialect contact in the formation of
Englishes. In Miriam A. Locher and Jürg Strässler, eds. *Standards and
Norms in the English Language*. Berlin: Mouton de Gruyter, 69–83.

Trudgill, Peter. 2009a. Sociolinguistic typology and complexification. In
Geoffrey Sampson, David Gil and Peter Trudgill, eds. *Language Complexity
as an Evolving Variable*. Oxford: Oxford University Press, 98–109.

Trudgill, Peter. 2009b. Vernacular universals and the sociolinguistic typology of English dialects. In Marrku Filppula, Juhani Klemola and
Heli Paulasto, eds. *Vernacular Universals and Language Contacts: Evidence
from Varieties of English and Beyond*. London: Routledge, 302–329.

Trudgill, Peter. 2010. Contact and sociolinguistic typology. In Raymond Hickey, ed. *The Handbook of Language Contact*. Malden, MA: Wiley-Blackwell, 299–319.

Trudgill, Peter. 2011. *Sociolinguistic Typology: Social Determinants of Linguistic Complexity*. Oxford: Oxford University Press.

Trudgill, Peter. 2016. The sociolinguistics of non-equicomplexity. In Raffaela Baechler and Guido Seiler, eds. *Complexity, Isolation, and Variation*. Berlin: Mouton de Gruyter, 159–170.

Trudgill, Peter, Elizabeth Gordon, Gillian Lewis and Margaret MacLagan. 2000. Determinism in new-dialect formation and the genesis of New Zealand English. *Journal of Linguistics* 36(2): 299–318.

Wohlgemuth, Jan and Michael Cysouw, eds. 2010. *Rara and Rarissima: Documenting the Fringes of Linguistic Diversity* (Empirical Approaches to Language Typology [EALT] 46). Berlin: de Gruyter Mouton.

24

Language Acquisition and World Englishes

Sarah Buschfeld

24.1 Introduction

English linguistics has developed various more or less related subdisciplines, of which Language Acquisition – itself again subdivided into subdisciplines such as First and Second Language Acquisition research – and World Englishes (WEs) research are only two of many. Over the years, both fields have developed their own, individual theoretical approaches, classifications, terminologies, and methodologies for investigation, as well as quite distinct perspectives on otherwise similar phenomena, viz. manifestations of acquiring/learning a language.[1] However, as early as 1986, Sridhar and Sridhar discerned "a lack of articulation between theories of SLA [second language acquisition] and research on the acquisition and use of IVEs [indigenized varieties of English]" (Sridhar and Sridhar 1986: 12) and prompted an integrated approach, a call largely unheard for about twenty years (see Hundt and Mukherjee 2011: 1; Nesselhauf 2009: 4). Since the beginning of the twenty-first century, only a few further studies have pointed to potential similarities and the connectedness of learner Englishes and WEs and the possibility, if not necessity, of an integrated approach to the two objects of inquiry (e.g. Ritchie 1986; Williams 1987, 1989). The majority of approaches from both fields, WEs and SLA, have disapproved of the idea of an integrated approach, with some of the

I thank the reviewers for their suggestions and comments on an earlier version of the manuscript, as well as Christiane M. Bongartz for sharing her expertise on some of the language acquisition aspects. All remaining shortcomings are my own.

[1] According to Krashen, a difference should be made between the notions of learning and acquisition. In his (1981) *Monitor Theory*, he differentiates between the two terms, with "acquisition" referring to unguided language acquisition in immersive, natural settings and the term "learning" to language learning in guided, classroom-based, formal instruction. Since his model and the two notions are not undisputed and have been criticized in recent years – and are ultimately not relevant for the discussion at hand – I use the term acquisition as a neutral denomination and cover term for the process of developing competence in a language, be it one's first language or any additional language, be it acquired in a natural immersive way or mainly through formal classroom instruction.

contributions openly stressing the alleged ESL/EFL dichotomy and consequently "the need for drawing a distinction between *English as a Foreign Language* (EFL) and *English as a Second Language* (ESL) varieties" (Szmrecsanyi and Kortmann 2011: 182; see also, e.g., Lowenberg 1986; Strevens 1992: 37). However, recently, first attempts have been made to "bridge" this paradigm gap by highlighting similarities in acquisitional route, mechanisms, and linguistic characteristics of second-language (L2) varieties and learner Englishes. The current chapter provides a state-of-the-art report of these developments, expanding the focus to the field of First Language Acquisition (FLA).

In a first step, Section 24.2.1 provides a summarizing account of the notions "learner English" and "second-language variety" and shows and discusses how the two concepts are related and what might set them apart. To underpin these theoretical reflections, I draw on findings from recent case studies. On this basis, I illustrate the need to bridge the paradigm gap long identified and discuss why the strict separation of WEs and SLA research does not meet linguistic realities and how the disciplines could profit from each other, in terms of both their findings and their methodologies (Section 24.2.2). Finally, I briefly present and discuss some recent theoretical reflections and attempts to integrate learner Englishes and second-language varieties (i.e. Schneider 2014; Edwards 2016; Buschfeld and Kautzsch 2017).

Section 24.3 extends the scope of this debate to the relationship of WEs and FLA research. To my knowledge, no explicit claim or empirical attempt has been made into this direction so far. Yet I argue that the same paradigm gap can be identified between these two subdisciplines and that the same line of reasoning is valid here, viz. that the acquisition of postcolonial Englishes as first languages (L1) – as, for example, found in Canada, Australia, New Zealand, but also recently developing in countries such as Singapore – underlies the same general mechanisms, strategies, and probably also developmental stages as English being acquired in the traditional native-speaker bases, viz. the UK and the USA. So far, FLA research often relies on data from monolingual speakers in these contexts – at least the major generative contributions that have produced many of the underlying theoretical approaches in the discipline.

To illustrate the need for an integration of the WEs and the FLA paradigms, Section 24.3.1 outlines an important recent change in the English Language Complex (Mesthrie and Bhatt 2008: 3–8) – a term that in my opinion is apt to capture the global spread and realities of the English language worldwide without a priori excluding any existing form of English – viz. the gradual development from ESL to ENL in some "Outer Circle" countries (e.g. in Singapore and Cameroon). Since this trend has been most prominently noted for Singapore (e.g. Bolton and Ng 2014; Gupta 1994, 1998; Lim 2007; Lim and Foley 2004; Schneider 2007; Tan 2014), Section 24.3.2 zooms in on this development and presents some findings from a pioneering, comprehensive empirical investigation of the acquisition of L1 Singapore English (see Buschfeld forthcoming b). I take a first step toward bridging the paradigm gap between the two disciplines and briefly discuss why the strict separation of WEs and FLA research does likewise not reflect linguistic realities and that the sole orientation on British (BrE) and American English (AmE) by FLA research is long outdated. In this respect, I also show how the two disciplines could profit from each other, again in terms of both their findings and their methodologies. With this in mind, I ultimately present and discuss some theoretical conclusions and methodological options for integrating the two fields of research (Section 24.3.3). Section 24.4 brings together the arguments and findings from the earlier sections and draws some final theoretical conclusions.

24.2 World Englishes Research Meets Second Language Acquisition

Apart from the few early attempts to raise an awareness of a potential interface between learner Englishes/EFL and second-language varieties of English/ESL (esp. Sridhar and Sridhar 1986; Williams 1987), the two concepts have traditionally been kept apart in the WEs paradigm and SLA research has not shown any particular interest in postcolonial second-language varieties of English. In fact, WEs research has mainly focused on the latter – as well as first-language varieties of English/ENL – and has largely neglected detailed analyses and an integration of EFL varieties in the WEs framework. Only recently has this potential interface experienced renewed research interest, especially by WEs researchers (e.g. Buschfeld 2013; Laporte 2012; Mukherjee and Hundt, 2011; Nesselhauf 2009), but learner Englishes and their acquisition are still largely treated as part of the SLA framework only; and this not only follows a very different methodological and often terminological approach but is also very different in its ideological orientation in that it traditionally has approached the nonnative types of English it deals with as deficient linguistic systems on their way toward native-like proficiency (with not too much hope that native-like proficiency can ever be reached)[2]. This difference in ideological orientation between WEs and SLA research is an important one and not only might be responsible for the strict separation of the two disciplines but is also hard to overcome. It is for this reason that WEs scholars have widely rejected the term "interlanguage," introduced and defined by Selinker (1969, 1972) as the individual's learning stages, including both their errors as well as non-errors, in their attempt to reach native-like proficiency. It is

---

[2] Note, however, that not all SLA approaches take such a negative orientation toward learner Englishes (e.g. the notions of "comparative fallacy" [Bley-Vroman 1983] and "multi-competence" [e.g. Cook 1999, 2007, 2010]).

precisely the orientation toward such external norms and the notion of "error" that, mostly for ideological reasons, is rejected in the WEs paradigm. Second-language varieties are considered language systems in their own right, often with their own (developing) norms and standards (see Hundt and Mukherjee 2011: 1–2; Mollin 2007: 171; Sridhar and Sridhar 1986: 8; Winford 2003: 245) and a comparison of the two concepts, let alone an integrated analysis, has thus "often [been] considered counter-productive to the acceptance of emergent norms in second-language varieties of English" (Götz and Schilk 2011: 80).

Yet this ideological stance seems to be rather unfounded for several reasons: First of all, the notion of interlanguage was not so much meant to highlight the deficiency of the learners' linguistic systems but primarily implies that it is a structured system independent of the target language or the speakers' mother tongue. In this respect, this notion even reminds us of the idea that WEs are speech systems in their own right (see also Laporte 2012: 266). What is more, the whole issue of norm-orientation and the ideological ideas revolving around this notion, that is, that second-language varieties are different from learner Englishes since they are independent systems that orient toward their own norms, often appears to be more of a scholarly figment than really representing linguistic realities. In many of the second-language varieties that researchers have described and identified as such, local linguistic norms are not fully accepted and speakers, though of course using local characteristics, still orient toward BrE or AmE as "good English" (see Kachru's notion of "linguistic schizophrenia"; e.g. Kachru [1977] 2009: 179; 1992: 60). On the other hand – and leaving the ideological side of this discussion – this chapter will show that, from a practical perspective, a convergence of the two disciplines would be advantageous for both and seems inevitable if we want to fully understand the nature of ESL and EFL, their relation-ship, and, most importantly, the global realities of the English Language Complex. Despite the discernible differences between ESL and EFL identi-fied in the following section (Section 24.2.1), recent case studies have shown that these differences are gradual (see Section 24.2.2) and that the categories have to be considered as two poles on a continuum (see Section 24.2.3).

24.2.1   Learner Englishes and Second-Language Varieties

The term "learner English" is closely connected to the notion of interlan-guage, which was first introduced by Selinker in 1972. It subsequently became one of the central notions in SLA research and has been taken up and discussed by various SLA researchers (e.g. Corder 1981; Gass and Selinker 2008). The term interlanguage (IL) describes the linguistic mental system of individual learners, that is, the individual stages and versions of the target language a learner passes through when acquiring a second or foreign language (Corder 1981: 66). This process is generally oriented toward a native-speaker norm, that is, the aim of the acquisition process is to achieve native-speaker competence on all linguistic levels, something achieved by only a small minority of language learners (Selinker 1972: 212–3). Selinker (1972) claims that the

> set of utterances for *most* learners of a second language is not identical to the hypothesized corresponding set of utterances which would have been produced by a native speaker of the TL [target language] had he attempted to express the same meaning as the learner.
>
> (Selinker 1972: 214; emphasis in original)

On the basis of this observation, he further hypothesizes that one has to assume separate linguistic systems in language learners, which strictly resemble neither the native language (henceforth NL) nor the target language (henceforth TL) systems of the learner (Selinker 1972: 214). With respect to the acquisition process itself, Selinker (1972: 215, 216–217) suggests that it is guided and influenced by five central mechanisms, viz. "language transfer," "transfer-of-training" (e.g. influence of how certain structures are taught, what is taught), "strategies of second-language learning," "strategies of second-language communication" (e.g. learners might stop improving their proficiency as soon as they think that they have mastered the TL sufficiently, i.e. that communication is ensured with respect to the needs given), and "overgeneralization of TL linguistic material." Since these mechanisms can also be clearly identified for the early stages in the development of second-language varieties, just because these also started as foreign languages being acquired by individuals, the crucial aspect that differentiates learner Englishes from second-language varieties is that the notion of learner language and the development of IL grammar apply to the idiolect of individual speakers. Second-language variety status is generally tied to language use in a speech community (see Buschfeld 2013; Mesthrie and Bhatt 2008: 157) and related criteria, viz. expansion in function of English, nativization of linguistic structures, institutionalization of these structures, and ways of language acquisition (see Kachru 1992: 55; Moag's 1992; Mollin 2006: 45–52, 2007: 170–173). As worked out in detail in Buschfeld (2013), the criterion "expansion in function" presupposes and at the same time causes widespread societal bilingualism and the intranational use of English in several domains (i.e. education, administration, media, and for intranational, interethnic communication). "Nativization of linguistic structures" is to be understood in Schneider's sense, that is, as "the emergence of locally distinctive linguistic forms and structures" (Schneider 2007: 71) on the different levels of language use (e.g. phonology, morphosyntax, lexis, or pragmatics). It involves the societal spread of these characteristics as well as a certain degree of systematicity in the use of them (for a detailed account of these characteristics, see Buschfeld 2013: 60–69). As a next step, an orientation toward a local norm may start to develop, which can ultimately result in "institutionalization," that is, the acceptance of characteristics as a local norm, the localization of usage domains (i.e. localization of creative writing, teaching, and the media), as well as codification. This last criterion has often been mentioned as characteristic of variety status. However, I do not consider it obligatory for variety status but as an indicator of a well-advanced developmental stage (e.g. phase 4, "endonormative stabilization," in Schneider's Dynamic Model) of a variety under investigation, because – as argued – many attested varieties still orient toward external norms but nevertheless employ nativized local features and are fully endorsed by their speakers (see Mollin 2007: 173). The last criterion of Buschfeld's (2013) criteria catalogue for variety status (for a similar catalogue, see Mollin 2006: 52, 2007: 173; see also Laporte 2012) is "ways of language acquisition," that is, the way in which English is acquired. In this respect, second-language varieties are normally acquired in a more natural, unguided way than English in EFL contexts, that is, often in direct interaction and before schooling starts, as opposed to mainly through formal language instruction.

Consequently – and not surprisingly in view of the fact that the strict differentiation between learner English and second-language variety has so long been upheld – certain criteria can be identified that differentiate second-language varieties from learner Englishes. However, these do not seem to be language internal, as the mechanisms at work at least in the early development of both types of English appear to be fundamentally similar, for example the mechanisms listed by Selinker (1972):[3] linguistic accommodation, simplification, overgeneralization, regularization, and language drift (e.g. Gilquin 2015: 97, 116–117; Mollin 2007: 171; Williams 1987; Winford 2003: 236, 243–245; see also Buschfeld 2013: 63, 72). The differences between the two types therefore evolve in the course of time due to extralinguistic factors and sociolinguistic developments in the respective speech community. Selinker (1972: 216) already suggested that fossilization[4] is not necessarily restricted to individual features but that it can occur for whole IL systems and – in this context – also for whole speaker communities, and he claims that fossilization was at work in the development of Indian English (Selinker 1972: 216). In other words, Selinker seems

---

[3] The influence of some of the mechanisms identified by Selinker on postcolonial Englishes certainly depends on the type of language policy pursued by the British and thus the overall acquisitional scenario in a territory. In this way, transfer-of-training, for example, is certainly stronger in territories where English is mainly introduced in education (e.g. in what Gupta 1997 has labeled multilingual scholastic English countries) than in speaker communities where English is mainly acquired through natural, direct interaction (e.g. in what Gupta 1997 has labeled monolingual ancestral English countries). However, the same considerations apply to those Englishes that fall within the realm of SLA research as there is a difference in acquiring English in a country where English is not the majority language (e.g. English acquired in Germany through mainly formal instruction) and acquiring English in a ENL country (e.g. in the USA in a mostly immersive way).

[4] Note that the notion of fossilization has experienced immense negative criticism since then (e.g. Long 2003). This cannot be discussed any further at this point and the notion is here considered in its sense of a more or less "stable" speech system that has developed over time.

to posit that the acquisition of English in the IDG strand first was subject to the typical mechanisms of language acquisition and started out as EFL, characterized by different interlanguage grammars. In the course of time, the linguistic repertoire became stabilized, systematized, and was culturally adapted – in other words, it underwent feature nativization; many of the structural characteristics of current Indian English have remained the same and originate from the initial interlanguage grammars (see Mollin 2007: 171; see also Williams 1987: 163; for a similar observation for Singapore Colloquial English, see Gupta 1994: 7). This observed continuity in feature quality of Indian English can be explained in terms of the acquisitional overlaps (i.e. the processes and mechanisms pointed out above) identified for the early development of second-language varieties and learner Englishes. As the following section argues, such overlaps in acquisitional processes and mechanisms must also be responsible for structural similarities between postcolonial and non-postcolonial non-native Englishes, in general, and those whose speakers share the same substrate language, in particular (see the studies by Buschfeld 2009 and Percillier 2016).

24.2.2 Bridging the Paradigm Gap: What Recent Case Studies Suggest About Linguistic Realities

Strong linguistic similarities between learner Englishes and second-language varieties were described as early as 1987, when Williams pointed to several morphosyntactic characteristics shared by or at least similar in learner productions and second-language varieties (Williams 1987). More recent research, mostly drawing on large-scale corpora, has reinforced this observation (e.g. Biewer 2011 on the use of modal auxiliaries; Laporte 2012 on the use of the verb *make*; Nesselhauf 2009 on co-selection phenomena).

Both synchronic and diachronic observations and case studies (to be outlined in the following) reinforce the idea that no clear-cut distinction can be drawn between second-language varieties and learner Englishes (and, consequently, WEs and SLA research) and that such a distinction cannot be made on the basis of the historical-political postcolonial/non-postcolonial divide. Two recent case studies (Buschfeld forthcoming a; Percillier 2016) empirically corroborate the above observation that learner Englishes and second-language varieties often share the same features, especially when their speakers have the same substrate language and thus acquire and use the English language in similar contact scenarios. Buschfeld (forthcoming a) compares English as spoken on Cyprus with English as spoken in Greece (henceforth CyE [Cypriot English] and GrE [Greek English], respectively)[5]. In both countries (for Cyprus the

---

[5] I use abbreviations for the label "X English" rather than the "English in X" here for reasons of economy and uniformity; I do not intend to imply anything about the status of these Englishes but use these labels as a neutral means of indication that they are spoken in the country under investigation as important additional languages.

investigation is limited to the Greek part), Greek is spoken as the first language by the majority of the population[6] and English is an important additional language.[7] The difference between the two contexts lies in the fact that Cyprus is a former colony of the British Empire, which exerted authority over the country between 1878 and 1960, while Greece is a country without a British colonial background. According to a survey of proficiency levels in English (European Commission 2012: 21), language proficiency is more widespread in Cyprus (73 percent) than in Greece (51 percent). A large-scale investigation by Buschfeld (2013) has revealed that, while in Cyprus English is widely used by all generations, in Greece it is mainly the young generation who has a good command of English. What is more, the situation in Cyprus is characterized by the existence of local and at least to some extent nativized characteristics of English on all levels of linguistic description, especially in the older group (Buschfeld 2013). When looking into the linguistic characteristics of GrE, many similarities are shared by the two Englishes, that is, GrE generally employs the same linguistic features as CyE (e.g. the use of zero subjects and objects, the use of definite and indefinite articles, intransitive usage of the verb *like*, and the time reference pattern *before X days/weeks/months/years*). Still, the question arises whether these features are as entrenched in Greece as they are in Cyprus. An exemplary quantification of two of the high-frequency morpho-syntactic features identified as characteristic for CyE in the mainland Greek data reveals clear and partially statistically significant differences between GrE and CyE (for details on the methodological procedure, see Buschfeld forthcoming a). Speakers of both communities employ the same local strategies for expressing hypothetical context, viz. they use *will*-future or simple present instead of conditional simple, as illustrated in Examples (1) and (2):

(1)   IE: What would you do if you won the lottery? [. . .]
       I: Uh uhm uh the first thing I **will make** with the first million, I **will take** it to the h& uh [//] to our house [. . .]. (CyE)
       [. . .] I **will have** the feeling that I'm save for the rest of my life, for the uh financial department. And uhm I'**ll give** some money to friends and relatives to make them feel better. And uhm I think I'**ll be traveling** a lot. (GrE)

(2)   I: Uh me, uh I **take** for myself one thousand-hundred. (CyE)
       I: I **give** some moneys to poor people. (GrE)

They also use the intensifier *too* + *much* instead of *very* + *much*, as illustrated in Example (3):

---

[6] Note that differences exist between the dialectal variants of Greek spoken in the two speech communities, viz. Standard Modern Greek and Cypriot Greek. These, however, are not fundamentally relevant when it comes to the question of feature nativization in the two countries and do not affect the comparison at hand.

[7] The "additional" here is used as a neutral means of describing the fact that English is spoken in addition to Greek, not suggesting anything about its status.

(3) I: [...] she love me **too much**, more than I. (CyE)

I2: I [...] told you ea& [/] earlier that uh I want to travel to& # [/] **too much**. (GrE)

Figure 24.1 illustrates the quantitative difference between the two contexts:

As both part (a) and part (b) in Figure 24.1 illustrate, the use of the local feature is clearly higher in Cyprus. In Greece, 58.3 percent and 91.32 percent of the participants employ the standard English variant, yet the percentage of nonconditional simple use is strikingly high in Greece as well and would surely pass as an entrenched form of local usage (for a discussion and suggestion on thresholds for feature nativization, see Buschfeld 2013: 63–66).

(a)

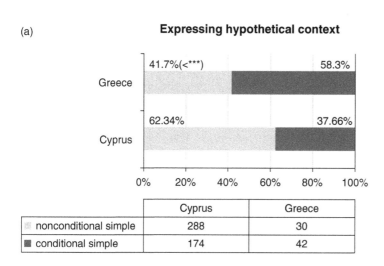

Expressing hypothetical context

	Cyprus	Greece
nonconditional simple	288	30
conditional simple	174	42

(b)

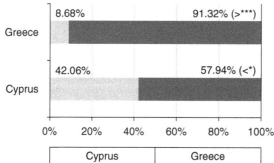

Use of intensifiers *very* and *too*

	Cyprus	Greece
too much	45	4
very much	62	42

Figures 24.1 Quantitative differences between CyE and GrE: (a) expressing hypothetical content; (b) use of intensifiers *very* and *too*

Percillier (2016) reveals some very similar trends by comparing three different Southeast Asian Englishes, viz. Singaporean (SingE), Malaysian (MalE), and Indonesian English (IndoE), which all have Malay (or a variety of it) as their substrate language. Percillier identifies thirty-four features from the different linguistic domains, of which only four occur in the nativized varieties but not in Indonesian learner English.[8] When reporting on and discussing the results in more detail, Percillier finds clear syntactic differences between IndoE, on the one hand, and SingE and MalE, on the other, with Singapore and Malaysia sharing "relatively similar frequencies of syntactic features" (p. 183). The phonological findings, however, reveal a different picture as MalE displays the highest rate of phonological local features, while feature frequency in IndoE lies between the formal and informal registers of SingE. Finally, his morphological findings show yet another tendency, viz. that MalE ranges between IndoE and SingE in terms of feature frequency. Different from his conclusion that "it is hard to fit morphology into any summarising maxim" (p. 184), this finding shows exactly what earlier research has argued, viz. that the differences between ESL and EFL cannot be as clear-cut as long assumed (something Percillier also concludes at a later point). What is more, the high rate of phonological features in all three varieties can be explained in terms of traditional SLA theorizing, which suggests (for learner Englishes) that native-like proficiency is most difficult to achieve on the level of pronunciation, which constitutes the greatest obstacle for learners. Such an explanation can also be valid for second-language varieties, when we assume that features originate in the interlanguage grammars of individual learners, are fed into a feature pool (for the notion of feature pool, see Mufwene 2001, 2005), and are then selected for systematization and widespread use on the community level, viz. undergo nativization. This should not deprive second-language varieties of their status as language systems in their own right or challenge the idea that they are not necessarily oriented toward some external standard.

A similar line of argument is pursued by Laporte (2012), who investigates the use and frequencies of the verb *make* in student writing in four second-language varieties of different evolutionary stages (Kenyan, Indian, Jamaican, and Singapore English) and in four learner Englishes (Japanese, Russian, French, and Dutch). Similar to the results of my comparison between CyE and GrE, Laporte (2012: 286) detects "significant qualitative similarities across both types of varieties . . . [d]espite quantitatively different trends" and concludes that this "further blurs the distinction between the concepts of EFL and ESL." The same has recently been confirmed by Koch et al. (2016), who investigate intrusive *as* in written second-language and learner English corpora.

---

[8] I here stick to the terminology used by Percillier. I would recommend using the distinction between "postcolonial" and "non-postcolonial," as this distinction does not make any presupposition about the status of English.

Looking into the developmental potential of some varieties, several scholars have pointed to their transitional character. Görlach (2002), for example, points to the ESL to ENL transition of Singapore English (pp. 107–108) and the ESL to EFL transition of Hong Kong English (pp. 109–110). Several later studies have reinforced this potential for transition from one category to the next (e.g. Buschfeld 2013 on the ESL to EFL transition in Cyprus, Buschfeld forthcoming b on the change from ESL to ENL in Singapore; Buschfeld and Kautzsch 2014 on the EFL to ESL development in Namibia; Edwards 2016 on the change from EFL to ESL in the Netherlands). In addition to that, some of these studies have revealed that development from or toward a specific variety type does not depend on whether a territory was under British colonial rule or not. Buschfeld and Kautzsch (2014), for example, show that, despite the fact that Namibia has never been a British colony, it has started to develop toward structural nativization and thus second-language variety status. On historically different grounds, Edwards (2016) traces a similar development for the Netherlands. When assessing both developments in terms of the criteria for variety status established by Buschfeld (2013), they show characteristics of both learner Englishes and second-language varieties and therefore have to be classified as hybrid cases to be located somewhere between EFL and ESL status.

Such fuzzy boundaries between EFL and ESL are also implied by the results of the Special Eurobarometer 386 (European Commission 2012: 21) for the use of English in the European member states. The survey has revealed important differences between the member states in terms of what their residents reported with respect to the role English plays when it comes to the "Languages that [they] speak well enough in order to be able to have a conversation." According to the results, proficiency varies greatly within the group of countries that would traditionally be classified as EFL territories, with Hungary coming in last with only 20 percent of its inhabitants feeling able to hold a conversation in English and the Netherlands at the top of this list with 90 percent. Cyprus and Malta, as the two member states with a colonial background, range in the upper third (with 73 percent and 89 percent, respectively) but below or on a par with non-postcolonial countries of the EU (see especially the Scandinavian countries, i.e. Sweden 86 percent, Denmark 86 percent, and Finland 70 percent). Even though it is not quite clear how exactly proficiency is measured here, these results certainly tell us something about current sociolinguistic realities in the EU and the status and roles of English worldwide – and are backed up by further empirical investigations: On the basis of an exemplary study into the use of the preposition *into* in the *International Corpus of Learner English* (ICLE), Gilquin and Granger (2011), for example, show that different types of learner English display different degrees of proximity to BrE, depending on extralinguistic factors such as type and degree of exposure to the target language (Gilquin and Granger 2011: 56,

74–75). On the basis of this finding, they convincingly argue that the concept "learner English" in itself is a complex one and opt for the term "learner English**es**," since this term more accurately reflects the diversity found among different types of learner English (Gilquin and Granger 2011: 74). In a similar vein, Biewer's (2011) study reveals such heterogeneity for ESL varieties as well, which she explains in terms of different degrees of nativization and cultural adaptation of the variety under scrutiny (Biewer 2011: 28).

24.2.3   Drawing Some Theoretical and Methodological Conclusions

Taken together, the above observations yield some important theoretical conclusions: The quantitative comparison of the two features in CyE and GrE and Percillier's (2016) findings on the differences and similarities between SingE, MalE, and IndoE show that differences in political and sociolinguistic background may indeed lead to differences in frequencies of use of local characteristics but that these differences are mainly quantitative and that the varieties under investigation are all very similar in terms of their qualitative properties. In general, the observed differences between ESL and EFL are rather unsystematic (see the differences Percillier observes with respect to the different levels of linguistic description and the findings for MalE as being located between IndoE and SingE; Section 24.2.2) and by no means large enough (also in quantitative terms) that they would justify a strict separation of EFL and ESL. The comparison of CyE and GrE has revealed that not every local characteristic we detect in a language variety is entrenched to the same extent. Feature frequency may vary among the individual features, depending on, for example, the level of linguistic description (e.g. phonological features may be more entrenched than syntactic features; see Percillier's [2016] findings on IndoE, MalE, and SingE) but probably also on factors such as overt or covert prestige of a form, salience, markedness, transparency, regularity (see also Schneider 2007: 110–112; Deshors et al. 2016: 139–140), and – often related to the other factors – the speaker's awareness of "correct" vs. "incorrect" language use, which is usually higher in the area of grammar than for pronunciation. Linguistic nativization within a variety therefore appears to proceed gradually with features to be located on a continuum of more or less entrenchment and indigenization. Together with the observation, made repeatedly, that speech communities may undergo changes in status from EFL to ESL or vice versa and that hybrid ESL-EFL varieties exist, this, too, corroborates the assumption that, when dealing with non-native Englishes, we are moving up and down a continuum of Englishes being more or less ESL or EFL in character (see also, e.g., Biewer 2011: 28; Buschfeld 2013: 74; Gilquin and Granger 2011: 76).

What the discussion so far has shown is that, even though well-defined differences between second-language varieties and learner Englishes do exist, the dichotomous distinction between the two types should not be considered as clear-cut as traditionally assumed. In reality, boundaries between the two concepts and thus between ESL and EFL are much more fuzzy. What this suggests in theoretical terms is that models and approaches building on this and similar classifications (also Kachru's categorization into Inner, Outer, and Expanding Circles) should be reconsidered (see also Hundt and Vogel 2011: 145). In order to grasp this fuzziness, the idea of an EFL-ESL-ENL continuum was already suggested by Platt et al. (1984: 22–23) as early as 1984 but was never really followed up on. The gradual change between the categories in their early EFL-ESL-ENL continuum is mainly attributed to an increase or decrease in functions.

In his 2003/2007 Dynamic Model, Schneider, however, convincingly shows that the picture is more complex and that not only the decrease in functions but the entirety of the sociopolitical, sociolinguistic forces that operate on the development of different Englishes have to be taken into consideration. Unfortunately, the Dynamic Model does not consider non-postcolonial Englishes, that is, it leaves out this segment of the English Language Complex that has traditionally been part of the SLA research paradigm but that has been shown to gradually and increasingly enter the WEs paradigm. Owing to this reason and on the basis of the assumption that understanding current developments of English worldwide and the English Language Complex in its entirety, an integrated approach toward postcolonial and non-postcolonial Englishes has been called for (e.g. Buschfeld and Kautzsch 2017; Gilquin 2015). Bringing together the idea of an EFL-ESL-ENL continuum, the major parameters and underlying conception of Schneider's Dynamic Model (especially the idea of a uniform process behind the development of different Englishes, along five characteristic stages, with the four parameters at work), and Schneider's (2014) conception of "transnational attraction," Buschfeld and Kautzsch (2017) have developed the Extra- and Intra-territorial Forces Model. To introduce the model in any detail here is beyond the scope of this chapter (for a detailed account, see Kautzsch and Buschfeld, Chapter 3, this volume; see also Buschfeld and Kautzsch 2017), but I would like to point out an important implication arising from such an integration: Treating postcolonial and non-postcolonial Englishes jointly, no matter how close or distant they are to the EFL/ESL poles, consequently requires the integration of SLA and WEs research – or at least strong collaboration – since conceptual borderlines are no longer easily drawn. As Biewer (2011: 29) has already poignantly pointed out: "SLA alone is not the answer, but without SLA we will never have an answer."

What can be concluded here is that, even if language acquisition is a psycholinguistic process in the first place (e.g. Gass and Selinker 2008: 279; Tarone 2000: 182), both fields should open up for the object of study of the other. Psycholinguists should increasingly ask "to what extent ... psycholinguistic processes [are] affected by social context" (Tarone 2000:

182; see also Gass and Selinker 2008: 279) and how research into second-language varieties could contribute to such a question (Williams 1987). WEs research, on the other hand, should turn to the following two questions: (1) How do WEs research and SLA tie in with each other and (2) how could WEs research benefit from what SLA theory has to offer, for example with respect to the psycholinguistic processes in the early phases of second-language varieties, the acquisitional stages taken by learners acquiring English as a second language under postcolonial conditions, and so on (see Biewer 2011)? As shown in Section 24.2, first important steps have already been taken in that direction. However, more detailed research is needed to answer these and related questions.

Having overcome the ideological barriers, the methodological options are manifold. A very promising approach lies in the comparison of large-scale corpora, which exist for both postcolonial and non-postcolonial Englishes. The latter are typically designated as "learner corpora" (e.g. the *International Corpus of Learner English* [ICLE] or the *Louvain International Database of Spoken English Interlanguage* [LINDSEI], both compiled at the Centre for English Corpus Linguistics at the Université catholique de Louvain, Belgium). These already have been compared to the huge amounts of ESL data we have and an increase in such a joint treatment of the different Englishes would be desirable (for a detailed account of how the corpus linguistic approach can be utilized for that purpose and potential limitations of such an approach, see Deshors et al. 2016). Apart from that, some other data collection procedures are similar between the two disciplines anyway (e.g. questionnaire studies) but WEs research could certainly also make use of psycholinguistic methodologies. This typically involves the validation of hypotheses or expectations by means of more formal procedures, often triggering specific linguistic constructions relevant to the investigation at hand by means of, for example, elicited narratives or acceptability judgment tasks.

Ultimately – and as a consequence of the above observations and conclusions – a quick note on terminology is required: Throughout this chapter, I have so far used the terms "learner Englishes" and "second-language varieties," "EFL," and "ESL," all of which, in principle, rely on a clear differentiation of these concepts. However, the preceding discussion has clearly shown that such denomination is often not accurate and that a premature labeling of a variety as learner English or second-language variety (or the respective corpora) is not adequate. The above discussion has shown that a categorization should definitely not be implemented on historical grounds only and that an in-depth empirical investigation of variety status (along the lines of, e.g., Buschfeld [2013] and Edwards [2016]) is mandatory; ultimately, one also has to keep in mind that hybrid forms exist, which defy classification as EFL or ESL altogether. For those varieties of unclear status, I would recommend approaching them as postcolonial or non-postcolonial when it comes to a first categorization, as this label is at least historically straightforward. However, one should keep in mind that this categorization does not suggest anything about their present-day status and that a comprehensive and empirical analysis is necessary that takes into consideration the entirety of the historical, political, sociolinguistic, and demographic factors at work in their development before one can really accurately assess their status. In my opinion, the ESL and EFL labels should only be used for those varieties of clear status and as points of reference when investigating, describing, and comparing varieties of English.

24.3 World Englishes and First Language Acquisition

The need to integrate postcolonial and non-postcolonial Englishes – and thus the WEs and Language Acquisition paradigms – is further reinforced by an interesting development in some of the postcolonial countries, viz. the acquisition of English as a first language in territories in which, for decades, people have spoken and used it as a second language (in addition to their respective native languages) for inter- and intranational communication. When treating these developments as manifestations of first-language acquisition[9] processes embedded in a WEs sociolinguistic framework – which they indisputably are – an in-depth understanding of these processes requires both an investigation and an understanding of the sociolinguistic realities of such speech communities as well as of the acquisitional aspects involved. The WEs paradigm, however, does not provide the methodological means for such an analysis and FLA research has mainly focused on the acquisition of British (BrE) and American English (AmE).

24.3.1 From ESL to ENL: Recent Changes in English Around the World

Today, more and more children who would not fall within the traditional category of "native speakers of English" acquire it as their first language, mostly in combination with one or more languages of their family's linguistic repertoires. This is particularly true for children growing up in some of the former colonies of the British Empire, for example Singapore or Cameroon. Referring to the latter case, Anchimbe (2012: 12) aptly notes that

> [o]ne criterion that changes the status of a second language is when it acquires native speakers, i.e. when it becomes a first language for many

---

[9] I use the term "first language acquisition" as a neutral means of denomination here. "First" here just refers to the fact that these languages are acquired by children as a language from birth and I do not intend to imply anything about language dominance in these mostly multilingual scenarios.

people. The New Englishes have not yet been elaborately described from this perspective, i.e. in relation to those who now speak them as their L1.

The reason for this, Anchimbe believes, "is the misconception that these Englishes are not yet *mature*" (2012: 13; emphasis in original; see also Anchimbe 2009). This assumption might indeed be true; yet I think there is more behind this research lag. What Anchimbe's line of reasoning again illustrates is the differences in orientation between the WEs and the Language Acquisition paradigms, with the former mainly focusing on the description of nativized language systems (see Section 24.2.1) at a particular point in time[10] and the latter interested in acquisitional stages in the development of a language system. Another factor that certainly plays a role here is that "linguists often shy away from cases which do not permit neat classifications" (Görlach 1998: 1–2), a reason that is also responsible for the neglect or too premature and superficial categorization of some of the non-native varieties (see, e.g., Buschfeld 2013 on the case of Cyprus and her argumentation in this respect). Postcolonial territories characterized by an increasing number of native speakers clearly defy such "neat classification," since such a development challenges the status traditionally applied to these speech communities, for example as English as a Second Language (ESL) or Outer Circle countries. The coexistence of native and non-native speakers in such territories again highlights the transitional character of some WEs territories, as outlined in Section 24.2.2, and the need for more flexible ways of categorization. Whatever the reasons may be, Anchimbe (2012) addresses an important development in WEs and identifies a research gap that urgently needs to be bridged in order to fully understand such new developments.

Another interesting, so far not comprehensively covered research area that indicates that a strict separation of the WEs and Language Acquisition paradigms is not always adequate is the acquisition of English by colonial immigrants and their children in the UK. This area of research also requires coverage from the two angles (WEs and Language Acquisition). On the one hand, the linguistic properties of their speech systems, the usage contexts, and issues of identity have been investigated and described to some extent (e.g. Sharma 2011; Rathore 2014). On the other hand, pertaining questions of acquisitional stages and the psycholinguistic processes behind the acquisition of these ethnolects to my knowledge have been underexplored in such contexts. How the children of such immigrant families acquire English, which particular type they acquire, and how they handle the lectal continuum they are often confronted with (between mainstream and ethnic varieties of English) again depend on a variety of factors such as their age of onset, their country of origin and their other L1,

---

[10] Even though most descriptions of varieties of English are indeed of synchronic nature, it has to be noted that diachronic accounts are on the rise and constitute a new research trend within the WEs paradigm (e.g. Brato 2018; Collins et al. 2014; Hickey 2009).

the proficiency of their parents, the dominant language of their home, and their embeddedness in the traditional native-speaker community. Related to that are, of course, issues of identity, part of which have been covered in the above approaches. Whatever the answers to these questions, what is important here is that it is by no means clear whether these Englishes should be investigated within the WEs framework – as they are offspring of colonial second-language varieties of English – or within the scope of Language Acquisition research. In the post-Chomskian paradigm, convergence is called for – in other words, an integration of first- and second-language acquisition and the WEs paradigm – as only such an integrative approach can shed full light on their emergence, usage contexts, and linguistic manifestations.

In the following, I exemplarily illustrate how such an integration might be accomplished, referring to the acquisition of L1 Singapore English, a case where English has gradually started to be acquired by child generations as their L1, in a multilingual and multilectal setting and initially mainly from L2 speakers who provide different ethnic and formal lects as input.

24.3.2 Bridging the Paradigm Gap: L1 Singapore English as a Case in Point

An increasing number of children acquiring English as a first language, and thus a gradual transformation from ESL to ENL, has been most prominently noted for Singapore (e.g. Bolton and Ng 2014; Gupta 1994, 1998; Lim 2007; Lim and Foley 2004; Schneider 2007; Tan 2014). Census data confirm this trend and have reported an increase of English as a home language for five-to-nine-year-olds from 34.1 percent in 2000 to 51.5 percent in 2010 (see Census of Population 2000; Census of Population 2010). Despite these far-reaching developments and the gradual change in status of Singapore English (SingE), this development has not been investigated in an empirical, comprehensive fashion, making use of adequate methodology. An approach that considers both the sociolinguistic realities of L1 SingE (i.e. the general WEs framework, the development of the L1 variety from an L2 speech form and related questions pertaining to language change, the description of characteristics of the L1 variety in comparison to the L2 variety, the stratification of colloquial and formal styles, etc.) and the psycholinguistic aspects of such a study (i.e. acquisitional issues such as acquisitional stages taken by the children, the role of input in such a multilingual setting, and the typical methodology to approach these aspects, e.g. hypotheses testing by means of psycholinguistic testing procedures) has been largely absent from the research agenda. I consider such an interdisciplinary approach as fundamental for fully grasping and describing such new developments. Precisely, for investigating the linguistic system of L1 SingE, that is, the linguistic forms the children use and, ultimately, understanding why the system is developing the way it is, one has to look into a number of factors:

the role input plays in a multilingual setting such as Singapore (including the influence of the different acro-, meso-, and basilectal variants in the input the children receive), questions of language transfer from the other first languages most children acquire as well as other psycholinguistic mechanisms at work in its acquisition, and the acquisitional stages the children go through. Investigating such aspects clearly belongs to the field of Language Acquisition research. On the other hand, the linguistic choices these children make and again which linguistic characteristics the children embrace cannot be understood and interpreted without considering the sociolinguistic context of SingE, that is, its current status in the WEs paradigm, issues of language policy, and, closely connected to that, questions of linguistic prestige, both overt and covert. This latter aspect relates to the lectal continuum the children are confronted with as part of their input and once more shows how the fields intersect in their research interests.

A first attempt in this direction is being taken by Buschfeld (forthcoming b), who investigates the acquisition of SingE as a first language by two-to-twelve-year-olds from the Chinese and Indian communities in Singapore. To that end, she combines the two frameworks conceptually and methodologically, taking into consideration the sociolinguistic framework of SingE and findings and methods from the WEs framework, on the one hand, and employing psycholinguistic methodology, that is, hypothesis testing by the means of psycholinguistic experiments, on the other. The data were elicited systematically in video-recorded task-directed dialogue between researcher and child. The data set consists of several parts: a grammar elicitation task, a story retelling task, elicited narratives and free interaction, and a picture naming task. Looking into three linguistic features in some detail, that is, the acquisition of subject pronouns (zero vs. realized), the acquisition of past tense inflections (zero vs. realized), and the acquisition of high vowel contrasts in the lexical sets KIT and FLEECE and FOOT and GOOSE (see Wells 1982), Buschfeld illustrates the acquisitional route taken by Singaporean children and compares the results to data collected in England (as representative for the acquisition of English in the traditionally investigated L1 countries) by the same methodological means. In that respect, the study of the two morphosyntactic characteristics has revealed the following (in a nutshell): First, important differences exist between the acquisition of English as an L1 in Singapore and in England; while British and American children produce zero subjects and bare verb forms in early acquisitional stages only (see also earlier findings by Roeper and Rohrbacher 2000 and Scott 2005 on zero subjects; and Marchman and Bates 1994 and Wexler 1998 on bare verb forms), the results of Buschfeld's study (forthcoming b) show that Singaporean children continue to variably omit subject pronouns and past tense inflections even at more advanced stages of first language acquisition. A merger of vowel length, as often suggested for L2 SingE, is only to be found for very few of the children.

What this tells us about the acquisition of L1 SingE in more general terms and about the sociolinguistic context of Singapore is that both

Singapore Standard and Singapore Colloquial English (SSE and SCE, respectively) serve as input varieties in the children's acquisition process. In this respect, SSE, as the name suggests, provides the more standard realizations from these binary feature choices (i.e. realized subject pronouns and past tense inflections)[11] for the feature pool the children choose from. The SCE input the children receive in more informal communicative situations, on the other hand, supplies the nonstandard realizations (i.e. zero subject pronouns and missing past tense marking). Apart from "age" having been identified as an important factor in the realization of subject pronouns and past tense endings, results have furthermore revealed that, in Singapore, "ethnicity" plays an important role for the use of the two grammatical features. Focusing on children of Indian and Chinese ethnic descent, the study has revealed that Indian children show a higher percentage of standard feature use, that is, realized subject pronouns and past tense endings. How this has to be interpreted cannot be discussed in detail here (for a more detailed account, see Buschfeld forthcoming b), as the difference might occur due to a variety of different factors (e.g. crosslinguistic influence, input, or task effects). For the realization of the long vs. short vowel contrasts, however, this ethnic difference could not be observed (for details, see Buschfeld forthcoming b).

What the results show in general, is that, at least in the young generation acquiring SingE as L1, the variety is not as homogeneous as is sometimes suggested by research on L2 SingE (but see, e.g., Leimgruber 2013 for a more differentiated approach to the L2 variety). Moreover, this variation is not only age- or ethnicity-based but also shows within individual speakers. I interpret this as indicative of the fact that L1 SingE is a very young speech form, which has not yet developed any stable characteristics and is therefore still "in the making"[12] (see Anchimbe's [2012: 13] notion of "maturation," though "in the making" is here meant strictly descriptively and explanatorily and not at all evaluatively) and that the children pick and mix features, as has also been reported as typical in polyglossic, multidialectal settings in research on new dialect formation (e.g. Schreier 2014: 232; see, e.g., Gordon et al. 2004; Hickey 2003 on the formation of New Zealand English). This variation may in parts be due to the lectal variants the children encounter in the adult input, which keeps available basilectal SCE/Singlish realizations of a particular characteristic (e.g. zero subject pronouns, uninflected verb forms, and reduced vowel contrasts) as well as

---

[11] Note, however, that even though the choice of realizations might be binary, it has to be kept in mind that a diglossic approach to the situation in Singapore, i.e. a dichotomic distinction between SSE and SCE, does not reflect linguistic realities in Singapore but that the situation is better captured in terms of a lectal continuum in which SSE and SCE constitute two extreme poles and in which more or less acro-, meso-, and basilectal variants of SingE are to be found (but see, for example, Gupta 1989 and Platt and Weber 1980 for further details on how to account for the heterogeneity found in SingE).

[12] Cf. Anchimbe's (2012: 13) notion of "maturation," though "in the making" here is strictly descriptive and explanatory and does not judge on the status or completeness of the speech system, as I assume that such an approach toward constantly changing and developing entities like language would not be adequate.

their standard realizations. However, whether for young children it is always fully assessable when to use what variant is questionable. This assumption is substantiated by the findings of Buschfeld's study since, especially, the investigation of long vs. short vowel contrasts have shown that internal variability is high in many of the children, that is, some children employ strong durational contrasts between KIT and FLEECE but not for FOOT and GOOSE or vice versa. While it might be arguable that they can deliberately control their grammatical realizations, it is certainly beyond their reach to make deliberate, spontaneous decisions about their vowel lengths. In this respect, it can further be argued that conscious orientation toward linguistic norms is largely absent in the linguistic behavior of young children; they might not care about governmental suggestions and attempts at linguistic regulations (as attempted in the so-called Speak Good English Movement by which Singaporeans should be encouraged to speak standard English) as adults do. This suggests that Singaporean children do not necessarily realize their speech styles along the lectal continuum found for adult SingE speech (see Footnote 11) – at least not to the same extent and likewise deliberately. In this regard, Buschfeld (forthcoming b) discusses the possibility of language change underway in SingE. This change has clearly not been initiated by the children (the adults started using the different variants and provide them as input) but Meisel (2011) convincingly argues that, if L2 speakers constitute the only or strongly predominant input for children acquiring the same language as an L1, the input they receive can contain the triggers for language change.

24.3.3   Drawing Some Theoretical Conclusions

Apart from the fresh insights that the findings in the previous section suggest for the current developments in SingE, the approach has implications for the relationship between WEs and FLA research. It shows that the paradigm gap exists not only between WEs and SLA research – as has repeatedly been observed in recent times – but between WEs and FLA and can thus be expanded to the general research field of Language Acquisition. Were it not for the psycholinguistic approach employed in the study, we would not have any insights into the acquisitional route the Singaporean children take, the differences from the English children, and ultimately the linguistic characteristics that make L1 SingE a system in its own right, certainly still developing, and influenced by different linguistic variants in the input. The choices these children make may, however, be differently motivated than adult choices and ultimately different in their outcome. It remains to be seen whether the system the children acquire fully mirrors the adult system or whether children make their own choices that will favor different variants over others, independent of usage context. Their linguistic choices and creativity may even yield further variants at the expense of existing ones or alongside the old ones. Again, the point here is that, for an insightful analysis of L1 SingE and for placing it among other L1 varieties of English (and the same would be true for other newly emerging L1 varieties), one has to draw on both disciplines.

24.4 Conclusions

English continues to spread around the globe, experiences entrenchment in contexts no longer limited to the former colonies of the British Empire, develops new, so far unprecedented forms of usage, no longer confined by national borders, and is undergoing changes in status, from learner language to second-language variety or vice versa, and in some cases even to first-language status. This brings new complexities to the already intricate framework of the English Language Complex and poses unprecedented challenges for WEs theorizing. Some have to do with questions of classification and membership assignment and the question of what should be (or rather must be) included in the WEs paradigm, revolving around geographical, historical, and political criteria, on the one hand, and general forces of globalization, on the other. Others deal with methodological issues, when, for example, aiming at capturing and describing these new realities. As Sections 24.2 and 24.3 have shown, recent linguistic realities and scientific accounts clearly show that a first crucial step in understanding and adequately depicting current linguistic developments is an integration of the WEs research paradigm with the field of Language Acquisition. In this respect, the two disciplines could finally profit from each other, not only in terms of their findings but also with respect to methodological approaches and techniques of data collection and analysis. For the investigation of the acquisition of newly evolving L1 Englishes in postcolonial societies, such an integrated approach appears to be inevitable, as argued in Section 24.3. For investigations of other postcolonial as well as non-postcolonial Englishes, it also appears promising to put a greater emphasis on the acquisitional side of the coin not only because both EFL and ESL varieties originate in the same mechanisms and initial strategies of language learning. From the methodological point of view, it would certainly be interesting to investigate these different types of non-native Englishes by means of the same methodologies. This would certainly help to shed further light on the relatedness of, for example, second-language varieties and learner Englishes and to better understand the continuum character of such categorizations. To capture and understand the intricate nature of the English Language Complex in its entirety, it is inevitable to investigate not only individual varieties and types of English (native or non-native, postcolonial and non-postcolonial alike) in isolation but their historical, political, and sociolinguistic relationship. The chapter has outlined some methodological and theoretical options for such a joint treatment; yet more research and theorizing are needed – and desirable – to fully come to terms with the major challenge of integrating some long-separated disciplines. Further rethinking of some of their central aims and long-established confines is a crucial task – and certainly a challenge – for future research.

References

Anchimbe, E. A. 2009. Revisiting the notion of maturation in new Englishes. *World Englishes 28*(3): 337–352.

Anchimbe, E. A. 2012. Language contact in a postcolonial setting: Research approaches to Cameroon English and Cameroon Pidgin English. In E. Anchimbe, ed. *Language Contact in a Postcolonial Setting: The Linguistic and Social Context of English and Pidgin in Cameroon*. New York: de Gruyter, 3–25.

Biewer, C. 2011. Modal auxiliaries in second language varieties of English: A learner's perspective. In J. Mukherjee and M. Hundt, eds. *Exploring Second-Language Varieties of English and Learner Englishes: Bridging a Paradigm Gap*. Amsterdam: John Benjamins, 7–33.

Bley-Vroman, R. 1983. The comparative fallacy in interlanguage studies: The case of systematicity. *Language Learning 33*(1): 1–17.

Bolton, K. and B. C. Ng. 2014. The dynamics of multilingualism in contemporary Singapore. *World Englishes 33*(3): 307–318.

Brato, T. 2018. "Outdooring" the Historical Corpus of English in Ghana. *English Today 34*(2): 25–34.

Buschfeld, S. forthcoming a. What Cyprus and Greece can tell us about the paradigm gap between World Englishes and Second Language Acquisition research. Manuscript.

Buschfeld, S. forthcoming b. *Children's English in Singapore: Acquisition, Properties, and Use*. London: Routledge.

Buschfeld, S. 2013. *English in Cyprus or Cyprus English? An Empirical Investigation of Variety Status*. Amsterdam: John Benjamins.

Buschfeld, S. and A. Kautzsch. 2014. English in Namibia: A first approach. *English World-Wide 35*(2): 121–160.

Buschfeld, S. and A. Kautzsch. 2017. Towards an integrated approach to postcolonial and non-postcolonial Englishes. *World Englishes 36*(1): 104–126.

Census of Population. 2000. *2000 Statistical Release 2*. www.singstat.gov.sg/pub lications/publications_and_papers/cop 192000/cop2000r2.html.

Census of Population. 2010. *2010 Statistical Release 1*. www.singstat.gov.sg /publications/publications_and_papers/cop   192010/census10_stat_re-lease1.html.

Collins, P. C., A. M. Borlongan and X. Yao. 2014. Modality in Philippine English: A diachronic study. *Journal of English Linguistics 42*(1): 68–88.

Cook, V. 1999. Going beyond the native speaker in language teaching. *TESOL Quarterly 33*(22): 185–209.

Cook, V. 2007. Multi-competence: Black hole or wormhole for SLA research? In Z. H. Han, ed. *Understanding Second Language Process*. Clevedon: Multilingual Matters, 16–26.

Cook, V. 2010. The relationship between first and second language acquisition revisited. In E. Macaro, ed. *The Continuum Companion to Second Language Acquisition*. London: Continuum, 137–157.

Corder, S. P. 1981. *Error Analysis and Interlanguage*. Oxford: Oxford University Press.

Deshors, S. C., S. Götz, and S. Laporte. 2016. Introduction. Linguistic innovations in EFL and ESL: Rethinking the linguistic creativity of non-native English speakers. *Linguistic Innovations: Rethinking linguistic creativity in non-native Englishes. Special Issue of the International Journal of Learner Corpus Research* 2(2): 131–150.

Edwards, A. 2016. *English in the Netherlands: Functions, Forms and Attitudes*. Amsterdam: John Benjamins.

European Commission. 2012. *Special Eurobarometer 386. Europeans and Their Languages*. http://ec.europa.eu/public_opinion/archives/ebs/ebs_386_en.pdf.

Gass, S. M. and L. Selinker. 2008. *Second Language Acquisition: An Introductory Course* (3rd ed.). London: Routledge.

Gilquin, G. 2015. At the interface of contact linguistics and second language acquisition research: New Englishes and Learner Englishes compared. *English World-Wide* 36(1): 91–124.

Gilquin, G. and S. Granger. 2011. From EFL to ESL: Evidence from the International Corpus of Learner English. In J. Mukherjee and M. Hundt, eds. *Exploring Second-Language Varieties of English and Learner Englishes: Bridging a Paradigm Gap*. Amsterdam: John Benjamins, 55–78.

Görlach, M. 1998. The origins and development of emigrant Englishes [1996]. In M. Görlach, ed. *Even More Englishes: Studies 1996–1997*. Amsterdam: John Benjamins, 19–38.

Görlach, M. 2002. English in Singapore, Malaysia, Hong Kong, Indonesia, the Philippines . . . a second or a foreign language? In M. Görlach, ed. *Still More Englishes*. Amsterdam: John Benjamins, 99–117.

Götz, S. and M. Schilk. 2011. Formulaic sequences in spoken ENL, ESL and EFL: Focus on British English, Indian English and learner English of advanced German learners. In J. Mukherjee and M. Hundt, eds. *Exploring Second-Language Varieties of English and Learner Englishes: Bridging a Paradigm Gap*. Amsterdam: John Benjamins, 79–100.

Gordon, E., L. Campbell, J. Hay, M. Maclagan, A. Sudbury and P. Trudgill. 2004. *New Zealand English: Its Origins and Evolution*. Cambridge: Cambridge University Press.

Gupta, A. F. 1989. Singapore Colloquial English and Standard English. *Singapore Journal of Education* 10(2): 33–39.

Gupta, A. F. 1994. *The Step-Tongue. Children's English in Singapore*. Clevedon: Multilingual Matters.

Gupta, A. F. 1997. Colonisation, migration, and functions of English. In E. W. Schneider, ed. *Englishes Around the World*. Vol. 1: *General Studies, British Isles, North America. Studies in Honour of Manfred Görlach*. Amsterdam: John Benjamins, 47–58.

Gupta, A. F. 1998. The situation of English in Singapore. In J. A. Foley, T. Kandiah, B. Zhiming, A. F. Gupta, L. Alsagoff, H. C. Lick, L. Wee, I. S. Talib and W. D. Bokhorst-Heng, eds. *English in New Cultural Contexts: Reflections from Singapore*. Singapore and Oxford: Singapore Institute of Management and Oxford University Press, 106–126.

Hickey, R. 2003. How do dialects get the features they have? On the process of new dialect formation. In R. Hickey, ed. *Motives for Language Change*. Cambridge: Cambridge University Press, 213–239.

Hickey, R., ed. 2019. *Listening to the Past: Audio Records of Accents of English*. Cambridge: Cambridge University Press.

Hundt, M. and J. Mukherjee. 2011. Introduction: Bridging a paradigm gap. In J. Mukherjee and M. Hundt, eds. *Exploring Second-Language Varieties of English and Learner Englishes: Bridging a Paradigm Gap*. Amsterdam: John Benjamins, 1–6.

Hundt, M. and K. Vogel. 2011. Overuse of the progressive in ESL and learner English – fact or fiction? In J. Mukherjee and M. Hundt, eds. *Exploring Second-Language Varieties of English and Learner Englishes: Bridging a Paradigm Gap*. Amsterdam: John Benjamins, 145–165.

Kachru, B. B. [1977] 2009. Linguistic Schizophrenia and Language Census: A Note on the Indian Situation. *Linguistics* 15(186): 17–32. doi:10.1515/ling.1977.15.186.17.

Kachru, B. B. 1992. Models for non-native Englishes. In B. B. Kachru, ed. *The Other Tongue: English across Cultures* (2nd ed.). Urbana: University of Illinois Press, 48–74.

Kachru, B. B., ed. 1992. *The Other Tongue: English across Cultures* (2nd ed.). Urbana IL: University of Illinois Press.

Koch, C., C. Lange and S. Leuckert. 2016. This hair-style called as "duck tail": The "intrusive *as*"-construction in South Asian varieties of English and Learner Englishes. *Linguistic Innovations: Rethinking linguistic creativity in non-native Englishes. Special Issue of the International Journal of Learner Corpus Research* 2(2): 151–176.

Krashen, S. D. 1981. *Second Language Acquisition and Second Language Learning*. Oxford: Pergamon Press.

Laporte, S. 2012. Mind the gap! Bridge between World Englishes and Learner Englishes in the making. *English Text Construction* 5(2): 264–291.

Leimgruber, J. R. E. 2013. *Singapore English: Structure, Variation, and Usage*. Cambridge: Cambridge University Press.

Lim, L. 2007. Mergers and acquisitions: On the ages and origins of Singapore English particles. *World Englishes* 26(4): 446–473.

Lim L. and J. A. Foley. 2004. English in Singapore and Singapore English. In L. Lim, ed. *Singapore English: A Grammatical Description*. Amsterdam: John Benjamins, 1–18.

Long, Michael H. 2003. Stabilization and fossilization in interlanguage development. In C. J. Doughty and M. H. Long, eds. *The Handbook of Second Language Acquisition*. Oxford: Blackwell, 487–535.

Lowenberg, P. H. 1986. Non-native varieties of English: Nativization, norms, and implications. *Studies in Second Language Acquisition 8*(1): 1–18.

Marchman, V. A. and E. Bates. 1994. Continuity in lexical and morphological development: A test of the critical mass hypothesis. *Journal of Child Language 21*(2): 339–366.

Meisel, J. M. 2011. Bilingual language acquisition and theories of diachronic change: Bilingualism as cause and effect of grammatical change. *Bilingualism: Language and Cognition 14*(2):121–145.

Mesthrie, R. and R. M. Bhatt. 2008. *World Englishes: The Study of New Varieties*. Cambridge: Cambridge University Press.

Moag, R. F. 1992. The life cycle of non-native Englishes: A case study. In B. B. Kachru, ed. *The Other Tongue: English across Cultures* (2nd ed.). Urbana: University of Illinois Press, 233–252.

Mollin, S. 2006. *Euro-English. Assessing Variety Status*. Tübingen: Gunter Narr.

Mollin, S. 2007. New variety or learner English? Criteria for variety status and the case of Euro-English. *English World-Wide 28*(2): 167–185.

Mufwene, Salikoko S. 2001. *The Ecology of Language Evolution*. Cambridge: Cambridge University Press.

Mufwene, Salikoko S. 2005. Language evolution: The population genetics way. In G. Hauska, ed. *Gene, Sprachen und ihre Evolution*. Regensburg: Universitätsverlag Regensburg, 30–52.

Mukherjee, J. and M. Hundt, eds. 2011. *Exploring Second-Language Varieties of English and Learner Englishes: Bridging a Paradigm Gap*. Amsterdam: John Benjamins.

Nesselhauf, N. 2009. Co-selection phenomena across New Englishes: Parallels (and differences) to foreign learner varieties. *English World-Wide 30*(1):1–26.

Percillier, M. 2016. *World Englishes and Second Language Acquisition: Insights from Southeast Asian Englishes*. Amsterdam: John Benjamins.

Platt, J. and H. Weber. 1980. *English in Singapore and Malaysia: Status, Features, Functions*. Kuala Lumpur: Oxford University Press.

Platt, J., H. Weber and M. L. Ho. 1984. *The New Englishes*. London: Routledge and Kegan Paul.

Rathore, C. 2014. East African Indian twice migrants in Britain: Phonological variation across generations. In M. Hundt and D. Sharma, eds. *English in the Indian Diaspora*. Amsterdam: John Benjamins, 55–83.

Ritchie, W. C. 1986. Second language acquisition research and the study of non-native varieties of English: Some issues in common. *World Englishes 5*(1): 15–30.

Roeper, T. and B. Rohrbacher. 2000. Null subjects in early child English and the theory of economy of projection. In S. M. Powers and C. Hamann, eds. *The Acquisition of Scrambling and Cliticization*. Dordrecht: Kluwer Academic Publishers, 345–396.

Schneider, E. W. 2003. The dynamics of New Englishes: From identity construction to dialect birth. *Language* 79(2): 233–281.

Schneider, E. W. 2007. *Postcolonial English: Varieties Around the World.* Cambridge: Cambridge University Press.

Schneider, E. W. 2014. New reflections on the evolutionary dynamics of World Englishes. *World Englishes* 33(1): 9–32.

Schreier, D. 2014. On cafeterias and new dialects: The role of primary transmitters. In S. Buschfeld, T. Hoffmann, M. Huber and A. Kautzsch, eds. *The Evolution of Englishes: The Dynamic Model and Beyond.* Amsterdam: John Benjamins, 231–248.

Scott, K. 2005. Child null subjects. *UCL Working Papers in Linguistics* 17, 1–25.

Selinker, L. 1972. Interlanguage. *IRAL – International Review of Applied Linguistics in Language Teaching* 10(3): 209–231.

Sharma, D. 2011. Style repertoire and social change in British Asian English. *Journal of Sociolinguistics* 15(4): 464–492.

Sridhar, K. K. and S. N. Sridhar. 1986. Bridging the paradigm gap: Second language acquisition theory and indigenized varieties of English. *World Englishes* 5(1):3–14.

Strevens, P. 1992. English as an international language: Directions in the 1990s. In B. B. Kachru, ed. *The Other Tongue: English across Cultures* (2nd ed.). Urbana: University of Illinois Press, 27–47.

Szmrecsanyi, B. and B. Kortmann. 2011. Typological profiling: learner Englishes versus indigenized L2 varieties of English. In J. Mukherjee and M. Hundt, eds. *Exploring Second-Language Varieties of English and Learner Englishes: Bridging a Paradigm Gap.* Amsterdam: John Benjamins, 167–187.

Tan, Y.-Y. 2014. English as a "mother tongue" in Singapore. *World Englishes* 33(3): 319–339.

Tarone, E. 2000. Still wrestling with "context" in interlanguage theory. *Annual Review of Applied Linguistics* 20: 182–198.

Wells, J. C. 1982. *Accents of English.* Cambridge: Cambridge University Press.

Wexler, K. 1998. Very early parameter setting and the unique checking constraint: A new explanation of the optional infinitive stage. *Lingua* 106(1–4): 23–79.

Williams, J. 1987. Non-native varieties of English: A special case of language acquisition. *English World-Wide* 8(2): 161–199.

Williams, J. 1989. Language acquisition, language contact and nativized varieties of English. *RELC Journal* 20(1): 39–67.

Winford, D. 2003. *An Introduction to Contact Linguistics.* Malden, MA: Blackwell.

Part IV

Current Challenges

25

Norms and Standards in World Englishes

Pam Peters

25.1 Introduction: Standards and Norms – Problems of Polysemy

Few words are subject to such ambiguity as *standards* and *norms* when applied in discussions of language. Both are polysemous with a variety of more and less specialized usages from *standard gauge railway* to *standard dress code*, and from the scientifically established "norms of apparent temperature" to the socially constructed "norms for cyberspace – Internet openness, security, and free speech." In each case, they can refer to precise quantitative measures or open-ended qualitative measures. Both terms can refer to particular kinds of social behavior, as when they substitute for each other in *Merriam-Webster's* (online) definition of *norms* as "*standards* of proper or acceptable behavior."

The terms *standard(s)* and *norm(s)* are often incorporated in discussions of the status and evolutionary development of World Englishes (WEs). Yet they need to be differentiated if they are to provide alternative perspectives on language usage in different regions of the English-speaking world and to complement each other rather than coincide in their reference. They can then be used to triangulate discussion of the types and levels of linguistic convergence and divergence in WEs and develop better insights into their advancement as new varieties of English.

Let us first review the linguistic issues inherent in the term "standard language," so as to operationalize it for the purposes of this analysis. We will then do the same for "language norms/norms of language," so as to anticipate the different kinds of data that can be brought to bear on individual WEs, both linguistic and sociolinguistic, to develop a full picture of their evolutionary status in multilingual habitats. Political factors and language management policies operating in the context need to be taken into account as the official framework for any World English. As case studies, we will focus on English in Singapore and in the Philippines. Both

are highly multilingual contexts for English but they differ on many parameters apart from their individual colonial histories, which introduced
British English (BrE) into Singapore and American English (AmE) into the
Philippines. In what follows, we shall be examining research on the standard forms of English that they adhere to, the divergence between their
language norms in spoken and written registers, and how those phenomena correlate with their evolutionary development. This contextual
approach to the standard language, combined with empirically based
appraisal of local norms of usage, provides a robust model for analyzing
the status of individual WEs.

25.2 Standard Language: Theoretical and Empirical Issues in Describing Regional Standards

The term *standard language* is used by researchers and scholars of different
persuasions, lending ambiguity to many linguistic discussions, except
where it is clearly associated with a given conceptual framework or empirical evidence from a focused inquiry. These are discussed in the following
four sections.

25.2.1 Evolutionary Models

Haugen's (1972) model of how a standard (national) language includes the
codification of its forms (its grammar and word-stock) and its elaboration
to serve widening functions within the nation. It accounts for the different
kinds of preoccupations with the standard language shown in newly
formed states and nations and in their well-established counterparts. In
younger and recently forged European nations such as Macedonia
(Gjurkova 2017), the main focus is on developing a functional framework
for the standard language, to ensure its inclusiveness, and language planning for education to sustain its use. By contrast, studies of the standard
language in long-established pluricentric nations (English, French,
Chinese, Russian) show their concentration on details of the form of the
language and standardizing it amid perceptible variation. Given the official and functional preeminence of these standard languages in their
respective birthplaces (England, France, China, Russia), their functions
can be taken for granted.

Haugen's model for the development of a national standard language
articulates its codification and the subsequent elaboration of its form(s) to
support widening national functions. It is helpfully extended by Schneider
in his five-stage model for the evolution of new dialects of English (2007),
in proposing that the codification of the standard variety in Stage 4 will
ultimately lead to its differentiation. The sociolinguistic convergence that
generates the new standardized variety of WEs, and gives it national

identity, also ushers the possibility of divergent forms evolving as subvarieties with their own sociolinguistic identity. This is evident in Settler (STL)/ Inner Circle Englishes such as Australian English, where urban Aboriginal English can be seen as the affirmation of Aboriginal identity against the mainstream (Peters 2014). It can also be seen in the periodic, often intense public discussion about what counts as standard forms of English language – as in the USA following the publication of *Webster's Third New International Dictionary* (1961), and in the UK following government reviews of the school English curriculum in the 1980s and 1990s. Hudson's dictionaries of "diseased English" (1977, 1983) were a symptom of this preoccupation with maintaining the standard, as was Honey's (1997) manifesto on *Language and Power: The Story of Standard English and Its Enemies*. Such publications are symptomatic of something like "moral panic" (Cameron 1995) about the state of the national language. It is clear that the makeup of standard English continues to be contested from within, long after the language has been codified and moved on to become an international standard of English. No doubt it reflects fresh social, ethnic, and cultural diversification within the UK (Gill 2017). Differentiation remains the final phase in Schneider's evolutionary model for WEs, but there is reason to ask whether these recurrent challenges to the forms and functions of the oldest established standard Englishes could herald a further phase of recalibration or "restandardization," as seems possible for much newer varieties of English, for example Black South African English (BSAE) in South Africa (Bowerman 2012).

25.2.2 Standardization as a Process and Degrees of Standardness

As Haugen's model indicated, a standard national language evolves in tandem with its gradual establishment as the common code for a range of sociocultural functions. With wider adoption of the language throughout the community, its natural variability in form is reduced with dialect leveling, a well-known phenomenon among the processes of standardization. Yet, within any language, individual modes and registers may be more or less resistant to standardization (Schreier 2012). This is clear in the case of writing (especially formal writing) whose diversity of forms and rate of change are much more constrained than those of speech. The circumstances in which writing is produced – the scope for conservative editorial intervention (Cameron 1995), its capacity for long-term storage, and revisiting by later generations of writers – all make it amenable to standardization. This supports the notion that variation in form is to be avoided within the standard language (to be discussed in Section 25.2.3). It also suggests that differing degrees of standardness are accorded to the written and spoken forms of a language. There can scarcely be a single *standard* encompassing both, as unmarked use of "the standard language" seems to imply.

Different aspects of standardization can be seen in different varieties of World English according to their developmental stage in the evolutionary model and whether they are used by Settler (STL) or Indigenous (IDG) speech communities. The focus of public and media discussions on (standard) Australian English is on its relationship to international Englishes, on resisting the influx of AmE elements through the media and other socioeconomic and political forces, and on a largely unspoken determination to affirm its European identity by maintaining British forms of English. Yet in multilingual settings such as the Philippines, regional English speakers may be indifferent to either form of international English and more responsive to influences from local languages, in a different kind of identity assertion. This may be conceptualized as allowing lesser degrees of standardness within a World English or as the impetus for dual standards or paths for standardization, as for BSAE among lower- and middle-class Black South Africans (Bowerman 2012).

In the opposite (top-down) direction, the possibility of supraregional standards of English crystallizing along with or out of individual regional Englishes has been flagged by several scholars of WEs. McArthur's (1998) compass model postulated major regional standards or "standardizing" forms of English in four quarters of the globe. Areal affinities that might generate more geographically based regional standards have been considered by some researchers, though based on limited numbers of features (Hickey 2012). Others argue against putative regional standards for the Caribbean (Devonish and Thomas 2012) or for the South Pacific (Biewer 2015) or for West Africa (Gut 2012). A different kind of areal standard English could conceivably emerge in Southeast Asia through ASEAN (Association of Southeast Asian Nations), the regional intergovernmental organization. It mandates the use of English for all ASEAN interchanges (written and spoken), because of the multiplicity of languages used by the regional governments participating (Kirkpatrick 2012). The language produced by ASEAN has until now been analyzed as an institutional form of ELF (English as a Lingua Franca), rather than a supraregional standard. But if it is taken up by participating governments within their own countries, it will serve to show how a supraregional form of English (other than ex-colonial forms British or American), can be established.

25.2.3 The Concept of a Standard Language

Theoretical challenges to the notion of the standard language have emerged, concomitant with the rise of empirical research on the evolution of WEs, and more evidence on the standardization processes. Originating with Milroy and Milroy's (1985) critique of the ideology of the standard language, other scholars in Britain and the USA have argued that standard English is an ideologically motivated abstraction, which lacks an identifiable speech community and operates as a form of cultural authority.

Kretzschmar and Meyer (2012) provide an extensive critique of the "idea of Standard American English." Others responding to their essay agree that rhetoric about the "standard language" represent something more like "a cultural practice of allegiance" (Chand 2014). The ideologizing of the "standard language" frequently morphs into the reification of "language standards," as notional reference points for the standard language, along with institutional statements that "standards are slipping" or "have fallen." The British media are inclined to endorse such statements without question (Gill 2017), and they are echoed in popular writing about the English language, for example Truss's (2003) manifesto on faulty punctuation, with the call to arms, zero tolerance, and aggressive action to stamp out variation in usage. These phenomena represent the ideologization of uniformity that goes with the rhetoric of the standard language – that its strength is in the convergence of its forms and that variation must be eliminated.

In predominantly monolingual English countries, the standard language thus acquires a symbolic function in "language = nation" thinking. Whereas, in multilingual countries, any incipient standard English simply functions alongside other official languages. The standardness of endonormative English is not so important, and there are no inhibitions about referring to exonormative standards of English in Fiji or India (Hundt et al. 2015; Bernaisch and Koch 2016). The idea of developing an endonormative English for the nation is not a widely held aspiration – perhaps only by the elite, as in the Philippines (see Section 25.4.2). So there is little motivation in either monolingual or multilingual countries to engage the community in critical thinking about the concept of standard English.

25.2.4 "Grassroots" Understandings of Standard Language

Recent sociolinguistic research in mono- and multilingual countries has raised issues about how ordinary citizens conceptualize the standard language and their orientations to it. How consistent is their understanding of what constitutes the standard language? Smakman's (2012) research shows that it varies considerably, in an empirical survey of more than 1,000 young adults in seven countries: England, Flanders (Dutch-speaking section of Belgium), Japan, the Netherlands, New Zealand, Poland, USA. The set of countries was chosen to represent cases where a given standard language becomes that of one or more secondary countries, for example Dutch in Flanders and English in New Zealand, as well as ones where the standard language is more or less confined to the country in which it originated (Japan, Poland). In all seven countries, the respondents' views clustered into inclusive and exclusive views of the standard: the inclusive view being that it was the lingua franca used by a majority of the community (defining it by its functions), while the exclusive view associated it with a select few speakers who put their stamp on its forms. The ratio between the two views in different English-speaking countries was remarkably polarized: The exclusive view prevailed by almost 3:1 in England, whereas in New Zealand it was the opposite, with those holding the inclusive view outnumbering the exclusive by almost 5:1. Smakman's explanation for this difference was that there has been relatively little time since English settlement of New Zealand for the notion of a distinctive national language to form (p. 51), whereas it had been cultivated much longer in England. In the USA (where the time depth for standard AmE to develop is much longer than for New Zealand English), the ratio between inclusive and exclusive views (2:3) was closer than in either of the other two anglophone countries. The closeness of that ratio aligns with other evidence of divergence among Americans about what counts as standard English (Peters and Young 1997). Their diversity is also underscored in Garner's (2009) language change index with its mix of democratic and elitist orientations to usage (Peters 2018).

The issues reviewed in Section 25.2 add to the complexities of discussing a standard language and underscore the diversity of approaches to researching the processes of language standardization. Yet the *norms* of a language may likewise be understood in different ways and researched by differing methodologies, to which we now turn.

25.3 Language Norms/Norms of Usage

The term *norm* occurs a good deal less often in research on WEs than *standard language* but it is still subject to ambiguity. From its origins in statistics, it refers to a numerical central tendency, a sense that is retained in quantitative research on variable features of WEs. Corpus-based research on WEs has supported numerous quantitative findings on their norms of grammar and usage, including multiword units and discourse-pragmatic features used by their speakers and writers. The statistical norms produced depend on the size and scope of the corpora used, their representativeness in relation to the linguistic variables under discussion, and the representation of the speech community as speakers and writers within the data. The perfect corpus, large enough to represent and balance all the known sociolinguistic factors affecting a given variable, may not exist, and the statistical ideal of a normal distribution ("bell curve," Gaussian curve) may therefore be elusive. When relevant data can be extracted from a set of different-sized corpora, the relative frequencies must include *normalized* frequencies, so that convergent and divergent patterns of distribution for the variables can be compared and allow statistically based *norms* of language usage to be extrapolated from them.

Yet the substance of *language norms* can also be nonquantitative, as the product of observation or conceptualization in linguistic argumentation. For example, sociolinguistic norms of usage are developed in discussions of different language-using groups, as when comparing the norms of English usage by ESL and EFL speakers, or hypothesizing similarities between them. Similar conceptualizations underlie comparisons of regional usage patterns that contribute to individual WEs and at the highest level of abstraction in established terms such as *exonormative* and *endonormative*. The implied norms are of course "top-down" rather than "bottom up" and useful generalizations though they could not claim to represent all the linguistic features that might be taken in under them. References to the norms of BrE or AmE are similarly top-down in their conceptualization and open to challenge in terms of the features they actually embrace, apart from their political, cultural, and ideological implications (cf. Section 15.2.3). References to BrE and AmE are nevertheless well established in the ELT industry (Peters 2012), as a way of indicating different native-speaker norms for the benefit of second-language learners. The same might be said of references to the language norms in geographically confined areas, so that the norms of *Southern British English* still evoke the old north/south division in English dialects, as shorthand for the traditional prestige enjoyed by the southern varieties (Wales 2006). Likewise, the norms of *Southern American English* may serve mostly to refer to "where the worst American English is spoken" (Preston 1996). Broad regional terms may effectively be folk-linguistic labels for stereotypical features of the region, rather than representing the multitude of linguistic variables they share, with adjacent dialects, whose norms may or may not have been carefully researched.

Regionally based language norms are also increasingly questioned by sociolinguists who draw attention to the complexity of social factors involved in language variation that do not coincide with geographical boundaries. Research on accent variation within Australia showed how the city/country divide was a major factor in the pronunciation norms of schoolchildren (Mitchell and Delbridge 1966), replicated in each state. Research into Australian written usage has consistently shown that the norms are generationally based, not conditioned by residence in a particular state (Peters 2014). The intricate interplay between other social variables of gender, education, and ethnicity are likely to affect norms of usage by speakers anywhere (Guy and Hinskens 2016) and need factorial analysis to be properly understood as elements of sociolinguistic identity. Norms of usage also need to be understood in terms of how monolingual or multilingual the speech community itself is. The language styles used by multilingual urban youth may include markers or features without them being proficient users of the languages from which the features are drawn.

The norms of multilingual usage and code-switching are especially challenging to describe, especially among proficient bi- or multilinguals who can make full use of their languages in conversation with others who share the same ones (*homolinguals*). So the deft use of their shared languages in mixed-code dialogues does not represent the norms of the local variety but is situation- and dyad-based. Speakers can creatively vary whether their "Taglish" consists of a Filipino-matrix clause or English-matrix (Thompson 2003), and the freely formed language of the latter could not be interpreted as any codified form of Philippine English. Yet the convergent forms of English (ELF – English as a Lingua Franca), which are generated among cohorts of *heterolingual* students in an English-medium university (Mauranen 2012), may present observable and quantifiable norms of usage because of their common communicative function.

In research on variation across genres, registers, and styles, normative statements are often made to inform hypotheses and to frame the discussion, for example that the norms of writing are more complex than speech. This assumption seems valid when you compare an academic or essay with social dialogue, no doubt because of the frequent use of nominalizations in the first and the lack of them in the second. Yet speech has been found to exhibit more complexity in its syntactic structures, with more frequent use of subordination (Halliday 1985). Thus the norms for phrase and clause construction in speech and writing contrast with each other and should not be subsumed into generalizations about complexity in discourse. Corpus-based studies by Biber (1988) show the great value of multidimensional research on a range of spoken and written text-types and the statistically based norms that can be extracted for different genres from it. Yet Biber et al.'s later (1994) research on the linguistic makeup of written genres across four centuries (including letter-writing, scientific writing, news writing, drama) showed that their respective linguistic norms are not constant over time. Scientific writing has become more impersonal in the last 150 years, while news writing has become more familiar/colloquial. Without quantitative norms to refer to in diachronic research like this, these not insubstantial changes in English usage would have remained impressionistic.

As we have seen, norms of usage may be more or less empirically based. Normative ideas and assumptions about language commonly are abundant in observation and generalizations about language and in language stereotypes. Using corpus linguistic techniques, empirically grounded norms can be extracted from large bodies of data, to test impression-based generalizations. Corpora come into their own in examining the extent to which external factors such as government and education policy impact on language usage and standardization of English in a given region. By documenting the changing norms of usage in diachronic corpora, we can describe the processes of standardization and the degrees of variation in individual WEs, review their evolutionary status, and gain better insights into the balance between endonormative and exonormative English within their speech communities.

Let us now put the spotlight on Singapore and the Philippines, first the historical and social contexts for their respective forms of English and the extent to which their use is formally standardized. We will draw on corpus-based research into some of their distinctive language norms and on socio-linguistic surveys for evidence of the status of the local English. Corpus evidence of the speech community's ways of referring to standards for English in Singapore, the Philippines, and other WEs will also be discussed.

25.4 Singapore English

25.4.1 English in Singapore: Language Policy and Reference Standards

English was used in Singapore from 1819, when it was acquired by Sir Stamford Raffles for the British East India Company as part of the Straits Settlements and then became a British Crown Colony in 1867 and subsequently one of the Federated Malay States in 1897. The island was originally inhabited by Malays, with an increasing proportion of Chinese settlers from southern China (Hokkien, Teochew) and from southern India during the nineteenth century. They contributed to the development of urban centers such as Singapore in the twentieth century; and, by 1931, the Chinese constituted 60 percent of the population. During World War II, Singapore fell to the Japanese in 1942, but British rule resumed afterwards and was maintained until Singapore became independent in 1965.

English has always been an official language in Singapore, endorsed since independence in government policy alongside Chinese and Malay as the major community languages, as well as Tamil in recognition of the Indian minority. The four languages used by Singaporean citizens are affirmed in government language policy. Yet, in relation to Chinese, the Singapore government mandates Mandarin Chinese as the Singaporean standard rather than the different regional forms of Chinese (Hokkien, Teochew), which are embedded in the community from the original settlements. The elevation of Mandarin can be seen as a sociopolitical strategy to achieve internal and external ends: to ensure cohesion among the Chinese citizens of Singapore and to secure Singapore's position in relation to global business involving mainland China. The importance of these goals was underscored as early as 1979 in an official government campaign urging citizens to "speak good Chinese" (i.e. Mandarin). It created an external (exonormative) standard for Singaporean Chinese, the ideological and aspirational aspects of this policy are evident. By implication, standard Mandarin becomes the acrolectal form for Singapore, with Singapore Mandarin and other Sinitic languages (e.g. Cantonese) positioned as if they constitute the mesolect and basilect of a notional trilectal scale, without forming a continuum (Ansaldo 2004: 146).

The subsequent positioning of exonormative and endonormative standards of English in Singapore is analogous to the standards established for

Chinese. BrE serves as an exonormative standard for official documents, already well established from more than a century of colonial management, and maintained after independence in 1965 as an international form of English, with some recent admixture from AmE media (Lim 2012). It sets the acrolectal standard for Singapore English (SingE), while endonormative Singaporean forms of English still occupy the lower positions on the notional lectal scale. The campaign to "speak good English," initiated by the government in 2000 to promote adjustments in the phonology, morphology, and lexis of Singaporean speech toward more "native"-speaker norms, may be seen as a managerial strategy to bridge the gap between the exonormative acrolect and the endonormative mesolect. However, it was also seen as a scarcely disguised attempt to combat the use of Singlish, the popular and widely used mixed form of Singapore English. It created considerable controversy, which may in fact have served to reinforce affiliation to Singlish (especially among younger Singaporeans) in a remarkable kind of "metadiscursive convergence" (Wee 2011).

Singapore's government-sanctioned education policy supports bilingualism, endorsing schools to teach in all four official languages, so that students can begin their education in home language (in keeping with best educational practice) and learn a second language there as well. Yet decreasing enrollments at Malay- and Tamil-medium schools from the later twentieth century, and increasing demand for Chinese-medium and English-medium schools both suggest early focus on exonormative standards of language for Singapore children. A continuing emphasis on "correct" written English emerges in discussions among educators about "standards and norms of SE" in the 1990s (Pakir 1993); and Gupta's later (2010) reflections on standards of English in Singapore suggest that international norms are still considered the relevant target for students.

In keeping with this exonormative emphasis, there's a dearth of locally produced instruments of codification for SingE and Singaporeans must refer to standard British dictionaries. One isolated example of a reference dictionary including Singaporean vocabulary was the *Times-Chambers Essential English Dictionary* (1993; 2nd ed. 1997), edited by Singaporean linguist Vincent Ooi. Yet the dictionary's matrix was an exonormative BrE word list into which Singaporeanisms were inserted, so did not represent a full codification of SingE. The most authentic locally produced reference to date is Lee's *Dictionary of Singlish and Singapore English*, published progressively online since 2004. It offers full, citation-based accounts of Singaporean words and is thus able to withstand skepticism about the origins of Singapore neologisms without appearing to be subversive. The same kind of situation holds in relation to SingE grammar. There is no reference grammar as such, since the acrolectal standard is exonormative; but Lim (2004) offers an empirically based collection of essays on the elements of Singapore colloquial English. It uses a purpose-built corpus of spoken Singaporean English to inform its description of the main syntactic constituents as well as common discourse markers.

As is evident, standard SingE is still a shifting concept in a multilingual language habitat where other languages, especially Chinese, are also salient and where government intervention in support of an exonormative standard is now juxtaposed to strong popular endorsement of endonormative forms of SingE. This is captured in Ansaldo's model (2004), which suggests two clusters of linguistic variation in Singapore: around standard/colloquial SingE, and around acrolectal/basilectal forms of Singlish with lesser and greater degrees of mixing with other languages/dialects spoken in Singapore. Ansaldo notes (pp. 148–189, n.19) that the Singlish cluster includes mixed language codes based on English (somewhat closer to standard Singaporean), as well as mixed codes based on Chinese.

These finer points of modeling the standard language in Singapore demonstrate some of the common challenges of identifying standard English in a multilingual postcolonial environment. Descriptions of the use of English in Singapore have variably represented it as a diglossia and as a post-creole continuum, neither of which works very well for Singapore. It lacks key features of the diglossic model (Ferguson 1972) since the Singapore habitat does not present strict compartmentalization of H(igh) and L(ow) applications of the exonormative and endonormative forms of English. It cannot be reduced to a binary system (Romaine 1995:145). The post-creole lectal continuum (Platt and Weber 1980) also seems an imperfect model, because of the discreteness of the speech communities whose usage could be identified as mesolectal and basilectal, and their own variability. The identification of Singlish with the basilectal has been a continuing problem because of the traditionally negative attitude toward it and how to accommodate it alongside more acceptable forms of SingE. Yet how could any account of English in Singapore be valid without it? Ansaldo (2004: 146) finds a place for it in his proposed "matrix" of languages in Singapore. It accommodates both exonormative and endonormative forms of English in a "polylectal system," without insisting on their being related according to the traditional post-creole continuum or having fixed functions and contexts of use, as in a di- or tri-glossia.

25.4.2 Corpus Data, Sociolinguistic Surveys, and the Norms of English Usage in Singapore

Empirical studies of SingE based on corpus evidence show that its grammatical norms are not as close to those of BrE as one might expect, despite it having long been the reference standard. For example, its overall use of the present perfect across comparable genres from the International Corpus of English (ICE) corpora was markedly lower than that of BrE and closer to the American norm (Yao and Collins, 2012). In its avoidance of contractions in present perfect, its rate was markedly lower than either British or American, and it patterned with other Outer Circle Englishes such as Hong Kong and Philippine English.

Differentiation from BrE norms also emerged in research on use of the mandative construction in WEs, again based on data from the ICE corpora. In Peters's (2009) study, SingE emerged as far more frequent in its use of the mandative (rather than paraphrases with *should*) than BrE, in both spoken and written genres. The use of the mandative declined in BrE through most of the twentieth century, while it continued to be used in AmE (Övergaard 1995). The strong presence of the mandative in SingE, and the wide range of lexical verbs that embody it (Peters 2009: 132), show its independence from BrE on this feature, perhaps because of recent American influence, or else retention of a grammatical resource from earlier (nineteenth-century) British input, that is, "colonial lag."

Corpus-based research studies like these demonstrate grammatical features where SingE differs from British in using the resources of standard grammar, which contribute to its endonormative profile. Other evidence comes from studies of nonstandard grammatical features that are accepted in SingE. Research on the ICE-SING corpus by Tan (2016) identified a set of distinctive multiword verb combinations: prepositional verbs such as *stressed on/discussed on* and phrasal verbs *list out, repay back*, which alternate in SingE with the transitive verbs of standard English, occurring in written as well as spoken genres, though more frequently in the spoken. This suggests a gradual nativization process from spoken to written usage, which Tan offers as evidence of how endonormative features become stabilized in regional standard Englishes.

These studies based on the ICE-SING corpus complement those carried out by Lim and colleagues on the corpus of spoken SingE (Lim 2004), which document multiple features of the verb cluster, and nouns and noun phrases in Singapore colloquial English, showing local divergences from the norms of standard English. They support other sociolinguistic evidence of endonormativity in SingE that must be associated with Stage 4 of Schneider's model, despite the dearth of formal codification. Sociolinguistic surveys of the usage of SingE among students show how fully it functions for them in everyday communication. Research by Siemund et al. (2014) on government census data showed that the use of English in the home grew from 23 percent to 32 percent between 2000 and 2010, while the use of Chinese (not including Chinese vernaculars) remained stable at 35 percent over the same period. Most students at university and the polytechnics were bilingual, all of them speaking English, usually alongside Mandarin. When questioned on the importance of their languages, all said that being proficient in English was more important than their mother tongue. In follow-up questions, most indicated that mother tongue knowledge and usage was not crucial for being a Singaporean. University students also tended to agree that Singlish was a critical part of their self-definition (pp. 355–357), an important indicator of their identification with it. However polytechnic students did not agree so strongly, suggesting that endorsement of Singlish as part of their identity is easier for those with higher social status. Widespread endorsement of Singlish as part of their identity was also found among primary school students (Tan and Tan 2008). The students found that use of Singlish makes the speaker sound "friendlier," though they knew it did not rate highly in terms of "fashionableness" (p. 476).

These sociolinguistic surveys provide insights into how Singaporean students identify with Singlish at lower and higher levels of education, while the university students recognize the instrumental value of standard English in their professional development. They provide triangulation on the textual evidence from corpora, of the integration of Singaporean features into their spoken and written discourse. The data confirm that SingE has reached Stage 4 (endonormative stabilization) in Schneider's model of evolutionary development, since its speakers embrace it as an expression of Singaporean identity.

25.5 Philippine English

25.5.1 English in the Philippines: Language Policy and Reference Standards

English was introduced into the Philippines in 1898, following its takeover from three centuries of Spanish rule by an American force. The American "Thomasite" teachers (so-called after the ship that first transported them from the USA) developed and implemented a comprehensive English curriculum in schools throughout the country. Within two decades, 47 percent of the population claimed to speak English and 56 percent to both read and write it (Bautista and Bolton 2008: 4). However, the percentage decreased amid the nationalist movement of the 1930s, including the first attempt to establish Tagalog as the national language in 1937. This was disrupted by the impacts of World War II in the Pacific, and resumed only in 1946 when the Philippines their gained independence.

The Philippine archipelago is the habitat for more than 130 different languages, including ten major ones, spoken by a population of more than 90 million people. The best-known Philippine language is Tagalog from the northern island of Luzon, which is strongly associated with the capital Manila and central government. This accounts for the fact that the national language developed after independence is based on Tagalog, though called Pilipino, then Filipino to articulate its national function. From 1970s, the Philippine government established a bilingual language policy, making Filipino and English its official languages. Both are used every day by many in Metro Manila, whereas Filipino is less acceptable further south (because of its associations with Tagalog), and English is used alongside other major local languages as a medium of communication. Taking all this into account, the sociolinguistic situation in the Philippines is polyglossic rather than diglossic, although English is the primary language in some quarters, such as the legal system.

In tandem with the national language policy, the Philippines government established a bilingual Filipino–English education policy in 1974. At its best it produced students proficient in both languages, but the supply of teaching materials and teachers competent in other Philippine languages was insufficient. Meanwhile the incentives to become proficient in English were evident as the government pursued the goal of internationalizing the Philippine workforce and preparing its citizens to work overseas, in Asia and the Middle East. The social inequality and dislocations caused by long-term absences of family members brought disenchantment with this policy; and, with a change of government in 1998, English was eclipsed for three years through President Estrada's refusal to use it for official purposes, prompting language riots by the English-using establishment. Since then, constructive work has been done to address the social and regional issues occasioned by the bilingual educational policy, through the Multilingual Language Education Policy (MLEP), which mandates the use of regional languages in primary schools, not just Filipino and English.

The complexity of multilingualism in the Philippines and its large, dispersed population contrast strongly with Singapore's compact linguistic habitat, not least in its impact on the role and functions of English. While English is the language of higher education, the mix of languages used in schools – now extended by the MLEP – means that students' proficiency in English is very variable. Teachers surveyed in both the 1990s (Thompson 2003) and the 2000s (Bautista 2001) reported the frequent use in the classroom of Taglish (a mixed language consisting of Filipino and English elements).

As with SingE, the written standard for English in the Philippines is exonormative – AmE rather than BrE. This also means that the reference materials are produced by overseas publishers, using their resources and editors. Webster's *Third New International Dictionary* (1961) was published in the Philippines, without providing codification for Philippine English (PhilE) itself. Since then a small dictionary for use in Philippine secondary schools was produced in partnership with an Australian publisher, titled the *Anvil-Macquarie Dictionary of Philippine English for High Schools* (2000). Yet, like the *Times-Chambers* dictionary produced in Singapore, it consists of an exonormative word list with a selection of Philippine words inserted into it. It does not provide codification of the range of vocabulary used in PhilE, to set the standard for it. There is no reference grammar of PhilE and, though there are increasing numbers of corpus-based studies to describe the grammatical norms of PhilE, they have yet to be compiled into a standard reference grammar.

Against the rather unstable sociopolitical conditions in the Philippines, the lack of resources or momentum to standardize the use of English is unsurprising. While its written standard is exonormative (AmE), what constitutes the spoken standard of English in the Philippines is elusive – probably not conceivable in unitary terms, given the diverse language habitats across the country. The most prevalent form of public speech, as Thompson (2003) observed in entertainment and broadcasting, was Taglish, which like Singlish is widely used but not esteemed. The unsettled relationship between Taglish and PhilE contributes to the difficulty of establishing a standard form of PhilE.

25.5.2   Corpus Data, Sociolinguistic Surveys, and the Norms of English Usage in Singapore

A number of corpus-based studies on elements of PhilE have shown its close relationship with the exonormative standard of AmE. In research on the frequencies of modals and quasimodals in WEs, Collins (2009) used ICE corpora to demonstrate how AmE is leading other varieties in its use of quasimodals and declining use of the core modals, and that PhilE showed the closest approximations to it among the nine varieties compared. In its use of the mandative construction (Peters 2009: 129), PhilE registered the highest number of mandative verbs among the six varieties examined, thus conspicuously in line with the strong American preference for mandatives, as opposed to BrE and most British-based varieties. PhilE use of the present perfect, again researched by Collins (2015) using ICE corpora, emerged close to that of AmE and lowest among the ten varieties examined – both in terms of actual frequency of occurrence and in the ratio between instances of the present perfect and the preterite. Yet the data also show that PhilE is much less inclined to contract the forms of the present perfect than AmE. This reluctance to emulate AmE in its more informal aspects also emerged in research on its use of the progressive (Collins 2015: 292), where the Philippine norms sometimes aligned with those of AmE but diverged especially in avoiding more colloquial uses of the progressive. This reluctance could be accounted for by the fact that AmE is used as the acrolect for PhilE and formality of style is maintained in it by Filipinos, despite it becoming more colloquial (Mair 2006).

The difficulties for Filipino teachers trained in standard AmE were eloquently expressed by Gonzales (1983) in his chapter "When does an *error* become a feature of *Philippine English*?" His anxieties about using PhilE do not seem to be shared by teachers a generation later. Those surveyed by Bautista (2001) were enthusiastic about PhilE and willing to admit that PhilE-Filipino mixed-code was used in their classes, without applying the label Taglish to it. Meanwhile teachers surveyed by Thompson (2003) both in Manila and in the Visayas, reported the use of Taglish in the classroom as part of their interactions with students. Some students and teachers even affirm its use and attach symbolic value to it, as a way of rejecting colonial hegemony (Bautista 2004). While Taglish is a well-known phenomenon, students in Borlongan's (2009) study were apparently less familiar with the term *Philippine English*, though willing to take on board the teacher's careful explanation of it – as involving grammatical forms that differed slightly from standard PhilE but without the code-switching typical of Taglish.

Students involved in a recent study of language usage in the Philippines (Lising, Peters, and Smith 2016) were ready to differentiate PhilE from AmE and to comment on their different functions, that is, AmE as the medium for writing and PhilE for speaking. Their understanding is the clearest evidence yet of how an exonormative standard of writing could complement endonormative ways of speaking in the Philippines (as found in Singapore). Yet this comes from a smallish group of students from a private university. What is lacking is widespread public endorsement of PhilE in Philippine society. Serious doubts about it have been expressed by Pefianco Martin (2014a: 57), as she represents the users of PhilE in terms of three circles like those of Kachru's well-known model:

> an Inner Circle of those who have embraced the English language (whether standard American of Philippine English), and actively promote it; an Outer Circle of Filipinos who may be aware of Philippine English as a distinct and legitimate variety, but who are either powerless to support it and/or ambivalent about its promotion; and an Expanding Circle of users of English in the Philippines to whom the language, of whatever variety, remains a requisite condition to upward mobility, but is often very difficult to access.

Pefianco Martin's regretful comments about the limited take-up of PhilE by its citizens do not support the suggestion that it has moved beyond the nativization stage of Schneider's model (2007: 143), on which she elsewhere expresses diffidence (Pefianco Martin 2014b).

25.6 Metalinguistic Awareness of Norms and Standards of English

Beyond the sociolinguistic surveys used above to explore the take-up of the new varieties of World English, let us turn to linguistic data for indications of their recognition and acceptance within the speech community. Happily, the GloWbE corpus of web-based WEs is a ready and very large source of data from 2012 on the terms and labels by which speakers of WEs refer to their own and other varieties, to give insights into which forms – and their implied standards and norms – are recognized by the speech community. GloWbE consists of more than two billion words of online English from the websites and blogs of twenty WEs. The discussion of standards and norms for English in Singapore and the Philippines in Sections 25.4 and 25.5 indicated much wider public endorsement of the endonormative variety in the first than the second. It is therefore of interest to see how far this is reflected in the set of terms mentioned for local and international forms of English, extracted from GloWbE's parallel corpora for SingE and PhilE. Those for Australian and New Zealand English are also provided by way of comparison for more fully evolved varieties of WEs, along with those for BrE (GB) and AmE (US). The latter are widely regarded as "international English" reference standards for other varieties or as "dual" standards (McArthur 2001), though increasingly it is AmE to which the international or "hyper-central" role is assigned (Mair 2013).

The data in Table 25.1 is suggestive of how speakers/Internet users in those six regions conceptualize their own and other varieties of English. The raw frequencies are paired (in brackets) with normalized figures per 10,000 relative to the size of each regional subcorpus, so as to allow horizontal comparisons across varieties. The two highest relative values in each column are marked in bold, to show which types of English are most often mentioned in the data for each variety.

These data present striking differences in the frequency with which the speakers refer to their own variety and other varieties or reference standards. The highest overall frequency of "self-reference" is to AmE in the US data, while the lowest is to New Zealand English in the NZ data – suggesting a low level of metalinguistic awareness or articulation of English

Table 25.1 *Reference forms of English used in six varieties of World Englishes (GloWbE corpus data)*

	SingE 42 million	PhilE 43 million	AusE 148 million	NZE 81 million	GB 387 million	US 386 million
Standard English	37 (0.88)	52 (1.21)	20 (1.35)	9 (0.1)	**300 (7.75)**	164 (4.2)
International English	4 (0.09)	17 (0.39)	**51 (3.45)**	38 (0.47)	44 (1.13)	7 (0.18)
Good English	**141 (3.36)**	**60 (1.39)**	91 (6.15)	**45 (0.56)**	263 (6.7)	106 (2.74)
British English	25 (0.59)	57 (1.33)	17 (1.15)	5 (0.06)	241 (6.23)	**191 (4.95)**
American English	32 (0.76)	**160 (3.73)**	41 (2.77)	26 (0.32)	255 (6.69)	**377 (8.77)**
Australian English	2 (0.05)	1 (0.02)	**91 (6.15)**	8 (0.09)	31 (1.01)	14 (0.36)
New Zealand English	0	0	0	**39 (0.48)**	7 (0.18)	1 (0.03)
Singapore English	19 (0.45)	1 (0.02)	0	0	3 (0.07)	0
Singlish	**247 (5.88)**	0	0	2 (0.02)	8 (0.21)	3 (0.08)
Philippines English	2 (0.05)	19 (0.44)	0	0	0	0
Taglish	0	**60 (1.39)**	0	0	1 (0.02)	2 (0.05)

varieties in its online discourse. In between and strikingly high frequency is the self-referencing to *Singlish* among Singaporeans, confirming the lively awareness of their own indigenized variety of English. Their recognition of more formal *Singapore English* is muted: Instead, it is the *good English* for which the Singapore government has campaigned, which is still a commonplace in Singaporean discourse. Thus the two highest frequency terms in Singapore both reflect locally endorsed, endonormative forms of English. Compare the Philippines data where the most frequent reference is exonormative to *American English*. References to *Taglish*, the indigenized variety, come second, well ahead of the still evolving concept of *Philippine English* and on a par with a notional *good English* (not grounded in any government language policy). The Philippine data reflect less developed metalinguistic awareness of English in a very multilingual country. Other points of interest in Table 25.1 are the high levels of self-referencing by Australians to *Australian English*, close to that shown in the GB data for *British English*. Yet the use of *British English* by GB web users is markedly lower than their use of *standard English*, echoing its powerful use in ideological British discussions about "the standard" (see Section 25.2.3) and continuing controversy over what constitutes *British English* in the twenty-first century (Peters 2012: 1888–1889). References to *international English* are remarkably few in both the GB and US data, that is, little used in self-reference, although the label is applied to them by speakers of the other four varieties, especially in Australia.

The data in Table 25.1 show how metalinguistic awareness of the identity and presumed norms of their own regional variety is strongest for Australians and Americans, helped no doubt by the numerous dictionaries that provide codification of their respective standards. Speakers of SingE are likewise confident of their indigenized variety, as well as the limits put on it by the officially mandated *good English*. The standards for SingE are thus locally defined, whereas those for PhilE are still far from convergent and largely exonormative in references to AmE. For all four varieties (Singapore, Philippines, Australia, the USA), the metalinguistic data coincide with their evolutionary status, ranging from Stages 3 to 5 (Schneider 2007: 56), in showing the extent to which speakers and Internet communicators in each region embrace their own variety and identify with it.

25.7 Conclusion

These various types of linguistic and sociolinguistic data brought to bear on the issues of standardization and the norms of language help to shed light on the relative endonormativity of two still evolving WEs and the ongoing relevance of exonormative standards even for the more advanced variety. As Gupta (2010) argued, exonormative standards (British or American) probably will continue to be the reference norms of writing for ESL varieties and remain their acrolect. This seems to hold even if endonormative varieties of English (standard, colloquial, and mixed-code) can provide speakers with rich means of expressing their local identity. In multilingual habitats, all such varieties will continue to evolve and their convergence or divergence will be influenced by other contextual factors, such as the size, linguistic makeup of speech community, official government language policy, and educational planning.

References

Ansaldo, Umberto. 2004. The evolution of Singapore English: Finding the matrix. In Lisa Lim, ed. *Singapore English: A Grammatical Description*. Amsterdam: Benjamins, 129–52.

Bautista, Maria (Ma.) Lourdes S. and Kingsley Bolton. 2008. *Philippine English: Linguistic and Literary Perspectives*. Hong Kong: Hong Kong University Press.

Bautista, Maria (Ma.) Lourdes S. 2001. Attitudes of selected Luzon university students and faculty towards Philippine English. In Maria (Ma.) Lourdes G. Tayao et al., eds. *Rosario E Maminta in Focus: Selected Writings in Applied Linguistics*. Quezon City: Philippine Association for Language Teaching, 236–73.

Bautista, Maria (Ma.) Lourdes S. 2004 Taglish-English code-switching as a mode of discourse. *Asia Pacific Education Review* 5(2): 226–233. doi:10.1007/BF03024960

Bernaisch, Tobias and Christopher Koch. 2016. Attitudes towards Englishes in India. *World Englishes* 35(1): 118–132.

Biber, Douglas, Edward Finegan and Dawn Atkinson. 1994. ARCHER and its challenges. In Udo Fries, Gunnel Tottie and Peter Schneider, eds. *Creating and Using English Language Corpora*. Amsterdam: Rodopi, 255–272.

Biber, Douglas. 1988. *Variation across Speech and Writing*. Cambridge: Cambridge University Press

Biewer, Carolin. 2015. *South Pacific Englishes: A Sociolinguistic and Morphosyntactic Profile of Fiji English, Samoan English and Cook Islands English*. Amsterdam: John Benjamins.

Borlongan, Ariane. 2009. A survey on language use, attitudes and identity in relation to Philippine English among young generation Filipinos. *Philippine ESL Journal* 3: 74–107.

Bowerman, Sean. 2012. Standard South African English. In Raymond Hickey, ed. *Standards of English. Codified Varieties Around the World*. Cambridge: Cambridge University Press, 198–212.

Cameron, Deborah. 1995. *Verbal Hygiene*. London: Routledge.

Chand, Vineeta. 2014. Review of Hickey *Standards of English: Codified Varieties around the World* (2012). *Journal of Sociolinguistics* 18(5): 708–719.

Collins, Peter. 2009. Modals and quasimodals in World Englishes. *World Englishes* 28: 281–292.

Collins, Peter. 2015. Recent diachronic change in the progressive in Philippine English. In Peter Collins, ed. *Grammatical Change in English World-Wide*. Amsterdam: Benjamins, 271–296.

Devonish, Hubert and Ewart A.C. Thomas. 2012. Standards of English in the Caribbean. In Raymond Hickey, ed. *Standards of English. Codified Varieties Around the World*. Cambridge: Cambridge University Press, 179–197.

Ferguson, Charles A. 1972. Diglossia. In Pier Paolo Giglioli, ed. *Language and Social Context: Selected Readings*. Harmondsworth: Penguin, 232–251.

Garner, Bryan. 2009. *Garner's Modern American Usage* (3rd ed.). New York: Oxford University Press.

Gill, Martin. 2017. "Goodbye, Sweet England": Language, nation and normativity in popular British news media. In Ingrid Tieken-Boon van Ostade and Carol Percy, eds. *Prescription and Tradition in Language: Establishing Standards across Space and Time*. Berlin: de Gruyter, 255–272.

Gjurkova, Aleksandra. 2017. Prescription and language management in Macedonia. In Ingrid Tieken-Boon van Ostade and Carol Percy, eds. *Prescription and Tradition in Language: Establishing Standards across Space and Time*. Berlin: de Gruyter, 318–330.

Gonzalez, Andrew. 1983. When does an *error* become a distinctive feature of *Philippine English*? In Richard B. Noss, ed. *Varieties of English in Southeast Asia*. Singapore: Singapore University Press, 150–172.

Gupta, Anthea Fraser. 2010. Singapore Standard English revisited. In Lisa Lim, Anne Pakir and Lionel Wee, eds. *English in Singapore: Unity and Utility*. Hong Kong: Hong Kong University Press, 57–89.

Gut, Ulrike. 2012. Standards of English in West Africa. In Raymond Hickey, ed. *Standards of English. Codified Varieties Around the World*. Cambridge: Cambridge University Press, 213–229.

Guy, Gregory and Frans Hinskens. 2016. Introduction to special issue. Linguistic coherence: Systems, repertoires and speech communities. *Lingua* 172(3): 1–9.

Halliday, M.A.K. 1985. *Spoken and Written Language*. Deakin University Press.

Haugen, Einar. 1972. Dialect, language, nation. In J.B. Pride and Janet Holmes, eds. *Sociolinguistics: Selected Readings*. Harmondsworth: Penguin, 97–111.

Hickey, Raymond, ed. 2012. *Areal Features of the Anglophone World*. Berlin: de Gruyter.

Honey, John. 1997. *Language and Power: The Story of Standard English and Its Enemies*. London: Faber & Faber.

Hundt, Marianne, Lena Zipp and André Huber. 2015. Attitudes towards varieties of English in Fiji. A shift to endonormativity? *World Englishes* 34(4): 688–707.

Kirkpatrick, Andy. 2012. English in ASEAN: Implications for regional multilingualism. *Journal of Multilingual and Multicultural Development* 33(4): 331–344.

Kretzschmar, William and Charles Meyer. 2012. The idea of Standard American English. In Raymond Hickey, ed. *Standards of English. Codified Varieties Around the World*. Cambridge: Cambridge University Press, 139–158.

Lee, J. 2004. *A Dictionary of Singlish and Singapore English*. www .Singlishdictionary.com

Lim, Lisa. 2012. Standards of English in South-East Asia. In Raymond Hickey, ed. *Standards of English. Codified Varieties Around the World*. Cambridge: Cambridge University Press, 274–293.

Lim, Lisa, ed. 2004 *Singapore English: A Grammatical Description*. Amsterdam: Benjamins.

Lising, Loy, Pam Peters and Adam Smith. 2016. Language use and language attitudes in multilingual habitats. Paper presented at the Australian Linguistic Society Conference, December 2016.

Mair, Christian. 2006. *Twentieth Century English*. Cambridge: Cambridge University Press.

Mair, Christian. 2013. The world system of Englishes: Accounting for the transnational importance of mobile and mediated vernaculars. *English World-Wide 34*(3): 253–278.

Mauranen, Anna. 2012. *Exploring ELF: Academic English Shaped by Non-native Speakers*. Cambridge: Cambridge University Press.

McArthur, Tom. 1998. *The English Languages*. Cambridge: Cambridge University Press.

McArthur, Tom. 2001. Review: World English and world Englishes: Trends, tensions, varieties, and standards. *Language Teaching 34*(1): 1–20.

Milroy, James and Lesley Milroy. 1985. *Authority in Language: Investigating Prescription and Language Standardization*. London: Routledge.

Mitchell, Alexander G. and Arthur Delbridge. 1966. *The Speech of Australian Adolescents*. Angus and Robertson.

Övergaard, Gert. 1995. *The Mandative Subjunctive in American and British English in the 20th Century*. Uppsala: Almquist and Wiksell.

Pakir, Anne. 1993. *The English Language in Singapore: Standards and Norms*. Singapore Association for Applied Linguistics.

Pefianco Martin, Isabel. 2014a. Philippine English revisited. *World Englishes 33*(1): 50–59.

Pefianco Martin, Isabel. 2014b. Philippine English: Beyond nativization? In Sarah Buschfeld, Thomas Hoffmann, Magnus Huber and Alexander Kautzsch, eds. The *Evolution of Englishes: The Dynamic Model and Beyond*. Amsterdam: Benjamins, 70–85.

Peters, Pam. 2009. The mandative subjunctive in spoken English. In Pam Peters, Peter Collins and Adam Smith, eds. *Comparative Studies of Australian and New Zealand English*. Amsterdam: Benjamins, 125–137.

Peters, Pam. 2012. Varieties of English: Standard British English. In Alexander Bergs and Laurel Brinton, eds. *HSK English Historical Linguistics* HSK 34.2. Berlin: de Gruyter, 1879–1899.

Peters, Pam. 2014. Differentiation in Australian English. In Sarah Buschfeld, Thomas Hoffmann, Magnus Huber and Alexander Kautzsch, eds. *The Evolution of Englishes: The Dynamic Model and Beyond*. Amsterdam: Benjamins, 107–125.

Peters, Pam. 2018. The lexicography of usage. In Ingrid Tieken-Boon van Ostade, ed. *English Usage Guides: History, Advice, Attitudes*. Oxford: Oxford University Press, 31–50.

Peters, Pam and Wendy Young. 1997. English grammar and the lexicography of usage. *Journal of English Linguistics* 25(4): 315–331.

Platt, John T. and Heidi Weber. 1980. *English in Singapore and Malaysia – Status, Features, Functions*. Amsterdam: Benjamins.

Preston, Dennis. 1996. Where the worst English is spoken. In Edgar W. Schneider, ed. *Focus on the USA*. Amsterdam: Benjamins, 279–360.

Romaine, Suzanne. 1995. *Bilingualism* (2nd ed.). Oxford: Oxford University Press.

Schneider, Edgar W. 2007. *Post-Colonial English*. Cambridge: Cambridge University Press.

Schreier, Daniel. 2012. Varieties resistant to standardization. In Raymond Hickey, ed. *Standards of English: Codified Varieties Around the World*. Cambridge: Cambridge University Press, 354–368.

Siemund, Peter, Monkia Schulz and Martin Schweinberger. 2014. Studying the linguistic ecology of Singapore: A comparison of college and university students. *World Englishes* 33(3): 340–362.

Smakman, Dirk. 2012. The definition of the standard language: A survey of seven countries. *International Journal of the Sociology of Language 218*: 25–58.

Tan, Peter K. W. and Daniel K. H. Tan. 2008. Attitudes towards non-standard English in Singapore. *World Englishes* 27(3–4): 465–479.

Tan, Siew Imm. 2016. Charting the endonormative stabilization of Singapore English. In Gerhard Leitner, Azirah Hashim and Hans-Georg Wolf, eds. *Communicating with Asia: The Future of English as a Global Language*. Cambridge: Cambridge University Press, 69–84.

Thompson, Roger M. 2003 *Filipino English and Taglish: Language Switching from Multiple Perspectives*. Amsterdam: Benjamins.

Truss, Lynne. 2003. *Eats, Shoots and Leaves*. Profile Books

Wales, Katie. 2006. *Northern English: A Social and Cultural History*. Cambridge: Cambridge University Press.

Wee, Lionel. 2011. Metadiscursive convergence in the Singlish debate. *Language and Communication 31*: 75–85.

Yao, Xinyue and Peter Collins. 2012. The present perfect in world Englishes. *World Englishes* 31(3): 386–403.

26

Identity and Indexicality in the Study of World Englishes

Erik Schleef

26.1 Introduction

In recent decades, identity has served a critical role in the study of World Englishes (WEs). At the core of this interest lies the idea that changing forms of identity construction may have played a crucial part among the groups involved in the development of New Englishes. Simply put, changes in identity construction, particularly regarding local, regional, or national identities, may be reflected in linguistic usage. However, not everyone agrees on the role identity may have played in the development of WEs (see, e.g., Trudgill 2008 and the various responses to his assertion that identity was irrelevant in the formation of new dialects). I argue in what follows that we still know much too little about where identity may matter and may have mattered in the development of WEs to dismiss the notion completely. This is especially true for the role of identity at the local interactional level. The concept of identity is rather undertheorized and often used somewhat vaguely in the study of WEs, and, in this chapter, I aim to locate this research strand in recent theoretically based ideas about identity. In particular, I would like to argue that indexicality is a useful concept that can provide more detail on some of the processes involved in the emergence and development of Englishes. It can serve as an important bridge that may help provide answers to many of the questions that have been only partially addressed or remain open. Specifically, we need to know:

(1) What happens at the interactional level of identity construction? Surely, a person's local/regional/national identity is not always fore-grounded. In fact, in most interactions, other identities matter more; for example, being a mother, a student, and a fun person.

(2) What precisely are the social meanings of a linguistic feature or a variety for different speakers and hearers in different contexts? Perceptual research suggests that these tend to have a whole host of different meanings (e.g. Campbell-Kibler 2007) rather than simply indexing "us" versus "them."

(3) What specifically is the link between identity construction and linguistic usage? Features that are associated with the local/regional/national level of identity construction probably also have other meanings that are linked ideologically to social meanings associated with these levels of identity. How does this work?

Many of these questions cannot yet be answered but indexicality theory provides a useful framework to understand and solve them in the future. This chapter provides the groundwork to do precisely this in the tradition of Variationist Sociolinguistics (VS). First, I give a brief overview of the different perspectives on identity within sociolinguistic work and relate this to the study of WEs. Then, I outline Third-Wave Variationist Sociolinguistics (TWVS) and some of its central issues pertaining to WEs, identity, and indexicality. I consider representative studies that provide empirical evidence on identity performance and indexicality in a variety of local and global contexts. These concern in particular (1) the social meanings of features of English at the micro-level of interaction, in which identity work is most transparent, and (2) the perception of linguistic features.

26.2 The First and Second Waves of Variationist Sociolinguistics

Eckert (2012) argues that VS developed through three successive waves of scholarship and I will use this idea to structure the first part of my review. Although one wave followed another, associated research for each continues to be conducted. One important aspect by which the waves differ is how they deal with the concept of identity. To a large degree, this is due to their different research foci and how and where they seek social meaning.

First-wave VS is based on large-scale surveys of populations, conducted with the goal of statistical representativeness, objectivity, and replicability. These studies result in stratified models of the speech of populations, particularly of urban areas in countries where English is the majority language. These include New York (Labov 1966), Detroit (Wolfram 1969), Norwich (Trudgill 1974), Glasgow (Macauley 1977), Sydney (Horvath 1985) and Montreal (Thibault and Sankoff 1993). The procedure in these is similar: Variation is identified and linguistic and social constraints are then determined alongside whether or not the variation is a reflection of language change. The social factors that this type of research may investigate tend to be of a relatively broad, census-type macrosociological nature, such as speaker sex, social class, age, and ethnicity. Filtered through a socioeconomic perspective on social space and, secondarily, some other salient social categories (see Eckert 2012: 90), first-wave studies provide a bird's-eye view of variation and the social and linguistic spread of language change (see D'Arcy, Chapter 19, this volume).

Identity does not and, considering the macrosociological orientation, cannot play a particularly large role here. It is rarely mentioned or even theorized. Occasionally, *indirect* arguments are made about identity when the behavior of people is to be explained that fall into the same macrosociological category, such as social class, gender, or ethnicity. When individuals in these groups are said to be influenced strongly by notions such as "prestige," "status," or "solidarity," researchers inevitably make assumptions about the type of people who hold these attitudes. For example, Trudgill (1972) argued that the speech of women in his sample was consistently more standard because of their strong desire for upward mobility and their more pronounced sensitivity to standard pressures. Similarly, he stated that male, middle-class speakers might adopt working-class innovations because of their association with masculinity. These macrosociological labels are conceptualized as *reflections* of language use. This implies their basis in identities that are stable, unified, and essential, as these identities are based on membership of individuals in particular social categories.

Where identity is evoked *directly*, this usually relates to particular individuals; for example, Labov (1972: 70–109) wrote about New York City identity in relation to one of his participants. The reason identity is seldom linked directly to the large category labels used in these studies is clear. Researchers working in the quantitative tradition, which is normally based on inferential statistics, are aware that claims about cause and effect must be considered carefully, especially since statistical models always explain only a portion of all variation. After all, individuals within descriptive categories do not have *one* unified, stable identity that has an essential link to language. Let us assume we find that male teenagers utilize a particular nonstandard feature in an urban community more than other groups. Is this due to an expression of adolescent masculinity? Perhaps for some but more data is required. We cannot turn immediately to identity as an explanation. This finding may be due to numerous reasons that may have no association with identity at all. Statistically motivated speculations about identity should be avoided. Instead, our explanation must be grounded in a principled linguistic or social theory and additional evidence, which may often be found in individual interactions. The second- and third-wave of VS developed refined methods to address many of these issues.

The second wave is characterized by:

A shift away from macrosociological categories to locally relevant groupings.
A shift from interview data to naturally occurring speech.
A focus on quantitative as well as qualitative data analysis.
A focus on the connections between identity work, local practice, and local forms of speech.

Although the level at which social categories are investigated changes (from macro- to meso-sociological, i.e. local categories), the view of identity is nonetheless one of fixedness and stability. The idea persists of linguistic varieties that comprise particular linguistic features, which define these varieties. So does the notion that these varieties mark specific social groups, albeit at a more localized level. Theoretically and methodologically, this shift was facilitated by ethnographic methods of data collection and analysis with the aim of finding out how certain linguistic forms are locally meaningful to specific social groupings that emerge in the fieldwork. These social groupings are, thus, not imposed on a community; rather, they arise from participant observation. They are based on participant beliefs of how the community is structured. This has a huge advantage when analyzing data: We are working with categories that we know are salient to community members in a particular locale and these classifications are likely those that influence language use. The use of particular linguistic features was increasingly seen as an expression of a distinct identity and the identity labels used are not of a macrosociological nature but refer to categories within local social networks or communities of practice (Lave and Wenger 1991; Eckert and McConnell-Ginet 1992).

For example, in Milroy's (1980) study of working-class neighborhoods in Belfast, the concept of the working class as a demographic category is thoroughly deconstructed and criticized. The crucial social variable and factor deemed most important when making predictions about language variation and change, for example of /a/-backing in a word such as *bad*, was the kind of social network speakers participate in. Milroy was interested in finding out why it is that nonstandard features, which have been criticized and condemned, continue to persist. First-wave research has revealed repeatedly that use of standard features is connected to higher social classes, status, and prestige. It could be argued that this is something people desire and strive for. Yet people do *not* start speaking like those socially above them on a grand scale. They want to belong to a group that has value to them. Ultimately, this is a debate about identity and Milroy provides ample statistical evidence for the claim that we tend to talk like the people with whom we interact, the people to whom we feel we belong.

This research and similar studies (e.g. Cheshire 1982; Gal 1979) may have changed their demographic categories but research in this tradition was not particularly specific about the identities that develop in social networks and how identity, social network, and the norms that this research strand argued are shared by network members relate to each other. Understanding these norms opens a door to understanding identity. Communities of practice are particularly suited to investigating norms and ideologies that relate to the social lives of speakers. Within a community of practice approach, an analysis of contextually dependent use of language goes hand in hand with an investigation of identity construction. The focus is on shared repertoires, values, and practices. Eckert (1989) was one of the first scholars to use this concept in linguistics, particularly in her study of language at a high school in suburban Detroit. The social order of this high school involved two mutually opposed social categories, "jocks" and "burnouts," which had multiple impacts on their speech.

26.3 Two Waves and World Englishes

The majority of work on WEs that deliberates the role of identity falls into waves one or two. Typically, identity construction is discussed at the national or regional level, and Schneider's (2003) Dynamic Model, in particular, incorporates both of these (see Hickey, Chapter 2, this volume, for details).

His model represents a crucial point of reference in how identity is thematized in this strand of research. Schneider outlines the processes involved in the development of New Englishes in several different stages: foundation, exonormative stabilization, nativization, endonormative stabilization, and differentiation. He argues that each of these is subject to changing forms of identity construction by the groups involved in the process, namely the settlers and the indigenous population. Group identities are reconstructed from an "us" identity to an "other" identity, from a perceived connection with the motherland to a subgroup within a new nation (other social identities are also constructed). These changes in identity construction are reflected in linguistic usage. The model is very honest about its macrosociological nature and the questions it raises.

We find similar discussions of the role of identity elsewhere about national identity (Moore 1999), local identity (Macaulay 2002: 239; Hickey 2003: 215), or to explain why it is that speakers accommodate to each other (Tuten 2003: 29). With the exception of Tuten, all of these discuss identity at a macro- or meso-sociological level. This applies also to those arguing against identity-based positions. Trudgill (2008) is very skeptical of the role that identity is supposed to have played in the formation of new colonial varieties, and he cites Labov (2001: 191), who argues that local identity may matter sometimes, for example in his Martha's Vineyard study, but qualifies that "we do not often find correlations between degrees of local identification and the progress of sound change."

Trudgill, on the basis of several case studies, contends that national identity, in particular, is unlikely to have played a role in identity construction, especially at times when there was no sense of a nation. According to him, identity is not needed as an explanatory factor for the development of new varieties. While he acknowledges that new identities do develop, he claims that they do not drive the process of variety formation; they are a consequence of accommodation and emerge after new mixed varieties have arisen by accommodation. For Trudgill (2008), dialect mixture is an inevitable outcome of colonial dialect contact. Accommodation in face-to-face interaction drives it. This, he argues, is a mechanism that is automatic and not driven by identity construction. He backs up his view with several sources claiming that accommodation is an automatic outcome of any interaction. It is merely due to behavioral coordination and a sense of self does not come into play here.

There are some interesting underlying similarities between pro and contra arguments: Identity is often undertheorized and arguments are based on unquestioned assumptions. It is this imprecise and common-sense manner of dealing with identity that allows this notion to be used rather vaguely. This may, in fact, represent an important cause of disagreement between scholars. In sum, the main assumptions are as follows:

1. Most arguments are made at a macrosociological level, yet identity construction happens at the interpersonal level. Arguments about identity are best made at this level as identity claims about groups of people are bound to be overgeneralizations. Thus, Labov (2001) and Trudgill (2008) have a point when criticizing macrosociological studies for jumping much too quickly onto the identity bandwagon. Nonetheless, their skepticism is also based on a concept of identity that is much too narrow.
2. Another similarity of the views of both "camps" is the concept of identity: It is seen as reflective, that is, particular language use reflects group membership; but linguistic features/styles/varieties can index not only a social group – they can have a variety of different meanings (in context and for different speakers).
3. Yet there is a tendency to focus on either whole varieties or individual features as (not) reflective of identity, and it is assumed that any potential link between an identity category and a linguistic feature is a direct one, that is, variants serving as identity markers. However, both of these assumptions deserve thorough investigation: The precise nature of any link often remains unclear.

Then there are assumptions about which different researchers do in fact hold different views.

4. There is a tendency among some to see identity as something that we can control and are conscious of. This is a particular view of agency. However, as I show in the next section, this assumption is not necessarily warranted and third-wave sociolinguistics has moved past it. Intentionality is not required.

5. Even if accommodation is automatic, identity construction may still be involved. The precise nature of accommodation and a wider notion of identity as co-constructed in context still needs closer scrutiny.

6. In some previous studies, identity construction in face-to-face conversation is not sufficiently separated from discourses about identity, particularly at a stage when certain varieties become enregistered (Johnstone 2010, see Section 26.4.2). How people then use these discourses and talk about the nation, identity, and language may be far removed from how language is used.

So what are some of the points where the two waves of research continue to help us along in our investigation of identity and WEs? Many studies suggest that aspects of our identity do influence how we speak in language contact situations, and some of these are local/regional/national identities. I do not think that identities are and can always be *linguistically* expressed, nor is the use of a specific form always an expression of a distinct identity. Nonetheless, when we are interactionally engaged, identity construction is ongoing and this construction process may involve linguistic features. Thus, even if we dismiss the claim that (national) identity may have been the driving force in the development of WEs, we cannot disregard other aspects of identity that may have impacted the process indirectly. I discuss some such aspects in what follows: They relate to peer adolescent identity; complex, local cultural alignments; and a variety of interactionally relevant identities that may result from them.

The role of children and adolescents in new dialect formation, especially when they turn their focus to their peers in adolescence, has been discussed by many scholars. Can this reorientation possibly happen without a reconstruction of their identities? Holmes and Kerswill (2008: 276) make a related point in regards to the evolution of the New Zealand accent:

> Rather than searching for evidence of the development of "New Zealand" identity at the early stages of dialect mixing, we should be looking for evidence on what it would mean to sound (locally) acceptable within any particular new, socially diverse community.

Many studies in the second wave of VS have demonstrated that it does not have to be local or national identities that move variation in a specific region into a certain direction. Acceptable gender, class roles, and so on in specific communities (of practice) seem to matter as well.

Similar arguments hold for complex contact situations. Yet the question of alignment with the local culture may also matter here, and it may matter more for some newcomers in an area than for others. Several studies show that some of L2 and heritage learners' linguistic output is influenced by their sense of who they are and who they want to be. For example, Sharma's (2005) research suggests that the use of phonological variables among speakers of Indian heritage in the USA was influenced significantly by their degree of alignment with American culture. Drummond's (2012) study of Polish migrants in Manchester, England, found that speakers who were planning on staying in England were less likely to use the most L1-influenced variant [ɪnk] (when compared with the other nonstandard yet local variant [ɪŋg]). Similarly, Schleef (2017a) examines t-glottalling in the speech of Polish migrant teenagers in London. He finds that once t-glottalling is available to them for stylistic practice in combination with other features (after about two years in London), it is used for the constitution of a *variety* of distinct identities at the interpersonal level. These range from a casual London adolescent identity to an identity construction of a middle-class, educated youth.

In Schleef (2017a), I caution against the danger of reading off alignment with one culture or another on the basis of nonstandard feature usage alone, t-glottalling in this case. Alignment with England need not be reflected in the use of t-glottalling: Nonuse can be a reflection of an intense connection with Poland but it can also be a reflection of alignment with that part of British culture that values standard language and frowns on the use of nonstandard features. While it is true that some pupils who align strongly with England use much t-glottalling, there are others who align with it just as strongly but use [t] almost exclusively rather than [ʔ].

Thus, national, colonial, local (and so on) identity can be expressed in a variety of ways. These findings appear particularly relevant in the light of research on multicultural London English, which has suggested that the language of immigrants may affect how English is used in inner-city London (Cheshire et al. 2011). Thus, if a sense of self influences language use of L2-immigrant arrivals to some degree and if such language, in turn, influences vernaculars in large, multicultural cities, interpersonal identity construction among immigrants can potentially influence aspects of a variety and may have done so in the past. It has become clear that the link between identity and linguistic features or varieties is rather more complex than previously assumed. These are valuable insights and TWVS is uniquely placed to follow up on them.

26.4 The Third Wave of Variationist Sociolinguistics

26.4.1 Identity in Third-Wave Variationist Sociolinguistics

The most crucial difference of the third wave in VS, when compared with previous waves, relates to the linguistic element and what precisely it is that it indexes: social categories in the former waves but social meanings in TWVS (e.g. Ochs 1992, Agha 2005, Podesva 2007, Eckert 2008, Kiesling 2009). The precise meanings of these linguistic (and other) elements emerge in the role they play in styles that individuals use to construct particular identities moment by moment and as they move from one identity and situation to another. This is a (partial) move away from con-crete demographic categories to concepts that are often more abstract and a view of social meaning not as stable and shared by the community but as emerging within particular conversational styles. Moore and Podesva (2009: 448–450) conceptualize social meanings as stances (e.g. critical, polite), personal characteristics (e.g. intelligent, educated), personae (e.g. "nerd," "jock"), and social types (e.g. "middle-class"). Thus, the categories we are familiar with from waves one and two *can* be social meanings of a linguistic element but often only alongside other social meanings and, crucially, they may be in an indexical relationship to each other. Before I explain what this means, however, I will outline some more innovations of the TW approach in VS.

A second important issue in this tradition concerns the role of identity. Identity here is not a reflection of language; instead, language is used to constitute identities through stylistic practice (Eckert 2012: 94). Language and identity cannot be separated; they are co-constitutive. The concept of identity in this sense is based on the assumption that identities are dynamic and changeable. They shift continually within interactions and across contexts as they are constructed and reconstructed between con-versationalists in discourse (see Bucholtz and Hall 2010: 25). We are unli-kely to fully grasp the concept if we limit ourselves to the quantitative study of language.

A variety of different identity levels matter in interactions. Bucholtz and Hall's (2005: 592; 2010: 21) concept of identity includes "(a) macro-level demographic categories; (b) local ethnographically-distinct cultural posi-tions; and (c) temporary and interactionally-specific stances and partici-pant roles" (see also Coupland 2007 and Kiesling 2013, for similar divisions). The latter are interactionally specific temporary roles and orien-tations that occur as our identity construction proceeds in a conversation, and they may include such fleeting identities as coffee "addict," empa-thetic conversationalist, or mountain enthusiast. These may take prece-dence over macro-level identities, such as male or Chinese-American or even occur at the same time. This reconceptualization of identity necessi-tates a significant methodological shift: a move toward ethnography and discourse analysis (broadly conceived) in the investigation of language, especially at the interpersonal level.

Third, agency continues to be an important concept, but agency here does not mean "at will." Agency need not be continuous, conscious inten-tion. Bucholtz and Hall (2010) consider the idea that agency can go beyond individual choice and deliberate action. Identity emerges in a variety of ways, ranging from deliberate action to routine practice and as the result of interactional processes. Thus, if face-to-face linguistic accommodation is, indeed, the primary process through which new dialects emerge (Trudgill 2008), then even "automatic" accommodation, as assumed by Trudgill, must involve identity construction. Trudgill's argument is, in any case, an enormous challenge to accommodation theory as initially conceived because identity construction and human motivation have been central concerns of accommodation theory, for example see Coupland's (2008: 268) defense of the role of identity in accommodation. At the same time, agency and identity are constrained. We are limited (also linguistically) in what kind of identities we can construct for ourselves.

Finally, how language relates to social meaning and ultimately identity is the most unique feature of the third wave. Linguistic features are meaningful as components of social styles. Eckert (2012) provides a very telling example of the variety of different meanings with which a single feature may be associated. Aspirated /t/ in intervocalic position has been found to be relevant in a variety of different styles in the USA; those of "geek" girls (Bucholtz 1996), Orthodox Jews (Benor 2001), and gay men (Podesva 2007). Aspirated intervocalic /t/ cannot possibly mean geek girl or Orthodox Jew or gay man. Instead, it must refer to something that all of the styles in which it occurs draw on, which, as Eckert (2008) argues, is a set of indexical values linked to extremely eloquent and clear speech. The social meanings of a linguistic feature or even a code enable us to constitute specific identities; in other words, linguistic features are combined into styles, style-specific social meanings emerge (based, to an extent, on those of individual features), and these enable us to constitute an identity in a specific conversational context. This must mean that social meanings of linguistic features are underspecified. They have not just one meaning but a somewhat broad meaning potential. Social meanings are also dynamic: The social meanings of a specific linguistic feature may alter as it is used in a specific style in a specific context by a specific person. Thus, an important goal of all third-wave research is uncovering the social meanings of a particular (linguistic) element in context and how these meanings emerge. One way to discover what a single variable may mean is to investigate its application in identity construction.

However, because social meanings of individual features may alter as they combine with other features and because changes in someone's identity (even within the same conversation) may result in a change in someone's (linguistic) practice, we must focus on more than just individual features. This is the reason why many variationists examine conversational style and changes therein (Eckert 2000; Moore 2011). A style may be viewed as "a socially meaningful clustering of features within and across linguistic levels and modalities" (Campbell-Kibler et al. 2006). This clustering need not only include linguistic features but any linguistic and nonlinguistic material that aids the construction of styles, such as makeup, clothing, and so on.

Thus far, I have made several important points: that linguistic elements index social meanings, that the notion of identity has been broadened and reconceptualized in TWVS, and that clusters of features (including non-linguistic ones) may index identities. The next section explores in more detail how indexing works.

26.4.2 Indexicality

It is best to conceive of indexicality as a mechanism that creates semiotic links between linguistic forms and social meanings (Silverstein 1985; Ochs 1992). For example, in London, a glottalled (t) in words such as *water* and *better* may be associated not only with social meanings, such as casualness, but also uneducatedness, and so on. Just as social meanings are under-specified and dynamic, the links between forms and social meanings, too, are vague and complex and not every member in a community may agree on them: They are contestable. For example, Meyerhoff and Niedzielski (2003: 547–549) conducted a study in which participants in New Zealand were asked to evaluate lexical items embedded in forty-one sentences on a scale that ranged from *Not at all New Zealand* to *Absolutely New Zealand*. Each of these lexical items (e.g. *torch*) was tested against an item that was often ascribed to an external source (e.g. *flashlight*). While participants agreed on the New Zealand-ness of some words, for example *jersey, lift,* and *biscuit*, there was considerable disagreement on others, including *lorry, elevator, truck, flashlight,* and *movies*. Social meanings of this latter category are contestable: While some spreading variants are perceived to be exotic, others are reinterpreted as local, and this may depend on varying paths of diffusion.

One important aspect of indexicality is that a linguistic element that has acquired social meaning in a particular context can gain new indexicalities by association. For example, if a linguistic feature is heard as uneducated, the speaker who uses it may also be heard as unintelligent. Of course, the speaker may not share the belief system of the hearer or even recognize a particular feature as relevant to an interaction. One important question in sociolinguistics is how social meanings come to be linked with specific linguistic forms, and how indexicality may constitute identities (on a more permanent basis). A variety of processes makes this possible. If identity is not indexed directly (simply by making reference to a category, e.g. as a man, I feel ... ; our local traditions are ...), it may be indexed indirectly. This is achieved through implicature and presupposition (i.e. by implying concepts such as gender and localness), stance-taking, and stylistic prac-tice, which is where indexicality matters.

The mechanisms by which indexicalities arise can be viewed from dif-ferent (yet relatively similar) perspectives. First, I will consider stance, followed by stylistic practice. Bucholtz and Hall (2010: 22) conceptualize stance as "evaluative, affective and epistemic orientations in discourse."

The focus here is on how the display of evaluation, affect, and epistemic orientation constitutes resources in identity construction. The link between a (linguistic) sign and social meaning is discussed usually in orders of indexicality (Silverstein 2003). A sign may index a speaker category in a first order, and some association with that category in a second order, and so on. These are interpretive orders, so there will be variability in interpretations.

Ochs (1992) identifies direct indexical links as those between language and stances, social acts, and activities. For example, we may use language and practice in such a way that it constitutes a particular aggressive stance directly, in a specific context. If this stance is extended ideologically to a social category, for example, men, an indirect indexicality has emerged. This can, of course, only happen if it is repeated often enough: if a particular social group repeatedly takes a particular stance in particular interactions and contexts. Under these circumstances, stance accretion (DuBois 2002; Rauniomaa 2003) may occur: stances grow into more enduring identity structures. By repeatedly taking the same stance, styles emerge (Kiesling 2009).

Johnstone's (2010) view of these processes is similar. Following Agha's (2005) notion of enregisterment, she describes how permanent links emerge between linguistic form(s) and social identity in Pittsburgh. Enregisterment is a process "through which a linguistic repertoire becomes differentiable [and] ... socially recognised" (Agha 2005: 231). In this context, the term register is similar to what Eckert (e.g. 2008) refers to as style. However, it is not identical: "a register may be associated with a situation or a set of social relations rather than or in addition to being linked to a social identity like 'jock' or 'burnout'" (Johnstone 2010: 34). The term enregisterment, then, is used once a form has become part of a register, that is, particular indexicalities are associated with each other. The form is now connected with a particular style and this style is associated with a particular identity, which in turn can be used to create further indexical links. For example, Moll (2014) in her study of the use of "Cyber-Jamaican" on an online discussion forum of Jamaicans in the diaspora, shows how forum members constitute their in-group identity as "Cyber-Jamaicans" by means of an informal, personal stance and the use of various enregistered "Cyber-Jamaican" features, which authenticate this "ethnolinguistic repertoire" (Hinrichs and Farquharson 2011: 6–7, cited in Moll 2014: 217). The a + infinitive progressive form and respellings with <aw> in words such as lord, start, gone have become an enregistered part of "Cyber-Jamaican." These forms index "Cyber-Jamaican" and this repertoire is associated with "Cyber-Jamaican" identity. In contrast to the a + infinitive progressive form, <aw> respelling is a feature not normally associated with "Jamaicaness" (Moll 2014: 238). Moll is able to show an increase in frequency of this respelling over the years, which may point to continuing conventionalization in "Cyber-Jamaican" and diffusion as a stylistic resource (also see Mair on Nigerian Pidgin in cyberspace, Chapter 16, this volume).

Eckert and associates hold similar views; yet they do not focus on stance-taking but the notion of style as a repertoire of linguistic forms with specific social meanings. Linguistic forms are not primarily associated with stances but the focus is on personae, social types, and social characteristics. Such links can be established through a noticeable linguistic form becoming first associated with particular groups of people that may stand out in a particular context. With time, a link may be created between feature and group and the linguistic form can index the specific population on its own. Then (and only then) the form becomes available for ideological positioning of the group: Its use can invoke certain characteristics and stereotypes of the group in question, and it can be used to align with and disalign from the group. The link between linguistic forms and social meaning has become conventionalized through repetition of these "indexical acts" (Eckert 2012: 94). These social meanings are the ones mentioned above – personal characteristics, personae or social types – and they can be used in conversational identity work to constitute particular identities.

In contrast to some scholars, which can be read as assuming that indexicality is a linear process, Eckert (2012: 94) argues that indexical order progresses in multiple directions. Meanings comprise what Eckert (2008) refers to as an indexical field: "a constellation of ideologically-linked meanings, any region of which can be invoked in context" (Eckert 2012: 94). Social meanings vary depending on social context (i.e. who is involved, where, when); in fact, social context helps create particular social meanings. This is what makes Eckert's concept of the indexical field so valuable. It provides an idea of the multiple *potential* meanings of which conversationalists may take advantage – either individually or simultaneously. In the following section, I explore how third-wave variationist research can contribute to the study of WEs by returning to the three questions outlined in the introduction.

26.5 Issues Concerning World Englishes

These three questions pertain to three issues in the study of identities:

(1) What happens at the local and interactional level of identity construction?
(2) What precisely are the social meanings of a linguistic feature/style/variety and so on for different speakers and hearers in different contexts?
(3) What is the link between identity construction and linguistic usage?

I have argued that indexicality theory provides a useful framework for investigating the third of these issues: It provides an explanatory framework for how identity construction (widely conceived) and linguistic usage may be linked via ideologically related social meanings. The next section focuses on the remaining two points while also providing examples for the third. First, I explore third-wave research that investigates social meanings and identity construction at the interactional level. Then, I consider research that aims to obtain a better idea of the social meanings of a linguistic feature, style, or stance by concentrating on the perceptual research strand of TWVS. I conclude that by incorporating interactional and perceptual research on the link between identity construction and language in WEs contexts, we will be able to understand better the emergence, evolution, and current use of WEs.

26.5.1   Interview and Interactional Data

If we want to discover whether identity matters in the emergence and development of WEs, we cannot limit ourselves to macrosociological studies of language use. We have to study language, identity, and social meaning in local stylistic practice. Such research has gained insights that are relevant to the study of WEs, namely that

- it is often difficult, if not impossible, to assign individual linguistic features to specific varieties and that doing so would result in an analytic loss;
- speakers may index multiple identities when using innovative linguistic features;
- indexicalities to place or nation develop through intermediate steps and a process of enregisterment may occur;
- ethnic styles may rapidly acquire new indexicalities and express localness, and these new indexicalities are more likely to hold in some populations than others.

These will be discussed in turn. Previously, I have argued that investigating the use of identity and WEs must include the micro-level of interaction, as identity is co-constructed at the conversational level. However, even this is somewhat oversimplified as many WEs contexts involve more than one language and code-switching. In studies of language use in Singapore, Leimgruber (2012, 2013) explores how switching and the resulting style that includes mixing can index particular social meanings. Many models of language variation in Singapore separate different varieties, which, Leimgruber (2012) argues, prevents them from accounting fully for the data complexity in Singapore. Many stretches of speech in Singapore do not appear to be utterance sections of Singlish, Hokkien, or Standard English but speech that draws from these to create a feature cluster in a particular exchange. The specific mix of features allows specific social meanings to be indexed. Although Leimgruber concentrates on linguistic variables rather than how these features co-occur in styles to create social meanings, the advantage of this framework in an investigation of social meaning at the local level becomes very apparent.

The difficulty of assigning individual linguistic features to specific varieties and the analytic loss that this would entail also became evident in Snell's research. Snell (2013) investigated the interactions of working-class children in two primary schools in Teesside, in the northeast of England. She argues that a more appropriate way to engage with this kind of interactional language is through a repertoire approach. She examines the use of nonstandard first-person objective singular *us* ("give us me shoe back") and demonstrates that the so-called standard version (e.g. "give me my shoe back") is not a direct alternative. The former contains indexical meanings of solidarity, alignment, and group identity lacking in the standard version. These insights are not limited to class-based concepts: Echoing Snell's (2013) work, Drummond (2016) demonstrates how young white British people in Manchester, England, have new uses for and understanding of what linguists assume to be ethnically salient variants. Several other studies have made similar arguments, highlighting the importance of understanding language use at the local, interactional level (e.g. Rampton 2006; Moore and Podesva 2009). The lesson, thus, for the study of WEs is that speakers are multiskilled language users and theoretical concepts from top-down models are often not reflected in actual language use. Investigating the repertoires of speakers and the social meanings of styles and linguistic features at the local, interactional level, therefore, is crucial to understanding the development of varieties in a locale.

This is even more so because identity is a complex notion. Speakers often index *multiple* identities. Any exclusive focus on just one identity aspect may be misplaced. Zipp and Staicov (2016) in their study of speech rhythm and identity construction in San Francisco Chinatown make this point very well. In a study of four speakers, it was those second-generation informants identifying with both ethnic and mainstream culture who exhibit flexible speech rhythm – rather than speakers with high ethnic Chinese identity scores.

TWVS also makes an important distinction between identity construction in interactions and identity as a metalinguistic category label. As I intimated in Section 26.3, in some previous studies, identity construction in face-to-face conversations is not sufficiently separated from discourses *about* identity. How people talk about the nation, identity, and language may be far removed from how language is used in interaction. For talk about a feature, a style, or a variety to even occur, it has to be enregistered. Enregisterment describes the process by which (a set of) linguistic features that were initially not noticed become perceived and used as markers of a particular group of speakers and, eventually, they become associated with yet another order of indexicality, for example place or a specific variety (see my discussion of indexicality in Section 26.4.2). For example, in Singapore English the phrase *where got*, as in Leimgruber's (2013: 79) example *Inflation? Where got inflation?*, indexes sarcasm but, in addition to this stance, the phrase has also acquired second-order indexicality: It indexes a local orientation to Singapore and Singlish.

Johnstone, Andrus, and Danielson (2006) take a historical perspective and provide a relevant example of how such processes have played out in the city of Pittsburgh with regard to the monophthongization of /aw/. Initially, nonmobile speakers in close-knit networks did not notice how their regional variants of /aw/ relate to social factors. The authors argue that the variation in /aw/ was imbued with second-order indexicality during World War II when a large number of working-class Pittsburgh men became geographically mobile. Interaction with people who sounded different resulted in an increased awareness of speech differences and /aw/ monphthongization became to be associated, for these individuals, with meanings that are shaped by ideologies involving social class and correctness. Second-order indexicality then transformed into third-order indexicality as monophthongized /aw/ becomes increasingly linked to Pittsburgh, drawing on a variety of more abstract ideologies – for example, the notion that each place has a dialect. At this stage, this feature is available for explicit metadiscourse to indicate how Pittsburghers talk, even by people who have never heard local Pittsburgh speech. This third-order indexicality was facilitated by the economic upheavals of the 1970s and 1980s and the resulting increase of outmigration. This study shows how, through intermediate steps, monophthongized /aw/ has shifted from not getting noticed to an association with social class and eventually a connection with Pittsburghese as this concept became enregistered in people's minds. It is likely that intermediate steps were also necessary for the enregisterment of (features of) national varieties of English. Metalinguistic comments in written or spoken media or from schoolteachers about features of local speech are an invaluable resource for tracking such developments in time (see Kytö on American English, Chapter 8; and Mair on English in cyberspace, Chapter 16, this volume). The other lesson we can learn for the study of WEs is that what outsiders regard as linguistically noticeable is, in fact, normative within the community.

Yet other developments are also possible. Based on interview narratives and participant observations in San Francisco's Sunset District, Hall-Lew (2014) investigates emerging indexicalities of Chinese cultural and linguistic practices from a style, rather than an enregisterment perspective. She argues that Chinese cultural and linguistic practices have become available as a resource to index local authenticity. Hall-Lew makes these observations by investigating personal reminiscences of FOB style. *FOB* is an acronym for *Fresh Off the Boat*. Its original meaning referred to immigrants who had arrived only very recently. FOB style was prevalent among San

Franciscan youths in the 1990s; it involved a specific way to dress, dye your hair, use language, and so on. White San Franciscans tend to orient positively to FOB style, which Hall-Lew (2014: 72) argues is due to it being a resource for local authentication. They can orient to "Chinese" social practice and construct "a cosmopolitan, transnational-yet-local identity" (Hall-Lew 2014: 57). A higher order indexicality has evolved over the years from FOB style first indexing ethnicity to it now (also) indexing local authenticity, "authentically San Franciscan" (Hall-Lew 2014: 57). However, it is harder for Chinese San Franciscans to access this new meaning as "bids for place-based authenticity are more likely to be interpreted as authentication of ethnicity" (Hall-Lew 2014: 73).

This study not only reveals the dynamic and context-dependent nature of social meaning but also demonstrates how formerly ethnic styles acquire new local meanings. Simultaneously, this study demonstrates that this new indexicality comes with constraints. Some speakers are more likely than others to be perceived as indexing local authenticity. Thus, early on and very quickly in contact situations, new meanings emerge and new social constellations appear, in addition to restricting who will be understood as saying what. If future studies can confirm these dynamics, we need certain preconditions for variables, styles, or varieties to be linked to local, regional, or national identities, once such identities are developing: contact with speakers of different varieties and time for these connections to become enregistered. Variables, styles, and varieties go through an extended process of indexical development before they may be used to constitute regional or national identities in actual conversation. Of course, even then, they may index more than one social meaning.

26.5.2 Perception Data

What the discussion of identity and WEs makes clear is that many an argument hinges on the perception of linguistic features, styles, varieties, and so on as representative of nations, locales, communities, and so forth. TWVS has made much use of experimental perception methods, as these represent an alternative manner in which to document the potential social meanings of a particular linguistic feature *in context*. Schneider (2008: 266), too, sees the need for exploring perception when he writes that "designing a study that will test a straightforward connection between socio-psychological attitudes (including national identity) and the use of specific linguistic forms in these contexts will clearly be a worthwhile task." This can be done but it is challenging as a lot of recent research has found that perception tasks are highly context-sensitive (e.g. Campbell-Kibler 2009; Hay, Drager, and Warren 2010; Johnstone and Kiesling 2008), as predicted by third-wave approaches to variation. Moreover, these perception tests highlight the fact that links between linguistic variants and social meanings are anything but straightforward as they have a *variety* of potential meanings.

TWVS has explored the associations certain features may trigger and under what conditions. When this method is applied to lexical or syntactic variables, text-based guises are sometimes used (e.g. Davydova, Tytus, and Schleef 2017). However, when the focus is on accent features, properties of recorded speech are manipulated. This results in resynthesized speech (e.g. Plichta and Preston 2005) or stimuli consisting of spliced linguistic cues (e.g. Campbell-Kibler 2007; Drummond and Schleef 2016; Schleef, Flynn, and Barras 2017; Schleef 2017b). A good deal of research is not only interested in how linguistic features are evaluated per se but also how they interact with other features or social information available in the surrounding context. The following section outlines briefly the extent to which perception tests have uncovered context-sensitivity. We must understand this if we want to devise methods to study the perception of variables or styles in WEs.

In many of her perception studies of the variable (ing), Campbell-Kibler (2007, 2009) finds that particular social meanings surface repeatedly. Such core meanings, particularly relating to education and intelligence, confirm findings made in production studies of this variable (Labov 1966; Trudgill 1974). Yet, at the same time, she shows that such meanings can be trumped by other factors such as perceived social class. For example, Campbell-Kibler (2009: 143–144) argued that the relationship between [ɪn]-guises and uneducatedness/lack of intelligence is indirect: A significant effect only emerges if speakers are heard as working class. Other studies support the idea that assumed speaker characteristics influence the evaluation of a feature. Hay, Warren, and Drager (2006) demonstrate that, when some listeners in New Zealand see a picture of an older rather than a younger speaker, they were better at distinguishing the NEAR and SQUARE vowels, which are merging in New Zealand, and younger speakers are more likely to merge than older speakers. Listener perception is influenced by the social information received (see also Niedzielski 1999).

Moreover, this line of research confirms that different groups within a locale may differ in their opinion about a variable feature. This is because each group has lived through different experiences and drifts toward different interpretations (Eckert 2016: 77). This variability in the evaluation also supports Eckert's (2008) idea that variables do not have fixed meanings but that they are associated with indexical fields of ideologically related meanings. Schleef and Flynn (2015) show that different subgroups of a population may evaluate a feature very differently in Manchester, England. This does not seem to hold for all variables, however. In a comparison of group-specific evaluations of (t) with those of (ing) in Greater Manchester, England, Schleef (2017b) found that, in contrast to findings for (ing), the social characteristics of listeners are not pertinent to the evaluation of (t) and its variants [t] and [ʔ]. The comparison was based on a set of perception surveys, in which participants listened to manipulated audio stimuli and rated them on a series of scales. Evaluations for (ing) also appear to differ from region to region, as suggested in Schleef, Flynn, and Barras's (2017) cross-regional study.

In conclusion, the social meaning of individual features, minimally, depends on other features with which they co-occur in a specific style: our perceptions of, and attitudes toward, certain speakers and groups of speakers; listener background; and region. Yet the evaluation of a linguistic feature may rely on much more, including listeners' prior experiences and various contextual conditions, such as eliciting conditions (Hay, Drager and Warren, 2010) and topic (see, e.g., Johnstone and Kiesling 2008; Campbell-Kibler 2009). Of course, this concerns perception rather than the production of styles. Nonetheless, similar factors are involved: we see (and hear) a person, perceive a cluster of linguistic and nonlinguistic signs (including speech, clothing, posture, demeanor), make assumptions about what kind of person our interlocutor is, and this may trigger social meanings. What does all of this mean for the study of WEs? I would like to highlight only two points. Social meanings are underspecified and dynamic. In dialect and language contact situations, these may be subject to very heterogeneous evaluation and relatively rapid change. Ultimately, the fate of any linguistic feature depends on its evaluation and its perceived role in the topography of social meaning within a community. Second, testing whether certain features are associated with national or other social categories is not an easy feat. These features may do this in one context, for some people in some regions, but not for/in others.

26.6 Conclusion

When constructing identities, we may constitute these by assembling specific features into styles. We select these features based on the social meanings they *can* have for us – in our region, social group, or specific context – and we do this with a view toward using a style that we think carries a particular social meaning in production and helps us constitute a specific individual identity. On the perception side, this may or may not be heard as intended since hearers, too, operate within a specific context: who they think a speaker is, their own social and regional background, and so on. The speaker may get a clue as to where the hearer stands once they respond in a specific manner. This is how identity is co-constructed, and the use of language may play a major role in constituting speaker and hearer identity. An indexical approach can highlight this multiplicity of meaning, identity construction, and possible linguistic usage. In the long run, these processes may influence the development of WEs. Language varies and new indexicalities of features, styles, or varieties develop, sometimes through intermediate steps, and these may index localness among some parts of the population. Indeed, some of these styles or varieties may become enregistered at a later stage.

Many debates about identity in the study of WEs are attributable to an unsatisfactory integration of social meaning, the micro- and the macro-level of investigation. It is clear that identities are constituted all the time, within certain constraints; but if we want to know whether identity matters in the emergence and development of WEs, we have to study identity and social meaning in local stylistic practice in the moment-to-moment development of practices and interaction. We also have to investigate meso- and macro-levels of social structure and relate meaning-making at the local level to larger social categories such as a community of practice, town, region, social class, and so on. Limiting the discussion of identity to macrosociological categories – be they social class, national, or regional identities – is abstracting the concept of identity away from where it matters the most: in local stylistic practice.

References

Agha, Asif. 2005. Voice, footing, enregisterment. *Journal of Linguistic Anthropology 15*, 38–59.

Benor, Sarah. 2001. Sounding learned: The gendered use of /t/ in Orthodox Jewish English. In Daniel Ezra Johnson and Tara Sanchez, eds. *Penn Working Papers in Linguistics: Selected Papers from NWAV 29*. Philadelphia: University of Pennsylvania, 1–16.

Bucholtz, Mary. 1996. Geek the girl: Language, femininity and female nerds. In Nancy Warner et al., eds. *Gender and Belief Systems*. Berkeley: Berkeley Women and Language Group, 119–131.

Bucholtz, Mary and Kira Hall. 2005. Identity and interaction: A socio-cultural linguistic approach. *Discourse Studies 7*: 585–614.

Bucholtz, Mary and Kira Hall. 2010. Locating identity in language. In Carmen Llamas and Dominic Watt, eds. *Language and Identities*. Edinburgh: Edinburgh University Press, 18–28.

Campbell-Kibler, Kathryn. 2007. Accent, (ING) and the social logic of listener perceptions. *American Speech 82*: 32–64.

Campbell-Kibler, Kathryn. 2009. The nature of sociolinguistic perception. *Language Variation and Change 21*: 135–156.

Campbell-Kibler, Kathryn, Penelope Eckert, Norma Mendoza-Denton and Emma Moore. 2006. The elements of style. Poster presented at New Ways of Analyzing Variation (NWAV) 35, Columbus.

Cheshire, Jenny. 1982. *Variation in an English Dialect*. Cambridge: Cambridge University Press.

Cheshire, Jenny, Paul Kerswill, Sue Fox and Eivind Torgersen. 2011. Contact, the feature pool and the speech community: The emergence of Multicultural London English. *Journal of Sociolinguistics* 15: 151–196.

Coupland, Nikolas. 2007. *Style: Language Variation and Identity*. Cambridge: Cambridge University Press.

Coupland, Nikolas. 2008. The delicate constitution of identity in face-to-face accommodation: A response to Trudgill. *Language in Society* 37: 267–270.

Davydova, Julia, Agnieszka Ewa Tytus and Erik Schleef. 2017. Acquisition of sociolinguistic awareness by German learners of English: A study in perceptions of quotative be like. *Linguistics* 55: 783–812.

Drummond, Rob. 2012. Aspects of identity in a second language: ING variation in the speech of Polish migrants living in Manchester, UK. *Language Variation and Change* 24: 107–133.

Drummond, Rob. 2016. (Mis)interpreting urban youth language: White kids sounding black? *Journal of Youth Studies* 20: 640–660.

Drummond, Rob and Erik Schleef. 2016. Identity in variationist sociolinguistics. In Siân Preece, ed. *The Routledge Handbook of Language and Identity*. London: Routledge, 50–65.

DuBois, John. 2002. Stance and consequence. Paper presented at the Annual Meeting of the American Anthropological Association, New Orleans, November.

Eckert, Penelope. 1989. *Jocks and Burnouts: Social Categories and Identity in the High School*. New York: Teachers' College Press.

Eckert, Penelope. 2000. *Linguistic Variation as Social Practice*. Malden, MA: Blackwell Publishing.

Eckert, Penelope. 2008. Variation and the indexical field. *Journal of Sociolinguistics* 12: 453–476.

Eckert, Penelope. 2012. Three waves of variation study: The emergence of meaning in the study of sociolinguistic variation. *Annual Review of Anthropology* 41: 87–100.

Eckert, Penelope. 2016. Variation, meaning and social change. In Nikolas Coupland, ed. *Sociolinguistics: Theoretical Debates*. Cambridge: Cambridge University Press, 68–85.

Eckert, Penelope and Sally McConnel-Ginet. 1992. Think practically and look locally: Language and gender as community-based practice. *Annual Review of Anthropology* 21: 461–490.

Gal, Susan. 1979. *Language Shift: Social Determinants of Linguistic Change in Bilingual Austria*. New York: Academic Press.

Hall-Lew, Lauren. 2014. Chinese social practice and San Franciscan authenticity. In Veronique Lacoste, Jakob Leimgruber and Thiemo Breyer, eds. *Indexing Authenticity: Sociolinguistic Perspectives*. Berlin: de Gruyter, 55–77.

Hay, Jennifer, Katie Drager and Paul Warren. 2010. Short-term exposure to one dialect affects processing of another. *Language and Speech* 53: 447–471.

Hay, Jennifer, Paul Warren and Katie Drager. 2006. Factors influencing speech perception in the context of a merger-in-progress. *Journal of Phonetics* 34: 458–484.

Hickey, Raymond. 2003. How do dialects get the features they have? In Raymond Hickey, ed., *Motives for Language Change*. Cambridge: Cambridge University Press, 213–239.

Hinrichs, Lars and Joseph T. Farquharson. 2011. Introduction. In Lars Hinrichs and Joseph T. Farquharson, eds. *Variation in the Caribbean: From Creole Continua to Individual Agency*. Amsterdam: John Benjamins, 1–9.

Holmes, Janet and Paul Kerswill. 2008. Contact is not enough: A response to Trudgill. *Language in Society* 37: 273–277.

Horvath, Barbara. 1985. *Variation in Australian English: The Sociolects of Sydney*. Cambridge: Cambridge University Press.

Johnstone, Barbara. 2010. Locating language in identity. In Carmen Llamas and Dominic Watt, eds. *Language and Identities*. Edinburgh: Edinburgh University Press, 29–36.

Johnstone, Barbara, Jennifer Andrus and Andrew E. Danielson. 2006. Mobility, indexicality, and the enregisterment of "Pittsburghese." *Journal of English Linguistics* 34: 77–104.

Johnstone, Barbara and Scott Kiesling. 2008. Indexicality and experience: Exploring the meanings of /aw/-monophthongization in Pittsburgh. *Journal of Sociolinguistics* 12: 5–33.

Kiesling, Scott F. 2009. Style as stance: Stance as the explanation for patterns of sociolinguistic variation. In Alexandra Jaffe, ed. *Stance: Sociolinguistic Perspectives*. Oxford: Oxford University Press, 171–194.

Kiesling, Scott F. 2013. Constructing identity. In J. K. Chambers and Natalie Schilling-Estes, eds. *The Handbook of Language Variation and Change* (2nd ed.). Malden, MA: John Wiley & Sons, 448–467.

Labov, William. 1966. *The Social Stratification of English in New York City*. Washington, DC: Cent. Appl. Ling.

Labov, William. 1972. *Sociolinguistic Patterns*. Philadelphia: University of Pennsylvania Press.

Labov, William. 2001. *Principles of Linguistic Change: Social Factors*. Oxford: Blackwell.

Lave, Jean and Etienne Wenger. 1991. *Situated Learning: Legitimate Peripheral Participation*. Cambridge: Cambridge University Press.

Leimgruber, Jakob. 2012. Singapore English: An indexical approach. *World Englishes* 31, 1–14.

Leimgruber, Jakob. 2013. *Singapore English: Structure, Variation, and Usage*. Cambridge: Cambridge University Press.

Macaulay, Ronald K. S. and Gavin D. Trevelyan. 1977. *Language, Social Class and Education: A Glasgow Study*. Edinburgh: Edinburgh University Press.

Macaulay, Ronald K. S. 2002. I'm off to Philadelphia in the morning. *American Speech* 77: 227–241.

Meyerhoff, Miriam and Nancy Niedzielski. 2003. The globalisation of vernacular variation. *Journal of Sociolinguistics* 7: 534–555.

Milroy, Lesley. 1980. *Language and Social Network*. Oxford: Blackwell.

Moll, Andrea. 2014. Authenticity in dialect performance? A case study of "Cyber-Jamaican." In Veronique Lacoste, Jakob Leimgruber and Thiemo Breyer, eds. *Indexing Authenticity: Sociolinguistic Perspectives*. Berlin: de Gruyter, 209–243.

Moore, Bruce. 1999. Australian English: Australian identity. *ABC*, November 27. www.abc.net.au/radionational/programs/linguafranca/australian-english-australian-identity/3562064

Moore, Emma. 2011. Variation and identity. In Warren Maguire and April McMahon, eds. *Analysing Variation in English*. Cambridge: Cambridge University Press, 219–236.

Moore, Emma and Robert Podesva. 2009. Style, indexicality, and the social meaning of tag questions. *Language in Society* 38: 447–485.

Niedzielski, Nancy. 1999. The effect of social information on the perception of sociolinguistic variables. *Journal of Language and Social Psychology* 18, 62–85.

Ochs, Elinor. 1992. Indexing gender. In Alessandro Duranti and Charles Goodwin, eds. *Rethinking Context: Language as an Interactive Phenomenon*. Cambridge: Cambridge University Press, 335–358.

Plichta, Bartek and Dennis R. Preston. 2005. The /ay/s have it: the perception of /ay/ as a North-South stereotype in US English. *Acta Linguistica Hafniensia* 37, 243–285.

Podesva, Robert. 2007. Phonation type as a stylistic variable: The use of falsetto in constructing a persona. *Journal of Sociolinguistics* 11, 478–504.

Rampton, Ben. 2006. *Language in Late Modernity: Interaction in an Urban School*. Cambridge: Cambridge University Press.

Rauniomaa, Mirka. 2003. Stance accretion. Paper presented at the Language, Interaction, and Social Organization Research Focus Group, University of California, Santa Barbara, February.

Schleef, Erik. 2017a. Developmental sociolinguistics and the acquisition of T-glottalling by immigrant teenagers in London. In Gunther de Vogelaer and Matthias Katerbow, eds. *Variation in Language Acquisition*. Amsterdam: John Benjamins, 311–347.

Schleef, Erik. 2017b. Social meanings across listener groups: When do social factors matter? *Journal of English Linguistics* 45: 28–59.

Schleef, Erik and Nicholas E. J. Flynn. 2015. Ageing meanings of (ing): Age and indexicality in Manchester, England. *English World-Wide* 36: 47–89.

Schleef, Erik, Nicholas E. J. Flynn and Will Barras. 2017. Regional diversity in social perceptions of (ing). *Language Variation and Change* 29: 29–56.

Schneider, Edgar W. 2003. The dynamics of New Englishes: From identity construction to dialect birth. *Language* 79: 233–81.

Schneider, Edgar W. 2008. Accommodation versus identity? A response to Trudgill. *Language in Society* 37: 262–267.

Sharma, Devyani. 2005. Dialect stabilization and speaker awareness in non-native varieties of English. *Journal of Sociolinguistics* 9: 194–224.

Silverstein, Michael. 1985. Language and the culture of gender: At the intersection of structure, usage, and ideology. In Elizabeth Mertz and Richard Parmentier, eds., *Semiotic Mediation: Socio-cultural and Psychological Perspectives*. Orlando, FL: Academic Press, 219–259.

Silverstein, Michael. 2003. Indexical order and the dialectics of sociolinguistic life. *Language and Communication* 23: 193–229.

Snell, Julia. 2013. Dialect, interaction and class positioning at school: From deficit to difference to repertoire. *Language and Education* 27: 110–128.

Thibault, Pierrette and Gillian Sankoff. 1993. Diverses facettes de l'insécurité linguistique: Vers une analyse comparative des attitudes et du français parlé par des Franco- et des Anglo-Montréalais. *Cahiers de l'institut de linguistique de Louvain* 19: 209–218.

Trudgill, Peter. 1972. Sex, covert prestige and linguistic change in the urban British English of Norwich. *Language in Society* 1: 179–195.

Trudgill, Peter. 1974. *The Social Differentiation of English in Norwich.* Cambridge: Cambridge University Press.

Trudgill, Peter. 2008. Colonial dialect contact in the history of European languages: On the irrelevance of identity to new-dialect formation. *Language in Society* 37: 241–254.

Tuten, Donald. 2003. *Koineization in Medieval Spanish.* Berlin: de Gruyter.

Wolfram, Walt. 1969. *A Sociolinguistic Description of Detroit Negro Speech.* Washington, DC: Center for Applied Linguistics.

Zipp, Lena and Adina Staicov. 2016. English in San Francisco Chinatown: Indexing identity with speech rhythm. In Elena Seoane and Cristina Suárez-Gómez, eds., *World Englishes: New Theoretical and Methodological Considerations*. Amsterdam: John Benjamins, 205–227.

27

The Politics of World Englishes

Mario Saraceni

Language is inherently political – the way we use it and the way we talk about it. In the field of World Englishes (henceforth WEs), the political character of language and language practice is particularly evident. Originating from 1960s and 1970s debates on the necessity (or not) of recognizing the validity of varieties other than British and American English, the egalitarian stance in the WEs paradigm is inherently political. Analogously, the positions of those who express different views with respect to the forms and functions of English in the world are political, too. This chapter provides an overview of the intrinsically political nature of WEs in relation to the history and geography of the spread of English, the study of varieties of English, and the different roles that this language plays for different people around the world.

27.1   Introduction

"Language," says Nash (1989: 6), "seems straightforwardly a piece of culture. But on reflection it is clear that language is often a political fact, at least as much as it is a cultural one." Even more radically, Joseph (2006: 17) sees language as being "political from top to bottom." Stemming from the fact that language is deeply embedded in and inextricable from the social context in which people use it, these statements encapsulate the fundamental premise of this chapter. As bare, decontextualized citations, however, they are a little generic and I will therefore focus on a more specific sense of this concept, that is, the idea that most discourse *about* language is inevitably political,[1] even when it purports not to be. More in particular, I

---

[1] This adjective here is to be intended both narrowly as referring to matters concerning the administration of the state and more broadly to the acquisition, maintenance, and exercise of power.

contend that this point is illustrated perfectly well by the development of WEs scholarship in the last fifty years.

The political nature of discourse about language is evident in everyday communication. Take, for example, the following comment in the section "below the line" to an article in the online edition of the *Guardian* (September 16, 2016), where a reader wrote:

> It would be nice if this story was actually written in English. You are a British newspaper after all. If the Americans want to have their own version of the language, good luck to them but it's not the NY Times I'm choosing to read.

It is obvious that this reader objected to, and felt quite strongly about, certain linguistic choices (possibly related to spelling or lexical items) that they considered "Americanisms" to be avoided by a British newspaper. It is equally obvious that to the reader this was not just a question of language but also one of nationhood and that it was in fact impossible to separate the two. So much so that the reader seemed to be resentful that the Americans should have "their own version of the language."

This kind of comment, appearing to be fueled by nationalistic sentiments rather than genuine preoccupations about language, is not rare or confined to twenty-first-century anonymous online commentators. In the first half of the nineteenth century, Thomas Hamilton, a British writer who visited the USA, remarked that "The amount of bad grammar in circulation is very great" (Hamilton 1833: 232) and that "the Americans have chosen arbitrarily to change the meaning of certain old and established English words, for reasons which they cannot explain" (p. 233). Therefore, he predicted, "the dialect of the Americans will become utterly unintelligible to an Englishman," and then reproached that "If they contemplate such an event with complacency, let them go on and prosper; they have only to '*progress*' in their present course, and their grandchildren bid fair to speak a jargon as novel and peculiar as the most patriotic American linguist can desire" (p. 235). Hamilton's feelings about American English, where language is discussed together with patriotism, are not dissimilar to those of the reader cited above. Even Prince Charles commented on American English having a corrupting effect on what he called "English English" (O'Leary 1995), typifying a widespread view of language as a national asset. Sometimes the language-as-national-asset idea is exploited for political purposes in very overt ways. On September 29, 2016, for example, a number of British newspapers, such as the *Daily Telegraph*, the *Daily Mail*, and others, ran a story that, misrepresenting a research report on language change in Britain (Watt and Gunn 2016), suggested that the "Queen's English" was about to be wiped out as a direct result of uncontrolled immigration.

Yet what is an adequate and informed response to this type of comment? With reference to Prince Charles's tirade, Pensalfini (2014, n.p.) quite rightly remarked that "for anyone to call [English] 'our' language is repugnantly colonial." Similarly, I characterized the suggestion that immigrants in Britain were destroying the English language as "essentially a xenophobic position" (Saraceni 2016, n.p.). Clearly, these observations are as political as the one they are meant to refute – language is talked about in wholly political terms.

Yet even when the political stance is not so overt, discussions on (in)equality among varieties of English are always and inevitably embedded within a wider discourse about (in)equality among *speakers* of English. That is to say, linguistic (in)equality is a proxy for social (in)equality. In this sense, for example, the argument that language change is entirely natural is ultimately political. This, I wish to clarify, is by no means a criticism. Rather, it is simply a way for me to begin to give substance to my claim that it is virtually impossible to talk about the forms and functions of English in the world in an entirely apolitical manner.

In order to begin to appreciate this, it is first necessary to consider that the worldwide spread of English and its establishment as global lingua franca are inextricably bound to (the imposition of) power. It was first through the expansion of the British Empire that the English language entered the linguistic environments of societies in all continents of the world and it has subsequently largely been the position of the USA as world superpower to have further secured its role as the preferred language of international communication. Consequently, the direct connection with positions of supremacy and power makes English not only a language that happened to find itself at "the right time at the right place" (Crystal 2003, pp. 120–122) through history but also a language that is deeply involved in the interplay of the (re-)establishment of power (im)balances, (in)equality, and national identities.

For this reason, as a sociolinguistic framework primarily developed for the study of postcolonial varieties of English, WEs is also very intimately concerned with such issues. Indeed, the theoretical framework of WEs rests on these three fundamental points: (1) as it spread around the world from the seventeenth century through to the twentieth, the English language went through a process of natural adaptation in the different cultural milieus to which the British Empire took it, and new forms of the language emerged as a result; (2) these new forms of English must therefore not be simplistically seen as imperfect deviations from their more illustrious counterparts, namely British English and American English, but as fully fledged varieties that are linguistically just as valid; (3) as a result, the English language is not the exclusive property of people in a handful of countries (Britain, the USA, Australia, etc.) but belongs to the hundreds of millions of people worldwide who speak it as an additional language.

27.2 Politics in the Prehistory of World Englishes

The legitimacy of varieties other than British English is an idea that can be traced to a time much earlier than the beginning of WEs, and particularly to the aftermath of independence in former British colonies. In the following two subsections, I provide a brief account of how these ideas were articulated both in *settlement* colonies and in *exploitation* colonies (Mufwene 2001), the former term referring to territories (such as North America and Australia) where European colonizers settled permanently in large numbers, having decimated and displaced the original inhabitants, and the latter to territories such as Nigeria, India, and British Malaya, "where Europeans had no, or little, interest in developing local roots" (Mufwene 2001: 208) but aimed primarily at exploiting local natural resources and manpower and controlling trade.

27.2.1 Settlement Colonies

Possibly the earliest time that an argument was decidedly put forward advocating the existence and legitimacy of a distinct national variety of English came at the end of the eighteenth century, when Noah Webster remarked that the language of North America was on a diverging path from that of Great Britain:

> several circumstances render a future separation of the American tongue from the English, necessary and unavoidable ... These causes will produce, in a course of time, a language in North America, as different from the future language of England, as the modern Dutch, Danish and Swedish are from the German, or from one another.   (Webster 1789: 22–23)

This citation comes from a book entitled *Dissertations on the English language*, which was as much about linguistic matters as about political ones. Indeed, Webster felt that Americans' linguistic independence was a necessary component of, and needed to complement, their newly gained political independence: "As an independent nation, our honor requires us to have a system of our own, in language as well as government" (1789: 20–21). It is very significant that Webster's thoughts were echoed by none other than Thomas Jefferson, the author of the first draft of America's Declaration of Independence and subsequently the third president of the USA (and also Webster's contemporary), who, commenting on a new grammar textbook,[2] described how Americans had to adapt the English language to its new environment: "The new circumstances under which we are placed, call for new words, new phrases, and for the transfer of old words to new objects. An American dialect will therefore be formed; so will a West-Indian and Asiatic, as a Scotch and an Irish are already formed"

---

[2] The textbook in question was by John Waldo, who had sent it to Jefferson asking for his opinion of it.

(Jefferson, 1813). Once again, Jefferson's words – whose spirit will resonate strikingly familiar to readers of WEs literature – were as much about language as about Americans' political independence from Great Britain.

At least a century and a half later, even without anything approaching the nationalistic fervor that animated Webster's and Jefferson's ideas about language, sentiments combining the need of local linguistic descriptions with an increased sense of independent national identity were similarly evident in Australia. As Damousi (2010: 216) notes, "Examining discussions about Australian speech from the 1920s to the early 1940s allows us to see how the preoccupation with the Australian accent had become a means of discussing Australianness." Indeed, "Most work on AusE ... has been done with the aim of establishing AusE as a distinct national variety of English worldwide, an important step in the construction of a national identity in a postcolonial context" (Horvath and Horvath, 2001: 352). From this point of view, the codification of Australian English into dictionaries – the *Macquarie Dictionary* and the *Australian National Dictionary* – was very much a matter of affirming an Australian national identity, besides being an endeavor in language description:

> there was a need for a dictionary that would serve Australians, as some of these foreign dictionaries had so imperfectly done, as a first-port-of-call reference book, for any and all the words that Australian users might want to look up in the course of their education, their occupation, their leisure reading. But it had to be focused on the usage of the Australian community itself, rather than on some other community.   (Delbridge, 2001: 306)

In the two contexts briefly looked at in this section, the USA and Australia, the claim of linguistic autonomy came from people – mainly the direct descendants of British settlers – for whom English was already *their* language. This meant that, in representing political and cultural independence, the marking of linguistic distinctiveness of the local varieties of English went hand in hand with decreased reverence toward British English and even a sense that the local variety of English was somehow superior to it.[3] As an illustration, consider the following anecdote where Margaret Hill, a British emigrant to Australia in the 1960s, recounts her experience of being openly antagonized on linguistic grounds:

> Local shopkeepers "used to pretend they couldn't understand what you were talking about", as when she [Margaret Hill] asked for ice cream: "we used to call them tubs and they call them dixies here – and I'd say, 'I'll have a tub' and they'd say, 'If you don't know what you're talking about, well take yourself off somewhere else, you Poms should learn to speak English.'"   (Hammerton and Thomson, 2005: 146)

---

[3] This was, of course, a gradual process. Self-consciousness about local varieties of English took some time to dissipate.

27.2.2 Exploitation Colonies

The situation was very different in *exploitation colonies*. On the one hand, the importance of a full legitimization of local varieties of English was expressed within the same general frame in which linguistic distinctiveness was seen as integral to cultural and political autonomy. On the other hand, however, the question of the relationship between language and national identity was considerably more complicated and thorny, since the sociolinguistic and historical contextual parameters were significantly different there in comparison to settlement colonies.

First, after independence, the sense of national identity was fragile at best in these countries, as the idea of nationally defined communities was far more "imagined" there than what Anderson (1983) discussed in relation to European nations. Most of the countries that gained their independence after the collapse of European empires were themselves creations of those empires rather than the outcome of actions driven by local national consciousness. The creation of Nigeria, for example, was documented in the *Times* of London in an article anonymously written by Flora Shaw on January 8, 1897: "The name 'Nigeria' applying to no other portion of Africa may, without offence to any neighbors, be accepted as co-extensive with the territories over which the Royal Niger Company has extended British influence" (Shaw 1897). As the article makes abundantly clear, the decision on the extent (i.e. its borders) and the name of Nigeria was a matter entirely in the hands of the British, whose only preoccupation was protecting their own interests and not offending their European neighbors also engaged in the scramble of Africa. As was the case elsewhere, "[t]he borders that Europeans drew were ... quite arbitrary and did not take into consideration the peoples living there" (Marks, 2007: 168) and so "[t]he new nations that replaced the old ethnic kingdoms and empires are a yoking together of sorts, and this accounts for the problems of identity at individual, local community and national levels" (Omoniyi, 2004: 10).

Second, in these regions, the vast majority of the population continued to speak local languages during colonial times, with little and rather uneven access to the English language.

As Brutt-Griffler (2002: 89) explains,

> the British policy limited the number of the students exposed to the formal teaching of English to meet the local demands for English-educated subjects of the empire. It left the bulk of the population to be educated in the local language or, at most, to acquire the rudimentary elements of the English language. In the main, economic interests within the colony controlled the spread of English. As a result, it created an uneven spread of English among different colonies within the British empire, and within a single colony.

This unevenness is very evident today, too, in Outer Circle countries, where the presence and the use of English vary significantly between urban and rural areas, as well as across different ethnic/cultural groups and social classes, ranging from being a virtually unknown foreign language for some people to being the main language of everyday life for others. Because of the absence of a widespread sense of national identity and the relatively limited and uneven spread of the language, the discourse on the importance of recognizing local varieties of English in connection to the development of independent nations was therefore significantly different in former exploitation colonies. The agents of that discourse were different and so were the (potential) stakeholders. In former African and Asian British colonies, that is, the debate on language largely remained confined within restricted circles of the intellectual elites, mainly composed of creative writers, while the vast majority of the population remained largely unaware of and unaffected by it. With reference to the Philippine context, for example, Tupas questions the agency of the appropriation of English: "'English is ours,' proclaims Filipino writer Gemino Abad (Abad et al. 1997: 170). 'We have colonized it too.' But who are the 'we' who have colonized English? Certainly not the majority of Filipinos" (Tupas, 2006: 169).

Finally, not only was English largely an elite language with very uneven penetration in society but it was also a heritage of imperial rule and hence "it came as part of a package deal which included many other items of doubtful value and the positive atrocity of racial arrogance and prejudice which may yet set the world on fire" (Achebe, 1965: 28). The choice of using the language that belonged to the former colonizers was bound to be controversial, and so the localization of English, its being different from British English, was a *condition* for its use. It was imperative that those who decided to take advantage of the international currency of English modified the language to such an extent as to be able to render it capable of expressing local cultural values. In the foreword to his 1938 novel *Kanthapura*, for example, Indian novelist Raja Rao commented on the use of English by Indian writers as a way of forging an Indian variety of the language:

> English is not really an alien language to us ... We cannot write like the English. We should not. We cannot write only as Indians. We have grown to look at the large world as part of us. Our method of expression therefore has to be a dialect which will some day prove to be as distinctive and colourful as the Irish or the American. Time alone will justify it.
>
> (Rao, 1938: vii)

In the same spirit, Nigerian writer Gabriel Okara believed that local varieties of the language were an obvious necessity:

> There are American, West Indian, Australian, Canadian, and New Zealand versions of English. All of them add life and vigour to the language while reflecting their own respective cultures. Why shouldn't there be a

> Nigerian or West African English which we can use to express our own
> ideas, thinking and philosophy in our own way?   (Okara 1963: 16)

Within a more explicit frame of postcolonial identity, fellow Nigerian Chinua Achebe (1965) discussed the same issue in a famous essay on the use of English by African writers. "The price a world language must be prepared to pay," he stated, "is submission to many different kinds of use" (p. 29) and therefore he felt that English was "able to carry the weight of [his] African experience," although it would have to be "a new English, still in full communion with its ancestral home but altered to suit its new African surroundings" (p. 30). The fundamental importance of decolonizing the language in decolonized countries was even more explicit, years later, in an article that Salman Rushdie wrote for the *Times*: "The [English] language, like much else in the newly independent societies, needs to be decolonized, to be remade in other images, if those of us who use it from positions outside Anglo-Saxon culture are to be more than Uncle Toms" (Rushdie, 1982). Confined to the intellectual elite as it may have been, it was the call for the full recognition of local varieties of English within the counter-discourse (Tiffin, 1987) enacted in postcolonial literature that was later embraced in WEs scholarship.

27.3 The Politics of Equality in the Inception of World Englishes

The WEs paradigm, which started to develop in the 1970s and flourished from the mid-1980s onward, was very much based on the ideas put forward by postcolonial writers as described in the previous section, addressing "a national desire for colonial closure through associating new and independent status with a recognizable and 'autonomous' variety of English toward which all within the boundaries of the nation-state can aspire" (Omoniyi, 2009: 173); and, as Omoniyi further elaborates,

> Arguably, nativization, indigenization, localization, or however else we choose to describe the process that transforms native into non-native English …, may be seen as part of the anti-imperial and anti-colonial apparatus engaged in the pursuit of self-determination and independence in postcolonial societies … Thus, from inception, non-native varieties of English as conceptualized in WE were ideologically and politically marked.   (p. 173)

The early stages of WEs, even before the term "World Englishes" acquired currency, was animated by debate. More than four decades ago, Braj Kachru (1976) wrote a position paper in response to a chapter in which Clifford Prator (1968) advocated the superiority of American and British English and criticized linguists such as Halliday, McIntosh, and Strevens (1964) for appearing to promote the acceptability of other international varieties of the language. In Prator's view, the suggestion that postcolonial varieties of English could be used in language education was a "heresy," and he expressed his exasperation particularly toward Indian English:

> I am firmly convinced that for the rest of the English-speaking world the most unintelligible educated variety is Indian English. The national group that profits least from the University's efforts to improve their intelligibility by classroom instruction also seems to be the Indians; they can almost never be brought to believe that there is any reason for trying to change their pronunciation.   (Prator, 1968: 464)

It was obvious that Prator's derogatory remarks were not simply about the linguistic features of a particular variety of English but also about the *speakers* of said variety. Kachru, who was originally from India, responded to Prator's paper by pointing out that postcolonial varieties of English were entirely valid as expressions of the sociocultural environments in which English had been transplanted and urged "native speakers of English [to] abandon the attitude of linguistic chauvinism and replace it with an attitude of linguistic tolerance ... appreciation and understanding" (Kachru, 1976: 236).

   Chauvinism and tolerance, sitting at opposite ends of a scale of attitudes, are not about language alone. They are about people and the recognition – or not – of their equality. So the discourse around English and its worldwide varieties that was developing in the second half of the 1970s (e.g. at conferences held in Honolulu and Urbana, Illinois, both in 1978 and the publications that ensued) was very firmly embedded in a conceptual-analytical frame in which the status of World Englishes was discussed as part of the wider discursive reconfiguration of power and cultural relations in the postcolonial globalizing world (e.g. in landmark publications such as Edward Said's [1978] *Orientalism*). In fact, to some extent it can be said that linguistic equality was a metaphor for social equality. In the editorial of the first issue of the *World Englishes* journal in 1985, for example, Braj Kachru and Larry Smith (1985: 211) explained that

> The editorial board considers the native and non-native users of English as equal partners in deliberations on users of English and its teaching internationally. *WE* is thus a vehicle which may be used to share the vast Western and non-Western expertise and experience for the benefit of all users of English ... The acronym *WE*, therefore aptly symbolises the underlying philosophy of the journal and the aspirations of the Editorial Board.

Significantly, with reference to the journal, Tom McArthur (1993: 334) later commented that its acronym WEs represented a "club of equals [and a] democratization of attitudes to English everywhere on the globe."

   The movement that started in the late 1970s and then led to the full development of the WEs field, with its own journal, annual international conference, and association – the International Association for World

Englishes (IAWE) – was an energetically revolutionary force that pushed for a paradigm shift in the way the English language was understood in the world. The boldly transgressive suffix *-es*, encapsulated the subversive power of WEs, whose expression was punctuated by *diversity* and *equality* as keywords and underpinned by the notion of appropriation and shared ownership of what was once the colonizers' language. This was indeed the spirit of much work by postcolonial writers, which the WEs ethos has always been very close to, and inspired by. *Depart white man*, exhorted Edwin Thumboo in "May 1954," *we know your language.* In "Listen Mr Oxford Don," John Agard warned:

> I slashing suffix in self-defence I bashing future wit present tense and if necessary
> I making de Queen's English accessory/ to my offence

On her part, Kamala Das, in "An introduction," claimed possession of the language:

> Don't write in English, they said, English is
> Not your mother-tongue. Why not leave
> Me alone, critics, friends, visiting cousins,
> Every one of you? Why not let me speak in
> Any language I like? The language I speak, Becomes mine, its distortions, its
>   queernesses All mine, mine alone.

A distorted and queer English epitomizes its appropriation and, in WEs, this also represents the most powerful response to those who consider the spread of English as serving the interests of Western capitalism and neoliberalism.

27.4 World Englishes vs. Linguistic Imperialism

The imperial origin of the spread of English worldwide could be said to be twofold: The British Empire literally took the language to its colonies but, after its collapse, it was the economic, financial, cultural, and military might of the USA – the imperialism of capitalism – that kept and boosted the global status of English. In the mid-1980s, the same period when WEs was developing into an established academic field, Naysmith (1986) warned about "the centrality of the English language in the maintenance of existing power relationships, as *the* language of capitalism" (p. 7, emphasis in original). The thesis that English is part and parcel of a neoliberal agenda emanating from the USA has been the core of what Robert Phillipson (1992) calls *linguistic imperialism*, whereby "global English [is] the capitalist neoimperial language that serves the interests of the corporate world and the governments that it influences so as to consolidate state and empire worldwide" (Phillipson, 2008b: 33). There are some important questions that Phillipson (2008a: 265) asks in relation to global English:

- Is the expansion and/or learning of English in any given context additive or subtractive?
- Is linguistic capital dispossession of national languages taking place?
- Is there a strengthening or a weakening of a balanced local language ecology?
- Where are our political and corporate leaders taking us in language policy?
- How can academics in English Studies contribute to public awareness and political change?
- If dominant norms are global, is English serving local needs or merely subordinating its users to the American empire project?

The WEs position with regard to these questions and to linguistic imperialism in general centers on the notions of appropriation and agency: (1) having been transplanted in so many different parts of the world, the English language has become embedded in, and has absorbed, the socio-cultural milieus of its new homes; and (2) thanks to this, users of English in these settings have been able to make the language their own and, therefore, (3) they are fully in control of their own decision whether to use English, when, with whom, and how. With regard to Indian English, for example, Bhatia (2008: 268) points out how "The fusion of the so-called Standard English and Indian cultures produces a distinct variety of English which reflects the identities and thought processes of Indians across the globe" and so "English is not accepted whole, nor has it blanketed its recipients with Westernisation. Instead, the 'collision of languages' has generated expressions that lead to the ability of people to 'shift seamlessly' between Hindi, Urdu, Punjabi, and English." Similarly, in an earlier riposte to Phillipson, Bisong (1995: 131) remarked how "Nigerians are sophisticated enough to know what is in their interest, and that their interest includes the ability to operate with two or more linguistic codes in a multilingual situation"; and, indeed, Nigerian writer Chimamanda Ngozi Adichie has no doubt that her relationship with English is by no means one of subordination:

> English is mine. Sometimes we talk about English in Africa as if Africans have no agency, as if there is not a distinct form of English spoken in Anglophone African countries. I was educated in it; I spoke it at the same time as I spoke Igbo. My English-speaking is rooted in a Nigerian experience and not in a British or American or Australian one. I have taken ownership of English.   (cited in Azodo, 2008)

Echoing those of her colleagues in Africa and Asia, the writer's words epitomize most powerfully the very essence of the anti-imperialist stance

in WEs and, simultaneously (and rather paradoxically), identify the limita-
tion of its counter-discursive force.

27.5 Between Equality and Diversity: The Political Conundrum of World Englishes

Specifically, there are two interrelated problems to consider. One is the
fact that, as was seen in the previous two sections, those who claim ownership of English in former exploitation colonies are a very restricted
group of intellectuals, whose sentiments and linguistic awareness are
unlikely to be shared by the majority of the population.[4] The other is
that, while regional changes in the language (phonological and/or lexico-
grammatical) represent *the* condition for these writers to be able to fully
make it their own, the new (African or Asian) reforged English, as we saw,
needs to be "still in full communion with its ancestral home" (Achebe
1965: 30) and so, in other words, the adaptation to the local surroundings
cannot go too far, lest the language become no longer recognizably
English. Kamala Das's English must not be *too* queer. The result is that
the Englishes in WEs need to simultaneously satisfy the opposite criteria of
difference and sameness and end up being versions of standard British or
American English, with just enough local flavor to make them interestingly exotic (Canagarajah, 2013: 59; Pennycook, 2007: 22–23; Saraceni,
2015: 88). Consequently, the "club of equals" is a collection of nationally
defined *elite* Englishes, while all other forms, to which the label "English"
does not easily attach, are dismissed as "colloquial," "basilectal," or given
names such as "Singlish," "Chinglish," and so on, to mark their (excessively) hybrid nature (see Lambert, 2018 for a discussion on the nomenclature of hybrid Englishes).

The underlying conceptual conundrum is the fact that descriptions and
classifications of Englishes operate within a conception of language deriving from "[t]he 'nation-state myth' – that basic view of the world as consisting naturally of nation-states" (Joseph, 2004: 98), which developed in the
eighteenth and nineteenth centuries in Europe and was "founded on a
biological continuity of blood relations, a spatial continuity of territory,
and linguistic commonality" (Hardt and Negri, 2000: 95). Within that
frame, language "has been successfully mobilized since the eighteenth
century as one among the symbolic resources recruited to construct
nations" (Andersen and Carter, 2016: 70). In particular, linguistic homogeneity has been of cardinal importance, while its opposite, linguistic diversity, "has been systematically erased from the historical record" (Piller,
2016: 26). As an illustration of this, Piller (2016: 28) describes what happened
when the Turkish Republic was instituted in 1923: "Languages other than

---

[4] See, for example, Joseph's (2004) discussion on the dismissal of "Hong Kong English" in public discourse.

Turkish started to be repressed ... Not only was Turkey going to have only one language – Turkish – but that language was going to be 'modernized,' that is, rid of the traces of other languages ...; such was the explicit aim of the Turkish Language Reform." Similar observations could be made about, for example, the language policies in France, which have traditionally sought to promote French as the only national language and to protect it from the interference of both local "dialects" and foreign languages (Ager, 1999). Or, even more evidently, about the academic discourse on the history of English, which has created the idea of a linear and uninterrupted geneal-ogy of the language all the way from the arrival of the "Anglo-Saxons" (Milroy, 2002), for example by removing the possibility of any influence from pre–Anglo-Saxon languages and by downplaying the profound linguis-tic transformation that took place as a result of the Norman Conquest simply as a shift from "Old English" to "Middle English."

Thus, rather paradoxically, the political impetus of the appropriation of English clashes with, and is thus tempered, restrained, and kept in check by, another political precept: that of linguistic homogeneity. In spite of the intention of promoting a more open-minded attitude toward diversity, in WEs the idea of the spread of English and its multiplication into distinct varieties is trapped in the same understanding of languages as homoge-neous entities. In this sense, therefore, the idea of many Englishes repre-sents little more than the "pluralization of singularity" (Makoni, 2011: 683), and the spread of English becomes just one more chapter in the supposedly long history of the language, and the WEs paradigm falls short of taking full account of the very linguistic diversity toward which it has the political desire to encourage better disposition.

This appears to be particularly problematic given that a trope of modern sociolinguistics – of which WEs is fully a part – is that the political imposi-tion of linguistic homogeneity creates inequality:

> the normalization of linguistic homogeneity continues to affect us today and constitutes a form of representational injustice as it has helped to create the linguistic homogeneity of the standard language as the ima-gined ideal against which the diverse repertoires of individual speakers are judged.   (Piller, 2016: 29)

Translated into the domain of WEs, this means that

> "legitimate" Englishes are "standard" Englishes inaccessible to majority of the Outer Circle. There are *inner circles* everywhere, in "native" and "non-native" English-speaking countries, whose speakers enjoy the privilege of having much access to Standard Englishes. Similarly, there are *outer circles* everywhere, whose speakers, because of positions of relative powerless-ness, are largely unable to gain access to such standards – and they are the much larger social groups.   (Tupas, 2006: 170)

The classification of (often nationally defined) Englishes and their being grouped into "circles" may have highlighted that English is not *one* language but this, on its own, does not guarantee the equal treatment of all its speakers. In fact, this creates a "hierarchy of Englishes, some of which are more equal than others" (Parakrama, 2012: 113). The fact that a few post-colonial creative writers have claimed "ownership" of their Englishes and that an entire academic field has developed on egalitarian principles about English in the world does not make this language, or its varieties, egalitarian. In fact, those declarations of ownership are often highly individualized: "English is mine" is hardly an expression of linguistic solidarity toward the community to which one belongs. Writers who claim ownership of English, observes Ngũgĩ wa Thiong'o (2013), "are a product of the metaphysical empire, which is when people now begin to claim 'this place is really mine'."

27.6 Concluding Remarks on English(es) and Social Inequality

As the limitations of the WEs paradigm in dealing with the ways in which the majority of people use English have become apparent, sociolinguistics has begun to look at language practices from a different perspective, paying particular attention to the ways in which, in communicating with one another, people draw from shared semiotic resources, without much regard to linguistic homogeneity. What is being brought to the fore more and more prominently is that this is "the normal mode of communication that, with some exceptions in some monolingual enclaves, characterizes communities throughout the world" (García, 2009: 44). This, indeed, has been the focus of much scholarship in the last few years (Canagarajah, 2013; García and Li Wei, 2014; Jørgensen, 2008; Li Wei, 2011; Otheguy, García and Reid, 2015; Pennycook, 2008; Rubdy and Alsagoff, 2013; Schneider, 2016), dubbed the "translanguaging turn" by García and Li Wei (2014: 19), the gist of which has been (1) a shift of focus on language as social practice rather than exclusively on language as a bounded system, (2) the recognition that, as a social practice, language use is not adequately described in terms of adherence to discrete, enumerable, and separate named languages, (3) but is best approached in terms of the ways in which people dynamically make use of shared linguistic and semiotic repertoires as a result of the social activities they are engaged in. In the words of Blommaert and Rampton (2011: 3), "rather than working with homogeneity, stability and boundedness as the starting assumptions, mobility, mixing, political dynamics and historical embedding are now central concerns in the study of languages, language groups and communication."

The expanded scope of investigation that this affords may represent greater democratization of the way in which global English is conceptualized but underlying questions relating to social (in)equality remain intact:

Do the apparent fluid and unhindered linguistic practices reflect individual freedom or are they enmeshed with ideology and unequal power relations? Who has resources and access to acquire hybrid English codes in the first place? What potential social consequences are imposed on hybrid language users and are such consequences unevenly experienced? Can all English users regardless of their racial, gender, socioeconomic, and other background equally transgress linguistic boundaries and engage in hybrid and fluid linguistic practices? (Kubota, 2015: 33)

Kubota's questions begin to make clear that perhaps the problem is not "English *per se*" (Bolton, 2008: 270), especially, "if by that, we mean a certain grammar and lexicon" (Pennycook, 2012: 26). The problem, instead, "is the *discourses* of English" (my emphasis), namely "the way that an idea of English is caught up," for example, in "all the exacerbations of inequality that go under the label of globalization" (p. 26). This, of course, includes discourses relating to socioeconomic advancement that English is often believed to guarantee (see, e.g., Hamid and Kirkpatrick, 2016; Parakrama, 2012; Park and Wee, 2012; Shin, 2012).

If inequality is not directly linked to English as such, or to how it is used or how it is described by sociolinguists, then power imbalance creating enormous socioeconomic disparities and a very uneven distribution of wealth should be taken much more seriously into account when considering the language choices made by individuals as well as groups. "Linguistics must address issues arising from the real world of socioeconomic inequality more globally and not just from the point of view of languages as maps of world views and illustrations of mental/cognitive variation" (Mufwene, 2010: 927). "[I]s it even possible," asks Block (2015: 14), "to develop a thorough understanding of the apparent choices made by people with regard to speaking one language or another, or speaking one variety or another, without acknowledging and exploring how ongoing communication is always enmeshed in the material existences of those making these choices?" Tupas and Rubdy (2015: 17) provide us with a sober reminder that "we have been seduced into celebrating our victories over English but forgetting the massive inequities sustained and perpetuated by the unbridled dominance of English today." Yet in a world where "the top 10% of the world population [owns] 86% of global wealth" (Credit Suisse, 2013: 4), which means that "the Inner Circle has more than 30% of the planet's wealth and only 6% of its population and where the figures for the Outer Circle are exactly reversed – 30% of the world's population owning 6% of the world's wealth" (Saraceni, 2015: 141), social equality is a fleeting illusion, let alone linguistic equality.

References

Abad, Gemino, Susan Butler, Marjorie Evasco, Francisco Sionil Jose and Cristina Pantoja-Hidalgo. (1997). Standards in Philippine English: The writers' forum. In Maria Lourdes S. Bautista, ed. *English Is an Asian language: The Philippine context*. Manila: The Macquarie Library, 163–176.

Achebe, Chinua. (1965). English and the African writer. *Transition 18*, 27–30.

Ager, Dennis. (1999). *Identity, Insecurity and Image: France and Language*. Clevedon: Multilingual Matters.

Andersen, Julie Tetel and Phillip. M. Carter (2016). *Languages in the World: How History, Culture, and Politics Shape Language*. Chichester: Wiley.

Anderson, Benedict. (1983). *Imagined Communities: Reflections on the Origin and Spread of Nationalism*. London: Verso.

Azodo, Ada Uzoamaka. (2008). Interview with Chimamanda Ngozi Adichie: Creative Writing and Literary Activism. www.iun.edu/minaua/interviews/interview chimamanda ngozi adichie.pdf

Bhatia, Aditi. (2008). Comment 1. *World Englishes 27*(2), 268–269.

Bisong, Joseph. (1995). Language choice and cultural imperialism: A Nigerian perspective. *ELT Journal 49*(2), 122–132.

Block, David. (2015). Social class in applied linguistics. *Annual Review of Applied Linguistics 35*, 1–19.

Blommaert, Jan and Ben Rampton. (2011). Language and superdiversity. *Diversities 13*(2), 1–21.

Bolton, Kingsley. (2008). Comment 2. *World Englishes 27*(2), 270–271.

Brutt-Griffler, Janina. (2002). *World English: A Study of Its Development*. Clevedon: Multilingual Matters.

Canagarajah, Suresh. (2013). *Translingual Practice: Global Englishes and Cosmopolitan Relations*. London: Routledge.

Credit Suisse. (2013). *Global Wealth Report 2013*. Zurich: Research Institute.

Crystal, David. (2003). *English as a Global Language* (2nd ed.). Cambridge: Cambridge University Press.

Damousi, Joy. (2010). *Colonial Voices: A Cultural History of English in Australia, 1840–1940*. Cambridge: Cambridge University Press.

Delbridge, Arthur. (2001). Lexicography and national identity: The Australian experience. In David Blair and Peter Collins, eds. *English in Australia*. Amsterdam: John Benjamins, 303–316.

García, Ofelia. (2009). *Bilingual Education in the 21st century: A Global Perspective*. Oxford: Wiley.

García, Ofelia. and Li Wei. (2014). *Translanguaging: Language, Bilingualism and Education*. Basingstoke: Palgrave Macmillan.

Halliday, M. A. K., Angus McIntosh and Peter Strevens. (1964). *The Linguistic Sciences and Language Teaching*. London: Longmans.

Hamid, M. Obaidul and Andy Kirkpatrick. (2016). Foreign language policies in Asia and Australia in the Asian century. *Language Problems and Language Planning* 40(1), 26–46.

Hamilton, Thomas. (1833). *Men and Manners in America*. Edinburgh: William Blackwood.

Hammerton, James and Alistair Thomson. (2005). *Ten pound Poms: Australia's invisible migrants*. Manchester: Manchester University Press.

Hardt, Michael and Antonio Negri. (2000). *Empire*. Cambridge, MA: Harvard University Press.

Horvath, Barbara. M. and Ronald J. Horvath. (2001). A Geolinguistics of short A in Australian English. In David Blair and Peter Collins, eds. *English in Australia*. Amsterdam: John Benjamins, 341–355.

Jefferson, Thomas. (1813). Thomas Jefferson to John Waldo [Manuscript/mixed material], August 13, 1813. www.loc.gov/item/mtjbib020982/

Jørgensen, J. Normann. (2008). Polylingual languaging around and among children and adolescents. *International Journal of Multilingualism* 5(3), 161–176.

Joseph, John E. (2004). *Language and Identity: National, Ethnic, Religious*. Basingstoke: Palgrave.

Joseph, John E. (2006). *Language and Politics*. Edinburgh: Edinburgh University Press.

Kachru, Braj B. (1976). Models of English for the third world: White man's linguistic burden or language pragmatics? *TESOL Quarterly* 10(2), 221–239.

Kachru, Braj B. and Larry E. Smith. (1985). Editorial. *World Englishes* 4(2), 209–212.

Kubota, Ryuko. (2015). Inequalities of Englishes, English speakers, and languages: A critical perspective on pluralist approaches to English. In Ruanni Tupas, ed. *Unequal Englishes: The Politics of Englishes Today*. Basingstoke: Palgrave, 21–42.

Lambert, James. (2018). A multitude of "lishes": The nomenclature of hybridity. *English World-Wide* 39(1), 1–33.

Li Wei. (2011). Moment analysis and translanguaging space: Discursive construction of identities by multilingual Chinese youth in Britain. *Journal of Pragmatics* 43(5), 1222–1235.

Makoni, Sinfree B. (2011). Sociolinguistics, colonial and postcolonial: An integrationist perspective. *Language Sciences* 33(4), 680–688.

Marks, Robert B. (2007). *The Origins of the Modern World: A Global and Ecological Narrative from the Fifteenth to the Twenty-first Century* (2nd ed.). Lanham, MD: Rowman & Littlefield.

McArthur, Tom. (1993). The English language or the English languages? In Whitney French Bolton and David Crystal, eds. *The English Language*. London: Penguin Books, 323–341.

Milroy, Jim. (2002). The legitimate language. In Richard Watts and Peter Trudgill, eds. *Alternative Histories of English*. London: Routledge, 7–25.

Mufwene, Salikoko. S. (2001). *The Ecology of Language Evolution*. Cambridge: Cambridge University Press.

Mufwene, Salikoko. S. (2010). The role of mother-tongue schooling in eradicating poverty: A response to Language and Poverty. *Language* 86(4), 901–932.

Nash, Manning. (1989). *The Cauldron of Ethnicity in the Modern World*. Chicago: University of Chicago Press.

Naysmith, John. (1986). English as imperialism? Paper presented at the IATEFL Annual Meeting, Brighton, April 1–4. https://files.eric.ed.gov/full text/ED274197.pdf

Ngũgĩ wa Thiong'o. (2013). HARDtalk with Ngũgĩ wa Thiong'o, *BBC*. www .bbc.co.uk/ programmes/p01d17d6

Okara, Gabriel. (1963). African Speech … English words. *Transition* 3(10), 15–16.

O'Leary, John. (1995). Prince says Americans are ruining the language. *The Times*, March 24.

Omoniyi, Tope. (2004). *The Sociolinguistics of Borderlands: Two Nations, One People*. Trenton, NJ: Africa World Press.

Omoniyi, Tope. (2009). West African Englishes. In Braj Kachru, Yamuna Kachru and Cecil Nelson, eds. *The Handbook of World Englishes*. Oxford: Wiley-Blackwell, 172–187.

Otheguy, Ricardo, Ofelia García and Wallis Reid. (2015). Clarifying translanguaging and deconstructing named languages: A perspective from linguistics. *Applied Linguistics Review* 6(3), 281–307.

Parakrama, Arjuna. (2012). The *Malchemy* of English in Sri Lanka: Reinforcing inequality through imposing extra-linguistic value. In Vaughan Rapatahana and Pauline Bunce, eds. *English Language as Hydra: Its Impacts on Non-English Language Cultures*. Bristol: Multilingual Matters, 107–132.

Park, Joseph Sung-Yul and Lionel Wee. (2012). *Markets of English: Linguistic Capital and Language Policy in a Globalizing World*. London: Routledge.

Pennycook, Alastair. (2007). *Global Englishes and Transcultural Flows*. London: Routledge.

Pennycook, Alastair. (2008). Translingual English. *Australian Review of Applied Linguistics* 31(3), 30.1–30.9.

Pennycook, Alastair. (2012). Afterword: Could Heracles have gone about things differently? In Vaughan Rapatahana and Pauline Bunce, eds. *English Language as Hydra: Its Impacts on Non-English Language Cultures*. Bristol: Multilingual Matters, 255–262.

Pensalfini, Rob. (2014). The Americans are destroying the English language – or are they? *The Conversation*, January 7. http://theconversation.com/the-americans-are-destroying-the-english-language-or-are-they-21461

Phillipson, Robert. (1992). *Linguistic Imperialism*. Oxford: Oxford University Press.

Phillipson, Robert. (2008a). Lingua franca or lingua frankensteinia? English in European integration and globalisation. *World Englishes 27*(2), 250–267.

Phillipson, Robert. (2008b). The linguistic imperialism of neoliberal empire. *Critical Inquiry in Language Studies 5*(1), 1–43.

Piller, Ingrid. (2016). *Linguistic Diversity and Social Justice: An Introduction to Applied Sociolinguistics*. Oxford: Oxford University Press.

Prator, Clifford H. (1968). The British heresy in TESL. In Joshua Fishman, Charles Ferguson and Jyotirindra Das Gupta, eds. *Language Problems of Developing Nations*. London: Wiley, 459–476.

Rao, Raja. (1938). *Kanthapura*. London: George Allen & Unwin.

Rubdy, Rani and Lubna Alsagoff, eds. (2013). *The Global-Local Interface and Hybridity: Exploring Language and Identity*. Bristol: Multilingual Matters.

Rushdie, Salman. (1982). The Empire writes back with a vengeance. *The Times*, July 3.

Said, Edward. (1978). *Orientalism*. London: Routledge and Kegan Paul.

Saraceni, Mario. (2015). *World Englishes: A Critical Analysis*. London: Bloomsbury.

Saraceni, Mario. (2016). Back to the 19th century: How language is being used to mark national borders. *The Conversation*, October 4. https:// the-conversation.com/back-to-the-19th-century-how-language-is-being-used-to-marknational-borders–66357

Schneider, Edgar. (2016). Hybrid Englishes: An exploratory survey. *World Englishes 35*, 339–354.

Shaw, Flora. (1897). Nigeria. *The Times*, January 8.

Shin, Hyunjung. (2012). From FOB to COOL: Transnational migrant students in Toronto and the styling of global linguistic capital. *Journal of Sociolinguistics 16*(2), 184–200.

Tiffin, Helen. (1987). Post-colonial literatures and counter-discourse. *Kunapipi 9*(3), 17–34.

Tupas, Ruanni. (2006). Standard Englishes, pedagogical paradigms and their conditions of (im)possibility. In R. Rubdy and M. Saraceni, eds. *English in the World: Global Rules, Global Roles*. London: Continuum, 169–185.

Tupas, Ruanni and Rani Rubdy. (2015). Introduction: From World Englishes to unequal Englishes. In Ruanni Tupas, ed. *Unequal Englishes: The Politics of Englishes Today*. Basingstoke: Palgrave, 1–17.

Watt, Dominic and Brendan Gunn. (2016). *The Sound of 2066*. HSBC. www.about.hsbc.co.uk//media/uk/en/news-and-media/160929-voice-biometricssounds-of-britain-2066.pdf?la=en-gb

Webster, Noah. (1789). *Dissertations on the English Language*. Boston: Isaiah Thomas.

28

World Englishes in the Media

Andrew Moody

28.1 Introduction

Sociolinguists have traditionally been reluctant, or at least hesitant, to draw linguistic data from the media in examination of linguistic variation. Given this general avoidance of data from the media, one might suppose that linguists would regard the mass media as one of the last places to find sociolinguistically relevant data demonstrating the depth and range of variation in World Englishes (WEs). In addition to the fact that media language is neither spontaneous nor naturally occurring – two features traditionally required for sociolinguistic data – the language of the media is also generally regarded as "standard English" and, as such, not normally expressive, or even tolerant, of variation. Consequently, variationist socio-linguists have come to regard the standard language as a "distractor" that masks or hides an individual speaker's performance of their natural and unedited style of speech. Labov (1972) identified systematic patterns of "style shifting" between what he calls the "vernacular" and other forms of speech that are more monitored, depending on the formality of the inter-view context (pp. 208–209). Labov hypothesizes that a speaker's shift between the vernacular and monitored speech is unavoidable and hence forms the "observer's paradox" where the goal of sociolinguists is to observe the speech individuals use when they are not being observed. While Labov's point in articulating the "observer's paradox" is to demon-strate that an examination of the "pure vernacular" is impossible and that focus should instead be on the systematic style switching between per-ceived targets of "vernacular" and monitored speech, the emphasis on collecting "spontaneous" and "naturally occurring" data has been general-ized into a dictum that virtually prohibits the examination of media language in variationist studies (see Chambers 1995; Tagliamonte 2006).

This bifurcation of the "vernacular" from "monitored speech" (usually operationalized as features that are more easily identified as "standard"), however, produces a false dichotomy in sociolinguistics, namely the belief that vernaculars are authentic languages and standards are not. Bucholtz (2003) discusses the origin of the dichotomy of "authentic language" and "standard language" in romanticized notions that rural cultures and vernaculars were disappearing as a result of industrialization:

> In its political guise, Romanticism sought to locate the underpinnings of the European nation in the spirit of its people – particularly the peasants whose culture supposedly remained untouched by urbanity. In its scholarly guise, Romanticism valorized the rural population as the authentic source of traditional cultural knowledge and practice, including language. Dialectology furthered both of these efforts. (p. 399)

Similarly, Coupland (2003: 418) complains that "sociolinguistics has invested very heavily – and arguably too heavily – in the view that some sorts of language and some sorts of speaker are authentic, and that it has thought them more valuable for being more authentic."

Although a rich tradition of scholarship examining media language as a form of linguistic practice has developed in sociolinguistics, the literature tends to focus on features of discourse or pragmatics much more often than on variation in phonology or grammar, and, as Queen (2015) notes, to be more often descriptive of language in the news media than in the "narrative media" (p. 20). Indeed, Queen argues that the study of language in the news media is taken at the expense of language in the narrative media precisely because the narrative media are assumed to be less "authentic." Noting the sociolinguistic value of scripted narrative media, Queen remarks that "the scripted media offer a fairly contained, and edited, microcosm of the places from which their plays come. In this sense, they are not more or less 'real' than the unscripted media" (p. 21). To the same degree, Lee and Moody (2012a) and Moody (2010) note that linguists have been reluctant to examine the languages of popular culture as media genres.

This chapter will strive to examine the various studies of media language that have been conducted from the WEs perspective. Although variationist sociolinguists tend to reject the study of media language as "inauthentic" varieties, the examination of media Englishes has become a staple component of descriptions of WEs and, as such, questioned the validity of claims that some languages are "authentic" and others are not. Instead, this chapter will demonstrate that "authenticity" is a feature of media Englishes that must be balanced against the "authority" of the standard language. Within this framework of thinking about media Englishes, then, the Three Circles of WEs varieties – the "Inner," "Outer," and "Expanding Circles" – show consistently different patterns of balancing concerns for "authenticity" and "authority" in media Englishes.

28.2   Prevalence of Media Studies in World Englishes

What exactly do we mean when we talk about "the media" and what justifies the discussion of media Englishes as functional varieties? As noted in the previous section, examination of the linguistic forms of a variety that appear within Inner, Outer, or Expanding Circle media is an accepted and somewhat expected feature of any description of a variety. Most of these descriptions focus on the free or low-cost broadcast and print media of radio, television, movies, newspapers, magazines, and so on. Within each one of these media genres, the value of any particular form is measured by the size of its audience. Hence radio and television stations spend great effort to compile reliable ratings data about the number of listeners or viewers. Likewise, newspapers and magazines measure success, vitality, and relevance with circulation and readership figures. Strong ratings or circulations figures, quite simply, are then easily translated into a price for advertising, where more expensive advertising is assumed to reach a greater number of individuals. This "profit-motivated" definition of the mass media describes the capitalistic practices of specific content providers (e.g. television or radio stations, newspapers, movie studios) and how they are able to offer free or low-cost content for mass consumption, and this model of consumption has functioned relatively well for a number of decades.

Although studies of media Englishes across multiple varieties of WEs are rare, descriptions of the roles, functions, and sometimes the forms of English in the media are a staple of descriptive work about individual varieties of WEs. These areal studies of English varieties typically include descriptions of English usage in mass media, and a review of these studies demonstrates how frequently media Englishes are described. Speech communities whose media are described in areal studies include Cameroon (Kouega 1999); China (Yong and Campbell 1995; Li 2012); Colombia (Martinez 2015); Costa Rica (Aguilar-Sanchez 2005); Ecuador (Alm 2003); Europe (Raedts et al. 2015); Finland (Leppanen 2007); France (Ruellot 2011); Ghana (Dolphyne 1997); Hong Kong (Luke and Richards 1982; Li 1999); Hungary (Petzold and Berns 2000); India (Dubey 1991; Philipson and Skutnabb-Kangas 1996); Iran (Baumgardner and Brown 2012); Japan (Dougill 1987); Jordan (Hamdan and Hatab 2009); the Maghreb (Battenburg 1996); Malawi (Matiki 2001); Mauritius (Foley 1995); Mexico (Baumgardner 1997); the Netherlands (Ridder 1995); Nigeria (Adekunle 1997); Pakistan (Abbas 1993); the Philippines (Dayag 2004); Russia (Ustinova 2005); Thailand (Masavisut, Sukiwat, and Wongmontha 1986); Tunisia (Battenburg 1997); and Turkey (Dogancay-Aktuna and Kiziltepe 2005). Each of these studies cites the local mass media as a source of data about the forms or functions of English varieties, and, as such, these studies document the rich variability of Englishes across varieties. At the same time, however, the media are notorious users and promoters of standard English. There is, therefore, an interesting and useful contradiction within the role of the mass media. While local media content providers may sometimes promote the language forms that are "local" and unique to a particular variety of English, media language is also more generally committed to the promotion of global standards of intelligibility. The tension between these two commitments within media Englishes – a commitment to both local and global forms – is essentially what defines the "authority" and the "authenticity" of media Englishes.

28.3 "Authority" and "Authenticity" in Media Englishes

Norms, standards, and codification have always been at the center of our understanding of WEs. In a very early description of the concentric circle model of WEs, Kachru (1985) describes the Outer Circle as possessing two clearly different sets of norms. Kachru writes that, in Outer Circle societies, "there has been a conflict between linguistic norm and linguistic behaviour … [and the varieties] are both endonormative and exonormative" (p. 17). The WEs perspective is one that recognizes and validates the pluricentricity of English varieties, including standard and standardizing varieties as well as varieties that might be characterized as "vernaculars" in the Inner Circle, "nativized varieties" in the Outer Circle or "learner varieties" in the Expanding Circle. Media Englishes in all three circles, however, demonstrate a consistent tension between two complementary impulses in language: the projection of "authority" and the production of "authenticity." Queen (2015) describes the sociolinguistic impact of the technological development of synchronized sound recording and moving pictures – a development that Bauman (2011) describes as having borrowed the authority of narrative storytelling into sound recordings – and the technological development of electronically broadcasting stories across commercialized networks. Queen (2015: 16) argues that the development and popularization of these technologies "linked authenticity and authority, especially in language, to the experience of consuming mass media products." While this occurred in the early to mid-twentieth century in most Inner Circle societies of English users, the linking of "authority" and "authenticity" – and especially the authority and authenticity *of English* – is still in stages of progressive development in Outer and Expanding Circle communities of English users.

28.3.1 "Authority" in Media Englishes

Although the WEs perspective celebrates the pluricentricity of English varieties, the fact of the matter is that content providers in mass media are generally committed to ideologies that affirm and strengthen the authority of standard languages, not the plurality of standards or varieties. McArthur (1997, 1999) and Gaskell (2000) each note that the degree of variation within the media internationally is relatively small because of the preference for what McArthur (1997) calls "International Standard English." From a historical perspective, Herbert (1997) argues that this language of broadcast has become increasingly "egalitarian" over the twentieth century but that this development never challenged the authority of the standard. In particular, a number of writers note that American English (AmE) is especially prevalent within the mass media and that, internationally, norms in the media have been influenced by this one variety (see Swan and Urdang 1985; Urdang 1990; Rindal 2013). While indigenous norms define speech styles in Inner and Outer Circle societies (and even in some Expanding Circle societies), the fact of the matter is that endonormative variation – and especially nonstandard variation – rarely dominates media texts. In the Inner and Outer Circles standardized varieties tend to dominate the media, and, in the Expanding Circle, media texts are especially committed to standardized varieties that are exonormative; and this is precisely the reason why a number of scholars advocate the use of locally produced English-language media texts from the Outer or Expanding Circles as authentic teaching texts – because these texts reinforce external Inner Circle norms (see, for Indonesia, Smith 1991; for Japan, Tanaka 1995; and, for Pakistan, Baumgardner 1987).

The primary mechanism by which media languages project authority is the "standard language ideology" (SLI), a term that was formally introduced in Milroy and Milroy's ([1985] 1999) definitive work on language standardization. While language ideologies are "sets of beliefs about language articulated by the users as a rationalization or justification of perceived language structure and use" (Silverstein, 1979: 193), the SLI functions specifically to preserve the authority of standard languages by obscuring the historical and sociological conditions that produce a standard language. While this happens most clearly in the written variety of standard English, Milroy and Milroy affirm that the SLI also works within the spoken standard. Not surprisingly, there is a particularly intimate connection between the development of standard languages and the media, and Milroy and Milroy note that "the media have successfully promoted an awareness of the standard spoken language (which is in fact popularly known as BBC English) without having much influence on the rate of adoption of that standard" (p. 25).

The close association of a standard language with the language of media is understandable; the impetus to codify English, both written and spoken standards, has historically come from the media (Millar 2012; Fitzmaurice 2000). Of course, media sources have played a role in all the processes of standardization (namely, *selection, restriction, elaboration,* and *codification*), but the final process of codification has historically been driven by the print media. During the stage of codification, texts of authority (e.g.

dictionaries, grammar books, learner materials) are produced to catalogue and formalize standard language forms, including pronunciations, word meanings and usages, punctuation, and grammatical usage. The standardization of Early Modern English (EModE) and Present-Day English (PDE) began (and, indeed, still continues) with the codification of standard English in print media. Beginning in the sixteenth century, printers began to use glossaries (i.e. lists of words), for example, to limit the number of variants in the spelling of various words, a purpose that is fundamentally consistent with one of the goals of standardization, to minimize the number of variants within the language (Leith 1983), and other forms of codification followed. Within the history of English, then, the publishing industry and related media were instrumental in developing codifications that defined the forms of standard English.

When English mass media were primarily in the form of print, the codification processes mainly applied to the written form of the language, and spoken varieties of English were allowed to diverge, develop, and thrive without much attention to the codification of spoken language. This, perhaps, explains in part how English developed as a pluricentric language during the colonial spread of the language in the seventeenth through nineteenth centuries. Although there was a single standard for written English, spoken varieties were allowed to diverge within the Inner and Outer Circles of WEs users. However, the early twentieth century saw the development of several media forms that were able to reproduce spoken languages, namely radio, phonographs, motion pictures (e.g. "talkies"), and, somewhat later, television. In North America, these new mass media genres drove the early adoption of the "Mid-Atlantic English" (MAE), an anglicized variety of AmE, as a spoken media standard (Labov 1998; Bolton 2010; Shytex BookVideo Training 2014). In the latter half of the twentieth century, the use of this specific dialect in spoken media began to decline as it was replaced by what is normally called "Broadcast Standard." Within the Inner Circle varieties of Englishes, two dominant varieties have emerged: BBC English from the UK and Broadcast Standard English (BSE) from the USA. The role of the mass media in defining these spoken standards is profound and it is no coincidence that they take their names from the media where they are used (Schwyter 2016). However, the SLI entails a belief that the standard language has always existed in its current form and that it is a pure version of the language (especially when compared to nonstandard variants). The ideology functions explicitly to obscure the dynamic nature of the standardization processes and standard English projects the authority of the standard language into media texts by reinforcing a belief in the purity and immutability of standard English. The authority of the standard language varieties (BBC English and BSE) originating from the Inner Circle is especially clear in international media. For example, several scholars have noted the worldwide adoption of English as an ex post facto official language of the media (Tillman 1986) and there is even some evidence that the promotion of English in the media represents a self-conscious expression of British (Howse 1979) or American (Demont-Heinrich 2008) hegemony in the developing world. It should also be mentioned here that there is some evidence that the dominance of English as an international media language may be responsible for language endangerment, loss of bilingualism, or loss of other languages within media domains (see, for Chamorro, Underwood 1989; for Danish Bilingualism, Christophersen 1991; for Diasporic Hindi, Pandharipande 2013; for European Spanish, Lujan-Garcia 2011; for Singlish, Rubdy 2001; and, for Turkmen, Sartor 2010).

28.3.2   "Authenticity" in Media Englishes

It was noted in Section 28.3.1 that, for much of the twentieth century, the "Mid-Atlantic English" (MAE) variety of AmE functioned as a media standard in North America, and particularly within the USA (Bolton 2010). This variety of English attempted to blend various features of British English as a prestige norm (most notably non-rhoticity) and, at the same, avoid many features of AmE that might be stigmatized (such as "*cot-caught* merger" or "intervocalic dental flapping"). The accent is still taught for use in theater and media performance training (Skinner 1990), but US BSE came to replace the MAE as a media standard as popular perceptions of MAE changed. The dialect retains some authority as a media variety, but principally just in the news media. As a language of "narrative media" (i.e. movies, television, radio dramas, etc.), MAE is frequently regarded as sounding "old-timey" and unlike contemporary ways of speaking (Drum 2011; Fallows 2015). In a word, the variety sounds "inauthentic" to contemporary AmE speakers.

Milroy's (2000) description of how the SLI functions in Britain and the USA explains how the change from MAE to BSE was institutionalized within the media. The primary difference between the SLI in Britain and the USA is the way that a spoken standard language functions within the two societies. Milroy notes that the SLI in Britain places a great deal of emphasis on a spoken standard, and that the consequences of this emphasis is a drive to use standard pronunciation within a number of different functional domains: education, media, politics, and law, to name a few. One way to think of the spoken standard in Great Britain is as a "productive standard," one that positively specifies the features of standard English pronunciation. Conversely, BSE is more of a "prohibitive standard," not specifying the forms that must be used to be standard but instead defining a set of stigmatized forms that should be avoided when speaking BSE. These ideological differences between the ways that a spoken standard is perceived in the UK and the USA, then, create functional differences in how the standard languages appear in various media within the two societies. Both societies posit "authority" to the standard languages when they are used in the media, but the complementary implementation of "authenticity" is relatively easier to produce within the spoken standard of US media, where broadcasters do not need to produce particular forms to be perceived as standard but must instead simply avoid those forms that are marked as "nonstandard." Finally, it should be noted that the ideological differences between the UK and the USA primarily pertain to the functions of English as a spoken standard language; the written standard in both societies functions similarly without many differences in how it is implemented within the print media.

Within media languages, therefore, a complex set of oppositions operates to define a standard that evokes both "authority" and "authenticity." Whereas MAE was able to evoke the authority of a standard language, it lacked authenticity, and the evolution of BSE effectively fulfilled the need for both authority and authenticity within a standard language. This is *not* to say that BSE is a more authentic language than BBC English, or that it might somehow have less authority. The media's need to project both "authority" and "authenticity" will not allow content providers to choose one over the other. Instead, "authority" and "authenticity" are complementary concerns that are in tension with one another and this tension may express itself in a number of different ways within the media. The tension certainly accounts for the variability that Labov (1972) notes between the "vernacular" and "self-monitored" speech but it is not limited to these variabilities. This tension might be realized as a contrast between, say, the "global" norms of the standard language and "local" norms.

Coupland (2001) describes a consistent style switch in Welsh radio broadcasting that is likely driven by the tension between "authority" and "authenticity" but expressed in terms of "global" and "local" norms of English. Coupland observed that Welsh radio announcers would consistently perform an Americanized accent when they announce the songs that they are playing. This performance of AmE, Coupland argues, is prompted by the content of the program: entertainment favors AmE as a "standard language" in these radio stations and, by performing AmE, the radio announcer manufactures both the "authority" and the "authenticity" related to being a competent and popular disk jockey. However, when the announcers delivered local information like news or weather, they shifted into the local form of Welsh-accented English. Coupland call this switch between AmE and Welsh-accented "dialect stylization," but it is related to a number of performative language strategies (e.g. audience design, crossing, and even code switching) that treat language performance as dynamic and interactive between multiple tensions and concerns.

How does Welsh DJs' performance of AmE fulfill the need for authenticity of language forms on the Welsh radio? Barker and Taylor (2007) describes two types of "authenticity" that can be produced in popular music: personal authenticity and cultural authenticity.[1] "Personal authenticity" refers to the language used when a performer is not trying to portray a character or alter ego, but themselves. While "personal authenticity" might appear to be related to the vernacular languages that dialectologists sought to isolate from monitored speech, in media texts the person is more closely related to what an audience actually knows about the individual. This means that the language variety related to "personal authenticity" must be performed in such a way that it manufactures authenticity that an audience will accept as accurately representing the person who is speaking. "Cultural authenticity" refers to the language used when a performer is trying to portray a character that is culturally appropriate to the media, genre, style, or register of the performance. This distinction between "personal" and "cultural authenticity" explains how the performance of both Welsh-accented English and AmE by the Welsh DJs is accepted by the listening audience as "authentic." While Welsh-accented English is probably "personally authentic" to the DJs, AmE in most cases is *not* a personally authentic language. Instead, the "cultural authenticity" of the two performances is most relevant here. Welsh-accented English is culturally appropriate for announcements from the local calendar, or the weather, because it indexes local culture. Likewise, AmE is culturally appropriate for announcing playlists or banter about music because it indexes global entertainment (especially pop music) culture.

28.3.3 "Authority" and "Authenticity" in World Englishes

Although "authority" and "authenticity" are presented here as existing in constant tension with one another in the media across all English varieties, there does seem to be a general pattern of emphasis or development that is easily described within Kachru's (1985) model of WEs varieties (i.e. "the Circles"). Kachru describes the defining features of the circles as their commitment to norms (whether they are "exonormative" or "endonormative") and this particular feature of Inner, Outer, and Expanding Circles influences whether a society's mass media content providers are more committed to ensuring the "authority" of English within their mass media or to developing the "authenticity" of English. Likewise, the developmental stages of "exonormative stabilization" and "endonormative stabilization" described within Schneider's Dynamic Model of postcolonial

---

[1] Barker and Taylor (2007) actually describe three types of authenticity but I have excluded from my discussion here the third type, representational authenticity. "Representational authenticity" refers to whether or not an artist is actually performing the work that is attributed to them. One of the better-known examples of a failure to produce "representational authenticity" is the musical performance attributed to the duet Milli Vanilli, who were sued for damages related to fraud when it was discovered that the two individuals who were represented as performing on their record did not actually perform the recordings. A more contemporary example of failure to produce "representational authority" is the hip-hop artist Drake, who was accused of using "ghost writers" to write rap lines (Britton 2015). See Moody (2012a) for a further discussion of how authenticity is manufactured within popular culture.

Englishes (Schneider 2007) are likely responsible, at least in part, for the differences observed within the Inner, Outer, and Expanding Circles.

The example of Welsh DJ speech (Coupland 2001) demonstrates how authenticity tends to be emphasized within Inner Circle varieties. The English used on the radio does not require much attention from the performers or the audience to accept its "authority," and this is due in large to the fact that Inner Circle varieties are endonormative, that is, the norms for these varieties are indigenous to the communities. Consequently, there is more explicit emphasis on "authenticity" within the Inner Circle, and this is demonstrated on a societal level in the USA by the decline in the use of MAE in the last half of the twentieth century as an authoritative media standard and the concurrent shift toward the non-fixed BSE. Although MAE evoked the prestige and authority of British English with its adoption of features like non-rhotic vowels or fully articu-lated (i.e. non-flapped) intervocalic dentals stops, the variety did not authentically represent the English that was spoken by the majority of Americans. When MAE was no longer regarded as the primary prestige variety, the broadcast standard that emerged was one that was not neces-sarily fixed to a single set of pronunciations, but would allow expression of variation (i.e. "authenticity") as long as variation avoided stigmatized forms (Milroy and Milroy 1999). In the Inner Circle of English users, there-fore, there is a tendency to emphasize "authenticity" over the "authority" of an English variety.

Expanding Circle varieties are, by definition, exonormative English vari-eties and as such rely on norms from Inner Circle varieties. While there may be an emphasis on the "authenticity" of native languages in the Expanding Circle, English varieties are usually portrayed using the stan-dard language to avoid any compromise of the "authority" of the standard. Moody (2006) and Moody and Matsumoto (2011), for example, examine various manifestations of English and English speakers on Japanese tele-vision within the genres of "language education" and "language entertain-ment" programs. In these programs, the portrayal of English – and especially the portrayal of Japanese English and Japanese speakers of English – is ideological and driven by the desire to present a specific set of positive characteristics of speakers and of speech. To this degree, English speech is often *not* authentic, but edited and manipulated in order to reinforce Inner Circle norms or to portray specific features of English or English speakers; and there is good reason to believe that this type of portrayal of English in the Expanding Circle takes place in other societies, too (Zhou and Moody 2017).

The pattern that emerges, then, is that Inner Circle Englishes are "endo-normative" and the media in those societies consequently spend greater effort to portray the "authenticity" of English rather than the "authority" of the language. Expanding Circle Englishes, however, are "exonormative" and instead spend greater effort to ensure that the standard language is delivered with "authority" – and variation that might portray authentic nonstandard usages in the Expanding Circle is frequently censored. The English varieties of the Outer Circle, as Kachru (1985) notes, are usually "mixed" in that both endonormative and exonormative varieties are used simultaneously in these societies (see the discussion in Section 28.3). A degree of mixing exists in all three circles, and this is because "authority" and "authenticity" are not necessarily emphasized in opposition to one another; the "authority" of the standard and the "authenticity" of the vernacular do not necessarily need to exclude one another. Yet linguistic practice in the Outer Circle, as Kachru (1985) notes, is in conflict with the espoused norms. Because Outer Circle societies have usually not completed the developmental stage "endonormative stabilization," described as "phase four" of the Dynamic Model (Schneider 2007), both endonormative and exonormative varieties can be found within the media; and studies of media and popular culture in the Outer Circle demonstrate that both endonormative and exonormative varieties are used simultaneously. For example, see Lin (2012) for a discussion of hybridity in Hong Kong's hip-hop music scene; see Moody (2012b) for a description of competing norms in print and radio advertising in Malaysia; and see Kirkpatrick and Moody (2009) for how two Outer Circle communities, Hong Kong and Singapore, present "authority" and "authenticity" very differently. Media Englishes within the Outer Circle of English users, then, are characterized by an equal emphasis on both "authority" and "authenticity."

28.4 World Englishes Perspectives on Popular Culture and Media Englishes

Within WEs scholarship there has been growing scholarly attention given to forms of popular culture that rely on the mass media for their presentation and development. While much of the scholarship presents findings that are consistent with analyses of language outside of popular culture, the assessment of Englishes in the media challenges the dictum that sociolinguistic data should be "spontaneous and naturally occurring" (see Moody 2010 for a full discussion of the dictum and how it has shaped the selection of linguistic data). Many of these discussions of forms within the media simply demonstrate how discriminatory language attitudes – and, of course, prejudice against ethnicities, races, regions, etc. – are recreated within media portrayals of stigmatized individuals. Dissanayake (1986) argues that the imaginative portrayal of Indian culture and identity in the movie A Passage to India is unable to rise above stereotypes and clichés. Similarly, Chan (2000) argues that colonial stereotypes about Chinese identity dominated the late-colonial press in Hong Kong in the dates before the handover of the territory to Chinese (i.e. People's Republic of China) rule. Mesthrie (2002) offers a particularly trenchant analysis of "mock English" accents in a South African radio program and demonstrates how the stereotyped portrayal of Indian South African English enhances the power of socially dominant groups. Each of these studies examines English in the postcolonial Outer Circle of English users, and Lippi-Green (1997) demonstrates how Disney, among other media content providers, exploits stereotypes of American, British, and "foreign-accented" English speakers in their portrayal of villains, heroes, and characters that change from villainous to heroic. Martin (2002a) also examines the stereotyping of American and other English accents in French advertising and Lee (2014) examines attitudes toward English on Korean TV, arguing that ageist discrimination toward older Koreans as non-English users is frequently expressed.

While these studies use data from popular culture and the mass media to demonstrate that societal language attitudes and prejudices can be identified within popular culture, they represent just one approach to English in the media or popular culture that has been supported within the WEs research frameworks. General examination of language in advertising (Bhatia 1987, 1992, 2000, 2006; Bhatia and Ritchie 2004; Chen 2006; Martin 1998, 2002b, 2006), pop music (Chan 2009, 2012; Chik 2010; Kachru 2006; Lee 2006, 2007; Lin 2012; Moody 2012a; Moody and Matsumoto 2003; Ominiyi 2006; Wang 2006), television (Moody and Matsumoto 2011; Park 2004; Thompson 2012), linguistic landscapes (Dimova 2008; Bolton 2012), and popular culture (Lee 2004; Lee and Moody 2012b; Moody 2006, 2011, 2012b, 2013; Park 2009; Park and Wee 2012) has begun to form a rich tradition of scholarship within WEs.

These approaches to English in the media are informed by larger, more comprehensive rejections of subjectivist constructions of language and identity in recent sociolinguistic thought. These rejections instead emphasize the performative aspects of language and identity (see Bucholtz and Hall 2004; Hill 1999; Pennycook 2003; Rampton 1995, 1999). The emphasis on the performative aspects of language – especially when used to examine data from the mass media – rejects the dictum that sociolinguistic data be "spontaneous and naturally occurring" and instead looks for language that is "authentic." There is a convincing argument to be made that the language of the media is intentionally designed to appeal to the greatest possible number of listeners, viewers, or readers. This intentional design of the mass media largely stems from the profit-oriented nature of the media; if language is inauthentic or if it fails to appeal to the public, the media content providers will not be able to earn from sponsorship or advertising. As a mechanism within capitalistic media systems, English functions internationally as a symbol of modernity in much of the Expanding Circle of English users: in Europe (Gerritsen et al. 2007); in Hungary (Petery 2011); in Italy (Vettorel 2016); in Korea (Baratta 2014); in Macedonia (Dimova 2012); and in Poland (Kasztalska 2014).

It should be further noted that "media language" has developed beyond the traditional media to include a number of new "social media" formats where Englishes can be explored. Many of the "content providers" of "new" or "social" media still work under the established paradigms to promote consumer (viewer, listener, reader) numbers in order to sell advertising within their media or the content. Nevertheless, much of the content in social media cannot yet be effectively sold to advertisers and there are frequent claims that the advent of "new" or "social media" has ushered in a new era where content is no longer directly linked to the motivations of sales and advertising.

The WEs commitment to examination of language in the media, therefore, derives from the paradigm's acknowledgment of plurality within varieties of the language and pluricentricity of standards. Localization of the media does not simply apply to the content of advertising, radio, television, or popular culture; localization also influences and determines the linguistic forms that appear within the media. This process of localization, which Kachru (1986) calls the "nativization" of Englishes, introduces new linguistic forms that may develop into established media languages. This process of endonormative development of media languages not only takes place in the USA and the UK but has also been described in the Inner Circle media of Australian English (Leitner 1984), Irish English (O'Sullivan 2013), and New Zealand English (Stadler 2016). Development of endonormative media standards in Outer and Expanding Circle languages include Cameroonian Pidgin English (Sala 2009); China English (Guo and Huang 2002; Alvaro 2015); East African Englishes (Schmied and Hudson-Ettle 1996); Igbo English (Ezejideaku and Ugwu 2009); Nigerian English (Nwoye 1992); Nigerian Pidgin English (Agheyisi 1984, 1988; Munzali 1997; Deuber 2002); Pakistan English (Baumgardner 1990); South African Black English (Makalela 2013); and West African Englishes (Huber and Görlach 1996)

28.5 English as a Linguistic Resource in the Development of Other Media Languages

"Nativization" is a typical effect of endonormative development of English varieties in the Outer and Expanding Circles, but it is just one of the effects that Kachru (1986) describes in the diaspora of English. The second effect is the "Englishization" of other languages used in these societies. Within the WEs literature, a fair amount of attention has been paid to the effects of English in the media when it is multilingually used alongside other languages. In the Expanding Circle, where English does not replace the native language as the dominant media language, a number of studies observe the presence of various forms of influence from English on a number of different languages: European languages (James 2016); Finnish (Taavitsainen and Pahta 2008); French (Martin 2002a); Hong Kong

Chinese (Chan 2009); Indian Languages (Bhatia 1987; Kathpalia and Ong 2015); Japanese (Geist 1991); Polish (Griffin 1997); Russian (Ustinova and Bhatia 2005); Taiwan Chinese (Chen 2006); Tamil (Krishnasamy 2007); and Thai (Snodin 2014).

While language mixing is the most commonly reported way in which English affects other languages in the media, a number of scholars have argued that English loanwords are being borrowed into other languages primarily within the language of the mass media. The media typically provide a "channel" through which the loanwords become more widely recognized and used within broader domains. In no language has this process been as thoroughly examined as in Japanese. Haarmann's (1989) and Loveday's (1996) early work on the source of loanwords in Japanese each point to the mass media as a significant source for the transmission of English etymons, and Stanlaw (2004) draws a clear connection between English and the Japanese used in popular culture. Likewise, Takashi (1990) examines the language of advertising to suggest that loanwords are borrowed more quickly in this genre than in others. Seargeant (2005) echoes these claims in an examination of English loanwords in the Japanese mass media. Several studies suggest that the rate of borrowing from mass media is unusually high in other languages, too, especially Chinese (Kang 1999), European Spanish (Smith 1997), Italian (Gani 2007), Korean (Shim 1994), and Mexican Spanish (Baumgardner 1997).

28.6 Conclusions: Media and Acquisition of Englishes

This chapter on WEs in the mass media began with the statement that sociolinguists traditionally do not regard media language as the best genre to find evidence of sociolinguistic variation. Nevertheless, descriptive work within the WEs perspective does not shy away from media and popular culture genres when collecting data demonstrating nativization or Englishization across the three WEs "Circles"; to the contrary, some linguists go so far as advocating these genres as authentic sources of linguistic data (Rose 2001; Walshe 2017). How, then, are we to respond to the more traditional prohibitions of using linguistic evidence from the mass media?

Chambers (1998: 124) summarizes the difference between popular opinion about the effect of the media on language change and sociolinguists' opinions:

> Television is the primary hypothesis for the motivation of any sound change for everyone, it seems, except the sociolinguists studying it. The sociolinguists see some evidence for the mass media playing a role in the spread of vocabulary items. But at the deeper reaches of language change – sound changes and grammatical changes – the media have no significant effect at all.

Chambers really only allows the possibility for media to influence the spread of lexicon, and there is indeed a rich examination of language in the media for evidence of neologisms within the WEs literature. Some of the studies examine new words that have been generated in specific contexts, such as Staczek's (1993) examination of new words in the media coined during the Gulf War. Studies may also focus on specific Englishes, such as Grant's (2012) study of neologisms in New Zealand English media, or Donlan's (2016) examination of new Australian colloquialisms in online media. Research in WEs has seen more extended studies examining the development of the term *queer* in the mass media (Jacobs 1998) and in the meanings and uses of the word *harmonious* in Chinese political discourse (Alvaro 2016).These examinations of media influence on the development of new words is consistent with Chambers (1993), where only two possible effects of media on language change are conceded: (1) the diffusion of "catch-phrases" that "belong for the moment of their currency to the most superficial linguistic level" (p. 139) and (2) the diffusion of "tolerance toward other accents and dialects" (p. 139). Chambers (1993) con- cludes – and in doing so expresses the majority opinion – that "speak- ers on our mass media, seeking no response and evoking none, make no impression on our dialects" (p. 140).

Although this has been a majority opinion among most sociolinguists about working with media data for a long time, recent years, however, have seen a number of challenges to this majority opinion. Sharbawi and Deterding (2010: 121) hypothesize that one reason why Brunei English is rhotic derives from the fact that "Brunei English is at an earlier stage of development than Singapore English and so it is more susceptible to outside influences, particularly from American media." Likewise, Leppanen (2007) examines youth culture in Finland to conclude that media has dynamically shaped the way that teens interact in English. These findings are echoed by Grau's (2009) examination of youth expo- sure to English in Germany, where the researcher concluded that expo- sure to English inside and outside the classroom occurred with very little interaction between the two domains. Lawson (2014) and Stuart-Smith et al. (2013) both introduce the feature of TH-Fronting (i.e. [f] for /θ/ in words like "think") in Scottish English. Both essays attribute the change to influence from the media, but Stuart-Smith and colleagues' discussion of this variant (in addition to L-Vocalization of coda /l/ in words like "milk" or "people") is extensive in scope and meticulous in attribution of the changes' origins. With more detailed analyses like this, along with theoretical constructs that understand the role of identity performance, WEs may be able to help understand how popular culture and mass media texts function more specifically in dialect acquisition and lan- guage change.

References

Abbas, Shemeem. 1993. The power of English in Pakistan. *World Englishes* 12(2): 147–156.

Adekunle, Mobolaji. 1997. English in Nigeria: Attitudes, policy and communicative realities. In Ayo Bamgbose, Ayo Banjo and Andrew Thomas, eds. *New Englishes: A West African Perspective*. Trenton, NJ: Africa World Press, 57–86.

Agheyisi, Rebecca N. 1984. Linguistic implications of the changing role of Nigerian Pidgin English. *English World-Wide* 5(2): 211–233.

Agheyisi, Rebecca N. 1988. The standardization of Nigerian Pidgin English. *English World-Wide* 9(2): 227–241.

Aguilar-Sanchez, Jorge. 2005. English in Costa Rica. *World Englishes* 24(2): 161–172.

Alm, Cecilia Ovesdotter. 2003. English in the Ecuadorian commercial context. *World Englishes* 22(2): 143–158.

Alvaro, Joseph James. 2015. Analysing China's English-language media. *World Englishes* 34(2): 260–77.

Alvaro, Joseph James. 2016. Political discourse in China's English language press. *World Englishes* 32(2): 147–168.

Baratta, Alex. 2014. The use of English in Korean TV drama to signal a modern identity. *English Today* 30(3): 54–60.

Barker, Hugh and Yuval Taylor. 2007. *Faking It: The Quest for Authenticity in Popular Music*. London: Faber & Faber.

Battenburg, John. 1996. English in the Maghreb. *English Today* 12(4): 3–14.

Battenburg, John. 1997. English versus French: Language rivalry in Tunisia. *World Englishes* 16(2): 281–290.

Bauman, Richard. 2011. The remediation of storytelling: Narrative performance on early commercial sound recordings. In Deborah Schiffrin, Anna De Fina and Anastasia Nylund, eds. *Telling Stories: Language, Narrative, and Social Life*, Washington, DC: Georgetown University Press, 23–43.

Baumgardner, Robert J. 1987. Utilizing Pakistani newspaper English to teach grammar. *World Englishes* 6(3): 241–252.

Baumgardner, Robert J. 1990. The indigenization of English in Pakistan. *English Today* 6(1): 59–65.

Baumgardner, Robert J. 1997. English in Mexican Spanish. *English Today* 13(4): 27–35.

Baumgardner, Robert J. and Kimberley Brown. 2012. English in Iranian magazine advertising. *World Englishes* 31(3): 292–311.

Bhatia, Tej K. 1987. English in advertising: Multiple mixing and media. *World Englishes* 6(1): 33–48.

Bhatia, Tej K. 1992. Discourse functions and pragmatics of mixing: Advertising across cultures. *World Englishes* 11(2–3): 195–215.

Bhatia, Tej K. 2000. *Advertising in Rural India: Language, Marketing Communication and Consumerism*. Tokyo: Tokyo University of Foreign Studies.

Bhatia, Tej K. 2006. World Englishes in global advertising. In Braj B. Kachru, Yamuna Kachru and Cecil L. Nelson, eds. *The Handbook of World Englishes*, Oxford: Blackwell, 609–619.

Bhatia, Tej K. and William C. Ritchie. 2004. Bilingualism in the global media and advertising. In Tej K. Bhatia and William C. Ritchie, eds. *The Handbook of Bilingualism*. Oxford: Blackwell, 513–546.

Bolton, Kingsley. 2010. Constructing the global vernacular: American English and the media. In Kingsley Bolton and Jan Olsson, eds. *Media, Popular Culture, and the American Century*. Stockholm: National Library of Sweden, 125–153.

Bolton, Kingsley. 2012. World Englishes and linguistic landscapes. *World Englishes* 31(1): 30–33.

Britton, Luke Morgan. 2015. Drake finally addresses ghostwriter claims: "Music can be a collaborative process." *NME*, September 25. www .nme.com/news/music/drake-133–1222920

Bucholtz, Mary. 2003. Sociolinguistic nostalgia and the authentication of identity. *Journal of Sociolinguistics* 7(3): 398–416.

Bucholtz, Mary and Kira Hall. 2004. Language and identity. In Alessandro Duranti, ed. *A Companion to Linguistic Anthropology*. Oxford: Basil Blackwell, 268–294.

Chambers, J. K. 1993. Sociolinguistic dialectology. In Dennis R. Preston, ed. *American Dialect Research*. Amsterdam: John Benjamins, 133–164.

Chambers, J. K. 1995. *Sociolinguistic Theory: Linguistic Variation and Its Social Significance*. Oxford: Blackwell.

Chambers, J. K. 1998. Myth 15: TV makes people sound the same. In Laurie Bauer and Peter Trudgill, eds. *Language Myths*. London: Penguin Books, 123–131.

Chan, Brian Hok-Shing. 2009. English in Hong Kong Cantopop: Language choice, code-switching and genre. *World Englishes* 28(1): 107–129.

Chan, Brian Hok-Shing. 2012. English in Cantopop: Code-switching, pop songs and the local identity of Hong Kong Chinese. In Jamie Shinhee Lee and Andrew Moody, eds. *English and Asian Popular Culture*. Hong Kong: Hong Kong University Press. 35–57.

Chan, Yuen-Ying. 2000. The English-language media in Hong Kong. *World Englishes* 19(3): 323–335.

Chen, Cheryl Wei-Yu. 2006. The mixing of English in magazine advertisements in Taiwan. *World Englishes* 25(3–4): 467–478.

Chik, Alice. 2010. Creative multilingualism in Hong Kong popular music. *World Englishes* 29(4): 508–522.

Christophersen, Paul. 1991. A bilingual Denmark. *English Today* 7(3): 7–10.

Coupland, Nikolas. 2001. Dialect stylization in radio talk. *Language in Society* 30(3): 345–375.

Coupland, Nikolas. 2003. Sociolinguistic authenticities. *Journal of Sociolinguistics* 7(3): 417–431.

Dayag, Danilo T. 2004. The English-language media in the Philippines. *World Englishes* 23(1): 33–45.

Demont-Heinrich, Christof. 2008. American "prestige press" representations of the global hegemony of English. *World Englishes* 27(2): 161–180.

Deuber, Dagmar. 2002. "First Year of Nation's Return to Government of Make You Talk Your Own Make I Talk My Own": Anglicisms versus Pidginization in news translations into Nigerian Pidgin. *English World-Wide* 23(2): 195–222.

Dimova, Slobodanka. 2008. English in Macedonian commercial nomenclature. *World Englishes* 27(1): 83–100.

Dimova, Slobodanka. 2012. English in Macedonian television commercials. *World Englishes* 31(1): 15–29.

Dissanayake, Wimal. 1986. Exotic Other: Western representation of India in English literature and film. *World Englishes* 5(2–3): 177–187.

Dogancay-Aktuna, Seran and Zeynep Kiziltepe. 2005. English in Turkey. *World Englishes* 24(2): 253–265.

Dolphyne, Florence. 1997. A note on the English language in Ghana. In Ayo Bamgbose, Ayo Banjo and Andrew Thomas, eds. *New Englishes: A West African Perspective*, Trenton, NJ: Africa World Press, 27–33.

Donlan, Lisa. 2016. Researching the etymology of Australian English colloquialisms in the digital age: Implications for 21st century lexicography. *English Today* 32(3): 40–44.

Dougill, John. 1987. English as a decorative language. *English Today* 12: 33–35.

Drum, Kevin. 2011. Oh, that old-timey movie accent! *Mother Jones*, August 9. www.motherjones.com/kevin-drum/2011/08/oh-old-timey-movie-voice/

Dubey, Vinod S. 1991. The lexical style of Indian English newspapers. *World Englishes* 10(1): 19–32.

Ezejideaku, Emma and Esther N. Ugwu. 2009. Igbo English in the Nigerian video film. *English World-Wide* 30(1): 52–67.

Fallows, James. 2015. That weirdo announcer-voice accent: Where it came from and why it went away. *The Atlantic*, June 7. www.theatlantic.com/national/archive/2015/06/that-weirdo-announcer-voice-accent-where-it-came-from-and-why-it-went-away/395141/

Fitzmaurice, Susan. 2000. *The Spectator*, the politics of social networks, and language standardisation in eighteenth century England. In Laura Wright, ed. *The Development of Standard English 1300–1800*, Cambridge: Cambridge University Press, 195–218.

Foley, Joseph. 1995. English in Mauritius. *World Englishes* 14(2): 205–222.

Gani, Martin. 2007. Anglicizing Italian. *English Today* 23(1): 40–41.

Gaskell, Philip. 2000. Standard written English. *English Today* 16(1): 48–52.

Geist, Kathe. 1991. English in Non-English-language films. *World Englishes* 10(3): 263–274.

Gerritsen, Marinel, Catherine Nickerson, Andreu van Hooft, Frank van Meurs, Ulrike Nederstigt, Marianne Starren and Rogier Crijns. 2007.

English in product advertisements in Belgium, France, Germany, the Netherlands and Spain. *World Englishes* 26(3): 291–315.

Grant, Lynn E. 2012. Culturally motivated lexis in New Zealand English. *World Englishes* 31(2): 162–176.

Grau, Maike. 2009. Worlds apart? English in German youth cultures and in educational settings. *World Englishes* 28(2): 160–174.

Griffin, Jeff. 1997. Global English Invades Poland. *English Today* 13(2): 34–41.

Guo, Zhongshi and Yu Huang. 2002. Hybridized discourse: Social openness and functions of English media in post-Mao China. *World Englishes* 21(2): 217–230.

Haarmann, Harold. 1989. *Symbolic Values of Foreign Language Use: From the Japanese Case to a General Sociolinguistic Perspective*. Berlin: Mouton de Gruyter.

Hamdan, Jihad M. and Wafa A. Abu Hatab. 2009. English in the Jordanian context. *World Englishes* 28(3): 394–405.

Herbert, John. 1997. The broadcast voice. *English Today* 13(2): 18–23.

Hill, Jane H. 1999. Styling locally, styling globally: What does it mean? *Journal of Sociolinguistics* 3(4): 542–556.

Howse, Hugh. 1979. BBC English by television and radio-news developments and new materials. *English Around the World* 20: 6–7.

Huber, Magnus and Manfred Görlach. 1996. West African Pidgin English. *English World-Wide* 17(2): 239–258.

Jacobs, Greg. 1998. The struggle over naming: A case study of "queer" in Toronto, 1990–1994. *World Englishes* 17(2): 193–201.

James, Allan. 2016. From code-mixing to mode-mixing in the European context. *World Englishes* 35(2): 259–275.

Kachru, Braj B. 1985. Standards, codification and sociolinguistic realism: The English language in the outer circle. In Randolph Quirk and H. G. Widdowson, eds. *English in the World: Teaching and Learning the Language and Literatures*. Cambridge: Cambridge University Press, 11–30.

Kachru, Braj. B. 1986. *The Alchemy of English: The Spread, Functions, and Models of Non-native Englishes*. Urbana: University of Illinois Press.

Kachru, Yamuna. 2006. Mixers lyricing in Hinglish: Blending and fusion in Indian pop culture. *World Englishes* 25(2): 223–233.

Kang, Jianxiu. 1999. English everywhere in China. *English Today* 15(2): 46–48.

Kasztalska, Aleksandra. 2014. English in contemporary Poland. *World Englishes* 33(2): 242–262.

Kathpalia, Sujata S. and Kenneth Keng Wee Ong. 2015. The use of code-mixing in Indian billboard advertising. *World Englishes* 34(4): 557–575.

Kirkpatrick, Andy and Andrew Moody. 2009. A tale of two songs: Singapore versus Hong Kong. *ELT Journal* 63(3): 265–271.

Kouega, Jean-Paul. 1999. Forty years of official bilingualism in Cameroon. *English Today* 15(4): 38–43.

Krishnasamy, Kanthimathi. 2007. English in Tamil: The language of advertising. *English Today* 23(3–4): 40–49.

Labov, William. 1972. *Sociolinguistic Patterns*. Philadelphia: University of Pennsylvania Press.

Labov, William. 1998. The three dialects of English. In Michael D. Linn, ed. *Handbook of Dialects and Language Variation* (2nd ed.). San Diego: Academic Press, 39–81.

Lawson, Robert. 2014. "Don't even [(theta)/f/h]ink aboot it": An ethnographic investigation of social meaning, social identity and ((theta)) variation in Glasgow. *English World-Wide 35*(1): 68–93.

Lee, Jamie Shinhee. 2004. Linguistic hybridization in K-pop: Discourse of self-assertion and resistance. *World Englishes 23*(3): 429–450.

Lee, Jamie Shinhee. 2006. Crossing and crossers in East Asian pop music: Korea and Japan. *World Englishes 25*(2): 235–250.

Lee, Jamie Shinhee. 2007. I'm the illest fucka: An analysis of African American English in South Korean hip hop. *English Today 23*(2): 54–60.

Lee, Jamie Shinhee. 2014. English on Korean television. *World Englishes 33*(1): 33–49.

Lee, Jamie Shinhee and Andrew Moody. 2012a. Sociolinguistics and the study of English in popular culture. In Jamie Shinhee Lee and Andrew Moody, eds. *English in Asian Popular Culture* (Asian Englishes Today Series). Hong Kong: Hong Kong University Press, 1–11.

Lee, Jamie Shinhee and Andrew Moody, eds. 2012b. *English in Asian Popular Culture*. Hong Kong: Hong Kong University Press.

Leith, Dick. 1983. *A Social History of English* (Language and Society Series). London: Routledge and Kegan Paul.

Leitner, G. 1984. Australian English or English in Australia-Linguistic identity or dependence in broadcast language. *English World-Wide 5*(1): 55–85.

Leppanen, Sirpa. 2007. Youth language in media contexts: insights into the functions of English in Finland. *World Englishes 26*(2): 149–169.

Li, David C. S. 1999. The functions and status of English in Hong Kong: A post-1997 update. *English World-Wide 20*(1): 67–110.

Li, Songqing. 2012. The use of English in China's real estate advertising. *English Today 28*(3): 53–59.

Lin, Angel. 2012. The hip hop music scene in Hong Kong: Hybridity and identity in youth culture. In Jamie Shinhee Lee and Andrew Moody, eds. *English in Asian Popular Culture*. Hong Kong: Hong Kong University Press, 59–73.

Lippi-Green, Rosina. 1997. *English with an Accent: Language, Ideology and Discrimination in the United States*. London: Routledge.

Loveday, Leo. 1996. *Language Contact in Japan: A Socio-Linguistic History*. New York: Oxford University Press.

Lujan-Garcia, Carmen. 2011. "English invasion" in Spain: An analysis of toys leaflets addressed to young children: Do toy advertisements introduce Spanish children to English? *English Today 27*(1): 3–9.

Luke, Kang-kwong and Jack C. Richards. 1982. English in Hong Kong: Functions and Status. *English World-Wide 3*(1): 47–64.

Makalela, Leketi. 2013. Black South African English on the radio. *World Englishes* 32(1): 93–107.

Martin, Elizabeth. 1998. The use of English in written French advertising: A study of code- switching, code-mixing, and borrowing in a commercial context. *Studies in the Linguistic Science* 28(1): 159–184.

Martin, Elizabeth. 2002a. Cultural images and different varieties of English in French television commercials. *English Today* 18(4): 8–20.

Martin, Elizabeth. 2002b. Mixing English in French advertising. *World Englishes* 21(3): 375–401.

Martin, Elizabeth. 2006. *Marketing Identities Through Language: English and Global Imagery in French Advertising*. Basingstoke: Palgrave Macmillan.

Martinez, Francia. 2015. English in advertising in Colombia. *World Englishes* 34(4): 600–619.

Masavisut, Nitaya, Mayuri Sukwiwat, and Seri Wongmontha. 1986. The power of the English language in Thai media. *World Englishes* 5(2–3): 197–207.

Matiki, Alfred J. 2001. The social significance of English in Malawi. *World Englishes* 20(2): 201–218.

McArthur, Tom. 1997. The printed word in the English-speaking world. *English Today* 13(1): 10–16.

McArthur, Tom. 1999. English in the World, in Africa, and in South Africa. *English Today* 15(1): 11–16.

Mesthrie, Rajend. 2002. Mock languages and symbolic power: The South African radio series "Applesammy and Naidoo." *World Englishes* 21(1): 99–112.

Millar, Robert McColl. 2012. *English Historical Sociolinguistics* (Edinburgh Textbooks on the English Language – Advanced Series). Edinburgh: Edinburgh University Press.

Milroy, Leslie. 2000. Britain and the United States: Two nations divided by the same language (and different language ideologies). *Journal of Linguistic Anthropology* 10(1): 56–89.

Milroy, James and Lesley Milroy. [1985] 1999. *Authority in Language: Investigating Standard English* (3rd ed.). London: Routledge.

Moody, Andrew. 2006. English in Japanese popular culture and J-pop Music. *World Englishes* 25(2): 209–222.

Moody, Andrew. 2010. The Englishes of popular cultures. In Andy Kirkpatrick, ed. *The Handbook of World Englishes*. London: Routledge, 535–549.

Moody, Andrew. 2011. Englishization in Japanese popular culture: Representation of ethnicity. In Kwok-kan Tam, ed., *Englishization in Asia: Language and Cultural Issues*. Hong Kong: Open University of Hong Kong Press, 183–206.

Moody, Andrew. 2012a. Authenticity of English in Asian popular music. In Andy Kirkpatrick and Roland Sussex, eds., *English as an International*

Language in Asia: Implications for Language Education. New York: Springer Science and Business Media Dordrecht, 209–222.

Moody, Andrew. 2012b. English in Southeast Asian pop culture. In Ee-Ling Low and Azirah Hashim, eds. *English in Southeast Asia: Features, Policy and Language in Use*. Amsterdam: John Benjamins, 307–324.

Moody, Andrew. 2013. Language ideology in the discourse of popular culture. In Carol A. Chapelle, ed. *The Encyclopedia of Applied Linguistics*, Vol. 5. Oxford: Wiley-Blackwell, 3009–3011.

Moody, Andrew and Yuko Matsumoto. 2003. "Don't touch my moustache": Language blending and code ambiguation by two J-pop artists. *Asian Englishes* 6(1): 4–33.

Moody, Andrew and Yuko Matsumoto. 2011. The ideal speaker of Japanese English as portrayed in "language entertainment" television. In P. Seargeant, ed. *English in Japan in the Era of Globalisation*. Houndmills: Palgrave Macmillan, 166–186.

Munzali, Jibril. 1997. The elaboration of the functions of Nigerian Pidgin. In Ayo Bamgbose, Ayo Banjo and Andrew Thomas, eds. *New Englishes: A West African Perspective*, Trenton, NJ: Africa World Press, 232–247.

Nwoye, Onuigbo. 1992. Obituary announcements as communicative events in Nigerian English. *World Englishes* 11(1): 15–27.

Omoniyi, Tope. 2006. Hip-hop through the world Englishes lens: A response to globalization. *World Englishes* 25(2): 195–208.

O'Sullivan, Joan. 2013. Advanced Dublin English in Irish radio advertising. *World Englishes* 32(3): 358–376.

Pandharipande, Rajeshwari. 2013. The language of Hinduism in the US diaspora. *World Englishes* 32(3): 417–428.

Park, Joseph Sung-Yul. 2004. "Baby, darling, honey!": Constructing a competence of English in South Korean TV shows. *Texas Linguistic Forum* 47: 143–154.

Park, Joseph Sung-Yul. 2009. *The Local Construction of a Global Language: Ideologies of English in South Korea*. Berlin: Mouton de Gruyter .

Park, Joseph Sung-Yul and Lionel Wee. 2012. *Markets of English: Linguistic Capital and Language Policy in a Globalizing World*. London: Routledge.

Pennycook, Alastair. 2003. Global Englishes, Rip Slyme and performativity. *Journal of Sociolinguistics* 7(4): 513–533.

Petery, Dorottya. 2011. English in Hungarian advertising. *World Englishes* 30(1): 21–40.

Petzold, Ruth and Margie Berns. 2000. Catching up with Europe: Speakers and functions of English in Hungary. *World Englishes* 19(1): 113–124.

Phillipson, Robert and Tove Skutnabb-Kangas. 1996. Is India throwing away its language resources? *English Today* 12(1): 23–27.

Queen, Robin. 2015. *Vox Popular: The Surprising Life of Language in the Media*. Chichester: Wiley Blackwell.

Raedts, Mariet, Natalie Dupre, Jef Hendrickx and Sophie Debrauwere. 2015. English in television commercials in Belgium, France, Italy, the Netherlands and Spain. *World Englishes* 34(4): 576–599.

Rampton, Ben. 1995. *Crossing: Language and Ethnicity among Adolescents.* London: Longman.

Rampton, Ben. 1999. Styling the other: Introduction. *Journal of Sociolinguistics* 3(4): 421–427.

Ridder, Susan. 1995. English in Dutch. *English Today* 11(4): 44–50.

Rindal, Ulrikke. 2013. Being "neutral"? English pronunciation among Norwegian learners. *World Englishes* 32(2): 211–229.

Rose, Kenneth R. 2001. Compliments and compliment responses in film: Implications for pragmatics research and language teaching. *IRAL: International Review of Applied Linguistics in Language Teaching* 39(4): 309–326.

Rubdy, Rani. 2001. Creative destruction: Singapore's Speak Good English Movement. *World Englishes* 20(3): 341–355.

Ruellot, Viviane. 2011. English in French print advertising from 1999 to 2007. *World Englishes* 30(1): 5–20.

Sala, Bonaventure M. 2009. Writing in Cameroon Pidgin English: Begging the question. *English Today* 25(2): 11–17.

Sartor, Valerie. 2010. Teaching English in Turkmenistan. *English Today* 26(4): 29–36.

Schmied, Josef and Diana Hudson-Ettle. 1996. Analyzing the style of East African newspapers in English. *World Englishes* 15(1): 103–113.

Schneider, Edgar W. 2007. *Postcolonial English: Varieties Around the World.* Cambridge: Cambridge University Press.

Schwyter, Jürg R. 2016. *Dictating to the Mob: The History of the BBC Advisory Committee on Spoken English.* Oxford: Oxford University Press.

Seargeant, Philip. 2005. Globalisation and reconfigured English in Japan. *World Englishes* 24(3): 309–319.

Sharbawi, Salbrina and David Deterding. 2010. Rhoticity in Brunei English. *English World-Wide* 31(2): 121–137.

Shim, Rosa Jinyoung. 1994. Englishized Korean: Structure, status, and attitudes. *World Englishes* 13(2): 225–244.

Shytex BookVideo Training. 2014. Video Course: Do You Speak American? Part 1. www.youtube.com/watch?v=kcx7khan180

Silverstein, Michael. 1979. Language structure and linguistic ideology. In Paul R. Clyne, William F. Hanks and Carol L. Hofbauer, eds., *The Elements: A Parasession on Linguistic Units and Levels, April 20–21, 1979: Including Papers from the Conference on Non-Slavic Languages of the USSR, April 18, 1979.* Chicago: Chicago Linguistic Society, 193–247.

Skinner, Edith. 1990. *Speak with Distinction* (rev. ed.; with new material added by Timothy Monich and Lilene Mansell). New York: Applause Theatre and Cinema Books.

Smith, Brian D. 1991. English in Indonesia. *English Today* 7(2): 39–43.

Smith, Ross. 1997. English in European Spanish. *English Today* 13(4): 22–26.

Snodin, Navaporn Sanpresert. 2014. English naming and code-mixing in Thai mass media. *World Englishes* 33(1): 100–11.

Staczek, John J. 1993. The English language and the Gulf War: Corpus linguistics, variations, and word-formation. *World Englishes* 12(1): 15–24.

Stadler, Stefanie. 2016. Televised political discourse in New Zealand. *World Englishes* 32(2): 243–260.

Stanlaw, James. 2004. *Japanese English: Language and Culture Contact.* Hong Kong: Hong Kong University Press.

Stuart-Smith, Jane, Gwilym Pryce, Claire Timmins and Barrie Gunter. 2013. Television can also be a factor in language change: Evidence from an urban dialect. *Language* 89(3) 501–536.

Swan, Michael and Laurence Urdang. 1985. Where is the language going? *English Today* 3: 6–10.

Taavitsainen, Irma and Paivi Pahta. 2008. From global language use to local meanings: English in Finnish public discourse. *English Today* 24(3): 25–38.

Tagliamonte, Sali A. 2006. *Analysing Sociolinguistic Variation.* Cambridge: Cambridge University Press.

Takashi, Kyoko. 1990. A sociolinguistic analysis of English borrowings in Japanese advertising texts. *World Englishes* 9(3): 327–341.

Tanaka, Sachiko Oda. 1995. The Japanese media and English. *World Englishes* 14(1): 37–53.

Thompson, Roger M. 2012. Colliding world-views: A night with Philippine television. In Jamie Shinhee Lee and Andrew Moody, eds. *English in Asian Popular Culture.* Hong Kong: Hong Kong University Press, 77–102.

Tillman, Frank. 1986. Film, thought and language *World Englishes* 5(2–3): 265–272.

Underwood, Robert. 1989. English and Chamorro on Guam. *World Englishes* 8(1): 73–82.

Urdang, Laurence. 1990. On observing World English. *English Today* 6(1): 11–16.

Ustinova, Irina. 2005. English in Russia. *World Englishes* 24(2): 239–251.

Ustinova, Irina P. and Tej K. Bhatia. 2005. Convergence of English in Russian TV commercials. *World Englishes* 24(4): 495–508.

Vettorel, Paola. 2016. English in Italian advertising. *World Englishes* 32(2): 261–278.

Walshe, Shane. 2017. The language of Irish Film. *World Englishes* 36(2): 283–299.

Wang, B. P. Y. 2006. English mixing in the lyrics of mandarin pop songs in Taiwan: A functional approach. *NCYU Inquiry of Applied Linguistics*: 211–240.

Yong, Zhao and Keith P. Campbell. 1995. English in China. *World Englishes* 14(3): 377–390.

Zhou, Sijing and Andrew Moody. 2017. English in *The Voice of China. World Englishes* 36(4): 554–570.

29

World Englishes and Transnationalism

Brook Bolander

29.1 Introduction

In 1916, the *Atlantic Monthly* published a piece by Randolph Bourne entitled "Trans-national America," in which "transnational" is used for the first time (Levitt 1996). In it, Bourne invokes the notion to counter the predominant model of the melting pot, specifically to underscore that America cannot be considered a single nation and to hence encourage reflection on the variety of possible meanings of "America" and "Americanisms." Many of the concerns raised by Bourne are still prominent today, including reflections on the degree of difference between present-day and past transnational ties (and by implication on the novelty of contemporary transnationalism), debates on whether ties are upheld beyond second-generation immigrants, and deliberations on how movement affects both sending and receiving states (Levitt 1996: 2).

Transnationalism's popularity though can be traced to the 1970s (Mahler 2009), when the term became prominent in political science, especially in international relations, and then, in the 1990s, in (qualitative) sociology and particularly anthropology (Hurrelmann and DeBardeleben 2011: 2). These two research traditions share a set of common interests, for example in migration and transboundary ties. Yet, whereas scholars in international relations tend to focus on how civil society actors influence state activities and international organizations, those in anthropology and (qualitative) sociology typically adopt a "bottom-up" approach, accompanied by an intense focus on identity, community, and spatial boundaries (Hurrelmann and DeBardeleben 2011: 2). It is because of these two separate histories that Hurrelmann and DeBardeleben (2011: 2) refer to transnationalism as involving "one concept, two literatures." This historical use of the term "in similar yet distinct ways" may have contributed to its "slipperiness" (Mahler 2009: 66). Indeed, today transnationalism is used to refer to such an expansive range of practices, processes and ties that "its explanatory power" has been "seriously diminishe[d]" (Levitt 2001: 196).

This concerted interest in transnationalism in international relations, sociology, and anthropology stems from a growing concern with globalization, or the increased "spacetime compression" (Harvey 1989) resulting from changes in domestic and international (air) travel, trade, migration, and the use of digital media. Within sociolinguistics, too, attention to transnationalism, emerged in connection with an upsurge in research on language and globalization in the early 2000s (see Coupland 2003b), although previous work on language and migration clearly predates this (see, e.g., Rampton 1995). This means that the history of transnationalism in sociolinguistics, whose social scientific roots mainly lie in the anthropology/sociology stream, is relatively recent. Much research has only appeared in the last decade, making it an evolving and dynamic field.

Against this backdrop, this chapter has three main aims: To delineate central concerns and ideas in the sociolinguistic study of transnationalism, to reflect on the implications of these concerns for research on World Englishes, and to address applications via examples of metatheoretical and empirical scholarship in sociolinguistics. The chapter begins by focusing on the polysemy of transnationalism (Section 29.2), before addressing the relationship between transnationalism and "methodological nationalism" (Section 29.3). These sections serve to highlight the pertinence of conceptual clarity and reflexivity for sociolinguistic research on language and transnationalism. The chapter then reviews metatheoretical and empirical sociolinguistic scholarship on language and transnationalism, with a focus on English (Section 29.4), before providing a brief conclusion and outlook (Section 29.5).

29.2 Conceptualizing Transnationalism

The literature on transnationalism highlights a common concern with "multiple ties and interactions linking people or institutions across the borders of nation-states" (Vertovec 1999: 447), and a concomitant view of transnationalism as a "multifaceted, multi-local process" (see, e.g., Guarnizo and Smith 2009: 6; Glick Schiller, Basch, and Blanc-Szanton 1992; Basch, Glick Schiller, and Blanc-Szanton 1994; Appadurai 1996; Hannerz 1996; Pries 1999; McEwan 2004; Iriye and Saunier 2009). Yet coexisting with this general shared understanding of transnationalism are a range of alternate, more specific approaches and conceptualizations. Indeed, the degree of "conceptual muddling" (Vertovec 1999) means that it is not always clear what or who is transnational, in what sense, and, by extension, how acting or imagining oneself as transnational is pertinent to language use and ideology, and thus also to the field of World Englishes.

Relatedly, it is often hard to tell how scholars conceive of the relationship between transnationalism and globalization. For Kearney (1995: 548), the distinction between the two is one of scale, with transnationalism seen as overlapping with globalization but as typically having "a more limited purview." From this perspective, "[w]hereas global processes are largely decentered from specific national territories and take place in a global space, transnational processes are anchored in and transcend one or more nation-states" (Kearney 1995: 548). However, this is evidently contingent on how both globalization and transnationalism are conceptualized: The two can overlap to greater or lesser degrees, depending on what is foregrounded, and in relation to approach and epistemology.[1] In this chapter, transnationalism is discussed and defined according to Vertovec's (1999) framework (introduced in the next paragraph). However, the chapter also recognizes that a sociolinguistics of both globalization and transnationalism is based on an understanding that "[g]lobalisation is proving to be the salient context for an increasing number of local sociolinguistic experiences" (Coupland 2003a: 466). Instead of perceiving the global and transnational as separate from the local, scholars now highlight their complex interrelation, prompting an intense engagement with how language becomes important to and, at the same time, influenced by this relationship. Central here are questions of how and where to research language, given the intensified movements of people, commodities, and ideas across geographical, social, virtual, and imagined spaces.

Vertovec (1999) provides a useful overview of six main ways transnationalism has been understood across numerous disciplines, including anthropology, sociology, and cultural studies. These comprise transnationalism as "social morphology," "type of consciousness," "mode of cultural reproduction," "avenue for capital," "site of political engagement," and "(re)construction of 'place' or locality." The term's variable application highlights differing interests in motivations and processes of transnationalism, concurrent with an appreciation of its situatedness, and the possible interplay between performing transnationalism (through migration) and imagining oneself as transnational. While sociolinguistics is not mentioned, a review of sociolinguistic research shows comparable foci (see Section 29.4).

The first of these – transnationalism as social morphology – is the most widespread, also in sociolinguistics. From this perspective, transnationalism is understood as a "social formation spanning borders" (Vertovec 1999: 449), brought about through migration and leading to the creation of

---

[1] While the chapter foregrounds research that explicitly refers to transnational ties, identities, and/or processes, by virtue of the polysemy of transnationalism and its overlaps with globalization, it also includes selected research on English and globalization.

diasporas and networks (see Zipp, Chapter 6, this volume, for case studies on English in the diaspora). Such definitions are among the oldest. As stated by Glick Schiller, Basch, and Blanc-Szanton (1992: ix),

> [i]n the course of the past few years, anthropologists have increasingly noted that immigrants live their lives across borders and maintain their ties to home, even when their countries of origin and settlements are geographically distant. To describe this new way of life, some social scientists have begun to use the term "transnational."

In this vein, transnationalism was increasingly applied to what was considered a new type of migration (Wimmer and Glick Schiller 2002: 322). Yet it also emerged as the term denoting the type of triadic relationship brought about through migration – between a sending state, a receiving state, and the migrant's networks (Pries 1999; Vertovec 1999).

A second type of transnationalism is what Vertovec (1999) terms "consciousness." From this perspective, transnationalism is not necessarily the result of migration and the formation of networks and diasporas. It emerges instead as a type of shared awareness or "subjectivity" (Dahinden 2009; see also Nonini and Ong 1997). From the vantage point of consciousness, transnationalism is intricately linked with issues of identity (Glick Schiller, Basch, and Szanton-Blanc 1992; see also, e.g., De Fina and Perrino 2013), where it complicates questions of belonging and underscores the pervasiveness of simultaneity.[2] As consciousness, transnationalism is not predicated on the basis of ties between two tangible geographical spaces or nation-states but emerges instead in the form of assumptions of commonality and connections beyond a "here," and the shared meanings these assumptions generate for individuals and communities.

From a third vantage point, transnationalism is conceptualized as a form of cultural reproduction. Invoked here are the dissemination, production, and consumption of "hybrid cultural phenomena" (Vertovec 1999) in fashion, film, music, the visual arts, and digital media. Cultural phenomena can be targeted at particular transnational communities, or transnationalism can be performed, for example, in situations where "facets of culture and identity are … selfconsciously selected, syncretised and elaborated from more than one heritage" (Vertovec 1999). These forms of cultural production are referred to using an array of related terms, including "bricolage," "syncretism," and "hybridity" (Vertovec 1999; for hybridity in sociolinguistics, see, e.g., Rubdy and Alsagoff 2013.).

Transnationalism is also understood as an opportunity for capital, epitomized by the emergence of transnational corporations (Vertovec 1999). Yet, in addition to an interest in an emerging "transnationalist capitalist

---

[2] As argued, for example, by Meinhof (2009, 149), it "is the simultaneity of multiple affiliations and identifications, made possible by the ease with which these can be globally upheld and strategically activated, which constitute the newness in transnational networks."

class" (Sklair 1998, cited in Vertovec 1999), transnationalism as capital also involves a focus on remittances and foreign exchange among individuals from lower social echelons (Vertovec 1999). Within sociolinguistics, a focus on transnationalism as capital is perhaps most closely linked to research on language and commodification in late capitalism (see, e.g., Heller and Duchêne 2012).

Transnationalism can also emerge as a site of political engagement, with alternate forms of civil action being facilitated through changes in publishing and communications technologies (Vertovec 1999). International NGOs and "Transnational Social Movement Organizations" (Vertovec 1999) might, for example, use these technologies to mobilize resources or attempt to obtain support for political activities. Alternately, political activities on the part of migrants as well as of political parties dominant in migrants' sending states might become active in receiving states, leading to the formation of what have been called "'deterritorialized' nation-states" (Basch, Glick Schiller, and Szanton Blanc 1994: 8). Nation-states, from this perspective, are no longer seen as confined within the bounds of a particular territory but as dispersed across them by virtue of the continued participation – political, but also social, cultural, and economic – and cross-border integration of migrants (Basch, Glick Schiller, and Szanton Blanc 1994: 8).

Finally, transnationalism has been conceptualized as the (re)construction of place or locality. At its core, this highlights the fact that all practices are grounded or "anchored in places" (Vertovec 1999). As Guarnizo and Smith (2009: 11) argue, "[t]ransnational practices, while connecting collectivities located in more than one national territory, are embodied in specific social relations established between specific people, situated in unequivocal localities, at historically determined times." Instead of viewing transnational individuals as "free-floating" (a viewpoint that encourages an unwarranted celebratory perspective on transnationalism), this approach calls attention to how practices (including face-to-face, written, or [digitally] mediated ones) are grounded in particular localities, while at the same time being part of the ways these localities are inter-subjectively (re)constructed.

Addressing transnationalism's range of meanings, Vertovec (1999) underscores that "[t]hese are obviously different phenomena of very different natures, requiring research and theorization on different scales and levels of abstraction." Qualifying what is meant by transnationalism should thus precede theorization. For research on transnationalism and World Englishes, engaging with transnationalism thus necessitates reflecting on which understanding/s is/are pertinent for describing and explaining the use of Englishes within particular localities, while, at the same time, recognizing that transnational spaces might be constructed as a locally viable frame for these same language practices and ideologies (see also Section 29.3).

29.3 Transnationalism as a Response to Methodological Nationalism

In their seminal paper, Wimmer and Glick Schiller (2002: 302) argue for a view of transnationalism as a "constant of modern life," which has been hidden by a perspective that assumed the primacy of the nation-state:

> What we discover ... is how transnational the modern world has always been, even in the high days when the nation-state bounded and bundled most social processes. Rather than a recent offspring of globalization, transnationalism appears as a constant of modern life, hidden from a view that was captured by methodological nationalism.

This is pertinent given that the literature on transnationalism has largely emerged as an offshoot of research on globalization. Without denying the relationship between transnationalism and globalization, this perspective thus encourages not assuming that the former derives from the latter. Importantly, too, it highlights that it is not so much the world that has changed with respect to the movement of ideas, people, and matter across space and time (although clearly the speed and scope of this movement has) but rather that a view of the world through the lens of methodological nationalism has hidden the ubiquity of transnationalism from sight.

From the perspective of methodological nationalism, the nation-state is the "natural social and political form of the modern world" (Wimmer and Glick Schiller 2002: 302). As a result of having been "naturalized," it has been rendered a kind of invisible context that frames and contains social actions and interactions. This has had widespread implications for the social sciences and humanities, encouraging research within nations, with the nation's imagined boundedness channeling decisions of what to focus on and where; and, in doing so, boosting work on centers at the expense of border regions and connections across borders.

These same tendencies have been highlighted in criticisms of World Englishes research (see, e.g., Krishnaswamy and Burde 1998; Bruthiaux 2003; Pennycook 2010a), which indeed suggest that the nation has not necessarily been as relevant for uses of English as previously assumed (e.g. for differentiation between varieties and for discussions of a variety's features). Moving away from methodological nationalism, then, encourages a focus on transnationalism as a form of connection across borders, while also prompting for a closer look at differences within nations, and at border regions.

In this sense, then, an increased focus on transnationalism as a constant, has both theoretical and methodological implications. With respect to theory, it encourages enhanced engagement with its polysemy (see Section 29.2) and the need to clarify in what sense the label is being applied and with what purpose vis-à-vis issues of language use and ideology. With respect to methodology, it encourages critical reflection on how an a priori delimitation of research to particular nation-states serve to shape perspective, that is, to variously highlight and hide issues of movement and boundedness. For World Englishes research, a fuller engagement with transnationalism thus calls for conceptual clarity in the first instance, coupled with an epistemological shift toward a view of the world as one in which cross-border movements and ties are not viewed as temporally succeeding a world made up of different nation-states, and thus as newer. This shift instead entails recognizing the pertinence of transnational ties for the structuring of social life, and thus for language use and ideologies. It includes exploring, in other words, how varieties of English are used as resources for constructing place and space, particularly in geographical territories where marking difference is/was coupled with drawing territorial distinctions. In this vein, a transnational approach to World Englishes might still focus on English in a particular nation if the nation is also analyzed as an object in its own right, and if the research includes an appreciation of the potential mobility of people, ideas, and materiality, and the possible concomitant pertinence of transnational subjectivity. This would entail an enhanced focus on a "linguistics of contact" (Rampton 2000, 2009), via analyses of situated language practices (in one or multiple sites).

29.4   Sociolinguistic Research on Language and Transnationalism, With a Focus on English

A review of the literature makes manifest that there is a growing body of metatheoretical literature on transnationalism that is of relevance to World Englishes and a range of empirical research illustrating various approaches to language and transnationalism, sometimes with an explicit focus on English or World Englishes. This work includes metatheoretical reflection on the concepts of "language" and "variety" as well as an increasing emphasis on multilingualism in World Englishes research (Section 29.4.1); methodological reflexivity pertaining to the empirical analysis of transnationalism (Section 29.4.2); and empirical research on transnationalism as social morphology and subjectivity (Section 29.4.3), on transnationalism in digital spaces (Section 29.4.4), and on transnationalism and language commodification (Section 29.4.5).

29.4.1   From "Language" and "Variety" to "Resources": Metatheoretical Reflection and the Importance of a Relational Perspective in World Englishes Research

In the conclusion to his discussion of English and globalization, Pennycook (2010a: 121) argues that, if it is clear that the ways we think about language are inevitably products of particular historical contexts, then an age of globalization suggests that we need both to reflect on how and why we look at languages as separate, countable, describable entities in the way we do and to consider that languages may be undergoing such forms of transition as to require new ways of conceptualization in terms of local activities, resources, or practices.

Conceptualized at its core as multiple border–spanning ties and interactions grounded in particular localities, communication is clearly central to the creation, maintenance, and intersubjective performance of transnationalism. Yet, rather than viewing these ties as being constructed through varieties of English, Pennycook's quote suggests the need for a stronger focus on activities, resources, and practices as a result of globalization.

A similar argument is made by Seargeant and Tagg (2011: 511), who question whether the concept of "variety" still has a "phenomenological reality," or should rather be treated as an "instrumental way of describing aspects or features of the discourse." Drawing on mediated data from Facebook and Blackberry exchanges among Thai-speaking participants in England and Thailand (see also Section 29.4.4), they argue for "a 'post-varieties' approach." While acknowledging the possibility of describing the observed digitally mediated linguistic phenomenon used by their participants according to "a terminology based around varieties," the discourse produced as a whole cannot be classified as a "variety" (Seargeant and Tagg 2011: 511). The notion of a post-varieties approach then serves as "an analytic apparatus that is sensitive to the dynamic communicative practices which use English-related forms and connotations as one part of a wider semiotic repertoire" (Seargeant and Tagg 2011: 498). Instead of beginning from a varieties perspective, the authors therefore suggest an initial focus on resources and their use, against the backdrop of issues of contextual appropriateness and framing (Seargeant and Tagg 2011: 511).

Facing comparable challenges in his ethnographic research on the Adriatic "ethno/mediascape," Jacquemet (2005: 264–265) introduces the notion of "transidiomatic practice" to refer to "the communicative practices of transnational groups that interact using different languages and communicative codes simultaneously present in a range of communicative channels, both local and distant." While he does not position his research in a World Englishes framework, by virtue of its global spread, resources drawn from English play an important role in the observed practices (Jacquemet 2005: 266). Drawing on Rampton's (2000: 125; see also Rampton 2009) emphasis on a "linguistics of contact," which is keenly interested in cross-border flows and boundaries, Jacquemet (2005: 274) argues for an increased parallel focus on the "disorderly recombinations and language mixings occurring simultaneously in local and distant environments," and thus for "a linguistics of xenoglossic becomings, transidiomatic mixing, and communicative recombinations."

Similarly, Li (2011) introduces the concepts of "translanguaging" and "translanguaging space" to do justice to the data he collected on multilingual Chinese youth in Britain. (Comparable concepts include "crossing," Rampton 1995; Rampton and Charalambous 2010; "polylanguaging," Jörgensen et al. 2011; "polylingualism," Jörgensen 2008; Creese and Blackledge 2010; "translingual practice," Canagarajah 2013; and "metrolingualism," Otsui and Pennycook 2010; see also Makoni and Pennycook 2007). For Li (2011: 1223), both "translanguaging" and "translanguaging space" can be traced back to a particular understanding of "languaging" taken from psycholinguistics, which views language as a means "to gain knowledge, to make sense, to articulate one's thought and to communicate about using language" (see also Li and Hua 2013). Translanguaging, then, refers to the process of "both going between different linguistic structures and systems, including different modalities (speaking, writing, signing, listening, reading, remembering) and going beyond them" (Li 2011: 1223); and "translanguaging space" denotes the social space in which translanguaging takes place, as well as the space constructed through translanguaging practices (see also Section 29.4.2).

The situatedness of language practices is consistently highlighted in this emergent research tradition. It is also epitomized in Pennycook's (1994: 34) concept of the "worldliness of English," which "refers both to its local and to its global position, both to the ways in which it reflects social relations and constitutes social relations." From this perspective, "the wordliness of English is always a question of cultural politics" (Pennycook 1994: 34); of how local differences are made manifest, of how local performances of language are made to relate to – to reflect, shape, and challenge – the existing social order, and to how these acts of doing language are indicative of particular interpretations of the meanings of places, while simultaneously reinforcing these interpretations (Pennycook 2010b: 2). This also involves stronger emphases on local language ideologies and hence a closer look at difference (Pennycook 2010c: 681), areas that have received less attention in World Englishes research relative to the study of phonological, morphosyntactic, and lexical features (Mair 2013: 254).

Critical consideration of the meaning of "language" and the concurrent emphasis on resources and situated practices has also entailed reflection on the relationship between varieties. As outlined by Mair (2013: 254), the field of World Englishes has been "regarded as an essentially monolingual enterprise." Whereas "[l]anguage contact was recognized as a force in the emergence of the New Englishes to the extent that it left structural residues, ... multilingual practices employed by individual agents were not usually at the centre of attention" (Mair 2013: 254). Applied to World Englishes research, concepts like "translanguaging" and "transidiomatic practices" suggest the importance of looking beyond Englishes to include resources drawn from other languages. This has brought about an increased interest in multilingualism.

This shift in focus has also been spurred on by the heightened movement of peoples, ideas, and matter across space, leading to intensified and new contact scenarios (both online and offline). Indeed, as a result of globalization "English, wherever it occurs in the world nowadays, occurs in a multilingual environment and as part of multilingual repertoires" (Blommaert 2012). For this reason, "whenever we look at English, we also need to look at the other languages with which it coexists and co-occurs" (Blommaert 2012). Acknowledging that "at least in principle, all Englishes are everywhere" (Mair 2013: 256) thus entails taking into account the ways individuals draw on resources in multilingual settings, and exploring how these linguistic ecologies are shaped by and are used to shape communicative practices. For World Englishes research, this then incites a relational perspective, as shown in the studies reviewed in Sections 29.4.2 to29.4.5.

29.4.2 Studying Transnationalism: Examples of Ethnography, Moment Analysis, and Maps

As highlighted in Section 29.3, a transnational perspective underscores problems with a model of the world in which language, nation, territory, and individual identity are united (Heller 2010a: 725). This model has been unsettled through changes brought about by globalization, as well as related processes of sociolinguistic "unthinking" and "rethinking" (Blommaert 2010: 1). These changes have, in turn, triggered new questions for sociolinguistic research, notably how to "identify … the local places and moments where processes occur, and their linkages across time and space with other heres and other nows" (Heller 2010a: 726; see also Martin-Jones and Gardner 2012: 5). As "practices of inquiry, shaped by the questions we ask, and by what we experience" (Heller 2012: 24), no one method is per se any better than any other. Yet, with respect to questions of language in the context of globalization and transnationalism, ethnography is widely considered a valuable approach (see, e.g., Blommaert, Collins, and Slembrouck 2005; Meinhof 2009; Baynham 2015). Within research on language and transnationalism, ethnography is emerging as a means to operationalize the study of the "trajectories of resources and of social actors across time and space" (Heller 2010a: 726).[3]

---

[3] As a method, ethnography typically entails a combination of techniques, including interviews, recordings, field notes, and participant observation, which is "based on relations of trust and a belief that data are produced in and of 'thick' interaction between researcher/s and researched" (Falzon 2009: 1; see, e.g., Copland and Creese 2015 for linguistic ethnography); and, as the phrase suggests, multisited ethnography, which is traced back to George Marcus (1995) and widely used in anthropological research on transnationalism, entails following people or things as they move across space, or studying the expression of a particular process in many sites at once (Heller 2010a, 726).

Examples of sociolinguistic research on transnationalism based on ethnographic fieldwork (in single or multiple sites, offline or online), or involving an ethnographic component (typically in the form of interviews and observations), include Farr's (2006) multisited ethnographic research on language and identity in a social network of Mexican families; Ek's (2009) ethnography of the language, identity, and transnationalism of a Pentecostal Guatemalan-American woman; Meinhof's (2009) ethnographic work on transnationalism and the life stories of African musicians from Madagascar in Paris; Heller's (2010a) multisited ethnography on transnational space and the commodification of Canadian francité in Canada and francophone Europe; Cressey's (2012) ethnographic research on English, identity, and processes of "translation" among British-born children and grandchildren of Pakistani or Kashmiri immigrants in Sparbrook, Birmingham; Song's (2012) ethnographic work on class, identity, and language in migrant South Korean families in a Midwestern US city; King's (2013) ethnographically informed study of language ideologies and identity in a bilingual, Ecuadorian-US family; and my own work on the importance of English for Ismaili Muslim transnationalism in northern Pakistan and eastern Tajikistan (Bolander 2016a, 2016b, 2017). While not the sole focus of this scholarship (see also Section 29.4.1), issues of English – language use, identity, ideology, and capital – feature widely in these examples.

My research on the role of English for the transnational Ismaili Muslim community, for instance, provides insight into striking similarities in ideologies of English between Ismailis living in different nation-states. While the community (which is dispersed in more than twenty-five countries) has adopted English as its official language, Ismailis in Hunza, northern Pakistan and Khorog, eastern Tajikistan typically learn English as a third or fourth language, respectively. Adopting a multisited ethnographic approach involving fieldwork (interviews, participant observation, living with local families), it became apparent that the Aga Khan IV, the community's spiritual leader, is central to the spread of both English and local ideologies of English. Without denying intercommunity variation resulting from the communities' embedding in different national and regional settings and intracommunity variation stratified according to various factors (including class, age and gender), fieldwork showed local Ismailis in both Hunza and Khorog striving to learn English. Key reasons include their wish to follow the edicts of the Aga Khan (who orders Ismailis to learn English) and to gain "direct access" to him (given that he uses English in his speeches), and ideologies of English as (economically) valuable. In both places, too, educational infrastructure providing English-language learning has been established by the Aga Khan Education Services, with Ismailis in Hunza and Khorog drawing a connection between quality English-language education and the set-up provided by the Aga Khan and his development network (Bolander 2016a, 2016b, 2017).

A complementary yet alternate approach is outlined in Li's (2011) research on transnationalism and identity among multilingual Chinese youth in Britain. Inspired by the MIT Community Innovation Lab's "Critical Moments Reflection Methodology," Li's (2011) paper introduces "Moment Analysis" as a means of empirically researching the concept of "translanguaging space" (introduced in Section 29.4.1). Theorized as an interactionally constructed site of "cultural translation" (Bhabha 1994), "translanguaging space" is seen to provide the context for and emerges as a result of individuals' "creative" and "critical" language practices. As argued by Li (2011: 1223), the space is thus not one "where different identities, values and practices simply co-exist." Rather, these "combine together to generate new ideas, values and practices" (Li 2011: 1223). Moment analysis, then, constitutes a means to study the performance of multilingual practices as "spontaneous, impromptu, and momentary actions," while at the same time, providing a possible means to subsequently analyze the shift from moments to patterns, through processes of recognition, adoption, and repetition (Li 2011: 1224). It does so by drawing on various sources of data, with observation and recording of naturally occurring interactions and metalanguage data (obtained through conversations, interviews, journals, and autobiographies in which participants are, for example, explicitly asked to reflect on crucial moments) being central (Li 2011: 1224). Results highlight the creative ways Li's three multilingual undergraduate student Chinese interlocutors draw on English and (varieties of) Chinese, the enjoyment they take from these practices, and their views on multilingualism, identity, and transnational connectedness. The analysis shows that the students do not view languages as discrete, separate entities to be used in distinct spaces for different purposes. They instead engage and wish to engage with practices of mixing, for example, for pleasure and for "personal and social gains" (Wei 2011: 1299). They see value in being multilingual, and their practices of multilingualism are intricately connected to the performance of multiple identities, the construction of "transnational space" (Li 2011: 1232), and the related idea of simultaneous belonging to multiple socio-cultural spaces (Li 2011: 1233).

In Mair (2013), the reader is presented with a methodology for digitally mapping vernacular language practices, as a means to study their transnational breadth and to explore questions of the relative importance of varieties of English. The research forms part of a broader interest in the increased multidialectality of online Englishes (Mair 2013: 257). Mair (2013: 257) refers here to "post-national uses of World Englishes," and the paper presents his adaptation of de Swann's (2002) "World Language System" to the study of pidgins and creoles in web fora that serve postcolonial West African and Caribbean diasporas. Using the example of Nigerian Pidgin and the Nairaland forum, and by mapping locations where individuals are posting onto a geographical map of the world,

Mair (2013: 275) is able to show the spread of "some non-traditional, displaced and mediated uses of vernaculars." Specifically, he is able to demonstrate (and visualize) that there is "no longer a supposedly natural link between Nigerian English and the territory of the nation state Nigeria, or between pidgin and its West African regional and social base" (Mair 2013: 257). Indeed, while the map shows a persistent community base for the vernaculars in Nigeria, it also highlights dense usage in London, the northeastern US seaboard, Toronto, and the Midwest/Great Lakes (Mair 2013: 267).

29.4.3 Transnationalism as Movement and Subjectivity

While there is extensive treatment of English in connection with migra-tion and diaspora (see Zipp, Chapter 6, this volume), there is comparatively less research on the importance of issues of identity, ideology, and atti-tudes toward English for the maintenance and local meanings of transna-tionalism. This section brings these two vantage points together. In doing so, it reviews research on three emerging areas: sociolinguistic scholarship on the relationship between transnationalism as movement and subjec-tivity; sociolinguistic scholarship on the heterogeneity of transnational-ism, and the persistence and importance of community-internal differences for its enactment and meanings; and sociolinguistic scholar-ship on diverse forms of movement beyond permanent and long-term migration.

There is increased recognition among both scholars of World Englishes and those working within the sociolinguistics of globalization that trans-nationalism needs to be explored in connection with questions of identity, language attitude, and language ideology. Some examples include Heller's (2010a) research on transnationalism and the circulation of commodified identity resources inside and outside francophone Canada; Song's (2012) article on the importance of transnational subjectivity and processes of distinction among Korean graduate student families in a Midwestern US city in relation to the relative value of English, Korean, and Chinese; Hundt's (2014) comparative work on zero articles in Indian Englishes in primary and secondary diaspora contexts, where transnationalism is con-ceptualized as social morphology, as a form of cultural reproduction and consciousness; Sharma's (2014) paper on the importance of transnational ties and social valuation with respect to Indian English among second-generation members of a British Punjabi community; and my own analysis of the role and importance of English with respect to both mobile and nonmobile local Ismailis in Hunza, northern Pakistan and Khorog, eastern Tajikistan (Bolander 2016a, 2017).

A second research trend involves recognition of and engagement with the heterogeneity of transnationalism, and the persistence and impor-tance of community-internal differences for its enactment and meanings (see also Section 29.2). Some examples include Harris, Leung, and Rampton's (2002: 29) reflections on widespread variation among immigrants to Britain (e.g. "newcomers" compared with "pupils with diaspora connections") and the implications of this variety for language education; Rampton's (2011) reflection on the persistence of "contemporary urban vernaculars" involving resources drawn from English, among post-adolescent and middle-aged informants with a migrant (South Asian) background in (west London) England; Song's (2012) study of the construction of distinction between different types of transnational Korean migrants (*jogi hunak*, or early stay abroad families, compared with graduate student families) for their children's envisaged language learning trajectories and the relative importance of English; and Sharma's (2014) discussion of differences in transnational ties and their valuation within second-generation members of a Punjabi community in West London with respect to the use of and attitudes toward Indian English.

Related to this is research that problematizes the role played by different types of migration for the formation of ties, for their social meanings at the individual and community level, and for issues of (English) language use and ideology. From this perspective, migration is no longer necessarily considered a permanent phenomenon. This point is made, for instance, by Harris, Leung, and Rampton (2002), who distinguish between long-term but not necessarily permanent migrants. It is also, for instance, exemplified by Meyerhoff and Walker's (2007) research on "urban sojourners," in which they compare copula/auxiliary BE between Bequians who have spent considerable time overseas and those who have not; in Park and Lo's (2012) edited special issue on *jogi yuhak*, where various papers address the role of this form of early study abroad migration for identity construction, ideology, and the value of particular languages on different markets and at various scales; and in my own research, which underscores the importance of English for the "imagined identities" (Norton 2013) of individual Ismailis, who envisage that their English-language skills will allow them to study abroad and then return home to help their own or other rural communities (see Bolander 2016a, 2017).

Song's (2012) research offers an illustration of all three trends. Her paper explores the role of transnational subjectivity in two Korean graduate families living in a Midwestern city in the USA, in connection with the intersection of class, identity, and capital with transnationalism. Both families went to the USA because one of the parents was studying in a doctoral program and both had a five-year-old child at the beginning of Song's research in 2004. Song's (2012: 205) main focus in the paper is on "how the participants implicitly constructed their subjectivities in interviews," particularly with respect to their children's language learning practices. This is set against the backdrop of an upsurge in *jogi yuhak*, which has led to tensions within the broader community of transnational Koreans. *Jogi yuhak* is "driven by the desire to acquire competence in

English and cosmopolitanism" (Song 2012: 202). For graduate families, *yogi juhak* families symbolize less educated, more materialistic, richer and unethical migrants, as compared with themselves (Song 2012: 204); and they thus attempt to distance themselves from these families. This process takes various forms, including, for example, an emphasis on Korean and Chinese over English, a declared indifference toward English, and the construction of a focus on English as un-Korean. More generally, emphases on differences serve to erase similarities in practices and trajectories (Song 2012: 214). Song's (2012: 203) focus on these discursive processes of distinction accentuates the importance of studying "transmigrant individual's subjective understandings of their situations," together with the enactment of this increasingly important type of South Korean migration. At the same time, it enables her to demonstrate the continued influence of the domestic linguistic market for views on English (e.g. how much English is needed for the South Korean market), and thus the persistent influence of the local. Indeed, as Song (2012: 215) maintains, "*jogi yuhak* and other modes of study abroad work to extend the struggle over domestic social reproduction of class, identity, and capital into transnational space."

My own research on the transnational Ismaili community also underscores the importance of taking into account transnationalism as migration and subjectivity. Basing my research on Dahinden's (2009) criticism that research on transnationalism tends to prioritize migrants at the expense of nonmigrants,[4] I explore how nonmigrant Ismailis become integrated into the transnational community. My interest here is primarily in English, since, as outlined in Section 29.4.2, official language policy gives English second-language status. In Bolander (2017), I thus distinguish between "movement from" and "movement to." In focusing on "movement to," I demonstrate that English becomes important for local constructions of Ismaili identity even among nonmobile Ismailis. My interviews with local Ismailis in Hunza, northern Pakistan and Khorog, eastern Tajikistan, highlight the pivotal role played by the Aga Khan IV – his visits to the region, the dissemination of his speeches in and on English, and the physical visibility of infrastructure in the form of schools and other institutes of higher education that provide quality English-medium instruction and English-language training. Focusing also on "movement from," I further highlight the role played by Aga Khan Education Services programs, which facilitate international exchange, and which provide the possibility for those competent in English to study abroad, for example at the Institute of Ismaili Studies in London.

---

[4] Exploring the different facets of transnationalism in a Swiss city, Dahinden (2009: 1366) draws a distinction between "network transnationalism" and "subjectivity," arguing that there is no necessary connection between migration and the creation or maintenance of transnational social relationships. Network transnationalism brought about through migration does not inevitably involve "thinking, feeling and belonging" (Dahinden 2009: 1367) transnational, nor, on the reverse, is transnational subjectivity predicated on having migrated.

In Sharma (2014), an exploration of community-internal variability is coupled with an interest in transnational migration and the social valuation of transnational ties. As part of her broader research on Indian English among second-generation members of a Punjabi community in West London, Sharma (2014: 216) poses two main questions: First "[d]oes a person's transnational activity influence their language use" and, second, "[w]hat ideologies are ascribed to distant varieties, in particular IndE, and can these influence language use as well" (Sharma 2014: 216)?. Her interest is, in other words, in both the "'material' and 'ideological' conduits of transnational influence" (Sharma 2014: abstract), and in how these change over time among second-generation members of a British Punjabi community. To answer her two questions, she applies quantitative and qualitative analysis: the former to explore the degree of postalveolar articulation of /t/ (obtained through sociolinguistic interviews) and the latter to interpret interview data on the individuals' biographies, social networks, degree of bilingualism, and personal cultural preferences (Sharma 2014: 224). Despite methodological challenges, her correlational analysis of transnational activity (measured, for example, on the basis of an individual's frequency of travel to India) and language use suggests "that a person's level of transnational social activity influences their use of an Asian-derived feature in English" (Sharma 2014: 217).

29.4.4 Transnationalism in Digital Spaces

As outlined by Jacquemet (2010), digital spaces constitute one of three dimensions of transnational space, together with "deterritorialization" and "reterritorialization." Whereas these first two concepts underscore the severing of straightforward links between a people, their practices, and a bounded territory (deterritorialization), and the processes whereby all translocal practices become locally anchored (reterritorialization), "digital spaces" refer to situated practices that take place in the "virtual reality of mediascapes" (Jacquemet 2010: 58). Compared with processes of deterritorialization and reterritorialization, digital spaces are relatively understudied (Jacquemet 2010: 58). Yet a review of the literature indicates that this is changing.

A growing body of literature on transnationalism in digital spaces includes critical metatheoretical reflection on the notion of variety and its applicability to various digital spaces (see also Section 29.4.1). Much of this research questions the validity of the notion of the "variety" given that mixing and creative language use are widespread in digital discourse. In this regard, see, for example Jacquemet's (2005, 2010) study of "transidiomatic practices" in the Adriadic ethno/mediascape; Seargeant and Tagg's (2011) previously discussed research on communication between Thai speakers via Facebook and MSN via Blackberry; You's (2011) work of Chinese white-collar workers' multilingual creativity on an electronic bulletin board; Mair's (2013) aforementioned research on Nigerian Pidgin mediated vernacular language practices; and Schreiber's (2015) analysis of the translanguaging writing practices of a Serbian university student on Facebook, with respect to identity construction and membership; see also Mair (Chapter 16, this volume).

Further critical research on digital spaces argues for the need to strike a balance between studying online language practices (including translanguaging) as creative acts without providing closer reflection on how these acts are also shaped by questions of power. Thus, Dovchin, Sultana, and Pennycook (2016: 14), for example, use data from offline and online (Facebook) ethnography in Mongolia and Bangladesh to demonstrate how "transnational linguistic flows are the outcome of complex uneven and unequal processes through which young adults manage to create their own linguistic and cultural texts in relation to the divisions of a society along lines of socio-economic differences." To do justice to issues of agency and creative language practices while also paying close attention to how these practices are shaped by differential access to Englishes, the researchers combine a focus on "translingual practices" (see Section 29.4.1) with "unequal Englishes" (Tupas and Rubdy 2015). (For a further example, see also Doan's [2015] critical discourse analytic approach to the construction of new class paradigms and competencies in a transnational space via the example of an Internet forum for international students in the UK.)

Like research on transnationalism offline, research on transnationalism in digital spaces has also begun to emphasize the relevance of the interplay between the local and the transnational, global or cosmopolitan. Such research thereby cautions from treating online transnationalism as despatialized, offering instead insight into how online practices become situated. This is exemplified by Schreiber's (2015) qualitative research on the multilingual practices and semiotic resources employed by Aleksandar (a student of English studying at a Serbian university). Based on observations, the analysis of Aleksandar's Facebook practices, and a semi-structured Facebook chat interview, Schreiber (2015: 72) sets out to "understand how this writer understands his own use of language and communicative purposes in his Facebook writing and how, for him, integrating these linguistic codes is related to his construction of local and global identities." By integrating resources from Serbian and English, for example to comment on links to multimodal content, Aleksandar is able to "jump scales," thereby creating an "online image of himself as firmly grounded in his local identity" and as a "knowledgeable member of the global hip-hop community" (Schreiber 2015: 82; see also Lam 2004; Sharma 2012).

29.4.5   Transnationalism and Language Commodification

A final theme emerging in sociolinguistic research on language and transnationalism is language commodification. The commodification of language generally and of particular languages can be linked to processes of new or late capitalism. These changes are seen as intricately connected with transformations in "the material processes of production and distribution, made possible by a combination of economic/financial deregulation and the availability of new information and communication technologies" (Cameron 2012: 353). Central repercussions for language entail its progressive "marketization" (typically from the 1980s), described by Cameron (2012: 353) as involving "a tendency for the values, logic, and language of capitalism and/or business to be applied in domains that were previously seen to lie at least partly outside their remit." As outlined by Heller (2010b: 103), as a result of the "expansion of markets and their progressive saturation," the importance of language grows with respect to (1) the "managing of the flow of resources over extended spatial relations and compressed space-time relations"; (2) "providing symbolic added value to industrially produced resources"; (3) "facilitating the construction of and access to niche markets"; and (4) "developing linguistically mediated knowledge and service industries." Viewed increasingly as a resource with an inherent "exchange value," the commodification of language thus involves a discursive shift toward the treatment of language (and also identity and culture) in mainly economic terms (Heller and Duchêne 2012: 7). Areas that aptly exemplify ties between late capitalism and the commodification of language include tourism, marketing and advertising, language teaching, translation, call centers, and performance art (Heller 2010b). (For examples of research within these fields, see Heller 2010b: 107–110.)

Sociolinguistics has responded to these changes, for example, through intense critical engagement with the notions of "value," "markets" (cf., e.g., Park and Wee 2012), and "commodification" (see, e.g., Heller and Duchêne 2012), and via sociolinguistic research on language and neoliberalism (see, e.g., Block, Gray, and Holborow 2012; Holborow 2015). For the purposes of this chapter, what is central is that processes of commodification involve a shift from national to transnational markets. Indeed, whereas the link between language, territory, and identity was key to the "legitimization of the nation-state as a particular historical mode of regulation of capital," the process of late capitalism "stretches the system of national regulation of markets to and possibly beyond its limits" (Heller and Duchêne 2012: 3). As a result, commodified languages and identities are circulated and marketed within but also across nation-state boundaries – with possibilities for the value of particular languages or varieties to be negotiated with respect to (sometimes simultaneous) local and/or trans-local markets. This means that both individuals (e.g. migrant reproductive workers; Piller and Pavlenko 2007) and practices (e.g. the placement of call centers) can circulate and be made to circulate across nation-state borders, leading to the creation of alternate transnational webs, opportunities, and dependencies.

Research addressing the commodification of language that incorporates a discussion of English (typically in relation to local and regional languages) and transnationalism includes Piller and Pavlenko's (2007) study of language and gender in global domestic scenarios; Rubdy and Tan's (2008) co-edited volume *Language as Commodity: Global Structures, Local Marketplaces*, which includes chapters on the relative value of English in various geographical and social spaces; Piller's (2010) research on the value of multilingualism (including usages of English) in sex tourism in Switzerland; Park and Lo's (2012) aforementioned edited special issue on "Transnational South Korea as a site for a sociolinguistics of globalization: Markets, timescales, neoliberalism"; Park and Wee's (2012) monograph on the *Markets of English: Linguistic Capital in a Globalizing World*; Blackledge and Creese's (2012) research on language, pride, profit, and distinction in two Bengali schools in Birmingham; Lorente's (2012) study of the instrumentalization of language for the construction of locally and globally marketable Filipino workers; and Lorente and Tupas's (2013) critical reflection on "hybridity" and its entanglement with "capitalist globalization," as seen in company websites offering training in English as a foreign language to Filipinos. Central points underscored in this literature include the prominence of multilingual ecologies and hence considerations of the relative value of English vis-à-vis local and regional languages; reflection on the interplay between opportunity and change, and difficulty, adversity, and the maintenance of the status quo; and the key role played by coexisting markets and multiple centers of authority (Blommaert 2007: 2) for (English) language use and ideologies.

29.5 Conclusion

Positioned against the backdrop of an increase in sociolinguistic research on language and globalization in the course of the last fifteen years, this chapter set out to focus on transnationalism. It thereby aimed to explore how central ideas framing the sociolinguistic study of transnationalism are pertinent for research on World Englishes, and to address applications via examples of metatheoretical and empirical scholarship in sociolinguistics. The latter includes research on transnationalism which explicitly positions itself within a World Englishes framework, as well as research on transnationalism with a focus on English which has implications for World Englishes research. For a chapter within Part IV, "Current Challenges," of this handbook, it seemed apt to address research from two areas that are both interested in the implications of the global spread of English and that might thus also benefit from enhanced engagement with one another despite epistemological, theoretical, and methodological distinctions.

Using English and transnationalism as the vantage point for this exploration is challenging in light of the multitude of understandings of transnationalism, the tendency for it to be treated as synonymous with globalization or as another type of migration, and the tendency for it not to be defined at all. To illustrate its range of meanings, Section 29.2 explicitly focused on the polysemy of transnationalism and the implications of this polysemy for World Englishes research. The chapter subsequently turned to address how a shift in perspective from "methodological nationalism" to transnationalism has implications for World Englishes research, particularly given the striking similarities between criticisms of "methodological nationalism" and criticisms of World Englishes research (Section 29.3). As the chapter underscores, a methodologically nationalistic viewpoint suggests an a priori relevance of the nation, and it steers expectations toward explanations based on national frameworks. This should not deter from World Englishes research in national contexts. It should rather prompt for the concurrent problematizing of the nation as an ideological and historical construct in its own right, in connection with a focus on how localized and localizing uses and ideologies of English become pertinent to the enactment of transnationalism, by whom and for what purposes (Bolander and Mostowlansky 2017; Britain 2017).

Turning then to metatheoretical and empirical research on language and transnationalism from a sociolinguistic perspective, Section 29.4 of the chapter focused on current conceptualizations of "language" and "variety," the growing importance of a relational perspective and of multilingualism in World Englishes research, and a discussion of methods for the study of transnationalism; and it addressed research on transnationalism as movement and subjectivity, on transnationalism in digital spaces, and on transnationalism and language commodification. In doing so, the section highlighted a growing emphasis on transnational subjectivity; an emerging interest in community-internal differences and the heterogeneity of transnationalism; and a continuous emphasis on the groundedness of transnationalism and its enactment as a practice that is local yet simultaneously also noncontiguous (for instance, in digital spaces). Some of these points are explicitly emphasized in research on World Englishes and transnationalism. Yet, as the review shows, many examples stem from related fields interested in the role of English for a sociolinguistics of globalization. As such, these points also highlight current challenges for World Englishes research and transnationalism, and offer an outlook to possible future research.

References

Appadurai, Arjun. 1996. *Modernity at Large: Cultural Dimensions of Globalization*. Minneapolis: University of Minnesota Press.

Basch, Linda, Nina Glick Schiller, and Cristina Szanton Blanc. 1994. *Nations Unbound: Transnational Projects, Postcolonial Predicaments, and Deterritorialized Nation-States*. London: Routledge.

Baynham, Mike. 2015. Narrative and space/time. In Anna De Fina and Alexandra Georgakopoulou, eds. *The Handbook of Narrative Analysis*. London: Wiley-Blackwell, 119–139.

Bhabha, Homi. 1994. *The Location of Culture*. London: Routledge.

Blackledge, Adrian and Angela Creese. 2012. Pride, profit and distinction: Negotiations across time and space in community language education. In Alexandre Duchêne and Monica Heller, eds. *Language in Late Capitalism*. London: Routledge, 116–141.

Block, David, John Gray, and Marnie Holborow. 2012. *Neoliberalism and Applied Linguistics*. London: Routledge.

Blommaert, Jan. 2007. Sociolinguistic scales. *Intercultural Pragmatics* 4(1): 1–19.

Blommaert, Jan. 2010. *The Sociolinguistics of Globalization*. Cambridge: Cambridge University Press.

Blommaert, Jan. 2012. Sociolinguistics and English language studies. Working Papers in Urban Language and Literacies, No. 85.

Blommaert, Jan, James Collins, and Stef Slembrouck. 2005. Spaces of multilingualism. *Language and Communication 25*: 197–216.

Bolander, Brook. 2016a. English and the transnational Ismaili Muslim community: Identity, the Aga Khan, and infrastructure. *Language in Society 45*: 583–604.

Bolander, Brook. 2016b. English language policy as ideology in multilingual Khorog, Tajikistan. In Elisabeth Barakos and Johann W. Unger, eds. *Discursive Approaches to Language Policy*. London: Palgrave Macmillan, 253–274.

Bolander, Brook. 2017. English, Motility and Ismaili Transnationalism. *International Journal of the Sociology of Language 247*: 71–88.

Bolander, Brook and Till Mostowlansky. 2017. Language and globalisation in South and Central Asian spaces. *International Journal of the Sociology of Language 247*: 1–11.

Britain, David. 2017. Language, mobility and scale in South and Central Asia: A commentary. *International Journal of the Sociology of Language 247*: 127–137 .

Bruthiaux, Paul. 2003. Squaring the circles: Issues in modeling English worldwide. *International Journal of Applied Linguistics 13*(2): 159–178.

Cameron, Deborah. 2012. The commodification of language: English as a global commodity. In Terttu Nevalainen and Elizabeth Closs Traugott, eds. *The Oxford Handbook of the History of English*. Oxford: Oxford University Press, 352–361.

Canagarajah, Suresh. 2013. *Translingual Practice: Global Englishes and Cosmopolitan Relations*. London: Routledge.

Copland, Fiona and Angela Creese. 2015. *Linguistic Ethnography: Collecting, Analysing and Presenting Data*. London: Sage.

Creese, Angela and Adrian Blackledge. 2010. Translanguaging in the bilingual classroom: A pedagogy for learning and teaching? *Modern Language Journal 49*(1): 103–115.

Coupland, Nikolas. 2003a. Introduction: Sociolinguistics and globalisation. *Journal of Sociolinguistics* 7(4): 465–472.

Coupland, Nikolas. 2003b. Sociolinguistics and globalization. *Journal of Sociolinguistics* 7(4): 465–637.

Cressey, Gill. 2012. Diaspora youth, ancestral languages and English as "translation" in multilingual space. In Sheena Gardner and Marilyn Martin-Jones, ed. *Multilingualism, Discourse and Ethnography*. London: Routledge, 131–141.

Dahinden, Janine. 2009. Are we all transnationals now? Network transnationalism and transnational subjectivity: The differing impacts of globalization on the inhabitants of a small Swiss city. *Ethnic and Racial Studies* 32(8): 1365–1386.

De Fina, Anna and Sabrina Perrino. 2013. Transnational identities. *Applied Linguistics* 34(5): 509–515.

de Swaan, Abram. 2002. *The World Language System: A Political Sociology and Political Economy of Language*. Cambridge: Polity.

Doan, Nguyen Quynh Tram. 2015. Neoliberal capitalism, transnationalism and networked individualism: Rethinking social class in international student mobility. London: MEDIA@LSE. www.lse.ac.uk/media@lse/research/mediaworkingpapers/mscdissertationseries/2015/nguyen-quynh-tram-doan.pdf

Dovchin, Sender, Shaila Sultana, and Alastair Pennycook. 2016. Unequal translingual Englishes in the Asian peripheries. *Asian Englishes* 18(2): 92–108.

Ek, Lucila D. 2009. "Allá en Guatemala": Transnationalism, language, and identity of a Pentecostal Guatemalan-American young woman. *The High School Journal* 92(4): 67–81.

Falzon, Mark-Anthony. 2009. Multi-sited ethnography: Theory, praxis and locality in contemporary research. In Mark-Anthony Falzon, ed. *Multi-Sited Ethnography: Theory, Praxis and Locality in Contemporary Research*. Surrey: Ashgate, 1–23.

Farr, Marcia. 2006. *Rancheros in Chicagoacán: Language and Identity in a Transnational Community*. Texas: University of Texas Press.

Glick Schiller, Nina Lina Basch and Cristina Blanc-Szanton. 1992. Towards a definition of transnationalism: Introductory remarks and research questions. *Annals of the New York Academy of Sciences 645*: ix–xiv.

Guarnizo, Luis Eduardo and Peter Michael Smith. 2009 [1998]. The locations of transnationalism. In Michael Peter Smith and Luis Eduardo Guarnizo, ed. *Transnationalism from Below, Vol. 6: Comparative Urban and Community Research*. New Brunswick, NJ: Transaction Publishers, 3–34.

Harris, Roxy, Constant Leung, and Ben Rampton. 2002. Globalisation, diaspora and language education in England. In David Block and Deborah Cameron, ed. *Globalisation and Language Teaching*. London: Routledge, 29–46.

Hannerz, Ulf. 1996. *Transnational Connections: Culture, People, Places*. London: Routledge.

Harvey, David. 1989. *The Condition of Postmodernity*. Oxford: Blackwell.

Heller, Monica. 2010a. Language as a process: A study on transnational spaces. In Peter Auer and Jürgen Erich Schmidt, eds. *Language and Space: An International Handbook of Linguistic Variation, Vol. 1: Theories and Methods*. Berlin: Walter de Gruyter, 724–740.

Heller, Monica. 2010b. The commodification of language. *Annual Review of Anthropology* 39: 101–114.

Heller, Monica. 2012. Rethinking sociolinguistic ethnography: From community and identity to process and practice. In Sheena Gardner and Marilyn Martin-Jones, eds. *Multilingualism, Discourse and Ethnography*. London: Routledge, 1–15.

Heller, Monica and Alexendre Duchêne. 2012. Pride and profit: Changing discourses of language, capital and nation-state. In Alexandre Duchêne and Monica Heller, eds. *Language in Late Capitalism*. London: Routledge, 116–141.

Hurrelmann, Adrian and Joan DeBardeleben. 2011. Introduction. In Joan DeBardeleben and Adrian Hurrelmann, eds.*Transnational Europe: Promise, Paradox, Limits*. London: Palgrave Macmillan, 1–16.

Holborow, Marnie. 2015. *Language and Neoliberalism*. London: Routledge.

Hundt, Marianne. 2014. Zero articles in Indian Englishes: A comparison of primary and secondary diaspora situations. In Marianne Hundt and Devyani Sharma, eds. *English in the Indian Diaspora*. Amsterdam: John Benjamims, 131–170.

Iriye, Akira and Pierre-Yves Saunier, eds. 2009. *The Palgrave Dictionary of Transnational History* (Palgrave MacMillan Transnational History). Houndmills: Palgrave Macmillan.

Jacquemet, Marco. 2005. Transidiomatic practices: Language and power in the age of globalization. *Language and Communication* 25(3): 257–277.

Jacquemet, Marco. 2010. Language and transnational Spaces. In Peter Auer and Jürgen Erich Schmidt, eds. *Language and Space: An International Handbook of Linguistic Variation, Vol. 1: Theories and Methods*. Berlin: Walter de Gruyter, 50–69.

Jörgensen, Jens Normann. 2008. Polylingual languaging around and among children and adolescents. *International Journal of Multilingualism* 5(3): 161–176

Jörgensen, Jens-Normann, Martha Karrebaek, Lian Madsen and Janus Möller. 2011. Polylanguaging in superdiversity. *Diversities* 13(2): 23–37.

Kearney, Michael. 1995. The local and the global: The anthropology of globalization and transnationalism. *Annual Review of Anthropology* 24: 547–565.

King, Kendall A. 2013. A tale of three sisters: Language ideologies, identities, and negotiations in a bilingual, transnational family. *International Multilingual Research Journal* 7(1): 49–65.

Krishnaswamy, N. and Archana S. Burde. 1998. *The Politics of Indians' English Linguistic Colonialism and the Expanding English Empire*. Oxford: Oxford University Press.

Lam, Wan Shun Eva. 2004 . Second language socialization in a bilingual chat room: Global and local considerations. *Language Learning and Technology* 8(3): 44–65.

Levitt, Peggy. 1996. Social remittances: A conceptual tool for understanding migration and development. Working Paper Series No. 96.04.

Levitt, Peggy. 2001. Transnational migration: Taking stock and future directions. *Global Networks* 1(3): 195–216.

Li, Wei. 2011. Moment analysis and translanguaging space: Discursive construction of identities by multilingual Chinese youth in Britain. *Journal of Pragmatics* 43: 1222–1235.

Li, Wei and Zhu Hua. 2013. Translanguaging identities: Creating transnational space through flexible multilingual practices amongst Chinese university students in the UK. *Applied Linguistics* 34(5): 516–535.

Lorente, Beatriz P. 2012. The making of "workers of the world": Language and the labor brokerage state. In Alexandre Duchêne and Monica Heller, eds. *Language in Late Capitalism*. London: Routledge, 183–206.

Lorente, Beatriz P. and T. Ruanni F. Tupas. 2013. (Un)emancipatory hybridity: Selling English in an unequal world. In Rani Rubdy and Lubna Alsagoff, eds. *The Global-Local Interface: Exploring Language and Identity*. Bristol: Multilingual Matters, 66–82.

Mahler, Sarah J. 2009 [1998]. Theoretical and empirical contributions toward a research agenda for transnationalism. In Michael Peter Smith and Luis Eduardo Guarnizo, eds. *Transnationalism from Below*. New Brunswick, NJ: Transaction Publishers, 64–100.

Mair, Christian. 2013.The World System of Englishes. Accounting for the transnational importance of mobile and mediated vernaculars. *English World-Wide* 34(3): 253–278.

Makoni, Sinfree and Alastair Pennycook. 2007. Disinventing and reconstituting languages. In Sinfree Makoni and Alastair Pennycook, eds. *Disinventing and Reconstituting Languages*. Bristol: Multilingual Matters, 1–42.

Marcus, George. 1995. Ethnography in/of the world system: The emergence of multi-sited ethnography. *Annual Review of Anthropology* 24: 95–117.

Martin-Jones, Marilyn and Sheena Gardner. 2012. Introduction: Multilingualism, discourse and ethnography. In Sheena Gardner and Marilyn Martin-Jones, eds. *Multilingualism, Discourse and Ethnography*. London: Routledge, 1–15.

McEwan, Cheryl. 2004. Transnationalism. In James S. Duncan, Nuala C. Johnson and Richard H. Schein, eds. *A Companion to Cultural Geography*. Malden, MA: Blackwell, 499–512.

Meinhof, Ulrike Hanna. 2009. Transnational flows, networks and "transcultural capital": Reflections on researching migrant networks through linguistic ethnography. In James Collins, Stef Slembrouck and Mike Baynham, eds. *Globalization and Language in Contact: Scale, Migration and Communicative Practices*. London: Continuum, 148–169.

Meyerhoff, Miriam and James A. Walker. 2007. The persistence of variation in individual grammars: Copula absence in "urban sojourners" and their stay-at-home peers, Bequia (St. Vincent and the Grenadines). *Journal of Sociolinguistics* 11(3): 346–366.

Nonini, Donald M. and Aihwa Ong. 1997. Chinese transnationalism as an alternative modernity. In Aihwa Ong and Donald M. Nonini, eds. *Ungrounded Empires: The Cultural Politics of Modern Chinese Transnationalism*. London: Routledge, 3–33.

Norton, Bonny. 2013. *Identity and Language Learning: Extending the Conversation*. Bristol: Multilingual Matters.

Otsuji, Emi and Alastair Pennycook. 2010. Metrolingualism: Fixity, fluidity and language in flux. *International Journal of Multilingualism* 7(3): 240–254.

Paolillo, John. 2007. How much multilingualism? Language diversity on the Internet. In Brenda Danet and Susan Herring, eds. *The Multilingual Internet: Language, Culture, and Communication Online*. Oxford: Oxford University Press, 408–430.

Park, Joseph Sung-Yul and Adrienne Lo. 2012. Transnational South Korea as a site for a sociolinguistics of globalization: Markets, timescales, neoliberalism. *Journal of Sociolinguistics* 16(2): 147–164.

Park, Joseph Sung-Yul and Lionel Wee. 2012. *Markets of English: Linguistic Capital and Language Policy in a Globalizing World*. London: Routledge.

Pennycook, Alastair. 1994. *The Cultural Politics of English as an International Language*. London: Longman.

Pennycook, Alastair. 2010a. English and globalization. In Janet Maybin and Joan Swann, eds. *The Routledge Companion to English Language Studies*. London: Routledge, 113–121.

Pennycook, Alastair. 2010b. *Language as a Local Practice*. London: Routledge.

Pennycook, Alastair. 2010c. The future of Englishes: One, many, or none? In Andy Kirkpatrick, ed. *The Routledge Handbook of World Englishes*. London: Routledge, 673–688.

Piller, Ingrid. 2010. Sex in the city: On making space and identity in travel spaces. In Adam Jaworski and Crispin Thurlow, eds. *Semiotic Landscapes: Language, Image, Space*. London: Continuum, 123–136.

Piller, Ingrid and Aneta Pavlenko. 2007. Globalization, gender, and multilingualism. In Laurenz Volkmann and Helene Decke-Cornill, eds. *Gender Studies and Foreign Language Teaching*. Tübingen: Narr, 15–30.

Pries, Ludger. 1999. *Migration and Transnational Social Spaces*. Aldershot: Ashgate.

Rampton, Ben. 1995. *Crossing: Language and Ethnicity among Adolescents*. London: Longman.

Rampton, Ben. 2000. Speech community. Working Papers in Urban Language and Literacies No. 15.

Rampton, Ben. 2009. Speech community and beyond. In Nikolas Coupland and Adam Jaworski, eds. *The New Sociolinguistics Reader*. Basingstoke: Palgrave Macmillan, 694–713.

Rampton, Ben. 2011. From "Multi-ethnic adolescent heteroglossia" to "Contemporary urban vernaculars." *Language and Communication* 31(4): 276–294.

Rampton, Ben and Constadina Charalambous. 2010. Crossing: A review of research. Working Papers in Urban Language and Literacies, No. 58.

Rubdy, Rani and Lubna Alsagoff, eds. 2013. *The Global-Local Interface: Exploring Language and Identity*. Bristol: Multilingual Matters.

Rubdy, Rani and Peter Tan, eds. 2008. *Language as Commodity: Global Structures, Local Marketplaces*. London: Bloomsbury.

Schreiber, Brooke R. 2015. "I am what I am": Multilingual identity and digital translanguaging. *Language Learning and Technology* 19: 69–87.

Seargeant, Philip and Caroline Tagg. 2011. English on the internet and a "post-varieties" approach to language. *World Englishes* 30(4): 496–514.

Sharma, Bal Krishna. 2012. Beyond social networking: Performing global Englishes in Facebook by college youth in Nepal. *Journal of Sociolinguistics* 16(4): 483–509.

Sharma, Devyani. 2014. Transnational flows, language variation, and ideology. In Marianne Hundt and Devyani Sharma, eds. *English in the Indian Diaspora*. Amsterdam: John Benjamims, 215–242.

Sklair, Leslie. 1995. *Sociology of the Global System*. London: Prentice Hall.

Song, Juyoung. 2012. The struggle over class, identity, and language: A case study of South Korean transnational families. *Journal of Sociolinguistics* 16(2): 201–217.

Tupas, Ruanni F. and Rani Rubdy, eds. 2015. *Unequal Englishes: The Politics of Englishes Today*. London: Palgrave Macmillan.

Vertovec, Steven. 1999. Conceiving and researching transnationalism. *Ethnic and Racial Studies* 22(2): 447–462.

Wimmer, Andreas and Nina Glick Schiller. 2002. Methodological nationalism and beyond: Nation-state building, migration and the social sciences. *Global Networks* 2(4): 301–334.

You, Xiaoye. 2011. Chinese white-collar workers and multilingual creativity in the diaspora. *World Englishes* 30(3): 409–427.

Index